MW01168584

NFPA® 13

Standard for the

Installation of Sprinkler Systems

2022 Edition

This edition of NFPA 13, *Standard for the Installation of Sprinkler Systems*, was prepared by the Technical Committees on Hanging and Bracing of Water-Based Fire Protection Systems, Private Water Supply Piping Systems, Sprinkler System Discharge Criteria, and Sprinkler System Installation Criteria, released by the Correlating Committee on Automatic Sprinkler Systems, and acted on by the NFPA membership during the 2021 NFPA Technical Meeting held June 14–July 2. It was issued by the Standards Council on August 26, 2021, with an effective date of September 15, 2021, and supersedes all previous editions.

This document has been amended by one or more Tentative Interim Amendments (TIAs) and/or Errata. See "Codes & Standards" at www.nfpa.org for more information.

This edition of NFPA 13 was approved as an American National Standard on September 15, 2021.

Origin and Development of NFPA 13

NFPA 13 represents the first standard published under the auspices of the NFPA Committee on Automatic Sprinklers. Originally titled *Rules and Regulations of the National Board of Fire Underwriters for Sprinkler Equipments, Automatic and Open Systems*, the standard has been continuously updated to keep in step with change.

Full information about the NFPA actions on various changes will be found in the NFPA Proceedings. The dates of successive editions are as follows: 1896, 1899, 1902, 1905, 1907, 1908, 1912, 1913, 1915, 1916, 1917, 1919, 1920, 1921, 1922, 1923, 1924, 1925, 1926, 1927, 1928, 1929. In 1930, a separate standard was published on Class B systems. This was integrated into the 1931 edition. Further revisions were adopted in 1934, 1935, and 1936. A two-step revision was presented in the form of a progress report in 1939 and finally adopted in 1940. Further amendments were made in 1947, 1950, 1953, 1956, 1958, 1960, 1961, 1963, 1964, 1965, 1966, 1968, 1969, 1971, 1972, 1973, 1974, 1975, 1976, 1978, 1980, 1982, 1984, 1986, and 1989.

The 1991 edition incorporated an entire rewrite of the standard to make the overall format user friendly. Substantive changes were made to numerous terms, definitions, and descriptions, with additional refinements made in 1994.

The centennial (1996) edition included a significant rework of the requirements pertaining to the application, placement, location, spacing, and use of various types of sprinklers. Other changes provided information on extended coverage sprinklers and recognized the benefits of fast-response sprinkler technology.

The 1999 edition encompassed a major reorganization of NFPA's Sprinkler Project that included the establishment of a Technical Correlating Committee on Automatic Sprinkler Systems and four new sprinkler systems technical committees, the consolidation of NFPA's sprinkler system design and installation requirements, and the implementation of numerous technical changes.

The scope of NFPA 13 was expanded to address all sprinkler system applications. The 1999 edition contained information on the installation of underground pipe from NFPA 24 and sprinkler system discharge criteria for on-floor and rack storage of Class I, II, III, IV, and plastic commodities, rubber tires, baled cotton, and roll paper that were previously located in NFPA 231, 231C, 231D, 231E, and 231F. Additionally, sprinkler system information for specialized hazards from over 40 NFPA documents was either brought into NFPA 13 using NFPA's extract policy or specifically referenced. A new chapter was also added to address the structural aspects of exposed and buried system piping. A table of cross-references to previous editions and material that was in other NFPA documents was included at the end of the 1999 edition.

Other specific changes included a new sprinkler identification marking system and the designation of sprinkler sizes by nominal K-factors. New criteria for the use of steel pipe in underground applications was added, as well as a new provision to guard against microbiologically influenced corrosion. Obstruction rules for specific sprinkler types and rules for locating sprinklers in concealed spaces were revised. New limitations were placed on the sprinkler sizes in storage applications, and criteria for the K-25 sprinkler was added. Additionally, the requirements for protecting sprinklers against seismic events also underwent significant revision.

The 2002 edition of NFPA 13 underwent style formatting and technical revisions. The style formatting was completed to comply with the *Manual of Style for NFPA Technical Committee Documents* and to reorganize many of the requirements in NFPA 13 into unique chapters. Editorially, NFPA 13 eliminated all the exceptions and reworded them as requirements where applicable, moved the mandatory references to Chapter 2, and relocated all the definitions to Chapter 3. In reorganizing NFPA 13, several new chapters were created to consolidate requirements including the following: Chapter 10 contained all of the applicable requirements for underground piping including materials, installation, and acceptance testing; Chapter 11 contained design approaches including pipe schedule, density/area method, room design method, special design areas, residential sprinklers, exposure protection, and water curtains; Chapter 12 contained the design approaches for the protection of storage, including idle pallets, miscellaneous storage, storage less than 12 ft, palletized, solid pile, bin box, and shelf storage, rack storage less than 25 ft, rack storage greater than 25 ft, rubber tire, baled cotton, rolled paper, and special storage designs; and Chapter 13 contained all of the design and installation requirements from all of the various documents that have been extracted into NFPA 13.

The 2002 edition made specific technical changes to address several key issues. Three major areas of irregular ceiling were addressed, including skylights, stepped ceilings, and ceiling pockets. The design requirements for ESFR sprinklers were expanded to allow the user to choose the storage height and then the building height for any allowable arrangement. Design requirements for the protection of storage on solid shelves were added. Requirements for the installation of residential sprinklers were added that parallel the requirements for other types of sprinklers.

For the 2007 edition, definitions were reorganized to place all the storage definitions in one area, and several new definitions addressing private water supply terms were added. The definitions and requirements of Ordinary Hazard Group 1 and 2 Occupancies were clarified where storage is present. The requirements for trapeze hangers were clarified and made consistent for all components, and the seismic bracing criteria were updated to ensure that NFPA 13 contains all the appropriate requirements for installation and design of seismic bracing of fire sprinkler systems. The requirements for storage were further reorganized and divided into separate chapters addressing general requirements for storage; miscellaneous storage; protection of Class I to Class IV commodities that are stored palletized, solid piled, bin boxes, or shelf storage; protection of plastic and rubber commodities that are stored palletized, solid piled, bin boxes, or shelf storage; protection of Class I through Class IV commodities that are stored on racks; protection of plastic and rubber commodities that are stored on racks; protection of rubber tire storage; protection of roll paper; and special designs of storage protection.

For the 2010 edition, many of the major changes related to the requirements for storage protection. First was the combination of large drop sprinkler and the specific application control mode sprinkler requirements and the revision of the terminology to identify them as Control Mode Specific Application sprinklers (CMSA). Next, new criteria for use of smoke vents were added to Chapter 12. The density/area curves in the storage chapters were reduced to a maximum 3000 ft^2 (278 m^2) operating area; this was a significant reduction of some curves that had extended up to 6000 ft^2 (557 m^2). Changes to rack storage in the 2010 edition included a new method to calculate the rack shelf area. Finally, the provisions for back-to-back shelf storage were added to the storage chapters.

Criteria for the protection of three new special storage arrangements were added to Chapter 20. These included protection of carton records storage with catwalk access; compact shelving of commodities consisting of paper files, magazines, books, and similar documents in folders and miscellaneous supplies with no more than 5 percent plastics up to 8 ft high; and protection of high bay record storage.

In Chapter 9, several changes occurred regarding sway bracing of sprinkler systems, including the introduction of new zone of influence tables for Schedule 5 steel pipe, CPVC, and Type M copper tube. Also the means for calculating the loads in the zone of influence were modified to correlate with SEI/ASCE-7, and a new Annex E was added that described this calculation.

Other areas of change included requirements for listed expansion chambers; clarification of ceiling pocket rules; and clarification of the formulas used in calculating large antifreeze systems.

The 2013 edition of NFPA 13 included changes to many technical requirements as well as the reorganization of multiple chapters. One significant change that was made to the administrative chapter of NFPA 13 was to clarify that watermist systems were not covered within NFPA 13 and that NFPA 750 should be used when looking for guidance on the design and installation of those systems. A series of new requirements addressed the need for a compatibility review where nonmetallic piping and fittings are installed in systems also using petroleum-based products such as cutting oils and corrosion inhibitors. Several modifications were made to the standard pertaining to freeze protection. The use of antifreeze in new NFPA 13 sprinkler systems was prohibited unless the solution use was listed, and the listing indicated the inability for the solution to ignite.

Other freeze protection modifications to the standard included clarification on the use of heat tracing, required barrel length for dry sprinklers, and the allowance for engineering analyses to be submitted to support an alternate freeze protection scheme. New sprinkler omission requirements were added for elevator machine rooms and other elevator associated spaces where certain criteria were met. Chapter 9 included updated information on shared support structures as well as a revised seismic bracing calculation form. Chapters 16 and 17 were reorganized to make the chapters easier to follow, to create more consistency between the various storage chapters. A new chapter on alternative approaches for storage applications was added to provide guidance on performance-based approaches dealing with storage arrangements.

One of the largest changes to the 2016 edition of NFPA 13 was the review of all metric conversions. Historically the document had used an "exact" conversion process, but in the 2016 edition an approximate conversion process was used. The intent of this change was to make the document more usable outside the United States. Another major change was the inclusion of a pipe venting requirement to eliminate as much air as possible from wet pipe systems. This requirement contemplates only a single vent in each wet system.

There were a significant number of changes to the storage chapters of NFPA 13. New design criteria were included for the protection of exposed, expanded Group A plastics stored in racks. Also, a ceiling and in-rack design approach, called an "alternative protection scheme," was added to Chapters 16 and 17. A similar concept had existed for sprinkler protection in NFPA 30 for several revision cycles.

A new section on sprinkler design where cloud ceilings are installed was added. This design scheme allows sprinklers to be omitted above cloud ceilings when the gap between clouds (or clouds and walls) meets a maximum allowable dimension based on the floor-to-cloud ceiling height. This new language was created based on a project conducted by the Fire Protection Research Foundation. Chapter 10, which is extracted from NFPA 24, was significantly revised based on the rewrite of NFPA 24. Most of the technical content remained the same, although the organization and structure were modified.

The 2019 edition of NFPA 13 has undergone a complete reorganization and is now fashioned in order of how one would approach the design of a sprinkler system. Users will now find hazard classifications, water supplies, and underground piping at the beginning of the standard. Chapter 8 has been divided into several new chapters, breaking out general rules for sprinkler locations into one chapter and several other chapters specific to sprinkler technology. The storage chapters have also been reorganized by sprinkler technology and address ceiling-only design. Chapter 25 has been revised and now contains all the requirements for in-rack sprinklers.

Requirements for vertical pipe chases have been clarified as have requirements for electrical equipment rooms where sprinklers can be omitted. Additionally, new beam rules for residential sprinklers have been added and details provided.

Due to the extensive reorganization of the 2019 edition, new features were added to help users locate requirements and identify sections with technical changes. The 2016–2019 Roadmap comparing the section numbers of the 2016 edition to the 2019 edition was compiled and is located after the index. It was provided for information only, to be used as a quick-reference locator. Technical changes from the last edition were also indicated and should be used as a guide. Shaded text identified requirements that were modified because of additions and deletions except for tables and figures. New requirements were marked with the N symbol. Users can view complete revision details in the First and Second Draft Reports in the NFPA 13 archived revision section at www.nfpa.org/docinfo.

Previous editions of this document have been translated into languages other than English, including French and Spanish.

The 2022 edition of NFPA 13 has undergone a philosophical change, moving away from the use of density/area curves in favor of single point density design options for new systems. Existing systems can still use the density/area curves. Many new definitions have been added and several existing definitions were modified. Several revisions to Chapter 4 delineate miscellaneous and low-piled storage requirements. As nitrogen generators are new to NFPA 13, supplementary requirements have been added throughout the standard. Considerations associated with water flow tests have been added to Chapter 5. Supervision requirements for dry pipe systems were added to Chapter 8. Requirements were added to Chapter 9 to address the use of intermediate temperature residential and quick response sprinklers. Also, a new section on small temporarily occupied spaces was added to address conditions where pods are installed. Obstruction criteria was added for suspended or floor-mounted obstructions in ordinary hazard occupancies. Chapter 14's ESFR sprinkler location criteria were modified, and obstruction requirements were revised to align with the results of a recent Fire Protection Research Foundation report.

In Chapter 16, the process for determining whether freeze protection is needed has been modified to require the use of the lowest mean temperature for 1 day, obtained for an approved source, and no longer permits the use of the isothermal map. Also, criteria were added to address the protection of piping subject to mechanical damage.

Criteria on multiple-row rack depth has been added to Chapter 20, and several tables throughout the storage chapters have been revised or reconfigured. New ESFR sprinklers with K-factors of K-28 (400) and K-33.6 (480) have been added to Chapter 23. Chapter 25 has been rewritten and reorganized completely. The chapter covers the single point density change and moves existing system criteria to its own sections and special design criteria for storage applications have all been combined into Chapter 26.

Correlating Committee on Automatic Sprinkler Systems

William E. Koffel, *Chair*
Koffel Associates, Inc, MD [SE]

Roland A. Asp, National Fire Sprinkler Association, Inc., MD [M]
Rep. National Fire Sprinkler Association

Jose R. Baz, JRB Associates Group Inc., FL [M]
Rep. NFPA Latin American Section

Kerry M. Bell, UL LLC, IL [RT]

Tracey D. Bellamy, Telgian Corporation, GA [U]
Rep. The Home Depot

Chase A. Browning, Medford Fire Department, OR [E]

Steven W. Dellasanta, Jensen Hughes Associates, Inc., RI [SE]

John August Denhardt, American Fire Sprinkler Association (AFSA), TX [IM]
Rep. American Fire Sprinkler Association

Michael J. Friedman, Friedman Consulting, Inc, MD [SE]

Alex Hoffman, Viking Fire Protection Inc., Canada [IM]
Rep. Canadian Automatic Sprinkler Association

Sultan M. Javeri, SC Engineering, France [IM]

Charles W. Ketner, National Automatic Sprinkler Fitters LU 669, MD [L]
Rep. United Assn. of Journeymen & Apprentices of the Plumbing & Pipe Fitting Industry

James D. Lake, Viking Corporation, MI [M]

John A. LeBlanc, FM Global, MA [I]

Kenneth W. Linder, Swiss Re, CT [I]

David O. Lowrey, City of Boulder Fire Rescue, CO [E]

Bryan Edwin Matthews, Liberty Mutual Group, NY [I]

Garner A. Palenske, Wiss Janney Elstner Associates, Inc., CA [SE]

Lawrence Richard Phillips, US Department of the Navy, VA [E]

Adam Seghi, Coda Risk Analysis, TX [I]

Joseph Su, National Research Council of Canada, Canada [RT]

J. Michael Thompson, GHD/The Protection Engineering Group, PC, VA [SE]

Alternates

Ralph E. Bless, Jr., Telgian Corporation, GA [U]
(Alt. to Tracey D. Bellamy)

Bruce H. Clarke, American International Group, Inc. (AIG), SC [I]
(Alt. to Adam Seghi)

Russell P. Fleming, Northeast Fire Suppression Associates, LLC, NH [SE]
(Alt. to Michael J. Friedman)

Scott T. Franson, The Viking Corporation, MI [M]
(Alt. to James D. Lake)

David B. Fuller, FM Approvals, RI [I]
(Alt. to John A. LeBlanc)

Jeffrey E. Harper, JENSEN HUGHES, IL [SE]
(Alt. to Steven W. Dellasanta)

Jeff Hebenstreit, UL LLC, IL [RT]
(Alt. to Kerry M. Bell)

Jeffrey M. Hugo, National Fire Sprinkler Association, Inc., MI [M]
(Alt. to Roland A. Asp)

Jack A. Medovich, Fire & Life Safety America, MD [IM]
(Alt. to John August Denhardt)

Donato A. Pirro, Electro Sistemas De Panama, S.A., Panama [M]
(Alt. to Jose R. Baz)

Jason W. Ryckman, Canadian Automatic Sprinkler Association, Canada [IM]
(Alt. to Alex Hoffman)

Douglas Paul Stultz, US Department of the Navy, VA [E]
(Alt. to Lawrence Richard Phillips)

Jeffrey J. Van Rhyn, Jr., Local 669 JATC, NV [L]
(Alt. to Charles W. Ketner)

Nonvoting

James B. Biggins, TUV SUD America Inc./Global Risk Consultants Corporation, IL [SE]
Rep. TC on Hanging & Bracing of Water-Based Systems

Christopher I. Deneff, FM Global, RI [I]
Rep. TC on Hanging & Bracing of Water-Based Systems

Raymond A. Grill, Arup, DC [SE]
Rep. TC on Sprinkler System Installation Criteria

Kenneth E. Isman, University of Maryland, MD [SE]
Rep. TC on Residential Sprinkler Systems

Russell B. Leavitt, Telgian Corporation, AZ [U]
Rep. TC on Sprinkler System Discharge Criteria

John J. Walsh, UA Joint Apprenticeship Committee Local 669, MD [SE]
Rep. United Assn. of Journeymen & Apprentices of the Plumbing & Pipe Fitting Industry
(Member Emeritus)

Chad Duffy, NFPA Staff Liaison

This list represents the membership at the time the Committee was balloted on the final text of this edition. Since that time, changes in the membership may have occurred. A key to classifications is found at the back of the document.

NOTE: Membership on a committee shall not in and of itself constitute an endorsement of the Association or any document developed by the committee on which the member serves.

Committee Scope: This Committee shall have overall responsibility for documents that pertain to the criteria for the design and installation of automatic, open and foam-water sprinkler systems including the character and adequacy of water supplies, and the selection of sprinklers, piping, valves, and all materials and accessories. This Committee does not cover the installation of tanks and towers, nor the installation, maintenance, and use of central station, proprietary, auxiliary, and local signaling systems for watchmen, fire alarm, supervisory service, nor the design of fire department hose connections.

Technical Committee on Hanging and Bracing of Water-Based Fire Protection Systems

Christopher I. Deneff, *Chair*
FM Global, RI [I]
Rep. FM Global

Joe Beagen, FlexHead Industries / Anvil International, RI [M]

Steve Berry, Raleigh Fire Department, NC [E]

James B. Biggins, TUV SUD America Inc./Global Risk Consultants Corporation, IL [SE]

Chase A. Browning, Medford Fire Department, OR [E]

Samuel S. Dannaway, Coffman Engineers, HI [SE]

John Deutsch, General Underground Fire Protection, CA [SE]

Daniel C. Duggan, Sr., Caddy/nVent, MO [M]

Thomas J. Forsythe, JENSEN HUGHES, CA [SE]

Jeff Hebenstreit, UL LLC, IL [RT]

Alan R. Laguna, Merit Sprinkler Company, Inc., LA [IM]

Ray Lambert, Schmidt Fire Protection, CA [IM]

Leslie "Chip" L. Lindley, II, Lindley Fire Protection Company Inc., CA [IM]

Wayne M. Martin, Wayne Martin & Associates Inc., CA [SE]

Michael Wade McDaniel, F Tech, Mexico [IM]
Rep. Mexican Fire Sprinkler Association (AMRACI)

J. Scott Mitchell, CNS Y-12/Pantex, TN [U]

Marco R. Nieraeth, Global Asset Protection Services, LLC, CA [I]

Michael A. Rothmier, UA Joint Apprenticeship Committee LU 669, CO [L]
Rep. United Assn. of Journeymen & Apprentices of the Plumbing & Pipe Fitting Industry

Daniel Sanchez, City of Los Angeles, CA [E]

Joseph R. Sanford, Liberty Mutual Property Risk Engineering, MA [I]

Peter T. Schwab, Wayne Automatic Fire Sprinklers, Inc., FL [IM]

John Silva, Hilti North America, CA [M]

Zeljko Sucevic, Vipond Fire Protection, Canada [IM]
Rep. Canadian Automatic Sprinkler Association

James Tauby, Mason Industries, Inc., NY [M]

Michael Tosunian, Eaton Tolco, CA [M]
Rep. National Fire Sprinkler Association

Victoria B. Valentine, Society of Fire Protection Engineers (SFPE), PA [SE]

Kenneth W. Wagoner, Parsley Consulting Engineers, CA [IM]
Rep. American Fire Sprinkler Association

Ronald N. Webb, S.A. Comunale Company, Inc., OH [IM]
Rep. National Fire Sprinkler Association

Warren Douglas Wilson, Scottsdale Fire Department, AZ [E]

Alternates

Scott Butler, Mason Industries, Inc., NY [M]
(Alt. to James Tauby)

Sheldon Dacus, Security Fire Protection Company, TN [IM]
(Alt. to Ronald N. Webb)

Todd A. Dillon, AXA XL/Global Asset Protection Services, LLC, OH [I]
(Alt. to Marco R. Nieraeth)

Daniel J. Duggan, Jr., Caddy/nVent, MO [M]
(Alt. to Daniel C. Duggan, Sr.)

Sorrel M. Hanson, FM Global, CA [I]
(Alt. to Christopher I. Deneff)

Jeffrey E. Harper, JENSEN HUGHES, IL [SE]
(Alt. to Thomas J. Forsythe)

Charles W. Ketner, National Automatic Sprinkler Fitters LU 669, MD [L]
(Alt. to Michael A. Rothmier)

Travis Mack, MFP Design LLC, AZ [IM]
(Voting Alt.)

Emil W. Misichko, UL LLC, IL [RT]
(Alt. to Jeff Hebenstreit)

Joseph Normandeau, XL Fire Protection, CA [IM]
(Alt. to Leslie "Chip" L. Lindley, II)

Gregory Nicholas Ohnemus, Anvil International, RI [M]
(Alt. to Joe Beagen)

Ryan Lee Peterson, Wayne Auto Fire Sprinklers, FL [IM]
(Alt. to Peter T. Schwab)

William Scott Roberts, Quick Response Fire Protection, NJ [M]
(Voting Alt.)

Jason W. Ryckman, Canadian Automatic Sprinkler Association, Canada [IM]
(Alt. to Zeljko Sucevic)

Scott Santos, Johnson Controls, CA [M]
(Alt. to Michael Tosunian)

Jack W. Thacker, Shambaugh and Sons, CA [IM]
(Voting Alt.)

Byron Weisz, Cen-Cal Fire Systems, Inc., CA [IM]
(Alt. to Kenneth W. Wagoner)

Chad Duffy, NFPA Staff Liaison

This list represents the membership at the time the Committee was balloted on the final text of this edition. Since that time, changes in the membership may have occurred. A key to classifications is found at the back of the document.

NOTE: Membership on a committee shall not in and of itself constitute an endorsement of the Association or any document developed by the committee on which the member serves.

Committee Scope: This Committee shall have the primary responsibility for those portions of NFPA 13 that pertain to the criteria for the use and installation of components and devices used for the support of water-based fire protection system piping including protection against seismic events.

Technical Committee on Private Water Supply Piping Systems

Robert G. Caputo, *Chair*
Fire & Life Safety America, AZ [IM]

Roland A. Asp, National Fire Sprinkler Association, Inc., MD [M]
　　Rep. National Fire Sprinkler Association

James B. Biggins, TUV SUD America Inc./Global Risk Consultants Corporation, IL [SE]

Dominic Bosco, Shambaugh & Son, NV [IM]
　　Rep. Illinois Fire Prevention Association

Marinus Both, API Group Inc., MA [IM]
　　Rep. National Fire Sprinkler Association

Flora F. Chen, Hayward Fire Department, California, CA [E]

Stephen A. Clark, Jr., Allianz, GA [I]

Jeffry T. Dudley, National Aeronautics & Space Administration, Kennedy Space Center (NASA), FL [U]

Byron E. Ellis, Entergy Corporation, LA [U]
　　Rep. Edison Electric Institute

Brandon W. Frakes, AXA XL/Global Asset Protection Services, LLC, NC [I]

Robert M. Gagnon, Gagnon Engineering, MD [SE]

LaMar Hayward, 3-D Fire Protection, Inc., ID [IM]

Jeff Hebenstreit, UL LLC, IL [RT]

Kevin J. Kelly, Victaulic, PA [M]
　　Rep. National Fire Sprinkler Association

Alan R. Laguna, Merit Sprinkler Company, Inc., LA [IM]

Michael Larsen, Amway Inc., MI [U]

Leslie "Chip" L. Lindley, II, Lindley Fire Protection Company Inc., CA [IM]

James M. Maddry, James M. Maddry, P.E., GA [SE]

Bob D. Morgan, Fort Worth Fire Department, TX [E]

Jason R. Olliges, Sprinkler Fitters Local 268, MO [L]
　　Rep. United Assn. of Journeymen & Apprentices of the Plumbing & Pipe Fitting Industry

Shawn C. Olson, Clackamas County Fire District #1, OR [E]

John H. Pecot, Johnson Controls, TX [M]
　　Rep. Johnson Controls

Dion Powell, Liberty Mutual, IL [I]

Martin Ramos, Environmental Systems Design, Inc., IL [SE]

James R. Richardson, Lisle Woodridge Fire District, IL [E]

Daniel Sanchez, City of Los Angeles, CA [E]

Peter T. Schwab, Wayne Automatic Fire Sprinklers, Inc., FL [IM]

Austin L. Smith, Consolidated Nuclear Security, LLC, Y-12, TN [U]

Kenneth W. Wagoner, Parsley Consulting Engineers, CA [SE]

Byron Weisz, Cen-Cal Fire Systems, Inc., CA [IM]

Alternates

Mark A. Bowman, Global Asset Protection Services, LLC, OH [I]
　　(Alt. to Brandon W. Frakes)

Christopher D Fulkerson, Local 669 Jatc, IN [L]
　　(Alt. to Jason R. Olliges)

William J. Gotto, TUV SUD America Inc./Global Risk Consultants Corporation, NJ [SE]
　　(Alt. to James B. Biggins)

Andrew C. Higgins, Allianz, NC [I]
　　(Alt. to Stephen A. Clark, Jr.)

Conor J. Kauffman, Kauffman Company, TX [IM]
　　(Alt. to Marinus Both)

Larry Keeping, PLC Fire Safety, Canada [SE]
　　(Voting Alt.)

Bryan Edwin Matthews, Liberty Mutual Group, NY [I]
　　(Alt. to Dion Powell)

Kevin D. Maughan, Victaulic/Globe Fire, MI [M]
　　(Alt. to Kevin J. Kelly)

Michael G. McCormick, UL LLC, IL [RT]
　　(Alt. to Jeff Hebenstreit)

Thomas William Noble, American Fire Sprinkler Association, TX [IM]
　　(Alt. to Byron Weisz)

William Overton, Consolidated Nuclear Security, LLC, Y-12, TN [U]
　　(Alt. to Austin L. Smith)

Ryan Lee Peterson, Wayne Auto Fire Sprinklers, FL [IM]
　　(Alt. to Peter T. Schwab)

Steven P. Rasch, Johnson Controls, OK [M]
　　(Alt. to John H. Pecot)

William Scott Roberts, Quick Response Fire Protection, NJ [M]
　　(Alt. to Roland A. Asp)

Craig M. Vesely, Alliant Energy, WI [U]
　　(Alt. to Byron E. Ellis)

James A. Zimmerman, JENSEN HUGHES, IL [SE]
　　(Voting Alt.)

Nonvoting

Frans Alferink, Wavin Overseas, Netherlands [U]

Chad Duffy, NFPA Staff Liaison

This list represents the membership at the time the Committee was balloted on the final text of this edition. Since that time, changes in the membership may have occurred. A key to classifications is found at the back of the document.

NOTE: Membership on a committee shall not in and of itself constitute an endorsement of the Association or any document developed by the committee on which the member serves.

Committee Scope: This Committee shall have the primary responsibility for documents on private piping systems supplying water for fire protection and for hydrants, hose houses, and valves. The Committee is also responsible for documents on fire flow testing and marking of hydrants.

Technical Committee on Sprinkler System Discharge Criteria

Russell B. Leavitt, *Chair*
Telgian Corporation, AZ [SE]

Carl P. Anderson, The Fire Protection International Consortium, WA [E]
    Rep. Washington State Association of Fire Marshals

Weston C. Baker, Jr., FM Global, RI [I]

Charles O. Bauroth, Liberty Mutual, MA [I]

Kerry M. Bell, UL LLC, IL [RT]

Jon Rodney Corbett, San Francisco Fire Department, CA [E]

John August Denhardt, American Fire Sprinkler Association (AFSA), TX [IM]
    Rep. American Fire Sprinkler Association

James Dockrill, J&S Fire Sprinkler Design & Consulting, Canada [IM]
    Rep. Canadian Automatic Sprinkler Association

James M. Fantauzzi, North East Fire Protection Systems Inc., NY [IM]
    Rep. American Fire Sprinkler Association

Abram Selim Fouad, Elite Consolidated Engineers, Egypt [SE]

Bo Hjorth, AlbaCon AB, Sweden [SE]

Donald Hopkins, Jr., JENSEN HUGHES, MD [SE]

Kenneth E. Isman, University of Maryland, MD [SE]

Sultan M. Javeri, SC Engineering, France [IM]

Michael J. Joanis, National Fire Sprinkler Association (NFSA), NH [M]
    Rep. National Fire Sprinkler Association

Larry Keeping, PLC Fire Safety Solutions, Canada [SE]

Kevin J. Kelly, Victaulic, PA [M]
    Rep. National Fire Sprinkler Association

Elham "Elley" Klausbruckner, Klausbruckner & Associates, Inc., CA [SE]

William E. Koffel, Koffel Associates, Inc., MD [SE]

Chris LaFleur, Sandia National Laboratories, NM [U]

Stuart Lloyd, Zurich Risk Engineering UK, Great Britain [I]

Joseph A. Lynch, Swiss Re, GA [I]

Brian Mosberian, Phoenix Fire Department, AZ [E]

Garner A. Palenske, Wiss Janney Elstner Associates, Inc. (WJE), CA [SE]

Richard Pehrson, Pehrson Fire PC, MN [E]
    Rep. International Fire Marshals Association

Kenneth R. Schneider, UA - ITF, MO [L]
    Rep. United Assn. of Journeymen & Apprentices of the Plumbing & Pipe Fitting Industry

Peter T. Schwab, Wayne Automatic Fire Sprinklers, Inc., FL [IM]

Michael D. Sides, Global Asset Protection Services, LLC, FL [I]

Manuel Silva, Johnson Controls, RI [M]

Michael Six, Bremerton Fire Department, WA [E]

Gary T. Smith, DACS, Inc., NJ [M]
    Rep. Rack Manufacturers Institute

William B. Smith, Code Consultants, Inc., MO [SE]

George W. Stanley, Wiginton Fire Protection Engineering, Inc., FL [IM]
    Rep. National Fire Sprinkler Association

Warren Douglas Wilson, Scottsdale Fire Department, AZ [E]

Steven D. Wolin, Reliable Automatic Sprinkler Company, Inc., SC [M]

Martin H. Workman, The Viking Corporation, MI [M]

Alternates

Joakim Bauer, AlbaCon AB, Sweden [SE]
    (Alt. to Bo Hjorth)

Tracey D. Bellamy, Telgian Corporation, GA [SE]
    (Alt. to Russell B. Leavitt)

Mark A. Bowman, Global Asset Protection Services, LLC, OH [I]
    (Alt. to Michael D. Sides)

John Desrosier, Globe Fire Sprinkler Corporation, MI [M]
    (Alt. to Kevin J. Kelly)

Skip Donnell, Liberty Mutual Insurance Company, IN [I]
    (Alt. to Charles O. Bauroth)

Thomas Larry Frank, Code Consultants, Inc., MO [SE]
    (Alt. to William B. Smith)

Richard A. Gallagher, Zurich Services Corporation, DE [I]
    (Alt. to Stuart Lloyd)

Pravinray D. Gandhi, UL LLC, IL [RT]
    (Alt. to Kerry M. Bell)

Jeffrey A. Hewitt, American Fire Protection, LLC, AL [M]
    (Alt. to Michael J. Joanis)

Robert C. Holliday, Sprinkler Fitters LU 268 JAC, MO [L]
    (Alt. to Kenneth R. Schneider)

Daniel A. Kaiser, Minnesota Department of Public Safety, MN [E]
    (Alt. to Richard Pehrson)

Shaun R. Kramer, The Viking Corporation, MI [M]
    (Alt. to Martin H. Workman)

James E. Lemanski, Swiss Re, IL [I]
    (Alt. to Joseph A. Lynch)

Ryan Lee Peterson, Wayne Auto Fire Sprinklers, FL [IM]
    (Alt. to Peter T. Schwab)

Milosh T. Puchovsky, Worcester Polytechnic Institute, MA [SE]
    (Alt. to Kenneth E. Isman)

Jason W. Ryckman, Canadian Automatic Sprinkler Association, Canada [IM]
    (Alt. to James Dockrill)

Tomas M. Sanchez, Sandia National Laboratories, NM [U]
    (Alt. to Chris LaFleur)

Steven J. Scandaliato, SDG, LLC, TX [IM]
    (Alt. to James M. Fantauzzi)

Gerald R. Schultz, The FPI Consortium, Inc., IL [M]
    (Alt. to Gary T. Smith)

Andrew J. Taggart, JENSEN HUGHES, CO [SE]
    (Alt. to Donald Hopkins, Jr.)

Jack W. Thacker, Shambaugh and Sons, CA [IM]
    (Alt. to George W. Stanley)

Terry L. Victor, Johnson Controls, MD [M]
    (Alt. to Manuel Silva)

Richard S. Wardak, FM Global, MA [I]
    (Alt. to Weston C. Baker, Jr.)

Cary M. Webber, Reliable Automatic Sprinkler, SC [M]
    (Alt. to Steven D. Wolin)

Chad Duffy, NFPA Staff Liaison

This list represents the membership at the time the Committee was balloted on the final text of this edition. Since that time, changes in the membership may have occurred. A key to classifications is found at the back of the document.

NOTE: Membership on a committee shall not in and of itself constitute an endorsement of the Association or any document developed by the committee on which the member serves.

Committee Scope: This Committee shall have primary responsibility for those portions of NFPA 13 that pertain to the classification of various fire hazards and the determination of associated discharge criteria for sprinkler systems employing automatic and open sprinklers, sprinkler system plans and calculations, and water supplies.

Technical Committee on Sprinkler System Installation Criteria

Raymond A. Grill, *Chair*
Arup, DC [SE]

Adam Seghi, *Secretary*
Coda Risk Analysis, TX [I]

Roland A. Asp, National Fire Sprinkler Association, Inc., MD [M]
Rep. National Fire Sprinkler Association

Hamid R. Bahadori, JENSEN HUGHES, FL [SE]

Weston C. Baker, Jr., FM Global, RI [I]

Cecil Bilbo, Jr., Academy of Fire Sprinkler Technology, Inc., IL [SE]

Chase A. Browning, Medford Fire Department, OR [E]

Robert G. Caputo, Fire & Life Safety America, AZ [IM]

Scott T. Franson, The Viking Corporation, MI [M]
Rep. National Fire Sprinkler Association

Jason Gill, Crews & Gregory Fire Sprinkler, Inc., VA [IM]
Rep. American Fire Sprinkler Association

Jeff Hebenstreit, UL LLC, IL [RT]

Elwin G. Joyce, II, Eastern Kentucky University, KY [U]
Rep. NFPA Industrial Fire Protection Section

Larry Keeping, PLC Fire Safety Solutions, Canada [SE]

John Kelly, Washington DC Fire & EMS Department, MD [E]

Charles W. Ketner, National Automatic Sprinkler Fitters LU 669, MD [L]
Rep. United Assn. of Journeymen & Apprentices of the Plumbing & Pipe Fitting Industry

Russell B. Leavitt, Telgian Corporation, AZ [SE]
Rep. Telgian Corporation

James E. Lemanski, Swiss Re, IL [I]

David O. Lowrey, City of Boulder Fire Rescue, CO [E]

Floyd Luinstra, Oklahoma State University, OK [SE]

Rodney A. McPhee, Canadian Wood Council, Canada [U]

Michael F. Meehan, VSC Fire & Security, VA [IM]
Rep. American Fire Sprinkler Association

Joe W. Noble, Noble Consulting Services, LLC, NV [E]
Rep. International Fire Marshals Association

Thomas A. Noble, City of North Las Vegas, NV [E]

Steven J. Scandaliato, SDG, LLC, TX [SE]

Peter T. Schwab, Wayne Automatic Fire Sprinklers, Inc., FL [IM]

Austin L. Smith, Consolidated Nuclear Security, LLC, Y-12, TN [U]

William B. Smith, Code Consultants, Inc., MO [SE]

Paul A. Statt, Eastman Kodak Company, NY [U]

Zeljko Sucevic, Vipond Fire Protection, Canada [IM]
Rep. Canadian Automatic Sprinkler Association

Lawrence M. Taylor, Schindler Elevator Corporation, TX [IM]
Rep. National Elevator Industry Inc.

Terry L. Victor, Johnson Controls, MD [M]

Robert Vincent, Shambaugh & Son, L.P., IN [IM]
Rep. National Fire Sprinkler Association

Daniel P. Wake, Victaulic Company of America, PA [M]

Jason E. Webb, Potter Electric Signal Company, MO [M]

Alternates

Kerry M. Bell, UL LLC, IL [RT]
(Alt. to Jeff Hebenstreit)

Ralph E. Bless, Jr., Telgian Corporation, GA [SE]
(Alt. to Russell B. Leavitt)

Johnathan C. Carl, Victaulic Company of America, PA [M]
(Alt. to Daniel P. Wake)

Virginia R. Charter, Oklahoma State University, OK [SE]
(Alt. to Floyd Luinstra)

Todd A. Dillon, AXA XL/Global Asset Protection Services, LLC, OH [I]
(Alt. to James E. Lemanski)

Jeffrey A. Hewitt, American Fire Protection, LLC, AL [M]
(Alt. to Roland A. Asp)

Mark G. Karr, Academy of Fire Sprinkler Technology, Inc., IL [SE]
(Alt. to Cecil Bilbo, Jr.)

Jim Kinslohr, Code Consultants, MO [SE]
(Alt. to William B. Smith)

Michael Wade McDaniel, F Tech, Mexico [SE]
(Alt. to Steven J. Scandaliato)

E. Parks Moore, S & S Sprinkler Company, LLC, AL [IM]
(Alt. to Michael F. Meehan)

Thomas William Noble, American Fire Sprinkler Association, TX [IM]
(Alt. to Jason Gill)

Patrick George Noble, City of North Las Vegas, NV [E]
(Alt. to Thomas A. Noble)

William Overton, Consolidated Nuclear Security, LLC, Y-12, TN [U]
(Alt. to Austin L. Smith)

Ryan Lee Peterson, Wayne Auto Fire Sprinklers, FL [IM]
(Alt. to Peter T. Schwab)

Michael A. Rothmier, UA Joint Apprenticeship Committee LU 669, CO [L]
(Alt. to Charles W. Ketner)

Jason W. Ryckman, Canadian Automatic Sprinkler Association, Canada [IM]
(Alt. to Zeljko Sucevic)

Manuel Silva, Johnson Controls, RI [M]
(Alt. to Terry L. Victor)

LeJay Slocum, JENSEN HUGHES, GA [SE]
(Alt. to Hamid R. Bahadori)

Richard S. Wardak, FM Global, MA [I]
(Alt. to Weston C. Baker, Jr.)

Ronald N. Webb, S.A. Comunale Company, Inc., OH [IM]
(Alt. to Robert Vincent)

Cary M. Webber, Reliable Automatic Sprinkler, SC [M]
(Alt. to Scott T. Franson)

Chad Duffy, NFPA Staff Liaison

This list represents the membership at the time the Committee was balloted on the final text of this edition. Since that time, changes in the membership may have occurred. A key to classifications is found at the back of the document.

NOTE: Membership on a committee shall not in and of itself constitute an endorsement of the Association or any document developed by the committee on which the member serves.

Committee Scope: This Committee shall have the primary responsibility for those portions of NFPA 13 that pertain to the criteria for the use and installation of sprinkler systems components (with the exception of those components used for supporting of piping), position of sprinklers, types of systems, and acceptance testing.

Contents

NFPA 13

Standard for the

Installation of Sprinkler Systems

2022 Edition

IMPORTANT NOTE: This NFPA document is made available for use subject to important notices and legal disclaimers. These notices and disclaimers appear in all publications containing this document and may be found under the heading "Important Notices and Disclaimers Concerning NFPA Standards." They can also be viewed at www.nfpa.org/disclaimers or obtained on request from NFPA.

UPDATES, ALERTS, AND FUTURE EDITIONS: New editions of NFPA codes, standards, recommended practices, and guides (i.e., NFPA Standards) are released on scheduled revision cycles. This edition may be superseded by a later one, or it may be amended outside of its scheduled revision cycle through the issuance of Tentative Interim Amendments (TIAs). An official NFPA Standard at any point in time consists of the current edition of the document, together with all TIAs and Errata in effect. To verify that this document is the current edition or to determine if it has been amended by TIAs or Errata, please consult the National Fire Codes® Subscription Service or the "List of NFPA Codes & Standards" at www.nfpa.org/docinfo. In addition to TIAs and Errata, the document information pages also include the option to sign up for alerts for individual documents and to be involved in the development of the next edition.

NOTICE: An asterisk (*) following the number or letter designating a paragraph indicates that explanatory material on the paragraph can be found in Annex A.

A reference in brackets [ ] following a section or paragraph indicates material that has been extracted from another NFPA document. Extracted text may be edited for consistency and style and may include the revision of internal paragraph references and other references as appropriate. Requests for interpretations or revisions of extracted text shall be sent to the technical committee responsible for the source document.

Information on referenced and extracted publications can be found in Chapter 2 and Annex F.

Chapter 1 Administration

1.1* Scope.

1.1.1 This standard shall provide the minimum requirements for the design and installation of automatic fire sprinkler systems and exposure protection sprinkler systems covered within this standard.

1.1.2* This standard shall not provide requirements for the design or installation of water mist fire protection systems.

1.1.2.1 Water mist fire protection systems shall not be considered fire sprinkler systems.

1.1.2.2 The design and installation of water mist fire protection systems shall comply with NFPA 750.

1.1.3* This standard is written with the assumption that the sprinkler system shall be designed to protect against a single fire originating within the building.

1.2* Purpose.

1.2.1 The purpose of this standard shall be to provide a reasonable degree of protection for life and property from fire through standardization of design, installation, and testing requirements for sprinkler systems, including private fire service mains, based on sound engineering principles, test data, and field experience.

1.2.2 Sprinkler systems and private fire service mains are specialized fire protection systems and shall require design and installation by knowledgeable and experienced personnel.

1.3 Application.

1.3.1 This standard shall apply to the following:

(1) Character and adequacy of water supplies
(2) Sprinklers
(3) Fittings
(4) Piping
(5) Valves
(6) All materials and accessories, including the installation of private fire service mains

1.3.2 Level of Protection. A building, where protected by an automatic sprinkler system installation, shall be provided with sprinklers in all areas except where specific sections of this standard permit the omission of sprinklers.

1.3.3 This standard shall also apply to "combined service mains" used to carry water for both fire service and other uses as well as to mains for fire service use only.

1.4 Retroactivity. The provisions of this standard reflect a consensus of what is necessary to provide an acceptable degree of protection from the hazards addressed in this standard at the time the standard was issued.

1.4.1 Unless otherwise specified, the provisions of this standard shall not apply to facilities, equipment, structures, or installations that existed or were approved for construction or installation prior to the effective date of the standard. Where specified, the provisions of this standard shall be retroactive.

1.4.2 In those cases where the authority having jurisdiction determines that the existing situation presents an unacceptable degree of risk, the authority having jurisdiction shall be permitted to apply retroactively any portions of this standard deemed appropriate.

1.4.3 The retroactive requirements of this standard shall be permitted to be modified if their application clearly would be impractical in the judgment of the authority having jurisdiction, and only where it is clearly evident that a reasonable degree of safety is provided.

1.5 Equivalency. Nothing in this standard is intended to prevent the use of systems, methods, or devices of equivalent or superior quality, strength, fire resistance, effectiveness, durability, and safety over those prescribed by this standard.

1.5.1 Technical documentation shall be submitted to the authority having jurisdiction to demonstrate equivalency.

1.5.2 The system, method, or device shall be approved for the intended purpose by the authority having jurisdiction.

1.6 Units and Symbols.

1.6.1 Units.

1.6.1.1 Metric units of measurement in this standard shall be in accordance with the modernized metric system known as the International System of Units (SI).

1.6.1.2 Two units (liter and bar), outside of but recognized by SI, are commonly used in international fire protection.

1.6.1.3 These units with conversion factors shall be used as listed in Table 1.6.1.3.

1.6.1.4* If a value for measurement as given in this standard is followed by an equivalent value in other units, the first stated shall be regarded as the requirement.

1.6.2 Hydraulic Symbols. The standard abbreviations in Table 1.6.2 shall be used on the hydraulic calculation form discussed in Chapter 28.

1.6.3* Some dimensions used in this standard are exact and some are not. Nominal dimension are often used, such as the dimensions used for pipe sizes. The metric equivalent shown in this standard might not be an exact conversion to the SI unit, but the nominal metric equivalent is typically used or a reasonably equivalent value or approximate conversion is used. It shall be acceptable to use the exact conversion or the conversions stated in the standard, even though they might not be exact.

1.7 New Technology.

1.7.1 Nothing in this standard shall be intended to restrict new technologies or alternate arrangements, provided the level of safety prescribed by this standard is not lowered.

1.7.2 Materials or devices not specifically designated by this standard shall be utilized in complete accord with all conditions, requirements, and limitations of their listings.

N **Table 1.6.1.3 Conversion Factors**

	Name of Unit	Unit Symbol	Conversion Factor
Length	Millimeter	mm	1 in. = 25 mm
	Meter	m	1 ft = 0.3048 m
Area	Square millimeters	mm^2	1 in.^{2} = 645.2 mm^2
	Square meter	m^2	1 ft^2 = 0.0929 m^2
Volume	Cubic millimeter	mm^3	1 in.^{3} = 16,387 mm^3
	Cubic meter	m^3	1 ft^3 = 0.02832 m^3
Fluid capacity	Liter	L	1 fl oz = 0.02957 L
	Liter	L	1 gal = 3.785 L
Flow	Liter per minute	L/min	1 gpm = 3.7848 L/min
Pressure	Bar	bar	1 psi = 0.0689 bar
Discharge density	Millimeter/minute	mm/min	1 gpm/ft^2 = 40.746 mm/min
	Liter/minute/m2	(L/min)/m^2	1 gpm/ft^2 = 40.746 (L/min)/m^2
k-factor	k-factor	L/min/(bar)^2	1 gpm/(psi)^2 = 14.285 L/min/(bar)^2
Weight	Kilogram	kg	1 lb = 0.4536 kg
Density	Kilogram/cubic meter	kg/m^3	1 lb/ft^3 = 16.02 kg/m^3
Temperature	Fahrenheit	°F	$F° = \frac{9}{5} \times C° + 32$
	Celsius	°C	$C° = \frac{5}{9} (F° - 32)$
Velocity	Kilometers per hour	km/h	1 mph = 1.609 km/h
Pound force	Newtons	N	1 lb force = 4.44822 N
Gauge (sheet steel)	Millimeter	mm	12 gauge = 2.8 mm
			14 gauge = 1.98 mm
			16 gauge = 1.57 mm
			22 gauge = 0.78 mm
			24 gauge = 0.63 mm

Note: For additional conversions and information, see ASTM SI 10, *IEEE/ASTM SI 10 American National Standard for Metric Practice.*

Δ **Table 1.6.2 Hydraulic Symbols**

Symbol or Abbreviation	Item
p	Pressure in psi
gpm	U.S. gallons per minute
q	Flow increment in gpm to be added at a specific location
Q	Summation of flow in gpm at a specific location
P_t	Total pressure in psi at a point in a pipe
P_f	Pressure loss due to friction between points indicated in location column
P_e	Pressure due to elevation difference between indicated points. This can be a plus value or a minus value. If minus, the (–) shall be used; if plus, no sign is needed.
P_v	Velocity pressure in psi at a point in a pipe
P_n	Normal pressure in psi at a point in a pipe
E	90-degree ell
EE	45-degree ell
Lt.E	Long-turn elbow
Cr	Cross
T	Tee-flow turned 90 degrees
GV	Gate valve
BV	Butterfly (wafer) valve
Del V	Deluge valve
ALV	Alarm valve
DPV	Dry pipe valve
CV	Swing check valve
WCV	Butterfly (wafer) check valve
St	Strainer
psi	Pounds per square inch
v	Velocity of water in pipe in feet per second
K	K-factor
C-factor	Friction loss coefficient

Chapter 2 Referenced Publications

2.1 General. The documents or portions thereof listed in this chapter are referenced within this standard and shall be considered part of the requirements of this document.

Δ **2.2 NFPA Publications.** National Fire Protection Association, 1 Batterymarch Park, Quincy, MA 02169-7471.

NFPA 11, *Standard for Low-, Medium-, and High-Expansion Foam*, 2021 edition.

NFPA 14, *Standard for the Installation of Standpipe and Hose Systems*, 2019 edition.

NFPA 20, *Standard for the Installation of Stationary Pumps for Fire Protection*, 2022 edition.

NFPA 22, *Standard for Water Tanks for Private Fire Protection*, 2018 edition.

NFPA 25, *Standard for the Inspection, Testing, and Maintenance of Water-Based Fire Protection Systems*, 2020 edition.

NFPA 30, *Flammable and Combustible Liquids Code*, 2021 edition.

NFPA 30B, *Code for the Manufacture and Storage of Aerosol Products*, 2019 edition.

NFPA 32, *Standard for Drycleaning Facilities*, 2021 edition.

NFPA 33, *Standard for Spray Application Using Flammable or Combustible Materials*, 2021 edition.

NFPA 34, *Standard for Dipping, Coating, and Printing Processes Using Flammable or Combustible Liquids*, 2021 edition.

NFPA 36, *Standard for Solvent Extraction Plants*, 2021 edition.

NFPA 37, *Standard for the Installation and Use of Stationary Combustion Engines and Gas Turbines*, 2021 edition.

NFPA 40, *Standard for the Storage and Handling of Cellulose Nitrate Film*, 2019 edition.

NFPA 45, *Standard on Fire Protection for Laboratories Using Chemicals*, 2019 edition.

NFPA 51, *Standard for the Design and Installation of Oxygen–Fuel Gas Systems for Welding, Cutting, and Allied Processes*, 2018 edition.

NFPA 51B, *Standard for Fire Prevention During Welding, Cutting, and Other Hot Work*, 2019 edition.

NFPA 55, *Compressed Gases and Cryogenic Fluids Code*, 2020 edition.

NFPA 59, *Utility LP-Gas Plant Code*, 2021 edition.

NFPA 59A, *Standard for the Production, Storage, and Handling of Liquefied Natural Gas (LNG)*, 2019 edition.

NFPA 70®, *National Electrical Code®*, 2020 edition.

NFPA 72®, *National Fire Alarm and Signaling Code®*, 2022 edition.

NFPA 75, *Standard for the Fire Protection of Information Technology Equipment*, 2020 edition.

NFPA 76, *Standard for the Fire Protection of Telecommunications Facilities*, 2020 edition.

NFPA 82, *Standard on Incinerators and Waste and Linen Handling Systems and Equipment*, 2019 edition.

NFPA 86, *Standard for Ovens and Furnaces*, 2019 edition.

NFPA 91, *Standard for Exhaust Systems for Air Conveying of Vapors, Gases, Mists, and Particulate Solids*, 2020 edition.

NFPA 96, *Standard for Ventilation Control and Fire Protection of Commercial Cooking Operations*, 2021 edition.

NFPA 99, *Health Care Facilities Code*, 2021 edition.

NFPA 101®, *Life Safety Code®*, 2021 edition.

NFPA 120, *Standard for Fire Prevention and Control in Coal Mines*, 2020 edition.

NFPA 122, *Standard for Fire Prevention and Control in Metal/Nonmetal Mining and Metal Mineral Processing Facilities*, 2020 edition.

NFPA 130, *Standard for Fixed Guideway Transit and Passenger Rail Systems*, 2020 edition.

NFPA 140, *Standard on Motion Picture and Television Production Studio Soundstages, Approved Production Facilities, and Production Locations*, 2018 edition.

NFPA 150, *Fire and Life Safety in Animal Housing Facilities Code*, 2022 edition.

NFPA 170, *Standard for Fire Safety and Emergency Symbols*, 2021 edition.

NFPA 214, *Standard on Water-Cooling Towers*, 2021 edition.

NFPA 259, *Standard Test Method for Potential Heat of Building Materials*, 2018 edition.

NFPA 307, *Standard for the Construction and Fire Protection of Marine Terminals, Piers, and Wharves*, 2021 edition.

NFPA 318, *Standard for the Protection of Semiconductor Fabrication Facilities*, 2021 edition.

NFPA 400, *Hazardous Materials Code*, 2022 edition.

NFPA 409, *Standard on Aircraft Hangars*, 2016 edition.

NFPA 415, *Standard on Airport Terminal Buildings, Fueling Ramp Drainage, and Loading Walkways*, 2016 edition.

NFPA 423, *Standard for Construction and Protection of Aircraft Engine Test Facilities*, 2016 edition.

NFPA 701, *Standard Methods of Fire Tests for Flame Propagation of Textiles and Films*, 2019 edition.

NFPA 703, *Standard for Fire-Retardant-Treated Wood and Fire-Retardant Coatings for Building Materials*, 2021 edition.

NFPA 750, *Standard on Water Mist Fire Protection Systems*, 2019 edition.

NFPA 780, *Standard for the Installation of Lightning Protection Systems*, 2020 edition.

NFPA 804, *Standard for Fire Protection for Advanced Light Water Reactor Electric Generating Plants*, 2020 edition.

NFPA 805, *Performance-Based Standard for Fire Protection for Light Water Reactor Electric Generating Plants*, 2020 edition.

NFPA 909, *Code for the Protection of Cultural Resource Properties — Museums, Libraries, and Places of Worship*, 2017 edition.

NFPA 1963, *Standard for Fire Hose Connections*, 2019 edition.

2.3 Other Publications.

2.3.1 ACI Publications. American Concrete Institute, 38800 Country Club Drive, Farmington Hills, MI 48331-3439.

ACI 318, *Building Code Requirements for Structural Concrete and Commentary*, 2014, errata 1, 2017, errata 2, 2018.

ACI 355.2, *Qualification of Post-Installed Mechanical Anchors in Concrete and Commentary*, 2019.

2.3.2 ASCE Publications. American Society of Civil Engineers, 1801 Alexander Bell Drive, Reston, VA 20191-4400.

ASCE/SEI 7, *Minimum Design Loads and Associated Criteria for Buildings and Other Structures*, 2016.

Δ 2.3.3 ASME Publications. ASME International, Two Park Avenue, New York, NY 10016-5990.

Boiler and Pressure Vessel Code, Section IX, "Welding, Brazing, and Fusing Qualifications," 2019.

ASME A17.1, *Safety Code for Elevators and Escalators*, 2019/CSA B44-16.

ASME B1.20.1, *Pipe Threads, General Purpose (Inch)*, 2013.

ASME B16.1, *Gray Iron Pipe Flanges and Flanged Fittings, Classes 25, 125, and 250*, 2015.

ASME B16.3, *Malleable Iron Threaded Fittings, Classes 150 and 300*, 2016.

ASME B16.4, *Gray Iron Threaded Fittings, Classes 125 and 250*, 2016.

ASME B16.5, *Pipe Flanges and Flanged Fittings, NPS 1/2 through NPS 24 Metric/Inch Standard*, 2017.

ASME B16.9, *Factory-Made Wrought Buttwelding Fittings*, 2018.

ASME B16.11, *Forged Fittings, Socket-Welding and Threaded*, 2016, errata, 2017.

ASME B16.15, *Cast Copper Alloy Threaded Fittings, Classes 125 and 250*, 2018.

ASME B16.18, *Cast Copper Alloy Solder Joint Pressure Fittings*, 2018.

ASME B16.22, *Wrought Copper and Copper Alloy Solder Joint Pressure Fittings*, 2018.

ASME B16.25, *Buttwelding Ends*, 2017.

ASME B36.10M, *Welded and Seamless Wrought Steel Pipe*, 2018.

Δ 2.3.4 ASTM Publications. ASTM International, 100 Barr Harbor Drive, P.O. Box C700, West Conshohocken, PA 19428-2959.

ASTM A53/A53M, *Standard Specification for Pipe, Steel, Black and Hot-Dipped, Zinc-Coated, Welded and Seamless*, 2018.

ASTM A106/A106M, *Standard Specification for Seamless Carbon Steel Pipe for High Temperature Service*, 2019.

ASTM A135/A135M, *Standard Specification for Electric-Resistance-Welded Steel Pipe*, 2009, reapproved 2014.

ASTM A234/A234M, *Standard Specification for Piping Fittings of Wrought Carbon Steel and Alloy Steel for Moderate and High Temperature Service*, 2019.

ASTM A312/A312M, *Standard Specification for Seamless, Welded, and Heavily Cold Worked Austenitic Stainless Steel Pipes*, 2019.

ASTM A403/A403M, *Standard Specification for Wrought Austenitic Stainless Steel Piping Fittings*, 2020.

ASTM A795/A795M, *Standard Specification for Black and Hot-Dipped Zinc-Coated (Galvanized) Welded and Seamless Steel Pipe for Fire Protection Use*, 2020.

ASTM B32, *Standard Specification for Solder Metal*, 2008, reapproved 2014.

ASTM B43, *Standard Specification for Seamless Red Brass Pipe, Standard Sizes*, 2020.

ASTM B75/B75M, *Standard Specification for Seamless Copper Tube*, 2020.

ASTM B88, *Standard Specification for Seamless Copper Water Tube*, 2020.

ASTM B251/B251M, *Standard Specification for General Requirements for Wrought Seamless Copper and Copper-Alloy Tube*, 2017.

ASTM B446, *Standard Specification for Nickel-Chromium-Molybdenum-Columbium Alloy (UNS N06625), Nickel-Chromium-Molybdenum-Silicon Alloy (UNS N06219), and Nickel-Chromium-Molybdenum-Tungsten Alloy (UNS N06625) Rod and Bar*, 2019.

ASTM B813, *Standard Specification for Liquid and Paste Fluxes for Soldering of Copper and Copper Alloy Tube*, 2016.

ASTM B828, *Standard Practice for Making Capillary Joints by Soldering of Copper and Copper Alloy Tube and Fittings*, 2016.

ASTM C635/C635M, *Standard Specification for Manufacture, Performance, and Testing of Metal Suspension Systems for Acoustical Tile and Lay-In Panel Ceilings*, 2017.

ASTM C636/C636M, *Standard Practice for Installation of Metal Ceiling Suspension Systems for Acoustical Tile and Lay-In Panels*, 2019.

ASTM E84, *Standard Test Method for Surface Burning Characteristics of Building Materials*, 2020.

ASTM E119, *Standard Test Methods for Fire Tests of Building Construction and Materials*, 2020.

ASTM E136, *Standard Test Method for Assessing Combustibility of Materials Using a Vertical Tube Furnace at 750°C*, 2019a.

ASTM E2652, *Standard Test Method for Assessing Combustibility of Materials Using a Tube Furnace with a Cone-shaped Airflow Stabilizer, at 750°C*, 2018.

ASTM E2768, *Standard Test Method for Extended Duration Surface Burning Characteristics of Building Materials (30 min Tunnel Test),*, reapproved 2018.

ASTM E2965, *Standard Test Method for Determination of Low Levels of Heat Release Rate for Materials and Products Using an Oxygen Combustion Calorimeter*, 2017.

ASTM F437, *Standard Specification for Threaded Chlorinated Poly(Vinyl Chloride) (CPVC) Plastic Pipe Fittings, Schedule 80*, 2015.

ASTM F438, *Standard Specification for Socket-Type Chlorinated Poly(Vinyl Chloride) (CPVC) Plastic Pipe Fittings, Schedule 40*, 2017.

ASTM F439, *Standard Specification for Chlorinated Poly(Vinyl Chloride) (CPVC) Plastic Pipe Fittings, Schedule 80*, 2019.

ASTM F442/F442M, *Standard Specification for Chlorinated Poly(Vinyl Chloride) (CPVC) Plastic Pipe (SDR-PR)*, 2019.

ASTM F1121, *Standard Specification for International Shore Connections for Marine Fire Applications*, 1987, 2019.

ASTM SI 10, *IEEE/ASTM SI 10 American National Standard for Metric Practice*, 2016.

2.3.5 AWS Publications. American Welding Society, 8669 NW 36 Street, Doral, FL 33166.

AWS A5.8M/A5.8, *Specification for Filler Metals for Brazing and Braze Welding*, 2019.

AWS B2.1/B2.1M, *Specification for Welding Procedure and Performance Qualification*, 2014.

Δ **2.3.6 AWWA Publications.** American Water Works Association, 6666 West Quincy Avenue, Denver, CO 80235.

AWWA C104/A21.4, *Cement-Mortar Lining for Ductile-Iron Pipe and Fittings*, 2016.

AWWA C105/A21.5, *Polyethylene Encasement for Ductile-Iron Pipe Systems,*2018.

AWWA C110/A21.10, *Ductile-Iron and Gray-Iron Fittings*, 2012.

AWWA C111/A21.11, *Rubber-Gasket Joints for Ductile-Iron Pressure Pipe and Fittings*, 2017.

AWWA C115/A21.15, *Flanged Ductile-Iron Pipe with Ductile-Iron or Gray-Iron Threaded Flanges*, 2011.

AWWA C150/A21.50, *Thickness Design of Ductile-Iron Pipe*, 2014.

AWWA C151/A21.51, *Ductile-Iron Pipe, Centrifugally Cast*, 2017, errata, 2018.

AWWA C153/A21.53, *Ductile-Iron Compact Fittings*, 2019.

AWWA C300, *Reinforced Concrete Pressure Pipe, Steel-Cylinder Type*, 2016.

AWWA C301, *Prestressed Concrete Pressure Pipe, Steel-Cylinder Type*, 2014, Reaffirmed without Revision 2019.

AWWA C302, *Reinforced Concrete Pressure Pipe, Non-Cylinder Type*, 2016.

AWWA C303, *Reinforced Concrete Pressure Pipe, Bar-Wrapped, Steel-Cylinder Type, Pretensioned*, 2017.

AWWA C600, *Installation of Ductile Iron Water Mains and Their Appurtenances*, 2017.

AWWA C602, *Cement-Mortar Lining of Water Pipe Lines in Place, 4 in. (100 mm) and Larger*, 2017.

AWWA C900, *Polyvinyl Chloride (PVC) Pressure Pipe and Fabricated Fittings, 4 in. Through 60 in. (100 mm Through 1,500 mm)*, 2016.

AWWA C906, *Polyethylene (PE) Pressure Pipe and Fittings, 4 in. (100 mm) Through 63 in. (1,650 mm), for Waterworks*, 2015.

AWWA C909, *Molecularly Oriented Polyvinyl Chloride (PVCO) Pressure Pipe, 4 in. (100 mm) and Larger,*, 2016.

AWWA M9, *Concrete Pressure Pipe*, 2008, errata, 2013.

AWWA M23, *PVC Pipe — Design and Installation*, 2002.

AWWA M55, *PE Pipe — Design and Installation*, 2006.

2.3.7 ICC-ES Publications. ICC Evaluation Service, 900 Montclair Road, Suite A, Birmingham, AL 35213.

ICC-ES AC446, *Acceptance Criteria for Headed Cast-in Specialty Inserts in Concrete*, 2018.

2.3.8 IEEE Publications. IEEE, Three Park Avenue, 17th Floor, New York, NY 10016-5997.

IEEE 45, *Recommended Practice for Electric Installations on Shipboard*, 2002.

Δ **2.3.9 UL Publications.** Underwriters Laboratories Inc., 333 Pfingsten Road, Northbrook, IL 60062-2096.

UL 263, *Standard for Fire Tests of Building Construction and Materials*, 2011, revised 2018.

UL 723, *Standard for Test for Surface Burning Characteristics of Building Materials*, 2018.

UL 2556, *Wire and Cable Test Methods*, 2015.

2.3.10 U.S. Government Publications. U.S. Government Publishing Office, 732 North Capitol Street, NW, Washington, DC 20401-0001.

Title 46, CFR, Parts 54.15-10 Safety and Relief Valves, 56.20 Valves, 56.20-5(a) Markings, 56.50-95 Overboard Discharges and Shore Connections, 56.60 Materials, and 58.01-40 Machinery, Angle of Inclination.

Title 46, CFR, Subchapter F, "Marine Engineering."

Title 46, CFR, Subchapter J, "Electrical Engineering."

2.3.11 Other Publications.

Merriam-Webster's Collegiate Dictionary, 11th edition, Merriam-Webster, Inc., Springfield, MA, 2003.

Δ **2.4 References for Extracts in Mandatory Sections.**

NFPA 1, *Fire Code*, 2021 edition.
NFPA 20, *Standard for the Installation of Stationary Pumps for Fire Protection*, 2022 edition.
NFPA 24, *Standard for the Installation of Private Fire Service Mains and Their Appurtenances*, 2022 edition.

NFPA 25, *Standard for the Inspection, Testing, and Maintenance of Water-Based Fire Protection Systems*, 2020 edition.

NFPA 5000®, *Building Construction and Safety Code®*, 2021 edition.

Chapter 3   Definitions

3.1 General. The definitions contained in this chapter shall apply to the terms used in this standard. Where terms are not defined in this chapter or within another chapter, they shall be defined using their ordinarily accepted meanings within the context in which they are used. *Merriam-Webster's Collegiate Dictionary*, 11th edition, shall be the source for the ordinarily accepted meaning.

3.2 NFPA Official Definitions.

3.2.1* Approved. Acceptable to the authority having jurisdiction.

3.2.2* Authority Having Jurisdiction (AHJ). An organization, office, or individual responsible for enforcing the requirements of a code or standard, or for approving equipment, materials, an installation, or a procedure.

3.2.3* Listed. Equipment, materials, or services included in a list published by an organization that is acceptable to the authority having jurisdiction and concerned with evaluation of products or services, that maintains periodic inspection of production of listed equipment or materials or periodic evaluation of services, and whose listing states that either the equipment, material, or service meets appropriate designated standards or has been tested and found suitable for a specified purpose.

3.2.4 Shall. Indicates a mandatory requirement.

3.2.5 Should. Indicates a recommendation or that which is advised but not required.

3.2.6 Standard. An NFPA Standard, the main text of which contains only mandatory provisions using the word "shall" to indicate requirements and that is in a form generally suitable for mandatory reference by another standard or code or for adoption into law. Nonmandatory provisions are not to be considered a part of the requirements of a standard and shall be located in an appendix, annex, footnote, informational note, or other means as permitted in the NFPA Manuals of Style. When used in a generic sense, such as in the phrase "standards development process" or "standards development activities," the term "standards" includes all NFPA Standards, including Codes, Standards, Recommended Practices, and Guides.

3.3 General Definitions.

3.3.1 A-Class Boundary. See 3.3.125.1.

3.3.2 Air Receiver. A chamber, compatible with an air compressor, that can store air under pressure that is higher in pressure than that in the dry pipe or preaction system piping. (AUT-SSI)

3.3.3 Air Reservoir. A chamber that can store air at the same pressure that is in the wet pipe system piping. (AUT-SSI)

3.3.4* Aisle Width. The horizontal dimension between the face of the loads in racks under consideration. (AUT-SSD)

3.3.5 Antifreeze Sprinkler System. See 3.3.216.1.

3.3.6 Appurtenance. An accessory or attachment that enables the private fire service main to perform its intended function. [24, 2022] (AUT-PRI)

3.3.7 Arm-Over. A horizontal pipe that extends from the branch line to a single sprinkler or a sprinkler above and below a ceiling. (AUT-SSI)

3.3.8 Array.

3.3.8.1 *Closed Array (Palletized, Solid-Piled, Bin Box, and Shelf Storage).* A storage arrangement where air movement through the pile is restricted because of 6 in. (150 mm) or less vertical flues. (AUT-SSD)

3.3.8.2 *Closed Array (Rolled Paper).* A vertical storage arrangement in which the distances between columns in both directions are short [not more than 2 in. (50 mm) in one direction and 1 in. (25 mm) in the other]. (AUT-SSD)

3.3.8.3* *Open Array (Palletized, Solid-Piled, Bin Box, and Shelf Storage).* A storage arrangement where air movement through the pile is enhanced because of vertical flues larger than 6 in. (150 mm). (AUT-SSD)

3.3.8.4 *Open Array (Rolled Paper).* A vertical storage arrangement in which the distance between columns in both directions is lengthy (all vertical arrays other than closed or standard). (AUT-SSD)

3.3.8.5* *Standard Array (Rolled Paper).* A vertical storage arrangement in which the distance between columns in one direction is short [1 in. (25 mm) or less] and is in excess of 2 in. (50 mm) in the other direction. (AUT-SSD)

3.3.9 Automated Inspection and Testing. The performance of inspections and tests at a distant location from the system or component being inspected or tested through the use of electronic devices or equipment installed for the purpose. (AUT-SSI)

3.3.10 Automatic Sprinkler. See 3.3.215.1.

3.3.11 Automotive Components on Portable Racks. All automotive components with or without expanded Group A plastic dunnage; excludes the storage of air bags, tires, and seats on portable racks. (AUT-SSD)

N **3.3.12 Average Roof Height.** See 3.3.21, Building Height. (AUT-HBS)

3.3.13* Back-to-Back Shelf Storage. Two solid or perforated shelves up to 30 in. (750 mm) in depth each, not exceeding a total depth of 60 in. (1.5 m), separated by a longitudinal vertical barrier such as plywood, particleboard, sheet metal, or equivalent, with a maximum 0.25 in. (6 mm) diameter penetrations and no longitudinal flue space and a maximum storage height of 15 ft (4.6 m). (AUT-SSD)

Δ **3.3.14* Baled Cotton.** A natural seed fiber wrapped and secured in industry-accepted materials, usually consisting of burlap, woven polypropylene, or sheet polyethylene, and secured with steel, synthetic or wire bands, or wire; also includes linters and motes. (AUT-SSD)

3.3.15 Banded Roll Paper Storage. See 3.3.188.1.

3.3.16 Banded Tires. A storage method in which a number of tires are strapped together. (AUT-SSD)

3.3.17* Bathroom. Within a dwelling unit, any room or compartment dedicated to personal hygiene, containing a toilet, sink, or bathing capability such as a shower or tub. (AUT-SSI)

3.3.18 B-Class Boundary. See 3.3.125.2.

3.3.19 Bin Box Storage. Storage in five-sided wood, metal, or cardboard boxes with open face on the aisles in which boxes are self-supporting or supported by a structure so designed that little or no horizontal or vertical space exists around boxes. (AUT-SSD)

3.3.20 Branch Lines. The pipes supplying sprinklers, either directly or through sprigs, drops, return bends, or arm-overs. (AUT-SSI)

N **3.3.21 Building Height.** For the purposes of seismic protection, the vertical distance from the grade plane to the average elevation of the highest roof surface. (AUT-HBS)

3.3.22 Bulkhead. A vertical barrier across the rack. (AUT-SSI)

3.3.23* Carton Records Storage. A Class III commodity consisting predominantly of paper records in cardboard cartons. (AUT-SSD)

3.3.24 Cartoned. A method of storage consisting of corrugated cardboard or paperboard containers fully enclosing the commodity. (AUT-SSD)

3.3.25 Catwalk. For the purposes of carton records storage, a storage aid consisting of either open metal grating or solid horizontal barriers supported from a rack storage system that is utilized as a walkway for access to storage at elevated levels. Catwalks are accessed using stairs and are not separate floors of a building. (AUT-SSD)

3.3.26 Ceiling Height. The distance between the floor and the underside of the ceiling above (or roof deck) within the area. (AUT-SSD)

3.3.27* Ceiling Pocket. An architectural ceiling feature that consists of a bounded area of ceiling located at a higher elevation than the attached lower ceiling. (AUT-SSI)

3.3.28 Ceiling Types.

3.3.28.1 *Flat Ceiling.* A continuous ceiling in a single plane. (AUT-SSI)

3.3.28.2 *Horizontal Ceiling.* A ceiling with a slope not exceeding 2 in 12 (16.7 percent). (AUT-SSI)

3.3.28.3 *Sloped Ceiling.* A ceiling with a slope exceeding 2 in 12 (16.7 percent). (AUT-SSI)

Δ **3.3.28.4** *Smooth Ceiling.* A continuous ceiling free from irregularities, lumps, or indentations greater than 4 in. (100 mm) in depth. (AUT-SSI)

3.3.29 Central Safety Station. See 3.3.125.3.

N **3.3.30 Check Valve.** See 3.3.235.1.

3.3.31 Clearance to Ceiling. The distance from the top of storage to the ceiling above. (AUT-SSD)

3.3.32 Closed Array (Palletized, Solid-Piled, Bin Box, and Shelf Storage). See 3.3.8.1.

3.3.33 Closed Array (Rolled Paper). See 3.3.8.2.

3.3.34 Cloud Ceiling. Any ceiling system, not including sloped ceilings, installed in the same plane with horizontal openings to the structure above on two or more sides. (AUT-SSI)

3.3.35 Column (Rolled Paper). A single vertical stack of rolls. (AUT-SSD)

3.3.36 Combined Dry Pipe Preaction Sprinkler System. See 3.3.216.2.

3.3.37 Commodity. The combination of products, packing material, and container that determines commodity classification. (AUT-SSD)

3.3.38 Compact Storage. Storage on solid shelves not exceeding 36 in. (900 mm) in total depth, arranged as part of a compact storage module, with no more than 30 in. (750 mm) between shelves vertically and with no internal vertical flue spaces other than those between individual shelving sections. (AUT-SSD)

3.3.39 Compact Storage Module. A type of shelving unit consisting of compact storage whereby the units move to allow for storage to be pushed together creating a storage unit with no flues or minimal spaces between units. Aisles are created by moving the shelving unit. Compact storage modules can be manual or electric in operation. (AUT-SSD)

3.3.40 Compartment. A space completely enclosed by walls and a ceiling. Each wall in the compartment is permitted to have openings to an adjoining space if the openings have a minimum lintel depth of 8 in. (200 mm) from the ceiling and the total width of the openings in each wall does not exceed 8 ft (2.4 m). A single opening of 36 in. (900 mm) or less in width without a lintel is permitted where there are no other openings to adjoining spaces. (AUT-SSI)

3.3.41* Compartmented. The rigid separation of the products in a container by dividers that form a stable unit under fire conditions. (AUT-SSD)

3.3.42 Concealed Sprinkler. See 3.3.215.3.1.

3.3.43 Construction Definitions.

3.3.43.1* *Obstructed Construction.* Panel construction and other construction where beams, trusses, or other members impede heat flow or water distribution in a manner that materially affects the ability of sprinklers to control or suppress a fire. (AUT-SSI)

3.3.43.2* *Unobstructed Construction.* Construction where beams, trusses, or other members do not impede heat flow or water distribution in a manner that materially affects the ability of sprinklers to control or suppress a fire. Unobstructed construction has horizontal structural members that are not solid, where the openings are at least 70 percent of the cross-section area and the depth of the member does not exceed the least dimension of the openings, or all construction types, with the exception of panel construction, where the spacing of structural members exceeds 7½ ft (2.3 m) on center. (AUT-SSI)

3.3.44* Container (Shipping, Master, or Outer Container). A receptacle strong enough, by reason of material, design, and construction, to be shipped safely without further packaging. (AUT-SSD)

3.3.45 Continuous Obstruction. See 3.3.140.1.

3.3.46 Control Mode Density/Area (CMDA) Sprinkler. See 3.3.215.4.1.

3.3.47 Control Mode Specific Application (CMSA) Sprinkler. See 3.3.215.4.2.

N **3.3.48 Control Valve.** See 3.3.235.2.

3.3.49 Conventional Pallet. See 3.3.154.1.

3.3.50 Core (Rolled Paper). The central tube around which paper is wound to form a roll. (AUT-SSD)

3.3.51 Corrosion-Resistant Piping. Piping that has the property of being able to withstand deterioration of its surface or its properties when exposed to its environment. [24, 2022] (AUT-PRI)

3.3.52 Corrosion-Resistant Sprinkler. See 3.3.215.4.3.

3.3.53 Corrosion-Retarding Material. A lining or coating material that when applied to piping or appurtenances has the property of reducing or slowing the deterioration of the object's surface or properties when exposed to its environment. [24, 2022] (AUT-PRI)

3.3.54 Cross Mains. The pipes supplying the branch lines, either directly or through riser nipples. (AUT-SSI)

3.3.55 Deluge Sprinkler System. See 3.3.216.3.

N **3.3.56 Differential Dry Pipe Valve.** See 3.3.235.4.1.

Δ **3.3.57 Distance Monitoring.** The monitoring of various conditions of a system or component from a distant location from the system or component through the use of electronic devices, meters, or equipment installed for the purpose. (AUT-SSI)

3.3.58 Double-Row Racks. Racks less than or equal to 12 ft (3.7 m) in depth or single-row racks placed back to back having an aggregate depth up to 12 ft (3.7 m), with aisles having an aisle width of at least 3.5 ft (1.1 m) between loads on racks. (AUT-SSD)

3.3.59* Draft Curtain. A fixed or deployable barrier that protrudes downward from the ceiling to channel, contain, or prevent the migration of smoke and/or heat. (AUT-SSD)

N **3.3.60 Drop.** A vertical pipe supplying one sprinkler from above. (AUT-SSI)

3.3.61 Drop-Out Ceiling. A suspended ceiling system, which is installed below the sprinklers, with listed translucent or opaque panels that are heat sensitive and fall from their setting when exposed to heat. (AUT-SSI)

3.3.62 Dry Barrel Hydrant (Frostproof Hydrant). See 3.3.107.1.

3.3.63 Dry Pipe Sprinkler System. See 3.3.216.4.

3.3.64 Dry Sprinkler. See 3.3.215.4.4.

3.3.65 Dwelling Unit (for sprinkler system installations). One or more rooms arranged for the use of one or more individuals living together, as in a single housekeeping unit normally having cooking, living, sanitary, and sleeping facilities that include, but are not limited to, hotel rooms, dormitory rooms, apartments, condominiums, sleeping rooms in nursing homes, and similar living units. (AUT-SSI)

3.3.66 Early Suppression Fast-Response (ESFR) Sprinkler. See 3.3.215.4.5.

N **3.3.67 Electrically Operated Sprinkler.** See 3.3.215.4.6.

3.3.68* Encapsulation. A method of packaging that either consists of a plastic sheet completely enclosing the sides and top of a pallet load containing a combustible commodity, a combustible package, or a group of combustible commodities or combustible packages, or consists of combustible commodities individually wrapped in plastic sheeting and stored exposed in a pallet load. (AUT-SSD)

3.3.69 Expanded (Foamed or Cellular) Plastics. Those plastics, the density of which is reduced by the presence of numerous small cavities (cells), interconnecting or not, dispersed throughout their mass. (AUT-SSD)

3.3.70 Exposed Group A Plastic Commodities. Those plastics not in packaging or coverings that absorb water or otherwise appreciably retard the burning hazard of the commodity. (Paper wrapped or encapsulated, or both, should be considered exposed.) (AUT-SSD)

3.3.71 Extended Coverage Sprinkler. See 3.3.215.4.7.

3.3.72 Extension Fitting. A male by female adapter intended to be used with a sprinkler to adjust the final fit where the sprinkler is installed in a finished ceiling or wall. (AUT-SSI)

N **3.3.73 Exterior Projection.** An extension beyond an exterior wall capable of collecting heat below. (AUT-SSI)

3.3.74 Extra Hazard (Group 1) (EH1). See 3.3.141.1.

3.3.75 Extra Hazard (Group 2) (EH2). See 3.3.141.2.

3.3.76* Face Sprinklers. Standard sprinklers that are located in transverse flue spaces along the aisle or in the rack, are within 18 in. (450 mm) of the aisle face of storage, and are used to oppose vertical development of fire on the external face of storage. (AUT-SSD)

3.3.77 Feed Mains. The pipes supplying cross mains, either directly or through risers. (AUT-SSI)

3.3.78 Fire Control. Limiting the size of a fire by distribution of water so as to decrease the heat release rate and pre-wet adjacent combustibles, while controlling ceiling gas temperatures to avoid structural damage. (AUT-SSD)

3.3.79 Fire Department Connection. A connection through which the fire department can pump supplemental water into the sprinkler system, standpipe, or other water-based fire protection systems, furnishing water for fire extinguishment to supplement existing water supplies. [24, 2022] (AUT-PRI)

3.3.80 Fire Pump. A pump that is a provider of liquid flow and pressure dedicated to fire protection. [20, 2022] (AUT-SSI)

3.3.81 Fire Suppression. Sharply reducing the heat release rate of a fire and preventing its regrowth by means of direct and sufficient application of water through the fire plume to the burning fuel surface. (AUT-SSD)

3.3.82 Flat Ceiling. See 3.3.28.1.

3.3.83 Flexible Coupling. A listed coupling or fitting that allows axial displacement, rotation, and at least 1 degree of angular movement of the pipe without inducing harm on the pipe. For pipe diameters of 8 in. (200 mm) and larger, the angular movement is permitted to be less than 1 degree but not less than 0.5 degree. (AUT-SSI)

3.3.84 Flow Hydrant. See 3.3.107.2.

3.3.85 Flow Test. A test performed by the flow and measurement of water from one hydrant and the static and residual pressures from an adjacent hydrant for the purpose of determining the available water supply at that location. [24, 2022] (AUT-PRI)

3.3.86 Flush Sprinkler. See 3.3.215.3.2.

3.3.87 Flushing Test. A test of a piping system using flowrates intended to remove debris from the piping system prior to it being placed in service. [24, 2022] (AUT-SSI)

3.3.88* Four-Way Bracing. Adjacent sway braces or a sway brace assembly intended to resist differential movement of the system piping in all horizontal directions. (AUT-HBS)

3.3.89* Free-Flowing Plastic Materials. Those plastics that fall out of their containers during a fire, fill flue spaces, and create a smothering effect on the fire. (AUT-SSD)

3.3.90 Fuel-Fired Heating Unit. An appliance that produces heat by burning fuel. (AUT-SSI)

3.3.91 General Sprinkler Characteristics. See 3.3.215.2.

N **3.3.92 Grade Plane.** A reference plane upon which vertical measurements of a building are based representing the average of the finished ground level adjoining the building at all exterior walls. *[See also 3.3.222, Finished Ground Level (Grade), of NFPA 5000.]* [5000, 2021] (AUT-HBS)

3.3.93 Gridded Sprinkler System. See 3.3.216.5.

3.3.94 Hanger. A device or assembly used to support the gravity load of the system piping. (AUT-HBS)

3.3.95 Heat-Sensitive Material. See 3.3.125.4.

3.3.96 Heel. See 3.3.125.5.

3.3.97 Heel Angle. See 3.3.125.6.

3.3.98 High Volume Low Speed Fan. A ceiling fan that is approximately 6 ft (1.8 m) to 24 ft (7.3 m) in diameter with a rotational speed of approximately 30 to 70 revolutions per minute. (AUT-SSD)

3.3.99 High-Challenge Fire Hazard. A fire hazard typical of that produced by fires in combustible high-piled storage. (AUT-SSD)

3.3.100* High-Piled Storage. Solid-piled, palletized, rack storage, bin box, and shelf storage of Class I through Class IV commodities more than 12 ft (3.7 m) in height and solid-piled, palletized, rack storage, bin box, and shelf storage of Group A plastic commodities more than 5 ft (1.5 m) in height. (AUT-SSD)

3.3.101 Horizontal Barrier. A solid barrier in the horizontal position covering the rack at certain height increments to prevent vertical fire spread. (AUT-SSD)

3.3.102 Horizontal Ceiling. See 3.3.28.2.

3.3.103 Horizontal Channel. Any uninterrupted space in excess of 5 ft (1.5 m) in length between horizontal layers of stored tires. Such channels can be formed by pallets, shelving, racks, or other storage arrangements. (AUT-SSD)

3.3.104 Horizontal Force, F_{pw}. The horizontal force due to seismic load acting on a brace at working stress levels. (AUT-HBS)

3.3.105 Horizontal Roll Paper Storage. See 3.3.188.2.

3.3.106 Hose House. An enclosure located over or adjacent to a hydrant or other water supply designed to contain the necessary hose nozzles, hose wrenches, gaskets, and spanners to be used in fire fighting in conjunction with and to provide aid to the local fire department. [24, 2022] (AUT-PRI)

3.3.107 Hydrant. An exterior valved connection to a water supply system that provides hose connections. [24, 2022] (AUT-PRI)

3.3.107.1 *Dry Barrel Hydrant (Frostproof Hydrant).* A type of hydrant with the main control valve below the frost line between the footpiece and the barrel. [24, 2022] (AUT-PRI)

3.3.107.2 *Flow Hydrant.* The hydrant that is used for the flow and flow measurement of water during a flow test. [24, 2022] (AUT-PRI)

3.3.107.3 *Private Fire Hydrant.* A valved connection on a water supply system having one or more outlets and that is used to supply hose and fire department pumpers with water on private property. [24, 2022] (AUT-PRI)

3.3.107.4 *Public Hydrant.* A valved connection on a water supply system having one or more outlets and that is used to supply hose and fire department pumpers with water. [24, 2022] (AUT-PRI)

3.3.107.5 *Residual Hydrant.* The hydrant that is used for measuring static and residual pressures during a flow test. [24, 2022] (AUT-PRI)

3.3.107.6 *Wet Barrel Hydrant.* A type of hydrant that is intended for use where there is no danger of freezing weather, where each outlet is provided with a valve and an outlet. [24, 2022] (AUT-PRI)

3.3.108 Hydrant Butt. The hose connection outlet of a hydrant. [24, 2022] (AUT-PRI)

3.3.109 Hydraulically Calculated Water Demand Flow Rate. The waterflow rate for a system or hose stream that has been calculated using accepted engineering practices. [24, 2022] (AUT-PRI)

3.3.110 Hydraulically Designed System. A calculated sprinkler system in which pipe sizes are selected on a pressure loss basis to provide a prescribed water density, in gallons per minute per square foot (mm/min), or a prescribed minimum discharge pressure or flow per sprinkler, distributed with a reasonable degree of uniformity over a specified area. (AUT-SSD)

3.3.111 Hydrostatic Test. A test of a closed piping system and its attached appurtenances consisting of subjecting the piping to an increased internal pressure for a specified period of duration to verify system integrity and leak rates. [24, 2022] (AUT-PRI)

N **3.3.112 Indicating Valve.** See 3.3.235.3.

3.3.113 Installation Orientation. See 3.3.215.3.

3.3.114 Institutional Sprinkler. See 3.3.215.4.8.

3.3.115 Intermediate-Level Sprinkler/Rack Storage Sprinkler. See 3.3.215.4.9.

3.3.116 International Shore Connection. See 3.3.125.7.

3.3.117 Laced Tire Storage. Tires stored where the sides of the tires overlap, creating a woven or laced appearance. *[See Figure A.3.3.191(g).]* (AUT-SSD)

3.3.118 Lateral Brace. A sway brace intended to resist differential movement perpendicular to the axis of the system piping. (AUT-HBS)

3.3.119 Light Hazard. See 3.3.141.3.

Δ **3.3.120* Limited-Combustible Material.** See Section 4.9.

3.3.121 Longitudinal Brace. A sway brace intended to resist differential movement parallel to the axis of the system piping. (AUT-HBS)

3.3.122* Longitudinal Flue Space. The space between rows of storage perpendicular to the direction of loading with a width not exceeding 24 in. (600 mm) between storage. (AUT-SSD)

3.3.123 Looped Sprinkler System. See 3.3.216.6.

3.3.124* Low-Piled Storage. Solid-piled, palletized, rack storage, bin box, and shelf storage of Class I through Class IV commodities up to 12 ft (3.7 m) in height and solid-piled, palletized, rack storage, bin box, and shelf storage of Group A plastic commodities up to 5 ft (1.5 m) in height. (AUT-SSD)

3.3.125 Marine Definitions. These definitions apply to Chapter 31 only. (AUT-SSI)

3.3.125.1 *A-Class Boundary.* A boundary designed to resist the passage of smoke and flame for 1 hour when tested in accordance with ASTM E119, *Standard Test Methods for Fire Tests of Building Construction and Materials,* or UL 263, *Standard for Fire Tests of Building Construction and Materials.* (AUT-SSI)

3.3.125.2 *B-Class Boundary.* A boundary designed to resist the passage of flame for ½ hour when tested in accordance with ASTM E119, *Standard Test Methods for Fire Tests of Building Construction and Materials,* or UL 263, *Standard for Fire Tests of Building Construction and Materials.* (AUT-SSI)

3.3.125.3 *Central Safety Station.* A continuously manned control station from which all of the fire control equipment is monitored. If this station is not the bridge, direct communication with the bridge must be provided by means other than the ship's service telephone. (AUT-SSI)

3.3.125.4* *Heat-Sensitive Material.* A material whose melting point is below 1700°F (927°C). (AUT-SSI)

3.3.125.5 *Heel.* The inclination of a ship to one side. (AUT-SSI)

3.3.125.6 *Heel Angle.* The angle defined by the intersection of a vertical line through the center of a vessel and a line perpendicular to the surface of the water. (AUT-SSI)

3.3.125.7* *International Shore Connection.* A universal connection to the vessel's fire main to which a shoreside fire-fighting water supply can be connected. (AUT-SSI)

3.3.125.8* *Marine System.* A sprinkler system installed on a ship, boat, or other floating structure that takes its supply from the water on which the vessel floats. (AUT-SSI)

3.3.125.9* *Marine Thermal Barrier.* An assembly that is constructed of noncombustible materials and made intact with the main structure of the vessel, such as shell, structural bulkheads, and decks; meets the requirements of a B-Class boundary; and is insulated such that, if tested in accordance with ASTM E119, *Standard Test Methods for Fire Tests of Building Construction and Materials,* or UL 263, *Standard for Fire Tests of Building Construction and Materials,* for 15 minutes, the average temperature of the unexposed side does not rise more than 250°F (139°C) above the original temperature, nor does the temperature at any one point, including any joint, rise more than 405°F (225°C) above the original temperature. (AUT-SSI)

3.3.125.10 *Marine Water Supply.* The supply portion of the sprinkler system from the water pressure tank or the sea suction of the designated sprinkler system pump up to and including the valve that isolates the sprinkler system from these two water sources. (AUT-SSI)

3.3.125.11 *Supervision.* A visual and audible alarm signal given at the central safety station to indicate when the system is in operation or when a condition that would impair the satisfactory operation of the system exists. Supervisory alarms must give a distinct indication for each individual system component that is monitored. (AUT-SSI)

3.3.125.12 *Survival Angle.* The maximum angle to which a vessel is permitted to heel after the assumed damage required by stability regulations is imposed. (AUT-SSI)

3.3.125.13 *Type 1 Stair.* A fully enclosed stair that serves all levels of a vessel in which persons can be employed. (AUT-SSI)

3.3.126 Marine System. See 3.3.125.8.

3.3.127 Marine Thermal Barrier. See 3.3.125.9.

3.3.128 Marine Water Supply. See 3.3.125.10.

N **3.3.129 Mechanical Dry Pipe Valve.** See 3.3.235.4.2.

3.3.130* Miscellaneous Storage. Storage that does not exceed 12 ft (3.7 m) in height, is incidental to another occupancy use group, does not constitute more than 10 percent of the building area or 4000 ft² (370 m²) of the sprinklered area, whichever is greater, does not exceed 1000 ft² (93 m²) in one pile or area, and is separated from other storage areas by at least 25 ft (7.6 m). (AUT-SSD)

3.3.131* Miscellaneous Tire Storage. The storage of rubber tires that is incidental to the main use of the building; storage areas do not exceed 2000 ft² (185 m²), and on-tread storage piles, regardless of storage method, do not exceed 25 ft (7.6 m) in the direction of the wheel holes. Acceptable storage arrangements include (a) on-floor, on-side storage up to 12 ft (3.7 m) high; (b) on-floor, on-tread storage up to 5 ft (1.5 m) high; (c) double-row or multirow fixed or portable rack storage on-side or on-tread up to 5 ft (1.5 m) high; (d) single-row fixed or portable rack storage on-side or on-tread up to 12 ft (3.7 m) high; and (e) laced tires in racks up to 5 ft (1.5 m) in height. (AUT-SSD)

3.3.132 Movable Racks. Racks on fixed rails or guides that can be moved back and forth only in a horizontal, two-dimensional plane. A moving aisle is created as abutting racks are either loaded or unloaded, then moved across the aisle to abut other racks. (AUT-SSD)

3.3.133 Multicycle System. See 3.3.216.7.

3.3.134 Multiple-Row Racks. Racks greater than 12 ft (3.7 m) in depth or single- or double-row racks separated by aisles less than 3.5 ft (1.1 m) wide having an overall width greater than 12 ft (3.7 m). (AUT-SSD)

3.3.135 Net Vertical Force. The vertical reaction due to the angle of installation of sway braces on system piping resulting from earthquake motion. (AUT-HBS)

3.3.136 Noncombustible Material. See Section 4.9.

3.3.137 Noncontinuous Obstruction. See 3.3.140.2.

3.3.138 Nozzle. See 3.3.215.4.10.

3.3.139 Obstructed Construction. See 3.3.43.1.

3.3.140 Obstruction.

3.3.140.1 *Continuous Obstruction.* An obstruction located at or below the level of sprinkler deflectors that affect the discharge pattern of two or more adjacent sprinklers. (AUT-SSI)

3.3.140.2 *Noncontinuous Obstruction.* An obstruction at or below the level of the sprinkler deflector that affects the discharge pattern of a single sprinkler. (AUT-SSI)

3.3.141 Occupancies.

3.3.141.1 *Extra Hazard (Group 1) (EH1).* Occupancies or portions of other occupancies where the quantity and combustibility of contents are very high or dust, lint, or other materials are present, introducing the probability of rapidly developing fires with high rates of heat release but with little or no combustible or flammable liquids. (AUT-SSD)

3.3.141.2 *Extra Hazard (Group 2) (EH2).* Occupancies or portions of other occupancies with moderate to substantial amounts of flammable or combustible liquids or occupancies where shielding of combustibles is extensive. (AUT-SSD)

Δ   **3.3.141.3** *Light Hazard.* Occupancies or portions of other occupancies where the quantity and/or combustibility of contents is low and fires with relatively low rates of heat release are expected. (AUT-SSD)

3.3.141.4 *Ordinary Hazard (Group 1) (OH1).* Occupancies or portions of other occupancies where combustibility is low, quantity of combustibles is moderate, stockpiles of contents do not exceed 8 ft (2.4 m), and fires with moderate rates of heat release are expected. (AUT-SSD)

3.3.141.5 *Ordinary Hazard (Group 2) (OH2).* Occupancies or portions of other occupancies where the quantity and combustibility of contents are moderate to high, stockpiles of contents with moderate rates of heat release do not exceed 12 ft (3.7 m), and stockpiles of contents with high rates of heat release do not exceed 8 ft (2.4 m). (AUT-SSD)

3.3.142 Old-Style/Conventional Sprinkler. See 3.3.215.4.11.

3.3.143 On-Side Tire Storage. Tires stored horizontally or flat. (AUT-SSD)

3.3.144 On-Tread Tire Storage. Tires stored vertically or on their treads. (AUT-SSD)

3.3.145 Open Array (Palletized, Solid-Piled, Bin Box, and Shelf Storage). See 3.3.8.3.

3.3.146 Open Array (Rolled Paper). See 3.3.8.4.

3.3.147 Open Rack. Racks without shelving or with shelving in racks that are fixed in place with shelves having a solid surface and a shelf area equal to or less than 20 ft² (1.9 m²) or with shelves having a wire mesh, slatted surface, or other material with openings representing at least 50 percent of the shelf area including the horizontal area of rack members and where the flue spaces are maintained. (AUT-SSD)

3.3.148 Open Sprinkler. See 3.3.215.4.12.

3.3.149* Open-Top Container. A container of any shape that is entirely or partially open on the top and arranged so as to allow for the collection of discharging sprinkler water cascading through the storage array. (AUT-SSD)

3.3.150 Ordinary Hazard (Group 1) (OH1). See 3.3.141.4.

3.3.151 Ordinary Hazard (Group 2) (OH2). See 3.3.141.5.

3.3.152 Ornamental/Decorative Sprinkler. See 3.3.215.4.13.

3.3.153 Packaging. A commodity wrapping, cushioning, or container. (AUT-SSD)

3.3.154 Pallet.

3.3.154.1* Conventional Pallet. A material-handling aid designed to support a unit load with openings to provide access for material-handling devices. *(See Figure A.3.3.154.1.)* (AUT-SSD)

3.3.154.2 *Plastic Pallet.* A pallet having any portion of its construction consisting of a plastic material. (AUT-SSD)

3.3.154.3* Reinforced Plastic Pallet. A plastic pallet incorporating a secondary reinforcing material (such as steel or fiberglass) within the pallet. (AUT-SSD)

3.3.154.4 *Slave Pallet.* A special pallet captive to a material-handling system. *(See Figure A.3.3.154.1.)* (AUT-SSD)

3.3.154.5 *Wood Pallet.* A pallet constructed entirely of wood with metal fasteners. (AUT-SSD)

3.3.155 Palletized Storage. Storage of commodities on pallets or other storage aids that form horizontal spaces between tiers of storage. (AUT-SSD)

3.3.156 Palletized Tire Storage. Storage on portable racks of various types utilizing a conventional pallet as a base. (AUT-SSD)

3.3.157 Paper (General Term). The term for all kinds of felted sheets made from natural fibrous materials, usually vegetable but sometimes mineral or animal, and formed on a fine wire screen from water suspension. (AUT-SSD)

3.3.158 Pendent Sprinkler. See 3.3.215.3.3.

3.3.159* Pile Stability, Stable Piles. Those arrays where collapse, spillage of content, or leaning of stacks across flue spaces is not likely to occur soon after initial fire development. (AUT-SSD)

3.3.160* Pile Stability, Unstable Piles. Those arrays where collapse, spillage of contents, or leaning of stacks across flue spaces occurs soon after initial fire development. (AUT-SSD)

3.3.161 Pilot Line Detector. See 3.3.215.4.14.

3.3.162 Pipe Schedule System. See 3.3.216.8.

3.3.163 Plastic Pallet. See 3.3.154.2.

3.3.164 Portable Racks. Racks that are not fixed in place and can be arranged in any number of configurations. (AUT-SSD)

3.3.165* Post-Installed Anchors. A device used for fastening pipe to the building structure, installed in hardened concrete. (AUT-HBS)

3.3.166 Preaction Sprinkler System. See 3.3.216.9.

3.3.167 Premixed Antifreeze Solution. A mixture of an antifreeze material with water that is prepared and factory-mixed by the manufacturer with a quality control procedure in place that ensures that the antifreeze solution remains homogeneous and that the concentration is as specified. (AUT-SSI)

3.3.168 Pressure Regulating Device. A device designed for the purpose of reducing, regulating, controlling, or restricting water pressure. [24, 2022] (AUT-PRI)

3.3.169 Private Fire Hydrant. See 3.3.107.3.

3.3.170* Private Fire Service Main. Private fire service main, as used in this standard, is that pipe and its appurtenances on private property (1) between a source of water and the base of the system riser for water-based fire protection systems, (2) between a source of water and inlets to foam-making systems, (3) between a source of water and the base elbow of private hydrants or monitor nozzles, and (4) used as fire pump suction and discharge piping, (5) beginning at the inlet side of the check valve on a gravity or pressure tank. [24, 2022] (AUT-PRI)

3.3.171* Prying Factor. A factor based on fitting geometry and brace angle from vertical that results in an increase in tension load due to the effects of prying between the upper seismic brace attachment fitting and the structure. (AUT-HBS)

3.3.172 Public Hydrant. See 3.3.107.4.

3.3.173 Pumper Outlet. The hydrant outlet intended to be connected to a fire department pumper for use in taking supply from the hydrant for pumpers. [24, 2022] (AUT-PRI)

3.3.174 Pyramid Tire Storage. On-floor storage in which tires are formed into a pyramid to provide pile stability. (AUT-SSD)

3.3.175 Quick-Response Extended Coverage Sprinkler. See 3.3.215.4.15.

3.3.176 Quick-Response (QR) Sprinkler. See 3.3.215.4.16.

3.3.177* Rack. Any combination of vertical, horizontal, and diagonal members that supports stored materials. [1, 2021] (AUT-SSD)

3.3.178 Rack Shelf Area. The area of the horizontal surface of a shelf in a rack defined by perimeter aisle(s) or nominal 6 in. (150 mm) flue spaces on all four sides, or by the placement of loads that block openings that would otherwise serve as the required flue spaces. (AUT-SSD)

3.3.179 Rated Capacity. The flow available from a hydrant at the designated residual pressure (rated pressure) either measured or calculated. [24, 2022] (AUT-PRI)

3.3.180* Raw Water Source. A water supply that has not been treated and could contain foreign material that could enter the sprinkler system. (AUT-SSD)

3.3.181 Recessed Sprinkler. See 3.3.215.3.4.

3.3.182 Reinforced Plastic Pallet. See 3.3.154.3.

3.3.183 Residential Sprinkler. See 3.3.215.4.17.

3.3.184 Residual Hydrant. See 3.3.107.5.

3.3.185 Residual Pressure. The pressure that exists in the distribution system, measured at the residual hydrant at the time the flow readings are taken at the flow hydrants. [24, 2022] (AUT-PRI)

3.3.186 Riser Nipple. A vertical pipe between the cross main and branch line. (AUT-SSI)

3.3.187 Risers. The vertical supply pipes in a sprinkler system. (AUT-SSI)

3.3.188 Roll Paper Storage.

3.3.188.1 *Banded Roll Paper Storage.* Rolls provided with a circumferential steel strap [⅜ in. (10 mm) or wider] at each end of the roll. (AUT-SSD)

3.3.188.2 *Horizontal Roll Paper Storage.* Rolls stored with the cores in the horizontal plane (on-side storage). (AUT-SSD)

3.3.188.3* *Roll Paper Storage Height.* The maximum vertical distance above the floor at which roll paper is normally stored. (AUT-SSD)

3.3.188.4 *Vertical Roll Paper Storage.* Rolls stored with the cores in the vertical plane (on-end storage). (AUT-SSD)

3.3.188.5* *Wrapped Roll Paper Storage.* Rolls provided with a complete heavy kraft covering around both sides and ends. (AUT-SSD)

3.3.189 Roll Paper Storage Height. See 3.3.188.3.

3.3.190 Roof Height. The distance between the floor and the underside of the roof deck within the storage area. (AUT-SSD)

3.3.191* Rubber Tire Rack Illustrations. See Figure A.3.3.191(a) through Figure A.3.3.191(g).

3.3.192 Rubber Tires. Pneumatic tires for passenger automobiles, aircraft, light and heavy trucks, trailers, farm equipment, construction equipment (off-the-road), and buses. (AUT-SSD)

Δ **3.3.193 Seismic Coefficient, C_p.** The seismic coefficient that combines ground motion and seismic response factors from ASCE/SEI 7, *Minimum Design Loads and Associated Criteria for Buildings and Other Structures.* (AUT-HBS)

3.3.194* Seismic Separation Assembly. An assembly of fittings, pipe, flexible pipe, and/or couplings that permits movement in all directions to accommodate seismic differential movement across building seismic separation joints. (AUT-HBS)

N **3.3.195* Shadow Area.** The floor area within the protection area of a sprinkler created by the portion of sprinkler discharge that is blocked by a wall, partition, or other obstruction. (AUT-SSI)

3.3.196* Shelf Storage. Storage on structures up to and including 30 in. (750 mm) deep and separated by aisles at least 30 in. (750 mm) wide. (AUT-SSD)

Δ **3.3.197 Shop-Welded.** Materials welded in a sprinkler contractor's or fabricator's premise or in an area specifically designed or authorized for welding, such as a detached outside location, maintenance shop, or other area. (AUT-SSI)

3.3.198 Short Period Spectral Response Acceleration Parameter, S_s. The maximum considered earthquake ground motion for 0.2-second spectral response acceleration (5 percent of critical damping), site Class B for a specific site. (AUT-HBS)

3.3.199 Sidewall Sprinkler. See 3.3.215.3.5.

3.3.200* Single-Row Racks. Racks that have no longitudinal flue space and that have a depth up to 6 ft (1.8 m) with aisles having a width of at least 3.5 ft (1.1 m) between loads on racks. (AUT-SSD)

N **3.3.201 Site Class.** A classification assigned to a site based on the types of soils present and their engineering properties as defined in Chapter 20 of ASCE/SEI 7, *Minimum Design Loads and Associated Criteria for Buildings and Other Structures.* [**ASCE/SEI 7**:11.2] (AUT-HBS)

3.3.202 Slatted Shelf Rack. A rack where shelves are fixed in place with a series of narrow individual solid supports used as the shelf material and spaced apart with regular openings. (AUT-SSD)

3.3.203 Slave Pallet. See 3.3.154.4.

3.3.204 Sloped Ceiling. See 3.3.28.3.

3.3.205* Small Openings. Openings in the ceiling or construction features of a concealed space that allow limited amounts of heat to enter the concealed space. (AUT-SSI)

3.3.206 Small Room. A compartment of light hazard occupancy classification having unobstructed construction and a floor area not exceeding 800 ft² (74 m²). (AUT-SSI)

3.3.207 Smooth Ceiling. See 3.3.28.4.

3.3.208 Solid Shelf Rack. A rack that is not defined as an open rack where shelves are fixed in place with a solid, slatted, or wire mesh barrier used as the shelf material and having limited openings in the shelf area. (AUT-SSD)

3.3.209* Solid Shelving. Shelving that is fixed in place, slatted, wire mesh, or other type of shelves located within racks. The area of a solid shelf is defined by perimeter aisle or flue space on all four sides or by the placement of loads that block openings that would otherwise serve as the required flue spaces. Solid shelves having an area equal to or less than 20 ft² (1.9 m²) are defined as open racks. Shelves of wire mesh, slats, or other materials more than 50 percent open and where the flue spaces are maintained are defined as open racks. (AUT-SSD)

3.3.210 Solid Unit Load of Nonexpanded Plastic (Either Cartoned or Exposed). A load that does not have voids (air) within the load and that burns only on the exterior of the load; water from sprinklers might reach most surfaces available to burn. (AUT-SSD)

3.3.211 Solid-Piled Storage. Storage of commodities stacked on each other. (AUT-SSD)

3.3.212 Special Sprinkler. See 3.3.215.4.18.

3.3.213 Spray Sprinkler. See 3.3.215.4.19.

3.3.214 Sprig. A pipe that rises vertically and supplies a single sprinkler. (AUT-SSI)

3.3.215 Sprinkler Definitions.

3.3.215.1 *Automatic Sprinkler.* A fire suppression or control device that operates automatically when its heat-activated element is heated to its thermal rating or above, allowing water to discharge over a specified area. (AUT-SSI)

3.3.215.2* *General Sprinkler Characteristics.* The following are characteristics of a sprinkler that define its ability to control or extinguish a fire. (1) Thermal sensitivity. A measure of the rapidity with which the thermal element operates as installed in a specific sprinkler or sprinkler assembly. One measure of thermal sensitivity is the response time index (RTI) as measured under standardized test conditions. (a) Sprinklers defined as fast response have a thermal element with an RTI of 50 (meters-seconds)$^{1/2}$ or less. (b) Sprinklers defined as standard response have a thermal element with an RTI of 80 (meters-seconds)$^{1/2}$ or more. (2) Temperature rating. (3) K-factor *(see Chapter 7)*. (4) Installation orientation *(see 3.3.215.3)*. (5) Water distribution characteristics (i.e., application rate, wall wetting). (6) Special service conditions. (AUT-SSI)

3.3.215.3 *Installation Orientation.* The following sprinklers are defined according to orientation. (AUT-SSI)

3.3.215.3.1 *Concealed Sprinkler.* A recessed sprinkler with cover plate. (AUT-SSI)

3.3.215.3.2 *Flush Sprinkler.* A sprinkler in which all or part of the body, including the shank thread, is mounted above the lower plane of the ceiling. (AUT-SSI)

3.3.215.3.3 *Pendent Sprinkler.* A sprinkler designed to be installed in such a way that the water stream is directed downward against the deflector. (AUT-SSI)

3.3.215.3.4 *Recessed Sprinkler.* A sprinkler in which all or part of the body, other than the shank thread, is mounted within a recessed housing. (AUT-SSI)

3.3.215.3.5 *Sidewall Sprinkler.* A sprinkler having special deflectors that are designed to discharge most of the water away from the nearby wall in a pattern resembling one-quarter of a sphere, with a small portion of the discharge directed at the wall behind the sprinkler. (AUT-SSI)

3.3.215.3.6 *Upright Sprinkler.* A sprinkler designed to be installed in such a way that the water spray is directed upwards against the deflector. (AUT-SSI)

3.3.215.4 *Sprinkler Types.* The following sprinklers are defined according to design and/or performance characteristics. (AUT-SSI)

3.3.215.4.1* *Control Mode Density/Area (CMDA) Sprinkler.* A type of spray sprinkler intended to provide fire control in storage applications using the design density/area criteria described in this standard. (AUT-SSI)

3.3.215.4.2* *Control Mode Specific Application (CMSA) Sprinkler.* A type of spray sprinkler that is capable of producing characteristic large water droplets and that is listed for its

Shaded text = Revisions.   Δ = Text deletions and figure/table revisions.   • = Section deletions.   *N* = New material.

2022 Edition

capability to provide fire control of specific high-challenge fire hazards. (AUT-SSI)

3.3.215.4.3 *Corrosion-Resistant Sprinkler.* A sprinkler fabricated with corrosion-resistant material, or with special coatings or platings, to be used in an atmosphere that would normally corrode sprinklers. (AUT-SSI)

3.3.215.4.4* *Dry Sprinkler.* A sprinkler secured in an extension nipple that has a seal at the inlet end to prevent water from entering the nipple until the sprinkler operates. (AUT-SSI)

3.3.215.4.5* *Early Suppression Fast-Response (ESFR) Sprinkler.* A type of fast-response sprinkler that has a thermal element with an RTI of 50 (meters-seconds)$^{1/2}$ or less and is listed for its capability to provide fire suppression of specific high-challenge fire hazards. (AUT-SSI)

N **3.3.215.4.6** *Electrically Operated Sprinkler.* A sprinkler equipped with an integral means of activation using electricity. (AUT-SSI)

3.3.215.4.7 *Extended Coverage Sprinkler.* A type of spray sprinkler with maximum coverage areas as specified in Sections 11.2 and 11.3. (AUT-SSI)

3.3.215.4.8 *Institutional Sprinkler.* A sprinkler specially designed for resistance to load-bearing purposes and with components not readily converted for use as weapons. (AUT-SSI)

3.3.215.4.9 *Intermediate-Level Sprinkler/Rack Storage Sprinkler.* A sprinkler equipped with integral shields to protect its operating elements from the discharge of sprinklers installed at higher elevations. (AUT-SSI)

3.3.215.4.10 *Nozzle.* A device for use in applications requiring special water discharge patterns, directional spray, or other unusual discharge characteristics. (AUT-SSI)

3.3.215.4.11 *Old-Style/Conventional Sprinkler.* A sprinkler that directs from 40 percent to 60 percent of the total water initially in a downward direction and that is designed to be installed with the deflector either upright or pendent. (AUT-SSI)

3.3.215.4.12 *Open Sprinkler.* A sprinkler that does not have actuators or heat-responsive elements. (AUT-SSI)

3.3.215.4.13 *Ornamental/Decorative Sprinkler.* A sprinkler that has been painted or plated by the manufacturer. (AUT-SSI)

3.3.215.4.14 *Pilot Line Detector.* A standard spray sprinkler or thermostatic fixed-temperature release device used as a detector to pneumatically or hydraulically release the main valve, controlling the flow of water into a fire protection system. (AUT-SSI)

3.3.215.4.15 *Quick-Response Extended Coverage Sprinkler.* A type of quick-response sprinkler that has a thermal element with an RTI of 50 (meter-seconds)$^{1/2}$ or less and complies with the extended protection areas defined in Chapter 11. (AUT-SSI)

3.3.215.4.16* *Quick-Response (QR) Sprinkler.* A type of spray sprinkler that has a thermal element with an RTI of 50 (meter-seconds)$^{1/2}$ or less and is listed as a quick-response sprinkler for its intended use. (AUT-SSI)

3.3.215.4.17 *Residential Sprinkler.* A type of fast-response sprinkler having a thermal element with an RTI of 50 (meters-seconds)$^{1/2}$ or less that has been specifically investigated for its ability to enhance survivability in the room of fire origin and that is listed for use in the protection of dwelling units. (AUT-SSI)

3.3.215.4.18 *Special Sprinkler.* A sprinkler that has been tested and listed as prescribed in Section 15.2. (AUT-SSI)

3.3.215.4.19 *Spray Sprinkler.* A type of sprinkler listed for its capability to provide fire control for a wide range of fire hazards. (AUT-SSI)

3.3.215.4.20 *Standard Spray Sprinkler.* A spray sprinkler with maximum coverage areas as specified in Sections 10.2 and 10.3. (AUT-SSI)

Δ **3.3.216*** **Sprinkler System.** A system, commonly activated by heat from a fire and discharges water over the fire area, that consists of an integrated network of piping designed in accordance with fire protection engineering standards that includes a water supply source, a control valve, a waterflow alarm, and a drain. The portion of the sprinkler system above ground is a network of specifically sized or hydraulically designed piping installed in a building, structure, or area, generally overhead, and to which sprinklers are attached in a systematic pattern. (AUT-SSI)

3.3.216.1 *Antifreeze Sprinkler System.* A wet pipe system using automatic sprinklers that contains a liquid solution to prevent freezing of the system, intended to discharge the solution upon sprinkler operation, followed immediately by water from a water supply. (AUT-SSI)

3.3.216.2 *Combined Dry Pipe Preaction Sprinkler System.* A sprinkler system employing automatic sprinklers attached to a piping system containing air under pressure with a supplemental detection system installed in the same areas as the sprinklers. Operation of the detection system actuates tripping devices that open dry pipe valves simultaneously and without loss of air pressure in the system. The detection system also serves as an automatic fire alarm system. (AUT-SSI)

3.3.216.3 *Deluge Sprinkler System.* A sprinkler system employing open sprinklers or nozzles that are attached to a piping system that is connected to a water supply through a valve that is opened by the operation of a detection system installed in the same areas as the sprinklers or the nozzles. When this valve opens, water flows into the piping system and discharges from all sprinklers or nozzles attached thereto. (AUT-SSI)

3.3.216.4 *Dry Pipe Sprinkler System.* A sprinkler system employing automatic sprinklers that are attached to a piping system containing air or nitrogen under pressure, the release of which (as from the opening of a sprinkler) permits the water pressure to open a valve known as a dry pipe valve, and the water then flows into the piping system and out the opened sprinklers. (AUT-SSI)

3.3.216.5* *Gridded Sprinkler System.* A sprinkler system in which parallel cross mains are connected by multiple branch lines, causing an operating sprinkler to receive water from both ends of its branch line while other branch lines help transfer water between cross mains. (AUT-SSD)

3.3.216.6* *Looped Sprinkler System.* A sprinkler system in which multiple cross mains are tied together so as to provide more than one path for water to flow to an operating sprinkler and branch lines are not tied together. (AUT-SSD)

3.3.216.7 *Multicycle System.* A type of sprinkler system capable of repeated on–off flow cycles in response to heat. (AUT-SSI)

3.3.216.8 *Pipe Schedule System.* A sprinkler system in which the pipe sizing is selected from a schedule that is determined by the occupancy classification and in which a given number of sprinklers are allowed to be supplied from specific sizes of pipe. (AUT-SSD)

3.3.216.9* *Preaction Sprinkler System.* A sprinkler system employing automatic sprinklers that are attached to a piping system that contains air that might or might not be under pressure, with a supplemental detection system installed in the same areas as the sprinklers. (AUT-SSI)

3.3.216.10 *Wet Pipe Sprinkler System.* A sprinkler system employing automatic sprinklers attached to a piping system containing water and connected to a water supply so that water discharges immediately from sprinklers opened by heat from a fire. (AUT-SSI)

N **3.3.217 Sprinkler Types.** See 3.3.215.4.

3.3.218 Standard Array (Rolled Paper). See 3.3.8.5.

3.3.219 Standard Spray Sprinkler. See 3.3.215.4.20.

3.3.220 Static Pressure. The pressure that exists at a given point under normal distribution system conditions measured at the residual hydrant with no hydrants flowing. [24, 2022] (AUT-PRI)

3.3.221 Storage Aids. Commodity storage devices, such as pallets, dunnage, separators, and skids. (AUT-SSD)

Δ **3.3.222 Supervision.** See 3.3.125.11.

3.3.223 Supervisory Device. A device arranged to supervise the operative condition of automatic sprinkler systems. (AUT-SSI)

3.3.224 Survival Angle. See 3.3.125.12.

3.3.225 System Riser. The aboveground horizontal or vertical pipe between the water supply and the mains (cross or feed) that contains a control valve (either directly or within its supply pipe), a pressure gauge, a drain, and a waterflow alarm device. (AUT-SSI)

3.3.226 System Working Pressure. The maximum anticipated static (nonflowing) or flowing pressure applied to sprinkler system components exclusive of surge pressures and exclusive of pressure from the fire department connection. (AUT-SSI)

3.3.227 Sway Brace. An assembly intended to be attached to the system piping to resist horizontal earthquake loads in two directions. (AUT-HBS)

3.3.228 Thermal Barrier. A material that limits the average temperature rise of the unexposed surface to not more than 250°F (139°C) above ambient for a specified fire exposure duration using the standard time–temperature curve of ASTM E119, *Standard Test Methods for Fire Tests of Building Construction and Materials*, or UL 263, *Standard for Fire Tests of Building Construction and Materials*. (AUT-SSI)

3.3.229* Tiered Storage (Baled Cotton). An arrangement in which bales are stored directly on the floor, two or more bales high. (AUT-SSD)

3.3.230 Transverse Flue Space. The space between rows of storage parallel to the direction of loading. *(See Figure A.3.3.122.)* (AUT-SSD)

3.3.231 Type 1 Stair. See 3.3.125.13.

3.3.232 Unit Load. A pallet load or module held together in some manner and normally transported by material-handling equipment. (AUT-SSD)

3.3.233 Unobstructed Construction. See 3.3.43.2.

3.3.234 Upright Sprinkler. See 3.3.215.3.6.

N **3.3.235 Valve.** A device for controlling the passage of fluid or gas through a pipe.

3.3.235.1 *Check Valve.* A valve that allows flow in one direction only. [24, 2022] (AUT-PRI)

3.3.235.2* *Control Valve.* A valve capable of stopping the flow of water to water-based fire protection systems and devices. (AUT-SSI)

3.3.235.3* *Indicating Valve.* A valve that has components that provide the valve operating position, open or closed. [24,2022] (AUT-PRI)

N **3.3.235.4*** *Water Control Valve.* A valve that activates to allow water flow to a water-based fire protection system. (AUT-SSI)

Δ **3.3.235.4.1** *Differential Dry Pipe Valve.* A water control valve that is held in the closed position by the system gas pressure exposed to the surface area on the air/nitrogen side of the clapper where such surface area is larger than the surface area on the water supply side, with an intermediate chamber between the two surface areas that is open to atmosphere. (AUT-SSI)

3.3.235.4.2 *Mechanical Dry Pipe Valve.* A water control valve that uses a series of mechanical devices such as levers, springs, diaphragms, and latches to hold the valve in the closed position with air/nitrogen pressure and without using the clapper surface areas to provide a differential between air/nitrogen and water pressures. (AUT-SSI)

3.3.236 Vertical Roll Paper Storage. See 3.3.188.4.

N **3.3.237 Water Control Valve.** See 3.3.235.4.

3.3.238 Waterflow Alarm Device. An attachment to the sprinkler system that detects a predetermined water flow and is connected to a fire alarm system to initiate an alarm condition or is used to mechanically or electrically initiate a fire pump or local audible or visual alarm. (AUT-SSI)

N **3.3.239 Wet Barrel Hydrant.** See 3.3.107.6.

N **3.3.240 Wet Pipe Sprinkler System.** See 3.3.216.10.

N **3.3.241 Wood Pallet.** See 3.3.154.5.

N **3.3.242 Wrapped Roll Paper Storage.** See 3.3.188.5.

Chapter 4   General Requirements

4.1 Level of Protection.

4.1.1 A building, where protected by an automatic sprinkler system installation, shall be provided with sprinklers in all areas except where specific sections of this standard permit the omission of sprinklers.

4.1.2 Limited Area Systems.

4.1.2.1 When partial sprinkler systems are installed, the requirements of this standard shall be used insofar as they are applicable.

4.1.2.2 The authority having jurisdiction shall be consulted in each case.

4.2* Owner's Certificate. The owner(s) of a building or structure where the fire sprinkler system is going to be installed or their authorized agent shall provide the sprinkler system installer with the following information prior to the layout and detailing of the fire sprinkler system [see Figure A.28.1(b)]:

(1) Intended use of the building, including the materials within the building and the maximum height of any storage
(2) A preliminary plan of the building or structure along with the design concepts necessary to perform the layout and detail for the fire sprinkler system
(3) Water supply information as identified in 5.2.2
(4)* Any special knowledge of the water supply, including known environmental conditions that might be responsible for corrosion, including microbiologically influenced corrosion (MIC)
(5) Whether seismic protection is required and the applicable short period response parameter

4.3* Classification of Hazard.

4.3.1 General.

4.3.1.1 Occupancy classifications for this standard shall relate to sprinkler design, installation, and water supply requirements only.

4.3.1.2 Occupancy classifications shall not be intended to be a general classification of occupancy hazards.

4.3.1.3 Commodity classification and storage arrangements for miscellaneous and low-piled storage specified in 4.3.1.5 through 4.3.1.8 shall be determined in accordance with Sections 20.3 through 20.5.

4.3.1.4* Miscellaneous Storage.

N **4.3.1.4.1** Miscellaneous storage shall not exceed 12 ft (3.7 m) in height.

4.3.1.4.2 Miscellaneous storage shall not constitute more than 10 percent of the building area or 4000 ft² (370 m²) of the sprinklered area, whichever is greater.

4.3.1.4.3 Miscellaneous storage shall not exceed 1000 ft² (93 m²) in one pile or area.

4.3.1.4.4 Miscellaneous storage shall be separated from other storage piles or areas by at least 25 ft (7.6 m).

N **4.3.1.4.5** Solid shelf racks in accordance with the requirements of Section 20.19 shall not apply to miscellaneous storage

of Class I through Class IV commodities up to 12 ft (3.7 m) and Group A plastics up to 5 ft (1.5 m).

4.3.1.5 Low-Piled Storage.

Δ **4.3.1.5.1** Low-piled storage of Class I through Class IV commodities shall not exceed 12 ft (3.7 m) in height.

Δ **4.3.1.5.2** Low-piled storage of Group A plastics shall not exceed 5 ft (1.5 m) in height.

4.3.1.6 Miscellaneous Tire Storage.

4.3.1.6.1 Miscellaneous tire storage shall not exceed 2000 ft² (185 m²).

4.3.1.6.2 Miscellaneous tire storage piles on-tread, regardless of storage method, shall not exceed 25 ft (7.6 m) in the direction of the wheel holes.

4.3.1.7 Protection Criteria for Miscellaneous and Low-Piled Storage.

N **4.3.1.7.1 Protection Criteria for Miscellaneous Storage.**

Δ **4.3.1.7.1.1** The protection criteria for miscellaneous storage protected by ceiling sprinklers only shall be selected from Table 4.3.1.7.1.1 and 19.2.3.1.1 in accordance with the density/area method of 19.2.3.

4.3.1.7.1.2 The protection criteria for miscellaneous storage with racks protected by in-rack sprinklers shall be in accordance with 25.2.1.

N **4.3.1.7.1.3** The maximum design area for miscellaneous storage shall not exceed 3000 ft² (280 m²).

N **4.3.1.7.2 Protection Criteria for Low-Piled Storage.**

N **4.3.1.7.2.1** The protection criteria for low-piled storage of Class I through Class IV commodities up to a maximum height of 12 ft (3.7 m) protected by ceiling sprinklers only shall be selected from Table 4.3.1.7.1.1 and 19.2.3.1.1 in accordance with the density/area method of 19.2.3.

N **4.3.1.7.2.2** The protection criteria for low-piled storage of Class I through Class IV commodities up to a maximum height of 12 ft (3.7 m) on open racks protected by in-rack sprinklers shall be in accordance with 25.2.2.

N **4.3.1.7.2.3** Low-piled storage of Class I through Class IV commodities up to a maximum height of 12 ft (3.7 m) on solid shelf racks shall be protected with in-rack sprinklers in accordance with Section 20.19 and 25.2.2.2, with corresponding ceiling sprinkler protection in accordance with 25.2.2.5.1.

N **4.3.1.7.2.4** The protection criteria for low-piled storage of Group A plastic commodities up to a maximum height of 5 ft (1.5 m) protected by ceiling sprinklers only shall be selected from Table 4.3.1.7.1.1 and 19.2.3.1.1 in accordance with the density/area method of 19.2.3.

N **4.3.1.7.2.5** The protection criteria for low-piled storage of Group A plastic commodities up to a maximum height of 5 ft (1.5 m) on open racks protected by in-rack sprinklers shall be in accordance with 25.2.2.

N **4.3.1.7.2.6** Low-piled storage of Group A plastic commodities up to a maximum height of 5 ft (1.5 m) on solid shelf racks shall be protected with in-rack sprinklers in accordance with Section 20.19 and 25.2.2.2, with corresponding ceiling sprinkler protection in accordance with 25.2.2.5.2.

Δ **Table 4.3.1.7.1.1 Discharge Criteria for Miscellaneous Storage Up to 12 ft (3.7 m) in Height**

Commodity		Type of Storage	Storage Height ft	Storage Height m	Maximum Ceiling Height ft	Maximum Ceiling Height m	Design from 19.2.3.1.1	Note	Inside Hose gpm	Inside Hose L/min	Total Combined Inside and Outside Hose gpm	Total Combined Inside and Outside Hose L/min	Duration (minutes)
Class I to Class IV													
Class I		Solid-piled, palletized, bin box, shelf, single-, double-, or multiple-row rack, and back-to-back shelf storage	≤12	≤3.7	—	—	OH1	—	0, 50, 100	0, 190, 380	250	950	90
Class II			≤10	≤3.0	—	—	OH1	—	0, 50, 100	0, 190, 380	250	950	90
Class II			>10 to ≤12	>3.0 to ≤3.7	—	—	OH2	—	0, 50, 100	0, 190, 380	250	950	90
Class III			≤12	≤3.7	—	—	OH2	—	0, 50, 100	0, 190, 380	250	950	90
Class IV			≤10	≤3.0	—	—	OH2	—	0, 50, 100	0, 190, 380	250	950	90
Class IV		Palletized, bin box, shelf, and solid-piled	>10 to ≤12	>3.0 to ≤3.7	32	9.8	OH2	—	0, 50, 100	0, 190, 380	250	950	90
		Single-, double-, or multiple-row rack, and back-to-back shelf storage	>10 to ≤12	>3.0 to ≤3.7	32	9.8	EH1	—	0, 50, 100	0, 190, 380	500	1900	120
		Single-, double-, or multiple-row rack	>10 to ≤12	>3.0 to ≤3.7	32	9.8	See Chapter 25.	+1 level of in-rack	0, 50, 100	0, 190, 380	250	950	90
Group A Plastic Storage													
Cartoned	Nonexpanded and expanded	Solid-piled, palletized, bin box, shelf, single-, double-, or multiple-row rack, and back-to-back shelf storage	≤5	≤1.5	—	—	OH2	—	0, 50, 100	0, 190, 380	250	950	90
			>5 to ≤10	>1.5 to ≤3.0	15	4.6	EH1	—	0, 50, 100	0, 190, 380	500	1900	120
			>5 to ≤10	>1.5 to ≤3.0	20	6.1	EH2	—	0, 50, 100	0, 190, 380	500	1900	120
			>10 to ≤12	>3.0 to ≤3.7	17	5.2	EH2	—	0, 50, 100	0, 190, 380	500	1900	120
		Solid-piled, palletized, bin box, shelf, and back-to-back shelf storage	>10 to ≤12	>3.0 to ≤3.7	32	9.8	EH2	—	0, 50, 100	0, 190, 380	500	1900	120
		Single-, double-, or multiple-row rack	>10 to ≤12	>3.0 to ≤3.7	32	9.8	See Chapter 25.	+ 1 level of in-rack	0, 50, 100	0, 190, 380	250	950	90

(continues)

Δ **Table 4.3.1.7.1.1** *Continued*

Commodity		Type of Storage	Storage Height		Maximum Ceiling Height		Design from 19.2.3.1.1	Note	Inside Hose		Total Combined Inside and Outside Hose		Duration (minutes)
			ft	m	ft	m			gpm	L/min	gpm	L/min	
Exposed	Nonexpanded and expanded	Solid-piled, palletized, bin box, shelf, single-, double-, or multiple-row rack, and back-to-back shelf storage	≤5	≤1.5	—	—	OH2	—	0, 50, 100	0, 190, 380	250	950	90
		Solid-piled, palletized, bin box, shelf, and back-to-back shelf storage	>5 to ≤8	>1.5 to ≤2.4	28	8.5	EH2	—	0, 50, 100	0, 190, 380	500	1900	120
		Solid-piled, palletized, bin box, shelf, single-, double-, or multiple-row rack, and back-to-back shelf storage	>5 to ≤10	>1.5 to ≤3.0	15	4.6	EH2	—	0, 50, 100	0, 190, 380	500	1900	120
	Nonexpanded	Solid-piled, palletized, shelf, bin box, single-, double-, or multiple-row rack, and back-to-back shelf storage	>5 to ≤10	>1.5 to ≤3.0	20	6.1	EH2	—	0, 50, 100	0, 190, 380	500	1900	120
	Expanded	Single-, double-, or multiple-row rack	>5 to ≤10	>1.5 to ≤3.0	20	6.1	See Chapter 25.	+1 level of in-rack	0, 50, 100	0, 190, 380	250	950	90
	Nonexpanded and expanded	Solid-piled, palletized, bin box, shelf, and back-to-back shelf storage	>10 to ≤12	>3.0 to ≤3.7	17	5.2	EH2	—	0, 50, 100	0, 190, 380	500	1900	120
		Single-, double-, or multiple-row rack	>10 to ≤12	>3.0 to ≤3.7	17	5.2	EH2	—	0, 50, 100	0, 190, 380	500	1900	120
			>10 to ≤12	>3.0 to ≤3.7	32	9.8	See Chapter 25.	+1 level of in-rack	0, 50, 100	0, 190, 380	250	950	90
Tire Storage													
Tires		On floor or on side	>5 to ≤12	>1.5 to ≤3.7	32	9.8	EH1	—	0, 50, 100	0, 190, 380	500	1900	120
		On floor, on tread, or on side	≤5	≤1.5	—	—	OH2	—	0, 50, 100	0, 190, 380	250	950	90
		Single-, double-, or multiple-row racks, on tread or on side	≤5	≤1.5	—	—	OH2	—	0, 50, 100	0, 190, 380	250	950	90
		Single-row rack, portable, on tread or on side	>5 to ≤12	>1.5 to ≤3.7	32	9.8	EH1	—	0, 50, 100	0, 190, 380	500	1900	120
		Single-row rack, fixed, on tread or on side	>5 to ≤12	>1.5 to ≤3.7	32	9.8	EH1	—	0, 50, 100	0, 190, 380	500	950	120
			>5 to ≤12	>1.5 to ≤3.7	32	9.8	See Chapter 25.	+1 level of in-rack	0, 50, 100	0, 190, 380	250	950	90
Rolled Paper Storage													
Heavyweight and mediumweight		On end	≤10	≤3.0	30	9.1	OH2	—	0, 50, 100	0, 190, 380	250	950	90
Tissue and lightweight		On end	≤10	≤3.0	30	9.1	EH1	—	0, 50, 100	0, 190, 380	250	950	120

Shaded text = Revisions.   Δ = Text deletions and figure/table revisions.   • = Section deletions.   *N* = New material.

Δ **4.3.1.7.2.7** The maximum design area for low-piled storage shall not exceed 3000 ft^2 (280 m^2).

4.3.1.7.3 Hose Connections. Hose connections shall not be required for the protection of miscellaneous storage.

4.3.1.8 In-Rack Sprinklers. Miscellaneous and low-piled storage in accordance with 4.3.1.4 through 4.3.1.7 that require in-rack sprinklers shall follow Chapter 25 for their installation and design requirements.

4.3.2* Light Hazard. The following shall be protected with light hazard occupancy criteria in this standard:

(1) Spaces with low quantity and combustibility of contents

N **4.3.3* Ordinary Hazard Occupancies.**

4.3.3.1* Ordinary Hazard (Group 1). The following shall be protected with OH1 occupancy criteria in this standard:

(1) Spaces with moderate quantity and low combustibility of contents
(2) Stockpiles of contents with low combustibility that do not exceed 8 ft (2.4 m)

4.3.3.2* Ordinary Hazard (Group 2). The following shall be protected with OH2 occupancy criteria in this standard:

(1) Spaces with moderate to high quantity and combustibility of contents
(2) Stockpiles of contents with moderate rates of heat release rate that do not exceed 12 ft (3.7 m) and stockpiles of contents with high rates of heat release that do not exceed 8 ft (2.4 m)

4.3.4* Extra Hazard (Group 1) (EH1). The following shall be protected with EH1 occupancy criteria in this standard:

(1) Spaces with very high quantity and combustibility of contents
(2) Spaces where dust, lint, or other materials are present, introducing the probability of rapidly developing fires

4.3.5* Extra Hazard (Group 2) (EH2). The following shall be protected with EH2 occupancy criteria in this standard:

(1) Spaces with very high quantity and combustibility of contents
(2) Spaces with substantial amounts of combustible or flammable liquids
(3) Spaces where shielding of combustibles is extensive

4.3.6 High-Piled Storage. Storage arrangements that do not meet the requirements of 4.3.1.4 through 4.3.1.8 shall be protected in accordance with Chapters 20 through 25.

Δ **4.3.7* Special Occupancy Hazards.** Special occupancies shall be in accordance with Chapter 27.

4.4 System Protection Area Limitations.

4.4.1 The maximum floor area on any one floor to be protected by sprinklers supplied by any one sprinkler system riser or combined system riser shall be as follows:

(1) Light hazard — 52,000 ft^2 (4830 m^2)
(2) Ordinary hazard — 52,000 ft^2 (4830 m^2)
(3)* Extra hazard — Hydraulically calculated — 40,000 ft^2 (3720 m^2)
(4) High-piled Storage — High-piled storage (as defined in 3.3.100) and storage covered by other NFPA standards — 40,000 ft^2 (3720 m^2)

(5) In-rack Storage — 40,000 ft^2 (3720 m^2)

4.4.2 The floor area occupied by mezzanines shall comply with 4.4.2.1, 4.4.2.2, or 4.4.2.3.

4.4.2.1 In a building with only one sprinkler system, the floor area occupied by mezzanines shall not be included in the area limits of 4.4.1.

4.4.2.2 In a building with more than one sprinkler system, if a mezzanine is located entirely within the same sprinkler system boundary as the sprinklers protecting the ceiling above, the floor area occupied by mezzanine(s) shall not be included in the area limits of 4.4.1.

Δ **4.4.2.3** In a building with more than one sprinkler system, if any portion of the mezzanine floor area is located outside the system boundary of the riser supplying the sprinklers under the mezzanine, the area of the mezzanine outside the boundary of the overhead system shall be added to the system area from which it is supplied, and the total system area shall meet the limits of 4.4.1.

Δ **4.4.3** Where single systems protect extra hazard, high-piled storage, or storage covered by other NFPA standards, and ordinary or light hazard areas, the extra hazard or storage area coverage shall not exceed the floor area specified for that hazard and the total area coverage shall not exceed the area specified for the lesser hazard.

4.4.4 The area protected by a single in-rack system includes all of the floor area occupied by the racks, including aisles, regardless of the number of levels of in-rack sprinklers.

4.4.5 Multiple buildings attached by canopies, covered breezeways, common roofs, or a common wall(s) shall be permitted to be supplied by a single fire sprinkler riser.

4.4.6* Detached Buildings.

4.4.6.1 Unless the requirements of 4.4.6.2 apply, detached buildings, regardless of separation distance, that do not meet the criteria of 4.4.4 shall be provided with separate fire sprinkler systems.

4.4.6.2 When acceptable to the authority having jurisdiction, detached structures shall be permitted to be supplied by the fire sprinkler system of an adjacent building.

4.5 Water Supply Information.

4.5.1 Water Supply Capacity Information. The following information shall be included:

(1) Location and elevation of static and residual test gauge with relation to the riser reference point
(2) Flow location
(3) Static pressure, psi (bar)
(4) Residual pressure, psi (bar)
(5) Flow, gpm (L/min)
(6) Date
(7) Time
(8) Name of person who conducted the test or supplied the information
(9) Other sources of water supply, with pressure or elevation

4.5.1.1* Where a waterflow test is used for the purposes of system design, the test shall be conducted no more than 12 months prior to working plan submittal unless otherwise approved by the authority having jurisdiction.

4.5.2 Water Supply Treatment Information. The following information shall be included when water supply treatment is provided in accordance with 5.1.4:

(1) Type of condition that requires treatment
(2) Type of treatment needed to address the problem
(3) Details of treatment plan

4.6* Additives. Additives or chemicals intended to stop leaks, such as sodium silicate or derivatives of sodium silicate, brine, or similar acting chemicals, shall not be used in sprinkler systems.

4.7 Air, Nitrogen, or Other Approved Gas. Where air is used to charge, maintain, or supervise sprinkler systems, nitrogen or other approved gas shall also be permitted to be used.

4.8* Support of Nonsprinkler System Components. Sprinkler system components shall not be used to support nonsprinkler system components unless expressly permitted by this standard.

4.9 Noncombustible Materials and Limited-Combustible Materials.

4.9.1* Noncombustible Material.

4.9.1.1 A material that complies with any of the following shall be considered a noncombustible material:

(1)* The material, in the form in which it is used, and under the conditions anticipated, will not ignite, burn, support combustion, or release flammable vapors when subjected to fire or heat.
(2) The material is reported as passing ASTM E136, *Standard Test Method for Assessing Combustibility of Materials Using a Vertical Tube Furnace at 750°C.*
(3) The material is reported as complying with the pass/fail criteria of ASTM E136 when tested in accordance with the test method and procedure in ASTM E2652, *Standard Test Method for Assessing Combustibility of Materials Using a Tube Furnace with a Cone-shaped Airflow Stabilizer, at 750°C.*
[**5000**:7.1.4.1.1]

4.9.1.2 Where the term *limited-combustible* is used in this standard, it shall also include the term *noncombustible*. [**5000**:7.1.4.1.2]

Δ **4.9.2* Limited-Combustible Material.** A material shall be considered a limited-combustible material where both of the following conditions of 4.9.2(1) and 4.9.2(2), and the conditions of either 4.9.2.1 or 4.9.2.2, are met:

(1) The material does not comply with the requirements for a noncombustible material in accordance with 4.9.1.
(2) The material, in the form in which it is used, exhibits a potential heat value not exceeding 3500 Btu/lb (8150 kJ/kg), when tested in accordance with NFPA 259.
[**5000**:7.1.4.2]

4.9.2.1 The material shall have a structural base of noncombustible material with a surfacing not exceeding a thickness of $\frac{1}{8}$ in. (3.2 mm) where the surfacing exhibits a flame spread index not greater than 50 when tested in accordance with ASTM E84, *Standard Test Method for Surface Burning Characteristics of Building Materials,* or UL 723, *Standard for Test for Surface Burning Characteristics of Building Materials.* [**5000**:7.1.4.2.1]

4.9.2.2 The material shall be composed of materials that in the form and thickness used, neither exhibit a flame spread index greater than 25 nor evidence of continued progressive combustion when tested in accordance with ASTM E84 or UL 723 and are of such composition that all surfaces that would be exposed by cutting through the material on any plane would neither exhibit a flame spread index greater than 25 nor exhibit evidence of continued progressive combustion when tested in accordance with ASTM E84 or UL 723. [**5000**:7.1.4.2.2]

4.9.2.3 Materials shall be considered limited-combustible materials where tested in accordance with ASTM E2965, *Standard Test Method for Determination of Low Levels of Heat Release Rate for Materials and Products Using an Oxygen Consumption Calorimeter,* at an incident flux of 75 kW/m^2 for a 20-minute exposure, and both the following conditions are met:

(1) The peak heat release rate shall not exceed 150 kW/m^2 for longer than 10 seconds.
(2) The total heat released shall not exceed 8 MJ/m^2.
[**5000**:7.1.4.2.3]

4.9.2.4 Where the term *limited-combustible* is used in this standard, it shall also include the term *noncombustible*. [**5000**:7.1.4.2.4]

Chapter 5 Water Supplies

5.1 General.

5.1.1 Number of Supplies. Every automatic sprinkler system shall have at least one automatic water supply.

5.1.2 Capacity. Water supplies shall be capable of providing the required flow and pressure for the remote design area determined using the requirements and procedures as specified in Chapters 19 through 27 including hose stream allowance where applicable for the required duration.

5.1.3* Size of Fire Mains.

5.1.3.1 Except as provided in 5.1.3.2 or 5.1.3.3, no pipe smaller than 6 in. (150 mm) in diameter shall be installed as a private service main.

Δ 5.1.3.2 Sizes smaller than 6 in. (150 mm) for fire mains that do not supply hydrants shall be permitted, provided that hydraulic calculations show the main will supply the total demand at the appropriate pressure.

5.1.3.3 Where a single main less than 4 in. (100 mm) in diameter serves both fire systems and other uses, the non-fire demand shall be added to the hydraulic calculations for the fire system at the point of connection unless provisions have been made to automatically isolate the non-fire demand during a fire event.

Δ 5.1.3.4 For pipe schedule systems, the underground supply pipe shall be at least as large as the system riser.

5.1.4* Water Supply Treatment.

Δ 5.1.4.1 Water Supplies and Environmental Conditions.

N 5.1.4.1.1 Water supplies and environmental conditions shall be evaluated for the existence of microbes and conditions that contribute to microbiologically influenced corrosion (MIC).

N 5.1.4.1.2 Where conditions that contribute to MIC are found, the owner(s) shall notify the sprinkler system installer and develop a plan to treat the system using one of the following methods:

(1) Install system piping that will not be affected by the MIC microbes
(2) Treat all water that enters the system using a listed bacterial inhibitor
(3) Implement an approved plan for monitoring the interior conditions of the pipe at established time intervals and locations
(4) Install a corrosion monitoring station and monitor at established intervals

Δ 5.1.4.2 Corrosion.

N 5.1.4.2.1 Water supplies and environmental conditions shall be evaluated for conditions that contribute to unusual corrosive properties.

N 5.1.4.2.2 Where conditions are found that contribute to unusual corrosive properties, the owner(s) shall notify the sprinkler system installer and a plan shall be developed to treat the system using at least one of the following methods:

(1) Install system piping that is corrosion resistant
(2) Treat water that enters the system using a listed corrosion inhibitor

(3) Implement an approved plan for monitoring the interior conditions of the pipe at established intervals and locations
(4) Install approved corrosion monitoring stations and monitor at established intervals
(5) Fill dry-pipe or preaction systems with at least 98 percent pure nitrogen in lieu of air to mitigate against corrosion
(6) Use a listed nitrogen generator that is sized and installed in accordance with the manufacturer's instructions

Δ 5.1.4.3 Inhibitors.

N 5.1.4.3.1 Where used, listed bacterial inhibitors and/or corrosion inhibitors shall be compatible with system components.

N 5.1.4.3.2 Where used together, listed bacterial inhibitors and corrosion inhibitors shall be compatible with each other.

5.1.5 Arrangement.

5.1.5.1 Connection Between Underground and Aboveground Piping.

Δ 5.1.5.1.1 The connection between the system piping and underground piping shall be made with a transition piece in accordance with 6.2.3 or 6.2.3.1that is properly strapped or fastened by approved devices.

5.1.5.1.2 Where required due to specific mechanical or environmental conditions, the transition piece shall be protected against possible damage from corrosive agents, solvent attack, or mechanical damage.

5.1.5.2* Connection Passing Through or Under Foundation Walls. When system piping pierces a foundation wall below grade or is located under the foundation wall, clearance shall be provided to prevent breakage of the piping due to building settlement.

5.1.6* Meters. Where meters are required by other authorities, they shall be listed.

5.1.7* Connection from Waterworks System.

5.1.7.1 The requirements of the public health authority having jurisdiction shall be determined and followed.

5.1.7.2 Where equipment is installed to guard against possible contamination of the public water system, such equipment and devices shall be listed for fire protection service.

5.2 Types.

5.2.1* Water supplies for sprinkler systems shall be one of the following or any combination:

(1) A connection to an approved public or private waterworks system in accordance with 5.2.2
(2) A connection including a fire pump in accordance with 5.2.3
(3) A connection to a water storage tank at grade or below grade installed in accordance with NFPA 22 and filled from an approved source
(4) A connection to a pressure tank in accordance with 5.2.4 and filled from an approved source
(5) A connection to a gravity tank in accordance with 5.2.5 and filled from an approved source
(6) A penstock, flume, river, lake, pond, or reservoir in accordance with 5.2.6
(7)* A source of recycled or reclaimed water where the building owner (or their agent) has analyzed the source of the

water and the treatment process (if any) that the water undergoes before being made available to the sprinkler system and determined that any materials, chemicals, or contaminants in the water will not be detrimental to the components of the sprinkler system it comes in contact with

5.2.2* Connections to Waterworks Systems.

5.2.2.1 A connection to a reliable waterworks system shall be an acceptable water supply source.

5.2.2.2* The volume and pressure of a public water supply shall be determined from waterflow test data or other approved method.

5.2.3* Pumps. A single automatically controlled fire pump installed in accordance with NFPA 20 shall be an acceptable water supply source.

5.2.4 Pressure Tanks.

5.2.4.1 Acceptability.

5.2.4.1.1 A pressure tank installed in accordance with NFPA 22 shall be an acceptable water supply source.

5.2.4.1.2 Pressure tanks shall be provided with an approved means for automatically maintaining the required air pressure.

5.2.4.1.3 Where a pressure tank is the sole water supply, an approved supervisory signal(s) shall be provided to indicate low air pressure and low water level with the signal supplied from an electrical branch circuit independent of the air compressor or, if the building has a fire alarm system, connected to the building's fire alarm system.

5.2.4.1.4 Pressure tanks shall not be used to supply other than sprinklers and hand hose attached to sprinkler piping.

5.2.4.2 Capacity.

5.2.4.2.1 In addition to the requirements of 5.1.2, the water capacity of a pressure tank shall include the extra capacity needed to fill dry pipe or preaction systems where installed.

5.2.4.2.2 The total volume shall be based on the water capacity plus the air capacity required by 5.2.4.3.

5.2.4.3* Water Level and Air Pressure.

5.2.4.3.1 Pressure tanks shall be kept with a sufficient supply of water to meet the demand of the fire protection system as calculated in Chapter 28 for the duration required by Chapter 19, Chapter 20, or Chapter 27.

5.2.4.3.2 The pressure shall be sufficient to push all of the water out of the tank while maintaining the necessary residual pressure (required by Chapter 28) at the top of the system.

5.2.5 Gravity Tanks. An elevated tank installed in accordance with NFPA 22 shall be an acceptable water supply source.

5.2.6 Penstocks, Flumes, Rivers, or Lakes. Water supply connections from penstocks, flumes, rivers, lakes, or reservoirs shall be arranged to avoid mud and sediment and shall be provided with approved double removable screens or approved strainers installed in an approved manner.

Chapter 6 Installation Underground Piping

6.1* Piping. [**24**:10.1]

6.1.1* All piping used in private fire service mains shall be in accordance with 6.1.1.1, 6.1.1.2, or 6.1.1.3. [**24**:10.1.1]

6.1.1.1 Use. Piping manufactured in accordance with Table 6.1.1.1 shall be permitted to be used. [**24**:10.1.1.1]

6.1.1.2 Piping specifically listed for use in private fire service mains shall be permitted to be used. [**24**:10.1.1.2]

6.1.1.2.1 Where listed pipe is used, it shall be installed in accordance with the listing limitations including installation instructions. [**24**:10.1.1.2.1]

6.1.1.2.2 Where listing limitations or installation instructions differ from the requirements of this standard, the listing limitations and installation instructions shall apply. [**24**:10.1.1.2.2]

6.1.1.3 Steel piping manufactured in accordance with Table 6.1.1.3 that is externally coated and wrapped and internally galvanized shall be permitted to be used between the hose coupling(s) on the fire department connection and the check valve installed in the fire department connection piping. [**24**:10.1.1.3]

6.1.1.3.1 External coating and wrapping as required by 6.1.1.3 shall be approved. [**24**:10.1.1.3.1]

6.1.1.4 Dry Pipe Underground.

6.1.1.4.1 Where necessary to place pipe that will be under air pressure underground, the pipe shall be protected against corrosion.

6.1.1.4.2 Unprotected cast-iron or ductile-iron pipe shall be permitted where joined with a gasketed joint listed for air service underground.

6.1.2* All piping used in private fire service mains shall be rated for the maximum system working pressure to which the piping is exposed to but shall not be rated at less than 150 psi (10.3 bar). [**24**:10.1.2]

Δ **Table 6.1.1.1 Manufacturing Standards for Underground Pipe**

Materials and Dimensions	Standard
Ductile Iron	
Cement-mortar lining for ductile-iron pipe and fittings	AWWA C104/A21.4
Polyethylene encasement for ductile-iron pipe systems	AWWA C105/A21.5
Rubber-gasket joints for ductile-iron pressure pipe and fittings	AWWA C111/A21.11
Flanged ductile-iron pipe with ductile-iron or gray-iron threaded flanges	AWWA C115/A21.15
Thickness design of ductile-iron pipe	AWWA C150/A21.50
Ductile-iron pipe, centrifugally cast	AWWA C151/A21.51
Ductile iron water mains and their appurtenances	AWWA C600
Concrete	
Reinforced concrete pressure pipe, steel-cylinder type	AWWA C300
Prestressed concrete pressure pipe, steel-cylinder type	AWWA C301
Reinforced concrete pressure pipe, non-cylinder type	AWWA C302
Reinforced concrete pressure pipe, steel-cylinder type, pretensioned	AWWA C303
Cement-mortar lining of water pipe lines in place, 4 in. (100 mm) and larger	AWWA C602
Plastic	
Polyvinyl chloride (PVC) pressure pipe and fabricated fittings, 4 in. through 60 in. (100 mm through 1,500 mm)	AWWA C900
Polyethylene (PE) pressure pipe and fittings, 4 in. (100 mm) through 63 in. (1575 mm) for waterworks	AWWA C906
Molecularly oriented polyvinyl chloride (PVCO), 4 in. through 24 in. (100 mm through 600 mm) for water, wastewater, and reclaimed water service	AWWA C909
Brass	
Seamless red brass pipe, standard sizes	ASTM B43
Copper	
Seamless copper tube	ASTM B75/B75M
Seamless copper water tube	ASTM B88
Wrought seamless copper and copper-alloy tube	ASTM B251
Stainless Steel	
Seamless, welded, and heavily cold worked austenitic stainless steel pipes	ASTM A312/312M

[**24**:Table 10.1.1.1]

Δ **Table 6.1.1.3 Steel Piping for Fire Department Connections**

Materials and Dimensions	Standard
Black and hot-dipped zinc-coated (galvanized) welded and seamless steel pipe for fire protection use	ASTM A795/A795M
Pipe, steel, black and hot-dipped, zinc-coated, welded and seamless	ASTM A53/A53M
Electric-resistance-welded steel pipe	ASTM A135/A135M

[**24**:Table 10.1.1.3]

6.1.3* When lined piping is used, the manufacturer's literature for internal diameter shall be used for all hydraulic calculations. [**24**:10.1.3]

6.1.4* Regardless of pipe type, underground piping shall be permitted to extend into the building through the slab or wall not more than 24 in. (600 mm). [**24**:10.1.4]

N **6.1.4.1** Underground piping extended vertically into the building through the slab shall be installed plumb. [**24**:10.1.4.1]

6.2 Fittings. [**24**:10.2]

6.2.1 All fittings used in private fire service mains shall be in accordance with 6.2.1.1 or 6.2.1.2. [**24**:10.2.1]

6.2.1.1 Fittings manufactured in accordance with Table 6.2.1.1 shall be permitted to be used. [**24**:10.2.1.1]

6.2.1.2 Special Listed Fittings. Fittings specifically listed for use in private fire service mains shall be permitted to be used. [**24**:10.2.1.2]

6.2.1.2.1 Where listed fittings are used, they shall be installed in accordance with their listing limitations including installation instructions. [**24**:10.2.1.2.1]

6.2.1.2.2 Where listing limitations or installation instructions differ from the requirements of this standard, the listing limitations and installation instructions shall apply. [**24**:10.2.1.2.2]

6.2.2 All fittings used in private fire service mains shall be rated for the maximum system working pressure to which the fittings are exposed, but shall not be rated at less than 150 psi (10.3 bar). [**24**:10.2.2]

6.2.3 Where fittings installed in a private fire service main must be installed above grade, the fittings shall conform to NFPA 13. [**24**:10.2.3]

6.2.3.1 Fittings in accordance with 6.2.1 shall be permitted for the transition to the above ground piping or fittings. [**24**:10.2.3.1]

6.3 Connection of Pipe, Fittings, and Appurtenances. [**24**:10.3]

6.3.1* Connection of all fittings and appurtenances to piping shall be in accordance with Section 6.3. [**24**:10.3.1]

Δ **Table 6.2.1.1 Fittings Materials and Dimensions**

Materials and Dimensions	Standard
Cast Iron	
Gray iron threaded fittings, classes 125 and 250	ASME B16.4
Gray iron pipe flanges and flanged fittings, classes 25, 125, and 250	ASME B16.1
Ductile Iron	
Ductile-iron and gray-iron fittings	AWWA C110/A21.10
Ductile-iron compact fittings	AWWA C153/A21.53
Malleable Iron	
Malleable iron threaded fittings, classes 150 and 300	ASME B16.3
Copper	
Wrought copper and copper alloy solder joint pressure fittings	ASME B16.22
Cast copper alloy solder joint pressure fitting	ASME B16.18
Bronze Fittings	
Cast copper alloy threaded fittings, classes 125 and 250	ASME B16.15
Stainless Steel	
Wrought austenitic stainless steel pipe fittings	ASTM A403/A403M

[**24**:Table 10.2.1.1]

6.3.2 Connections of pipe and fittings indicated in Table 6.1.1.1 and Table 6.2.1.1 shall be in accordance with the referenced standard in the table. [**24**:10.3.2]

6.3.3 Listed Connections. Connections utilizing listed products shall be in accordance with the listing limitations and the manufacturer's installation instructions. [**24**:10.3.3]

6.3.3.1 Where listing limitations or installation instructions differ from the requirements of this standard, the listing limitations and installation instructions shall apply. [**24**:10.3.3.1]

6.3.4 Threaded Pipe and Fittings. Where pipe, fittings or appurtenances are connected using threads, all threads shall be in accordance with ASME B1.20.1, *Pipe Threads, General Purpose (Inch)*. [**24**:10.3.4]

6.3.5 Grooved Connections. Where pipe, fittings, or appurtenances are connected using grooves, they shall be connected in accordance with 6.3.5.1 through 6.3.5.3. [**24**:10.3.5]

6.3.5.1 Pipe, fittings, and appurtenances to be joined with grooved couplings shall contain cut, rolled, or cast grooves that are dimensionally compatible with the couplings. [**24**:10.3.5.1]

6.3.5.2 Pipe, fittings, and appurtenances that are connected with grooved couplings and are part of a listed assembly shall be permitted to be used. [**24**:10.3.5.2]

6.3.5.3* Pipe joined with grooved fittings shall be joined by a listed combination of fittings, gaskets, and grooves. [**24**:10.3.5.3]

6.3.6 Copper Tube. All joints for the connection of copper tube shall be brazed or joined using pressure fittings as specified in Table 6.2.1.1. [**24**:10.3.6]

6.4 Protection of Private Fire Service Mains. [24:10.4]

6.4.1 Protection from Corrosion. [24:10.4.1]

6.4.1.1 Coatings. All bolted joint accessories shall be cleaned and thoroughly coated with asphalt or other corrosion-retarding material after installation. [24:10.4.1.1]

6.4.1.2 The requirements of 6.3.5.3 shall not apply to epoxy-coated fittings, valves, glands, or other accessories. [24:10.4.1.2]

6.4.1.3* Where it is necessary to join metal pipe with pipe of dissimilar metal, the joint shall be insulated against the passage of an electric current using an approved method. [24:10.4.1.3]

Δ **6.4.2* Protection of Piping.** [24:10.4.2]

6.4.2.1 Protection from Freezing. The depth of cover for private fire service mains and their appurtenances to protect against freezing shall be in accordance with 6.4.2. [24:10.4.2.1]

6.4.2.1.1* The top of the pipe shall be buried not less than 1 ft (300 mm) below the frost line for the locality. [24:10.4.2.1.1]

6.4.2.1.2 The depth of piping shall be measured from the top of the piping to the final grade. [24:10.4.2.1.2]

6.4.2.1.3 Where listed piping is used and the bury depth differs from this standard, the listing limitations shall apply. [24:10.4.2.1.3]

6.4.2.1.4 Where private fire service mains are installed above ground, they shall be protected from freezing in accordance with NFPA 13. [24:10.4.2.1.4]

6.4.2.1.5 Private fire service mains installed in water raceways or shallow streams shall be installed so that the piping will remain in the running water throughout the year. [24:10.4.2.1.5]

6.4.2.1.6 Where piping is installed adjacent to a vertical face, it shall be installed from the vertical face at the same distance as if the piping were buried. [24:10.4.2.1.6]

6.4.2.1.7 Protection of private fire service mains from freezing using heat tracing shall be permitted when the heat tracing is specifically listed for underground use. [24:10.4.2.1.7]

6.4.2.1.7.1 Heat tracing not listed for underground use shall be permitted when piping is installed in accordance with 6.1.4. [24:10.4.2.1.7.1]

6.4.2.2 Protection from Mechanical Damage. The depth of cover for private fire service mains and their appurtenances to protect against mechanical damage shall be in accordance with 6.4.2.2. [24:10.4.2.2]

6.4.2.2.1 The depth of piping shall be measured from the top of the piping to the final grade. [24:10.4.2.2.1]

6.4.2.2.2 In locations where freezing is not a factor, the depth of cover shall be not less than 30 in. (750 mm) below grade to prevent mechanical damage. [24:10.4.2.2.2]

6.4.2.2.2.1 Where listed piping is used and the bury depth differs from this standard, the listing limitations shall apply. [24:10.4.2.2.2.1]

6.4.2.2.3 Private fire service mains installed under driveways or roadways shall be buried at a minimum depth of 36 in. (900 mm). [24:10.4.2.2.3]

6.4.2.2.3.1 Sidewalks, walkways, and other paved or concrete pedestrian passageways shall not be required to comply with 6.4.2.2.3. [24:10.4.2.2.3.1]

6.4.2.2.4 Private fire service mains installed under railroad tracks shall be buried at a minimum depth of 4 ft (1.2 m). [24:10.4.2.2.4]

6.4.2.2.4.1 Where railroad operators require a greater depth of bury, the greater depth shall apply. [24:10.4.2.2.4.1]

6.4.2.2.5 Private fire service mains installed under large piles of heavy commodities or subject to heavy shock and vibrations shall be buried at a minimum depth of 4 ft (1.2 m). [24:10.4.2.2.5]

6.4.2.2.6 Where private fire service mains are installed above ground, they shall be protected with bollards or other means as approved by the AHJ when subject to mechanical damage. [24:10.4.2.2.6]

6.4.3 Private Fire Service Mains Beneath Buildings. Except as permitted by 6.4.3, private fire service mains shall not be installed beneath buildings. [24:10.4.3]

6.4.3.1* Private fire service mains supplying fire protection systems within the building shall be permitted to extend horizontally no more than 10 ft (3.0 m) cumulatively, as measured from the outside of the building, under the building to the riser location. [24:10.4.3.1]

6.4.3.1.1* Pipe joints shall not be located directly under foundation footings. [24:10.4.3.1.1]

6.4.3.1.2* Piping shall be installed a minimum of 12 in. (300 mm) below the bottom of building foundations or footers. [24:10.4.3.1.2]

6.4.3.1.2.1 The requirements of 6.4.3.1.2 shall not apply when the piping is sleeved with an approved material. [24:10.4.3.1.2.1]

6.4.3.2* Private fire service mains shall not be permitted to extend more than 10 ft (3 m) under the building except as allowed in 6.4.3.2.1. [24:10.4.3.2]

6.4.3.2.1* Where private fire service mains extend more than 10 ft (3 m) into the building, they shall be run in a covered trench. [24:10.4.3.2.1]

6.4.3.2.1.1* The trench shall be accessible from within the building. [24:10.4.3.2.1.1]

6.4.3.2.1.2 The trench shall have rigid walls and a base. [24:10.4.3.2.1.2]

6.4.3.2.1.3 The trench shall be constructed of noncombustible materials. [24:10.4.3.2.1.3]

6.4.3.2.1.4* Provisions for draining water shall be provided for the trench. [24:10.4.3.2.1.4]

6.4.3.2.1.5 Where the piping in the trench is installed under foundations or footers, clearance shall be provided in accordance with 6.4.3.1.2 or 6.4.3.1.2.1. [24:10.4.3.2.1.5]

6.4.3.2.2 Piping in the trench shall be permitted to be in accordance with 6.1.1. [**24**:10.4.3.2.2]

6.4.3.2.2.1 Aboveground piping in accordance with NFPA 13 shall be permitted to be used. [**24**:10.4.3.2.2.1]

6.4.3.2.2.2 Where piping installed in the trench is in accordance with 6.1.1, all joints shall be restrained in accordance with 6.6.2 or 6.6.3. [**24**:10.4.3.2.2.2]

6.4.3.2.3* Where piping is installed in a trench as permitted by 6.4.3.2.1, a valve shall be provided where the underground piping enters the trench. [**24**:10.4.3.2.3]

6.4.3.2.4 When piping is installed in a trench, bury depths of 6.4.2.2 shall not apply. [**24**:10.4.3.2.4]

6.4.3.2.4.1 Piping in the trench shall be protected from freezing in accordance with 6.4.2.1.4. [**24**:10.4.3.2.4.1]

6.5 Grounding and Bonding. [**24**:10.5]

6.5.1* In no case shall the underground piping be used as a grounding electrode for electrical systems. [**24**:10.5.1]

6.5.1.1* The requirement of 6.5.1 shall not preclude the bonding of the underground piping to the lightning protection grounding system as required by NFPA 780 in those cases where lightning protection is provided for the structure. [**24**:10.5.1.1]

6.6* Restraint. Private fire service mains shall be restrained against movement at changes in direction in accordance with 6.6.1, 6.6.2, or 6.6.3. [**24**:10.6]

6.6.1* Thrust Blocks.

6.6.1.1 Thrust blocks shall be permitted where soil is stable and capable of resisting the anticipated thrust forces. [**24**:10.6.1.1]

6.6.1.2 Thrust blocks shall be concrete of a mix not leaner than one part cement, two and one-half parts sand, and five parts stone. [**24**:10.6.1.2]

6.6.1.3 Thrust blocks shall be placed between undisturbed earth and the fitting to be restrained and shall be capable of resisting the calculated thrust forces. [**24**:10.6.1.3]

6.6.1.4 Wherever possible, thrust blocks shall be located so that the joints are accessible for repair. [**24**:10.6.1.4]

6.6.2* Restrained Joint Systems. Private fire service mains using restrained joint systems shall include one or more of the following:

(1) Listed locking mechanical or push-on joints
(2) Listed mechanical joints utilizing setscrew retainer glands
(3) Listed bell joint restraints
(4) Bolted flange joints
(5) Pipe clamps and tie rods in accordance with 6.6.2.1
(6) Other approved methods or devices
[**24**:10.6.2]

6.6.2.1* Sizing Clamps, Rods, Bolts, and Washers. [**24**:10.6.2.1]

6.6.2.1.1 Clamps. [**24**:10.6.2.1.1]

6.6.2.1.1.1 Clamps shall have the following dimensions:

(1) ½ in. × 2 in. (13 mm × 50 mm) for 4 in. (100 mm) to 6 in. (150 mm) pipe

(2) ⅝ in. × 2½ in. (16 mm × 65 mm) for 8 in. (200 mm) to 10 in. (250 mm) pipe
(3) ⅝ in. × 3 in. (16 mm × 75 mm) for 12 in. (300 mm) pipe
[**24**:10.6.2.1.1.1]

6.6.2.1.1.2 The diameter of a bolt hole shall be ⅛ in. (3.2 mm) larger than that of the corresponding bolt. [**24**:10.6.2.1.1.2]

6.6.2.1.2 Rods. [**24**:10.6.2.1.2]

6.6.2.1.2.1 Rods shall be not less than ⅝ in. (16 mm) in diameter. [**24**:10.6.2.1.2.1]

6.6.2.1.2.2 Table 6.6.2.1.2.2 provides the numbers of various diameter rods that shall be used for a given pipe size. [**24**:10.6.2.1.2.2]

6.6.2.1.2.3 When using bolting rods, the diameter of mechanical joint bolts shall limit the diameter of rods to ¾ in. (20 mm). [**24**:10.6.2.1.2.3]

6.6.2.1.2.4 Threaded sections of rods shall not be formed or bent. [**24**:10.6.2.1.2.4]

6.6.2.1.2.5 Where using clamps, rods shall be used in pairs for each clamp. [**24**:10.6.2.1.2.5]

6.6.2.1.2.6 Assemblies in which a restraint is made by means of two clamps canted on the barrel of the pipe shall be permitted to use one rod per clamp if approved for the specific installation by the AHJ. [**24**:10.6.2.1.2.6]

6.6.2.1.2.7 Where using combinations of rods, the rods shall be symmetrically spaced. [**24**:10.6.2.1.2.7]

6.6.2.1.3 Clamp Bolts. Clamp bolts shall have the following diameters:

(1) ⅝ in. (16 mm) for pipe 4 in. (100 mm), 6 in. (150 mm), and 8 in. (200 mm)
(2) ¾ in. (20 mm) for 10 in. (250 mm) pipe
(3) ⅞ in. (22 mm) for 12 in. (300 mm) pipe
[**24**:10.6.2.1.3]

6.6.2.1.4 Washers. [**24**:10.6.2.1.4]

6.6.2.1.4.1 Washers shall be permitted to be cast iron or steel and round or square. [**24**:10.6.2.1.4.1]

Δ **Table 6.6.2.1.2.2 Rod Number — Diameter Combinations**

Nominal Pipe Size		⅝ in.	¾ in.	⅞ in.	1 in.
in.	mm	(16 mm)	(20 mm)	(22 mm)	(25 mm)
4	100	2	—	—	—
6	150	2	—	—	—
8	200	3	2	—	—
10	250	4	3	2	—
12	300	6	4	3	2
14	350	8	5	4	3
16	400	10	7	5	4

Note: This table has been derived using pressure of 225 psi (15.5 bar) and design stress of 25,000 psi (172.4 MPa).
[**24**:Table 10.6.2.1.2.2]

6.6.2.1.4.2 Cast-iron washers shall have the following dimensions:

(1) ⅝ in. × 3 in. (16 mm × 75 mm) for 4 in. (100 mm), 6 in. (150 mm), 8 in. (200 mm), and 10 in. (250 mm) pipe
(2) ¾ in. × 3½ in. (20 mm × 90 mm) for 12 in. (300 mm) pipe
[**24:**10.6.2.1.4.2]

6.6.2.1.4.3 Steel washers shall have the following dimensions:

(1) ½ in. × 3 in. (12 mm × 75 mm) for 4 in. (100 mm), 6 in. (150 mm), 8 in. (200 mm), and 10 in. (250 mm) pipe
(2) ½ in. × 3½ in. (12 mm × 90 mm) for 12 in. (300 mm) pipe
[**24:**10.6.2.1.4.3]

6.6.2.1.4.4 The diameter of holes shall be ⅛ in. (3 mm) larger than that of bolts or rods. [**24:**10.6.2.1.4.4]

6.6.2.2 Sizes of Restraint Straps for Tees. [**24:**10.6.2.2]

6.6.2.2.1 Restraint straps for tees shall have the following dimensions:

(1) ⅝ in. (16 mm) thick and 2½ in. (65 mm) wide for 4 in. (100 mm), 6 in. (150 mm), 8 in. (200 mm), and 10 in. (250 mm) pipe
(2) ⅝ in. (16 mm) thick and 3 in. (75 mm) wide for 12 in. (300 mm) pipe
[**24:**10.6.2.2.1]

6.6.2.2.2 The diameter of rod holes shall be 1/16 in. (1.6 mm) larger than that of rods. [**24:**10.6.2.2.2]

6.6.2.2.3 Figure 6.6.2.2.3 and Table 6.6.2.2.3 shall be used in sizing the restraint straps for both mechanical and push-on joint tee fittings. [**24:**10.6.2.2.3]

6.6.2.3 Sizes of Plug Strap for Bell End of Pipe. [**24:**10.6.2.3]

6.6.2.3.1 The strap shall be ¾ in. (20 mm) thick and 2½ in. (65 mm) wide. [**24:**10.6.2.3.1]

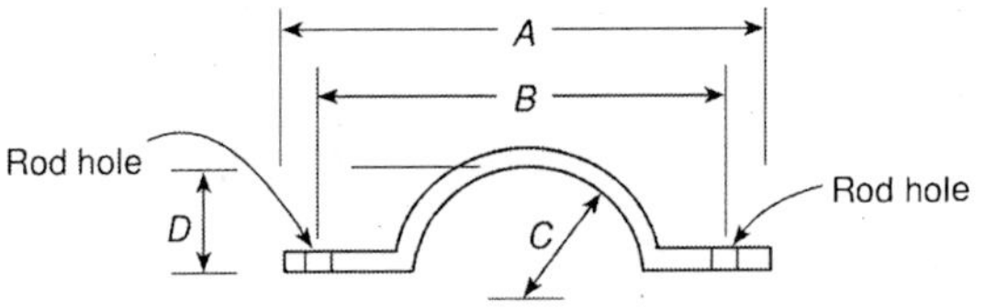

FIGURE 6.6.2.2.3 Restraint Straps for Tees. [24:Figure 10.6.2.2.3]

6.6.2.3.2 The strap length shall be the same as dimension *A* for tee straps as shown in Figure 6.6.2.2.3. [**24:**10.6.2.3.2]

6.6.2.3.3 The distance between the centers of rod holes shall be the same as dimension *B* for tee straps as shown in Figure 6.6.2.2.3. [**24:**10.6.2.3.3]

6.6.2.4 Material. Clamps, rods, rod couplings or turnbuckles, bolts, washers, restraint straps, and plug straps shall be of a material that has physical and chemical characteristics that indicate its deterioration under stress can be predicted with reliability. [**24:**10.6.2.4]

Δ **6.6.2.5 Corrosion Resistance.** After installation, rods, nuts, bolts, washers, clamps, and other restraining devices shall be cleaned and thoroughly coated with a corrosion-retarding material. [**24:**10.6.2.5]

6.6.2.5.1 The requirements of 6.6.2.5 shall not apply to epoxy-coated fittings, valves, glands, or other accessories. [**24:**10.6.2.5.1]

6.6.3* Private fire service mains utilizing one or more of the following connection methods shall not require additional restraint, provided that such joints can pass the hydrostatic test of 6.10.2.2 without shifting of piping.

(1) Threaded connections
(2) Grooved connections
(3) Welded connections
(4) Heat-fused connections
(5) Chemical or solvent cemented connections
[**24:**10.6.3]

6.7 Steep Grades. [**24:**10.7]

6.7.1 On steep grades, mains shall be additionally restrained to prevent slipping. [**24:**10.7.1]

6.7.1.1 Pipe shall be restrained at the bottom of a hill and at any turns (lateral or vertical). [**24:**10.7.1.1]

6.7.1.1.1 The restraint specified in 6.7.1.1 shall be to natural rock or to piles or piers built on the downhill side of the bell. [**24:**10.7.1.1.1]

6.7.1.2 Bell ends shall be installed facing uphill. [**24:**10.7.1.2]

6.7.1.3 Straight runs on hills shall be restrained as determined by a design professional. [**24:**10.7.1.3]

Δ **Table 6.6.2.2.3 Restraint Straps for Tees**

Nominal Pipe Size		A		B		C		D	
in.	mm	in.	mm	in.	mm	in.	mm	in.	mm
4	100	12½	315	10⅛	255	2½	65	1¾	45
6	150	14½	365	12⅛	305	3 9/16	90	2 13/16	70
8	200	16¾	420	14⅜	360	4 21/32	115	3 29/32	100
10	250	19 1/16	475	16 11/16	415	5¾	145	5	125
12	300	22 5/16	560	19 3/16	480	6¾	170	5⅞	145

[**24:**Table 10.6.2.2.3]

6.8 Installation Requirements. [24:10.8]

6.8.1 Piping, valves, hydrants, gaskets, and fittings shall be inspected for damage when received and shall be inspected prior to installation. [24:10.8.1]

6.8.2 The tightness of bolted joints shall be verified by the bolt torque or by the method described in the listing information or manufacturer's installation instructions. [24:10.8.2]

6.8.3 Pipe, valves, hydrants, and fittings shall be clean and free from internal debris. [24:10.8.3]

6.8.4 When work is stopped, the open ends of piping, valves, hydrants, and fittings shall be plugged or covered to prevent foreign materials from entering. [24:10.8.4]

6.8.5 All piping, fittings, valves, and hydrants shall be examined for cracks or other defects while suspended above the trench and lowered into the trench using equipment designed for such use. [24:10.8.5]

6.8.6 Plain ends shall be inspected for signs of damage prior to installation. [24:10.8.6]

6.8.7 Piping, fittings, valves, hydrants, and appurtenances shall not be dropped, dumped or rolled or skidded against other materials. [24:10.8.7]

6.8.8 Pipes shall be supported in the trench throughout their full length and shall not be supported by the bell ends only or by blocks. [24:10.8.8]

6.8.9 If the ground is soft, other means shall be provided to support the pipe. [24:10.8.9]

6.8.10 Valves and fittings used with nonmetallic pipe shall be supported and restrained in accordance with the manufacturer's installation instructions. [24:10.8.10]

6.9 Backfilling. [24:10.9]

6.9.1 Backfill material shall be tamped in layers or in puddles under and around pipes to prevent settlement or lateral movement and shall contain no ashes, cinders, refuse, organic matter, or other corrosive materials. [24:10.9.1]

6.9.2 Backfill material shall not contain ash, cinders, refuse, organic matter or other corrosive materials. [24:10.9.2]

6.9.3* In the absence of specific guidelines or specifications, the maximum allowable particle size for backfill within 1 ft (300 mm) of the pipe shall not be larger than 1½ in. (40 mm). [24:10.9.3]

6.9.3.1 Nominal pipe sizes of 4 in. (100 mm) or smaller shall not exceed ½ in. (13 mm) maximum particle size. [24:10.9.3.1]

6.9.3.2 Nominal pipe sizes of 6 in. to 12 in. (150 mm to 300 mm) shall not exceed ¾ in. (19 mm) maximum particle size. [24:10.9.3.2]

6.9.4 Frozen earth shall not be used as backfill material. [24:10.9.4]

6.9.5 In trenches cut through rock, tamped backfill shall be used for at least 6 in. (150 mm) under and around the pipe and for at least 2 ft (600 mm) above the pipe. [24:10.9.5]

6.9.6 Where using piping listed for private fire service mains, the manufacturer's installation instructions for backfill shall be followed. [24:10.9.6]

6.10 Testing and Acceptance. [24:10.10]

Δ 6.10.1 Approval of Underground Piping. [24:10.10.1]

N 6.10.1.1 The installing contractor shall be responsible for the following:

(1) Notifying the AHJ and the owner's representative of the time and date testing is to be performed
(2) Performing all required acceptance tests
(3) Completing and signing a contractor's material and test certificate(s) shown in Figure 6.10.1.1

[24:10.10.1.1]

N 6.10.1.2 Alternate forms or electronic records providing at minimum the required information found in Figure 6.10.1.1 shall be permitted. [24:10.10.1.2]

6.10.2 Acceptance Requirements. [24:10.10.2]

6.10.2.1* Flushing of Piping. [24:10.10.2.1]

6.10.2.1.1 Underground piping, from the water supply to the system riser, and lead-in connections to the system riser, including all hydrants, shall be completely flushed before connection is made to downstream fire protection system piping. [24:10.10.2.1.1]

6.10.2.1.2 The flushing operation shall continue until water flow is verified to be clear of debris. [24:10.10.2.1.2]

6.10.2.1.3* The minimum rate of flow shall be in accordance with Table 6.10.2.1.3. [24:10.10.2.1.3]

6.10.2.1.3.1 Where the flow rates established in Table 6.10.2.1.3 are not attainable, the maximum allowable flow rate at the minimum allowable residual pressure to the system shall be acceptable. [24:10.10.2.1.3.1]

N 6.10.2.1.3.2 Suction piping supplying fire pump(s) shall be flushed prior to connecting to the fire pump(s) based on the requirements of NFPA 20. [24:10.10.2.1.3.2]

N 6.10.2.1.4* In lieu of flushing with the waterflow rates prescribed in 6.10.2.1.3 and 6.10.2.1.3.1, water main cleaning of the piping by the forceful introduction of swabs through the pipe shall be permitted. [24:10.10.2.1.4]

N 6.10.2.1.4.1 Water main swabbing shall be repeated, as necessary, until the last swab that has fully penetrated the pipe is clean and the discharge water is clear. [24:10.10.2.1.4.1]

Δ 6.10.2.1.5 Provision shall be made for the disposal of water used for flushing or testing to minimize any water damage caused by the discharge. [24:10.10.2.1.5]

6.10.2.2 Hydrostatic Test. [24:10.10.2.2]

6.10.2.2.1* All piping and attached appurtenances subjected to system working pressure shall be hydrostatically tested at gauge pressure of 200 psi (14 bar) or 50 psi (3.4 bar) in excess of the system working pressure, whichever is greater, and shall maintain that pressure at gauge pressure of ±5 psi (0.3 bar) for 2 hours. [24:10.10.2.2.1]

Contractor's Material and Test Certificate for Underground Piping

PROCEDURE

Upon completion of work, inspection and tests shall be made by the contractor's representative and witnessed by an owner's representative. All defects shall be corrected and system left in service before contractor's personnel finally leave the job.

A certificate shall be filled out and signed by both representatives. Copies shall be prepared for approving authorities, owners, and contractor. It is understood the owner's representative's signature in no way prejudices any claim against contractor for faulty material, poor workmanship, or failure to comply with approving authority's requirements or local ordinances.

Property name		Date

Property address	

Plans	Accepted by approving authorities (names)	
	Address	
	Installation conforms to accepted plans	☐ Yes ☐ No
	Equipment used is approved If no, state deviations	☐ Yes ☐ No
Instructions	Has person in charge of fire equipment been instructed as to location of control valves and care and maintenance of this new equipment? If no, explain	☐ Yes ☐ No
	Have copies of appropriate instructions and care and maintenance charts been provided to the owner or owner's representative? If no, explain	☐ Yes ☐ No
Location	Supplies buildings	

Underground pipes and joints	Pipe types and class	Type joint
	Pipe conforms to _____ standard	☐ Yes ☐ No
	Fittings conform to _____ standard If no, explain	☐ Yes ☐ No
	Joints needing anchorage clamped, strapped, or blocked in accordance with _____ standard If no, explain	☐ Yes ☐ No

Test description

Flushing: Flow the required rate until water is verified to be clear of debris at outlets such as hydrants and blow-offs. Flush at one of the flow rates as specified in 6.10.2.1.3.

Hydrostatic: All piping and attached appurtenances subjected to system working pressure shall be hydrostatically tested at 200 psi (13.8 bar) or 50 psi (3.4 bar) in excess of the system working pressure, whichever is greater, and shall maintain that pressure ±5 psi (0.34 bar) for 2 hours.

Hydrostatic Testing Allowance: Where additional water is added to the system to maintain the test pressures required by 6.10.2.2.1, the amount of water shall be measured and shall not exceed the limits of the following equation (for metric equation, see 6.10.2.2.6):

$$L = \frac{SD\sqrt{P}}{148,000}$$

L = testing allowance (makeup water), in gallons per hour (lpm)
S = length of pipe tested, in feet (m)
D = nominal diameter of the pipe, in inches (mm)
P = average test pressure during the hydrostatic test, in pounds per square inch (gauge) (bar)

Flushing tests	New underground piping flushed according to _____ standard by (company) If no, explain	☐ Yes ☐ No
	How flushing flow was obtained ☐ Public water ☐ Tank or reservoir ☐ Fire pump	Through what type opening ☐ Hydrant butt ☐ Open pipe
	Lead-ins flushed according to _____ standard by (company) If no, explain	☐ Yes ☐ No
	How flushing flow was obtained ☐ Public water ☐ Tank or reservoir ☐ Fire pump	Through what type opening ☐ Y connection to flange and spigot ☐ Open pipe

© 2021 National Fire Protection Association

NFPA 13 (p. 1 of 2)

N **FIGURE 6.10.1.1** Sample of Contractor's Material and Test Certificate for Underground Piping. [24:Figure 10.10.1.1]

Hydrostatic test	All new underground piping hydrostatically tested at _____ psi (bar) for _____ hours		Joints covered ☐ Yes ☐ No
Leakage test	Total amount of leakage measured _____ gallons (liters) _____ hours		
	Allowable leakage _____ gallons (liters) _____ hours		
Forward flow test of backflow preventer	Forward flow test performed in accordance with 6.10.2.5.2:		☐ Yes ☐ No
Hydrants	Number installed	Type and make	All operate satisfactorily ☐ Yes ☐ No
Control valves	Water control valves left wide open If no, state reason		☐ Yes ☐ No
	Hose threads of fire department connections and hydrants interchangeable with those of fire department answering alarm		☐ Yes ☐ No
Remarks	Date left in service		

Signatures	Name of installing contractor		
	Tests witnessed by		
	For property owner (signed)	Title	Date
	For installing contractor (signed)	Title	Date

Additional explanation and notes

NFPA 13 (p. 2 of 2)

N **FIGURE 6.10.1.1**   *Continued*

Δ **Table 6.10.2.1.3 Flow Required to Produce Velocity of 10 ft/sec (3.0 m/sec) in Pipes**

Nominal Pipe Size (in.)	Flow Rate (gpm)	Nominal Pipe Size (mm)	Flow Rate (L/min)
2	100	50	380
2½	150	65	570
3	220	75	833
4	390	100	1,500
5	610	125	2,300
6	880	150	3,350
8	1,560	200	5,900
10	2,440	250	9,250
12	3,520	300	13,300

[**24**:Table 10.10.2.1.3]

6.10.2.2.2 Successful test results shall be determined by indication of either a pressure loss less than gauge pressure of 5 psi (0.3 bar) or by no visual leakage. [**24**:10.10.2.2.2]

6.10.2.2.3 The test pressure shall be read from one of the following, located at the lowest elevation of the system or the portion of the system being tested:

(1) A gauge located at one of the hydrant outlets
(2) A gauge located at the lowest point where no hydrants are provided

[**24**:10.10.2.2.3]

6.10.2.2.4* The trench shall be backfilled between joints before testing to prevent movement of pipe. [**24**:10.10.2.2.4]

6.10.2.2.5 Where required for safety measures presented by the hazards of open trenches, the pipe and joints shall be permitted to be backfilled, provided the installing contractor takes the responsibility for locating and correcting leakage. [**24**:10.10.2.2.5]

6.10.2.2.6* Hydrostatic Testing Allowance. Where additional water is added to the system to maintain the test pressures required by 6.10.2.2.1, the amount of water shall be measured and shall not exceed the limits of Table 6.10.2.2.6, which are based upon the following equations:

U.S. Customary Units:

[6.10.2.2.6a]

$$L = \frac{SD\sqrt{P}}{148,000}$$

where:
L = testing allowance (makeup water) [gph (gal/hr)]
S = length of pipe tested (ft)
D = nominal diameter of pipe (in.)
P = average test pressure during hydrostatic test (gauge psi)

Metric Units:

[6.10.2.2.6b]

$$L = \frac{SD\sqrt{P}}{794,797}$$

where:
L = testing allowance (makeup water) (L/hr)
S = length of pipe tested (m)
D = nominal diameter of pipe (mm)
P = average test pressure during hydrostatic test (kPa)
[**24**:10.10.2.2.6]

Δ **Table 6.10.2.2.6 Hydrostatic Testing Allowance at 200 psi (14 bar)**

Nominal Pipe Diameter		Testing Allowance	
in.	mm	Gal/hr/100 ft	L/hr/100 m
2	50	0.019	0.236
4	100	0.03	0.472
6	150	0.057	0.708
8	200	0.076	0.944
10	250	0.096	1.19
12	300	0.115	1.43
14	350	0.134	1.66
16	400	0.153	1.90
18	450	0.172	2.14
20	500	0.191	2.37
24	600	0.229	2.84

Notes:
(1) For other length, diameters, and pressures, utilize Equation 6.10.2.2.6a or 6.10.2.2.6b to determine the appropriate testing allowance.
(2) For test sections that contain various sizes and sections of pipe, the testing allowance is the sum of the testing allowances for each size and section.
[**24**:Table 10.10.2.2.6]

6.10.2.3* Other Means of Hydrostatic Tests. Where acceptable to the AHJ, hydrostatic tests shall be permitted to be completed in accordance with the guidelines provided in AWWA C600, *Installation of Ductile Iron Water Mains and Their Appurtenances,* AWWA M9, *Concrete Pressure Pipe,* AWWA M23, *PVC Pipe — Design and Installation,* or AWWA M55, *PE Pipe — Design and Installation,* as long as the test pressure and test duration requirements of 6.10.2.2.1 are still employed. [**24**:10.10.2.3]

N **6.10.2.3.1*** For existing system modifications or repairs that cannot be isolated, hydrostatic testing shall be limited to visual evidence of leakage at system working pressure. [**24**:10.10.2.3.1]

6.10.2.4 Operating Test. [**24**:10.10.2.4]

6.10.2.4.1 Each hydrant shall be fully opened and closed under system water pressure. [**24**:10.10.2.4.1]

Δ **6.10.2.4.2** Dry barrel hydrants shall be checked for drainage. [**24**:10.10.2.4.2]

Δ **6.10.2.4.3** All control valves shall be fully closed and opened under system water pressure to ensure operation. [**24**:10.10.2.4.3]

6.10.2.4.4 Where fire pumps supply the private fire service main, the operating tests required by 6.10.2.4 shall be completed with the pumps running. [**24**:10.10.2.4.4]

6.10.2.5 Backflow Prevention Assemblies. [**24**:10.10.2.5]

Δ **6.10.2.5.1** The backflow prevention assembly shall be forward flow tested. [**24**:10.10.2.5.1]

6.10.2.5.2 The minimum flow rate tested in 6.10.2.5.1 shall be the system demand, including hose stream demand where applicable. [**24**:10.10.2.5.2]

Chapter 7   Requirements for System Components and Hardware

7.1 General. This chapter shall provide requirements for correct use of sprinkler system components and hardware.

7.1.1* Listing.

7.1.1.1 Materials or devices not specifically designated by this standard shall be used in accordance with all conditions, requirements, and limitations of their special listing.

7.1.1.1.1 All special listing requirements shall be included and identified in the product submittal literature and installation instructions.

7.1.1.2 Unless the requirements of 7.1.1.3, 7.1.1.4, or 7.1.1.5 are met, all materials and devices essential to successful system operation shall be listed.

7.1.1.2.1 Valve components (including valve trim, internal parts, gaskets, and the like) shall not be required to be individually listed.

7.1.1.3 Equipment as permitted in Table 7.3.1.1 and Table 7.4.1 shall not be required to be listed.

7.1.1.3.1 Nonmetallic pipe and fittings included in Table 7.3.1.1 and Table 7.4.1 shall be listed.

7.1.1.4 Materials meeting the requirements of 17.1.2, 17.1.6.2, 17.1.6.3, and 17.1.7.3 shall not be required to be listed.

7.1.1.5* Components that do not affect system performance shall not be required to be listed.

7.1.2 Rated Pressure. System components shall be rated for the maximum system working pressure to which they are exposed but shall not be rated at less than 175 psi (12 bar) for components installed above ground and 150 psi (10 bar) for components installed underground.

7.2 Sprinklers.

7.2.1* Sprinkler Identification. All sprinklers shall be permanently marked with one or two English uppercase alphabetic characters to identify the manufacturer, immediately followed by three or four numbers, to uniquely identify a sprinkler as to K-factor, deflector characteristic, pressure rating, and thermal sensitivity.

7.2.2 Sprinkler Discharge Characteristics.

7.2.2.1* General. Unless the requirements of 7.2.2.2, 7.2.2.3, or 7.2.2.4 are met, the K-factor, relative discharge, and marking identification for sprinklers having different K-factors shall be in accordance with Table 7.2.2.1.

7.2.2.2 Pipe Threads. Listed sprinklers having pipe threads different from those shown in Table 7.2.2.1 shall be permitted.

7.2.2.3 K-Factors Greater than K-28.0 (400). Sprinklers listed with nominal K-factors greater than K-28.0 (400) shall increase the flow by 100 percent increments when compared with a nominal K-5.6 (80) sprinkler.

7.2.2.4 Residential Sprinklers. Residential sprinklers shall be permitted with K-factors other than those specified in Table 7.2.2.1.

7.2.2.5 CMSA and ESFR K-Factors. Control mode specific application (CMSA) and early suppression fast-response (ESFR) sprinklers shall have a minimum nominal K-factor of K-11.2 (160).

7.2.2.6 ESFR K-Factor. ESFR sprinkler K-factor shall be selected as appropriate for the hazard. *(See Chapter 20.)*

7.2.3 Occupancy Limitations. Unless the requirements of 7.2.3.1 or 7.2.3.2 are met, sprinklers shall not be listed for protection of a portion of an occupancy classification.

Δ **Table 7.2.2.1 Sprinkler Discharge Characteristics Identification**

Nominal K-Factor [gpm/(psi)$^{1/2}$]	Nominal K-Factor [L/min/(bar)$^{1/2}$]	K-Factor Range [gpm/(psi)$^{1/2}$]	K-Factor Range [L/min/(bar)$^{1/2}$]	Percent of Nominal K-5.6 Discharge	Thread Type
1.4	20	1.3–1.5	19–22	25	½ in. (15 mm) NPT
1.9	27	1.8–2.0	26–29	33.3	½ in. (15 mm) NPT
2.8	40	2.6–2.9	38–42	50	½ in. (15 mm) NPT
4.2	60	4.0–4.4	57–63	75	½ in. (15 mm) NPT
5.6	80	5.3–5.8	76–84	100	½ in. (15 mm) NPT
8.0	115	7.4–8.2	107–118	140	¾ in. (20 mm) NPT or ½ in. (15 mm) NPT
11.2	160	10.7–11.7	159–166	200	½ in. (15 mm) NPT or ¾ in. (20 mm) NPT
14.0	200	13.5–14.5	195–209	250	¾ in. (20 mm) NPT
16.8	240	16.0–17.6	231–254	300	¾ in. (20 mm) NPT
19.6	280	18.6–20.6	272–301	350	1 in. (25 mm) NPT
22.4	320	21.3–23.5	311–343	400	1 in. (25 mm) NPT
25.2	360	23.9–26.5	349–387	450	1 in. (25 mm) NPT
28.0	400	26.6–29.4	389–430	500	1 in. (25 mm) NPT
33.6	480	31.9–35.3	456–504	600	1¼ in. (32 mm) NPT

Note: The nominal K-factor for dry-type sprinklers are used for sprinkler selection. See 28.2.4.10.3 for use of adjusted dry-type sprinkler K-factors for hydraulic calculation purposes.

7.2.3.1 Residential Sprinklers. Residential sprinklers shall be permitted to be listed for portions of residential occupancies as defined in 12.1.1.

7.2.3.2 Special Sprinklers. Special sprinklers shall be permitted to be listed for protection of a specific construction feature in a portion of an occupancy classification. *(See Section 15.2.)*

7.2.4* Temperature Characteristics.

7.2.4.1* Automatic sprinklers shall have their frame arms, deflector, coating material, or liquid bulb colored in accordance with the requirements of Table 7.2.4.1(a) and Table 7.2.4.1(b) or the requirements of 7.2.4.2, 7.2.4.3, 7.2.4.4, or 7.2.4.5.

7.2.4.2 A dot on the top of the deflector, the color of the coating material, or colored frame arms shall be permitted for color identification of corrosion-resistant sprinklers.

7.2.4.3 Color identification shall not be required for ornamental sprinklers such as factory-plated or factory-painted sprinklers or for recessed, flush, or concealed sprinklers.

7.2.4.4 The frame arms of bulb-type sprinklers shall not be required to be color coded.

7.2.4.5 The liquid in bulb-type sprinklers shall be color coded in accordance with Table 7.2.4.1(a).

7.2.5 Special Coatings.

7.2.5.1* Corrosion Resistant.

7.2.5.2* Painting. Sprinklers shall only be painted by the sprinkler manufacturer.

7.2.5.3 Ornamental Finishes.

7.2.5.3.1 Ornamental finishes shall only be applied to sprinklers and, if applicable, their concealed cover plates, by the sprinkler manufacturer.

Δ **7.2.5.3.2** Sprinklers with ornamental finishes shall be specifically listed.

7.2.6 Escutcheons and Cover Plates.

7.2.6.1 Plates, escutcheons, or other devices used to cover the annular space around a sprinkler shall be metallic or shall be listed for use around a sprinkler.

7.2.6.2* Escutcheons used with recessed, flush-type, or concealed sprinklers shall be part of a listed sprinkler assembly.

7.2.6.3 Cover plates used with concealed sprinklers shall be part of the listed sprinkler assembly.

7.3 Aboveground Pipe and Tube.

7.3.1 General.

7.3.1.1 Pipe or tube shall meet or exceed one of the standards in Table 7.3.1.1 or be in accordance with 7.3.3.

7.3.2* Nonmetallic Pipe and Tubing.

7.3.2.1 Nonmetallic pipe in accordance with Table 7.3.1.1 shall be investigated for suitability in automatic sprinkler installations and listed for this service.

Δ Table 7.2.4.1(a) Temperature Ratings, Classifications, and Color Codings for Glass Bulbs

Maximum Ceiling Temperature		Temperature Rating		Temperature Classification	Glass Bulb Colors
°F	°C	°F	°C		
100	38	135	57	Ordinary	Orange
120	49	155	68	Ordinary	Red
150	66	175	79	Intermediate	Yellow
150	66	200	93	Intermediate	Green
225	107	250–300	121–149	High	Blue
300	149	325–375	163–191	Extra high	Purple
375	191	400–475	204–246	Very extra high	Black
475	246	500–575	260–302	Ultra high	Black
625	329	650	343	Ultra high	Black

N Table 7.2.4.1(b) Temperature Ratings, Classifications, and Color Codings for Fusible Links

Maximum Ceiling Temperature		Temperature Rating		Temperature Classification	Color Code
°F	°C	°F	°C		
100	38	135–170	57–77	Ordinary	Uncolored or black
150	66	175–225	79–107	Intermediate	White
225	107	250–300	121–149	High	Blue
300	149	325–375	163–191	Extra high	Red
375	191	400–475	204–246	Very extra high	Green
475	246	500–575	260–302	Ultra high	Orange
625	329	650	343	Ultra high	Orange

7.3.2.1.1 Other types of nonmetallic pipe or tube investigated for suitability in automatic sprinkler installations and listed for this service, including but not limited to CPVC, and differing from that provided in Table 7.3.1.1 shall be permitted where installed in accordance with their listing limitations.

7.3.2.1.2 Manufacturer's installation instructions shall include its listing limitations.

Table 7.3.1.1 Pipe or Tube Materials and Dimensions

Materials and Dimensions	Standard
Ferrous Piping (Welded and Seamless)	
Standard Specification for Black and Hot-Dipped Zinc-Coated (Galvanized) Welded and Seamless Steel Pipe for Fire Protection Use	ASTM A795/A795M
Standard Specification for Pipe, Steel, Black and Hot-Dipped, Zinc-Coated, Welded and Seamless	ASTM A53/A53M
Welded and Seamless Wrought Steel Pipe	ASME B36.10M
Standard Specification for Electric-Resistance-Welded Steel Pipe	ASTM A135/A135M
Copper Tube (Drawn, Seamless)	
Standard Specification for Seamless Copper Tube	ASTM B75/B75M
Standard Specification for Seamless Copper Water Tube	ASTM B88
Standard Specification for General Requirements for Wrought Seamless Copper and Copper-Alloy Tube	ASTM B251
Standard Specification for Liquid and Paste Fluxes for Soldering of Copper and Copper Alloy Tube	ASTM B813
Specification for Filler Metals for Brazing and Braze Welding (Classification BCuP-3 or BCuP-4)	AWS A5.8M/A5.8
Standard Specification for Solder Metal, Section 1: Solder Alloys Containing Less Than 0.2% Lead and Having Solidus Temperatures Greater than 400°F	ASTM B32
Alloy Materials	ASTM B446
CPVC	
Standard Specification for Chlorinated Poly(Vinyl Chloride) (CPVC) Plastic Pipe (SDR-PR)	ASTM F442/F442M
Brass Pipe	
Standard Specification for Seamless Red Brass Pipe, Standard Sizes	ASTM B43
Stainless Steel	
Standard Specification for Seamless, Welded, and Heavily Cold Worked Austenitic Stainless Steel Pipes	ASTM A312/A312M

7.3.2.2 Nonmetallic pipe shall not be listed for portions of an occupancy classification.

7.3.3* Listed Metallic Pipe and Tubing.

7.3.3.1 Other types of pipe or tube investigated for suitability in automatic sprinkler installations and listed for this service, including steel, and differing from that provided in Table 7.3.1.1 shall be permitted where installed in accordance with their listing limitations, including installation instructions.

7.3.3.2 Pipe or tube shall not be listed for portions of an occupancy classification.

7.3.4 Pipe and Tube Identification.

7.3.4.1* All pipe shall be marked along its length by the manufacturer in such a way as to properly identify the type of pipe.

7.3.4.2 The marking shall be visible on every piece of pipe over 2 ft (600 mm) long.

7.3.4.3 Pipe identification shall include the manufacturer's name, model designation, or schedule.

7.4 Fittings.

7.4.1 Fittings used in sprinkler systems shall meet or exceed the standards in Table 7.4.1 or be in accordance with 7.4.2 or 7.4.4.

7.4.2 In addition to the standards in Table 7.4.1, nonmetallic fittings shall also be in accordance with 7.4.4.

7.4.3 Nonmetallic Fittings. Nonmetallic fittings in accordance with Table 7.4.1 shall be investigated for suitability in automatic sprinkler installations and listed for this service. Listed nonmetallic fittings shall be installed in accordance with their listing limitations, including installation instructions.

7.4.4* Other types of fittings investigated for suitability in automatic sprinkler installations and listed for this service, including but not limited to CPVC and steel, and differing from that provided in Table 7.4.1 shall be permitted when installed in accordance with their listing limitations, including installation instructions.

7.5 Joining of Pipe and Fittings.

7.5.1 Threaded Pipe and Fittings.

7.5.1.1 All threaded pipe and fittings shall have threads cut to ASME B1.20.1, *Pipe Threads, General Purpose (Inch)*.

7.5.1.2* Steel pipe with wall thicknesses less than Schedule 30 [in sizes 8 in. (200 mm) and larger] or Schedule 40 [in sizes less than 8 in. (200 mm)] shall only be permitted to be joined by threaded fittings where the threaded assembly is investigated for suitability in automatic sprinkler installations and listed for this service.

7.5.1.3 Joint compound or tape shall be applied only to male threads.

7.5.2 Welded Pipe and Fittings.

7.5.2.1 General.

7.5.2.1.1 Welding shall be permitted as a means of joining sprinkler piping in accordance with 7.5.2.2 through 7.5.2.6.

Table 7.4.1 Fittings Materials and Dimensions

Materials and Dimensions	Standard
Cast Iron	
Gray Iron Threaded Fittings, Classes 125 and 250	ASME B16.4
Gray Iron Pipe Flanges and Flanged Fittings, Classes 25, 125, and 250	ASME B16.1
Malleable Iron	
Malleable Iron Threaded Fittings, Classes 150 and 300	ASME B16.3
Steel	
Factory-Made Wrought Buttwelding Fittings	ASME B16.9
Buttwelding Ends	ASME B16.25
Standard Specification for Piping Fittings of Wrought Carbon Steel and Alloy Steel for Moderate and High Temperature Service	ASTM A234/A234M
Pipe Flanges and Flanged Fittings, NPS-1/2 through NPS 24 Metric/Inch Standard	ASME B16.5
Forged Fittings, Socket-Welding and Threaded	ASME B16.11
Copper	
Wrought Copper and Copper Alloy Solder Joint Pressure Fittings	ASME B16.22
Cast Copper Alloy Solder Joint Pressure Fittings	ASME B16.18
CPVC	
Standard Specification for Threaded Chlorinated Poly(Vinyl Chloride) (CPVC) Plastic Pipe Fittings, Schedule 80	ASTM F437
Standard Specification for Socket-Type Chlorinated Poly(Vinyl Chloride) (CPVC) Plastic Pipe Fittings, Schedule 40	ASTM F438
Standard Specification for Chlorinated Poly(Vinyl Chloride) (CPVC) Plastic Pipe Fittings, Schedule 80	ASTM F439
Bronze Fittings	
Cast Copper Alloy Threaded Fittings, Classes 125 and 250	ASME B16.15
Stainless Steel	
Standard Specification for Wrought Austenitic Stainless Steel Piping Fittings	ASTM A403/A403M

7.5.2.2* Fabrication.

7.5.2.2.1 When welding sprinkler pipe, the pipe shall be shop welded unless the requirements of 7.5.2.2 or 7.5.2.3 are met.

N **7.5.2.2.1.1** Repair of weld leaks on site shall be permitted provided the repairs are performed in accordance with 7.5.2.2.2 and 7.5.2.5.

Δ **7.5.2.2.2** Where the design specifications require any part of the piping system to be welded in place, welding of sprinkler piping shall be permitted where the welding process is performed in accordance with NFPA 51B and the fittings required by Section 16.6 are provided.

7.5.2.2.3 Tabs for longitudinal earthquake bracing shall be permitted to be welded to in-place piping where the welding process is performed in accordance with NFPA 51B.

7.5.2.2.4 Welding shall not be performed where there is impingement of rain, snow, sleet, or high wind on the weld area of the pipe product.

7.5.2.2.5 Torch cutting and welding shall not be permitted as a means of modifying or repairing sprinkler systems.

7.5.2.3 Fittings.

7.5.2.3.1* Welded fittings used to join pipe shall be listed fabricated fittings or manufactured in accordance with Table 7.4.1.

7.5.2.3.2 Fittings referenced in 7.5.2.3.1 shall be joined in conformance with a qualified welding procedure as set forth in this section and shall be an acceptable product under this standard, provided that materials and wall thickness are compatible with other sections of this standard.

7.5.2.3.3 Fittings shall not be required where pipe ends are buttwelded in accordance with the requirements of 7.5.2.4.3.

7.5.2.3.4 When the pipe size in a run of piping is reduced, a reducing fitting designed for that purpose shall be used in accordance with the requirements of 7.5.2.3.1.

7.5.2.4 Welding Requirements.

7.5.2.4.1* Welds between pipe and welding outlet fittings shall be permitted to be attached by full penetration welds, partial penetration groove welds, or fillet welds.

7.5.2.4.2* Where fillet welded joints are used, the minimum throat thickness shall be not less than the thickness of the pipe, the thickness of the welding fitting, or 3/16 in. (5 mm), whichever is least.

7.5.2.4.3* Circumferential butt joints shall be cut, beveled, and fit so that full penetration is achievable.

7.5.2.4.4 Full penetration welding shall not be required.

7.5.2.4.5 Where slip-on flanges are welded to pipe with a single fillet weld, the weld shall be on the hub side of the flange and the minimum throat weld thickness shall not be less than 1.25 times the pipe wall thickness or the hub thickness, whichever is less.

7.5.2.4.6 Face welds on the internal face of the flange shall be permitted as a water seal in addition to the hub weld required in 7.5.2.4.5.

7.5.2.4.7 Tabs for longitudinal earthquake bracing shall have minimum throat weld thickness not less than 1.25 times the pipe wall thickness and welded on both sides of the longest dimension.

7.5.2.4.8* When welding is performed, the following shall apply:

(1) Holes in piping for outlets shall be cut to the full inside diameter of fittings prior to welding in place of the fittings.
(2) Coupons shall be retrieved.
(3) Openings cut into piping shall be smooth bore, and all internal slag and welding residue shall be removed.
(4) Fittings shall not penetrate the internal diameter of the piping.
(5) Steel plates shall not be welded to the ends of piping or fittings.
(6) Fittings shall not be modified.
(7) Nuts, clips, eye rods, angle brackets, or other fasteners shall not be welded to pipe or fittings, except as permitted in 7.5.2.2.3 and 7.5.2.4.7.
(8) Completed welds shall be free from cracks, incomplete fusion, surface porosity greater than $\frac{1}{16}$ in. (1.6 mm) diameter, and undercut deeper than 25 percent of the wall thickness or $\frac{1}{32}$ in. (0.8 mm), whichever is less.
(9) Completed circumferential butt weld reinforcement shall not exceed $\frac{3}{32}$ in. (2 mm).

7.5.2.5 Qualifications.

7.5.2.5.1 A welding procedure shall be prepared and qualified by the contractor or fabricator before any welding is done.

7.5.2.5.2 Qualification of the welding procedure to be used and the performance of all welders and welding operators shall be required and shall meet or exceed the requirements of AWS B2.1/B2.1M, *Specification for Welding Procedure and Performance Qualification;* ASME *Boiler and Pressure Vessel Code,* Section IX, "Welding, Brazing, and Fusing Qualifications"; or other applicable qualification standard as required by the authority having jurisdiction, except as permitted by 7.5.2.5.3.

7.5.2.5.3 Successful procedure qualification of complete joint penetration groove welds shall qualify partial joint penetration (groove/fillet) welds and fillet welds in accordance with the provisions of this standard.

7.5.2.5.4 Welding procedures qualified under standards recognized by previous editions of this standard shall be permitted to be continued in use.

7.5.2.5.5 Contractors or fabricators shall be responsible for all welding they produce.

7.5.2.5.6 Each contractor or fabricator shall have available to the authority having jurisdiction an established written quality assurance procedure ensuring compliance with the requirements of 7.5.2.4.

7.5.2.6 Records.

7.5.2.6.1 Welders or welding machine operators shall, upon completion of each welded pipe, place their identifiable mark or label onto each piece adjacent to a weld.

7.5.2.6.2 Contractors or fabricators shall maintain certified records, which shall be available to the authority having jurisdiction, of the procedures used and the welders or welding machine operators employed by them, along with their welding identification.

7.5.2.6.3 Records shall show the date and the results of procedure and performance qualifications.

7.5.3 Groove Joining Methods.

7.5.3.1* Pipe, fittings, valves, and devices to be joined with grooved couplings shall contain cut, rolled, or cast grooves that are dimensionally compatible with the couplings.

7.5.3.1.1* Pipe, fittings, valves, devices, and couplings that conform with or are listed in compliance with standardized groove specifications shall be considered compatible.

7.5.3.1.2 Other groove dimensions and grooving methods shall be acceptable in accordance with 7.5.5.1.

7.5.3.2 Grooved couplings, including gaskets used on dry pipe, preaction, and deluge systems, shall be listed for dry service.

7.5.4* Brazed and Soldered Joints.

7.5.4.1 Solder joints, where permitted, shall be fabricated in accordance with the methods and procedures listed in ASTM B828, *Standard Practice for Making Capillary Joints by Soldering of Copper and Copper Alloy Tube and Fittings.*

7.5.4.2 Unless the requirements of 7.5.4.3 or 7.5.4.4 are met, joints for the connection of copper tube shall be brazed.

7.5.4.3 Solder joints shall be permitted for exposed wet pipe systems in light hazard occupancies where the temperature classification of the installed sprinklers is of the ordinary- or intermediate-temperature classification.

7.5.4.4 Solder joints shall be permitted for wet pipe systems in light hazard and ordinary hazard (Group 1) occupancies where the piping is concealed, irrespective of sprinkler temperature ratings.

7.5.4.5* Soldering fluxes shall be in accordance with Table 7.3.1.1.

7.5.4.6 Brazing fluxes, if used, shall not be of a highly corrosive type.

7.5.5 Other Joining Methods.

7.5.5.1 Other joining methods investigated for suitability in sprinkler installations and listed for this service shall be permitted where installed in accordance with their listing limitations, including installation instructions.

7.5.5.2 Outlet Fittings. Rubber-gasketed outlet fittings that are used on sprinkler systems shall meet the following requirements:

(1) Be installed in accordance with the listing and manufacturer's installation instructions
(2) Have all coupons retrieved
(3) Have smooth bores cut into the pipe, with all cutting residue removed
(4) Not be modified

7.5.6 End Treatment.

7.5.6.1 After cutting, pipe ends shall have burrs and fins removed.

7.5.6.2 Pipe used with listed fittings and its end treatment shall be in accordance with the fitting manufacturer's installation instructions and the fitting's listing.

7.6 Valves.

7.6.1 Valve Closure Time. Listed indicating control valves shall not close in less than 5 seconds when operated at maximum possible speed from the fully open position.

N **7.6.2 Automated Valves.** A listed indicating control valve with automated controls shall be permitted.

N **7.6.2.1** A listed automated water control valve assembly with a reliable position indication connected to a remote supervisory station shall be permitted.

N **7.6.2.2** An automated water control valve shall be able to be operated manually as well as automatically.

Δ **7.7 Waterflow Alarm Devices.**

N **7.7.1*** Mechanical waterflow alarm devices shall be listed for the service and so constructed and installed that any flow of water from a sprinkler system equal to or greater than that from a single automatic sprinkler of the smallest K-factor installed on the system will result in an audible alarm on the premises within 5 minutes after such flow begins and until such flow stops.

N **7.7.2*** Electrical waterflow alarm devices shall be listed for the service and so constructed and installed that any flow of water from a sprinkler system equal to or greater than that from a single automatic sprinkler of the smallest K-factor installed on the system will result in an audible alarm on the premises within 100 seconds after such flow begins and until such flow stops.

7.8 Additives and Coatings.

7.8.1 Additives to the water supply intended for control of microbiological or other corrosion shall be listed for use within fire sprinkler systems.

7.8.2 Internal pipe coatings, excluding galvanizing, intended for control of microbiological or other corrosion shall be listed for use within fire sprinkler systems.

N **7.9 Automated Inspection and Testing Devices and Equipment.**

N **7.9.1** Automated inspection devices and equipment shall be shown to be as effective as a manual examination.

N **7.9.2** Automated testing devices and equipment shall produce the same action required by this standard and NFPA 25 to test a device.

N **7.9.2.1** The installation of testing device or component shall be arranged to discharge water where required by this standard and NFPA 25.

N **7.9.3** Failure of automated inspection and testing devices and equipment shall not impair the operation of the system unless indicated by an audible and visual supervisory signal in accordance with *NFPA 72* or other approved fire alarm code.

N **7.9.4** Failure of a system or component to pass automated inspection and testing devices and equipment shall result in an audible and visual supervisory signal in accordance with *NFPA 72* or other approved fire alarm code.

N **7.9.5** Failure of automated inspection and testing devices and equipment shall result in an audible and visual trouble signal in accordance with *NFPA 72* or other approved fire alarm code.

Chapter 8   System Types and Requirements

8.1 Wet Pipe Systems.

8.1.1 Pressure Gauges.

8.1.1.1 An approved pressure gauge conforming to Section 16.13 shall be installed in each system riser.

8.1.1.2* Pressure gauges shall be installed above and below each alarm check valve or system riser check valve where such devices are present.

8.1.1.2.1 A single pressure gauge shall be permitted to be installed on a manifold below multiple riser check valves or alarm check valves.

8.1.1.2.2 Pressure gauges below check valves required by 16.9.10 and 16.15.2.2(1) shall not be required.

8.1.2 Relief Valves.

8.1.2.1 Unless the requirements of 8.1.2.2 are met, a wet pipe system shall be provided with a listed relief valve not less than ½ in. (15 mm) in size and set to operate at 175 psi (12 bar) or 10 psi (0.7 bar) in excess of the maximum system pressure, whichever is greater.

8.1.2.2 Where auxiliary air reservoirs are installed to absorb pressure increases, a relief valve shall not be required.

8.1.2.3 A relief valve per 8.1.2.1 shall be required downstream of check valves required by 16.15.2.2(1).

8.1.3 Auxiliary Systems. A wet pipe system shall be permitted to supply an auxiliary dry pipe, preaction, or deluge system, provided the water supply is adequate.

8.1.4 Heat tracing shall not be used in lieu of heated valve enclosures to protect the valve and supply pipe from freezing.

8.1.5 Air Venting. A single air vent with a connection conforming to Section 16.7 shall be provided on each wet pipe system utilizing metallic pipe. *(See A.16.7.)*

8.1.5.1 Venting from multiple points on each system shall not be required.

8.2* Dry Pipe Systems.

8.2.1 Pressure Gauges. Approved pressure gauges in accordance with Section 16.13 shall be connected as follows:

(1) On the water side and air side of the dry pipe valve
(2) At the air pump supplying the air receiver where one is provided
(3) At the air receiver where one is provided
(4) In each independent pipe from air supply to dry pipe system
(5) At quick-opening devices

Δ 8.2.2 Sprinklers.

8.2.2.1 Residential sprinklers installed on dry pipe systems shall be listed for dry pipe applications.

N **8.2.2.2** The following sprinkler orientations and arrangements shall be permitted for dry pipe systems:

(1) Upright sprinklers
(2)* Listed dry sprinklers
(3) Pendent sprinklers and sidewall sprinklers installed on return bends, where the sprinklers, return bend, and branch line piping are in an area maintained at or above 40°F (4°C)
(4) Horizontal sidewall sprinklers installed so that water is not trapped
(5) Pendent sprinklers and sidewall sprinklers, where the sprinklers and branch line piping are in an area maintained at or above 40°F (4°C), the water supply is potable, and the piping for the dry pipe system is copper or CPVC specifically listed for dry pipe applications

8.2.3* Size of Systems.

8.2.3.1* The system capacity (volume) controlled by a dry pipe valve shall be determined by 8.2.3.2, 8.2.3.3, 8.2.3.4, 8.2.3.5, or 8.2.3.7.

8.2.3.1.1 For dry pipe systems protecting dwelling unit portions of any occupancy, system size shall be such that initial water is discharged from the system test connection in not more than 15 seconds, starting at the normal air pressure on the system and at the time of fully opened inspection test connection.

8.2.3.1.1.1 Dry pipe systems protecting dwelling unit portions of any occupancy shall not be permitted to use the options outlined in 8.2.3.2, 8.2.3.3, or 8.2.3.4.

8.2.3.2 System size shall be such that initial water is discharged from the system test connection in not more than 60 seconds, starting at the normal air pressure on the system and at the time of fully opened inspection test connection.

8.2.3.3 A system size of not more than 500 gal (1900 L) shall be permitted without a quick-opening device and shall not be required to meet any specific water delivery requirement to the inspection test connection.

8.2.3.4 A system size of not more than 750 gal (2850 L) shall be permitted with a quick-opening device and shall not be required to meet any specific water delivery requirement to the inspection test connection.

8.2.3.5 System size shall be based on dry pipe systems being calculated for water delivery in accordance with 8.2.3.6.

8.2.3.6 Dry Pipe System Water Delivery.

8.2.3.6.1 Calculations for dry pipe system water delivery shall be based on the hazard shown in Table 8.2.3.6.1.

8.2.3.6.2 The calculation program and method shall be listed by a nationally recognized testing laboratory.

Δ Table 8.2.3.6.1 Dry Pipe System Water Delivery

Hazard	Number of Most Remote Sprinklers Initially Open	Maximum Time of Water Delivery (seconds)
Dwelling unit	1	15
Light	1	60
Ordinary I	2	50
Ordinary II	2	50
Extra I	4	45
Extra II	4	45
High piled	4	40

N **8.2.3.6.3** Calculations of water delivery time shall be based on the time interval between the following:

(1) Calculated point in time when the selected most remote sprinkler(s) open
(2) Calculated point in time when pressure at the most remote sprinkler reaches or surpasses and maintains the design pressure

8.2.3.6.4 For dry pipe systems protecting dwelling unit portions of any occupancy, the sprinklers in the dwelling unit shall have a maximum water delivery time of 15 seconds to the single most remote sprinkler.

Δ **8.2.3.7* Manifold Test Connection.**

N **8.2.3.7.1** System size shall be such that initial water discharge from the system trip test connection or manifold outlets is not more than the maximum time of water delivery specified in Table 8.2.3.6.1, starting at normal air pressure on the system and at the time of fully opened test connection.

8.2.3.7.2 When flow is from four sprinklers, the test manifold shall be arranged to simulate two sprinklers on the most remote sprinkler branch line and two sprinklers on the next adjacent branch line.

8.2.3.7.3 When flow is from three sprinklers, the test manifold shall be arranged to simulate two sprinklers on the most remote branch line and one sprinkler on the next adjacent branch line.

8.2.3.7.4 When flow is from two sprinklers, the test manifold shall be arranged to simulate two sprinklers on the most remote branch line.

8.2.3.7.5 When flow is from one sprinkler, the test manifold shall be installed as per the requirements for a trip test connection in accordance with 16.14.2.

8.2.3.7.6 A system meeting the requirements of this section shall not be required to also meet the requirements of 8.2.3.2 or 8.2.3.5.

8.2.3.8 Dry pipe systems with water delivery times other than 8.2.3.2, 8.2.3.5, and 8.2.3.7 shall be acceptable where listed by a nationally recognized testing laboratory.

8.2.3.9 Dry Pipe System Subdivision. Unless installed in a heated enclosure, check valves shall not be used to subdivide the dry pipe systems.

8.2.3.9.1 When check valves are used to subdivide dry pipe systems in accordance with 8.2.3.9, a hole ⅛ in. (3 mm) in diameter shall be drilled in the clapper of each check valve to permit equalization of air pressure among the various parts of the system.

8.2.3.9.2 Where auxiliary drains are not provided for each subdivided section, an approved indicating drain valve supervised in the closed position in accordance with 16.9.3.3, connected to a bypass around each check valve, shall be provided as a means for draining the system.

8.2.3.10 Gridded dry pipe systems shall not be installed.

8.2.4 Quick-Opening Devices.

8.2.4.1 A listed quick-opening device shall be permitted to help meet the requirements of 8.2.3.2, 8.2.3.5, 8.2.3.7, or 8.2.3.8.

8.2.4.2 The quick-opening device shall be located as close as practical to the dry pipe valve.

8.2.4.3 To protect the restriction orifice and other operating parts of the quick-opening device against submergence, the connection to the riser shall be above the point at which water (priming water and back drainage) is expected when the dry pipe valve and quick-opening device are set, except where design features of the particular quick-opening device make these requirements unnecessary.

8.2.4.4 Where a valve is installed in the connection between a dry pipe sprinkler riser and a quick-opening device, it shall be an indicating-type valve that is sealed, locked, or electrically supervised in the open position.

8.2.4.5 A check valve shall be installed between the quick-opening device and the intermediate chamber of the dry pipe valve, where the quick-opening device requires protection against submergence after system operation.

8.2.4.6 If the quick-opening device requires pressure feedback from the intermediate chamber, a valve type that will clearly indicate whether it is opened or closed shall be permitted in place of that check valve.

8.2.4.7 Where a valve is utilized in accordance with 8.2.4.6, the valve shall be constructed so that it can be locked or sealed in the open position.

8.2.4.8 Antiflooding Device.

8.2.4.8.1 Unless the requirements of 8.2.4.8.2 are met, a listed antiflooding device shall be installed in the connection between the dry pipe sprinkler riser and the quick-opening device.

8.2.4.8.2 A listed antiflooding device shall not be required where the quick-opening device has built-in antiflooding design features or the quick-opening device is listed or approved without the use of an antiflooding device.

8.2.5* Location and Protection of Dry Pipe Valve.

8.2.5.1* General. The dry pipe valve and supply pipe shall be protected against freezing and mechanical injury.

8.2.5.2 Valve Rooms.

8.2.5.2.1 Valve rooms shall be lighted and heated.

8.2.5.2.2 The source of heat shall be of a permanently installed type.

8.2.5.2.3 Heat tape shall not be used in lieu of heated valve enclosures to protect the dry pipe valve and supply pipe against freezing.

8.2.5.3 Supply. The supply for the sprinkler in the dry pipe valve enclosure shall be either from the dry side of the system or from a wet pipe sprinkler system that protects the area where the dry pipe valve is located.

8.2.5.4 High Water Level Protection.

8.2.5.4.1 Where it is possible to reseat the dry valve after actuation without first draining the system, a high water level device in accordance with 8.2.5.4.3 shall be provided.

8.2.5.4.2 Differential Dry Pipe Valve. Protection against accumulation of water above the clapper shall be provided for differential dry pipe valves in accordance with 8.2.5.4.3.

8.2.5.4.3 High Water Level Device. An automatic high water level signaling device or an automatic drain shall be permitted.

8.2.6 Air Pressure and Supply.

8.2.6.1 Where the term *air* is used throughout this standard, it shall also include the use of nitrogen or other approved gas.

8.2.6.2 Maintenance of Air Pressure. Air or nitrogen or other approved gas pressure shall be maintained on dry pipe systems throughout the year.

8.2.6.3* Air Supply.

8.2.6.3.1 The compressed air supply shall be from a source available at all times.

8.2.6.3.2* The air supply shall have a capacity capable of restoring normal air pressure in the system within 30 minutes.

8.2.6.3.3 The requirements of 8.2.6.3.2 shall not apply in refrigerated spaces maintained below 5°F (−15°C), where normal system air pressure shall be permitted to be restored within 60 minutes.

8.2.6.4 Air Supply Connections.

8.2.6.4.1* The connection from the air supply to the dry pipe valve shall not be less than ½ in. (15 mm) in diameter and shall enter the system above the priming water level of the dry pipe valve.

8.2.6.4.2 A check valve shall be installed in the air filling connection.

8.2.6.4.2.1 A listed or approved shutoff valve of either the renewable disc or ball valve type shall be installed on the supply side of this check valve.

8.2.6.5 Relief Valve. An approved relief valve shall be provided between the air supply and the shutoff valve and shall be set to relieve pressure no less than 10 psi (0.7 bar) in excess of system air pressure provided in 8.2.6.7.1 and shall not exceed the manufacturer's limitations.

8.2.6.6 Automatic Air Maintenance.

8.2.6.6.1* Unless the requirements of 8.2.6.6.2 are met, where the air supply to a dry pipe system is maintained automatically, the air supply shall be from a dependable plant system or an air compressor with an air receiver, and shall utilize an air maintenance device specifically listed for such service and capable of controlling the required air pressure on, and maximum airflow to, the dry pipe system.

Δ **8.2.6.6.2** Where the air compressor supplying a single dry pipe system has a capacity less than 5.5 ft³/min (160 L/min), an air receiver or air maintenance device shall not be required.

8.2.6.6.3 The automatic air supply to more than one dry pipe system shall be connected to enable individual maintenance of air pressure in each system.

8.2.6.6.3.1 Each dry pipe system shall have a dedicated air maintenance device.

8.2.6.6.4 A check valve or other positive backflow prevention device shall be installed in the air supply to each system to prevent airflow or waterflow from one system to another.

8.2.6.6.5 Where an air compressor is the dedicated air supply, it shall be installed in accordance with *NFPA 70,* Article 430.

8.2.6.6.5.1 The disconnecting means for an automatic air compressor shall not be a general-use light switch or a cord-and-plug connected motor.

8.2.6.7 System Air Pressure.

8.2.6.7.1 The system air pressure shall be maintained in accordance with the instruction sheet furnished with the dry pipe valve, or shall be 20 psi (1.4 bar) in excess of the calculated trip pressure of the dry pipe valve, based on the highest normal water pressure of the system supply.

N **8.2.6.7.2** Each dry pipe valve shall have a low/high supervisory pressure switch that provides a supervisory signal when the air pressure within the system is out of the ranges specified in 8.2.6.7.2.1 and 8.2.6.7.2.2.

N **8.2.6.7.2.1** The low pressure signal shall be set at a minimum of 5 psi (0.3 bar) above the calculated trip pressure of the dry pipe valve.

N **8.2.6.7.2.2** The high pressure signal shall be set at 5 psi (0.3 bar) above the system air pressure specified in 8.2.6.7.1.

N **8.2.6.7.2.3** When a low or high air pressure condition is detected, notification shall be by either of the following:

(1) An audible signal at a location that will be heard by building maintenance staff
(2) Through the fire alarm control unit as a supervisory condition

8.2.6.7.3 The permitted rate of air leakage shall be as specified in 29.2.2.

8.2.6.8 Nitrogen or Other Approved Gas.

8.2.6.8.1* Where nitrogen or other approved gas is used, the supply shall be from a reliable source.

8.2.6.8.2 Where stored nitrogen or other approved gas is used, the gas shall be introduced through a pressure regulator and shall be in accordance with 8.2.6.6.

8.2.6.8.3 A low pressure alarm shall be provided on gas storage containers to notify the need for refilling.

8.2.6.8.4* When nitrogen or other approved gas is the only source of gas for pressurizing a system, it shall have a capacity capable of restoring normal gas pressure in the system within 30 minutes.

8.2.6.8.5 The requirements of 8.2.6.8.4 shall not apply in refrigerated spaces maintained below 5°F (−15°C), where normal system air pressure shall be permitted to be restored within 60 minutes.

N **8.2.6.9* Nitrogen Supply for Increased C Value.**

N **8.2.6.9.1** Where nitrogen is used to allow for increased C value in accordance with Table 28.2.4.8.1, the nitrogen supply shall be in accordance with 8.2.6.9.2 through 8.2.6.9.6.

N **8.2.6.9.2** Nitrogen shall be from a listed nitrogen generator permanently installed.

N **8.2.6.9.3** The generator shall be capable of supplying and maintaining at least 98 percent nitrogen concentration throughout the system at a minimum leakage rate of 1.5 psi (0.1 bar) per hour.

N **8.2.6.9.4** A means of verifying nitrogen concentration shall be provided for each system where increased C value is used.

N **8.2.6.9.5** The nitrogen generator shall be installed per the manufacturer's instruction.

N **8.2.6.9.6** The nitrogen generator shall be maintained in accordance with Chapter 32.

8.3 Preaction Systems and Deluge Systems.

8.3.1* General.

8.3.1.1* All components of pneumatic, hydraulic, or electrical systems shall be compatible.

8.3.1.2 The automatic water control valve shall be provided with hydraulic, pneumatic, or mechanical manual means for operation that is independent of detection devices and of the sprinklers.

8.3.1.2.1 Actuator Supervision. Effective January 1, 2021, removal of an electric actuator from the preaction or deluge valve that it controls shall result in an audible and visual indication of system impairment at the system releasing control panel.

8.3.1.3 Pressure Gauges. Approved pressure gauges conforming with Section 16.13 shall be installed as follows:

(1) Above and below preaction valve and below deluge valve
(2) On air supply to preaction and deluge valves

8.3.1.4 A supply of spare fusible elements for heat-responsive devices, not less than two of each temperature rating, shall be maintained on the premises for replacement purposes.

8.3.1.5 Hydraulic release systems shall be designed and installed in accordance with manufacturer's requirements and listing for height limitations above deluge valves or deluge valve actuators to prevent water column.

8.3.1.6 Location and Spacing of Releasing Devices.

8.3.1.6.1 Spacing of releasing devices, including automatic sprinklers used as releasing devices, shall be in accordance with their listing and manufacturer' specifications.

8.3.1.6.2 The release system shall serve all areas that the preaction system protects.

8.3.1.6.3 Where thermal activation is utilized, the activation temperature of the release system shall be lower than the activation temperature of the sprinkler.

8.3.1.7 Devices for Test Purposes and Testing Apparatus.

8.3.1.7.1 Where detection devices installed in circuits are located where not accessible for testing, an additional detection device shall be provided on each circuit for test purposes at an accessible location and shall be connected to the circuit at a point that will ensure a proper test of the circuit.

8.3.1.7.2 Testing apparatus capable of producing the heat or impulse necessary to operate any normal detection device shall be furnished to the owner of the property with each installation.

8.3.1.7.3 Where explosive vapors or materials are present, hot water, steam, or other methods of testing not involving an ignition source shall be used.

8.3.1.7.4* A separate additional indicating control valve, supervised in accordance with 16.9.3.3, shall be permitted to be installed in the riser assembly above a preaction or deluge valve to permit full function trip testing as required by NFPA 25, without flooding the system.

8.3.1.8 Location and Protection of System Water Control Valves.

8.3.1.8.1 System water control valves and supply pipes shall be protected against freezing and mechanical injury.

8.3.1.8.2 Valve Rooms.

8.3.1.8.2.1 Valve rooms shall be lighted and heated.

8.3.1.8.2.2 The source of heat shall be of a permanently installed type.

8.3.1.8.2.3 Heat tracing shall not be used in lieu of heated valve enclosure rooms to protect preaction and deluge valves and supply pipe against freezing.

8.3.2 Preaction Systems.

8.3.2.1 Preaction systems shall be one of the following types:

(1) A single interlock system, which admits water to sprinkler piping upon operation of detection devices
(2) A non-interlock system, which admits water to sprinkler piping upon operation of detection devices or automatic sprinklers
(3) A double interlock system, which admits water to sprinkler piping upon operation of both detection devices and automatic sprinklers

8.3.2.2 Size of Systems — Single and Non-Interlock Preaction Systems. Not more than 1000 automatic sprinklers shall be controlled by any one preaction valve.

8.3.2.3 Size of Systems — Double Interlock Preaction Systems.

8.3.2.3.1 The system size controlled by a double interlock preaction valve shall be determined by either 8.3.2.3.1.1, 8.3.2.3.1.2, 8.3.2.3.1.3, or 8.3.2.3.1.4.

8.3.2.3.1.1 A system size for double interlock preaction systems of not more than 500 gal (1900 L) shall be permitted and shall not be required to meet any specific water delivery requirement to the trip test connection.

8.3.2.3.1.2 The system size for double interlock preaction systems shall be designed to deliver water to the system test connection in no more than 60 seconds, starting at the normal air pressure on the system, with the detection system activated and the inspection test connection fully opened simultaneously.

8.3.2.3.1.3 The system size for double interlock preaction systems shall be based on calculating water delivery in accordance with 8.2.3.6, anticipating that the detection system activation and sprinkler operation will be simultaneous.

8.3.2.3.1.4* The system size for double interlock preaction systems shall be designed to deliver water to the system trip test connection or manifold outlets in not more than the maximum time of water delivery specified in Table 8.2.3.6.1, starting at the normal air pressure on the system, with the detection system activated and the inspection trip test connection or manifold opened simultaneously.

8.3.2.3.2 A listed quick-opening device shall be permitted to be used to help meet the requirements of 8.3.2.3.1.2, 8.3.2.3.1.3, and 8.3.2.3.1.4.

8.3.2.4* Supervision. Sprinkler piping and fire detection devices shall be automatically supervised where more than 20 sprinklers are on the system.

• **8.3.2.5 Air Pressure** Except as provided by 8.3.2.5.1 through 8.3.2.5.3, air or nitrogen supervising pressure for preaction systems shall be installed in conformance with the dry pipe system air pressure and supply rules of 8.2.6.

8.3.2.5.1 The relief valves required by 8.2.6 shall be permitted to be omitted for the type of preaction system described in 8.3.2.1(1) when the air pressure is supplied from a source that is not capable of developing pressures in excess of 15 psi (1.0 bar).

8.3.2.5.2 A preaction system type described in 8.3.2.1(2) and 8.3.2.1(3) shall maintain a minimum supervising air or nitrogen pressure of 7 psi (0.5 bar).

N **8.3.2.5.3** The air pressure values for the type of preaction system described in 8.3.2.1(1) shall be set in accordance with the manufacturer's installation instructions.

8.3.2.6 Sprinklers. The following sprinkler orientations and arrangements shall be permitted for preaction systems:

(1) Upright sprinklers
(2)* Listed dry sprinklers
(3) Pendent sprinklers and sidewall sprinklers installed on return bends, where the sprinklers, return bend, and branch line piping are in an area maintained at or above 40°F (4°C)
(4) Horizontal sidewall sprinklers, installed so that water is not trapped
(5) Pendent sprinklers and sidewall sprinklers, where the sprinklers and branch line piping are in an area maintained at or above 40°F (4°C), the water supply is potable, and the piping for the preaction system is copper or CPVC specifically listed for dry pipe applications

8.3.2.7 System Configuration. Preaction systems of the type described in 8.3.2.1(3) and all preaction systems protecting storage occupancies, excluding miscellaneous storage, shall not be gridded.

8.3.3* Deluge Systems.

8.3.3.1 The detection devices or systems shall be automatically supervised.

8.3.3.2 Deluge systems shall be hydraulically calculated.

8.4 Combined Dry Pipe and Preaction Systems for Piers, Terminals, and Wharves.

8.4.1 In addition to the requirements of Section 8.4, design and installation requirements for piers, terminals, and wharves shall be in accordance with Section 27.27.

8.4.2* General.

8.4.2.1* Combined automatic dry pipe and preaction systems shall be so constructed that failure of the detection system shall not prevent the system from functioning as a conventional automatic dry pipe system.

8.4.2.2 Combined automatic dry pipe and preaction systems shall be so constructed that failure of the dry pipe system of automatic sprinklers shall not prevent the detection system from properly functioning as an automatic fire alarm system.

8.4.2.3 Provisions shall be made for the manual operation of the detection system at locations requiring not more than 200 ft (61 m) of travel.

8.4.2.4 Sprinklers. The following types of sprinklers and arrangements shall be permitted for combined dry pipe and preaction systems:

(1) Upright sprinklers
(2)* Listed dry sprinklers
(3) Pendent sprinklers and sidewall sprinklers installed on return bends, where both the sprinklers and the return bends are located in a heated area
(4) Horizontal sidewall sprinklers, installed so that water is not trapped

8.4.3 Dry Pipe Valves in Combined Systems.

8.4.3.1 Where the system consists of more than 600 sprinklers or has more than 275 sprinklers in any fire area, the entire system shall be controlled through two 6 in. (150 mm) dry pipe valves connected in parallel and shall feed into a common feed main.

8.4.3.2* Where parallel dry pipe valves are required by 8.4.3.1, these valves shall be checked against each other.

8.4.3.3 Each dry pipe valve shall be provided with a listed tripping device actuated by the detection system.

8.4.3.4 Dry pipe valves shall be cross-connected through a 1 in. (25 mm) pipe connection to permit simultaneous tripping of both dry pipe valves.

8.4.3.5 The 1 in. (25 mm) cross-connection pipe shall be equipped with an indicating valve so that either dry pipe valve can be shut off and worked on while the other remains in service.

8.4.3.6 The check valves between the dry pipe valves and the common feed main shall be equipped with ½ in. (15 mm) bypasses so that a loss of air from leakage in the trimmings of a dry pipe valve will not cause the valve to trip until the pressure in the feed main is reduced to the tripping point.

8.4.3.7 An indicating valve shall be installed in each of these bypasses so that either dry pipe valve can be completely isolated from the main riser or feed main and from the other dry pipe valve.

8.4.3.8 Each combined dry pipe and preaction system shall be provided with listed quick-opening devices at the dry pipe valves.

8.4.4 Subdivision of System Using Check Valves.

8.4.4.1 Where more than 275 sprinklers are required in a single fire area, the system shall be divided into sections of 275 sprinklers or fewer by means of check valves.

8.4.4.2 Where the system is installed in more than one fire area or story, not more than 600 sprinklers shall be supplied through any one check valve.

8.4.4.3 Each section shall have a 1¼ in. (32 mm) drain on the system side of each check valve supplemented by a dry pipe system auxiliary drain.

8.4.4.4 Section drain lines and dry pipe system auxiliary drains shall be located in heated areas or inside heated cabinets to enclose drain valves and auxiliary drains for each section.

8.4.5 Time Limitation.

8.4.5.1 The sprinkler system shall be so constructed and the number of sprinklers controlled shall be so limited that water shall reach the farthest sprinkler within a period of time not exceeding 1 minute for each 400 ft (120 m) of common feed main from the time the heat-responsive system operates.

8.4.5.2 The maximum time permitted shall not exceed 3 minutes.

8.4.6 System Test Connection. The end section shall have a system test connection as required for dry pipe systems.

8.5 Multi-Cycle Systems.

8.5.1 All multi-cycle systems shall be specifically tested and listed as systems.

8.5.2 All multi-cycle systems shall be installed in compliance with the manufacturer's installation instructions.

8.6* Antifreeze Systems.

8.6.1* General.

8.6.1.1 The use of antifreeze solutions shall be in conformity with state and local health regulations.

8.6.1.2 Antifreeze shall not be used in ESFR systems unless the ESFR sprinkler is listed for use with the antifreeze solution.

8.6.1.3* Where pendent sprinklers are utilized, the water shall be drained from the entire system after hydrostatic testing with water.

8.6.1.3.1 The requirements of 8.6.1.3 shall not apply where the system is hydrostatically tested with a listed antifreeze solution.

8.6.1.4 Where antifreeze systems are remote from the system riser, a placard shall be mounted on the system riser that indicates the number and location of all remote antifreeze systems supplied by that riser.

8.6.1.5 A placard shall be placed on the antifreeze system main valve that indicates the manufacture type and brand of the antifreeze solution, the minimum use temperature of the antifreeze solution used, and the volume of the antifreeze solution used in the system.

8.6.2* Antifreeze Solutions.

8.6.2.1* Except as permitted in 8.6.2.2, antifreeze solutions shall be listed for use in sprinkler systems.

8.6.2.2 Premixed antifreeze solutions of propylene glycol shall be permitted to be used with ESFR sprinklers where the ESFR sprinklers are listed for such use in a specific application.

8.6.3 Arrangement of Supply Piping and Valves.

8.6.3.1 Where the connection between the antifreeze system and the supply piping does not incorporate a backflow preven-

tion device, and the conditions of 8.6.3.5 are not met, piping and valves shall be installed as illustrated in Figure 8.6.3.1.

8.6.3.2* Where the connection between the antifreeze system and the supply piping incorporates a backflow prevention device, and the conditions of 8.6.3.5 are not met, piping and valves shall be installed as illustrated in Figure 8.6.3.3 or Figure 8.6.3.4.

8.6.3.2.1 A means shall be provided to perform a full forward flow test in accordance with 16.14.5.

8.6.3.3* Where the connection between the antifreeze system and supply pipe incorporates a backflow prevention device, and the conditions of 8.6.3.5 are not met, a listed expansion chamber shall be provided to compensate for thermal expansion of the antifreeze solution as illustrated in Figure 8.6.3.3.

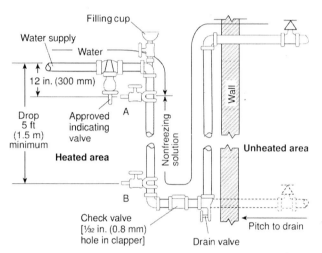

Notes:
1. Check valves are permitted to be omitted where sprinklers are below the level of valve A.
2. The ½₂ in. (0.8 mm) hole in the check valve clapper is needed to allow for expansion of the solution during a temperature rise, thus preventing damage to sprinklers.

FIGURE 8.6.3.1   Arrangement of Supply Piping and Valves.

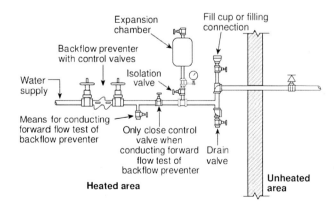

△ FIGURE 8.6.3.3   Arrangement of Supply Piping with Backflow Device.

8.6.3.3.1 When determining the size of the expansion chamber, the precharge air temperature and precharge air pressure shall be included.

8.6.3.3.2 The size of the expansion chamber shall be such that the maximum system pressure does not exceed the rated pressure for any components of the antifreeze system.

8.6.3.4 A listed ½ in. (15 mm) relief valve shall be permitted in lieu of the expansion chamber required in 8.6.3.3, and as illustrated in Figure 8.6.3.4, provided the antifreeze system volume does not exceed 40 gal (150 L).

8.6.3.5 The requirements of 8.6.3.1, 8.6.3.2, and 8.6.3.3 shall not apply where the following three conditions are met:

(1) The antifreeze system is provided with an automatic pressure pump or other device or apparatus to automatically maintain a higher pressure on the system side than on the supply side of the water supply check valve separating the antifreeze system from the water supply.
(2) Provision is made to automatically release solution to prevent overpressurization due to thermal expansion of the solution.
(3) Provision is made to automatically supply premixed solution as needed to restore system pressure due to thermal contraction.

8.6.3.6* A drain/test connection shall be installed at the most remote portion of the system.

8.6.3.7 For systems with a capacity larger than 150 gal (570 L), an additional test connection shall be provided for every additional 150 gal (570 L).

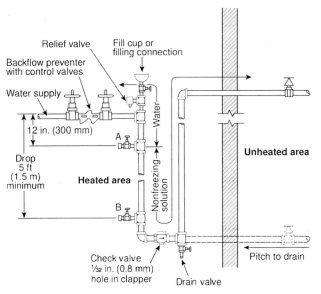

Notes:
1. Check valve can be omitted where sprinklers are below the level of valve A.
2. The ¹⁄₃₂ in. (0.8 mm) hole in the check valve clapper is needed to allow for expansion of the solution during a temperature rise, thus preventing damage to sprinklers.

Δ **FIGURE 8.6.3.4** Arrangement of Supply Piping with Relief Valve and Backflow Device.

8.7 Outside Sprinklers for Protection Against Exposure Fires (Exposure Protection Sprinkler Systems).

8.7.1 Applications.

8.7.1.1 Exposure protection sprinkler systems shall be permitted on buildings and structures regardless of whether the building's interior is protected by a sprinkler system.

8.7.1.2 Where exposure protection systems are required, they shall be installed to provide protection of windows and other openings within masonry walls, complete protection of walls, protection of roofs, or any combination thereof.

8.7.2 Water Supply and Control.

8.7.2.1 Unless the requirements of 8.7.2.2 are met, sprinklers installed for protection against exposure fires shall be supplied from a standard water supply as outlined in Chapter 5.

8.7.2.2 Where approved, other supplies, such as manual valves or pumps or fire department connections, shall be permitted to supply water to sprinklers for exposure protection.

8.7.2.3 Where fire department connections are used for water supply, they shall be so located that they will not be affected by the exposing fire.

8.7.3 Control.

8.7.3.1 Each system of outside sprinklers shall have an independent control valve.

8.7.3.2 Manually controlled open sprinklers shall be used only where constant supervision is present.

8.7.3.3 Sprinklers shall be of the open or automatic type.

8.7.3.4 Automatic sprinklers in areas subject to freezing shall be on dry pipe systems conforming to Section 8.2 or antifreeze systems conforming to Section 8.6, or be dry sprinklers of an adequate length connected to wet pipe systems located in heated areas.

8.7.3.5 Automatic systems of open sprinklers shall be controlled by the operation of fire detection devices designed for the specific application.

8.7.4 System Components.

8.7.4.1 Drain Valves. Each system of outside sprinklers shall have a separate drain valve installed on the system side of each control valve, except where an open sprinkler, top-fed system is arranged to facilitate drainage.

8.7.4.2 Check Valves.

8.7.4.2.1* Where sprinklers are installed on two adjacent sides of a building, protecting against two separate and distinct exposures, with separate control valves for each side, the end lines shall be connected with check valves located so that one sprinkler around the corner will operate.

8.7.4.2.2 The intermediate pipe between the two check valves shall be arranged to drain.

8.7.4.2.3* As an alternate solution, an additional sprinkler shall be installed on each system located around the corner from the system involved.

8.7.4.3 System Arrangement. Where one exposure affects two sides of the protected structure, the system shall not be subdivided between the two sides but rather shall be arranged to operate as a single system.

8.7.5 Pipe and Fittings. Pipe and fittings installed on the exterior of the building or structure shall be corrosion resistant.

8.7.6 Strainers. A listed strainer shall be provided in the riser or feed main that supplies sprinklers having nominal K-factors smaller than K-2.8 (40).

8.7.7 Gauge Connections. A pressure gauge conforming to Section 16.13 shall be installed immediately below the control valve of each system.

8.7.8 Sprinklers.

8.7.8.1 A single line of sprinklers is permitted to protect a maximum of two stories of wall area or two levels of vertically aligned windows where architectural features are sufficiently flush to allow rundown.

8.7.8.2 Where window sills or similar features result in recesses or projections exceeding 1 in. (25 mm) in depth, separate sprinklers shall be provided for each window on each level, regardless of whether protection is being provided for windows or complete walls.

8.7.8.3 For wall protection systems, sprinklers shall be located 6 in. to 12 in. (150 mm to 300 mm) from the wall surface and within 6 in. (150 mm) of the top of the wall, with maximum spacing of 8 ft (2.4 m) or as indicated in the sprinkler listing for exposure protection use.

8.7.8.4 For protection of window and similar openings, listed window sprinklers shall be positioned within 2 in. (50 mm) of the top of the window sash in accordance with Table 8.7.8.4.

8.7.8.5 Where exposure protection sprinkler systems are installed, listed cornice sprinklers shall be used to protect combustible cornices exceeding 12 in. (300 mm) in depth.

8.7.8.5.1 Cornice sprinklers shall be installed in each bay formed by cornice features and shall be spaced up to a maximum distance of 10 ft (3.0 m) apart, with deflectors 8 in. (200 mm) below the underside of the roof sheathing.

8.7.8.6 Open spray sprinklers (upright, pendent, or sidewall) shall be permitted for application in roof protection when installed in accordance with ordinary hazard Group 1 protection areas and discharge criteria, with deflectors aligned paral-

lel to the slope and positioned a minimum 18 in. (450 mm) above the roof surface.

8.7.8.6.1 Upright sprinklers positioned as ridge pole sprinklers shall be permitted with their deflectors horizontal and minimum 6 in. (150 mm) above the ridge, with their maximum spacing and protection areas determined in the plan view rather than along the slope.

8.7.9* Exposure Protection Sprinkler Systems.

8.7.9.1 Exposure protection sprinkler systems shall be hydraulically calculated using Table 8.7.9.1 based on severity of exposure as indicated by a relative classification of guide number or other approved source.

8.7.9.2 In no case shall compliance with Table 8.7.9.1 result in a sprinkler discharge pressure below 7 psi (0.5 bar).

8.7.9.3 Only half of the flow from upright, pendent, and other nondirectional sprinklers shall be used in determining the minimum average application rate over the protected surface.

8.7.9.4 The water supply shall be capable of simultaneously supplying the total demand of sprinklers along an exposure to a maximum length of 300 ft (91 m). Where systems of open sprinklers are used, the water supply shall be capable of simultaneously flowing all sprinklers that would flow as part of all systems that could be actuated within any 300 ft (91 m) length.

8.7.9.5 The water supply duration for an exposure protection sprinkler system shall be a minimum of 60 minutes.

8.7.9.6 A level of window sprinklers as described in Table 8.7.9.1 shall be defined as a floor level of the building being protected.

8.7.9.7 Window sprinklers shall be permitted to cover more than 25 ft² (2.3 m²) of window area per level.

8.7.9.7.1 The starting pressure shall be calculated based on the application rate over 25 ft² (2.3 m²) of window area as indicated in Table 8.7.9.1.

8.7.9.7.2 The maximum spacing between window sprinklers shall not exceed 8 ft (2.4 m) unless listed for a greater distance.

8.8* Refrigerated Spaces.

8.8.1 Spaces Maintained at Temperatures Above 32°F (0°C). Where temperatures are maintained above 32°F (0°C) in refrigerated spaces, the requirements in this section shall not apply.

8.8.2* Spaces Maintained at Temperatures Below 32°F (0°C).

8.8.2.1 General.

8.8.2.1.1* Where sprinkler pipe passes through a wall or floor into the refrigerated space, a section of pipe arranged for removal shall be provided immediately inside the space.

8.8.2.1.2 The removable length of pipe required in 8.8.2.1.1 shall be a minimum of 30 in. (750 mm).

8.8.2.2 Low Air Pressure Alarm.

8.8.2.2.1 Unless the requirements of 8.8.2.2.2 are met, a low air pressure alarm to a constantly attended location shall be installed.

Table 8.7.8.4 Position of Window Sprinklers

Width of Window (ft)	Nominal K-Factor		Nominal Distance from Window	
	U.S.	Metric	in.	mm
Up to 3	2.8	40	7	175
>3 to 4	2.8	40	8	200
>4 to 5	2.8	40	9	225
	5.6	80	12	300
>5 to 7	11.2	160	12	300
	Two 2.8	40	7	175
>7 to 9.5	14.0	200	12	300
	Two 2.8	40	9	225
>9.5 to 12	Two 5.6	80	12	300

For SI units, 1 ft = 0.3048 m.

Table 8.7.9.1 Exposure Protection

Section A — Wall and Window Sprinklers

Exposure Severity	Guide Number	Level of Wall or Window Sprinklers	Minimum Nominal K-Factor	Discharge Coefficient (K-Factor)	Minimum Average Application Rate Over Protected Surface	
					gpm/ft²	mm/min
Light	1.50 or less	Top 2 levels	2.8 (40)	2.8 (40)	0.20	8.1
		Next lower 2 levels	1.9 (27)	1.9 (27)	0.15	6.1
		Next lower 2 levels	1.4 (20)	1.4 (20)	0.10	4.1
Moderate	1.5–2.20	Top 2 levels	5.6 (80)	5.6 (80)	0.30	12.2
		Next lower 2 levels	4.2 (60)	4.2 (60)	0.25	10.2
		Next lower 2 levels	2.8 (40)	2.8 (40)	0.20	8.2
Severe	>2.20	Top 2 levels	11.2 (161)	11.2 (161)	0.40	16.3
		Next lower 2 levels	8.0 (115)	8.0 (115)	0.35	14.3
		Next lower 2 levels	5.6 (80)	5.6 (80)	0.30	12.2

Section B — Cornice Sprinklers

Guide Number	Cornice Sprinkler Minimal Nominal K-Factor	Application Rate per Lineal Foot (gpm)	Application Rate per Lineal Meter (L/min)
1.50 or less	2.8 (40)	0.75	9.3
>1.51–2.20	5.6 (80)	1.50	18.6
>2.20	11.2 (161)	3.00	37.3

8.8.2.2.2 Systems equipped with local low pressure alarms and an automatic air maintenance device shall not be required to alarm to a constantly attended location.

8.8.2.3 Piping Pitch. Piping in refrigerated spaces shall be installed with pitch as outlined in 16.10.3.3.

8.8.2.4* Air or Nitrogen Supply. Air or nitrogen supply for systems shall be one of the following:

(1) Air from the room of lowest temperature to reduce the moisture content
(2) Air compressor/dryer package listed for the application utilizing ambient air
(3) Compressed nitrogen gas from cylinders used in lieu of compressed air

8.8.2.5* Control Valve. An indicating-type control valve for operational testing of the system shall be provided on each sprinkler riser outside of the refrigerated space.

8.8.2.6* Check Valve.

8.8.2.6.1 Unless the requirements of 8.8.2.6.2 are met, a check valve with a 3/32 in. (2 mm) diameter hole in the clapper shall be installed in the system riser below the test valve required in 8.8.2.5.

8.8.2.6.2 Check valves shall not be required where dry pipe or preaction valves are used and designed to completely drain all water above the seat and that are listed for installation without priming water remaining and where priming water is not used in the system riser.

8.8.2.7 Air or Nitrogen Supply Piping.

8.8.2.7.1* The air or nitrogen supply piping entering the freezer area shall be as stated in 8.8.2.7.1.1 and 8.8.2.7.1.2.

8.8.2.7.1.1 Air Supply. The supply piping shall be equipped with two easily removable supply lines at least 6 ft (1.8 m) long

and at least 1 in. (25 mm) in diameter as shown in Figure 8.8.2.7.1.1(a) or Figure 8.8.2.7.1.1(b).

8.8.2.7.1.2 Nitrogen Supply. The supply piping shall be equipped with a single easily removable supply line at least 6 ft (1.8 m) long and at least 1 in. (25 mm) in diameter.

8.8.2.7.2 Each supply line shall be equipped with control valves located in the warm area.

8.8.2.7.3 Only one air supply line shall be open to supply the system air at any one time.

8.8.2.8 Fire Detection for Preaction Release.

8.8.2.8.1 Detectors for Preaction Systems.

8.8.2.8.1.1* The release system shall be designed to operate prior to sprinkler operation, unless detectors meet the requirements of 8.8.2.8.1.2.

(A) Detectors shall be electric or pneumatic fixed temperature type with temperature ratings less than that of the sprinklers.

(B) Detection devices shall not be rate-of-rise type.

8.8.2.8.1.2 Where the system is a double interlock preaction system or single interlock preaction antifreeze system, detection devices shall be permitted to be any type specifically approved for use in a refrigerated area if installed in accordance with their listing requirements and *NFPA 72* or other approved fire alarm code.

8.8.2.8.2 Detector Location at Ceiling.

8.8.2.8.2.1 Under smooth ceilings, detectors shall be spaced not exceeding their listed spacing.

8.8.2.8.2.2 For other than smooth ceilings, detectors shall not exceed one-half of the listed linear detector spacing or full allowable sprinkler spacing, whichever is greater.

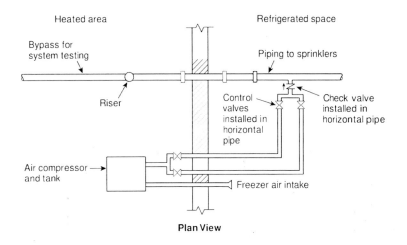

Plan View

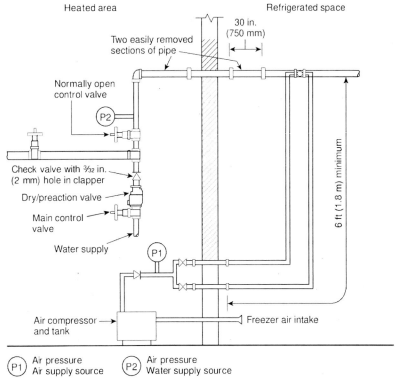

Elevation View

Notes:

1. Check valve with ³⁄₃₂ in. (2 mm) hole in clapper not required if prime water not used.

2. Supply air to be connected to top or side of system pipe.

3. Each removable air line to be a minimum of 1 in. (25 mm) diameter and a minimum of 6 ft (1.8 m) long.

△ **FIGURE 8.8.2.7.1.1(a)   Refrigerator Area Sprinkler System Used to Minimize the Chances of Developing Ice Plugs.**

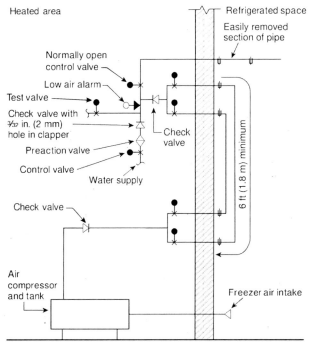

Notes:
1. Check valve with ³⁄₃₂ in. (2 mm) hole in clapper not required if prime water not used.
2. Each removable air line is to be installed a minimum of 1 in. (25 mm) in diameter and a minimum of 6 ft (1.8 m) long.

Δ FIGURE 8.8.2.7.1.1(b)   Preaction System Arrangement.

8.8.2.8.3 Detector Location in Racks.

8.8.2.8.3.1 Unless conditions in 8.8.2.8.4 are met, one level of detectors shall be installed for each level of sprinklers.

8.8.2.8.3.2 Detectors shall be installed vertically within one storage level of the rack sprinklers and as follows:

(1) Detectors shall be located in the transverse flue in single-row racks and in the longitudinal flue in double-row racks.
(2) For multiple-row racks, detectors shall be located in either longitudinal or transverse flue space and shall be within 5 ft (1.5 m) horizontally of each sprinkler.
(3) Separate detection systems shall be installed for ceiling sprinkler systems and in-rack sprinkler systems.
(4) Where system is double interlock preaction type, ceiling detection system shall operate solenoid valves on both ceiling and in-rack preaction systems.

8.8.2.8.4 Single Detection System for Ceiling and In-Rack Sprinklers. Ceiling detection only shall be permitted where all of the following conditions are met:

(1) Maximum storage height is 35 ft (11 m).
(2) Maximum ceiling height is 40 ft (12.0 m).
(3) Maximum hazard of storage is Class III.
(4) No solid shelves are present.
(5) One preaction valve is used for both ceiling and in-rack sprinklers protecting the same area, with separate indicating control valves and check valves provided downstream as shown in Figure 8.8.2.8.4.

(6) Detectors at the ceiling are spaced at a maximum of one-half the listed detector spacing but not less than the sprinkler spacing.

8.9 Commercial-Type Cooking Equipment and Ventilation.

8.9.1 General. In cooking areas protected by automatic sprinklers, additional sprinklers or automatic spray nozzles shall be provided to protect commercial-type cooking equipment and ventilation systems that are designed to carry away grease-laden vapors unless otherwise protected.

8.9.2* Sprinklers and Automatic Spray Nozzles.

8.9.2.1 Standard spray sprinklers or automatic spray nozzles shall be so located as to provide for the protection of exhaust ducts, hood exhaust duct collars, and hood exhaust plenum chambers.

8.9.2.2 Unless the requirements of 8.9.2.4 are met, standard spray sprinklers or automatic spray nozzles shall be so located as to provide for the protection of cooking equipment and cooking surfaces.

8.9.2.3 Hoods containing automatic fire-extinguishing systems are protected areas; therefore, these hoods are not considered obstructions to overhead sprinkler systems and shall not require floor coverage underneath.

8.9.2.4 Cooking equipment below hoods that contain automatic fire-extinguishing equipment is protected and shall not require protection from the overhead sprinkler system.

8.9.3 Sprinkler and Automatic Spray Nozzle Location — Ducts.

8.9.3.1 Unless the requirements of 8.9.3.2 or 8.9.3.4 are met, exhaust ducts shall have one sprinkler or automatic spray nozzle located at the top of each vertical riser and at the midpoint of each offset.

8.9.3.2 Sprinklers or automatic spray nozzles shall not be required in a vertical riser located outside of a building, provided the riser does not expose combustible material or provided the interior of the building and the horizontal distance between the hood outlet and the vertical riser is at least 25 ft (7.6 m).

8.9.3.3 Unless the requirements of 8.9.3.4 are met, horizontal exhaust ducts shall have sprinklers or automatic spray nozzle devices located on 10 ft (3.0 m) centers beginning no more than 5 ft (1.5 m) from the duct entrance.

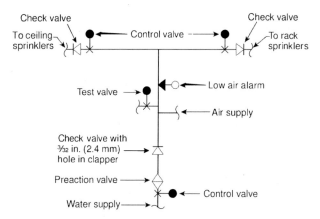

FIGURE 8.8.2.8.4   Valve Arrangement.

8.9.3.4 Sprinklers or automatic spray nozzles shall be required in ducts.

8.9.3.4.1 Where ducts do not exceed 75 ft (23 m) in length and the entire exhaust duct is protected in accordance with NFPA 96, sprinkler(s) or automatic spray nozzle(s) shall not be required.

8.9.3.5 A sprinkler(s) or an automatic spray nozzle(s) in exhaust ducts subject to freezing shall be properly protected against freezing by approved means. *(See 16.4.1.)*

8.9.4 Sprinkler and Automatic Spray Nozzle Location — Duct Collar.

8.9.4.1 Each hood exhaust duct collar shall have one sprinkler or automatic spray nozzle located 1 in. minimum to 12 in. maximum (25 mm minimum to 300 mm maximum) above the point of duct collar connection in the hood plenum.

8.9.4.2 Hoods that have listed fire dampers located in the duct collar shall be protected with a sprinkler or automatic spray nozzle located on the discharge side of the damper and shall be so positioned as not to interfere with damper operation.

8.9.5 Sprinkler and Automatic Spray Nozzle Location — Exhaust Plenum Chambers.

8.9.5.1 Hood exhaust plenum chambers shall have one sprinkler or automatic spray nozzle centered in each chamber not exceeding 10 ft (3.0 m) in length.

8.9.5.2 Plenum chambers greater than 10 ft (3.0 m) in length shall have two sprinklers or automatic spray nozzles evenly spaced, with the maximum distance between the two sprinklers not to exceed 10 ft (3.0 m).

8.9.6 Sprinkler and Automatic Spray Nozzle Temperature Ratings and K-Factors.

8.9.6.1 Where the exposed temperature is expected to be 300°F (149°C) or less, sprinklers or automatic spray nozzles being used in duct, duct collar, and plenum areas shall be of the extra high–temperature classification [325°F to 375°F (163°C to 191°C)].

8.9.6.2 When use of a temperature-measuring device indicates temperatures above 300°F (149°C), a sprinkler or automatic spray nozzle of higher classification shall be used.

8.9.6.3 Sprinklers or automatic spray nozzles being used in duct, duct collar, and plenum areas shall have orifices with K-factors not less than K-1.4 (20) and not more than K-5.6 (80).

8.9.7 Sprinkler and Automatic Spray Nozzle. Access shall be provided to all sprinklers or automatic spray nozzles for examination and replacement.

8.9.8 Cooking Equipment.

8.9.8.1 General. Cooking equipment (such as deep fat fryers, ranges, griddles, and broilers) that is considered to be a source of ignition shall be protected in accordance with the provisions of 8.9.1.

8.9.8.2 Deep Fat Fryers.

8.9.8.2.1 A sprinkler or automatic spray nozzle used for protection of deep fat fryers shall be listed for that application.

8.9.8.2.2 The position, arrangement, location, and water supply for each sprinkler or automatic spray nozzle shall be in accordance with its listing.

8.9.8.3 Fuel and Heat Shutoff.

8.9.8.3.1 The operation of any cooking equipment sprinkler or automatic spray nozzle shall automatically shut off all sources of fuel and heat to all equipment requiring protection.

8.9.8.3.2 Any gas appliance not requiring protection but located under ventilating equipment shall also be shut off.

8.9.8.3.3 All shutdown devices shall be of the type that requires manual resetting prior to fuel or power being restored.

8.9.9 Indicating Valves. A listed indicating valve shall be installed in the water supply line to the sprinklers and spray nozzles protecting the cooking and ventilating system.

8.9.10 Strainers. A listed line strainer shall be installed in the main water supply preceding sprinklers or automatic spray nozzles having nominal K-factors smaller than K-2.8 (40).

8.9.11 Test Connection. A system test connection shall be provided to verify proper operation of equipment specified in 8.9.8.3.

8.10 Pilot Line Detectors.

8.10.1 Pilot line detectors and related components including pipe and fittings shall be corrosion resistant when installed in areas exposed to weather or corrosive conditions.

8.10.2 Where subject to mechanical or physical damage, pilot line detectors and related detection system components shall be protected.

8.10.3 Where spray sprinklers are used as pilot line detectors, they shall be installed in accordance with Section 8.10 and the spacing and location rules of Section 10.2, except that the obstruction to water distribution rules for automatic sprinklers shall not be required to be followed.

8.10.3.1 Where located under a ceiling, pilot sprinklers shall be positioned in accordance with the requirements of Section 10.2.

8.10.4 The temperature rating of spray sprinklers utilized as pilot line detectors shall be selected in accordance with 9.4.2.

8.10.5 Maximum horizontal spacing for indoor locations shall not exceed 12 ft (3.7 m).

8.10.6 Pilot line detectors shall be permitted to be spaced more than 22 in. (550 mm) below a ceiling or deck where the maximum spacing between pilot line detectors is 10 ft (3.0 m) or less.

8.10.6.1 Other maximum horizontal spacing differing from those required in 8.10.5 shall be permitted where installed in accordance with their listing.

8.10.7 Pilot line detectors located outdoors, such as in open process structures, shall be spaced such that the elevation of a single level of pilot line detectors and between additional levels of pilot line detectors shall not exceed 17 ft (5.2 m).

8.10.8 The maximum distance between pilot line detectors installed outdoors shall not exceed 8 ft (2.4 m).

8.10.8.1 The horizontal distance between pilot line detectors installed outdoors on a given level shall be permitted to be increased to 10 ft (3.0 m) when all of the following conditions are met:

(1) The elevation of the first level does not exceed 15 ft (4.6 m).
(2) The distance between additional levels does not exceed 12 ft (3.7 m).
(3) The pilot line actuators are staggered vertically.

8.10.8.2 Alternate vertical spacing of pilot line detectors differing from those required in 8.10.8.1 shall be permitted where installed in accordance with their listing.

8.10.9 Pilot line detectors located in open-sided buildings shall follow the indoor spacing rules.

8.10.9.1 A row of pilot line detectors spaced in accordance with the outdoor pilot line detector spacing rules shall be located along the open sides of open-sided buildings.

8.10.9.2 Pilot line detectors located under open gratings shall be spaced in accordance with the outdoor rules.

8.10.9.3 Where two or more adjacent water spray systems in one fire area are controlled by separate pilot line detector systems, the detectors on each system shall be spaced independently as if the dividing line between the systems were a wall or draft curtain.

8.10.9.4 Where pilot line detectors are installed in water cooling tower applications, they shall be in accordance with Section 27.26.

8.10.10 Pipe supplying pilot line detectors shall be permitted to be supported from the same points of hanger attachment as the piping system it serves.

8.10.10.1 Pipe supplying pilot line detectors shall not be required to meet the requirements of Section 18.5.

Chapter 9   Sprinkler Location Requirements

9.1* Basic Requirements.

9.1.1* The requirements for spacing, location, and position of sprinklers shall be based on the following principles:

(1) Sprinklers shall be installed throughout the premises.
(2) Sprinklers shall be located so as not to exceed the maximum protection area per sprinkler.
(3)* Sprinklers shall be positioned and located so as to provide satisfactory performance with respect to activation time and distribution.
(4) Sprinklers shall be permitted to be omitted from areas specifically allowed by this standard.
(5) When sprinklers are specifically tested and test results demonstrate that deviations from clearance requirements to structural members do not impair the ability of the sprinkler to control or suppress a fire, their positioning and locating in accordance with the test results shall be permitted.
(6) Clearance between sprinklers and ceilings exceeding the maximums specified in this standard shall be permitted, provided that tests or calculations demonstrate comparable sensitivity and performance of the sprinklers to those installed in conformance with these sections.

9.2 Allowable Sprinkler Omission Locations.

9.2.1* Concealed Spaces Not Requiring Sprinkler Protection.

9.2.1.1* Concealed spaces of noncombustible and limited-combustible construction with minimal combustible loading having no access shall not require sprinkler protection.

9.2.1.1.1 The space shall be considered a concealed space even with small openings such as those used as return air for a plenum.

9.2.1.1.2* Small openings with both of the following limits shall be permitted:

(1) A combined total area of not more than 20 percent of the ceiling, construction feature, or plane shall be used to determine the boundaries of the concealed space.
(2) Gaps greater than 4 ft (1.2 m) long shall not be more than 8 in. (200 mm) wide.

9.2.1.2 Concealed spaces of noncombustible and limited-combustible construction with limited access and not permitting occupancy or storage of combustibles shall not require sprinkler protection.

9.2.1.2.1 The space shall be considered a concealed space even with small openings such as those used as return air for a plenum.

N **9.2.1.2.2*** The space shall be considered a concealed space even with non-fuel-fired equipment and access panels.

9.2.1.3 Concealed spaces formed by studs or joists with less than 6 in. (150 mm) between the inside or near edges of the studs or joists shall not require sprinkler protection. *(See Figure 10.2.6.1.5.1.)*

9.2.1.4 Concealed spaces formed by bar joists with less than 6 in. (150 mm) between the roof or floor deck and ceiling shall not require sprinkler protection.

9.2.1.5* Concealed spaces formed by ceilings attached directly to or within 6 in. (150 mm) of wood joist or similar solid member construction shall not require sprinkler protection.

9.2.1.6* Concealed spaces formed by ceilings attached to composite wood joist construction either directly or onto metal channels not exceeding 1 in. (25 mm) in depth, provided the joist channels as measured from the top of the batt insulation are separated into volumes each not exceeding 160 ft³ (4.5 m³) using materials equivalent to the web construction and at least 3½ in. (90 mm) of batt insulation is installed at the bottom of the joist channels when the ceiling is attached utilizing metal channels, shall not require sprinkler protection.

9.2.1.7 Concealed spaces filled with noncombustible insulation shall not require sprinkler protection.

9.2.1.7.1 A maximum 2 in. (50 mm) air gap at the top of the space shall be permitted.

9.2.1.8 Concealed spaces within wood joist construction having noncombustible insulation filling the space from the ceiling up to the bottom edge of the joist of the roof or floor deck shall not require sprinkler protection.

9.2.1.9 Concealed spaces within composite wood joist construction having noncombustible insulation filling the space from the ceiling up to the bottom edge of the composite wood joist of the roof or floor deck and with the joist channels separated into volumes each not exceeding 160 ft³ (4.5 m³) to the full depth of the composite wood joist, with material equivalent to the web construction, shall not require sprinkler protection.

9.2.1.10 Concealed spaces over isolated small compartments not exceeding 55 ft² (5.1 m²) in area shall not require sprinkler protection.

N **9.2.1.11*** Concealed spaces created by soffits of combustible construction below noncombustible or limited combustible ceilings separated into volumes each not exceeding 160 ft³ (4.5 m³) by noncombustible or limited combustible materials shall not require sprinkler protection.

9.2.1.12 Concealed spaces where rigid materials are used and the exposed surfaces, in the form in which they are installed, comply with one of the following shall not require sprinkler protection:

(1) The surface materials have a flame spread index of 25 or less, and the materials have been demonstrated not to propagate fire more than 10.5 ft (3.2 m) when tested in accordance with ASTM E84, *Standard Test Method for Surface Burning Characteristics of Building Materials,* or UL 723, *Standard for Test for Surface Burning Characteristics of Building Materials,* extended for an additional 20 minutes.
(2) The surface materials comply with the requirements of ASTM E2768, *Standard Test Method for Extended Duration Surface Burning Characteristics of Building Materials (30 min Tunnel Test).*

9.2.1.13* Concealed spaces in which the exposed materials are constructed entirely of fire retardant–treated wood as defined by NFPA 703 shall not require sprinkler protection.

9.2.1.14 Noncombustible concealed spaces having exposed combustible insulation where the heat content of the facing and substrate of the insulation material does not exceed

1000 Btu/ft^2 (11,400 kJ/m^2) shall not require sprinkler protection.

9.2.1.15 Concealed spaces below insulation that is laid directly on top of or within wood joists or composite wood joists used as ceiling joists in an otherwise sprinklered concealed space, with the ceiling attached directly to the bottom of the joists, shall not require sprinkler protection.

9.2.1.16 Sprinklers shall not be required in vertical pipe chases under 10 ft^2 (0.9 m^2).

9.2.1.16.1 Pipe chases in accordance with 9.2.1.16 shall contain no sources of ignition.

9.2.1.16.2 In buildings having more than a single story, pipe penetrations at each floor shall be firestopped using materials equivalent to the floor construction.

9.2.1.17 Exterior columns under 10 ft^2 (0.9 m^2) in area, formed by studs or wood joist supporting exterior canopies that are fully protected with a sprinkler system, shall not require sprinkler protection.

9.2.1.18* Concealed spaces formed by noncombustible or limited-combustible ceilings suspended from the bottom of wood joists, composite wood joists, wood bar joists, or wood trusses that have insulation filling all of the gaps between the bottom of the trusses or joists, and where sprinklers are present in the space above the insulation within the trusses or joists, shall not require sprinkler protection.

9.2.1.18.1 The heat content of the facing, substrate, and support of the insulation material shall not exceed 1000 Btu/ft^2 (11,400 kJ/m^2).

9.2.1.19* Concealed spaces formed by noncombustible or limited-combustible ceilings suspended from the bottom of wood joists and composite wood joists with a maximum nominal chord width of 2 in. (50 mm), where joist spaces are full of noncombustible batt insulation with a maximum 2 in. (50 mm) air space between the decking material and the top of the batt insulation shall not require sprinklers.

9.2.1.19.1 Facing that meets the requirements for noncombustible or limited-combustible material covering the surface of the bottom chord of each joist and secured in place per the manufacturer's recommendations shall not require sprinklers.

9.2.1.20 Exterior Soffits, Eaves, Overhangs, and Decorative Frame Elements.

9.2.1.20.1 Sprinklers shall be permitted to be omitted from within combustible soffits, eaves, overhangs, and decorative frame elements that are constructed in accordance with 9.2.1.20.2 through 9.2.1.20.5.

9.2.1.20.2 Combustible soffits, eaves, overhangs, and decorative frame elements shall not exceed 4 ft 0 in. (1.2 m) in width.

9.2.1.20.3 Combustible soffits, eaves, overhangs, and decorative frame elements shall be draftstopped, with a material equivalent to that of the soffit, into volumes not exceeding 160 ft^3 (4.5 m^3).

9.2.1.20.4 Combustible soffits, eaves, overhangs, and decorative frame elements shall be separated from the interior of the building by walls or roofs of noncombustible or limited-combustible construction.

9.2.1.20.5 Combustible soffits, eaves, overhangs, and decorative frame elements shall have no openings or unprotected penetrations directly into the building.

9.2.2 Spaces Under Ground Floors, Exterior Docks, and Exterior Platforms. Sprinklers shall be permitted to be omitted from spaces under ground floors, exterior docks, and exterior platforms where all of the following conditions exist:

(1) The space is not accessible for storage purposes and is protected against accumulation of wind-borne debris.
(2) The space contains no equipment such as conveyors or fuel-fired heating units.
(3) The floor over the space is of tight construction.
(4) No combustible or flammable liquids or materials that under fire conditions would convert into combustible or flammable liquids are processed, handled, or stored on the floor above the space.

9.2.3* Exterior Projections.

9.2.3.1* Sprinklers shall be permitted to be omitted where the exterior canopies, roofs, porte-cocheres, balconies, decks, and similar projections are constructed with materials that are noncombustible, limited-combustible, or fire retardant–treated wood as defined in NFPA 703, or where the projections are constructed utilizing a noncombustible frame, limited-combustibles, or fire retardant–treated wood with an inherently flame-resistant fabric overlay as demonstrated by Test Method 2 in accordance with NFPA 701.

9.2.3.2 Sprinklers shall be permitted to be omitted from below the exterior projections of combustible construction, provided the exposed finish material on the exterior projections are noncombustible, limited-combustible, or fire retardant–treated wood as defined in NFPA 703, and the exterior projections contain only sprinklered concealed spaces or any of the following unsprinklered combustible concealed spaces:

(1) Combustible concealed spaces filled entirely with noncombustible insulation
(2) Light or ordinary hazard occupancies where noncombustible or limited-combustible ceilings are directly attached to the bottom of solid wood joists so as to create enclosed joist spaces 160 ft^3 (4.5 m^3) or less in volume, including space below insulation that is laid directly on top or within the ceiling joists in an otherwise sprinklered attic [see 19.2.3.1.5.2(4)]
(3) Concealed spaces over isolated small exterior projections not exceeding 55 ft^2 (5.1 m^2) in area

N **9.2.3.2.1** Sprinklers shall be required for porte-cocheres that are located directly below floors intended for occupancy.

9.2.3.3 Sprinklers shall be permitted to be omitted from an exterior exit corridor where the exterior wall of the corridor is at least 50 percent open and where the corridor is entirely of noncombustible construction.

9.2.3.4 Sprinklers shall be installed under all exterior projections greater than 4 ft (1.2 m) where combustibles are stored.

9.2.4 Dwelling Units.

9.2.4.1 Bathrooms.

9.2.4.1.1* Unless sprinklers are required by 9.2.4.1.2 or 9.2.4.1.3, sprinklers shall not be required in bathrooms that are located within dwelling units, that do not exceed 55 ft^2 (5.1 m^2) in area, and that have walls and ceilings of noncombustible or limited-combustible materials with a 15-minute thermal barrier rating, including the walls and ceilings behind any shower enclosure or tub.

N **9.2.4.1.1.1** Bathrooms in accordance with 9.2.4.1.1 that are located under stairs that are part of the path of egress shall not be required to be protected provided that the bathroom is separated from the stairs by fire-resistive construction in accordance with the local building code.

9.2.4.1.2 Sprinklers shall be required in bathrooms of limited care facilities and nursing homes, as defined in NFPA *101*.

9.2.4.1.3 Sprinklers shall be required in bathrooms opening directly onto public corridors or exitways.

Δ **9.2.5 Closets and Pantries.**

N **9.2.5.1** Sprinklers shall not be required in clothes closets, linen closets, and pantries within dwelling units in hotels and motels where the area of the space does not exceed 24 ft^2 (2.2 m^2) and the walls and ceilings are surfaced with noncombustible or limited-combustible materials.

9.2.5.2* Hospital Clothes Closets. Sprinklers shall not be required in clothes closets of patient sleeping rooms in hospitals where the area of the closet does not exceed 6 ft^2 (0.6 m^2), provided the distance from the sprinkler in the patient sleeping room to the back wall of the closet does not exceed the maximum distance permitted by 9.5.3.2.

N **9.2.5.3** Sprinklers shall not be required in closets and pantries where other governing laws, codes, or standards permit their omission.

9.2.6* Electrical Equipment Rooms. Sprinklers shall not be required in electrical equipment rooms where all of the following conditions are met:

(1) The room is dedicated to electrical equipment only.
(2) Only dry-type or liquid-type with listed K-class fluid electrical equipment is used.
(3) Equipment is installed in a 2-hour fire-rated enclosure including protection for penetrations.
(4) Storage is not permitted in the room.

9.2.7 Cloud Ceilings.

9.2.7.1* Sprinklers shall be permitted to be omitted above cloud ceilings where all of the following apply:

(1)* The combined total area of the openings around the cloud are less than or equal to 20 percent of the area of the ceiling, construction feature, or plane used to determine the boundaries of the compartment.
(2) The width of the gap and the maximum sprinkler protection area are in accordance with Table 9.2.7.1.
(3) The requirements of 9.2.7.2 are met.
(4) Spaces above cloud ceilings contain either noncombustible or limited-combustible construction with minimal combustible loading.

9.2.7.2 When sprinklers are omitted from above a cloud ceiling in accordance with 9.2.7.1, the requirements of this section shall apply.

9.2.7.2.1 All sprinklers shall be quick response standard spray or extended coverage pendent or upright sprinklers.

9.2.7.2.2 Maximum cloud ceiling height shall not exceed 20 ft (6.1 m).

Table 9.2.7.1 Maximum Sprinkler Protection Area Based on Ceiling Cloud Width and Opening Width

Ceiling Cloud — Minimum Width Dimension (ft)	Maximum Area (ft^2) — Opening Width ≤0.5 in./ft of Ceiling Height	Maximum Area (ft^2) — Opening Width ≤0.75 in./ft of Ceiling Height	Maximum Area (ft^2) — Opening Width ≤1 in./ft of Ceiling Height
2–<2.5	175	70	NP
2.5–4	225	120	70
>4	225	150	150

9.2.7.2.3 Maximum spacing and area of protection shall not exceed the maximum requirements of Table 10.2.4.2.1(a) for light hazard and Table 10.2.4.2.1(b) for ordinary hazard.

9.2.7.2.3.1 Where extended coverage sprinklers are used, the maximum distance between sprinklers shall not exceed 16 ft (4.9 m).

9.2.7.2.4 Cloud ceilings shall be of smooth ceiling construction.

9.2.7.2.5* For irregular shaped ceiling clouds (not rectangular) the minimum width dimension shall be the smallest width dimension of the cloud and for the gap shall be the greatest dimension between clouds or adjacent walls as applicable.

9.2.8 Revolving Doors Enclosures. Sprinkler protection shall not be required within revolving door enclosures.

Δ **9.2.9* Furniture and Cabinets.**

N **9.2.9.1** Sprinklers shall not be required to be installed in furniture, cabinets, and similar items not intended for occupancy.

N **9.2.9.2** This type of feature shall be permitted to be attached to the finished structure.

N **9.2.9.3** Where sprinklers are omitted from furniture, sprinklers in the surrounding area shall be located based on covering the area to the wall behind the furniture.

N **9.2.10 Small Temporarily Occupied Enclosures.**

N **9.2.10.1*** Sprinklers shall not be required in small isolated temporarily occupied enclosures that do not extend to the ceiling.

N **9.2.10.2** The maximum area of the small temporarily occupied enclosures shall not exceed 24 ft^2 (2.2 m^2), and storage shall not be permitted.

9.2.11* Equipment Enclosures. Sprinklers shall not be required to be installed within electrical equipment, mechanical equipment, or air handling units not intended for occupancy.

9.2.12 Noncombustible Vertical Shafts. Sprinklers shall not be required at the top of noncombustible or limited-combustible, nonaccessible vertical duct, electric, and mechanical shafts as permitted by 9.3.3.1.1 and 9.3.3.1.2.

9.2.13 Noncombustible Stairways.

9.2.13.1 Sprinklers shall not be required at the bottom of stairwells complying with the provisions of 9.3.4.2.3.1.

9.2.13.2 Sprinklers shall not be required for exterior stair towers complying with the provisions of 9.3.4.2.4.

9.2.14 Elevator Hoistways and Machine Rooms. Sprinklers shall not be required in locations complying with 9.3.6.3, 9.3.6.6, or 9.3.6.7.2.

9.2.15 Duct Protection. Sprinklers shall not be required in vertical duct risers complying with 9.3.9.1.2.

9.2.16 Open-Grid Ceilings. Sprinklers shall not be required below open grid ceiling installations complying with 9.3.10.

9.2.17 Drop-Out Ceilings. Sprinklers shall not be required below drop-out ceilings complying with 9.3.11.

9.2.18 Skylights. Sprinklers shall not be required in skylights complying with 9.3.16.

9.3 Special Situations.

9.3.1 Heat-Producing Devices with Composite Wood Joist Construction. Where heat-producing devices such as furnaces or process equipment are located in the joist channels above a ceiling attached directly to the underside of composite wood joist construction that would not otherwise require sprinkler protection of the spaces, the joist channel containing the heat-producing devices shall be sprinklered by installing sprinklers in each joist channel, on each side, adjacent to the heat-producing device.

Δ **9.3.2 Special Sprinklers for Horizontal Combustible Concealed Spaces.** Unless the requirements of 9.2.1.19 are met, sprinklers used in horizontal combustible concealed spaces (with a slope not exceeding 2 in 12) with wood truss, wood joist construction, or bar joist construction having a combustible upper surface and where the depth of the space is less than 36 in. (900 mm) from deck to deck, from deck to ceiling, or with double wood joist construction with a maximum of 36 in. (900 mm) between the top of the bottom joist and the bottom of the upper joist shall be listed for such use.

Δ **9.3.2.1** Sprinklers specifically listed to provide protection of combustible concealed spaces described in 9.3.2 shall be permitted to be used in accordance with 9.4.1.2 where the space is less than 12 in. (300 mm) from deck to deck or deck to ceiling

9.3.2.2 Sprinklers specifically listed to provide protection of combustible concealed spaces described in 9.3.2 shall be permitted to be used in accordance with 9.4.1.2 throughout the area when a portion of the area exceeds a depth of 36 in. (900 mm).

N **9.3.2.3** Sprinklers specifically listed to provide protection of combustible concealed spaces described in 9.3.2 shall be permitted to be used in accordance with 9.4.1.2 to protect composite wood joist construction.

9.3.3 Vertical Shafts.

9.3.3.1 General. Unless the requirements of 9.3.3.1.1 or 9.3.3.1.2 are met, one sprinkler shall be installed at the top of shafts.

9.3.3.1.1 Noncombustible or limited-combustible, nonaccessible vertical duct shafts shall not require sprinkler protection.

9.3.3.1.2 Noncombustible or limited-combustible, nonaccessible vertical electrical or mechanical shafts shall not require sprinkler protection.

9.3.3.2* Shafts with Combustible Surfaces.

9.3.3.2.1 Where vertical shafts have combustible surfaces, one sprinkler shall be installed at each alternate floor level.

9.3.3.2.2 Where a shaft having combustible surfaces is trapped, an additional sprinkler shall be installed at the top of each trapped section.

9.3.3.3 Accessible Shafts with Noncombustible Surfaces. Where accessible vertical shafts have noncombustible surfaces, one sprinkler shall be installed near the bottom.

9.3.4 Stairways.

9.3.4.1 Combustible Construction. Sprinklers shall be installed beneath all stairways of combustible construction.

9.3.4.1.1 Sprinklers shall be installed at the top of combustible stair shafts to protect the entire footprint of the shaft.

9.3.4.1.2* Sprinklers shall be installed under the landings at each floor level.

9.3.4.1.3 Sprinklers shall be installed beneath the lowest intermediate landing.

9.3.4.2 Noncombustible Construction.

9.3.4.2.1 In noncombustible stair shafts having noncombustible stairs with noncombustible or limited-combustible finishes, sprinklers shall be installed at the top of the shaft to protect the entire footprint of the shaft and under the first accessible landing above the bottom of the shaft.

9.3.4.2.2 Where noncombustible stair shafts are divided by walls or doors, sprinklers shall be provided on each side of the separation.

9.3.4.2.3 Sprinklers shall be installed beneath landings or stairways where the area beneath is used for storage.

9.3.4.2.3.1* Sprinklers shall be permitted to be omitted from the bottom of the stairwell when the space under the stairs at the bottom is blocked off so that storage cannot occur.

9.3.4.2.4 Sprinklers shall be permitted to be omitted from exterior stair towers when the exterior walls of the stair tower are at least 50 percent open and when the stair tower is entirely of noncombustible construction.

9.3.4.3* Stairs Serving Two or More Areas. When stairs have openings to each side of a fire wall(s), sprinklers shall be installed in the stair shaft at each floor landing with multiple openings.

9.3.5* Vertical Openings.

9.3.5.1* General. Unless the requirements of 9.3.5.4 are met, where moving stairways, staircases, or similar floor openings are unenclosed and where sprinkler protection is serving as the alternative to enclosure of the vertical opening, the floor openings involved shall be protected by closely spaced sprinklers in combination with draft curtains in accordance with 9.3.5.2 and 9.3.5.3.

9.3.5.2 Draft Curtains. Draft curtains shall meet all of the following criteria:

(1) The draft curtains shall be located immediately adjacent to the opening.
(2) The draft curtains shall be at least 18 in. (450 mm) deep.
(3) The draft curtains shall be of noncombustible or limited-combustible material that will stay in place before and during sprinkler operation.

9.3.5.3 Sprinklers.

9.3.5.3.1 Sprinklers shall be spaced not more than 6 ft (1.8 m) apart and placed 6 in. to 12 in. (150 mm to 300 mm) from the draft curtain on the side away from the opening.

9.3.5.3.2 Where sprinklers are closer than 6 ft (1.8 m), cross baffles shall be provided in accordance with 10.2.5.4.2.

9.3.5.4 Large Openings. Closely spaced sprinklers and draft curtains are not required around large openings such as those found in shopping malls, atrium buildings, and similar structures where all adjoining levels and spaces are protected by automatic sprinklers in accordance with this standard and where the openings have all horizontal dimensions between opposite edges of 20 ft (6.1 m) or greater and an area of 1000 ft² (93 m²) or greater.

9.3.6 Elevator Machine Rooms, Machinery Spaces, Control Rooms, Control Spaces, and Hoistways.

𝑁 9.3.6.1* Sidewall spray sprinklers shall be installed at the bottom of each elevator hoistway not more than 2 ft (600 mm) above the floor of the pit.

𝑁 9.3.6.2 The sprinkler required at the bottom of the elevator hoistway by 9.3.6.1 shall not be required for enclosed, noncombustible elevator shafts that do not contain combustible hydraulic fluid.

Δ 9.3.6.3 Automatic fire sprinklers shall not be required in elevator machine rooms, machinery spaces, control rooms, control spaces, or hoistways of traction elevators installed in accordance with the applicable provisions in NFPA *101*, or the applicable building code, where all of the following conditions are met:

(1) The elevator machine room, machinery space, control room, control space, or hoistway of traction elevator is dedicated to elevator equipment only.
(2) The elevator machine room, machinery space, control room, control space, or hoistway of traction elevators are protected by smoke detectors, or other automatic fire detection, installed in accordance with *NFPA 72* or other approved fire alarm code.
(3) The elevator machinery space, control room, control space, or hoistway of traction elevators is separated from the remainder of the building by walls and floor/ceiling or roof/ceiling assemblies having a fire resistance rating of not less than that specified by the applicable building code.
(4) No materials unrelated to elevator equipment are permitted to be stored in elevator machine rooms, machinery spaces, control rooms, control spaces, or hoistways of traction elevators.
(5) The elevator machinery is not of the hydraulic type.

9.3.6.4* Automatic sprinklers in elevator machine rooms, machinery spaces, control rooms, control spaces, or hoistways shall be standard response.

9.3.6.5 Upright, pendent, or sidewall spray sprinklers shall be installed at the top of elevator hoistways.

9.3.6.6* The sprinklers required at the top of the elevator hoistway by 9.3.6.5 shall not be required where the hoistway for passenger elevators is noncombustible or limited-combustible and the car enclosure materials meet the requirements of ASME A17.1, *Safety Code for Elevators and Escalators.*

9.3.6.7 Combustible Suspension in Elevators.

9.3.6.7.1 Sprinklers shall be installed at the top and bottom of elevator hoistways where elevators utilize combustible suspension means such as noncircular elastomeric-coated or polyurethane-coated steel belts.

Δ 9.3.6.7.2 The sprinklers in the elevator hoistway shall not be required when the suspension means provide not less than an FT-1 rating when tested to the vertical burn test requirements of UL 2556, *Wire and Cable Test Methods*, where the suspension means shall not continue to burn for more than 60 seconds, nor shall the indicator flag be burned more than 25 percent.

9.3.7* Library Stack Areas and Record Storage. Where books or records are stored in fixed open book shelves, sprinklers shall be installed in accordance with one of the following:

(1) Sprinklers shall be permitted to be installed without regard to aisles where clearance between sprinkler deflectors and tops of stacks is 18 in. (450 mm) or more.
(2) Where the 18 in. (450 mm) clearance between sprinkler deflectors and tops of stacks cannot be maintained, sprinklers shall be installed in every aisle and at every tier of stacks with distance between sprinklers along aisles not to exceed 12 ft (3.7 m) in accordance with Figure 9.3.7(a).
(3) Where the 18 in. (450 mm) clearance between sprinkler deflectors and tops of stacks cannot be maintained and where vertical shelf dividers are incomplete and allow water distribution to adjacent aisles, sprinklers shall be permitted to be omitted in alternate aisles on each tier, and where ventilation openings are also provided in tier floors, sprinklers shall be staggered vertically in accordance with Figure 9.3.7(b).

9.3.8* Industrial Ovens and Furnaces.

9.3.9 Duct Protection. Duct protection shall be required to meet the requirements of 9.3.9 where required by the authority having jurisdiction or the applicable referenced code or standard.

9.3.9.1 Sprinkler Location.

9.3.9.1.1 Unless the requirements of 9.3.9.1.2 or 9.3.9.1.3 are met, ducts shall have one sprinkler located at the top of each vertical riser and at the midpoint of each offset.

9.3.9.1.2 Sprinklers shall not be required in a vertical riser located outside of a building, provided the riser does not expose combustible material or provided the interior of the building and the horizontal distance between the hood outlet and the vertical riser is at least 25 ft (7.6 m).

9.3.9.1.3 Horizontal exhaust ducts shall have sprinklers located on 10 ft (3.0 m) centers beginning no more than 5 ft (1.5 m) from the duct entrance.

9.3.9.2 Protection Against Freezing. Sprinklers in exhaust ducts subject to freezing shall be properly protected against freezing. *(See 16.4.1.)*

9.3.9.3 Sprinkler Access. Access shall be provided to all sprinklers for inspection, testing, and maintenance.

9.3.9.4 Strainers. A listed line strainer shall be installed in the main water supply preceding sprinklers having nominal K-factors smaller than K-2.8 (40).

9.3.10* Open-Grid Ceilings. Open-grid ceilings shall only be installed beneath sprinklers where one of the following is met:

(1) Open-grid ceilings in which the openings are ¼ in. (6 mm) or larger in the least dimension, where the thickness or depth of the material does not exceed the least dimension of the opening, and where such openings constitute 70 percent of the area of the ceiling material.

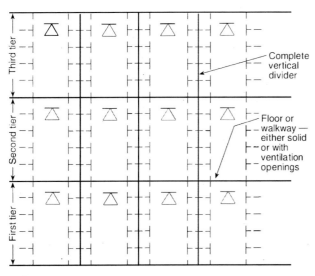

FIGURE 9.3.7(a)   Sprinklers in Multitier Bookstacks with Complete Vertical Dividers.

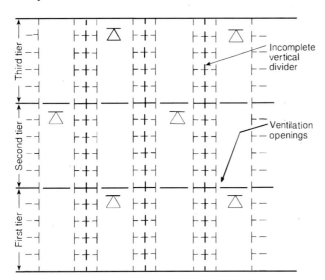

FIGURE 9.3.7(b)   Sprinklers in Multitier Bookstacks with Incomplete Vertical Dividers.

The spacing of the sprinklers over the open-grid ceiling shall then comply with the following:

(a) In light hazard occupancies where sprinkler spacing (either spray or old-style sprinklers) is less than 10 ft × 10 ft (3 m × 3 m), a minimum clearance of at least 18 in. (450 mm) shall be provided between the sprinkler deflectors and the upper surface of the open-grid ceiling. Where spacing is greater than 10 ft × 10 ft (3 m × 3 m) but less than 10 ft × 12 ft (3 m × 3.7 m), a clearance of at least 24 in. (600 mm) shall be provided from spray sprinklers and at least 36 in. (900 mm) from old-style sprinklers. Where spacing is greater than 10 ft × 12 ft (3 m × 3.7 m), a clearance of at least 48 in. (1.2 m) shall be provided.

(b) In ordinary hazard occupancies, open-grid ceilings shall be permitted to be installed beneath spray sprinklers only. Where sprinkler spacing is less than 10 ft × 10 ft (3 m × 3 m), a minimum clearance of at least 24 in. (600 mm) shall be provided between the sprinkler deflectors and the upper surface of the open-grid ceiling. Where spacing is greater than 10 ft × 10 ft (3 m × 3 m), a clearance of at least 36 in. (900 m) shall be provided.

(2) Other types of open-grid ceilings shall be permitted to be installed beneath sprinklers where they are listed for such service and are installed in accordance with instructions contained in each package of ceiling material.

9.3.11 Drop-Out Ceilings and Ceiling Materials.

9.3.11.1* Drop-out ceilings and ceiling materials shall be permitted to be installed beneath sprinklers where the ceiling panels or ceiling materials are listed for that service and are installed in accordance with their listings.

9.3.11.2 Drop-out ceilings and ceiling materials meeting the criteria in 9.3.11.1 shall not be installed below quick-response or extended coverage sprinklers unless specifically listed for that application.

9.3.11.3 Drop-out ceilings and ceiling materials meeting the criteria in 9.3.11.1 shall not be considered ceilings within the context of this standard.

9.3.11.4* Piping installed above drop-out ceilings and ceiling materials meeting the criteria in 9.3.11.1 shall not be considered concealed piping.

9.3.11.5* Sprinklers shall not be installed beneath drop-out ceilings or ceiling materials meeting the criteria in 9.3.11.1.

9.3.12* Old-style sprinklers shall be installed in fur storage vaults.

9.3.13 Stages.

9.3.13.1 Sprinklers shall be installed under the roof at the ceiling, in spaces under the stage either containing combustible materials or constructed of combustible materials, and in all adjacent spaces and dressing rooms, storerooms, and workshops.

9.3.13.2 Where proscenium opening protection is required, a deluge system shall be provided with open sprinklers located not more than 3 ft (900 mm) away from the stage side of the proscenium arch and spaced up to a maximum of 6 ft (1.8 m) on center. *(See Chapter 19 for design criteria.)*

9.3.14 Spaces Above Ceilings.

9.3.14.1 Where spaces have ceilings that are lower than the rest of the area, the space above this lower ceiling shall be sprinklered unless it complies with the rules of 9.2.1 for allowable unsprinklered concealed spaces.

9.3.14.2 Where the space above a drop ceiling is sprinklered, the sprinkler system shall conform to the rules of 19.1.2 and Section 20.13.

9.3.14.3* Where there is a noncombustible space above a noncombustible or limited-combustible drop ceiling that is sprinklered because it is open to an adjacent sprinklered space and where there is no possibility for storage above the drop ceiling, the sprinkler system shall be permitted to extend only as far into the space as 0.6 times the square root of the design area of the sprinkler system in the adjacent space.

9.3.14.3.1 The sprinkler system shall extend at least 24 ft (7.3 m) into the space above the ceiling.

9.3.15* Sprinkler-Protected Glazing. Where sprinklers are used in combination with glazing as an alternative to a required fire-rated wall or window assembly, the sprinkler-protected assembly shall comply with the following:

(1) Sprinklers shall be listed as specific application window sprinklers unless the standard spray sprinklers are specifically permitted by the building code.
(2) Sprinklers shall be supplied by a wet pipe system.
(3) Glazing shall be heat-strengthened, tempered, or glass ceramic and shall be fixed.
(4) Where the assembly is required to be protected from both sides, sprinklers shall be installed on both sides of the glazing.
(5) The use of sprinkler-protected glazing shall be limited to non-load-bearing walls.
(6) The glazed assembly shall not have any horizontal members that would interfere with uniform distribution of water over the surface of the glazing, and there shall be no obstructions between sprinklers and glazing that would obstruct water distribution.
(7) The water supply duration for the design area that includes the window sprinklers shall not be less than the required rating of the assembly

9.3.16 Skylights.

9.3.16.1 Sprinklers shall be permitted to be omitted from skylights not exceeding 32 ft² (3.0 m²) in area, regardless of hazard classification, that are separated by at least 10 ft (3.0 m) horizontally from any other unprotected skylight or unprotected ceiling pocket.

9.3.16.1.1 When a sprinkler is installed directly beneath a skylight that does not allow venting and does not exceed 32 ft² (3.0 m²), the distance to the ceiling shall be measured to the plane of the ceiling as if the skylight was not present.

9.3.16.2 Skylights not exceeding 32 ft² (3.0 m²) shall be permitted to have a plastic cover.

9.3.16.3 Skylights that allow venting, other than smoke and heat venting per 20.9.5, shall be provided with sprinkler protection installed in the skylight.

9.3.17 Concealed Spaces.

9.3.17.1 Concealed Spaces Requiring Sprinkler Protection. Concealed spaces of exposed combustible construction shall be protected by sprinklers except in concealed spaces where sprinklers are not required to be installed by 9.2.1.1 through 9.2.1.20 and 9.2.2.

9.3.17.1.1* Concealed Space Design Requirements. Sprinklers in concealed spaces having no access for storage or other use shall be installed in accordance with the requirements for light hazard occupancy.

9.3.17.1.2 Localized Protection of Exposed Combustible Construction or Exposed Combustibles. When otherwise noncombustible or limited-combustible concealed spaces that would not require sprinkler protection have localized exposed combustible construction, or contain localized areas of exposed combustibles, the combustibles shall be permitted to be protected as follows:

(1) If the exposed combustibles are in the vertical partitions or walls around all or a portion of the enclosure, a single row of sprinklers spaced not over 12 ft (3.7 m) apart nor more than 6 ft (1.8 m) from the inside of the partition shall be permitted to protect the surface. The first and last sprinklers in such a row shall not be over 5 ft (1.5 m) from the ends of the partitions.
(2) If the exposed combustibles are in the horizontal plane, the area of the combustibles shall be permitted to be protected with sprinklers on a light hazard spacing. Additional sprinklers shall be installed no more than 6 ft (1.8 m) outside the outline of the area and not more than 12 ft (3.7 m) on center along the outline. When the outline returns to a wall or other obstruction, the last sprinkler shall not be more than 6 ft (1.8 m) from the wall or obstruction.

9.3.18 Spaces Under Ground Floors, Exterior Docks, and Platforms.

9.3.18.1 Unless the requirements of 9.2.2 are met, sprinklers shall be installed in spaces under all combustible ground floors and combustible exterior docks and platforms.

9.3.19 Exterior Projections.

9.3.19.1* Unless the requirements of 9.2.3.1, 9.2.3.2, or 9.2.3.3 are met, sprinklers shall be installed under exterior projections exceeding 4 ft (1.2 m) in width.

9.3.19.2* Sprinklers shall be installed under all exterior projections greater than 4 ft (1.2 m) where combustibles are stored.

N 9.3.20* Balconies and Decks Serving Dwelling Units.

N 9.3.20.1* Where a roof, deck, or balcony greater than 4 ft (1.2 m) wide is provided above, sprinklers shall be installed to protect attached exterior balconies, attached exterior decks, and ground floor patios directly serving dwelling units in buildings of Type V construction.

N 9.3.20.2 Where sprinklers are installed beneath roofs, overhangs, decks, or balconies, sprinklers shall be permitted to be installed with deflectors positioned in accordance with 9.3.20.3 or 9.3.20.4 or the manufacturer's installation instructions.

N **9.3.20.3** Sidewall sprinklers shall not be less than 4 in. (100 mm) or more than 6 in. (150 mm) below structural members under a smooth ceiling and not less than 1 in. (25 mm) or more than 6 in. (150 mm) below exposed structural members, provided that the deflector is not more than 14 in. (350 mm) below the underside surface of the deck above the exposed structural members.

N **9.3.20.4** Pendent sprinklers shall be positioned in accordance with the requirements of NFPA 13 for the sprinkler type installed.

9.3.21 Electrical Equipment.

9.3.21.1 Unless the requirements of 9.2.6 are met, sprinkler protection shall be required in electrical equipment rooms.

9.4 Use of Sprinklers.

9.4.1 General.

9.4.1.1* Sprinklers shall be installed in accordance with their listing.

9.4.1.2 Where no sprinklers are specifically listed for construction features or other special situations that require unusual water distribution, the requirements of 9.4.1.1 shall not apply and listed sprinklers shall be permitted to be installed in positions other than anticipated by their listing to achieve specific results.

9.4.1.3* Upright sprinklers shall be installed with the frame arms parallel to the branch line, unless specifically listed for other orientation.

9.4.1.4 Where solvent cement is used as the pipe and fittings bonding agent, sprinklers shall not be installed in the fittings prior to the fittings being cemented in place.

9.4.1.5 Protective Caps and Straps.

9.4.1.5.1* Protective caps and straps shall be removed using means that are in accordance with the manufacturer's installation instructions.

9.4.1.5.2* Protective caps and straps shall be removed from all sprinklers prior to the time when the sprinkler system is placed in service.

9.4.1.5.3 Protective caps and straps on all upright sprinklers or on any sprinklers installed more than 10 ft (3.0 m) above the floor shall be permitted to be removed from sprinklers immediately following their installation.

9.4.2 Temperature Ratings.

9.4.2.1* Unless the requirements of 9.4.2.2, 9.4.2.3, 9.4.2.4, or 9.4.2.5 are met, ordinary or intermediate-temperature sprinklers shall be permitted to be used throughout buildings.

9.4.2.2 Where maximum ceiling temperatures exceed 100°F (38°C), sprinklers with temperature ratings in accordance with the maximum ceiling temperatures of Table 7.2.4.1(a) shall be used.

9.4.2.3 High-temperature sprinklers shall be permitted to be used throughout ordinary and extra hazard occupancies, storage occupancies, and as allowed in this standard and other NFPA codes and standards.

9.4.2.4 Sprinklers of intermediate- and high-temperature classifications shall be installed in specific locations as required by 9.4.2.5.

Δ **9.4.2.5*** The following practices shall be observed to provide sprinklers of other than ordinary-temperature classification unless other temperatures are determined or unless high-temperature sprinklers are used throughout, and temperature selection shall be in accordance with Table 9.4.2.5(a), Table 9.4.2.5(b), and Figure 9.4.2.5:

(1)* Sprinklers in the high-temperature zone shall be of the high-temperature classification, and sprinklers in the intermediate-temperature zone shall be of the intermediate-temperature classification.

(2) Sprinklers located within 12 in. (300 mm) to one side or 30 in. (750 mm) above an uncovered steam main, heating coil, or radiator shall be of the intermediate-temperature classification.

(3) Sprinklers within 7 ft (2.1 m) of a low-pressure blowoff valve that discharges free in a large room shall be of the high-temperature classification.

(4) Sprinklers under glass or plastic skylights exposed to the direct rays of the sun shall be of the intermediate-temperature classification.

(5) Sprinklers in attics (peaked or flat) shall be of the intermediate-temperature classification.

(6) Sprinklers in enclosed show windows shall be of the intermediate-temperature classification.

(7) Sprinklers protecting commercial-type cooking equipment and ventilation systems shall be of the high- or extra-high-temperature classification as determined by use of a temperature-measuring device. *(See 8.9.6.)*

(8) Sprinklers protecting residential areas installed near specific heat sources identified in Table 9.4.2.5(b) shall be installed in accordance with Table 9.4.2.5(b).

(9) Ordinary-temperature sprinklers located adjacent to a heating duct that discharges air that is less than 100°F (38°C) are not required to be separated in accordance with Table 9.4.2.5(a) or Table 9.4.2.5(b).

(10) Sprinklers in walk-in type coolers and freezers with automatic defrosting shall be of the intermediate-temperature classification or higher.

(11) Sprinklers in closets containing ventless clothes dryers shall be of the intermediate-temperature classification or higher.

9.4.2.6 In case of occupancy change involving temperature change, the sprinklers shall be changed accordingly.

9.4.2.7* The minimum temperature rating of ceiling sprinklers in general storage, rack storage, rubber tire storage, roll paper storage, and baled cotton storage applications shall be 150°F (66°C).

N **9.4.2.8** Listed residential sprinklers of intermediate temperature rating shall be permitted to be installed throughout areas where residential sprinklers are required or permitted.

N **9.4.2.9** Listed quick response sprinklers of ordinary and/or intermediate temperature rating shall be permitted to be installed throughout areas where quick response sprinklers are required or permitted.

Table 9.4.2.5(a) Temperature Ratings of Sprinklers Based on Distance from Heat Sources

Type of Heat Condition	Ordinary-Temperature Rating	Intermediate-Temperature Rating	High-Temperature Rating
(1) Heating ducts			
(a) Above	More than 2 ft 6 in. (750 mm)	2 ft 6 in. or less (750 mm)	
(b) Side and below	More than 1 ft 0 in. (300 mm)	1 ft 0 in. or less (300 mm)	
(c) Diffuser	Any distance except as shown under Intermediate-Temperature Rating column	*Downward discharge:* Cylinder with 1 ft 0 in. (300 mm) radius from edge extending 1 ft 0 in. (300 mm) below and 2 ft 6 in. (750 mm) above *Horizontal discharge:* Semicylinder or cylinder with 2 ft 6 in. (750 mm) radius in direction of flow extending 1 ft 0 in. (300 mm) below and 2 ft 6 in. (750 mm) above	
(2) Unit heater and radiant heater			
(a) Horizontal discharge		*Discharge side:* 7 ft 0 in. (2.1 m) to 20 ft 0 in. (6.1 m) radius pie-shaped cylinder *(see Figure 9.4.2.5)* extending 7 ft 0 in. (2.1 m) above and 2 ft 0 in. (600 mm) below heater; also 7 ft 0 in. (2.1 m) radius cylinder more than 7 ft 0 in. (2.1 m) above unit heater	7 ft 0 in. (2.1 m) radius cylinder extending 7 ft 0 in. (2.1 m) above and 2 ft 0 in. (600 mm) below unit heater
(b) Vertical downward discharge *(for sprinklers below unit heater, see Figure 9.4.2.5)*		7 ft 0 in. (2.1 m) radius cylinder extending upward from an elevation 7 ft 0 in. (2.1 m) above unit heater	7 ft 0 in. (2.1 m) radius cylinder extending from the top of the unit heater to an elevation 7 ft 0 in. (2.1 m) above unit heater
(3) Steam mains (uncovered)			
(a) Above	More than 2 ft 6 in. (750 mm)	2 ft 6 in. or less (750 mm)	
(b) Side and below	More than 1 ft 0 in. (300 mm)	1 ft 0 in. or less (300 mm)	
(c) Blowoff valve	More than 7 ft 0 in. (2.1 m)		7 ft 0 in. or less (2.1 m)

9.4.3 Thermal Sensitivity.

9.4.3.1 Sprinklers in light hazard occupancies shall be one of the following:

(1)   Quick-response type as defined in 3.3.215.4.16
(2)   Residential sprinklers in accordance with the requirements of Chapter 12
(3)   Quick response CMSA sprinklers
(4)   ESFR sprinklers
(5)   Standard-response sprinklers used for modifications or additions to existing light hazard systems equipped with standard-response sprinklers
(6)   Standard-response sprinklers used where individual standard-response sprinklers are replaced in existing light hazard systems

9.4.3.2 Where quick-response sprinklers are installed, all sprinklers within a compartment shall be quick-response unless otherwise permitted in 9.4.3.3, 9.4.3.4, or 9.4.3.5.

9.4.3.3 Where there are no listed quick-response sprinklers in the temperature range required, standard-response sprinklers shall be permitted to be used.

9.4.3.4 The provisions of 9.4.3.2 shall not apply to in-rack sprinklers.

9.4.3.5 In other than light hazard occupancies, where a sprinkler carries a listing for both standard-response protection and quick-response protection at different coverage areas, that sprinkler shall be permitted to be installed within a compartment at the spacing for both the quick-response and standard-response listings without any separation between the areas so covered.

9.4.3.6 When existing light hazard systems are converted to use quick-response or residential sprinklers, all sprinklers in a compartment shall be changed.

Table 9.4.2.5(b) Temperature Ratings of Sprinklers in Specified Residential Areas

Heat Source	Minimum Distance from Edge of Source to Ordinary-Temperature Sprinkler		Minimum Distance from Edge of Source to Intermediate-Temperature Sprinkler	
	in.	mm	in.	mm
Side of open or recessed fireplace	36	900	12	300
Front of recessed fireplace	60	1500	36	900
Coal- or wood-burning stove	42	1050	12	300
Kitchen range	18	450	9	225
Wall oven	18	450	9	225
Hot air flues	18	450	9	225
Uninsulated heat ducts	18	450	9	225
Uninsulated hot water pipes	12	300	6	150
Side of ceiling- or wall-mounted hot air diffusers	24	600	12	300
Front of wall-mounted hot air diffusers	36	900	18	450
Hot water heater or furnace	6	150	3	75
Light fixture:				
0 W–250 W	6	150	3	75
250 W–499 W	12	300	6	150

9.4.4 Sprinklers with K-Factors Less than K-5.6 (80).

9.4.4.1 Sprinklers shall have a minimum nominal K-factor of 5.6 (80) unless otherwise permitted by 9.4.4.

9.4.4.2 For light hazard occupancies, sprinklers having a nominal K-factor smaller than K-5.6 (80) shall be permitted, subject to the following restrictions:

(1) The system shall be hydraulically calculated.
(2) Sprinklers with nominal K-factors of less than K-5.6 (80) shall be installed only in wet pipe sprinkler systems or in accordance with the limitations of 9.4.4.3 or 9.4.4.4.
(3) A listed strainer shall be provided on the supply side of sprinklers with nominal K-factors of less than K-2.8 (40).

9.4.4.3 Sprinklers with nominal K-factors of less than K-5.6 (80) shall be permitted to be installed in conformance with 19.3.2 for protection against exposure fires.

9.4.4.4 Sprinklers with nominal K-factors of K-4.2 (57) shall be permitted to be installed on dry pipe and preaction systems protecting light hazard occupancies where piping is corrosion resistant or internally galvanized.

9.4.5 Thread Size Limitations. Sprinklers having a K-factor exceeding K-5.6 (80) and having ½ in. (15 mm) National Pipe Thread (NPT) shall not be installed in new sprinkler systems.

9.5 Position, Location, Spacing, and Use of Sprinklers.

9.5.1 General.

9.5.1.1 Sprinklers shall be located, spaced, and positioned in accordance with the requirements of Section 9.5.

9.5.1.2 Sprinklers shall be positioned to provide protection of the area consistent with the overall objectives of this standard by controlling the positioning and allowable area of coverage for each sprinkler.

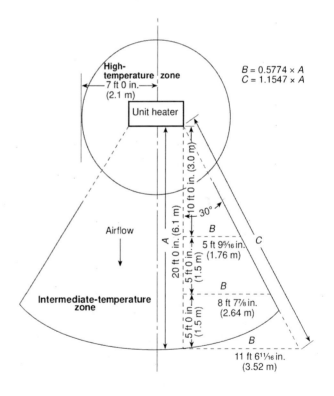

FIGURE 9.4.2.5 High-Temperature and Intermediate-Temperature Zones at Unit Heaters and Radiant Heaters.

N **9.5.1.3*** In light and ordinary hazard occupancies, small areas created by architectural features shall be evaluated as follows:

(1) Where no additional floor area is created by the architectural features, no additional sprinkler protection is required.

(2) Where additional floor area is created by an architectural feature, no additional sprinkler protection is required, provided all of the following conditions are met:

    (a) The floor area does not exceed 18 ft^2 (1.7 m^2).

    (b) The floor area is not greater than 2 ft (0.61 m) in depth at the deepest point of the architectural feature to the plane of the primary wall where measured along the finished floor.

    (c) The floor area is not greater than 9 ft (2.7 m) in length where measured along the plane of the primary wall.

    (d) Measurement from the deepest point of the architectural feature shall not exceed the maximum listed spacing of the sprinkler.

(3) The hydraulic design is not required to consider the area created by the architectural feature.

9.5.1.4 The requirements of 9.5.2 through 9.5.5 shall apply to all sprinkler types unless modified by more restrictive rules in Chapters 10 through 15.

9.5.2 Protection Areas per Sprinkler.

9.5.2.1 Determination of Protection Area of Coverage.

9.5.2.1.1 The protection area of coverage per sprinkler (A_s) shall be determined as follows:

(1) Along branch lines as follows:

    (a) Determine distance between sprinklers (or to wall or obstruction in the case of the end sprinkler on the branch line) upstream and downstream

    (b) Choose the larger of either twice the distance to the wall or the distance to the next sprinkler

    (c) Define dimension as *S*

(2) Between branch lines as follows:

    (a) Determine perpendicular distance to the sprinkler on the adjacent branch line (or to a wall or obstruction in the case of the last branch line) on each side of the branch line on which the subject sprinkler is positioned

    (b) Choose the larger of either twice the distance to the wall or obstruction or the distance to the next sprinkler

    (c) Define dimension as *L*

9.5.2.1.2 The protection area of coverage of the sprinkler shall be established by multiplying the *S* dimension by the *L* dimension, as follows:

[9.5.2.1.2]

$$A_s = S \times L$$

9.5.2.2 Maximum Protection Area of Coverage.

9.5.2.2.1 The maximum allowable protection area of coverage for a sprinkler (A_s) shall be in accordance with the value indicated in the section for each type or style of sprinkler.

9.5.2.2.2 The maximum area of coverage of any sprinkler shall not exceed 400 ft^2 (37 m^2).

9.5.3 Sprinkler Spacing.

9.5.3.1 Maximum Distance Between Sprinklers.

9.5.3.1.1 The maximum distance permitted between sprinklers shall be based on the centerline distance between adjacent sprinklers.

9.5.3.1.2 The maximum distance shall be measured along the slope of the ceiling.

9.5.3.1.3 The maximum distance permitted between sprinklers shall comply with the value indicated in the applicable section for each type or style of sprinkler.

9.5.3.2 Maximum Distance from Walls.

9.5.3.2.1 The distance from sprinklers to walls shall not exceed one-half of the allowable maximum distance between sprinklers.

9.5.3.2.2 The distance from the wall to the sprinkler shall be measured perpendicular to the wall.

Δ **9.5.3.2.3*** The distance from the wall to the sprinkler shall be measured to the wall behind furniture.

9.5.3.2.4 The distance from the wall to the sprinkler shall be measured to the wall when sprinklers are spaced near windows and no additional floor space is created.

9.5.3.3 Minimum Distance from Walls.

9.5.3.3.1 The minimum distance permitted between a sprinkler and the wall shall comply with the value indicated in the applicable section for each type or style of sprinkler.

9.5.3.3.2 The distance from the wall to the sprinkler shall be measured perpendicular to the wall.

9.5.3.4 Minimum Distance Between Sprinklers.

9.5.3.4.1 A minimum distance shall be maintained between sprinklers to prevent operating sprinklers from wetting adjacent sprinklers and to prevent skipping of sprinklers.

9.5.3.4.2 The minimum distance permitted between sprinklers shall comply with the value indicated in the applicable section for each type or style of sprinkler.

N **9.5.3.4.3** The minimum distance to be maintained between sprinklers shall not apply when either one of the affected sprinklers is capable of protecting the room or space without the other sprinkler having to operate.

9.5.4 Deflector Position.

9.5.4.1* Distance Below Ceilings.

9.5.4.1.1 The distances between the sprinkler deflector and the ceiling above shall be selected based on the type of sprinkler and the type of construction.

9.5.4.1.2 Corrugated Metal Deck Roofs.

9.5.4.1.2.1 For corrugated metal deck roofs up to 3 in. (75 mm) in depth, the distance shall be measured to the sprinkler from the bottom of the deck.

9.5.4.1.2.2 For decks deeper than 3 in. (75 mm), the distance shall be measured to the highest point on the deck.

9.5.4.1.3 For ceilings that have insulation installed directly against underside of the ceiling or roof structure, the deflector distance shall be measured from the bottom of the insulation and shall be in accordance with 9.5.4.1.3.1, 9.5.4.1.3.2, and 9.5.4.1.3.3.

9.5.4.1.3.1 Insulation used to measure sprinkler deflector distance shall be batt insulation or insulation that withstands $3 \, lb/ft^2$ $(0.13 \, kg/m^2)$ uplift force.

9.5.4.1.3.2 For insulation that is installed directly against the ceiling or roof structure and is installed flat and parallel to the ceiling or roof structure, the deflector distance shall be measured to the underside of the insulation.

9.5.4.1.3.3 For insulation that is installed in a manner that causes it to deflect or sag down from the ceiling or roof structure, the deflector distance shall be measured as half of the distance of the deflection from the insulation high point to the insulation low point.

(A) If the deflection or sag in the insulation exceeds 6 in. (150 mm), the deflector distance shall be measured to the high point of the insulation.

(B) The deflector shall not be positioned above the low point of the insulation.

9.5.4.1.4* Heat collectors shall not be used as a means to assist the activation of a sprinkler.

9.5.4.2 Deflector Orientation. Deflectors of sprinklers shall be aligned parallel to ceilings, roofs, or the incline of stairs.

9.5.5 Obstructions to Sprinkler Discharge.

9.5.5.1* Performance Objective. Sprinklers shall be located so as to minimize obstructions to discharge as defined in 9.5.5.2 and 9.5.5.3, or additional sprinklers shall be provided to ensure adequate coverage of the hazard. *(See Figure A.9.5.5.1.)*

9.5.5.2* Obstructions to Sprinkler Discharge Pattern Development.

9.5.5.2.1 Continuous or noncontinuous obstructions less than or equal to 18 in. (450 mm) below the sprinkler deflector that prevent the pattern from fully developing shall comply with 9.5.5.2.

9.5.5.2.2 Sprinklers shall be positioned in accordance with the minimum distances and special requirements of Section 10.2 through Section 14.2 so that they are located sufficiently away from obstructions such as truss webs and chords, pipes, columns, and fixtures.

9.5.5.3* Obstructions that Prevent Sprinkler Discharge from Reaching Hazard. Continuous or noncontinuous obstructions that interrupt the water discharge in a horizontal plane more than 18 in. (450 mm) below the sprinkler deflector in a manner to limit the distribution from reaching the protected hazard shall comply with 9.5.5.3.

9.5.5.3.1* Sprinklers shall be installed below fixed obstructions over 4 ft (1.2 m) in width.

9.5.5.3.1.1* Open grate flooring over 4 ft (1.2 m) in width shall require sprinkler protection below the grating.

9.5.5.3.1.2* Sprinklers located below obstructions shall comply with one of the following, regardless of the geometry of obstruction:

(1) Installed below the obstruction
(2) Installed adjacent to the obstruction not more than 3 in. (75 mm) from the outside edge of the obstruction

9.5.5.3.1.3 Where sprinklers are located adjacent to the obstruction, they shall be of the intermediate level rack type.

9.5.5.3.1.4 The deflector of automatic sprinklers installed below fixed obstructions shall be positioned no more than 12 in. (300 mm) below the bottom of the obstruction.

9.5.5.3.1.5 Sprinklers shall not be required below noncombustible obstructions over 4 ft (1.2 m) wide where the bottom of the obstruction is 24 in. (600 mm) or less above the floor or deck.

Δ **9.5.5.3.2*** Sprinklers shall not be required below obstructions that are not fixed in place.

9.5.5.3.3 Sprinklers installed below obstructions shall be of the same type (spray, CMSA, ESFR, residential) as installed at the ceiling except as permitted by 9.5.5.3.3.1.

9.5.5.3.3.1 Spray sprinklers shall be permitted to be utilized under overhead doors.

9.5.5.3.4* Sprinklers installed under open gratings shall be of the intermediate level/rack storage type or otherwise shielded from the discharge of overhead sprinklers.

9.5.5.4 Closets. In all closets and compartments, including those closets housing mechanical equipment, that are not larger than 400 ft^3 (11 m^3) in size, a single sprinkler at the highest ceiling level shall be sufficient without regard to obstructions or minimum distance to the wall.

Chapter 10   Installation Requirements for Standard Pendent, Upright, and Sidewall Spray Sprinklers

10.1 General. Standard pendent, upright, and sidewall sprinklers shall be selected for use and installation as indicated in this chapter and shall be positioned and spaced in accordance with Section 9.5.

10.2 Standard Pendent and Upright Spray Sprinklers.

10.2.1 General. All requirements of Section 9.5 shall apply to standard pendent and upright spray sprinklers except as modified in Section 10.2.

10.2.2 Upright and pendent spray sprinklers shall be permitted in all occupancy hazard classifications and building construction types unless the requirements of 9.3.2 apply.

10.2.3 Quick-response sprinklers shall not be permitted for use in extra hazard occupancies under the density/area design method.

10.2.4 Protection Areas per Sprinkler (Standard Pendent and Upright Spray Sprinklers).

10.2.4.1 Determination of Protection Area of Coverage.

10.2.4.1.1 Except as permitted by 10.2.4.1.2, the protection area of coverage per sprinkler (A_s) shall be determined in accordance with 9.5.2.1.

10.2.4.1.2 The requirements of 10.2.4.1.1 shall not apply in a small room as defined in 3.3.206.

10.2.4.1.2.1 The protection area of coverage for each sprinkler in the small room shall be the area of the room divided by the number of sprinklers in the room.

10.2.4.2 Maximum Protection Area of Coverage.

10.2.4.2.1* The maximum allowable protection area of coverage for a sprinkler (A_s) shall be in accordance with the value indicated in Table 10.2.4.2.1(a) through Table 10.2.4.2.1(d).

10.2.4.2.2 In any case, the maximum area of coverage of a sprinkler shall not exceed 225 ft² (20 m²).

Table 10.2.4.2.1(a) Protection Areas and Maximum Spacing of Standard Pendent and Upright Spray Sprinklers for Light Hazard

Construction Type	System Type	Maximum Protection Area		Maximum Spacing	
		ft²	m²	ft	m
Noncombustible unobstructed	Hydraulically calculated	225	20	15	4.6
Noncombustible unobstructed	Pipe schedule	200	18	15	4.6
Noncombustible obstructed	Hydraulically calculated	225	20	15	4.6
Noncombustible obstructed	Pipe schedule	200	18	15	4.6
Combustible unobstructed with no exposed members	Hydraulically calculated	225	20	15	4.6
Combustible unobstructed with no exposed members	Pipe schedule	200	18	15	4.6
Combustible unobstructed with exposed members 3 ft (910 mm) or more on center	Hydraulically calculated	225	20	15	4.6
Combustible unobstructed with exposed members 3 ft (910 mm) or more on center	Pipe schedule	200	18	15	4.6
Combustible unobstructed with members less than 3 ft (910 mm) on center	All	130	12	15	4.6
Combustible obstructed with exposed members 3 ft (910 mm) or more on center	All	168	16	15	4.6
Combustible obstructed with members less than 3 ft (910 mm) on center	All	130	12	15	4.6
Combustible concealed spaces in accordance with 10.2.6.1.4	All	120	11	15 parallel to the slope 10 perpendicular to the slope*	4.6 parallel to the slope 3.0 perpendicular to the slope*

*See 10.2.6.1.4.4.

Table 10.2.4.2.1(b) Protection Areas and Maximum Spacing of Standard Pendent and Upright Spray Sprinklers for Ordinary Hazard

Construction Type	System Type	Protection Area		Maximum Spacing	
		ft²	m²	ft	m
All	All	130	12	15	4.6

Table 10.2.4.2.1(c) Protection Areas and Maximum Spacing of Standard Pendent and Upright Spray Sprinklers for Extra Hazard

Construction Type	System Type	Protection Area		Maximum Spacing	
		ft²	m²	ft	m
All	Pipe schedule	90	8.4	12*	3.7*
All	Hydraulically calculated with density ≥0.25 gpm/ft² (10.2 mm/min)	100	9	12*	3.7*
All	Hydraulically calculated with density <0.25 gpm/ft² (10.2 mm/min)	130	12	15	4.6

*In buildings where solid structural members create bays up to 25 ft (7.6 m) wide, maximum spacing between sprinklers is permitted up to 12 ft 6 in. (3.8 m).

Table 10.2.4.2.1(d) Protection Areas and Maximum Spacing of Standard Pendent and Upright Spray Sprinklers for High-Piled Storage

Construction Type	System Type	Protection Area		Maximum Spacing	
		ft²	m²	ft	m
All	Hydraulically calculated with density ≥0.25 gpm/ft² (10.2 mm/min)	100	9	12*	3.7*
All	Hydraulically calculated with density <0.25 gpm/ft² (10.2 mm/min)	130	12	15	4.6

*In buildings where solid structural members create bays up to 25 ft (7.6 m) wide, maximum spacing between sprinklers is permitted up to 12 ft 6 in. (3.8 m).

10.2.5 Sprinkler Spacing (Standard Pendent and Upright Spray Sprinklers).

10.2.5.1 Maximum Distance Between Sprinklers. The maximum distance permitted between sprinklers shall comply with Table 10.2.4.2.1(a) through Table 10.2.4.2.1(d).

10.2.5.2 Maximum Distance from Walls.

10.2.5.2.1 The distance from sprinklers to walls shall not exceed one-half of the allowable distance between sprinklers as indicated in Table 10.2.4.2.1(a) through Table 10.2.4.2.1(d).

10.2.5.2.2* The requirements of 10.2.5.2.1 shall not apply where walls are angled or irregular, and the maximum horizontal distance between a sprinkler and any point of floor area protected by that sprinkler shall not exceed 0.75 times the allowable distance permitted between sprinklers, provided the maximum perpendicular distance is not exceeded.

10.2.5.2.3* The requirements of 10.2.5.2.1 shall not apply within small rooms as defined in 3.3.206.

10.2.5.2.3.1 Sprinklers shall be permitted to be located not more than 9 ft (2.7 m) from any single wall.

10.2.5.2.3.2 Sprinkler spacing limitations of 10.2.5 and area limitations of Table 10.2.4.2.1(a) shall not be exceeded.

10.2.5.2.4 Under curved surfaces, the horizontal distance shall be measured at the floor level from the wall, or the intersection of the curved surface and the floor to the nearest sprinkler shall not be greater than one-half the allowable distance between sprinklers.

10.2.5.3 Minimum Distances from Walls. Sprinklers shall be located a minimum of 4 in. (100 mm) from a wall.

10.2.5.4 Minimum Distances Between Sprinklers.

10.2.5.4.1 Unless the requirements of 10.2.5.4.2 or 10.2.5.4.3 are met, sprinklers shall be spaced not less than 6 ft (1.8 m) on center.

10.2.5.4.2 Sprinklers shall be permitted to be placed less than 6 ft (1.8 m) on center where the following conditions are satisfied:

(1) Baffles shall be arranged to protect the actuating elements.
(2) Baffles shall be of solid and rigid material that will stay in place before and during sprinkler operation.
(3) Baffles shall be not less than 8 in. (200 mm) long and 6 in. (150 mm) high.
(4) The tops of baffles shall extend between 2 in. and 3 in. (50 mm and 75 mm) above the deflectors of upright sprinklers.
(5) The bottoms of baffles shall extend downward to a level at least even with the deflectors of pendent sprinklers.

10.2.5.4.3 In-rack sprinklers shall be permitted to be placed less than 6 ft (1.8 m) on center.

10.2.6 Deflector Position (Standard Pendent and Upright Spray Sprinklers).

10.2.6.1 Distance Below Ceilings.

10.2.6.1.1 Unobstructed Construction.

10.2.6.1.1.1 Under unobstructed construction, the distance between the sprinkler deflector and the ceiling shall be a minimum of 1 in. (25 mm) and a maximum of 12 in. (300 mm) throughout the area of coverage of the sprinkler.

10.2.6.1.1.2 The requirements of 10.2.6.1.1.1 shall not apply where ceiling-type sprinklers (concealed, recessed, and flush types) have the operating element above the ceiling and the deflector located nearer to the ceiling where installed in accordance with their listing.

10.2.6.1.1.3 The requirements of 10.2.6.1.1.1 shall not apply for light and ordinary hazard occupancies with ceilings of noncombustible or limited-combustible construction where either 10.2.6.1.1.3(A) or 10.2.6.1.1.3(B) applies.

(A) Where a vertical change in ceiling elevation within the area of coverage of the sprinkler creates a distance of more than 36 in. (900 mm) between the upper ceiling and the sprinkler deflector, a vertical plane extending down from the ceiling at the change in elevation shall be considered a wall for the purpose of sprinkler spacing as shown in Figure 10.2.6.1.1.3(A).

(B) Where the distance between the upper ceiling and the sprinkler deflector is less than or equal to 36 in. (900 mm), the sprinklers shall be permitted to be spaced as though the ceiling was flat, provided the obstruction rules are observed as shown in Figure 10.2.6.1.1.3(B).

10.2.6.1.2 Obstructed Construction. Under obstructed construction, the sprinkler deflector shall be located in accordance with one of the following arrangements:

(1) Installed with the deflectors within the horizontal planes of 1 in. to 6 in. (25 mm to 150 mm) below the structural members and a maximum distance of 22 in. (550 mm) below the ceiling/roof deck

(2) Installed with the deflectors at or above the bottom of the structural member to a maximum of 22 in. (550 mm) below the ceiling/roof deck where the sprinkler is installed in conformance with 10.2.7.2

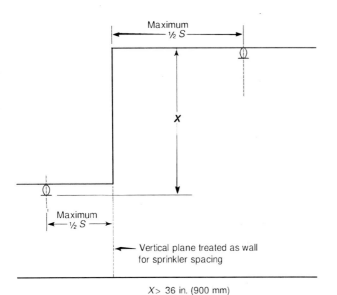

X> 36 in. (900 mm)
S = maximum allowable distance between sprinklers

FIGURE 10.2.6.1.1.3(A)   Vertical Change in Ceiling Elevation Greater Than 36 in. (900 mm).

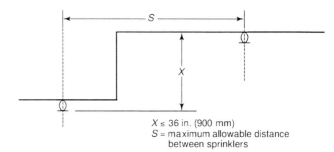

X ≤ 36 in. (900 mm)
S = maximum allowable distance between sprinklers

FIGURE 10.2.6.1.1.3(B)   Vertical Change in Ceiling Elevation Less Than or Equal to 36 in. (900 mm).

(3) Installed in each bay of obstructed construction, with the deflectors located a minimum of 1 in. (25 mm) and a maximum of 12 in. (300 mm) below the ceiling

(4) Installed with the deflectors within the horizontal planes 1 in. to 6 in. (25 mm to 150 mm) below composite wood joists to a maximum distance of 22 in. (550 mm) below the ceiling/roof deck only where joist channels are fire-stopped to the full depth of the joists with material equivalent to the web construction so that individual channel areas do not exceed 300 ft² (28 m²)

(5)* Installed with deflectors of sprinklers under concrete tee construction with stems spaced less than 7½ ft (2.3 m) on centers, regardless of the depth of the tee, located at or above a horizontal plane 1 in. (25 mm) below the bottom of the stems of the tees and complying with Table 10.2.7.2(a) or Table 10.2.7.2(b)

10.2.6.1.3 Peaked Roofs and Ceilings.

10.2.6.1.3.1 Unless the requirements of 10.2.6.1.3.2 or 10.2.6.1.3.3 are met, sprinklers under or near the peak of a roof or ceiling shall have deflectors located not more than 36 in. (900 mm) vertically down from the peak as indicated in Figure 10.2.6.1.3.1(a) and Figure 10.2.6.1.3.1(b).

10.2.6.1.3.2* Under saw-toothed roofs, sprinklers at the highest elevation shall not exceed a distance of 36 in. (900 mm) measured down the slope from the peak.

10.2.6.1.3.3* Under a steeply pitched surface, the distance from the peak to the deflectors shall be permitted to be increased to maintain a horizontal clearance of not less than 24 in. (600 mm) from other structural members as indicated in Figure 10.2.6.1.3.3.

10.2.6.1.4 Sprinklers under a roof or ceiling in combustible concealed spaces of wood joist or wood truss construction with members less than 3 ft (900 mm) on center with a slope having a pitch of 4 in 12 or greater shall be positioned in accordance with Figure 10.2.6.1.4 and the requirements of 10.2.6.1.4.1 through 10.2.6.1.4.6.

10.2.6.1.4.1 Sprinklers shall be quick-response.

10.2.6.1.4.2 Sprinklers shall be installed so that a row of sprinklers is installed within 12 in. (300 mm) horizontally of the peak and between 1 in. and 12 in. (25 mm and 300 mm) down from the bottom of the top chord member.

10.2.6.1.4.3* Sprinklers shall be installed so that the sprinklers installed along the eave are located not less than 5 ft (1.5 m) from the intersection of the upper and lower truss chords or the wood rafters and ceiling joists.

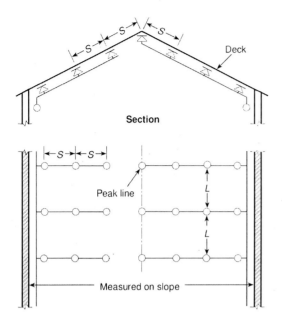

FIGURE 10.2.6.1.3.1(a)   Sprinklers Under Pitched Roof with Sprinkler Directly Under Peak; Branch Lines Run Up Slopes.

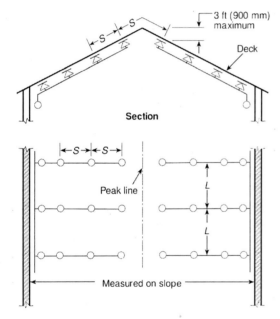

FIGURE 10.2.6.1.3.1(b)   Sprinklers at Pitched Roof; Branch Lines Run Up Slopes.

10.2.6.1.4.4* Sprinklers installed where the dimension perpendicular to the slope exceeds 8 ft (2.4 m) shall have a minimum pressure of 20 psi (1.4 bar).

10.2.6.1.4.5* The requirements of 10.2.6.1.4.3 or 10.2.6.1.4.4 shall not apply to sprinklers installed at the corner of the eave of a hip type roof where located directly under the hip line spaced in accordance with 10.2.5.2.2 or located on the slope plane not less than 5 ft (1.5 m) from the intersection of the upper and lower truss chords or the wood rafters and ceiling

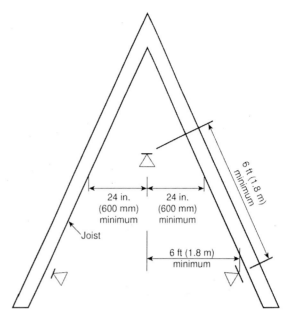

Δ FIGURE 10.2.6.1.3.3   Horizontal Clearance for Sprinkler at Peak of Pitched Roof.

joists on the eave and no more than 5 ft (1.5 m) from the hip line.

10.2.6.1.4.6 The special requirements of 10.2.4.2.1 and 10.2.6.1.4 shall not apply when the exposed combustible sheathing in the roof or ceiling space are constructed of pressure impregnated fire retardant–treated wood as defined by NFPA 703.

10.2.6.1.5 Double Joist Obstructions.

10.2.6.1.5.1 Unless the requirements of 10.2.6.1.5.2 are met, where two sets of joists are under a roof or ceiling, and no flooring is over the lower set, sprinklers shall be installed above and below the lower set of joists where a clearance of 6 in. (150 mm) or more is between the top of the lower joist and the bottom of the upper joist as indicated in Figure 10.2.6.1.5.1.

10.2.6.1.5.2 Sprinklers shall be permitted to be omitted from below the lower set of joists where at least 18 in. (450 mm) is maintained between the sprinkler deflector and the top of the lower joist.

10.2.6.2 Deflector Orientation.

10.2.6.2.1 Unless the requirements of 10.2.6.2.2 or 10.2.6.2.3 are met, deflectors of sprinklers shall be aligned parallel to ceilings, roofs, hips, or the incline of stairs.

10.2.6.2.2 Where sprinklers are installed in the peak below a sloped ceiling or roof surface, the sprinkler shall be installed with the deflector horizontal.

10.2.6.2.3 Roofs having a pitch not exceeding 2 in 12 (16.7 percent) are considered horizontal in the application of 10.2.6.2, and sprinklers shall be permitted to be installed with deflectors horizontal.

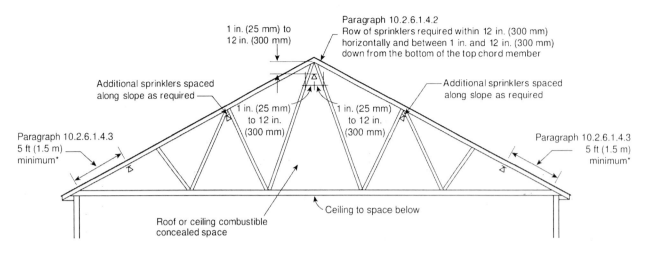

*The 5 ft minimum dimension is measured from the intersection of the upper and lower truss chords or the wood rafters and ceiling joists.

Δ **FIGURE 10.2.6.1.4** **Sprinklers Under Roof or Ceiling in Combustible Concealed Spaces of Wood Joist or Wood Truss Construction with Members Less Than 3 ft (900 mm) on Center with a Slope Having a Pitch of 4 in 12 or Greater.**

10.2.7 Obstructions to Sprinkler Discharge (Standard Pendent and Upright Spray Sprinklers).

10.2.7.1 General. Sprinklers shall be located so as to minimize obstructions to discharge as defined in 10.2.7, or additional sprinklers shall be provided to ensure adequate coverage of the hazard.

10.2.7.2* Obstructions to Sprinkler Discharge Pattern Development. Sprinklers shall be arranged to comply with one of the following arrangements:

(1) Subsection 9.5.5.2, Table 10.2.7.2(a) or Table 10.2.7.2(b), and Figure 10.2.7.2(a) shall be followed.
(2) Sprinklers shall be permitted to be spaced on opposite sides of obstructions not exceeding 4 ft (1.2 m) in width, provided the distance from the centerline of the obstruction to the sprinklers does not exceed one-half the allowable distance permitted between sprinklers.
(3) Obstructions located against the wall and that are not over 30 in. (750 mm) in width shall be permitted to be protected in accordance with Figure 10.2.7.2(b).
(4) Obstructions located against the wall and that are not over 24 in. (600 mm) in width shall be permitted to be protected in accordance with Figure 10.2.7.2(c). The maximum distance between the sprinkler and the wall shall be measured from the sprinkler to the wall behind the obstruction and not to the face of the obstruction.
(5) Obstructions no greater than 12 in. (300 mm) in width in hallways up to 6 ft (1.8 m) in width shall be permitted in accordance with Figure 10.2.7.2(d) when the sprinkler is located within the allowable obstruction zone and the closest edge of the obstruction is a minimum of 12 in. (300 mm) away from the centerline of the sprinkler.
(6) Sprinklers shall be installed below fixed obstructions over 4 ft (1.2 m) wide.
(7) Sprinklers shall not be required under obstructions 4 ft. (1.2 m) or less wide when the provisions of Table 10.2.7.2(a) or Table 10.2.7.2(b) and Figure 10.2.7.2(a) are maintained.

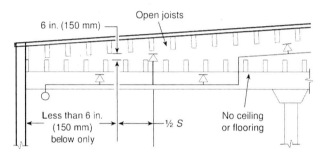

FIGURE 10.2.6.1.5.1 **Arrangement of Sprinklers Under Two Sets of Open Joists — No Sheathing on Lower Joists.**

N **Table 10.2.7.2(a) Positioning of Sprinklers to Avoid Obstructions to Discharge [Standard Spray Upright/Standard Spray Pendent (SSU/SSP)]**

Distance from Sprinkler to Side of Obstruction (A) (ft)	Allowable Distance of Deflector Above Bottom of Obstruction (B) (in.)
Less than 1	0
1 or more	2½ or less
1½ or more	3½ or less
2 or more	5½ or less
2½ or more	7½ or less
3 or more	9½ or less
3½ or more	12 or less
4 or more	14 or less
4½ or more	16½ or less
5 or more	18 or less
5½ or more	20 or less
6 or more	24 or less
6½ or more	30 or less
7 or more	35 or less

Note: For A and B, refer to Figure 10.2.7.2(a).

N Table 10.2.7.2(b) Positioning of Sprinklers to Avoid Obstructions to Discharge [Standard Spray Upright/Standard Spray Pendent (SSU/SSP)]

Distance from Sprinkler to Side of Obstruction (A) (mm)	Allowable Distance of Deflector Above Bottom of Obstruction (B) (mm)
Less than 300	0
300 or more	65 or less
450 or more	90 or less
600 or more	140 or less
750 or more	190 or less
900 or more	240 or less
1100 or more	300 or less
1200 or more	350 or less
1400 or more	420 or less
1500 or more	450 or less
1700 or more	510 or less
1800 or more	600 or less
2000 or more	750 or less
2100 or more	875 or less

Note: For A and B, refer to Figure 10.2.7.2(a).

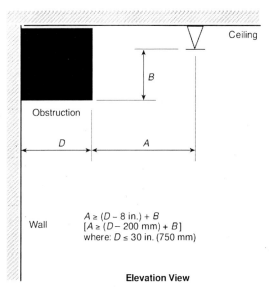

Elevation View

$A \geq (D - 8 \text{ in.}) + B$
$[A \geq (D - 200 \text{ mm}) + B]$
where: $D \leq 30 \text{ in. } (750 \text{ mm})$

FIGURE 10.2.7.2(b)   Obstruction Against Wall (SSU/SSP).

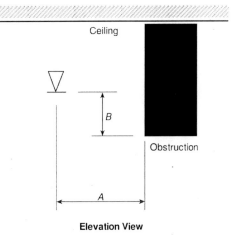

Elevation View

FIGURE 10.2.7.2(a)   Positioning of Sprinkler to Avoid Obstruction to Discharge (SSU/SSP).

10.2.7.3 Obstructions to Sprinkler Discharge Pattern Development.

10.2.7.3.1 General.

10.2.7.3.1.1 Continuous or noncontinuous obstructions less than or equal to 18 in. (450 mm) below the sprinkler deflector that prevent the pattern from fully developing shall comply with 10.2.7.3.

10.2.7.3.1.2 Regardless of the rules of 10.2.7.3, solid continuous obstructions, where the top of the obstruction is level with or above the plane of the deflector, shall meet the applicable requirements of 10.2.7.2.

10.2.7.3.1.3* Minimum Distance from Obstructions. Unless the requirements of 10.2.7.3.1.4 through 10.2.7.3.1.9 are met, sprinklers shall be positioned away from obstructions a minimum distance of three times the maximum dimension of the

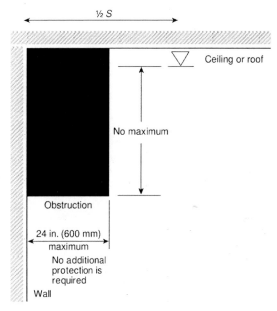

Δ **FIGURE 10.2.7.2(c)   Obstructions Against Walls (SSU/SSP).**

obstruction (e.g., structural members, pipe, columns, and fixtures) in accordance with Figure 10.2.7.3.1.3(a) and Figure 10.2.7.3.1.3(b).

(A) The maximum clear distance required shall be 24 in. (600 mm).

(B) The maximum clear distance shall not be applied to obstructions in the vertical orientation (e.g., columns).

10.2.7.3.1.4* For light and ordinary hazard occupancies, structural members only shall be considered when applying the requirements of 10.2.7.3.1.3.

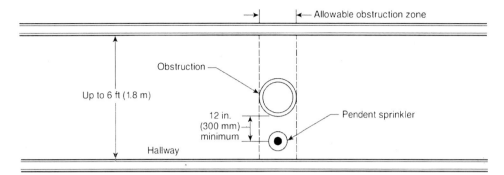

N **FIGURE 10.2.7.2(d)   Obstruction in Hallway.**

10.2.7.3.1.5 Sprinklers shall be permitted to be spaced on opposite sides of the obstruction not exceeding 4 ft (1.2 m) in width, where the distance from the centerline of the obstruction to the sprinklers does not exceed one-half the allowable distance between sprinklers.

10.2.7.3.1.6 Sprinklers shall be permitted to be located one-half the distance between the obstructions where the obstruction consists of open trusses 20 in. (500 mm) or greater apart [24 in. (600 mm) on center], provided that all truss members are not greater than 4 in. (100 mm) (nominal) in width.

10.2.7.3.1.7 Sprinklers shall be permitted to be installed on the centerline of a truss or bar joist or directly above a beam, provided that the truss chord or beam dimension is not more than 8 in. (200 mm) and the sprinkler deflector is located at least 6 in. (150 mm) above the structural member and where the sprinkler is positioned at a distance three times greater than the maximum dimension of the web members away from the web members.

10.2.7.3.1.8 The requirements of 10.2.7.3.1.3 shall not apply to sprinkler system piping less than 3 in. (80 mm) in diameter.

10.2.7.3.1.9 The requirements of 10.2.7.3.1.3 shall not apply to sprinklers positioned with respect to obstructions in accordance with 10.2.7.2.

10.2.7.3.1.10* Sprinklers shall be permitted to be placed without regard to the blades of ceiling fans less than 60 in. (1.5 m) in diameter, provided the plan view of the fan is at least 50 percent open.

Δ **10.2.7.3.2 Suspended or Floor-Mounted Vertical Obstructions.**

N **10.2.7.3.2.1** The distance from sprinklers to privacy curtains, freestanding partitions, room dividers, and similar obstructions in light hazard occupancies shall be in accordance with Table 10.2.7.3.2.1(a) or Table 10.2.7.3.2.1(b) and Figure 10.2.7.3.2.1.

10.2.7.3.2.2* In light hazard occupancies, privacy curtains, as shown in Figure 10.2.7.3.2.1, shall not be considered obstructions where all of the following are met:

(1) The curtains are supported by fabric mesh on ceiling track.
(2) Openings in the mesh are equal to 70 percent or greater.
(3) The mesh extends a minimum of 22 in. (550 mm) down from ceiling.

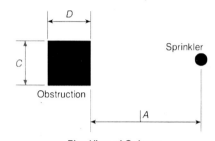

Plan View of Column
(Obstruction in vertical orientation)

$A \geq 3C$ or $3D$
(Use dimension *C* or *D*, whichever is greater)

Δ **FIGURE 10.2.7.3.1.3(a)   Minimum Distance from an Obstruction in the Vertical Orientation (SSU/SSP).**

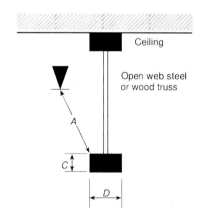

Elevation View of Truss
(Obstruction in horizontal orientation)

$A \geq 3C$ or $3D$
$A \leq 24$ in. (600 mm)
(Use dimension *C* or *D*, whichever is greater)

FIGURE 10.2.7.3.1.3(b)   Minimum Distance from an Obstruction in the Horizontal Orientation (SSU/SSP).

N Table 10.2.7.3.2.1(a) Suspended or Floor-Mounted Obstructions in Light Hazard Occupancies Only (SSU/SSP)

Horizontal Distance *(A)* (in.)	Minimum Vertical Distance Below Deflector *(B)* (in.)
6 or less	3 or more
9 or less	4 or more
12 or less	6 or more
15 or less	8 or more
18 or less	9½ or more
24 or less	12½ or more
30 or less	15½ or more
More than 30	18 or more

Note: For *A* and *B*, refer to Figure 10.2.7.3.2.1.

N Table 10.2.7.3.2.1(b) Suspended or Floor-Mounted Obstructions in Light Hazard Occupancies Only (SSU/SSP)

Horizontal Distance *(A)* (mm)	Minimum Vertical Distance Below Deflector *(B)* (mm)
150 or less	75 or more
225 or less	100 or more
300 or less	150 or more
375 or less	200 or more
450 or less	240 or more
600 or less	315 or more
750 or less	390 or more
More than 750	450 or more

Note: For *A* and *B*, refer to Figure 10.2.7.3.2.1.

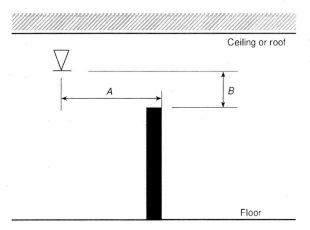

FIGURE 10.2.7.3.2.1   Suspended or Floor-Mounted Obstruction in Light Hazard Occupancies Only (SSU/SSP).

N 10.2.7.3.2.3 In ordinary hazard occupancies, where sprinklers are installed above freestanding partitions, room dividers, and similar obstructions, the distance from the sprinkler deflector to the top of the obstruction shall be 18 in. (450 mm) or greater per Figure 10.2.7.3.2.3.

N 10.2.7.3.2.4 In ordinary hazard occupancies, where sprinklers are installed within 6 in. (150 mm) horizontally of the center-line of freestanding partitions, room dividers, and similar

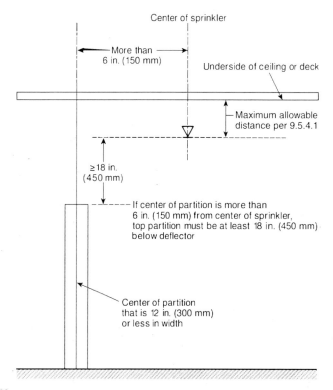

N FIGURE 10.2.7.3.2.3   Location of Suspended or Floor-Mounted Obstruction in Ordinary Hazard Occupancies (Sprinkler Located to the Side) (SSU/SSP).

obstructions no greater than 12 in. (300 mm) in width, the distance from the sprinkler deflector to the top of the obstruction shall be permitted to be installed 6 in. (150 mm) or greater vertically per Figure 10.2.7.3.2.4.

10.2.7.4* Obstructions that Prevent Sprinkler Discharge from Reaching Hazard.

10.2.7.4.1 Continuous or noncontinuous obstructions that interrupt the water discharge in a horizontal plane more than 18 in. (450 mm) below the sprinkler deflector in a manner to limit the distribution from reaching the protected hazard shall comply with 10.2.7.4.

10.2.7.4.2* Sprinklers shall be installed under fixed obstructions over 4 ft (1.2 m) wide.

10.2.7.4.3 Sprinklers installed under open gratings shall be of the intermediate level/rack storage type or otherwise shielded from the discharge of overhead sprinklers.

10.2.7.4.4 The deflector of automatic sprinklers installed under fixed obstructions shall be positioned no more than 12 in. (300 mm) below the bottom of the obstruction.

10.2.7.4.5 Sprinklers installed under round ducts shall be of the intermediate level/rack storage type or otherwise shielded from the discharge of overhead sprinklers.

10.2.8 Clearance to Storage (Standard Pendent and Upright Spray Sprinklers).

10.2.8.1* The clearance between the deflector and the top of storage shall be 18 in. (450 mm) or greater.

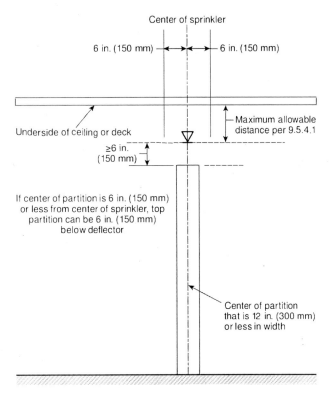

FIGURE 10.2.7.3.2.4   Location of Suspended or Floor-Mounted Obstruction in Ordinary Hazard Occupancies (Sprinkler Located Directly Above) (SSU/SSP).

Δ **10.2.8.2** The 18 in. (450 mm) dimension shall not limit the height of shelving on a wall or shelving against a wall in accordance with 10.2.8.1.

10.2.8.2.1 Where shelving is installed on a wall and is not directly below sprinklers, the shelves, including storage thereon, shall be permitted to extend above the level of a plane located 18 in. (450 mm) below ceiling sprinkler deflectors.

10.2.8.2.2 Shelving, and any storage thereon, directly below the sprinklers shall not extend above a plane located 18 in. (450 mm) below the ceiling sprinkler deflectors.

N **10.2.8.3** The clearance between the top of storage to sprinkler deflectors shall not be less than 36 in. (900 mm) where rubber tires are stored.

10.2.8.4 Where other standards specify greater clearance to storage minimums, they shall be followed.

10.2.9 Ceiling Pockets (Standard Pendent and Upright Spray Sprinklers).

10.2.9.1* Except as provided in 10.2.9.2 and 10.2.9.3, sprinklers shall be required in all ceiling pockets.

10.2.9.2 Sprinklers shall not be required in ceiling pockets where all of the following are met:

(1)   The total volume of the unprotected ceiling pocket does not exceed 1000 ft³ (28 m³).
(2)   The depth of the unprotected ceiling pocket does not exceed 36 in. (900 mm).

(3)   The entire floor under the unprotected ceiling pocket is protected by sprinklers at the lower ceiling elevation.
(4)* The total size of all unprotected ceiling pockets in the same compartment within 10 ft (3 m) of each other does not exceed 1000 ft³ (28 m³).
(5)   The unprotected ceiling pocket has noncombustible or limited-combustible finishes.
(6)   Quick-response sprinklers are utilized throughout the compartment.

10.2.9.3 Sprinklers shall not be required in skylights and similar pockets in accordance with 9.3.16.

10.3 Sidewall Standard Spray Sprinklers.

10.3.1 General. All requirements of Section 9.5 shall apply to sidewall standard spray sprinklers except as modified in Section 10.3.

Δ **10.3.2 Sidewall Spray Sprinklers.** Sidewall sprinklers shall only be installed as follows:

(1)   In light hazard occupancies with smooth, horizontal ceilings
(2)   In light hazard occupancies with sloped, flat ceilings
(3)   In ordinary hazard occupancies with smooth, flat ceilings where specifically listed for such use
(4)   To protect areas below overhead doors
(5)   At the top and bottom of elevator hoistways
(6)   For the protection of steel building columns
(7)   Under obstructions that require sprinklers
(8)   For the protection of exterior projections and similar structures
(9)* Under cars in car stackers and car lift systems with cars stacked vertically placed under each level of cars

N **10.3.2.1** For purposes of 10.3.2(1) and 10.3.2(2), corrugated metal deck with channel depths up to 3 in. (75 mm) shall be considered as smooth ceilings.

10.3.3 Protection Areas per Sprinkler (Standard Sidewall Spray Sprinklers).

10.3.3.1 Determination of Protection Area of Coverage.

10.3.3.1.1 The protection area of coverage per sprinkler (A_s) shall be determined as follows:

(1)   Along the wall as follows:

   (a)   Determine the distance between sprinklers along the wall (or to the end wall or obstruction in the case of the end sprinkler on the branch line) upstream and downstream
   (b)   Choose the larger of either twice the distance to the end wall or the distance to the next sprinkler
   (c)   Define dimension as S

(2)   Across the room as follows:

   (a)   Determine the distance from the wall on which the sprinkler is installed to the wall opposite the sprinklers or to the midpoint of the room where sprinklers are installed on two opposite walls (see 10.3.4.1.5 and 10.3.4.1.6)
   (b)   Define dimension as L

10.3.3.1.2 The protection area of the sprinkler shall be established by multiplying the S dimension by the L dimension, as follows:

[10.3.3.1.2]

$$A_s = S \times L$$

10.3.3.2 Maximum Protection Area of Coverage.

10.3.3.2.1 The maximum allowable protection area of coverage for a sprinkler (A_s) shall be in accordance with the value indicated in Table 10.3.3.2.1.

10.3.3.2.2 In any case, the maximum area of coverage of a sprinkler shall not exceed 196 ft² (18 m²).

10.3.4 Sprinkler Spacing (Standard Sidewall Spray Sprinklers).

10.3.4.1 Maximum Distance Between Sprinklers.

10.3.4.1.1 The maximum distance permitted between sidewall spray sprinklers shall be based on the centerline distance between sprinklers on the branch line.

10.3.4.1.2 The maximum distance between sidewall spray sprinklers or to a wall shall be measured along the slope of the ceiling.

10.3.4.1.3 Where sidewall spray sprinklers are installed along the length of a single wall of rooms or bays, they shall be spaced in accordance with the maximum spacing provisions of Table 10.3.3.2.1.

10.3.4.1.4 Sidewall spray sprinklers shall not be installed back-to-back without being separated by a continuous lintel or soffit.

10.3.4.1.4.1 The maximum width of the lintel or soffit shall not exceed 16 in. (400 mm).

N **10.3.4.1.4.2** The lintel or soffit shall project a minimum of 4 in. (100 mm) below the deflector of the back-to-back horizontal sidewall sprinklers.

10.3.4.1.4.3 The maximum width of the lintel or soffit can exceed 16 in. (400 mm) when a pendent sprinkler is installed under the lintel or soffit.

10.3.4.1.5 Where sidewall spray sprinklers are installed on two opposite walls or sides of bays, the maximum width of the room or bay shall be permitted to be up to 24 ft (7.3 m) for light hazard occupancy or 20 ft (6.1 m) for ordinary hazard occupancy, with spacing as required by Table 10.3.3.2.1.

10.3.4.1.6 Sidewall spray sprinklers shall be permitted to be installed on opposing or adjacent walls, provided no sprinkler is located within the maximum protection area of another sprinkler.

10.3.4.1.7 Where sidewall standard spray sprinklers are installed to protect areas below overhead doors within ordinary hazard occupancy spaces or rooms, protection area and maximum sprinkler spacing for light hazard as specified in Table 10.3.3.2.1 shall be permitted under the overhead doors.

10.3.4.2 Maximum Distance from Walls. The distance from sprinklers to the end walls shall not exceed one-half of the allowable distance permitted between sprinklers as indicated in Table 10.3.3.2.1.

10.3.4.3 Minimum Distance from Walls.

10.3.4.3.1 Sprinklers shall be located a minimum of 4 in. (100 mm) from an end wall.

10.3.4.4 Minimum Distance Between Sprinklers. Sprinklers shall be spaced not less than 6 ft (1.8 m) on center unless required by 10.3.5.1.3.1 or unless the sprinklers are separated by baffles that comply with the following:

(1) Baffles shall be arranged to protect the actuating elements.
(2) Baffles shall be of solid and rigid material that will stay in place before and during sprinkler operation.
(3) Baffles shall be not less than 8 in. (200 mm) long and 6 in. (150 mm) high.
(4) The tops of baffles shall extend between 2 in. and 3 in. (50 mm and 75 mm) above the deflectors.
(5) The bottoms of baffles shall extend downward to a level at least even with the deflectors.

10.3.5 Deflector Position from Ceilings and Walls (Standard Sidewall Spray Sprinklers).

10.3.5.1 Distance Below Ceilings and from Walls.

10.3.5.1.1 Ceilings.

10.3.5.1.1.1 Unless the requirements of 10.3.5.1.1.2 are met, sidewall sprinkler deflectors shall be located not more than 6 in. (150 mm) or less than 4 in. (100 mm) from ceilings.

10.3.5.1.1.2 Horizontal sidewall sprinklers shall be permitted to be located in a zone 6 in. to 12 in. (150 mm to 300 mm) or 12 in. to 18 in. (300 mm to 450 mm) below noncombustible and limited-combustible ceilings where listed for such use.

10.3.5.1.2 Walls.

10.3.5.1.2.1* Vertical sidewall sprinkler deflectors shall be located not more than 6 in. (150 mm) or less than 4 in. (100 mm) from the wall from which they are projecting.

Table 10.3.3.2.1 Protection Areas and Maximum Spacing (Standard Sidewall Spray Sprinkler)

	Light Hazard		Ordinary Hazard	
	Combustible Ceiling Finish	Noncombustible or Limited-Combustible Ceiling Finish	Combustible Ceiling Finish	Noncombustible or Limited-Combustible Ceiling Finish
Maximum distance along the wall (S) (ft) [m]	14 [4.3]	14 [4.3]	10 [3.0]	10 [3.0]
Maximum room width (L) (ft) [m]	12 [3.7]	14 [4.3]	10 [3.0]	10 [3.0]
Maximum protection area (ft²) [m²]	120 [11]	196 [18]	80 [7.4]	100 [9.3]

10.3.5.1.2.2 Horizontal sidewall sprinkler deflectors shall be located no more than 6 in. (150 mm), and shall be permitted to be located with their deflectors less than 4 in. (100 mm) from the wall on which they are mounted.

10.3.5.1.3 Lintels and Soffits.

10.3.5.1.3.1 Where soffits used for the installation of sidewall sprinklers exceed 8 in. (200 mm) in width or projection from the wall, additional sprinklers shall be installed below the soffit.

10.3.5.1.3.2* Where soffits used for the installation of sidewall sprinklers are less than or equal to 8 in. (200 mm) in width or projection from the wall, additional sprinklers shall not be required below the soffit when the sidewall sprinkler is installed on the soffit.

10.3.5.1.3.3* A sidewall sprinkler shall be permitted to be installed under a soffit when both the minimum distance from the sprinkler deflector to the bottom of the soffit and maximum distance from the sprinkler deflector to the high ceiling is maintained.

10.3.5.1.4* Soffits and Cabinets. Where soffits are used for the installation of sidewall sprinklers, the sprinklers and soffits shall be installed in accordance with 10.3.5.1.4.1, 10.3.5.1.4.2, or 10.3.5.1.4.3.

10.3.5.1.4.1 Where soffits exceed more than 8 in. (200 mm) in width or projection from the wall, pendent sprinklers shall be installed under the soffit.

10.3.5.1.4.2 Sidewall sprinklers shall be permitted to be installed in the face of a soffit located directly over cabinets, without requiring additional sprinklers below the soffit or cabinets, where the soffit does not project horizontally more than 12 in. (300 mm) from the wall.

10.3.5.1.4.3 Where sidewall sprinklers are more than 36 in. (900 mm) above the top of cabinets, the sprinkler shall be permitted to be installed on the wall above the cabinets where the cabinets are no greater than 12 in. (300 mm) from the wall.

10.3.5.2 Deflector Orientation.

10.3.5.2.1 Sidewall sprinklers, where installed under a sloped ceiling with a slope exceeding 2 in 12, shall be located at the high point of the slope and positioned to discharge downward along the slope.

10.3.6 Obstructions to Sprinkler Discharge (Standard Sidewall Spray Sprinklers).

10.3.6.1 Performance Objective.

10.3.6.1.1 Sprinklers shall be located so as to minimize obstructions to discharge as defined in 9.5.5.2 and 9.5.5.3, or additional sprinklers shall be provided to ensure adequate coverage of the hazard.

10.3.6.1.2 Sidewall sprinklers shall not be installed less than 4 ft (1.2 m) from light fixtures or similar obstructions unless the requirements of 10.3.6.1.2.1 or 10.3.6.1.2.2 are met.

10.3.6.1.2.1 For obstructions such as light fixtures, where the greatest dimension of the obstruction is less than 2 ft (0.6 m), sidewall sprinklers shall be permitted to be installed at a minimum distance of three times the greatest dimension.

10.3.6.1.2.2 The bottom of light fixtures and similar obstructions located less than 4 ft (1.2 m) from the sprinkler shall be above the plane of the sprinkler deflector.

10.3.6.1.3 The distance between light fixtures or similar obstructions located 4 ft (1.2 m) or greater from the sprinkler shall be in conformity with Table 10.3.6.1.3(a) or Table 10.3.6.1.3(b) and Figure 10.3.6.1.3.

N **Table 10.3.6.1.3(a) Positioning of Sprinklers to Avoid Obstructions to Discharge (Standard Spray Sidewall)**

Distance from Sprinkler to Side of Obstruction (A) (ft)	Allowable Distance of Deflector Above Bottom of Obstruction (B) (in.)
Less than 4	0
4 or more	1 or less
5 or more	2 or less
5½ or more	3 or less
6 or more	4 or less
6½ or more	6 or less
7 or more	7 or less
7½ or more	9 or less
8 or more	11 or less
8½ or more	14 or less

Note: For *A* and *B*, refer to Figure 10.3.6.1.3.

N **Table 10.3.6.1.3(b) Positioning of Sprinklers to Avoid Obstructions to Discharge (Standard Spray Sidewall)**

Distance from Sprinkler to Side of Obstruction (A) (mm)	Allowable Distance of Deflector Above Bottom of Obstruction (B) (mm)
Less than 1200	0
1200 or more	25 or less
1500 or more	50 or less
1700 or more	75 or less
1800 or more	100 or less
2000 or more	150 or less
2100 or more	175 or less
2300 or more	225 or less
2400 or more	275 or less
2600 or more	350 or less

Note: For *A* and *B*, refer to Figure 10.3.6.1.3.

10.3.6.1.4 Obstructions projecting from the same wall as the one on which the sidewall sprinkler is mounted shall be in accordance with Table 10.3.6.1.4(a) or Table 10.3.6.1.4(b) and Figure 10.3.6.1.4.

10.3.6.1.4.1 Isolated obstructions projecting from the same wall as the one on which the sidewall sprinkler is mounted shall be located a minimum of 4 in. (100 mm) from the sidewall sprinkler.

10.3.6.1.5 Sprinklers shall be permitted to be spaced on opposite sides of obstructions less than 4 ft (1.2 m) in width where the distance from the centerline of the obstruction to the sprinklers does not exceed one-half the allowable distance between sprinklers.

10.3.6.1.6 Obstructions on the wall opposite from the sidewall sprinkler shall be permitted in accordance with Figure 10.3.6.1.6.

N **10.3.6.1.7** Obstructions up to 12 in. (300 mm) in width in hallways up to 6 ft (1.8 m) in width shall be permitted in accordance with Figure 10.3.6.1.7 when the sprinkler is located in the allowable obstruction zone and the closest edge of the obstruction is a minimum of 12 in. (300 mm) away from the deflector.

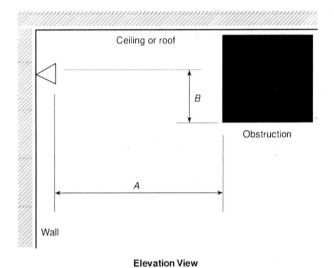

Elevation View

FIGURE 10.3.6.1.3   Positioning of Sprinkler to Avoid Obstruction (Standard Sidewall Spray Sprinklers).

N **Table 10.3.6.1.4(a) Positioning of Sprinklers to Avoid Obstructions Along Wall (Standard Spray Sidewall Sprinklers)**

Distance from Sprinkler to Side of Obstruction *(A)*	Allowable Distance of Deflector Above Bottom of Obstruction *(B)* (in.)
Less than 4 in.	0
4 in. or more	1 or less
6 in. or more	2 or less
1 ft or more	3 or less
1½ ft or more	4½ or less
2 ft or more	5¾ or less
2½ ft or more	7 or less
3 ft or more	8 or less
3½ ft or more	9¼ or less
4 ft or more	10 or less
4½ ft or more	11½ or less
5 ft or more	12¾ or less
5½ ft or more	14 or less
6 ft or more	15 or less
6½ ft or more	16¼ or less
7 ft or more	17½ or less

Note: For *A* and *B*, refer to Figure 10.3.6.1.4.

N **Table 10.3.6.1.4(b) Positioning of Sprinklers to Avoid Obstructions Along Wall (Standard Spray Sidewall Sprinklers)**

Distance from Sprinkler to Side of Obstruction *(A)* (mm)	Allowable Distance of Deflector Above Bottom of Obstruction *(B)* (mm)
Less than 100	0
100 or more	25 or less
150 or more	50 or less
300 or more	75 or less
450 or more	115 or less
600 or more	145 or less
750 or more	175 or less
900 or more	200 or less
1100 or more	230 or less
1200 or more	250 or less
1400 or more	290 or less
1500 or more	320 or less
1700 or more	350 or less
1800 or more	375 or less
2000 or more	410 or less
2200 or more	440 or less

Note: For *A* and *B*, refer to Figure 10.3.6.1.4.

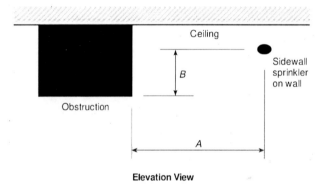

Elevation View

FIGURE 10.3.6.1.4   Positioning of Sprinkler to Avoid Obstruction Along Wall (Standard Sidewall Spray Sprinklers).

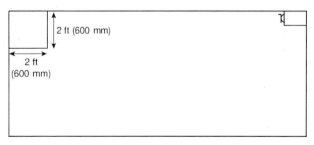

N **FIGURE 10.3.6.1.6   Permitted Obstruction on Wall Opposite Sidewall Sprinkler.**

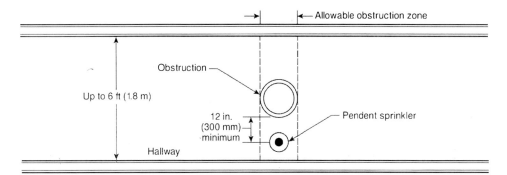

N FIGURE 10.3.6.1.7   Sprinkler Obstruction in Hallways (Standard Spray Sidewall Sprinklers).

10.3.6.2 Obstructions to Sprinkler Discharge Pattern Development.

10.3.6.2.1 General.

10.3.6.2.1.1 Continuous or noncontinuous obstructions less than or equal to 18 in. (450 mm) below the sprinkler deflector that prevent the pattern from fully developing shall comply with this section.

10.3.6.2.1.2 Regardless of the rules of this section, solid continuous obstructions shall meet the requirements of 10.3.6.1.2 and 10.3.6.1.3.

10.3.6.2.1.3* Unless the requirements of 10.3.6.2.1.4 or 10.3.6.2.1.5 are met, sprinklers shall be positioned away from obstructions a minimum distance of three times the maximum dimension of the obstruction (e.g., truss webs and chords, pipe, columns, and fixtures) in accordance with Figure 10.3.6.2.1.3(a) and Figure 10.3.6.2.1.3(b).

(A) The maximum clear distance required to obstructions in the horizontal orientation (e.g., light fixtures and truss chords) shall be 24 in. (600 mm).

(B) The maximum clear distance shall not be applied to obstructions in the vertical orientation (e.g., columns).

10.3.6.2.1.4 The requirements of 10.3.6.2.1.3 shall not apply to sprinkler system piping less than 3 in. (80 mm) in diameter.

10.3.6.2.1.5 The requirements of 10.3.6.2.1.3 shall not apply where sprinklers are positioned with respect to obstructions in accordance with 10.3.6.1.2, 10.3.6.1.3, and 10.3.6.1.4.

10.3.6.2.1.6* Sprinklers shall be permitted to be placed without regard to the blades of ceiling fans less than 60 in. (1.5 m) in diameter, provided the plan view of the fan is at least 50 percent open.

10.3.6.2.2 Suspended or Floor-Mounted Vertical Obstructions. The distance from sprinklers to privacy curtains, free-standing partitions, room dividers, and similar obstructions in light hazard occupancies shall be in accordance with Table 10.3.6.2.2(a) or Table 10.3.6.2.2(b) and Figure 10.3.6.2.2.

10.3.6.2.2.1* In light hazard occupancies, privacy curtains, as shown in Figure 10.3.6.2.2, shall not be considered obstructions where all of the following are met:

(1)   The curtains are supported by fabric mesh on ceiling track.
(2)   Openings in the mesh are equal to 70 percent or greater.

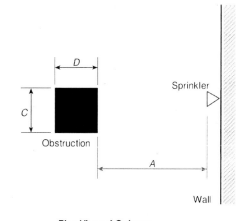

Plan View of Column
(Obstruction in vertical orientation)

$A \geq 3C$ or $3D$
(Use dimension C or D, whichever is greater)

FIGURE 10.3.6.2.1.3(a)   Minimum Distance from an Obstruction in the Vertical Orientation (Standard Sidewall Spray Sprinklers).

(3)   The mesh extends a minimum of 22 in. (550 mm) down from ceiling.

10.3.6.3* Obstructions that Prevent Sprinkler Discharge from Reaching Hazard.

10.3.6.3.1 Continuous or noncontinuous obstructions that interrupt the water discharge in a horizontal plane more than 18 in. (450 mm) below the sprinkler deflector in a manner to limit the distribution from reaching the protected hazard shall comply with this section.

10.3.6.3.2* Sprinklers shall be installed under fixed obstructions over 4 ft (1.2 m) wide.

10.3.7* Clearance to Storage (Standard Sidewall Spray Sprinklers).

10.3.7.1 The clearance between the deflector and the top of storage shall be 18 in. (450 mm) or greater.

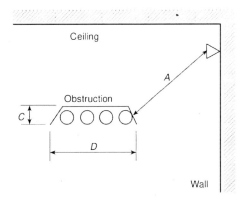

Elevation View of Pipe Conduit or Light Fixture

$A \geq 3C$ or $3D$
$A \leq 24$ in. (600 mm)
(Use dimension C or D, whichever is greater)

FIGURE 10.3.6.2.1.3(b) Minimum Distance from an Obstruction in the Horizontal Orientation (Standard Sidewall Spray Sprinklers).

N **Table 10.3.6.2.2(a) Suspended or Floor-Mounted Obstructions in Light Hazard Occupancies Only (Standard Spray Sidewalls)**

Horizontal Distance (A) (in.)	Minimum Vertical Distance Below Deflector (B) (in.)
6 or less	3 or more
9 or less	4 or more
12 or less	6 or more
15 or less	8 or more
18 or less	9½ or more
24 or less	12½ or more
30 or less	15½ or more
More than 30	18 or more

Note: For A and B, refer to Figure 10.3.6.2.2.

N **Table 10.3.6.2.2(b) Suspended or Floor-Mounted Obstructions in Light Hazard Occupancies Only (Standard Spray Sidewalls)**

Horizontal Distance (A) (mm)	Minimum Vertical Distance Below Deflector (B) (mm)
150 or less	75 or more
225 or less	100 or more
300 or less	150 or more
375 or less	200 or more
450 or less	240 or more
600 or less	315 or more
750 or less	390 or more
More than 750	450 or more

Note: For A and B, refer to Figure 10.3.6.2.2.

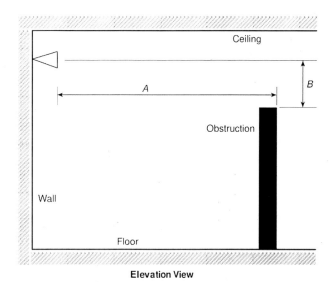

Elevation View

FIGURE 10.3.6.2.2 Suspended or Floor-Mounted Obstruction (Standard Sidewall Spray Sprinklers) in Light Hazard Occupancy Only.

10.3.7.2 The 18 in. (450 mm) dimension shall not limit the height of shelving on a wall or shelving against a wall in accordance with 10.3.7.1.

10.3.7.2.1 Where shelving is installed on a wall and is not directly below sprinklers, the shelves, including storage thereon, shall be permitted to extend above the level of a plane located 18 in. (450 mm) below ceiling sprinkler deflectors.

10.3.7.2.2 Shelving, and any storage thereon, directly below the sprinklers shall not extend above a plane located 18 in. (450 mm) below the ceiling sprinkler deflectors.

N **10.3.7.3** Where other standards specify greater clearance to storage minimums, they shall be followed.

Chapter 11   Installation Requirements for Extended Coverage Upright, Pendent, Sidewall Spray Sprinkler

11.1 General. Extended coverage pendent, upright, and sidewall sprinklers shall be selected for use and installation as indicated in this chapter and shall be positioned and spaced in accordance with Section 9.5.

11.2 Extended Coverage Upright and Pendent Spray Sprinklers.

11.2.1 Extended Coverage Sprinklers. Extended coverage sprinklers shall only be installed as follows:

(1) In unobstructed construction consisting of flat, smooth ceilings with a slope not exceeding a pitch of 1 in 6 (a rise of 2 units in a run of 12 units, a roof slope of 16.7 percent)

(2) In unobstructed or noncombustible obstructed construction, where specifically listed for such use

(3) Within trusses or bar joists having web members not greater than 1 in. (25 mm) maximum dimension or where trusses are spaced greater than 7½ ft (2.3 m) on center and where the ceiling slope does not exceed a pitch of 1 in 6 (a rise of 2 units in a run of 12 units, a roof slope of 16.7 percent)

(4) Extended coverage upright and pendent sprinklers installed under smooth, flat ceilings that have slopes not exceeding a pitch of 1 in 3 (a rise of 4 units in a run of 12 units, a roof slope of 33.3 percent), where specifically listed for such use

(5) Extended coverage sidewall sprinklers installed in accordance with 11.3.5.2.1 in slopes exceeding a ceiling pitch of 2 in 12

(6) In each bay of obstructed construction consisting of solid structural members that extend below the deflector of the sprinkler

(7) Extended coverage sprinklers installed to protect areas below a single overhead door(s)

11.2.2 Protection Areas per Sprinkler (Extended Coverage Upright and Pendent Spray Sprinklers).

11.2.2.1* Determination of Protection Area of Coverage.

11.2.2.1.1 The protection area of coverage (A_s) for extended coverage sprinklers shall be not less than that prescribed by the listing.

11.2.2.1.2 Listing dimensions shall be even-numbered square protection areas as shown in Table 11.2.2.1.2.

11.2.2.1.3 Determination of the protection area of coverage and sprinkler spacing for sprinklers listed for extended coverage extra hazard or high-piled storage shall be permitted to be spaced in accordance with the requirements of 9.5.2 and 9.5.3 and shall not exceed 14 ft (4.3 m) maximum spacing and 196 ft² (18 m²) maximum area per sprinkler or 15 ft (4.6 m) maximum spacing and 144 ft² (13 m²) maximum area per sprinkler.

11.2.2.2 Maximum Protection Area of Coverage.

11.2.2.2.1* The maximum allowable area of coverage for a sprinkler (A_s) shall be in accordance with the value indicated in Table 11.2.2.1.2.

11.2.2.2.2 In any case, the maximum area of coverage of a sprinkler shall not exceed 400 ft² (37 m²).

11.2.3 Sprinkler Spacing (Extended Coverage Upright and Pendent Spray Sprinklers).

11.2.3.1 Maximum Distance Between Sprinklers.

11.2.3.1.1 The maximum distance permitted between sprinklers shall be based on the centerline distance between sprinklers on the branch line or on adjacent branch lines.

11.2.3.1.2 The maximum distance shall be measured along the slope of the ceiling.

11.2.3.1.3 The maximum distance permitted between sprinklers shall comply with Table 11.2.2.1.2.

Δ **Table 11.2.2.1.2 Protection Areas and Maximum Spacing (Extended Coverage Upright and Pendent Spray Sprinklers)**

Construction Type	Light Hazard Protection Area [ft² (m²)]	Spacing [ft (m)]	Ordinary Hazard Protection Area [ft² (m²)]	Spacing [ft (m)]	Extra Hazard Protection Area [ft² (m²)]	Spacing [ft (m)]	High-Piled Storage Protection Area [ft² (m²)]	Spacing [ft (m)]
Unobstructed	400 (37)	20 (6.1)	400 (37)	20 (6.1)	—	—	—	—
	324 (30)	18 (5.5)	324 (30)	18 (5.5)	—	—	—	—
	256 (24)	16 (4.9)	256 (24)	16 (4.9)	—	—	—	—
	—	—	196 (18)	14 (4.3)	196 (18)	14 (4.3)	196 (18)	14 (4.3)
	—	—	144 (13)	12 (3.7)	144 (13)	15 (4.6)	144 (13)	15 (4.6)
Obstructed noncombustible (when specifically listed for such use)	400 (37)	20 (6.1)	400 (37)	20 (6.1)	—	—	—	—
	324 (30)	18 (5.5)	324 (30)	18 (5.5)	—	—	—	—
	256 (24)	16 (4.9)	256 (24)	16 (4.9)	—	—	—	—
	—	—	196 (18)	14 (4.3)	196 (18)	14 (4.3)	196 (18)	14 (4.3)
	—	—	144 (13)	12 (3.7)	144 (13)	15 (4.6)	144 (13)	15 (4.6)
Obstructed combustible	N/A	N/A	N/A	N/A	N/A	N/A	N/A	N/A

11.2.3.2 Maximum Distance from Walls.

11.2.3.2.1 The distance from sprinklers to walls shall not exceed one-half of the allowable distance permitted between sprinklers as indicated in Table 11.2.2.1.2.

11.2.3.2.2 The distance from the wall to the sprinkler shall be measured perpendicular to the wall.

11.2.3.2.3 Where walls are angled or irregular, the maximum horizontal distance between a sprinkler and any point of floor area protected by that sprinkler shall not exceed 0.75 times the allowable distance permitted between sprinklers.

11.2.3.3 Minimum Distance from Walls. Sprinklers shall be located a minimum of 4 in. (100 mm) from a wall unless listed for distances less than 4 in. (100 mm).

11.2.3.4 Minimum Distance Between Sprinklers.

11.2.3.4.1 Unless the requirements of 11.2.3.4.2 are met, sprinklers shall be spaced not less than 8 ft (2.4 m) on center.

11.2.3.4.2 Sprinklers shall be permitted to be placed less than 8 ft (2.4 m) on center where the following conditions are satisfied:

(1)   Baffles shall be arranged to protect the actuating elements.
(2)   Baffles shall be of solid and rigid material that will stay in place before and during sprinkler operation.
(3)   Baffles shall be not less than 8 in. (200 mm) long and 6 in. (150 mm) high.
(4)   The tops of baffles shall extend between 2 in. and 3 in. (50 mm and 75 mm) above the deflectors of upright sprinklers.
(5)   The bottoms of baffles shall extend downward to a level at least even with the deflectors of pendent sprinklers.

11.2.4 Deflector Position (Extended Coverage Upright and Pendent Spray Sprinklers).

11.2.4.1 Distance Below Ceilings.

11.2.4.1.1 Unobstructed Construction.

11.2.4.1.1.1 Under unobstructed construction, the distance between the sprinkler deflector and the ceiling shall be a minimum of 1 in. (25 mm) and a maximum of 12 in. (300 mm) throughout the area of coverage of the sprinkler.

11.2.4.1.1.2 The requirements of 11.2.4.1.1.1 shall not apply where ceiling-type sprinklers (concealed, recessed, and flush types) have the operating element above the ceiling and the deflector located nearer to the ceiling where installed in accordance with their listing.

11.2.4.1.1.3 The requirements of 11.2.4.1.1.1 shall not apply where sprinklers are listed for use under other ceiling construction features or for different distances where they shall be permitted to be installed in accordance with their listing.

11.2.4.1.1.4 The requirements of 11.2.4.1.1.1 shall not apply for light and ordinary hazard occupancies with ceilings of noncombustible or limited-combustible construction.

(A)* Where a vertical change in ceiling elevation within the area of coverage of the sprinkler creates a distance of more than 36 in. (900 mm) between the upper ceiling and the sprinkler deflector, a vertical plane extending down from the ceiling at the change in elevation shall be considered a wall for the purpose of sprinkler spacing.

(B)* Where the distance between the upper ceiling and the sprinkler deflector is less than or equal to 36 in. (900 mm), the sprinklers shall be permitted to be spaced as though the ceiling were flat, provided the obstruction rules are observed.

11.2.4.1.2 Obstructed Construction. Under obstructed construction, the sprinkler deflector shall be located in accordance with one of the following arrangements:

(1)   Installed with the deflectors within the horizontal planes of 1 in. to 6 in. (25 mm to 150 mm) below noncombustible structural members and a maximum distance of 22 in. (550 mm) below the ceiling/roof deck
(2)   Installed with the deflectors at or above the bottom of noncombustible structural member to a maximum of 22 in. (550 mm) below the noncombustible ceiling/roof deck where the sprinkler is installed in conformance with 11.2.5.1.2
(3)   Installed in each bay of combustible or noncombustible obstructed construction, with the deflectors located a minimum of 1 in. (25 mm) and a maximum of 12 in. (300 mm) below the ceiling
(4)   Installed in accordance with their listing where sprinklers are listed for use under other ceiling construction features or for different distances

11.2.4.1.3* Peaked Roofs and Ceilings. Sprinklers under or near the peak of a roof or ceiling shall have deflectors located not more than 3 ft (900 mm) vertically down from the peak in accordance with Figure 10.2.6.1.3.1(a) and Figure 10.2.6.1.3.1(b).

11.2.4.2 Deflector Orientation. Deflectors of sprinklers shall be aligned parallel to ceilings or roofs.

11.2.4.2.1 Roofs and ceilings having a pitch not exceeding 2 in 12 (16.7 percent) are considered horizontal in the application of 11.2.4.2, and sprinklers shall be permitted to be installed with deflectors horizontal.

11.2.5 Obstructions to Sprinkler Discharge (Extended Coverage Upright and Pendent Spray Sprinklers).

11.2.5.1 Performance Objective.

11.2.5.1.1 Sprinklers shall be located so as to minimize obstructions to discharge as defined in 11.2.5.2 and 11.2.5.3, or additional sprinklers shall be provided to ensure adequate coverage of the hazard.

11.2.5.1.2* Sprinklers shall be arranged to comply with one of the following arrangements:

(1)   Sprinklers shall be in accordance with 9.5.5.2, Table 11.2.5.1.2(a) or Table 11.2.5.1.2(b), and Figure 11.2.5.1.2(a).
(2)   Sprinklers shall be permitted to be spaced on opposite sides of obstructions not exceeding 4 ft (1.2 m) in width provided the distance from the centerline of the obstruction to the sprinklers does not exceed one-half the allowable distance permitted between sprinklers.
(3)   Obstructions located against the wall and that are not over 30 in. (750 mm) in width shall be permitted to be protected in accordance with Figure 11.2.5.1.2(b).

(4) Obstructions located against the wall and that are not over 24 in. (600 mm) in width shall be permitted to be protected in accordance with Figure 11.2.5.1.2(c). The maximum distance between the sprinkler and the wall shall be measured from the sprinkler to the wall behind the obstruction and not to the face of the obstruction.

(5) Obstructions up to 12 in. (300 mm) in width in hallways up to 6 ft (1.8 m) in width shall be permitted in accordance with Figure 11.2.5.1.2(d) when the sprinkler is located in the allowable obstruction zone and the closest edge of the obstruction is a minimum of 12 in. (300 mm) away from the centerline of the sprinkler.

11.2.5.2 Obstructions to Sprinkler Discharge Pattern Development.

11.2.5.2.1 General.

11.2.5.2.1.1 Continuous or noncontinuous obstructions less than or equal to 18 in. (450 mm) below the sprinkler deflector that prevent the pattern from fully developing shall comply with 11.2.5.2.

N **Table 11.2.5.1.2(a) Positioning of Sprinklers to Avoid Obstructions to Discharge (Extended Coverage Upright and Pendent Sprinklers)**

Distance from Sprinkler to Side of Obstruction (A) (ft)	Allowable Distance of Deflector Above Bottom of Obstruction (B)(in.)
Less than 1½	0
1½ or more	1 or less
3 or more	3 or less
4 or more	5 or less
4½ or more	7 or less
6 or more	9 or less
6½ or more	11 or less
7 or more	14 or less
8 or more	15 or less
8½ or more	17 or less
9 or more	19 or less
9½ or more	21 or less

Note: For A and B, refer to Figure 11.2.5.1.2(a).

N **Table 11.2.5.1.2(b) Positioning of Sprinklers to Avoid Obstructions to Discharge (Extended Coverage Upright and Pendent Sprinklers)**

Distance from Sprinkler to Side of Obstruction (A) (mm)	Allowable Distance of Deflector Above Bottom of Obstruction (B) (mm)
Less than 450	0
450 or more	25 or less
900 or more	75 or less
1200 or more	125 or less
1400 or more	175 or less
1800 or more	225 or less
2000 or more	275 or less
2100 or more	350 or less
2400 or more	375 or less
2600 or more	425 or less
2700 or more	475 or less
2900 or more	525 or less

Note: For A and B, refer to Figure 11.2.5.1.2(a).

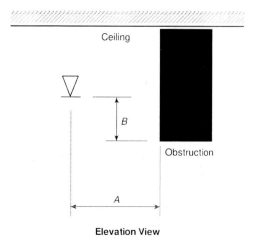

Elevation View

FIGURE 11.2.5.1.2(a)   Position of Sprinkler to Avoid Obstruction to Discharge (Extended Coverage Upright and Pendent Spray Sprinklers).

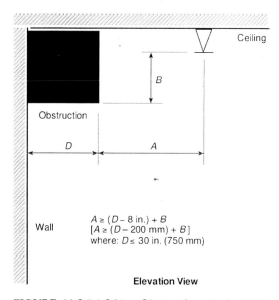

$$A \geq (D - 8 \text{ in.}) + B$$
$$[A \geq (D - 200 \text{ mm}) + B]$$
where: $D \leq 30$ in. (750 mm)

Elevation View

FIGURE 11.2.5.1.2(b)   Obstructions Against Walls (Extended Coverage Upright and Pendent Spray Sprinklers).

11.2.5.2.1.2 Regardless of the rules of this section, solid continuous obstructions shall meet the applicable requirements of 11.2.5.1.2.

11.2.5.2.1.3* Unless the requirements of 11.2.5.2.1.4 through 11.2.5.2.1.8 are met, sprinklers shall be positioned away from obstructions a minimum distance of four times the maximum dimension of the obstruction (e.g., truss webs and chords, pipe, columns, and fixtures) in accordance with Figure 11.2.5.2.1.3(a) and Figure 11.2.5.2.1.3(b).

(A) The maximum clear distance required to obstructions in the horizontal orientation (e.g., light fixtures and truss chords) shall be 36 in. (900 mm).

(B) The maximum clear distance shall not be applied to obstructions in the vertical orientation (e.g., columns).

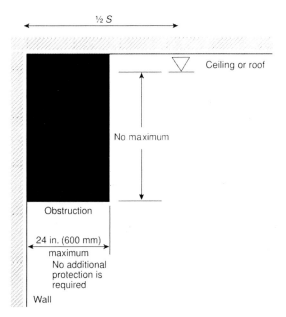

△ **FIGURE 11.2.5.1.2(c)   Obstructions Against Walls (Extended Coverage Upright and Pendent Spray Sprinklers).**

11.2.5.2.1.4 Sprinklers shall be permitted to be spaced on opposite sides of the obstruction where the distance from the centerline of the obstruction to the sprinklers does not exceed one-half the allowable distance between sprinklers.

11.2.5.2.1.5 Sprinklers shall be permitted to be located one-half the distance between the obstructions where the obstruction consists of wood bar joists 20 in. (500 mm) or greater apart, provided that the top and bottom chords of the wood bar joist are not greater than 4 in. (100 mm) (nominal) in width and bar members do not exceed 1 in. (25 mm) in width.

11.2.5.2.1.6 Sprinklers shall be permitted to be installed on the centerline of a truss or bar joist or directly above a beam, provided that the truss chord or beam, dimension is not more than 8 in. (200 mm) and the sprinkler deflector is located at least 6 in. (150 mm) above the structural member and where the sprinkler is positioned at a distance four times greater than the maximum dimension of the web members away from the web members.

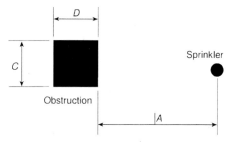

Plan View of Column
(Obstruction in vertical orientation)

$A \geq 4C$ or $4D$
(Use dimension C or D, whichever is greater)

△ **FIGURE 11.2.5.2.1.3(a)   Minimum Distance from an Obstruction in the Vertical Orientation (Extended Coverage Upright and Pendent Spray Sprinkler).**

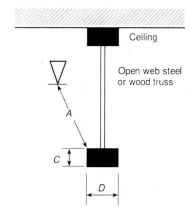

Elevation View of Truss
(Obstruction in horizontal orientation)

$A \geq 4C$ or $4D$
$A \leq 36$ in. (900 mm)
(Use dimension C or D, whichever is greater)

FIGURE 11.2.5.2.1.3(b)   Minimum Distance from an Obstruction in the Horizontal Orientation (Extended Coverage Upright and Pendent Spray Sprinkler).

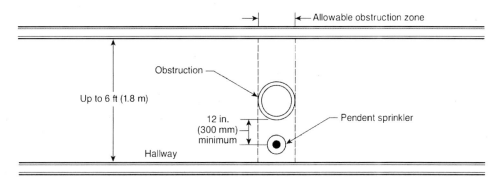

N **FIGURE 11.2.5.1.2(d)   Obstruction in Hallway**

11.2.5.2.1.7 The requirements of 11.2.5.2.1.3 shall not apply to sprinkler system piping less than 3 in. (80 mm) in diameter.

11.2.5.2.1.8 The requirements of 11.2.5.2.1.3 shall not apply to sprinklers positioned with respect to obstructions in accordance with 11.2.5.1.2.

11.2.5.2.1.9* Sprinklers shall be permitted to be placed without regard to the blades of ceiling fans less than 60 in. (1.5 m) in diameter, provided the plan view of the fan is at least 50 percent open.

11.2.5.2.2 Suspended or Floor-Mounted Vertical Obstructions. The distance from sprinklers to privacy curtains, freestanding partitions, room dividers, and similar obstructions in light hazard occupancies shall be in accordance with Table 11.2.5.2.2(a)or Table 11.2.5.2.2(b)and Figure 11.2.5.2.2.

N Table 11.2.5.2.2(a) Suspended or Floor-Mounted Obstructions in Light Hazard Occupancies Only (Extended Coverage Upright and Pendent Sprinklers)

Horizontal Distance *(A)* (in.)	Minimum Vertical Distance Below Deflector *(B)* (in.)
6 or less	3 or more
9 or less	4 or more
12 or less	6 or more
15 or less	8 or more
18 or less	9½ or more
24 or less	12½ or more
30 or less	15½ or more
More than 30	18 or more

Note: For *A* and *B*, refer to Figure 11.2.5.2.2.

N Table 11.2.5.2.2(b) Suspended or Floor-Mounted Obstructions in Light Hazard Occupancies Only (Extended Coverage Upright and Pendent Sprinklers)

Horizontal Distance *(A)* (mm)	Minimum Vertical Distance Below Deflector *(B)* (mm)
150 or less	75 or more
225 or less	100 or more
300 or less	150 or more
375 or less	200 or more
450 or less	240 or more
600 or less	315 or more
750 or less	390 or more
More than 750	450 or more

Note: For *A* and *B*, refer to Figure 11.2.5.2.2.

11.2.5.2.2.1 In light hazard occupancies, privacy curtains, as shown in Figure 11.2.5.2.2, shall not be considered obstructions where all of the following are met:

(1) The curtains are supported by fabric mesh on ceiling track.
(2) Openings in the mesh are equal to 70 percent or greater.
(3) The mesh extends a minimum of 22 in. (550 mm) down from ceiling.

N **11.2.5.2.2.2** In ordinary hazard occupancies, where sprinklers are installed above freestanding partitions, room dividers, and similar obstructions, the distance from the sprinkler deflector to the top of the obstruction shall be 18 in. (450 mm) or greater per Figure 11.2.5.2.2.2.

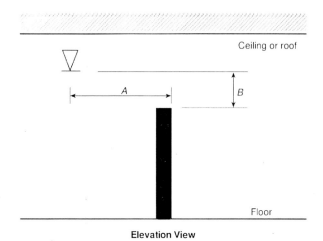

FIGURE 11.2.5.2.2 Suspended or Floor-Mounted Obstruction (Extended Coverage Upright and Pendent Spray Sprinklers) in Light Hazard Occupancy Only.

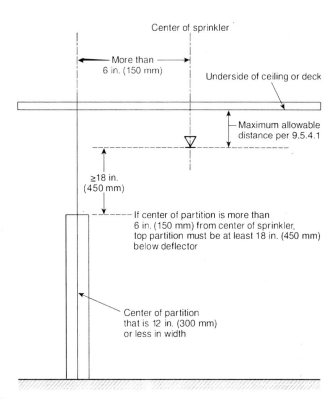

N **FIGURE 11.2.5.2.2.2** Location of Suspended or Floor-Mounted Obstruction in Ordinary Hazard Occupancies (Sprinkler Located to the Side) (ECU/ECP).

N 11.2.5.2.2.3 In ordinary hazard occupancies, where sprinklers are installed within 6 in. (150 mm) horizontally of the centerline of freestanding partitions, room dividers, and similar obstructions no greater than 12 in. (300 mm) in width, the distance from the sprinkler deflector to the top of the obstruction shall be permitted to be installed 6 in. (150 mm) or greater vertically per Figure 11.2.5.2.2.3.

11.2.5.3* Obstructions that Prevent Sprinkler Discharge from Reaching Hazard.

11.2.5.3.1 Continuous or noncontinuous obstructions that interrupt the water discharge in a horizontal plane more than 18 in. (450 mm) below the sprinkler deflector in a manner to limit the distribution from reaching the protected hazard shall comply with 11.2.5.3.

11.2.5.3.2* Sprinklers shall be installed under fixed obstructions over 4 ft (1.2 m) wide.

11.2.5.3.3 Sprinklers shall not be required under obstructions that are not fixed in place such as conference tables.

11.2.5.3.4 Sprinklers installed under open gratings shall be of the intermediate level/rack storage type or otherwise shielded from the discharge of overhead sprinklers.

11.2.5.3.5 Sprinklers installed under round ducts shall be of the intermediate level/rack storage type or otherwise shielded from the discharge of overhead sprinklers.

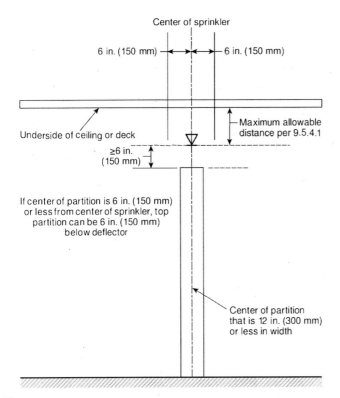

N **FIGURE 11.2.5.2.2.3 Location of Suspended or Floor-Mounted Obstruction in Ordinary Hazard Occupancies (Sprinkler Located Directly Above) (ECU/ECP).**

11.2.6 Clearance to Storage (Extended Coverage Upright and Pendent Spray Sprinklers).

11.2.6.1* The clearance between the deflector and top of storage shall be 18 in. (450 mm) or greater.

11.2.6.2 The 18 in. (450 mm) dimension shall not limit the height of shelving on a wall or shelving against a wall in accordance with 11.2.6.

11.2.6.2.1 Where shelving is installed on a wall and is not directly below sprinklers, the shelves, including storage thereon, shall be permitted to extend above the level of a plane located 18 in. (450 mm) below ceiling sprinkler deflectors.

11.2.6.2.2 Shelving, and any storage thereon, directly below the sprinklers shall not extend above a plane located 18 in. (450 mm) below the ceiling sprinkler deflectors.

N **11.2.6.3** The clearance from the top of storage to sprinkler deflectors shall not be less than 36 in. (900 mm) where rubber tires are stored.

N **11.2.6.4** Where other standards specify greater clearance to storage minimums, they shall be followed.

11.2.7 Ceiling Pockets (Extended Coverage Upright and Pendent Spay Sprinklers).

11.2.7.1* Except as allowed in 11.2.7.2 and 11.2.7.3, sprinklers shall be required in all ceiling pockets.

11.2.7.2 Sprinklers shall not be required in ceiling pockets where all of the following are met:

(1) The total volume of the unprotected ceiling pocket does not exceed 1000 ft³ (28 m³).
(2) The depth of the unprotected ceiling pocket does not exceed 36 in. (900 mm).
(3) The entire floor under the unprotected ceiling pocket is protected by sprinklers at the lower ceiling elevation.
(4)* The total size of all unprotected ceiling pockets in the same compartment within 10 ft (3 m) of each other does not exceed 1000 ft³ (28 m³).
(5) The unprotected ceiling pocket has noncombustible or limited-combustible finishes.
(6) Quick-response sprinklers are utilized throughout the compartment.

11.2.7.3 Sprinklers shall not be required in skylights and similar pockets in accordance with 9.3.16.

11.3* Extended Coverage Sidewall Spray Sprinklers.

11.3.1 General. All requirements of Section 9.5 shall apply to extended coverage sidewall spray sprinklers except as modified in Section 11.3.

11.3.2 Extended coverage sidewall spray sprinklers shall only be installed as follows:

(1) Light hazard occupancies with smooth, horizontal or sloped, flat ceilings
(2) Ordinary hazard occupancies with smooth, flat ceilings where specifically listed for such use
(3) In unobstructed construction consisting of flat, smooth ceilings with a slope not exceeding a pitch of 1 in 6 (a rise of 2 units in a run of 12 units, a roof slope of 16.7 percent)
(4) In unobstructed or noncombustible obstructed construction, where specifically listed for such use

(5) Within trusses or bar joists having web members not greater than 1 in. (25 mm) maximum dimension or where trusses are spaced greater than 7½ ft (2.3 m) on center and where the ceiling slope does not exceed a pitch of 1 in 6 (a rise of 2 units in a run of 12 units, a roof slope of 16.7 percent)

(6) Extended coverage sidewall sprinklers installed in accordance with 11.3.6.2.2 in slopes exceeding a ceiling pitch of 2 in 12

(7) In each bay of obstructed construction consisting of solid structural members that extend below the deflector of the sprinkler

(8) Extended coverage sprinklers installed to protect areas below a single overhead door(s)

11.3.3 Protection Areas per Sprinkler (Extended Coverage Sidewall Spray Sprinklers).

11.3.3.1* Determination of Protection Area of Coverage.

11.3.3.1.1 The protection area of coverage per sprinkler (A_s) for extended coverage sidewall sprinklers shall be not less than that prescribed by the listing.

11.3.3.1.2 Listing dimensions shall be in 2 ft (600 mm) increments up to 28 ft (8.5 m).

11.3.3.2 Maximum Protection Area of Coverage.

11.3.3.2.1 The maximum allowable protection area of coverage for a sprinkler (A_s) shall be in accordance with the value indicated in Table 11.3.3.2.1.

11.3.3.2.2 In any case, the maximum area of coverage of a sprinkler shall not exceed 400 ft² (37 m²).

11.3.4 Sprinkler Spacing (Extended Coverage Sidewall Spray Sprinklers).

11.3.4.1 Maximum Distance Between Sprinklers.

11.3.4.1.1 The maximum distance permitted between sprinklers shall be based on the centerline distance between sprinklers on the branch line along the wall.

11.3.4.1.2 Where sprinklers are installed along the length of a single wall of rooms or bays, they shall be spaced in accordance with the maximum spacing provisions of Table 11.3.3.2.1.

11.3.4.1.3 Sidewall sprinklers shall not be installed back-to-back without being separated by a continuous lintel, soffit, or baffle.

11.3.4.1.4 Sidewall sprinklers shall be permitted to be installed on opposing or adjacent walls, provided no sprinkler is located within 12 ft (3.7 m) of the opposing sprinkler.

N **11.3.4.1.5** Where sidewall extended spray sprinklers are installed to protect areas below overhead doors within ordinary hazard occupancy spaces or rooms, listed light hazard sidewall extended coverage spray sprinklers shall be permitted and the protection area and maximum sprinkler spacing for light hazard as specified in Table 11.3.3.2.1 shall be permitted.

11.3.4.2 Maximum Distance from Walls. The distance from sprinklers to the end walls shall not exceed one-half of the allowable distance permitted between sprinklers as indicated in Table 11.3.3.2.1.

11.3.4.3 Minimum Distance from Walls.

11.3.4.3.1 Sprinklers shall be located a minimum of 4 in. (100 mm) from an end wall.

11.3.4.3.2 The distance from the wall to the sprinkler shall be measured perpendicular to the wall.

11.3.4.4 Minimum Distance Between Sprinklers. Sprinklers shall be not located within the maximum protection area of any other sprinkler unless required by 11.3.5.1.4.1 or separated by baffles that comply with the following:

(1) Baffles shall be arranged to protect the actuating elements.

(2) Baffles shall be of solid and rigid material that will stay in place before and during sprinkler operation.

(3) Baffles shall be not less than 8 in. (200 mm) long and 6 in. (150 mm) high.

(4) The tops of baffles shall extend between 2 in. and 3 in. (50 mm and 75 mm) above the deflectors.

(5) The bottoms of baffles shall extend downward to a level at least even with the deflectors.

11.3.5 Deflector Position from Ceilings and Walls (Extended Coverage Sidewall Spray Sprinklers).

11.3.5.1 Distance Below Ceilings and from Walls to Which Sprinklers Are Mounted.

11.3.5.1.1 Ceilings.

11.3.5.1.1.1 Unless the requirements of 11.3.5.1.1.2 are met, sidewall sprinkler deflectors shall be located not more than 6 in. (150 mm) nor less than 4 in. (100 mm) from ceilings.

11.3.5.1.1.2 Horizontal sidewall sprinklers shall be permitted to be located in a zone 6 in. to 12 in. (150 mm to 300 mm) or 12 in. to 18 in. (300 mm to 450 mm) below noncombustible or limited-combustible ceilings where listed for such use.

11.3.5.1.2 Walls.

11.3.5.1.2.1* Sidewall sprinkler deflectors shall be located not more than 6 in. (150 mm) or less than 4 in. (100 mm) from walls on which they are mounted.

11.3.5.1.2.2 Horizontal sidewall sprinklers shall be permitted to be located with their deflectors less than 4 in. (100 mm) from the wall on which they are mounted.

Table 11.3.3.2.1 Protection Area and Maximum Spacing for Extended Coverage Sidewall Spray Sprinklers

| | Light Hazard | | | | Ordinary Hazard | | | |
| | Protection Area | | Spacing | | Protection Area | | Spacing | |
Construction Type	ft²	m²	ft	m	ft²	m²	ft	m
Unobstructed, smooth, flat	400	37	28	8.5	400	37	24	7.3

11.3.5.1.3 Lintels and Soffits.

11.3.5.1.3.1* Where soffits used for the installation of sidewall sprinklers are less than or equal to 8 in. (200 mm) in width or projection from the wall, additional sprinklers shall not be required below the soffit.

11.3.5.1.3.2* A sidewall sprinkler shall be permitted to be installed under a soffit when both the minimum distance from the sprinkler deflector to the bottom of the soffit and the maximum distance from the sprinkler deflector to the high ceiling are maintained.

11.3.5.1.4* Soffits and Cabinets in Residential Areas/Occupancies. Where soffits are used for the installation of sidewall sprinklers, the sprinklers and soffits shall be installed in accordance with 11.3.5.1.4.1, 11.3.5.1.4.2, or 11.3.5.1.4.3.

11.3.5.1.4.1 Where soffits exceed more than 8 in. (200 mm) in width or projection from the wall, pendent sprinklers shall be installed under the soffit.

11.3.5.1.4.2 Sidewall sprinklers shall be permitted to be installed in the face of a soffit located directly over cabinets, without requiring additional sprinklers below the soffit or cabinets, where the soffit does not project horizontally more than 12 in. (300 mm) from the wall.

11.3.5.1.4.3 Where sidewall sprinklers are more than 3 ft (900 mm) above the top of cabinets, the sprinkler shall be permitted to be installed on the wall above the cabinets where the cabinets are no greater than 12 in. (300 mm) from the wall.

11.3.5.2 Deflector Orientation.

11.3.5.2.1 Sidewall sprinklers, where installed under a sloped ceiling with a slope exceeding 2 in 12, shall be located at the high point of the slope and positioned to discharge downward along the slope.

11.3.5.2.2 Sidewall sprinklers specifically listed for other ceiling configurations shall be permitted to be installed in accordance with the listing requirements.

11.3.6 Obstructions to Sprinkler Discharge (Extended Coverage Sidewall Spray Sprinklers).

11.3.6.1 Performance Objective.

11.3.6.1.1 Sprinklers shall be located so as to minimize obstructions to discharge as defined in 9.5.5.2 and 9.5.5.3, or additional sprinklers shall be provided to ensure adequate coverage of the hazard.

11.3.6.1.2 Sidewall sprinklers shall not be installed less than 8 ft (2.4 m) from light fixtures or similar obstructions unless the requirements of 11.3.6.1.2.1 or 11.3.6.1.2.2 are met.

11.3.6.1.2.1 For obstructions such as light fixtures, where the greatest dimension of the obstruction is less than 2 ft (0.6 m), sidewall sprinklers shall be permitted to be installed at a minimum distance of four times the greatest dimension.

11.3.6.1.2.2 For obstructions located 4 in. or greater above the plane of the sprinkler deflector the sprinkler shall be permitted to be located less than 8 ft (2.4 m) from the obstruction.

11.3.6.1.3 The distance between light fixtures or similar obstructions located 8 ft (2.4 m) or greater from the sprinkler shall be in conformance with Table 11.3.6.1.3(a) or Table 11.3.6.1.3(b) and Figure 11.3.6.1.3.

N Table 11.3.6.1.3(a) Positioning of Sprinklers to Avoid Obstructions to Discharge (Extended Coverage Sidewall)

Distance from Sprinkler to Side of Obstruction (A) (ft)	Allowable Distance of Deflector Above Bottom of Obstruction (B) (in.)
Less than 8	0
8 or more	1 or less
10 or more	2 or less
11 or more	3 or less
12 or more	4 or less
13 or more	6 or less
14 or more	7 or less
15 or more	9 or less
16 or more	11 or less
17 or more	14 or less

Note: For A and B, refer to Figure 11.3.6.1.3.

N Table 11.3.6.1.3(b) Positioning of Sprinklers to Avoid Obstructions to Discharge (Extended Coverage Sidewall)

Distance from Sprinkler to Side of Obstruction (A) (mm)	Allowable Distance of Deflector Above Bottom of Obstruction (B) (mm)
Less than 2400	0
2400 or more	25 or less
3000 or more	50 or less
3400 or more	75 or less
3700 or more	100 or less
4000 or more	150 or less
4300 or more	175 or less
4600 or more	225 or less
4900 or more	275 or less
5200 or more	350 or less

Note: For A and B, refer to Figure 11.3.6.1.3.

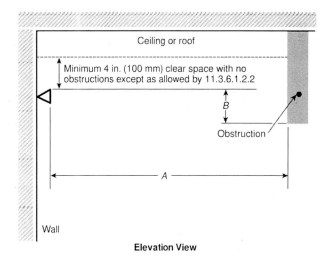

Elevation View

Δ FIGURE 11.3.6.1.3   Positioning of Sprinkler to Avoid Obstruction (Extended Coverage Sidewall Spray Sprinklers).

11.3.6.1.4 Continuous obstructions projecting from the same wall as the one on which the sidewall sprinkler is mounted shall be in accordance with one of the following arrangements:

(1) Sprinklers shall be installed in accordance with Table 11.3.6.1.4(a)or Table 11.3.6.1.4(b) and Figure 11.3.6.1.4(a).

(2) Sprinklers shall be permitted to be spaced on opposite sides of obstructions less than 4 ft (1.2 m) in width where the distance from the centerline of the obstruction to the sprinklers does not exceed one-half the allowable distance between sprinklers.

(3) Obstructions located against the wall and that are not over 30 in. (750 mm) in width shall be permitted to be protected in accordance with Figure 11.3.6.1.4(b).

(4) Obstructions located against the wall and that are not over 24 in. (600 mm) in width shall be permitted to be protected in accordance with Figure 11.3.6.1.4(c). The maximum distance between the sprinkler and the wall shall be measured from the sprinkler to the wall behind the obstruction and not to the face of the obstruction.

(5) Obstructions with a maximum width of 12 in. (300 mm) in hallways up to 6 ft (1.8 m) in width shall be permitted in accordance with Figure 11.3.6.1.4(d) when the sprinkler is located in the allowable obstruction zone and the closest edge of the obstruction is a minimum of 12 in. (300 mm) away from the deflector.

N **Table 11.3.6.1.4(a) Positioning of Sprinklers to Avoid Obstructions Along Wall (Extended Coverage Sidewall)**

Distance from Sprinkler to Side of Obstruction (A) (ft)	Allowable Distance of Deflector Above Bottom of Obstruction (B) (in.)
Less than 1½	0
1½ or more	1 or less
3 ft or more	3 or less
4 ft or more	5 or less
4½ or more	7 or less
6 ft or more	9 or less
6½ or more	11 or less
7 or more	14 or less

Note: For A and B, refer to Figure 11.3.6.1.4(a).

N **Table 11.3.6.1.4(b) Positioning of Sprinklers to Avoid Obstructions Along Wall (Extended Coverage Sidewall)**

Distance from Sprinkler to Side of Obstruction (A) (mm)	Allowable Distance of Deflector Above Bottom of Obstruction (B) (mm)
Less than 450	0
450 or more	25 or less
900 or more	75 or less
1200 or more	125 or less
1400 or more	175 or less
1800 or more	225 or less
2000 or more	275 or less
2100 or more	350 or less

Note: For A and B, refer to Figure 11.3.6.1.4(a).

11.3.6.1.5 Isolated Obstructions. Isolated obstructions projecting from the same wall as the one on which the extended coverage sidewall sprinkler is mounted shall be located a minimum of 6 in. (150 mm) from the sidewall sprinkler.

11.3.6.1.6 Obstructions on the wall opposite from the sidewall sprinkler shall be permitted in accordance with Figure 11.3.6.1.6.

11.3.6.2 Obstructions to Sprinkler Discharge Pattern Development.

11.3.6.2.1 General.

11.3.6.2.1.1 Continuous or noncontinuous obstructions less than or equal to 18 in. (450 mm) below the sprinkler deflector that prevent the pattern from fully developing shall comply with this section.

11.3.6.2.1.2 Regardless of the rules of this section, solid continuous obstructions shall meet the requirements of 11.3.6.1.2 and 11.3.6.1.3.

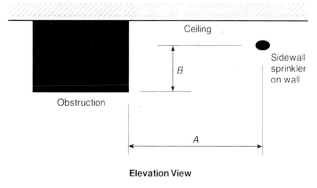

FIGURE 11.3.6.1.4(a)   Positioning of Sprinkler to Avoid Obstruction Along Wall (Extended Coverage Sidewall Spray Sprinklers).

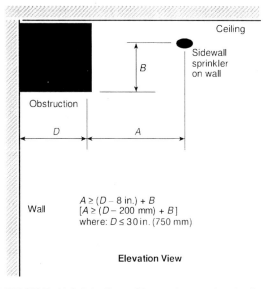

Δ **FIGURE 11.3.6.1.4(b)   Obstruction Against Wall (Extended Coverage Sidewall Spray Sprinklers).**

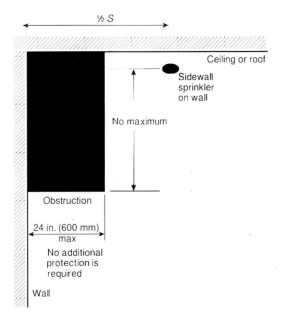

FIGURE 11.3.6.1.4(c)   Obstruction Against Wall (Extended Coverage Sidewall Spray Sprinklers).

11.3.6.2.1.3* Unless the requirements of 11.3.6.2.1.4 and 11.3.6.2.1.5 are met, sprinklers shall be positioned away from obstructions a minimum distance of four times the maximum dimension of the obstruction (e.g., truss webs and chords, pipe, columns, and fixtures) in accordance with Figure 11.3.6.2.1.3(a) and Figure 11.3.6.2.1.3(b).

(A) The maximum clear distance required to obstructions in the horizontal orientation (e.g., light fixtures and truss chords) shall be 36 in. (900 mm).

(B) The maximum clear distance shall not be applied to obstructions in the vertical orientation (e.g., columns).

11.3.6.2.1.4 The requirements of 11.3.6.2.1.3 and 11.3.6.2.1.4 shall not apply where sprinklers are positioned with respect to obstructions in accordance with 11.3.6.1.2 and 11.3.6.1.3.

11.3.6.2.1.5 The requirements of 11.3.6.2.1.3 shall not apply to sprinkler system piping less than 3 in. (80 mm) in diameter.

11.3.6.2.1.6* Sprinklers shall be permitted to be placed without regard to the blades of ceiling fans less than 60 in. (1.5 m)

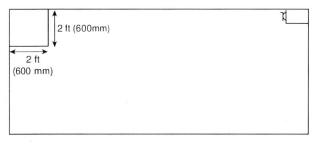

N **FIGURE 11.3.6.1.6   Permitted Obstruction on Wall Opposite EC Sidewall Sprinkler.**

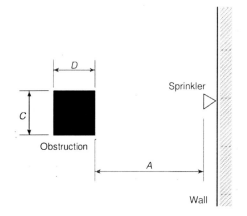

Plan View of Column
(Obstruction in vertical orientation)
$A \geq 4C$ or $4D$
(Use dimension C or D, whichever is greater)

FIGURE 11.3.6.2.1.3(a)   Minimum Distance from an Obstruction in the Vertical Orientation (Extended Coverage Sidewall).

in diameter, provided the plan view of the fan is at least 50 percent open.

11.3.6.2.2 Suspended or Floor-Mounted Vertical Obstructions. The distance from sprinklers to privacy curtains, freestanding partitions, room dividers, and similar obstructions in light hazard occupancies shall be in accordance with Table 11.3.6.2.2(a) or Table 11.3.6.2.2(b) and Figure 11.3.6.2.2.

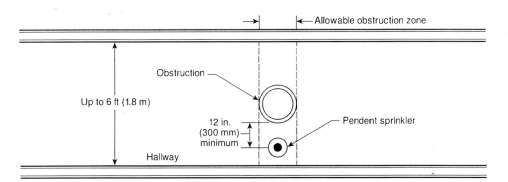

N **FIGURE 11.3.6.1.4(d)   Obstruction in Hallway (Extended Coverage Sidewall Spray Sprinklers).**

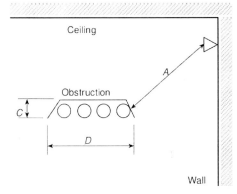

Elevation View of Pipe Conduit or Light Fixture
(Obstruction in horizontal orientation)

$A \geq 4\,C$ or $4D$
$A \leq 36$ in. (900 mm)
(Use dimension C or D, whichever is greater)

FIGURE 11.3.6.2.1.3(b)   Minimum Distance from an Obstruction in the Horizontal Orientation (Extended Coverage Sidewall).

N **Table 11.3.6.2.2(a) Suspended or Floor-Mounted Obstructions in Light Hazard Occupancies Only (Extended Coverage Sidewall Sprinklers)**

Horizontal Distance *(A)* (in.)	Minimum Vertical Distance Below Deflector *(B)* (in.)
6 or less	3 or more
9 or less	4 or more
12 or less	6 or more
15 or less	8 or more
18 or less	9½ or more
24 or less	12½ or more
30 or less	15½ or more
More than 30	18 or more

Note: For *A* and *B*, refer to Figure 11.3.6.2.2.

N **Table 11.3.6.2.2(b) Suspended or Floor-Mounted Obstructions in Light Hazard Occupancies Only (Extended Coverage Sidewall Sprinklers)**

Horizontal Distance *(A)* (mm)	Minimum Vertical Distance Below Deflector *(B)* (mm)
150 or less	75 or more
225 or less	100 or more
300 or less	150 or more
375 or less	200 or more
450 or less	240 or more
600 or less	315 or more
750 or less	390 or more
More than 750	450 or more

Note: For *A* and *B*, refer to Figure 11.3.6.2.2.

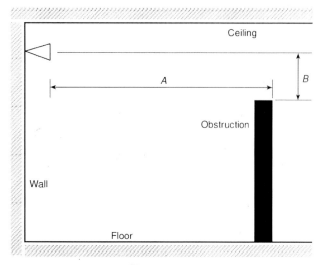

Elevation View

FIGURE 11.3.6.2.2   Suspended or Floor-Mounted Obstruction (Extended Coverage Sidewall Sprinklers) in Light Hazard Occupancy Only.

11.3.6.2.2.1* In light hazard occupancies, privacy curtains, as shown in Figure 11.3.6.2.2, shall not be considered obstructions where all of the following are met:

(1) The curtains are supported by fabric mesh on ceiling track.
(2) Openings in the mesh are equal to 70 percent or greater.
(3) The mesh extends a minimum of 22 in. (550 mm) down from ceiling.

11.3.6.3* Obstructions that Prevent Sprinkler Discharge from Reaching Hazard.

11.3.6.3.1 Continuous or noncontinuous obstructions that interrupt the water discharge in a horizontal plane more than 18 in. (450 mm) below the sprinkler deflector in a manner to limit the distribution from reaching the protected hazard shall comply with this section.

11.3.6.3.2* Sprinklers shall be installed under fixed obstructions over 4 ft (1.2 m) wide.

11.3.6.3.3 Sprinklers shall not be required under obstructions that are not fixed in place, such as conference tables.

11.3.7 Clearance to Storage (Extended Coverage Sidewall Spray Sprinklers). The clearance between the deflector and the top of storage shall be 18 in. (450 mm) or greater.

N **11.3.7.1** The 18 in. (450 mm) dimension shall not limit the height of shelving on a wall in accordance with 11.3.7.1.1.

N **11.3.7.1.1** Where shelving is installed on a wall and is not directly below the sprinklers, the shelves, including storage thereon, shall be permitted to extend above the level of a plane located 18 in. (450 mm) below the sprinkler deflectors.

N **11.3.7.1.2** Shelving, and any storage thereon, directly below the sprinklers shall not extend above a plane located 18 in. (450 mm) below the ceiling sprinkler deflectors.

N **11.3.7.2** Where other standards specify greater clearance to storage minimums, they shall be followed.

Chapter 12 Installation Requirements for Residential Sprinklers

12.1 General. Residential sprinklers shall be selected for use and installation as indicated in this Chapter and shall be positioned and spaced in accordance with Section 9.5.

12.1.1* Residential sprinklers shall be permitted in dwelling units and their adjoining corridors, provided they are installed in conformance with their listing and when installed under the following conditions:

(1) A flat, smooth, horizontal ceiling with no beams up to a maximum of 24 ft (7.3 m) above the floor.
(2) A flat, horizontal, beamed ceiling, with a maximum ceiling height of 24 ft (7.3 m), with beams up to 14 in. (355 mm) deep with pendent sprinklers under the beams. The compartment containing the beamed ceiling shall be a maximum of 600 ft^2 (56 m^2) in area. The highest sprinkler in the compartment shall be above all openings from the compartment into any communicating spaces.
(3) A smooth, flat, sloped ceiling with no beams up to a maximum slope of 8 in 12. The highest portion of the ceiling shall not be more than 24 ft (7.3 m) above the floor. The highest sprinkler in the sloped portion of the ceiling shall be above all openings from the compartment containing the sloped ceiling into any communicating spaces.
(4) A sloped ceiling with beams up to 14 in. (350 mm) deep with pendent sprinklers under the beams. The compartment containing the sloped, beamed ceiling shall be a maximum of 600 ft^2 (56 m^2) in area. The slope of the ceiling shall be between 2 in 12 and 8 in 12. The highest portion of the ceiling shall not be more than 24 ft (7.3 m) above the floor. The highest sprinkler in the sloped portion of the ceiling shall be above all openings from the compartment containing the sloped ceiling into any communicating spaces.
(5) A sloped ceiling with beams of any depth with sidewall or pendent sprinklers in each pocket formed by the beams. The compartment containing the sloped, beamed ceiling shall be a maximum of 600 ft^2 (56 m^2) in area. The slope of the ceiling shall be between 2 in 12 and 8 in 12. The highest portion of the ceiling shall not be more than 24 ft (7.3 m) above the floor.

12.1.2 Where construction features or other special conditions exist that are outside the scope of sprinkler listings, listed sprinklers shall be permitted to be installed beyond their listing limitations when acceptable to the authority having jurisdiction.

12.1.3 Residential sprinklers shall be used only in wet systems unless specifically listed for use in dry systems or preaction systems.

12.1.4 Where residential sprinklers are installed in a compartment as defined in 3.3.40, all sprinklers within the compartment shall be residential sprinklers.

N **12.1.4.1** Residential sprinklers shall be permitted to be installed in corridors of residential occupancies that are adjacent to areas protected by quick-response sprinklers.

12.1.5 Reserved.

12.1.6* Listings.

12.1.6.1 Areas of coverage shall be in accordance with the manufacturer's listing.

12.1.7 Distances Between Sprinklers.

12.1.7.1 Maximum distances between sprinklers shall be in accordance with the manufacturer's listing.

12.1.7.2 The distance between the sprinkler and the wall shall not exceed half the maximum allowable distance between sprinklers per the manufacturer's listing.

12.1.7.3 The minimum distance between sprinklers within a compartment shall be 8 ft (2.4 m), unless the listing of the sprinkler requires a greater distance, unless required by 12.1.11.1.5.1, or unless separated by baffles that comply with the following:

(1) Baffles shall be arranged to protect the actuating elements.
(2) Baffles shall be of solid and rigid material that will stay in place before and during sprinkler operation.
(3) Baffles shall be not less than 8 in. (200 mm) long and 6 in. (150 mm) high.
(4) The tops of baffles shall extend between 2 in. and 3 in. (50 mm and 75 mm) above the deflectors of upright sprinklers.
(5) The bottoms of baffles shall extend downward to a level at least even with the deflectors of pendent sprinklers.

12.1.7.4 Residential sidewall sprinklers shall be permitted to be installed on opposing or adjacent walls, provided no sprinkler is located within the maximum protection area of another sprinkler or unless separated by baffles that comply with the following:

(1) Baffles shall be arranged to protect the actuating elements.
(2) Baffles shall be of solid and rigid material that will stay in place before and during sprinkler operation.
(3) Baffles shall be not less than 8 in. (200 mm) long and 6 in. (150 mm) high.
(4) The tops of baffles shall extend between 2 in. and 3 in. (50 mm and 75 mm) above the deflectors.
(5) The bottoms of baffles shall extend downward to a level at least even with the deflectors.

12.1.7.5 The maximum distance shall be measured along the slope of the ceiling as shown in Figure 12.1.7.5(a) and Figure 12.1.7.5(b), and the maximum vertical distance from the peak shall be no more than 3 ft (900 mm).

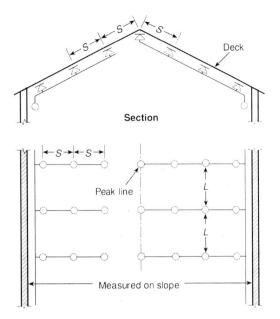

FIGURE 12.1.7.5(a)   Maximum Distance Between Sprinklers with Sloped Ceilings — Arrangement A.

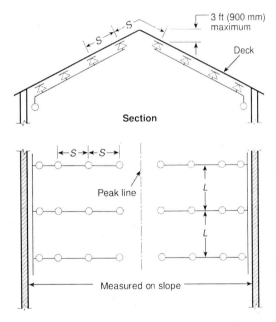

FIGURE 12.1.7.5(b)   Maximum Distance Between Sprinklers with Sloped Ceilings — Arrangement B.

Δ **12.1.7.6** Where sprinklers are installed along sloped ceilings, a sprinkler shall be installed within 3 ft (900 mm) of the peak and the sprinklers shall maintain the minimum listed spacing, but no less than 8 ft (2.4 m), measured in the plan view from one sprinkler to another as shown in Figure 12.1.7.6 unless separated by baffles that comply with the following:

(1)   Baffles shall be arranged to protect the actuating elements.

(2)   Baffles shall be of solid and rigid material that will stay in place before and during sprinkler operation.
(3)   Baffles shall be not less than 8 in. (200 mm) long and 6 in. (150 mm) high.
(4)   The tops of baffles shall extend between 2 in. (50 mm) and 3 in. (75 mm) above the deflectors of upright sprinklers.
(5)   The bottoms of baffles shall extend downward to a level at least even with the deflectors of pendent sprinklers.

12.1.8 Deflector Position from Ceilings and Walls.

12.1.8.1 Pendent and upright sprinklers shall be positioned so that the deflectors are 1 in. to 4 in. (25 mm to 100 mm) from the ceiling unless the listing allows a greater distance.

12.1.8.1.1 Pendent and upright sprinklers installed under beamed or beamed and sloped ceilings shall be permitted to be installed where all of the following apply:

(1)   Maximum beam depth of 14 in. (350 mm)
(2)   Maximum ceiling height of 24 ft (7.3 m)
(3)   Maximum ceiling slope of 8 in 12
(4)   Maximum compartment size of 600 ft² (56 m²)

12.1.8.1.2 Pendent-type residential sprinklers located under or adjacent to beams shall be installed in accordance with one of the following:

(1)   Pendent, recessed pendent, concealed, and flush-type pendent sprinklers shall be permitted to be installed directly under a beam having a maximum depth of 14 in. (350 mm) with the sprinkler deflector 1 in. to 2 in. (25 mm to 50 mm) below the beam, or in accordance with the manufacturer's instructions for recessed or flush sprinklers if the deflector is less than 1 in. (25 mm) below the beam, as shown in Figure 12.1.8.1.2(a).
(2)   Pendent sprinklers shall be permitted to be installed adjacent to beams where the vertical centerline of the sprinkler is no greater than 2 in. (50 mm) from the edge of the beam and with the sprinkler deflector 1 in. to 2 in. (25 mm to 50 mm) below the beam, or in accordance with the manufacturer's instructions for flush sprinklers if the deflector is less than 1 in. (25 mm) below the beam, as shown in Figure 12.1.8.1.2(b).

12.1.8.1.3 The highest sprinkler in the compartment shall be above all openings from the compartment into any communicated spaces.

12.1.8.2 Sidewall sprinklers shall be positioned so that the deflectors are within 4 in. to 6 in. (100 mm to 150 mm) from the ceiling unless the listing allows greater distances.

12.1.8.3 Where soffits used for the installation of sidewall sprinklers exceed 8 in. (200 mm) in width or projection from the wall, additional sprinklers shall be installed below the soffit.

12.1.8.4 Residential horizontal sidewall sprinkler deflectors shall be located no more than 6 in. (150 mm) from the wall on which they are mounted unless listed for greater distances.

12.1.8.5 The distance from sprinklers to the end walls shall not exceed one-half of the allowable distance permitted between sprinklers as indicated in the sprinkler listing.

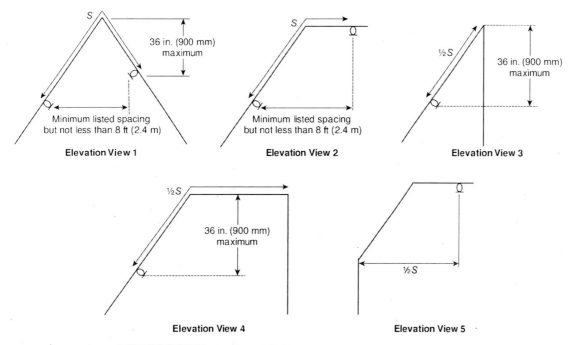

△ FIGURE 12.1.7.6   Sprinkler Spacing with Sloped Ceilings.

12.1.8.6 Minimum Distance from Walls.

12.1.8.6.1 Sprinklers shall be located a minimum of 4 in. (100 mm) from an end wall.

12.1.8.7 Deflector Orientation (Residential Upright and Pendent Spray).

12.1.8.7.1 Unless the requirements of 12.1.8.7.2 or 12.1.8.7.3 are met, deflectors of upright and pendent sprinklers shall be aligned parallel to ceilings, roofs, or the incline of stairs.

12.1.8.7.2 Where upright or pendent sprinklers are installed at the peak below a sloped ceiling or roof surface, the sprinkler shall be installed with the deflector horizontal.

12.1.8.7.3 Roofs and ceilings having a pitch not exceeding 2 in 12 (16.7 percent) are considered horizontal in the application of 12.1.8.7, and upright and pendent sprinklers shall be permitted to be installed with deflectors horizontal.

12.1.9 Residential sprinklers installed in conformance with this standard shall follow the sprinkler obstruction rules of 12.1.10 or 12.1.11 as appropriate for their installation orientation (upright, pendent, or sidewall) and the obstruction criteria specified in the manufacturer's installation instructions.

12.1.10 Obstructions to Sprinkler Discharge (Residential Upright and Pendent Spray Sprinklers).

12.1.10.1 Performance Objective.

12.1.10.1.1 Sprinklers shall be located so as to minimize obstructions to discharge as defined in 12.1.10.2 and 12.1.10.3, or additional sprinklers shall be provided to ensure adequate coverage of the hazard.

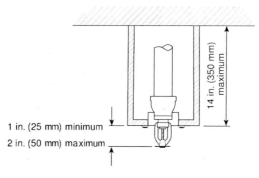

FIGURE 12.1.8.1.2(a)   Position of Sprinkler Under Beam.

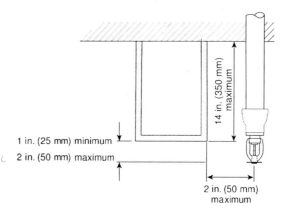

FIGURE 12.1.8.1.2(b)   Position of Sprinkler Adjacent to Beam.

12.1.10.1.2 Sprinklers shall be arranged to comply with one of the following arrangements:

(1) Sprinklers shall be in accordance with 9.5.5.2, Table 12.1.10.1.2(a) or Table 12.1.10.1.2(b), and Figure 12.1.10.1.2(a).

(2) Sprinklers shall be permitted to be spaced on opposite sides of obstructions not exceeding 4 ft (1.2 m) in width, provided the distance from the centerline of the obstruction to the sprinklers does not exceed one-half the allowable distance permitted between sprinklers.

(3) Obstructions located against the wall and that are not over 30 in. (750 mm) in width shall be permitted to be protected in accordance with Figure 12.1.10.1.2(b).

(4) Obstructions that are located against the wall and that are not over 24 in. (600 mm) in width shall be permitted to be protected in accordance with Figure 12.1.10.1.2(c). The maximum distance between the sprinkler and the wall shall be measured from the sprinkler to the wall behind the obstruction and not to the face of the obstruction.

(5) Obstructions 12 in. (300 mm) in width in hallways up to 6 ft (1.8 m) in width shall be permitted in accordance with Figure 12.1.10.1.2(d) when the sprinkler is located in the allowable obstruction zone and the closest edge of the obstruction is a minimum of 12 in. (300 mm) away from the centerline of the sprinkler.

12.1.10.2 Obstructions to Sprinkler Discharge Pattern Development.

12.1.10.2.1 General.

12.1.10.2.1.1 Continuous or noncontinuous obstructions less than or equal to 18 in. (450 mm) below the sprinkler deflector that prevent the pattern from fully developing shall comply with 12.1.10.2.

12.1.10.2.1.2 Regardless of the rules of this section, solid continuous obstructions shall meet the applicable requirements of 12.1.10.1.2.

N **Table 12.1.10.1.2(a) Positioning of Sprinklers to Avoid Obstructions to Discharge (Residential Upright and Pendent Sprinklers)**

Distance from Sprinkler to Side of Obstruction (A) (ft)	Allowable Distance of Deflector Above Bottom of Obstruction (B) (in.)
Less than 1½	0
1½ or more	1 or less
3 or more	3 or less
4 or more	5 or less
4½ or more	7 or less
6 or more	9 or less
6½ or more	11 or less
7 or more	14 or less
8 or more	15 or less
8½ or more	17 or less
9 or more	19 or less

Note: For A and B, refer to Figure 12.1.10.1.2(a).

N **Table 12.1.10.1.2(b) Positioning of Sprinklers to Avoid Obstructions to Discharge (Residential Upright and Pendent Sprinklers)**

Distance from Sprinkler to Side of Obstruction (A) (mm)	Allowable Distance of Deflector Above Bottom of Obstruction (B) (mm)
Less than 450	0
450 or more	25 or less
900 or more	75 or less
1200 or more	125 or less
1400 or more	175 or less
1800 or more	225 or less
2000 or more	275 or less
2100 or more	350 or less
2400 or more	375 or less
2600 or more	425 or less
2700 or more	475 or less

Note: For A and B, refer to Figure 12.1.10.1.2(a).

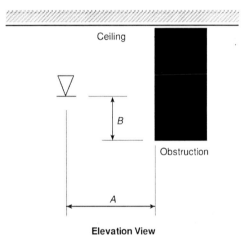

Elevation View

FIGURE 12.1.10.1.2(a)   Positioning of Sprinkler to Avoid Obstruction to Discharge (Residential Upright and Pendent Spray Sprinklers).

12.1.10.2.1.3* Unless the requirements of 12.1.10.2.1.4 through 12.1.10.2.1.8 are met, sprinklers shall be positioned away from obstructions a minimum distance of four times the maximum dimension of the obstruction (e.g., truss webs and chords, pipe, columns, and fixtures) in accordance with Figure 12.1.10.2.1.3(a) and Figure 12.1.10.2.1.3(b).

(A) The maximum clear distance required to obstructions in the horizontal orientation (e.g., light fixture and truss chords) shall be 36 in. (900 mm).

(B) The maximum clear distance shall not be applied to obstructions in the vertical orientation (e.g., columns).

12.1.10.2.1.4 Sprinklers shall be permitted to be spaced on opposite sides of the obstruction where the distance from the centerline of the obstruction to the sprinklers does not exceed one-half the allowable distance between sprinklers.

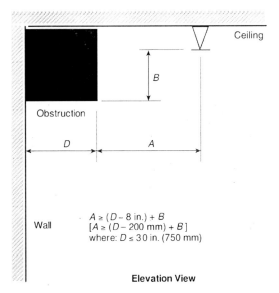

$A \geq (D - 8 \text{ in.}) + B$
$[A \geq (D - 200 \text{ mm}) + B]$
where: $D \leq 30$ in. (750 mm)

Elevation View

FIGURE 12.1.10.1.2(b)   Obstructions Against Wall (Residential Upright and Pendent Spray Sprinklers).

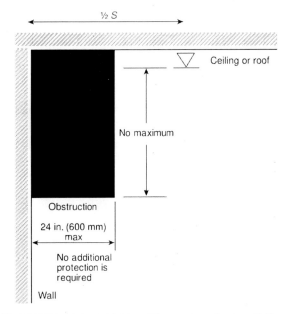

Δ **FIGURE 12.1.10.1.2(c)   Obstructions Against Wall (Measurements for Residential Upright and Pendent Spray Sprinklers).**

12.1.10.2.1.5 Sprinklers shall be permitted to be located one-half the distance between the obstructions where the obstruction consists of open trusses 20 in. (500 mm) or greater apart [24 in. (600 mm) on center], provided that all truss members are not greater than 4 in. (100 mm) (nominal) in width and web members do not exceed 1 in. (25 mm) in width.

12.1.10.2.1.6 Sprinklers shall be permitted to be installed on the centerline of a truss or bar joist or directly above a beam provided that the truss chord or beam dimension is not more than 8 in. (200 mm) and the sprinkler deflector is located at

least 6 in. (150 mm) above the structural member and where the sprinkler is positioned at a distance four times greater than the maximum dimension of the web members away from the web members.

12.1.10.2.1.7 The requirements of 12.1.10.2.1.3 shall not apply to sprinkler system piping less than 3 in. (80 mm) in diameter.

12.1.10.2.1.8 The requirements of 12.1.10.2.1.3 shall not apply to sprinklers positioned with respect to obstructions in accordance with 12.1.10.1.2.

12.1.10.2.1.9* Sprinklers shall be permitted to be placed without regard to the blades of a ceiling fan, provided the plan view of the fan is at least 50 percent open.

12.1.10.2.2 Suspended or Floor-Mounted Vertical Obstructions. The distance from sprinklers to privacy curtains, free-standing partitions, room dividers, and similar obstructions shall be in accordance with Table 12.1.10.2.2(a) or Table 12.1.10.2.2(b) and Figure 12.1.10.2.2.

Δ **12.1.10.2.3*** **Shadow Areas.** Shadow areas created by walls and partitions shall be permitted in the protection area of a sprinkler as long as the cumulative areas do not exceed 15 ft² (1.4 m²) per sprinkler.

12.1.10.3* **Obstructions that Prevent Sprinkler Discharge from Reaching Hazard.**

12.1.10.3.1 Continuous or noncontinuous obstructions that interrupt the water discharge in a horizontal plane more than 18 in. (450 mm) below the sprinkler deflector in a manner to limit the distribution from reaching the protected hazard shall comply with 12.1.10.3.

12.1.10.3.2 Sprinklers shall be installed under fixed obstructions over 4 ft (1.2 m) wide.

12.1.10.3.3 Sprinklers installed under open gratings shall be shielded from the discharge of overhead sprinklers.

12.1.11 Obstructions to Sprinkler Discharge (Residential Sidewall Spray Sprinklers).

12.1.11.1 Performance Objective.

12.1.11.1.1 Sprinklers shall be located so as to minimize obstructions to discharge as defined in 9.5.5.2 and 9.5.5.3, or additional sprinklers shall be provided to ensure adequate coverage of the hazard.

12.1.11.1.2 Sidewall sprinklers shall not be installed less than 8 ft (2.4 m) from light fixtures or similar obstructions unless the requirements of 12.1.11.1.2.1 or 12.1.11.1.2.2 are met.

12.1.11.1.2.1 For obstructions such as light fixtures, where the greatest dimension of the obstruction is less than 2 ft (0.6 m), sidewall sprinklers shall be permitted to be installed at a minimum distance of four times the greatest dimension.

12.1.11.1.2.2 For obstructions located at least 4 in. (100 mm) above the plane of the sprinkler deflector, the sprinkler shall be permitted to be located less than 8 ft (2.4 m) from the obstruction.

12.1.11.1.3 The distance between light fixtures or similar obstructions located 8 ft (2.4 m) or greater from the sprinkler shall be in conformance with Table 12.1.11.1.3(a) or Table 12.1.11.1.3(b) and Figure 12.1.11.1.3.

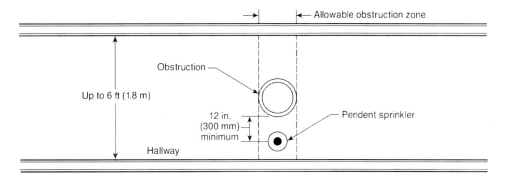

N **FIGURE 12.1.10.1.2(d)   Obstruction in Hallway.**

12.1.11.1.4 Continuous obstructions projecting from the same wall as the one on which the sidewall sprinkler is mounted shall be in accordance with one of the following arrangements:

(1) Sprinklers shall be in accordance with Table 12.1.11.1.4(a) or Table 12.1.11.1.4(b) and Figure 12.1.11.1.4(a).

(2) Sprinklers shall be permitted to be spaced on opposite sides of obstructions less than 4 ft (1.2 m) in width where the distance from the centerline of the obstruction to the sprinklers does not exceed one-half the allowable distance between sprinklers.

(3) Obstructions located against the wall and that are not over 30 in. (750 mm) in width shall be permitted to be protected in accordance with Figure 12.1.11.1.4(b).

(4) Obstructions located against the wall and that are not over 24 in. (600 mm) in width shall be permitted to be protected in accordance with Figure 12.1.11.1.4(c). The maximum distance between the sprinkler and the wall shall be measured from the sprinkler to the wall behind the obstruction and not to the face of the obstruction.

(5) Obstructions 12 in. (300 mm) in width in hallways up to 6 ft (1.8 m) in width shall be permitted in accordance with Figure 12.1.11.1.4(d) when the sprinkler is located in the allowable obstruction zone and the closest edge of the obstruction is a minimum of 12 in. (300 mm) away from the deflector.

12.1.11.1.5* Soffits and Cabinets. Where soffits are used for the installation of sidewall sprinklers, the sprinklers and soffits shall be installed in accordance with 12.1.11.1.5.1, 12.1.11.1.5.2, or 12.1.11.1.5.3.

12.1.11.1.5.1 Where soffits exceed more than 8 in. (200 mm) in width or projection from the wall, pendent sprinklers shall be installed under the soffit.

12.1.11.1.5.2 Sidewall sprinklers shall be permitted to be installed in the face of a soffit located directly over cabinets, without requiring additional sprinklers below the soffit or cabinets, where the soffit does not project horizontally more than 12 in. (300 mm) from the wall.

12.1.11.1.5.3 Where sidewall sprinklers are more than 3 ft (900 mm) above the top of cabinets, the sprinkler shall be permitted to be installed on the wall above the cabinets where the cabinets are no greater than 12 in. (300 mm) from the wall.

12.1.11.1.6 Obstructions on the wall opposite from the sidewall sprinkler shall be permitted in accordance with Figure 12.1.11.1.6.

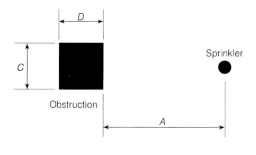

Plan View of Column
(Obstruction in vertical orientation)

$A \geq 4C$ or $4D$
(Use dimension C or D, whichever is greater)

FIGURE 12.1.10.2.1.3(a)   Minimum Distance from an Obstruction in the Vertical Orientation (Residential Upright and Pendent Spray Sprinkler).

12.1.11.2 Obstructions to Sprinkler Discharge Pattern Development.

12.1.11.2.1 General.

12.1.11.2.1.1 Continuous or noncontinuous obstructions less than or equal to 18 in. (450 mm) below the sprinkler deflector that prevent the pattern from fully developing shall comply with this section.

12.1.11.2.1.2 Regardless of the rules of this section, solid continuous obstructions shall meet the requirements of 12.1.11.1.2 and 12.1.11.1.3.

12.1.11.2.1.3* Unless the requirements of 12.1.11.2.1.4 through 12.1.11.2.1.7 are met, sprinklers shall be positioned away from obstructions a minimum distance of four times the maximum dimension of the obstruction (e.g., truss webs and chords, pipe, columns, and fixtures).

(A) The maximum clear distance required from obstructions in the horizontal orientation (e.g., light fixtures and truss chords) shall be 36 in. (900 mm).

(B) The maximum clear distance shall not be applied to obstructions in the vertical orientation (e.g., columns).

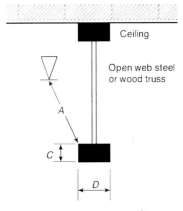

Elevation View of Truss
(Obstruction in horizontal orientation)

$A \geq 4\,C$ or $4D$
$A \leq 36$ in. (900 mm)
(Use dimension C or D, whichever is greater)

FIGURE 12.1.10.2.1.3(b) Minimum Distance from an Obstruction in the Horizontal Orientation (Residential Upright and Pendent Spray Sprinkler).

N Table 12.1.10.2.2(a) Suspended or Floor-Mounted Obstructions in Light Hazard Occupancies Only (Residential Upright and Pendent Sprinklers)

Horizontal Distance *(A)* (in.)	Minimum Vertical Distance Below Deflector *(B)* (in.)
6 or less	3 or more
9 or less	4 or more
12 or less	6 or more
15 or less	8 or more
18 or less	9½ or more
24 or less	12½ or more
30 or less	15½ or more
More than 30	18 or more

Note: For *A* and *B*, refer to Figure 12.1.10.2.2.

N Table 12.1.10.2.2(b) Suspended or Floor-Mounted Obstructions in Light Hazard Occupancies Only (Residential Upright and Pendent Sprinklers)

Horizontal Distance *(A)* (mm)	Minimum Vertical Distance Below Deflector *(B)* (mm)
150 or less	75 or more
225 or less	100 or more
300 or less	150 or more
375 or less	200 or more
450 or less	240 or more
600 or less	315 or more
750 or less	390 or more
More than 750	450 or more

Note: For *A* and *B*, refer to Figure 12.1.10.2.2.

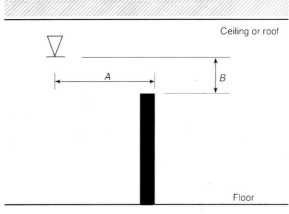

Elevation View

FIGURE 12.1.10.2.2 Suspended or Floor-Mounted Obstruction (Residential Upright and Pendent Spray Sprinklers).

N Table 12.1.11.1.3(a) Positioning of Sprinklers to Avoid Obstructions to Discharge (Residential Sidewall)

Distance from Sprinkler to Side of Obstruction *(A)* (ft)	Allowable Distance of Deflector Above Bottom of Obstruction *(B)* (in.)
Less than 8	0
8 or more	1 or less
10 or more	2 or less
11 or more	3 or less
12 or more	4 or less
13 or more	6 or less
14 or more	7 or less
15 or more	9 or less
16 or more	11 or less
17 or more	14 or less

Note: For *A* and *B*, refer to Figure 12.1.11.1.3.

N Table 12.1.11.1.3(b) Positioning of Sprinklers to Avoid Obstructions to Discharge (Residential Sidewall)

Distance from Sprinkler to Side of Obstruction *(A)* (mm)	Allowable Distance of Deflector Above Bottom of Obstruction *(B)* (mm)
Less than 2400	0
2400 or more	1 or less
3000 or more	50 or less
3400 or more	75 or less
3700 or more	100 or less
4000 or more	150 or less
4300 or more	175 or less
4600 or more	225 or less
4900 or more	275 or less
5200 or more	350 or less

Note: For *A* and *B*, refer to Figure 12.1.11.1.3.

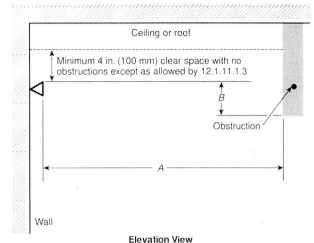

Δ FIGURE 12.1.11.1.3 Positioning of Sprinkler to Avoid Obstruction (Residential Sidewall Sprinklers).

N Table 12.1.11.1.4(a) Positioning of Sprinklers to Avoid Obstructions Along Wall (Residential Sidewall)

Distance from Sprinkler to Side of Obstruction (A) (ft)	Allowable Distance of Deflector Above Bottom of Obstruction (B) (in.)
Less than 1½	0
1½ or more	1 or less
3 or more	3 or less
4 or more	5 or less
4½ or more	7 or less
6 or more	9 or less
6½ or more	11 or less
7 or more	14 or less

Note: For A and B, refer to Figure 12.1.11.1.4(a).

N Table 12.1.11.1.4(b) Positioning of Sprinklers to Avoid Obstructions Along Wall (Residential Sidewall)

Distance from Sprinkler to Side of Obstruction (A) (mm)	Allowable Distance of Deflector Above Bottom of Obstruction (B) (mm)
Less than 450	0
450 or more	25 or less
900 or more	75 or less
1200 or more	125 or less
1400 or more	175 or less
1800 or more	225 or less
2000 or more	275 or less
2100 or more	350 or less

Note: For A and B, refer to Figure 12.1.11.4(a).

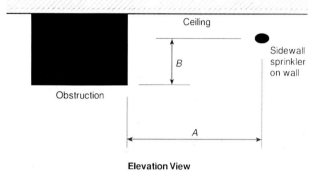

FIGURE 12.1.11.1.4(a) Positioning of Sprinkler to Avoid Obstruction Along Wall (Residential Sidewall Sprinklers).

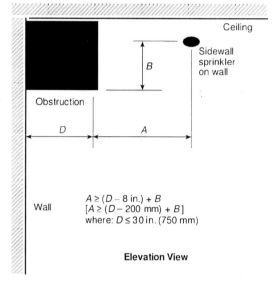

$A \geq (D - 8 \text{ in.}) + B$
$[A \geq (D - 200 \text{ mm}) + B]$
where: $D \leq 30$ in. (750 mm)

Δ FIGURE 12.1.11.1.4(b) Obstruction Against Wall (Residential Sidewall Spray Sprinklers).

12.1.11.2.1.4 Sidewall sprinklers shall be positioned in accordance with Figure 12.1.11.2.1.4(a) and Figure 12.1.11.2.1.4(b) when obstructions are present.

12.1.11.2.1.5 The requirements of 12.1.11.2.1.3 and 12.1.11.2.1.4 shall not apply where sprinklers are positioned with respect to obstructions in accordance with 12.1.11.1.2 and 12.1.11.1.3.

12.1.11.2.1.6 The requirements of 12.1.11.2.1.3 shall not apply to sprinkler system piping less than 3 in. (80 mm) in diameter.

12.1.11.2.1.7* Sprinklers shall be permitted to be placed without regard to the blades of a ceiling fan, provided the plan view of the fan is at least 50 percent open.

12.1.11.2.2* Suspended or Floor-Mounted Vertical Obstructions. The distance from sprinklers to privacy curtains, freestanding partitions, room dividers, and similar obstructions shall be in accordance with Table 12.1.11.2.2(a) or Table 12.1.11.2.2(b), Figure 12.1.11.2.2(a), and Figure 12.1.11.2.2(b).

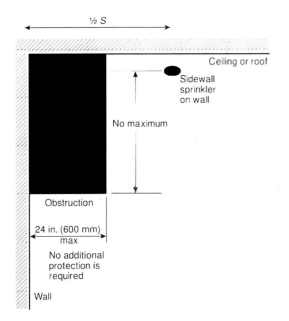

FIGURE 12.1.11.1.4(c)   Obstruction Against Wall (Residential Sidewall Spray Sprinklers).

Δ **12.1.11.3* Obstructions that Prevent Sprinkler Discharge from Reaching Hazard.**

12.1.11.3.1 Continuous or noncontinuous obstructions that interrupt the water discharge in a horizontal plane more than 18 in. (450 mm) below the sprinkler deflector in a manner to limit the distribution from reaching the protected hazard shall comply with this section.

12.1.11.3.2* Sprinklers shall be installed under fixed obstructions over 4 ft (1.2 m) wide.

12.1.11.3.3 Sprinklers installed under open gratings shall be shielded from the discharge of overhead sprinklers.

12.1.11.3.4 The deflector of automatic sprinklers installed under fixed obstructions shall be positioned below the bottom of the obstruction in accordance with their listed distance below ceilings.

12.1.11.3.5 Sprinklers installed under round ducts shall be shielded from the discharge of overhead sprinklers.

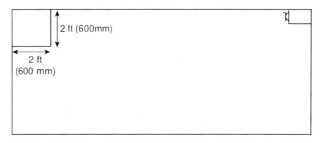

N **FIGURE 12.1.11.1.6   Permitted Obstruction on Wall Opposite Residential Sidewall Sprinkler.**

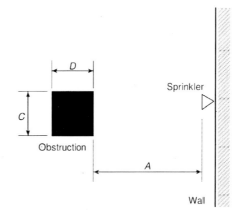

Plan View of Column
(Obstruction in vertical orientation)

$A \geq 4C$ or $4D$
(Use dimension C or D, whichever is greater)

FIGURE 12.1.11.2.1.4(a)   Minimum Distance from an Obstruction in the Vertical Orientation (Residential Sidewall Sprinkler).

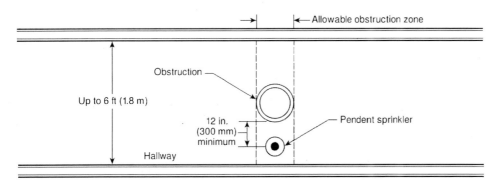

N **FIGURE 12.1.11.1.4(d)   Obstruction in Hallway (Residential Sidewall Spray Sprinklers).**

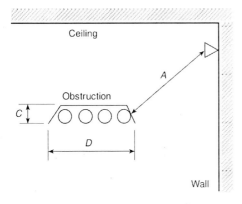

Elevation View of Pipe Conduit or Light Fixture
(Obstruction in horizontal orientation)
$A \geq 4C$ or $4D$
$A \leq 36$ in. (900 mm)
(Use dimension C or D, whichever is greater)

FIGURE 12.1.11.2.1.4(b)   Minimum Distance from an Obstruction in the Horizontal Orientation (Residential Sidewall Sprinkler).

N **Table 12.1.11.2.2(a) Suspended or Floor-Mounted Obstructions (Residential Sidewall Sprinklers)**

Horizontal Distance (A) (in.)	Minimum Vertical Distance Below Deflector (B) (in.)
6 or less	3 or more
9 or less	4 or more
12 or less	6 or more
15 or less	8 or more
18 or less	9½ or more
24 or less	12½ or more
30 or less	15½ or more
More than 30	18 or more

Note: For A and B, refer to Figure 12.1.11.2.2(a).

N **Table 12.1.11.2.2(b) Suspended or Floor-Mounted Obstructions (Residential Sidewall Sprinklers)**

Horizontal Distance (A) (mm)	Minimum Vertical Distance Below Deflector (B) (mm)
150 or less	75 or more
225 or less	100 or more
300 or less	150 or more
375 or less	200 or more
450 or less	240 or more
600 or less	315 or more
750 or less	390 or more
More than 750	450 or more

Note: For A and B, refer to Figure 12.1.11.2.2(a).

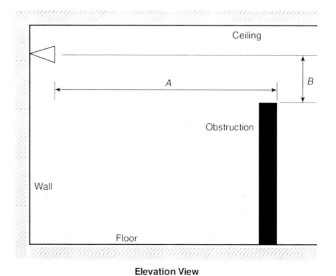

Elevation View

FIGURE 12.1.11.2.2(a)   Suspended or Floor-Mounted Obstruction (Residential Sidewall Sprinklers).

12.1.12 Ceiling Pockets.

12.1.12.1 Sprinklers shall be required in all ceiling pockets.

12.1.12.2 The requirement of 12.1.12.1 shall not apply where all of the following requirements are met:

(1) The total volume of the unprotected ceiling pocket does not exceed 100 ft³ (2.8 m³).
(2) The depth of the unprotected ceiling pocket does not exceed 12 in. (300 mm).
(3) The entire floor area under the unprotected ceiling pocket is protected by listed residential sprinklers at the lower ceiling elevation.
(4) The interior finish of the unprotected ceiling pocket is noncombustible or limited-combustible construction.

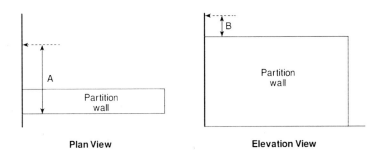

Plan View   **Elevation View**

FIGURE 12.1.11.2.2(b)   Suspended or Floor-Mounted Obstructions (Residential Sprinklers).

Chapter 13   Installation Requirements for CMSA Sprinklers

13.1 General. Control mode specific application (CMSA) sprinklers shall be selected for use and installation as indicated in this chapter and shall be positioned and spaced in accordance with Section 9.5.

13.2 CMSA Sprinklers.

13.2.1 General. All requirements of Section 9.5 shall apply to CMSA sprinklers except as modified in Section 13.2.

13.2.1.1 CMSA pendent sprinklers shall be installed in accordance with Section 9.5 and the manufacturer's installation instructions in lieu of the requirements in Section 13.2.

13.2.2 CMSA sprinklers shall be permitted to be used in wet, dry, or preaction systems and shall be installed in accordance with their listing.

13.2.3 Temperature Ratings.

13.2.3.1 Unless the requirements of 13.2.3.2, 13.2.3.3, or 13.2.3.4 are met, sprinkler temperature ratings shall be the same as those indicated in Table 9.4.2.5(a) and Table 9.4.2.5(b) or those used in large-scale fire testing to determine the protection requirements for the hazard involved.

13.2.3.2 Sprinklers of intermediate- and high-temperature ratings shall be installed in specific locations as required by 9.4.2.

13.2.3.3 In storage occupancies, ordinary, intermediate, or high temperature–rated sprinklers shall be used for wet pipe systems.

13.2.3.4 In storage occupancies, high temperature–rated sprinklers shall be used for dry pipe systems.

13.2.4 Occupancy and Hazard.

13.2.4.1 Quick-response CMSA sprinklers designed to meet any criteria in Chapter 12 through Chapter 20 shall be permitted to protect light and ordinary hazard occupancies.

13.2.4.2 Standard-response CMSA sprinklers designed to meet any criteria in Chapter 12 through Chapter 20 shall be permitted to protect ordinary hazard occupancies.

13.2.5* Protection Areas per Sprinkler (CMSA Sprinklers).

13.2.5.1 Determination of Protection Area of Coverage. The protection area of coverage per sprinkler (A_s) shall be determined in accordance with 9.5.2.1.

13.2.5.2 Maximum Protection Area of Coverage.

13.2.5.2.1 The maximum allowable protection area of coverage for a sprinkler (A_s) shall be in accordance with the value indicated in Table 13.2.5.2.1.

13.2.5.2.2 In any case, the maximum area of coverage of any sprinkler shall not exceed 130 ft^2 (12 m^2).

13.2.5.3 Minimum Protection Area of Coverage. The minimum allowable protection area of coverage for a sprinkler (A_s) shall be not less than 80 ft^2 (7.4 m^2).

Table 13.2.5.2.1 Protection Areas and Maximum Spacing for CMSA Sprinklers

Construction Type	Protection Area		Maximum Spacing	
	ft^2	m^2	ft	m
Noncombustible unobstructed	130	12	12	3.7
Noncombustible obstructed	130	12	12	3.7
Combustible unobstructed	130	12	12	3.7
Combustible obstructed	100	9	10	3.0
Rack storage combustible obstructed	100	9	10	3.0
Rack storage unobstructed and noncombustible obstructed	100	9	12	3.7

13.2.6 Sprinkler Spacing (CMSA Sprinklers).

13.2.6.1* Maximum Distance Between Sprinklers.

13.2.6.1.1 Under unobstructed and obstructed noncombustible construction and unobstructed combustible construction, the distance between sprinklers shall be limited to not more than 12 ft (3.7 m) between sprinklers, as shown in Table 13.2.5.2.1.

13.2.6.1.2 Under obstructed combustible construction, the maximum distance shall be limited to 10 ft (3 m).

13.2.6.2 Maximum Distance from Walls. The distance from sprinklers to walls shall not exceed one-half of the allowable distance permitted between sprinklers as indicated in Table 13.2.5.2.1.

13.2.6.3 Minimum Distance from Walls. Sprinklers shall be located a minimum of 4 in. (100 mm) from a wall.

13.2.6.4 Minimum Distance Between Sprinklers. Sprinklers shall be spaced not less than 8 ft (2.4 m) on center.

N **13.2.6.4.1** Sprinklers shall be permitted to be placed less than 8 ft (2.4 m) on center where the following conditions are satisfied:

(1)   Baffles shall comply with the criteria in 13.2.8.1.2.
(2)   Baffles shall be solid and rigid material that will stay in place before and during sprinkler operation.
(3)   Baffles shall be not less than 8 in. (200 mm) long and 6 in. (150 mm) high.
(4)   The tops of baffles shall extend between 2 in. (50 mm) and 3 in. (75 mm) above the deflectors of upright sprinklers.
(5)   The bottoms of baffles shall extend downward to a level at least even with the deflectors of pendent sprinklers.

13.2.7 Deflector Position (CMSA Sprinklers).

13.2.7.1* Distance Below Ceilings.

13.2.7.1.1 Unobstructed Construction. Under unobstructed construction, the distance between the sprinkler deflector and the ceiling shall be a minimum of 6 in. (150 mm) and a maximum of 8 in. (200 mm).

13.2.7.1.2 Obstructed Construction. Under obstructed construction, the sprinkler deflector shall be located in accordance with one of the following arrangements:

(1) Installed with the deflectors located a minimum of 6 in. (150 mm) and a maximum of 12 in. (300 mm) from the ceiling.

(2) Installed with the deflectors within the horizontal planes 1 in. to 6 in. (25 mm to 150 mm) below wood joist, composite wood joist, solid obstructed noncombustible, or solid obstructed limited combustible construction, to a maximum distance of 22 in. (550 mm) below the ceiling/roof or deck. Where CMSA sprinklers are installed under open wood joist construction, their minimum operating pressure shall be 50 psi (3.4 bar) for a K-11.2 (160) sprinkler or 22 psi (1.5 bar) for a K-16.8 (240) sprinkler in accordance with 22.1.5.1.

(3) Installed with deflectors of sprinklers under concrete tee construction with stems spaced less than 7 ft 6 in. (2.3 m) but more than 3 ft (900 mm) on centers, regardless of the depth of the tee, located at or above a horizontal plane 1 in. (25 mm) below the bottom of the stems of the tees and in compliance with Table 13.2.8.1.2(a) or Table 13.2.8.1.2(b).

13.2.8* Obstructions to Sprinkler Discharge (CMSA Sprinklers).

13.2.8.1 Performance Objective.

13.2.8.1.1 Sprinklers shall be located so as to minimize obstructions to discharge as defined in 9.5.5.2 and 9.5.5.3, or additional sprinklers shall be provided to ensure adequate coverage of the hazard.

13.2.8.1.2 Sprinklers shall be arranged to comply with 9.5.5.2, Table 13.2.8.1.2(a) or Table 13.2.8.1.2(b), and Figure 13.2.8.1.2.

Table 13.2.8.1.2(a) Positioning of Sprinklers to Avoid Obstructions to Discharge (CMSA Sprinklers)

Distance from Sprinkler to Side of Obstruction (A) (ft)	Allowable Distance of Deflector Above Bottom of Obstruction (B) (in.)
Less than 1	0
1 or more	1½ or less
1½ or more	3 or less
2 ft or more	5½ or less
2½ or more	8 or less
3 or more	10 or less
3½ or more	12 or less
4 or more	15 or less
4½ or more	18 or less
5 or more	22 or less
5½ or more	26 or less
6 or more	31 or less

Note: For A and B, refer to Figure 13.2.8.1.2.

Table 13.2.8.1.2(b) Positioning of Sprinklers to Avoid Obstructions to Discharge (CMSA Sprinklers)

Distance from Sprinkler to Side of Obstruction (A) (mm)	Allowable Distance of Deflector Above Bottom of Obstruction (B) (mm)
Less than 300	0
300 or more	40 or less
450 or more	75 or less
600 or more	140 or less
750 or more	200 or less
900 or more	250 or less
1100 or more	300 or less
1200 or more	375 or less
1400 or more	450 or less
1500 or more	550 or less
1700 or more	650 or less
1800 or more	775 or less

Note: For A and B, refer to Figure 13.2.8.1.2.

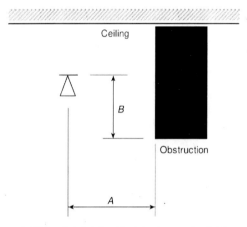

FIGURE 13.2.8.1.2 Positioning of Sprinkler to Avoid Obstruction to Discharge (CMSA Sprinklers).

13.2.8.1.3 The requirements of 13.2.8.1.2 shall not apply where sprinklers are positioned on opposite sides of the obstruction.

13.2.8.2 Obstructions to Sprinkler Discharge Pattern Development.

13.2.8.2.1 General.

13.2.8.2.1.1 Continuous or noncontinuous obstructions less than or equal to 36 in. (900 mm) below the sprinkler deflector that prevent the pattern from fully developing shall comply with 13.2.8.2.

13.2.8.2.1.2 Regardless of the rules of this section, solid continuous obstructions shall meet the requirements of 13.2.8.1.2 or 13.2.8.1.3.

13.2.8.2.1.3* Unless the requirements of 13.2.8.1.2 or 13.2.8.1.3 are met, for obstructions 8 in. (200 mm) or less in width, as shown in Figure 13.2.8.2.1.3, sprinklers shall be positioned such that they are located at least a distance three times greater than the maximum dimension of the obstruction from the sprinkler (e.g., webs and chord members, pipe, columns, and fixtures).

13.2.8.2.2 Branch Lines. Upright sprinklers shall be positioned with respect to branch lines in accordance with one of the following:

(1) Upright sprinklers shall be permitted to be attached directly to branch lines less than or equal to 4 in. (100 mm) nominal in diameter.
(2) Upright sprinklers shall be permitted to be offset horizontally a minimum of 12 in. (300 mm) from the pipe.
(3) Upright sprinklers shall be permitted to be supplied by a riser nipple (sprig) to elevate the sprinkler deflector a minimum of 12 in. (300 mm) from the centerline of any pipe over 4 in. (100 mm) nominal in diameter.

13.2.8.3* Obstructions that Prevent Sprinkler Discharge from Reaching Hazard.

13.2.8.3.1 Continuous or noncontinuous obstructions that interrupt the water discharge in a horizontal plane below the sprinkler deflector in a manner to limit the distribution from reaching the protected hazard shall comply with 13.2.8.3.

13.2.8.3.2 Sprinklers shall be positioned with respect to fluorescent lighting fixtures, ducts, and obstructions more than 24 in. (600 mm) wide and located entirely below the sprinklers so that the minimum horizontal distance from the near side of the obstruction to the center of the sprinkler is not less than the value specified in Table 13.2.8.3.2(a) or Table 13.2.8.3.2(b) and Figure 13.2.8.3.2.

N Table 13.2.8.3.2(a) Obstructions Entirely Below Sprinkler (CMSA Sprinklers)

Distance from Sprinkler to Side of Obstruction (A) (ft)	Allowable Distance of Deflector Above Bottom of Obstruction (B) (in.)
1½ or more	Less than 6
3 or more	Less than 12
4 or more	Less than 18
5 or more	Less than 24
5½ or more	Less than 30
6 or more	Less than 36

Note: For *A* and *B*, refer to Figure 13.2.8.3.2.

N Table 13.2.8.3.2(b) Obstructions Entirely Below Sprinkler (CMSA Sprinklers)

Distance from Sprinkler to Side of Obstruction (A) (mm)	Allowable Distance of Deflector Above Bottom of Obstruction (B) (mm)
450 or more	Less than 150
900 or more	Less than 300
1200 or more	Less than 450
1500 or more	Less than 600
1700 or more	Less than 750
1800 or more	Less than 900

Note: For *A* and *B*, refer to Figure 13.2.8.3.2.

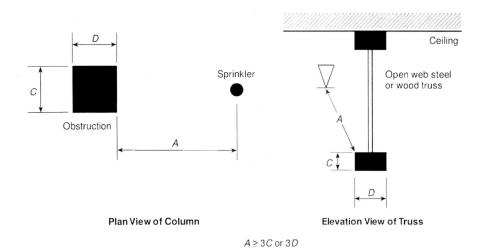

Plan View of Column   **Elevation View of Truss**

$A \geq 3C$ or $3D$
(Use dimension *C* or *D*, whichever is greater)

FIGURE 13.2.8.2.1.3   Minimum Distance from Obstruction (CMSA Sprinklers).

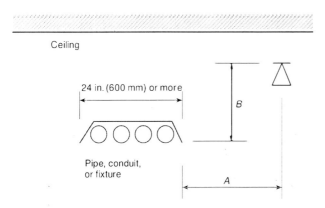

FIGURE 13.2.8.3.2   Obstruction Entirely Below Sprinkler (CMSA Sprinklers).

13.2.8.3.3 Sprinklers installed under open gratings shall be shielded from the discharge of overhead sprinklers.

13.2.8.3.4 Where the bottom of the obstruction is located 24 in. (600 mm) or more below the sprinkler deflectors, the following shall occur:

(1) Sprinklers shall be positioned so that the obstruction is centered between adjacent sprinklers in accordance with Figure 13.2.8.3.4.
(2) The obstruction width shall meet the following requirements:

    (a) The obstruction shall be limited to a maximum width of 24 in. (600 mm) in accordance with Figure 13.2.8.3.4.

(b) Where the obstruction is greater than 24 in. (600 mm) wide, one or more lines of sprinklers shall be installed below the obstruction.

(3) The obstruction extension shall meet the following requirements:

    (a) The obstruction shall not extend more than 12 in. (300 mm) to either side of the midpoint between sprinklers in accordance with Figure 13.2.8.3.4.
    (b) Where the extensions of the obstruction exceed 12 in. (300 mm), one or more lines of sprinklers shall be installed below the obstruction.

(4) At least 18 in. (450 mm) clearance shall be maintained between the top of storage and the bottom of the obstruction in accordance with Figure 13.2.8.3.4.

13.2.8.3.5 In the special case of an obstruction running parallel to or directly below a branch line, the following shall occur:

(1) The sprinkler shall be located at least 36 in. (900 mm) above the top of the obstruction in accordance with Figure 13.2.8.3.5.
(2) The obstruction shall be limited to a maximum width of 12 in. (300 mm) in accordance with Figure 13.2.8.3.5.
(3) The obstruction shall be limited to a maximum extension of 6 in. (150 mm) to either side of the centerline of the branch line in accordance with Figure 13.2.8.3.5.

13.2.9 Clearance to Storage (CMSA Sprinklers). The clearance between the deflector and the top of storage shall be 36 in. (900 mm) or greater.

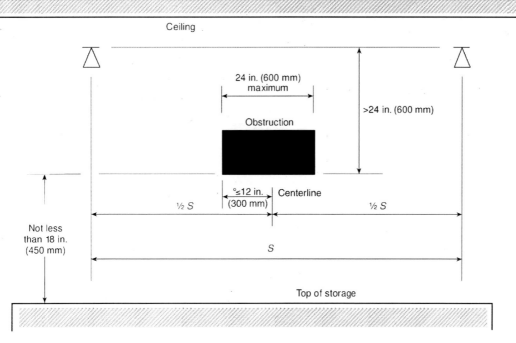

FIGURE 13.2.8.3.4   Obstruction More Than 24 in. (600 mm) Below Sprinklers (CMSA Sprinklers).

Shaded text = Revisions.   Δ = Text deletions and figure/table revisions.   • = Section deletions.   *N* = New material.   2022 Edition

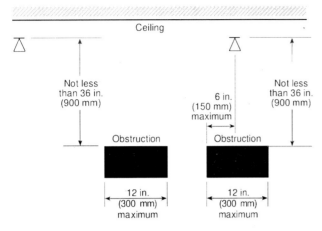

FIGURE 13.2.8.3.5   Obstruction More Than 36 in. (900 mm) Below Sprinklers (CMSA Sprinklers).

Shaded text = Revisions.   Δ = Text deletions and figure/table revisions.   • = Section deletions.   *N* = New material.

Chapter 14 Installation Requirements for Early Suppression Fast-Response Sprinklers

14.1 General. Early suppression fast-response (ESFR) sprinklers shall be selected for use and installation as indicated in this chapter and shall be positioned and spaced in accordance with Section 9.5.

14.2 Early Suppression Fast-Response Sprinklers.

14.2.1 General. All requirements of Section 9.5 shall apply except as modified in Section 14.2.

14.2.2 ESFR sprinklers shall be used only in wet pipe systems unless specifically listed for use in dry systems or preaction systems.

14.2.3 ESFR sprinklers shall be installed only in buildings where roof or ceiling slope above the sprinklers does not exceed a pitch of 2 in 12 (a rise of 2 units in a run of 12 units, a roof slope of 16.7 percent).

14.2.4* ESFR sprinklers shall be permitted for use in buildings with unobstructed or obstructed construction.

14.2.4.1 In buildings with obstructed construction where the depths of the solid structural members (beams, stem, and so forth) exceed 12 in. (300 mm), ESFR sprinklers shall be installed in each channel formed by the solid structural members.

N 14.2.4.2 In buildings with obstructed construction where ESFR sprinklers are installed in accordance with 14.2.4.1, the minimum requirements for sprinkler spacing and area of coverage shall comply with the requirements of 14.2.8 and 14.2.9.

N 14.2.4.3 In buildings with obstructed construction where ESFR sprinklers are installed in accordance with 14.2.4.1 and the sprinklers are located entirely above the bottom plane of the adjacent solid structural members (beams, stem, and so forth), the requirements for minimum sprinkler spacing per 14.2.9.4 shall apply within each channel formed by the solid structural members, but the requirements for minimum sprinkler area spacing per 14.2.8.3 and minimum sprinkler linear spacing per 14.2.9.4 for sprinklers between channels formed by the solid structural members shall not apply.

14.2.4.4 Where sprinklers are not located entirely above the horizontal plane created by any adjacent solid structural member, the minimum sprinkler spacing and area of coverage shall comply with the requirements of 14.2.8 and 14.2.9.

14.2.5 Draft Curtains.

14.2.5.1 Where ESFR sprinkler systems are installed adjacent to sprinkler systems with standard-response sprinklers, a draft curtain of noncombustible construction and at least 2 ft (600 mm) in depth shall be required to separate the two areas.

14.2.5.2 A clear aisle of at least 4 ft (1.2 m) centered below the draft curtain shall be maintained for separation.

Δ 14.2.6 Temperature Ratings. Sprinkler temperature ratings for ESFR sprinklers shall be ordinary or intermediate unless 9.4.2 requires intermediate-temperature ratings.

14.2.7* Occupancy and Hazard. ESFR sprinklers designed to meet any criteria in Chapter 23 or Chapter 24 shall be permitted to protect light and ordinary hazard occupancies.

N 14.2.7.1 When ESFR sprinklers are used for the protection of light or ordinary hazard occupancies, 14.2.7.1.1 through 14.2.7.1.3 shall be permitted.

N 14.2.7.1.1 In light hazard occupancies, the protection area limitations of ESFR sprinklers shall be permitted to meet the protection area requirements of Table 10.2.4.2.1(a).

N 14.2.7.1.2 In light and ordinary hazard occupancies, the sprinkler spacing of ESFR sprinklers shall be permitted to meet the sprinkler spacing requirements of 10.2.5.

N 14.2.7.1.3 In light and ordinary hazard occupancies, the obstruction to the sprinkler discharge pattern of ESFR sprinklers shall be permitted to meet the obstruction discharge requirements of 10.2.7.2.

14.2.8 Protection Areas per Sprinkler (Early Suppression Fast-Response Sprinklers).

14.2.8.1 Determination of Protection Area of Coverage. The protection area of coverage per sprinkler (A_s) shall be determined in accordance with 9.5.2.1.

14.2.8.2 Maximum Protection Area of Coverage.

14.2.8.2.1 The maximum allowable protection area of coverage for a sprinkler (A_s) shall be in accordance with the value indicated in Table 14.2.8.2.1.

14.2.8.2.2 Unless the requirements of 14.2.8.2.3 are met, the maximum area of coverage of any sprinkler shall not exceed 100 ft² (9.3 m²).

Table 14.2.8.2.1 Protection Areas and Maximum Spacing of ESFR Sprinklers

| | Ceiling/Roof Heights Up to 30 ft (9.1 m) | | | | Ceiling/Roof Heights Over 30 ft (9.1 m) | | | |
| | Protection Area | | Spacing | | Protection Area | | Spacing | |
Construction Type	ft²	m²	ft	m	ft²	m²	ft	m
Noncombustible unobstructed	100	9	12	3.7	100	9	10	3.0
Noncombustible obstructed	100	9	12	3.7	100	9	10	3.0
Combustible unobstructed	100	9	12	3.7	100	9	10	3.0
Combustible obstructed	100	9	12	3.7	100	9	10	3.0

14.2.8.2.3* Deviations from the maximum sprinkler spacing shall be permitted to eliminate obstructions created by structural elements (such as trusses, bar joists, and wind bracing) by moving a sprinkler along the branch line a maximum of 1 ft (300 mm) from its allowable spacing, provided coverage for that sprinkler does not exceed 110 ft^2 (10 m^2) per sprinkler where all of the following conditions are met:

(1) The average actual floor area protected by the moved sprinkler and the adjacent sprinklers shall not exceed 100 ft^2 (9 m^2).
(2) Adjacent branch lines shall maintain the same pattern.
(3) In no case shall the distance between sprinklers exceed 12 ft (3.7 m).

14.2.8.2.4 Deviations from the maximum sprinkler spacing shall be permitted to eliminate obstructions created by structural elements (such as trusses, bar joists, and wind bracing) by moving a single branch line a maximum of 1 ft (300 mm) from its allowable spacing, provided coverage for the sprinklers on that branch line and the sprinklers on the branch line it is moving away from does not exceed 110 ft^2 (10 m^2) per sprinkler where all of the following conditions are met:

(1) The average actual floor area protected by the sprinklers on the moved branch line and the sprinklers on the adjacent branch lines shall not exceed 100 ft^2 (9 m^2) per sprinkler.
(2) In no case shall the distance between sprinklers exceed 12 ft (3.7 m).
(3) It shall not be permitted to move a branch line where there are moved sprinklers on a branch line that exceed the maximum sprinkler spacing.

14.2.8.3 Minimum Protection Area of Coverage. The minimum allowable protection area of coverage for a sprinkler (A,) shall not be less than 64 ft^2 (5.9 m^2).

N **14.2.8.3.1*** In buildings with unobstructed construction where sprinklers are located entirely above the bottom plane of an adjacent solid structural member, the requirements of 14.2.8.3 shall not apply to the sprinklers on either side of the solid structural member.

14.2.9 Sprinkler Spacing (Early Suppression Fast-Response Sprinklers).

14.2.9.1 Maximum Distance Between Sprinklers. The maximum distance between sprinklers shall be in accordance with the following:

(1) Where the storage height is less than or equal to 25 ft (7.6 m) and the ceiling height is less than or equal to 30 ft (9.1 m), the distance between sprinklers shall be limited to not more than 12 ft (3.7 m) between sprinklers as shown in Table 14.2.8.2.1.
(2) Unless the requirements of 14.2.9.1(3) or 14.2.9.1(4) are met, where the storage height exceeds 25 ft (7.6 m) or the ceiling height exceeds 30 ft (9.1 m), the distance between sprinklers shall be limited to not more than 10 ft (3.0 m) between sprinklers.
(3)* Regardless of the storage or ceiling height arrangement, deviations from the maximum sprinkler spacing shall be permitted to eliminate obstructions created by structural elements (such as trusses, bar joists, and wind bracing) by moving a sprinkler along the branch line a maximum of 1 ft (300 mm) from its allowable spacing, provided cover-

age for that sprinkler does not exceed 110 ft^2 (10 m^2) where all of the following conditions are met:

(a) The average actual floor area protected by the moved sprinkler and the adjacent sprinklers shall not exceed 100 ft^2 (9 m^2).
(b) Adjacent branch lines shall maintain the same pattern.
(c) In no case shall the distance between sprinklers exceed 12 ft (3.7 m).

(4) Where branch lines are parallel to trusses and bar joists, deviations from the maximum sprinkler spacing shall be permitted to eliminate obstructions created by structural elements (such as trusses, bar joists, and wind bracing) by moving a single branch line a maximum of 1 ft (300 mm) from its allowable spacing, provided coverage for the sprinklers on that branch line and the sprinklers on the branch line it is moving away from does not exceed 110 ft^2 (10 m^2) per sprinkler where all of the following conditions are met:

(a) The average actual floor area protected by the sprinklers on the moved branch line and the sprinklers on the adjacent branch lines shall not exceed 100 ft^2 (9 m^2) per sprinkler.
(b) In no case shall the distance between sprinklers exceed 12 ft (3.7 m).
(c) It shall not be permitted to move a branch line where there are moved sprinklers on a branch line that exceed the maximum sprinkler spacing.

14.2.9.2 Maximum Distance from Walls. The distance from sprinklers to walls shall not exceed one-half of the allowable distance permitted between sprinklers as indicated in Table 14.2.8.2.1.

14.2.9.3 Minimum Distance from Walls. Sprinklers shall be located a minimum of 4 in. (100 mm) from a wall.

14.2.9.4 Minimum Distance Between Sprinklers. Sprinklers shall be spaced not less than 8 ft (2.4 m) on center.

N **14.2.9.4.1*** In buildings with unobstructed construction where sprinklers are located entirely above the bottom plane of an adjacent solid structural member, the requirements of 14.2.9.4 shall not apply to the sprinklers on either side of the solid structural member.

N **14.2.9.4.2** Sprinklers shall be permitted to be placed less than 8 ft (2.4 m) on center where the following conditions are satisfied:

(1) Baffles shall comply with the criteria in 14.2.11.1.1.
(2) Baffles shall be of solid and rigid materials that will stay in place before and during sprinkler operation.
(3) Baffles shall not be less than 8 in. (200 mm) long and 6 in. (150 mm) high.
(4) The tops of baffles shall extend between 2 in. (50 mm) and 3 in. (75 mm) above the deflectors of upright sprinklers.
(5) The bottoms of baffles shall extend downward to a level at least even with the deflectors of pendent sprinklers.

14.2.10 Deflector Position (Early Suppression Fast-Response Sprinklers).

14.2.10.1 Distance Below Ceilings.

14.2.10.1.1 Pendent sprinklers with a nominal K-factor of K-14.0 (K-200), K-16.8 (K-240), and K-28.0 (K-400) shall be positioned so that deflectors are a maximum 14 in. (350 mm) and a minimum 6 in. (150 mm) below the ceiling.

14.2.10.1.2 Pendent sprinklers with a nominal K-factor of K-22.4 (K-320), K-25.2 (K-360), and K-33.6 (K-480) shall be positioned so that deflectors are a maximum 18 in. (450 mm) and a minimum 6 in. (150 mm) below the ceiling.

Δ **14.2.10.1.3** Upright sprinklers with a nominal K-factor of K-14.0 (K-200) and K-16.8 (K-240) shall be positioned so that the deflector is 3 in. (75 mm) to 12 in. (300 mm) below the ceiling.

14.2.10.1.4 With obstructed construction, the branch lines shall be permitted to be installed across the beams, but sprinklers shall be located in the bays and not under the beams.

14.2.10.2 Deflector Orientation. Deflectors of sprinklers shall be aligned parallel to ceilings or roofs.

14.2.11* Obstructions to Sprinkler Discharge (Early Suppression Fast-Response Sprinklers).

14.2.11.1 Obstructions at or Near Ceiling.

14.2.11.1.1 Sprinklers shall be arranged to comply with Table 14.2.11.1.1(a) or Table 14.2.11.1.1(b) and Figure 14.2.11.1.1 for obstructions at the ceiling, such as beams, ducts, lights, and top chords of trusses and bar joists.

14.2.11.1.2 The requirements of 14.2.11.1.1 shall not apply where sprinklers are spaced on opposite sides of obstructions less than 24 in. (600 mm) wide, provided the distance from the centerline on the obstructions to the sprinklers does not exceed one-half the allowable distance between sprinklers.

14.2.11.1.3 Sprinklers with a special obstruction allowance shall be installed according to their listing.

Δ **14.2.11.2* Isolated Obstructions Below Elevation of Sprinklers.** Sprinklers shall be arranged with respect to obstructions in accordance with one of the following:

(1) Sprinklers shall be installed below isolated noncontinuous obstructions that restrict only one sprinkler and are located below the elevation of sprinklers such as light fixtures and unit heaters.

N **Table 14.2.11.1.1(a) Positioning of Sprinklers to Avoid Obstructions to Discharge (ESFR Sprinklers)**

Distance from Sprinkler to Side of Obstruction (A) (ft)	Allowable Distance of Deflector Above Bottom of Obstruction (B) (in.)
Less than 1	0
1 or more	1½ or less
1½ or more	3 or less
2 or more	5½ or less
2½ or more	8 or less
3 or more	10 or less
3½ or more	12 or less
4 or more	15 or less
4½ or more	18 or less
5 or more	22 or less
5½ or more	26 or less
6 or more	31 or less

Note: For A and B, refer to Figure 14.2.11.1.1.

N **Table 14.2.11.1.1(b) Positioning of Sprinklers to Avoid Obstructions to Discharge (ESFR Sprinklers)**

Distance from Sprinkler to Side of Obstruction (A) (mm)	Allowable Distance of Deflector Above Bottom of Obstruction (B) (mm)
Less than 300	0
300 or more	40 or less
450 or more	75 or less
600 or more	140 or less
750 or more	200 or less
900 or more	250 or less
1100 or more	300 or less
1200 or more	375 or less
1400 or more	450 or less
1500 or more	550 or less
1700 or more	650 or less
1800 or more	775 or less

Note: For A and B, refer to Figure 14.2.11.1.1.

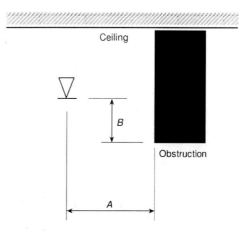

FIGURE 14.2.11.1.1 Positioning of Sprinkler to Avoid Obstruction to Discharge (ESFR Sprinklers).

(2) Additional sprinklers shall not be required below isolated noncontiguous obstructions where the obstruction is 1½ in. (38 mm) or less in width and is located horizontally a minimum of 12 in. (300 mm) below the elevation of the sprinkler deflector.

(3) Additional sprinklers shall not be required below isolated noncontiguous obstructions where the obstruction is 6 in. (150 mm) or less in width and is located a minimum of 6 in. (150 mm) horizontally from the sprinkler.

(4) Additional sprinklers shall not be required below isolated noncontiguous obstructions where the obstruction is 24 in. (600 mm) or less in width and is located a minimum of 12 in. (300 mm) horizontally from the sprinkler.

(5) Additional sprinklers shall not be required below isolated noncontiguous obstructions where sprinklers are positioned with respect to the bottom of obstructions in accordance with 14.2.11.1.

(6) Sprinklers with a special obstruction allowance shall be installed according to their listing.

(7) Additional sprinklers shall not be required where the occupancy is protected in accordance with 14.2.7 and obstructions comply with 9.5.5.3.

(8)* Where high-piled storage is not physically separated from an adjacent light or ordinary hazard area, the sprinkler obstruction criteria of 14.2.11.2 shall apply to all ceiling sprinklers located within 6 ft (1.8 m) horizontally of any high-piled storage.

14.2.11.3 Continuous Obstructions Below Sprinklers.

Δ **14.2.11.3.1 General Continuous Obstructions.** Sprinklers shall be arranged with respect to obstructions in accordance with one of the following:

(1) Sprinklers shall be installed below continuous obstructions, or they shall be arranged to comply with Table 14.2.11.1.1(a) or Table 14.2.11.1.1(b) for horizontal obstructions entirely below the elevation of sprinklers that restrict sprinkler discharge pattern for two or more adjacent sprinklers such as ducts, lights, and pipes.

(2) Additional sprinklers shall not be required where the obstruction is 1½ in. (38 mm) or less in width and is located a minimum of 12 in. (300 mm) below the elevation of the sprinkler deflector.

(3) Additional sprinklers shall not be required where the obstruction is 6 in. (150 mm) or less in width and located a minimum of 6 in. (150 mm) horizontally from the sprinkler.

(4) Additional sprinklers shall not be required where the obstruction is 24 in. (600 mm) or less in width and located a minimum of 12 in. (300 mm) horizontally from the sprinkler.

(5) Ceiling sprinklers shall not be required to comply with Table 14.2.11.1.1(a) or Table 14.2.11.1.1(b) where a row of sprinklers is installed under the obstruction.

(6) Additional sprinklers shall not be required where the occupancy is protected in accordance with 14.2.7 and obstructions comply with 9.5.5.3.

14.2.11.3.2 Bottom Chords of Bar Joists or Open Trusses. ESFR sprinklers shall be arranged with respect to the bottom chord of a bar joist or open truss in accordance with the following:

(1) Where the bottom cord is 6 in. (150 mm) or less in width, the sprinkler shall be located a minimum 6 in. (150 mm) horizontally from the nearest edge of the bottom chord.

(2) Where the bottom cord is 24 in. (600 mm) or less in width, the sprinkler shall be located a minimum 12 in. (300 mm) horizontally from the nearest edge of the bottom chord.

14.2.11.3.2.1 The requirements of 14.2.11.3.2 shall not apply where upright sprinklers are located over the bottom chords of bar joists or open trusses that are 4 in. (100 mm) maximum in width.

N **14.2.11.3.3 Branchlines.** Upright sprinklers shall be positioned with respect to branch lines in accordance with one of the following:

(1) Attached directly to branch lines less than or equal to 4 in. (100 mm) nominal diameter

(2) Offset horizontally a minimum of 12 in. (300 mm) from the pipe

(3) Supplied by a riser nipple (sprig) to elevate the sprinkler deflector a minimum of 12 in. (300 mm) from the centerline of any pipe over 4 in. (100 mm) nominal in diameter

14.2.11.3.4* For pipes, conduits, or groups of pipes and conduit to be considered individual, they shall be separated from the closest adjacent pipe, conduit, cable tray, or similar obstructions by a minimum of three times the width of the adjacent pipe, conduit, cable tray, or similar obstruction.

14.2.11.3.5 Open Gratings. Sprinklers installed under open gratings shall be of the intermediate level/rack storage type or otherwise shielded from the discharge of overhead sprinklers.

14.2.11.3.6 Overhead Doors. Quick-response spray sprinklers shall be permitted to be utilized under overhead doors.

14.2.11.3.7 Special Obstruction Allowance. Sprinklers with a special obstruction allowance shall be installed according to their listing.

N **14.2.11.4 Conveyors.** Sprinklers shall be arranged with respect to conveyors in accordance with one of the following:

(1) Quick-response standard spray sprinklers shall be permitted to be installed below conveyors without high-piled storage located underneath.

(2) Ceiling level sprinklers shall be installed below conveyors with high-piled storage located underneath.

(3) Additional sprinklers shall not be required below belt or similar type conveyors where the conveyor in a horizontal profile is a minimum 70 percent open.

(4) Additional sprinklers shall not be required below belt conveyors up to 4 ft (1.2 m) wide where the area below the conveyor is void of high-piled storage.

(5) Additional sprinklers shall not be required below roller conveyors where the horizontal opening between rollers equals or exceeds the width of the roller.

(6) Additional sprinklers shall not be required below roller conveyors where the area below the conveyor is void of high-piled storage.

14.2.12 Clearance to Storage (Early Suppression Fast-Response Sprinklers). The clearance between the deflector and the top of storage shall be 36 in. (900 mm) or greater.

Chapter 15 Installation Requirements for Special Sprinklers

15.1 Open Sprinklers.

15.1.1 Open sprinklers shall be permitted to be used in deluge systems to protect special hazards or exposures or in other special locations.

15.1.2 Open sprinklers shall be installed in accordance with all applicable requirements of this standard for their automatic counterpart.

15.2 Special Sprinklers.

15.2.1 Special sprinklers that are intended for the protection of specific hazards or construction features shall be permitted where such devices have been evaluated and listed for performance under the following conditions:

(1) Fire tests related to the intended hazard
(2) Distribution of the spray pattern with respect to wetting of floors and walls
(3) Distribution of the spray pattern with respect to obstructions
(4) Evaluation of the thermal sensitivity of the sprinkler
(5) Performance under horizontal or sloped ceilings
(6) Area of design
(7) Allowable clearance to ceilings

15.2.2 Special sprinklers shall maintain the following characteristics:

(1) K-factor size shall be in accordance with 7.2.2.
(2) Temperature ratings shall be in accordance with Table 7.2.4.1(a).
(3) The protection area of coverage shall not exceed 400 ft^2 (37 m^2) for light hazard and ordinary hazard occupancies.
(4) The protection area of coverage shall not exceed 196 ft^2 (18 m^2) for extra hazard and high-piled storage occupancies.

15.3 Dry Sprinklers.

15.3.1* Where dry sprinklers are connected to wet pipe sprinkler systems protecting areas subject to freezing temperatures, the minimum exposed length of the barrel of the dry sprinkler shall be in accordance with Table 15.3.1(a) or Table 15.3.1(b).

15.3.2 The minimum exposed length shall be measured along the length of the dry sprinkler from the face of the fitting to which the dry sprinkler is installed to the inside surface of the insulation, wall, or ceiling leading to the cold space, whichever is closest to the fitting.

15.3.3* Where dry sprinklers are connected to wet pipe sprinkler systems protecting insulated freezer structures, the clearance space around the sprinkler barrel shall be sealed.

15.3.4* Dry sprinklers shall only be installed in fittings as specified by the sprinkler manufacturer.

15.4 Old-Style Sprinklers.

15.4.1 Unless required by 9.3.12 or 15.4.2, old-style sprinklers shall not be used in a new installation.

Table 15.3.1(a) Exposed Barrel Lengths for Dry Sprinklers (U.S. Customary Units)

Ambient Temperature Exposed to Discharge End of Sprinkler (°F)	Minimum Exposed Barrel Length when Exposed to 40°F (in.)	Minimum Exposed Barrel Length when Exposed to 50°F (in.)	Minimum Exposed Barrel Length when Exposed to 60°F (in.)
40	0	0	0
30	0	0	0
20	4	0	0
10	8	1	0
0	12	3	0
−10	14	4	1
−20	14	6	3
−30	16	8	4
−40	18	8	4
−50	20	10	6
−60	20	10	6

Table 15.3.1(b) Exposed Barrel Lengths for Dry Sprinklers (Metric Units)

Ambient Temperature Exposed to Discharge End of Sprinkler (°C)	Minimum Exposed Barrel Length when Exposed to 4°C (mm)	Minimum Exposed Barrel Length when Exposed to 10°C (mm)	Minimum Exposed Barrel Length when Exposed to 16°C (mm)
4	0	0	0
−1	0	0	0
−7	100	0	0
−12	200	25	0
−18	300	75	0
−23	350	100	25
−29	350	150	75
−34	400	200	100
−40	450	200	100
−46	500	250	150
−51	500	250	150

15.4.2 Use of old-style sprinklers shall be permitted where construction features or other special situations require unique water distribution.

15.4.3 Old-style sprinklers protecting fur storage vaults shall be permitted to be placed less than 6 ft (1.8 m) on center.

N **15.5 Attic Sprinklers.** Attic sprinklers shall be permitted to be used for protecting areas of an attic and shall be installed in accordance with their listing.

N **15.6 Electrically Operated Sprinklers.** Electrically operated sprinklers shall be permitted where such devices have been evaluated and listed for performance under the following conditions:

(1) Fire tests related to the intended hazard
(2) Distribution of the spray pattern with respect to wetting of floors and walls
(3) Distribution of the spray pattern with respect to obstructions
(4) Performance under horizontal or sloped ceilings
(5) Area of design
(6) Allowable clearance to ceilings

Chapter 16   Installation of Piping, Valves, and Appurtenances

16.1 Basic Requirements.

16.1.1* System valves and gauges shall be accessible for operation, inspection, tests, and maintenance.

16.1.2 Materials and components shall be installed in accordance with material compatibility information that is available as a part of a listing or manufacturer's published information.

16.1.3 Reconditioned Components.

16.1.3.1 The use of reconditioned valves and devices as replacement equipment in existing systems shall be permitted.

16.1.3.2 Reconditioned sprinklers shall not be permitted to be utilized on any new or existing system.

16.2 Sprinkler Installation.

16.2.1 Only new sprinklers shall be installed.

16.2.1.1* When a threaded sprinkler is removed from a fitting or welded outlet, it shall not be reinstalled except as permitted by 16.2.1.1.1.

16.2.1.1.1 Dry sprinklers shall be permitted to be reinstalled when removed in accordance with the manufacturer's installation and maintenance instructions.

16.2.2 Corrosion Resistant.

16.2.2.1 Listed corrosion-resistant sprinklers shall be installed in locations where chemicals, moisture, or other corrosive vapors sufficient to cause corrosion of such devices exist.

16.2.2.1.1* Unless the requirements of 16.2.2.1.2 are met, corrosion-resistant coatings shall be applied only by the manufacturer of the sprinkler and in accordance with the requirements of 16.2.2.1.2.

16.2.2.1.2 Any damage to the protective coating occurring at the time of installation shall be repaired at once using only the coating of the manufacturer of the sprinkler in the approved manner so that no part of the sprinkler will be exposed after installation has been completed.

16.2.3 Painting.

16.2.3.1 Where sprinklers have had paint applied by other than the sprinkler manufacturer, they shall be replaced with new listed sprinklers of the same characteristics, including K-factor, thermal response, and water distribution.

16.2.3.2 Where cover plates on concealed sprinklers have been painted by other than the sprinkler manufacturer, the cover plate shall be replaced.

16.2.4 Protective Coverings.

16.2.4.1 Sprinklers protecting spray areas and mixing rooms in resin application areas shall be protected against overspray residue so that they will operate in the event of fire.

16.2.4.2* Where protected in accordance with 16.2.4.1, cellophane bags having a thickness of 0.003 in. (0.08 mm) or less or thin paper bags shall be used.

16.2.4.3 Sprinklers that have been painted or coated shall be replaced in accordance with the requirements of 16.2.3.

16.2.5 Escutcheons and Cover Plates.

16.2.5.1 Plates, escutcheons, or other devices used to cover the annular space around a sprinkler shall be metallic or shall be listed for use around a sprinkler.

16.2.5.2* Recessed and flush sprinklers shall be installed with the escutcheon that is part of its listing.

16.2.5.3 Concealed sprinklers shall be installed with the cover assembly that is part of its listing.

16.2.5.4 The use of caulking or glue to seal the penetration or to affix the components of a recessed escutcheon or concealed cover plate shall not be permitted.

16.2.6 Sprinklers subject to mechanical injury shall be protected with listed guards.

16.2.7 Stock of Spare Sprinklers.

16.2.7.1* A supply of at least six spare sprinklers shall be maintained on the premises so that any sprinklers that have operated or been damaged in any way can be promptly replaced.

16.2.7.2* The sprinklers shall correspond to the types and temperature ratings of the sprinklers in the property.

16.2.7.3 The sprinklers shall be kept in a cabinet located where the temperature to which they are subjected will at no time exceed the maximum ceiling temperatures specified in Table 7.2.4.1 for each of the sprinklers within the cabinet.

16.2.7.4 Where dry sprinklers of different lengths are installed, spare dry sprinklers shall not be required, provided that a means of returning the system to service is furnished.

16.2.7.5 The stock of spare sprinklers shall include all types and ratings installed and shall be as follows:

(1) For protected facilities having under 300 sprinklers — no fewer than six sprinklers
(2) For protected facilities having 300 to 1000 sprinklers — no fewer than 12 sprinklers
(3) For protected facilities having over 1000 sprinklers — no fewer than 24 sprinklers

16.2.7.6* One sprinkler wrench as specified by the sprinkler manufacturer shall be provided in the cabinet for each type of sprinkler installed to be used for the removal and installation of sprinklers in the system.

16.2.7.7 A list of the sprinklers installed in the property shall be posted in the sprinkler cabinet.

16.2.7.7.1* The list shall include the following:

(1) Sprinkler Identification Number (SIN) if equipped; or the manufacturer, model, K-factor, deflector type, thermal sensitivity, and pressure rating
(2) General description
(3) Quantity of each type to be contained in the cabinet
(4) Issue or revision date of the list

16.3 Piping Installation.

16.3.1 General.

16.3.1.1 Steel pipe shall be in accordance with 16.3.2, 16.3.3, or 16.3.4.

16.3.1.2 Copper tube shall be in accordance with 16.3.5.

16.3.1.3 Nonmetallic pipe shall be in accordance with 16.3.9.

16.3.1.4 Brass pipe shall be in accordance with 16.3.6.

16.3.1.5 Stainless steel pipe shall be in accordance with 16.3.7.

16.3.2* Steel Pipe — Welded or Roll-Grooved. When steel pipe referenced in Table 7.3.1.1 is used and joined by welding as referenced in 7.5.2 or by roll-grooved pipe and fittings as referenced in 7.5.3, the minimum nominal wall thickness for pressures up to 300 psi (21 bar) shall be in accordance with Schedule 10 for pipe sizes up to 5 in. (125 mm), 0.134 in. (3.4 mm) for 6 in. (150 mm) pipe, 0.188 in. (4.8 mm) for 8 in. and 10 in. (200 mm and 250 mm) pipe, and 0.330 in. (8.4 mm) for 12 in. (300 mm) pipe.

16.3.3 Steel Pipe — Threaded. When steel pipe referenced in Table 7.3.1.1 is joined by threaded fittings referenced in 7.5.1 or by fittings used with pipe having cut grooves, the minimum wall thickness shall be in accordance with Schedule 30 pipe [in sizes 8 in. (200 mm) and larger] or Schedule 40 pipe [in sizes less than 8 in. (200 mm)] for pressures up to 300 psi (21 bar).

16.3.4 Specially Listed Steel Pipe. Pressure limitations and wall thickness for steel pipe specially listed in accordance with 7.3.3 shall be permitted to be in accordance with the pipe listing requirements.

16.3.5* Copper Tube. Copper tube as specified in the standards listed in Table 7.3.1.1 shall have a wall thickness of Type K, Type L, or Type M where used in sprinkler systems.

16.3.6 Brass Pipe. Brass pipe specified in Table 7.3.1.1 shall be permitted in the standard weight in sizes up to 6 in. (150 mm) for pressures up to 175 psig (12 bar) and in the extra strong weight in sizes up to 8 in. (200 mm) for pressures up to 300 psig (21 bar).

16.3.7 Stainless Steel Pipe. Stainless steel pipe as referenced in the standards listed in Table 7.3.1.1 shall be in accordance with Schedules 10S or 40S pipe.

16.3.8 Metallic Pipe and Tube Bending.

16.3.8.1 Bending of Schedule 10 steel pipe, or any steel pipe of wall thickness equal to or greater than Schedule 10 and Types K and L copper tube, shall be permitted when bends are made with no kinks, ripples, distortions, or reductions in diameter or any noticeable deviations from round.

16.3.8.2 For Schedule 40 and copper tubing, the minimum radius of a bend shall be six pipe diameters for pipe sizes 2 in. (50 mm) and smaller and five pipe diameters for pipe sizes 2½ in. (65 mm) and larger.

16.3.8.3 For all other steel pipe, the minimum radius of a bend shall be 12 pipe diameters for all sizes.

16.3.8.4 Bending of listed pipe and tubing shall be permitted as allowed by the listing.

16.3.9 Nonmetallic Pipe and Tubing.

16.3.9.1 Listed nonmetallic pipe shall be installed in accordance with its listing limitations, including installation instructions.

16.3.9.2 When nonmetallic pipe is used in systems utilizing steel piping internally coated with corrosion inhibitors, the steel pipe coating shall be listed for compatibility with the nonmetallic pipe materials.

16.3.9.3 When nonmetallic pipe is used in systems utilizing steel pipe that is not internally coated with corrosion inhibitors, no additional evaluations shall be required.

16.3.9.4* When nonmetallic pipe is used in systems utilizing steel pipe, cutting oils and lubricants used for fabrication of the steel piping shall be compatible with the nonmetallic pipe materials in accordance with 16.1.2.

16.3.9.5 Fire-stopping materials intended for use on nonmetallic piping penetrations shall be compatible with the nonmetallic pipe materials in accordance with 16.1.2.

16.3.9.6 Nonmetallic pipe listed for light hazard occupancies shall be permitted to be installed in ordinary hazard rooms of otherwise light hazard occupancies where the room does not exceed 400 ft² (37 m²).

16.3.9.6.1 Nonmetallic pipe installed in accordance with 16.3.9.6 shall be permitted to be installed exposed, in accordance with the listing.

16.3.9.6.2 Where nonmetallic pipe installed in accordance with 16.3.9.6 supplies sprinklers in a private garage within a dwelling unit, and the garage does not exceed 1000 ft² (93 m²) in area, the nonmetallic piping shall be permitted to be protected from the garage compartment by not less than the same wall or ceiling sheathing that is required by the applicable building code.

16.3.9.7 Bending of listed nonmetallic pipe or tubing shall be permitted as allowed by the listing.

16.3.10 Listed Metallic Pipe and Tubing.

16.3.10.1 Pipe or tube listed only for light hazard occupancies shall be permitted to be installed in ordinary hazard rooms of otherwise light hazard occupancies where the room does not exceed 400 ft² (37 m²).

16.3.10.1.1 Pipe or tube installed in accordance with 16.3.10.1 shall be permitted to be installed exposed, in accordance with the listing.

16.3.10.2 Bending of listed pipe and tubing shall be permitted as allowed by the listing.

16.3.11 Return Bends.

16.3.11.1 Unless the requirements of 16.3.11.3, 16.3.11.4, or 16.3.11.5 are met, return bends shall be used where pendent sprinklers are supplied from a raw water source, a mill pond, or open-top reservoirs.

16.3.11.2 Return bends shall be connected to the top of branch lines in order to avoid accumulation of sediment in the drop nipples in accordance with Figure 16.3.11.2.

16.3.11.3 Return bends shall not be required for deluge systems.

16.3.11.4 Return bends shall not be required where dry pendent sprinklers are used.

16.3.11.5 Return bends shall not be required for wet pipe systems where sprinklers with a nominal K-factor of K-11.2 (160) or larger are used.

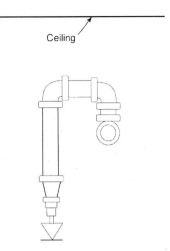

FIGURE 16.3.11.2   Return Bend Arrangement.

16.3.12 Piping to Sprinklers Below Ceilings.

16.3.12.1* In new installations expected to supply sprinklers below a ceiling, minimum 1 in. (25 mm) outlets shall be provided.

16.3.12.2* In new installations, it shall be permitted to provide minimum 1 in. (25 mm) outlets with hexagonal bushings to accommodate sprinklers attached directly to branch line fittings to allow for future system modifications.

16.4 Protection of Piping.

16.4.1 Protection of Piping Against Freezing.

16.4.1.1* Where any portion of a system is subject to freezing and the temperatures cannot be reliably maintained at or above 40°F (4°C), the system shall be installed as a dry pipe or preaction system.

N **16.4.1.1.1** The weather temperature used to determine if an unheated portion of a system is subject to freezing and required to be protected in accordance with 16.4.1.1 shall be the lowest mean temperature for one day, obtained from an approved source.

16.4.1.1.2 The requirements of 16.4.1.1 shall not apply where alternate methods of freeze prevention are provided in accordance with one of the methods described in 16.4.1.2 through 16.4.1.4.2.

16.4.1.2 Unheated areas shall be permitted to be protected by antifreeze systems or by other systems specifically listed for the purpose.

16.4.1.3 Where aboveground water-filled supply pipes, risers, system risers, or feed mains pass through open areas, cold rooms, passageways, or other areas exposed to temperatures below 40°F (4°C), the pipe shall be permitted to be protected against freezing by insulating coverings, frostproof casings, or other means of maintaining a minimum temperature between 40°F and 120°F (4°C and 49°C).

16.4.1.4* Listed heat-tracing systems shall be permitted in accordance with 16.4.1.4.1 and 16.4.1.4.2.

16.4.1.4.1 Where used to protect branch lines, the heat-tracing system shall be specifically listed for use on branch lines.

16.4.1.4.2 Electric supervision of the heat-tracing system shall provide positive confirmation that the circuit is energized.

16.4.1.5 Water-filled piping shall be permitted to be installed in areas where the temperature is less than 40°F (4°C) when heat loss calculations performed by a professional engineer verify that the system will not freeze.

16.4.2* Protection of Piping Against Corrosion.

16.4.2.1* Where corrosive conditions are known to exist due to moisture or fumes from corrosive chemicals or both, special types of fittings, pipes, and hangers that resist corrosion shall be used, or a protective coating shall be applied to all unprotected exposed surfaces of the sprinkler system.

16.4.2.2 Where water supplies or environmental conditions are known to have unusual corrosive properties, piping shall have a corrosion resistance ratio (CRR) of 1 or more, and the system shall be treated in accordance with 5.1.4.

16.4.2.3 Where corrosive conditions exist or piping is exposed to the weather, corrosion-resistant types of pipe, fittings, and hangers or protective corrosion-resistant coatings shall be used.

16.4.2.4 Where steel pipe is used underground, the pipe shall be protected against corrosion.

16.4.3* Protection of Piping in Hazardous Areas.

16.4.3.1 Private service main aboveground piping shall not pass through hazardous areas and shall be located so that it is protected from mechanical and fire damage.

16.4.3.2 Private service main aboveground piping shall be permitted to be located in hazardous areas protected by an automatic sprinkler system.

N **16.4.4 Protection of Piping Subject to Mechanical Damage.** Where pipe other than steel is run horizontally or vertically through wood or metal studs the following provisions shall apply:

(1) Steel shield plates shall be provided where the face of the piping is less than 1.25 in. (32 mm) from the nearest edge of the member.
(2) Steel shield plates shall have a minimum thickness of 0.0575 in. (1.463 mm) (No. 16 gauge).
(3) Steel shield plates shall cover the area of the pipe where the member is notched or bored.

16.5 Protection of Risers Subject to Mechanical Damage. Sprinkler risers subject to mechanical damage shall be protected by steel posts, concrete barriers, or other approved means.

16.6 Provision for Flushing Systems.

16.6.1 All sprinkler systems shall be arranged for flushing.

16.6.2 Readily removable fittings shall be provided at the end of all cross mains.

16.6.3 All cross mains shall terminate in 1¼ in. (32 mm) or larger pipe.

16.6.4 All branch lines on gridded systems shall be arranged to facilitate flushing.

16.7* Air Venting. The vent required by 8.1.5 shall be located near a high point in the system to allow air to be removed from that portion of the system by one of the following methods:

(1) Manual valve, minimum ½ in. (15 mm) size
(2) Automatic air vent
(3) Remote inspector's test valve
(4) Other approved means

16.8 Fitting Installation.

16.8.1 Metallic Fittings. (Reserved)

16.8.2 Nonmetallic Fittings.

16.8.2.1* When nonmetallic fittings are used in systems utilizing internally coated steel piping, the steel pipe shall be listed for compatibility with the nonmetallic fittings.

16.8.2.2* When nonmetallic fittings are used in systems utilizing steel pipe that is not internally coated with corrosion inhibitors, no additional evaluations are required.

16.8.2.3 When nonmetallic fittings are used in systems utilizing steel pipe, cutting oils and lubricants used for fabrication of the steel piping shall be compatible with the nonmetallic fittings in accordance with 16.1.2.

16.8.2.4 Fire-stopping materials intended for use on nonmetallic fitting penetrations shall be investigated for compatibility with the nonmetallic fitting materials in accordance with 16.1.2.

16.8.3* Fitting Pressure Limits.

16.8.3.1 Standard weight pattern cast-iron fittings 2 in. (50 mm) in size and smaller shall be permitted where pressures do not exceed 300 psi (21 bar).

16.8.3.2 Standard weight pattern malleable iron fittings 6 in. (150 mm) in size and smaller shall be permitted where pressures do not exceed 300 psi (21 bar).

16.8.3.3 Fittings not meeting the requirements of 16.8.3.1 and 16.8.3.2 shall be extra-heavy pattern where pressures exceed 175 psi (12 bar).

16.8.3.4 Cast bronze threaded fittings in accordance with ASME B16.15, *Cast Copper Alloy Threaded Fittings, Classes 125 and 250*, shall be permitted where pressures do not exceed 200 psi (14 bar) for Class 125 fittings and 400 psi (28 bar) for Class 250 fittings.

16.8.3.5 Listed fittings shall be permitted for system pressures up to the limits specified in their listings.

16.8.4* Couplings and Unions.

16.8.4.1 Screwed unions shall not be used on pipe larger than 2 in. (50 mm).

16.8.4.2 Couplings and unions of other than screwed-type shall be of types listed specifically for use in sprinkler systems.

16.8.5 Reducers and Bushings.

16.8.5.1 Unless the requirements of 16.8.5.2 or 16.8.5.3 are met, a one-piece reducing fitting shall be used wherever a change is made in the size of the pipe.

16.8.5.2 Hexagonal or face bushings shall be permitted in reducing the size of openings of fittings when standard fittings of the required size are not available.

16.8.5.3 Hexagonal bushings as permitted in 16.3.12.2 shall be permitted to be used.

16.8.5.4 The requirements of 16.8.5.1 and 16.8.5.2 shall not apply to CPVC fittings.

16.8.6 Extension Fitting.

16.8.6.1 Extension fittings shall be permitted to be used with sprinklers K-8.0 or smaller.

16.8.6.2 Extension fittings shall be permitted to be used with sprinklers in light hazard and ordinary hazard occupancies only.

16.8.6.3 The internal diameter of extension fittings shall have the same nominal inlet diameter of the attached sprinkler.

16.8.6.4 A single extension fitting up to a maximum of 2 in. (50 mm) in length shall be permitted to be installed with a sprinkler.

16.8.6.4.1 Extension fittings longer than 2 in. (50 mm) shall not be permitted unless specifically listed.

16.8.6.5 Extension fittings shall be included in the hydraulic calculations.

16.8.6.5.1 Extension fittings 2 in. (50 mm) and less shall not be required to be included in the hydraulic calculations.

16.8.7 Threaded Pipe and Fittings.

16.9 Valves.

16.9.1 General.

16.9.1.1 Drain Valves and Test Valves. Drain valves and test valves shall be approved.

16.9.1.2 Valve Pressure Requirements. When water pressures exceed 175 psi (12 bar), valves shall be used in accordance with their pressure ratings.

16.9.2 Wafer-Type Valves. Wafer-type valves with components that extend beyond the valve body shall be installed in a manner that does not interfere with the operation of any system components.

16.9.3* Control Valves.

16.9.3.1* General.

16.9.3.1.1 Each sprinkler system shall be provided with a listed indicating valve in an accessible location, so located as to control all automatic sources of water supply.

16.9.3.1.2 At least one listed indicating valve shall be installed in each source of water supply.

16.9.3.1.3 The requirements of 16.9.3.1.2 shall not apply to the fire department connection, and there shall be no shutoff valve in the fire department connection.

16.9.3.2 Listed Indicating Valves. Unless the requirements of 16.9.3.2.1, 16.9.3.2.2, or 16.9.3.2.3 are met, all valves controlling connections to water supplies and to supply pipes to sprinklers shall be listed indicating valves.

16.9.3.2.1 A listed underground gate valve equipped with a listed indicator post shall be permitted.

16.9.3.2.2 A listed water control valve assembly with a reliable position indication connected to a remote supervisory station shall be permitted.

16.9.3.2.3 A nonindicating valve, such as an underground gate valve with approved roadway box, complete with T-wrench, and where accepted by the authority having jurisdiction, shall be permitted.

16.9.3.3* Supervision.

16.9.3.3.1 Valves on connections to water supplies, sectional control and isolation valves, and other valves in supply pipes to sprinklers and other fixed water-based fire suppression systems shall be supervised by one of the following methods:

(1) Central station, proprietary, or remote station signaling service
(2) Local signaling service that will cause the sounding of an audible signal at a constantly attended point
(3) Valves locked in the correct position
(4) Valves located within fenced enclosures under the control of the owner, sealed in the open position, and inspected weekly as part of an approved procedure

16.9.3.3.2 Floor control valves in high-rise buildings shall comply with 16.9.3.3.1(1) or 16.9.3.3.1(2).

16.9.3.3.3 The requirements of 16.9.3.3.1 shall not apply to underground gate valves with roadway boxes.

16.9.3.3.4 Where control valves are installed overhead, they shall be positioned so that the indicating feature is visible from the floor below.

16.9.3.3.5 A listed backflow prevention assembly shall be permitted to be considered a control valve, provided both control valves are listed for fire protection system use and an additional control valve shall not be required.

16.9.3.4* Control Valve Accessibility. All control valves shall be located where accessible and free of obstructions.

16.9.3.5 Control Valve Identification. Identification signs shall be provided at each valve to indicate its function and what it controls.

16.9.4* Check Valves.

16.9.4.1 Where there is more than one source of water supply, a check valve shall be installed in each connection.

16.9.4.2 A listed backflow prevention device shall be considered a check valve, and an additional check valve shall not be required.

16.9.4.3 Where cushion tanks are used with automatic fire pumps, no check valve is required in the cushion tank connection.

16.9.4.4 Check valves shall be installed in a vertical (flow upwards) or horizontal position in accordance with their listing.

16.9.4.5* Where a single wet pipe sprinkler system is equipped with a fire department connection, the alarm valve is considered a check valve, and an additional check valve shall not be required.

16.9.5* Control Valves with Check Valves.

16.9.5.1 In a connection serving as one source of supply, listed indicating valves or post-indicator valves shall be installed on both sides of all check valves required in 16.9.4.

16.9.5.2 The city services control valve (non-indicating control valve) shall be permitted to serve as the supply side control valve.

16.9.5.3 The requirements of 16.9.5.1 shall not apply to the check valve located in the fire department connection piping, and there shall be no control valves in the fire department connection piping.

16.9.5.4 The requirements of 16.9.5.1 shall not apply where the city connection serves as the only automatic source of supply to a wet pipe sprinkler system; a control valve is not required on the system side of the check valve or the alarm check valve.

16.9.5.5* Control Valves for Gravity Tanks. Gravity tanks shall have listed indicating valves installed on both sides of the check valve.

16.9.6* Pumps. When a pump is located in a combustible pump house or exposed to danger from fire or falling walls, or when a tank discharges into a private fire service main fed by another supply, either the check valve in the connection shall be located in a pit or the control valve shall be of the post-indicator type located a safe distance outside buildings.

16.9.7 Pressure-Reducing Valves.

Δ **16.9.7.1** In portions of systems where the potential exists for normal (nonfire condition) water pressure in excess of 175 psi (12 bar) and all components are not listed for pressures equal to or greater than the maximum potential water pressure, a listed pressure-reducing valve shall be installed and set for an outlet pressure not exceeding 10 psi (0.7 bar) below the minimum rated pressure of any component within that portion of the system at the maximum inlet pressure.

N **16.9.7.1.1** The pressure on the inlet side of the pressure-regulating device shall not exceed the rated working pressure of the device.

16.9.7.2 Pressure gauges shall be installed on the inlet and outlet sides of each pressure-reducing valve.

16.9.7.3* A listed relief valve of not less than ½ in. (15 mm) in size shall be provided on the discharge side of the pressure-reducing valve set to operate at a pressure not exceeding the rated pressure of the components of the system.

16.9.7.4 A listed indicating valve shall be provided on the inlet side of each pressure-reducing valve, unless the pressure-reducing valve meets the listing requirements for use as an indicating valve.

16.9.7.5 A test connection shall be provided downstream of all pressure-reducing valves for the performance of flow tests at sprinkler system demand as required by this standard and NFPA 25.

N **16.9.7.5.1** A 2 ½ in. (65 mm) hose valve shall be provided downstream of the pressure reducing valve for every 250 gpm (950 L/min) of flow rate required by the system demand.

N **16.9.7.5.2*** Existing hose connections downstream of the pressure reducing valve shall be allowed to be utilized.

N **16.9.7.5.3*** Other means shall be permitted as long as the system doesn't require modification to perform the test and it is sized to meet the system demand.

16.9.8* Post-Indicator Valves.

16.9.8.1 Where post-indicator valves are used, they shall be set so that the top of the post is 32 in. to 40 in. (800 mm to 1000 mm) above the final grade.

16.9.8.2 Post-indicator valves shall be properly protected against mechanical damage where needed.

16.9.8.3 The requirements of 16.9.8.1 shall not apply to wall post-indicator valves.

16.9.9 Valves in Pits.

16.9.9.1 Where it is impractical to provide a post-indicator valve, valves shall be permitted to be placed in pits with permission of the authority having jurisdiction.

16.9.9.2* Valve Pit Construction.

16.9.9.2.1 When used, valve pits shall be of adequate size and accessible for inspection, operation, testing, maintenance, and removal of equipment contained therein.

16.9.9.2.2 Valve pits shall be constructed and arranged to properly protect the installed equipment from movement of earth, freezing, and accumulation of water.

16.9.9.2.3 Poured-in-place or precast concrete, with or without reinforcement, or brick (all depending upon soil conditions and size of pit) shall be appropriate materials for construction of valve pits.

16.9.9.2.4 Other approved materials shall be permitted to be used for valve pit construction.

16.9.9.2.5 Where the water table is low and the soil is porous, crushed stone or gravel shall be permitted to be used for the floor of the pit.

16.9.9.2.6 Valve pits located at or near the base of the riser of an elevated tank shall be designed in accordance with NFPA 22.

16.9.9.3 Valve Pit Marking. The location of the valve shall be clearly marked, and the cover of the pit shall be kept free of obstructions.

16.9.10 Floor Control Valve Assemblies.

16.9.10.1 Multistory buildings exceeding two stories in height shall be provided with a floor control valve, check valve, pressure gauge, main drain valve, and flow switch for isolation, control, and annunciation of water flow for each individual floor level.

16.9.10.2 The floor control valve, check valve, pressure gauge, main drain valve, and flow switch required by 16.9.10.1 shall not be required where sprinklers on the top level of a multi-story building are supplied by piping on the floor below.

16.9.10.3 The floor control valve, check valve, pressure gauge, main drain valve, and flow switch required by 16.9.10.1 shall not be required where the total area of all floors combined does not exceed the system protection area limitations of 4.4.1.

16.9.10.4 The requirements of 16.9.10 shall not apply to dry systems in parking garages.

16.9.11* Identification of Valves.

16.9.11.1 All control, drain, venting, and test connection valves shall be provided with permanently marked weatherproof metal or rigid plastic identification signs.

16.9.11.2 The identification sign shall be secured with corrosion-resistant wire, chain, or other approved means.

16.9.11.3 The control valve sign shall identify the portion of the building served.

16.9.11.3.1* Systems that have more than one control valve that must be closed to work on a system or space shall have a sign referring to existence and location of other valves.

16.10 Drainage.

16.10.1* General. All sprinkler pipe and fittings shall be installed so that the system can be drained.

16.10.2 Wet Pipe Systems.

16.10.2.1 On wet pipe systems, sprinkler pipes shall be permitted to be installed level.

16.10.2.2 Trapped piping shall be drained in accordance with 16.10.5.

16.10.3 Dry Pipe and Preaction Systems. Piping shall be pitched to drain as stated in 16.10.3.1 through 16.10.3.3.

16.10.3.1 Dry Pipe Systems in Nonrefrigerated Areas. In dry pipe system, branch lines shall be pitched at least ½ in. per 10 ft (4 mm/m), and mains shall be pitched at least ¼ in. per 10 ft (2 mm/m) in nonrefrigerated areas.

16.10.3.2 Preaction Systems. In preaction systems, branch lines shall be pitched at least ½ in. per 10 ft (4 mm/m), and mains shall be pitched at least ¼ in. per 10 ft (2 mm/m).

16.10.3.3 Dry Pipe and Preaction Systems in Refrigerated Areas. Branch lines shall be pitched at least ½ in. per 10 ft (4 mm/m), and mains shall be pitched at least ½ in. per 10 ft (4 mm/m) in refrigerated areas.

16.10.4* System, Main Drain, or Sectional Drain Connections.

16.10.4.1 Provisions shall be made to properly drain all parts of the system.

16.10.4.2* Drain connections for system supply risers and mains shall be sized as shown in Table 16.10.4.2.

16.10.4.3 Where an interior sectional or floor control valve(s) is provided, it shall be provided with a drain connection having a minimum size as shown in Table 16.10.4.2 to drain that portion of the system controlled by the sectional valve.

16.10.4.4 Drains shall discharge outside or to a drain connection capable of handling the flow of the drain.

Δ **Table 16.10.4.2 Drain Size**

Riser or Main Size		Size of Drain Connection	
in.	mm	in.	mm
Up to 2	Up to 50	¾ or larger	20 or larger
2½, 3, 3½	65, 80, 90	1¼ or larger	32 or larger
4 and larger	100 and larger	2 or larger	50 or larger

16.10.4.5 For those drains serving pressure-reducing valves, the drain, drain connection, and all other downstream drain piping shall be sized to permit a flow of at least the greatest system demand supplied by the pressure-reducing valve.

16.10.4.6 Main Drain Test Connections.

16.10.4.6.1 Main drain test connections shall be provided at locations that will permit flow tests of water supplies and connections.

16.10.4.6.2 Main drain test connections shall be installed so that the valve can be opened wide for a sufficient time to assure a proper test without causing water damage.

16.10.4.6.3 Main drain connections shall be sized in accordance with 16.10.4.2.

16.10.4.7 The test connections required by 16.10.4.6 shall be permitted to be used as main drain connections.

16.10.4.8 Where drain connections for floor control valves are tied into a common drain riser, the drain riser shall be one pipe size larger downstream of each size drain connection tying into it.

16.10.4.9 Where subject to freezing, a minimum 4 ft (1.2 m) of exposed drain pipe shall be in a heated area between the drain valve and the exterior wall when drain piping extends through the wall to the outside.

16.10.5 Auxiliary Drains.

16.10.5.1 Auxiliary drains shall be provided where a change in piping direction prevents drainage of system piping through the main drain valve.

16.10.5.2 Auxiliary Drains for Wet Pipe Systems and Preaction Systems in Areas Not Subject to Freezing.

16.10.5.2.1* Where the capacity of isolated trapped sections of pipe is 50 gal (200 L) or more, the auxiliary drain shall consist of a valve not smaller than 1 in. (25 mm), piped to an accessible location.

16.10.5.2.2 Where the capacity of isolated trapped sections of pipe is more than 5 gal (20 L) and less than 50 gal (200 L), the auxiliary drain shall consist of a valve ¾ in. (20 mm) or larger and a plug or a nipple and cap.

16.10.5.2.3 Where the capacity of trapped sections of pipes in wet systems is less than 5 gal (20 L), one of the following arrangements shall be provided:

(1) An auxiliary drain shall consist of a nipple and cap or plug not less than ½ in. (15 mm) in size.
(2) An auxiliary drain shall not be required for trapped sections less than 5 gal (20 L) where the system piping can be drained by removing a single pendent sprinkler.
(3) Where flexible couplings, flexible hose connections, or other easily separated connections are used, the nipple and cap or plug shall be permitted to be omitted.

16.10.5.2.4 Tie-in drains shall not be required on wet pipe systems and preaction systems protecting nonfreezing environments.

16.10.5.3 Auxiliary Drains for Dry Pipe Systems and Preaction Systems.

16.10.5.3.1 Auxiliary drains located in areas subject to freezing shall be accessible.

16.10.5.3.2 Auxiliary drains located in areas maintained at freezing temperatures shall be accessible and shall consist of a valve not smaller than 1 in. (25 mm) and a plug or a nipple and cap.

16.10.5.3.3 Where the capacity of trapped sections of pipe is less than 5 gal (20 L), the auxiliary drain shall consist of a valve not smaller than ½ in. (15 mm) and a plug or a nipple and cap.

16.10.5.3.4* Auxiliary drains shall not be required for pipe drops supplying dry pendent sprinklers installed in accordance with 8.2.2, 8.3.2.6, and 8.7.3.4.

16.10.5.3.5 Where the capacity of isolated trapped sections of system piping is more than 5 gal (20 L), the auxiliary drain shall consist of two 1 in. (25 mm) valves and one 2 in. × 12 in. (50 mm × 300 mm) condensate nipple or equivalent, accessibly located in accordance with Figure 16.10.5.3.5, or a device listed for this service.

16.10.5.3.6 Tie-in drains shall be provided for multiple adjacent trapped branch pipes and shall be only 1 in. (25 mm). Tie-in drain lines shall be pitched a minimum of ½ in. per 10 ft (4 mm/m).

16.10.5.3.7 Systems with low point drains shall have a sign at the dry pipe or preaction valve indicating the number of low point drains and the location of each individual drain.

16.10.6 Discharge of Drain Valves.

16.10.6.1* Direct interconnections shall not be made between sprinkler drains and sewers.

16.10.6.2 The drain discharge shall conform to any health or water department regulations.

16.10.6.3 Where drain pipes are buried underground, approved corrosion-resistant pipe shall be used.

16.10.6.4 Drain pipes shall not terminate in blind spaces under the building.

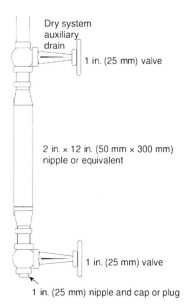

Dry system auxiliary drain

1 in. (25 mm) valve

2 in. × 12 in. (50 mm × 300 mm) nipple or equivalent

1 in. (25 mm) valve

1 in. (25 mm) nipple and cap or plug

FIGURE 16.10.5.3.5   Dry System Auxiliary Drain.

16.10.6.5 Where exposed to the atmosphere, drain pipes shall be fitted with a turned-down elbow.

16.10.6.6 Drain pipes shall be arranged to avoid exposing any of the water-filled portion of the sprinkler system to freezing conditions.

16.11 System Attachments.

16.11.1 Attachments — General.

16.11.1.1* An alarm unit shall include a listed mechanical alarm, horn, or siren or a listed electric gong, bell, speaker, horn, or siren.

16.11.1.2* Exterior water motor-operated or electrically operated bells shall be weatherproofed and guarded.

16.11.1.3 All piping to water motor-operated devices shall be galvanized steel, brass, copper, or other approved metallic corrosion-resistant material of not less than ¾ in. (20 mm) nominal pipe size.

16.11.1.4 Piping between the sprinkler system and a pressure-actuated alarm-initiating device shall be galvanized steel, brass, copper, or other approved metallic corrosion-resistant material of not less than ⅜ in. (10 mm) nominal pipe size.

16.11.2* Sprinkler Alarms/Waterflow Alarms.

16.11.2.1 Local Waterflow Alarms. A local waterflow alarm shall be provided on every sprinkler system having more than 20 sprinklers.

16.11.3 Waterflow Detection Devices.

16.11.3.1 Wet Pipe Systems. The alarm apparatus for a wet pipe system shall consist of a listed alarm check valve or other listed waterflow detection alarm device with the necessary attachments required to give an alarm.

16.11.3.2 Dry Pipe Systems.

16.11.3.2.1 The alarm apparatus for a dry pipe system shall consist of listed alarm attachments to the dry pipe valve.

16.11.3.2.2 Where a dry pipe valve is located on the system side of an alarm valve, connection of the actuating device of the alarms for the dry pipe valve to the alarms on the wet pipe system shall be permitted.

16.11.3.3 Preaction and Deluge Systems. The alarm apparatus for deluge and preaction systems shall consist of alarms actuated independently by the detection system and the flow of water.

16.11.3.3.1 Deluge and preaction systems activated by pilot sprinklers shall not require an independent detection system alarm.

16.11.3.4* Paddle-Type Waterflow Devices. Paddle-type waterflow alarm indicators shall be installed in wet systems only.

16.11.4 Retarding Devices. On each alarm check valve used under conditions of variable water pressure, a retarding device shall be installed.

16.11.5 Alarm Bypass Test Connections.

16.11.5.1 Alarm, dry pipe, preaction, and deluge valves shall be fitted with an alarm bypass test connection for an electric alarm switch, water motor gong, or both.

16.11.5.2 The alarm bypass test connection for alarm, dry pipe, preaction, and deluge valves shall be made on the water supply side of the system and provided with a control valve and drain for the alarm piping.

16.11.5.3 The alarm bypass test connection for alarm valves at the riser shall be permitted to be made on the system side of an alarm valve.

16.11.5.4 A check valve shall be installed between the intermediate chamber of a dry pipe valve and the waterflow alarm device so as to prevent flow from the alarm bypass test connection from entering the intermediate chamber of a dry pipe valve during an alarm test via the alarm bypass test connection.

16.11.6 Indicating Control Valves.

16.11.6.1 Where a control valve is installed in the connection to pressure-type contactors or water motor-operated alarm devices, it shall be of the indicating type.

16.11.6.2 Such valves shall be sealed, locked, or electrically supervised in the open position.

16.11.7* Attachments — Electrically Operated.

16.11.7.1 Electrically operated alarm attachments forming part of an auxiliary, central station, local protective, proprietary, or remote station signaling system shall be installed in accordance with *NFPA 72* or other approved fire alarm code.

16.11.7.2 Sprinkler waterflow alarm systems that are not part of a required protective signaling system shall not be required to be supervised and shall be installed in accordance with *NFPA 70*, Article 760.

16.11.7.3 Exterior electric alarm devices shall be listed for outdoor use.

16.11.8* Attachments — Mechanically Operated.

16.11.8.1 For all types of sprinkler systems employing water motor-operated alarms, a listed ¾ in. (20 mm) strainer shall be installed at the alarm outlet of the waterflow detecting device.

16.11.8.2 Where a retarding chamber is used in connection with an alarm valve, the strainer shall be located at the outlet of the retarding chamber unless the retarding chamber is provided with an approved integral strainer in its outlet.

16.11.9 Alarm Device Drains. Drains from alarm devices shall be arranged so that there will be no overflowing at the alarm apparatus, at domestic connections, or elsewhere with the sprinkler drains wide open and under system pressure. *(See 16.10.6.)*

16.11.10* Alarm Attachments — High-Rise Buildings. When a fire must be fought internally due to the height of a building, the following additional alarm apparatus shall be provided:

(1)	Each sprinkler system on each floor shall be equipped with a separate waterflow device. The waterflow device shall be connected to an alarm system in such a manner that operation of one sprinkler will actuate the alarm system, and the location of the operated flow device shall be indicated on an annunciator and/or register. The annunciator or register shall be located at grade level at the normal point of fire department access, at a constantly attended building security control center, or at both locations.

(2) Where the location within the protected buildings where supervisory or alarm signals are received is not under constant supervision by qualified personnel in the employ of the owner, a connection shall be provided to transmit a signal to a remote central station.

(3) A distinct trouble signal shall be provided to indicate a condition that will impair the satisfactory operation of the sprinkler system.

16.12* Fire Department Connections.

16.12.1* Unless the requirements of 16.12.2 are met, a fire department connection shall be provided as described in Section 16.12 in accordance with Figure 16.12.1.

16.12.2 The following systems shall not require a fire department connection:

(1) Buildings located in remote areas that are inaccessible for fire department support

(2) Large-capacity deluge systems exceeding the pumping capacity of the fire department

(3) Single-story buildings not exceeding 2000 ft² (185 m²) in area

Δ 16.12.3 Fire Department Connection Types.

16.12.3.1* Unless the requirements of 16.12.3.1.1, 16.12.3.1.2, or 16.12.3.1.3 are met, the fire department connection(s) shall consist of two 2½ in. (65 mm) connections using NH internal threaded swivel fitting(s) with "2.5–7.5 NH standard thread," as specified in NFPA 1963.

16.12.3.1.1 Where local fire department connections do not conform to NFPA 1963, the authority having jurisdiction shall be permitted to designate the connection to be used.

16.12.3.1.2 The use of threadless couplings shall be permitted where required by the authority having jurisdiction and where listed for such use.

16.12.3.1.3 A single-outlet fire department connection shall be acceptable where piped to a 3 in. (80 mm) or smaller riser.

16.12.3.2 Fire department connections shall be equipped with approved plugs or caps, properly secured and arranged for easy removal by fire departments.

16.12.3.3 Fire department connections shall be of an approved type.

16.12.4* **Size.** The size of the pipe for the fire department connection shall be in accordance with one of the following:

(1) Pipe size shall be a minimum of 4 in. (100 mm) for fire engine connections.

(2) Pipe size shall be a minimum of 6 in. (150 mm) for fire boat connections.

(3) For hydraulically calculated systems, the pipe size shall be permitted to be less than 4 in. (100 mm), but not less than the largest riser being served by that connection.

16.12.5* **Arrangement.** The fire department connection shall be arranged in accordance with Figure 16.12.1.

16.12.5.1* The fire department connection shall be on the system side of the water supply check valve.

16.12.5.1.1 The fire department connection shall not be attached to branch line piping.

16.12.5.1.2 The fire department connection shall be located not less than 18 in. (450 mm) and not more than 4 ft (1.2 m) above the level of the adjacent grade or access level.

16.12.5.2 For single systems, the fire department connection shall be installed as follows:

(1) Wet system — on the system side of system control, check, and alarm valves *(see Figure A.16.9.3)*

(2) Dry system — between the system control valve and the dry pipe valve

(3) Preaction system — between the preaction valve and the check valve on the system side of the preaction valve

(4) Deluge system — on the system side of the deluge valve

16.12.5.3 The fire department connection shall be permitted to be connected to the main piping on the wet pipe or deluge system it serves.

16.12.5.4 For multiple systems, the fire department connection shall be connected between the supply control valves and the system control valves.

16.12.5.5* The requirements of 16.12.5.2 and 16.12.5.4 shall not apply where the fire department connection is connected to the underground piping.

16.12.5.6 Where a fire department connection services only a portion of a building, a sign shall be attached indicating the portions of the building served.

16.12.5.7* Fire department connections shall be located at the nearest point of fire department apparatus accessibility or at a location approved by the authority having jurisdiction.

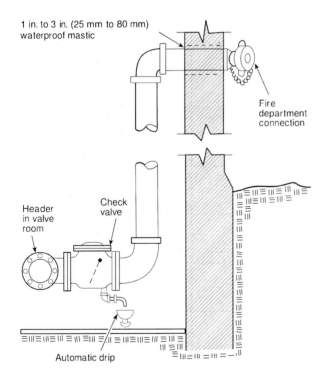

1 in. to 3 in. (25 mm to 80 mm) waterproof mastic

Fire department connection

Header in valve room

Check valve

Automatic drip

FIGURE 16.12.1   Fire Department Connection.

16.12.5.8 Signs.

16.12.5.8.1 Each fire department connection to sprinkler systems shall be designated by a sign having raised or engraved letters at least 1 in. (25 mm) in height on plate or fitting reading service design — for example, AUTOSPKR., OPEN SPKR., AND STANDPIPE.

16.12.5.8.2 A sign shall also indicate the pressure required at the inlets to deliver the greatest system demand.

16.12.5.8.3 The sign required in 16.12.5.8.2 shall not be required where the system demand pressure is less than 150 psi (10.3 bar).

16.12.5.9 Fire department connections shall not be connected on the suction side of fire pumps.

16.12.5.10 Fire department connections shall be properly supported.

16.12.6 Valves.

16.12.6.1 A listed check valve shall be installed in each fire department connection and shall be located in an accessible location.

16.12.6.2 There shall be no shutoff valve in the fire department connection piping.

16.12.7* Drainage. The piping between the check valve and the outside hose coupling shall be equipped with an approved automatic drain valve in areas subject to freezing.

16.12.7.1 The automatic drain valve shall be installed in a location that permits inspection and testing as required by NFPA 25.

16.13 Gauges.

16.13.1 A pressure gauge with a connection not smaller than ¼ in. (6 mm) shall be installed at the system main drain, at each main drain associated with a floor control valve, and on the inlet and outlet side of each pressure-reducing valve.

16.13.2 Each gauge connection shall be equipped with a shut-off valve and provisions for draining.

16.13.3 The required pressure gauges shall be approved and shall have a maximum limit not less than twice the normal system working pressure at the point where installed.

16.13.4 Gauges shall be installed to permit removal and shall be located where they will not be subject to freezing.

16.14 System Connections.

16.14.1* Wet Pipe Systems.

16.14.1.1 An alarm test connection not less than 1 in. (25 mm) in diameter, terminating in a smooth bore corrosion-resistant orifice, giving a flow equal to or less than one sprinkler of a type having the smallest K-factor installed on the particular system, shall be provided to test each waterflow alarm device for each system.

16.14.1.2 The test connection valve shall be accessible.

16.14.1.3 The discharge shall be to the outside, to a drain connection capable of accepting full flow under system pressure, or to another location where water damage will not result.

16.14.1.4 The alarm test connection shall be permitted to be installed in any location on the fire sprinkler system downstream of the waterflow alarm.

Δ 16.14.2* Dry Pipe Systems.

16.14.2.1 A trip test connection or manifold not less than 1 in. (25 mm) in diameter, terminating in a smooth bore corrosion-resistant orifice, to provide a flow equivalent to one sprinkler of a type installed on the particular system, shall be installed.

16.14.2.2 The trip test connection or manifold shall be located on the end of the most distant sprinkler pipe in the upper story and shall be equipped with an accessible shutoff valve and a plug not less than 1 in. (25 mm), of which at least one shall be brass.

16.14.2.3 In lieu of a plug, a nipple and cap shall be acceptable.

16.14.2.4 When the capacity (volume) of the dry pipe system has been determined in accordance with 8.2.3.2, 8.2.3.3, 8.2.3.4, or 8.2.3.5, a trip test connection shall be permitted to provide a flow equivalent to one sprinkler in accordance with 16.14.2.1 through 16.14.2.3.

16.14.2.5 When the capacity (volume) of the dry pipe system has been determined in accordance with 8.2.3.7, the following shall apply:

(1) When flow is from four sprinklers, the trip test manifold shall be arranged to simulate two sprinklers on each of two sprinkler branch lines.
(2) When flow is from three sprinklers, the test manifold shall be arranged to simulate two sprinklers on the most remote branch line and one sprinkler on the next adjacent branch line.
(3) When flow is from two sprinklers, the test manifold shall be arranged to simulate two sprinklers on the most remote branch line.
(4) When flow is from one sprinkler, the test manifold shall be installed per the requirements for a trip test connection in accordance with 16.14.2.1 through 16.14.2.3.

16.14.3 Preaction Systems.

16.14.3.1 A test connection shall be provided on a preaction system using supervisory air.

16.14.3.2 The connection used to control the level of priming water shall be considered adequate to test the operation of the alarms monitoring the supervisory air pressure.

16.14.3.3 For double interlock preaction systems, a trip test connection or manifold not less than 1 in. (25 mm) in diameter, terminating in a smooth bore corrosion-resistant orifice to provide a flow equivalent to one sprinkler of a type installed on the particular system, shall be installed.

16.14.3.4 For double interlock preaction systems, the trip test connection or manifold shall be located on the end of the most distant sprinkler pipe in the upper story and shall be equipped with an accessible shutoff valve and a plug not less than 1 in. (25 mm), of which at least one shall be brass.

16.14.3.5 In lieu of a plug, a nipple and cap shall be acceptable.

16.14.3.6 When the capacity (volume) of the double interlock preaction system has been determined in accordance with

8.3.2.3.1.1, 8.3.2.3.1.2, or 8.3.2.3.1.3, a trip test connection shall be permitted to provide a flow equivalent to one sprinkler in accordance with 16.14.3.3 through 16.14.3.5.

16.14.3.7 When the capacity (volume) of the double interlock preaction system has been determined in accordance with 8.3.2.3.1.4, the following shall apply:

(1) When flow is from four sprinklers, the trip test manifold shall be arranged to simulate two sprinklers on each of two sprinkler branch lines.
(2) When flow is from three sprinklers, the test manifold shall be arranged to simulate two sprinklers on the most remote branch line and one sprinkler on the next adjacent branch line.
(3) When flow is from two sprinklers, the test manifold shall be arranged to simulate two sprinklers on the most remote branch line.
(4) When flow is from one sprinkler, the test manifold shall be installed as per the requirements for a trip test connection in accordance with 16.14.3.3 through 16.14.3.5.

16.14.4 Deluge Systems. A test connection shall not be required on a deluge system.

16.14.5* Backflow Devices.

16.14.5.1* Backflow Prevention Valves. A test connection shall be provided downstream of all backflow prevention valves for the performance of forward flow tests required by this standard and NFPA 25 at a minimum flow rate of the system demand including hose allowance where applicable.

N **16.14.5.1.1** A 2 ½ in. (65 mm) hose valve shall be provided downstream of the backflow prevention valve for every 250 gpm (950 L/min) of flow rate required by the system demand including hose allowance where applicable.

N **16.14.5.1.2*** Existing hose connections downstream of the backflow prevention valve shall be allowed to be utilized.

N **16.14.5.1.3*** Other means shall be permitted as long as the system doesn't require modification to perform the test and it is sized to meet the system demand.

16.15 Hose Connections.

16.15.1 Small [1½ in. (40 mm)] Hose Connections. See Section C.5.

16.15.1.1* Where required, small [1½ in. (40 mm)] hose connections shall be installed.

16.15.1.1.1 Valves shall be available to reach all portions of the area with 100 ft (30 m) of hose plus 30 ft (9.1 m) of hose stream distance.

16.15.1.1.2 Where the building is protected throughout by an approved automatic sprinkler system, the presence of 1½ in. (40 mm) hose lines for use by the building occupants shall not be required, subject to the approval of the authority having jurisdiction.

16.15.1.1.3 Where approved by the authority having jurisdiction, the location of valves shall be permitted to exceed the distances specified in 16.15.1.1.1.

16.15.1.2 The hose connections shall not be required to meet the requirements of Class II hose systems defined by NFPA 14.

16.15.1.3 Hose connections shall be supplied from one of the following:

(1) Outside hydrants
(2) Separate piping system for small hose connections
(3) Valved hose connections on sprinkler risers where such connections are made upstream of all sprinkler control valves
(4) Adjacent sprinkler systems
(5) In rack storage areas, the ceiling sprinkler system in the same area (as long as in-rack sprinklers are provided in the same area and are separately controlled)
(6) In nonstorage occupancies that are not a part of a standpipe system, ceiling sprinkler piping in the same area as the hose connection

16.15.1.4* Hose connections used for fire purposes only shall be permitted to be connected to wet pipe sprinkler systems only, subject to the following restrictions:

(1) Hose connection's supply pipes shall not be connected to any pipe smaller than 2½ in. (65 mm) in diameter.
(2) The requirements of 16.15.1.4(1) shall not apply to hydraulically designed loops and grids, where the minimum size pipe between the hose connection's supply pipe and the source shall be permitted to be 2 in. (50 mm).
(3) For piping serving a single hose connection, pipe shall be a minimum of 1 in. (25 mm) for horizontal runs up to 20 ft (6.1 m), a minimum of 1¼ in. (32 mm) for the entire run for runs between 20 ft and 80 ft (6.1 m and 24 m), and a minimum of 1½ in. (40 mm) for the entire run for runs greater than 80 ft (24 m). For piping serving multiple hose connections, runs shall be a minimum of 1½ in. (40 mm) throughout.
(4) Piping shall be at least 1 in. (25 mm) for vertical runs.
(5) Where the residual pressure at a 1½ in. (40 mm) outlet on a hose connection exceeds 100 psi (7 bar), an approved pressure-regulating device shall be provided to limit the residual pressure at the outlet to 100 psi (7 bar).
(6) Where the static pressure at a 1½ in. (40 mm) hose connection exceeds 175 psi (12 bar), an approved pressure-regulating device shall be provided to limit static and residual pressures at the outlet to 100 psi (7 bar).

16.15.2 Hose Connections for Fire Department Use.

16.15.2.1 In buildings of light or ordinary hazard occupancy, 2½ in. (65 mm) hose valves for fire department use shall be permitted to be attached to wet pipe sprinkler system risers.

16.15.2.2* The following restrictions shall apply:

(1) Each connection from a standpipe that is part of a combined system to a sprinkler system shall have an individual control valve and check valve of the same size as the connection.
(2) The minimum size of the riser shall be 4 in. (100 mm) unless hydraulic calculations indicate that a smaller size riser will satisfy sprinkler and hose stream allowances.
(3) Each combined sprinkler and standpipe riser shall be equipped with a riser control valve to permit isolating a riser without interrupting the supply to other risers from the same source of supply. *(For fire department connections serving standpipe and sprinkler systems, refer to Section 16.12.)*

16.16 Electrical Bonding and Grounding.

16.16.1 In no case shall sprinkler system piping be used for the grounding of electrical systems.

16.16.2* The requirement of 16.16.1 shall not preclude the bonding of the sprinkler system piping to the lightning protection grounding system as required by NFPA 780 in those cases where lightning protection is provided for the structure.

16.17* Signs. (Reserved)

Chapter 17 Installation Requirements for Hanging and Support of System Piping

17.1* General.

17.1.1 Unless the requirements of 17.1.2 are met, types of hangers shall be in accordance with the requirements of Chapter 17.

17.1.2 Hangers certified by a registered professional engineer to include all of the following shall be an acceptable alternative to the requirements of Chapter 17:

(1) Hangers shall be designed to support five times the weight of the water-filled pipe plus 250 lb (115 kg) at each point of piping support.
(2) These points of support shall be adequate to support the system.
(3) The spacing between hangers shall not exceed the value given for the type of pipe as indicated in Table 17.4.2.1(a) or Table 17.4.2.1(b).
(4) Hanger components shall be ferrous.
(5) Detailed calculations shall be submitted, when required by the reviewing authority, showing stresses developed in hangers, piping, and fittings, and safety factors allowed.

17.1.3 Support of Non-System Components.

17.1.3.1* Sprinkler piping or hangers shall not be used to support non-system components.

17.1.3.2 Sprinkler piping shall be permitted to utilize shared support assemblies in accordance with 17.1.4.

17.1.4 Shared support assemblies shall be certified by a registered professional engineer in accordance with 17.1.2 and 17.1.4.

17.1.4.1* The design of a shared support assembly shall be based on either 17.1.4.1.1 or 17.1.4.1.2.

17.1.4.1.1 Sprinkler pipe and other distribution systems shall be permitted to be supported from a shared support assembly designed to support five times the weight of water-filled sprinkler pipe and other supported distribution systems plus 250 lb (115 kg), based on the allowable ultimate stress.

17.1.4.1.2 Sprinkler pipe and other distribution systems shall be permitted to be supported from a shared support assembly designed to support five times the weight of the water-filled sprinkler pipe plus 250 lb (115 kg), and one and one-half times the weight of all other supported distribution systems.

17.1.4.1.3 The building structure shall not be considered a shared support assembly.

17.1.4.1.4* The requirements of 17.1.4.1 shall not apply to 17.4.1.3.3.

17.1.4.1.5 Systems that are incompatible with the fire sprinkler systems based on vibration, thermal expansion and contraction, or other factors shall not share support assemblies.

17.1.5 Where water-based fire protection systems are required to be protected against damage from earthquakes, hangers shall also meet the requirements of Section 18.7.

17.1.6 Listing.

17.1.6.1* Unless permitted by 17.1.6.2 or 17.1.6.3, the components of hanger assemblies that directly attach to the pipe, building structure, or racking structure shall be listed.

17.1.6.2* Mild steel hanger rods and hangers formed from mild steel rods shall be permitted to be not listed.

17.1.6.3* Fasteners as specified in 17.2.2, 17.2.3, and 17.2.4 shall be permitted to be not listed.

17.1.6.4 Other fasteners shall be permitted as part of a hanger assembly that has been tested, listed, and installed in accordance with the listing requirements.

17.1.7 Component Material.

17.1.7.1 Unless permitted by 17.1.7.2 or 17.1.7.3, hangers and their components shall be ferrous metal.

17.1.7.2 Nonferrous components that have been proven by fire tests to be adequate for the hazard application, that are listed for this purpose, and that are in compliance with the other requirements of this section shall be acceptable.

17.1.7.3 Holes through solid structural members shall be permitted to serve as hangers for the support of system piping, provided such holes are permitted by applicable building codes and the spacing and support provisions for hangers of this standard are satisfied.

17.2 Hanger Components.

17.2.1 Hanger Rods.

17.2.1.1 Unless the requirements of 17.2.1.2 are met, hanger rod size shall be the same as that approved for use with the hanger assembly, and the size of rods shall not be less than that given in Table 17.2.1.1.

Table 17.2.1.1 Hanger Rod Sizes

Pipe Size		Diameter of Rod	
in.	mm	in.	mm
Up to and including 4	100	$\frac{3}{8}$	10
5	125	$\frac{1}{2}$	13
6	150		
8	200		
10	250	$\frac{5}{8}$	16
12	300	$\frac{3}{4}$	20

17.2.1.2 Rods of smaller diameters than indicated in Table 17.2.1.1 shall be permitted where the hanger assembly has been tested and listed by a testing laboratory and installed within the limits of pipe sizes expressed in individual listings.

17.2.1.3 Where the pitch of the branch line is 6 in 12 or greater, a reduction in the lateral loading on branch line hanger rods shall be done by one of the following:

(1)* Second hanger installed in addition to the required main hangers
(2) Lateral sway brace assemblies on the mains
(3) Branch line hangers utilizing an articulating structural attachment

Table 17.2.1.4 U-Hook Rod Sizes

Pipe Size		Hook Material Diameter	
in.	mm	in.	mm
Up to and including 2	50	5/16	8
2½ to 6	65 to 150	3/8	10
8	200	½	13

Table 17.2.1.5.1 Eye Rod Sizes

Pipe Size		Diameter of Rod			
		With Bent Eye		With Welded Eye	
in.	mm	in.	mm	in.	mm
Up to and including 4	100	3/8	10	3/8	10
5	125	½	13	½	13
6	150	½	13	½	13
8	200	3/4	20	½	13

(4) Equivalent means providing support to the branch line hanger rods

17.2.1.4 U-Hooks. The size of the rod material of U-hooks shall not be less than that given in Table 17.2.1.4.

17.2.1.5 Eye Rods.

17.2.1.5.1 The size of the rod material for eye rods shall not be less than specified in Table 17.2.1.5.1.

17.2.1.5.2 Eye rods shall be secured with lock washers to prevent lateral motion.

17.2.1.5.3 Where eye rods are fastened to wood structural members, the eye rod shall be backed with a large flat washer bearing directly against the structural member, in addition to the lock washer.

17.2.1.6 Threaded Sections of Rods. Threaded sections of rods shall not be formed or bent.

17.2.2* Fasteners in Concrete.

17.2.2.1 Unless prohibited by 17.2.2.2 or 17.2.2.3, the use of listed inserts set in concrete and listed post-installed anchors to support hangers shall be permitted for mains and branch lines.

17.2.2.2 Post-installed anchors shall not be used in cinder concrete, except for branch lines where the post-installed anchors are alternated with through-bolts or hangers attached to beams.

17.2.2.3 Post-installed anchors shall not be used in ceilings of gypsum or other similar soft material.

17.2.2.4 Unless the requirements of 17.2.2.5 are met, post-installed anchors shall be installed in a horizontal position in the sides of concrete beams.

17.2.2.5 Post-installed anchors shall be permitted to be installed in the vertical position under any of the following conditions:

(1) When used in concrete having gravel or crushed stone aggregate to support pipes 4 in. (100 mm) or less in diameter
(2) When post-installed anchors are alternated with hangers connected directly to the structural members, such as trusses and girders, or to the sides of concrete beams [to support pipe 5 in. (125 mm) or larger]
(3) When post-installed anchors are spaced not over 10 ft (3 m) apart [to support pipe 4 in. (100 mm) or larger]

17.2.2.6 Holes for post-installed anchors in the side of beams shall be above the centerline of the beam or above the bottom reinforcement steel rods.

17.2.2.7 Holes for post-installed anchors used in the vertical position shall be drilled to provide uniform contact with the shield over its entire circumference.

17.2.2.8 The depth of the post-installed anchor hole shall not be less than specified for the type of shield used.

17.2.2.9 Powder-Driven Studs.

17.2.2.9.1 Powder-driven studs, welding studs, and the tools used for installing these devices shall be listed.

17.2.2.9.2 Pipe size, installation position, and construction material into which they are installed shall be in accordance with individual listings.

17.2.2.9.3* Where test records indicating the strength of the concrete into which studs are being driven are not available, representative samples of the concrete shall be tested to determine that the studs will hold a minimum load of 750 lb (340 kg) for 2 in. (50 mm) or smaller pipe; 1000 lb (454 kg) for 2½ in., 3 in., or 3½ in. (65 mm, 80 mm, or 90 mm) pipe; and 1200 lb (544 kg) for 4 in. or 5 in. (100 mm or 125 mm) pipe.

17.2.2.9.4 Increaser couplings shall be attached directly to the powder-driven studs.

17.2.2.10 Minimum Bolt or Rod Size for Concrete.

17.2.2.10.1 The size of a bolt or rod used with a hanger and installed through concrete shall not be less than specified in Table 17.2.2.10.1.

Table 17.2.2.10.1 Minimum Bolt or Rod Size for Concrete

Pipe Size		Size of Bolt or Rod	
in.	mm	in.	mm
Up to and including 4	100	3/8	10
5	125	½	13
6	150		
8	200		
10	250	5/8	16
12	300	3/4	20

17.2.2.10.2 Holes for bolts or rods shall not exceed $\frac{1}{16}$ in. (1.6 mm) greater than the diameter of the bolt or rod.

17.2.2.10.3 Bolts and rods shall be provided with flat washers and nuts.

17.2.3 Fasteners in Steel.

17.2.3.1* Powder-driven studs, welding studs, and the tools used for installing these devices shall be listed.

17.2.3.2 Pipe size, installation position, and construction material into which they are installed shall be in accordance with individual listings.

17.2.3.3 Increaser couplings shall be attached directly to the powder-driven studs or welding studs.

17.2.3.4 Welding studs or other hanger parts shall not be attached by welding to steel less than U.S. Standard, 12 gauge (2.8 mm).

17.2.3.5 Minimum Bolt or Rod Size for Steel.

17.2.3.5.1 The size of a bolt or rod used with a hanger and installed through steel shall not be less than specified in Table 17.2.3.5.1.

17.2.3.5.2 Holes for bolts or rods shall not exceed $\frac{1}{16}$ in. (1.6 mm) greater than the diameter of the bolt or rod.

17.2.3.5.3 Bolts and rods shall be provided with flat washers and nuts.

17.2.4 Fasteners in Wood.

17.2.4.1 Drive Screws.

17.2.4.1.1 Drive screws shall be used only in a horizontal position as in the side of a beam and only for 2 in. (50 mm) or smaller pipe.

17.2.4.1.2 Drive screws shall only be used in conjunction with hangers that require two points of attachments.

17.2.4.2 Ceiling Flanges and U-Hooks with Screws.

17.2.4.2.1 Unless the requirements of 17.2.4.2.2 or 17.2.4.2.3 are met, for ceiling flanges and U-hooks, screw dimensions shall not be less than those given in Table 17.2.4.2.1.

17.2.4.2.2 When the thickness of planking and thickness of flange do not permit the use of screws 2 in. (50 mm) long, screws $1\frac{3}{4}$ in. (45 mm) long shall be permitted with hangers spaced not over 10 ft (3 m) apart.

Table 17.2.3.5.1 Minimum Bolt or Rod Size for Steel

Pipe Size		Size of Bolt or Rod	
in.	mm	in.	mm
Up to and including 4	100	$\frac{3}{8}$	10
5	125	$\frac{1}{2}$	13
6	150		
8	200		
10	250	$\frac{5}{8}$	15
12	300	$\frac{3}{4}$	20

Table 17.2.4.2.1 Screw Dimensions for Ceiling Flanges and U-Hooks

Pipe Size		
in.	mm	**Two Screw Ceiling Flanges**
Up to and including 2	50	Wood screw No. 18 × 1½ in. or Lag screw $\frac{5}{16}$ in. × 1½ in. (8 mm × 40 mm)
		Three Screw Ceiling Flanges
Up to and including 2	50	Wood screw No. 18 × 1½ in.
2½	65	Lag screw $\frac{3}{8}$ in. × 2 in. (10 mm × 50 mm)
3	80	
3½	90	
4	100	Lag screw $\frac{1}{2}$ in. × 2 in. (13 mm × 50 mm)
5	125	
6	150	
8	200	Lag screw $\frac{5}{8}$ in. × 2 in. (16 mm × 50 mm)
		Four Screw Ceiling Flanges
Up to and including 2	50	Wood screw No. 18 × 1½ in.
2½	65	Lag screw $\frac{3}{8}$ in. × 1½ in. (10 mm × 40 mm)
3	80	
3½	90	
4	100	Lag screw $\frac{1}{2}$ in. × 2 in. (13 mm × 50 mm)
5	125	
6	150	
8	200	Lag screw $\frac{5}{8}$ in. × 2 in. (16 mm × 50 mm)
		U-Hooks
Up to and including 2	50	Drive screw No. 16 × 2 in.
2½	65	Lag screw $\frac{3}{8}$ in. × 2½ in. (10 mm × 65 mm)
3	80	
3½	90	
4	100	Lag screw $\frac{1}{2}$ in. × 3 in. (13 mm × 75 mm)
5	125	
6	150	
8	200	Lag screw $\frac{5}{8}$ in. × 3 in. (16 mm × 75 mm)

17.2.4.2.3 When the thickness of beams or joists does not permit the use of screws 2½ in. (65 mm) long, screws 2 in. (50 mm) long shall be permitted with hangers spaced not over 10 ft (3 m) apart.

17.2.4.3 Bolts, Rods, or Lag Screws.

17.2.4.3.1 Unless the requirements of 17.2.4.3.2 are met, the size of bolt, rod, or lag screw used with a hanger and installed on the side of the beam shall not be less than specified in Table 17.2.4.3.1.

17.2.4.3.2 Where the thickness of beams or joists does not permit the use of screws 2½ in. (65 mm) long, screws 2 in. (50 mm) long shall be permitted with hangers spaced not over 10 ft (3 m) apart.

17.2.4.3.3 All holes for lag screws shall be pre-drilled ⅛ in. (3 mm) less in diameter than the maximum root diameter of the lag screw thread.

17.2.4.3.4 Holes for bolts or rods shall not exceed 1/16 in. (1.6 mm) greater than the diameter of the bolt or rod.

17.2.4.3.5 Bolts and rods shall be provided with flat washers and nuts.

17.2.4.4 Wood Screws. Wood screws shall be installed with a screwdriver.

17.2.4.5 Nails. Nails shall not be acceptable for fastening hangers.

17.2.4.6 Screws in Side of Timber or Joists.

17.2.4.6.1 Screws in the side of a timber or joist shall be not less than 2½ in. (65 mm) from the lower edge where supporting pipe is up to and including nominal 2½ in. (65 mm) and not less than 3 in. (75 mm) where supporting pipe is greater than nominal 2½ in. (65 mm).

17.2.4.6.2 The requirements of 17.2.4.6.1 shall not apply to 2 in. (50 mm) or thicker nailing strips resting on top of steel beams.

17.2.4.7 Coach Screw Rods.

17.2.4.7.1 Minimum Coach Screw Rod Size. The size of coach screw rods shall not be less than the requirements of Table 17.2.4.7.1.

17.2.4.7.2 The minimum plank thickness and the minimum width of the lower face of beams or joists in which coach screw rods are used shall be not less than that specified in Table 17.2.4.7.2 and shown in Figure 17.2.4.7.2.

Table 17.2.4.3.1 Minimum Bolt, Rod, or Lag Screw Sizes for Side of Beam Installation

Pipe Size		Size of Bolt, Rod or Lag Screw		Length of Lag Screw Used with Wood Beams	
in.	mm	in.	mm	in.	mm
Up to and including 2	50	⅜	10	2½	65
2½ to 6 (inclusive)	65 to 150	½	13	3	75
8	200	⅝	16	3	75

Table 17.2.4.7.1 Minimum Coach Screw Rod Size

Pipe Size		Diameter of Rod		Minimum Penetration	
in.	mm	in.	mm	in.	mm
Up to and including 4	100	⅜	10	3	75
Larger than 4	100	NP	NP	NP	NP

NP: Not permitted.

Table 17.2.4.7.2 Minimum Plank Thicknesses and Beam or Joist Widths

Pipe Size		Nominal Plank Thickness		Nominal Width of Beam or Joist Face	
in.	mm	in.	mm	in.	mm
Up to and including 2	50	3	75	2	50
2½	65	4	100	2	50
3	80	4	100	3	75
3½	90				
4	100				

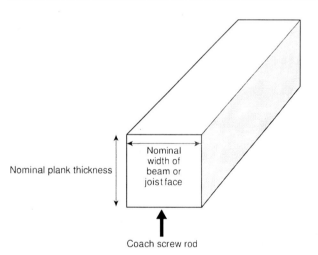

FIGURE 17.2.4.7.2   Dimensions for Structural Members with Coach Screw Rods.

17.2.4.7.3 Coach screw rods shall not be used for support of pipes larger than 4 in. (100 mm) in diameter.

17.2.4.7.4 All holes for coach screw rods shall be predrilled ⅛ in. (3 mm) less in diameter than the maximum root diameter of the wood screw thread.

17.3* Trapeze Hangers.

17.3.1 For trapeze hangers, the minimum size of steel angle or pipe span between structural members shall be such that the section modulus required in Table 17.3.1(a) or Table 17.3.1(b) does not exceed the available section modulus of the trapeze member in Table 17.3.1(c) or Table 17.3.1(d).

Δ Table 17.3.1(a) Section Modulus Required for Trapeze Members (in.^{3})

Span (ft)	Nominal Diameter of Pipe Being Supported — Schedule 10 Steel											
	1	1.25	1.5	2	2.5	3	3.5	4	5	6	8	10
1.5	0.08	0.08	0.09	0.09	0.10	0.11	0.12	0.13	0.15	0.18	0.26	0.34
2.0	0.11	0.11	0.12	0.13	0.14	0.15	0.16	0.17	0.20	0.24	0.34	0.45
2.5	0.14	0.14	0.15	0.16	0.17	0.18	0.20	0.21	0.25	0.30	0.43	0.56
3.0	0.16	0.17	0.18	0.19	0.20	0.22	0.24	0.26	0.31	0.36	0.51	0.67
3.5	0.19	0.20	0.21	0.22	0.24	0.26	0.28	0.30	0.36	0.42	0.60	0.78
4.0	0.22	0.22	0.24	0.25	0.27	0.30	0.32	0.34	0.41	0.48	0.68	0.89
4.5	0.24	0.25	0.27	0.28	0.30	0.33	0.36	0.38	0.46	0.54	0.77	1.01
5.0	0.27	0.28	0.30	0.31	0.34	0.37	0.40	0.43	0.51	0.60	0.85	1.12
5.5	0.30	0.31	0.33	0.34	0.37	0.41	0.44	0.47	0.56	0.66	0.94	1.23
6.0	0.33	0.34	0.35	0.38	0.41	0.44	0.48	0.51	0.61	0.71	1.02	1.34
6.5	0.35	0.36	0.38	0.41	0.44	0.48	0.52	0.56	0.66	0.77	1.11	1.45
7.0	0.38	0.39	0.41	0.44	0.47	0.52	0.56	0.60	0.71	0.83	1.19	1.56
7.5	0.41	0.42	0.44	0.47	0.51	0.55	0.60	0.64	0.76	0.89	1.28	1.68
8.0	0.43	0.45	0.47	0.50	0.54	0.59	0.63	0.68	0.82	0.95	1.36	1.79
8.5	0.46	0.48	0.50	0.53	0.58	0.63	0.67	0.73	0.87	1.01	1.45	1.90
9.0	0.49	0.50	0.53	0.56	0.61	0.66	0.71	0.77	0.92	1.07	1.53	2.01
9.5	0.52	0.53	0.56	0.60	0.64	0.70	0.75	0.81	0.97	1.13	1.62	2.12
10.0	0.54	0.56	0.59	0.63	0.68	0.74	0.79	0.85	1.02	1.19	1.70	2.23
10.5	0.57	0.59	0.62	0.66	0.71	0.78	0.83	0.90	1.07	1.25	1.79	2.35
11.0	0.60	0.62	0.65	0.69	0.74	0.81	0.87	0.94	1.12	1.31	1.87	2.46
11.5	0.63	0.64	0.68	0.72	0.78	0.85	0.91	0.98	1.17	1.37	1.96	2.57
12.0	0.65	0.67	0.71	0.75	0.81	0.89	0.95	1.02	1.22	1.43	2.04	2.68
12.5	0.68	0.70	0.74	0.78	0.85	0.92	0.99	1.07	1.27	1.49	2.13	2.79
13.0	0.71	0.73	0.77	0.81	0.88	0.96	1.03	1.11	1.33	1.55	2.21	2.90
13.5	0.73	0.76	0.80	0.85	0.91	1.00	1.07	1.15	1.38	1.61	2.30	3.02
14.0	0.76	0.78	0.83	0.88	0.95	1.03	1.11	1.20	1.43	1.67	2.38	3.13
14.5	0.79	0.81	0.86	0.91	0.98	1.07	1.15	1.24	1.48	1.73	2.47	3.24
15.0	0.82	0.84	0.89	0.94	1.02	1.11	1.19	1.28	1.53	1.79	2.56	3.35
15.5	0.84	0.87	0.92	0.97	1.05	1.14	1.23	1.32	1.58	1.85	2.64	3.46
16.0	0.87	0.90	0.95	1.00	1.08	1.18	1.27	1.37	1.63	1.91	2.73	3.58

Span (ft)	Nominal Diameter of Pipe Being Supported — Schedule 40 Steel											
	1	1.25	1.5	2	2.5	3	3.5	4	5	6	8	10
1.5	0.08	0.09	0.09	0.1	0.11	0.12	0.14	0.15	0.18	0.22	0.30	0.41
2.0	0.11	0.11	0.12	0.13	0.15	0.16	0.18	0.20	0.24	0.29	0.40	0.55
2.5	0.14	0.14	0.15	0.16	0.18	0.21	0.23	0.25	0.30	0.36	0.50	0.69
3.0	0.16	0.17	0.18	0.20	0.22	0.25	0.27	0.30	0.36	0.43	0.60	0.82
3.5	0.19	0.20	0.21	0.23	0.26	0.29	0.32	0.35	0.42	0.51	0.70	0.96
4.0	0.22	0.23	0.24	0.26	0.29	0.33	0.36	0.40	0.48	0.58	0.80	1.10
4.5	0.25	0.26	0.27	0.29	0.33	0.37	0.41	0.45	0.54	0.65	0.90	1.23
5.0	0.27	0.29	0.30	0.33	0.37	0.41	0.45	0.49	0.60	0.72	1.00	1.37
5.5	0.30	0.31	0.33	0.36	0.40	0.45	0.50	0.54	0.66	0.79	1.10	1.51
6.0	0.33	0.34	0.36	0.39	0.44	0.49	0.54	0.59	0.72	0.87	1.20	1.64
6.5	0.36	0.37	0.40	0.42	0.48	0.54	0.59	0.64	0.78	0.94	1.31	1.78
7.0	0.38	0.40	0.43	0.46	0.52	0.58	0.63	0.69	0.84	1.01	1.41	1.92
7.5	0.41	0.43	0.46	0.49	0.55	0.62	0.68	0.74	0.90	1.08	1.51	2.06
8.0	0.44	0.46	0.49	0.52	0.59	0.66	0.72	0.79	0.96	1.16	1.61	2.19
8.5	0.47	0.48	0.52	0.56	0.63	0.70	0.77	0.84	1.02	1.23	1.71	2.33
9.0	0.49	0.51	0.55	0.59	0.66	0.74	0.81	0.89	1.08	1.30	1.81	2.47
9.5	0.52	0.54	0.58	0.62	0.70	0.78	0.86	0.94	1.14	1.37	1.91	2.60
10.0	0.55	0.57	0.61	0.65	0.74	0.82	0.90	0.99	1.20	1.45	2.01	2.74
10.5	0.58	0.60	0.64	0.69	0.77	0.86	0.95	1.04	1.26	1.52	2.11	2.88
11.0	0.60	0.63	0.67	0.72	0.81	0.91	0.99	1.09	1.32	1.59	2.21	3.01
11.5	0.63	0.66	0.70	0.75	0.85	0.95	1.04	1.14	1.38	1.66	2.31	3.15
12.0	0.66	0.68	0.73	0.78	0.88	0.99	1.08	1.19	1.44	1.73	2.41	3.29
12.5	0.69	0.71	0.76	0.82	0.92	1.03	1.13	1.24	1.5	1.81	2.51	3.43
13.0	0.71	0.74	0.79	0.85	0.96	1.07	1.17	1.29	1.56	1.88	2.61	3.56
13.5	0.74	0.77	0.82	0.88	0.99	1.11	1.22	1.34	1.62	1.95	2.71	3.70
14.0	0.77	0.80	0.85	0.91	1.03	1.15	1.26	1.39	1.68	2.02	2.81	3.84
14.5	0.80	0.83	0.88	0.95	1.07	1.19	1.31	1.43	1.74	2.1	2.91	3.97
15.0	0.82	0.86	0.91	0.98	1.10	1.24	1.35	1.48	1.8	2.17	3.01	4.11
15.5	0.85	0.88	0.94	1.01	1.14	1.28	1.4	1.53	1.86	2.24	3.11	4.25
16.0	0.88	0.91	0.97	1.05	1.18	1.32	1.44	1.58	1.92	2.31	3.21	4.39

Note: The table is based on a maximum bending stress of 15 ksi and a midspan concentrated load from 15 ft of water-filled pipe, plus 250 lb.

N Table 17.3.1(b) Section Modulus Required for Trapeze Members (mm³)

Span (m)	Nominal Diameter of Pipe Being Supported — Schedule 10 Steel											
	25	32	40	50	65	80	90	100	125	150	200	250
0.5	1310	1310	1470	1470	1640	1800	1970	2130	2460	2950	4260	5570
0.6	1800	1800	1970	2130	2290	2460	2620	2790	3280	3930	5570	7370
0.8	2290	2290	2460	2620	2790	2950	3280	3440	4100	4920	7050	9180
0.9	2620	2790	2950	3110	3280	3610	3930	4260	5080	5900	8360	10980
1.1	3110	3280	3440	3610	3930	4260	4590	4920	5900	6880	9830	12780
1.2	3610	3610	3930	4100	4420	4920	5240	5570	6720	7870	11140	14580
1.4	3930	4100	4420	4590	4920	5410	5900	6230	7540	8850	12620	16550
1.5	4420	4590	4920	5080	5570	6060	6550	7050	8360	9830	13930	18350
1.7	4920	5080	5410	5570	6060	6720	7210	7700	9180	10820	15400	20160
1.8	5410	5570	5740	6230	6720	7210	7870	8360	10000	11630	16710	21960
2.0	5740	5900	6230	6720	7210	7870	8520	9180	10820	12620	18190	23760
2.1	6230	6390	6720	7210	7700	8520	9180	9830	11630	13600	19500	25560
2.3	6720	6880	7210	7700	8360	9010	9830	10490	12450	14580	20980	27530
2.4	7050	7370	7700	8190	8850	9670	10320	11140	13440	15570	22290	29330
2.6	7540	7870	8190	8690	9500	10320	10980	11960	14260	16550	23760	31140
2.7	8030	8190	8690	9180	10000	10820	11630	12620	15080	17530	25070	32940
2.9	8520	8690	9180	9830	10490	11470	12290	13270	15900	18520	26550	34740
3.0	8850	9180	9670	10320	11140	12130	12950	13930	16710	19500	27860	36540
3.2	9340	9670	10160	10820	11630	12780	13600	14750	17530	20480	29330	38510
3.4	9830	10160	10650	11310	12130	13270	14260	15400	18350	21470	30640	40310
3.5	10320	10490	11140	11800	12780	13930	14910	16060	19170	22450	32120	42110
3.7	10650	10980	11630	12290	13270	14580	15570	16710	19990	23430	33430	43920
3.8	11140	11470	12130	12780	13930	15080	16220	17530	20810	24420	34900	45720
4.0	11630	11960	12620	13270	14420	15730	16880	18190	21790	25400	36220	47520
4.1	11960	12450	13110	13930	14910	16390	17530	18850	22610	26380	37690	49490
4.3	12450	12780	13600	14420	15570	16880	18190	19660	23430	27370	39000	51290
4.4	12950	13270	14090	14910	16060	17530	18850	20320	24250	28350	40480	53090
4.6	13440	13770	14580	15400	16710	18190	19500	20980	25070	29330	41950	54900
4.7	13770	14260	15080	15900	17210	18680	20160	21630	25890	30320	43260	56700
4.9	14260	14750	15570	16390	17700	19340	20810	22450	26710	31300	44740	58670

Span (m)	Nominal Diameter of Pipe Being Supported — Schedule 40 Steel											
	25	32	40	50	65	80	90	100	125	150	200	250
0.5	1310	1470	1470	1640	1800	1970	2290	2460	2950	3610	4920	6720
0.6	1800	1800	1970	2130	2460	2620	2950	3280	3930	4750	6550	9010
0.8	2290	2290	2460	2620	2950	3440	3770	4100	4920	5900	8190	11310
0.9	2620	2790	2950	3280	3610	4100	4420	4920	5900	7050	9830	13440
1.1	3110	3280	3440	3770	4260	4750	5240	5740	6880	8360	11470	15730
1.2	3610	3770	3930	4260	4750	5410	5900	6550	7870	9500	13110	18030
1.4	4100	4260	4420	4750	5410	6060	6720	7370	8850	10650	14750	20160
1.5	4420	4750	4920	5410	6060	6720	7370	8030	9830	11800	16390	22450
1.7	4920	5080	5410	5900	6550	7370	8190	8850	10820	12950	18030	24740
1.8	5410	5570	5900	6390	7210	8030	8850	9670	11800	14260	19660	26870
2.0	5900	6060	6550	6880	7870	8850	9670	10490	12780	15400	21470	29170
2.1	6230	6550	7050	7540	8520	9500	10320	11310	13770	16550	23110	31460
2.3	6720	7050	7540	8030	9010	10160	11140	12130	14750	17700	24740	33760
2.4	7210	7540	8030	8520	9670	10820	11800	12950	15730	19010	26380	35890
2.6	7700	7870	8520	9180	10320	11470	12620	13770	16710	20160	28020	38180
2.7	8030	8360	9010	9670	10820	12130	13270	14580	17700	21300	29660	40480
2.9	8520	8850	9500	10160	11470	12780	14090	15400	18680	22450	31300	42610
3.0	9010	9340	10000	10650	12130	13440	14750	16220	19660	23760	32940	44900
3.2	9500	9830	10490	11310	12620	14090	15570	17040	20650	24910	34580	47190
3.4	9830	10320	10980	11800	13270	14910	16220	17860	21630	26060	36220	49330
3.5	10320	10820	11470	12290	13930	15570	17040	18680	22610	27200	37850	51620
3.7	10820	11140	11960	12780	14420	16220	17700	19500	23600	28350	39490	53910

(continues)

N Table 17.3.1(b)   *Continued*

Span (m)	Nominal Diameter of Pipe Being Supported — Schedule 10 Steel											
	25	32	40	50	65	80	90	100	125	150	200	250
3.8	11310	11630	12450	13440	15080	16880	18520	20320	24580	29660	41130	56210
4.0	11630	12130	12950	13930	15730	17530	19170	21140	25560	30810	42770	58340
4.1	12130	12620	13440	14420	16220	18190	19990	21960	26550	31950	44410	60630
4.3	12620	13110	13930	14910	16880	18850	20650	22780	27530	33100	46050	62930
4.4	13110	13600	14420	15570	17530	19500	21470	23430	28510	34410	47690	65060
4.6	13440	14090	14910	16060	18030	20320	22120	24250	29500	35560	49330	67350
4.7	13930	14420	15400	16550	18680	20980	22940	25070	30480	36710	50960	69650
4.9	14420	14910	15900	17210	19340	21630	23600	25890	31460	37850	52600	71940

Note: The table is based on a maximum bending stress of 103.4 MPa and a midspan concentrated load from 4.6 m of water-filled pipe, plus 114 kg.

17.3.2 Any other sizes or shapes giving equal or greater section modulus shall be acceptable.

17.3.3 All angles shall be installed with the longer leg vertical.

17.3.4 The trapeze member shall be secured to prevent slippage.

17.3.5* All components of each hanger assembly that attach to a trapeze member shall conform to 17.1.6 and be sized to support the suspended sprinkler pipe.

17.3.6 The ring, strap, or clevis installed on a pipe trapeze shall be manufactured to fit the pipe size of the trapeze member.

17.3.7 Holes for bolts or rods shall not exceed $\frac{1}{16}$ in. (1.6 mm) greater than the diameter of the bolt or rod.

17.3.8 Bolts and rods shall be provided with flat washers and nuts.

17.3.9 Where angles are used for trapeze hangers and slotted holes are used, the slotted holes shall meet all of the following:

(1) The length of each slotted hole shall not exceed 3 in. (75 mm).
(2) The width of the slotted hole shall not exceed $\frac{1}{16}$ in. (1.6 mm) greater than the bolt or rod diameter.
(3) The minimum distance between slotted holes shall be 3 in. (75 mm) edge to edge.
(4) The minimum distance from the end of the angle to the edge of the slotted hole shall be 3 in. (75 mm).
(5) The number of slots shall be limited to three per section of angle.
(6) The washer(s) required by 17.3.8 shall have a minimum thickness of one-half the thickness of the angle.
(7) Washers and nuts required by 17.3.8 shall be provided on both the top and bottom of the angle.

17.4* Installation of Pipe Hangers.

17.4.1 General.

17.4.1.1 Ceiling Sheathing.

17.4.1.1.1* Unless the requirements of 17.4.1.1.2 are met, sprinkler piping shall be supported independently of the ceiling sheathing.

17.4.1.1.2 Toggle hangers shall be permitted only for the support of pipe 1½ in. (40 mm) or smaller in size under ceilings of hollow tile or metal lath and plaster.

17.4.1.2 Storage Racks. Where sprinkler piping is installed in storage racks, piping shall be supported from the storage rack structure or building in accordance with all applicable provisions of Section 17.4 and Chapter 18.

17.4.1.3* Building Structure.

17.4.1.3.1 Sprinkler piping shall be substantially supported from the building structure, which must support the added load of the water-filled pipe plus 250 lb (115 kg) applied at the point of hanging, except where permitted by 17.4.1.1.2, 17.4.1.3.3, and 17.4.1.4.1.

17.4.1.3.2 Trapeze hangers shall be used where necessary to transfer loads to appropriate structural members.

17.4.1.3.3* Flexible Sprinkler Hose Fittings.

17.4.1.3.3.1 Listed flexible sprinkler hose fittings and their anchoring components intended for use in installations connecting the sprinkler system piping to sprinklers shall be installed in accordance with the requirements of the listing, including any installation instructions.

Δ **17.4.1.3.3.2** When installed and supported by suspended ceilings, the ceiling shall meet ASTM C635/C635M, *Standard Specification for Manufacture, Performance, and Testing of Metal Suspension Systems for Acoustical Tile and Lay-In Panel Ceilings*, and shall be installed in accordance with ASTM C636/C636M, *Standard Practice for Installation of Metal Ceiling Suspension Systems for Acoustical Tile and Lay-In Panels*.

17.4.1.3.3.3* Where flexible sprinkler hose fittings exceed 6 ft (1.8 m) in length and are supported by a suspended ceiling in accordance with 17.4.1.3.3.2, a hanger(s) attached to the structure shall be required to ensure that the maximum unsupported length does not exceed 6 ft (1.8 m).

17.4.1.3.3.4* Where flexible sprinkler hose fittings are used to connect sprinklers to branch lines in suspended ceilings, a label limiting relocation of the sprinkler shall be provided on the anchoring component.

17.4.1.4 Metal Deck.

17.4.1.4.1* Branch line hangers attached to metal deck shall be permitted only for the support of pipe 1 in. (25 mm) or smaller in size, by drilling or punching the vertical portion of the metal deck and using through bolts.

17.4.1.4.2 The distance from the bottom of the bolt hole to the bottom of the vertical member shall be not less than $\frac{3}{8}$ in. (10 mm).

Δ Table 17.3.1(c) Available Section Modulus of Common Trapeze Hangers (in.^{3})

Pipe (in.)	Modulus (in.^{3})	Angles (in.)	Modulus (in.^{3})
Schedule 10			
1	0.12	1½ × 1½ × 3/16	0.10
1¼	0.19	2 × 2 × 1/8	0.13
1½	0.26	2 × 1½ × 3/16	0.18
2	0.42	2 × 2 × 3/16	0.19
2½	0.69	2 × 2 × ¼	0.25
3	1.04	2½ × 1½ × 3/16	0.28
3½	1.38	2½ × 2 × 3/16	0.29
4	1.76	2 × 2 × 5/16	0.30
5	3.03	2½ × 2½ × 3/16	0.30
6	4.35	2 × 2 × 3/8	0.35
		2½ × 2½ × ¼	0.39
		3 × 2 × 3/16	0.41
Schedule 40			
1	0.13	3 × 2½ × 3/16	0.43
1¼	0.23	3 × 3 × 3/16	0.44
1½	0.33	2½ × 2½ × 5/16	0.48
2	0.56	3 × 2 × ¼	0.54
2½	1.06	2½ × 2 × 3/8	0.55
3	1.72	2½ × 2½ × 3/8	0.57
3½	2.39	3 × 3 × ¼	0.58
4	3.21	3 × 3 × 5/16	0.71
5	5.45	2½ × 2½ × ½	0.72
6	8.50	3½ × 2½ × ¼	0.75
		3 × 2½ × 3/8	0.81
		3 × 3 × 3/8	0.83
		3½ × 2½ × 5/16	0.93
		3 × 3 × 7/16	0.95
		4 × 4 × ¼	1.05
		3 × 3 × ½	1.07
		4 × 3 × 5/16	1.23
		4 × 4 × 5/16	1.29
		4 × 3 × 3/8	1.46
		4 × 4 × 3/8	1.52
		5 × 3½ × 5/16	1.94
		4 × 4 × ½	1.97
		4 × 4 × 5/8	2.40
		4 × 4 × ¾	2.81
		6 × 4 × 3/8	3.32
		6 × 4 × ½	4.33
		6 × 4 × ¾	6.25
		6 × 6 × 1	8.57

17.4.1.5 Where sprinkler piping is installed below ductwork, piping shall be supported from the building structure or from the ductwork supports, provided such supports are capable of handling both the load of the ductwork and the load specified in 17.4.1.3.1.

17.4.2* Maximum Distance Between Hangers.

17.4.2.1 The maximum distance between hangers shall not exceed that specified in Table 17.4.2.1(a) or Table 17.4.2.1(b), except where the provisions of 17.4.4 apply.

Δ Table 17.3.1(d) Available Section Modulus of Common Trapeze Hangers (mm^3)

Pipe (mm)	Modulus (mm^3)	Angles (mm)	Modulus (mm^3)
Schedule 10			
25	19.7	40 × 40 × 5	1640
32	31.1	50 × 50 × 3	2130
40	42.6	50 × 40 × 5	2950
50	68.8	50 × 50 × 5	3110
65	113	50 × 50 × 6	4100
80	170	65 × 40 × 5	4590
90	226	65 × 50 × 5	4750
100	288	50 × 50 × 8	4920
125	497	65 × 65 × 5	4920
150	713	50 × 50 × 10	5740
		65 × 65 × 6	6390
		80× 50 × 5	6720
Schedule 40			
25	21.0	80 × 65 × 10	7050
32	38.0	80 × 80 × 5	7210
40	54.0	65 × 65 × 8	7870
50	92.0	80 × 50 × 6	8850
65	174.0	65 × 50 × 10	9010
80	282.0	65 × 65 × 10	9340
90	392.0	80 × 80 × 6	9500
100	526.0	80 × 80 × 8	11,600
125	893.0	65 × 65 ×15	11,800
150	1393.0	90 × 65 ×6	12,300
		80 × 65 × 10	13,300
		80 × 80 × 10	13,600
		90 × 65 × 8	15,200
		80 × 80 × 11	15,600
		100 × 100 × 6	17,200
		80 × 80 × 15	17,500
		100 × 80 × 8	20,200
		100 × 100 × 8	21,100
		100 × 80 × 10	23,900
		100 ×100 × 10	24,900
		125 × 90 × 8	31,800
		100 × 100 × 16	32,300
		100 × 100 × 8	39,300
		100 × 100 × 20	46,000
		150 × 100 × 10	54,400
		150 × 100 × 15	71,000
		150 × 100 × 20	102,000
		150 × 150 × 25	140,000

17.4.2.2 The maximum distance between hangers for listed nonmetallic pipe shall be modified as specified in the individual product listings.

17.4.3 Location of Hangers on Branch Lines.

17.4.3.1 Subsection 17.4.3 shall apply to the support of steel pipe or copper tube as specified in 7.3.1 and subject to the provisions of 17.4.2.

17.4.3.2* Minimum Number of Hangers.

17.4.3.2.1 Unless the requirements of 17.4.3.2.2 through 17.4.3.2.5 are met, there shall be not less than one hanger for each section of pipe.

Table 17.4.2.1(a) Maximum Distance Between Hangers (ft-in.)

	Nominal Pipe Size (in.)											
	¾	1	1¼	1½	2	2½	3	3½	4	5	6	8
Steel pipe except threaded lightwall	NA	12-0	12-0	15-0	15-0	15-0	15-0	15-0	15-0	15-0	15-0	15-0
Threaded lightwall steel pipe	NA	12-0	12-0	12-0	12-0	12-0	12-0	NA	NA	NA	NA	NA
Copper tube	8-0	8-0	10-0	10-0	12-0	12-0	12-0	15-0	15-0	15-0	15-0	15-0
CPVC	5-6	6-0	6-6	7-0	8-0	9-0	10-0	NA	NA	NA	NA	NA
Ductile-iron pipe	NA	NA	NA	NA	NA	NA	15-0	NA	15-0	NA	15-0	15-0

NA: Not applicable.

Table 17.4.2.1(b) Maximum Distance Between Hangers (m)

	Nominal Pipe Size (mm)											
	20	25	32	40	50	65	80	90	100	125	150	200
Steel pipe except threaded lightwall	NA	3.7	3.7	4.6	4.6	4.6	4.6	4.6	4.6	4.6	4.6	4.6
Threaded lightwall steel pipe	NA	3.7	3.7	3.7	3.7	3.7	3.7	NA	NA	NA	NA	NA
Copper tube	2.4	2.4	3.0	3.0	3.7	3.7	3.7	4.6	4.6	4.6	4.6	4.6
CPVC	1.7	1.8	2.0	2.1	2.4	2.7	3.0	NA	NA	NA	NA	NA
Ductile-iron pipe	NA	NA	NA	NA	NA	NA	4.6	NA	4.6	NA	4.6	4.6

NA: Not applicable.

17.4.3.2.2* Unless the requirements of 17.4.3.2.3 are met, where sprinklers are spaced less than 6 ft (1.8 m) apart, hangers spaced up to a maximum of 12 ft (3.7 m) shall be permitted.

17.4.3.2.3 For welded or mechanical outlets on a continuous section of pipe, hanger spacing shall be according to Table 17.4.2.1(a) or Table 17.4.2.1(b).

17.4.3.2.4* Starter lengths less than 6 ft (1.8 m) shall not require a hanger, unless on the end line of a sidefeed system or where an intermediate cross main hanger has been omitted.

17.4.3.2.5* A single section of pipe shall not require a hanger when the cumulative distance between hangers on the branch line does not exceed the spacing required by Table 17.4.2.1(a) and Table 17.4.2.1(b).

17.4.3.3 Clearance to Hangers. The distance between a hanger and the centerline of an upright sprinkler shall not be less than 3 in. (75 mm).

17.4.3.4* Unsupported Lengths.

17.4.3.4.1 For steel pipe, the unsupported horizontal length between the end sprinkler and the last hanger on the line shall not be greater than 36 in. (900 mm) for 1 in. (25 mm) pipe, 48 in. (1200 mm) for 1¼ in. (32 mm) pipe, and 60 in. (1500 mm) for 1½ in. (40 mm) or larger pipe.

17.4.3.4.2 For copper tube, the unsupported horizontal length between the end sprinkler and the last hanger on the line shall not be greater than 18 in. (450 mm) for 1 in. (25 mm) pipe, 24 in. (600 mm) for 1¼ in. (32 mm) pipe, and 30 in. (750 mm) for 1½ in. (40 mm) or larger pipe.

17.4.3.4.3 Where the limits of 17.4.3.4.1 and 17.4.3.4.2 are exceeded, the pipe shall be extended beyond the end sprinkler and shall be supported by an additional hanger.

17.4.3.4.4* Unsupported Length with Maximum Pressure Exceeding 100 psi (6.9 bar) and Branch Line Above Ceiling Supplying Sprinklers in Pendent Position Below Ceiling.

17.4.3.4.4.1 Where the maximum static or flowing pressure, whichever is greater at the sprinkler, applied other than through the fire department connection, exceeds 100 psi (6.9 bar) and a branch line above a ceiling supplies sprinklers in a pendent position below the ceiling, the hanger assembly supporting the pipe supplying an end sprinkler in a pendent position shall be of a type that restrains upward movement of the pipe.

17.4.3.4.4.2 The unsupported length between the end sprinkler in a pendent position or drop nipple and the last hanger on the branch line shall not be greater than 12 in. (300 mm) for steel pipe or 6 in. (150 mm) for copper pipe.

17.4.3.4.4.3 When the limit of 17.4.3.4.4.2 is exceeded, the pipe shall be extended beyond the end sprinkler and supported by an additional hanger.

17.4.3.4.4.4 Unless flexible hose fittings in accordance with 17.4.1.3.3.1 and ceilings in accordance with 17.4.1.3.3.2 are used, the hanger closest to the sprinkler shall be of a type that restrains the pipe from upward movement.

17.4.3.5* Unsupported Armover Length.

17.4.3.5.1 The cumulative horizontal length of an unsupported armover to a sprinkler, sprinkler drop, or sprig shall not exceed 24 in. (600 mm) for steel pipe or 12 in. (300 mm) for copper tube.

17.4.3.5.2* Unsupported Armover Length with Maximum Pressure Exceeding 100 psi (6.9 bar) and Branch Line Above Ceiling Supplying Sprinklers in Pendent Position Below Ceiling.

17.4.3.5.2.1 Where the maximum static or flowing pressure, whichever is greater at the sprinkler, applied other than through the fire department connection, exceeds 100 psi (6.9 bar) and a branch line above a ceiling supplies sprinklers in a pendent position below the ceiling, the cumulative horizontal length of an unsupported armover to a sprinkler or sprinkler drop shall not exceed 12 in. (300 mm) for steel pipe and 6 in. (150 mm) for copper tube.

17.4.3.5.2.2 Unless flexible sprinkler hose fittings in accordance with 17.4.1.3.3.1 are used, the hanger closest to the sprinkler shall be of a type that restrains upward movement of the pipe.

17.4.3.5.2.3 Where the armover exceeds the maximum unsupported length of 17.4.3.5.2.1, a hanger shall be installed so that the distance from the end sprinkler or drop nipple to the hanger is not greater than 12 in. (300 mm) for steel or 6 in. (150 mm) for copper, or the pipe shall be extended beyond the end sprinkler and shall be supported by an additional hanger.

17.4.3.6* Wall-mounted sidewall sprinklers shall be restrained to prevent movement.

17.4.3.7 Sprigs. Sprigs 4 ft (1.2 m) or longer shall be restrained against lateral movement.

17.4.4 Location of Hangers on Mains.

17.4.4.1 Unless any of the requirements of 17.4.4.2 through 17.4.4.7 are met, hangers for mains shall be in accordance with 17.4.2, between each branch line, or on each section of pipe, whichever is the lesser dimension.

17.4.4.2 For welded or mechanical outlets on a continuous section of pipe, hanger spacing shall be according to Table 17.4.2.1(a) or Table 17.4.2.1(b).

17.4.4.3 For cross mains in steel pipe systems in bays having two branch lines, the intermediate hanger shall be permitted to be omitted, provided that a hanger attached to a purlin is installed on each branch line located as near to the cross main as the location of the purlin permits.

17.4.4.3.1 The remaining branch line hangers shall be installed in accordance with 17.4.3.

17.4.4.4 For cross mains in steel pipe systems only in bays having three branch lines, either side or center feed, one (only) intermediate hanger shall be permitted to be omitted, provided that a hanger attached to a purlin is installed on each branch line located as near to the cross main as the location of the purlin permits.

17.4.4.4.1 The remaining branch line hangers shall be installed in accordance with 17.4.3.

17.4.4.5 For cross mains in steel pipe systems only in bays having four or more branch lines, either side or center feed, two intermediate hangers shall be permitted to be omitted, provided the maximum distance between hangers does not exceed the distances specified in 17.4.2 and a hanger attached to a purlin on each branch line is located as near to the cross main as the purlin permits.

17.4.4.6 The unsupported length of the end of a main shall be no greater than one half the maximum allowable hanger spacing per Table 17.4.2.1(a) and Table 17.4.2.1(b).

17.4.4.7 At the end of the main, intermediate trapeze hangers shall be installed unless the main is extended to the next fram-

ing member with a hanger installed at this point, in which event an intermediate hanger shall be permitted to be omitted in accordance with 17.4.4.3, 17.4.4.4, and 17.4.4.5.

17.4.4.8* A single section of pipe shall not require a hanger when the cumulative distance between hangers on the main does not exceed the spacing required by Table 17.4.2.1(a) and Table 17.4.2.1(b).

17.4.5 Support of Risers.

17.4.5.1 Risers shall be supported by riser clamps or by hangers located on the horizontal connections within 24 in. (600 mm) of the centerline of the riser.

17.4.5.2 Riser clamps supporting risers by means of set screws shall not be used.

17.4.5.3* Riser clamps anchored to walls using hanger rods in the horizontal position shall not be permitted to vertically support risers.

17.4.5.4 Multistory Buildings.

17.4.5.4.1 In multistory buildings, riser supports shall be provided at the lowest level, at each alternate level above, above and below offsets, and at the top of the riser.

17.4.5.4.2* Supports above the lowest level shall also restrain the pipe to prevent movement by an upward thrust where flexible fittings are used.

17.4.5.4.3 Where risers are supported from the ground, the ground support shall constitute the first level of riser support.

17.4.5.4.4 Where risers are offset or do not rise from the ground, the first ceiling level above the offset shall constitute the first level of riser support.

17.4.5.5 Distance between supports for risers shall not exceed 25 ft (7.6 m).

17.5* Pipe Stands.

17.5.1 General.

17.5.1.1 Where pipe stands are used to support system piping, the requirements of Section 17.5 shall apply unless the requirements of 17.5.1.2 are met.

17.5.1.2 Pipe stands certified by a registered professional engineer to include all of the following shall be an acceptable alternative to the requirements of Section 17.5:

(1) Pipe stands shall be designed to support five times the weight of water-filled pipe plus 250 lb (115 kg) at each point of piping support.
(2) These points of support shall be adequate to support the system.
(3) The spacing between pipe stands shall not exceed the value given for the type of pipe as indicated in Table 17.4.2.1(a) or Table 17.4.2.1(b).
(4) Pipe stand components shall be ferrous.
(5) Detailed calculations shall be submitted, when required by the reviewing authority, showing stresses developed in the pipe stand, the system piping and fittings, and safety factors allowed.

17.5.1.3 Where water-based fire protection systems are required to be protected against damage from earthquakes, pipe stands shall also meet the requirements of Section 18.8.

17.5.2 Component Material.

17.5.2.1 Pipe stands and their components shall be ferrous unless permitted by 17.5.2.2.

17.5.2.2 Nonferrous components that have been proven by fire tests to be adequate for the hazard application and that are in compliance with the other requirements of this section shall be acceptable.

17.5.3 Sizing.

17.5.3.1* The maximum heights for pipe stands shall be in accordance with Table 17.5.3.1(a) or Table 17.5.3.1(b) unless the requirements of 17.5.3.2 are met.

17.5.3.2* Pipe diameters up to and including 10 in. (250 mm) Schedule 40 are permitted to be supported by 2 in. (50 mm) Schedule 40 diameter pipe stands when all of the following conditions are met:

(1)   The maximum height shall be 4 ft (1.2 m), as measured from the base of the pipe stand to the centerline of the pipe being supported.
(2)* The pipe stand shall be axially loaded.

17.5.3.3 The distance between pipe stands shall not exceed the values in Table 17.4.2.1(a) or Table 17.4.2.1(b).

17.5.4 Pipe Stand Base.

17.5.4.1 The pipe stand base shall be secured by an approved method.

Δ **Table 17.5.3.1(a) Maximum Pipe Stand Heights (ft)**

System Pipe Diameter (in.)†	Pipe Stand Diameter (in.)*					
	1½	2	2½	3	4	6
1½	6.6	9.4	11.3	13.8	18.0	26.8
2	4.4	9.4	11.3	13.8	18.0	26.8
2½	—	8.1	11.3	13.8	18.0	26.8
3	—	5.2	11.3	13.8	18.0	26.8
4 up to and including 8	—	—	—	—	14.7	26.8

*Pipe stands are Schedule 40 pipe.
†System piping is assumed to be Schedule 40 (8 in. is Schedule 30).

N **Table 17.5.3.1(b) Maximum Pipe Stand Heights (m)**

System Pipe Diameter (mm)†	Pipe Stand Diameter (mm)*					
	40	50	65	80	100	150
40	2	2.9	3.4	4.2	5.5	8.2
50	1.3	2.9	3.4	4.2	5.5	8.2
65	—	2.5	3.4	4.2	5.5	8.2
80	—	1.6	3.4	4.2	5.5	8.2
100 up to and including 200	—	—	—	—	4.5	8.2

*Pipe stands are Schedule 40 pipe.
†System piping is assumed to be Schedule 40 (200 mm is Schedule 30).

17.5.4.2* Pipe stand base plates shall be threaded malleable iron flanges or welded steel flanges in accordance with Table 7.4.1.

17.5.4.2.1 Pipes stands installed in accordance with 17.5.3.2 shall be permitted to use a welded steel plate.

17.5.4.3* Pipe stands shall be fastened to a concrete floor or footing using listed concrete anchors or other approved means.

17.5.4.4 A minimum of four anchors shall be used to attach the base plate to the floor.

17.5.4.4.1 Pipe stands installed in accordance with 17.5.3.2 shall be permitted to use a minimum of two anchors to attach the base plate to the floor.

17.5.4.5 The minimum diameter for the anchors shall be ½ in. (15 mm) for pipe stand diameters up to and including 3 in. (80 mm) and ⅝ in. (16 mm) for pipe stands 4 in. (100 mm) diameter and larger.

17.5.4.5.1 Where the pipe stand complies with 17.5.3.2, ⅜ in. (10 mm) anchors shall be permitted.

17.5.5 Attaching to System Piping.

17.5.5.1 Piping shall be attached to the pipe stand with U-bolts or equivalent attachment, unless the requirements of 17.5.5.2 are met.

N **17.5.5.2** When a saddle-type pipe stand is utilized and the pipe is not subject to a net vertical upward force, a through-bolt or equivalent attachment is not required.

17.5.5.3* Where a horizontal bracket is used to attach the system piping to the pipe stand, it shall not be more than 1 ft (0.3 m) as measured horizontally from the centerline of the pipe stand to the centerline of the supported pipe.

17.5.5.4 Horizontal support brackets shall be sized such that the section modulus required in Table 17.5.5.4 does not exceed the available section modulus from Table 17.3.1(c).

17.5.6 Thrust.

17.5.6.1* System piping shall be supported and restrained to restrict movement due to sprinkler/nozzle reaction and water surges.

17.5.6.2* Where thrust forces are anticipated to be high, a pipe ring or clamp shall secure the system piping to the pipe stand.

17.5.7 Exterior Applications.

17.5.7.1 Where required, pipe stands used in exterior applications shall be made of galvanized steel or other suitable corrosion-resistant materials.

17.5.7.2 A welded, threaded, grooved, or other approved cap shall be securely attached to the top of the pipe stand.

Table 17.5.5.4 Required Section Modulus for Pipe Stand Horizontal Support Arms (in.^{3})

Nominal Diameter of Pipe Being Supported (in.)	1	1¼	1½	2	2½	3	3½	4	5	6	8
Section Modulus – Schedule 10 Steel	0.22	0.23	0.24	0.25	0.30	0.36	0.42	0.49	0.66	0.85	1.40
Section Modulus – Schedule 40 Steel	0.22	0.24	0.24	0.27	0.36	0.45	0.54	0.63	0.86	1.13	1.64

For SI units, 1 in. = 25.4 mm.

Note: The table is based on the controlling section modulus determined for a concentrated load at a 1 ft (0.3 m) cantilever using: a) a maximum bending stress of 15 ksi (103 MPa) and a concentrated load equal to the weight of 15 ft (4.6 m) of water-filled pipe plus 250 lb (115 kg), or b) a maximum bending stress of 28 ksi (193 MPa) and a concentrated load equal to five times the weight of 15 ft (4.6 m) of water-filled pipe plus 250 lb (115 kg).

Chapter 18 Installation Requirements for Seismic Protection

18.1* Protection of Piping Against Damage Where Subject to Earthquakes.

18.1.1 Where water-based fire protection systems are required to be protected against damage from earthquakes, the requirements of Chapter 18 shall apply, unless the requirements of 18.1.2 are met.

18.1.2 Alternative methods of providing earthquake protection of sprinkler systems based on a seismic analysis certified by a registered professional engineer such that system performance will be at least equal to that of the building structure under expected seismic forces shall be permitted.

18.1.3 Obstructions to Sprinklers. Braces and restraints shall not obstruct sprinklers and shall comply with the obstruction rules of Chapters 10 through 14.

18.2* Flexible Couplings.

18.2.1 Flexible couplings joining grooved end pipe shall be provided as flexure joints to allow individual sections of piping 2½ in. (65 mm) or larger to move differentially with the individual sections of the building to which it is attached.

18.2.2 Flexible couplings shall be arranged to coincide with structural separations within a building.

18.2.3 Systems having more flexible couplings than required by this section shall be provided with additional sway bracing as required in 18.5.5.9.

18.2.3.1 The flexible couplings shall be installed as follows:

(1)* Within 24 in. (600 mm) of the top and bottom of all risers, unless the following provisions are met:

    (a) In risers less than 3 ft (900 mm) in length, flexible couplings shall be permitted to be omitted.
    (b) In risers 3 ft to 7 ft (900 mm to 2100 mm) in length, one flexible coupling shall be adequate.

(2) Within 12 in. (300 mm) above and within 24 in. (600 mm) below the floor in multistory buildings, unless the following provision is met:

    (a)* In risers up to 7 ft (2.1 m) in length terminating above the roof assembly or top landing, the flexible coupling shall not be required above the landing or roof assembly.

(3) On both sides of concrete or masonry walls within 1 ft (300 mm) of the wall surface, unless clearance is provided in accordance with Section 18.4
(4)* Within 24 in. (600 mm) of building expansion joints
(5) Within 24 in. (600 mm) of the top of drops exceeding 15 ft (4.6 m) in length to portions of systems supplying more than one sprinkler, regardless of pipe size
(6) Within 24 in. (600 mm) above and 24 in. (600 mm) below any intermediate points of support for a riser or other vertical pipe

18.2.3.2 When the flexible coupling below the floor is above the tie-in main to the main supplying that floor, a flexible coupling shall be provided in accordance with one of the following:

(1)* On the horizontal portion within 24 in. (600 mm) of the tie-in where the tie-in is horizontal
(2)* On the vertical portion of the tie-in where the tie-in incorporates a riser

18.2.4* Flexible Couplings for Drops. Flexible couplings for drops to hose lines, rack sprinklers, mezzanines, and free-standing structures shall be installed regardless of pipe sizes as follows:

(1) Within 24 in. (600 mm) of the top of the drop
(2) Within 24 in. (600 mm) above the uppermost drop support attachment, where drop supports are provided to the structure, rack, or mezzanine
(3) Within 24 in. (600 mm) above the bottom of the drop where no additional drop support is provided

18.3* Seismic Separation Assembly.

18.3.1 An approved seismic separation assembly shall be installed where sprinkler piping, regardless of size, crosses building seismic separation joints at ground level and above.

18.3.2 Seismic separation assemblies shall consist of flexible fittings or flexible piping so as to allow movement sufficient to accommodate closing of the separation, opening of the separation to twice its normal size, and movement relative to the separation in the other two dimensions in an amount equal to the separation distance.

18.3.3* The seismic separation assembly shall include a four-way brace upstream and downstream within 6 ft (1.8 m) of the seismic separation assembly.

18.3.4 Bracing shall not be attached to the seismic separation assembly.

18.4* Clearance.

18.4.1* Clearance shall be provided around all piping extending through walls, floors, platforms, and foundations, including drains, fire department connections, and other auxiliary piping.

18.4.2 Unless any of the requirements of 18.4.3 through 18.4.7 or 18.4.10 are met, where pipe passes through holes in platforms, foundations, walls, or floors, the holes shall be sized such that the diameter of the holes is nominally 2 in. (50 mm) larger than the pipe for pipe 1 in. (25 mm) nominal to 3½ in. (90 mm) nominal and 4 in. (100 mm) larger than the pipe for pipe 4 in. (100 mm) nominal and larger.

18.4.3 Where clearance is provided by a pipe sleeve, a nominal diameter 2 in. (50 mm) larger than the nominal diameter of the pipe shall be acceptable for pipe sizes 1 in. (25 mm) through 3½ in. (90 mm), and the clearance provided by a pipe sleeve of nominal diameter 4 in. (100 mm) larger than the nominal diameter of the pipe shall be acceptable for pipe sizes 4 in. (100 mm) and larger.

18.4.4 No clearance shall be required for piping passing through gypsum board or equally frangible construction.

18.4.5 No clearance shall be required if flexible couplings are located within 1 ft (300 mm) of each side of a wall or if the requirements of 18.2.3.1 (2) are met.

18.4.6 No clearance shall be required where horizontal piping passes perpendicularly through successive studs or joists that form a wall or floor/ceiling assembly.

18.4.7 No clearance shall be required where nonmetallic pipe has been demonstrated to have inherent flexibility equal to or greater than the minimum provided by flexible couplings located within 1 ft (300 mm) of each side of a wall, floor, platform, or foundation.

18.4.8 Where required, the clearance shall be filled with a flexible material that is compatible with the piping material.

18.4.9 The installed horizontal and upward vertical clearance between horizontal sprinkler piping and structural members not penetrated or used, collectively or independently, to support the piping shall be at least 2 in. (50 mm).

18.4.10* No clearance shall be required where piping is supported by holes through structural members as permitted by 17.1.7.3.

18.4.11* The installed clearance between a sprinkler and structural elements not used collectively or independently to support the sprinklers shall be at least 3 in. (75 mm).

18.4.11.1 Where sprinklers are installed using flexible sprinkler hose, clearance for the sprinkler shall not be required.

18.4.12 Clearance shall not be required for piping that is vertically supported by the bottom edge of holes through structural members as permitted by 17.1.7.3.

18.4.13 No horizontal clearance (tight fit) shall be provided for piping that is laterally supported by the side edges of holes through structural members.

18.4.13.1 Clearance shall be permitted where piping is secured to the structural member with an approved hanger or restraint.

18.5* Sway Bracing.

18.5.1 General.

18.5.1.1 The system piping shall be braced to resist both lateral and longitudinal horizontal seismic loads and to prevent vertical motion resulting from seismic loads.

18.5.1.2 The structural components to which bracing is attached shall be determined to be capable of resisting the added applied seismic loads.

18.5.1.3* Horizontal loads on system piping shall be determined in accordance with 18.5.9.

18.5.1.4* A shared support assembly shall be permitted to support both the gravity loads addressed in 17.1.4.1 and the seismic loads addressed in 18.5.9.

18.5.1.4.1 When a shared support assembly is used to support gravity and seismic loads, the structure shall be designed to support these loads for all pipe and distribution systems on the structure using either 18.5.9.3 or 18.5.9.4 with an importance factor, *Ip*, of 1.5 being applied to all of the distribution systems.

18.5.1.5* If a shared support assembly is used to support sprinkler pipe and other distribution systems per 17.1.4.1 and that assembly does not provide seismic resistance as required in 18.5.1.4, the following shall be met:

(1) The sprinkler pipe shall be braced using the method in 18.5.6 with the zone of influence including the water-filled sprinkler pipe and all other distribution systems that are not independently equipped with seismic protection and attached to the shared support assembly.
(2) The sprinkler sway bracing attachment shall be connected to the same building or structure as the shared support assembly.

18.5.1.6 Bracing requirements of Section 18.5 shall not apply to drain piping downstream of the drain valve.

18.5.2 Listing.

18.5.2.1 Sway bracing assemblies shall be listed for a maximum load rating, unless the requirements of 18.5.2.2 are met.

18.5.2.2 Where sway bracing utilizing pipe, angles, flats, or rods as shown in Table 18.5.11.8(a) through Table 18.5.11.8(f) is used, the components shall not require listing.

18.5.2.2.1 Bracing fittings and connections used with those specific materials shall be listed.

18.5.2.3* The listed load rating shall be reduced as shown in Table 18.5.2.3 to determine the allowable load for installations where the brace is less than 90 degrees from vertical.

Table 18.5.2.3 Listed Horizontal Load Adjustment

Brace Angle Degrees from Vertical	Allowable Horizontal Load
30 to 44	Listed load rating divided by 2.000
45 to 59	Listed load rating divided by 1.414
60 to 89	Listed load rating divided by 1.155
90	Listed load rating

18.5.2.3.1* Maximum allowable horizontal loads shall be determined by testing at angles of 30, 45, 60, and 90 degrees from vertical and confirmed to be equal to or greater than those calculated using 18.5.2.3.

18.5.2.3.2 For attachments to structures, additional tests shall be performed at 0 degrees.

18.5.3 Component Material.

18.5.3.1 Unless permitted by 18.5.3.2, components of sway brace assemblies shall be ferrous.

18.5.3.2 Nonferrous components that have been proven by fire tests to be adequate for the hazard application, that are listed for this purpose, and that are in compliance with the other requirements of this section shall be acceptable.

18.5.4 Sway Bracing Design.

18.5.4.1 Sway braces shall be designed to withstand forces in tension and compression, unless the requirements of 18.5.4.2 are met.

18.5.4.2* Tension-only bracing systems shall be permitted for use where listed for this service and where installed in accordance with their listing limitations, including installation instructions.

18.5.4.3 For all braces, whether or not listed, the maximum allowable load shall be based on the weakest component of the brace with safety factors.

18.5.5 Lateral Sway Bracing.

18.5.5.1* Lateral sway bracing shall be provided on all feed and cross mains regardless of size and all branch lines and other piping with a diameter of 2½ in. (65 mm) and larger.

Shaded text = Revisions. Δ = Text deletions and figure/table revisions. • = Section deletions. *N* = New material.

18.5.5.1.1 Where branch lines are not provided with lateral sway bracing, they shall be provided with restraint in accordance with Section 18.6.

18.5.5.2* The spacing between lateral sway braces shall be in accordance with either Table 18.5.5.2(a) through Table 18.5.5.2(n) or 18.5.5.3, based on the piping material of the sprinkler system.

18.5.5.2.1 Specially listed nonstandard pipe shall be permitted using the values in Table 18.5.5.2(e) and Table 18.5.5.2(f) or with values provided by the manufacturer.

18.5.5.2.2 Spacing shall not exceed a maximum interval of 40 ft (12 m) on center.

Table 18.5.5.2(a) Maximum Load (F_{pw}) in Zone of Influence (lb), (F_y = 30 ksi) Schedule 10 Steel Pipe

Diameter of Pipe (in.) Being Braced	Lateral Sway Brace Spacing (ft)				
	20	25	30	35	40
1	111	89	73	63	52
1¼	176	141	116	99	83
1½	241	193	158	136	114
2	390	312	256	219	183
2½	641	513	420	360	301
3	966	773	633	543	454
3½	1281	1025	840	720	603
4	1634	1307	1071	918	769
5	2814	2251	1844	1581	1324
6 and larger*	4039	3231	2647	2269	1900

Note: ASTM A106 Grade B or ASTM A53 Grade B has an F_y = 35 ksi. An F_y = 30 ksi was used as a conservative value to account for differences in material properties as well as other operational stresses.
*Larger diameter pipe can be used when justified by engineering analysis.

Table 18.5.5.2(b) Maximum Load (F_{pw}) in Zone of Influence (kg), (F_y = 207 N/mm²) Schedule 10 Steel Pipe

Diameter of Pipe (mm) Being Braced	Lateral Sway Brace Spacing (m)				
	6.1	7.6	9.1	11	12
25	50	40	33	29	24
32	80	64	53	45	38
40	109	88	72	62	52
50	177	142	116	99	83
65	291	233	191	163	137
80	438	351	287	246	206
90	581	465	381	327	273
100	741	593	486	416	349
125	1276	1021	836	717	601
150*	1832	1466	1201	1029	862

Note: ASTM A106 Grade B or ASTM A53 Grade B has an F_y = 241 N/mm². An F_y = 207 N/mm² was used also as a conservative value to account for differences in material properties as well as other operational stresses.
*Larger diameter pipe can be used when justified by engineering analysis.

Table 18.5.5.2(c) Maximum Load (F_{pw}) in Zone of Influence (lb), (F_y = 30 ksi) Schedule 40 Steel Pipe

Diameter of Pipe (in.) Being Braced	Lateral Sway Brace Spacing (ft)				
	20	25	30	35	40
1	121	97	79	68	57
1¼	214	171	140	120	100
1½	306	245	201	172	144
2	520	416	341	292	245
2½	984	787	645	553	463
3	1597	1278	1047	897	751
3½	2219	1775	1455	1247	1044
4	2981	2385	1954	1675	1402
5	5061	4049	3317	2843	2381
6 and larger*	7893	6314	5173	4434	3713

Note: ASTM A106 Grade B or ASTM A53 Grade B has an F_y = 35 ksi. An F_y = 30 ksi was used as a conservative value to account for differences in material properties as well as other operational stresses.
*Larger diameter pipe can be used when justified by engineering analysis.

Table 18.5.5.2(d) Maximum Load (F_{pw}) in Zone of Influence (kg), (F_y = 207 N/mm²) Schedule 40 Steel Pipe

Diameter of Pipe (in.) Being Braced	Lateral Sway Brace Spacing (m)				
	6.1	7.6	9.1	11	12
25	55	44	36	31	26
32	97	78	63	54	45
40	139	111	91	78	65
50	236	189	155	132	111
65	446	357	293	251	210
80	724	580	475	407	341
90	1007	805	660	566	474
100	1352	1082	886	760	636
125	2296	1837	1505	1290	1080
150*	3580	2864	2346	2011	1684

Note: ASTM A106 Grade B or ASTM A53 Grade B has an F_y = 241 N/mm². An F_y = 207 N/mm² was used also as a conservative value to account for differences in material properties as well as other operational stresses.
*Larger diameter pipe can be used when justified by engineering analysis.

18.5.5.2.3 The maximum permissible load in the zone of influence of a sway brace shall not exceed the values given in Table 18.5.5.2(a) through Table 18.5.5.2(n) or the values calculated in accordance with 18.5.5.3.

18.5.5.2.4 When determining permissible loads in accordance with 18.5.5.2 or 18.5.5.2.1 on a main with varying sizes, the allowable load shall be based on the smallest pipe size within the zone of influence.

18.5.5.3 The maximum load (F_{pw}) in the zone of influence for specially listed pipe shall be calculated. *(See Annex E.)*

18.5.5.4 The requirements of 18.5.5.1 shall not apply to 2½ in. (65 mm) starter pieces that do not exceed 12 ft (3.7 m) in length.

Table 18.5.5.2(e) Maximum Load (F_{pw}) in Zone of Influence (lb), (F_y = 30 ksi) Schedule 5 Steel Pipe

Diameter of Pipe (in.) Being Braced	Lateral Sway Brace Spacing (ft)				
	20	25	30	35	40
1	71	56	46	40	33
1¼	116	93	76	65	55
1½	154	124	101	87	73
2	246	197	161	138	116
2½	459	367	301	258	216
3	691	552	453	388	325
3½	910	728	597	511	428
4*	1160	928	760	652	546

Note: ASTM A106 Grade B or ASTM A53 Grade B has an F_y = 35 ksi. An F_y = 30 ksi was used as a conservative value to account for differences in material properties as well as other operational stresses.
*Larger diameter pipe can be used when justified by engineering analysis.

Table 18.5.5.2(f) Maximum Load (F_{pw}) in Zone of Influence (kg), (F_y = 207 N/mm²) Schedule 5 Steel Pipe

Diameter of Pipe (mm) Being Braced	Lateral Sway Brace Spacing (m)				
	6.1	7.6	9.1	11	12
25	32	25	21	18	15
32	53	42	34	29	25
40	70	56	46	39	33
50	112	89	73	63	53
65	208	166	137	117	98
80	313	250	205	176	147
90	413	330	271	232	194
100*	526	421	345	296	248

Note: ASTM A106 Grade B or ASTM A53 Grade B has an F_y = 241 N/mm². An F_y = 207 N/mm² was used also as a conservative value to account for differences in material properties as well as other operational stresses.
*Larger diameter pipe can be used when justified by engineering analysis.

Table 18.5.5.2(g) Maximum Load (F_{pw}) in Zone of Influence (lb), (F_y = 8 ksi) CPVC Pipe

Diameter of Pipe (in.) Being Braced	Lateral Sway Brace Spacing (ft)				
	20	25	30	35	40
¾	15	12	10	8	7
1	28	22	18	15	13
1¼	56	45	37	30	26
1½	83	67	55	45	39
2	161	129	105	87	76
2½	286	229	188	154	135
3	516	413	338	278	243

Table 18.5.5.2(h) Maximum Load (F_{pw}) in Zone of Influence (kg), (F_y = 55 N/mm²) CPVC Pipe

Diameter of Pipe (in.) Being Braced	Lateral Sway Brace Spacing (m)				
	6.1	7.6	9.1	11	12
20	7	5	5	4	3
25	13	10	8	7	6
32	25	20	17	14	12
40	38	30	25	20	18
50	73	59	48	39	34
65	130	104	85	70	61
80	234	187	153	126	110

Table 18.5.5.2(i) Maximum Load (F_{pw}) in Zone of Influence (lb), (F_y = 30 ksi) Type M Copper Tube (with Soldered Joints)

Diameter of Pipe (in.) Being Braced	Lateral Sway Brace Spacing (ft)				
	20	25	30	35	40
¾	16	13	10	9	8
1	29	24	19	16	14
1¼	53	42	35	28	25
1½	86	69	56	46	41
2*	180	144	118	97	85

*Larger diameter pipe can be used when justified by engineering analysis.

Table 18.5.5.2(j) Maximum Load (F_{pw}) in Zone of Influence (kg), (F_y = 3207 N/mm²) Type M Copper Tube (with Soldered Joints)

Diameter of Pipe (in.) Being Braced	Lateral Sway Brace Spacing (m)				
	6.1	7.6	9.1	11	12
20	7.3	5.9	5	4.1	3.6
25	13.2	10.9	8.6	7.3	6.4
32	24	19.1	15.9	12.7	11.3
40	39	31.3	25.4	20.9	18.6
50*	81.6	65.3	53	44	38.6

*Larger diameter pipe can be used when justified by engineering analysis.

Table 18.5.5.2(k) Maximum Load (F_{pw}) in Zone of Influence (lb), (F_y = 9 ksi) Type M Copper Tube (with Brazed Joints)

Diameter of Pipe (in.) Being Braced	Lateral Sway Spacing (ft)				
	20	25	30	35	40
¾	6	5	4	3	3
1	11	9	7	6	5
1¼	20	16	13	12	10
1½	33	27	22	19	16
2*	70	56	46	39	33

*Larger diameter pipe can be used when justified by engineering analysis.

N **Table 18.5.5.2(l) Maximum Load (F_{pw}) in Zone of Influence (kg), (F_y = 62 N/mm²) Type M Copper Tube (with Brazed Joints)**

Diameter of Pipe (mm) Being Braced	Lateral Sway Spacing (m)				
	6.1	7.6	9.1	11	12
20	3	2	2	1	1
25	5	4	3	3	2
32	9	7	6	5	5
40	15	12	10	9	7
50*	32	25	21	18	15

*Larger diameter pipe can be used when justified by engineering analysis.

Table 18.5.5.2(m) Maximum Load (F_{pw}) in Zone of Influence (lb), (F_y = 9 ksi) Red Brass Pipe (with Brazed Joints)

Diameter of Pipe (in.) Being Braced	Lateral Sway Spacing (ft)				
	20	25	30	35	40
¾	34	27	22	19	16
1	61	49	40	35	29
1¼	116	93	76	65	55
1½	161	129	105	90	76
2*	272	218	178	153	128

*Larger diameter pipe can be used when justified by engineering analysis.

N **Table 18.5.5.2(n) Maximum Load (F_{pw}) in Zone of Influence (lb), (F_y = 62 N/mm²) Red Brass Pipe (with Brazed Joints)**

Diameter of Pipe (mm) Being Braced	Lateral Sway Spacing (m)				
	6.1	7.6	9.1	11	12
20	15	12	10	9	7
25	28	22	18	16	13
32	53	42	35	30	25
40	73	59	48	41	35
50*	124	99	81	70	58

*Larger diameter pipe can be used when justified by engineering analysis.

18.5.5.5 The distance between the last brace and the end of the pipe shall not exceed 6 ft (1.8 m).

18.5.5.6 Where there is a change in direction of the piping, the cumulative distance between consecutive lateral sway braces shall not exceed the maximum permitted distance in accordance with 18.5.5.2.2.

18.5.5.7 The last length of pipe at the end of a feed or cross main shall be provided with a lateral brace.

18.5.5.8 Lateral braces shall be allowed to act as longitudinal braces if they are within 24 in. (600 mm) of the centerline of the piping braced longitudinally and the lateral brace is on a pipe of equal or greater size than the pipe being braced longitudinally.

18.5.5.9 Where flexible couplings are installed on mains other than as required in Section 18.2, a lateral brace shall be provided within 24 in. (600 mm) of every other coupling, including flexible couplings at grooved fittings, but not more than 40 ft (12 m) on center.

18.5.5.10* The lateral sway bracing required by 18.5.5 shall be permitted to be omitted when 18.5.5.10.1 for branch lines or 18.5.5.10.2 for mains is met.

18.5.5.10.1 Branch lines shall comply with the following:

(1)* The branch lines shall be individually supported within 6 in. (150 mm) of the structure, measured between the top of the pipe and the point of attachment to the building structure.
(2) At least 75 percent of all the hangers on the branch line shall meet the requirements of 18.5.5.10.1(1).
(3) Consecutive hangers on the branch line shall not be permitted to exceed the limitation in 18.5.5.10.1(1).

18.5.5.10.2 Mains shall comply with all the following:

(1)* The main piping shall be individually supported within 6 in. (150 mm) of the structure, measured between the top of the pipe and the point of attachment to the building structure.
(2) At least 75 percent of all the hangers on the main shall meet the requirements of 18.5.5.10.2(1).
(3) Consecutive hangers on the main shall not be permitted to exceed the limitation in 18.5.5.10.2(1)
(4) The seismic coefficient (C_p) shall not exceed 0.5.
(5) The nominal pipe diameter shall not exceed 6 in. (150 mm) for feed mains and 4 in. (100 mm) for cross mains.
(6) Hangers shall not be omitted in accordance with 17.4.4.3, 17.4.4.4, or 17.4.4.5.

18.5.5.10.3 Branch lines permitted to omit lateral sway bracing by 18.5.5.10 shall not be omitted from load calculations for the mains serving them in 18.5.9.6.

18.5.5.11 The lateral sway bracing required by 18.5.5 shall be permitted to be omitted when 18.5.5.11.1 for branch lines or 18.5.5.11.2 for mains is met.

18.5.5.11.1 Branch lines shall comply with the following:

(1) The branch lines shall be individually supported by wrap-around u-hooks or u-hooks arranged to keep pipe tight to the structural element, provided the legs are bent out at least 30 degrees from the vertical and the maximum length of each leg and the rod size satisfies the conditions of Table 18.5.11.8(a) through Table 18.5.11.8(f), or the length of the rod shall be calculated.
(2) At least 75 percent of all the hangers on the branch line shall meet the requirements of 18.5.5.11.1(1).
(3) Consecutive hangers on the branch line shall not be permitted to exceed the limitation in 18.5.5.11.1(1).

18.5.5.11.2 Mains shall comply with all the following:

(1) The main piping shall be individually supported by wrap-around u-hooks or u-hooks arranged to keep pipe tight to the structural element provided the legs are bent out at least 30 degrees from the vertical and the maximum length of each leg and rod size satisfies the conditions of Table 18.5.11.8(a) through Table 18.5.11.8(f).
(2) At least 75 percent of all the hangers on the main shall meet the requirements of 18.5.5.11.2(1).

(3) Consecutive hangers on the main shall not be permitted to exceed the limitation in 18.5.5.11.2(1).
(4) The seismic coefficient (C_p) shall not exceed 0.5.
(5) The nominal pipe diameter shall not exceed 6 in. (150 mm) for feed mains and 4 in. (100 mm) for cross mains.
(6) Hangers shall not be omitted in accordance with 17.4.4.3, 17.4.4.4, or 17.4.4.5.

18.5.6 Longitudinal Sway Bracing.

18.5.6.1 Longitudinal sway bracing spaced at a maximum of 80 ft (24 m) on center shall be provided for feed and cross mains.

N **18.5.6.2** Unless the requirements of 18.5.9.6 are met, longitudinal sway bracing shall be provided on branch lines at a maximum spacing of 80 ft (24 m) on center.

18.5.6.3 Longitudinal braces shall be allowed to act as lateral braces if they are within 24 in. (600 mm) of the centerline of the piping braced laterally.

18.5.6.4 The distance between the last brace and the end of the pipe or a change in direction shall not exceed 40 ft (12 m).

18.5.7 Pipe with Change(s) in Direction.

18.5.7.1 Each run of pipe between changes in direction shall be provided with both lateral and longitudinal bracing, unless the requirements of 18.5.7.2 are met.

18.5.7.2* Pipe runs less than 12 ft (3.7 m) in length shall be permitted to be supported by the braces on adjacent runs of pipe.

18.5.8 Sway Bracing of Risers.

18.5.8.1* Tops of risers exceeding 36 in. (900 mm) in length shall be provided with a four-way brace located on the topmost section of vertical piping, but not more than 24 in. (600 mm) below the top coupling.

18.5.8.1.1* The four-way brace shall not be required for risers up to 7 ft (2.1 m) in length that terminate above the roof assembly or top landing.

18.5.8.2 Riser nipples shall be permitted to omit the four-way brace required by 18.5.8.1.

18.5.8.3 When a four-way brace at the top of a riser is attached on the horizontal piping, it shall be within 24 in. (600 mm) of the centerline of the riser and the loads for that brace shall include both the vertical and horizontal pipe.

18.5.8.4 Distance between four-way braces for risers shall not exceed 25 ft (7.6 m).

18.5.8.5 Four-way bracing shall not be required where risers penetrate intermediate floors in multistory buildings where the clearance does not exceed the limits of Section 18.4.

18.5.9* Horizontal Seismic Loads.

18.5.9.1* The horizontal seismic load for the braces shall be as determined in 18.5.9.6 or 18.5.9.7, or as required by the authority having jurisdiction.

18.5.9.2 The weight of the system being braced (W_p) shall be taken as 1.15 times the weight of the water-filled piping. *(See A.18.5.9.1.)*

18.5.9.3 The horizontal force, F_{pw}, acting on the brace shall be taken as $F_{pw} = C_p W_p$, where C_p is the seismic coefficient selected in Table 18.5.9.3 utilizing the short period response parameter, S_s.

18.5.9.3.1 The value of S_s from Table 18.5.9.3 shall be obtained from the authority having jurisdiction or from seismic hazard maps.

N **18.5.9.3.2** The default value of C_p from Table 18.5.9.3 shall be used unless 18.5.9.3.2.1 is met.

N **18.5.9.3.2.1*** The use of a site class–specific C_p, obtained from the authority having jurisdiction, from Table 18.5.9.3 shall be permitted.

N **Table 18.5.9.3 Seismic Coefficient Table**

S_s	Default C_p	Site Class–Specific C_p			
		A	B	C	D
0.33 or less	0.24	0.13	0.14	0.21	0.24
0.4	0.28	0.15	0.17	0.25	0.28
0.5	0.33	0.19	0.21	0.31	0.33
0.6	0.37	0.23	0.26	0.36	0.37
0.7	0.41	0.27	0.30	0.40	0.41
0.8	0.45	0.30	0.34	0.45	0.45
0.9	0.51	0.34	0.38	0.51	0.48
1.0	0.56	0.38	0.42	0.56	0.52
1.1	0.62	0.42	0.47	0.62	0.55
1.2	0.68	0.45	0.51	0.68	0.58
1.3	0.73	0.49	0.55	0.73	0.61
1.4	0.79	0.53	0.59	0.79	0.66
1.5	0.84	0.56	0.63	0.84	0.70
1.6	0.90	0.60	0.68	0.90	0.75
1.7	0.96	0.64	0.72	0.96	0.80
1.8	1.01	0.68	0.76	1.01	0.84
1.9	1.07	0.71	0.80	1.07	0.89
2.0	1.12	0.75	0.84	1.12	0.94
2.1	1.18	0.79	0.89	1.18	0.98
2.2	1.24	0.83	0.93	1.24	1.03
2.3	1.29	0.86	0.97	1.29	1.08
2.4	1.35	0.90	1.01	1.35	1.12
2.5	1.40	0.94	1.05	1.40	1.17
2.6	1.46	0.98	1.10	1.46	1.22
2.7	1.52	1.01	1.14	1.52	1.26
2.8	1.57	1.05	1.18	1.57	1.31
2.9	1.63	1.09	1.22	1.63	1.36
3.0	1.68	1.12	1.26	1.68	1.40
3.1	1.74	1.16	1.31	1.74	1.45
3.2	1.80	1.20	1.35	1.80	1.50
3.3	1.85	1.24	1.39	1.85	1.54
3.4	1.91	1.27	1.43	1.91	1.59
3.5	1.96	1.31	1.47	1.96	1.64
3.6	2.02	1.35	1.52	2.02	1.68
3.7	2.08	1.39	1.56	2.08	1.73
3.8	2.13	1.42	1.60	2.13	1.78
3.9	2.19	1.46	1.64	2.19	1.82
4.0	2.24	1.50	1.68	2.24	1.87

N **18.5.9.3.2.2*** Where site class E or F is applicable, the authority having jurisdiction shall confirm whether it is acceptable to use the method outlined in 18.5.9.3 and 18.5.9.4 or an alternative method in accordance with 18.1.2 to determine F_{pw}.

18.5.9.3.3* Linear interpolation shall be permitted to be used for intermediate values of S_s.

N **18.5.9.3.4*** Where the height of the component attachment to the structure is between 51 percent and 75 percent of the average roof height, the C_p value shall be permitted to be multiplied by a factor of 0.875.

N **18.5.9.3.5** Where the height of the component attachment to the structure is less than 50 percent of the average roof height, the C_p value shall be permitted to be multiplied by a factor of 0.75. *(See Figure A.18.5.9.3.4.)*

18.5.9.4* The horizontal force, F_{pw}, acting on the brace shall be permitted to be determined in accordance with 13.3.1 of ASCE/SEI 7, *Minimum Design Loads and Associated Criteria for Buildings and Other Structures*, multiplied by 0.7 to convert to allowable stress design (ASD).

18.5.9.5* Where data for determining C_p are not available, the horizontal seismic force acting on the braces shall be determined as specified in 18.5.9.3 with $C_p = 0.5$.

△ **18.5.9.6*** The zone of influence for lateral braces shall include all branch lines, drops, sprigs, and mains tributary to the brace, except branch lines that are provided with longitudinal bracing.

△ **18.5.9.6.1*** When riser nipples are provided in systems requiring seismic protection, they shall satisfy the requirements of 18.5.9.6.2 unless the following requirements are met:

(1) Where riser nipples are 4 ft (1.2 m) or less in length and C_p is 0.50 or less
(2) Where riser nipples are 3 ft (900 mm) or less in length and C_p is less than 0.67
(3) Where riser nipples are 2 ft (600 mm) or less in length and C_p is less than is 1.0

18.5.9.6.2 If the calculated value as determined by the following equation is equal to or greater than the allowable yield strength of the riser nipple, F_y, the longitudinal seismic load of each line shall be evaluated individually, and branch lines shall be provided with longitudinal sway bracing in accordance with 18.5.6:

[18.5.9.6.2]

$$\frac{\left(H_r \cdot W_p \cdot C_p\right)}{S} \leq F_y$$

where:
H_r = length of riser nipple piping (in.)
W_p = tributary weight (lb) for the branch line or portion of branch line within the zone of influence including the riser nipple
C_p = seismic coefficient
S = sectional modulus of the riser nipple pipe
F_y = allowable yield strength of 30,000 psi (2070 bar) for steel, 30,000 psi (2070 bar) for copper (soldered), and 8000 psi (550 bar) for CPVC

18.5.9.7 The zone of influence for longitudinal braces shall include all mains tributary to the brace.

△ **18.5.10 Net Vertical Forces.** Where the horizontal seismic load used exceeds 0.5 W_p and the brace angle is less than 45 degrees from vertical or where the horizontal seismic load used exceeds 1.0 W_p and the brace angle is less than 60 degrees from vertical, the braces shall be arranged to resist the net vertical force produced by the horizontal load.

18.5.11* Sway Brace Installation.

18.5.11.1* Bracing shall be attached directly to the system pipe.

18.5.11.2 Sway bracing shall be tight.

18.5.11.3 For individual braces, the slenderness ratio *(l/r)* shall not exceed 300, where *l* is the length of the brace and *r* is the least radius of gyration.

18.5.11.4 Where threaded pipe is used as part of a sway brace assembly, it shall not be less than Schedule 30.

18.5.11.5 All parts and fittings of a brace shall lie in a straight line to avoid eccentric loadings on fittings and fasteners.

18.5.11.6 For longitudinal braces only, the brace shall be permitted to be connected to a tab welded to the pipe in conformance to 7.5.2.

18.5.11.7 For tension-only braces, two tension-only brace components opposing each other must be installed at each lateral or longitudinal brace location.

18.5.11.8 The loads determined in 18.5.9 shall not exceed the lesser of the maximum allowable loads provided in Table 18.5.11.8(a) through Table 18.5.11.8(f), and the manufacturer's certified maximum allowable horizontal loads for brace angles of 30 to 44 degrees, 45 to 59 degrees, 60 to 89 degrees, or 90 degrees.

18.5.11.9* Other pipe schedules and materials not specifically included in Table 18.5.11.8(a) through Table 18.5.11.8(f) shall be permitted to be used if certified by a registered professional engineer to support the loads determined in accordance with the criteria in the tables.

18.5.11.9.1 Calculations shall be submitted where required by the authority having jurisdiction.

18.5.11.10 C-type clamps including beam and large flange clamps, with or without restraining straps, shall not be used to attach braces to the building structure.

18.5.11.11 Powder-driven fasteners shall not be used to attach braces to the building structure, unless they are specifically listed for service in resisting lateral loads in areas subject to earthquakes.

18.5.12* Fasteners.

18.5.12.1 The designated angle category for the fastener(s) used in the sway brace installation shall be determined in accordance with Figure 18.5.12.1.

18.5.12.2* For individual fasteners, unless alternative allowable loads are determined and certified by a registered professional engineer, the loads determined in 18.5.9 shall not exceed the allowable loads provided in Table 18.5.12.2(a) through Table 18.5.12.2(m) or 18.5.12.7.

Table 18.5.11.8(a) Maximum Horizontal Loads for Sway Braces with $l/r = 100$ for Steel Braces with $F_y = 36$ ksi

Brace Shape and Size (in.)		Area (in.²)	Least Radius of Gyration (r) (in.)	Maximum Length for $l/r = 100$		Maximum Horizontal Load (lb) Brace Angle		
				ft	in.	30° to 44° Angle from Vertical	45° to 59° Angle from Vertical	60° to 90° Angle from Vertical
Pipe Schedule 40	1	0.494	0.421	3	6	3,150	4,455	5,456
	1¼	0.669	0.540	4	6	4,266	6,033	7,389
	1½	0.799	0.623	5	2	5,095	7,206	8,825
	2	1.07	0.787	6	6	6,823	9,650	11,818
Angles	1½ × 1½ × ¼	0.688	0.292	2	5	4,387	6,205	7,599
	2 × 2 × ¼	0.938	0.391	3	3	5,982	8,459	10,360
	2½ × 2 × ¼	1.06	0.424	3	6	6,760	9,560	11,708
	2½ × 2½ × ¼	1.19	0.491	4	1	7,589	10,732	13,144
	3 × 2½ × ¼	1.31	0.528	4	4	8,354	11,814	14,469
	3 × 3 × ¼	1.44	0.592	4	11	9,183	12,987	15,905
Rods (all thread)	⅜	0.07	0.075	0	7	446	631	773
	½	0.129	0.101	0	10	823	1,163	1,425
	⅝	0.207	0.128	1	0	1,320	1,867	2,286
	¾	0.309	0.157	1	3	1,970	2,787	3,413
	⅞	0.429	0.185	1	6	2,736	3,869	4,738
Rods (threaded at ends only)	⅜	0.11	0.094	0	9	701	992	1,215
	½	0.196	0.125	1	0	1,250	1,768	2,165
	⅝	0.307	0.156	1	3	1,958	2,769	3,391
	¾	0.442	0.188	1	6	2,819	3,986	4,882
	⅞	0.601	0.219	1	9	3,833	5,420	6,638
Flats	1½ × ¼	0.375	0.0722	0	7	2,391	3,382	4,142
	2 × ¼	0.5	0.0722	0	7	3,189	4,509	5,523
	2 × ⅜	0.75	0.1082	0	10	4,783	6,764	8,284

Table 18.5.11.8(b) Maximum Horizontal Loads for Sway Braces with $l/r = 200$ for Steel Braces with $F_y = 36$ ksi

Brace Shape and Size (in.)		Area (in.²)	Least Radius of Gyration (r) (in.)	Maximum Length for $l/r = 200$		Maximum Horizontal Load (lb) Brace Angle		
				ft	in.	30° to 44° Angle from Vertical	45° to 59° Angle from Vertical	60° to 90° Angle from Vertical
Pipe Schedule 40	1	0.494	0.421	7	0	926	1310	1604
	1¼	0.669	0.540	9	0	1254	1774	2173
	1½	0.799	0.623	10	4	1498	2119	2595
	2	1.07	0.787	13	1	2006	2837	3475
Angles	1½ × 1½ × ¼	0.688	0.292	4	10	1290	1824	2234
	2 × 2 × ¼	0.938	0.391	6	6	1759	2487	3046
	2½ × 2 × ¼	1.06	0.424	7	0	1988	2811	3442
	2½ × 2½ × ¼	1.19	0.491	8	2	2231	3155	3865
	3 × 2½ × ¼	1.31	0.528	8	9	2456	3474	4254
	3 × 3 × ¼	1.44	0.592	9	10	2700	3818	4677
Rods (all thread)	⅜	0.07	0.075	1	2	131	186	227
	½	0.129	0.101	1	8	242	342	419
	⅝	0.207	0.128	2	1	388	549	672
	¾	0.309	0.157	2	7	579	819	1004
	⅞	0.429	0.185	3	0	804	1138	1393
Rods (threaded at ends only)	⅜	0.11	0.094	1	6	206	292	357
	½	0.196	0.125	2	0	368	520	637
	⅝	0.307	0.156	2	7	576	814	997
	¾	0.442	0.188	3	1	829	1172	1435
	⅞	0.601	0.219	3	7	1127	1594	1952
Flats	1½ × ¼	0.375	0.0722	1	2	703	994	1218
	2 × ¼	0.5	0.0722	1	2	938	1326	1624
	2 × ⅜	0.75	0.1082	1	9	1406	1989	2436

Table 18.5.11.8(c) Maximum Horizontal Loads for Sway Braces with $l/r = 300$ for Steel Braces with $F_y = 36$ ksi

Brace Shape and Size (in.)		Area (in.^{2})	Least Radius of Gyration (r) (in.)	Maximum Length for $l/r = 300$		Maximum Horizontal Load (lb)		
						Brace Angle		
				ft	in.	30°to 44°Angle from Vertical	45°to 59°Angle from Vertical	60°to 90°Angle from Vertical
Pipe Schedule 40	1	0.494	0.421	10	6	412	582	713
	1¼	0.669	0.540	13	6	558	788	966
	1½	0.799	0.623	15	6	666	942	1153
	2	1.07	0.787	19	8	892	1261	1544
Angles	1½ × 1½ × ¼	0.688	0.292	7	3	573	811	993
	2 × 2 × ¼	0.938	0.391	9	9	782	1105	1354
	2½ × 2 × ¼	1.06	0.424	10	7	883	1249	1530
	2½ × 2½ × ¼	1.19	0.491	12	3	992	1402	1718
	3 × 2½ × ¼	1.31	0.528	13	2	1092	1544	1891
	3 × 3 × ¼	1.44	0.592	14	9	1200	1697	2078
Rods (all thread)	⅜	0.07	0.075	1	10	58	82	101
	½	0.129	0.101	2	6	108	152	186
	⅝	0.207	0.128	3	2	173	244	299
	¾	0.309	0.157	3	11	258	364	446
	⅞	0.429	0.185	4	7	358	506	619
Rods (threaded at ends only)	⅜	0.11	0.094	2	4	92	130	159
	½	0.196	0.125	3	1	163	231	283
	⅝	0.307	0.156	3	10	256	362	443
	¾	0.442	0.188	4	8	368	521	638
	⅞	0.601	0.219	5	5	501	708	867
Flats	1½ × ¼	0.375	0.0722	1	9	313	442	541
	2 × ¼	0.5	0.0722	1	9	417	589	722
	2 × ⅜	0.75	0.1082	2	8	625	884	1083

Table 18.5.11.8(d) Maximum Horizontal Loads for Sway Braces with $l/r = 100$ for Steel Braces with $F_y = 248$ N/mm^2

Brace Shape and Size (mm)		Area (mm^2)	Least Radius of Gyration (r) (mm)	Maximum Length for $l/r = 100$		Maximum Horizontal Load (kg)		
						Brace Angle		
				meters	mm	30°to 44°Angle from Vertical	45°to 59°Angle from Vertical	60°to 90°Angle from Vertical
Pipe Schedule 40	25	318.7	11	1.0	150	1,429	2,021	2,475
	32	431.6	14	1.2	150	1,935	2,737	3,352
	40	515.5	16	1.5	50	2,311	3,269	4,003
	50	690.3	20	1.8	150	3,095	4,377	5,361
Angles	40 × 40 × 6	443.9	7	0.6	125	1,990	2,815	3,447
	50 × 50 × 6	605.2	10	1.0	75	2,713	3,837	4,699
	65 × 50 × 6	683.9	11	1.0	150	3,066	4,336	5,311
	65 × 65 × 6	767.7	12	1.2	25	3,442	4,868	5,962
	80 × 65 × 6	845.2	13	1.2	100	3,789	5,359	6,563
	80 × 80 × 6	929.0	15	1.2	275	4,165	5,891	7,214
Rods (all thread)	10	45.2	2	0.0	175	202	286	351
	15	83.2	3	0.0	250	373	528	646
	16	133.5	3	0.3	0	599	847	1,037
	20	199.4	4	0.3	75	894	1,264	1,548
	22	276.8	5	0.3	150	1,241	1,755	2,149
Rods (threaded at ends only)	10	71.0	2	0.0	225	318	450	551
	15	126.5	3	0.3	0	567	802	982
	16	198.1	4	0.3	75	888	1,256	1,538
	20	285.2	5	0.3	150	1,279	1,808	2,214
	22	387.7	5	0.3	225	1,739	2,458	3,011
Flats	40 × 6	241.9	2	0.0	175	1,085	1,534	1,879
	50 × 6	322.6	2	0.0	175	1,447	2,045	2,505
	50 × 10	483.9	3	0.0	250	2,170	3,068	3,758

Shaded text = Revisions. Δ = Text deletions and figure/table revisions.   • = Section deletions. N = New material.

Table 18.5.11.8(e) Maximum Horizontal Loads for Sway Braces with $l/r = 200$ for Steel Braces with $F_y = 248$ N/mm^2

Brace Shape and Size (nun)		Area (mm^2)	Least Radius of Gyration (r) (mm)	Maximum Length for $l/r = 200$		Maximum Horizontal Load (kg)		
						Brace Angle		
				meters	nun	30°to 44°Angle from Vertical	45°to 59°Angle from Vertical	60°to 90°Angle from Vertical
Pipe Schedule 40	25	318.7	11	2.1	0	420	594	728
	32	431.6	14	2.7	0	569	805	986
	40	515.5	16	3	100	679	961	1177
	50	690.3	20	4.0	25	910	1287	1576
Angles	40 × 40 × 6	443.9	7	1.2	250	585	827	1013
	50 × 50 × 6	605.2	10	1.8	150	798	1128	1382
	65 × 50 × 6	683.9	11	2.1	0	902	1275	1561
	65 × 65 × 6	767.7	12	2.4	50	1012	1431	1753
	80 × 65 × 6	845.2	13	2.4	225	1114	1576	1930
	80 × 80 × 6	929.0	15	2.7	250	1225	1732	2121
Rods (all thread)	10	45.2	2	0.3	50	59	84	103
	15	83.2	3	0.3	200	110	155	190
	16	133.5	3	0.6	25	176	249	305
	20	199.4	4	0.6	175	263	371	455
	22	276.8	5	0.9	0	365	516	632
Rods (threaded at ends only)	10	71.0	2	0.3	150	93	132	162
	15	126.5	3	0.6	0	167	236	289
	16	198.1	4	0.6	175	261	369	452
	20	285.2	5	0.9	25	376	532	651
	22	387.7	5	0.9	175	511	723	885
Flats	40 × 6	241.9	2	0.3	50	319	451	552
	50 × 6	322.6	2	0.3	50	425	601	737
	50 × 10	483.9	3	0.3	225	638	902	1105

Table 18.5.11.8(f) Maximum Horizontal Loads for Sway Braces with $l/r = 300$ for Steel Braces with $F_y = 248$ N/mm^2

Brace Shape and Size (nun)		Area (nun^2)	Least Radius of Gyration (r) (nun)	Maximum Length for $l/r = 300$		Maximum Horizontal Load (kg)		
						Brace Angle		
				meters	mm	30°to 44°Angle from Vertical	45°to 59°Angle from Vertical	60°to 90°Angle from Vertical
Pipe Schedule 40	25	318.7	10.5	3	150	187	264	323
	32	431.6	13.5	4	150	253	357	438
	40	515.5	15.6	4.6	150	302	427	523
	50	690.3	19.7	5.8	200	405	572	700
Angles	40 × 40 × 6	443.9	7.3	2.1	75	260	368	450
	50 × 50 × 6	605.2	9.8	2.7	225	355	501	614
	65 × 50 × 6	683.9	10.6	3	175	401	567	694
	65 × 65 × 6	767.7	12.3	3.7	75	450	636	779
	80 × 65 × 6	845.2	13.2	4	50	495	700	858
	80 × 80 × 6	929.0	14.8	4.3	225	544	770	943
Rods (all thread)	10	45.2	1.9	0.3	250	26	37	46
	15	83.2	2.5	0.6	150	49	69	84
	16	133.5	3.2	0.9	50	79	111	136
	20	199.4	3.9	0.9	275	117	165	202
	22	276.8	4.6	1.2	175	162	230	281
Rods (threaded at ends only)	10	71.0	2.4	0.6	100	42	59	72
	15	126.5	3.1	0.9	25	74	105	128
	16	198.1	3.9	0.9	250	116	164	201
	20	285.2	4.7	1.2	200	167	236	289
	22	387.7	5.5	1.5	125	227	321	393
Flats	40 × 6	241.9	1.8	0.3	225	142	200	245
	50 × 6	322.6	1.8	0.3	225	189	267	327
	50 × 10	483.9	2.7	0.6	200	283	401	491

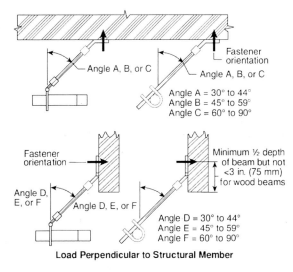

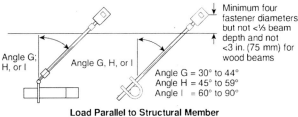

Load Parallel to Structural Member

△ **FIGURE 18.5.12.1 Designation of Angle Category Based on Angle of Sway Brace and Fastener Orientation.**

18.5.12.3* The type of fasteners used to secure the bracing assembly to the structure shall be limited to those shown in Table 18.5.12.2(a) through Table 18.5.12.2(m) or to listed devices.

18.5.12.4* For connections to wood, through-bolts with washers on each end shall be used, unless the requirements of 18.5.12.5 are met.

18.5.12.5 Where it is not practical to install through-bolts due to the thickness of the wood member in excess of 12 in. (300 mm) or inaccessibility, lag screws shall be permitted and holes shall be pre-drilled ⅛ in. (3 mm) smaller than the maximum root diameter of the lag screw.

18.5.12.6 Holes for through-bolts and similar listed attachments shall be ¹⁄₁₆ in. (1.6 mm) greater than the diameter of the bolt.

18.5.12.6.1 The requirements of 18.5.12 shall not apply to other fastening methods, which shall be acceptable for use if certified by a registered professional engineer to support the loads determined in accordance with the criteria in 18.5.9.

18.5.12.6.2 Calculations shall be submitted where required by the authority having jurisdiction.

18.5.12.7* Concrete Anchors.

18.5.12.7.1* Post-installed concrete anchors shall be prequalified for seismic applications in accordance with ACI 355.2, *Qualification of Post-Installed Mechanical Anchors in Concrete and Commentary*, and installed in accordance with the manufacturer's instructions.

18.5.12.7.2 Unless the requirements of 18.5.12.7.3 are met, concrete anchors shall be based on concrete strength, anchor type, designated angle category A through I, prying factor (*Pr*) range, and allowable maximum load.

18.5.12.7.2.1 Sway brace manufacturers shall provide prying factors (*Pr*) based on the geometry of the structure attachment fitting and the designated angle category A through I as shown in Figure 18.5.12.1.

△ **18.5.12.7.2.2** Where the prying factor (*Pr*) for the fitting is unknown, the largest *Pr* range in Table 18.5.12.2(a) through Table 18.5.12.2(j) for the concrete strength and designated angle category A through I shall be used.

18.5.12.7.3 The allowable maximum load shall be permitted to be calculated.

18.5.12.7.3.1 Allowable concrete anchor loads shall be permitted to be determined using approved software that considers the effects of prying for concrete anchors.

18.5.12.7.3.2 Anchors shall be seismically prequalified per 18.5.12.7.1.

△ **18.5.12.7.3.3** Allowable maximum loads shall be based on anchor capacities given in approved evaluation service reports, where the calculation of allowable stress design (ASD) allowable shear and tension values are determined in accordance with Chapter 17 of ACI 318, *Building Code Requirements for Structural Concrete and Commentary*, and include the effects of prying, the brace angle, and the over strength factor ($\Omega = 2.0$).

△ **18.5.12.7.3.4*** The shear and tension values determined in 18.5.12.7.3.3 shall be multiplied by 0.43.

18.5.12.7.4 Concrete anchors shall be acceptable for use where designed in accordance with the requirements of the applicable building code and certified by a registered professional engineer.

18.5.12.7.5 Headed cast-in specialty inserts (i.e., concrete inserts) as prescribed in Table 18.5.12.2(a) through Table 18.5.12.2(j) shall be prequalified for seismic applications in accordance with ICC-ES AC446, *Acceptance Criteria for Headed Cast-in Specialty Inserts in Concrete*, and installed in accordance with the manufacturer's instructions.

18.5.13 Braces to Buildings with Differential Movement. A length of pipe shall not be braced to sections of the building that will move differentially.

Δ Table 18.5.12.2(a) Maximum Load for Wedge Anchors in 3000 psi (207 bar) Lightweight Cracked Concrete on Metal Deck

				A	B	C	D	E	F	G	H	I
Diameter (in.)	Min. Nom. Embedment (in.)	Min. Slab Thickness (in.)	Max. Flute Center Offset (in.)	$Pr \le 2.0$	$Pr \le 1.1$	$Pr \le 0.7$	$Pr \le 1.2$	$Pr \le 1.1$	$Pr \le 1.1$	$Pr \le 1.4$	$Pr \le 0.9$	$Pr \le 0.8$
⅜	2.375	6.25	1	123	183	233	—	—	—	—	—	—
½	3.750	6.25	1	147	231	310	—	—	—	—	—	—
⅝	3.875	6.25	1	188	292	387	—	—	—	—	—	—
¾	4.500	6.25	1	255	380	486	—	—	—	—	—	—
Diameter (in.)	Min. Nom. Embedment (in.)	Min. Slab Thickness (in.)	Max. Flute Center Offset (in.)	$2.0 < Pr \le 3.5$	$1.1 < Pr \le 1.8$	$0.7 < Pr \le 1.0$	$1.2 < Pr \le 1.7$	$1.1 < Pr \le 1.8$	$1.1 < Pr \le 2.0$	$1.4 < Pr \le 1.9$	$0.9 < Pr \le 1.3$	$0.8 < Pr \le 1.1$
⅜	2.375	6.25	1	79	133	193	—	—	—	—	—	—
½	3.750	6.25	1	86	160	247	—	—	—	—	—	—
⅝	3.875	6.25	1	113	204	311	—	—	—	—	—	—
¾	4.500	6.25	1	165	275	402	—	—	—	—	—	—
Diameter (in.)	Min. Nom. Embedment (in.)	Min. Slab Thickness (in.)	Max. Flute Center Offset (in.)	$3.5 < Pr \le 5.0$	$1.8 < Pr \le 2.5$	$1.0 < Pr \le 1.3$	$1.7 < Pr \le 2.2$	$1.8 < Pr \le 2.5$	$2.0 < Pr \le 2.9$	$1.9 < Pr \le 2.4$	$1.3 < Pr \le 1.7$	$1.1 < Pr \le 1.4$
⅜	2.375	6.25	1	56	104	165	—	—	—	—	—	—
½	3.750	6.25	1	60	121	205	—	—	—	—	—	—
⅝	3.875	6.25	1	79	157	260	—	—	—	—	—	—
¾	4.500	6.25	1	116	216	343	—	—	—	—	—	—
Diameter (in.)	Min. Nom. Embedment (in.)	Min. Slab Thickness (in.)	Max. Flute Center Offset (in.)	$5.0 < Pr \le 6.5$	$2.5 < Pr \le 3.2$	$1.3 < Pr \le 1.6$	$2.2 < Pr \le 2.7$	$2.5 < Pr \le 3.2$	$2.9 < Pr \le 3.8$	$2.4 < Pr \le 2.9$	$1.7 < Pr \le 2.1$	$1.4 < Pr \le 1.7$
⅜	2.375	6.25	1	43	85	144	—	—	—	—	—	—
½	3.750	6.25	1	46	94	175	—	—	—	—	—	—
⅝	3.875	6.25	1	60	124	224	—	—	—	—	—	—
¾	4.500	6.25	1	89	177	299	—	—	—	—	—	—

Pr: Prying factor range *(see A.18.5.12.2 for additional information).*

Δ Table 18.5.12.2(b) Maximum Load for Wedge Anchors in 3000 psi (207 bar) Lightweight Cracked Concrete

Wedge Anchors in 3000 psi Lightweight Cracked Concrete (lb)												
				A	B	C	D	E	F	G	H	I
Diameter (in.)	Min. Nom. Embedment (in.)	Min. Slab Thickness (in.)	Min. Edge Distance (in.)	*Pr* ≤ 2.0	*Pr* ≤ 1.1	*Pr* ≤ 0.7	*Pr* ≤ 1.2	*Pr* ≤ 1.1	*Pr* ≤ 1.1	*Pr* ≤ 1.4	*Pr* ≤ 0.9	*Pr* ≤ 0.8
3/8	2.375	5	4	142	216	280	162	216	256	139	208	244
1/2	3.750	6	6	200	314	419	243	314	362	209	312	365
5/8	3.875	6	6	259	394	512	297	394	467	255	380	446
3/4	4.500	7	8	356	552	731	424	552	641	365	544	636
				A	B	C	D	E	F	G	H	I
Diameter (in.)	Min. Nom. Embedment (in.)	Min. Slab Thickness (in.)	Min. Edge Distance (in.)	2.0 < *Pr* ≤ 3.5	1.1 < *Pr* ≤ 1.8	0.7 < *Pr* ≤ 1.0	1.2 < *Pr* ≤ 1.7	1.1 < *Pr* ≤ 1.8	1.1 < *Pr* ≤ 2.0	1.4 < *Pr* ≤ 1.9	0.9 < *Pr* ≤ 1.3	0.8 < *Pr* ≤ 1.1
3/8	2.375	5	4	89	154	229	133	154	157	117	170	204
1/2	3.750	6	6	119	218	335	195	218	209	172	250	299
5/8	3.875	6	6	163	281	418	244	281	286	215	311	373
3/4	4.500	7	8	214	386	588	343	386	376	303	438	525
				A	B	C	D	E	F	G	H	I
Diameter (in.)	Min. Nom. Embedment (in.)	Min. Slab Thickness (in.)	Min. Edge Distance (in.)	3.5 < *Pr* ≤ 5.0	1.8 < *Pr* ≤ 2.5	1.0 < *Pr* ≤ 1.3	1.7 < *Pr* ≤ 2.2	1.8 < *Pr* ≤ 2.5	2.0 < *Pr* ≤ 2.9	1.9 < *Pr* ≤ 2.4	1.3 < *Pr* ≤ 1.7	1.1 < *Pr* ≤ 1.4
3/8	2.375	5	4	62	119	194	113	119	108	101	144	175
1/2	3.750	6	6	83	167	279	163	167	144	147	208	254
5/8	3.875	6	6	113	218	354	207	218	197	186	263	320
3/4	4.500	7	8	150	297	492	288	297	259	259	367	447
				A	B	C	D	E	F	G	H	I
Diameter (in.)	Min. Nom. Embedment (in.)	Min. Slab Thickness (in.)	Min. Edge Distance (in.)	5.0 < *Pr* ≤ 6.5	2.5 < *Pr* ≤ 3.2	1.3 < *Pr* ≤ 1.6	2.2 < *Pr* ≤ 2.7	2.5 < *Pr* ≤ 3.2	2.9 < *Pr* ≤ 3.8	2.4 < *Pr* ≤ 2.9	1.7 < *Pr* ≤ 2.1	1.4 < *Pr* ≤ 1.7
3/8	2.375	5	4	47	97	168	98	97	82	89	125	154
1/2	3.750	6	6	63	130	239	140	130	109	128	178	220
5/8	3.875	6	6	87	178	306	179	178	150	163	228	281
3/4	4.500	7	8	115	234	422	248	234	197	226	315	389

Pr: Prying factor range *(see A.18.5.12.2 for additional information)*.

Δ Table 18.5.12.2(c) Maximum Load for Wedge Anchors in 3000 psi (207 bar) Normal Weight Cracked Concrete

				Wedge Anchors in 3000 psi Normal Weight Cracked Concrete (lb)								
Diameter (in.)	Min. Nom. Embedment (in.)	Min. Slab Thickness (in.)	Min. Edge Distance (in.)	A $Pr<2.0$	B $Pr<1.1$	C $Pr<0.7$	D $Pr<1.2$	E $Pr<1.1$	F $Pr<1.1$	G $Pr<1.4$	H $Pr<0.9$	I $Pr<0.8$
⅜	2.375	5	4	189	274	342	197	274	340	170	251	297
½	3.750	6	6	272	423	563	326	423	490	281	419	490
⅝	3.875	6	6	407	623	814	472	623	733	406	605	709
¾	4.500	7	8	613	940	1232	715	940	1104	615	916	1073
Diameter (in.)	Min. Nom. Embedment (in.)	Min. Slab Thickness (in.)	Min. Edge Distance (in.)	A $2.0<Pr\le3.5$	B $1.1<Pr\le1.8$	C $0.7<Pr\le1.0$	D $1.2<Pr\le1.7$	E $1.1<Pr\le1.8$	F $1.1<Pr\le2.0$	G $1.4<Pr\le1.9$	H $0.9<Pr\le1.3$	I $0.8<Pr\le1.1$
⅜	2.375	5	4	125	203	288	167	203	219	147	212	256
½	3.750	6	6	162	295	451	263	295	285	233	337	403
⅝	3.875	6	6	252	441	662	386	441	442	341	492	590
¾	4.500	7	8	378	665	999	583	665	662	515	744	892
Diameter (in.)	Min. Nom. Embedment (in.)	Min. Slab Thickness (in.)	Min. Edge Distance (in.)	A $3.5<Pr\le5.0$	B $1.8<Pr\le2.5$	C $1.0<Pr\le1.3$	D $1.7<Pr\le2.2$	E $1.8<Pr\le2.5$	F $2.0<Pr\le2.9$	G $1.9<Pr\le2.4$	H $1.3<Pr\le1.7$	I $1.1<Pr\le1.4$
⅜	2.375	5	4	92	162	249	145	162	159	130	184	225
½	3.750	6	6	113	226	377	220	226	196	199	281	342
⅝	3.875	6	6	176	341	557	326	341	304	293	415	506
¾	4.500	7	8	264	514	841	493	514	456	443	627	763
Diameter (in.)	Min. Nom. Embedment (in.)	Min. Slab Thickness (in.)	Min. Edge Distance (in.)	A $5.0<Pr\le6.5$	B $2.5<Pr\le3.2$	C $1.3<Pr\le1.6$	D $2.2<Pr\le2.7$	E $2.5<Pr\le3.2$	F $2.9<Pr\le3.8$	G $2.4<Pr\le2.9$	H $1.7<Pr\le2.1$	I $1.4<Pr\le1.7$
⅜	2.375	5	4	70	134	220	128	134	121	116	162	200
½	3.750	6	6	87	178	323	190	178	149	173	241	298
⅝	3.875	6	6	135	276	481	283	276	232	258	359	442
¾	4.500	7	8	203	413	725	426	413	348	389	541	667

Pr: Prying factor range (see A.18.5.12.2 for additional information).

Δ **Table 18.5.12.2(d) Maximum Load for Wedge Anchors in 4000 psi (276 bar) Normal Weight Cracked Concrete**

				Wedge Anchors in 4000 psi Normal Weight Cracked Concrete (lb)								
Diameter (in.)	Min. Nom. Embedment (in.)	Min. Slab Thickness (in.)	Min. Edge Distance (in.)	A	B	C	D	E	F	G	H	I
				$Pr \leq 2.0$	$Pr \leq 1.1$	$Pr \leq 0.7$	$Pr \leq 1.2$	$Pr \leq 1.1$	$Pr \leq 1.1$	$Pr \leq 1.4$	$Pr \leq 0.9$	$Pr \leq 0.8$
⅜	2.375	5	4	206	293	360	208	293	370	179	264	313
½	3.750	6	6	304	466	610	353	466	548	304	453	531
⅝	3.875	6	6	469	716	935	542	716	844	467	694	814
¾	4.500	7	8	657	997	1293	750	997	1182	646	959	1125
Diameter (in.)	Min. Nom. Embedment (in.)	Min. Slab Thickness (in.)	Min. Edge Distance (in.)	A	B	C	D	E	F	G	H	I
				$2.0 < Pr \leq 3.5$	$1.1 < Pr \leq 1.8$	$0.7 < Pr \leq 1.0$	$1.2 < Pr \leq 1.7$	$1.1 < Pr \leq 1.8$	$1.1 < Pr \leq 2.0$	$1.4 < Pr \leq 1.9$	$0.9 < Pr \leq 1.3$	$0.8 < Pr \leq 1.1$
⅜	2.375	5	4	138	221	307	178	221	242	157	226	272
½	3.750	6	6	188	330	495	289	330	330	255	368	442
⅝	3.875	6	6	291	508	761	444	508	511	392	566	678
¾	4.500	7	8	414	711	1057	617	711	725	544	786	942
Diameter (in.)	Min. Nom. Embedment (in.)	Min. Slab Thickness (in.)	Min. Edge Distance (in.)	A	B	C	D	E	F	G	H	I
				$3.5 < Pr \leq 5.0$	$1.8 < Pr \leq 2.5$	$1.0 < Pr \leq 1.3$	$1.7 < Pr \leq 2.2$	$1.8 < Pr \leq 2.5$	$2.0 < Pr \leq 2.9$	$1.9 < Pr \leq 2.4$	$1.3 < Pr \leq 1.7$	$1.1 < Pr \leq 1.4$
⅜	2.375	5	4	103	177	268	156	177	179	139	197	241
½	3.750	6	6	131	255	417	244	255	227	219	310	378
⅝	3.875	6	6	203	393	641	375	393	352	337	477	582
¾	4.500	7	8	289	553	894	524	553	500	470	665	810
Diameter (in.)	Min. Nom. Embedment (in.)	Min. Slab Thickness (in.)	Min. Edge Distance (in.)	A	B	C	D	E	F	G	H	I
				$5.0 < Pr \leq 6.5$	$2.5 < Pr \leq 3.2$	$1.3 < Pr \leq 1.6$	$2.2 < Pr \leq 2.7$	$2.5 < Pr \leq 3.2$	$2.9 < Pr \leq 3.8$	$2.4 < Pr \leq 2.9$	$1.7 < Pr \leq 2.1$	$1.4 < Pr \leq 1.7$
⅜	2.375	5	4	80	148	237	139	148	138	125	175	216
½	3.750	6	6	100	205	360	211	205	173	192	268	330
⅝	3.875	6	6	156	319	554	325	319	268	296	413	509
¾	4.500	7	8	222	452	774	455	452	381	414	577	711

Pr: Prying factor range *(see A.18.5.12.2 for additional information).*

Δ Table 18.5.12.2(e) Maximum Load for Wedge Anchors in 6000 psi (414 bar) Normal Weight Cracked Concrete

Diameter (in.)	Min. Nom. Embedment (in.)	Min. Slab Thickness (in.)	Min. Edge Distance (in.)	A	B	C	D	E	F	G	H	I
				$Pr \leq 2.0$	$Pr \leq 1.1$	$Pr \leq 0.7$	$Pr \leq 1.2$	$Pr \leq 1.1$	$Pr \leq 1.1$	$Pr \leq 1.4$	$Pr \leq 0.9$	$Pr \leq 0.8$
⅜	2.375	5	4	225	313	379	219	313	402	189	277	329
½	3.750	6	6	354	529	676	392	529	637	337	500	589
⅝	3.875	6	6	546	812	1036	601	812	981	517	766	902
¾	4.500	7	8	763	1127	1429	829	1127	1370	714	1055	1243
Diameter (in.)	Min. Nom. Embedment (in.)	Min. Slab Thickness (in.)	Min. Edge Distance (in.)	A	B	C	D	E	F	G	H	I
				$2.0 < Pr \leq 3.5$	$1.1 < Pr \leq 1.8$	$0.7 < Pr \leq 1.0$	$1.2 < Pr \leq 1.7$	$1.1 < Pr \leq 1.8$	$1.1 < Pr \leq 2.0$	$1.4 < Pr \leq 1.9$	$0.9 < Pr \leq 1.3$	$0.8 < Pr \leq 1.1$
⅜	2.375	5	4	153	240	327	190	240	267	167	240	289
½	3.750	6	6	228	382	559	326	382	400	287	414	498
⅝	3.875	6	6	353	589	859	500	589	617	441	636	764
¾	4.500	7	8	496	822	1190	693	822	868	611	881	1058
Diameter (in.)	Min. Nom. Embedment (in.)	Min. Slab Thickness (in.)	Min. Edge Distance (in.)	A	B	C	D	E	F	G	H	I
				$3.5 < Pr \leq 5.0$	$1.8 < Pr \leq 2.5$	$1.0 < Pr \leq 1.3$	$1.7 < Pr \leq 2.2$	$1.8 < Pr \leq 2.5$	$2.0 < Pr \leq 2.9$	$1.9 < Pr \leq 2.4$	$1.3 < Pr \leq 1.7$	$1.1 < Pr \leq 1.4$
⅜	2.375	5	4	115	194	288	168	194	200	149	211	258
½	3.750	6	6	161	299	477	279	299	278	250	354	431
⅝	3.875	6	6	249	462	733	429	462	431	384	544	663
¾	4.500	7	8	354	647	1019	596	647	612	534	756	921
Diameter (in.)	Min. Nom. Embedment (in.)	Min. Slab Thickness (in.)	Min. Edge Distance (in.)	A	B	C	D	E	F	G	H	I
				$5.0 < Pr \leq 6.5$	$2.5 < Pr \leq 3.2$	$1.3 < Pr \leq 1.6$	$2.2 < Pr \leq 2.7$	$2.5 < Pr \leq 3.2$	$2.9 < Pr \leq 3.8$	$2.4 < Pr \leq 2.9$	$1.7 < Pr \leq 2.1$	$1.4 < Pr \leq 1.7$
⅜	2.375	5	4	91	163	257	150	163	157	135	189	233
½	3.750	6	6	123	246	415	243	246	212	221	308	380
⅝	3.875	6	6	192	380	639	375	380	329	341	475	585
¾	4.500	7	8	272	533	891	523	533	467	475	662	815

Pr: Prying factor range *(see A.18.5.12.2 for additional information).*

Δ **Table 18.5.12.2(f) Maximum Load for Metal Deck Inserts in 3000 psi (207 bar) Lightweight Cracked Concrete on Metal Deck**

Metal Deck Inserts in 3000 psi Sand Lightweight Cracked Concrete on 4½ in. Flute Width Metal Deck (lb)

Diameter (in.)	Min. Effect. Embedment (in.)	Min. Slab Thickness (in.)	Max. Flute Center Offset (in.)	A $Pr \le 2.0$	B $Pr \le 1.1$	C $Pr \le 0.7$	D $Pr \le 1.2$	E $Pr \le 1.1$	F $Pr \le 1.1$	G $Pr \le 1.4$	H $Pr \le 0.9$	I $Pr \le 0.8$
⅜	1.750	6.25	1	135	192	236	—	—	—	—	—	—
½	1.750	6.25	1	138	199	247	—	—	—	—	—	—
⅝	1.750	6.25	1	138	199	247	—	—	—	—	—	—
¾	1.750	6.25	1	164	257	344	—	—	—	—	—	—

Diameter (in.)	Min. Effect. Embedment (in.)	Min. Slab Thickness (in.)	Max. Flute Center Offset (in.)	A $2.0 < Pr \le 3.5$	B $1.1 < Pr \le 1.8$	C $0.7 < Pr \le 1.0$	D $1.2 < Pr \le 1.7$	E $1.1 < Pr \le 1.8$	F $1.1 < Pr \le 2.0$	G $1.4 < Pr \le 1.9$	H $0.9 < Pr \le 1.3$	I $0.8 < Pr \le 1.1$
⅜	1.750	6.25	1	90	144	201	—	—	—	—	—	—
½	1.750	6.25	1	91	148	209	—	—	—	—	—	—
⅝	1.750	6.25	1	91	148	209	—	—	—	—	—	—
¾	1.750	6.25	1	97	178	275	—	—	—	—	—	—

Diameter (in.)	Min. Effect. Embedment (in.)	Min. Slab Thickness (in.)	Max. Flute Center Offset (in.)	A $3.5 < Pr \le 5.0$	B $1.8 < Pr \le 2.5$	C $1.0 < Pr \le 1.3$	D $1.7 < Pr \le 2.2$	E $1.8 < Pr \le 2.5$	F $2.0 < Pr \le 2.9$	G $1.9 < Pr \le 2.4$	H $1.3 < Pr \le 1.7$	I $1.1 < Pr \le 1.4$
⅜	1.750	6.25	1	67	115	175	—	—	—	—	—	—
½	1.750	6.25	1	67	118	181	—	—	—	—	—	—
⅝	1.750	6.25	1	67	118	181	—	—	—	—	—	—
¾	1.750	6.25	1	67	136	229	—	—	—	—	—	—

Diameter (in.)	Min. Effect. Embedment (in.)	Min. Slab Thickness (in.)	Max. Flute Center Offset (in.)	A $5.0 < Pr \le 6.5$	B $2.5 < Pr \le 3.2$	C $1.3 < Pr \le 1.6$	D $2.2 < Pr \le 2.7$	E $2.5 < Pr \le 3.2$	F $2.9 < Pr \le 3.8$	G $2.4 < Pr \le 2.9$	H $1.7 < Pr \le 2.1$	I $1.4 < Pr \le 1.7$
⅜	1.750	6.25	1	52	96	155	—	—	—	—	—	—
½	1.750	6.25	1	52	98	160	—	—	—	—	—	—
⅝	1.750	6.25	1	52	98	160	—	—	—	—	—	—
¾	1.750	6.25	1	52	106	196	—	—	—	—	—	—

Pr: Prying factor range (see A.18.5.12.2 for additional information).

Δ **Table 18.5.12.2(g) Maximum Load for Wood Form Inserts in 3000 psi (207 bar) Lightweight Cracked Concrete**

				Wood Form Inserts in 3000 psi Lightweight Cracked Concrete (lb)								
Diameter (in.)	Min. Effect. Embedment (in.)	Min. Slab Thickness (in.)	Min. Edge Distance (in.)	A	B	C	D	E	F	G	H	I
				$Pr \leq 2.0$	$Pr \leq 1.1$	$Pr \leq 0.7$	$Pr \leq 1.2$	$Pr \leq 1.1$	$Pr \leq 1.1$	$Pr \leq 1.4$	$Pr \leq 0.9$	$Pr \leq 0.8$
⅜	1.100	4	6	224	316	387	223	316	401	193	283	336
½	1.690	4	6	252	376	480	278	376	454	239	355	418
⅝	1.750	4	8	252	376	480	278	376	454	239	355	418
¾	1.750	4	8	252	376	480	278	376	454	239	355	418
Diameter (in.)	Min. Effect. Embedment (in.)	Min. Slab Thickness (in.)	Min. Edge Distance (in.)	A	B	C	D	E	F	G	H	I
				$2.0 < Pr \leq 3.5$	$1.1 < Pr \leq 1.8$	$0.7 < Pr \leq 1.0$	$1.2 < Pr \leq 1.7$	$1.1 < Pr \leq 1.8$	$1.1 < Pr \leq 2.0$	$1.4 < Pr \leq 1.9$	$0.9 < Pr \leq 1.3$	$0.8 < Pr \leq 1.1$
⅜	1.100	4	6	150	239	331	192	239	264	169	243	293
½	1.690	4	6	163	272	398	231	272	286	204	294	354
⅝	1.750	4	8	163	272	398	231	272	286	204	294	354
¾	1.750	4	8	163	272	398	231	272	286	204	294	354
Diameter (in.)	Min. Effect. Embedment (in.)	Min. Slab Thickness (in.)	Min. Edge Distance (in.)	A	B	C	D	E	F	G	H	I
				$3.5 < Pr \leq 5.0$	$1.8 < Pr \leq 2.5$	$1.0 < Pr \leq 1.3$	$1.7 < Pr \leq 2.2$	$1.8 < Pr \leq 2.5$	$2.0 < Pr \leq 2.9$	$1.9 < Pr \leq 2.4$	$1.3 < Pr \leq 1.7$	$1.1 < Pr \leq 1.4$
⅜	1.100	4	6	113	193	290	169	193	196	150	213	260
½	1.690	4	6	115	213	339	198	213	199	178	251	307
⅝	1.750	4	8	115	213	339	198	213	199	178	251	307
¾	1.750	4	8	115	213	339	198	213	199	178	251	307
Diameter (in.)	Min. Effect. Embedment (in.)	Min. Slab Thickness (in.)	Min. Edge Distance (in.)	A	B	C	D	E	F	G	H	I
				$5.0 < Pr \leq 6.5$	$2.5 < Pr \leq 3.2$	$1.3 < Pr \leq 1.6$	$2.2 < Pr \leq 2.7$	$2.5 < Pr \leq 3.2$	$2.9 < Pr \leq 3.8$	$2.4 < Pr \leq 2.9$	$1.7 < Pr \leq 2.1$	$1.4 < Pr \leq 1.7$
⅜	1.100	4	6	88	161	257	150	161	152	135	190	234
½	1.690	4	6	88	175	296	173	175	152	157	219	271
⅝	1.750	4	8	88	175	296	173	175	152	157	219	271
¾	1.750	4	8	88	175	296	173	175	152	157	219	271

Pr: Prying factor range *(see A.18.5.12.2 for additional information).*

Δ **Table 18.5.12.2(h) Maximum Load for Wood Form Inserts in 3000 psi (207 bar) Normal Weight Cracked Concrete**

Wood Form Inserts in 3000 psi Normal Weight Cracked Concrete (lb)												
Diameter (in.)	Min. Effect. Embedment (in.)	Min. Slab Thickness (in.)	Min. Edge Distance (in.)	A	B	C	D	E	F	G	H	I
				$Pr \le 2.0$	$Pr \le 1.1$	$Pr \le 0.7$	$Pr \le 1.2$	$Pr \le 1.1$	$Pr \le 1.1$	$Pr \le 1.4$	$Pr \le 0.9$	$Pr \le 0.8$
3/8	1.100	4	6	248	342	411	237	342	444	205	300	357
1/2	1.690	4	6	297	443	565	327	443	535	282	418	492
5/8	1.750	4	8	297	443	565	327	443	535	282	418	492
3/4	1.750	4	8	297	443	565	327	443	535	282	418	492
Diameter (in.)	Min. Effect. Embedment (in.)	Min. Slab Thickness (in.)	Min. Edge Distance (in.)	A	B	C	D	E	F	G	H	I
				$2.0 < Pr \le 3.5$	$1.1 < Pr \le 1.8$	$0.7 < Pr \le 1.0$	$1.2 < Pr \le 1.7$	$1.1 < Pr \le 1.8$	$1.1 < Pr \le 2.0$	$1.4 < Pr \le 1.9$	$0.9 < Pr \le 1.3$	$0.8 < Pr \le 1.1$
3/8	1.100	4	6	170	264	357	207	264	298	182	261	315
1/2	1.690	4	6	192	321	468	272	321	336	240	347	416
5/8	1.750	4	8	192	321	468	272	321	336	240	347	416
3/4	1.750	4	8	192	321	468	272	321	336	240	347	416
Diameter (in.)	Min. Effect. Embedment (in.)	Min. Slab Thickness (in.)	Min. Edge Distance (in.)	A	B	C	D	E	F	G	H	I
				$3.5 < Pr \le 5.0$	$1.8 < Pr \le 2.5$	$1.0 < Pr \le 1.3$	$1.7 < Pr \le 2.2$	$1.8 < Pr \le 2.5$	$2.0 < Pr \le 2.9$	$1.9 < Pr \le 2.4$	$1.3 < Pr \le 1.7$	$1.1 < Pr \le 1.4$
3/8	1.100	4	6	129	215	315	184	215	224	163	231	282
1/2	1.690	4	6	135	251	399	233	251	235	209	296	361
5/8	1.750	4	8	135	251	399	233	251	235	209	296	361
3/4	1.750	4	8	135	251	399	233	251	235	209	296	361
Diameter (in.)	Min. Effect. Embedment (in.)	Min. Slab Thickness (in.)	Min. Edge Distance (in.)	A	B	C	D	E	F	G	H	I
				$5.0 < Pr \le 6.5$	$2.5 < Pr \le 3.2$	$1.3 < Pr \le 1.6$	$2.2 < Pr \le 2.7$	$2.5 < Pr \le 3.2$	$2.9 < Pr \le 3.8$	$2.4 < Pr \le 2.9$	$1.7 < Pr \le 2.1$	$1.4 < Pr \le 1.7$
3/8	1.100	4	6	104	181	282	165	181	179	148	208	256
1/2	1.690	4	6	104	207	348	204	207	179	185	258	319
5/8	1.750	4	8	104	207	348	204	207	179	185	258	319
3/4	1.750	4	8	104	207	348	204	207	179	185	258	319

Pr: Prying factor range *(see A.18.5.12.2 for additional information).*

Δ **Table 18.5.12.2(i) Maximum Load for Wood Form Inserts in 4000 psi (276 bar) Normal Weight Cracked Concrete**

				Wood Form Inserts in 4000 psi Normal Weight Cracked Concrete (lb)								
Diameter (in.)	Min. Effect. Embedment (in.)	Min. Slab Thickness (in.)	Min. Edge Distance (in.)	A	B	C	D	E	F	G	H	I
				$Pr \le 2.0$	$Pr \le 1.1$	$Pr \le 0.7$	$Pr \le 1.2$	$Pr \le 1.1$	$Pr \le 1.1$	$Pr \le 1.4$	$Pr \le 0.9$	$Pr \le 0.8$
⅜	1.100	4	6	270	364	431	249	364	482	215	313	374
½	1.690	4	6	335	493	623	361	493	602	311	459	541
⅝	1.750	4	8	344	511	653	378	511	618	326	482	568
¾	1.750	4	8	344	511	653	378	511	618	326	482	568
Diameter (in.)	Min. Effect. Embedment (in.)	Min. Slab Thickness (in.)	Min. Edge Distance (in.)	A	B	C	D	E	F	G	H	I
				$2.0 < Pr \le 3.5$	$1.1 < Pr \le 1.8$	$0.7 < Pr \le 1.0$	$1.2 < Pr \le 1.7$	$1.1 < Pr \le 1.8$	$1.1 < Pr \le 2.0$	$1.4 < Pr \le 1.9$	$0.9 < Pr \le 1.3$	$0.8 < Pr \le 1.1$
⅜	1.100	4	6	188	287	379	220	287	330	193	277	334
½	1.690	4	6	218	361	520	303	361	382	266	384	462
⅝	1.750	4	8	222	371	541	315	371	389	278	400	481
¾	1.750	4	8	222	371	541	315	371	389	278	400	481
Diameter (in.)	Min. Effect. Embedment (in.)	Min. Slab Thickness (in.)	Min. Edge Distance (in.)	A	B	C	D	E	F	G	H	I
				$3.5 < Pr \le 5.0$	$1.8 < Pr \le 2.5$	$1.0 < Pr \le 1.3$	$1.7 < Pr \le 2.2$	$1.8 < Pr \le 2.5$	$2.0 < Pr \le 2.9$	$1.9 < Pr \le 2.4$	$1.3 < Pr \le 1.7$	$1.1 < Pr \le 1.4$
⅜	1.100	4	6	145	236	338	197	236	251	175	247	302
½	1.690	4	6	157	284	446	261	284	271	233	330	403
⅝	1.750	4	8	157	290	461	270	290	271	242	342	417
¾	1.750	4	8	157	290	461	270	290	271	242	342	417
Diameter (in.)	Min. Effect. Embedment (in.)	Min. Slab Thickness (in.)	Min. Edge Distance (in.)	A	B	C	D	E	F	G	H	I
				$5.0 < Pr \le 6.5$	$2.5 < Pr \le 3.2$	$1.3 < Pr \le 1.6$	$2.2 < Pr \le 2.7$	$2.5 < Pr \le 3.2$	$2.9 < Pr \le 3.8$	$2.4 < Pr \le 2.9$	$1.7 < Pr \le 2.1$	$1.4 < Pr \le 1.7$
⅜	1.100	4	6	117	201	305	178	201	202	160	224	275
½	1.690	4	6	120	234	390	229	234	207	207	290	357
⅝	1.750	4	8	120	239	402	236	239	207	214	299	368
¾	1.750	4	8	120	239	402	236	239	207	214	299	368

Pr: Prying factor range (see A.18.5.12.2 for additional information).

Shaded text = Revisions.   Δ = Text deletions and figure/table revisions.   • = Section deletions.   *N* = New material.

Δ Table 18.5.12.2(j) Maximum Load for Wood Form Inserts in 6000 psi (414 bar) Normal Weight Cracked Concrete

				Wood Form Inserts in 6000 psi Normal Weight Cracked Concrete (lb)								
Diameter (in.)	Min. Effect. Embedment (in.)	Min. Slab Thickness (in.)	Min. Edge Distance (in.)	A $Pr \le 2.0$	B $Pr \le 1.1$	C $Pr \le 0.7$	D $Pr \le 1.2$	E $Pr \le 1.1$	F $Pr \le 1.1$	G $Pr \le 1.4$	H $Pr \le 0.9$	I $Pr \le 0.8$
3/8	1.100	4	6	302	395	458	264	395	537	228	332	397
1/2	1.690	4	6	385	551	680	394	551	690	339	499	591
5/8	1.750	4	8	421	627	800	463	627	756	399	591	696
3/4	1.750	4	8	421	627	800	463	627	756	399	591	696
Diameter (in.)	Min. Effect. Embedment (in.)	Min. Slab Thickness (in.)	Min. Edge Distance (in.)	A $2.0 < Pr \le 3.5$	B $1.1 < Pr \le 1.8$	C $0.7 < Pr \le 1.0$	D $1.2 < Pr \le 1.7$	E $1.1 < Pr \le 1.8$	F $1.1 < Pr \le 2.0$	G $1.4 < Pr \le 1.9$	H $0.9 < Pr \le 1.3$	I $0.8 < Pr \le 1.1$
3/8	1.100	4	6	216	319	409	237	319	379	207	297	360
1/2	1.690	4	6	256	413	578	336	413	449	296	426	512
5/8	1.750	4	8	272	454	662	386	454	476	340	491	589
3/4	1.750	4	8	272	454	662	386	454	476	340	491	589
Diameter (in.)	Min. Effect. Embedment (in.)	Min. Slab Thickness (in.)	Min. Edge Distance (in.)	A $3.5 < Pr \le 5.0$	B $1.8 < Pr \le 2.5$	C $1.0 < Pr \le 1.3$	D $1.7 < Pr \le 2.2$	E $1.8 < Pr \le 2.5$	F $2.0 < Pr \le 2.9$	G $1.9 < Pr \le 2.4$	H $1.3 < Pr \le 1.7$	I $1.1 < Pr \le 1.4$
3/8	1.100	4	6	169	267	370	215	267	292	190	270	329
1/2	1.690	4	6	192	330	503	293	330	332	262	371	452
5/8	1.750	4	8	192	356	565	331	356	332	296	419	511
3/4	1.750	4	8	192	356	565	331	356	332	296	419	511
Diameter (in.)	Min. Effect. Embedment (in.)	Min. Slab Thickness (in.)	Min. Edge Distance (in.)	A $5.0 < Pr \le 6.5$	B $2.5 < Pr \le 3.2$	C $1.3 < Pr \le 1.6$	D $2.2 < Pr \le 2.7$	E $2.5 < Pr \le 3.2$	F $2.9 < Pr \le 3.8$	G $2.4 < Pr \le 2.9$	H $1.7 < Pr \le 2.1$	I $1.4 < Pr \le 1.7$
3/8	1.100	4	6	138	229	337	196	229	238	176	246	303
1/2	1.690	4	6	147	275	445	260	275	253	235	328	405
5/8	1.750	4	8	147	293	493	289	293	253	263	366	451
3/4	1.750	4	8	147	293	493	289	293	253	263	366	451

Pr: Prying factor range *(see A.18.5.12.2 for additional information).*

Table 18.5.12.2(k) Maximum Load for Connections to Steel Using Unfinished Steel Bolts

Connections to Steel (Values Assume Bolt Perpendicular to Mounting Surface)																	
Diameter of Unfinished Steel Bolt (in.)																	
1/4									3/8								
A	B	C	D	E	F	G	H	I	A	B	C	D	E	F	G	H	I
400	500	600	300	500	650	325	458	565	900	1200	1400	800	1200	1550	735	1035	1278
Diameter of Unfinished Steel Bolt (in.)																	
1/2									5/8								
A	B	C	D	E	F	G	H	I	A	B	C	D	E	F	G	H	I
1600	2050	2550	1450	2050	2850	1300	1830	2260	2500	3300	3950	2250	3300	4400	2045	2880	3557

Table 18.5.12.2(1) Maximum Load for Through-Bolts in Sawn Lumber or Glue-Laminated Timbers

Length of Bolt in Timber (in.)		Through-Bolts in Sawn Lumber or Glue-Laminated Timbers (Load Perpendicular to Grain)																									
		Bolt Diameter (in.)																									
		½									⅝									¾								
		A	B	C	D	E	F	G	H	I	A	B	C	D	E	F	G	H	I	A	B	C	D	E	F	G	H	I
	1½	115	165	200	135	230	395	130	215	310	135	190	235	155	270	460	155	255	380	155	220	270	180	310	530	170	300	450
	2½	140	200	240	160	280	480	165	275	410	160	225	280	185	320	550	190	320	495	180	255	310	205	360	615	215	365	575
	3½	175	250	305	200	350	600	200	330	485	200	285	345	230	400	685	235	405	635	220	310	380	255	440	755	260	455	730
	5½	—	—	—	—	—	—	—	—	—	280	395	485	325	560	960	315	515	735	310	440	535	360	620	1065	360	610	925

Note: Wood fastener maximum capacity values are based on the 2001 National Design Specifications (NDS) for wood with a specific gravity of 0.35. Values for other types of wood can be obtained by multiplying the above values by the factors in Table 18.5.12.2(n).

Δ **Table 18.5.12.2(m) Maximum Load for Lag Screws and Lag Bolts in Wood**

Length of Bolt in Timber (in.)		Lag Screws and Lag Bolts in Wood (Load Perpendicular to Grain — Holes Predrilled Using Good Practice)																									
		Lag Bolt Diameter (in.)																									
		⅜									½									⅝								
		A	B	C	D	E	F	G	H	I	A	B	C	D	E	F	G	H	I	A	B	C	D	E	F	G	H	I
	3½	165	190	200	170	220	310	80	120	170	—	—	—	—	—	—	—	—	—	—	—	—	—	—	—	—	—	—
	4½	180	200	200	175	235	350	80	120	170	300	355	380	315	400	550	145	230	325	—	—	—	—	—	—	—	—	—
	5½	190	200	200	175	245	380	80	120	170	320	370	380	320	420	610	145	230	325	435	525	555	425	550	775	195	320	460
	6½	195	205	200	175	250	400	80	120	170	340	375	380	325	435	650	145	230	325	465	540	555	430	570	840	195	320	460

Note: Wood fastener maximum capacity values are based on the 2001 National Design Specifications (NDS) for wood with a specific gravity of 0.35. Values for other types of wood can be obtained by multiplying the above values by the factors in Table 18.5.12.2(n).

18.6 Restraint of Branch Lines.

18.6.1* Restraint is considered a lesser degree of resisting loads than bracing and shall be provided by use of one of the following:

(1) Listed sway brace assembly
(2) Wraparound U-hook satisfying the requirements of 18.5.5.11
(3) No. 12, 440 lb (200 kg) wire installed at least 45 degrees from the vertical plane and anchored on both sides of the pipe
(4) CPVC hangers listed to provide restraint
(5)* Hanger not less than 45 degrees from vertical installed within 6 in. (150 mm) of the vertical hanger arranged for restraint against upward movement, provided it is utilized such that l/r does not exceed 400, where the rod extends to the pipe or a surge clip has been installed
(6) Other approved means

18.6.2 Wire Restraint.

18.6.2.1 Wire used for restraint shall be located within 2 ft (600 mm) of a hanger.

18.6.2.2 The hanger closest to a wire restraint shall be of a type that resists upward movement of a branch line.

18.6.3 The end sprinkler on a branch line shall be restrained.

18.6.3.1 The location of the restraint from end of the line shall not be greater than 36 in. (900 mm) for 1 in. (25 mm) pipe, 48 in. (1200 mm) for 1¼ in. (32 mm) pipe, and 60 in. (1.5 m) for 1½ in. (40 mm) or larger pipe.

Table 18.5.12.2(n) Factors for Wood Based on Specific Gravity

Specific Gravity of Wood	Multiplier
0.36 thru 0.49	1.17
0.50 thru 0.65	1.25
0.66 thru 0.73	1.50

18.6.4* Branch lines shall be laterally restrained at intervals not exceeding those specified in Table 18.6.4(a) or Table 18.6.4(b) based on branch line diameter and the value of C_p.

18.6.5 Where the branch lines are supported by rods less than 6 in. (150 mm) long measured between the top of the pipe and the point of attachment to the building structure, the requirements of 18.6.1 through 18.6.4 shall not apply and additional restraint shall not be required for the branch lines.

18.6.6* Sprigs 4 ft (1.2 m) or longer shall be restrained against lateral movement.

18.6.7 Drops and armovers shall not require restraint.

18.7 Hangers and Fasteners Subject to Earthquakes.

18.7.1 Where seismic protection is provided, C-type clamps (including beam and large flange clamps) used to attach hangers to the building structure shall be equipped with a restraining strap unless the provisions of 18.7.1.1 are satisfied.

18.7.1.1 As an alternative to the installation of a required restraining strap, a device investigated and specifically listed to restrain the clamp to the structure is permitted where the intent of the device is to resist the worst-case expected horizontal load.

18.7.2 The restraining strap shall be listed for use with a C-type clamp or shall be a steel strap of not less than 16 gauge (1.57 mm) thickness and not less than 1 in. (25 mm) wide for pipe diameters 8 in. (200 mm) or less and 14 gauge (1.98 mm) thickness and not less than 1¼ in. (32 mm) wide for pipe diameters greater than 8 in. (200 mm).

18.7.3 The restraining strap shall wrap around the beam flange not less than 1 in. (25 mm).

18.7.4 A lock nut on a C-type clamp shall not be used as a method of restraint.

18.7.5 A lip on a "C" or "Z" purlin shall not be used as a method of restraint.

18.7.6 Where purlins or beams do not provide a secure lip to a restraining strap, the strap shall be through-bolted or secured by a self-tapping screw.

18.7.7 In areas where the horizontal force factor exceeds 0.50 W_p, powder-driven studs shall be permitted to attach hangers to the building structure where they are specifically listed for use in areas subject to earthquakes.

18.7.8* Where seismic protection is provided, concrete anchors used to secure hangers to the building structure shall be in accordance with ACI 355.2, *Qualification of Post-Installed Mechanical Anchors in Concrete and Commentary*, and installed in accordance with manufacturer's instructions.

18.7.9 Where seismic protection is provided, cast-in-place anchors used to secure hangers to the building structure shall be in accordance with ICC-ES AC446, *Acceptance Criteria for Headed Cast-in Specialty Inserts in Concrete*, and installed in accordance with manufacturer's instructions.

18.8* Pipe Stands Subject to Earthquakes.

18.8.1 In areas where the horizontal force factor exceeds 0.5 W_p, pipe stands over 4 ft (1.2 m) in height shall be certified by a registered professional engineer to be adequate for the seismic forces.

18.8.2 Where seismic protection is provided, concrete anchors used to secure pipe stands to their bases shall be in accordance with ACI 355.2, *Qualification of Post-Installed Mechanical Anchors in Concrete and Commentary*, and shall be installed in accordance with manufacturer's instructions.

Δ **Table 18.6.4(a) Maximum Spacing [ft (m)] of Steel Pipe Restraints**

Pipe [in. (mm)]	Seismic Coefficient, C_p			
	$C_p \leq 0.50$	$0.5 < C_p \leq 0.71$	$0.71 < C_p \leq 1.40$	$C_p > 1.40$
½ (15)	34 (10.3)	29 (8.8)	20 (6.1)	18 (5.5)
¾ (20)	38 (11.6)	32 (9.7)	23 (7.0)	20 (6.1)
1 (25)	43 (13.1)	36 (11.0)	26 (7.9)	22 (6.7)
1¼ (32)	46 (14.0)	39 (11.9)	27 (8.2)	24 (7.3)
1½ (40)	49 (14.9)	41 (12.5)	29 (8.8)	25 (7.6)
2 (50)	53 (16.1)	45 (13.7)	31 (9.4)	27 (8.2)

Δ **Table 18.6.4(b) Maximum Spacing [ft (m)] of CPVC, Copper, and Red Brass Pipe Restraints**

Pipe [in. (mm)]	Seismic Coefficient, C_p			
	$C_p \leq 0.50$	$0.5 < C_p \leq 0.71$	$0.71 < C_p \leq 1.40$	$C_p > 1.40$
½ (15)	26 (7.9)	22 (6.7)	16 (4.9)	13 (4.0)
¾ (20)	31 (9.4)	26 (7.9)	18 (5.5)	15 (4.6)
1 (25)	34 (10.3)	28 (8.5)	20 (6.1)	17 (5.2)
1¼ (32)	37 (11.3)	31 (9.4)	22 (6.7)	19 (5.8)
1½ (40)	40 (12.2)	34 (10.3)	24 (7.3)	20 (6.1)
2 (50)	45 (13.7)	38 (11.6)	27 (8.2)	23 (7.0)

Chapter 19 Design Approaches

Δ **19.1 General.** The requirements of Section 19.1 shall apply to all sprinkler systems unless modified by a specific section of Chapter 19 or Chapter 20.

19.1.1* A building or portion thereof shall be permitted to be protected in accordance with any applicable design approach at the discretion of the designer.

19.1.2* Adjacent Hazards or Design Methods. For buildings with two or more adjacent hazards or design methods, the following shall apply:

(1) Where areas are not physically separated by a draft curtain, barrier, or partition capable of delaying heat from a fire in one area from fusing sprinklers in the adjacent area, the required sprinkler protection for the more demanding design basis shall extend 15 ft (4.6 m) beyond its perimeter.

(2) The requirements of 19.1.2(1) shall not apply where the areas are separated by a draft curtain, or barrier located above an aisle, where the aisle has a minimum 2 ft (600 mm) horizontal separation from the adjacent hazard on each side, or a partition that is capable of delaying heat from a fire in one area from fusing sprinklers in the adjacent area.

(3) The requirements of 19.1.2(1) shall not apply to the extension of more demanding criteria from an upper ceiling level to beneath a lower ceiling level where the difference in height between the ceiling levels is at least 2 ft (600 mm), located above an aisle, where the aisle has a minimum 2 ft (600 mm) horizontal separation from the adjacent hazard on each side.

19.1.3 For hydraulically calculated systems, the total system water supply requirements for each design basis shall be determined in accordance with the procedures of Section 28.2 unless modified by a section of Chapter 19 or Chapter 20.

19.1.4 Water Demand.

19.1.4.1* The water demand requirements shall be determined from the following:

(1) Occupancy hazard fire control approach and special design approaches of Chapter 19
(2) Storage design approaches of Chapter 20 through Chapter 25
(3) Special occupancy approaches of Chapter 27

19.1.4.2* The minimum water demand requirements for a sprinkler system shall be determined by adding the hose stream allowance to the water demand for sprinklers.

19.1.5 Water Supplies.

19.1.5.1 The minimum water supply shall be available for the minimum duration specified in Chapter 19.

19.1.5.2* Tanks shall be sized to supply the equipment that they serve.

19.1.5.3* Pumps shall be sized to supply the equipment that they serve.

19.1.6 Hose Allowance.

19.1.6.1 Systems with Multiple Hazard Classifications. For systems with multiple hazard classifications, the hose stream allowance and water supply duration shall be in accordance with one of the following:

(1) The water supply requirements for the highest hazard classification within the system shall be used.
(2) The water supply requirements for each individual hazard classification shall be used in the calculations for the design area for that hazard.
(3)* For systems with multiple hazard classifications where the higher classification only lies within single rooms less than or equal to 400 ft^2 (37 m^2) in area with no such rooms adjacent, the water supply requirements for the principal occupancy shall be used for the remainder of the system.

19.1.6.2* Water allowance for outside hose shall be added to the sprinkler requirement at the connection to the city main or a private fire hydrant, whichever is closer to the system riser.

19.1.6.3 Where inside hose connections are planned or are required, the following shall apply:

(1) A total water allowance of 50 gpm (190 L/min) for a single hose connection installation shall be added to the sprinkler requirements.
(2) A total water allowance of 100 gpm (380 L/min) for a multiple hose connection installation shall be added to the sprinkler requirements.
(3) The water allowance shall be added in 50 gpm (190 L/min) increments beginning at the most remote hose connection, with each increment added at the pressure required by the sprinkler system design at that point.

19.1.6.3.1 Where the system is a combined sprinkler/standpipe system (Class I or Class III) and the building is fully sprinklered in accordance with NFPA 13, no inside hose demand shall be required at any of the standpipe outlets.

19.1.6.4* When hose valves for fire department use are attached to wet pipe sprinkler system risers in accordance with 16.15.2, the following shall apply:

(1) The sprinkler system demand shall not be required to be added to standpipe demand as determined from NFPA 14.
(2) Where the combined sprinkler system demand and hose stream allowance of Table 19.2.3.1.2 exceeds the requirements of NFPA 14, this higher demand shall be used.
(3) For partially sprinklered buildings, the sprinkler demand, not including hose stream allowance, as indicated in Figure 19.2.3.1.1 shall be added to the requirements given in NFPA 14.

Δ **19.1.7* High Volume Low Speed (HVLS) Fans.**

N **19.1.7.1** The installation of HVLS fans in buildings equipped with sprinklers, including ESFR sprinklers, shall comply with the following:

(1) The maximum fan diameter shall be 24 ft (7.3 m).
(2) The HVLS fan shall be centered approximately between four adjacent sprinklers.
(3) The vertical clearance from the HVLS fan to sprinkler deflector shall be a minimum of 36 in. (900 mm).
(4) All HVLS fans shall be interlocked to shut down immediately upon a waterflow alarm.

N **19.1.7.2** Where a building is protected with a fire alarm system, the interlock required by 19.1.7.1(4) shall be in accordance with the requirements of *NFPA 72* or other approved fire alarm code.

19.2 Occupancy Hazard Fire Control Approach for Spray Sprinklers.

19.2.1 General.

19.2.1.1* The water demand requirements shall be determined by either the pipe schedule method in accordance with 19.2.2 or the hydraulic calculation method in accordance with 19.2.3.

19.2.1.2 Occupancy Classifications.

19.2.1.2.1 Occupancy classifications for this standard shall relate to sprinkler installations and their water supplies only.

19.2.1.2.2 Occupancy classifications shall not be used as a general classification of occupancy hazards.

19.2.1.2.3 Occupancies or portions of occupancies shall be classified according to the quantity and combustibility of contents, the expected rates of heat release, the total potential for energy release, the heights of stockpiles, and the presence of flammable and combustible liquids, using the definitions contained in 4.3.2 through 4.3.6.

19.2.1.2.4 Classifications shall be as follows:

(1) Light hazard
(2) Ordinary hazard (Groups 1 and 2)
(3) Extra hazard (Groups 1 and 2)
(4) Special occupancy hazard (*see Chapter 27*)

19.2.2 Water Demand Requirements — Pipe Schedule Method.

19.2.2.1 Table 19.2.2.1 shall be used in determining the minimum water supply requirements for light and ordinary hazard occupancies protected by systems with pipe sized according to the pipe schedules of Section 28.5.

19.2.2.2 Pressure and flow requirements for extra hazard occupancies shall be based on the hydraulic calculation methods of 19.2.3, except as permitted by 19.2.2.3(2).

19.2.2.3 The pipe schedule method shall be permitted as follows:

(1) Additions or modifications to existing pipe schedule systems sized according to the pipe schedules of Section 28.5
(2) Additions or modifications to existing extra hazard pipe schedule systems
(3) New systems of 5000 ft² (465 m²) or less
(4) New systems exceeding 5000 ft² (465 m²) where the flows required in Table 19.2.2.1 are available at a minimum

Δ **Table 19.2.2.1 Water Supply Requirements for Pipe Schedule Sprinkler Systems**

Occupancy Classification	Minimum Residual Pressure Required psi	bar	Acceptable Flow at Base of Riser (Including Hose Stream Allowance) gpm	L/min	Duration (minutes)
Light hazard	15	1	500–750	1900–2850	30 or 60
Ordinary hazard	20	1.4	850–1500	3200–5700	60 or 90

residual pressure of 50 psi (3.4 bar) at the highest elevation of sprinkler

19.2.2.4 The lower duration value of Table 19.2.2.1 shall be acceptable only where the sprinkler system waterflow alarm device(s) and supervisory device(s) are electrically supervised and such supervision is monitored at an approved, constantly attended location.

19.2.2.5* Residual Pressure.

19.2.2.5.1 The residual pressure requirement of Table 19.2.2.1 shall be met at the elevation of the highest sprinkler.

19.2.2.5.2 Friction Loss Due to Backflow Prevention Valves.

19.2.2.5.2.1 When backflow prevention valves are installed on pipe schedule systems, the friction losses of the device shall be accounted for when determining acceptable residual pressure at the top level of sprinklers.

19.2.2.5.2.2 The friction loss of this device [in psi (bar)] shall be added to the elevation loss and the residual pressure at the top row of sprinklers to determine the total pressure needed at the water supply.

19.2.2.6 The lower flow figure of Table 19.2.2.1 shall be permitted only where the building is of noncombustible construction or the potential areas of fire are limited by building size or compartmentation such that no open areas exceed 3000 ft² (280 m²) for light hazard or 4000 ft² (370 m²) for ordinary hazard.

19.2.3 Water Demand Requirements — Hydraulic Calculation Methods.

19.2.3.1 General.

19.2.3.1.1 The water demand for sprinklers shall be determined only from one of the following, at the discretion of the designer:

(1) For new systems, the density/area selected from Table 19.2.3.1.1 in accordance with the density/area method of 19.2.3.2
(2) For the evaluation or modification of existing systems, the density/area curves of Figure 19.2.3.1.1 in accordance with the density/area method of 19.2.3.2
(3) The room that creates the greatest demand in accordance with the room design method of 19.2.3.3
(4) Special design areas in accordance with 19.2.3.4

N **Table 19.2.3.1.1 Density/Area**

Hazard	Density/Area [gpm/ft²/ft² (mm/min/m²)]
Light	0.1/1500 or 0.07/3000* (4.1/140 or 2.9/280)
Ordinary Group 1	0.15/1500 or 0.12/3000* (6.1/140 or 4.9/280)
Ordinary Group 2	0.2/1500 or 0.17/3000* (8.1/140 or 6.9/280)
Extra Group 1	0.3/2500 or 0.28/3000* (12.2/230 or 11.4/280)
Extra Group 2	0.4/2500 or 0.38/3000* (16.3/230 or 15.5/280)

*When required by 19.2.3.1.5.

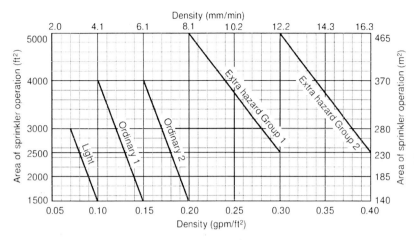

Δ **FIGURE 19.2.3.1.1 Density/Area Curves for the Evaluation or Modification of Existing Systems.**

Δ **Table 19.2.3.1.2 Hose Stream Allowance and Water Supply Duration Requirements for Hydraulically Calculated Systems**

Occupancy	Inside Hose		Total Combined Inside and Outside Hose		Duration (minutes)
	gpm	L/min	gpm	L/min	
Light hazard	0, 50, or 100	0, 190, or 380	100	380	30
Ordinary hazard	0, 50, or 100	0, 190, or 380	250	950	60 or 90
Extra hazard	0, 50, or 100	0, 190, or 380	500	1900	90 or 120

19.2.3.1.2 The minimum water supply shall be available for the minimum duration specified in Table 19.2.3.1.2.

19.2.3.1.3 The lower duration values in Table 19.2.3.1.2 shall be permitted where the sprinkler system waterflow alarm device(s) and supervisory device(s) are electrically supervised and such supervision is monitored at an approved, constantly attended location.

19.2.3.1.4 Restrictions. When either the density/area method or room design method is used, the following shall apply:

(1)* For areas of sprinkler operation less than 1500 ft² (140 m²) used for light and ordinary hazard occupancies, the density for 1500 ft² (140 m²) shall be used.
(2) For areas of sprinkler operation less than 2500 ft² (230 m²) for extra hazard occupancies, the density for 2500 ft² (230 m²) shall be used.

19.2.3.1.5 Unsprinklered Combustible Concealed Spaces.

19.2.3.1.5.1* When using the density/area or room design method, unless the requirements of 19.2.3.1.5.2 are met for buildings having unsprinklered combustible concealed spaces, as described in 9.2.1 and 9.2.2, the minimum area of sprinkler operation for that portion of the building shall be 3000 ft² (280 m²).

(A) The design area of 3000 ft² (280 m²) shall be applied only to the sprinkler system or portions of the sprinkler system that are adjacent to the qualifying combustible concealed space.

(B) The term *adjacent* shall apply to any sprinkler system protecting a space above, below, or next to the qualifying concealed space except where a barrier with a fire resistance rating at least equivalent to the water supply duration completely separates the concealed space from the sprinklered area.

Δ **19.2.3.1.5.2** The following unsprinklered concealed spaces shall not require a minimum area of sprinkler operation of 3000 ft² (280 m²):

(1) Noncombustible and limited-combustible concealed spaces with minimal combustible loading having no access, including those with small openings such as those used as return air for a plenum
(2) Noncombustible and limited-combustible concealed spaces with limited access and not permitting occupancy or storage of combustibles, including those with small openings such as those used as return air for a plenum
(3) Combustible concealed spaces filled entirely with noncombustible insulation
(4)* Light or ordinary hazard occupancies where noncombustible or limited-combustible ceilings are directly attached to the bottom of solid wood joists or solid limited-combustible construction or noncombustible construction to create enclosed joist spaces 160 ft³ (4.5 m³) or less in volume, including space below insulation that is laid directly on top or within the ceiling joists in an otherwise sprinklered concealed space
(5) Concealed spaces where rigid materials are used and the exposed surfaces comply with one of the following in the form in which they are installed in the space:

(a) The surface materials have a flame spread index of 25 or less and the materials have been demonstrated to not propagate fire more than 10.5 ft (3.2 m) when tested in accordance with ASTM E84, *Standard Test Method for Surface Burning Characteristics of Building Materials*, or UL 723, *Standard for Test for Surface Burning Characteristics of Building Materials,* extended for an additional 20 minutes in the form in which they are installed in the space

(b) The surface materials comply with the requirements of ASTM E2768, *Standard Test Method for Extended Duration Surface Burning Characteristics of Building Materials (30 min Tunnel Test)*

(6) Concealed spaces in which the exposed materials are constructed entirely of fire-retardant-treated wood as defined by NFPA 703

(7) Concealed spaces over isolated small rooms not exceeding 55 ft² (5.1 m²) in area

(8) Vertical pipe chases under 10 ft² (0.9 m²), provided that in multifloor buildings the chases are firestopped at each floor using materials equivalent to the floor construction and pipe penetrations at each floor are properly sealed, and where such pipe chases contain no sources of ignition, and piping is noncombustible

(9) Exterior columns under 10 ft² (0.9 m²) in area formed by studs or wood joists, supporting exterior canopies that are fully protected with a sprinkler system

(10)* Light or ordinary hazard occupancies where noncombustible or limited-combustible ceilings are attached to the bottom of composite wood joists either directly or on to metal channels not exceeding 1 in. (25 mm) in depth, provided the adjacent joist channels are firestopped into volumes not exceeding 160 ft³ (4.5 m³) using materials equivalent to ½ in. (13 mm) gypsum board, and at least 3½ in. (90 mm) of batt insulation is installed at the bottom of the joist channels when the ceiling is attached utilizing metal channels

(11) Cavities within unsprinklered wall spaces

(12) Exterior soffits, eaves, overhangs, and decorative frame elements complying with 9.2.1.20.

19.2.3.2 Density/Area Method.

19.2.3.2.1 Water Supply.

19.2.3.2.1.1 The water supply requirement for sprinklers only shall be calculated from Table 19.2.3.1.1 for new systems and from the density/area curves of Figure 19.2.3.1.1 for the evaluation or modification of existing systems, or from Chapter 27 where density/area criteria are specified for special occupancy hazards.

19.2.3.2.1.2 When using Figure 19.2.3.1.1, the calculations shall satisfy any single point on the appropriate density/area curve.

19.2.3.2.1.3 When using Figure 19.2.3.1.1, it shall not be necessary to meet all points on the selected curves.

19.2.3.2.2 Sprinklers.

19.2.3.2.2.1 The densities and areas provided in Table 19.2.3.1.1 or Figure 19.2.3.1.1 shall be for use only with spray sprinklers.

19.2.3.2.2.2 Quick-response sprinklers shall not be permitted for use in extra hazard occupancies or other occupancies where there are substantial amounts of flammable liquids or combustible dusts.

19.2.3.2.2.3 For extended coverage sprinklers, the minimum design area shall be that corresponding to the hazard in Table 19.2.3.1.1 or Figure 19.2.3.1.1 or the area protected by five sprinklers, whichever is greater.

Δ **19.2.3.2.2.4** Extended coverage sprinklers shall be listed with and designed for the minimum flow corresponding to the density selected from the smallest design area of Table 19.2.3.1.1 for the hazard as specified.

19.2.3.2.3 Quick-Response Sprinklers.

19.2.3.2.3.1 Where listed quick-response sprinklers, including extended coverage quick-response sprinklers, are used throughout a system or portion of a system having the same hydraulic design basis, the system area of operation shall be permitted to be reduced without revising the density as indicated in Figure 19.2.3.2.3.1 when all of the following conditions are satisfied:

(1) Wet pipe system
(2) Light hazard or ordinary hazard occupancy
(3) 20 ft (6.1 m) maximum ceiling height
(4) No unprotected ceiling pockets as allowed by 10.2.9 and 11.2.7 exceeding 32 ft² (3.0 m²)
(5) No unprotected areas above cloud ceilings as allowed by 9.2.7

19.2.3.2.3.2 The number of sprinklers in the design area shall never be less than five.

19.2.3.2.3.3 Where quick-response sprinklers are used on a sloped ceiling or roof, the maximum ceiling or roof height shall be used for determining the percent reduction in design area.

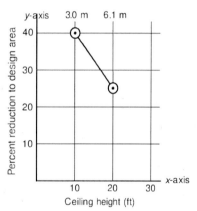

Note: $y = \dfrac{-3x}{2} + 55$ for U.S. Customary Units

Note: $y = -4.8x + 54.6$ for S.I. Units

For ceiling height ≥10 ft and ≤20 ft, $y = \dfrac{-3x}{2} + 55$

For ceiling height <10 ft, $y = 40$

For ceiling height >20, $y = 0$

For SI units, 1 ft = 0.31 m.

Δ **FIGURE 19.2.3.2.3.1   Design Area Reduction for Quick-Response Sprinklers.**

Shaded text = Revisions.   Δ = Text deletions and figure/table revisions.   • = Section deletions.   *N* = New material.

2022 Edition

19.2.3.2.4 Sloped Ceilings. The system area of operation shall be increased by 30 percent without revising the density when the following types of sprinklers are used on sloped ceilings with a pitch exceeding 1 in 6 (a rise of 2 units in a run of 12 units, a roof slope of 16.7 percent) in nonstorage applications:

(1) Spray sprinklers, including extended coverage sprinklers listed in accordance with 11.2.1(4), and quick-response sprinklers
(2) CMSA sprinklers

19.2.3.2.5* Dry Pipe and Double Interlock Preaction Systems. For dry pipe systems and double interlock preaction systems, the area of sprinkler operation shall be increased by 30 percent without revising the density.

19.2.3.2.6 High-Temperature Sprinklers. Where high-temperature sprinklers are used for extra hazard occupancies, the area of sprinkler operation shall be permitted to be reduced by 25 percent without revising the density, but not to less than 2000 ft^2 (185 m^2).

19.2.3.2.7 Where K-11.2 (160) or larger sprinklers are used with Extra Hazard Group 1 or Extra Hazard Group 2 design curves and 19.2.3.1.1, the design area shall be permitted to be reduced by 25 percent but not below 2000 ft^2 (185 m^2), regardless of temperature rating.

19.2.3.2.8* Multiple Adjustments.

19.2.3.2.8.1 Where multiple adjustments to the area of operation are required to be made in accordance with 19.2.3.2.3, 19.2.3.2.4, 19.2.3.2.5, or 19.2.3.2.6, these adjustments shall be compounded based on the area of operation originally selected from Table 19.2.3.1.1 or Figure 19.2.3.1.1.

19.2.3.2.8.2 If the building has unsprinklered combustible concealed spaces, the rules of 19.2.3.1.5 shall be applied after all other modifications have been made.

19.2.3.3 Room Design Method.

19.2.3.3.1* The water supply requirements for sprinklers only shall be based upon the room that creates the greatest demand.

19.2.3.3.2 The density selected shall be that from Table 19.2.3.1.1 or Figure 19.2.3.1.1 corresponding to the occupancy hazard classification and room size.

19.2.3.3.3 All interior walls enclosing the room shall have a fire resistance rating equal to the water supply duration indicated in Table 19.2.3.1.2.

19.2.3.3.4 If the room is smaller than the area specified in Table 19.2.3.1.1 or Figure 19.2.3.1.1, the provisions of 19.2.3.1.4(1) and 19.2.3.1.4(2) shall apply.

19.2.3.3.5 The minimum protection required for openings in interior walls shall be as follows:

(1) Light hazard — Nonrated automatic or self-closing doors shall be required.
(2) Light hazard with no opening protection — Calculations shall include the sprinklers in the room and two sprinklers in the communicating space nearest each such unprotected opening unless the communicating space has only one sprinkler, in which case calculations extend to the operation of that sprinkler. The selection of the room and communicating space sprinklers to be calcula-

ted shall be that which produces the greatest hydraulic demand. A minimum lintel depth of 8 in. (200 mm) shall be required for openings and openings shall not exceed 8 ft (2.4 m) in width. It shall be permitted to have a single opening of 36 in. (900 mm) or less without a lintel, provided there are no other openings to adjoining spaces.
(3) Ordinary and extra hazard — Automatic or self-closing doors with appropriate fire resistance ratings for the enclosure shall be required.

19.2.3.3.6 Where the room design method is used and the area under consideration is a corridor protected by a single row of sprinklers with protected openings in accordance with 19.2.3.3.5, the maximum number of sprinklers that needs to be calculated is five or, when extended coverage sprinklers are installed, all sprinklers contained within 75 linear feet (23 linear meters) of the corridor.

19.2.3.3.7 Where the area under consideration is a corridor protected by a single row of sprinklers with unprotected openings, in a light hazard occupancy, the design area shall include all sprinklers in the corridor to a maximum of five or, when extended coverage sprinklers are installed, all sprinklers within 75 linear feet (23 linear meters) of the corridor.

19.2.3.4 Special Design Areas.

19.2.3.4.1 Where the design area consists of a building service chute supplied by a separate riser, the maximum number of sprinklers that needs to be calculated is three, each with a minimum discharge of 15 gpm (57 L/min).

19.2.3.4.2* Where an area is to be protected by a single line of sprinklers, the design area shall include all sprinklers on the line up to a maximum of seven.

19.2.3.4.3 Sprinklers in ducts as described in Section 8.9 and 9.3.9 shall be hydraulically designed to provide a discharge pressure of not less than 7 psi (0.5 bar) at each sprinkler with all sprinklers within the duct flowing.

19.2.3.4.4 Stair Towers. Stair towers, or other construction with incomplete floors, if piped on independent risers, shall be treated as one area with reference to pipe sizes.

19.3 Special Design Approaches.

19.3.1 Residential Sprinklers.

19.3.1.1* The design area shall be the area that includes the four adjacent sprinklers that produce the greatest hydraulic demand.

_N_ **19.3.1.1.1** The room design method, in accordance with 19.2.3.3 and using light hazard criteria, shall be permitted.

19.3.1.2* Unless the requirements of 19.2.3.1.5.2 are met for buildings having unsprinklered combustible concealed spaces, as described in 9.2.1 and 9.3.18, the minimum design area of sprinkler operation for that portion of the building shall be eight sprinklers.

19.3.1.2.1* The design area of eight sprinklers shall be applied only to the portion of the residential sprinklers that are adjacent to the qualifying combustible concealed space.

19.3.1.2.2 The term _adjacent_ shall apply to any sprinkler system protecting a space above, below, or next to the qualifying concealed space except where a barrier with a fire resistance rating at least equivalent to the water supply duration completely separates the concealed space from the sprinklered area.

19.3.1.3 Unless the requirements of 19.3.1.4 are met, the minimum required discharge from each design area sprinkler shall be the greater of the following:

(1) In accordance with minimum flow rates indicated in the sprinkler listings
(2) In rooms or compartments greater than 800 ft² (74 m²), calculated based on delivering a minimum of 0.1 gpm/ft² (4.1 mm/min) over the design area in accordance with the provisions of 9.5.2.1
(3) In rooms or compartments 800 ft² (74 m²) or less calculated based on delivering a minimum of 0.1 gpm/ft² (4.1 mm/min) over the room or the compartment using the area of the room divided by the number of sprinklers in the room

19.3.1.4 For modifications or additions to existing systems equipped with residential sprinklers, the listed discharge criteria less than 0.1 gpm/ft² (4.1 mm/min) shall be permitted to be used.

19.3.1.4.1 Where replacing residential sprinklers manufactured prior to 2003 that are no longer available from the manufacturer and that are installed using a design density less than 0.05 gpm/ft² (2.0 mm/min), a residential sprinkler with an equivalent K-factor (± 5 percent) shall be permitted to be used provided the currently listed coverage area for the replacement sprinkler is not exceeded.

19.3.1.5 Where areas such as attics, basements, or other types of occupancies are outside of dwelling units but within the same structure, these areas shall be protected as a separate design basis in accordance with Section 19.1.

19.3.1.6 Hose stream allowance and water supply duration requirements shall be in accordance with those for light hazard occupancies in Table 19.2.3.1.2.

19.3.2 Exposure Protection.

19.3.2.1* Piping shall be hydraulically calculated in accordance with Section 28.2 to furnish a minimum of 7 psi (0.5 bar) at any sprinkler with all sprinklers facing the exposure operating.

19.3.2.2 Where the water supply feeds other fire protection systems, it shall be capable of furnishing total demand for such systems as well as the exposure system demand.

19.3.3 Water Curtains.

Δ **19.3.3.1** Sprinklers in a water curtain, such as that described in 9.3.5 or 9.3.13.2, shall be hydraulically designed to provide a discharge of 3 gpm per lineal foot (37 L/min per lineal meter) of water curtain with no sprinklers discharging less than 15 gpm (57 L/min).

19.3.3.2 For water curtains employing automatic sprinklers, the number of sprinklers calculated in this water curtain shall correspond to the length parallel to the branch lines in the area determined by 28.2.4.2.

Δ **19.3.3.3** If a single fire is expected to operate sprinklers within the water curtain and within the design area of a hydraulically calculated system, the water supply to the water curtain shall be added to the water demand of the hydraulic calculations and balanced to the calculated area demand.

N **19.3.3.4** Hydraulic design calculations shall include a design area selected to include ceiling sprinklers adjacent to the water curtain.

19.3.3.5 For a deluge system water curtain providing proscenium opening protection in accordance with 9.3.13.2, the water curtain shall be calculated to supply all of the open sprinklers attached thereto.

19.3.4 Sprinklers Under Roof or Ceiling in Combustible Concealed Spaces of Wood Joist or Wood Truss Construction with Members 3 ft (0.9 m) or Less on Center and Slope Having Pitch of 4 in 12 (33.3 percent) or Greater.

19.3.4.1 Where sprinkler spacing does not exceed 8 ft (2.4 m) measured perpendicular to the slope, the minimum sprinkler discharge pressure shall be 7 psi (0.5 bar).

19.3.4.2 Where sprinkler spacing exceeds 8 ft (2.4 m) measured perpendicular to the slope, the minimum sprinkler discharge pressure shall be 20 psi (1.4 bar).

19.3.4.3 Hose stream allowance and water supply duration requirements shall be in accordance with those for light hazard occupancies in Table 19.2.3.1.2.

19.3.5 Sprinkler-Protected Glazing. Where the sprinkler-protected glazing is required to comply with 9.3.15, the water supply duration for the design area that includes the window sprinklers shall be not less than the required rating of the assembly.

19.3.5.1 For sprinkler-protected glazing, the number of sprinklers calculated for the glazing shall be the number in the length corresponding to the length parallel to the branch lines in the area determined by 28.2.4.2.

19.3.5.2 If a single fire can be expected to operate sprinklers for the sprinkler-protected glazing and within the design area of a hydraulically calculated system, the water supply to the sprinkler-protected glazing shall be added to the water demand of the hydraulic calculations and shall be balanced to the calculated area demand.

19.3.5.3 Hydraulic design calculations shall include a design area selected to include ceiling sprinklers adjacent to the sprinkler-protected glazing.

N **19.3.6** Where special sprinklers are listed for protection of features, system design shall be based on the listing requirements identified in the manufacturer's instructions for the individual sprinkler being used, unless otherwise approved.

19.4 Deluge Systems. Open sprinkler and deluge systems shall be hydraulically calculated according to applicable standards.

Chapter 20 General Requirements for Storage

20.1 General. This chapter shall provide the necessary steps for identifying commodity, storage arrangements, storage heights, and clearances as well as general protection criteria for storage conditions relative to Chapters 21 through 25.

20.1.1 Miscellaneous and low-piled storage, meeting the criteria of Chapter 4, shall be protected in accordance with the relative occupancy hazard criteria reference in that section.

20.2 Protection of Storage. Protection of storage shall follow the following criteria:

(1) Identify the storage commodity class in accordance with Sections 20.3 and 20.4.
(2) Identify the method of storage in accordance with Section 20.5.
(3) Establish storage height, building height, and associated clearances in accordance with Section 20.9.
(4) Define the general protection criteria that are common to all storage protection options in accordance with Sections 20.10 through 20.18.
(5) Select the appropriate system/sprinkler technology for protection criteria (Chapters 21 through 25).
(6) Design and install system in accordance with the remainder of this document.
(7) Design and install sprinklers in accordance with the sections to which they apply or in accordance with their specific application listing.

Δ **20.2.1*** Protection criteria for Group A plastics shall be permitted for the protection of the same storage height and configuration of Class I through Class IV commodities.

20.2.2 CMSA and ESFR sprinklers shall be permitted to protect storage of Class I through Class IV commodities, Group A plastic commodities, miscellaneous storage, and other storage as specified in Chapters 20 through 25 or by other NFPA standards.

20.2.3 Systems with Multiple Hazard Classifications. For systems with multiple hazard classifications, the hose stream allowance and water supply duration shall be in accordance with 20.15.2 as well as one of the following:

(1) The water supply requirements for the highest hazard classification within the system shall be used.
(2) The water supply requirements for each individual hazard classification shall be used in the calculations for the design area for that hazard.
(3)* For systems with multiple hazard classifications where the higher classification only lies within single rooms less than or equal to 400 ft² (37 m²) in area with no such rooms adjacent, the water supply requirements for the principal occupancy shall be used for the remainder of the system.

20.3* Classification of Commodities.

20.3.1* Commodity classification and the corresponding protection requirements shall be determined based on the makeup of individual storage units. *(See Section C.2.)*

20.3.1.1 The type and amount of materials used as part of the product and its primary packaging as well as the storage pallet shall be considered in the classification of the commodity.

20.3.1.2 When specific test data of commodity classification by a nationally recognized testing agency are available, the data shall be permitted to be used in determining classification of commodities.

N **20.3.1.3** For the same storage arrangement, the following commodity classification ranking shall apply from lowest (Class I) to highest (exposed expanded plastic) severity as follows:

(1) Class I
(2) Class II
(3) Class III
(4) Class IV
(5) Cartoned nonexpanded plastic
(6) Cartoned expanded plastic
(7) Exposed nonexpanded plastic
(8) Exposed expanded plastic

N **20.3.1.4** Protection criteria for commodities listed in 20.3.1.3 shall be permitted to protect lower commodities in the same list.

20.3.2 Pallet Types.

20.3.2.1 General. When loads are palletized, the use of wood or metal pallets, or listed pallets equivalent to wood, shall be assumed in the classification of commodities.

20.3.2.2 Plastic Pallet. A pallet having any portion of its construction consisting of a plastic material that has not been listed as equivalent to wood shall increase the class of commodity determined for a storage load in accordance with 20.3.2.2.1 or 20.3.2.2.2.

20.3.2.2.1* Unreinforced Plastic Pallets. Plastic pallets that have no secondary reinforcing shall be treated as unreinforced plastic pallets.

20.3.2.2.1.1 For Class I through Class IV commodities, when unreinforced polypropylene or unreinforced high-density polyethylene plastic pallets are used, the classification of the commodity unit shall be increased one class.

20.3.2.2.1.2 Unreinforced polypropylene or unreinforced high-density polyethylene plastic pallets shall be marked with a permanent symbol to indicate that the pallet is unreinforced.

20.3.2.2.2 Reinforced Plastic Pallet. A plastic pallet incorporating a secondary reinforcing material (such as steel or fiberglass) within the pallet shall be considered a reinforced plastic pallet.

20.3.2.2.2.1* For Class I through Class IV commodities, when reinforced polypropylene or reinforced high-density polyethylene plastic pallets are used, the classification of the commodity unit shall be increased two classes except for Class IV commodity, which shall be increased to a cartoned nonexpanded Group A plastic commodity.

20.3.2.2.2.2 Pallets shall be assumed to be reinforced if no permanent marking or manufacturer's certification of nonreinforcement is provided.

20.3.2.2.3 No increase in the commodity classification shall be required for Group A plastic commodities stored on plastic pallets.

20.3.2.2.4 For ceiling-only sprinkler protection, the requirements of 20.3.2.2.1 and 20.3.2.2.2.1 shall not apply where plastic pallets are used and where the sprinkler system uses spray sprinklers with a minimum K-factor of K-16.8 (240).

20.3.2.3 The requirements of 20.3.2.2.1 through 20.3.2.4 shall not apply to nonwood pallets that have demonstrated a fire hazard that is equal to or less than wood pallets and are listed as such.

Δ **20.3.2.4 Plastic Pallets Other Than Polypropylene or High-Density Polyethylene.**

N **20.3.2.4.1** For Class I through Class III commodities stored on plastic pallets other than polypropylene or high-density polyethylene, the classification of the commodity unit shall be determined by specific testing conducted by an approved testing laboratory or shall be increased two classes.

N **20.3.2.4.2** For Class IV commodities stored on plastic pallets other than polypropylene or high-density polyethylene, the classification shall be increased to a cartoned nonexpanded Group A plastic commodity.

20.3.2.5 Slave Pallet. Where solid, flat-bottom, combustible pallets are used for rack storage of Class I through IV commodity up to 25 ft (7.6 m) in height in combination with CMDA sprinklers, 21.4.1.7.2 shall apply. *(See Figure A.3.3.154.1.)*

Δ **20.3.3 Open-Top Container.** A container of any shape that is entirely or partially open on the top and arranged to allow for the collection of discharging sprinkler water cascading through the storage array shall be considered outside the criteria of rack storage protection outlined in Chapters 21 through 25. *(See Section C.12.)*

20.3.4 Solid Unit Load of Nonexpanded Plastic (Either Cartoned or Exposed). A load that does not have voids (air) within the load and that burns only on the exterior of the load and that water from sprinklers will reach most surfaces available to burn shall allow a reduction in design density of CMDA sprinklers. *[See Table 21.3.3(a).]*

20.4* Commodity Classes.

20.4.1* Class I. A Class I commodity shall be defined as a noncombustible product that meets one of the following criteria:

(1) Placed directly on wood pallets
(2) Placed in single-layer corrugated cartons, with or without single-thickness cardboard dividers, with or without pallets
(3) Shrink-wrapped or paper-wrapped as a unit load with or without pallets

20.4.2* Class II. A Class II commodity shall be defined as a noncombustible product that is in slatted wooden crates, solid wood boxes, multiple-layered corrugated cartons, or equivalent combustible packaging material, with or without pallets.

20.4.3* Class III.

20.4.3.1 A Class III commodity shall be defined as a product fashioned from wood, paper, natural fibers, or Group C plastics with or without cartons, boxes, or crates and with or without pallets.

20.4.3.2 A Class III commodity shall be permitted to contain a limited amount (5 percent or less by weight of nonexpanded

plastic or 5 percent or less by volume of expanded plastic) of Group A or Group B plastics.

20.4.3.3 Class III commodities containing a mix of both Group A expanded and nonexpanded plastics shall comply with Figure 20.4.3.3(a) where they are within cartons, boxes, or crates or with Figure 20.4.3.3(b) where they are exposed.

20.4.4* Class IV.

20.4.4.1 A Class IV commodity shall be defined as a product, with or without pallets, that meets one of the following criteria:

(1) Constructed partially or totally of Group B plastics
(2) Consists of free-flowing Group A plastic materials
(3) Cartoned, or within a wooden container, that contains greater than 5 percent and up to 15 percent by weight of Group A nonexpanded plastic
(4) Cartoned, or within a wooden container, that contains greater than 5 percent and up to 25 percent by volume of expanded Group A plastics
(5) Cartoned, or within a wooden container, that contains a mix of Group A expanded and nonexpanded plastics and complies with Figure 20.4.3.3(a)
(6) Exposed, that contains greater than 5 percent and up to 15 percent by weight of Group A nonexpanded plastic
(7) Exposed, that contains a mix of Group A expanded and nonexpanded plastics and complies with Figure 20.4.3.3(b)

20.4.4.2 The remaining materials shall be permitted to be noncombustible, wood, paper, natural fibers, or Group B or Group C plastics.

20.4.5* Classification of Plastics, Elastomers, and Rubber. Plastics, elastomers, and rubber shall be classified as Group A, Group B, or Group C.

20.4.5.1* Group A. The following materials shall be classified as Group A:

(1) ABS (acrylonitrile-butadiene-styrene copolymer)
(2) Acetal (polyformaldehyde)
(3) Acrylic (polymethyl methacrylate)
(4) Butyl rubber
(5) Cellulosics (cellulose acetate, cellulose acetate butyrate, ethyl cellulose)
(6) EPDM (ethylene-propylene rubber)
(7) FRP (fiberglass-reinforced polyester)
(8) Natural rubber
(9) Nitrile-rubber (acrylonitrile-butadiene-rubber)
(10) Nylon (nylon 6, nylon 6/6)
(11) PET (thermoplastic polyester)
(12) Polybutadiene
(13) Polycarbonate
(14) Polyester elastomer
(15) Polyethylene
(16) Polypropylene
(17) Polystyrene
(18) Polyurethane
(19) PVC (polyvinyl chloride — highly plasticized, with plasticizer content greater than 20 percent) (rarely found)
(20) PVF (polyvinyl fluoride)
(21) SAN (styrene acrylonitrile)
(22) SBR (styrene-butadiene rubber)

20.4.5.2* Group A plastics shall be further subdivided as either expanded or nonexpanded.

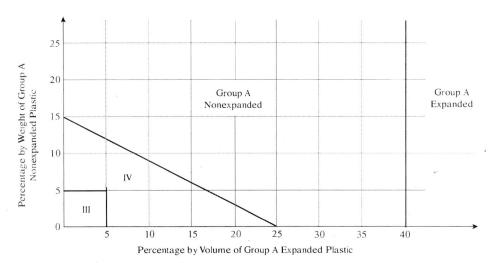

III - Class III Commodity. Refer to 20.3.2 if a plastic pallet is used.

IV - Class IV Commodity. Refer to 20.3.2 if a plastic pallet is used.

Δ **FIGURE 20.4.3.3(a)   Commodities, Cartoned or Within a Wooden Container, Containing a Mixture of Expanded and Nonexpanded Group A Plastics.**

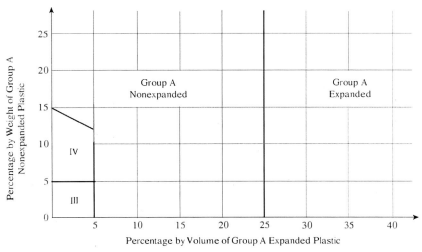

III - Class III Commodity. Refer to 20.3.2 if a plastic pallet is used.

IV - Class IV Commodity. Refer to 20.3.2 if a plastic pallet is used.

Δ **FIGURE 20.4.3.3(b)   Exposed Commodities Containing a Mixture of Expanded and Nonexpanded Group A Plastics.**

20.4.5.3 A Group A expanded plastic commodity shall be defined as a product, with or without pallets, that meets one of the following criteria:

(1) Cartoned, or within a wooden container, that contains greater than 40 percent by volume of Group A expanded plastic

(2) Exposed, that contains greater than 25 percent by volume of Group A expanded plastic

20.4.5.4 A Group A nonexpanded plastic commodity shall be defined as a product, with or without pallets, that meets one of the following criteria:

(1) Cartoned, or within a wooden container, that contains greater than 15 percent by weight of Group A nonexpanded plastic

(2) Cartoned, or within a wooden container, that contains greater than 25 percent and up to 40 percent by volume of Group A expanded plastic

(3) Cartoned, or within a wooden container, that contains a mix of Group A nonexpanded and expanded plastics, in compliance with Figure 20.4.3.3(a)

(4) Exposed, that contains greater than 15 percent by weight of Group A nonexpanded plastic

(5) Exposed, that contains greater than 5 percent and up to 25 percent by volume of Group A expanded plastic

(6) Exposed, that contains a mix of Group A nonexpanded and expanded plastics, in compliance with Figure 20.4.3.3(b)

20.4.5.5 The remaining materials shall be permitted to be noncombustible, wood, paper, natural or synthetic fibers, or Group A, Group B, or Group C plastics.

20.4.6 Group B. The following materials shall be classified as Group B:

(1) Chloroprene rubber

(2) Fluoroplastics (ECTFE — ethylene-chlorotrifluoro-ethylene copolymer; ETFE — ethylene-tetrafluoroethylene-copolymer; FEP — fluorinated ethylene-propylene copolymer)

(3) Silicone rubber

20.4.7 Group C. The following materials shall be classified as Group C:

(1) Fluoroplastics (PCTFE — polychlorotrifluoroethylene; PTFE — polytetrafluoroethylene)

(2) Melamine (melamine formaldehyde)

(3) Phenolic

(4) PVC (polyvinyl chloride — flexible — PVCs with plasticizer content up to 20 percent)

(5) PVDC (polyvinylidene chloride)

(6) PVDF (polyvinylidene fluoride)

(7) Urea (urea formaldehyde)

20.4.8* Plastic commodities shall be protected in accordance with Figure 20.4.8. *(See Section C.21.)*

20.4.8.1 Group B plastics and free-flowing Group A plastics shall be protected the same as Class IV commodities.

20.4.8.2 Group C plastics shall be protected the same as Class III commodities.

Δ **20.4.9 Rubber Tires.** Pneumatic tires for passenger automobiles, aircraft, light and heavy trucks, trailers, farm equipment, construction equipment (off-the-road), and buses shall be

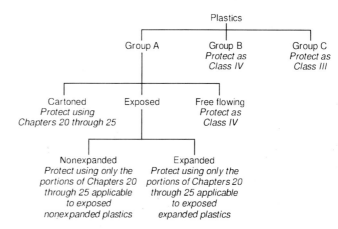

Δ **FIGURE 20.4.8   Decision Tree.**

protected as rubber tire storage in accordance with Chapters 20 through 25.

Δ **20.4.10* Classification of Rolled Paper Storage.** For the purposes of this standard, the classifications of paper described in 20.4.10.1 through 20.4.10.4 shall apply and shall be used to determine the sprinkler system design criteria in accordance with Chapters 20 through 25.

20.4.10.1 Heavyweight Class. Heavyweight class shall be defined so as to include paperboard and paper stock having a basis weight [weight per 1000 ft^2 (93 m^2)] of 20 lb (100 g/m^2).

20.4.10.2 Mediumweight Class. Mediumweight class shall be defined so as to include all the broad range of papers having a basis weight [weight per 1000 ft^2 (93 m^2)] of 10 lb to 20 lb (50 g/m^2 to 100 g/m^2).

20.4.10.3 Lightweight Class. Lightweight class shall be defined so as to include all papers having a basis weight [weight per 1000 ft^2 (93 m^2)] of 10 lb (50 g/m^2).

20.4.10.4 Tissue.

20.4.10.4.1 Tissue shall be defined so as to include the broad range of papers of characteristic gauzy texture, which, in some cases, are fairly transparent.

20.4.10.4.2 For the purposes of this standard, tissue shall be defined as the soft, absorbent type, regardless of basis weight — specifically, crepe wadding and the sanitary class including facial tissue, paper napkins, bathroom tissue, and toweling.

Δ **20.4.11 Display/Storage of Up to Group A Plastics.** Group A plastics combined with Class I through Class IV commodities in a display/storage arrangement shall be permitted to be protected as display/storage of up to Group A plastics in accordance with Section 26.3.

Δ **20.4.11.1 Baled Cotton.** Baled cotton shall be protected in accordance with Section 26.5. *(See Table A.3.3.14.)*

Δ **20.4.12 Carton Records Storage.** A Class III commodity consisting predominantly of paper records in cardboard cartons shall be permitted to be protected as cartoned record storage in accordance with Section 26.6.

20.4.13 Mixed Commodities.

20.4.13.1 Protection requirements shall not be based on the overall commodity mix in a fire area.

20.4.13.2 Unless the requirements of 20.4.13.3 or 20.4.13.4 are met, mixed commodity storage shall be protected by the requirements for the highest classified commodity and storage arrangement.

20.4.13.3 The protection requirements for the lower commodity class shall be permitted to be utilized where all of the following are met:

(1) Up to 10 pallet loads of a higher hazard commodity, as described in 20.4.1 through 20.4.7, shall be permitted to be present in an area not exceeding 40,000 ft^2 (3720 m^2).
(2) The higher hazard commodity shall be randomly dispersed with no adjacent loads in any direction (including diagonally).
(3) Where the ceiling protection is based on Class I or Class II commodities, the allowable number of pallet loads for Class IV or Group A plastics shall be reduced to five.

20.4.13.4 Mixed Commodity Segregation. The protection requirements for the lower commodity class shall be permitted to be utilized in the area of lower commodity class, where the higher hazard material is confined to a designated area and the area is protected to the higher hazard in accordance with the requirements of this standard.

20.5 Storage Arrangement.

20.5.1 Movable Racks. Rack storage in movable racks shall be protected in the same manner as multiple-row racks.

N **20.5.2 Portable Racks.** Except where otherwise allowed in this standard, portable rack storage shall be protected in the same manner as multiple-row racks.

Δ **20.5.3* Rack Storage.**

20.5.3.1 Shelving.

20.5.3.1.1 Shelving material that is less than 50 percent open, or placement of loads that block openings that would otherwise serve as the required flue spaces, greater than 20 ft^2 (1.9 m^2) in area shall be treated as solid shelf racks.

Δ **20.5.3.1.2 Double-Row Racks.**

N **20.5.3.1.2.1** Unless the requirements of 20.5.3.1.2.2 are met, double-row racks without solid shelves shall be considered racks with solid shelves where longitudinal flue spaces are not provided.

N **20.5.3.1.2.2** Double-row racks without solid shelves and a longitudinal flue space shall be considered open racks where the storage height does not exceed 25 ft (7.6 m) and transverse flue spaces are provided at maximum 5 ft (1.5 m) intervals.

N **20.5.3.1.3 Multiple-Row Racks.** Unless the requirements of 20.5.3.1.3.1 or 20.5.3.1.3.2 are met, multiple-row racks without solid shelves shall be considered racks with solid shelves.

N **20.5.3.1.3.1** Multiple-row racks without solid shelves shall be considered open racks where both transverse and longitudinal flue spaces are provided at maximum 5 ft (1.5 m) intervals.

N **20.5.3.1.3.2** Multiple-row racks without solid shelves shall be considered open racks where transverse flue spaces are provi-

ded at maximum 5 ft (1.5 m) intervals and the rack depth does not exceed 20 ft (6.1 m) between aisles that are a minimum width of 3.5 ft (1.1 m).

N **20.5.3.2* Slatted Shelves.** Slatted rack shelves shall be considered equivalent to solid rack shelves where the shelving is not considered open rack shelving or where the requirements of 26.4.1.2 or 26.4.1.3 are not met. *(See Section C.20.)*

20.5.3.3 Aisles.

20.5.3.3.1 Aisles required by Chapters 21 through 25 shall not be obstructed unless Chapters 21 through 25 include specific guidance allowing obstructions over the aisle.

20.5.3.4 Flues.

20.5.3.4.1 Longitudinal Flue Space.

Δ **20.5.3.4.1.1** For Class I through Class IV and Group A plastic commodities in double-row open racks, a longitudinal flue space shall not be required for storage up to and including 25 ft (7.6 m). *(See Section C.13.)*

20.5.3.4.1.2 For Class I through IV and Group A plastic nominal 6 in. (150 mm) longitudinal flue spaces shall be provided in double-row racks for storage over 25 ft (7.6 m).

20.5.3.4.2 Transverse Flue Space.

20.5.3.4.2.1 Nominal 6 in. (150 mm) transverse flue spaces between loads and at rack uprights shall be maintained in single-row, double-row, and multiple-row racks.

20.5.3.4.2.2 Random variations in the width of flue spaces or in their vertical alignment shall be permitted. *(See Section C.26.)*

20.5.4 Plastic Motor Vehicle Components. Group A plastic automotive components and associated packaging material consisting of exposed, expanded Group A plastic dunnage, instrument panels, and plastic bumper fascia shall be permitted to be protected in accordance with Section 26.2.

20.6 Protection Criteria for Roll Paper Storage.

20.6.1 Wet pipe systems shall be used in tissue storage areas.

20.6.2 Horizontal storage of heavyweight or mediumweight paper shall be protected as a closed array.

20.6.3 Lightweight paper or tissue paper shall be permitted to be protected as mediumweight paper where wrapped completely on the sides and both ends, or where wrapped on the sides only with steel bands, with the wrapping material being either a single layer of heavyweight paper with a basis weight of 40 lb (18 kg) or two layers of heavyweight paper with a basis weight of less than 40 lb (18 kg).

20.6.4 For purposes of sprinkler system design criteria, lightweight class paper shall be protected as tissue.

20.6.5 Mediumweight paper shall be permitted to be protected as heavyweight paper where wrapped completely on the sides and both ends, or where wrapped on the sides only with steel bands, with the wrapping material being either a single layer of heavyweight paper with a basis weight of 40 lb (18 kg) or two layers of heavyweight paper with a basis weight of less than 40 lb (18 kg).

Δ 20.7* Plastic Motor Vehicle Components.

N **20.7.1** Group A plastic automotive components and associated packaging material consisting of exposed, expanded Group A plastic dunnage, instrument panels, and plastic bumper fascia shall be permitted to be protected as provided in Section 26.2.

20.7.2 Automotive components covered in this section shall not include the storage of air bags, tires, and seats on portable racks.

20.8* High Volume Low Speed (HVLS) Fans.

Δ **20.8.1** The installation of HVLS fans in buildings equipped with sprinklers, including ESFR sprinklers, shall comply with the following:

(1) The maximum fan diameter shall be 24 ft (7.3 m).
(2) The HVLS fan shall be centered approximately between four adjacent sprinklers.
(3) The vertical clearance from the HVLS fan to sprinkler deflector shall be a minimum of 36 in. (900 mm).
(4) All HVLS fans shall be interlocked to shut down immediately upon a waterflow alarm.

N **20.8.2** Where a building is protected with a fire alarm system, the interlock required by 20.8.1(4) shall be in accordance with the requirements of *NFPA 72* or other approved fire alarm code.

20.9 Building Construction and Storage: Heights and Clearance.

Δ **20.9.1 Ceiling Slope.** Except as permitted by 20.9.1.1, the sprinkler system criteria specified in Chapters 20 through 25 shall apply to buildings with ceiling slopes not exceeding 2 in 12 (16.7 percent).

N **20.9.1.1** The following situations shall permit storage under ceilings with slope exceeding 2 in 12 (16.7 percent):

(1) Where a specific section in Chapters 20 through 25 permits ceiling slope in excess of 2 in 12 (16.7 percent).
(2) Where storage is protected with in-rack sprinklers in accordance with one of the options in Section 25.6, provided no storage is placed above the highest level of in-rack sprinklers.

Δ 20.9.2* Building Height.

20.9.2.1 The maximum building height shall be measured to the underside of the roof deck or ceiling in the storage area or in accordance with 20.9.2.4.1 through 20.9.2.4.2.

20.9.2.2 For corrugated metal deck roofs up to 3 in. (75 mm) in depth, the maximum roof height shall be measured from floor to the bottom of the deck.

20.9.2.3 For decks deeper than 3 in. (75 mm), the maximum roof height shall be measured to the highest point on the deck.

20.9.2.4 For ceilings that have insulation installed directly against underside of the ceiling or roof structure, the maximum roof height shall be measured to the bottom of insulation and shall be in accordance with 20.9.2.4.1 or 20.9.2.4.2.

20.9.2.4.1 For insulation that is installed directly against the ceiling or roof structure and is installed flat and parallel to the ceiling or roof structure, the maximum roof height shall be measured to the underside of the insulation.

20.9.2.4.2 For insulation that is installed in a manner that causes it to deflect or sag down from the ceiling or roof structure, the maximum roof height shall be measured as half of the distance of the deflection from the insulation high point to the insulation low point. If the deflection or sag in the insulation exceeds 6 in. (150 mm), the maximum roof height shall be measured to the high point of the insulation.

20.9.2.5* Where the building height changes within a compartment, the sprinklers directly over the storage shall be capable of protecting storage directly beneath.

20.9.2.5.1 Where a barrier to heat and smoke in accordance with 20.13.1(2) or 20.13.1(3) is not present, the sprinkler criteria 15 ft (4.6 m) into the perimeter of the lower ceiling area shall be the same as the sprinkler protection for the high ceiling area.

20.9.2.6 ESFR sprinklers shall be used only in buildings equal to, or less than, the height of the building for which they have been listed.

20.9.3 Storage Height.

20.9.3.1 The sprinkler system design shall be based on the storage height that routinely or periodically exists in the building and creates the greatest water demand.

20.9.3.2 Where storage is placed above doors, the storage height shall be calculated from the base of storage above the door.

20.9.4 Clearance to Ceiling.

20.9.4.1* The clearance to ceiling shall be measured in accordance with 20.9.4.1.1 through 20.9.4.1.3.

20.9.4.1.1 For corrugated metal deck roofs up to 3 in. (75 mm) in depth, the clearance to ceiling shall be measured from the top of storage to the bottom of the deck.

20.9.4.1.2 For corrugated metal deck roofs deeper than 3 in. (75 mm), the clearance to ceiling shall be measured to the highest point on the deck.

20.9.4.1.3 For ceilings that have insulation attached directly to underside of the ceiling or roof structure, the clearance to ceiling shall be measured from the top of storage to the bottom of the insulation and shall be in accordance with 20.9.4.1.3.1 or 20.9.4.1.3.2.

20.9.4.1.3.1 For insulation that is attached directly to the ceiling or roof structure and is installed flat and parallel to the ceiling or roof structure, the clearance to ceiling shall be measured from the top of storage to the underside of the insulation.

20.9.4.1.3.2 For insulation that is installed in a manner that causes it to deflect or sag down from the ceiling or roof structure, the clearance to ceiling shall be measured from the top of storage to a point half of the distance of the deflection from the insulation high point to the insulation low point. If the deflection or sag in the insulation exceeds 6 in. (150 mm), the clearance to ceiling shall be measured from the top of storage to the high point of the insulation.

20.9.4.2 For CMDA criteria where the clearance to ceiling exceeds those identified in Table 20.9.4.2, the requirements of Table 20.9.4.3 and Table 20.9.4.4 shall apply.

Δ **Table 20.9.4.2 Maximum Clearance from Top of Storage to Ceiling for CMDA Protection Criteria**

Commodity	Class I to IV	Group A Plastic
Palletized, solid-piled, bin box, shelf, or back-to-back shelf storage	20 ft (6.1 m)	20 ft (6.1 m)
Rack storage up to 25 ft (7.6 m)	20 ft (6.1 m)	10 ft (3.0 m)
Rack storage >25 ft (7.6 m)	10 ft (3.0 m)	10 ft (3.0 m)

20.9.4.3 Protection of Class I through Class IV commodities using CMDA criteria that exceed the maximum allowable clearance in Table 20.9.4.2 shall be in accordance with Table 20.9.4.3.

20.9.4.4 Protection of plastic and rubber commodities with CMDA criteria having clearance exceeding the allowable limits of Table 20.9.4.3 shall be in accordance with Table 20.9.4.4.

20.9.4.5 If in-rack sprinklers are required for the actual storage height with an acceptable clearance to ceiling, in-rack sprinklers shall be installed as indicated by that criteria.

20.9.5 Roof Vents and Draft Curtains. See Section C.6.

20.9.5.1* Manually operated roof vents or automatic roof vents with operating elements that have a higher temperature classification than the automatic sprinklers shall be permitted.

20.9.5.2 Early suppression fast-response (ESFR) sprinklers shall not be used in buildings with automatic heat or smoke vents unless the vents use a high-temperature rated, standard-response operating mechanism.

20.9.5.3* Draft curtains shall not be used within ESFR sprinkler systems.

20.9.5.3.1 Draft curtains separating ESFR sprinklers at system breaks or from control mode sprinklers or between hazards shall be permitted. *(See 14.2.5.)*

Δ **Table 20.9.4.3 Class I Through Class IV Commodities**

Storage Configuration	Where the clearance to ceiling exceeds	Protection is based upon the storage height that would result in a clearance to ceiling of...	In-rack Sprinklers*
Palletized, solid-piled, bin box, shelf, or back-to-back shelf storage	20 ft (6.1 m)	20 ft (6.1 m)	N/A
Rack storage up to and including 25 ft (7.6 m) in height	20 ft (6.1 m)	20 ft (6.1 m)	Permitted as alternative to presumed clearance of 20 ft (6.1 m)
Rack storage over 25 ft (7.6 m) in height	10 ft (3.0 m)	10 ft (3.0 m)	Permitted as alternative to presumed clearance of 10 ft (3.0 m)

*When applying the supplemental in-rack sprinkler option, the ceiling density is based upon the given storage height with an assumed acceptable clearance to ceiling. Provide one level of supplemental, quick response in-rack sprinklers located directly below the top tier of storage and at every flue space intersection.

Δ **Table 20.9.4.4 Plastics and Rubber Commodities**

Storage Configuration	Where the clearance to ceiling exceeds	Protection is based upon the storage height that would result in a clearance to ceiling of...	In-rack Sprinklers*
Palletized, solid-piled, bin box, shelf, or back-to-back shelf storage	20 ft (6.1 m)	20 ft (6.1 m)	N/A
Rack storage up to and including 25 ft (7.6 m) in height	10 ft (3.0 m)	10 ft (3.0 m)	Permitted as alternative to presumed clearance of 10 ft (3.0 m)
Rack storage over 25 ft (7.6 m) in height	10 ft (3.0 m)	N/A	Required

*If in-rack sprinklers are required for the actual storage height with an acceptable clearance to ceiling, in-rack sprinklers are installed as indicated by that criteria. Provide one level of supplemental, quick response in-rack sprinklers located directly below the top tier of storage and at every flue space intersection.

20.9.5.3.2 Where ESFR sprinkler systems are installed adjacent to sprinkler systems with standard-response sprinklers, a draft curtain of noncombustible construction and at least 2 ft (600 mm) in depth shall be required to separate the two areas.

20.9.5.3.3 A clear aisle of at least 4 ft (1.2 m) centered below the draft curtain shall be maintained for separation.

20.9.6 Clearance from Deflector to Storage.

20.9.6.1 Unless the requirements of 20.9.6.2 through 20.9.6.4 are met, the clearance between the deflector and the top of storage or contents of the room shall be 18 in. (450 mm) or greater.

20.9.6.2 Greater clearance to storage minimums specified by other standards or sprinkler listings shall be followed.

20.9.6.3 A minimum clearance to storage of less than 18 in. (450 mm) between the top of storage and ceiling sprinkler deflectors shall be permitted where proven by successful large-scale fire tests for the particular hazard.

20.9.6.4 The clearance from the top of storage to sprinkler deflectors shall be not less than 36 in. (900 mm) where rubber tires are stored.

20.9.6.5 A minimum clearance to storage of 36 in. (900 mm) shall be provided for ESFR and CMSA sprinklers.

20.10 Unsprinklered Combustible Concealed Spaces.

20.10.1* When using the density/area method or room design method, unless the requirements of 20.10.2 are met for buildings having unsprinklered combustible concealed spaces as described in 9.2.1 and 9.3.18, the minimum area of sprinkler operation for that portion of the building shall be 3000 ft² (280 m²).

20.10.1.1 The design area of 3000 ft² (280 m²) shall be applied only to the sprinkler system or portions of the sprinkler system that are adjacent to the qualifying combustible concealed space.

20.10.1.2 The term *adjacent* shall apply to any sprinkler system protecting a space above, below, or next to the qualifying concealed space except where a barrier with a fire resistance rating at least equivalent to the water supply duration completely separates the concealed space from the sprinklered area.

20.10.2 The following unsprinklered combustible concealed spaces shall not require a minimum design area of sprinkler operation of 3000 ft² (280 m²):

(1) Noncombustible and limited-combustible concealed spaces with minimal combustible loading having no access. The space shall be considered a concealed space even with small openings such as those used as return air for a plenum.

(2) Noncombustible and limited-combustible concealed spaces with limited access and not permitting occupancy or storage of combustibles. The space shall be considered a concealed space even with small openings such as those used as return air for a plenum.

(3) Combustible concealed spaces filled entirely with noncombustible insulation.

(4) Concealed spaces where rigid materials are used and the exposed surfaces have a flame spread index of 25 or less and the materials have been demonstrated to not propa-

gate fire more than 10.5 ft (3.2 m) when tested in accordance with ASTM E84, *Standard Test Method for Surface Burning Characteristics of Building Materials*, or UL 723, *Standard for Test for Surface Burning Characteristics of Building Materials*, extended for an additional 20 minutes in the form in which they are installed in the space.

(5) Concealed spaces in which the exposed materials are constructed entirely of fire retardant–treated wood as defined by NFPA 703.

(6) Concealed spaces over isolated small compartments not exceeding 55 ft² (5.1 m²) in area.

(7) Vertical pipe chases under 10 ft² (0.9 m²), provided that in multifloor buildings the chases are firestopped at each floor using materials equivalent to the floor construction. Such pipe chases shall contain no sources of ignition, piping shall be noncombustible, and pipe penetrations at each floor shall be properly sealed.

(8) Exterior columns under 10 ft² (0.9 m²) in area formed by studs or wood joists, supporting exterior canopies that are fully protected with a sprinkler system.

(9) Cavities within unsprinklered wall spaces.

20.11 Room Design Method.

20.11.1* The water supply requirements for sprinklers only shall be based upon the room that creates the greatest demand.

20.11.2 To utilize the room design method, all rooms shall be enclosed with walls having a fire resistance rating equal to the required water supply duration.

20.11.2.1 Minimum protection of openings shall include automatic- or self-closing doors with the appropriate fire protection rating for the enclosure.

20.11.3* Where the room design method is used, the density shall correspond to that required for the smallest area acceptable under the density/area method.

20.12* High-Expansion Foam Systems.

20.12.1 General: High Expansion Foam Systems.

20.12.1.1 High-expansion foam systems that are installed in addition to automatic sprinklers shall be installed in accordance with NFPA 11.

20.12.1.2 High-expansion foam systems shall be automatic in operation.

20.12.1.3 High-expansion foam used to protect the idle pallet shall have a maximum fill time of 4 minutes.

20.12.1.4 Detectors for high-expansion foam systems shall be listed and shall be installed at no more than one-half the listed spacing.

20.12.1.5 The release system for the high expansion foam deluge system shall be designed to operate prior to the sprinklers installed in the area.

20.12.1.5.1 The maximum submergence time for the high-expansion foam shall be 5 minutes for Class I, Class II, or Class III commodities and 4 minutes for Class IV commodities.

20.12.2 High-Expansion Foam: Reduction in Ceiling Density.

20.12.2.1 Using CMDA sprinkler protection criteria for palletized, solid-piled, bin box, shelf, or back-to-back shelf storage of Class I through Class IV commodities, idle pallets, or plastics, where high-expansion foam systems are used in combination with ceiling sprinklers, a reduction in ceiling density to one-half that required for Class I through Class IV commodities, idle pallets, or plastics shall be permitted without revising the design area, but the density shall be no less than 0.15 gpm/ft² (6.1 mm/min).

20.12.2.2 Using CMDA sprinkler protection criteria for rack storage, where high-expansion foam systems are used in combination with ceiling sprinklers, the minimum ceiling sprinkler design density shall be 0.2 gpm/ft² (8.2 mm/min) for Class I, Class II, or Class III commodities or 0.25 gpm/ft² (10.2 mm/min) for Class IV commodities for the most hydraulically remote 2000 ft² (185 m²) operating area.

20.12.2.3 Where high-expansion foam systems are used in combination with ceiling sprinklers, the maximum submergence time shall be 7 minutes for Class I, Class II, or Class III commodities and 5 minutes for Class IV commodities.

20.12.2.4 Where high-expansion foam systems are used for rack storage of Class I through IV commodities over 25 ft (7.6 m) high up to and including 35 ft (10.7 m) high, they shall be used in combination with ceiling sprinklers.

20.12.2.5 Reduced-Discharge Density. Where high-expansion foam systems for rubber tire protection are installed in accordance with NFPA 11, a reduction in sprinkler discharge density to one-half the density specified in Table 21.7.1(a) or 0.24 gpm/ft² (9.8 mm/min), whichever is higher, shall be permitted.

20.12.2.6 In-rack sprinklers for the protection of Class I through IV commodities shall not be required where high-expansion foam systems are used in combination with ceiling sprinklers.

20.12.2.7 Detectors for High-Expansion Foam Systems.

20.12.2.7.1 Detectors shall be listed and shall be installed in one of the following configurations:

(1) At the ceiling only where installed at one-half the listed linear spacing [e.g., 15 ft × 15 ft (4.6 m × 4.6 m) rather than at 30 ft × 30 ft (9.1 m × 9.1 m)]; at the ceiling at the listed spacing and in racks at alternate levels
(2) Where listed for rack storage installation and installed in accordance with the listing to provide response within 1 minute after ignition using an ignition source that is equivalent to that used in a rack storage testing program

20.12.2.7.2 Ceiling detectors alone shall not be used where the clearance to ceiling exceeds 10 ft (3.0 m) or the height of the storage exceeds 25 ft (7.6 m).

20.12.2.7.3 Detectors for preaction systems shall be installed in accordance with 20.12.2.7.

20.13* Adjacent Hazards or Design Methods.

20.13.1 For buildings with two or more adjacent hazards or design methods, the following shall apply:

(1) Where areas are not physically separated by a barrier or partition capable of delaying heat from a fire in one area from fusing sprinklers in the adjacent area, the required sprinkler protection for the more demanding design basis shall extend 15 ft (4.6 m) beyond its perimeter.
(2) The requirements of 20.13.1(1) shall not apply where the areas are separated by a draft curtain or barrier located

above an aisle, horizontally a minimum of 24 in. (600 mm) from the adjacent hazard on each side, or a partition that is capable of delaying heat from a fire in one area from fusing sprinklers in the adjacent area.
(3) The requirements of 20.13.1(1) shall not apply to the extension of more demanding criteria from an upper ceiling level to beneath a lower ceiling level where the difference in height between the ceiling levels is at least 24 in. (600 mm), located above an aisle, horizontally a minimum 24 in. (600 mm) from the adjacent hazard on each side.

20.14* Hose Connections.

20.14.1 Small [1½ in. (40 mm)] Hose Connections. See Section C.5.

20.14.1.1 Hose Connection. Small hose connections [1½ in. (40 mm)] shall be provided where required by the authority having jurisdiction in accordance with Section 16.15 for first-aid, fire-fighting, and overhaul operations.

20.14.1.2 Small hose connections shall not be required for the protection of Class I, II, III, and IV commodities stored 12 ft (3.7 m) or less in height.

20.15 Hose Stream Allowance and Water Supply Duration.

20.15.1 Hose stream allowance and water supply duration for Chapters 20 through 25 shall be in accordance with Section 20.15.

20.15.2 Hose Stream Allowance and Water Supply Duration.

20.15.2.1* Tanks shall be sized to supply the equipment that they serve.

20.15.2.2* Pumps shall be sized to supply the equipment that they serve.

20.15.2.3 Water allowance for outside hose shall be added to the sprinkler requirement at the connection to the city main or a yard hydrant, whichever is closer to the system riser.

20.15.2.4 Where inside hose connections are planned or are required, the following shall apply:

(1) A total water allowance of 50 gpm (190 L/min) for a single hose connection installation shall be added to the sprinkler requirements.
(2) A total water allowance of 100 gpm (380 L/min) for a multiple hose connection installation shall be added to the sprinkler requirements.
(3) The water allowance shall be added in 50 gpm (190 L/min) increments beginning at the most remote hose connection, with each increment added at the pressure required by the sprinkler system design at that point.

Δ **20.15.2.5** When hose valves for fire department use are attached to wet pipe sprinkler system risers in accordance with 16.15.2, the following shall apply:

(1) The water supply shall not be required to be added to standpipe demand as determined from NFPA 14.
(2) Where the combined sprinkler system demand and hose stream allowance of Chapters 20 through 25 exceeds the requirements of NFPA 14, this higher demand shall be used.
(3) For partially sprinklered buildings, the sprinkler demand, not including hose stream allowance, as indicated in

Chapters 20 through 25 shall be added to the requirements given in NFPA 14.

20.15.2.6 Unless indicated otherwise, the minimum water supply requirements for a hydraulically designed sprinkler system shall be determined by adding the hose stream allowance from Table 20.15.2.6 to the water demand for sprinklers.

20.15.2.7 For the protection of baled cotton, the total water supply available shall be sufficient to provide the recommended sprinkler discharge density over the area to be protected, plus a minimum of 500 gpm (1900 L/min) for hose streams.

20.15.2.7.1 Water supplies shall be capable of supplying the total demand for sprinklers and hose streams for not less than 2 hours.

20.15.2.8 For roll paper storage, the water supply design shall include the demand of the automatic sprinkler system plus the hose stream allowance plus, where provided, the high-expansion foam system for the duration specified in Table 20.15.2.6.

N **20.15.2.9** For the protection of rubber tires, the total water supply available shall be capable of providing flow sufficient for the recommended sprinkler discharge density over the protected area, hose streams, and foam systems (if provided) for the duration required in Table 20.15.2.6.

Δ **20.15.3** The minimum water supply requirements shall be determined by adding the hose stream allowance from 20.15.2 to the water supply for sprinklers as determined by Chapters 20 through 25.

20.15.4 The minimum water supply requirements determined from 20.15.3 shall be available for the minimum duration specified in 20.15.2.

20.15.5 Total system water supply requirements shall be determined in accordance with the hydraulic calculation procedures of Chapter 28.

20.16 Discharge Considerations: General.

20.16.1 Multiple Adjustments.

20.16.1.1 Where multiple adjustments to the area of operation are required to be made, these adjustments shall be compounded based on the area of operation originally selected.

20.16.1.2 If the building has unsprinklered combustible concealed spaces, the rules of Section 20.10 shall be applied after all other modifications have been made.

20.16.2* Wet Pipe Systems.

20.16.2.1 Sprinkler systems shall be wet pipe systems.

20.16.2.2* In areas that are subject to freezing or where special conditions exist, dry pipe systems and preaction systems shall be permitted to protect storage occupancies.

20.16.3 Dry Pipe and Preaction Systems. For dry pipe systems and preaction systems using control mode density/area (CMDA) criteria, the area of sprinkler operation shall be increased by 30 percent without revising the density.

20.17* Protection of Idle Pallets.

20.17.1 Wood Pallets.

20.17.1.1* Wood pallets shall be permitted to be stored in the following arrangements:

(1) Stored outside
(2) Stored in a detached structure
(3) Stored indoors where arranged and protected in accordance with 20.17.1.2

Δ **20.17.1.2** Wood pallets, where stored indoors, shall be protected in accordance with one of the following:

(1) Control mode density/area sprinkler protection as specified in Table 20.17.1.2(a)
(2) CMSA sprinkler protection in accordance with Table 20.17.1.2(b)
(3) ESFR sprinkler protection in accordance with Table 20.17.1.2(c)
(4) Control mode density/area sprinkler protection in accordance with the Ordinary Hazard Group 2 curve and Figure 19.2.3.1.1 with a hose stream demand of at least 250 gpm (950 L/min) for a duration of at least 60 minutes when pallets are stored no higher than 6 ft (1.8 m) and each pile of no more than four stacks is separated from other pallet piles by at least 8 ft (2.4 m) of clear space or 25 ft (7.6 m) of commodity

20.17.1.2.1 The maximum clearance to ceiling of 20 ft (6.1 m) specified in 20.9.4 shall not apply to arrangement 20.17.1.2(4).

20.17.1.3 Idle wood pallets shall not be stored in racks unless they are protected in accordance with the appropriate requirements of Table 20.17.1.2(a) or Table 20.17.1.2(c). *(See Section C.7.)*

20.17.2 Plastic Pallets.

20.17.2.1 Plastic pallets shall be permitted to be stored in the following manner:

(1) Plastic pallets shall be permitted to be stored outside.
(2) Plastic pallets shall be permitted to be stored in a detached structure.
(3) Plastic pallets shall be permitted to be stored indoors where arranged and protected in accordance with the requirements of 20.17.2.2.

20.17.2.2 Protection Criteria for Plastic Pallets Stored Indoors.

20.17.2.2.1 Plastic pallets having a demonstrated fire hazard that is equal to or less than idle wood pallets and is listed for such equivalency shall be permitted to be protected in accordance with 20.17.1.

20.17.2.2.2 When specific test data are available, the data shall take precedence in determining the required protection of idle plastic pallets.

20.17.2.2.3 Protection with ESFR sprinklers shall be in accordance with the requirements of Table 20.17.2.2.3.

20.17.2.2.4 Protection with spray sprinklers shall be in accordance with one of the scenarios in 20.17.2.2.4.1 through 20.17.2.2.4.3.

Δ **Table 20.15.2.6 Hose Stream Allowance and Water Supply Duration**

Commodity	Sprinkler Type	Sprinkler Spacing Type	Number of Ceiling Sprinklers in Design Area[a]	Size of Design Area at Ceiling	Hose Stream Allowance		Water Supply Duration (minutes)
					gpm	L/min	
Class I–IV commodities, Group A plastics, idle wood pallets, and idle plastic pallets	Control mode density/area (CMDA)	Standard and extended-coverage	NA	Up to 1200 ft² (112 m²)	250	950	60
				Over 1200 ft² (112 m²) up to 1500 ft² (140 m²)	500	1900	90
				Over 1500 ft² (140 m²) up to 2600 ft² (240 m²)	500	1900	120
				Over 2600 ft² (240 m²)	500	1900	150
	Control mode specific application (CMSA)	Standard	Up to 12	NA	250	950	60
			Over 12 to 15	NA	500	1900	90
			Over 15 to 25	NA	500	1900	120
			Over 25	NA	500	1900	150
		Extended-coverage	Up to 6	NA	250	950	60
			Up to 8[b]	NA	250	950	60
			Over 6 to 8	NA	500	1900	90
			Over 8 to 12	NA	500	1900	120
			Over 12	NA	500	1900	150
	Early suppression fast response (ESFR)	Standard	Up to 12	NA	250	950	60
			Over 12 to 15	NA	500	1900	90
			Over 15 to 25	NA	500	1900	120
			Over 25	NA	500	1900	150
On-floor rubber tire storage up to 5 ft (1.5 m) in height	CMDA & CMSA	Standard and extended-coverage	Any	Any	250	950	120
Rubber tire storage	CMDA	Standard and extended-coverage	NA	Up to 5000 ft² (465 m²)	750	2850	180
	CMSA	Standard	Up to 15	NA	500	1900	180
	ESFR	Standard	Up to 12	NA	250	950	60
			Over 12 to 20	NA	500	1900	120[c]
Roll paper	CMDA	Standard	NA	Up to 4000 ft² (370 m²)	500	1900	120
	CMSA	Standard	Up to 25	NA	500	1900	120
	ESFR	Standard	Up to 12	NA	250	950	60
Alternative protection in accordance with Section 25.6	NA	NA	NA	NA	250	950	60

NA: Not applicable.

[a]For CMSA and ESFR sprinklers, the additional sprinklers included in the design area for obstructions do not need to be considered in determining the total number of sprinklers in this column.

[b]Limited to a maximum of 144 ft² (13 m²) per sprinkler.

[c]For storage on-tread, on-side, and laced tires in open portable steel racks or palletized portable racks, with pile height up to 25 ft (7.6 m) and building height up to 30 ft (9.1 m) with K-14.0 (K-200) or K-16.8 (K-240) ESFR sprinklers, the water supply duration is 180 minutes.

Δ Table 20.17.1.2(a) Control Mode Density/Area Sprinkler Protection for Indoor Storage of Idle Wood Pallets

Type of Sprinkler	Location of Storage	Nominal K-Factor	Maximum Storage Height		Maximum Ceiling/Roof Height		Sprinkler Density		Areas of Operation	
			ft	m	ft	m	gpm/ft²	mm/min	ft²	m²
Control mode density/area	On floor	8 (115) or larger	Up to 6	Up to 1.8	20	6.1	0.20	8.2	3000*	280*
	On floor	11.2 (160) or larger	Up to 8	Up to 2.4	30	9.1	0.45	18.3	2500	230
	On floor or rack without solid shelves	11.2 (160) or larger	8 to 12	2.4 to 3.7	30	9.1	0.6	24.5	3500	325
			12 to 20	3.7 to 6.1	30	9.1	0.6	24.5	4500	420
	On floor	16.8 (240) or larger	Up to 20	Up to 6.1	30	9.1	0.6	24.5	2000	185

*The area of sprinkler operation should be permitted to be reduced to 2000 ft² (185 m²) when sprinklers having a nominal K-factor of 11.2 (160) or larger are used or if high-temperature-rated sprinklers with a nominal K-factor of 8.0 (115) are used.

Δ Table 20.17.1.2(b) CMSA Sprinkler Protection for Indoor Storage of Idle Wood Pallets

Storage Arrangement	Commodity Class	Maximum Storage Height		Maximum Ceiling/ Roof Height		K-Factor/ Orientation	Type of System	Number of Design Sprinklers	Minimum Operating Pressure	
		ft	m	ft	m				psi	bar
On floor	Idle wood pallets	20	6.1	30	9.1	11.2 (160) Upright	Wet	15	25	1.7
							Dry	25	25	1.7
						16.8 (240) Upright	Wet	15	15	1.0
							Dry	25	15	1.0
						19.6 (280) Pendent	Wet	15	16	1.1
				35	10.7	19.6 (280) Pendent	Wet	15	25	1.7
				40	12.2	19.6 (280) Pendent	Wet	15	30	2.1

Δ **20.17.2.2.4.1** Where plastic pallets are stored in dedicated rooms, the following shall apply:

(1) The rooms shall have at least one exterior wall.
(2) The plastic pallet storage shall be separated from the remainder of the building by 3-hour-rated fire walls.
(3) The storage shall be protected by sprinklers designed to deliver 0.6 gpm/ft² (24.5 mm/min) for the entire room or by high-expansion foam and sprinklers designed to deliver 0.3 gpm/ft² (12.2 mm/min) for the entire room.
(4) The storage shall be piled no higher than 12 ft (3.7 m).
(5) Any steel columns shall be protected by 1-hour fireproofing or a sidewall sprinkler directed to one side of the column at the top or at the 15 ft (4.6 m) level, whichever is lower. Flow from these sprinklers shall be permitted to be omitted from the sprinkler system demand for hydraulic calculations.

20.17.2.2.4.2 Where plastic pallets are not separated from other storage, the following shall apply:

(1) Maximum storage height of 10 ft (3.0 m)
(2) Maximum ceiling height of 30 ft (9.1 m)
(3) Sprinkler density 0.6 gpm/ft² over 2000 ft² (24.5 mm/min over 185 m²)
(4) Minimum sprinkler K-factor of 16.8 (240)

20.17.2.2.4.3 Plastic pallets shall have no impact on the required sprinkler protection when stored as follows:

(1) Storage shall be piled no higher than 4 ft (1.2 m).
(2) Sprinkler protection shall employ high temperature–rated sprinklers.
(3) Each pallet pile of no more than two stacks shall be separated from other pallet piles by at least 8 ft (2.4 m) of clear space or 25 ft (7.6 m) of stored commodity.
(4) Minimum ceiling design of OH2 shall be used.

20.17.2.3 Idle plastic pallets shall be stored only in racks where protected in accordance with the requirements of Table 20.17.2.2.3.

20.17.2.3.1 When specific test data and a product listing are available, the data shall take precedence in determining the required protection of idle plastic pallets stored in racks.

20.17.3 Idle Pallets Stored on Racks, on Shelves, and Above Doors.

20.17.3.1 Idle pallets shall not be stored on racks or shelves, except where permitted in 20.17.1.3, 20.17.2.3, and 20.17.3.2.

Shaded text = Revisions.   Δ = Text deletions and figure/table revisions.   • = Section deletions.   N = New material.

2022 Edition

Δ Table 20.17.1.2(c) ESFR Sprinkler Protection for Indoor Storage of Idle Wood Pallets

Type of Sprinkler (Orientation)	Location of Storage	Nominal K-Factor	Maximum Storage Height		Maximum Ceiling/Roof Height		Minimum Operating Pressure	
			ft	m	ft	m	psi	bar
ESFR (pendent)	On floor or rack without solid shelves	14.0 (200)	25	7.6	30	9.1	50	3.4
			25	7.6	32	9.8	60	4.1
		16.8 (240)	25	7.6	30	9.1	35	2.4
			25	7.6	32	9.8	42	2.9
			35	10.7	40	12.2	52	3.6
		22.4 (320)	25	7.6	30	9.1	25	1.7
			30	9.1	35	10.7	35	2.4
			35	10.7	40	12.2	40	2.8
		25.2 (360)	25	7.6	30	9.1	15	1.0
			30	9.1	35	10.7	20	1.4
			35	10.7	40	12.2	25	1.7
ESFR (upright)	On floor	14.0 (200)	20	6.1	30	9.1	50	3.4
			20	6.1	35	10.7	75	5.2
		16.8 (240)	20	6.1	30	9.1	35	2.4
			20	6.1	35	10.7	52	3.6

20.17.3.2 Idle pallets shall be permitted to be stored on the lowest level of storage only where no storage or shelves are located above the stored pallets and the applicable protection criteria referenced for on-floor storage in Section 20.17 are applied.

20.17.3.3 Where idle pallet storage is above a door, the idle pallet storage height and ceiling height shall be calculated from the base of storage above the door using the applicable protection criteria referenced in Section 20.17.

20.18 Column Protection: Rack Storage and Rubber Tire Storage.

20.18.1* Where fireproofing of building columns is not provided and storage heights are in excess of 15 ft (4.6 m), protection of building columns located wholly or partially within the rack footprint inclusive of flue spaces or within 12 in. (300 mm) of the footprint shall be protected in accordance with one of the following (see Section C.10):

(1) In-rack sprinklers
(2) Sidewall sprinklers at the 15 ft (4.6 m) elevation, pointed toward one side of the steel column
(3) Provision of ceiling sprinkler density for a minimum of 2000 ft² (185 m²) with ordinary-temperature-rated [165°F (74°C)] or high-temperature-rated[286°F (140°C)] sprinklers as shown in Table 20.18.1 for storage heights above 15 ft (4.6 m), up to and including 20 ft (6.1 m)
(4) Provision of CMSA or ESFR ceiling sprinkler protection

Δ **20.18.1.1** Where storage heights are in excess of 15 ft (4.6 m) and vertical rack members support the building structure, the vertical rack members shall be protected in accordance with 20.18.1.

N **Table 20.17.2.2.3 ESFR Pendent Sprinkler Protection for Indoor Storage of Idle Plastic Pallets on Floor or Open Frame Racks**

Maximum Ceiling Height		Minimum Operating Pressure [psi (bar)]			
ft	m	K14 (200)	K168 (240)	K22.4 (320)	K25.2 (360)
30	9.1	50 (3.4)	35 (2.4)	35 (2.4)	35 (2.4)
40	12.2	Racked options available, but in-rack sprinklers required.*		75 (5.2)	60 (4.1)
>40	>12.2			Racked options available, but in-rack sprinklers required.*	

*See Chapter 25 for exposed nonexpanded Group A plastic commodities.

Table 20.18.1 Ceiling Sprinkler Densities for Protection of Steel Building Columns

Commodity Classification	Aisle Width			
	4 ft (1.2 m)		8 ft (2.4 m)	
	gpm/ft²	mm/min	gpm/ft²	mm/min
Class I	0.37	15.1	0.33	13.4
Class II	0.44	17.9	0.37	15.1
Class III	0.49	20.0	0.42	17.1
Class IV and Group A plastics	0.68	27.7	0.57	23.2

20.18.1.2 The flow from a column sprinkler(s) shall be permitted to be omitted from the sprinkler system hydraulic calculations.

20.18.2 Columns Within Rubber Tire Storage.

20.18.2.1 Where fireproofing is not provided, steel columns shall be protected as follows:

(1) Storage exceeding 15 ft through 20 ft (4.6 m through 6.1 m) in height — one sidewall sprinkler directed to one side of the column at a 15 ft (4.6 m) level
(2) Storage exceeding 20 ft (6.1 m) in height — two sidewall sprinklers, one at the top of the column and the other at a 15 ft (4.6 m) level, both directed to the side of the column

20.18.2.2 The flow from a column sprinkler(s) shall be permitted to be omitted from the sprinkler system hydraulic calculations.

20.18.2.3 The protection specified in 20.18.2.1(1) and 20.18.2.1(2) shall not be required where storage in fixed racks is protected by in-rack sprinklers.

20.18.2.4 The protection specified in 20.18.2.1 shall not be required where ESFR or CMSA sprinkler systems that are approved for rubber tire storage are installed.

20.18.2.5 The rate of water supply shall be sufficient to provide the required sprinkler discharge density over the required area of application plus provision for generation of high-expansion foam and in-rack sprinklers where used.

N 20.19 Protection of Racks with Solid Shelves.

N 20.19.1 General. The requirements in this chapter for the installation of in-rack sprinklers shall apply to racks with solid shelves except as modified in this section. *(See Section C.8.)*

N 20.19.2 Open Racks Combined with In-Rack Sprinklers. Ceiling-level sprinkler design criteria for CMDA, CMSA, and ESFR sprinklers shall be an applicable option for open racks combined with in-rack sprinklers installed in accordance with the criteria for solid shelving.

N 20.19.3 Vertical Spacing and Location of In-Rack Sprinklers in Racks with Solid Shelves.

N 20.19.3.1 Where CMDA sprinklers are at ceiling level protecting racks with solid shelving that exceeds 20 ft² (1.9 m²) but

not 64 ft² (5.9 m²) in area, in-rack sprinklers shall not be required below every shelf but shall be installed below shelves at intermediate levels not more than 6 ft (1.8 m) apart vertically. *(See Section C.11.)*

N 20.19.3.2 Where CMDA sprinklers are at ceiling level protecting racks with solid shelving that exceeds 64 ft² (5.9 m²) in area or where the levels of storage exceed 6 ft (1.8 m), in-rack sprinklers shall be installed below each level of shelving.

N 20.19.3.3 Where CMSA sprinklers are at ceiling level and protect racks with solid shelving, in-rack sprinklers shall be installed beneath all tiers under the highest solid shelf.

N 20.19.3.4 Where ESFR sprinklers are at ceiling level and protect racks with solid shelving, in-rack sprinklers shall be installed beneath all tiers under the highest solid shelf.

N 20.19.3.5 Where racks with solid shelves obstruct only a portion of an open rack, in-rack sprinklers shall be installed vertically as follows:

(1) In accordance with 20.19.3.1 and 20.19.3.2 where CMDA sprinklers are installed at ceiling level
(2) In accordance with 20.19.3.3 where CMSA sprinklers are installed at ceiling level
(3) In accordance with 20.19.3.4 where ESFR sprinklers are installed at ceiling level

N 20.19.4 Horizontal Location and Spacing of In-Rack Sprinklers in Racks with Solid Shelves.

N 20.19.4.1 Where racks with solid shelves contain storage of Class I through Class IV commodities, the maximum allowable horizontal spacing of in-rack sprinklers shall be 10 ft (3.0 m).

N 20.19.4.2 Where racks with solid shelves contain storage of Group A plastic commodities, the maximum allowable horizontal spacing of in-rack sprinklers shall be 5 ft (1.5 m).

N 20.19.4.3 Where racks with solid shelves obstruct only a portion of an open rack, in-rack sprinklers shall be extended beyond the end of the solid shelf a minimum of 4 ft (1.2 m) to the nearest flue space intersection.

Chapter 21   Protection of High Piled Storage Using Control Mode Density Area (CMDA) Sprinklers

21.1 General.

Δ **21.1.1** The criteria in Chapter 20 shall apply to storage protected with CMDA sprinklers.

21.1.2* For storage applications with densities of 0.2 gpm/ft² (8.2 mm/min) or less, standard-response sprinklers with a K-factor of K-5.6 (80) or larger shall be permitted.

21.1.3 For general storage applications, rack storage, rubber tire storage, roll paper storage, and baled cotton storage being protected with upright and pendent spray sprinklers with required densities of greater than 0.2 gpm/ft² to 0.34 gpm/ft² (8.2 mm/min to 13.9 mm/min), standard-response sprinklers with a nominal K-factor of K-8.0 (115) or larger shall be used.

21.1.4 For general storage applications, rack storage, rubber tire storage, roll paper storage, and baled cotton storage being protected with upright and pendent spray sprinklers with required densities greater than 0.34 gpm/ft² (13.9 mm/min), standard-response spray sprinklers with a K-factor of K-11.2 (K-160) or larger that are listed for storage applications shall be used.

21.1.5* Unless the requirements of 21.1.6 are met, the requirements of Table 21.5.1.1 shall not apply to modifications to existing storage application systems, using sprinklers with K-factors of K-8.0 (115) or less.

21.1.6 Where applying the requirements of Table 21.5.1.1 utilizing the design criteria of 0.6 gpm/ft² per 2000 ft² (24.5 mm/min per 185 m²) to existing storage applications, the requirements of 21.1.4 shall apply.

21.1.7 The use of quick-response spray sprinklers for storage applications shall be permitted when listed for such use.

21.1.8 The design figures indicate water demands for ordinary-temperature-rated and nominal high-temperature-rated sprinklers at the ceiling.

Δ **21.1.8.1** The ordinary-temperature design densities shall be used for sprinklers with ordinary- and intermediate-temperature classification.

Δ **21.1.8.2** The high-temperature design densities shall be used for sprinklers with high-temperature classification.

21.1.9 Ordinary- and intermediate-temperature sprinklers with K-factors of K-11.2 (K-160) or larger, where listed for storage, shall be permitted to use the densities for high-temperature sprinklers.

21.1.10 Discharge Considerations.

21.1.10.1 The water supply for sprinklers only shall be determined either from the density/area requirements of Chapter 20, Chapter 24, and Chapter 25 or shall be based upon the room design method in accordance with Section 20.11, at the discretion of the designer.

21.1.10.2 The calculations shall satisfy any single point on appropriate density/area curves for the evaluation or modification of existing systems.

21.1.10.3 When using the density/area method, the design area shall meet the requirements of 28.2.4.2.1.

21.1.10.4 The minimum design density shall be not less than 0.15 gpm/ft² (6.1 mm/min) after all adjustments are made.

21.2* **Control Mode Density/Area Sprinkler Protection Criteria for Palletized, Solid-Piled, Bin Box, Shelf, or Back-to-Back Shelf Storage of Class I Through Class IV Commodities.**

21.2.1 Protection for Class I through Class IV commodities in the following configurations shall be provided in accordance with this section:

(1) Nonencapsulated commodities that are solid-piled, palletized, or bin box storage up to 30 ft (9.1 m) in height

(2) Nonencapsulated commodities on shelf storage up to 15 ft (4.6 m) in height

(3)* Encapsulated commodities that are solid-piled, palletized, bin box, or shelf storage up to 15 ft (4.6 m) in height

(4) Back-to-back shelf storage up to 15 ft (4.6 m) in height

(5) Encapsulated storage of solid-piled and palletized Class I through IV commodities permitted in accordance with 21.2.3 for storage heights over 15 ft (4.6 m) up to and including 20 ft (6.1 m)

21.2.2 Protection Criteria for Palletized, Solid-Piled, Bin Box, Shelf, or Back-to-Back Shelf Storage of Class I Through Class IV Commodities Stored Over 12 ft (3.7 m) in Height.

N **21.2.2.1 General.**

N **21.2.2.1.1** For new systems, 21.2.2.2 shall be used.

N **21.2.2.1.2** For the evaluation or modification of existing systems, 21.2.2.3 shall be permitted to be used.

N **21.2.2.2 New System Criteria.**

N **21.2.2.2.1** Densities shall be selected from Table 21.2.2.2.1 with a design area of 2000 ft² (185 m²).

N **21.2.2.2.2** For back-to-back shelf storage greater than 12 ft (3.7 m) and up to 15 ft (4.6 m), the design density shall be taken from Table 21.2.2.2.1 for storage greater than 18 ft (5.5 m) and up to 20 ft (6.1 m) using ordinary temperature sprinklers.

N **21.2.2.3 Evaluation or Modification of Existing Systems.**

21.2.2.3.1 For the evaluation or modification of existing systems, where using ordinary temperature–rated sprinklers, a single point shall be selected from the appropriate commodity curve on Figure 21.2.2.3.1.

21.2.2.3.2 For the evaluation or modification of existing systems, where using high temperature–rated sprinklers, a single point shall be selected from the appropriate commodity curve on Figure 21.2.2.3.2.

21.2.2.3.3 The densities selected in accordance with 21.2.2.3.1 or 21.2.2.3.2 shall be modified in accordance with Figure 21.2.2.3.3 without revising the design area.

21.2.2.3.4 In the case of metal bin boxes with face areas not exceeding 16 ft² (1.5 m²) and metal closed shelves with face areas not exceeding 16 ft² (1.5 m²), the area of application shall be permitted to be reduced by 33 percent, provided the minimum requirements of 21.2.2.3.5 and 21.2.2.3.6 are met.

N Table 21.2.2.2.1 Sprinkler System Design Density, Storage 12 ft to 30 ft (3.7 m to 9.1 m) High [gpm/ft^2 (mm/min)]

Storage Height		Commodity Class	High-Temperature-Rated Sprinkler	Ordinary-Temperature-Rated Sprinkler
ft	m			
12 to 15	3.7 to 4.6	I	0.15 (6.1)	0.15 (6.1)
		II	0.15 (6.1)	0.16 (6.5)
		III	0.20 (8.2)	0.20 (8.2)
		IV	0.21 (8.6)	0.27 (11.0)
>15 to 18	>4.6 to 5.5	I	0.15 (6.1)	0.19 (7.7)
		II	0.15 (6.1)	0.21 (8.6)
		III	0.20 (8.2)	0.26 (10.6)
		IV	0.27 (11.0)	0.35 (14.3)
>18 to 20	>5.5 to 6.1	I	0.15 (6.1)	0.21 (8.6)
		II	0.17 (6.9)	0.23 (9.4)
		III	0.21 (8.6)	0.29 (11.8)
		IV	0.30 (12.2)	0.39 (15.9)
>20 to 22	>6.1 to 6.7	I	0.17 (6.9)	0.23 (9.4)
		II	0.19 (7.7)	0.25 (10.2)
		III	0.23 (9.4)	0.32 (13.0)
		IV	0.33 (13.4)	0.43 (17.5)
>22 to 25	>6.7 to 7.6	I	0.20 (8.2)	0.28 (11.4)
		II	0.23 (9.4)	0.31 (12.6)
		III	0.28 (11.4)	0.39 (15.9)
		IV	0.41 (16.7)	0.53 (21.6)
>25 to 28	>7.6 to 8.5	I	0.25 (10.2)	0.35 (14.3)
		II	0.28 (11.4)	0.38 (15.5)
		III	0.35 (14.3)	0.48 (19.6)
		IV	0.50 (20.4)	0.64 (26.1)
>28 to 30	>8.5 to 9.1	I	0.29 (11.8)	0.40 (16.3)
		II	0.32 (13.0)	0.44 (17.9)
		III	0.40 (16.3)	0.55 (22.4)
		IV	0.57 (23.2)	0.74 (30.2)

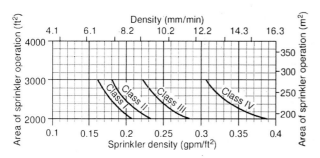

FIGURE 21.2.2.3.1   For the Evaluation or Modification of Existing Systems, Sprinkler System Design Curves for 20 ft (6.1 m) High Storage — Ordinary Temperature–Rated Sprinklers.

21.2.2.3.5 For storage greater than 12 ft (3.7 m), the design density shall not be less than 0.15 gpm/ft^2 (6.1 mm/min), and the design area shall not be less than 2000 ft^2 (185 m^2) for wet systems or 2600 ft^2 (240 m^2) for dry systems for any commodity, class, or group.

21.2.2.3.6 For storage greater than 12 ft (3.7 m), the sprinkler design density for any given area of operation for a Class III or Class IV commodity, calculated in accordance with 21.2.2, shall not be less than the density for the corresponding area of operation for ordinary hazard Group 2.

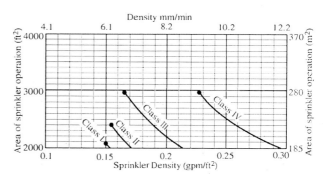

Δ FIGURE 21.2.2.3.2   For the Evaluation or Modification of Existing Systems, Sprinkler System Design Curves for 20 ft (6.1 m) High Storage — High Temperature–Rated Sprinklers.

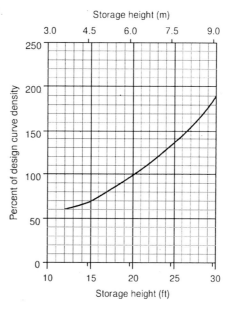

FIGURE 21.2.2.3.3   For the Evaluation or Modification of Existing Systems, Ceiling Sprinkler Density vs. Storage Height.

21.2.2.3.7 For back-to-back shelf storage, the design density shall be taken from Figure 21.2.2.3.1 for storage greater than 12 ft (3.7 m) and up to 15 ft (4.6 m) with no reduction for design density referenced in Figure 21.2.2.3.3.

21.2.3 Encapsulated Storage Over 15 ft (4.6 m) in Height Up to and Including 20 ft (6.1 m) in Height.

21.2.3.1 Encapsulated storage over 15 ft (4.6 m) in height up to and including 20 ft (6.1 m) in height shall be limited to solid-piled and palletized storage.

21.2.3.2 Encapsulated storage over 15 ft (4.6 m) in height up to and including 20 ft (6.1 m) in height shall be protected by sprinklers with a K-factor of 11.2 (160) or larger.

21.2.3.3 Encapsulated storage over 15 ft (4.6 m) in height up to and including 20 ft (6.1 m) in height of Class I commodity shall be protected with a density/area of at least 0.46 gpm/ft^2 over 2000 ft^2 (18.7 mm/min over 185 m^2).

21.2.3.4 Encapsulated storage over 15 ft (4.6 m) in height up to and including 20 ft (6.1 m) in height of Class II commodity shall be protected with a density/area of at least 0.53 gpm/ft² over 2000 ft² (21.6 mm/min over 185 m²).

21.2.3.5 Encapsulated storage over 15 ft (4.6 m) in height up to and including 20 ft (6.1 m) in height of Class III and Class IV commodity shall be protected with a density/area of at least 0.6 gpm/ft² over 2000 ft² (24.5 mm/min over 185 m²).

21.3 Control Mode Density/Area Sprinkler Protection Criteria for Palletized, Solid-Piled, Bin Box, Shelf, or Back-to-Back Shelf Storage of Plastic and Rubber Commodities.

21.3.1 Protection for plastic and rubber commodities shall be in accordance with Section 21.3. The decision tree shown in Figure 21.3.1 shall be used to determine the protection in each specific situation, subject to the following limitations:

(1) Commodities that are stored palletized, solid piled, or in bin boxes up to 25 ft (7.6 m) in height.
(2) Commodities that are stored in shelf storage up to 15 ft (4.6 m) in height.
(3) Commodities that are stored using back-to-back shelf storage up to 15 ft (4.6 m) in height. The minimum aisle width shall be 5 ft (1.5 m). The design criteria shall be in accordance with Table 21.3.1. The back-to-back shelf shall have a full height solid vertical transverse barrier of ⅜ in. (10 mm) plywood or particleboard, .78 mm sheet metal, or equivalent, from face of aisle to face of aisle, spaced at a maximum 45 ft (14 m) interval. The transverse barrier shall be permitted to terminate at the longitudinal barrier.

21.3.2* Factors affecting protection requirements such as closed/open array, clearance to ceiling, and stable/unstable piles shall be applicable only to storage of Group A plastics. This decision tree also shall be used to determine protection for commodities that are not wholly Group A plastics but contain such quantities and arrangements of the same that they are deemed more hazardous than Class IV commodities.

21.3.3* Design areas and densities for the appropriate storage configuration shall be selected from Table 21.3.3(a) or Table 21.3.3(b) as appropriate.

Δ **21.3.3.1*** For Table 21.3.3(a) and Table 21.3.3(b), the design areas shall be as follows:

(1) The area shall be a minimum of 2500 ft² (230 m²).
(2) Where Table 21.3.3(a) and Table 21.3.3(b) allow densities and areas to be selected in accordance with Extra Hazard Group 1 and Group 2, including 19.2.3.1.1, the following area reductions shall be permitted:

(a) For K-8.0 (115) sprinklers used with Extra Hazard Group 1, the design area shall be permitted to be reduced by 25 percent, but not below 2000 ft² (185 m²), where high temperature–sprinklers are used.
(b) For K-11.2 (160) or larger sprinklers, the design area shall be permitted to be reduced by 25 percent, but not below 2000 ft² (185 m²), regardless of sprinkler temperature rating.

(3) For closed arrays, the area shall be permitted to be reduced to 2000 ft² (185 m²).

Table 21.3.1 Back-to-Back Shelf Storage of Cartoned Nonexpanded Group A Plastics

Storage Height		Ceiling Height		Protection
ft	m	ft	m	
Over 5 up to 8	1.5/2.4	Up to 14	4.3	Ordinary Hazard Group 2
Up to 12	3.7	Up to 15	4.6	0.45 gpm/ft² over 2500 ft² 18.3 mm/min/230 m²
Up to 12	3.7	Up to 30	9.1	0.6 gpm/ft² over 2500 ft² 24.5 mm/min/232 m²
Up to 15	4.6	Up to 30	9.1	0.7 gpm/ft² over 2500 ft² 28.5 mm/min/230 m²

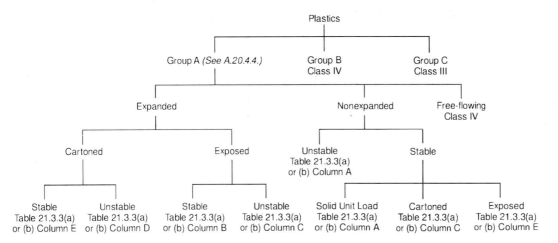

Δ **FIGURE 21.3.1   Decision Tree.**

Δ Table 21.3.3(a) Design Densities for Palletized, Solid-Piled, Bin Box, or Shelf Storage of Group A Plastic Commodities (U.S. Customary Units)

Maximum Storage Height (ft)	Roof/Ceiling Height (ft)	Density (gpm/ft²)				
		A	B	C	D	E
>5 to ≤12	Up to 15	0.2	EH2	0.3	EH1	EH2
	>15 to 20	0.3	0.6	0.5	EH2	EH2
	>20 to 32	0.4	0.8	0.6	0.45	0.7
15	Up to 20	0.3	0.6	0.5	0.4	0.45
	>20 to 25	0.4	0.8	0.6	0.45	0.7
	>25 to 35	0.45	0.9	0.7	0.55	0.85
20	Up to 25	0.4	0.8	0.6	0.45	0.7
	>25 to 30	0.45	0.9	0.7	0.55	0.85
	>30 to 35	0.6	1.2	0.85	0.7	1.1
25	Up to 30	0.45	0.9	0.7	0.55	0.85
	>30 to 35	0.6	1.2	0.85	0.7	1.1

Notes:
(1) Minimum clearance between sprinkler deflector and top of storage shall be maintained as required.
(2) Column designations correspond to the configuration of plastics storage as follows:
  A: (1) Nonexpanded, unstable
    (2) Nonexpanded, stable, solid unit load
  B: Expanded, exposed, stable
  C: (1) Expanded, exposed, unstable
    (2) Nonexpanded, stable, cartoned
  D: Expanded, cartoned, unstable
  E: (1) Expanded, cartoned, stable
    (2) Nonexpanded, stable, exposed
(3) EH1 = Density required by Extra Hazard Group 1 and 19.3.3.1.1
  EH2 = Density required by Extra Hazard Group 2 and 19.3.3.1.1
(4) Roof/ceiling height greater than 35 ft is not permitted.

21.3.3.2* Interpolation of densities between storage heights shall be permitted.

21.3.3.2.1 Interpolation of ceiling/roof heights shall not be permitted.

Δ 21.3.4 The ceiling-only protection criteria specified in Chapter 21 for rack storage of Group A plastic commodities shall be permitted to be used for solid-piled and palletized storage of the same commodity at the same height and clearance to ceiling.

21.3.5 For storage of Group A plastics between 5 ft (1.5 m) and 12 ft (3.7 m) in height, the installation requirements for extra hazard systems shall apply.

21.4 Control Mode Density/Area Sprinkler Protection Criteria for Rack Storage of Class I Through Class IV Commodities.

21.4.1 Protection Criteria for Rack Storage of Class I Through Class IV Commodities Stored Over 12 ft (3.7 m) Up to and Including 25 ft (7.6 m) in Height.

Δ 21.4.1.1* General.

N 21.4.1.1.1 Ceiling sprinkler water demand for new systems shall be determined in accordance with 21.4.1.2.2.1 for single- and double-row racks or 21.4.1.6 and 21.4.1.3.2.1 for multiple-row racks. *(See Section C.14.)*

N 21.4.1.1.2 Ceiling sprinkler water demand for the evaluation or modification of existing systems shall be permitted to be determined in accordance with 21.4.1.2.3 for single- and double-row racks or 21.4.1.3.1.2 and 21.4.1.3.2.2 for multiple-row racks. *(See Section C.14.)*

N 21.4.1.2 Protection Criteria for Single- or Double-Row Rack Storage of Class I Through Class IV Commodities Stored Over 12 ft (3.7 m) Up to and Including 25 ft (7.6 m) in Height.

N 21.4.1.2.1 New Systems Criteria for Single- or Double-Row Rack Storage of Class I Through Class IV Commodities Stored Over 12 ft (3.7 m) Up to and Including 25 ft (7.6 m) in Height.

N 21.4.1.2.1.1 For single- or double-row racks for Class I, Class II, Class III, or Class IV commodities, encapsulated or nonencapsulated, the ceiling sprinkler water demand in terms of density [gpm/ft² (mm/min)] and area of sprinkler operation [ft² (m²) of ceiling or roof] shall be selected from the criteria in Table 21.4.1.2.1.1(a) through Table 21.4.1.2.1.1(e) that are appropriate for each commodity and configuration and shall be modified as appropriate by 21.4.1.4.

Δ Table 21.3.3(b) Design Densities for Palletized, Solid-Piled, Bin Box, or Shelf Storage of Group A Plastic Commodities (S.I. Units)

Maximum Storage Height (m)	Roof/Ceiling Height (m)	Density (mm/min)				
		A	B	C	D	E
>1.5 to ≤3.6	Up to 4.6	8.2	EH2	12.2	EH1	EH2
	>4.6 to 6.1	12.2	24.5	20.4	EH2	EH2
	>6.1 to 9.7	16.3	32.6	24.5	18.3	28.5
4.6	Up to 6.1	12.2	24.5	20.4	16.3	18.3
	>6.1 to 7.6	16.3	32.6	24.5	18.3	28.5
	>7.6 to 10.7	18.3	36.7	28.5	22.4	34.6
6.1	Up to 7.6	16.3	32.6	24.5	18.3	28.5
	>7.6 to 9.1	18.3	36.7	28.5	22.4	34.6
	>9.1 to 10.7	24.5	48.9	34.6	28.5	44.8
7.6	Up to 9.1	18.3	36.7	28.5	22.4	34.6
	>9.1 to 10.7	24.5	48.9	34.6	28.5	44.8

Notes:

(1) Minimum clearance between sprinkler deflector and top of storage shall be maintained as required.

(2) Column designations correspond to the configuration of plastics storage as follows:

   A: (1) Nonexpanded, unstable
      (2) Nonexpanded, stable, solid unit load
   B: Expanded, exposed, stable
   C: (1) Expanded, exposed, unstable
      (2) Nonexpanded, stable, cartoned
   D: Expanded, cartoned, unstable
   E: (1) Expanded, cartoned, stable
      (2) Nonexpanded, stable, exposed

(3) EH1 = Density required by Extra Hazard Group 1 and 19.3.3.1.1
    EH2 = Density required by Extra Hazard Group 2 and 19.3.3.1.1

(4) Roof/ceiling height greater than 11 m is not permitted.

N Table 21.4.1.2.1.1(a) Single- or Double-Row Racks — Storage Height Up to and Including 15 ft (4.6 m) [gpm/ft² (mm/min)]

Commodity Class	Encapsulated	In-Rack Sprinklers Mandatory	Aisles ft (m)	High-Temperature-Rated Sprinkler	Ordinary-Temperature-Rated Sprinkler
I	No	No	4 (1.2)	0.19 (7.7)	0.22 (9.0)
			8 (2.4)	0.17 (6.9)	0.20 (8.1)
	Yes	No	4 (1.2)	0.33 (13.4)[a]	0.33 (13.4)[b]
			8 (2.4)	0.28 (11.4)	0.32 (13.0)
II	No	No	4 (1.2)	0.23 (9.4)	0.26 (10.6)
			8 (2.4)	0.20 (8.2)	0.22 (9.0)
	Yes	No	4 (1.2)	0.33 (13.4)[a]	0.33 (13.4)[b]
			8 (2.4)	0.28 (11.4)	0.32 (13.0)
III	No	No	4 (1.2)	0.26 (10.6)	0.29 (11.8)
			8 (2.4)	0.22 (9.0)	0.25 (10.2)
	Yes	Yes	4 (1.2) 8 (2.4)	See Chapter 25.	
IV	No	No	4 (1.2)	0.35 (14.3)	0.36 (14.7)[c]
			8 (2.4)	0.30 (12.2)	0.34 (13.9)
	Yes	Yes	4 (1.2) 8 (2.4)	See Chapter 25.	

[a]Design area is 2400 ft² (220 m²).
[b]Design area is 4000 ft² (370 m²).
[c]Design area is 3000 ft² (280 m²).

N Table 21.4.1.2.1.1(b) Single- or Double-Row Racks —Storage Height Greater Than 15 ft (4.6 m) Up to and Including 18 ft (5.5 m) [gpm/ft² (mm/min)]

Commodity Class	Encapsulated	In-Rack Sprinklers Mandatory	Aisles ft (m)	High-Temperature-Rated Sprinkler	Ordinary-Temperature-Rated Sprinkler
I	No	No	4 (1.2)	0.27 (11.0)	0.31 (12.6)
			8 (2.4)	0.25 (10.2)	0.28 (11.4)
	Yes	No	4 (1.2)	0.47 (19.2)[a]	0.47 (19.2)[b]
			8 (2.4)	0.40 (16.3)	0.46 (18.7)
II	No	No	4 (1.2)	0.32 (13.0)	0.37 (15.1)
			8 (2.4)	0.28 (11.4)	0.31 (12.6)
	Yes	No	4 (1.2)	0.47 (19.2)[a]	0.47 (19.2)[b]
			8 (2.4)	0.40 (16.3)	0.46 (18.7)
III	No	No	4 (1.2)	0.37 (15.1)	0.42 (17.1)
			8 (2.4)	0.31 (12.6)	0.36 (14.7)
	Yes	Yes	4 (1.2)	See Chapter 25.	
			8 (2.4)		
IV	No	No	4 (1.2)	0.49 (20.0)	0.51 (20.8)[c]
			8 (2.4)	0.42 (17.1)	0.48 (19.6)
	Yes	Yes	4 (1.2)	See Chapter 25.	
			8 (2.4)		

[a]Design area is 2400 ft² (220 m²).
[b]Design area is 4000 ft² (370 m²).
[c]Design area is 3000 ft² (280 m²).

N Table 21.4.1.2.1.1(c) Single- or Double-Row Racks — Storage Height Greater Than 18 ft (5.5 m) Up to and Including 20 ft (6.1 m) [gpm/ft² (mm/min)]

Commodity Class	Encapsulated	In-Rack Sprinklers Mandatory	Aisles ft (m)	High-Temperature-Rated Sprinkler	Ordinary-Temperature-Rated Sprinkler
I	No	No	4 (1.2)	0.32 (13.0)	0.37 (15.1)
			8 (2.4)	0.29 (11.8)	0.33 (13.4)
	Yes	No	4 (1.2)	0.55 (22.4)[a]	0.55 (22.4)[b]
			8 (2.4)	0.47 (19.1)	0.54 (21.9)
II	No	No	4 (1.2)	0.38 (15.5)	0.44 (17.9)
			8 (2.4)	0.33 (13.5)	0.37 (15.1)
	Yes	No	4 (1.2)	0.55 (22.4)[a]	0.55 (22.4)[b]
			8 (2.4)	0.47 (19.1)	0.54 (21.9)
III	No	No	4 (1.2)	0.43 (17.5)	0.49 (19.9)
			8 (2.4)	0.37 (15.1)	0.42 (17.1)
	Yes	Yes	4 (1.2)	See Chapter 25.	
			8 (2.4)		
IV	No	No	4 (1.2)	0.58 (23.7)	0.60 (24.5)[c]
			8 (2.4)	0.50 (20.4)	0.57 (23.2)
	Yes	Yes	4 (1.2)	See Chapter 25.	
			8 (2.4)		

[a]Design area is 2400 ft² (220 m²).
[b]Design area is 4000 ft² (370 m²).
[c]Design area is 3000 ft² (280 m²).

N Table 21.4.1.2.1.1(d) Single- or Double-Row Racks — Storage Height Greater Than 20 ft (6.1 m)
Up to and Including 22 ft (6.7 m) [gpm/ft² (mm/min)]

Commodity Class	Encapsulated	In-Rack Sprinklers Mandatory	Aisles ft (m)	High-Temperature-Rated Sprinkler	Ordinary-Temperature-Rated Sprinkler
I	No	No	4 (1.2)	0.42 (17.1)	0.48 (19.6)
			8 (2.4)	0.38 (15.5)	0.43 (17.5)
	Yes	Yes	4 (1.2)	See Chapter 25.	
			8 (2.4)		
II	No	No	4 (1.2)	0.49 (20.0)	0.57 (23.2)
			8 (2.4)	0.43 (17.5)	0.48 (19.6)
	Yes	Yes	4 (1.2)	See Chapter 25.	
			8 (2.4)		
III	No	No	4 (1.2)	0.56 (22.8)	0.64 (26.1)
			8 (2.4)	0.48 (19.6)	0.55 (22.4)
	Yes	Yes	4 (1.2)	See Chapter 25.	
			8 (2.4)		
IV	No	No	4 (1.2)	0.75 (30.5)	0.78 (31.7)*
			8 (2.4)	0.65 (26.5)	0.74 (30.1)
	Yes	Yes	4 (1.2)	See Chapter 25.	
			8 (2.4)		

*Design area is 3000 ft² (280 m²).

N Table 21.4.1.2.1.1(e) Single- or Double-Row Racks — Storage Height Greater Than 22 ft (6.7 m)
Up to and Including 25 ft (7.6 m) [gpm/ft² (mm/min)]

Commodity Class	Encapsulated	In-Rack Sprinklers Mandatory	Aisles ft (m)	High-Temperature-Rated Sprinkler	Ordinary-Temperature-Rated Sprinkler
I	No	No	4 (1.2)	0.56 (22.8)	0.65 (26.9)
			8 (2.4)	0.51 (20.8)	0.58 (23.6)
	Yes	Yes	4 (1.2)	See Chapter 25.	
			8 (2.4)		
II	No	No	4 (1.2)	0.67 (27.3)	0.77 (31.3)
			8 (2.4)	0.58 (23.7)	0.65 (26.5)
	Yes	Yes	4 (1.2)	See Chapter 25.	
			8 (2.4)		
III	No	No	4 (1.2)	0.75 (30.5)	0.86 (34.9)
			8 (2.4)	0.65 (26.5)	0.74 (30.1)
	Yes	Yes	4 (1.2)	See Chapter 25.	
			8 (2.4)		
IV	No	Yes	4 (1.2)	See Chapter 25.	
			8 (2.4)		
	Yes	Yes	4 (1.2)		
			8 (2.4)		

N **21.4.1.2.1.2** The requirements in 21.4.1.2.1.1 shall apply to portable racks arranged in the same manner as single- or double-row racks.

N **21.4.1.2.1.3** Unless otherwise indicated in Table 21.4.1.2.1.1(a) through Table 21.4.1.2.1.1(e), the minimum design area shall be 2000 ft² (185 m²).

N **21.4.1.2.2 Evaluation or Modification of Existing Systems for Single- or Double-Row Rack Storage of Class I Through Class IV Commodities Stored Over 12 ft (3.7 m) Up to and Including 25 ft (7.6 m) in Height.**

Δ **21.4.1.2.2.1*** For single- or double-row racks for Class I, Class II, Class III, or Class IV commodities, encapsulated or nonencapsulated in single- or double-row racks, ceiling sprinkler water demand in terms of density [gpm/ft² (mm/min)] and area of sprinkler operation [ft² (m²) of ceiling or roof] shall be selected from the density/area curves of Figure 21.4.1.2.2.1(a) through Figure 21.4.1.2.2.1(e) that are appropriate for each commodity and configuration as shown in Table 21.4.1.2.2.1 and shall be modified as appropriate by 21.4.1.7.

N **21.4.1.2.2.2** The requirements in 21.4.1.2.2.1 shall apply to portable racks arranged in the same manner as single- or double-row racks.

21.4.1.2.3* Design densities for single- and double-row racks shall be selected to correspond to aisle width in 21.4.1.2. (*See Section C.15.*)

21.4.1.2.3.1 For aisle widths between 4 ft (1.2 m) and 8 ft (2.4 m), the rules for 4 ft (1.2 m) aisle width shall be used or direct linear interpolation between the densities shall be permitted.

21.4.1.2.3.2 The density given for 8 ft (2.4 m) wide aisles shall be applied to aisles wider than 8 ft (2.4 m).

21.4.1.2.3.3 The density given for 4 ft (1.2 m) wide aisles shall be applied to aisles more narrow than 4 ft (1.2 m) down to 3½ ft (1.1 m).

21.4.1.2.3.4 Where aisles are more narrow than 3½ ft (1.1 m), racks shall be considered to be multiple-row racks.

N **21.4.1.3 Protection for Multiple-Row Racks — Rack Depth Up to and Including 16 ft (4.9 m), Aisles 8 ft (2.4 m) or Wider, Storage Height Over 12 ft (3.7 m) Up to and Including 25 ft (7.6 m).**

N **21.4.1.3.1 New System Criteria — Rack Depth Up to and Including 16 ft (4.9 m), Aisles 8 ft (2.4 m) or Wider, Storage Height Over 12 ft (3.7 m) Up to and Including 25 ft (7.6 m).**

N **21.4.1.3.1.1** For Class I, Class II, Class III, or Class IV commodities, encapsulated or nonencapsulated, ceiling sprinkler water demand in terms of density [gpm/ft² (mm/min)] and area of sprinkler operation [ft² (m²) of ceiling or roof] shall be selected from the criteria in Table 21.4.1.3.1.1(a) through Table 21.4.1.3.1.1(e) that are appropriate for each commodity and configuration and shall be modified as appropriate by 21.4.1.4.

N **21.4.1.3.1.2** The protection criteria in accordance with 21.4.1.3.1.1 shall apply to portable racks arranged in the same manner as multiple-row racks.

N **21.4.1.3.1.3** Unless otherwise indicated in Table 21.4.1.3.1.1(a) through Table 21.4.1.3.1.1(e), the minimum design area shall be 2000 ft² (185 m²).

N **21.4.1.3.2 Evaluation or Modification of Existing Systems — Rack Depth Up to and Including 16 ft (4.9), Aisles 8 ft (2.4) or Wider, Storage Height Over 12 ft (3.7 m) Up to and Including 25 ft (7.6 m).**

Δ **21.4.1.3.2.1 Multiple-Row Racks — Rack Depth Up to and Including 16 ft (4.9 m) with Aisles 8 ft (2.4 m) or Wider.** For Class I, Class II, Class III, or Class IV commodities, encapsulated or nonencapsulated, ceiling sprinkler water demand in terms of density [gpm/ft² (mm/min)] and area of sprinkler operation [ft² (m²) of ceiling or roof] shall be selected from the density/area curves of Figure 21.4.1.2.2.1(a) through Figure 21.4.1.2.2.1(e) that are appropriate for each commodity and configuration as shown in Table 21.4.1.3.2.1 and shall be modified as appropriate by 21.4.1.7.

N **21.4.1.3.2.2** The protection criteria in accordance with 21.4.1.3.2.1 shall apply to portable racks arranged in the same manner as multiple-row racks.

N **21.4.1.4 Protection for Multiple-Row Racks — Rack Depth Over 16 ft (4.9 m) or Aisles Narrower Than 8 ft (2.4 m), Storage Height Over 12 ft (3.7 m) Up to and Including 25 ft (7.6 m).**

N **21.4.1.4.1 New System Criteria — Rack Depth Over 16 ft (4.9 m) or Aisles More Narrow Than 8 ft (2.4 m), Storage Height Over 12 ft (3.7 m) Up to and Including 25 ft (7.6 m).**

N **21.4.1.4.1.1** For Class I, Class II, Class III, or Class IV commodities, encapsulated or nonencapsulated, storage height up to and including 15 ft. (4.6 m), the ceiling sprinkler water demand in terms of density [gpm/ft² (mm/min)] and area of sprinkler operation [ft² (m²) of ceiling or roof] appropriate for each commodity and configuration shall be selected from Table 21.4.1.4.1.1 and shall be modified as appropriate by 21.4.1.4.

N **21.4.1.4.1.2** Encapsulated or nonencasulated Class I through Class IV commodities stored over 15 ft (4.6 m) shall be in accordance with Chapter 25.

N **21.4.1.4.1.3** The protection criteria in accordance with 21.4.1.4.1.1 shall apply to portable racks arranged in the same manner as multiple-row racks.

Δ **21.4.1.5 Evaluation or Modification of Existing Systems — Rack Depth Over 16 ft (4.9 m) or Aisles More Narrow Than 8 ft (2.4 m), Storage Height Over 12 ft (3.7 m) Up to and Including 25 ft (7.6 m).**

N **21.4.1.5.1** For Class I, Class II, Class III, or Class IV commodities, encapsulated or nonencapsulated, ceiling sprinkler water demand in terms of density [gpm/ft² (mm/min)] and area of sprinkler operation [ft² (m²) of ceiling or roof] shall be selected from the density/area curves of Figure 21.4.1.2.2.1(a) through Figure 21.4.1.2.2.1(e) that are appropriate for each commodity and configuration as shown in Table 21.4.1.5.1 and shall be modified as appropriate by 21.4.1.7.

N **21.4.1.5.2** The protection criteria in accordance with 21.4.1.5.1 shall apply to portable racks arranged in the same manner as multiple-row racks.

Δ Table 21.4.1.2.2.1 Single- or Double-Row Racks — Storage Height Over 12 ft (3.7 m) Up to and Including 25 ft (7.6 m)

Height	Commodity Class	Encapsulated	Aisles*		Ceiling Sprinkler Water Demand		Apply Figure 21.4.1.4.1
			ft	m	Figure	Curves	
Over 12 ft (3.7 m) up to and including 20 ft (6.1 m)	I	No	4	1.2	21.4.1.2.2.1(a)	B and D	Yes
			8	2.4		A and C	
		Yes	4	1.2	21.4.1.2.2.1(e)	C and D	Yes
			8	2.4		A and B	
	II	No	4	1.2	21.4.1.2.2.1(b)	C and D	Yes
			8	2.4		A and B	
		Yes	4	1.2	21.4.1.2.2.1(e)	C and D	Yes
			8	2.4		A and B	
	III	No	4	1.2	21.4.1.2.2.1(c)	C and D	Yes
			8	2.4		A and B	
		Yes	4	1.2	In-rack sprinklers required. See Chapter 25.	NA	NA
			8	2.4			
	IV	No	4	1.2	21.4.1.2.2.1(d)	C and D	Yes
			8	2.4		A and B	
		Yes	4	1.2	In-rack sprinklers required. See Chapter 25.	NA	NA
			8	2.4			
Over 20 ft (6.1 m) up to and including 22 ft (6.7 m)	I	No	4	1.2	21.4.1.2.2.1(a)	A and C	Yes
			8	2.4		B and D	
		Yes	4	1.2	In-rack sprinklers required. See Chapter 25.	NA	NA
			8	2.4			
	II	No	4	1.2	21.4.1.2.2.1(b)	C and D	Yes
			8	2.4		A and B	
		Yes	4	1.2	In-rack sprinklers required. See Chapter 25.	NA	NA
			8	2.4			
	III	No	4	1.2	21.4.1.2.2.1(c)	C and D	Yes
			8	2.4		A and B	
		Yes	4	1.2	In-rack sprinklers required. See Chapter 25.	NA	NA
			8	2.4			
	IV	No	4	1.2	21.4.1.2.2.1(d)	C and D	Yes
			8	2.4		A and B	
		Yes	4	1.2	In-rack sprinklers required. See Chapter 25.	NA	NA
			8	2.4			

(continues)

Shaded text = Revisions.   Δ = Text deletions and figure/table revisions.   • = Section deletions.   *N* = New material.

Δ Table 21.4.1.2.2.1   *Continued*

Height	Commodity Class	Encapsulated	Aisles*		Ceiling Sprinkler Water Demand		Apply Figure 21.4.1.4.1
			ft	m	Figure	Curves	
Over 22 ft (6.7 m) up to and including 25 ft (7.6 m)	I	No	4	1.2	21.4.1.2.2.1(a)	A and C	Yes
			8	2.4		B and D	
		Yes	4	1.2	In-rack sprinklers required. See Chapter 25.	NA	NA
			8	2.4			
	II	No	4	1.2	21.4.1.2.2.1(b)	C and D	Yes
			8	2.4		A and B	
		Yes	4	1.2	In-rack sprinklers required. See Chapter 25.	NA	NA
			8	2.4			
	III	No	4	1.2	21.4.1.2.2.1(c)	C and D	Yes
			8	2.4		A and B	
		Yes	4	1.2	In-rack sprinklers required. See Chapter 25.	NA	NA
			8	2.4			
	IV	No	4	1.2	In-rack sprinklers required. See Chapter 25.	NA	NA
			8	2.4			
		Yes	4	1.2	In-rack sprinklers required. See Chapter 25.	NA	NA
			8	2.4			

NA: Not applicable.
*See 21.4.1.2.3 for interpolation of aisle widths.

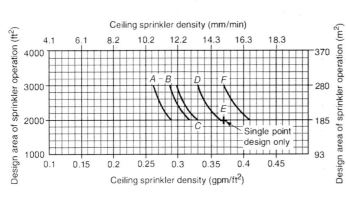

Curve   Legend

A — Single- or double-row racks with 8 ft (2.4 m) aisles and high-temperature ceiling sprinklers

B — Single- or double-row racks with 4 ft (1.2 m) aisles and high-temperature ceiling sprinklers

C — Single- or double-row racks with 8 ft (2.4 m) aisles and ordinary-temperature ceiling sprinklers

D — Single- or double-row racks with 4 ft (1.2 m) aisles and ordinary-temperature ceiling sprinklers

E — Multiple-row racks with 8 ft (2.4 m) or wider aisles and high-temperature ceiling sprinklers

F — Multiple-row racks with 8 ft (2.4 m) or wider aisles and ordinary-temperature ceiling sprinklers

FIGURE 21.4.1.2.2.1(a)   Sprinkler System Design Curves — 20 ft (6.1 m) High Rack Storage — Class I Nonencapsulated Commodities — Conventional Pallets.

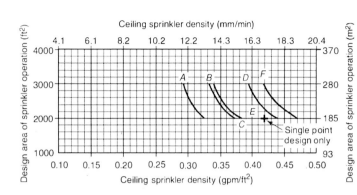

Curve   Legend

A — Single- or double-row racks with 8 ft (2.4 m) aisles and high-temperature ceiling sprinklers

B — Single- or double-row racks with 8 ft (2.4 m) aisles and ordinary-temperature ceiling sprinklers

C — Single- or double-row racks with 4 ft (1.2 m) aisles and high-temperature ceiling sprinklers

D — Single- or double-row racks with 4 ft (1.2 m) aisles and ordinary-temperature ceiling sprinklers

E — Multiple-row racks with 8 ft (2.4 m) or wider aisles and high-temperature ceiling sprinklers

F — Multiple-row racks with 8 ft (2.4 m) or wider aisles and ordinary-temperature ceiling sprinklers

FIGURE 21.4.1.2.2.1(b)   Sprinkler System Design Curves — 20 ft (6.1 m) High Rack Storage — Class II Nonencapsulated Commodities — Conventional Pallets.

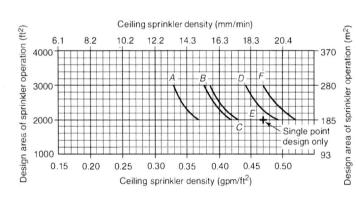

Curve   Legend

A — Single- or double-row racks with 8 ft (2.4 m) aisles and high-temperature ceiling sprinklers

B — Single- or double-row racks with 8 ft (2.4 m) aisles and ordinary-temperature ceiling sprinklers

C — Single- or double-row racks with 4 ft (1.2 m) aisles and high-temperature ceiling sprinklers

D — Single- or double-row racks with 4 ft (1.2 m) aisles and ordinary-temperature ceiling sprinklers

E — Multiple-row racks with 8 ft (2.4 m) or wider aisles and high-temperature ceiling sprinklers

F — Multiple-row racks with 8 ft (2.4 m) or wider aisles and ordinary-temperature ceiling sprinklers

FIGURE 21.4.1.2.2.1(c)   Sprinkler System Design Curves — 20 ft (6.1 m) High Rack Storage — Class III Nonencapsulated Commodities — Conventional Pallets.

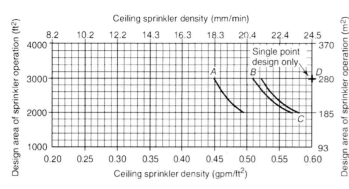

Note: Curves *C* and *D* also apply to ceiling sprinklers only for multiple-row rack storage up to and including 15 ft (4.6 m) high, and Figure 21.4.1.4.1 shall not be applied.

Δ **FIGURE 21.4.1.2.2.1(d)** Sprinkler System Design Curves — 20 ft (6.1 m) High Rack Storage — Class IV Nonencapsulated Commodities — Conventional Pallets.

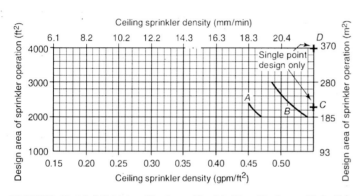

FIGURE 21.4.1.2.2.1(e) Single- or Double-Row Racks — 20 ft (6.1 m) High Rack Storage — Sprinkler System Design Curves — Class I and Class II Encapsulated Commodities — Conventional Pallets.

N Table 21.4.1.3.1.1(a) Multiple-Row Racks — Rack Depth Up to and Including 16 ft (4.9 m), Aisles 8 ft (2.4 m) or Wider, Storage Height Up to and Including 15 ft (4.6 m) [gpm/ft² (mm/min)]

Commodity Class	Encapsulated	In-Rack Sprinklers Mandatory	High-Temperature-Rated Sprinkler	Ordinary-Temperature-Rated Sprinkler
I	No	No	0.22 (9.0)	0.25 (10.2)
	Yes	No	0.28 (11.4)	0.31 (12.6)
II	No	No	0.25 (10.2)	0.28 (11.4)
	Yes	No	0.32 (13.0)	0.35 (14.3)
III	No	No	0.28 (11.4)	0.31 (12.6)
	Yes	Yes	See Chapter 25.	
IV	No	Yes	See Chapter 25.	
	Yes	Yes	See Chapter 25.	

N Table 21.4.1.3.1.1(b) Multiple-Row Racks — Rack Depth Up to and Including 16 ft (4.9 m), Aisles 8 ft (2.4 m) or Wider, Storage Height Above 15 ft (4.6 m) Up to and Including 18 ft (5.5 m) [gpm/ft² (mm/min)]

Commodity Class	Encapsulated	In-Rack Sprinklers Mandatory	High-Temperature-Rated Sprinkler	Ordinary-Temperature-Rated Sprinkler
I	No	No	0.31 (12.6)	0.35 (14.3)
	Yes	No	0.39 (15.9)	0.44 (17.9)
II	No	No	0.36 (14.7)	0.40 (16.3)
	Yes	No	0.45 (18.3)	0.50 (20.4)
III	No	No	0.40 (16.3)	0.44 (17.9)
	Yes	Yes	See Chapter 25.	
IV	No	Yes	See Chapter 25.	
	Yes	Yes	See Chapter 25.	

N Table 21.4.1.3.1.1(c) Multiple-Row Racks — Rack Depth Up to and Including 16 ft (4.9 m), Aisles 8 ft (2.4 m) or Wider, Storage Height Above 18 ft (5.5 m) Up to and Including 20 ft (6.1 m) [gpm/ft² (mm/min)]

Commodity Class	Encapsulated	In-Rack Sprinklers Mandatory	High-Temperature-Rated Sprinkler	Ordinary-Temperature-Rated Sprinkler
I	No	No	0.37 (15.1)	0.41 (16.7)
	Yes	No	0.46 (18.7)	0.51 (20.8)
II	No	No	0.42 (17.1)	0.47 (19.2)
	Yes	No	0.53 (21.6)	0.59 (24.0)
III	No	No	0.47 (19.1)	0.52 (21.2)
	Yes	Yes	See Chapter 25.	
IV	No	Yes	See Chapter 25.	
	Yes	Yes	See Chapter 25.	

N Table 21.4.1.3.1.1(d) Multiple-Row Racks — Rack Depth Up to and Including 16 ft (4.9 m), Aisles 8 ft (2.4 m) or Wider, Storage Height Above 20 ft (6.1 m) Up to and Including 22 ft (6.7 m) [gpm/ft² (mm/min)]

Commodity Class	Encapsulated	In-Rack Sprinklers Mandatory	High-Temperature-Rated Sprinkler	Ordinary-Temperature-Rated Sprinkler
I	No	No	0.48 (19.6)	0.53 (21.6)
	Yes	Yes	See Chapter 25.	
II	No	Yes	See Chapter 25.	
	Yes	Yes	See Chapter 25.	
III	No	Yes	See Chapter 25.	
	Yes	Yes	See Chapter 25.	
IV	No	Yes	See Chapter 25.	
	Yes	Yes	See Chapter 25.	

N Table 21.4.1.3.1.1(e) Multiple-Row Racks — Rack Depth Up to and Including 16 ft (4.9 m), Aisles 8 ft (2.4 m) or Wider, Storage Height Above 22 ft (6.7 m) Up to and Including 25 ft (7.6 m) [gpm/ft^2 (mm/min)]

Commodity Class	Encapsulated	In-Rack Sprinklers Mandatory	High-Temperature-Rated Sprinkler	Ordinary-Temperature-Rated Sprinkler
I	No	No	0.65 (26.5)	0.72 (29.3)
	Yes	Yes	See Chapter 25.	
II	No	Yes	See Chapter 25.	
	Yes	Yes	See Chapter 25.	
III	No	Yes	See Chapter 25.	
	Yes	Yes	See Chapter 25.	
IV	No	Yes	See Chapter 25.	
	Yes	Yes	See Chapter 25.	

Δ **21.4.1.6 Multiple-Row Racks — Storage Height Over 12 ft (3.7 m) Up to and Including 25 ft (7.6 m).**

21.4.1.6.1 Where Class I, Class II, and Class III commodities are encapsulated, ceiling sprinkler density shall be 25 percent greater than for nonencapsulated.

21.4.1.6.2 Where Class IV commodities are encapsulated, ceiling sprinkler density shall be 50 percent greater than for nonencapsulated.

21.4.1.7 Ceiling Sprinkler Density Adjustments.

21.4.1.7.1 For the evaluation or modification of an existing system with storage height over 12 ft (3.7 m) up to and including 25 ft (7.6 m) protected with ceiling sprinklers only, densities obtained from design curves shall be adjusted in accordance with Figure 21.4.1.7.1.

Δ **21.4.1.7.2** Where solid, flat-bottom, combustible pallets (slave pallets) are used with storage height up to and including 25 ft (7.6 m), the densities that are indicated based on conventional pallets shall be increased 20 percent for the given area.

21.4.1.7.2.1 The percentage shall be applied to the density determined in accordance with 21.4.1.7.

21.4.1.7.2.2 The increase in density shall not apply where in-rack sprinklers are utilized in the design.

21.4.2 Control Mode Density/Area Sprinkler Protection Criteria for Rack Storage of Class I Through Class IV Commodities Stored Over 25 ft (7.6 m) in Height.

21.4.2.1* The protection criteria requirements for rack storage of Class I through Class IV commodities stored over 25 ft (7.6 m) in height protected by CMDA sprinklers shall be in accordance with Chapter 25.

21.4.2.2 Where such storage is encapsulated, ceiling sprinkler density shall be 25 percent greater than for nonencapsulated storage.

21.5 Control Mode Density/Area Sprinkler Protection Criteria for Single-, Double-, and Multiple-Row Racks for Group A Plastic Commodities Stored Up to and Including 25 ft (7.6 m) in Height.

21.5.1 Plastic commodities shall be protected in accordance with this section. *(See Section C.21.)*

21.5.1.1 For Group A plastic commodities in cartons, encapsulated or nonencapsulated in single-, double-, and multiple-row racks and with a clearance to ceiling up to and including 10 ft (3.1 m), ceiling sprinkler water demand in terms of density [gpm/ft^2 (mm/min)] and area of operation [ft^2 (m^2)] shall be selected from Table 21.5.1.1. *(See Section C.22.)*

21.5.1.2 Linear interpolation of design densities and areas of application shall be permitted between storage heights with the same clearance to ceiling.

21.5.1.3 No interpolation between clearance to ceiling shall be permitted.

21.5.1.4 An option shall be selected from Table 21.5.1.1 given the storage height and clearance being protected.

21.5.2 Exposed nonexpanded Group A plastics protected with control mode density/area sprinklers shall be protected in accordance with Table 21.5.2.

21.6 Control Mode Density/Area Sprinkler Protection Criteria for Rack Storage of Group A Plastic Commodities Stored Over 25 ft (7.6 m) in Height for Single-, Double-, and Multiple-Row Racks. The protection criteria requirements for rack storage of Group A plastic commodities stored over 25 ft (7.6 m) in height protected by CMDA sprinklers shall be in accordance with Chapter 25.

Δ **21.7* Control Mode Density/Area Sprinkler Protection Criteria for Storage of Rubber Tires.**

21.7.1 Ceiling Systems. Protection of rubber tire storage by ceiling-only sprinkler arrangements shall be selected from Table 21.7.1(a) or Table 21.7.1(b) or in accordance with Chapter 25 using ceiling and in-rack sprinkler arrangements.

21.8 Control Mode Density/Area Sprinkler Protection Criteria for Roll Paper Storage.

21.8.1 Storage of heavyweight or mediumweight classes of rolled paper up to 10 ft (3.0 m) in height shall be protected by sprinklers designed for ordinary hazard Group 2 densities.

21.8.2 Storage of tissue and lightweight classes of paper up to 10 ft (3.0 m) in height shall be protected by sprinklers in accordance with extra hazard Group 1 densities.

Δ Table 21.4.1.3.2.1 Multiple-Row Racks — Rack Depth Up to and Including 16 ft (4.9 m), Aisles 8 ft (2.4 m) or Wider, and Storage Height Over 12 ft (3.7 m) Up to 25 ft (7.6 m)

| Height | Commodity Class | Encapsulated | Ceiling Sprinkler Water Demand | | | |
			Figure	Curves	Apply Figure 21.4.1.4.1	1.25 × Density
Over 12 ft (3.7 m) up to and including 15 ft (4.6 m)	I	No	21.4.1.2.2.1(a)	E and F	Yes	No
		Yes	21.4.1.2.2.1(a)	E and F		Yes
	II	No	21.4.1.2.2.1(b)	E and F	Yes	No
		Yes	21.4.1.2.2.1(b)	E and F		Yes
	III	No	21.4.1.2.2.1(c)	E and F	Yes	No
		Yes	In-rack sprinklers required. See Chapter 25.	NA	NA	NA
	IV	No	In-rack sprinklers required. See Chapter 25.	NA	No	No
		Yes	In-rack sprinklers required. See Chapter 25.	NA	NA	NA
Over 15 ft (4.6 m) up to and including 20 ft (6.1 m)	I	No	21.4.1.2.2.1(a)	E and F	Yes	No
		Yes	21.4.1.2.2.1(a)	E and F		Yes
	II	No	21.4.1.2.2.1(b)	E and F	Yes	No
		Yes	21.4.1.2.2.1(b)	E and F		Yes
	III	No	21.4.1.2.2.1(c)	E and F	Yes	No
		Yes	In-rack sprinklers required. See Chapter 25.	NA	NA	NA
	IV	No				
		Yes				
Over 20 ft (6.1 m) up to and including 25 ft (7.6 m)	I	No	21.4.1.2.2.1(a)	E and F	Yes	No
		Yes	In-rack sprinklers required. See Chapter 25.	NA	NA	NA
	II	No				
		Yes				
	III	No				
		Yes				
	IV	No				
		Yes				

NA: Not applicable.

N Table 21.4.1.4.1.1 Multiple-Row Racks — Rack Depth Over 16 ft (4.9 m) or Aisles Narrower Than 8 ft (2.4 m), Storage Height Up to and Including 15 ft (4.6 m)

Commodity Class	Encapsulated	In-Rack Sprinklers Mandatory	High-Temperature-Rated Sprinkler	Ordinary-Temperature-Rated Sprinkler
I	No	No	0.22 (9.0)	0.25 (10.2)
	Yes	No	0.28 (11.4)	0.31 (12.6)
II	No	No	0.25 (10.2)	0.28 (11.4)
	Yes	No	0.32 (13.0)	0.35 (14.3)
III	No	No	0.28 (11.4)	0.31 (12.6)
	Yes	Yes	See Chapter 25.	
IV	No	Yes	See Chapter 25.	
	Yes	Yes	See Chapter 25.	

21.8.3 Sprinkler design criteria for storage of roll paper 10 ft (3.0 m) high and higher in buildings or structures with roof or ceilings up to 30 ft (9.1 m) shall be in accordance with Table 21.8.3(a) and Table 21.8.3(b).

21.8.4* High-temperature sprinklers shall be used for installations protecting roll paper stored 15 ft (4.6 m) or higher.

21.8.5 The protection area per sprinkler shall not exceed 100 ft² (9.3 m²) or be less than 70 ft² (6.5 m²).

21.8.6 Where high-expansion foam systems are installed in heavyweight class and mediumweight class storage areas, sprinkler discharge design densities shall be permitted to be reduced to not less than 0.24 gpm/ft² (9.8 mm/min) with a minimum operating area of 2000 ft² (185 m²).

21.8.7 Where high-expansion foam systems are installed in tissue storage areas, sprinkler discharge densities and areas of application shall not be reduced below those provided in Table 21.8.3(a) and Table 21.8.3(b).

Δ Table 21.4.1.5.1 Multiple-Row Racks — Rack Depth Over 16 ft (4.9 m) or Aisles Narrower Than 8 ft (2.4 m), Storage Height Over 12 ft (3.7 m) Up to and Including 25 ft (7.6 m)

Height	Commodity Class	Encapsulated	Ceiling Sprinkler Water Demand			
			Figure	Curves	Apply Figure 21.4.1.4.1	1.25 × Density
Over 12 ft (3.7 m) up to and including 15 ft (4.6 m)	I	No	21.4.1.2.2.1(a)	E and F	Yes	No
	I	Yes	21.4.1.2.2.1(a)	E and F		Yes
	II	No	21.4.1.2.2.1(b)	E and F	Yes	No
	II	Yes	21.4.1.2.2.1(b)	E and F		Yes
	III	No	21.4.1.2.2.1(c)	E and F	Yes	No
	III	Yes	In-rack sprinklers required. See Chapter 25.	NA	NA	NA
	IV	No	In-rack sprinklers required. See Chapter 25.	NA	No	No
	IV	Yes	In-rack sprinklers required. See Chapter 25.	NA	NA	NA
Over 15 ft (4.6 m) up to and including 20 ft (6.1 m)	I	No	In-rack sprinklers required. See Chapter 25.	NA	NA	NA
	I	Yes				
	II	No				
	II	Yes				
	III	No				
	III	Yes				
	IV	No				
	IV	Yes				
Over 20 ft (6.1 m) up to and including 25 ft (7.6 m)	I	No	In-rack sprinklers required. See Chapter 25.	NA	NA	NA
	I	Yes				
	II	No				
	II	Yes				
	III	No				
	III	Yes				
	IV	No				
	IV	Yes				

NA: Not applicable.

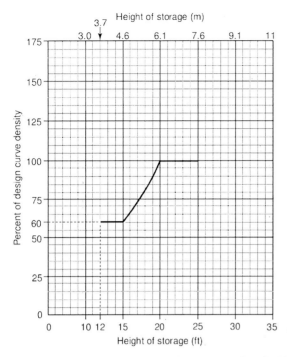

Δ **FIGURE 21.4.1.7.1** **Evaluation or Modification of Existing System's Ceiling Sprinkler Density vs. Storage Height.**

Δ **Table 21.5.1.1 Control Mode Density/Area Sprinkler Protection Criteria for Single-, Double-, and Multiple-Row Racks for Group A Plastic Commodities in Cartons Stored Up to and Including 25 ft (7.6 m) in Height**

Commodity	Storage Height ft (m)	Maximum Clearance from Top of Storage to Ceiling ft (m)	Maximum Ceiling Height ft (m)	Ceiling Sprinklers Density Clearance to Ceiling Up to 10 ft (3.0 m) gpm/ft² (mm/min)	Ceiling Sprinkler Operating Area ft² (m²)
Group A plastic commodities in cartons, encapsulated or nonencapsulated	5 to 10 (1.5 to 3.0)	<5 (<1.5)	<15 (<4.6)	0.30 (12.2)	2000 (185)
		5 to 10 (1.5 to 3.0)	20 (6.1)	0.45 (18.3)	
	15 (4.6)	5 to 10 (1.5 to 3.0)	22 (6.7)	0.45 (18.3)	
		≤10 (≤3.0)	25 (7.7)	0.60 (24.5)	
	20 (6.1)	<5 (<1.5)	<25 (<7.7)	0.60 (24.5)[a]	
		5 to 10 (1.5 to 3.0)	27 (8.2)	0.60 (24.5)	
		≤10 (≤3.0)	30 (9.1)	0.8 (32.6)[b,c]	
	25 (7.7)	5 to 10 (1.5 to 3.0)	35 (11)	See Chapter 25.	

[a]For the protection of single- and double-row racks only.
[b]Ceiling-only protection is not permitted for this storage configuration except where K-16.8 (K-240) spray sprinklers listed for storage use are installed.
[c]For dry systems, the operating area is increased to 4500 ft² (420 m²).

Table 21.5.2 Control Mode Density/Area Sprinkler Protection Criteria for Exposed Nonexpanded Group A Plastics

Commodity	Storage height ft (m)	Maximum Ceiling Height ft (m)	Ceiling Sprinklers Density Clearance to Ceiling Up to 10 ft gpm/ft² (mm/min)	Ceiling Sprinkler Operating Area ft² (m²)
Exposed nonexpanded Group A plastic	10 ft (3.1 m)	20 ft (6.1 m)	0.80 gpm/ft² (32.6 mm/min)	2500 ft² (230 m²)

Δ **Table 21.7.1(a) Protection Criteria for Rubber Tire Storage Using Control Mode Density/Area Sprinklers**

Piling Method	Pile Height [ft (m)]	Sprinkler Discharge Density[a] [gpm/ft² (mm/min)]	Areas of Application[a] [ft² (m²)]	
			Ordinary Temperature	High Temperature
(1) On-floor storage	Up to 5 (1.5)	0.19 (7.7)	2000 (185)	2000 (185)
(a) Pyramid piles, on-side	Over 5 (1.5) to 12 (3.7)	0.30 (12.2)	2500 (230)	2500 (230)
(b) Other arrangements such that no horizontal channels are formed[b]	Over 12 (3.7) to 18 (5.5)	0.60 (24.5)	Not allowed	2500 (230)
(2) On-floor storage	Up to 5 (1.5)	0.19 (7.7)	2000 (185)	2000 (185)
Tires, on-tread	Over 5 (1.5) to 12 (3.7)	0.30 (12.2)	2500 (230)	2500 (230)
(3) Palletized portable rack storage	Up to 5 (1.5)	0.19 (7.7)	2000 (185)	2000 (185)
On-side or on-tread	Over 5 (1.5) to 20 (6.1)	See Table 21.7.1(b).	—	—
	Over 20 (6.1) to 30 (9.1)	0.30 (12.2) plus high-expansion foam	3000 (280)	3000 (280)
(4) Palletized portable rack storage, on-side	Up to 5 (1.5)	0.19 (7.7)	2000 (185)	2000 (185)
	Over 5 (1.5) to 20 (6.1)	See Table 21.7.1(b).	—	—
	Over 20 (6.1) to 25 (7.6)	0.60 (24.5) and	Not allowed	5000 (465)
		0.90 (36.7)[c] or	Not allowed	3000 (280)
		0.75 (2.8) with 1-hour fire-resistive rating of roof and ceiling assembly	Not allowed	4000 (370)
(5) Open portable rack storage, on-side or on-tread	Up to 5 (1.5)	0.19 (7.7)	2000 (185)	2000 (185)
	Over 5 (1.5) to 12 (3.7)	0.60 (24.5)	5000 (465)	3000 (280)
	Over 12 (3.7) to 20 (6.1)	0.60 (24.5) and	Not allowed	5000 (465)
		0.90 (36.7)[c] or	Not allowed	3000 (280)
		0.30 (12.2) plus high-expansion foam	3000 (280)	3000 (280)
(6) Open portable rack storage, laced	Over 12 (3.7) to 20 (6.1)	0.60 (24.5) and	Not allowed	5000 (465)
		0.90 (36.7)[c,d]	Not allowed	3000 (280)
(7) Single-, double-, and multiple-row fixed rack storage on pallets, on-side, or on-tread without shelves	Up to 5 (1.5)	0.19 (7.7)	2000 (185)	2000 (185)
	Over 5 (1.5) to 20 (6.1)	See Table 21.7.1(b) or 0.30 (12.2) plus high-expansion foam	3000 (280) —	3000 (280) —
	Over 20 (6.1) to 30 (9.1)	0.30 (12.2) plus high-expansion foam	Not allowed	3000 (280)
(8) Single-, double-, and multiple-row fixed rack storage without pallets or shelves, on-side or on-tread	Up to 5 (1.5)	0.19 (7.7)	2000 (185)	2000 (185)
	Over 5 (1.5) to 12 (3.7)	0.60 (24.5)	5000 (465)	3000 (280)
	Over 12 (3.7) to 20 (6.1)	0.60 (24.5) and	Not allowed	5000 (465)
		0.90 (36.7)[c] or	Not allowed	3000 (280)
		0.30 (12.2) plus high-expansion foam	3000 (280)	3000 (280)
	Over 20 (6.1) to 30 (9.1)	0.30 (12.2) plus high-expansion foam	Not allowed	3000 (280)

Note: Shelf storage of rubber tires is protected as solid rack shelving.

[a]Sprinkler discharge densities and areas of application are based on a maximum clearance to ceiling of 10 ft (3.0 m) with the maximum height of storage anticipated.

[b]Laced tires on-floor, vertical stacking on-side (typical truck tires), and off-road tires. Laced tires are not stored to a significant height by this method due to the damage inflicted on the tire (i.e., bead).

[c]Water supply fulfills both requirements.

[d]This protection scheme is for use with K-16.8 (K-240) or larger control mode sprinklers only. Maximum clearance to ceiling can be increased to 14 ft (4.3 m) with this scheme.

Δ Table 21.7.1(b) Control Mode Density/Area Sprinklers System Density [gpm/ft^2 (mm/min)] for Palletized Portable Rack Storage and Fixed Rack Storage of Rubber Tires with Pallets Over 5 ft (1.5 m) to 20 ft (3.7 m) in Height

	Sprinkler Temperature	
Storage Height [ft (m)]	High Temperature	Ordinary Temperature
>5 to 10 (>1.5 to 3.0)	0.32/2000 (13.0/185)	0.32/2000 (13.0/185)
>10 to 12 (>3.0 to 3.7)	0.39/2000 (15.9/185)	0.39/2600 (15.9/270)
>12 to 14 (>3.7 to 4.3)	0.45/2000 (18.3/185)	0.45/3200 (18.3/280)
>14 to 16 (>4.3 to 4.9)	0.5/2300 (20.4/215)	0.5/3700 (20.4/320)
>16 to 18 (>4.9 to 5.5)	0.55/2600 (22.4/270)	0.55/4400 (22.4/380)
>18 to 20 (>5.5 to 6.1)	0.6/3000 (24.5/260)	0.6/5000 (24.5/465)

Table 21.8.3(a) Control Mode Density/Area Sprinkler Protection Criteria for Roll Paper Storage for Buildings or Structures with Roof or Ceilings Up to 30 ft (Discharge Densities are gpm/ft^2 over ft^2)

Storage Height (ft)	Ceiling (ft)	Heavyweight					Mediumweight				Tissue All Storage Arrays
		Closed Array Banded or Unbanded	Standard Array		Open Array		Closed Array Banded or Unbanded	Standard Array		Open Array Banded or Unbanded	
			Banded	Unbanded	Banded	Unbanded		Banded	Unbanded		
10	≤5	0.3/2000	0.3/2000	0.3/2000	0.3/2000	0.3/2000	0.3/2000	0.3/2000	0.3/2000	0.3/2000	0.45/2000
10	>5	0.3/2000	0.3/2000	0.3/2000	0.3/2000	0.3/2000	0.3/2000	0.3/2000	0.3/2000	0.3/2000	0.45/2500
15	≤5	0.3/2000	0.3/2000	0.3/2000	0.3/2500	0.3/3000	0.3/2000	0.3/2000	0.45/2500	0.45/2500	0.60/2000
15	>5	0.3/2000	0.3/2000	0.3/2000	0.3/3000	0.3/3500	0.3/2000	0.3/2500	0.45/3000	0.45/3000	0.60/3000
20	≤5	0.3/2000	0.3/2000	0.3/2500	0.45/3000	0.45/3500	0.3/2000	0.45/2500	0.6/2500	0.6/2500	0.75/2500
20	>5	0.3/2000	0.3/2500	0.3/3000	0.45/3500	0.45/4000	0.3/2500	0.45/3000	0.6/3000	0.6/3000	0.75/3000
25	≤5	0.45/2500	0.45/3000	0.45/3500	0.6/2500	0.6/3000	0.45/3000	0.6/3000	0.75/2500	0.75/2500	*see Note 1*

Notes:
(1) Sprinkler protection requirements for tissue stored above 20 ft have not been determined.
(2) Densities or areas, or both, shall be permitted to be interpolated between any 5 ft storage height increment.

Table 21.8.3(b) Control Mode Density/Area Sprinkler Protection Criteria for the Protection of Roll Paper Storage for Buildings or Structures with Roof or Ceilings Up to 9.1 m (Discharge Densities are mm/min over m^2)

Storage Height (m)	Ceiling (m)	Heavyweight					Mediumweight				Tissue All Storage Arrays
		Closed Array Banded or Unbanded	Standard Array		Open Array		Closed Array Banded or Unbanded	Standard Array		Open Array Banded or Unbanded	
			Banded	Unbanded	Banded	Unbanded		Banded	Unbanded		
3.0	≤1.5	12.2/185	12.2/185	12.2/185	12.2/185	12.2/185	12.2/185	12.2/185	12.2/185	12.2/185	18.3/185
3.0	>1.5	12.2/185	12.2/185	12.2/185	12.2/185	12.2/185	12.2/185	12.2/185	12.2/185	12.2/185	18.3/230
4.6	≤1.5	12.2/185	12.2/185	12.2/185	12.2/230	12.2/280	12.2/185	12.2/185	18.3/230	18.3/230	24.5/185
4.6	>1.5	12.2/185	12.2/185	12.2/185	12.2/280	12.2/330	12.2/185	12.2/230	18.3/280	18.3/280	24.5/280
6.1	≤1.5	12.2/185	12.2/185	12.2/230	18.3/280	18.3/325	12.2/185	18.3/230	24.5/230	24.5/230	31.0/230
6.1	>1.5	12.2/185	12.2/185	12.2/280	18.3/230	18.3/230	12.2/230	18.3/280	24.5/280	24.5/280	30.6/280
7.6	≤1.5	18.3/230	18.3/230	18.3/230	24.5/230	24.5/280	18.3/280	24.5/280	31.0/230	31.0/230	*see Note 1*

Notes:
(1) Sprinkler protection requirements for tissue stored above 6.1 m have not been determined.
(2) Densities or areas, or both, shall be permitted to be interpolated between any 1.5 m storage height increment.

Chapter 22 CMSA Requirements for Storage Applications

22.1 General. The criteria in Chapter 20 shall apply to storage protected with CMSA sprinklers.

22.1.1 Quick-response CMSA sprinklers designed to meet any criteria in Chapter 20 through Chapter 25 shall be permitted to protect any of the following:

(1) Light hazard occupancies
(2) Ordinary hazard occupancies

22.1.2 Standard-response CMSA sprinklers designed to meet any criteria in Chapter 20 through Chapter 25 shall be permitted to protect ordinary hazard occupancies.

22.1.3 When using CMSA, the design area shall meet the requirements of 28.2.4.3.1.

22.1.4 Protection shall be provided as specified in this chapter or appropriate NFPA standards in terms of minimum operating pressure and the number of sprinklers to be included in the design area.

22.1.5 Open Wood Joist Construction.

22.1.5.1 Where CMSA sprinklers are installed under open wood joist construction, one of the following shall be provided:

(1) A minimum pressure of 50 psi (3.4 bar) for K-11.2 (160) sprinklers
(2) A minimum pressure of 22 psi (1.5 bar) for K-16.8 (240) sprinklers
(3) The pressure from Table 22.4 for K-19.6 (280) or larger sprinkler.
(4) The pressure from Table 22.4 for K-11.2 (160) or K-16.8 (240) where each joist channel is fully separated with material equal to the joist material to its full depth at intervals not exceeding 20 ft (6.1 m).

22.1.5.2 Preaction Systems.

22.1.5.2.1 For the purpose of using Table 22.2, preaction systems shall be classified as dry pipe systems.

22.1.5.3 Building steel shall not require special protection where Table 22.2 are applied as appropriate for the storage configuration.

22.1.5.4* Storage Conditions. The design of the sprinkler system shall be based on those conditions that routinely or periodically exist in a building and create the greatest water demand, which include the following:

(1) Pile height
(2) Clearance to ceiling
(3) Pile stability
(4) Array

Δ **22.1.6*** The ceiling design criteria for single-, double-, and multiple-row racks in Chapter 22 shall be based on open rack configurations as defined in 3.3.147.

22.1.7 Protection criteria for Group A plastics shall be permitted for the protection of the same storage height and configuration of Class I, II, III, and IV commodities.

22.2 Palletized and Solid-Piled Storage of Class I Through Class IV Commodities. Protection of palletized and solid-piled storage of Class I through Class IV commodities shall be in accordance with Table 22.2.

22.3 Palletized and Solid-Piled Storage of Nonexpanded and Expanded Group A Plastic Commodities. Protection of palletized and solid-piled storage of nonexpanded and expanded Group A plastic commodities shall be in accordance with Table 22.3.

22.4 Single-, Double-, and Multiple-Row Rack Storage for Class I Through Class IV Commodities. Protection of single-, double-, and multiple-row rack storage for Class I through Class IV commodities shall be in accordance with Table 22.4.

22.5 RackStorage of Group A Plastic Commodities. Protection of single-, double-, and multiple-row rack storage for nonexpanded Group A plastic commodities shall be in accordance with Table 22.5.

22.6 Rubber Tires. Protection of rubber tires with CMSA sprinklers shall be in accordance with Table 22.6.

22.7 Roll Paper Storage. Protection of roll paper storage with CMSA sprinklers shall be in accordance with Table 22.7.

Δ Table 22.2 CMSA Sprinkler Design Criteria for Palletized and Solid-Piled Storage of Class I Through Class IV Commodities (Encapsulated and Nonencapsulated)

Configuration	Commodity Class	Maximum Storage Height		Maximum Ceiling/Roof Height		K-Factor/Orientation	Type of System	Number of Design Sprinklers	Minimum Operating Pressure	
		ft	m	ft	m				psi	bar
Palletized	Class I or II	25	7.6	30	9.1	11.2 (160) Upright	Wet	15	25	1.7
							Dry	25	25	1.7
						16.8 (240) Upright	Wet	15	10	0.7
							Dry	25	15	1.0
						19.6 (280) Pendent	Wet	15	16	1.1
						25.2 (360) Pendent	Wet	15	10	0.7
				35	10.7	11.2 (160) Upright	Wet	15	25	1.7
							Dry	25	25	1.7
						16.8 (240) Upright	Wet	15	15	1.0
							Dry	25	15	1.0
				40	12.2	25.2 (360) Pendent	Wet	15	23	1.6
		30	9.1	35	10.7	19.6 (280) Pendent	Wet	15	25	1.7
				40	12.2	25.2 (360) Pendent	Wet	15	23	1.6
		35	10.7	40	12.2	19.6 (280) Pendent	Wet	15	30	2.1
				40	12.2	25.2 (360) Pendent	Wet	15	23	1.6
	Class III	25	7.6	30	9.1	11.2 (160) Upright	Wet	15	25	1.7
							Dry	25	25	1.7
						16.8 (240) Upright	Wet	15	15	1.0
							Dry	25	15	1.0
						19.6 (280) Pendent	Wet	15	16	1.1
						25.2 (360) Pendent	Wet	15	10	0.7
				35	10.7	11.2 (160) Upright	Wet	15	25	1.7
							Dry	25	25	1.7
						16.8 (240) Upright	Wet	15	15	1.0
							Dry	25	15	1.0
				40	12.2	25.2 (360) Pendent	Wet	15	23	1.6
		30	9.1	35	10.7	19.6 (280) Pendent	Wet	15	25	1.7
				40	12.2	25.2 (360) Pendent	Wet	15	23	1.6
		35	10.7	40	12.2	19.6 (280) Pendent	Wet	15	30	2.1
				40	12.2	25.2 (360) Pendent	Wet	15	23	1.6

(continues)

Δ **Table 22.2**   *Continued*

Configuration	Commodity Class	Maximum Storage Height		Maximum Ceiling/ Roof Height		K-Factor/ Orientation	Type of System	Number of Design Sprinklers	Minimum Operating Pressure	
		ft	m	ft	m				psi	bar
	Class IV	20	6.1	30	9.1	11.2 (160) Upright	Wet	20	25	1.7
								15	50	3.4
						16.8 (240) Upright	Wet	20	15	1.0
								15	22	1.5
						19.6 (280) Pendent	Wet	15	16	1.1
						25.2 (360) Pendent	Wet	15	10	0.7
				40	12.2	25.2 (360) Pendent	Wet	15	23	1.6
		25	7.6	30	9.1	16.8 (240) Upright	Wet	15	22	1.5
						19.6 (280) Pendent	Wet	15	16	1.1
						25.2 (360) Pendent	Wet	15	10	0.7
				40	12.2	25.2 (360) Pendent	Wet	15	23	1.6
		30	9.1	35	10.7	19.6 (280) Pendent	Wet	15	25	1.7
				40	12.2	25.2 (360) Pendent	Wet	15	23	1.6
		35	10.7	40	12.2	19.6 (280) Pendent	Wet	15	30	2.1
						25.2 (360) Pendent	Wet	15	23	1.6
Solid piled	Class I or II	20	6.1	30	9.1	11.2 (160) Upright	Wet	15	25	1.7
							Dry	25	25	1.7
						16.8 (240) Upright	Wet	15	10	0.7
							Dry	25	15	1.0
						19.6 (280) Pendent	Wet	15	16	1.1
						25.2 (360) Pendent	Wet	15	10	0.7
				40	12.2	25.2 (360) Pendent	Wet	15	23	1.6
		25	7.6	30	9.1	16.8 (240) Upright	Wet	15	10	0.7
						19.6 (280) Pendent	Wet	15	16	1.1
						25.2 (360) Pendent	Wet	15	10	0.7
				40	12.2	25.2 (360) Pendent	Wet	15	23	1.6
		30	9.1	35	10.7	19.6 (280) Pendent	Wet	15	25	1.7
				40	12.2	25.2 (360) Pendent	Wet	15	23	1.6
		35	10.7	40	12.2	19.6 (280) Pendent	Wet	15	30	2.1
						25.2 (360) Pendent	Wet	15	23	1.6

(continues)

Shaded text = Revisions.   Δ = Text deletions and figure/table revisions.   • = Section deletions.   *N* = New material.

Δ **Table 22.2** *Continued*

Configuration	Commodity Class	Maximum Storage Height		Maximum Ceiling/ Roof Height		K-Factor/ Orientation	Type of System	Number of Design Sprinklers	Minimum Operating Pressure	
		ft	m	ft	m				psi	bar
	Class III	20	6.1	30	9.1	11.2 (160) Upright	Wet	15	25	1.7
							Dry	25	25	1.7
						16.8 (240) Upright	Wet	15	15	1.0
							Dry	25	15	1.0
						19.6 (280) Pendent	Wet	15	16	1.1
						25.2 (360) Pendent	Wet	15	10	0.7
				40	12.2	25.2 (360) Pendent	Wet	15	23	1.6
		25	7.6	30	9.1	16.8 (240) Upright	Wet	15	22	1.5
						19.6 (280) Pendent	Wet	15	16	1.1
						25.2 (360) Pendent	Wet	15	10	0.7
				40	12.2	25.2 (360) Pendent	Wet	15	23	1.6
		30	9.1	35	10.7	19.6 (280) Pendent	Wet	15	25	1.7
				40	12.2	25.2 (360) Pendent	Wet	15	23	1.6
		35	10.7	40	12.2	19.6 (280) Pendent	Wet	15	30	2.1
						25.2 (360) Pendent	Wet	15	23	1.6
	Class IV	20	6.1	30	9.1	11.2 (160) Upright	Wet	15	50	3.4
						16.8 (240) Upright	Wet	15	22	1.5
						19.6 (280) Pendent	Wet	15	16	1.1
						25.2 (360) Pendent	Wet	15	10	0.7
				40	12.2	25.2 (360) Pendent	Wet	15	23	1.6
		25	7.6	30	9.1	16.8 (240) Upright	Wet	15	22	1.5
						19.6 (280) Pendent	Wet	15	16	1.1
						25.2 (360) Pendent	Wet	15	10	0.7
				40	12.2	25.2 (360) Pendent	Wet	15	23	1.6
		30	9.1	35	10.7	19.6 (280) Pendent	Wet	15	25	1.7
				40	12.2	25.2 (360) Pendent	Wet	15	23	1.6
		35	10.7	40	12.2	19.6 (280) Pendent	Wet	15	30	2.1
						25.2 (360) Pendent	Wet	15	23	1.6

Δ **Table 22.3 CMSA Sprinkler Design Criteria for Palletized and Solid-Piled Storage of Group A Plastic Commodities**

Storage Arrangement	Commodity Class	Maximum Storage Height		Maximum Ceiling/ Roof Height		K-Factor/Orientation	Type of System	Number of Design Sprinklers	Minimum Operating Pressure	
		ft	m	ft	m				psi	bar
Palletized	Cartoned nonexpanded plastics	20	6.1	30	9.1	11.2 (160) Upright	Wet	25	25	1.7
						16.8 (240) Upright	Wet	15	22	1.5
						19.6 (280) Pendent	Wet	15	16	1.1
						25.2 (360) Pendent	Wet	15	10	0.7
				40	12.2	25.2 (360) Pendent	Wet	15	23	1.6
		25	7.6	30	9.1	16.8 (240) Upright	Wet	15	22	1.5
						19.6 (280) Pendent	Wet	15	16	1.1
						25.2 (360) Pendent	Wet	15	10	0.7
				40	12.2	25.2 (360) Pendent	Wet	15	23	1.6
		30	9.1	35	10.7	19.6 (280) Pendent	Wet	15	25	1.7
				40	12.2	25.2 (360) Pendent	Wet	15	23	1.6
		35	10.7	40	12.2	19.6 (280) Pendent	Wet	15	30	2.1
						25.2 (360) Pendent	Wet	15	23	1.6
Solid piled	Cartoned nonexpanded plastics	20	6.1	30	9.1	11.2 (160) Upright	Wet	15	50	3.4
						16.8 (240) Upright	Wet	15	22	1.5
						19.6 (280) Pendent	Wet	15	16	1.1
						25.2 (360) Pendent	Wet	15	10	0.7
				40	12.2	25.2 (360) Pendent	Wet	15	23	1.6
		25	7.6	30	9.1	16.8 (240) Upright	Wet	15	22	1.5
						19.6 (280) Pendent	Wet	15	16	1.1
						25.2 (360) Pendent	Wet	15	10	0.7
				40	12.2	25.2 (360) Pendent	Wet	15	23	1.6
		30	9.1	35	10.7	19.6 (280) Pendent	Wet	15	25	1.7
				40	12.2	25.2 (360) Pendent	Wet	15	23	1.6
		35	10.7	40	12.2	19.6 (280) Pendent	Wet	15	30	2.1
						25.2 (360) Pendent	Wet	15	23	1.6
Palletized	Exposed nonexpanded plastics	20	6.1	30	9.1	11.2 (160) Upright	Wet	25	25	1.7
						16.8 (240) Upright	Wet	15	22	1.5
		25	7.6	30	9.1	16.8 (240) Upright	Wet	15	22	1.5
	Cartoned or exposed expanded plastics	18	5.5	26	7.9	11.2 (160) Upright	Wet	15	50	3.4
						16.8 (240) Upright	Wet	15	22	1.5
Solid piled	Cartoned or exposed nonexpanded plastics	20	6.1	30	9.1	11.2 (160) Upright	Wet	15	50	3.4
		25	7.6	30	9.1	16.8 (240) Upright	Wet	15	22	1.5

Δ Table 22.4 CMSA Sprinkler Design Criteria for Rack Storage of Class I Through Class IV Commodities (Encapsulated and Nonencapsulated)

Storage Arrangement	Commodity Class	Maximum Storage Height		Maximum Ceiling/Roof Height		K-Factor/Orientation	Type of System	Number of Design Sprinklers	Minimum Operating Pressure	
		ft	m	ft	m				psi	bar
Single, double, and multiple-row racks	Class I or II	20	6.1	30	9.1	11.2 (160) Upright	Wet	15	25	1.7
							Dry	25	25	1.7
						16.8 (240) Upright	Wet	15	10	0.7
							Dry	25	15	1.0
						19.6 (280) Pendent	Wet	15	16	1.1
						25.2 (360) Pendent	Wet	15	10	0.7
				40	12.2	25.2 (360) Pendent	Wet	15	23	1.6
		25	7.6	30	9.1	11.2 (160) Upright	Wet	20	25	1.7
							Dry	30	25	1.7
						16.8 (240) Upright	Wet	15	10	0.7
							Dry	30	15	1.0
						19.6 (280) Pendent	Wet	15	16	1.1
						25.2 (360) Pendent	Wet	15	10	0.7
				40	12.2	25.2 (360) Pendent	Wet	15	23	1.6
		30	9.1	35	10.7	11.2 (160) Upright	Wet	In-rack sprinklers required. See Chapter 25.	NA	NA
							Dry	In-rack sprinkler option available. See Chapter 25.	NA	NA
							Dry*	36	55	3.8
						16.8 (240) Upright	Wet	In-rack sprinklers required. See Chapter 25.	NA	NA
							Dry	In-rack sprinkler option available. See Chapter 25.	NA	NA
							Dry*	36	22	1.5
						19.6 (280) Pendent	Wet	15	25	1.7
		35	10.7	40	12.2	11.2 (160) Upright	Dry*	36	55	3.8
						16.8 (240) Upright	Dry*	36	22	1.5
						19.6 (280) Pendent	Wet	15	30	2.1
						25.2 (360) Pendent	Wet	15	23	1.6

(continues)

Shaded text = Revisions.   Δ = Text deletions and figure/table revisions.   • = Section deletions.   N = New material.

2022 Edition

Δ **Table 22.4**   *Continued*

Storage Arrangement	Commodity Class	Maximum Storage Height		Maximum Ceiling/Roof Height		K-Factor/Orientation	Type of System	Number of Design Sprinklers	Minimum Operating Pressure	
		ft	m	ft	m				psi	bar
		20	6.1	30	9.1	11.2 (160) Upright	Wet	15	25	1.7
							Dry	25	25	1.7
						16.8 (240) Upright	Wet	15	15	1.0
							Dry	25	15	1.0
						19.6 (280) Pendent	Wet	15	16	1.1
						25.2 (360) Pendent	Wet	15	10	0.7
				40	12.2	25.2 (360) Pendent	Wet	15	23	1.6
	Class III	25	7.6	30	9.1	11.2 (160) Upright	Wet	In-rack sprinklers required. See Chapter 25.	NA	NA
							Dry	In-rack sprinklers required. See Chapter 25.	NA	NA
						16.8 (240) Upright	Wet	15	22	1.5
							Dry	In-rack sprinklers required. See Chapter 25.	NA	NA
						19.6 (280) Pendent	Wet	15	16	1.1
						25.2 (360) Pendent	Wet	15	10	0.7
				35	10.7	11.2 (160) Upright	Wet	In-rack sprinklers required. See Chapter 25.	NA	NA
							Dry	In-rack sprinklers required. See Chapter 25.	NA	NA
						16.8 (240) Upright	Wet	In-rack sprinklers required. See Chapter 25.	NA	NA
							Dry	In-rack sprinklers required. See Chapter 25.	NA	NA
						19.6 (280) Pendent	Wet	15	25	1.7
				40	12.2	19.6 (280) Pendent	Wet	15	30	2.1
						25.2 (360) Pendent	Wet	15	23	1.6
		30	9.1	35	10.7	19.6 (280) Pendent	Wet	15	25	1.7
		35	10.7	40	12.2	19.6 (280) Pendent	Wet	15	30	2.1
						25.2 (360) Pendent	Wet	15	23	1.6

(continues)

Δ Table 22.4 *Continued*

Storage Arrangement	Commodity Class	Maximum Storage Height		Maximum Ceiling/Roof Height		K-Factor/Orientation	Type of System	Number of Design Sprinklers	Minimum Operating Pressure	
		ft	m	ft	m				psi	bar
	Class IV	20	6.1	25	7.6	11.2 (160) Upright	Wet	15	50	3.4
						16.8 (240) Upright	Wet	15	22	1.5
						19.6 (280) Pendent	Wet	15	16	1.1
				30	9.1	11.2 (160) Upright	Wet	20	50	3.4
						11.2 (160) Upright	Wet	15	75	5.2
						16.8 (240) Upright	Wet	15	22	1.5
						19.6 (280) Pendent	Wet	15	16	1.1
						25.2 (360) Pendent	Wet	15	10	0.7
				40	12.2	25.2 (360) Pendent	Wet	15	23	1.6
		25	7.6	30	9.1	11.2 (160) Upright	Wet	In-rack sprinklers required. See Chapter 25.	NA	NA
						16.8 (240) Upright	Wet	15	22	1.5
						19.6 (280) Pendent	Wet	15	16	1.1
						25.2 (360) Pendent	Wet	15	10	0.7
				35	10.7	11.2 (160) Upright	Wet	In-rack sprinklers required. See Chapter 25.	NA	NA
							Wet	In-rack sprinklers required. See Chapter 25.	NA	NA
						16.8 (240) Upright	Wet	In-rack sprinklers required. See Chapter 25.	NA	NA
							Wet	In-rack sprinklers required. See Chapter 25.	NA	NA
						19.6 (280) Pendent	Wet	15	25	1.7
				40	12.2	19.6 (280) Pendent	Wet	15	30	2.1
						25.2 (360) Pendent	Wet	15	23	1.6
		30	9.1	35	10.7	19.6 (280) Pendent	Wet	15	25	1.7
		35	10.7	40	12.2	19.6 (280) Pendent	Wet	15	30	2.1
						25.2 (360) Pendent	Wet	15	23	1.6

NA: Not applicable.

*High temperature-rated sprinklers are used. Dry system water delivery is required in accordance with 8.2.3.6 with a maximum time of water delivery of 30 seconds with four sprinklers initially open.

Δ Table 22.5 CMSA Sprinkler Design Criteria for RackStorage of Group A Plastic Commodities Stored Up to and Including 35 ft (10.7 m) in Height

Storage Arrangement	Commodity Class	Maximum Storage Height		Maximum Ceiling/Roof Height		K-Factor/ Orientation	Type of System	Number of Design Sprinklers	Minimum Operating Pressure	
		ft	m	ft	m				psi	bar
Single-, double-, and multiple-row racks	Cartoned nonexpanded plastics	20	6.1	25	7.6	11.2 (160) Upright	Wet	15	50	3.4
						16.8 (240) Upright	Wet	15	22	1.5
						19.6 (280) Pendent	Wet	15	16	1.1
				30	9.1	11.2 (160) Upright	Wet	30	50	3.4
							Wet	20	75	5.2
						16.8 (240) Upright	Wet	15*	22	1.5
						19.6 (280) Pendent	Wet	15	16	1.1
		25	7.6	30	9.1	11.2 (160) Upright	Wet	In-rack sprinklers required. See Chapter 25.	NA	NA
						16.8 (240) Upright	Wet	15*	22	1.5
						19.6 (280) Pendent	Wet	15	16	1.1
						25.2 (360) Pendent	Wet	15	10	0.7
		25	7.6	35	10.7	11.2 (160) Upright	Wet	In-rack sprinklers required. See Chapter 25.	NA	NA
							Wet	In-rack sprinklers required. See Chapter 25.	NA	NA
						16.8 (240) Upright	Wet	In-rack sprinklers required. See Chapter 25.	NA	NA
							Wet	In-rack sprinklers required. See Chapter 25.	NA	NA
						19.6 (280) Pendent	Wet	15	25	1.7
		30	9.1	35	10.7	19.6 (280) Pendent	Wet	15	25	1.7
		35	10.6	40	12.2	19.6 (280) Pendent	Wet	15	30	2.1
						25.2 (360) Pendent	Wet	15	23	1.6

(continues)

Δ **Table 22.5** *Continued*

Storage Arrangement	Commodity Class	Maximum Storage Height		Maximum Ceiling/Roof Height		K-Factor/Orientation	Type of System	Number of Design Sprinklers	Minimum Operating Pressure	
		ft	m	ft	m				psi	bar
	Exposed nonexpanded plastics	20	6.1	25	7.6	11.2 (160) Upright	Wet	15	50	3.4
						16.8 (240) Upright	Wet	15	22	1.5
		20	6.1	30	9.1	11.2 (160) Upright	Wet	30	50	3.4
						11.2 (160) Upright	Wet	20	75	5.2
						16.8 (240) Upright	Wet	15*	22	1.5
		25	7.6	30	9.1	11.2 (160) Upright	Wet	In-rack sprinklers required. See Chapter 25.	NA	NA
						16.8 (240) Upright	Wet	15*	22	1.5
		25	7.6	35	10.7	11.2 (160) Upright	Wet	In-rack sprinklers required. See Chapter 25.	NA	NA
						11.2 (160) Upright	Wet	In-rack sprinklers required. See Chapter 25.	NA	NA
						16.8 (240) Upright	Wet	In-rack sprinklers required. See Chapter 25.	NA	NA
						16.8 (240) Upright	Wet	In-rack sprinklers required. See Chapter 25.	NA	NA

NA: Not applicable.

*Limited to single- and double-row racks with minimum 8 ft (2.4 m) aisles.

Δ **Table 22.6 Control Mode Specific Application (CMSA) Protection for Rubber Tires**

Piling Method	Maximum Storage Height		Maximum Ceiling/Roof Height		K-Factor	Type of System	Number of Sprinklers	Operating Pressure
	ft	m	ft	m				
Rubber tire storage, on-side or on-tread, in palletized portable racks, or open portable racks, or fixed racks without solid shelves	25	7.6	32	9.8	11.2 (160)	Wet	15	75 psi (5.2 bar)
	25	7.6	32	9.8	16.8 (240)	Wet	15	35 psi (2.4 bar)

Δ **Table 22.7 Control Mode Specific Application (CMSA) Protection of Roll Paper Storage [Number of Sprinklers at Operating Pressure, psi (bar)]**

Storage Height		Maximum Building Height		Nominal K-Factor	Type of System	Heavyweight					Mediumweight					Tissue All Storage Arrays
						Closed Array	Standard Array		Open Array		Closed Array	Standard Array		Open Array		
ft	m	ft	m			Banded or Unhanded	Banded	Unhanded	Banded	Unhanded	Banded or Unhanded	Banded	Unhanded	Banded	Unhanded	
20	6.1	30	9.1	11.2 (160)	Wet	15 at 50(3.4)	15 at 50(3.4)	15 at 50(3.4)	15 at 50(3.4)	NA	15 at 50(3.4)	15 at 50(3.4)	15 at 50(3.4)	NA	NA	See Note
20	6.1	30	9.1	11.2 (160)	Dry	25 at 50(3.4)	25 at 50(3.4)	25 at 50(3.4)	NA	NA	25 at 50(3.4)	25 at 50(3.4)	25 at 50(3.4)	NA	NA	NA
26	7.9	60	18.3	11.2 (160)	Wet	15 at 50(3.4)	15 at 50(3.4)	15 at 50(3.4)	15 at 50(3.4)	NA	NA	NA	NA	NA	NA	NA
20	6.1	30	9.1	16.8 (240)	Wet	15 at 22(1.5)	15 at 22(1.5)	15 at 22(1.5)	15 at 22(1.5)	NA	15 at 22(1.5)	15 at 22(1.5)	15 at 22(1.5)	NA	NA	See Note
20	6.1	30	9.1	16.8 (240)	Dry	25 at 22(1.5)	25 at 22(1.5)	25 at 22(1.5)	NA	NA	25 at 22(1.5)	25 at 22(1.5)	25 at 22(1.5)	NA	NA	NA
26	7.9	60	18.3	16.8 (240)	Wet	15 at 22(1.5)	15 at 22(1.5)	15 at 22(1.5)	15 at 22(1.5)	NA	NA	NA	NA	NA	NA	NA

Note: Base design on 25 sprinklers at 75 psi (5.2 bar) for K-11.2 (160) sprinklers or 25 sprinklers at 35 psi (240) for K-16.8 (240) sprinklers when storage is in closed or standard array; other arrays not applicable (NA).

Shaded text = Revisions. Δ = Text deletions and figure/table revisions. • = Section deletions. *N* = New material.

Chapter 23 ESFR Requirements for Storage Applications

23.1 General. The criteria in Chapter 20 shall apply to storage protected with ESFR sprinklers.

23.1.1 ESFR sprinklers designed to meet any criteria in this chapter shall be permitted to protect any of the following:

(1) Light hazard occupancies
(2) Ordinary hazard occupancies
(3) Any storage arrangement with OH1, OH2, EH1, and EH2 design criteria

23.1.2 Draft Curtains.

23.1.2.1 Where ESFR sprinkler systems are installed adjacent to sprinkler systems with standard-response sprinklers, a draft curtain of noncombustible construction and at least 2 ft (600 mm) in depth shall be required to separate the two areas.

23.1.2.2 A clear aisle of at least 4 ft (1.2 m) centered below the draft curtain shall be maintained for separation.

23.1.3 The ceiling design criteria for single-, double-, and multiple-row racks in this chapter shall be based on open-rack configurations as defined in 3.3.147.

23.1.3.1 ESFR sprinklers shall not be permitted to protect storage on solid shelf racks unless the solid shelf racks are protected with in-rack sprinklers in accordance with Chapter 25.

23.1.3.2 ESFR sprinklers shall not be permitted to protect storage with open-top containers.

23.1.3.3 ESFR sprinkler systems shall be designed such that the minimum operating pressure is not less than that indicated in this chapter for type of storage, commodity, storage height, and building height involved.

Δ 23.2 ESFR Design Criteria.

N 23.2.1 ESFR design criteria shall be selected from Section 23.3 through Section 23.6.

N 23.2.2 All design areas shall consist of the most hydraulically demanding 12 sprinklers, with four sprinklers on each of three branch lines, unless otherwise specified.

23.3 ESFR Sprinklers for Palletized, Solid-Piled, or Rack Storage of Class I Through Class IV and Group A Plastic Commodities.

23.3.1 Protection of palletized, solid-piled, or rack storage of Class I through Class IV and Group A commodities shall be in accordance with Table 23.3.1.

23.4* Protection of Exposed Expanded Group A Plastics.

23.4.1 Protection of single-, double-, and multiple-row rack storage of exposed expanded Group A plastics shall be permitted to be in accordance with 23.4.2 through 23.4.7.

23.4.2 The maximum storage height shall be 35 ft (10.7 m).

23.4.3 The maximum ceiling height shall be 40 ft (12.2 m).

23.4.4 Sprinklers shall be intermediate temperature–rated ESFR pendent sprinklers with a nominal K-factor of K-25.2 (360).

23.4.4.1 The maximum sprinkler deflector distance below the ceiling shall be 14 in. (350 mm).

Δ 23.4.5 The minimum operating pressure shall be as follows, based upon the applicable storage and ceiling height for the installation:

(1) 30 psi (2.0 bar) for storage heights up to 25 ft (7.6 m) with a maximum ceiling height of 30 ft (9.1 m)
(2) 60 psi (4.1 bar) for storage heights up to 35 ft (10.7 m) with a maximum ceiling height of 40 ft (12.2 m)

23.4.6 The minimum aisle width shall be 8 ft (2.4 m).

23.4.7 The rack shall have a solid vertical barrier of ⅜ in. (10 mm) plywood or particleboard, 0.013 in. (0.78 mm) sheet metal, or equivalent, from face of rack to face of rack, spaced at a maximum of 16.5 ft (5.0 m) intervals.

23.4.7.1 The vertical barrier shall extend from a maximum of 4 in. (100 mm) above the floor to the maximum storage height.

23.4.7.2 The plan area of storage between vertical barriers and aisles shall not exceed 124 ft² (12 m²).

23.4.7.3 The vertical barrier shall extend across the longitudinal flue.

23.4.7.4 The commodity shall be permitted to extend a nominal 4 in. (100 mm) beyond the vertical barrier at the aisle.

23.5 ESFR Protection of Rack Storage of Rubber Tires. The sprinkler discharge and area of application shall be in accordance with Table 23.5.

Δ 23.6 ESFR Sprinklers for Protection of Roll Paper Storage. Where automatic sprinkler system protection utilizes ESFR sprinklers, hydraulic design criteria shall be as specified in Table 23.6.

N Table 23.3.1 ESFR Sprinkler Ceiling-Only Options for Solid Pile; Palletized; and Single-, Double-, and Multiple-Row Rack Storage

Commodity[a]	Maximum Ceiling/Roof Height		ESFR Sprinklers — Pendent Orientation Minimum Operating Pressure psi (bar)				ESFR Sprinklers — Upright Orientation Minimum Operating Pressure psi (bar)	
			Nominal K-Factors				Nominal K-Factors	
	ft	m	14 (200)	16.8 (240)	22.4 (320)	25.2 (360)	14 (200)	16.8 (240)
Class I through	25	7.6	50 (3.4)	35 (2.4)	25 (1.7)	15 (1.0)	50 (3.4)	35 (2.4)
Class IV and	30	9.1	50 (3.4)	35 (2.4)	25 (1.7)	15 (1.0)	50 (3.4)	35 (2.4)
cartoned	35	10.7	75 (5.2)	52 (3.6)	35 (2.4)	20 (1.4)	75 (5.2)	52 (3.6)
nonexpanded	40	12.2	—	52 (3.6)	—	25 (1.7)	—	—
Group A plastics	45	13.7	—	—	40 (2.8)	40 (2.8)	—	—
Cartoned	25	7.6	50 (3.4)	35 (2.4)	—	—	50 (3.4)	35 (2.4)
expanded	30	9.1	50 (3.4)	35 (2.4)	—	—	50 (3.4)	35 (2.4)
Group A plastics	35	10.7	—	—	—	—	—	—
	40	12.2	—	—	—	—	—	—
	45	13.7	—	—	—	—	—	—
Exposed	25	7.6	50 (3.4)	35 (2.4)	—	—	—	—
nonexpanded,	30	9.1	50 (3.4)	35 (2.4)	—	—	—	—
Group A plastics	35	10.7	—	—	—	—	—	—
	40	12.2	—	—	75 (5.2)	60 (4.1)	—	—
	45	13.7	In-rack sprinklers required. See Chapter 25.	—	—	—	—	—
Exposed	25	7.6	—	—	—	—	—	—
expanded	30	9.1	—	—	—	30 (2.0)[b]	—	—
Group A plastics	32	9.8	—	—	—	—	—	—
	35	10.7	—	—	—	—	—	—
	40	12.2	—	—	—	60 (4.1)[b,c]	—	—
	45	13.7	—	—	—	—	—	—

[a]See 20.3.2 for information regarding protection of lower hazard commodities with higher hazard criteria.
[b]These options apply when all requirements in Section 27.4 are applied including vertical barriers.
[c]This option applies to palletized and solid pile storage in a closed array.

Shaded text = Revisions.   Δ = Text deletions and figure/table revisions.   • = Section deletions.   N = New material.

Δ Table 23.5 ESFR Sprinklers for Protection of Rubber Tires

Piling Method	Pile Height	Maximum Building Height ft	Maximum Building Height m	Nominal K-factor	Orientation	Number of Sprinklers	Minimum Operating Pressure psi	Minimum Operating Pressure bar
Rubber tire storage, on-side or on-tread, in palletized portable racks, open portable racks, or fixed racks without solid shelves	Up to 25 ft (7.6 m)	30	9.1	14.0 (200)	Upright/pendent	12[a]	50	3.4
				16.8 (240)	Upright/pendent	12[a]	35	2.4
				22.4 (320)	Pendent	12[a]	25	1.7
				25.2 (360)	Pendent	12[a]	15	1.0
Rubber tire storage, on-side, in palletized portable racks, open portable racks, or fixed racks without solid shelves	Up to 25 ft (7.6 m)	35	10.7	14.0 (200)	Upright/pendent	12[a]	75	5.2
				16.8 (240)	Pendent	12[a]	52	3.6
				22.4 (320)	Pendent	12[a]	35	2.4
				25.2 (360)	Pendent	12[a]	25	1.7
On-tread, on-side, and laced tires in open portable steel racks or palletized portable racks	Up to 25 ft (7.6 m)	30	9.1	14.0 (200)	Pendent	20[b,c]	75	5.2
				16.8 (240)	Pendent	20[b,c]	52	3.6
Rubber tire storage, on-side, in palletized portable racks	Up to 25 ft (7.6 m)	40	12.2	16.8 (240)	Pendent	12[a]	52	3.6
Rubber tire storage, on-tread or laced in open portable steel racks	Up to 25 ft (7.6 m)	40	12.2	25.2 (360)	Pendent	12[a]	40	2.8
On-tread, on-side, and laced tires in open portable steel racks or palletized portable racks	Up to 30 ft (9.1 m)	40	12.2	25.2 (360)	Pendent	12[a]	75	5.2

Note: This table is applicable to wet systems only.
[a]The shape of the design area is in accordance with 23.2.2.
[b]Where used in this application, ESFR protection is expected to control rather than suppress the fire.
[c]The design area consists of the most hydraulically demanding 20 sprinklers, with five sprinklers on each of four branch lines. The design includes a minimum operating area of 1600 ft² (150 m²).

Δ Table 23.6 ESFR Sprinklers for Protection of Roll Paper Storage (Maximum Height of Storage Permitted)

ESFR K-Factor	Orientation	System Type	Pressure psi	Pressure bar	Building Height ft	Building Height m	Heavyweight Closed ft	Heavyweight Closed m	Heavyweight Standard ft	Heavyweight Standard m	Heavyweight Open ft	Heavyweight Open m	Mediumweight Closed ft	Mediumweight Closed m	Mediumweight Standard ft	Mediumweight Standard m	Mediumweight Open ft	Mediumweight Open m	Tissue All Arrays
14.0 (200)	Upright/pendent	Wet	50	3.4	30	9.1	25	7.6	25	7.6	25	7.6	25	7.6	25	7.6	25	7.6	NA
16.8 (240)	Upright/pendent	Wet	35	2.4															
22.4 (320)	Pendent	Wet	25	1.7															
25.2 (360)	Pendent	Wet	15	1.0															
14.0 (200)	Upright/pendent	Wet	75	5.2	35	10.7	30	9.1	30	9.1	30	9.1	NA		NA		NA		NA
16.8 (240)	Upright/pendent	Wet	52	3.6															
16.8 (240)	Pendent	Wet	52	3.6	40	12.2	30	9.1	30	9.1	30	9.1	NA		NA		NA		NA
22.4 (320)	Pendent	Wet	40	2.7															
25.2 (360)	Pendent	Wet	25	1.7															
22.4 (320)	Pendent	Wet	50	3.4	45	13.7	30	9.1	30	9.1	30	9.1	NA		NA		NA		NA
25.2 (360)	Pendent	Wet	50	3.4															

NA: Not applicable.

Chapter 24 Alternative Sprinkler System Designs for Chapters 20 Through 25

24.1* General.

24.1.1 Sprinklers intended to protect storage fire risks shall be permitted to be installed using water supply design criteria that are different from the design criteria specified for the sprinklers described in Chapters 20 through 23 and 25 when specifically listed for such use within the limitations described in this chapter.

24.1.2 The requirements of Chapters 20 through 23 and 25 shall apply unless modified by this chapter.

24.1.2.1 Sprinklers having standard coverage areas that require up to 20 sprinklers to be included in the hydraulic calculation shall be installed in accordance with 14.2.3, 14.2.4, 14.2.4.1, and 20.9.5.

24.1.2.1.1 Quick-response sprinklers shall also be installed in accordance with 14.2.5.1 and 14.2.5.2.

24.1.2.2 Sprinklers having extended coverage areas that require up to 10 sprinklers to be included in the hydraulic calculation shall be installed in accordance with 14.2.3, 14.2.4, 14.2.4.1, and 20.9.5.

24.1.2.2.1 Quick-response sprinklers shall also be installed in accordance with 14.2.5.1 and 14.2.5.2.

24.1.3 The in-rack protection requirements of Chapter 25 shall apply when storage racks are equipped with solid shelves, and in-rack sprinklers are required per the applicable chapter.

24.1.4 The requirements of the applicable chapter shall apply when ceiling-only protection options are not available per this chapter.

24.1.5 The design criteria in this chapter shall not be used to permit a reduction in the water supply requirements for in-rack sprinkler protection.

24.1.6 A series of large-scale fire tests involving challenging test scenarios that address the range of variables associated with the intended application of the sprinkler shall be conducted to evaluate the ability of the sprinkler to protect storage fire risks that are representative of those described in the manufacturer's installation and design parameter instructions and referenced in the listing.

24.1.7 The manufacturer's installation and design parameter instructions for these sprinklers shall specify in a standardized manner the end-use limitations and sprinkler system design criteria including at least the following:

(1) Commodity or commodities to be protected
(2) Storage arrangements allowed
(3) Installation guidelines including obstruction and ceiling construction limitations
(4) Maximum ceiling and storage heights with associated minimum operating pressures and number of sprinklers required to be included in the hydraulic calculation
(5) Hose stream allowance and duration

24.1.8 The number of sprinklers to be used in the sprinkler system design shall be based on the worst-case result obtained from the full-scale fire test series increased by a minimum 50 percent.

24.1.8.1 Regardless of the number of sprinklers that operated during the worst-case full-scale fire test, the number in the sprinkler system demand shall be no less than one of the following:

(1) Twelve sprinklers for standard coverage sprinklers
(2) Eight sprinklers for extended-coverage sprinklers based on a spacing of 12 ft × 12 ft (3.7 × 3.7 m)
(3) Six sprinklers for extended-coverage sprinklers based on a spacing of 14 ft × 14 ft (4.3 m × 4.3 m)

24.1.8.2 Once the number of sprinklers for a demand area has been established, the minimum operating area, based on the proposed sprinkler spacing, shall not be less than 768 ft² (71 m²).

24.1.8.3 The design area and number of sprinklers calculated on a branch line shall be in accordance with 28.2.4.2 using an area of sprinkler operation equal to the required number of operating sprinklers and the maximum allowable coverage for the specific design criteria being utilized.

24.1.9 Listed storage sprinklers that are not specifically referenced in Sections 24.2 and 24.3 but are tested in accordance with Chapter 24 with system design criteria based upon Sections 24.1, 24.4, and 24.5 shall be permitted to be used in accordance with their listing limitations, where approved.

24.2* Sprinkler Design Criteria for Palletized and Solid-Piled, Storage of Class I Through Class IV and Plastic Commodities.

24.2.1 Protection of palletized and solid-piled storage of Class I through Class IV and cartoned nonexpanded plastic commodities shall be permitted to be protected in accordance with Table 24.2.1.

24.3* Sprinkler Protection Criteria for Open-Frame Rack Storage of Class I Through Class IV and Plastic Commodities.

24.3.1 Protection of single-, double-, and multiple-row racks without solid shelves of Class I through Class IV and cartoned nonexpanded plastic commodities shall be permitted to be protected in accordance with Table 24.3.1.

24.3.2 Protection of Class I through Class IV and cartoned nonexpanded plastic commodities stored on single-, double-, or multiple-row racks without solid shelves or solid-piled, palletized, storage arrangements shall be permitted to be protected in accordance with Table 24.3.2(a) or Table 24.3.2(b).

24.3.3 Protection of open rack storage of Class I through Class III commodities with dry pipe systems using standard response upright sprinkler design criteria and high-temperature-rated sprinklers shall be in accordance with Table 24.3.3.

24.3.3.1 For protection criteria using a minimum operating pressure of 15 psi (1 bar), a maximum water delivery time of 25 seconds shall be used.

24.3.3.2 For protection criteria using a minimum operating pressure of 50 psi (3.4 bar), a maximum water delivery time of 20 seconds shall be used.

Δ Table 24.2.1 Extended Coverage, CMSA [K-factor 25.2 (360)] Sprinkler Design Criteria for Palletized and Solid-Piled Storage of Class I Through Class IV and Cartoned Nonexpanded Plastic Commodities

Storage Arrangement	Commodity Class	Maximum Storage Height		Maximum Ceiling/Roof Height		K-Factor/ Orientation	Type of System	Number of Design Sprinklers	Minimum Operating Pressure	Maximum Coverage Area
		ft	m	ft	m					
Palletized and solid-piled	Class I through Class IV, encapsulated and nonencapsulated, and cartoned nonexpanded plastics	20	6.1	30	9.1	25.2 (360) Upright/ pendent	Wet	6	30 psi (2.1 bar)	12 ft × 12 ft (3.7 m × 3.7 m) 144 ft² (13 m²)
		20	6.1	30	9.1	25.2 (360) Upright/ pendent	Wet	6	30 psi (2.1 bar)	14 ft × 14 ft (4.3 m × 4.3 m) 196 ft² (18 m²)
		25	7.6	30	9.1	25.2 (360) Upright/ pendent	Wet	6	30 psi (2.1 bar)	12 ft × 12 ft (3.7 m × 3.7 m) 144 ft² (13 m²)
		25	7.6	30	9.1	25.2 (360) Upright/ pendent	Wet	6	30 psi (2.1 bar)	14 ft × 14 ft (4.3 m × 4.3 m) 196 ft² (18 m²)
		25	7.6	35	10.7	25.2 (360) Upright/ pendent	Wet	8	40 psi (2.8 bar)	12 ft × 12 ft (3.7 m × 3.7 m) 144 ft² (13 m²)
		25	7.6	35	10.7	25.2 (360) Upright	Wet	8	40 psi (2.8 bar)	14 ft × 14 ft (4.3 m × 4.3 m) 196 ft² (18 m²)
		30	9.1	35	10.7	25.2 (360) Upright/ pendent	Wet	8	40 psi (2.8 bar)	12 ft × 12 ft (3.7 m × 3.7 m) 144 ft² (13 m²)
		30	9.1	35	10.7	25.2 (360) Upright	Wet	8	40 psi (2.8 bar)	14 ft × 14 ft (4.3 m × 4.3 m) 196 ft² (18 m²)

Δ Table 24.3.1 Extended Coverage, CMSA [K-Factor 25.2 (360)] Sprinkler Design Criteria for Single-, Double-, and Multiple-Row Racks Without Solid Shelves of Class I Through Class IV and Cartoned Nonexpanded Plastic Commodities

Storage Arrangement	Commodity Class	Maximum Storage Height		Maximum Ceiling/Roof Height		K-Factor/ Orientation	Type of System	Number of Design Sprinklers	Minimum Operating Pressure	Maximum Coverage Area
		ft	m	ft	m					
Single-, double-, and multiple-row racks without solid shelves (no open-top containers)	Class I through Class IV, encapsulated and nonencapsulated, and cartoned nonexpanded plastics	20	6.1	30	9.1	25.2 (360) Upright/ pendent	Wet	6	30 psi (2.1 bar)	12 ft × 12 ft (3.7 m × 3.7 m) 144 ft² (13 m²)
		20	6.1	30	9.1	25.2 (360) Upright/ pendent	Wet	6	30 psi (2.1 bar)	14 ft × 14 ft (4.3 m × 4.3 m) 196 ft² (18 m²)
		25	7.6	30	9.1	25.2 (360) Upright/ pendent	Wet	6	30 psi (2.1 bar)	12 ft × 12 ft (3.7 m × 3.7 m) 144 ft² (13 m²)
		25	7.6	30	9.1	25.2 (360) Upright/ pendent	Wet	6	30 psi (2.1 bar)	14 ft × 14 ft (4.3 m × 4.3 m) 196 ft² (18 m²)
		25	7.6	35	10.7	25.2 (360) Upright/ pendent	Wet	8	40 psi (2.8 bar)	12 ft × 12 ft (3.7 m × 3.7 m) 144 ft² (13 m²)
		25	7.6	35	10.7	25.2 (360) Upright	Wet	8	40 psi (2.8 bar)	14 ft × 14 ft (4.3 m × 4.3 m) 196 ft² (18 m²)
		30	9.1	35	10.7	25.2 (360) Upright/ pendent	Wet	8	40 psi (2.8 bar)	12 ft × 12 ft (3.7 m × 3.7 m) 144 ft² (13 m²)
		30	9.1	35	10.7	25.2 (360) Upright	Wet	8	40 psi (2.8 bar)	14 ft × 14 ft (4.3 m × 4.3 m) 196 ft² (18 m²)

Shaded text = Revisions.   Δ = Text deletions and figure/table revisions.   • = Section deletions.   N = New material.

2022 Edition

Δ Table 24.3.2(a) CMSA K-25.2 (K-360) Upright Standard Coverage Sprinkler Design Criteria for Single-, Double-, and Multiple-Row Racks Without Solid Shelves and Solid-Piled, Palletized Storage Arrangement of Class I Through IV and Cartoned Nonexpanded Plastic Commodities

Storage Arrangement	Commodity Class	Maximum Storage Height		Maximum Ceiling/Roof Height		K-Factor/ Orientation	System Type	Number of Design Sprinklers	Minimum Operating Pressure	Sprinkler Linear Spacing		Sprinkler Area Spacing	
		ft	m	ft	m					Min	Max	Min	Max
Solid-piled, palletized, and single-, double-, and multiple-row racks without solid shelves (no open-top containers)	Class I–IV encapsulated and nonencapsulated, and cartoned nonexpanded plastics	25	7.6	30	9.1	25.2 (360) Upright	Wet	12	20 psi (1.4 bar)	8 ft (2.4 m)	12 ft (3.7 m)	80 ft² (7.4 m²)	100 ft² (9.0 m²)

Δ Table 24.3.2(b) CMSA K-25.2 (K-360) Pendent Standard Coverage Sprinkler Design Criteria for Single-, Double-, and Multiple-Row Racks Without Solid Shelves and Solid-Piled, Palletized Storage Arrangement of Class I Through IV and Cartoned Nonexpanded Plastic Commodities

Storage Arrangement	Commodity Class	Maximum Storage Height		Maximum Ceiling/Roof Height		K-Factor/ Orientation	System Type	Number of Design Sprinklers	Minimum Operating Pressure	Sprinkler Linear Spacing		Sprinkler Area Spacing	
		ft	m	ft	m					Min	Max	Min	Max
Solid-piled, palletized, and single-, double-, and multiple-row racks without solid shelves (no open-top containers)	Class I–IV encapsulated and nonencapsulated, and cartoned nonexpanded plastics	25	7.6	30	9.1	25.2 (360) Pendent	Wet	12	15 psi (1.0 bar)	8 ft (2.4 m)	12 ft (3.7 m)	80 ft² (7.5 m²)	100 ft² (9.0 m²)

Δ Table 24.3.3 Standard Response Upright Sprinkler Design Criteria for Open Rack Storage of Class I Through Class III Commodities (Using High-Temperature-Rated Sprinklers)

Storage Arrangement	Commodity Class	Maximum Storage Height		Maximum Ceiling/ Roof Height		K-Factor	Type of System	Number of Design Sprinklers	Minimum Operating Pressure	
		ft	m	ft	m				psi	bar
Rack storage without solid shelves (no open-top containers)	Class I, Class II, or Class III	35	10.7	40	12.2	25.2 (360)	Dry	24	15*	1.0*
		40	12.2	45	13.7	25.2 (360)	Dry	12	50†	3.4†
		45	13.7	50	15.2	33.6 (480)	Dry	15	50†	3.4†
		50	15.2	55	16.7	33.6 (480)	Dry	16	50†	3.4†

*25-second water delivery time maximum.
†20-second water delivery time maximum.

Δ **24.4 Hose Stream Allowance and Water Supply Duration.**

Δ **24.4.1** The minimum water supply requirements for a hydraulically designed sprinkler system shall be determined by adding the hose stream allowance from Table 20.15.2.6 to the water supply for sprinklers obtained from this chapter.

Δ **24.4.1.1** The water supply requirements for a hydraulically designed sprinkler system shall be available for the minimum duration specified in Table 20.15.2.6.

24.5 Minimum Obstruction Criteria.

24.5.1 General. The installation guidelines for obstructions to ceiling-level sprinklers shall be in accordance with the requirements of Section 24.5 for sprinkler system designs obtained from this chapter.

Δ **24.5.2 Standard Coverage Sprinklers.**

24.5.2.1 Sprinklers having standard coverage areas requiring up to 20 sprinklers to be included in the hydraulic calculation shall be installed in accordance with the obstruction criteria described in 14.2.11, unless large-scale fire testing is conducted with a representative obstruction below the sprinkler that demonstrates equivalent performance.

24.5.2.2 CMDA and CMSA sprinklers having standard coverage areas requiring more than 20 sprinklers in the design area shall be installed in accordance with the obstructions to sprinkler discharge criteria described in 13.2.8.

24.5.2.3 ESFR sprinklers having standard-coverage areas requiring more than 20 sprinklers in the design area shall be installed in accordance with the obstructions to sprinkler discharge criteria described in 14.2.11.

24.5.2.4 Other obstruction criteria shall be acceptable if large-scale fire testing is conducted with a representative obstruction below the sprinkler that demonstrates equivalent performance.

Δ **24.5.3 Extended Coverage Sprinklers.**

24.5.3.1 Sprinklers having extended coverage areas requiring up to 10 sprinklers to be included in the hydraulic calculation shall be installed in accordance with the obstruction criteria described in 11.2.5.1, 14.2.11.2, and 14.2.11.3, unless large-scale fire testing is conducted with a representative obstruction below the sprinkler that demonstrates equivalent performance.

24.5.3.2 CMDA and CMSA sprinklers having extended coverage areas requiring more than 10 sprinklers in the design area shall be installed in accordance with the obstructions to sprinkler discharge criteria described in 13.2.8 and 11.2.5.1.

24.5.3.3 Other obstruction criteria shall be acceptable if large-scale fire testing is conducted with a representative obstruction below the sprinkler that demonstrates equivalent performance.

24.5.3.4 When utilizing upright CMSA, CMDA, or ESFR sprinklers, any continuous obstruction 4 in. (100 mm) or less shall be permitted to be ignored.

Chapter 25 Protection of Rack Storage Using In-Rack Sprinklers

25.1 General Requirements for Ceiling and In-Rack Sprinklers Protecting Rack Storage.

N **25.1.1 Scope.**

N **25.1.1.1*** This chapter shall apply to the storage of Class I through Class IV and Group A plastic commodities as well as rubber tires representing the broad range of combustibles stored in racks that will be protected by in-rack sprinklers.

N **25.1.1.2** The requirements of Chapter 20 shall apply unless modified by this chapter. *(See Section C.9).*

N **25.1.2 Chapter Organization.** This chapter is organized as follows:

(1) Section 25.1 contains general requirements for the entire chapter.

(2) Section 25.2 contains requirements for the protection of miscellaneous and low-piled rack storage using in-rack sprinklers.

(3) Section 25.3 contains requirements for in-rack sprinkler protection in combination with CMDA ceiling-level sprinklers.

(4) Section 25.4 contains requirements for in-rack sprinkler protection in combination with CMSA ceiling-level sprinklers.

(5) Section 25.5 contains requirements for in-rack sprinkler protection in combination with ESFR ceiling-level sprinklers.

(6) Section 25.6 contains requirements for in-rack sprinkler protection independent of ceiling-level sprinklers.

(7) Section 25.7 contains requirements for the evaluation or modification of existing protection for miscellaneous and low-piled rack storage using in-rack sprinklers.

(8) Section 25.8 contains requirements for the evaluation or modification of existing protection for CMDA ceiling-level sprinkler rack storage protection of Class I through Class IV commodities over 12 ft (3.7 m) and up to and including 25 ft (7.6 m) using in-rack sprinklers.

N **25.1.3 Building Steel Protection.** Where in-rack sprinklers are installed in accordance with this chapter, building steel shall not require special protection.

N **25.1.4 In-Rack Sprinkler System.**

N **25.1.4.1 In-Rack Sprinkler System Size.** An area protected by a single in-rack sprinkler system shall not exceed 40,000 ft² (3,720 m²) of floor area occupied by the racks, including aisles, regardless of the number of in-rack sprinkler levels.

N **25.1.4.2* In-Rack Sprinkler System Control Valves.**

N **25.1.4.2.1** Unless the requirements of 25.1.4.2.2 or 25.1.4.2.3 are met, separate indicating control valves and drains shall be provided and arranged so that ceiling and in-rack sprinkler systems can be controlled independently.

N **25.1.4.2.2** A separate indicating control valve shall not be required where 20 or fewer in-rack sprinklers are supplied by any one ceiling sprinkler system.

N **25.1.4.2.3** The separate indicating valves shall be permitted to be arranged as sectional control valves supplied from the ceiling sprinkler system where in-rack sprinklers are required and

the racks, including the adjacent aisles, occupy 8000 ft² (745 m²) or less of the area protected by the ceiling sprinklers.

N **25.1.4.3* In-Rack Sprinkler Waterflow Alarm. (Reserved)**

N **25.1.5* Open Rack Storage.** The in-rack sprinkler arrangements as well as the ceiling and in-rack sprinkler design criteria for rack storage in this chapter shall be based on open rack configurations as defined in 3.3.147 unless indicated otherwise.

N **25.1.6 In-Rack Sprinkler Characteristics.**

N **25.1.6.1** In-rack sprinklers shall be pendent or upright, standard- or quick-response, ordinary-temperature-rated and have a minimum nominal K-factor of K-5.6 (80) unless indicated otherwise.

N **25.1.6.2** In-rack sprinklers with intermediate- and high-temperature ratings shall be used near heat sources as required by 9.4.2.

N **25.1.6.3** In-rack sprinklers shall be permitted to have a different RTI rating from the ceiling sprinklers under which they are installed.

N **25.1.6.4** Where in-rack sprinklers are not shielded by horizontal barriers, either water shields shall be provided above the sprinklers or listed intermediate level/rack storage sprinklers shall be used. *(See Section C.3.)*

N **25.1.7 Horizontal Location of In-Rack Sprinklers.**

N **25.1.7.1** The horizontal location and spacing of in-rack sprinklers shall be as shown in the figures of the applicable section of this chapter, and as follows:

(1) The rack plan view shall be considered in determining the maximum area covered by each sprinkler when protecting multiple-row racks.

(2) The aisles shall not be included in the area calculations.

N **25.1.7.2** In-rack sprinklers shall not be required to meet the obstruction criteria and clearance from storage requirements of Section 9.5.

N **25.1.7.3*** Where in-rack sprinklers are installed in longitudinal flues, they shall be located at an intersection of transverse and longitudinal flues while not exceeding the maximum horizontal spacing rules.

N **25.1.7.4** Where horizontal distances between transverse flues exceed the maximum allowable horizontal linear spacing for in-rack sprinklers, in-rack sprinklers shall be installed at the intersection of the transverse and longitudinal flues, and additional in-rack sprinklers shall be installed between transverse flues to meet the maximum allowable horizontal linear spacing rules for in-rack sprinklers.

N **25.1.7.5** In-rack sprinklers shall be permitted to be installed horizontally less than 6 ft (1.8 m) apart.

N **25.1.7.6 Higher-Hazard Commodities.**

N **25.1.7.6.1** Where in-rack sprinklers are installed to protect a higher-hazard commodity that occupies only a portion of the length of a rack, in-rack sprinklers shall be extended a minimum of 8 ft (2.4 m) or one bay, whichever is greater, in each direction along the rack on either side of the higher hazard.

N **25.1.7.6.2** In-rack sprinklers protecting a higher-hazard commodity shall not be required to extend across the aisle.

N **25.1.7.7** Where rack storage of Class I through Class IV commodities is up to and including 25 ft (7.6 m), in-rack sprinklers shall be permitted to be installed horizontally without regard to rack uprights. *(See Section C.17.)*

N **25.1.7.8*** Where rack storage is over 25 ft (7.6 m) in height, in-rack sprinklers shall be a minimum 3 in. (75 mm) radially from the side of rack uprights.

N **25.1.7.9** Where rack storage is over 25 ft (7.6 m) in height and will be protected by face sprinklers, the face sprinklers shall be located within the rack a minimum 3 in. (75 mm) from rack uprights and no more than 18 in. (450 mm) from the aisle face of storage.

N **25.1.7.10 In-Rack Sprinklers for Single-Row Racks.**

N **25.1.7.10.1** Unless indicated otherwise, in-rack sprinklers protecting single-row racks shall be installed in the transverse flue space at any point between the load faces.

N **25.1.7.10.2*** Where the horizontal distance between a single-row rack and an adjacent full-height wall does not exceed 2 ft (0.6 m), in-rack sprinklers shall be permitted to be installed within this space as if it were a longitudinal flue of a double-row rack.

N **25.1.8 Vertical Location of In-Rack Sprinklers.**

N **25.1.8.1*** Where one level of in-rack sprinklers is required by the guidelines of this chapter and the vertical location of the in-rack sprinklers is not indicated in an applicable figure, in-rack sprinklers shall be installed at the first tier level at or above one-half of the highest expected storage height.

N **25.1.8.2** Where two levels of in-rack sprinklers are required by the guidelines of this chapter and the vertical location of the in-rack sprinklers is not indicated in an applicable figure, in-rack sprinklers shall be installed at the first tier level at or above one-third and two-thirds of the highest expected storage height.

N **25.1.8.3 Vertical Clear Space Between Top of Storage and In-Rack Sprinkler Deflectors.**

N **25.1.8.3.1*** A minimum 6 in. (150 mm) vertical clear space shall be maintained between in-rack sprinkler deflectors and the top of storage located below them.

N **25.1.8.3.2*** Where in-rack sprinklers are being installed within single- and double-row racks of Class I through Class IV commodities up to and including 20 ft (6.1 m) in height, the vertical clear space of in-rack sprinkler deflectors with respect to the top of storage located below them shall be permitted to be less than 6 in. (150 mm). *(See Section C.16.)*

N **25.1.8.4** In-rack sprinklers shall not be required to meet the obstruction criteria and clearance from storage requirements of Section 9.5.

N **25.1.8.5** In-rack sprinkler discharge shall not be obstructed by horizontal rack members.

N **25.1.8.6** All in-rack sprinkler vertical spacings shown in the applicable figures start from the floor.

N **25.1.9 Horizontal Barriers in Combination with In-Rack Sprinklers.**

N **25.1.9.1*** Where required by sections of this chapter, horizontal barriers used in combination with in-rack sprinklers to impede vertical fire development shall be constructed of sheet metal, wood, or similar material and shall extend the full length and depth of the rack.

N **25.1.9.2** Barriers shall be fitted within 3 in. (75 mm) horizontally around rack uprights.

N **25.1.10 Design Criteria for In-Rack Sprinklers in Combination with Ceiling-Level Sprinklers.**

N **25.1.10.1** The design pressure for the most remote in-rack sprinkler shall not be less than 7 psi (0.5 bar).

N **25.1.10.2** In-rack sprinkler design criteria for Group A plastic commodities shall be permitted for the protection of the same storage height and configuration of Class I, Class II, Class III, and Class IV commodities.

N **25.1.10.3** Pipe sizing of an in-rack sprinkler system shall be permitted to be based on hydraulic calculations and not restricted by any pipe schedule.

N **25.1.10.4** Where in-rack sprinklers are being installed to protect a storage rack and, due to the length of the rack, fewer in-rack sprinklers will be installed than the number of in-rack sprinklers specified in the design, the in-rack sprinkler design shall be based on only those in-rack sprinklers installed within the protected rack.

N **25.1.10.5** Where in-rack sprinkler arrangements have been installed in accordance with this chapter, except for those specified in Section 25.6, the flow and pressure requirements of both the ceiling and in-rack sprinkler systems over the same protected area shall be hydraulically balanced together to the higher sprinkler system pressure requirement at their point of connection.

N **25.1.11 Aisle Width for Group A Plastic Commodities.**

N **25.1.11.1** Unless indicated otherwise in this chapter, ceiling-level sprinkler design criteria for single- and double-row rack storage of Group A plastic commodities shall be applicable where aisles are 3.5 ft (1.1 m) or greater in width.

N **25.1.11.2** Unless indicated otherwise in this chapter, ceiling-level sprinkler design criteria for rack storage of Group A plastic commodities shall be protected as multiple-row racks where aisles are less than 3.5 ft (1.1 m) in width.

N **25.1.12* Group A Plastic Commodity Protection for Class I, Class II, Class III, or Class IV Commodities.** Ceiling-level sprinkler design criteria as well as in-rack sprinkler design criteria for Group A plastic commodities in this chapter shall be permitted for the protection of the same storage height and configuration of Class I, Class II, Class III, or Class IV commodities.

N **25.1.13 Water Supply Requirements.** Unless indicated otherwise in this chapter, the minimum water supply requirements for a hydraulically designed ceiling and in-rack sprinkler system shall be determined by adding the hose stream allowance from Table 20.15.2.6 to the water demand for sprinklers.

N **25.2 Protection of Miscellaneous and Low-Piled Rack Storage Using In-Rack Sprinklers.**

N **25.2.1 Miscellaneous Rack Storage.**

N **25.2.1.1 Scope.** This section shall apply to miscellaneous rack storage up to and including 12 ft (3.7 m) in height of Class I through Class IV commodities, Group A plastic commodities, and rubber tires.

N 25.2.1.2 In-Rack Sprinkler Design for Miscellaneous Storage. Where in-rack sprinklers are installed in accordance with this section to protect miscellaneous rack storage of Class I through Class IV commodities, Group A plastic commodities, and rubber tires up to and including 12 ft (3.7 m) in height, the in-rack sprinkler design shall be based on the hydraulically most demanding four adjacent in-rack sprinklers using a minimum flow of 22 gpm (83 L/min) from the hydraulically most remote in-rack sprinkler.

N 25.2.1.3 Horizontal Spacing of In-Rack Sprinklers for Miscellaneous Storage. The maximum allowable horizontal spacing of in-rack sprinklers is 10 ft (3.0 m).

N 25.2.1.4 Ceiling Sprinkler Design in Combination with In-Rack Sprinklers for Miscellaneous Storage.

N 25.2.1.4.1 Where in-rack sprinklers are installed in accordance with this chapter to protect miscellaneous rack storage of Class I through Class IV commodities, Group A plastic commodities, and rubber tires up to and including 12 ft (3.7 m) in height under a maximum 32 ft (9.8 m) high ceiling, the ceiling-level sprinkler design criteria shall be a 0.20 gpm/ft² (0.8.2 mm/min) density over a 1500 ft² (140 m²) area of ceiling-level sprinkler operation.

N 25.2.1.4.2 Installation criteria as permitted by this standard and design criteria and modifiers as permitted by the density/area method of Section 19.1 for ordinary hazard Group 2 occupancies shall be applicable.

N 25.2.1.4.3 The sprinkler system criteria specified in this chapter for miscellaneous storage shall not be limited to a ceiling slope of 2 in 12 (16.7 percent).

N 25.2.1.5 Hose Connections. Hose connections shall not be required for the protection of miscellaneous storage.

N 25.2.2 Low-Piled Rack Storage.

N 25.2.2.1 Scope. This section shall apply to any of the following situations:

(1) Rack storage of Class I through Class IV commodities up to and including 12 ft (3.7 m) in height
(2)* Rack storage of Group A plastic commodities up to and including 5 ft (1.5 m) in height

N 25.2.2.2 In-Rack Sprinkler Design for Low-Piled Storage. Where in-rack sprinklers are installed in accordance with this section to protect low-piled rack storage of Class I through Class IV commodities up to and including 12 ft (3.7 m) in height and low-piled rack storage of Group A plastic commodities up to and including 5 ft (1.5 m) in height, the in-rack sprinkler design shall be based on the hydraulically most demanding four adjacent in-rack sprinklers using a minimum flow of 22 gpm (83 L/min) from the hydraulically most remote in-rack sprinkler.

N 25.2.2.3 Horizontal Spacing of In-Rack Sprinklers for Low-Piled Storage. The maximum allowable horizontal spacing of in-rack sprinklers is 10 ft (3.0 m).

N 25.2.2.4 Ceiling Sprinkler Design in Combination with In-Rack Sprinklers for Low-Piled Storage.

N 25.2.2.4.1 Where in-rack sprinklers are installed in accordance with this section to protect low-piled rack storage of Class I through Class IV and Group A plastic commodities, that does not meet the definition of miscellaneous storage, the ceiling-level design shall be a 0.20 gpm/ft² (0.8.2 mm/min) density over a 1500 ft² (140 m²) area of ceiling-level sprinkler operation.

N 25.2.2.4.2 The sprinkler system criteria specified in this chapter for low-piled storage shall not be limited to a ceiling slope of 2 in 12 (16.7 percent).

N 25.2.2.5 Ceiling Sprinkler Design in Combination with In-Rack Sprinklers for Low-Piled Storage with Solid Shelves.

N 25.2.2.5.1 For low-piled rack storage with solid shelves of Class I through Class IV commodities up to and including 12 ft (3.7 m) in height that does not meet the definition of miscellaneous storage, the ceiling-level sprinkler design shall be permitted to be a 0.20 gpm/ft² (0.8.2 mm/min) density over a 1500 ft² (140 m²) area of ceiling-level sprinkler operation where the in-rack sprinklers are installed in accordance with Section 20.19.

N 25.2.2.5.2 For low-piled rack storage with solid shelves of Group A plastic commodities up to and including 5 ft (1.5 m) in height that does not meet the definition of miscellaneous storage, the ceiling-level sprinkler design shall be permitted to be a 0.20 gpm/ft² (0.8.2 mm/min) density over a 1500 ft² (140 m²) area of ceiling-level sprinkler operation where the in-rack sprinklers are installed in accordance with Section 20.19.

N 25.3 In-Rack Sprinkler Protection in Combination with CMDA Ceiling-Level Sprinklers.

N 25.3.1 General.

N 25.3.1.1 In-Rack Sprinkler Design Criteria in Combination with CMDA Ceiling-Level Sprinklers. The in-rack sprinkler system design, in terms of the number of operating sprinklers at a minimum flow from the most remote in-rack sprinkler, in combination with CMDA ceiling-level sprinklers shall be in accordance with Table 25.3.1.1. *(See Sections C.18 and C.19.)*

N 25.3.1.2 CMDA Ceiling-Level Sprinkler Design Criteria in Combination with In-Rack Sprinklers.

N 25.3.1.2.1 CMDA Ceiling-level sprinkler design criteria, in combination with in-rack sprinklers, for rack storage over 12 ft (3.7 m) and up to and including 25 ft (7.6 m) in height of Class I through Class IV commodities and rubber tires shall be in accordance with the following:

(1) For the storage of exposed nonencapsulated Class I through Class IV commodities, see 25.3.2.1.2
(2) For the storage of exposed encapsulated, or cartoned (nonencapsulated or encapsulated) Class I through Class IV commodities, see 25.3.2.2.2
(3) For the storage of rubber tires see 25.3.2.5.2

N Table 25.3.1.1 Design Criteria for In-Rack Sprinklers in Combination with CMDA Ceiling-Level Sprinklers for Storage Not Meeting the Definition of Miscellaneous

Commodity Classification	Rack Type	Storage Height ft (m)	No. of IRAS Levels	IRAS Design, No. of IRAS @ gpm (L/min)
Class I, Class II or Class III	Open	Up to 25 (7.6)	1	6 @ 22 (83)
			More than 1	10 (5 in-rack sprinklers on top 2 in-rack sprinkler levels) @ 22 (83)
		Over 25 (7.6)	1	6 @ 30 (114)
			More than 1	10 (5 in-rack sprinklers on top 2 in-rack sprinkler levels) @ 30 (114)
	Solid shelves	Up to 25 (7.6)	1	6 @ 30 (114)
			More than 1	10 (5 in-rack sprinklers on top 2 in-rack sprinkler levels) @ 30 (114)
		Over 25 (7.6)	1	6 @ 30 (114)
			More than 1	10 (5 in-rack sprinklers on top 2 in-rack sprinkler levels) @ 30 (114)
Class IV	Open	Up to 25 (7.6)	1	8 @ 22 (83)
			More than 1	10 (5 in-rack sprinklers on top 2 in-rack sprinkler levels) @ 22 (83)
		Over 25 (7.6)	1	8 @ 30 (114)
			More than 1	10 (5 in-rack sprinklers on top 2 in-rack sprinkler levels) @ 30 (114)
	Solid shelves	Up to 25 (7.6)	1	8 @ 30 (114)
			More than 1	14 (7 in-rack sprinklers on top 2 in-rack sprinkler levels) @ 30 (114)
		Over 25 (7.6)	1	8 @ 30 (114)
			More than 1	14 (7 in-rack sprinklers on top 2 in-rack sprinkler levels) @ 30 (114)
Group A plastics	Open	Up to 25 (7.6)	1	8 @ 22 (83)
			More than 1	14 (7 in-rack sprinklers on top 2 in-rack sprinkler levels) @ 22 (83)
		Over 25 (7.6)	1	8 @ 30 (114)
			More than 1	14 (7 in-rack sprinklers on top 2 in-rack sprinkler levels) @ 30 (114)
	Solid shelves	Up to 25 (7.6)	1	8 @ 30 (114)
			More than 1	14 (7 in-rack sprinklers on top 2 in-rack sprinkler levels) @ 30 (114)
		Over 25 (7.6)	1	8 @ 30 (114)
			More than 1	14 (7 in-rack sprinklers on top 2 in-rack sprinkler levels) @ 30 (114)
Rubber tires	Open	Up to 20 (6.1)	1	12 @ 30 (114)

N **25.3.1.2.2** CMDA Ceiling-level sprinkler design criteria, in combination with in-rack sprinklers, for rack storage over 5 ft (1.5 m) and up to and including 25 ft (7.6 m) in height of Group A plastic commodities shall be in accordance with the following:

(1) For the storage of cartoned Group A plastic commodities, see 25.3.2.3.2

(2) For the storage of exposed nonexpanded Group A plastic commodities, see 25.3.2.4.2

N **25.3.1.2.3** CMDA Ceiling-level sprinkler design criteria, in combination with in-rack sprinklers, for rack storage over 25 ft (7.6 m) in height of Class I through Class IV and Group A plastic commodities shall be in accordance with the following:

(1) For the storage of exposed nonexpanded Class I through Class IV commodities, see 25.3.3.1.2

(2) For the storage of exposed encapsulated, or cartoned (nonencapsulated or encapsulated) Class I through Class IV commodities, see 25.3.3.2.2

(3) For the storage of cartoned Group A plastic commodities, see 25.3.3.3.2

(4) For the storage of exposed nonexpanded Group A plastic commodities, see 25.3.3.3.2

N **25.3.1.2.4** The water supply for CMDA ceiling-level sprinklers in combination with in-rack sprinklers shall be determined from the CMDA ceiling-level sprinkler design requirements of Section 25.3.

N **25.3.1.2.5** The ceiling-level sprinkler system design area shall meet the requirements of 28.2.4.2.1.

N **25.3.1.3 CMDA Ceiling-Level Sprinkler Characteristics.** CMDA Ceiling-level sprinkler characteristics in combination with in-rack sprinklers shall be in accordance with Figure 25.3.1.3.

N **25.3.2 Ceiling and In-Rack Sprinkler Protection for Rack Storage Heights Up to and Including 25 ft (7.6 m).**

N **25.3.2.1 Exposed Nonencapsulated Class I, Class II, Class III, or Class IV Commodities.**

N **25.3.2.1.1* In-Rack Sprinkler Arrangements and Designs for Exposed Nonencapsulated Class I, Class II, Class III, or Class IV Commodities Stored Up to and Including 25 ft (7.6 m) in Height.**

N **25.3.2.1.1.1** Where rack storage of exposed nonencapsulated Class I through Class IV commodities stored over 12 ft (3.7 m) and up to and including 25 ft (7.6 m) in height will be protected by in-rack sprinklers, the following levels of in-rack sprinklers shall be required:

(1) One level of in-rack sprinklers where Class I through Class IV commodities are stored in single- or double-row racks up to and including 25 ft (7.6 m)

(2) One level of in-rack sprinklers where Class IV commodities are stored in multiple-row racks up to and including 20 ft (6.1 m)

(3) Two levels of in-rack sprinklers where Class IV commodities are stored in multiple-row racks over 20 ft (6.1 m) and up to and including 25 ft (7.6 m)

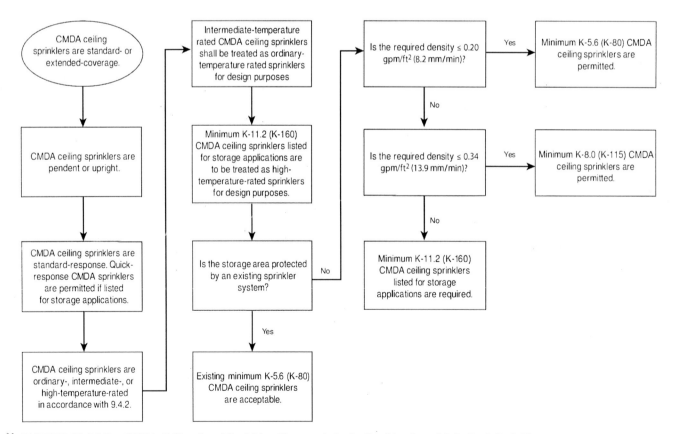

N **FIGURE 25.3.1.3   CMDA Ceiling-Level Sprinkler Characteristics in Combination with In-Rack Sprinklers.**

N **25.3.2.1.1.2** Where rack storage of exposed nonencapsulated Class I or Class II commodities stored over 12 ft (3.7 m) and up to and including 25 ft (7.6 m) in height will be protected by in-rack sprinklers, in-rack sprinkler arrangements and designs shall be selected from Figure 25.3.2.1.1.2(a) through Figure 25.3.2.1.1.2(c). *(See Section 20.19 for racks with solid shelving.)*

N **25.3.2.1.1.3** Where rack storage of exposed nonencapsulated Class III commodities stored over 12 ft (3.7 m) and up to and including 25 ft (7.6 m) in height will be protected by in-rack sprinklers, in-rack sprinkler arrangements and designs shall be

selected from Figure 25.3.2.1.1.3(a) through Figure 25.3.2.1.1.3(c). *(See Section 20.19 for racks with solid shelving.)*

N **25.3.2.1.1.4** Where rack storage of exposed nonencapsulated Class IV commodities stored over 12 ft (3.7 m) and up to and including 25 ft (7.6 m) in height in single- and double-row racks will be protected by in-rack sprinklers, in-rack sprinkler arrangements and designs shall be selected from Figure 25.3.2.1.1.4(a) through Figure 25.3.2.1.1.4(c). *(See Section 20.19 for racks with solid shelving.)*

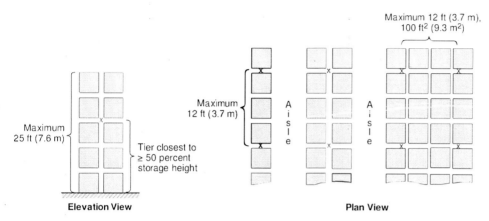

Notes:
(1) See 25.3.2.1.2 for the ceiling-level sprinkler design.
(2) In-rack sprinklers are ordinary-temperature-rated, quick-or standard-response, pendent or upright, minimum K-5.6 (K-80), and designed for a minimum of six (6) in-rack sprinklers operating at 22 gpm (83 L/min).
(3) The symbol X represents in-rack sprinklers.
(4) Each square represents a storage cube measuring 4 ft to 5 ft (1.2 m to 1.5 m) on a side.

N **FIGURE 25.3.2.1.1.2(a)** In-Rack Sprinkler Arrangements for Exposed Nonencapsulated Class I or Class II Commodities Stored to a Maximum Height of 25 ft (7.6 m) with One Level of In-Rack Sprinklers.

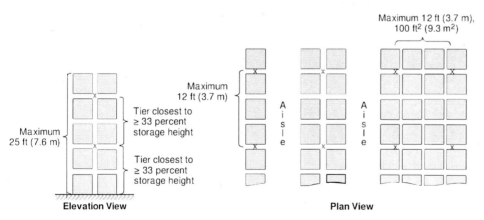

Notes:
(1) See 25.3.2.1.2 for the ceiling-level sprinkler design.
(2) In-rack sprinklers are ordinary-temperature-rated, quick-or standard-response, pendent or upright, minimum K-5.6 (K-80), and designed for a minimum of ten (10) in-rack sprinklers [five (5) in-rack sprinklers on top two levels] operating at 22 gpm (83 L/min).
(3) The symbol X represents in-rack sprinklers.
(4) Each square represents a storage cube measuring 4 ft to 5 ft (1.2 m to 1.5 m) on a side.

N **FIGURE 25.3.2.1.1.2(b)** In-Rack Sprinkler Arrangements for Exposed Nonencapsulated Class I or Class II Commodities Stored to a Maximum Height of 25 ft (7.6 m) with More Than One Level of In-Rack Sprinklers (Not at Each Tier Level).

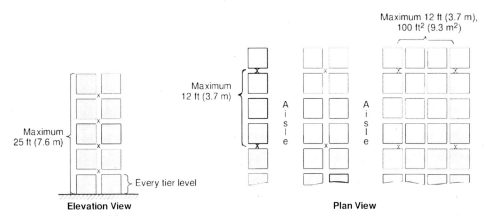

Notes:
(1) See 25.3.2.1.2 for the ceiling-level sprinkler design.
(2) In-rack sprinklers are ordinary-temperature-rated, quick-or standard-response, pendent or upright, minimum K-5.6 (K-80), and designed for a minimum of ten (10) in-rack sprinklers [five (5) in-rack sprinklers on top two levels] operating at 22 gpm (83 L/min).
(3) The symbol X represents in-rack sprinklers.
(4) Each square represents a storage cube measuring 4 ft to 5 ft (1.2 m to 1.5 m) on a side.

N **FIGURE 25.3.2.1.1.2(c)   In-Rack Sprinkler Arrangements for Exposed Nonencapsulated Class I or Class II Commodities Stored to a Maximum Height of 25 ft (7.6 m) with In-Rack Sprinklers at Each Tier Level.**

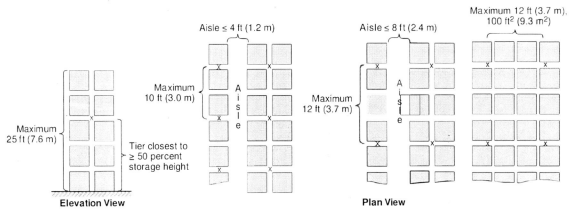

Notes:
(1) See 25.3.2.1.2 for the ceiling-level sprinkler design.
(2) In-rack sprinklers are ordinary-temperature-rated, quick-or standard-response, pendent or upright, minimum K-5.6 (K-80), and designed for a minimum of six (6) in-rack sprinklers operating at 22 gpm (83 L/min).
(3) The symbol X represents in-rack sprinklers.
(4) Each square represents a storage cube measuring 4 ft to 5 ft (1.2 m to 1.5 m) on a side.

N **FIGURE 25.3.2.1.1.3(a)   In-Rack Sprinkler Arrangements for Exposed Nonencapsulated Class III Commodities Stored to a Maximum Height of 25 ft (7.6 m) with One Level of In-Rack Sprinklers.**

N **25.3.2.1.1.5** Where rack storage of exposed nonencapsulated Class IV commodities stored over 12 ft (3.7 m) and up to and including 20 ft (6.1 m) in height in multiple-row racks will be protected by in-rack sprinklers, in-rack sprinkler arrangements and designs shall be selected from Figure 25.3.2.1.1.5(a) through Figure 25.3.2.1.1.5(c). *(See Section 20.19 for racks with solid shelving.)*

N **25.3.2.1.1.6** Where rack storage of exposed nonencapsulated Class IV commodities stored over 20 ft (6.1 m) and up to and including 25 ft (7.6 m) in height in multiple-row racks will be protected by in-rack sprinklers, in-rack sprinkler arrangements and designs shall be selected from Figure 25.3.2.1.1.6(a) or Figure 25.3.2.1.1.6(b). *(See Section 20.19 for racks with solid shelving.)*

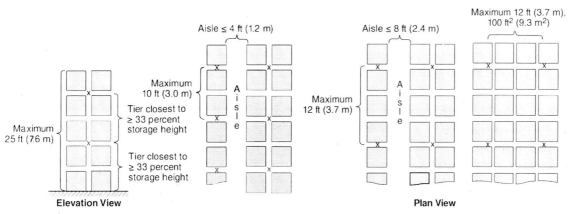

Notes:
(1) See 25.3.2.1.2 for the ceiling-level sprinkler design.
(2) In-rack sprinklers are ordinary-temperature-rated, quick-or standard-response, pendent or upright, minimum K-5.6 (K-80), and designed for a minimum of ten (10) in-rack sprinklers [five (5) in-rack sprinklers on top two levels] operating at 22 gpm (83 L/min).
(3) The symbol X represents in-rack sprinklers.
(4) Each square represents a storage cube measuring 4 ft to 5 ft (1.2 m to 1.5 m) on a side.

N FIGURE 25.3.2.1.1.3(b) In-Rack Sprinkler Arrangements for Exposed Nonencapsulated Class III Commodities Stored to a Maximum Height of 25 ft (7.6 m) with More Than One Level of In-Rack Sprinklers (Not at Each Tier Level).

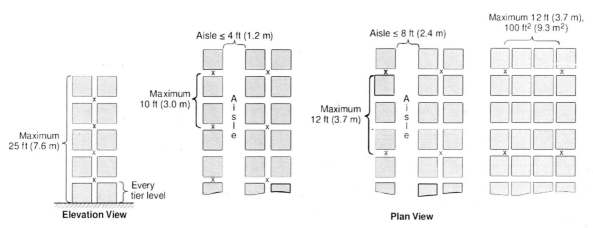

Notes:
(1) See 25.3.2.1.2 for the ceiling-level sprinkler design.
(2) In-rack sprinklers are ordinary-temperature-rated, quick-or standard-response, pendent or upright, minimum K-5.6 (K-80), and designed for a minimum of ten (10) in-rack sprinklers [five (5) in-rack sprinklers on top two levels] operating at 22 gpm (83 L/min).
(3) The symbol X represents in-rack sprinklers.
(4) Each square represents a storage cube measuring 4 ft to 5 ft (1.2 m to 1.5 m) on a side.

N FIGURE 25.3.2.1.1.3(c) In-Rack Sprinkler Arrangements for Exposed Nonencapsulated Class III Commodities Stored to a Maximum Height of 25 ft (7.6 m) with In-Rack Sprinklers at Each Tier Level.

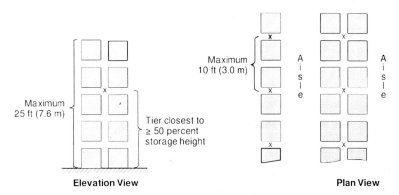

Elevation View   **Plan View**

Notes:
(1) See 25.3.2.1.2 for the ceiling-level sprinkler design.
(2) In-rack sprinklers are ordinary-temperature-rated, quick- or standard-response, pendent or upright, minimum
    K-5.6 (K-80), and designed for a minimum of eight (8) in-rack sprinklers operating at 22 gpm (83 L/min).
(3) The symbol X represents in-rack sprinklers.
(4) Each square represents a storage cube measuring 4 ft to 5 ft (1.2 m to 1.5 m) on a side.

N **FIGURE 25.3.2.1.1.4(a)   In-Rack Sprinkler Arrangements for Exposed Nonencapsulated Class IV Commodities Stored to a Maximum Height of 25 ft (7.6 m) in Single- and Double-Row Racks with One Level of In-Rack Sprinklers.**

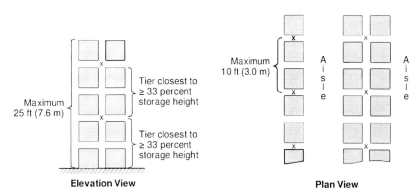

Elevation View   **Plan View**

Notes:
(1) See 25.3.2.1.2 for the ceiling-level sprinkler design.
(2) In-rack sprinklers are ordinary-temperature-rated, quick- or standard-response, pendent or upright, minimum
    K-5.6 (K-80), and designed for a minimum of 14 in-rack sprinklers [seven (7) in-rack sprinklers on top two levels]
    operating at 22 gpm (83 L/min).
(3) The symbol X represents in-rack sprinklers.
(4) Each square represents a storage cube measuring 4 ft to 5 ft (1.2 m to 1.5 m) on a side.

N **FIGURE 25.3.2.1.1.4(b)   In-Rack Sprinkler Arrangements for Exposed Nonencapsulated Class IV Commodities Stored to a Maximum Height of 25 ft (7.6 m) in Single- and Double-Row Racks with More Than One Level of In-Rack Sprinklers (Not at Each Tier Level).**

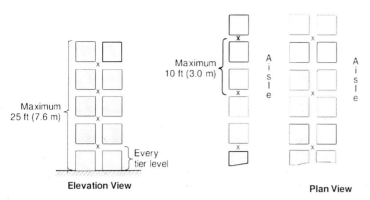

Elevation View

Plan View

Notes:
(1) See 25.3.2.1.2 for the ceiling-level sprinkler design.
(2) In-rack sprinklers are ordinary-temperature-rated, quick-or standard-response, pendent or upright, minimum K-5.6 (K-80), and designed for a minimum of 14 in-rack sprinklers [seven (7) in-rack sprinklers on top two levels] operating at 22 gpm (83 L/min).
(3) The symbol X represents in-rack sprinklers.
(4) Each square represents a storage cube measuring 4 ft to 5 ft (1.2 m to 1.5 m) on a side.

N **FIGURE 25.3.2.1.1.4(c)   In-Rack Sprinkler Arrangements for Exposed Nonencapsulated Class IV Commodities Stored to a Maximum Height of 25 ft (7.6 m) in Single- and Double-Row Racks with In-Rack Sprinklers at Each Tier Level.**

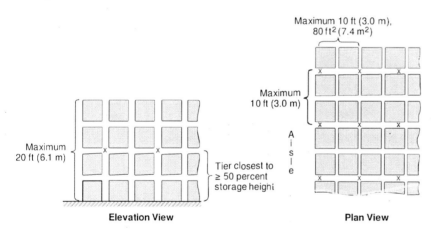

Elevation View

Plan View

Notes:
(1) See 25.3.2.1.2 for the ceiling-level sprinkler design.
(2) In-rack sprinklers are ordinary-temperature-rated, quick-or standard-response, pendent or upright, minimum K-5.6 (K-80), and designed for a minimum of eight (8) in-rack sprinklers operating at 22 gpm (83 L/min).
(3) The symbol X represents in-rack sprinklers.
(4) Each square represents a storage cube measuring 4 ft to 5 ft (1.2 m to 1.5 m) on a side.

N **FIGURE 25.3.2.1.1.5(a)   In-Rack Sprinkler Arrangements for Exposed Nonencapsulated Class IV Commodities Stored to a Maximum Height of 20 ft (6.1 m) in Multiple-Row Racks with One Level of In-Rack Sprinklers.**

Shaded text = Revisions.   Δ = Text deletions and figure/table revisions.   • = Section deletions.   *N* = New material.

2022 Edition

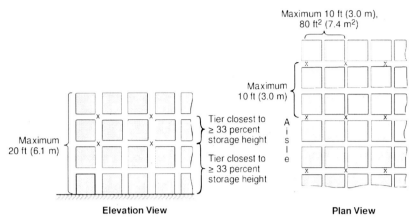

Notes:
(1) See 25.3.2.1.2 for the ceiling-level sprinkler design.
(2) In-rack sprinklers are ordinary-temperature-rated, quick-or standard-response, pendent or upright, minimum K-5.6 (K-80), and designed for a minimum of 14 in-rack sprinklers [seven (7) in-rack sprinklers on top two levels] operating at 22 gpm (83 L/min).
(3) The symbol X represents in-rack sprinklers.
(4) Each square represents a storage cube measuring 4 ft to 5 ft (1.2 m to 1.5 m) on a side.

N FIGURE 25.3.2.1.1.5(b)   In-Rack Sprinkler Arrangements for Exposed Nonencapsulated Class IV Commodities Stored to a Maximum Height of 20 ft (6.1 m) in Multiple-Row Racks with More Than One Level of In-Rack Sprinklers.

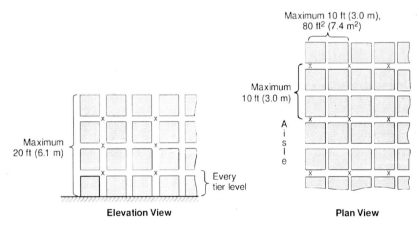

Notes:
(1) See 25.3.2.1.2 for the ceiling-level sprinkler design.
(2) In-rack sprinklers are ordinary-temperature-rated, quick-or standard-response, pendent or upright, minimum K-5.6 (K-80), and designed for a minimum of 14 in-rack sprinklers [seven (7) in-rack sprinklers on top two levels] operating at 22 gpm (83 L/min).
(3) The symbol X represents in-rack sprinklers.
(4) Each square represents a storage cube measuring 4 ft to 5 ft (1.2 m to 1.5 m) on a side.

N FIGURE 25.3.2.1.1.5(c)   In-Rack Sprinkler Arrangements for Exposed Nonencapsulated Class IV Commodities Stored to a Maximum Height of 20 ft (6.1 m) in Multiple-Row Racks with In-Rack Sprinklers at Each Tier Level.

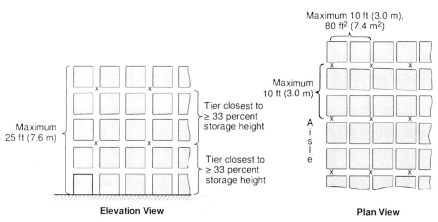

Notes:
(1) See 25.3.2.1.2 for the ceiling-level sprinkler design.
(2) In-rack sprinklers are ordinary-temperature-rated, quick-or standard-response, pendent or upright, minimum K-5.6 (K-80), and designed for a minimum of 14 in-rack sprinklers [seven (7) in-rack sprinklers on top two levels] operating at 22 gpm (83 L/min).
(3) The symbol X represents in-rack sprinklers.
(4) Each square represents a storage cube measuring 4 ft to 5 ft (1.2 m to 1.5 m) on a side.

N FIGURE 25.3.2.1.1.6(a) In-Rack Sprinkler Arrangements for Exposed Nonencapsulated Class IV Commodities Stored Over 20 ft (6.1 m) and up to a Maximum Height of 25 ft (7.6 m) in Multiple-Row Racks with Two Levels of In-Rack Sprinklers.

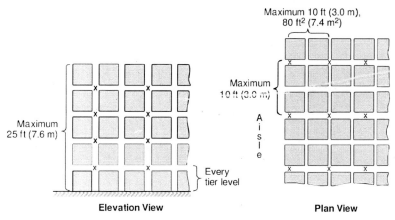

Notes:
(1) See 25.3.2.1.2 for the ceiling-level sprinkler design.
(2) In-rack sprinklers are ordinary-temperature-rated, quick-or standard-response, pendent or upright, minimum K-5.6 (K-80), and designed for a minimum of 14 in-rack sprinklers [seven (7) in-rack sprinklers on top two levels] operating at 22 gpm (83 L/min).
(3) The symbol X represents in-rack sprinklers.
(4) Each square represents a storage cube measuring 4 ft to 5 ft (1.2 m to 1.5 m) on a side.

N FIGURE 25.3.2.1.1.6(b) In-Rack Sprinkler Arrangements for Exposed Nonencapsulated Class IV Commodities Stored Over 20 ft (6.1 m) and up to a Maximum Height of 25 ft (7.6 m) in Multiple-Row Racks with In-Rack Sprinklers at Each Tier Level.

Shaded text = Revisions.   Δ = Text deletions and figure/table revisions.   • = Section deletions.   N = New material.

2022 Edition

N **25.3.2.1.2 CMDA Ceiling-Level Sprinkler Designs for Exposed Nonencapsulated Class I, Class II, Class III, or Class IV Commodities Stored Up to and Including 25 ft (7.6 m) in Height in Combination with In-Rack Sprinklers.**

N **25.3.2.1.2.1* Single-, Double-, and Multiple-Row Rack Storage of Exposed Nonencapsulated Class I Through Class IV Commodities.**

N **(A)** For single-, double-, and multiple-row rack storage of exposed nonencapsulated Class I through Class IV commodities stored over 12 ft (3.7 m) and up to and including 25 ft (7.6 m) in height, the ceiling-level sprinkler design in terms of density [gpm/ft^2 (mm/min)] over a 2000 ft^2 (186 m^2) area of ceiling-level sprinkler operation, with the provision of in-rack sprinklers, shall be in accordance with the following:

(1) For exposed nonencapsulated Class I commodities, see Table 25.3.2.1.2.1(A)(a)
(2) For exposed nonencapsulated Class II commodities, see Table 25.3.2.1.2.1(A)(b)
(3) For exposed nonencapsulated Class III commodities, see Table 25.3.2.1.2.1(A)(c)
(4) For exposed nonencapsulated Class IV commodities, see Table 25.3.2.1.2.1(A)(d)

N **(B)*** Design densities obtained from Table 25.3.2.1.2.1(A)(a) through Table 25.3.2.1.2.1(A)(d) for single- and double-row racks shall be selected to correspond to aisle width *(see Section C.15)*:

(1) The density given for 8 ft (2.4 m) wide aisles shall be applied to aisles wider than 8 ft (2.4 m).
(2) For aisle widths between 4 ft (1.2 m) and 8 ft (2.4 m), the rules for 4 ft (1.2 m) aisle width shall be used or direct linear interpolation between the densities shall be permitted.
(3) The density given for 4 ft (1.2 m) wide aisles shall be applied to aisles narrower than 4 ft (1.2 m) down to 3½ ft (1.1 m).
(4) Where aisles narrower than 3½ ft (1.1 m), racks shall be considered to be multiple-row racks.

N **25.3.2.1.2.2 Clearance.**

N **(A)** The ceiling-level sprinkler design obtained from Table 25.3.2.1.2.1(A)(a) through Table 25.3.2.1.2.1(A)(d) shall be based on a maximum clearance from top of storage to ceiling of 20 ft (6.1 m).

N **(B)** Where the clearance for 25.3.2.1.2.2(A) exceeds 20 ft (6.1 m), one of the following two options shall be implemented:

(1) The ceiling design shall be determined from Table 25.3.2.1.2.1(A)(a) through Table 25.3.2.1.2.1(A)(d) using a theoretical storage height that does not exceed 25 ft (7.6 m) and results in a clearance to ceiling of 20 ft (6.1 m).
(2) If not already provided, the in-rack sprinkler arrangement shall be supplemented with one level of quick-response in-rack sprinklers located directly below the top tier level of storage and at every flue space intersection.

N **25.3.2.2 Exposed Encapsulated, or Cartoned (Nonencapsulated or Encapsulated) Class I, Class II, Class III, or Class IV Commodities.**

N **25.3.2.2.1* In-Rack Sprinkler Arrangements and Designs for Exposed Encapsulated, or Cartoned (Nonencapsulated or Encapsulated) Class I, Class II, Class III, or Class IV Commodities Stored Up to and Including 25 ft (7.6 m) in Height.**

N **25.3.2.2.1.1** Where rack storage of exposed encapsulated, or cartoned (nonencapsulated or encapsulated) Class I through Class IV commodities stored over 12 ft (3.7 m) and up to and including 25 ft (7.6 m) in height will be protected by in-rack sprinklers, the following levels of in-rack sprinklers shall be required:

(1) One level of in-rack sprinklers where Class I through Class IV commodities are stored in single- or double-row racks up to and including 25 ft (7.6 m)
(2) One level of in-rack sprinklers where Class IV commodities are stored in multiple-row racks up to and including 20 ft (6.1 m)
(3) Two levels of in-rack sprinklers where Class IV commodities are stored in multiple-row racks over 20 ft (6.1 m) and up to and including 25 ft (7.6 m)

N **25.3.2.2.1.2** Where rack storage of exposed encapsulated, or cartoned (nonencapsulated or encapsulated) Class I or Class II commodities stored over 12 ft (3.7 m) and up to and including 25 ft (7.6 m) in height will be protected by in-rack sprinklers, in-rack sprinkler arrangements and designs shall be selected from Figure 25.3.2.2.1.2(a) through Figure 25.3.2.2.1.2(c). *(See Section 20.19 for racks with solid shelving.)*

N **25.3.2.2.1.3** Where rack storage of exposed encapsulated, or cartoned (nonencapsulated or encapsulated) Class III commodities stored over 12 ft (3.7 m) and up to and including 25 ft (7.6 m) in height will be protected by in-rack sprinklers, in-rack sprinkler arrangements and designs shall be selected from Figure 25.3.2.2.1.3(a) through Figure 25.3.2.2.1.3(c). *(See Section 20.19 for racks with solid shelving.)*

N **25.3.2.2.1.4** Where rack storage of exposed encapsulated, or cartoned (nonencapsulated or encapsulated) Class IV commodities stored over 12 ft (3.7 m) and up to and including 25 ft (7.6 m) in height in single- and double-row racks will be protected by in-rack sprinklers, in-rack sprinkler arrangements and designs shall be selected from Figure 25.3.2.2.1.4(a) through Figure 25.3.2.2.1.4(c). *(See Section 20.19 for racks with solid shelving.)*

N **25.3.2.2.1.5** Where rack storage of exposed encapsulated, or cartoned (nonencapsulated or encapsulated) Class IV commodities stored over 12 ft (3.7 m) and up to and including 20 ft (6.1 m) in height in multiple-row racks will be protected by in-rack sprinklers, in-rack sprinkler arrangements and designs shall be selected from Figure 25.3.2.2.1.5(a) through Figure 25.3.2.2.1.5(c). *(See Section 20.19 for racks with solid shelving.)*

N **25.3.2.2.1.6** Where rack storage of exposed encapsulated, or cartoned (nonencapsulated or encapsulated) Class IV commodities stored over 20 ft (6.1 m) and up to and including 25 ft (7.6 m) in height in multiple-row racks will be protected by in-rack sprinklers, in-rack sprinkler arrangements and designs shall be selected from Figure 25.3.2.2.1.6(a) or Figure 25.3.2.2.1.6(b). *(See Section 20.19 for racks with solid shelving.)*

N Table 25.3.2.1.2.1(A)(a) CMDA Ceiling-Level Sprinkler Design Requirements for Exposed Nonencapsulated Class I Commodities Stored Over 12 ft (3.7 m) and Up to 25 ft (7.6 m) in Height Supplemented with In-Rack Sprinklers

Maximum Storage Height ft (m)	Maximum Ceiling Height ft (m)	Storage Arrangement	Aisle Width ft (m)	No. of In-Rack Sprinkler Levels Installed	Ceiling Sprinkler System Design [gpm/ft²/2000 ft² (mm/min/186 m²)]	
					High-Temperature-Rated Sprinklers	Ordinary- or Intermediate-Temperature-Rated Sprinklers
15 (4.6)	35 (10.7)	Single- and double-row racks	8 (2.4)	1	0.15 (6.1)	0.15 (6.1)
				More than 1 but not every tier level	0.15 (6.1)	0.15 (6.1)
				Every tier level	0.15 (6.1)	0.15 (6.1)
			4 (1.2)	1	0.15 (6.1)	0.15 (6.2)
				More than 1 but not every tier level	0.15 (6.1)	0.15 (6.1)
				Every tier level	0.15 (6.1)	0.15 (6.1)
		Multiple-row racks	Any	1	0.15 (6.1)	0.15 (6.2)
				More than 1 but not every tier level	0.15 (6.1)	0.15 (6.1)
				Every tier level	0.15 (6.1)	0.15 (6.1)
18 (5.5)	38 (11.6)	Single- and double-row racks	8 (2.4)	1	0.16 (6.5)	0.18 (7.4)
				More than 1 but not every tier level	0.15 (6.1)	0.15 (6.1)
				Every tier level	0.15 (6.1)	0.15 (6.1)
			4 (1.2)	1	0.20 (8.2)	0.22 (8.8)
				More than 1 but not every tier level	0.16 (6.5)	0.17 (7.0)
				Every tier level	0.15 (6.1)	0.15 (6.1)
		Multiple-row racks	Any	1	0.20 (8.2)	0.22 (8.8)
				More than 1 but not every tier level	0.16 (6.5)	0.18 (7.3)
				Every tier level	0.15 (6.1)	0.15 (6.1)
25 (7.6)	45 (13.7)	Single- and double-row racks	8 (2.4)	1	0.19 (7.7)	0.22 (8.8)
				More than 1 but not every tier level	0.15 (6.1)	0.17 (7.0)
				Every tier level	0.15 (6.1)	0.15 (6.1)
			4 (1.2)	1	0.23 (9.4)	0.26 (10.6)
				More than 1 but not every tier level	0.18 (7.3)	0.20 (8.2)
				Every tier level	0.15 (6.1)	0.15 (6.1)
		Multiple-row racks	Any	1	0.23 (9.4)	0.26 (10.6)
				More than 1 but not every tier level	0.18 (7.3)	0.20 (8.2)
				Every tier level	0.15 (6.1)	0.15 (6.1)

Shaded text = Revisions.   Δ = Text deletions and figure/table revisions.   • = Section deletions.   N = New material.

2022 Edition

N **Table 25.3.2.1.2.1(A)(b) CMDA Ceiling-Level Sprinkler Design Requirements for Exposed Nonencapsulated Class II Commodities Stored Over 12 ft (3.7 m) and Up to 25 ft (7.6 m) in Height Supplemented with In-Rack Sprinklers**

Maximum Storage Height ft (m)	Maximum Ceiling Height ft (m)	Storage Arrangement	Aisle Width ft (m)	No. of In-Rack Sprinkler Levels Installed	Ceiling Sprinkler System Design [gpm/ft²/2000 ft² (mm/min/186 m²)]	
					High-Temperature-Rated Sprinklers	Ordinary- or Intermediate-Temperature-Rated Sprinklers
15 (4.6)	35 (10.7)	Single- and double-row racks	8 (2.4)	1	0.15 (6.1)	0.15 (6.1)
				More than 1 but not every tier level	0.15 (6.1)	0.15 (6.1)
				Every tier level	0.15 (6.1)	0.15 (6.1)
			4 (1.2)	1	0.15 (6.1)	0.18 (7.3)
				More than 1 but not every tier level	0.15 (6.1)	0.15 (6.1)
				Every tier level	0.15 (6.1)	0.15 (6.1)
		Multiple-row racks	Any	1	0.15 (6.1)	0.18 (7.3)
				More than 1 but not every tier level	0.15 (6.1)	0.15 (6.1)
				Every tier level	0.15 (6.1)	0.15 (6.1)
18 (5.5)	38 (11.6)	Single- and double-row racks	8 (2.4)	1	0.18 (7.3)	0.20 (8.2)
				More than 1 but not every tier level	0.15 (6.1)	0.16 (6.5)
				Every tier level	0.15 (6.1)	0.15 (6.1)
			4 (1.2)	1	0.21 (8.6)	0.26 (10.6)
				More than 1 but not every tier level	0.17 (7.0)	0.20 (8.2)
				Every tier level	0.15 (6.1)	0.15 (6.1)
		Multiple-row racks	Any	1	0.21 (8.6)	0.26 (10.6)
				More than 1 but not every tier level	0.17 (7.0)	0.20 (8.2)
				Every tier level	0.15 (6.1)	0.15 (6.1)
25 (7.6)	45 (13.7)	Single- and double-row racks	8 (2.4)	1	0.21 (8.6)	0.24 (9.8)
				More than 1 but not every tier level	0.17 (7.0)	0.19 (7.7)
				Every tier level	0.15 (6.1)	0.15 (6.1)
			4 (1.2)	1	0.25 (10.2)	0.30 (12.2)
				More than 1 but not every tier level	0.20 (8.2)	0.24 (9.8)
				Every tier level	0.15 (6.1)	0.18 (7.3)
		Multiple-row racks	Any	1	0.25 (10.2)	0.30 (12.2)
				More than 1 but not every tier level	0.20 (8.2)	0.24 (9.8)
				Every tier level	0.15 (6.1)	0.18 (7.3)

Shaded text = Revisions.   Δ = Text deletions and figure/table revisions.   • = Section deletions.   N = New material.

N Table 25.3.2.1.2.1(A)(c) CMDA Ceiling-Level Sprinkler Design Requirements for Exposed Nonencapsulated Class III Commodities Stored Over 12 ft (3.7 m) and Up to 25 ft (7.6 m) in Height Supplemented with In-Rack Sprinklers

Maximum Storage Height ft (m)	Maximum Ceiling Height ft (m)	Storage Arrangement	Aisle Width ft (m)	No. of In-Rack Sprinkler Levels Installed	Ceiling Sprinkler System Design [gpm/ft²/2000 ft² (mm/min/186 m²)]	
					High-Temperature-Rated Sprinklers	Ordinary- or Intermediate-Temperature-Rated Sprinklers
15 (4.6)	35 (10.7)	Single- and double-row racks	8 (2.4)	1	0.15 (6.1)	0.17 (7.0)
				More than 1 but not every tier level	0.15 (6.1)	0.15 (6.1)
				Every tier level	0.15 (6.1)	0.15 (6.1)
			4 (1.2)	1	0.17 (7.0)	0.20 (8.2)
				More than 1 but not every tier level	0.15 (6.1)	0.16 (6.5)
				Every tier level	0.15 (6.1)	0.15 (6.1)
		Multiple-row racks	Any	1	0.17 (7.0)	0.20 (8.2)
				More than 1 but not every tier level	0.15 (6.1)	0.16 (6.5)
				Every tier level	0.15 (6.1)	0.15 (6.1)
18 (5.5)	38 (11.6)	Single- and double-row racks	8 (2.4)	1	0.21 (8.6)	0.23 (9.3)
				More than 1 but not every tier level	0.17 (7.0)	0.19 (7.7)
				Every tier level	0.15 (6.1)	0.15 (6.1)
			4 (1.2)	1	0.24 (9.8)	0.28 (11.4)
				More than 1 but not every tier level	0.19 (7.7)	0.22 (9.0)
				Every tier level	0.15 (6.1)	0.17 (7.0)
		Multiple-row racks	Any	1	0.24 (9.8)	0.28 (11.4)
				More than 1 but not every tier level	0.19 (7.7)	0.22 (9.0)
				Every tier level	0.15 (6.1)	0.17 (7.0)
25 (7.6)	45 (13.7)	Single- and double-row racks	8 (2.4)	1	0.25 (10.2)	0.28 (11.4)
				More than 1 but not every tier level	0.20 (8.2)	0.22 (9.0)
				Every tier level	0.15 (6.1)	0.17 (7.0)
			4 (1.2)	1	0.29 (11.8)	0.33 (13.4)
				More than 1 but not every tier level	0.23 (9.3)	0.26 (10.6)
				Every tier level	0.17 (7.0)	0.20 (8.2)
		Multiple-row racks	Any	1	0.29 (11.8)	0.33 (13.4)
				More than 1 but not every tier level	0.23 (9.3)	0.26 (10.6)
				Every tier level	0.17 (7.0)	0.20 (8.2)

N Table 25.3.2.1.2.1(A)(d) CMDA Ceiling-Level Sprinkler Design Requirements for Exposed Nonencapsulated Class IV Commodities Stored Over 12 ft (3.7 m) and Up to 25 ft (7.6 m) in Height Supplemented with In-Rack Sprinklers

Maximum Storage Height ft (m)	Maximum Ceiling Height ft (m)	Storage Arrangement	Aisle Width ft (m)	No. of In-Rack Sprinkler Levels Installed	Ceiling Sprinkler System Design [gpm/ft²/2000 ft² (mm/min/186 m²)]	
					High-Temperature-Rated Sprinklers	Ordinary- or Intermediate-Temperature-Rated Sprinklers
15 (4.6)	35 (10.7)	Single- and double-row racks	8 (2.4)	1	0.19 (7.7)	0.22 (9.0)
				More than 1 but not every tier level	0.15 (6.1)	0.18 (7.3)
				Every tier level	0.15 (6.1)	0.15 (6.1)
			4 (1.2)	1	0.23 (9.3)	0.27 (11.0)
				More than 1 but not every tier level	0.18 (7.3)	0.21 (8.6)
				Every tier level	0.15 (6.1)	0.16 (6.5)
		Multiple-row racks	Any	1	0.23 (9.3)	0.27 (11.0)
				More than 1 but not every tier level	0.18 (7.3)	0.21 (8.6)
				Every tier level	0.15 (6.1)	0.16 (6.5)
18 (5.5)	38 (11.6)	Single- and double-row racks	8 (2.4)	1	0.27 (11.0)	0.31 (12.6)
				More than 1 but not every tier level	0.22 (9.0)	0.25 (10.2)
				Every tier level	0.16 (6.5)	0.19 (7.7)
			4 (1.2)	1	0.33 (13.4)	0.38 (15.5)
				More than 1 but not every tier level	0.26 (10.6)	0.30 (12.2)
				Every tier level	0.20 (8.2)	0.23 (9.3)
		Multiple-row racks	Any	1	0.33 (13.4)	0.38 (15.5)
				More than 1 but not every tier level	0.26 (10.6)	0.30 (12.2)
				Every tier level	0.20 (8.2)	0.23 (9.3)
25 (7.6)	45 (13.7)	Single- and double-row racks	8 (2.4)	1	0.32 (13.0)	0.37 (15.1)
				More than 1 but not every tier level	0.26 (10.6)	0.30 (12.2)
				Every tier level	0.19 (7.7)	0.22 (8.9)
			4 (1.2)	1	0.39 (15.9)	0.45 (18.3)
				More than 1 but not every tier level	0.31 (12.6)	0.36 (14.7)
				Every tier level	0.23 (9.3)	0.27 (10.9)
		Multiple-row racks	Any	2	0.39 (15.9)	0.45 (18.3)
				More than 2 but not every tier level	0.31 (12.6)	0.36 (14.7)
				Every tier level	0.23 (9.3)	0.27 (10.9)

Shaded text = Revisions.   Δ = Text deletions and figure/table revisions.   • = Section deletions.   N = New material.

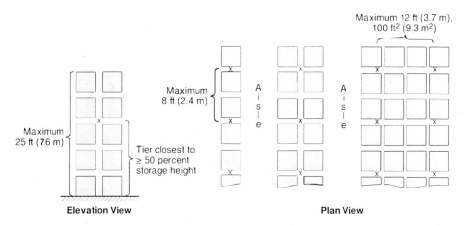

Notes:
(1) See 25.3.2.2.2 for the ceiling-level sprinkler design.
(2) In-rack sprinklers are ordinary-temperature-rated, quick-or standard-response, pendent or upright, minimum
    K-5.6 (K-80), and designed for a minimum of six (6) in-rack sprinklers operating at 22 gpm (83 L/min).
(3) The symbol X represents in-rack sprinklers.
(4) Each square represents a storage cube measuring 4 ft to 5 ft (1.2 m to 1.5 m) on a side.

N **FIGURE 25.3.2.2.1.2(a)   In-Rack Sprinkler Arrangements for Exposed Encapsulated, or Cartoned (Nonencapsulated or Encapsulated) Class I or Class II Commodities Stored to a Maximum Height of 25 ft (7.6 m) With One Level of In-Rack Sprinklers.**

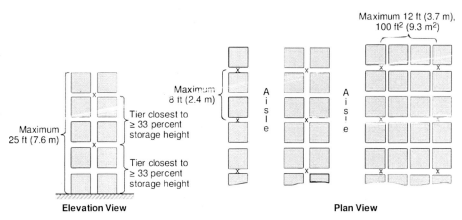

Notes:
(1) See 25.3.2.2.2 for the ceiling-level sprinkler design.
(2) In-rack sprinklers are ordinary-temperature-rated, quick-or standard-response, pendent or upright, minimum
    K-5.6 (K-80), and designed for a minimum of ten (10) in-rack sprinklers [five (5) in rack sprinklers on top two
    levels] operating at 22 gpm (83 L/min).
(3) The symbol X represents in-rack sprinklers.
(4) Each square represents a storage cube measuring 4 ft to 5 ft (1.2 m to 1.5 m) on a side.

N **FIGURE 25.3.2.2.1.2(b)   In-Rack Sprinkler Arrangements for Exposed Encapsulated, or Cartoned (Nonencapsulated or Encapsulated) Class I or Class II Commodities Stored to a Maximum Height of 25 ft (7.6 m) With More Than One Level of In-Rack Sprinklers (Not at Each Tier Level).**

Shaded text = Revisions.   Δ = Text deletions and figure/table revisions.   • = Section deletions.   *N* = New material.

2022 Edition

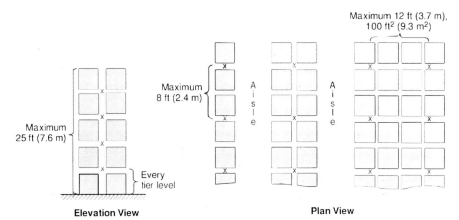

Notes:
(1) See 25.3.2.2.2 for the ceiling-level sprinkler design.
(2) In-rack sprinklers are ordinary-temperature-rated, quick-or standard-response, pendent or upright, minimum K-5.6 (K-80), and designed for a minimum of 10 in-rack sprinklers [five (5) in-rack sprinklers on top two levels] operating at 22 gpm (83 L/min).
(3) The symbol X represents in-rack sprinklers.
(4) Each square represents a storage cube measuring 4 ft to 5 ft (1.2 m to 1.5 m) on a side.

N **FIGURE 25.3.2.2.1.2(c)   In-Rack Sprinkler Arrangements for Exposed Encapsulated, or Cartoned (Nonencapsulated or Encapsulated) Class I or Class II Commodities Stored to a Maximum Height of 25 ft (7.6 m) With In-Rack Sprinklers at Each Tier Level.**

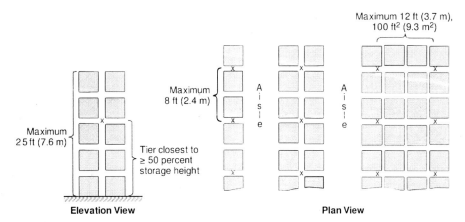

Notes:
(1) See 25.3.2.2.2 for the ceiling-level sprinkler design.
(2) In-rack sprinklers are ordinary-temperature-rated, quick-or standard-response, pendent or upright, minimum K-5.6 (K-80), and designed for a minimum of six (6) in-rack sprinklers operating at 22 gpm (83 L/min).
(3) The symbol X represents in-rack sprinklers.
(4) Each square represents a storage cube measuring 4 ft to 5 ft (1.2 m to 1.5 m) on a side.

N **FIGURE 25.3.2.2.1.3(a)   In-Rack Sprinkler Arrangements for Exposed Encapsulated, or Cartoned (Nonencapsulated or Encapsulated) Class III Commodities Stored to a Maximum Height of 25 ft (7.6 m) With One Level of In-Rack Sprinklers.**

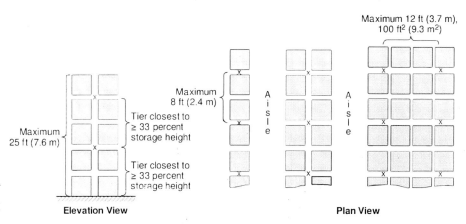

Notes:
(1) See 25.3.2.2.2 for the ceiling-level sprinkler design.
(2) In-rack sprinklers are ordinary-temperature-rated, quick-or standard-response, pendent or upright, minimum K-5.6 (K-80), and designed for a minimum of ten (10) in-rack sprinklers [five (5) in rack sprinklers on top two levels] operating at 22 gpm (83 L/min).
(3) The symbol X represents in-rack sprinklers.
(4) Each square represents a storage cube measuring 4 ft to 5 ft (1.2 m to 1.5 m) on a side.

N **FIGURE 25.3.2.2.1.3(b)   In-Rack Sprinkler Arrangements for Exposed Encapsulated, or Cartoned (Nonencapsulated or Encapsulated) Class III Commodities Stored to a Maximum Height of 25 ft (7.6 m) With More Than One Level of In-Rack Sprinklers (Not at Each Tier Level).**

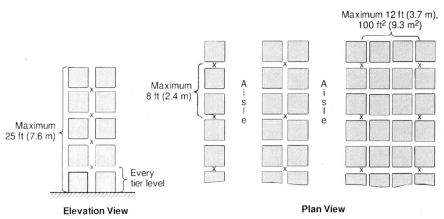

Notes:
(1) See 25.3.2.2.2 for the ceiling-level sprinkler design.
(2) In-rack sprinklers are ordinary-temperature-rated, quick-or standard-response, pendent or upright, minimum K-5.6 (K-80), and designed for a minimum of 10 in-rack sprinklers [five (5) in-rack sprinklers on top two levels] operating at 22 gpm (83 L/min).
(3) The symbol X represents in-rack sprinklers.
(4) Each square represents a storage cube measuring 4 ft to 5 ft (1.2 m to 1.5 m) on a side.

N **FIGURE 25.3.2.2.1.3(c)   In-Rack Sprinkler Arrangements for Exposed Encapsulated, or Cartoned (Nonencapsulated or Encapsulated) Class III Commodities Stored to a Maximum Height of 25 ft (7.6 m) With In-Rack Sprinklers at Each Tier Level.**

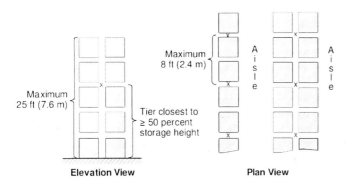

Notes:
(1) See 25.3.2.2.2 for the ceiling-level sprinkler design.
(2) In-rack sprinklers are ordinary-temperature-rated, quick- or standard-response, pendent or upright, minimum K-5.6 (K-80), and designed for a minimum of eight (8) in-rack sprinklers operating at 22 gpm (83 L/min).
(3) The symbol X represents in-rack sprinklers.
(4) Each square represents a storage cube measuring 4 ft to 5 ft (1.2 m to 1.5 m) on a side.

N FIGURE 25.3.2.2.1.4(a)   In-Rack Sprinkler Arrangements for Exposed Encapsulated or Cartoned (Nonencapsulated or Encapsulated) Class IV Commodities Stored to a Maximum Height of 25 ft (7.6 m) in Single- and Double-Row Racks with One Level of In-Rack Sprinklers.

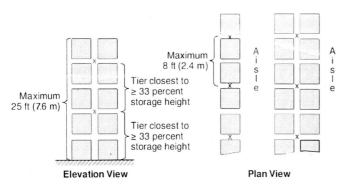

Notes:
(1) See 25.3.2.2.2 for the ceiling-level sprinkler design.
(2) In-rack sprinklers are ordinary-temperature-rated, quick- or standard-response, pendent or upright, minimum K-5.6 (K-80), and designed for a minimum of 14 in-rack sprinklers [seven (7) in-rack sprinklers on top two levels] operating at 22 gpm (83 L/min).
(3) The symbol X represents in-rack sprinklers.
(4) Each square represents a storage cube measuring 4 ft to 5 ft (1.2 m to 1.5 m) on a side.

N FIGURE 25.3.2.2.1.4(b)   In-Rack Sprinkler Arrangements for Exposed Encapsulated or Cartoned (Nonencapsulated or Encapsulated) Class IV Commodities Stored to a Maximum Height of 25 ft (7.6 m) in Single- and Double-Row Racks with More Than One Level of In-Rack Sprinklers (Not at Each Tier Level).

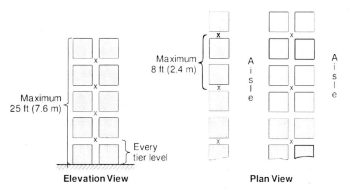

Notes:
(1) See 25.3.2.2.2 for the ceiling-level sprinkler design.
(2) In-rack sprinklers are ordinary-temperature-rated, quick-or standard-response, pendent or upright, minimum K-5.6 (K-80), and designed for a minimum of 14 in-rack sprinklers [seven (7) in-rack sprinklers on top two levels] operating at 22 gpm (83 L/min).
(3) The symbol X represents in-rack sprinklers.
(4) Each square represents a storage cube measuring 4 ft to 5 ft (1.2 m to 1.5 m) on a side.

N **FIGURE 25.3.2.2.1.4(c)** **In-Rack Sprinkler Arrangements for Exposed Encapsulated or Cartoned (Nonencapsulated or Encapsulated) Class IV Commodities Stored to a Maximum Height of 25 ft (7.6 m) in Single- and Double-Row Racks with In-Rack Sprinklers at Each Tier Level.**

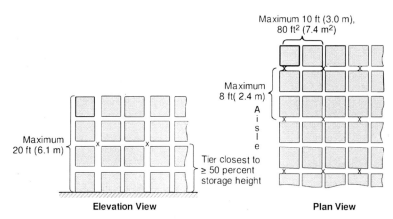

Notes:
(1) See 25.3.2.2.2 for the ceiling-level sprinkler design.
(2) In-rack sprinklers are ordinary-temperature-rated, quick-or standard-response, pendent or upright, minimum K-5.6 (K-80), and designed for a minimum of eight (8) in-rack sprinklers operating at 22 gpm (83 L/min).
(3) The symbol X represents in-rack sprinklers.
(4) Each square represents a storage cube measuring 4 ft to 5 ft (1.2 m to 1.5 m) on a side.

N **FIGURE 25.3.2.2.1.5(a)** **In-Rack Sprinkler Arrangements for Exposed Encapsulated or Cartoned (Nonencapsulated or Encapsulated) Class IV Commodities Stored to a Maximum Height of 20 ft (6.1 m) in Multiple-Row Racks with One Level of In-Rack Sprinklers.**

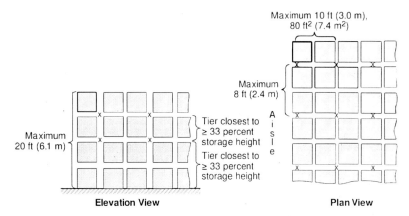

Notes:
(1) See 25.3.2.2.2 for the ceiling-level sprinkler design.
(2) In-rack sprinklers are ordinary-temperature-rated, quick-or standard-response,
    pendent or upright, minimum K-5.6 (K-80), and designed for a minimum of
    14 in-rack sprinklers [seven (7) in-rack sprinklers on top two levels] operating at
    22 gpm (83 L/min).
(3) The symbol X represents in-rack sprinklers.
(4) Each square represents a storage cube measuring 4 ft to 5 ft (1.2 m to 1.5 m) on a side.

N **FIGURE 25.3.2.2.1.5(b)   In-Rack Sprinkler Arrangements for Exposed Encapsulated or Cartoned (Nonencapsulated or Encapsulated) Class IV Commodities Stored to a Maximum Height of 20 ft (6.1 m) in Multiple-Row Racks with More Than One Level of In-Rack Sprinklers.**

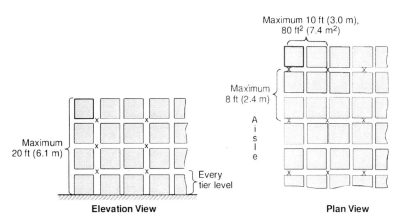

Notes:
(1) See 25.3.2.2.2 for the ceiling-level sprinkler design.
(2) In-rack sprinklers are ordinary-temperature-rated, quick-or standard-response,
    pendent or upright, minimum K-5.6 (K-80), and designed for a minimum of
    14 in-rack sprinklers [seven (7) in-rack sprinklers on top two levels] operating at
    22 gpm (83 L/min).
(3) The symbol X represents in-rack sprinklers.
(4) Each square represents a storage cube measuring 4 ft to 5 ft (1.2 m to 1.5 m) on a side.

N **FIGURE 25.3.2.2.1.5(c)   In-Rack Sprinkler Arrangements for Exposed Encapsulated or Cartoned (Nonencapsulated or Encapsulated) Class IV Commodities Stored to a Maximum Height of 20 ft (6.1 m) in Multiple-Row Racks with In-Rack Sprinklers at Each Tier Level.**

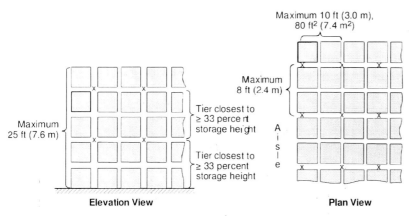

Notes:
(1) See 25.3.2.2.2 for the ceiling-level sprinkler design.
(2) In-rack sprinklers are ordinary-temperature-rated, quick-or standard-response,
    14 in-rack sprinklers [seven (7) in-rack sprinklers on top two levels] operating at
    22 gpm (83 L/min).
(3) The symbol X represents in-rack sprinklers.
(4) Each square represents a storage cube measuring 4 ft to 5 ft (1.2 m to 1.5 m) on a side.

N FIGURE 25.3.2.2.1.6(a)   In-Rack Sprinkler Arrangements for Exposed Encapsulated or
Cartoned (Nonencapsulated or Encapsulated) Class IV Commodities Stored Over 20 ft (6.1 m)
and Up to a Maximum Height of 25 ft (7.6 m) in Multiple-Row Racks with Two Levels of In-Rack
Sprinklers.

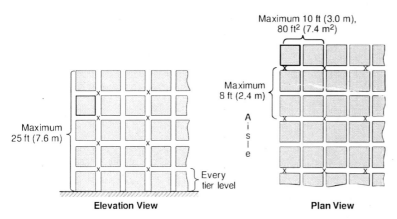

Notes:
(1) See 25.3.2.2.2 for the ceiling-level sprinkler design.
(2) In-rack sprinklers are ordinary-temperature-rated, quick-or standard-response,
    pendent or upright, minimum K-5.6 (K-80), and designed for a minimum of
    14 in-rack sprinklers [seven (7) in-rack sprinklers on top two levels] operating at
    22 gpm (83 L/min).
(3) The symbol X represents in-rack sprinklers.
(4) Each square represents a storage cube measuring 4 ft to 5 ft (1.2 m to 1.5 m) on a side.

N FIGURE 25.3.2.2.1.6(b)   In-Rack Sprinkler Arrangements for Exposed Encapsulated or
Cartoned (Nonencapsulated or Encapsulated) Class IV Commodities Stored Over 20 ft (6.1 m)
and Up to a Maximum Height of 25 ft (7.6 m) in Multiple-Row Racks with In-Rack Sprinklers at
Each Tier Level.

N **25.3.2.2.2 CMDA Ceiling-Level Sprinkler Designs for Exposed Encapsulated, or Cartoned (Nonencapsulated or Encapsulated) Class I through Class IV Commodities Stored Up to and Including 25 ft (7.6 m) in Height in Combination with In-Rack Sprinklers.**

N **25.3.2.2.2.1* Single-, Double-, and Multiple-Row Rack Storage of Exposed Encapsulated, or Cartoned (Nonencapsulated or Encapsulated) Class I Through Class IV Commodities.**

N **(A)** For single-, double-, and multiple-row rack storage of exposed encapsulated, or cartoned (nonencapsulated or encapsulated) Class I, Class II, Class III, or Class IV commodities stored over 12 ft (3.7 m) and up to and including 25 ft (7.6 m) in height, the ceiling-level sprinkler design in terms of density [gpm/ft^2 (mm/min)] over a 2000 ft^2 (185 m^2) area of ceiling-level sprinkler operation, with the provision of in-rack sprinklers, shall be in accordance with the following:

(1) For exposed encapsulated, or cartoned (nonencapsulated or encapsulated) Class I commodities, see Table 25.3.2.2.2.1(A)(a)

(2) For exposed encapsulated, or cartoned (nonencapsulated or encapsulated) Class II commodities, see Table 25.3.2.2.2.1(A)(b)

(3) For exposed encapsulated, or cartoned (nonencapsulated or encapsulated) Class III commodities, see Table 25.3.2.2.2.1(A)(c)

(4) For exposed encapsulated, or cartoned (nonencapsulated or encapsulated) Class IV commodities, see Table 25.3.2.2.2.1(A)(d)

N **(B)*** Design densities obtained from Table 25.3.2.2.2.1(A)(a) through Table 25.3.2.2.2.1(A)(d) for single- and double-row racks shall be selected to correspond to aisle width as follows *(See Section C.15)*:

(1) For aisle widths between 4 ft (1.2 m) and 8 ft (2.4 m), the rules for 4 ft (1.2 m) aisle width shall be used or direct linear interpolation between the densities shall be permitted.

(2) The density given for 8 ft (2.4 m) wide aisles shall be applied to aisles wider than 8 ft (2.4 m).

(3) The density given for 4 ft (1.2 m) wide aisles shall be applied to aisles narrower than 4 ft (1.2 m) down to 3½ ft (1.1 m).

(4) Where aisles are narrower than 3½ ft (1.1 m), racks shall be considered to be multiple-row racks.

N **25.3.2.2.2.2 Clearance.**

N **(A)** The ceiling-level sprinkler design obtained from Table 25.3.2.2.2.1(A)(a) through Table 25.3.2.2.2.1(A)(d) shall be based on a maximum clearance from top of storage to ceiling of 20 ft (6.1 m).

N **(B)** Where the clearance for 25.3.2.2.2.2(A) exceeds 20 ft (6.1 m), one of the following two options shall be implemented:

(1) The ceiling design shall be determined from Table 25.3.2.2.2.1(A)(a) through Table 25.3.2.2.2.1(A)(d) using a theoretical storage height that does not exceed 25 ft (7.6 m) and results in a clearance to ceiling of 20 ft (6.1 m).

(2) If not already provided, the in-rack sprinkler arrangement shall be supplemented with one level of quick-response in-rack sprinklers located directly below the top tier level of storage and at every flue space intersection.

N **25.3.2.3 Cartoned Group A Plastic Commodities.**

N **25.3.2.3.1 In-Rack Sprinkler Arrangements and Designs for Cartoned Group A Plastic Commodities Stored Up to and Including 25 ft (7.6 m) in Height.**

N **25.3.2.3.1.1** Where rack storage of cartoned Group A plastic commodities, encapsulated or nonencapsulated, stored over 5 ft (1.5 m) and up to and including 25 ft (7.6 m) in height will be protected by in-rack sprinklers, in-rack sprinkler arrangements and designs shall be selected from Figure 25.3.2.3.1.1(a) through Figure 25.3.2.3.1.1(g). *(See Section 20.19 for racks with solid shelving.)*

N **25.3.2.3.1.2*** Any notes provided in Figure 25.3.2.3.1.1(a) through Figure 25.3.2.3.1.1(g) shall be permitted to clarify options.

N **25.3.2.3.2 CMDA Ceiling-Level Sprinkler Designs for Cartoned Group A Plastic Commodities Stored Up to and Including 25 ft (7.6 m) in Height in Combination with In-Rack Sprinklers.**

N **25.3.2.3.2.1** For single-, double-, and multiple-row rack storage of cartoned Group A plastic commodities, encapsulated or nonencapsulated, stored over 5 ft (1.5 m) and up to and including 25 ft (7.6 m) in height, the ceiling-level sprinkler design in terms of density [gpm/ft^2 (mm/min)] and area of sprinkler operation [ft^2 (m^2) of ceiling or roof sprinklers] with the provision of in-rack sprinklers shall be in accordance with Figure 25.3.2.3.1.1(a) through Figure 25.3.2.3.1.1(g).

N **25.3.2.3.2.2** Linear interpolation of design densities and areas shall be permitted between storage heights with the same ceiling height.

N **25.3.2.3.2.3** No interpolation between ceiling heights shall be permitted.

N **25.3.2.3.2.4 Clearance.**

N **(A)** The ceiling-level sprinkler design obtained from Figure 25.3.2.3.1.1(a) through Figure 25.3.2.3.1.1(g) shall be based on a maximum clearance from top of storage to ceiling of 10 ft (3.0 m).

N **(B)** Where the clearance of 25.3.2.3.2.4(A) exceeds 10 ft (3.0 m), one of the following two options shall be implemented:

(1) The ceiling design shall be determined from Figure 25.3.2.3.1.1(a) through Figure 25.3.2.3.1.1(g) using a theoretical storage height that results in a clearance to ceiling of 10 ft (3.0 m).

(2) If not already provided, the in-rack sprinkler arrangement shall be supplemented with one level of quick-response in-rack sprinklers located directly below the top tier level of storage and at every flue space intersection.

N Table 25.3.2.2.2.1(A)(a) CMDA Ceiling-Level Sprinkler Design Requirements for Exposed Encapsulated, or Cartoned (Nonencapsulated or Encapsulated) Class I Commodities Stored Over 12 ft (3.7 m) and Up to and Including 25 ft (7.6 m) in Height Supplemented with In-Rack Sprinklers

Maximum Storage Height ft (m)	Maximum Ceiling Height ft (m)	Storage Arrangement	Aisle Width ft (m)	No. of In-Rack Sprinkler Levels Installed	Ceiling Sprinkler System Design [gpm/ft²/2000 ft² (mm/min/185 m²)]	
					High-Temperature-Rated Sprinklers	Ordinary- or Intermediate-Temperature-Rated Sprinklers
15 (4.6)	35 (10.7)	Single- and double-row racks	8 (2.4)	1	0.15 (6.1)	0.17 (7.0)
				More than 1 but not every tier level	0.15 (6.1)	0.15 (6.1)
				Every tier level	0.15 (6.1)	0.15 (6.1)
			4 (1.2)	1	0.18 (7.3)	0.21 (8.6)
				More than 1 but not every tier level	0.15 (6.1)	0.17 (7.0)
				Every tier level	0.15 (6.1)	0.15 (6.1)
		Multiple-row racks	Any	1	0.17 (7.0)	0.20 (8.2)
				More than 1 but not every tier level	0.15 (6.1)	0.16 (6.5)
				Every tier level	0.15 (6.1)	0.15 (6.1)
18 (5.5)	38 (11.6)	Single- and double-row racks	8 (2.4)	1	0.21 (8.6)	0.23 (9.3)
				More than 1 but not every tier level	0.17 (7.0)	0.19 (7.7)
				Every tier level	0.15 (6.1)	0.15 (6.1)
			4 (1.2)	1	0.26 (10.6)	0.30 (12.2)
				More than 1 but not every tier level	0.20 (8.2)	0.24 (9.8)
				Every tier level	0.15 (6.1)	0.18 (7.3)
		Multiple-row racks	Any	1	0.24 (9.8)	0.28 (11.4)
				More than 1 but not every tier level	0.20 (8.2)	0.22 (9.0)
				Every tier level	0.15 (6.1)	0.17 (7.0)
25 (7.6)	45 (13.7)	Single- and double-row racks	8 (2.4)	1	0.25 (10.2)	0.28 (11.4)
				More than 1 but not every tier level	0.20 (8.2)	0.22 (9.0)
				Every tier level	0.15 (6.1)	0.17 (7.0)
			4 (1.2)	1	0.30 (12.2)	0.35 (14.3)
				More than 1 but not every tier level	0.24 (9.8)	0.28 (11.4)
				Every tier level	0.18 (7.3)	0.21 (8.6)
		Multiple-row racks	Any	1	0.29 (11.8)	0.33 (13.4)
				More than 1 but not every tier level	0.23 (9.3)	0.26 (10.6)
				Every tier level	0.17 (7.0)	0.20 (8.2)

N Table 25.3.2.2.2.1(A)(b) CMDA Ceiling-Level Sprinkler Design Requirements for Exposed Encapsulated, or Cartoned (Nonencapsulated or Encapsulated) Class II Commodities Stored Over 12 ft (3.7 m) and Up to and Including 25 ft (7.6 m) in Height Supplemented with In-Rack Sprinklers

Maximum Storage Height ft (m)	Maximum Ceiling Height ft (m)	Storage Arrangement	Aisle Width ft (m)	No. of In-Rack Sprinkler Levels Installed	Ceiling Sprinkler System Design [gpm/ft²/2000 ft² (mm/min/185 m²)]	
					High-Temperature-Rated Sprinklers	Ordinary- or Intermediate-Temperature-Rated Sprinklers
15 (4.6)	35 (10.7)	Single- and double-row racks	8 (2.4)	1	0.15 (6.1)	0.17 (7.0)
				More than 1 but not every tier level	0.15 (6.1)	0.15 (6.1)
				Every tier level	0.15 (6.1)	0.15 (6.1)
			4 (1.2)	1	0.18 (7.3)	0.21 (8.6)
				More than 1 but not every tier level	0.15 (6.1)	0.17 (7.0)
				Every tier level	0.15 (6.1)	0.15 (6.1)
		Multiple-row racks	Any	1	0.19 (7.7)	0.23 (9.3)
				More than 1 but not every tier level	0.15 (6.1)	0.18 (7.3)
				Every tier level	0.15 (6.1)	0.15 (6.1)
18 (5.5)	38 (11.6)	Single- and double-row racks	8 (2.4)	1	0.21 (8.6)	0.23 (9.3)
				More than 1 but not every tier level	0.17 (7.0)	0.19 (7.7)
				Every tier level	0.15 (6.1)	0.15 (6.1)
			4 (1.2)	1	0.26 (10.6)	0.30 (12.2)
				More than 1 but not every tier level	0.20 (8.2)	0.24 (9.8)
				Every tier level	0.15 (6.1)	0.18 (7.3)
		Multiple-row racks	Any	1	0.27 (11.0)	0.32 (13.0)
				More than 1 but not every tier level	0.21 (8.6)	0.26 (10.6)
				Every tier level	0.16 (6.5)	0.19 (7.7)
25 (7.6)	45 (13.7)	Single- and double-row racks	8 (2.4)	1	0.25 (10.2)	0.28 (11.4)
				More than 1 but not every tier level	0.20 (8.2)	0.22 (9.0)
				Every tier level	0.15 (6.1)	0.17 (7.0)
			4 (1.2)	1	0.30 (12.2)	0.35 (14.3)
				More than 1 but not every tier level	0.24 (9.8)	0.28 (11.4)
				Every tier level	0.18 (7.3)	0.21 (8.6)
		Multiple-row racks	Any	1	0.31 (12.6)	0.38 (15.5)
				More than 1 but not every tier level	0.25 (10.2)	0.30 (12.2)
				Every tier level	0.19 (7.7)	0.23 (9.3)

N Table 25.3.2.2.2.1(A)(c) CMDA Ceiling-Level Sprinkler Design Requirements for Exposed Encapsulated, or Cartoned (Nonencapsulated or Encapsulated) Class III Commodities Stored Over 12 ft (3.7 m) and Up to and Including 25 ft (7.6 m) in Height Supplemented with In-Rack Sprinklers

Maximum Storage Height ft (m)	Maximum Ceiling Height ft (m)	Storage Arrangement	Aisle Width ft (m)	No. of In-Rack Sprinkler Levels Installed	Ceiling Sprinkler System Design [gpm/ft²/2000 ft² (mm/min/185 m²)]	
					High-Temperature-Rated Sprinklers	Ordinary- or Intermediate-Temperature-Rated Sprinklers
15 (4.6)	35 (10.7)	Single- and double-row racks	8 (2.4)	1	0.17 (7.0)	0.19 (7.7)
				More than 1 but not every tier level	0.15 (6.1)	0.15 (6.1)
				Every tier level	0.15 (6.1)	0.15 (6.1)
			4 (1.2)	1	0.21 (8.6)	0.23 (9.3)
				More than 1 but not every tier level	0.17 (7.0)	0.19 (7.7)
				Every tier level	0.15 (6.1)	0.15 (6.1)
		Multiple-row racks	Any	1	0.22 (9.0)	0.25 (10.2)
				More than 1 but not every tier level	0.17 (7.0)	0.20 (8.2)
				Every tier level	0.15 (6.1)	0.15 (6.1)
18 (5.5)	38 (11.6)	Single- and double-row racks	8 (2.4)	1	0.24 (9.8)	0.27 (11.0)
				More than 1 but not every tier level	0.19 (7.7)	0.22 (9.0)
				Every tier level	0.15 (6.1)	0.16 (6.5)
			4 (1.2)	1	0.29 (11.8)	0.33 (13.4)
				More than 1 but not every tier level	0.23 (9.3)	0.27 (11.0)
				Every tier level	0.18 (7.3)	0.20 (8.2)
		Multiple-row racks	Any	1	0.31 (12.6)	0.35 (14.3)
				More than 1 but not every tier level	0.25 (10.2)	0.28 (11.4)
				Every tier level	0.18 (7.3)	0.21 (8.6)
25 (7.6)	45 (13.7)	Single- and double-row racks	8 (2.4)	1	0.28 (11.4)	0.32 (13.0)
				More than 1 but not every tier level	0.22 (9.0)	0.26 (10.6)
				Every tier level	0.17 (7.0)	0.19 (7.7)
			4 (1.2)	1	0.35 (14.3)	0.39 (15.9)
				More than 1 but not every tier level	0.28 (11.4)	0.31 (12.6)
				Every tier level	0.21 (8.6)	0.23 (9.3)
		Multiple-row racks	Any	1	0.36 (14.7)	0.41 (16.7)
				More than 1 but not every tier level	0.29 (11.8)	0.33 (13.4)
				Every tier level	0.22 (9.0)	0.25 (10.2)

N Table 25.3.2.2.2.1(A)(d) CMDA Ceiling-Level Sprinkler Design Requirements for Exposed Encapsulated, or Cartoned (Nonencapsulated or Encapsulated) Class IV Commodities Stored Over 12 ft (3.7 m) and Up to and Including 25 ft (7.6 m) in Height Supplemented with In-Rack Sprinklers

Maximum Storage Height ft (m)	Maximum Ceiling Height ft (m)	Storage Arrangement	Aisle Width ft (m)	No. of In-Rack Sprinkler Levels Installed	Ceiling Sprinkler System Design [gpm/ft² /2000 ft² (mm/min/185 m²)]	
					High-Temperature-Rated Sprinklers	Ordinary- or Intermediate-Temperature-Rated Sprinklers
15 (4.6)	35 (10.7)	Single- and double-row racks	8 (2.4)	1	0.23 (9.3)	0.27 (11.0)
				More than 1 but not every tier level	0.19 (7.7)	0.22 (9.0)
				Every tier level	0.15 (6.1)	0.16 (6.5)
			4 (1.2)	1	0.29 (11.8)	0.33 (13.4)
				More than 1 but not every tier level	0.23 (9.3)	0.26 (10.6)
				Every tier level	0.17 (7.0)	0.20 (8.2)
		Multiple-row racks	≥8 (≥2.4)	1	0.29 (11.8)	0.33 (13.4)
				More than 1 but not every tier level	0.23 (9.3)	0.27 (11.0)
				Every tier level	0.17 (7.0)	0.20 (8.1)
			<8 (<2.4)	1	0.35 (14.3)	0.40 (16.3)
				More than 1 but not every tier level	0.28 (11.4)	0.32 (13.0)
				Every tier level	0.21 (8.6)	0.24 (9.8)
18 (5.5)	38 (11.6)	Single- and double-row racks	8 (2.4)	1	0.33 (13.4)	0.39 (15.9)
				More than 1 but not every tier level	0.27 (11.0)	0.31 (12.6)
				Every tier level	0.20 (8.2)	0.23 (9.3)
			4 (1.2)	1	0.40 (16.3)	0.47 (19.1)
				More than 1 but not every tier level	0.32 (13.0)	0.37 (15.1)
				Every tier level	0.24 (9.8)	0.28 (11.4)
		Multiple-row racks	≥8 (≥2.4)	1	0.41 (16.7)	0.47 (19.1)
				More than 1 but not every tier level	0.33 (13.4)	0.38 (15.5)
				Every tier level	0.24 (9.8)	0.28 (11.4)
			<8 (<2.4)	1	0.50 (20.4)	0.56 (22.8)
				More than 1 but not every tier level	0.40 (16.3)	0.45 (18.3)
				Every tier level	0.30 (12.2)	0.34 (13.9)

(continues)

Shaded text = Revisions.   Δ = Text deletions and figure/table revisions.   • = Section deletions.   N = New material.

N Table 25.3.2.2.2.1(A)(d) *Continued*

Maximum Storage Height ft (m)	Maximum Ceiling Height ft (m)	Storage Arrangement	Aisle Width ft (m)	No. of In-Rack Sprinkler Levels Installed	Ceiling Sprinkler System Design [gpm/ft²/2000 ft² (mm/min/185 m²)]	
					High-Temperature-Rated Sprinklers	Ordinary- or Intermediate-Temperature-Rated Sprinklers
25 (7.6)	45 (13.7)	Single- and double-row racks	8 (2.4)	1	0.39 (15.9)	0.46 (18.7)
				More than 1 but not every tier level	0.31 (12.6)	0.36 (14.7)
				Every tier level	0.23 (9.3)	0.27 (11.0)
			4 (1.2)	1	0.48 (19.6)	0.55 (22.4)
				More than 1 but not every tier level	0.38 (15.5)	0.44 (17.9)
				Every tier level	0.29 (11.8)	0.33 (13.4)
		Multiple-row racks	≥8 (≥2.4)	2	0.48 (19.5)	0.56 (22.8)
				More than 2 but not every tier level	0.38 (15.5)	0.44 (17.9)
				Every tier level	0.29 (11.8)	0.33 (13.4)
			<8 (<2.4)	2	0.59 (24.1)	0.66 (26.9)
				More than 2 but not every tier level	0.47 (19.1)	0.53 (21.6)
				Every tier level	0.35 (14.3)	0.40 (16.3)

N **25.3.2.4 Exposed Nonexpanded Group A Plastic Commodities.**

N **25.3.2.4.1* In-Rack Sprinkler Arrangements and Designs for Exposed Nonexpanded Group A Plastic Commodities Stored Up to and Including 25 ft (7.6 m) in Height.** Where rack storage of exposed nonexpanded Group A plastic commodities, encapsulated or nonencapsulated, stored over 5 ft (1.5 m) and up to and including 25 ft (7.6 m) in height will be protected by in-rack sprinklers, in-rack sprinkler arrangements and designs shall be selected from Figure 25.3.2.4.1(a) through Figure 25.3.2.4.1(e). *(See Section 20.19 for racks with solid shelving.)*

N **25.3.2.4.2 CMDA Ceiling-Level Sprinkler Designs for Exposed Nonexpanded Group A Plastic Commodities Stored Up to and Including 25 ft (7.6 m) in Height in Combination with In-Rack Sprinklers.**

N **25.3.2.4.2.1** For single-, double-, and multiple-row rack storage of exposed nonexpanded Group A plastic commodities, encapsulated or nonencapsulated, stored over 5 ft (1.5 m) and up to and including 25 ft (7.6 m) in height, the ceiling-level sprinkler design in terms of density [gpm/ft² (mm/min)] and area of sprinkler operation [ft² (m²) of ceiling or roof sprinklers] with the provision of in-rack sprinklers shall be in accordance with Figure 25.3.2.4.1(a) through Figure 25.3.2.4.1(e).

N **25.3.2.4.2.2 Clearance.**

N **(A)** The ceiling-level sprinkler design obtained from Figure 25.3.2.4.1(a) through Figure 25.3.2.4.1(e) shall be based on a maximum clearance from top of storage to ceiling of 10 ft (3.0 m).

N **(B)** Where the clearance of 25.3.2.4.2.2(A) exceeds 10 ft (3.0 m), one of the following two options shall be implemented:

(1) The ceiling design shall be determined from Figure 25.3.2.4.1(a) through Figure 25.3.2.4.1(e) using a theoretical storage height that results in a clearance to ceiling of 10 ft (3.0 m).

(2) If not already provided, the in-rack sprinkler arrangement shall be supplemented with one level of quick-response in-rack sprinklers located directly below the top tier level of storage and at every flue space intersection.

N **25.3.2.5 Rubber Tire Commodities.**

N **25.3.2.5.1 In-Rack Sprinkler Arrangements for Rubber Tire Commodities Stored Up to and Including 20 ft (6.1 m) in Height.** Where rack storage of rubber tires stored over 12 ft (3.7 m) and up to and including 20 ft (6.1 m) in height will be protected by in-rack sprinklers, in-rack sprinkler arrangements and designs shall be selected from Figure 25.3.2.5.1(a) and Figure 25.3.2.5.1(b). *(See Section 20.19 for racks with solid shelving.)*

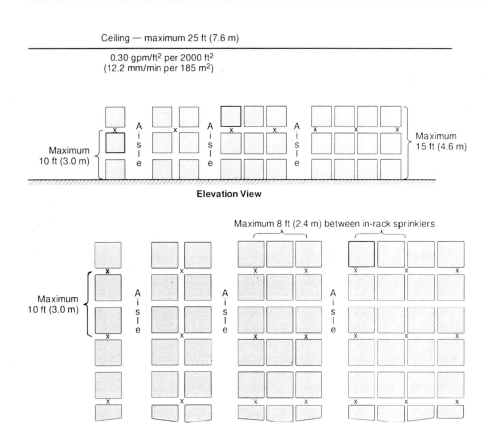

Elevation View

Plan View

Notes:
(1) In-rack sprinklers are ordinary-temperature-rated, quick- or standard-response, pendent or upright, minimum K-5.6 (K-80), and designed for a minimum of eight (8) in-rack sprinklers operating at 22 gpm (83 L/min).
(2) The storage height above the top level of in-rack sprinklers is limited to a maximum of 5 ft (1.5 m).
(3) The symbol X represents in-rack sprinklers.
(4) Each square represents a storage cube measuring 4 ft to 5 ft (1.2 m to 1.5 m) on a side. Actual load heights can vary from approximately 18 in. (450 mm) to 10 ft (3.0 m). Therefore, there could be as few as one load or as many as six loads between in-rack sprinklers that are spaced 10 ft (3.0 m) apart vertically.

N **FIGURE 25.3.2.3.1.1(a)   Ceiling Design Criteria and In-Rack Sprinkler Arrangement and Design Criteria for Cartoned Group A Plastic Commodities Stored to a Maximum Height of 15 ft (4.6 m) Under a Maximum 25 ft (7.6 m) Ceiling in Open Racks.**

N **25.3.2.5.2 CMDA Ceiling-Level Sprinkler Designs for Rubber Tire Commodities Stored Up to and Including 20 ft (6.1 m) in Height in Combination with In-Rack Sprinklers.**

N **25.3.2.5.2.1** For single-, double-, and multiple-row rack storage of rubber tires stored over 12 ft (3.7 m) and up to and including 20 ft (6.1 m) in height, the ceiling-level sprinkler design in terms of density [gpm/ft² (mm/min)] and area of sprinkler operation [ft² (m²) of ceiling or roof sprinklers] with the provision of in-rack sprinklers shall be in accordance with Figure 25.3.2.5.1(a) and Figure 25.3.2.5.1(b). (*See A.21.7.*)

N **25.3.2.5.2.2 Clearance.**

N **(A)** The ceiling-level sprinkler design obtained from Figure 25.3.2.5.1(a) and Figure 25.3.2.5.1(b) shall be based on a maximum clearance from top of storage to ceiling of 10 ft (3.0 m).

N **(B)** Where the clearance of 25.3.2.5.2.2(A) exceeds 10 ft (3.0 m), one of the following two options shall be implemented.

(1) The ceiling design shall be determined from Figure 25.3.2.5.1(a) and Figure 25.3.2.5.1(b) using a theoretical storage height that results in a clearance to ceiling of 10 ft (3.0 m).

(2) If not already provided, the in-rack sprinkler arrangement shall be supplemented with one level of quick-response in-rack sprinklers located directly below the top tier level of storage and at every flue space intersection.

N **25.3.2.5.2.3** The minimum water supply requirements for a hydraulically designed ceiling and in-rack sprinkler system, including foam systems (if provided), shall be determined by adding the hose stream allowance from Table 20.15.2.6 to the water demand for sprinklers.

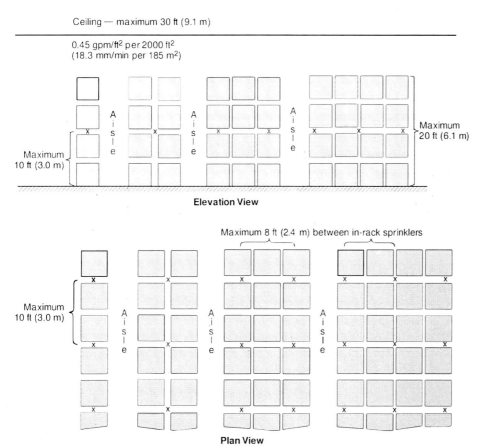

Notes:
(1) In-rack sprinklers are ordinary-temperature-rated, quick-or standard-response, pendent or upright, minimum K-5.6 (K-80), and designed for a minimum of eight (8) in-rack sprinklers operating at 22 gpm (83 L/min).
(2) The storage height above the top level of in-rack sprinklers is limited to a maximum of 10 ft (3.0 m).
(3) The symbol X represents in-rack sprinklers.
(4) Each square represents a storage cube measuring 4 ft to 5 ft (1.2 m to 1.5 m) on a side. Actual load heights can vary from approximately 18 in. (450 mm) to 10 ft (3.0 m). Therefore, there could be as few as one load or as many as six loads between in-rack sprinklers that are spaced 10 ft (3.0 m) apart vertically.

N **FIGURE 25.3.2.3.1.1(b)   Ceiling Design Criteria and In-Rack Sprinkler Arrangement and Design Criteria for Cartoned Group A Plastic Commodities Stored to a Maximum Height of 20 ft (6.1 m) Under a Maximum 30 ft (9.1 m) Ceiling in Open Racks — Option 1.**

Shaded text = Revisions.   Δ = Text deletions and figure/table revisions.   • = Section deletions.   *N* = New material.

2022 Edition

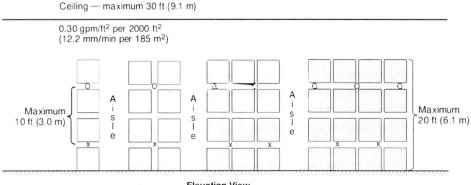

Elevation View

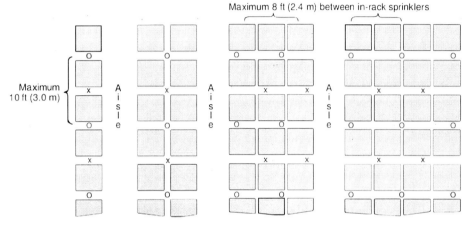

Plan View

Notes:
(1) In-rack sprinklers are ordinary-temperature-rated, quick-or standard-response, pendent or upright, minimum K-5.6 (K-80), and designed for a minimum of 14 in-rack sprinklers [seven (7) in-rack sprinklers on each level] operating at 22 gpm (83 L/min).
(2) The storage height above the top level of in-rack sprinklers is limited to a maximum of 5 ft (1.5 m).
(3) The symbols X and O represent in-rack sprinklers that are staggered both horizontally and vertically.
(4) Each square represents a storage cube measuring 4 ft to 5 ft (1.2 m to 1.5 m) on a side. Actual load heights can vary from approximately 18 in. (450 mm) to 10 ft (3.0 m). Therefore, there could be as few as one load or as many as six loads between in-rack sprinklers that are spaced 10 ft (3.0 m) apart vertically.

N **FIGURE 25.3.2.3.1.1(c)   Ceiling Design Criteria and In-Rack Sprinkler Arrangement and Design Criteria for Cartoned Group A Plastic Commodities Stored to a Maximum Height of 20 ft (6.1 m) Under a Maximum 30 ft (9.1 m) Ceiling in Open Racks — Option 2.**

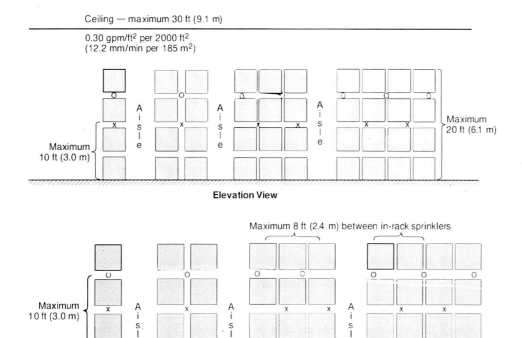

Elevation View

Plan View

Notes:
(1) In-rack sprinklers are ordinary-temperature-rated, quick-or standard-response, pendent or upright, minimum K-5.6 (K-80), and designed for a minimum of 14 in-rack sprinklers [seven (7) in-rack sprinklers on each level] operating at 22 gpm (83 L/min).
(2) The storage height above the top level of in-rack sprinklers is limited to a maximum of 5 ft (1.5 m).
(3) The symbols X and O represent in-rack sprinklers that are staggered both horizontally and vertically.
(4) Each square represents a storage cube measuring 4 ft to 5 ft (1.2 m to 1.5 m) on a side. Actual load heights can vary from approximately 18 in. (450 mm) to 10 ft (3.0 m). Therefore, there could be as few as one load or as many as six loads between in-rack sprinklers that are spaced 10 ft (3.0 m) apart vertically.

N **FIGURE 25.3.2.3.1.1(d)   Ceiling Design Criteria and In-Rack Sprinkler Arrangement and Design Criteria for Cartoned Group A Plastic Commodities Stored to a Maximum Height of 20 ft (6.1 m) Under a Maximum 30 ft (9.1 m) Ceiling in Open Racks — Option 3.**

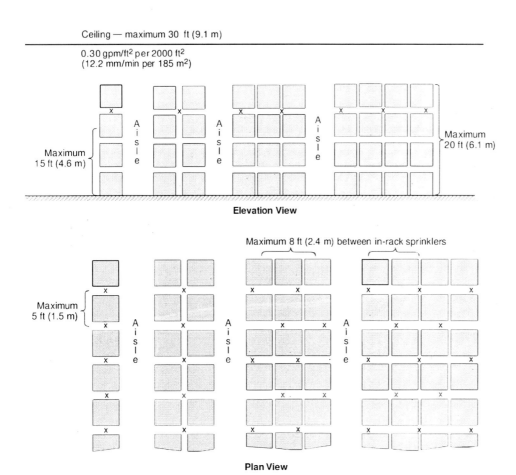

Ceiling — maximum 30 ft (9.1 m)

0.30 gpm/ft² per 2000 ft²
(12.2 mm/min per 185 m²)

Elevation View

Maximum 8 ft (2.4 m) between in-rack sprinklers

Plan View

Notes:
(1) In-rack sprinklers are ordinary-temperature-rated, quick-or standard-response, pendent or upright, minimum K-5.6 (K-80), and designed for a minimum of eight (8) in-rack sprinklers operating at 30 gpm (114 L/min).
(2) The storage height above the top level of in-rack sprinklers is limited to a maximum of 5 ft (1.5 m).
(3) The symbol X represents in-rack sprinklers.
(4) Each square represents a storage cube measuring 4 ft to 5 ft (1.2 m to 1.5 m) on a side. Actual load heights can vary from approximately 18 in. (450 mm) to 10 ft (3.0 m). Therefore, there could be as few as one load or as many as ten loads between in-rack sprinklers that are spaced 15 ft (4.5 m) apart vertically.

N **FIGURE 25.3.2.3.1.1(e)   Ceiling Design Criteria and In-Rack Sprinkler Arrangement and Design Criteria for Cartoned Group A Plastic Commodities Stored to a Maximum Height of 20 ft (6.1 m) Under a Maximum 30 ft (9.1 m) Ceiling in Open Racks — Option 4.**

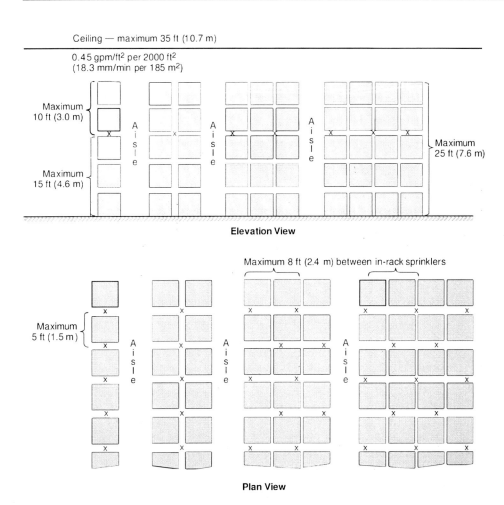

Elevation View

Plan View

Notes:
(1) In-rack sprinklers are ordinary-temperature-rated, quick- or standard-response, pendent or upright, minimum K-5.6 (K-80), and designed for a minimum of eight (8) in-rack sprinklers operating at 30 gpm (114 L/min).
(2) The storage height above the top level of in-rack sprinklers is limited to a maximum of 10 ft (3.0 m).
(3) The symbol X represents in-rack sprinklers.
(4) Each square represents a storage cube measuring 4 ft to 5 ft (1.2 m to 1.5 m) on a side. Actual load heights can vary from approximately 18 in. (450 mm) to 10 ft (3.0 m). Therefore, there could be as few as one load or as many as ten loads between in-rack sprinklers that are spaced 15 ft (4.6 m) apart vertically.

N **FIGURE 25.3.2.3.1.1(f)   Ceiling Design Criteria and In-Rack Sprinkler Arrangement and Design Criteria for Cartoned Group A Plastic Commodities Stored to a Maximum Height of 25 ft (7.6 m) Under a Maximum 35 ft (10.7 m) Ceiling in Open Racks — Option 1.**

Shaded text = Revisions.   Δ = Text deletions and figure/table revisions.   • = Section deletions.   *N* = New material.

2022 Edition

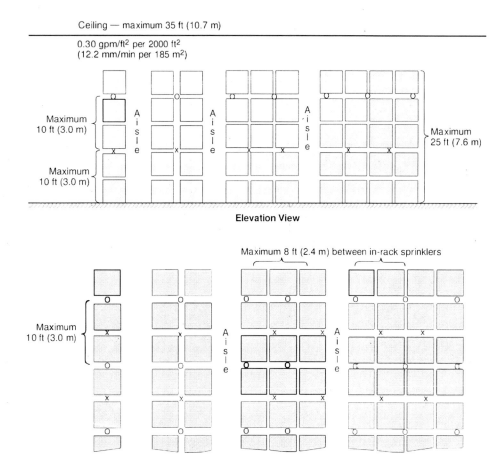

Ceiling — maximum 35 ft (10.7 m)

0.30 gpm/ft² per 2000 ft²
(12.2 mm/min per 185 m²)

Maximum 10 ft (3.0 m)

Maximum 10 ft (3.0 m)

Maximum 25 ft (7.6 m)

Aisle

Elevation View

Maximum 8 ft (2.4 m) between in-rack sprinklers

Maximum 10 ft (3.0 m)

Aisle

Plan View

Notes:
(1) In-rack sprinklers are ordinary-temperature-rated, quick-or standard-response, pendent or upright, minimum K-5.6 (K-80), and designed for a minimum of 14 in-rack sprinklers [seven (7) in-rack sprinklers on each level] operating at 22 gpm (83 L/min).
(2) The storage height above the top level of in-rack sprinklers is limited to a maximum of 5 ft (1.5 m).
(3) The symbols X and O represent in-rack sprinklers that are staggered both horizontally and vertically.
(4) Each square represents a storage cube measuring 4 ft to 5 ft (1.2 m to 1.5 m) on a side. Acutal load heights can vary from approximately 18 in. (450 mm) to 10 ft (3.0 m). Therefore, there could be as few as one load or as many as six loads between in-rack sprinklers that are spaced 10 ft (3.0 m) apart vertically.

N **FIGURE 25.3.2.3.1.1(g)   Ceiling Design Criteria and In-Rack Sprinkler Arrangement and Design Criteria for Cartoned Group A Plastic Commodities Stored to a Maximum Height of 25 ft (7.6 m) Under a Maximum 35 ft (10.7 m) Ceiling in Open Racks — Option 2.**

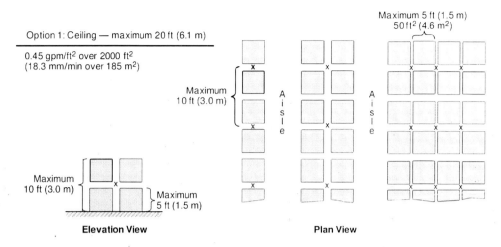

Notes:
(1) In-rack sprinklers are ordinary-temperature-rated, quick- or standard-response, pendent or upright, minimum K-5.6 (K-80), and designed for a minimum of eight in-rack sprinklers operating at 30 gpm (114 L/min).
(2) The symbol X represents in-rack sprinklers.
(3) Each square represents a storage cube measuring 4 ft to 5 ft (1.2 m to 1.5 m) on a side. Actual load heights can vary from approximately 18 in. to 5 ft (450 mm to 1.5 m). Therefore, there could be as few as one load or as many as three loads between in-rack sprinklers that are spaced 5 ft (1.5 m) apart vertically.

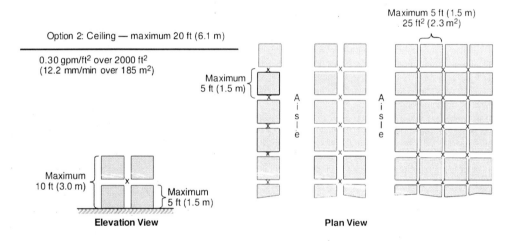

Notes:
(1) In-rack sprinklers are ordinary-temperature-rated, quick- or standard-response, pendent or upright, minimum K-5.6 (K-80), and designed for a minimum of eight in-rack sprinklers operating at 30 gpm (114 L/min).
(2) The symbol X represents in-rack sprinklers.
(3) Each square represents a storage cube measuring 4 ft to 5 ft (1.2 m to 1.5 m) on a side. Actual load heights can vary from approximately 18 in. to 5 ft (450 mm to 1.5 m). Therefore, there could be as few as one load or as many as three loads between in-rack sprinklers that are spaced 5 ft (1.5 m) apart vertically.

N FIGURE 25.3.2.4.1(a)   In-Rack Sprinkler Arrangement and Design, Exposed Nonexpanded Group A Plastic Commodities Up to 10 ft (3.0 m) in Height in Up to a 20 ft (6.1 m) High Building.

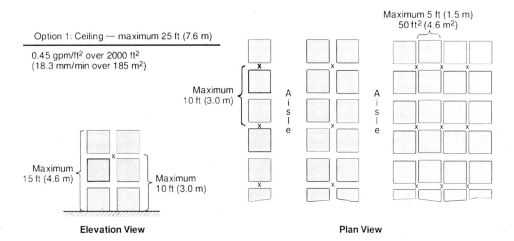

Elevation View   **Plan View**

Notes:
(1) In-rack sprinklers are ordinary-temperature-rated, quick- or standard-response, pendent or upright, minimum K-5.6 (K-80), and designed for a minimum of eight in-rack sprinklers operating at 30 gpm (114 L/min).
(2) The symbol X represents in-rack sprinklers.
(3) Each square represents a storage cube measuring 4 ft to 5 ft (1.2 m to 1.5 m) on a side. Actual load heights can vary from approximately 18 in. to 10 ft (450 mm to 3.0 m). Therefore, there could be as few as one load or as many as six loads between in-rack sprinklers that are spaced 10 ft (3.0 m) apart vertically.

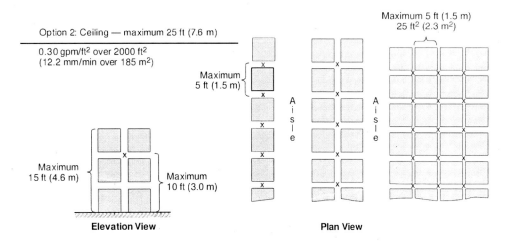

Elevation View   **Plan View**

Notes:
(1) In-rack sprinklers are ordinary-temperature-rated, quick- or standard-response, pendent or upright, minimum K-5.6 (K-80), and designed for a minimum of eight in-rack sprinklers operating at 30 gpm (114 L/min).
(2) The symbol X represents in-rack sprinklers.
(3) Each square represents a storage cube measuring 4 ft to 5 ft (1.2 m to 1.5 m) on a side. Actual load heights can vary from approximately 18 in. to 10 ft (450 mm to 3.0 m). Therefore, there could be as few as one load or as many as six loads between in-rack sprinklers that are spaced 10 ft (3.0 m) apart vertically.

N **FIGURE 25.3.2.4.1(b)   In-Rack Sprinkler Arrangement and Design, Exposed Nonexpanded Group A Plastic Commodities Up to 15 ft (4.6 m) in Height in Up to a 25 ft (7.6 m) High Building.**

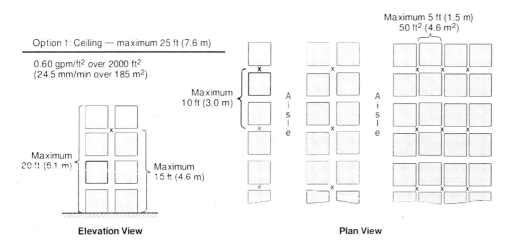

Notes:
(1) In-rack sprinklers are ordinary-temperature-rated, quick- or standard-response, pendent or upright, minimum K-5.6 (K-80), and designed for a minimum of eight in-rack sprinklers operating at 30 gpm (114 L/min).
(2) The symbol X represents in-rack sprinklers.
(3) Each square represents a storage cube measuring 4 ft to 5 ft (1.2 m to 1.5 m) on a side. Actual load heights can vary from approximately 18 in. to 10 ft (450 mm to 3.0 m). Therefore, there could be as few as one load or as many as 10 loads between in-rack sprinklers that are spaced 15 ft (4.6 m) apart vertically.

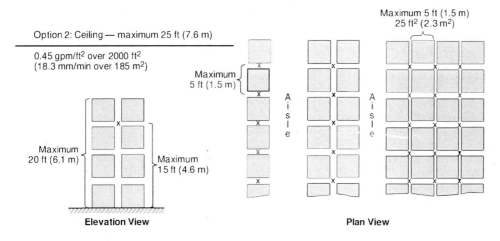

Notes:
(1) In-rack sprinklers are ordinary-temperature-rated, quick- or standard-response, pendent or upright, minimum K-5.6 (K-80), and designed for a minimum of eight in-rack sprinklers operating at 30 gpm (114 L/min).
(2) The symbol X represents in-rack sprinklers.
(3) Each square represents a storage cube measuring 4 ft to 5 ft (1.2 m to 1.5 m) on a side. Actual load heights can vary from approximately 18 in. to 10 ft (450 mm to 3.0 m). Therefore, there could be as few as one load or as many as 10 loads between in-rack sprinklers that are spaced 15 ft (4.8 m) apart vertically.

N **FIGURE 25.3.2.4.1(c)   In-Rack Sprinkler Arrangement and Design, Exposed Nonexpanded Group A Plastic Commodities Up to 20 ft (6.1 m) in Height in Up to a 25 ft (7.6 m) High Building.**

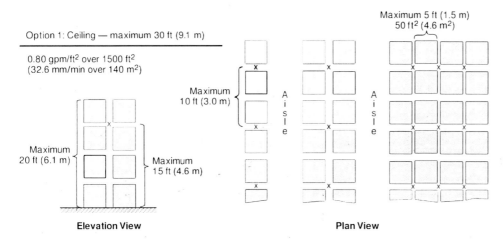

Notes:
(1) In-rack sprinklers are ordinary-temperature-rated, quick- or standard-response, pendent or upright, minimum K-5.6 (K-80), and designed for a minimum of eight in-rack sprinklers operating at 30 gpm (114 L/min) when one level of in-rack sprinklers is installed or a minimum of 14 in-rack sprinklers (seven in-rack sprinklers on each level) operating at 30 gpm (114 L/min) when more than one level of in-rack sprinklers are installed.
(2) The symbol X represents in-rack sprinklers.
(3) Each square represents a storage cube measuring 4 ft to 5 ft (1.2 m to 1.5 m) on a side. Actual load heights can vary from approximately 18 in. to 10 ft (450 mm to 3.0 m). Therefore, there could be as few as one load or as many as 10 loads between in-rack sprinklers that are spaced 15 ft (4.6 m) apart vertically.

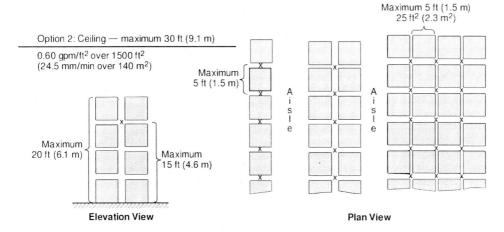

Notes:
(1) In-rack sprinklers are ordinary-temperature-rated, quick- or standard-response, pendent or upright, minimum K-5.6 (K-80), and designed for a minimum of eight in-rack sprinklers operating at 30 gpm (114 L/min) when one level of in-rack sprinklers is installed or a minimum of 14 in-rack sprinklers (seven in-rack sprinklers on each level) operating at 30 gpm (114 L/min) when more than one level of in-rack sprinklers is installed.
(2) The symbol X represents in-rack sprinklers.
(3) Each square represents a storage cube measuring 4 ft to 5 ft (1.2 m to 1.5 m) on a side. Acutal load heights can vary from approximately 18 in. to 10 ft (450 mm to 3.0 m). Therefore, there could be as few as one load or as many as 10 loads between in-rack sprinklers that are spaced 15 ft (4.6 m) apart vertically.

N   **FIGURE 25.3.2.4.1(d)   In-Rack Sprinkler Arrangement and Design, Exposed Nonexpanded Group A Plastic Commodities Up to 20 ft (6.1 m) in Height in Up to a 30 ft (9.1 m) High Building.**

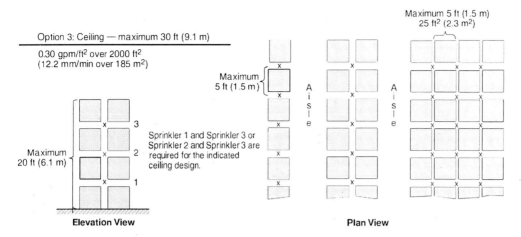

Elevation View   **Plan View**

Notes:
(1) In-rack sprinklers are ordinary-temperature-rated, quick- or standard-response, pendent or upright, minimum K-5.6 (K-80), and designed for a minimum of eight in-rack sprinklers operating at 30 gpm (114 L/min) when one level of in-rack sprinklers is installed or a minimum of 14 in-rack sprinklers (seven in-rack sprinklers on each level) operating at 30 gpm (114 L/min) when more than one level of in-rack sprinklers are installed.
(2) The symbol X represents in-rack sprinklers.
(3) Each square represents a storage cube measuring 4 ft to 5 ft (1.2 m to 1.5 m) on a side. Actual load heights can vary from approximately 18 in. to 10 ft (450 mm to 3.0 m). Therefore, there could be as few as one load or as many as 10 loads between in-rack sprinklers that are spaced 15 ft (4.6 m) apart vertically.

N **FIGURE 25.3.2.4.1(d)**   *Continued*

Shaded text = Revisions.   Δ = Text deletions and figure/table revisions.   • = Section deletions.   *N* = New material.

2022 Edition

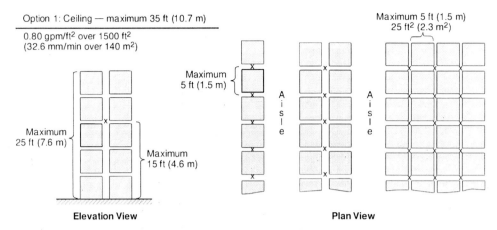

Notes:
(1) In-rack sprinklers are ordinary-temperature-rated, quick- or standard-response, pendent or upright, minimum K-5.6 (K-80), and designed for a minimum of eight in-rack sprinklers operating at 30 gpm (114 L/min) when one level of in-rack sprinklers is installed.
(2) The symbol X represents in-rack sprinklers.
(3) Each square represents a storage cube measuring 4 ft to 5 ft (1.2 m to 1.5 m) on a side. Actual load heights can vary from approximately 18 in. to 10 ft (450 mm to 3.0 m). Therefore, there could be as few as one load or as many as 10 loads between in-rack sprinklers that are spaced 15 ft (4.6 m) apart vertically.

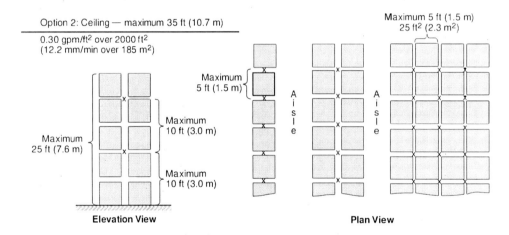

Notes:
(1) In-rack sprinklers are ordinary-temperature-rated, quick- or standard-response, pendent or upright, minimum K-5.6 (K-80), and designed for a minimum of 14 in-rack sprinklers (seven in-rack sprinklers on each level) operating at 30 gpm (114 L/min) when one level of in-rack sprinklers is installed.
(2) The symbol X represents in-rack sprinklers.
(3) Each square represents a storage cube measuring 4 ft to 5 ft (1.2 m to 1.5 m) on a side. Actual load heights can vary from approximately 18 in. to 10 ft (450 mm to 3.0 m). Therefore, there could be as few as one load or as many as six loads between in-rack sprinklers that are spaced 10 ft (3.0 m) apart vertically.

N   **FIGURE 25.3.2.4.1(e)   In-Rack Sprinkler Arrangement and Design, Exposed Nonexpanded Group A Plastic Commodities Up to 25 ft (7.6 m) in Height in Up to a 35 ft (10.7 m) High Building.**

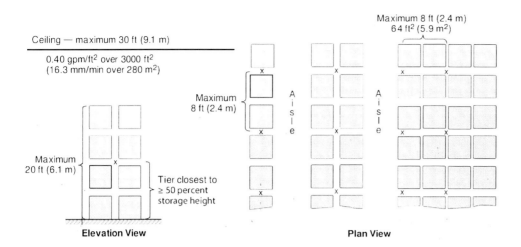

Notes:
(1) In-rack sprinklers are ordinary-temperature-rated, quick- or standard-response, pendent or upright, minimum K-5.6 (K-80), and designed for a minimum of 12 in-rack sprinklers operating at 30 gpm (114 L/min).
(2) The symbol X represents in-rack sprinklers.
(3) Each square represents a storage cube measuring 4 ft to 5 ft (1.2 m to 1.5 m) on a side.

N FIGURE 25.3.2.5.1(a)   In-Rack Sprinkler Arrangement and Design, Rubber Tires on Pallets, Either On-Side or On-Tread, Up to 20 ft (6.1 m) in Height in Up to a 30 ft (9.1 m) High Building.

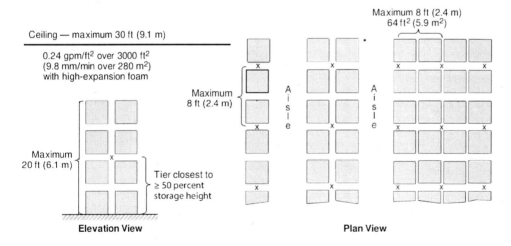

Notes:
(1) In-rack sprinklers are ordinary-temperature-rated, quick- or standard-response, pendent or upright, minimum K-5.6 (K-80), and designed for a minimum of 12 in-rack sprinklers operating at 30 gpm (114 L/min).
(2) The symbol X represents in-rack sprinklers.
(3) Each square represents a storage cube measuring 4 ft to 5 ft (1.2 m to 1.5 m) on a side.

N FIGURE 25.3.2.5.1(b)   In-Rack Sprinkler Arrangement and Design Supplemented with High-Expansion Foam, Rubber Tires on Pallets, Either On-Side or On-Tread, Up to 20 ft (6.1 m) in Height in Up to a 30 ft (9.1 m) High Building.

N **25.3.3 Rack Storage Arrangements with Storage Heights Over 25 ft (7.6 m).**

N **25.3.3.1 Exposed Nonencapsulated Class I, Class II, Class III, or Class IV Commodities.**

N **25.3.3.1.1 In-Rack Sprinkler Arrangements and Designs for Exposed Nonencapsulated Class I, Class II, Class III, or Class IV Commodities Stored Over 25 ft (7.6 m) in Height.**

N **25.3.3.1.1.1** Where rack storage of exposed nonencapsulated Class I commodities stored over 25 ft (7.6 m) in height will be protected by in-rack sprinklers, in-rack sprinkler arrangements and designs shall be selected from Figure 25.3.3.1.1.1(a) through Figure 25.3.3.1.1.1(f). *(See Section 20.19 for racks with solid shelving. See also Section C.23.)*

N **25.3.3.1.1.2** Where rack storage of exposed nonencapsulated Class II or Class III commodities stored over 25 ft (7.6 m) in height will be protected by in-rack sprinklers, in-rack sprinkler arrangements and designs shall be selected from Figure 25.3.3.1.1.2(a) through Figure 25.3.3.1.1.2(g). *(See Section 20.19 for racks with solid shelving.)*

N **25.3.3.1.1.3** Where rack storage of exposed nonencapsulated Class IV commodities stored over 25 ft (7.6 m) in height will be protected by in-rack sprinklers, in-rack sprinkler arrangements

and designs shall be selected from Figure 25.3.3.1.1.3(a) through Figure 25.3.3.1.1.3(f). *(See Section 20.19 for racks with solid shelving.)*

N **25.3.3.1.1.4** The in-rack sprinkler arrangements of 25.3.3.1.1.1 through 25.3.3.1.1.3 for single- and double-row racks shall result in a maximum storage height of 10 ft (3.0 m) above the top level of in-rack sprinklers.

N **25.3.3.1.1.5** The in-rack sprinkler arrangements of 25.3.3.1.1.1 through 25.3.3.1.1.3 for multiple-row racks shall result in a maximum storage height of 10 ft (3.0 m) above the top level of in-rack sprinklers for Class I, Class II, or Class III commodities, and a maximum storage height of 5 ft (1.5 m) for Class IV commodities.

N **25.3.3.1.1.6 Excessive Clearance to Ceiling.**

N **(A)*** Where the clearance to ceiling exceeds 10 ft (3.0 m), the in-rack sprinkler arrangements required for the protection of exposed nonencapsulated Class I, Class II, Class III, or Class IV commodities shall be supplemented with one level of supplemental quick-response in-rack sprinklers installed directly below the top tier of storage and at every flue space intersection.

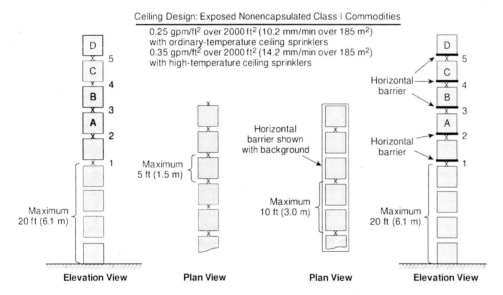

Notes:
(1) In-rack sprinklers are ordinary-temperature-rated, quick- or standard-response, pendent or upright, minimum K-5.6 (K-80), and designed for a minimum of six in-rack sprinklers operating at 30 gpm (114 L/min) when only one level of in-rack sprinklers is installed or a minimum of 10 in-rack sprinklers (five in-rack sprinklers on the top two levels) operating at 30 gpm (114 L/min) when more than one level is installed.
(2) Sprinkler 1 or Sprinkler 1 and Sprinkler 2 are required when Load A represents the top of storage.
(3) Sprinkler 1 and Sprinkler 2 or Sprinkler 1 and Sprinkler 3 are required when Load B represents the top of storage.
(4) Sprinkler 1 and Sprinkler 3 or Sprinkler 1 and Sprinkler 4 are required when Load C represents the top of storage.
(5) Sprinkler 1 and Sprinkler 4 or Sprinkler 1 and Sprinkler 5 are required when Load D represents the top of storage.
(6) For storage higher than represented by Load D, the cycle defined by Note 2 through Note 5 above is repeated.
(7) The storage height above the top level of in-rack sprinklers is limited to a maximum of 10 ft (3.0 m).
(8) In-rack sprinklers in the transverse flue space are permitted to be at any point between load faces.
(9) The symbol X represents in-rack sprinklers.
(10) Each square represents a storage cube measuring 4 ft to 5 ft (1.2 m to 1.5 m) on a side. Actual load heights can vary from approximately 18 in. to 10 ft (450 mm to 3.0 m). Therefore, there could be as few as two loads or as many as 13 loads between in-rack sprinklers that are spaced 20 ft (6.1 m) apart vertically.

N **FIGURE 25.3.3.1.1.1(a)**   **In-Rack Sprinkler Arrangements for Exposed Nonencapsulated Class I Commodities Stored Over 25 ft (7.6 m) in Height in Single-Row Racks.**

Ceiling Design: Exposed Nonencapsulated Class I Commodities

0.25 gpm/ft² over 2000 ft² (10.2 mm/min over 185 m²)
with ordinary-temperature ceiling sprinklers
0.35 gpm/ft² over 2000 ft² (14.2 mm/min over 185 m²)
with high-temperature ceiling sprinklers

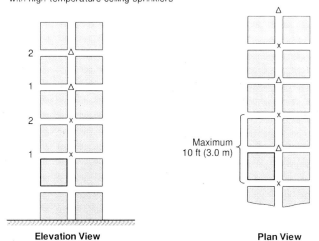

Elevation View   **Plan View**

Notes:
(1) In-rack sprinklers are ordinary-temperature-rated, quick- or standard-response, pendent or upright, minimum K-5.6 (K-80), and designed for a minimum of 10 in-rack sprinklers (five in-rack sprinklers on two levels) operating at 30 gpm (114 L/min).
(2) Sprinkler 1 or Sprinkler 2 is required where the maximum storage height is 30 ft (9.1 m).
(3) The storage height above the top level of in-rack sprinklers is limited to a maximum of 10 ft (3.0 m).
(4) The symbols X and Δ represent in-rack sprinklers that are to be staggered both horizontally and vertically.
(5) Each square represents a storage cube measuring 4 ft to 5 ft (1.2 m to 1.5 m) on a side. Actual load heights can vary from approximately 18 in. to 10 ft (450 mm to 3.0 m). Therefore, there could be as few as one load or as many as six loads between in-rack sprinklers that are spaced 10 ft (3.0 m) apart vertically.

N **FIGURE 25.3.3.1.1.1(b)** **In-Rack Sprinkler Arrangements for Exposed Nonencapsulated Class I Commodities Stored Over 25 ft (7.6 m) and Up to 30 ft (9.1 m) in Height in Double-Row Racks — Option 1.**

N **(B)** Where supplemental in-rack sprinklers have been installed in accordance with 25.3.3.1.1.6(A), the required ceiling-level sprinkler system design shall be based on a ceiling clearance of 10 ft (3.0 m).

N **25.3.3.1.2*** **CMDA Ceiling-Level Sprinkler Designs for Exposed Nonencapsulated Class I, Class II, Class III, or Class IV Commodities Stored Over 25 ft (7.6 m) in Height in Combination with In-Rack Sprinklers.**

N **25.3.3.1.2.1** Where rack storage of exposed nonencapsulated Class I commodities stored over 25 ft (7.6 m) in height will be protected by in-rack sprinklers, the ceiling-level sprinkler design in terms of density [gpm/ft² (mm/min)] and area of sprinkler operation [ft² (m²) of ceiling or roof sprinklers] shall be in accordance with Figure 25.3.3.1.1.1(a) through Figure 25.3.3.1.1.1(f).

N **25.3.3.1.2.2** Where rack storage of exposed nonencapsulated Class II or Class III commodities stored over 25 ft (7.6 m) in height will be protected by in-rack sprinklers, the ceiling-level sprinkler design in terms of density [gpm/ft² (mm/min)] and

Ceiling Design: Exposed Nonencapsulated Class I Commodities

0.25 gpm/ft² over 2000 ft² (10.2 mm/min over 185 m²)
with ordinary-temperature ceiling sprinklers
0.35 gpm/ft² over 2000 ft² (14.3 mm/min over 185 m²)
with high-temperature ceiling sprinklers

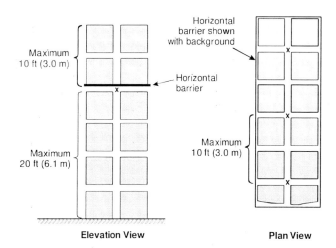

Elevation View   **Plan View**

Notes:
(1) In-rack sprinklers are ordinary-temperature-rated, quick- or standard-response, pendent or upright, minimum K-5.6 (K-80), and designed for a minimum of six in-rack sprinklers operating at 30 gpm (114 L/min).
(2) The storage height above the top level of in-rack sprinklers is limited to a maximum of 10 ft (3.0 m).
(3) The symbol X represents in-rack sprinklers.
(4) Each square represents a storage cube measuring 4 ft to 5 ft (1.2 m to 1.5 m) on a side. Actual load heights can vary from approximately 18 in. to 10 ft (450 mm to 3.0 m). Therefore, there could be as few as two loads or as many as 13 loads between in-rack sprinklers that are spaced 20 ft (6.1 m) apart vertically.

N **FIGURE 25.3.3.1.1.1(c)** **In-Rack Sprinkler Arrangements for Exposed Nonencapsulated Class I Commodities Stored Over 25 (7.6 m) and Up to 30 ft (9.1 m) in Height in Double-Row Racks — Option 2.**

area of sprinkler operation [ft² (m²) of ceiling or roof sprinklers] shall be in accordance with Figure 25.3.3.1.1.2(a) through Figure 25.3.3.1.1.2(g).

N **25.3.3.1.2.3** Where rack storage of exposed nonencapsulated Class IV commodities stored over 25 ft (7.6 m) in height will be protected by in-rack sprinklers, the ceiling-level sprinkler design in terms of density [gpm/ft² (mm/min)] and area of sprinkler operation [ft² (m²) of ceiling or roof sprinklers] shall be in accordance with Figure 25.3.3.1.1.3(a) through Figure 25.3.3.1.1.3(f).

N **25.3.3.2 Exposed Encapsulated, or Cartoned (Nonencapsulated or Encapsulated) Class I, Class II, Class III, or Class IV Commodities.**

N **25.3.3.2.1 In-Rack Sprinkler Arrangements and Designs for Exposed Encapsulated, or Cartoned (Nonencapsulated or Encapsulated) Class I, Class II, Class III, or Class IV Commodities Stored Over 25 ft (7.6 m) in Height.**

N **25.3.3.2.1.1** Where rack storage of exposed encapsulated, or cartoned (nonencapsulated or encapsulated) Class I commodi-

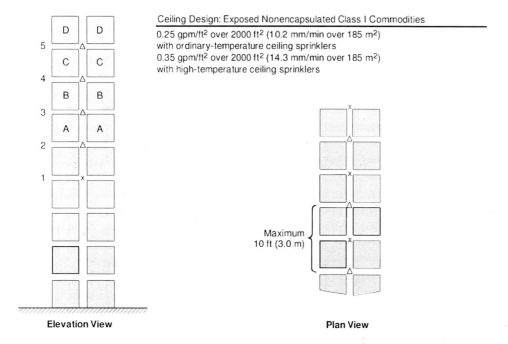

Ceiling Design: Exposed Nonencapsulated Class I Commodities

0.25 gpm/ft² over 2000 ft² (10.2 mm/min over 185 m²)
with ordinary-temperature ceiling sprinklers
0.35 gpm/ft² over 2000 ft² (14.3 mm/min over 185 m²)
with high-temperature ceiling sprinklers

Elevation View

Plan View

Maximum 10 ft (3.0 m)

Notes:
(1) In-rack sprinklers are ordinary-temperature-rated, quick- or standard-response, pendent or upright, minimum K-5.6 (K-80), and designed for a minimum of 10 in-rack sprinklers (five in-rack sprinklers on top two levels) operating at 30 gpm (114 L/min).
(2) Face sprinklers are to be a minimum of 3 in. (75 mm) from rack uprights and a maximum of 18 in. (450 mm) from the aisle face of storage.
(3) Sprinkler 1 or Sprinkler 1 and Sprinkler 2 are required where Load A represents the top of storage.
(4) Sprinkler 1 and Sprinkler 2 or Sprinkler 1 and Sprinkler 3 are required where Load B represents the top of storage.
(5) Sprinkler 1 and Sprinkler 3 or Sprinkler 1 and Sprinkler 4 are required where Load C represents the top of storage.
(6) Sprinkler 1 and Sprinkler 4 or Sprinkler 1 and Sprinkler 5 are required where Load D represents the top of storage.
(7) For storage higher than represented by Load D, the cycle defined by Note 3 through Note 6 above is repeated, with stagger as indicated.
(8) The storage height above the top level of in-rack sprinklers is limited to a maximum of 10 ft (3.0 m).
(9) The symbols X and Δ represent in-rack sprinklers that are to be staggered both horizontally and vertically.
(10) Each square represents a storage cube measuring 4 ft to 5 ft (1.2 m to 1.5 m) on a side. Actual load heights can vary from approximately 18 in. to 10 ft (450 mm to 3.0 m). Therefore, there could be as few as two loads or as many as 13 loads between in-rack sprinklers that are spaced 20 ft (6.1 m) apart vertically.

N **FIGURE 25.3.3.1.1.1(d)   In-Rack Sprinkler Arrangements for Exposed Nonencapsulated Class I Commodities Stored Over 25 ft (7.6 m) in Height in Double-Row Racks — Option 1.**

ties stored over 25 ft (7.6 m) in height will be protected by in-rack sprinklers, in-rack sprinkler arrangements and designs shall be selected from Figure 25.3.3.2.1.1(a) through Figure 25.3.3.2.1.1(f). *(See Section 20.19 for racks with solid shelving. See also Section C.23.)*

N **25.3.3.2.1.2** Where rack storage of exposed encapsulated, or cartoned (nonencapsulated or encapsulated) Class II or Class III commodities stored over 25 ft (7.6 m) in height will be protected by in-rack sprinklers, in-rack sprinkler arrangements and designs shall be selected from Figure 25.3.3.2.1.2(a) through Figure 25.3.3.2.1.2(g). *(See Section 20.19 for racks with solid shelving.)*

N **25.3.3.2.1.3** Where rack storage of exposed encapsulated, or cartoned (nonencapsulated or encapsulated) Class IV commodities stored over 25 ft (7.6 m) in height will be protected by in-rack sprinklers, in-rack sprinkler arrangements and designs shall be selected from Figure 25.3.3.2.1.3(a) through Figure 25.3.3.2.1.3(f). *(See Section 20.19 for racks with solid shelving.)*

N **25.3.3.2.1.4** The in-rack sprinkler arrangements of 25.3.3.2.1.1 through 25.3.3.2.1.3 for single- and double-row racks shall result in a maximum storage height of 10 ft (3.0 m) above the top level of in-rack sprinklers.

N **25.3.3.2.1.5** The in-rack sprinkler arrangements of 25.3.3.2.1.1 through 25.3.3.2.1.3 for multiple-row racks shall result in a maximum storage height of 10 ft (3.0 m) above the top level of in-rack sprinklers for Class I, Class II, or Class III commodities, and a maximum storage height of 5 ft (1.5 m) for Class IV commodities.

N **25.3.3.2.1.6 Excessive Clearance to Ceiling.**

N **(A)*** Where the clearance to ceiling exceeds 10 ft (3.0 m), the in-rack sprinkler arrangements required for the protection of exposed encapsulated, or cartoned (nonencapsulated or encapsulated) Class I, Class II, Class III, or Class IV commodities shall be supplemented with one level of supplemental quick-response in-rack sprinklers installed directly below the top tier of storage and at every flue space intersection.

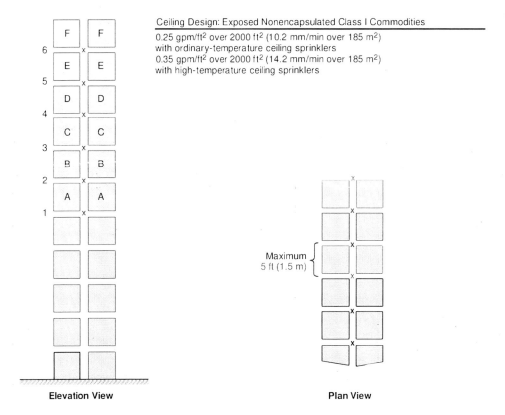

Ceiling Design: Exposed Nonencapsulated Class I Commodities

0.25 gpm/ft² over 2000 ft² (10.2 mm/min over 185 m²)
with ordinary-temperature ceiling sprinklers
0.35 gpm/ft² over 2000 ft² (14.2 mm/min over 185 m²)
with high-temperature ceiling sprinklers

Elevation View   **Plan View**

Maximum 5 ft (1.5 m)

Notes:
(1) In-rack sprinklers are ordinary-temperature-rated, quick- or standard-response, pendent or upright, minimum K-5.6 (K-80), and designed for a minimum of six in-rack sprinklers operating at 30 gpm (114 L/min) when only one level of in-rack sprinklers is installed or a minimum of 10 in-rack sprinklers (five in-rack sprinklers on top two levels) operating at 30 gpm (114 L/min) when more than one level of in-rack sprinklers is installed.
(2) Face sprinklers are to be a minimum of 3 in. (75 mm) from rack uprights and a maximum of 18 in. (450 mm) from the aisle face of storage.
(3) Sprinkler 1 is required where Load A represents the top of storage.
(4) Sprinkler 1 or Sprinkler 1 and Sprinkler 2 are required where Load B represents the top of storage.
(5) Sprinkler 1 and Sprinkler 2 or Sprinkler 1 and Sprinkler 3 are required where Load C represents the top of storage.
(6) Sprinkler 1 and Sprinkler 3 or Sprinkler 1 and Sprinkler 4 are required where Load D represents the top of storage.
(7) Sprinkler 1 and Sprinkler 4 or Sprinkler 1 and Sprinkler 5 are required where Load E represents the top of storage.
(8) Sprinkler 1 and Sprinkler 5 or Sprinkler 1 and Sprinkler 6 are required where Load F represents the top of storage.
(9) For storage higher than represented by Load F, the cycle defined by Note 3 through Note 8 above is repeated.
(10) The storage height above the top level of in-rack sprinklers is limited to a maximum of 10 ft (3.0 m).
(11) The symbol X represents in-rack sprinklers.
(12) Each square represents a storage cube measuring 4 ft to 5 ft (1.2 m to 1.5 m) on a side. Actual load heights can vary from approximately 18 in. to 10 ft (450 mm to 3.0 m). Therefore, there could be as few as two loads or as many as 16 loads between in-rack sprinklers that are spaced 25 ft (7.6 m) apart vertically.

N FIGURE 25.3.3.1.1.1(e)   In-Rack Sprinkler Arrangements for Exposed Nonencapsulated Class I Commodities Stored Over 25 ft (7.6 m) in Height in Double-Row Racks — Option 2.

N **(B)** Where supplemental in-rack sprinklers have been installed in accordance with 25.3.3.2.1.6(A), the required ceiling-level sprinkler system design shall be based on a ceiling clearance of 10 ft (3.0 m).

N **25.3.3.2.2* CMDA Ceiling-Level Sprinkler Designs for Exposed Encapsulated, or Cartoned (Nonencapsulated or Encapsulated) Class I, Class II, Class III, or Class IV Commodities Stored Over 25 ft (7.6 m) in Height in Combination with In-Rack Sprinklers.**

N **25.3.3.2.2.1** Where rack storage of exposed encapsulated, or cartoned (nonencapsulated or encapsulated) Class I commodities stored over 25 ft (7.6 m) in height will be protected by in-

rack sprinklers, the ceiling-level sprinkler design in terms of density [gpm/ft² (mm/min)] and area of sprinkler operation [ft² (m²) of ceiling or roof sprinklers] shall be in accordance with Figure 25.3.3.2.1.1(a) through Figure 25.3.3.2.1.1(f).

N **25.3.3.2.2.2** Where rack storage of exposed encapsulated, or cartoned (nonencapsulated or encapsulated) Class II or Class III commodities stored over 25 ft (7.6 m) in height will be protected by in-rack sprinklers, the ceiling-level sprinkler design in terms of density [gpm/ft² (mm/min)] and area of sprinkler operation [ft² (m²) of ceiling or roof sprinklers] shall be in accordance with Figure 25.3.3.2.1.2(a) through Figure 25.3.3.2.1.2(g).

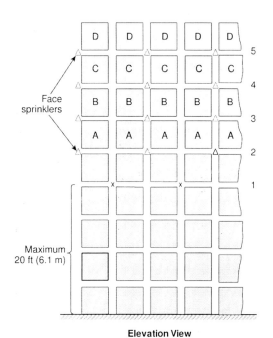

Elevation View

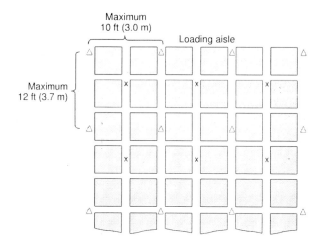

Plan View

Ceiling Design: Exposed Nonencapsulated Class I Commodities

0.25 gpm/ft² over 2000 ft² (10.2 mm/min over 185 m²)
with ordinary-temperature ceiling sprinklers
0.35 gpm/ft² over 2000 ft² (14.3 mm/min over 185 m²)
with high-temperature ceiling sprinklers

Notes:
(1) In-rack sprinklers are ordinary-temperature-rated, quick- or standard-response, pendent or upright, minimum K-5.6 (K-80), and designed for a minimum of six in-rack sprinklers operating at 30 gpm (114 L/min) when only one level of in-rack sprinklers is installed or a minimum of 10 in-rack sprinklers (five in-rack sprinklers on the top two levels) operating at 30 gpm (114 L/min) when more than one level of in-rack sprinklers are installed.
(2) Face sprinklers are to be a minimum of 3 in. (75 mm) from rack uprights and a maximum of 18 in. (450 mm) from the aisle face of storage.
(3) Sprinkler 1 or Sprinkler 1 and Sprinkler 2 are required where Load A represents the top of storage.
(4) Sprinkler 1 and Sprinkler 2 or Sprinkler 1 and Sprinkler 3 are required where Load B represents the top of storage.
(5) Sprinkler 1 and Sprinkler 3 or Sprinkler 1 and Sprinkler 4 are required where Load C represents the top of storage.
(6) Sprinkler 1 and Sprinkler 4 or Sprinkler 1 and Sprinkler 5 are required where Load D represents the top of storage.
(7) For storage higher than represented by Load D, the cycle defined by Note 3 through Note 6 above is repeated, with stagger as indicated.
(8) The storage height above the top level of in-rack sprinklers is limited to a maximum of 10 ft (3.0 m).
(9) The symbols X and △ represent in-rack sprinklers that are to be staggered both horizontally and vertically.
(10) Each square represents a storage cube measuring 4 ft to 5 ft (1.2 m to 1.5 m) on a side. Actual load heights can vary from approximately 18 in. to 10 ft (450 mm to 3.0 m). Therefore, there could be as few as two loads or as many as 13 loads between in-rack sprinklers that are spaced 20 ft (6.1 m) apart vertically.

N **FIGURE 25.3.3.1.1.1(f) In-Rack Sprinkler Arrangements for Exposed Nonencapsulated Class I Commodities Stored Over 25 ft (7.6 m) in Height in Multiple-Row Racks.**

N **25.3.3.2.2.3** Where rack storage of exposed encapsulated, or cartoned (nonencapsulated or encapsulated) Class IV commodities stored over 25 ft (7.6 m) in height will be protected by in-rack sprinklers, the ceiling-level sprinkler design in terms of density [gpm/ft² (mm/min)] and area of sprinkler operation [ft² (m²) of ceiling or roof sprinklers] shall be in accordance with Figure 25.3.3.2.1.3(a) through Figure 25.3.3.2.1.3(f).

N **25.3.3.3 Cartoned Group A Plastic Commodities.**

N **25.3.3.3.1 In-Rack Sprinkler Arrangements and Designs for Cartoned Group A Plastic Commodities Stored Over 25 ft (7.6 m) in Height.**

N **25.3.3.3.1.1** Where rack storage of cartoned Group A plastic commodities stored over 25 ft (7.6 m) in height will be protected by in-rack sprinklers, in-rack sprinkler arrangements and designs shall be selected from Figure 25.3.3.3.1.1(a) through Figure 25.3.3.3.1.1(g). *(See Section 20.19 for racks with solid shelving.)*

N **25.3.3.3.1.2** The in-rack sprinkler arrangements of 25.3.3.3.1.1 shall result in a maximum storage height of 10 ft (3.0 m) above the top level of in-rack sprinklers.

N **25.3.3.3.1.3 Excessive Clearance to Ceiling.**

N **(A)** Where the clearance to ceiling exceeds 10 ft (3.0 m), the existing in-rack sprinkler arrangements indicated in Figure 25.3.3.3.1.1(a) through Figure 25.3.3.3.1.1(g) for cartoned Group A plastic commodities shall be supplemented with one level of supplemental quick-response in-rack sprinklers installed directly below the top tier of storage and at every flue space intersection.

N **(B)** Where supplemental in-rack sprinklers have been installed in accordance with 25.3.3.3.1.3(A), the required ceiling-level sprinkler system design shall be based on a ceiling clearance of 10 ft (3.0 m).

N **25.3.3.3.2* CMDA Ceiling-Level Sprinkler Designs for Cartoned Group A Plastic Commodities Stored Over 25 ft (7.6 m) in Height in Combination with In-Rack Sprinklers.** Where rack storage of cartoned Group A plastic commodities

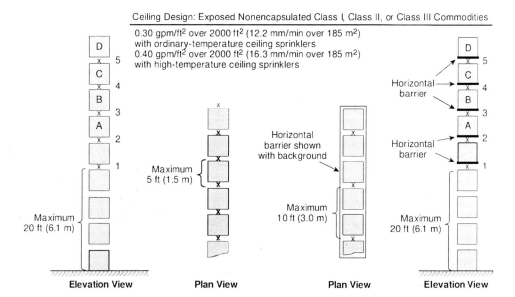

Ceiling Design: Exposed Nonencapsulated Class I, Class II, or Class III Commodities

0.30 gpm/ft² over 2000 ft² (12.2 mm/min over 185 m²) with ordinary-temperature ceiling sprinklers
0.40 gpm/ft² over 2000 ft² (16.3 mm/min over 185 m²) with high-temperature ceiling sprinklers

Notes:
(1) In-rack sprinklers are ordinary-temperature-rated, quick- or standard-response, pendent or upright, minimum K-5.6 (K-80), and designed for a minimum of six in-rack sprinklers operating at 30 gpm (114 L/min) when only one level of in-rack sprinklers is installed or a minimum of 10 in-rack sprinklers (five in-rack sprinklers on the top two levels) operating at 30 gpm (114 L/min) when more than one level is installed.
(2) Sprinkler 1 or Sprinkler 1 and Sprinkler 2 are required when Load A represents the top of storage.
(3) Sprinkler 1 and Sprinkler 2 or Sprinkler 1 and Sprinkler 3 are required when Load B represents the top of storage.
(4) Sprinkler 1 and Sprinkler 3 or Sprinkler 1 and Sprinkler 4 are required when Load C represents the top of storage.
(5) Sprinkler 1 and Sprinkler 4 or Sprinkler 1 and Sprinkler 5 are required when Load D represents the top of storage.
(6) For storage higher than represented by Load D, the cycle defined by Note 2 through Note 5 above is repeated.
(7) The storage height above the top level of in-rack sprinklers is limited to a maximum of 10 ft (3.0 m).
(8) In-rack sprinklers in the transverse flue space are permitted to be at any point between load faces.
(9) The symbol X represents in-rack sprinklers.
(10) Each square represents a storage cube measuring 4 ft to 5 ft (1.2 m to 1.5 m) on a side. Actual load heights can vary from approximately 18 in. to 10 ft (450 mm to 3.0 m). Therefore, there could be as few as two loads or as many as 13 loads between in-rack sprinklers that are spaced 20 ft (6.1 m) apart vertically.

N FIGURE 25.3.3.1.1.2(a) In-Rack Sprinkler Arrangements for Exposed Nonencapsulated Class I, Class II, or Class III Commodities Stored Over 25 ft (7.6 m) in Height in Single-Row Racks.

stored over 25 ft (7.6 m) in height will be protected by in-rack sprinklers, the ceiling-level sprinkler design in terms of density [gpm/ft² (mm/min)] and area of sprinkler operation [ft² (m²) of ceiling or roof sprinklers] shall be in accordance with Figure 25.3.3.3.1.1(a) through Figure 25.3.3.3.1.1(g).

N 25.3.3.4 Exposed Nonexpanded Group A Plastic Commodities.

N 25.3.3.4.1 In-Rack Sprinkler Arrangements and Designs for Exposed Nonexpanded Group A Plastic Commodities Stored Over 25 ft (7.6 m) in Height.

N 25.3.3.4.1.1 Where rack storage of exposed nonexpanded Group A plastic commodities stored over 25 ft (7.6 m) in height will be protected by in-rack sprinklers, in-rack sprinkler arrangements and designs shall be selected from Figure 25.3.3.4.1.1(a) through Figure 25.3.3.4.1.1(d). (See Section 20.19 for racks with solid shelving.)

N 25.3.3.4.1.2 The in-rack sprinkler arrangements of 25.3.3.4.1.1 shall result in a maximum storage height of 10 ft (3.0 m) above the top level of in-rack sprinklers.

N 25.3.3.4.1.3 Excessive Clearance to Ceiling.

N (A) Where the clearance to ceiling exceeds 10 ft (3.0 m), the existing in-rack sprinkler arrangements indicated in Figure 25.3.3.4.1.1(a) through Figure 25.3.3.4.1.1(d) for exposed nonexpanded Group A plastic commodities shall be supplemented with one level of supplemental quick-response in-rack sprinklers installed directly below the top tier of storage and at every flue space intersection.

N (B) Where supplemental in-rack sprinklers have been installed in accordance with 25.3.3.4.1.3(A), the required ceiling-level sprinkler system design shall be based on a ceiling clearance of 10 ft (3.0 m).

N 25.3.3.4.2* CMDA Ceiling-Level Sprinkler Designs for Exposed Nonexpanded Group A Plastic Commodities Stored Over 25 ft (7.6 m) in Height in Combination with In-Rack Sprinklers. Where rack storage of exposed nonexpanded Group A plastic commodities stored over 25 ft (7.6 m) in height will be protected by in-rack sprinklers, the ceiling-level sprinkler design in terms of density [gpm/ft² (mm/min)] and area of sprinkler operation [ft² (m²) of ceiling or roof sprinklers] shall be in accordance with Figure 25.3.3.4.1.1(a) through Figure 25.3.3.4.1.1(d).

Ceiling Design: Exposed Nonencapsulated Class I, Class II, or Class III Commodities

0.30 gpm/ft² over 2000 ft² (12.2 mm/min over 185 m²)
with ordinary-temperature ceiling sprinklers
0.40 gpm/ft² over 2000 ft² (16.3 mm/min over 185 m²)
with high-temperature ceiling sprinklers

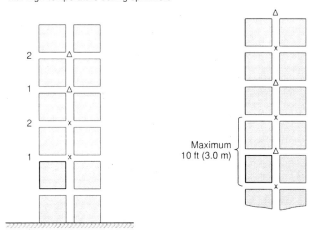

Elevation View   **Plan View**

Notes:
(1) In-rack sprinklers are ordinary-temperature-rated, quick- or
standard-response, pendent or upright, minimum K-5.6 (K-80), and
designed for a minimum of 10 in-rack sprinklers (five in-rack
sprinklers on two levels) operating at 30 gpm (114 L/min).
(2) Sprinkler 1 or Sprinkler 2 is required where the maximum storage
height is 30 ft (9.1 m).
(3) The storage height above the top level of in-rack sprinklers is limited to a
maximum of 10 ft (3.0 m).
(4) The symbols X and △ represent in-rack sprinklers that are to be
staggered both horizontally and vertically.
(5) Each square represents a storage cube measuring 4 ft to 5 ft (1.2 m to
1.5 m) on a side. Actual load heights can vary from approximately 18 in.
to 10 ft (450 mm to 3.0 m). Therefore, there could be as few as one load
or as many as six loads between in-rack sprinklers that are spaced
10 ft (3.0 m) apart vertically.

N FIGURE 25.3.3.1.1.2(b)   In-Rack Sprinkler Arrangements for Exposed Nonencapsulated
Class I, Class II, or Class III Commodities Stored Over 25 ft (7.6 m) and Up to 30 ft (9.1 m) in
Height in Double-Row Racks.

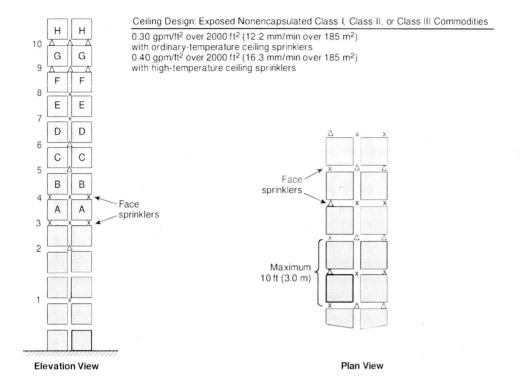

Ceiling Design: Exposed Nonencapsulated Class I, Class II, or Class III Commodities

0.30 gpm/ft² over 2000 ft² (12.2 mm/min over 185 m²)
with ordinary-temperature ceiling sprinklers
0.40 gpm/ft² over 2000 ft² (16.3 mm/min over 185 m²)
with high-temperature ceiling sprinklers

Elevation View   **Plan View**

Notes:
(1) In-rack sprinklers are ordinary-temperature-rated, quick- or standard-response, pendent or upright, minimum K-5.6 (K-80), and designed for a minimum of 10 in-rack sprinklers (five in-rack sprinklers on top two levels) operating at 30 gpm (114 L/min).
(2) Face sprinklers are to be a minimum of 3 in. (75 mm) from rack uprights and a maximum of 18 in. (450 mm) from the aisle face of storage.
(3) Sprinkler 1 and Sprinkler 2 or Sprinkler 1, Sprinkler 2, and Sprinkler 3 are required where Load A represents the top of storage.
(4) Sprinkler 1, Sprinkler 2, and Sprinkler 3 or Sprinkler 1, Sprinkler 2, and Sprinkler 4 are required where Load B represents the top of storage.
(5) Sprinkler 1, Sprinkler 2, and Sprinkler 4 or Sprinkler 1, Sprinkler 2, Sprinkler 4, and Sprinkler 5 are required where Load C represents the top of storage.
(6) Sprinkler 1 and Sprinkler 4 or Sprinkler 1 and Sprinkler 5 are required where Load D represents the top of storage.
(7) Sprinkler 1, Sprinkler 2, Sprinkler 4, and Sprinkler 6 or Sprinkler 1, Sprinkler 2, Sprinkler 4, and Sprinkler 7 are required where Load E represents the top of storage.
(8) Sprinkler 1, Sprinkler 2, Sprinkler 4, Sprinkler 6, and Sprinkler 7 or Sprinkler 1, Sprinkler 2, Sprinkler 4, Sprinkler 6, and Sprinkler 8 are required where Load F represents the top of storage.
(9) Sprinkler 1, Sprinkler 2, Sprinkler 4, Sprinkler 6, and Sprinkler 8 or Sprinkler 1, Sprinkler 2, Sprinkler 4, Sprinkler 6, Sprinkler 8, and Sprinkler 9 are required where Load G represents the top of storage.
(10) Sprinkler 1, Sprinkler 2, Sprinkler 4, Sprinkler 6, Sprinkler 8, and Sprinkler 9 or Sprinkler 1, Sprinkler 2, Sprinkler 4, Sprinkler 6, Sprinkler 8, and Sprinkler 10 are required where Load H represents the top of storage.
(11) For storage higher than represented by Load H, the cycle defined by Note 3 through Note 10 above is repeated, with stagger as indicated.
(12) The storage height above the top level of in-rack sprinklers is limited to a maximum of 10 ft (3.0 m).
(13) The symbols X and △ represent in-rack sprinklers that are to be staggered both horizontally and vertically.
(14) Each square represents a storage cube measuring 4 ft to 5 ft (1.2 m to 1.5 m) on a side. Actual load heights can vary from approximately 18 in. to 10 ft (450 mm to 3.0 m). Therefore, there could be as few as one load or as many as six loads between in-rack sprinklers that are spaced 10 ft (3.0 m) apart vertically.

𝑁 **FIGURE 25.3.3.1.1.2(c)   In-Rack Sprinkler Arrangements for Exposed Nonencapsulated Class I, Class II, or Class III Commodities Stored Over 25 ft (7.6 m) in Height in Double-Row Racks — Option 1.**

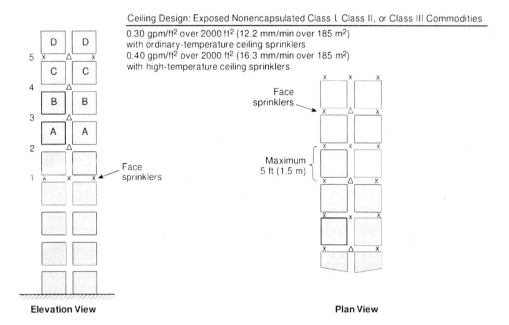

Ceiling Design: Exposed Nonencapsulated Class I, Class II, or Class III Commodities

0.30 gpm/ft² over 2000 ft² (12.2 mm/min over 185 m²)
with ordinary-temperature ceiling sprinklers
0.40 gpm/ft² over 2000 ft² (16.3 mm/min over 185 m²)
with high-temperature ceiling sprinklers

Elevation View   **Plan View**

Notes:

(1) In-rack sprinklers are ordinary-temperature-rated, quick- or standard-response, pendent or upright, minimum K-5.6 (K-80), and designed for a minimum of six in-rack sprinklers operating at 30 gpm (114 L/min) when only one level of in-rack sprinklers is installed or a minimum of 10 in-rack sprinklers (five in-rack sprinklers on top two levels) operating at 30 gpm (114 L/min) when more than one level of in-rack sprinklers are installed.

(2) Face sprinklers are to be a minimum of 3 in. (75 mm) from rack uprights and a maximum of 18 in. (450 mm) from the aisle face of storage.

(3) Sprinkler 1 or Sprinkler 1 and Sprinkler 2 are required where Load A represents the top of storage.

(4) Sprinkler 1 and Sprinkler 2 or Sprinkler 1 and Sprinkler 3 are required where Load B represents the top of storage.

(5) Sprinkler 1 and Sprinkler 3 or Sprinkler 1 and Sprinkler 4 are required where Load C represents the top of storage.

(6) Sprinkler 1 and Sprinkler 4 or Sprinkler 1 and Sprinkler 5 are required where Load D represents the top of storage.

(7) For storage higher than represented by Load D, the cycle defined by Note 3 through Note 6 above is repeated, with stagger as indicated.

(8) The storage height above the top level of in-rack sprinklers is limited to a maximum of 10 ft (3.0 m).

(9) The symbols X and △ represent in-rack sprinklers that are to be staggered both horizontally and vertically.

(10) Each square represents a storage cube measuring 4 ft to 5 ft (1.2 m to 1.5 m) on a side. Actual load heights can vary from approximately 18 in. to 10 ft (450 mm to 3.0 m). Therefore, there could be as few as two loads or as many as 13 loads between in-rack sprinklers that are spaced 10 ft (3.0 m) apart vertically.

N **FIGURE 25.3.3.1.1.2(d)   In-Rack Sprinkler Arrangements for Exposed Nonencapsulated Class I, Class II, or Class III Commodities Stored Over 25 ft (7.6 m) in Height in Double-Row Racks — Option 2.**

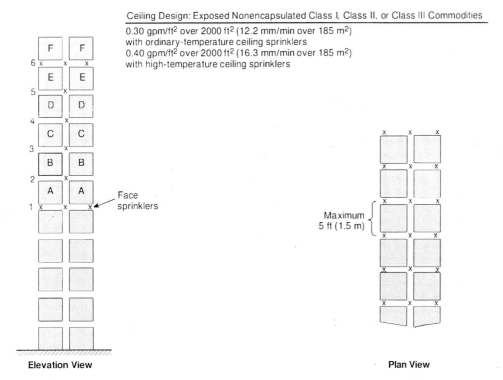

Ceiling Design: Exposed Nonencapsulated Class I, Class II, or Class III Commodities

0.30 gpm/ft² over 2000 ft² (12.2 mm/min over 185 m²)
with ordinary-temperature ceiling sprinklers
0.40 gpm/ft² over 2000 ft² (16.3 mm/min over 185 m²)
with high-temperature ceiling sprinklers

Elevation View

Plan View

Notes:
(1) In-rack sprinklers are ordinary-temperature-rated, quick- or standard-response, pendent or upright, minimum K-5.6 (K-80), and designed for a minimum of six in-rack sprinklers operating at 30 gpm (114 L/min) when only one level of in-rack sprinklers is installed or a minimum of 10 in-rack sprinklers (five in-rack sprinklers on top two levels) operating at 30 gpm (114 L/min) when more than one level of in-rack sprinklers are installed.
(2) Face sprinklers are to be a minimum of 3 in. (75 mm) from rack uprights and a maximum of 18 in. (450 mm) from the aisle face of storage.
(3) Sprinkler 1 is required where Load A represents the top of storage.
(4) Sprinkler 1 or Sprinkler 1 and Sprinkler 2 are required where Load B represents the top of storage.
(5) Sprinkler 1 and Sprinkler 2 or Sprinkler 1 and Sprinkler 3 are required where Load C represents the top of storage.
(6) Sprinkler 1 and Sprinkler 3 or Sprinkler 1 and Sprinkler 4 are required where Load D represents the top of storage.
(7) Sprinkler 1 and Sprinkler 4 or Sprinkler 1 and Sprinkler 5 are required where Load E represents the top of storage.
(8) Sprinkler 1 and Sprinkler 5 or Sprinkler 1 and Sprinkler 6 are required where Load F represents the top of storage.
(9) For storage higher than represented by Load F, the cycle defined by Note 3 through Note 8 above is repeated.
(10) The storage height above the top level of in-rack sprinklers is limited to a maximum of 10 ft (3.0 m).
(11) The symbol X represents in-rack sprinklers.
(12) Each square represents a storage cube measuring 4 ft to 5 ft (1.2 m to 1.5 m) on a side. Actual load heights can vary from approximately 18 in. to 10 ft (450 mm to 3.0 m). Therefore, there could be as few as two loads or as many as 16 loads between in-rack sprinklers that are spaced 25 ft (7.6 m) apart vertically.

N **FIGURE 25.3.3.1.1.2(e)   In-Rack Sprinkler Arrangements for Exposed Nonencapsulated Class I, Class II, or Class III Commodities Stored Over 25 ft (7.6 m) in Height in Double-Row Racks — Option 3.**

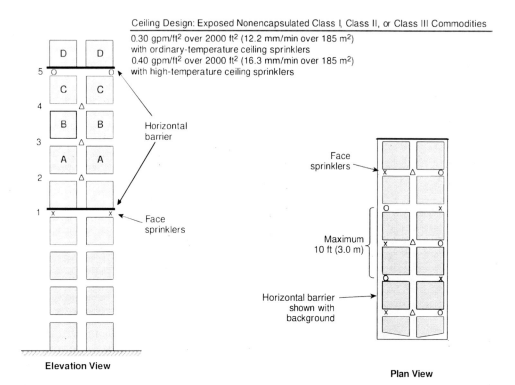

Ceiling Design: Exposed Nonencapsulated Class I, Class II, or Class III Commodities

0.30 gpm/ft² over 2000 ft² (12.2 mm/min over 185 m²)
with ordinary-temperature ceiling sprinklers
0.40 gpm/ft² over 2000 ft² (16.3 mm/min over 185 m²)
with high-temperature ceiling sprinklers

Elevation View   **Plan View**

Notes:
(1) In-rack sprinklers are ordinary-temperature-rated, quick- or standard-response, pendent or upright, minimum K-5.6 (K-80), and designed for a minimum of six in-rack sprinklers operating at 30 gpm (114 L/min) when only one level of in-rack sprinklers is installed or a minimum of 10 in-rack sprinklers (five in-rack sprinklers on top two levels) operating at 30 gpm (114 L/min) when more than one level of in-rack sprinklers are installed.
(2) Face sprinklers are to be a minimum of 3 in. (75 mm) from rack uprights and a maximum of 18 in. (450 mm) from the aisle face of storage.
(3) Sprinkler 1 or Sprinkler 1 and Sprinkler 2 are required where Load A represents the top of storage.
(4) Sprinkler 1 and Sprinkler 2 or Sprinkler 1 and Sprinkler 3 are required where Load B represents the top of storage.
(5) Sprinkler 1 and Sprinkler 3 or Sprinkler 1 and Sprinkler 4 are required where Load C represents the top of storage.
(6) Sprinkler 1 and Sprinkler 4 or Sprinkler 1 and Sprinkler 5 are required where Load D represents the top of storage.
(7) For storage higher than represented by Load D, the cycle defined by Note 3 through Note 6 above is repeated, with stagger as indicated.
(8) The storage height above the top level of in-rack sprinklers is limited to a maximum of 10 ft (3.0 m).
(9) The symbols X, O, and △ represent in-rack sprinklers that are to be staggered both horizontally and vertically.
(10) Each square represents a storage cube measuring 4 ft to 5 ft (1.2 m to 1.5 m) on a side. Actual load heights can vary from approximately 18 in. to 10 ft (450 mm to 3.0 m). Therefore, there could be as few as two loads or as many as 13 loads between in-rack sprinklers that are spaced 20 ft (6.1 m) apart vertically.

N **FIGURE 25.3.3.1.1.2(f) In-Rack Sprinkler Arrangements for Exposed Nonencapsulated Class I, Class II, or Class III Commodities Stored Over 25 ft (7.6 m) in Height in Double-Row Racks — Option 4.**

Ceiling Design: Exposed Nonencapsulated Class I, Class II, or Class III Commodities

0.30 gpm/ft² over 2000 ft² (12.2 mm/min over 185 m²)
with ordinary-temperature ceiling sprinklers
0.40 gpm/ft² over 2000 ft² (16.3 mm/min over 185 m²)
with high-temperature ceiling sprinklers

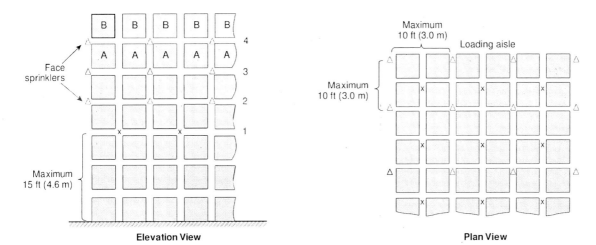

Elevation View **Plan View**

Notes:
(1) In-rack sprinklers are ordinary-temperature-rated, quick- or standard-response, pendent or upright, minimum K-5.6 (K-80), and designed for a minimum of 10 in-rack sprinklers (five in-rack sprinklers on the top two levels) operating at 30 gpm (114 L/min).
(2) Face sprinklers are to be a minimum of 3 in. (75 mm) from rack uprights and a maximum of 18 in. (450 mm) from the aisle face of storage.
(3) Sprinkler 1 and Sprinkler 2 or Sprinkler 1 and Sprinkler 3 are required where Load A represents the top of storage.
(4) Sprinkler 1 and Sprinkler 3 or Sprinkler 1 and Sprinkler 4 are required where Load B represents the top of storage.
(5) For storage higher than represented by Load B, the cycle defined by Note 3 and Note 4 above is repeated, with stagger as indicated.
(6) The storage height above the top level of in-rack sprinklers is limited to a maximum of 10 ft (3.0 m).
(7) The symbols X and △ represent in-rack sprinklers that are to be staggered both horizontally and vertically.
(8) Each square represents a storage cube measuring 4 ft to 5 ft (1.2 m to 1.5 m) on a side. Actual load heights can vary from approximately 18 in. to 10 ft (450 mm to 3.0 m). Therefore, there could be as few as two loads or as many as 10 loads between in-rack sprinklers that are spaced 15 ft (4.6 m) apart vertically.

N **FIGURE 25.3.3.1.1.2(g)** **In-Rack Sprinkler Arrangements for Exposed Nonencapsulated Class I, Class II, or Class III Commodities Stored Over 25 ft (7.6 m) in Height in Multiple-Row Racks.**

Ceiling Design: Exposed Nonencapsulated Class I, Class II, Class III, or Class IV Commodities

0.35 gpm/ft² over 2000 ft² (14.2 mm/min over 185 m²)
with ordinary-temperature ceiling sprinklers
0.45 gpm/ft² over 2000 ft² (18.3 mm/min over 185 m²)
with high-temperature ceiling sprinklers

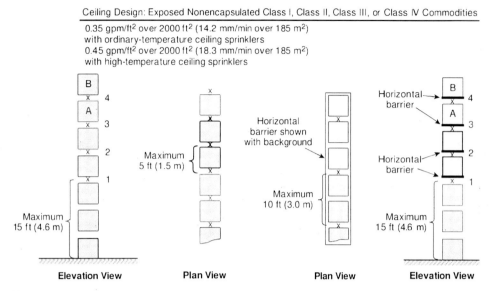

Notes:
(1) In-rack sprinklers are ordinary-temperature-rated, quick- or standard-response, pendent or upright, minimum K-5.6 (K-80), and designed for a minimum of 10 in-rack sprinklers (five in-rack sprinklers on the top two levels) operating at 30 gpm (114 L/min).
(2) Sprinkler 1 and Sprinkler 2 or Sprinkler 1 and Sprinkler 3 are required when Load A represents the top of storage.
(3) Sprinkler 1 and Sprinkler 3 or Sprinkler 1 and Sprinkler 4 are required when Load B represents the top of storage.
(4) For storage higher than represented by Load B, the cycle defined by Note 2 and Note 3 above is repeated.
(5) The storage height above the top level of in-rack sprinklers is limited to a maximum of 10 ft (3.0 m).
(6) In-rack sprinklers in the transverse flue space are permitted to be at any point between load faces.
(7) The symbol X represents in-rack sprinklers.
(8) Each square represents a storage cube measuring 4 ft to 5 ft (1.2 m to 1.5 m) on a side. Actual load heights can vary from approximately 18 in. to 10 ft (450 mm to 3.0 m). Therefore, there could be as few as one load or as many as 10 loads between in-rack sprinklers that are spaced 15 ft (4.6 m) apart vertically.

N **FIGURE 25.3.3.1.1.3(a)   In-Rack Sprinkler Arrangements for Exposed Nonencapsulated Class I, Class II, Class III, or Class IV Commodities Stored Over 25 ft (7.6 m) in Height in Single-Row Racks — Option 1.**

Ceiling Design: Exposed Nonencapsulated Class I, Class II, Class III, or Class IV Commodities

0.35 gpm/ft² over 2000 ft² (14.2 mm/min over 185 m²)
with ordinary-temperature ceiling sprinklers
0.45 gpm/ft² over 2000 ft² (18.3 mm/min over 185 m²)
with high-temperature ceiling sprinklers

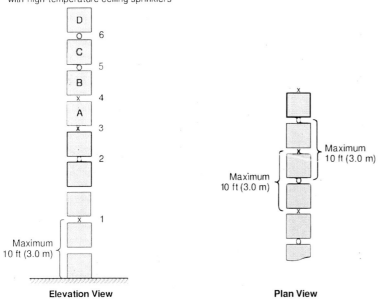

Elevation View　　　　　**Plan View**

Notes:
(1) In-rack sprinklers are ordinary-temperature-rated, quick- or standard-response, pendent or upright, minimum K-5.6 (K-80), and designed for a minimum of 10 in-rack sprinklers (five in-rack sprinklers on the top two levels) operating at 30 gpm (114 L/min).
(2) Sprinkler 1 and Sprinkler 2 or Sprinkler 1, Sprinkler 2, and Sprinkler 3 are required where Load A represents the top of storage.
(3) Sprinkler 1, Sprinkler 2, and Sprinkler 3 or Sprinkler 1, Sprinkler 2, and Sprinkler 4 are required where Load B represents the top of storage.
(4) Sprinkler 1, Sprinkler 2, and Sprinkler 4 or Sprinkler 1, Sprinkler 2, Sprinkler 4, and Sprinkler 5 are required where Load C represents the top of storage.
(5) Sprinkler 1, Sprinkler 2, Sprinkler 4, and Sprinkler 5 or Sprinkler 1, Sprinkler 2, Sprinkler 4, and Sprinkler 6 are required where Load D represents the top of storage.
(6) For storage higher than represented by Load D, the cycle defined by Note 2 through Note 5 above is repeated.
(7) The storage height above the top level of in-rack sprinklers is limited to a maximum of 10 ft (3.0 m).
(8) In-rack sprinklers in the transverse flue space are permitted to be at any point between load faces.
(9) The symbols X and O represent in-rack sprinklers that are to be staggered vertically.
(10) Each square represents a storage cube measuring 4 ft to 5 ft (1.2 m to 1.5 m) on a side. Actual load heights can vary from approximately 18 in. to 10 ft (450 mm to 3.0 m). Therefore, there could be as few as one load or as many as six loads between in-rack sprinklers that are spaced 10 ft (3.0 m) apart vertically.

N **FIGURE 25.3.3.1.1.3(b)** **In-Rack Sprinkler Arrangements for Exposed Nonencapsulated Class I, Class II, Class III, or Class IV Commodities Stored Over 25 ft (7.6 m) in Height in Single-Row Racks — Option 2.**

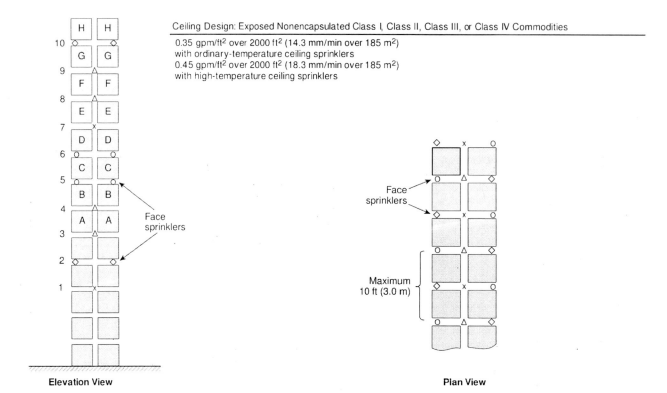

Ceiling Design: Exposed Nonencapsulated Class I, Class II, Class III, or Class IV Commodities

0.35 gpm/ft^2 over 2000 ft^2 (14.3 mm/min over 185 m^2)
with ordinary-temperature ceiling sprinklers
0.45 gpm/ft^2 over 2000 ft^2 (18.3 mm/min over 185 m^2)
with high-temperature ceiling sprinklers

Elevation View

Plan View

Notes:
(1) In-rack sprinklers are ordinary-temperature-rated, quick- or standard-response, pendent or upright, minimum K-5.6 (K-80), and designed for a minimum of 10 in-rack sprinklers (five in-rack sprinklers on the top two levels) operating at 30 gpm (114 L/min).
(2) Face sprinklers are to be a minimum of 3 in. (75 mm) from rack uprights and a maximum of 18 in. (450 mm) from the aisle face of storage.
(3) Sprinkler 1 and Sprinkler 2 or Sprinkler 1, Sprinkler 2, and Sprinkler 3 are required where Load A represents the top of storage.
(4) Sprinkler 1, Sprinkler 2, and Sprinkler 3 or Sprinkler 1, Sprinkler 2, and Sprinkler 4 are required where Load B represents the top of storage.
(5) Sprinkler 1, Sprinkler 2, and Sprinkler 4 or Sprinkler 1, Sprinkler 2, Sprinkler 4, and Sprinkler 5 are required where Load C represents the top of storage.
(6) Sprinkler 1, Sprinkler 2, Sprinkler 4, and Sprinkler 5 or Sprinkler 1, Sprinkler 2, Sprinkler 4, and Sprinkler 6 are required where Load D represents the top of storage.
(7) Sprinkler 1, Sprinkler 2, Sprinkler 4, and Sprinkler 6 or Sprinkler 1, Sprinkler 2, Sprinkler 4, Sprinkler 6, and Sprinkler 7 are required where Load E represents the top of storage.
(8) Sprinkler 1, Sprinkler 2, Sprinkler 4, Sprinkler 6, and Sprinkler 7 or Sprinkler 1, Sprinkler 2, Sprinkler 4, Sprinkler 6, Sprinkler 7, and Sprinkler 8 are required where Load F represents the top of storage.
(9) Sprinkler 1, Sprinkler 2, Sprinkler 4, Sprinkler 6, Sprinkler 7, and Sprinkler 8 or Sprinkler 1, Sprinkler 2, Sprinkler 4, Sprinkler 6, Sprinkler 7, and Sprinkler 9 are required where Load G represents the top of storage.
(10) Sprinkler 1, Sprinkler 2, Sprinkler 4, Sprinkler 6, Sprinkler 7, and Sprinkler 9 or Sprinkler 1, Sprinkler 2, Sprinkler 4, Sprinkler 6, Sprinkler 7, Sprinkler 9, and Sprinkler 10 are required where Load H represents the top of storage.
(11) For storage higher than represented by Load H, the cycle defined by Note 3 through Note 10 above is repeated, with stagger as indicated.
(12) The storage height above the top level of in-rack sprinklers is limited to a maximum of 10 ft (3.0 m).
(13) The symbols X, O, ◇, and △ represent in-rack sprinklers that are to be staggered both horizontally and vertically.
(14) Each square represents a storage cube measuring 4 ft to 5 ft (1.2 m to 1.5 m) on a side. Actual load heights can vary from approximately 18 in. to 10 ft (450 mm to 3.0 m). Therefore, there could be as few as one load or as many as 10 loads between in-rack sprinklers that are spaced 15 ft (4.6 m) apart vertically.

N FIGURE 25.3.3.1.1.3(c)   In-Rack Sprinkler Arrangements for Exposed Nonencapsulated Class I, Class II, Class III, or Class IV Commodities Stored Over 25 ft (7.6 m) in Height in Double-Row Racks — Option 1.

Ceiling Design: Exposed Nonencapsulated Class I through Class IV Commodities

0.35 gpm/ft² over 2000 ft² (15.1 mm/min over 185 m²)
with ordinary-temperature ceiling sprinklers
0.45 gpm/ft² over 2000 ft² (18.3 mm/min over 185 m²)
with high-temperature ceiling sprinklers

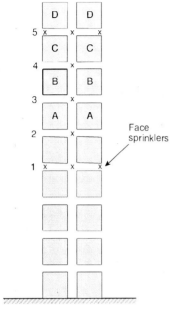

Elevation View

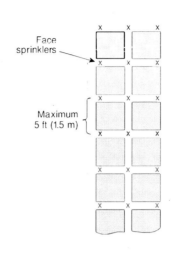

Plan View

Notes:
(1) In-rack sprinklers are ordinary-temperature-rated, quick- or standard-response, pendent or upright, minimum K-5.6 (K-80), and designed for a minimum of six in-rack sprinklers operating at 30 gpm (114 L/min) when only one level of in-rack sprinklers is installed or a minimum of 10 in-rack sprinklers (five in-rack sprinklers on the top two levels) operating at 30 gpm (114 L/min) when more than one level of in-rack sprinklers are installed.
(2) Face sprinklers are to be a minimum of 3 in. (75 mm) from rack uprights and a maximum of 18 in. (450 mm) from the aisle face of storage.
(3) Sprinkler 1 or Sprinkler 1 and Sprinkler 2 are required where Load A represents the top of storage.
(4) Sprinkler 1 and Sprinkler 2 or Sprinkler 1 and Sprinkler 3 are required where Load B represents the top of storage.
(5) Sprinkler 1 and Sprinkler 3 or Sprinkler 1 and Sprinkler 4 are required where Load C represents the top of storage.
(6) Sprinkler 1 and Sprinkler 4 or Sprinkler 1 and Sprinkler 5 are required where Load D represents the top of storage.
(7) For storage higher than represented by Load D, the cycle defined by Note 3 through Note 6 above is repeated.
(8) The storage height above the top level of in-rack sprinklers is limited to a maximum of 10 ft (3.0 m).
(9) The symbol X represents in-rack sprinklers.
(10) Each square represents a storage cube measuring 4 ft to 5 ft (1.2 m to 15 m) on a side. Actual load heights can vary from approximately 18 in. to 10 ft (450 mm to 3.0 m). Therefore, there could be as few as two loads or as many as 13 loads between in-rack sprinklers that are spaced 20 ft (6.1 m) apart vertically.

N FIGURE 25.3.3.1.1.3(d)   In-Rack Sprinkler Arrangements for Exposed Nonencapsulated Class I, Class II, Class III, or Class IV Commodities Stored Over 25 ft (7.6 m) in Height in Double-Row Racks — Option 2.

Shaded text = Revisions.   Δ = Text deletions and figure/table revisions.   • = Section deletions.   N = New material.

2022 Edition

Ceiling Design: Exposed Nonencapsulated Class I, Class II, Class III, or Class IV Commodities

0.35 gpm/ft^2 over 2000 ft^2 (14.3 mm/min over 185 m^2)
with ordinary-temperature ceiling sprinklers
0.45 gpm/ft^2 over 2000 ft^2 (18.3 mm/min over 185 m^2)
with high-temperature ceiling sprinklers

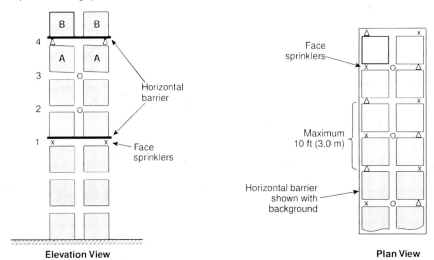

Elevation View   **Plan View**

Notes:
(1) In-rack sprinklers are ordinary-temperature-rated, quick- or standard-response, pendent or upright, minimum K-5.6 (K-80), and designed for a minimum of 10 in-rack sprinklers (five in-rack sprinklers on the top two levels) operating at 30 gpm (114 L/min).
(2) Face sprinklers are to be a minimum of 3 in. (75 mm) from rack uprights and a maximum of 18 in. (450 mm) from the aisle face of storage.
(3) Sprinkler 1 and Sprinkler 2 or Sprinkler 1 and Sprinkler 3 are required where Load A represents the top of storage.
(4) Sprinkler 1 and Sprinkler 3 or Sprinkler 1 and Sprinkler 4 are required where Load B represents the top of storage.
(5) For storage higher than represented by Load B, the cycle defined by Note 3 and Note 4 above is repeated, with stagger as indicated.
(6) The storage height above the top level of in-rack sprinklers is limited to a maximum of 10 ft (3.0 m).
(7) The symbols X, O, and Δ represent in-rack sprinklers that are to be staggered both horizontally and vertically.
(8) Each square represents a storage cube measuring 4 ft to 5 ft (1.2 m to 1.5 m) on a side. Actual load heights can vary from approximately 18 in. to 10 ft (450 mm to 3.0 m). Therefore, there could be as few as two loads or as many as 13 loads between in-rack sprinklers that are spaced 20 ft (6.1 m) apart vertically.

N **FIGURE 25.3.3.1.1.3(e)   In-Rack Sprinkler Arrangements for Exposed Nonencapsulated Class I, Class II, Class III, or Class IV Commodities Stored Over 25 ft (7.6 m) in Height in Double-Row Racks — Option 3.**

Ceiling Design: Exposed Nonencapsulated Class I, Class II, Class III, or Class IV Commodities

0.35 gpm/ft^2 over 2000 ft^2 (14.3 mm/min over 185 m^2)
with ordinary-temperature ceiling sprinklers
0.45 gpm/ft^2 over 2000 ft^2 (18.3 mm/min over 185 m^2)
with high-temperature ceiling sprinklers

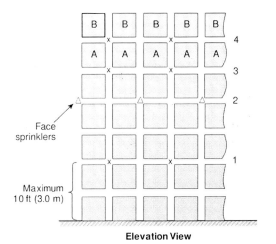

Elevation View

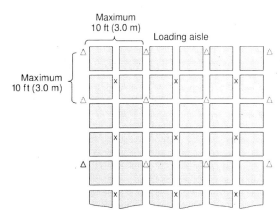

Plan View

Notes:
(1) In-rack sprinklers are ordinary-temperature-rated, quick- or standard-response, pendent or upright, minimum K-5.6 (K-80), and designed for a minimum of 10 in-rack sprinklers (five in-rack sprinklers on the top two levels) operating at 30 gpm (114 L/min).
(2) Face sprinklers are to be a minimum of 3 in. (75 mm) from rack uprights and a maximum of 18 in. (450 mm) from the aisle face to storage.
(3) Sprinkler 1, Sprinkler 2, and Sprinkler 3 are required where Load A represents the top of storage.
(4) Sprinkler 1, Sprinkler 2, and Sprinkler 4 are required where Load B represents the top of storage.
(5) For storage higher than represented by Load B, the cycle defined by Note 3 and Note 4 above is repeated, with stagger as indicated.
(6) The storage height above the top level of in-rack sprinklers is limited to a maximum of 5 ft (1.5 m).
(7) The symbols X and △ represent in-rack sprinklers that are to be staggered both horizontally and vertically.
(8) Each square represents a storage cube measuring 4 ft to 5 ft (1.2 m to 1.5 m) on a side. Actual load heights can vary from approximately 18 in. to 10 ft (450 mm to 3.0 m). Therefore, there could be as few as one load or as many as six loads between in-rack sprinklers that are spaced 10 ft (3.1 m) apart vertically.

N **FIGURE 25.3.3.1.1.3(f)   In-Rack Sprinkler Arrangements for Exposed Nonencapsulated Class I, Class II, Class III, or Class IV Commodities Stored Over 25 ft (7.6 m) in Height in Multiple-Row Racks.**

Shaded text = Revisions.   **Δ** = Text deletions and figure/table revisions.   • = Section deletions.   *N* = New material.

2022 Edition

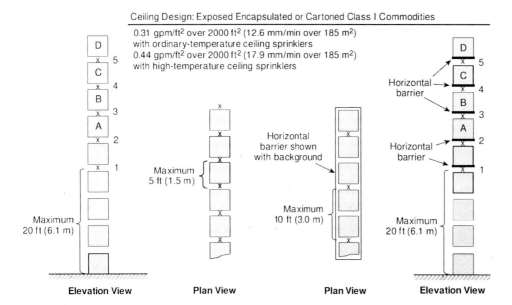

Notes:

(1) In-rack sprinklers are ordinary-temperature-rated, quick- or standard-response, pendent or upright, minimum K-5.6 (K-80), and designed for a minimum of six in-rack sprinklers operating at 30 gpm (114 L/min) when only one level of in-rack is installed or a minimum of 10 in-rack sprinklers (five in-rack sprinklers on the top two levels) operating at 30 gpm (114 L/min) when more than one level of in-rack sprinklers are installed.

(2) Sprinkler 1 or Sprinkler 1 and Sprinkler 2 are required when Load A represents the top of storage.

(3) Sprinkler 1 and Sprinkler 2 or Sprinkler 1 and Sprinkler 3 are required where Load B represents the top of storage.

(4) Sprinkler 1 and Sprinkler 3 or Sprinkler 1 and Sprinkler 4 are required where Load C represents the top of storage.

(5) Sprinkler 1 and Sprinkler 4 or Sprinkler 1 and Sprinkler 5 are required where Load D represents the top of storage.

(6) For storage higher than represented by Load D, the cycle defined by Note 2 through Note 5 above is repeated.

(7) The storage height above the top level of in-rack sprinklers is limited to a maximum of 10 ft (3.0 m).

(8) In-rack sprinklers in the transverse flue space are permitted to be at any point between load faces.

(9) The symbol X represents in-rack sprinklers.

(10) Each square represents a storage cube measuring 4 ft to 5 ft (1.2 m to 1.5 m) on a side. Actual load heights can vary from approximately 18 in. to 10 ft (450 mm to 3.0 m). Therefore, there could be as few as two loads or as many as 13 loads between in-rack sprinklers that are spaced 20 ft (6.1 m) apart vertically.

N **FIGURE 25.3.3.2.1.1(a)   In-Rack Sprinkler Arrangements for Exposed Encapsulated, or Cartoned (Nonencapsulated or Encapsulated) Class I Commodities Stored Over 25 ft (7.6 m) in Height in Single-Row Racks.**

Ceiling Design: Exposed Encapsulated or Cartoned Class I Commodities

0.31 gpm/ft^2 over 2000 ft^2 (12.6 mm/min over 185 m^2)
with ordinary-temperature ceiling sprinklers
0.44 gpm/ft^2 over 2000 ft^2 (17.9 mm/min over 185 m^2)
with high-temperature ceiling sprinklers

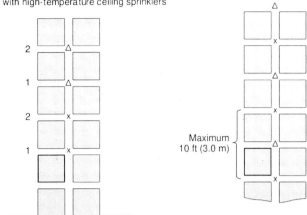

Elevation View   **Plan View**

Notes:
(1). In-rack sprinklers are ordinary-temperature-rated, quick- or
    standard-response, pendent or upright, minimum K-5.6 (K-80), and
    designed for a minimum of 10 in-rack sprinklers (five in-rack
    sprinklers on two levels) operating at 30 gpm (114 L/min).
(2) Sprinkler 1 or Sprinkler 2 is required where the maximum storage height
    is 30 ft (9.1 m).
(3) The storage height above the top level of in-rack sprinklers is limited to
    a maximum of 10 ft (3.0 m).
(4) The symbols X and △ represent in-rack sprinklers that are to be
    staggered both horizontally and vertically.
(5) Each square represents a storage cube measuring 4 ft to 5 ft (1.2 m to
    1.5 m) on a side. Actual load heights can vary from approximately 18 in.
    to 10 ft (450 mm to 3.0 m). Therefore, there could be as few as one load
    or as many as six loads between in-rack sprinklers that are spaced
    10 ft (3.0 m) apart vertically.

N **FIGURE 25.3.3.2.1.1(b)   In-Rack Sprinkler Arrangements for Exposed Encapsulated, or
Cartoned (Nonencapsulated or Encapsulated) Class I Commodities Stored Over 25 ft (7.6 m) and
Up to 30 ft (9.1 m) in Height in Double-Row Racks — Option 1.**

Ceiling Design: Exposed Encapsulated or Cartoned Class I Commodities

0.31 gpm/ft^2 over 2000 ft^2 (12.6 mm/min over 185 m^2)
with ordinary-temperature ceiling sprinklers
0.44 gpm/ft^2 over 2000 ft^2 (17.9 mm/min over 185 m^2)
with high-temperature ceiling sprinklers

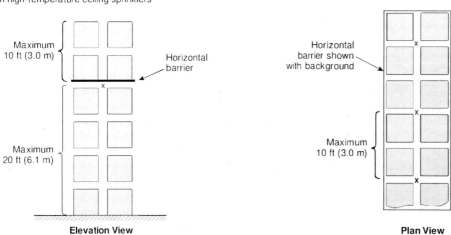

Notes:
(1) In-rack sprinklers are ordinary-temperature-rated, quick- or standard-response, pendent or upright, minimum K-5.6 (K-80), and designed for a minimum of six in-rack sprinklers operating at 30 gpm (114 L/min).
(2) The storage height above the top level of in-rack sprinklers is limited to a maximum of 10 ft (3.0 m).
(3) The symbol X represents in-rack sprinklers.
(4) Each square represents a storage cube measuring 4 ft to 5 ft (1.2 m to 1.5 m) on a side. Actual load heights can vary from approximately 18 in. to 10 ft (450 mm to 3.0 m). Therefore, there could be as few as two loads or as many as 13 loads between in-rack sprinklers that are spaced 20 ft (6.1 m) apart vertically.

N **FIGURE 25.3.3.2.1.1(c)   In-Rack Sprinkler Arrangements for Exposed Encapsulated, or Cartoned (Nonencapsulated or Encapsulated) Class I Commodities Stored Over 25 ft (7.6 m) and Up to 30 ft (9.1 m) in Height in Double-Row Racks — Option 2.**

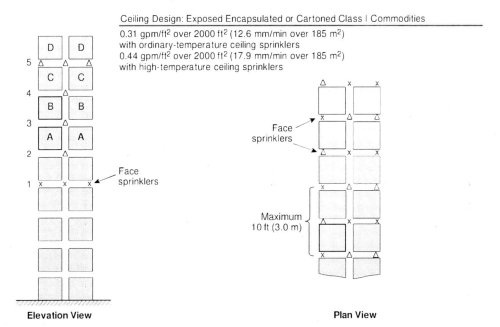

Ceiling Design: Exposed Encapsulated or Cartoned Class I Commodities

0.31 gpm/ft² over 2000 ft² (12.6 mm/min over 185 m²) with ordinary-temperature ceiling sprinklers
0.44 gpm/ft² over 2000 ft² (17.9 mm/min over 185 m²) with high-temperature ceiling sprinklers

Elevation View   **Plan View**

Notes:
(1) In-rack sprinklers are ordinary-temperature-rated, quick- or standard-response, pendent or upright, minimum K-5.6 (K-80), and designed for a minimum of 10 in-rack sprinklers (five in-rack sprinklers on top two levels) operating at 30 gpm (114 L/min).
(2) Face sprinklers are to be a minimum of 3 in. (75 mm) from rack uprights and a maximum of 18 in. (450 mm) from the aisle face of storage.
(3) Sprinkler 1 or Sprinkler 1 and Sprinkler 2 are required where Load A represents the top of storage.
(4) Sprinkler 1 and Sprinkler 2 or Sprinkler 1 and Sprinkler 3 are required where Load B represents the top of storage.
(5) Sprinkler 1 and Sprinkler 3 or Sprinkler 1 and Sprinkler 4 are required where Load C represents the top of storage.
(6) Sprinkler 1 and Sprinkler 4 or Sprinkler 1 and Sprinkler 5 are required where Load D represents the top of storage.
(7) For storage higher than represented by Load D, the cycle defined by Note 3 through Note 6 above is repeated.
(8) The storage height above the top level of in-rack sprinklers is limited to a maximum of 10 ft (3.0 m).
(9) The symbols X and △ represent in-rack sprinklers that are to be staggered both horizontally and vertically.
(10) Each square represents a storage cube measuring 4 ft to 5 ft (1.2 m to 1.5 m) on a side. Actual load heights can vary from approximately 18 in. to 10 ft (450 mm to 3.0 m). Therefore, there could be as few as two loads or as many as 13 loads between in-rack sprinklers that are spaced 20 ft (6.1 m) apart vertically.

N FIGURE 25.3.3.2.1.1(d)   In-Rack Sprinkler Arrangements for Exposed Encapsulated, or Cartoned (Nonencapsulated or Encapsulated) Class I Commodities Stored Over 25 ft (7.6 m) in Height in Double-Row Racks — Option 1.

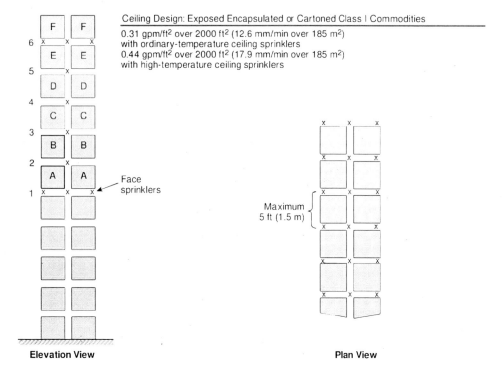

Ceiling Design: Exposed Encapsulated or Cartoned Class I Commodities

0.31 gpm/ft^2 over 2000 ft^2 (12.6 mm/min over 185 m^2)
with ordinary-temperature ceiling sprinklers
0.44 gpm/ft^2 over 2000 ft^2 (17.9 mm/min over 185 m^2)
with high-temperature ceiling sprinklers

Elevation View   **Plan View**

Notes:
(1) In-rack sprinklers are ordinary-temperature-rated, quick- or standard-response, pendent or upright, minimum K-5.6 (K-80), and designed for a minimum of six in-rack sprinklers operating at 30 gpm (114 L/min) when only one level of in-rack sprinklers is installed or a minimum of 10 in-rack sprinklers (five in-rack sprinklers on the top two levels) operating at 30 gpm (114 L/min) when more than one level of in-rack sprinklers are installed.
(2) Face sprinklers are to be a minimum of 3 in. (75 mm) from rack uprights and a maximum of 18 in. (450 mm) from the aisle face to storage.
(3) Sprinkler 1 is required where Load A represents the top of storage.
(4) Sprinkler 1 or Sprinkler 1 and Sprinkler 2 are required where Load B represents the top of storage.
(5) Sprinkler 1 and Sprinkler 2 or Sprinkler 1 and Sprinkler 3 are required where Load C represents the top of storage.
(6) Sprinkler 1 and Sprinkler 3 or Sprinkler 1 and Sprinkler 4 are required where Load D represents the top of storage.
(7) Sprinkler 1 and Sprinkler 4 or Sprinkler 1 and Sprinkler 5 are required where Load E represents the top of storage.
(8) Sprinkler 1 and Sprinkler 5 or Sprinkler 1 and Sprinkler 6 are required where Load F represents the top of storage.
(9) For storage higher than represented by Load F, the cycle defined by Note 3 through Note 8 above is repeated.
(10) The storage height above the top level of in-rack sprinklers is limited to a maximum of 10 ft (3.0 m).
(11) The symbol X represents in-rack sprinklers.
(12) Each square represents a storage cube measuring 4 ft to 5 ft (1.2 m to 1.5 m) on a side. Actual load heights can vary from approximately 18 in. to 10 ft (450 mm to 3.0 m). Therefore, there could be as few as two loads or as many as 16 loads between in-rack sprinklers that are spaced 25 ft (7.6 m) apart vertically.

N FIGURE 25.3.3.2.1.1(e)   In-Rack Sprinkler Arrangements for Exposed Encapsulated, or Cartoned (Nonencapsulated or Encapsulated) Class I Commodities Stored Over 25 ft (7.6 m) in Height in Double-Row Racks — Option 2.

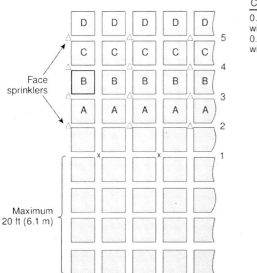

Elevation View

Ceiling Design: Exposed Encapsulated or Cartoned Class I Commodities

0.31 gpm/ft² over 2000 ft² (12.6 mm/min over 185 m²)
with ordinary-temperature ceiling sprinklers
0.44 gpm/ft² over 2000 ft² (17.9 mm/min over 185 m²)
with high-temperature ceiling sprinklers

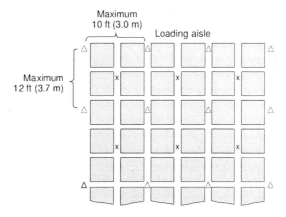

Plan View

Notes:
(1) In-rack sprinklers are ordinary-temperature-rated, quick- or standard-response, pendent or upright, minimum K-5.6 (K-80), and designed for a minimum of six in-rack sprinklers operating at 30 gpm (114 L/min) when only one level of in-rack sprinklers is installed or a minimum of 10 in-rack sprinklers (five in-rack sprinklers on the top two levels) operating at 30 gpm (114 L/min) when more than one level of in-rack sprinklers are installed.
(2) Face sprinklers are to be a minimum of 3 in. (75 mm) from rack uprights and a maximum of 18 in. (450 mm) from the aisle face to storage.
(3) Sprinkler 1 or Sprinkler 1 and Sprinkler 2 are required where Load A represents the top of storage.
(4) Sprinkler 1 and Sprinkler 2 or Sprinkler 1 and Sprinkler 3 are required where Load B represents the top of storage.
(5) Sprinkler 1 and Sprinkler 3 or Sprinkler 1 and Sprinkler 4 are required where Load C represents the top of storage.
(6) Sprinkler 1 and Sprinkler 4 or Sprinkler 1 and Sprinkler 5 are required where Load D represents the top of storage.
(7) For storage higher than represented by Load D, the cycle defined by Note 3 through Note 6 above is repeated.
(8) The storage height above the top level of in-rack sprinklers is limited to a maximum of 10 ft (3.0 m).
(9) The symbols X and △ represent in-rack sprinklers that are to be staggered both horizontally and vertically.
(10) Each square represents a storage cube measuring 4 ft to 5 ft (1.2 m to 1.5 m) on a side. Actual load heights can vary from approximately 18 in. to 10 ft (450 mm to 3.0 m). Therefore there could be as few as two loads or as many as 13 loads between in-rack sprinklers that are spaced 20 ft (6.1 m) apart vertically.

N **FIGURE 25.3.3.2.1.1(f)** In-Rack Sprinkler Arrangements for Exposed Encapsulated, or Cartoned (Nonencapsulated or Encapsulated) Class I Commodities Stored Over 25 ft (7.6 m) in Height in Multiple-Row Racks.

Shaded text = Revisions. △ = Text deletions and figure/table revisions. • = Section deletions. *N* = New material.

2022 Edition

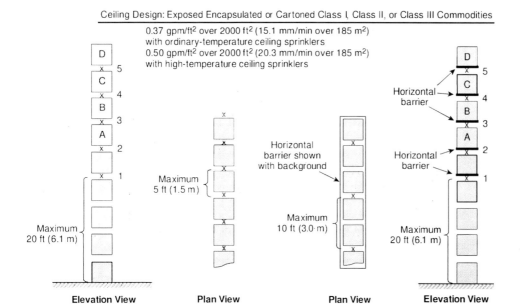

Notes:
(1) In-rack sprinklers are ordinary-temperature-rated, quick- or standard-response, pendent or upright, minimum K-5.6 (K-80), and designed for a minimum of six in-rack sprinklers operating at 30 gpm (114 L/min) when only one level of in-rack is installed or a minimum of 10 in-rack sprinklers (five in-rack sprinklers on the top two levels) operating at 30 gpm (114 L/min) when more than one level of in-rack sprinklers are installed.
(2) Sprinkler 1 or Sprinkler 1 and Sprinkler 2 are required when Load A represents the top of storage.
(3) Sprinkler 1 and Sprinkler 2 or Sprinkler 1 and Sprinkler 3 are required where Load B represents the top of storage.
(4) Sprinkler 1 and Sprinkler 3 or Sprinkler 1 and Sprinkler 4 are required where Load C represents the top of storage.
(5) Sprinkler 1 and Sprinkler 4 or Sprinkler 1 and Sprinkler 5 are required where Load D represents the top of storage.
(6) For storage higher than represented by Load D, the cycle defined by Note 2 through Note 5 above is repeated.
(7) The storage height above the top level of in-rack sprinklers is limited to a maximum of 10 ft (3.0 m).
(8) In-rack sprinklers in the transverse flue space are permitted to be at any point between load faces.
(9) The symbol X represents in-rack sprinklers.
(10) Each square represents a storage cube measuring 4 ft to 5 ft (1.2 m to 1.5 m) on a side. Actual load heights can vary from approximately 18 in. to 10 ft (450 mm to 3.0 m). Therefore, there could be as few as two loads or as many as 13 loads between in-rack sprinklers that are spaced 20 ft (6.1 m) apart vertically.

N FIGURE 25.3.3.2.1.2(a) In-Rack Sprinkler Arrangements for Encapsulated Exposed, or Cartoned (Nonencapsulated or Encapsulated) Class I, Class II, or Class III Commodities Stored Over 25 ft (7.6 m) in Height in Single-Row Racks.

Ceiling Design: Exposed Encapsulated or Cartoned Class I, Class II, or Class III Commodities

0.37 gpm/ft^2 over 2000 ft^2 (15.1 mm/min over 185 m^2)
with ordinary-temperature ceiling sprinklers
0.50 gpm/ft^2 over 2000 ft^2 (20.4 mm/min over 185 m^2)
with high-temperature ceiling sprinklers

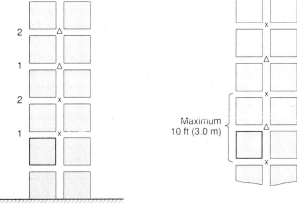

Elevation View   **Plan View**

Notes:
(1) In-rack sprinklers are ordinary-temperature-rated, quick- or standard-response, pendent or upright, minimum K-5.6 (K-80), and designed for a minimum of 10 in-rack sprinklers (five in-rack sprinklers on two levels) operating at 30 gpm (114 L/min).
(2) Sprinkler 1 or Sprinkler 2 is required where the maximum storage height is 30 ft (9.1 m).
(3) The storage height above the top level of in-rack sprinklers is limited to a maximum of 10 ft (3.0 m).
(4) The symbols X and △ represent in-rack sprinklers that are to be staggered both horizontally and vertically.
(5) Each square represents a storage cube measuring 4 ft to 5 ft (1.2 m to 1.5 m) on a side. Actual load heights can vary from approximately 18 in. to 10 ft (450 mm to 3.0 m). Therefore, there could be as few as one load or as many as six loads between in-rack sprinklers that are spaced 10 ft (3.0 m) apart vertically.

N FIGURE 25.3.3.2.1.2(b)   In-Rack Sprinkler Arrangements for Encapsulated Exposed, or Cartoned (Nonencapsulated or Encapsulated) Class I, Class II, or Class III Commodities Stored Over 25 ft (7.6 m) and Up to 30 ft (9.1 m) in Height in Double-Row Racks.

Shaded text = Revisions.   Δ = Text deletions and figure/table revisions.   • = Section deletions.   N = New material.

2022 Edition

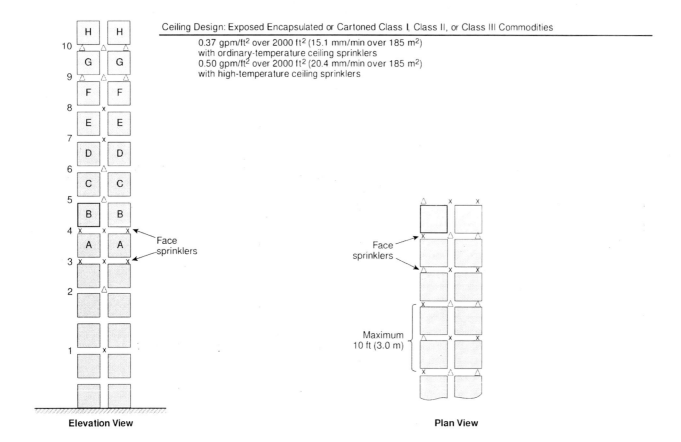

Ceiling Design: Exposed Encapsulated or Cartoned Class I, Class II, or Class III Commodities

0.37 gpm/ft^2 over 2000 ft^2 (15.1 mm/min over 185 m^2)
with ordinary-temperature ceiling sprinklers
0.50 gpm/ft^2 over 2000 ft^2 (20.4 mm/min over 185 m^2)
with high-temperature ceiling sprinklers

Elevation View   **Plan View**

Notes:
(1) In-rack sprinklers are ordinary-temperature-rated, quick- or standard-response, pendent or upright, minimum K-5.6 (K-80), and designed for a minimum of 10 in-rack sprinklers (five in-rack sprinklers on the top two levels) operating at 30 gpm (114 L/min).
(2) Face sprinklers are to be a minimum of 3 in. (75 mm) from rack uprights and a maximum of 18 in. (450 mm) from the aisle face of storage.
(3) Sprinkler 1 and Sprinkler 2 or Sprinkler 1, Sprinkler 2, and Sprinkler 3 are required where Load A represents the top of storage.
(4) Sprinkler 1, Sprinkler 2, and Sprinkler 3 or Sprinkler 1, Sprinkler 2, and Sprinkler 4 are required where Load B represents the top of storage.
(5) Sprinkler 1, Sprinkler 2, and Sprinkler 4 or Sprinkler 1, Sprinkler 2, Sprinkler 4, and Sprinkler 5 are required where Load C represents the top of storage.
(6) Sprinkler 1, Sprinkler 2, Sprinkler 4, and Sprinkler 5 or Sprinkler 1, Sprinkler 2, Sprinkler 4, and Sprinkler 6 are required where Load D represents the top of storage.
(7) Sprinkler 1, Sprinkler 2, Sprinkler 4, and Sprinkler 6 or Sprinkler 1, Sprinkler 2, Sprinkler 4, and Sprinkler 7 are required where Load E represents the top of storage.
(8) Sprinkler 1, Sprinkler 2, Sprinkler 4, Sprinkler 6, and Sprinkler 7 or Sprinkler 1, Sprinkler 2, Sprinkler 4, Sprinkler 6, and Sprinkler 8 are required where Load F represents the top of storage.
(9) Sprinkler 1, Sprinkler 2, Sprinkler 4, Sprinkler 6, and Sprinkler 8 or Sprinkler 1, Sprinkler 2, Sprinkler 4, Sprinkler 6, Sprinkler 8, and Sprinkler 9 are required where Load G represents the top of storage.
(10) Sprinkler 1, Sprinkler 2, Sprinkler 4, Sprinkler 6, Sprinkler 8, and Sprinkler 9 or Sprinkler 1, Sprinkler 2, Sprinkler 4, Sprinkler 6, Sprinkler 8, and Sprinkler 10 are required where Load H represents the top of storage.
(11) For storage higher than represented by Load H, the cycle defined by Note 3 through Note 10 above is repeated, with stagger as indicated.
(12) The storage height above the top level of in-rack sprinklers is limited to a maximum of 10 ft (3.0 m).
(13) The symbols X and △ represent in-rack sprinklers that are to be staggered both horizontally and vertically.
(14) Each square represents a storage cube measuring 4 ft to 5 ft (1.2 m to 1.5 m) on a side. Actual load heights can vary from approximately 18 in. to 10 ft (450 mm to 3.0 m). Therefore, there could be as few as one load or as many as six loads between in-rack sprinklers that are spaced 10 ft (3.0 m) apart vertically.

N **FIGURE 25.3.3.2.1.2(c)   In-Rack Sprinkler Arrangements for Encapsulated Exposed, or Cartoned (Nonencapsulated or Encapsulated) Class I, Class II, or Class III Commodities Stored Over 25 ft (7.6 m) in Height in Double-Row Racks — Option 1.**

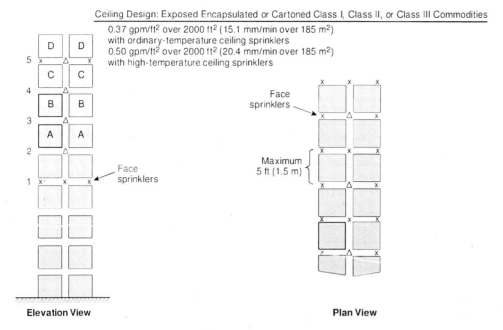

Ceiling Design: Exposed Encapsulated or Cartoned Class I, Class II, or Class III Commodities

0.37 gpm/ft² over 2000 ft² (15.1 mm/min over 185 m²) with ordinary-temperature ceiling sprinklers
0.50 gpm/ft² over 2000 ft² (20.4 mm/min over 185 m²) with high-temperature ceiling sprinklers

Elevation View

Plan View

Notes:
(1) In-rack sprinklers are ordinary-temperature-rated, quick- or standard-response, pendent or upright, minimum K-5.6 (K-80), and designed for a minimum of six in-rack sprinklers operating at 30 gpm (114 L/min) when only one level of in-rack sprinklers is installed or a minimum of 10 in-rack sprinklers (five in-rack sprinklers on top two levels) operating at 30 gpm (114 L/min) when more than one level of in-rack sprinklers are installed.
(2) Face sprinklers are to be a minimum of 3 in. (75 mm) from rack uprights and a maximum of 18 in. (450 mm) from the aisle face to storage.
(3) Sprinkler 1 or Sprinkler 1 and Sprinkler 2 are required where Load A represents the top of storage.
(4) Sprinkler 1 and Sprinkler 2 or Sprinkler 1 and Sprinkler 3 are required where Load B represents the top of storage.
(5) Sprinkler 1 and Sprinkler 3 or Sprinkler 1 and Sprinkler 4 are required where Load C represents the top of storage.
(6) Sprinkler 1 and Sprinkler 4 or Sprinkler 1 and Sprinkler 5 are required where Load D represents the top of storage.
(7) For storage higher than represented by Load D, the cycle defined by Note 3 through Note 6 above is repeated.
(8) The storage height above the top level of in-rack sprinklers is limited to a maximum of 10 ft (3.0 m).
(9) The symbols X and △ represent in-rack sprinklers that are to be staggered both horizontally and vertically.
(10) Each square represents a storage cube measuring 4 ft to 5 ft (1.2 m to 1.5 m) on a side. Actual load heights can vary from approximately 18 in. to 10 ft (450 mm to 3.0 m). Therefore, there could be as few as two loads or as many as 13 loads between in-rack sprinklers that are spaced 20 ft (6.1 m) apart vertically.

N **FIGURE 25.3.3.2.1.2(d)   In-Rack Sprinkler Arrangements for Encapsulated Exposed, or Cartoned (Nonencapsulated or Encapsulated) Class I, Class II, or Class III Commodities Stored Over 25 ft (7.6 m) in Height in Double-Row Racks — Option 2.**

Shaded text = Revisions.   △ = Text deletions and figure/table revisions.   • = Section deletions.   N = New material.

2022 Edition

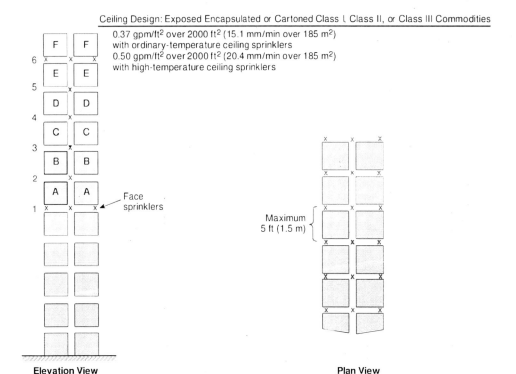

Ceiling Design: Exposed Encapsulated or Cartoned Class I, Class II, or Class III Commodities

0.37 gpm/ft² over 2000 ft² (15.1 mm/min over 185 m²)
with ordinary-temperature ceiling sprinklers
0.50 gpm/ft² over 2000 ft² (20.4 mm/min over 185 m²)
with high-temperature ceiling sprinklers

Elevation View

Plan View

Notes:
(1) In-rack sprinklers are ordinary-temperature-rated, quick- or standard-response, pendent or upright, minimum K-5.6 (K-80), and designed for a minimum of six in-rack sprinklers operating at 30 gpm (114 L/min) when only one level of in-rack sprinklers is installed or a minimum of 10 in-rack sprinklers (five in-rack sprinklers on top two levels) operating at 30 gpm (114 L/min) when more than one level of in-rack sprinklers are installed.
(2) Face sprinklers are to be a minimum of 3 in. (75 mm) from rack uprights and a maximum of 18 in. (450 mm) from the aisle face to storage.
(3) Sprinkler 1 is required where Load A represents the top of storage.
(4) Sprinkler 1 or Sprinkler 1 and Sprinkler 2 are required where Load B represents the top of storage.
(5) Sprinkler 1 and Sprinkler 2 or Sprinkler 1 and Sprinkler 3 are required where Load C represents the top of storage.
(6) Sprinkler 1 and Sprinkler 3 or Sprinkler 1 and Sprinkler 4 are required where Load D represents the top of storage.
(7) Sprinkler 1 and Sprinkler 4 or Sprinkler 1 and Sprinkler 5 are required where Load E represents the top of storage.
(8) Sprinkler 1 and Sprinkler 5 or Sprinkler 1 and Sprinkler 6 are required where Load F represents the top of storage.
(9) For storage higher than represented by Load F, the cycle defined by Note 3 through Note 8 above is repeated.
(10) The storage height above the top level of in-rack sprinklers is limited to a maximum of 10 ft (3.0 m).
(11) The symbol X represents in-rack sprinklers.
(12) Each square represents a storage cube measuring 4 ft to 5 ft (1.2 m to 1.5 m) on a side. Actual load heights can vary from approximately 18 in. to 10 ft (450 mm to 3.0 m). Therefore, there could be as few as two loads or as many as 16 loads between in-rack sprinklers that are spaced 25 ft (7.6 m) apart vertically.

N FIGURE 25.3.3.2.1.2(e)   In-Rack Sprinkler Arrangements for Encapsulated Exposed, or Cartoned (Nonencapsulated or Encapsulated) Class I, Class II, or Class III Commodities Stored Over 25 ft (7.6 m) in Height in Double-Row Racks — Option 3.

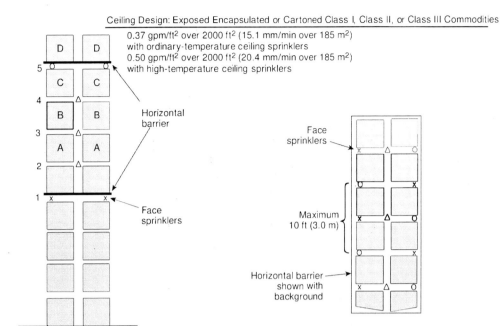

Ceiling Design: Exposed Encapsulated or Cartoned Class I, Class II, or Class III Commodities

0.37 gpm/ft² over 2000 ft² (15.1 mm/min over 185 m²) with ordinary-temperature ceiling sprinklers
0.50 gpm/ft² over 2000 ft² (20.4 mm/min over 185 m²) with high-temperature ceiling sprinklers

Elevation View

Plan View

Notes:
(1) In-rack sprinklers are ordinary-temperature-rated, quick- or standard-response, pendent or upright, minimum K-5.6 (K-80), and designed for a minimum of six in-rack sprinklers operating at 30 gpm (114 L/min) when only one level of in-rack sprinklers is installed or a minimum of 10 in-rack sprinklers (five in-rack sprinklers on the top two levels) operating at 30 gpm (114 L/min) when more than one level of in-rack sprinklers are installed.
(2) Face sprinklers are to be a minimum of 3 in. (75 mm) from rack uprights and a maximum of 18 in. (450 mm) from the aisle face of storage.
(3) Sprinkler 1 or Sprinkler 1 and Sprinkler 2 are required where Load A represents the top of storage.
(4) Sprinkler 1 and Sprinkler 2 or Sprinkler 1 and Sprinkler 3 are required where Load B represents the top of storage.
(5) Sprinkler 1 and Sprinkler 3 or Sprinkler 1 and Sprinkler 4 are required where Load C represents the top of storage.
(6) Sprinkler 1 and Sprinkler 4 or Sprinkler 1 and Sprinkler 5 are required where Load D represents the top of storage.
(7) For storage higher than represented by Load D, the cycle defined by Note 3 through Note 6 above is repeated, with stagger as indicated.
(8) The storage height above the top level of in-rack sprinklers is limited to a maximum of 10 ft (3.0 m).
(9) The symbols X, O, and Δ represent in-rack sprinklers that are to be staggered both horizontally and vertically.
(10) Each square represents a storage cube measuring 4 ft to 5 ft (1.2 m to 1.5 m) on a side. Actual load heights can vary from approximately 18 in. to 10 ft (450 mm to 3.0 m). Therefore, there could be as few as two loads or as many as 13 loads between in-rack sprinklers that are spaced 20 ft (6.1 m) apart vertically.

N **FIGURE 25.3.3.2.1.2(f)   In-Rack Sprinkler Arrangements for Encapsulated Exposed, or Cartoned (Nonencapsulated or Encapsulated) Class I, Class II, or Class III Commodities Stored Over 25 ft (7.6 m) in Height in Double-Row Racks — Option 4.**

Ceiling Design: Exposed Encapsulated or Cartoned Class I, Class II, or Class III Commodities

0.37 gpm/ft² over 2000 ft² (15.1 mm/min over 185 m²)
with ordinary-temperature ceiling sprinklers
0.50 gpm/ft² over 2000 ft² (20.4 mm/min over 185 m²)
with high-temperature ceiling sprinklers

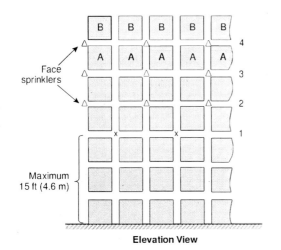

Elevation View

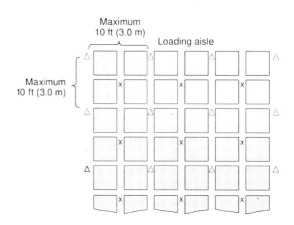

Plan View

Notes:
(1) In-rack sprinklers are ordinary-temperature-rated, quick- or standard-response, pendent or upright, minimum K-5.6 (K-80), and designed for a minimum of 10 in-rack sprinklers (five in-rack sprinklers on the top two levels) operating at 30 gpm (114 L/min).
(2) Face sprinklers are to be a minimum of 3 in. (75 mm) from rack uprights and a maximum of 18 in. (450 mm) from the aisle face of storage.
(3) Sprinkler 1 and Sprinkler 2 or Sprinkler 1 and Sprinkler 3 are required where Load A represents the top of storage.
(4) Sprinkler 1 and Sprinkler 3 or Sprinkler 1 and Sprinkler 4 are required where Load B represents the top of storage.
(5) For storage higher than represented by Load B, the cycle defined by Note 3 and Note 4 above is repeated, with stagger as indicated.
(6) The storage height above the top level of in-rack sprinklers is limited to a maximum of 10 ft (3.0 m).
(7) The symbols X and △ represent in-rack sprinklers that are to be staggered both horizontally and vertically.
(8) Each square represents a storage cube measuring 4 ft to 5 ft (1.2 m to 1.5 m) on a side. Actual load heights can vary from approximately 18 in. to 10 ft (450 mm to 3.0 m). Therefore, there could be as few as two loads or as many as 10 loads between in-rack sprinklers that are spaced 15 ft (4.6 m) apart vertically.

N FIGURE 25.3.3.2.1.2(g)   In-Rack Sprinkler Arrangements for Encapsulated Exposed, or Cartoned (Nonencapsulated or Encapsulated) Class I, Class II, or Class III Commodities Stored Over 25 ft (7.6 m) in Height in Multiple-Row Racks.

Ceiling Design: Exposed Encapsulated or Cartoned Class I, Class II, Class III, or Class IV Commodities

0.44 gpm/ft² over 2000 ft² (17.9 mm/min over 185 m²)
with ordinary-temperature ceiling sprinklers
0.56 gpm/ft² over 2000 ft² (22.8 mm/min over 185 m²)
with high-temperature ceiling sprinklers

Elevation View   Plan View   Plan View   Elevation View

Notes:
(1) In-rack sprinklers are ordinary-temperature-rated, quick- or standard-response, pendent or upright, minimum K-5.6 (K-80), and designed for a minimum of 10 in-rack sprinklers (five in-rack sprinklers on the top two levels) operating at 30 gpm (114 L/min).
(2) Sprinkler 1 and Sprinkler 2 or Sprinkler 1 and Sprinkler 3 are required where Load A represents the top of storage.
(3) Sprinkler 1 and Sprinkler 3 or Sprinkler 1 and Sprinkler 4 are required where Load B represents the top of storage.
(4) For storage higher than represented by Load B, the cycle defined by Note 2 and Note 3 above is repeated.
(5) The storage height above the top level of in-rack sprinklers is limited to a maximum of 10 ft (3.0 m).
(6) In-rack sprinklers in the transverse flue space are permitted to be at any point between load faces.
(7) The symbol X represents in-rack sprinklers.
(8) Each square represents a storage cube measuring 4 ft to 5 ft (1.2 m to 1.5 m) on a side. Actual load heights can vary from approximately 18 in. to 10 ft (450 mm to 3.0 m). Therefore, there could be as few as one load or as many as 10 loads between in-rack sprinklers that are spaced 15 ft (4.6 m) apart vertically.

N **FIGURE 25.3.3.2.1.3(a)   In-Rack Sprinkler Arrangements for Encapsulated Exposed, or Cartoned (Nonencapsulated or Encapsulated) Class I, Class II, Class III, or Class IV Commodities Stored Over 25 ft (7.6 m) in Height in Single-Row Racks — Option 1.**

Ceiling Design: Exposed Encapsulated or Cartoned Class I, Class II, Class III, or Class IV Commodities

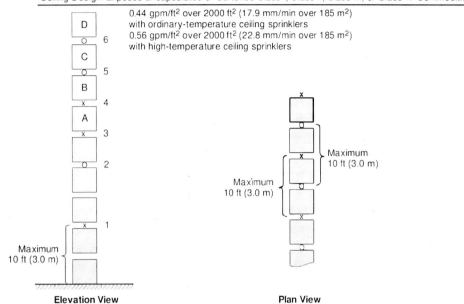

0.44 gpm/ft² over 2000 ft² (17.9 mm/min over 185 m²)
with ordinary-temperature ceiling sprinklers
0.56 gpm/ft² over 2000 ft² (22.8 mm/min over 185 m²)
with high-temperature ceiling sprinklers

Elevation View   **Plan View**

Notes:
(1) In-rack sprinklers are ordinary-temperature-rated, quick- or standard-response, pendent or upright, minimum K-5.6 (K-80), and designed for a minimum of 10 in-rack sprinklers (five in-rack sprinklers on the top two levels) operating at 30 gpm (114 L/min).
(2) Sprinkler 1 and Sprinkler 2 or Sprinkler 1, Sprinkler 2, and Sprinkler 3 are required when Load A represents the top of storage.
(3) Sprinkler 1, Sprinkler 2, and Sprinkler 3 or Sprinkler 1, Sprinkler 2, and Sprinkler 4 are required when Load B represents the top of storage.
(4) Sprinkler 1, Sprinkler 2, and Sprinkler 4 or Sprinkler 1, Sprinkler 2, Sprinkler 4, and Sprinkler 5 are required where Load C represents the top of storage.
(5) Sprinkler 1, Sprinkler 2, Sprinkler 4, and Sprinkler 5 or Sprinkler 1, Sprinkler 2, Sprinkler 4, and Sprinkler 6 are required where Load D represents the top of storage.
(6) For storage higher than represented by Load D, the cycle defined by Note 2 through Note 5 above is repeated.
(7) The storage height above the top level of in-rack sprinklers is limited to a maximum of 10 ft (3.0 m).
(8) In-rack sprinklers in the transverse flue space are permitted to be at any point between load faces.
(9) The symbols X and O represent in-rack sprinklers that are to be staggered vertically.
(10) Each square represents a storage cube measuring 4 ft to 5 ft (1.2 m to 1.5 m) on a side. Actual load heights can vary from approximately 18 in. to 10 ft (450 mm to 3.0 m). Therefore, there could be as few as one load or as many as six loads between in-rack sprinklers that are spaced 10 ft (3.0 m) apart vertically.

N **FIGURE 25.3.3.2.1.3(b)   In-Rack Sprinkler Arrangements for Encapsulated Exposed, or Cartoned (Nonencapsulated or Encapsulated) Class I, Class II, Class III, or Class IV Commodities Stored Over 25 ft (7.6 m) in Height in Single-Row Racks — Option 2.**

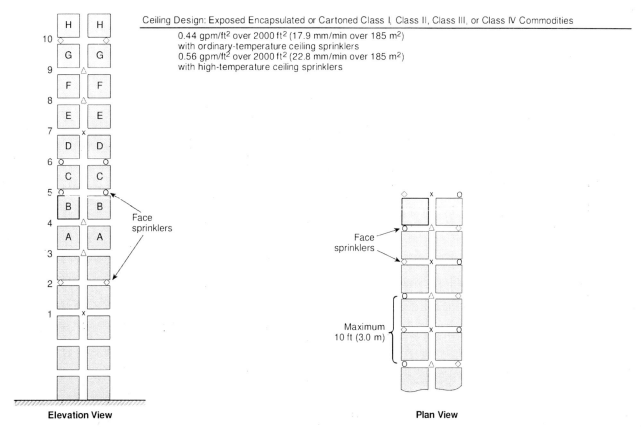

Ceiling Design: Exposed Encapsulated or Cartoned Class I, Class II, Class III, or Class IV Commodities

0.44 gpm/ft² over 2000 ft² (17.9 mm/min over 185 m²)
with ordinary-temperature ceiling sprinklers
0.56 gpm/ft² over 2000 ft² (22.8 mm/min over 185 m²)
with high-temperature ceiling sprinklers

Elevation View   **Plan View**

Notes:

(1) In-rack sprinklers are ordinary-temperature-rated, quick- or standard-response, pendent or upright, minimum K-5.6 (K-80), and designed for a minimum of 10 in-rack sprinklers (five in-rack sprinklers on the top two levels) operating at 30 gpm (114 L/min).

(2) Face sprinklers are to be a minimum of 3 in. (75 mm) from rack uprights and a maximum of 18 in. (450 mm) from the aisle face of storage.

(3) Sprinkler 1 and Sprinker 2 or Sprinkler 1, Sprinkler 2, and Sprinkler 3 are required where Load A represents the top of storage.

(4) Sprinkler 1, Sprinkler 2, and Sprinkler 3 or Sprinkler 1, Sprinkler 2, and Sprinkler 4 are required where Load B represents the top of storage.

(5) Sprinkler 1, Sprinkler 2, and Sprinkler 4 or Sprinkler 1, Sprinkler 2, Sprinkler 4, and Sprinkler 5 are required where Load C represents the top of storage.

(6) Sprinkler 1, Sprinkler 2, Sprinkler 4, and Sprinkler 5 or Sprinkler 1, Sprinkler 2, Sprinkler 4, and Sprinkler 6 are required where Load D represents the top of storage.

(7) Sprinkler 1, Sprinkler 2, Sprinkler 4, and Sprinkler 6 or Sprinkler 1, Sprinkler 2, Sprinkler 4, Sprinkler 6, and Sprinkler 7 are required where Load E represents the top of storage.

(8) Sprinkler 1, Sprinkler 2, Sprinkler 4, Sprinkler 6, and Sprinkler 7 or Sprinkler 1, Sprinkler 2, Sprinkler 4, Sprinkler 6, Sprinkler 7, and Sprinkler 8 are required where Load F represents the top of storage.

(9) Sprinkler 1, Sprinkler 2, Sprinkler 4, Sprinkler 6, Sprinkler 7, and Sprinkler 8 or Sprinkler 1, Sprinkler 2, Sprinkler 4, Sprinkler 6, Sprinkler 7, and Sprinkler 9 are required where Load G represents the top of storage.

(10) Sprinkler 1, Sprinkler 2, Sprinkler 4, Sprinkler 6, Sprinkler 7, and Sprinkler 9 or Sprinkler 1, Sprinkler 2, Sprinkler 4, Sprinkler 6, Sprinkler 7, Sprinkler 9, and Sprinkler 10 are required where Load H represents the top of storage.

(11) For storage higher than represented by Load H, the cycle defined by Note 3 through Note 10 above is repeated, with stagger as indicated.

(12) The storage height above the top level of in-rack sprinklers is limited to a maximum of 10 ft (3.0 m).

(13) The symbols X, O, ◇, and △ represent in-rack sprinklers that are to be staggered both horizontally and vertically.

(14) Each square represents a storage cube measuring 4 ft to 5 ft (1.2 m to 1.5 m) on a side. Actual load heights can vary from approximately 18 in. to 10 ft (450 mm to 3.0 m). Therefore, there could be as few as one load or as many as 10 loads between in-rack sprinklers that are spaced 15 ft (4.6 m) apart vertically.

N **FIGURE 25.3.3.2.1.3(c)   In-Rack Sprinkler Arrangements for Encapsulated Exposed, or Cartoned (Nonencapsulated or Encapsulated) Class I, Class II, Class III, or Class IV Commodities Stored Over 25 ft (7.6 m) in Height in Double-Row Racks — Option 1.**

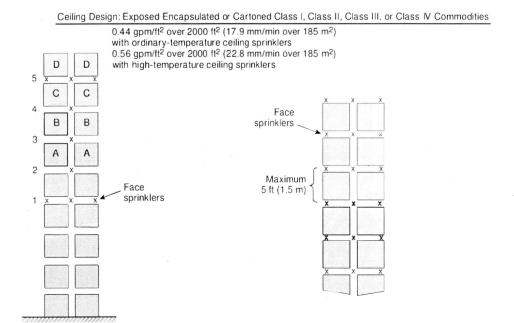

Ceiling Design: Exposed Encapsulated or Cartoned Class I, Class II, Class III, or Class IV Commodities

0.44 gpm/ft² over 2000 ft² (17.9 mm/min over 185 m²)
with ordinary-temperature ceiling sprinklers
0.56 gpm/ft² over 2000 ft² (22.8 mm/min over 185 m²)
with high-temperature ceiling sprinklers

Elevation View   **Plan View**

Notes:
(1) In-rack sprinklers are ordinary-temperature-rated, quick- or standard-response, pendent or upright, minimum K-5.6 (K-80), and designed for a minimum of six in-rack sprinklers operating at 30 gpm (114 L/min) when only one level of in-rack sprinklers is installed or a minimum of 10 in-rack sprinklers (five in-rack sprinklers on the top two levels) operating at 30 gpm (114 L/min) when more than one level of in-rack sprinklers are installed.
(2) Face sprinklers are to be a minimum of 3 in. (75 mm) from rack uprights and a maximum of 18 in. (450 mm) from the aisle face to storage.
(3) Sprinkler 1 or Sprinkler 1 and Sprinkler 2 are required where Load A represents the top of storage.
(4) Sprinkler 1 and Sprinkler 2 or Sprinkler 1 and Sprinkler 3 are required where Load B represents the top of storage.
(5) Sprinkler 1 and Sprinkler 3 or Sprinkler 1 and Sprinkler 4 are required where Load C represents the top of storage.
(6) Sprinkler 1 and Sprinkler 4 or Sprinkler 1 and Sprinkler 5 are required where Load D represents the top of storage.
(7) For storage higher than represented by Load D, the cycle defined by Note 3 through Note 6 above is repeated.
(8) The storage height above the top level of in-rack sprinklers is limited to a maximum of 10 ft (3.0 m).
(9) The symbol X represents in-rack sprinklers.
(10) Each square represents a storage cube measuring 4 ft to 5 ft (1.2 m to 1.5 m) on a side. Actual load heights can vary from approximately 18 in. to 10 ft (450 mm to 3.0 m). Therefore, there could be as few as two loads or as many as 13 loads between in-rack sprinklers that are spaced 20 ft (6.1 m) apart vertically.

N **FIGURE 25.3.3.2.1.3(d)   In-Rack Sprinkler Arrangements for Encapsulated Exposed, or Cartoned (Nonencapsulated or Encapsulated) Class I, Class II, Class III, or Class IV Commodities Stored Over 25 ft (7.6 m) in Height in Double-Row Racks — Option 2.**

Ceiling Design: Exposed Encapsulated or Cartoned Class I, Class II, Class III, or Class IV Commodities

0.44 gpm/ft^2 over 2000 ft^2 (17.9 mm/min over 185 m^2)
with ordinary-temperature ceiling sprinklers
0.56 gpm/ft^2 over 2000 ft^2 (22.8 mm/min over 185 m^2)
with high-temperature ceiling sprinklers

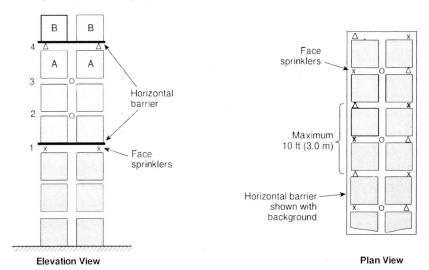

Elevation View   **Plan View**

Notes:
(1) In-rack sprinklers are ordinary-temperature-rated, quick- or standard-response, pendent or upright, minimum K-5.6 (K-80), and designed for a minimum of 10 in-rack sprinklers (five in-rack sprinklers on the top two levels) operating at 30 gpm (114 L/min).
(2) Face sprinklers are to be a minimum of 3 in. (75 mm) from rack uprights and a maximum of 18 in. (450 mm) from the aisle face of storage.
(3) Sprinkler 1 and Sprinkler 2 or Sprinkler 1 and Sprinkler 3 are required where Load A represents the top of storage.
(4) Sprinkler 1 and Sprinkler 3 or Sprinkler 1 and Sprinkler 4 are required where Load B represents the top of storage.
(5) For storage higher than represented by Load B, the cycle defined by Note 3 and Note 4 above is repeated.
(6) The storage height above the top level of in-rack sprinklers is limited to a maximum of 10 ft (3.0 m).
(7) The symbols X, O, and Δ represent in-rack sprinklers that are to be staggered both horizontally and vertically.
(8) Each square represents a storage cube measuring 4 ft to 5 ft (1.2 m to 1.5 m) on a side. Actual load heights can vary from approximately 18 in. to 10 ft (450 mm to 3.0 m). Therefore, there could be as few as two loads or as many as 13 loads between in-rack sprinklers that are spaced 20 ft (6.1 m) apart vertically.

N **FIGURE 25.3.3.2.1.3(e)   In-Rack Sprinkler Arrangements for Encapsulated Exposed, or Cartoned (Nonencapsulated or Encapsulated) Class I, Class II, Class III, or Class IV Commodities Stored Over 25 ft (7.6 m) in Height in Double-Row Racks — Option 3.**

Ceiling Design: Exposed Encapsulated or Cartoned Class I, Class II, Class III, or Class IV Commodities
0.44 gpm/ft² over 2000 ft² (117.9 mm/min over 185 m²)
with ordinary-temperature ceiling sprinklers
0.56 gpm/ft² over 2000 ft² (22.8 mm/min over 185 m²)
with high-temperature ceiling sprinklers

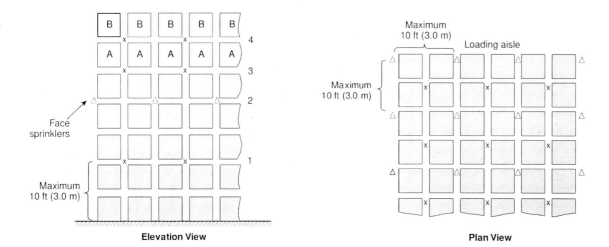

Elevation View   **Plan View**

Notes:
(1) In-rack sprinklers are ordinary-temperature-rated, quick- or standard-response, pendent or upright, minimum K-5.6 (K-80), and designed for a minimum of 10 in-rack sprinklers (five in-rack sprinklers on the top two levels) operating at 30 gpm (114 L/min).
(2) Face sprinklers are to be a minimum of 3 in. (75 mm) from rack uprights and a maximum of 18 in. (450 mm) from the aisle face of storage.
(3) Sprinkler 1, Sprinkler 2, and Sprinkler 3 are required where Load A represents the top of storage.
(4) Sprinkler 1, Sprinkler 2, and Sprinkler 4 are required where Load B represents the top of storage.
(5) For storage higher than represented by Load B, the cycle defined by Note 3 and Note 4 above is repeated, with stagger as indicated.
(6) The storage height above the top level of in-rack sprinklers is limited to a maximum of 5 ft (1.5 m).
(7) The symbols X and △ represent in-rack sprinklers that are to be staggered both horizontally and vertically.
(8) Each square represents a storage cube measuring 4 ft to 5 ft (1.2 m to 1.5 m) on a side. Actual load heights can vary from approximately 18 in. to 10 ft (450 mm to 3.0 m). Therefore, there could be as few as one load or as many as six loads between in-rack sprinklers that are spaced 10 ft (3.1 m) apart vertically.

N   FIGURE 25.3.3.2.1.3(f)   In-Rack Sprinkler Arrangements for Encapsulated Exposed, or Cartoned (Nonencapsulated or Encapsulated) Class I, Class II, Class III, or Class IV Commodities Stored Over 25 ft (7.6 m) in Height in Multiple-Row Racks.

Ceiling Design: Cartoned Group A Plastic Commodities

0.30 gpm/ft² over 2000 ft² (12.2 mm/min over 185 m²)
where maximum storage height over top of in-rack sprinklers is 5 ft (1.5 m)
0.45 gpm/ft² over 2000 ft² (18.3 mm/min over 185 m²)
where maximum storage height over top of in-rack sprinklers is over 5 ft (1.5 m) and up to 10 ft (3.0 m)

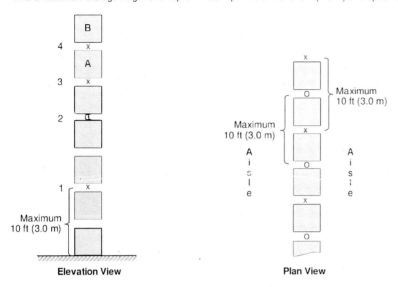

Elevation View   **Plan View**

Notes:
(1) In-rack sprinklers are ordinary-temperature-rated, quick- or standard-response, pendent or upright, minimum K-5.6 (K-80), and designed for a minimum of 14 in-rack sprinklers (seven in-rack sprinklers on the top two levels) operating at 30 gpm (114 L/min).
(2) Sprinkler 1 and Sprinkler 2 or Sprinkler 1, Sprinkler 2, and Sprinkler 3 are required when Load A represents the top of storage.
(3) Sprinkler 1, Sprinkler 2, and Sprinkler 3 or Sprinkler 1, Sprinkler 2, and Sprinkler 4 are required when Load B represents the top of storage.
(4) For storage higher than represented by Load B, the cycle defined by Note 2 and Note 3 above is repeated.
(5) The storage height above the top level of in-rack sprinklers is limited to a maximum of 10 ft (3.0 m).
(6) The symbols X and O represent in-rack sprinklers that are to be staggered vertically.
(7) Each square represents a storage cube measuring 4 ft to 5 ft (1.2 m to 1.5 m) on a side. Actual load heights can vary from approximately 18 in. to 10 ft (450 mm to 3.0 m). Therefore, there could be as few as one load or as many as six loads between in-rack sprinklers that are spaced 10 ft (3.0 m) apart vertically.

N **FIGURE 25.3.3.3.1.1(a) In-Rack Sprinkler Arrangements for Cartoned Group A Plastic Commodities Stored Over 25 ft (7.6 m) in Height — Option 1.**

Shaded text = Revisions.   Δ = Text deletions and figure/table revisions.   • = Section deletions.   *N* = New material.

2022 Edition

Ceiling Design: Cartoned Group A Plastic Commodities

0.30 gpm/ft² over 2000 ft² (12.2 mm/min over 185 m²)
where maximum storage height over top of in-rack sprinklers is 5 ft (1.5 m)
0.45 gpm/ft² over 2000 ft² (18.3 mm/min over 185 m²)
where maximum storage height over top of in-rack sprinklers is over 5 ft (1.5 m)
and up to 10 ft (3.0 m)

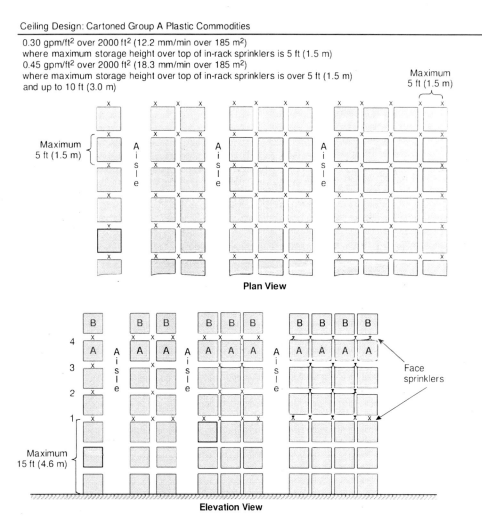

N FIGURE 25.3.3.3.1.1(b)   In-Rack Sprinkler Arrangements for Cartoned Group A Plastic
Commodities Stored Over 25 ft (7.6 m) in Height — Option 2.

Notes:
(1) In-rack sprinklers are ordinary-temperature-rated, quick- or standard-response, pendent or upright, minimum K-5.6
    (K-80), and designed for a minimum of 14 in-rack sprinklers (seven in-rack sprinklers on the top two levels)
    operating at 30 gpm (114 L/min).
(2) Face sprinklers are to be a minimum of 3 in. (75 mm) from rack uprights and a maximum of 18 in. (450 mm) from
    the aisle face of storage.
(3) Sprinkler 1 and Sprinkler 2 or Sprinkler 1 and Sprinkler 3 are required where Load A represents the top of storage.
(4) Sprinkler 1 and Sprinkler 2 or Sprinkler 1 and Sprinkler 4 are required where Load B represents the top of storage.
(5) For storage higher than represented by Load B, the cycle defined by Note 3 and Note 4 above is repeated.
(6) The storage height above the top level of in-rack sprinklers is limited to a maximum of 10 ft (3.0 m).
(7) The symbol X represents in-rack sprinklers.
(8) Each square represents a storage cube measuring 4 ft to 5 ft (1.2 m to 1.5 m) on a side. Actual load heights can
    vary from approximately 18 in. to 10 ft (450 mm to 3.0 m). Therefore, there could be as few as one load or as
    many as 10 loads between in-rack sprinklers that are spaced 15 ft (4.6 m) apart vertically.

Ceiling Design: Cartoned Group A Plastic Commodities

0.30 gpm/ft² over 2000 ft² (12.2 mm/min over 185 m²)
where maximum storage height over top of in-rack sprinklers is 5 ft (1.5 m)
0.45 gpm/ft² over 2000 ft² (18.3 mm/min over 185 m²)
where maximum storage height over top of in-rack sprinklers is over 5 ft (1.5 m)
and up to 10 ft (3.0 m)

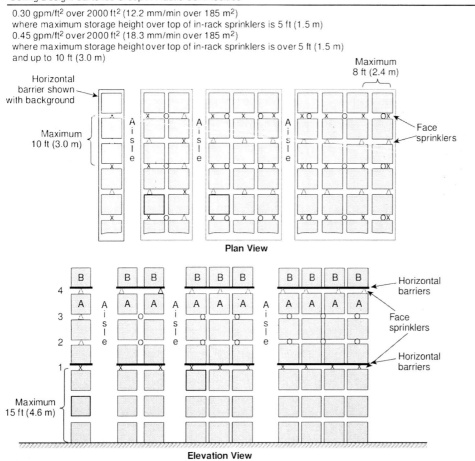

Notes:
(1) In-rack sprinklers are ordinary-temperature-rated, quick- or standard-response, pendent or upright, minimum K-5.6 (K-80), and designed for a minimum of 14 in-rack sprinklers (seven in-rack sprinklers on the top two levels) operating at 30 gpm (114 L/min).
(2) Face sprinklers are to be a minimum of 3 in. (75 mm) from rack uprights and a maximum of 18 in. (450 mm) from the aisle face of storage.
(3) Sprinkler 1 and Sprinkler 2 or Sprinkler 1 and Sprinkler 3 are required where Load A represents the top of storage.
(4) Sprinkler 1 and Sprinkler 3 or Sprinkler 1 and Sprinkler 4 are required where Load B represents the top of storage.
(5) For storage higher than represented by Load B, the cycle defined by Note 3 and Note 4 above is repeated, with stagger as indicated.
(6) The storage height above the top level of in-rack sprinklers is limited to a maximum of 10 ft (3.0 m).
(7) The symbols X, O, and △ represent in-rack sprinklers that are to be staggered both horizontally and vertically.
(8) Each square represents a storage cube measuring 4 ft to 5 ft (1.2 m to 1.5 m) on a side. Actual load heights can vary from approximately 18 in. to 10 ft (450 mm to 3.0 m). Therefore, there could be as few as two loads or as many as 13 loads between in-rack sprinklers that are spaced 20 ft (6.1 m) apart vertically.

N FIGURE 25.3.3.3.1.1(c)   In-Rack Sprinkler Arrangements for Cartoned Group A Plastic Commodities Stored Over 25 ft (7.6 m) in Height — Option 3.

Shaded text = Revisions.   **Δ** = Text deletions and figure/table revisions.   • = Section deletions.   *N* = New material.

2022 Edition

Ceiling Design: Cartoned Group A Plastic Commodities

0.30 gpm/ft² over 2000 ft² (12.2 mm/min over 185 m²)
where maximum storage height over top of in-rack sprinklers is 5 ft (1.5 m)
0.45 gpm/ft² over 2000 ft² (18.3 mm/min over 185 m²)
where maximum storage height over top of in-rack sprinklers is over 5 ft (1.5 m)
and up to 10 ft (3.0 m)

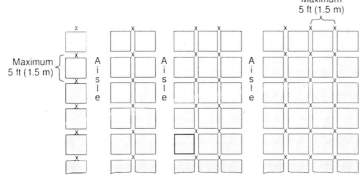

Plan View

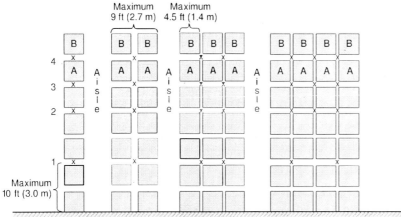

Elevation View

Notes:
(1) In-rack sprinklers are ordinary-temperature-rated, quick- or standard-response, pendent or upright, minimum K-5.6 (K-80), and designed for a minimum of 14 in-rack sprinklers (seven in-rack sprinklers on the top two levels) operating at 30 gpm (114 L/min).
(2) Sprinkler 1 and Sprinkler 2 or Sprinkler 1, Sprinkler 2, and Sprinkler 3 are required where Load A represents the top of storage.
(3) Sprinkler 1, Sprinkler 2, and Sprinkler 3 or Sprinkler 1, Sprinkler 2, and Sprinkler 4 are required where Load B represents the top of storage.
(4) For storage higher than represented by Load B, the cycle defined by Note 2 and Note 3 above is repeated.
(5) The storage height above the top level of in-rack sprinklers is limited to a maximum of 10 ft (3.0 m).
(6) In-rack sprinklers in the transverse flue space are permitted to be at any point between load faces.
(7) The symbol X represents in-rack sprinklers.
(8) Each square represents a storage cube measuring 4 ft to 5 ft (1.2 m to 1.5 m) on a side. Actual load heights can vary from approximately 18 in. to 10 ft (450 mm to 3.0 m). Therefore, there could be as few as one load or as many as six loads between in-rack sprinklers that are spaced 10 ft (3.0 m) apart vertically.

N   **FIGURE 25.3.3.3.1.1(d)**   **In-Rack Sprinkler Arrangements for Cartoned Group A Plastic Commodities Stored Over 25 ft (7.6 m) in Height — Option 4.**

Ceiling Design: Cartoned Group A Plastic Commodities

0.30 gpm/ft^2 over 2000 ft^2 (12.2 mm/min over 185 m^2)
where maximum storage height over top of in-rack sprinklers is 5 ft (1.5 m)
0.45 gpm/ft^2 over 2000 ft^2 (18.3 mm/min over 185 m^2)
where maximum storage height over top of in-rack sprinklers is over 5 ft (1.5 m)
and up to 10 ft (3.0 m)

Plan View

Elevation View

Notes:
(1) In-rack sprinklers are ordinary-temperature-rated, quick- or standard-response, pendent or upright, minimum K-5.6 (K-80), and designed for a minimum of 14 in-rack sprinklers (seven in-rack sprinklers on the top two levels) operating at 30 gpm (114 L/min).
(2) Face sprinklers are to be a minimum of 3 in. (75 mm) from rack uprights and a maximum of 18 in. (450 mm) from the aisle face of storage.
(3) Sprinkler 1 and Sprinkler 2 or Sprinkler 1, Sprinkler 2, and Sprinkler 3 are required where Load A represents the top of storage.
(4) Sprinkler 1, Sprinkler 2, and Sprinkler 3 or Sprinkler 1, Sprinkler 2, and Sprinkler 4 are required where Load B represents the top of storage.
(5) For storage higher than represented by Load B, the cycle defined by Note 3 and Note 4 above is repeated.
(6) The storage height above the top level of in-rack sprinklers is limited to a maximum of 10 ft (3.0 m).
(7) The symbol X represents in-rack sprinklers.
(8) Each square represents a storage cube measuring 4 ft to 5 ft (1.2 m to 1.5 m) on a side. Actual load heights can vary from approximately 18 in. to 10 ft (450 mm to 3.0 m). Therefore, there could be as few as one load or as many as six loads between in-rack sprinklers that are spaced 10 ft (3.0 m) apart vertically.

N **FIGURE 25.3.3.3.1.1(e)   In-Rack Sprinkler Arrangements for Cartoned Group A Plastic Commodities Stored Over 25 ft (7.6 m) in Height — Option 5.**

Ceiling Design: Cartoned Group A Plastic Commodities

0.30 gpm/ft^2 over 2000 ft^2 (12.2 mm/min over 185 m^2)
where maximum storage height over top of in-rack sprinklers is 5 ft (1.5 m)
0.45 gpm/ft^2 over 2000 ft^2 (18.3 mm/min over 185 m^2)
where maximum storage height over top of in-rack sprinklers is over 5 ft (1.5 m)
and up to 10 ft (3.0 m)

Plan View

Elevation View

Notes:
(1) In-rack sprinklers are ordinary-temperature-rated, quick- or standard-response, pendent or upright, minimum K-5.6 (K-80), and designed for a minimum of 14 in-rack sprinklers (seven in-rack sprinklers on the top two levels) operating at 30 gpm (114 L/min).
(2) Face sprinklers are to be a minimum of 3 in. (75 mm) from rack uprights and a maximum of 18 in. (450 mm) from the aisle face of storage.
(3) Sprinkler 1 and Sprinkler 2 or Sprinkler 1, Sprinkler 2, and Sprinkler 3 are required where Load A represents the top of storage.
(4) Sprinkler 1, Sprinkler 2, and Sprinkler 3 or Sprinkler 1, Sprinkler 2, and Sprinkler 4 are required where Load B represents the top of storage.
(5) For storage higher than represented by Load B, the cycle defined by Note 3 and Note 4 above is repeated.
(6) The storage height above the top level of in-rack sprinklers is limited to a maximum of 10 ft (3.0 m).
(7) The symbol X represents in-rack sprinklers.
(8) Each square represents a storage cube measuring 4 ft to 5 ft (1.2 m to 1.5 m) on a side. Actual load heights can vary from approximately 18 in. to 10 ft (450 mm to 3.0 m). Therefore, there could be as few as one load or as many as six loads between in-rack sprinklers that are spaced 10 ft (3.0 m) apart vertically.

N **FIGURE 25.3.3.3.1.1(f)   In-Rack Sprinkler Arrangements for Cartoned Group A Plastic Commodities Stored Over 25 ft (7.6 m) in Height — Option 6.**

Ceiling Design: Cartoned Group A Plastic Commodities

0.30 gpm/ft^2 over 2000 ft^2 (12.2 mm/min over 185 m^2)
where maximum storage height over top of in-rack sprinklers is 5 ft (1.5 m)
0.45 gpm/ft^2 over 2000 ft^2 (18.3 mm/min over 185 m^2)
where maximum storage height over top of in-rack sprinklers is over 5 ft (1.5 m)
and up to 10 ft (3.0 m)

Plan View

Elevation View

Notes:
(1) In-rack sprinklers are ordinary-temperature-rated, quick- or standard-response, pendent or upright, minimum K-5.6 (K-80), and designed for a minimum of 14 in-rack sprinklers (seven in-rack sprinklers on the top two levels) operating at 30 gpm (114 L/min).
(2) Face sprinklers are to be a minimum of 3 in. (75 mm) from rack uprights and a maximum of 18 in. (450 mm) from the aisle face of storage.
(3) Sprinkler 1, Sprinkler 2, Sprinkler 3, and Sprinkler 4 or Sprinkler 1, Sprinkler 2, Sprinkler 3, Sprinkler 4, and Sprinkler 5 are required where Load A represents the top of storage.
(4) Sprinkler 1, Sprinkler 2, Sprinkler 3, Sprinkler 4, and Sprinkler 5 or Sprinkler 1, Sprinkler 2, Sprinkler 3, Sprinkler 4, and Sprinkler 6 are required where Load B represents the top of storage.
(5) For storage higher than represented by Load B, the cycle defined by Note 3 and Note 4 above is repeated.
(6) The storage height above the top level of in-rack sprinklers is limited to a maximum of 10 ft (3.0 m).
(7) The symbols X and △ represent in-rack sprinklers that are to be staggered both horizontally and vertically.
(8) Each square represents a storage cube measuring 4 ft to 5 ft (1.2 m to 1.5 m) on a side. Actual load heights can vary from approximately 18 in. to 10 ft (450 mm to 3.0 m). Therefore, there could be as few as one load or as many as six loads between in-rack sprinklers that are spaced 10 ft (3.0 m) apart vertically.

N **FIGURE 25.3.3.3.1.1(g)   In-Rack Sprinkler Arrangements for Cartoned Group A Plastic Commodities Stored Over 25 ft (7.6 m) in Height — Option 7.**

Shaded text = Revisions.   Δ = Text deletions and figure/table revisions.   • = Section deletions.   *N* = New material.

2022 Edition

Ceiling Design: Exposed, Nonexpanded Group A Plastic Commodities

0.45 gpm/ft² over 2000 ft² (18.3 mm/min over 185 m²)
where maximum storage height over top of in-rack sprinklers is up to 10 ft (3.0 m)

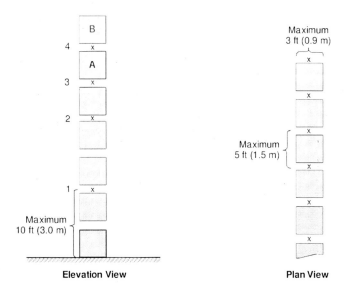

Elevation View   **Plan View**

Notes:
(1) In-rack sprinklers are ordinary-temperature-rated, quick- or standard-response, pendent or upright, minimum K-5.6 (K-80), and designed for a minimum of 14 in-rack sprinklers (seven in-rack sprinklers on the top two levels) operating at 30 gpm (114 L/min).
(2) Sprinkler 1 and Sprinkler 2 or Sprinkler 1, Sprinkler 2, and Sprinkler 3 are required when Load A represents the top of storage.
(3) Sprinkler 1, Sprinkler 2, and Sprinkler 3 or Sprinkler 1, Sprinkler 2, and Sprinkler 4 are required where Load B represents the top of storage.
(4) For storage higher than represented by Load B, the cycle defined by Note 2 and Note 3 above is repeated.
(5) The storage height above the top level of in-rack sprinklers is limited to a maximum of 10 ft (3.0 m).
(6) The symbol X represents in-rack sprinklers.
(7) Each square represents a storage cube measuring 4 ft to 5 ft (1.2 m to 1.5 m) on a side. Actual load heights can vary from approximately 18 in. to 10 ft (450 mm to 3.0 m). Therefore, there could be as few as one load or as many as six loads between in-rack sprinklers that are spaced 10 ft (3.0 m) apart vertically.

N **FIGURE 25.3.3.4.1.1(a)   In-Rack Sprinkler Arrangements for Exposed Nonexpanded Group A Plastic Commodities Stored Over 25 ft (7.6 m) in Height — Option 1.**

Ceiling Design: Exposed Nonexpanded Group A Plastic Commodities

0.30 gpm/ft² over 2000 ft² (12.2 mm/min over 185 m²)
where maximum storage height over top of in-rack sprinklers is 5 ft (1.5 m)
0.45 gpm/ft² over 2000 ft² (18.3 mm/min over 185 m²)
where maximum storage height over top of in-rack sprinklers is over 5 ft (1.5 m)
and up to 10 ft (3.0 m)

Plan View

Elevation View

Notes:
(1) In-rack sprinklers are ordinary-temperature-rated, quick- or standard-response, pendent or upright, minimum K-5.6 (K-80), and designed for a minimum of 14 in-rack sprinklers (seven in-rack sprinklers on the top two levels) operating at 30 gpm (114 L/min).
(2) Face sprinklers are to be a minimum of 3 in. (75 mm) from rack uprights and a maximum of 18 in. (450 mm) from the aisle face of storage.
(3) Sprinkler 1 and Sprinkler 2 or Sprinkler 1, Sprinkler 2, and Sprinkler 3 are required where Load A represents the top of storage.
(4) Sprinkler 1, Sprinkler 2, and Sprinkler 3 or Sprinkler 1, Sprinkler 2, and Sprinkler 4 are required where Load B represents the top of storage.
(5) For storage higher than represented by Load B, the cycle defined by Note 3 and Note 4 above is repeated.
(6) The storage height above the top level of in-rack sprinklers is limited to a maximum of 10 ft (3.0 m).
(7) The symbol X represents in-rack sprinklers.
(8) Each square represents a storage cube measuring 4 ft to 5 ft (1.2 m to 1.5 m) on a side. Actual load heights can vary from approximately 18 in. to 10 ft (450 mm to 3.0 m). Therefore, there could be as few as one load or as many as six loads between in-rack sprinklers that are spaced 10 ft (3.0 m) apart vertically.

N **FIGURE 25.3.3.4.1.1(b)   In-Rack Sprinkler Arrangements for Exposed Nonexpanded Group A Plastic Commodities Stored Over 25 ft (7.6 m) in Height — Option 2.**

Ceiling Design: Exposed Nonexpanded Group A Plastic Commodities

0.30 gpm/ft² over 2000 ft² (12.2 mm/min over 185 m²)
where maximum storage height over top of in-rack sprinklers is 5 ft (1.5 m)
0.45 gpm/ft² over 2000 ft² (18.3 mm/min over 185 m²)
where maximum storage height over top of in-rack sprinklers is over 5 ft (1.5 m)
and up to 10 ft (3.0 m)

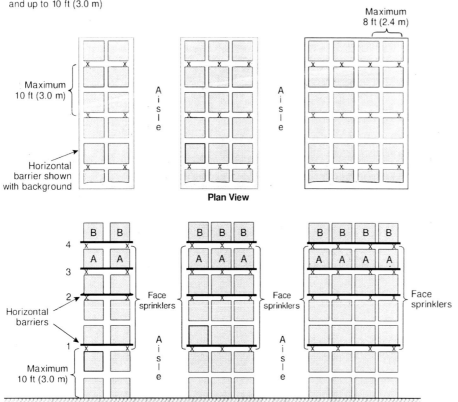

Plan View

Elevation View

Notes:
(1) In-rack sprinklers are ordinary-temperature-rated, quick- or standard-response, pendent or upright, minimum K-5.6 (K-80), and designed for a minimum of 14 in-rack sprinklers (seven in-rack sprinklers on the top two levels) operating at 30 gpm (114 L/min).
(2) Face sprinklers are to be a minimum of 3 in. (75 mm) from rack uprights and a maximum of 18 in. (450 mm) from the aisle face of storage.
(3) Sprinkler 1 and Sprinkler 2 or Sprinkler 1, Sprinkler 2, and Sprinkler 3 are required where Load A represents the top of storage.
(4) Sprinkler 1, Sprinkler 2, and Sprinkler 3 or Sprinkler 1, Sprinkler 2, and Sprinkler 4 are required where Load B represents the top of storage.
(5) For storage higher than represented by Load B, the cycle defined by Note 3 and Note 4 above is repeated.
(6) The storage height above the top level of in-rack sprinklers is limited to a maximum of 10 ft (3.0 m).
(7) The symbol X represents in-rack sprinklers.
(8) Each square represents a storage cube measuring 4 ft to 5 ft (1.2 m to 1.5 m) on a side. Actual load heights can vary from approximately 18 in. to 10 ft (450 mm to 3.0 m). Therefore, there could be as few as one load or as many as six loads between in-rack sprinklers that are spaced 10 ft (3.0 m) apart vertically.

N **FIGURE 25.3.3.4.1.1(c)   In-Rack Sprinkler Arrangements for Exposed Nonexpanded Group A Plastic Commodities Stored Over 25 ft (7.6 m) in Height — Option 3.**

Ceiling Design: Exposed Nonexpanded Group A Plastic Commodities

0.30 gpm/ft^2 over 2000 ft^2 (12.2 mm/min over 185 m^2)
where maximum storage height over top of in-rack sprinklers is 5 ft (1.5 m)
0.45 gpm/ft^2 over 2000 ft^2 (18.3 mm/min over 185 m^2)
where maximum storage height over top of in-rack sprinklers is over 5 ft (1.5 m)
and up to 10 ft (3.0 m)

Plan View

Elevation View

Notes:
(1) In-rack sprinklers are ordinary-temperature-rated, quick- or standard-response, pendent or upright, minimum K-5.6 (K-80), and designed for a minimum of 14 in-rack sprinklers (seven in-rack sprinklers on the top two levels) operating at 30 gpm (114 L/min).
(2) Face sprinklers are to be a minimum of 3 in. (75 mm) from rack uprights and a maximum of 18 in. (450 mm) from the aisle face of storage.
(3) Sprinkler 1, Sprinkler 2, Sprinkler 3, and Sprinkler 4 or Sprinkler 1, Sprinkler 2, Sprinkler 3, Sprinkler 4, and Sprinkler 5 are required where Load A represents the top of storage.
(4) Sprinkler 1, Sprinkler 2, Sprinkler 3, Sprinkler 4, and Sprinkler 5 or Sprinkler 1, Sprinkler 2, Sprinkler 3, Sprinkler 4, and Sprinkler 6 are required where Load B represents the top of storage.
(5) For storage higher than represented by Load B, the cycle defined by Note 3 and Note 4 above is repeated.
(6) The storage height above the top level of in-rack sprinklers is limited to a maximum of 10 ft (3.0 m).
(7) The symbols X and △ represent in-rack sprinklers that are to be staggered both horizontally and vertically.
(8) Each square represents a storage cube measuring 4 ft to 5 ft (1.2 m to 1.5 m) on a side. Actual load heights can vary from approximately 18 in. to 10 ft (450 mm to 3.0 m). Therefore, there could be as few as one load or as many as six loads between in-rack sprinklers that are spaced 10 ft (3.0 m) apart vertically.

N **FIGURE 25.3.3.4.1.1(d) In-Rack Sprinkler Arrangements for Exposed Nonexpanded Group A Plastic Commodities Stored Over 25 ft (7.6 m) in Height — Option 4.**

N **25.4 In-Rack Sprinkler Protection in Combination with CMSA Ceiling-Level Sprinklers.**

N **25.4.1 Protection of Racks with Solid Shelves.**

N **25.4.1.1 General.**

N **25.4.1.1.1** The requirements of this chapter for the installation of in-rack sprinklers within open rack configurations shall apply to racks with solid shelves except as modified in this section.

N **25.4.1.1.2** CMSA ceiling-level sprinkler design criteria shall be an applicable option for open racks combined with in-rack sprinklers installed in accordance with the criteria for solid shelving.

N **25.4.1.2 Horizontal Location and Spacing of In-Rack Sprinklers in Racks with Solid Shelves.**

N **25.4.1.2.1** Where racks with solid shelves contain storage of Class I through Class IV commodities, the maximum allowable horizontal spacing of in-rack sprinklers shall be 10 ft (3.0 m).

N **25.4.1.2.2** Where racks with solid shelves contain storage of Group A plastic commodities, the maximum allowable horizontal spacing of in-rack sprinklers shall be 5 ft (1.5 m).

N **25.4.1.2.3*** Where racks with solid shelves obstruct only a portion of an open rack, in-rack sprinklers shall be extended beyond the end of the solid shelf a minimum of 4 ft (1.2 m) to the nearest flue space intersection.

N **25.4.1.3 Vertical Location and Spacing of In-Rack Sprinklers in Racks with Solid Shelves.**

N **25.4.1.3.1** Where CMSA ceiling-level sprinklers protect racks with solid shelving, in-rack sprinklers shall be installed beneath all tiers under the highest solid shelf.

N **25.4.1.3.2** Where racks with solid shelves obstruct only a portion of an open rack, in-rack sprinklers shall be installed in accordance with 25.4.1.3.1. *(See Figure A.25.4.1.2.3.)*

N **25.4.2 In-Rack Sprinkler Arrangements and Designs for Class I, Class II, Class III, Class IV, or Group A Plastic Commodities Protected by CMSA Ceiling-Level Sprinklers.**

N **25.4.2.1 In-Rack Sprinkler Arrangements and Designs.** Where rack storage of encapsulated or nonencapsulated Class I, Class II, Class III, Class IV, or Group A plastic commodities will be protected by in-rack sprinklers, the in-rack sprinkler arrangements and designs shall be selected from Figure 25.4.2.1(a) through Figure 25.4.2.1(c). *(See 25.4.1 for racks with solid shelving.)*

N **25.4.2.2 Horizontal Spacing of In-Rack Sprinklers in Combination with CMSA Ceiling-Level Sprinklers.**

N **25.4.2.2.1** Where rack storage of encapsulated or nonencapsulated Class I through Class IV commodities is up to and including 25 ft (7.6 m) in height and protected by CMSA ceiling-level sprinklers, the maximum allowable horizontal spacing of in-rack sprinklers shall be 8 ft (2.4 m).

N **25.4.2.2.2** Where rack storage of Group A plastic commodities is protected by CMSA ceiling-level sprinklers, the maximum allowable horizontal spacing of in-rack sprinklers shall be 5 ft (1.5 m).

N **25.4.2.2.3** Where rack storage of encapsulated or nonencapsulated Class I through Class IV commodities is over 25 ft (7.6 m) in height and protected by CMSA ceiling-level sprinklers, the maximum allowable horizontal spacing of in-rack sprinklers shall be 5 ft (1.5 m).

N **25.4.2.3 Design Criteria for In-Rack Sprinklers in Combination with CMSA Ceiling-Level Sprinklers.** The in-rack sprinkler system design, in terms of number of operating sprinklers at a minimum flow from the most remote in-rack sprinkler, in combination with CMSA ceiling-level sprinklers shall be in accordance with Table 25.4.2.3.

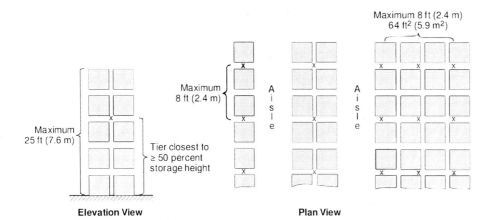

Notes:
(1) See Table 25.4.3.1 for the CMSA ceiling sprinkler design in combination with one level of in-rack sprinklers.
(2) In-rack sprinklers are ordinary-temperature-rated, quick- or standard-response, pendent or upright, minimum K-5.6 (K-80), and designed for a minimum of eight (8) in-rack sprinklers operating at 22 gpm (83 L/min).
(3) The symbol X represents in-rack sprinklers.
(4) Each square represents a storage cube measuring 4 ft to 5 ft (1.2 m to 1.5 m) on a side.

N **FIGURE 25.4.2.1(a)   In-Rack Sprinkler Arrangements for Encapsulated or Nonencapsulated Class I through Class IV Commodities Stored Up to and Including 25 ft (7.6 m) in Height.**

N **25.4.3 Ceiling-Level CMSA Sprinkler Designs for Rack Storage of Class I, Class II, Class III, Class IV, and Group A Plastic Commodities in Combinations with In-Rack Sprinklers.**

N **25.4.3.1* Ceiling-Level CMSA Sprinkler Designs in Combination with In-Rack-Sprinklers.** Where rack storage of encapsulated or nonencapsulated Class I, Class II, Class III, Class IV, and Group A plastic commodities will be protected by one or more levels of in-rack sprinklers, unless 25.4.3.2 applies, the ceiling-level sprinkler design in terms of minimum operating pressure [psi (bar)] and the number of ceiling-level sprinklers shall be in accordance with Table 25.4.3.1.

N **25.4.3.2 Open Wood Joist Construction with CMSA Ceiling-Level Sprinklers.**

N **25.4.3.2.1** Where CMSA ceiling-level sprinklers are installed under open wood joist construction, firestopping in accordance with 25.4.3.2.2 shall be provided or the minimum operating pressure of the sprinklers shall be 50 psi (3.4 bar) for a K-11.2 (K-160) sprinkler or 22 psi (1.5 bar) for a K-16.8 (K240) sprinkler.

N **25.4.3.2.2** Where each joist channel of open wood joist construction is fully firestopped to its full depth at intervals not exceeding 20 ft (6.1 m), the design pressures specified in Table 25.4.3.1 shall be permitted to be used.

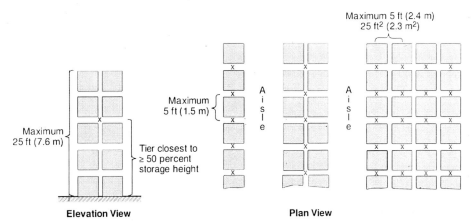

Notes:
(1) See Table 25.4.3.1 for the CMSA ceiling sprinkler design in combination with one level of in-rack sprinklers.
(2) In-rack sprinklers are ordinary-temperature-rated, quick- or standard-response, pendent or upright, minimum K-5.6 (K-80), and designed for a minimum of eight (8) in-rack sprinklers operating at 22 gpm (83 L/min).
(3) The symbol X represents in-rack sprinklers.
(4) Each square represents a storage cube measuring 4 ft to 5 ft (1.2 m to 1.5 m) on a side.

N **FIGURE 25.4.2.1(b)   In-Rack Sprinkler Arrangements for Nonexpanded, Cartoned or Exposed, Group A Plastic Commodities Stored Up to and Including 25 ft (7.6 m) in Height.**

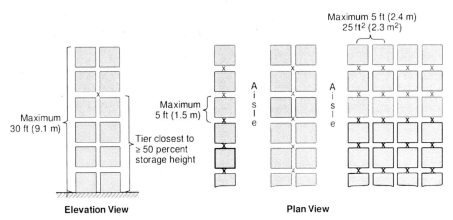

Notes:
(1) See Table 25.4.3.1 for the CMSA ceiling sprinkler design in combination with one level of in-rack sprinklers.
(2) In-rack sprinklers are ordinary-temperature-rated, quick- or standard-response, pendent or upright, minimum K-5.6 (K-80), and designed for a minimum of eight (8) in-rack sprinklers operating at 22 gpm (83 L/min).
(3) The symbol X represents in-rack sprinklers.
(4) Each square represents a storage cube measuring 4 ft to 5 ft (1.2 m to 1.5 m) on a side.

N **FIGURE 25.4.2.1(c)   In-Rack Sprinkler Arrangements for Encapsulated or Nonencapsulated Class I or Class II Commodities Stored Over 25 ft (7.6 m) in Height.**

Shaded text = Revisions.   **Δ** = Text deletions and figure/table revisions.   • = Section deletions.   *N* = New material.   2022 Edition

N Table 25.4.2.3 Design Criteria for In-Rack Sprinklers in Combination with CMSA Ceiling-Level Sprinklers

Commodity Classification	Maximum Storage Height ft (m)	Maximum Ceiling Height ft (m)	Rack Type	No. of IRAS Levels	IRAS Design, No. of IRAS @ gpm (L/min)
Class I and Class II	30 (9.1)	35 (10.7)	Open	1	8 @ 22 (83)
			Solid shelves	1	6 @ 30 (114)
			More than 1		10 (5 on 2 levels) @ 30 (114)
Class III	25 (7.6)	35 (10.7)	Open	1	8 @ 22 (83)
			Solid shelves	1	6 @ 30 (114)
			More than 1		10 (5 on 2 levels) @ 30 (114)
Class IV and Group A plastics	25 (7.6)	35 (10.7)	Open	1	8 @ 22 gpm (83 L/min)
			Solid Shelves	1	8 @ 30 (114)
			More than 1		14 (7 on 2 levels) @ 30 (114)

N Table 25.4.3.1 CMSA Ceiling-Level Sprinkler Design Criteria for Rack Storage of Encapsulated or Nonencapsulated Class I Through Class IV and Nonexpanded, Cartoned or Exposed, Group A Plastic Commodities Supplemented with In-Rack Sprinklers

Commodity Classification	Maximum Storage Height		Maximum Ceiling Height		K-Factor / Orientation	Type of System	No. of Ceiling Sprinklers in the Design	No. of Required IRAS Levels	Minimum Ceiling Sprinkler Operating Pressure	
	ft	m	ft	m					bar	psi
Class I or Class II	30	9.1	35	10.7	11.2 (160) Upright	Wet	20	One level	25	1.7
						Dry	30	One level	25	1.7
					16.8 (240) Upright	Wet	20	One level	15	1.0
						Dry	30	One level	15	1.0
Class III	25	7.6	30	9.1	11.2 (160) Upright	Wet	15	One level	25	1.7
						Dry	25	One level	25	1.7
					16.8 (240) Upright	Dry	25	One level	15	1.0
			35	10.7	11.2 (160) Upright	Wet	15	One level	25	1.7
						Dry	25	One level	25	1.7
					16.8 (240) Upright	Wet	15	One level	15	1.0
						Dry	25	One level	15	1.0
Class IV	25	7.6	30	9.1	11.2 (160) Upright	Wet	15	One level	50	3.4
			35	10.7	11.2 (160) Upright	Wet	20	One level	50	3.4
							15	One level	75	5.2
					16.8 (240) Upright	Wet	20	One level	22	1.5
							15	One level	22	1.5
Nonexpanded, cartoned and exposed, Group A plastics	25	7.6	30	9.1	11.2 (160) Upright	Wet	15	One level	50	3.4
			35	10.7	11.2 (160) Upright	Wet	30	One level	50	3.4
						Wet	20	One level	75	5.2
					16.8 (240) Upright	Wet	30	One level	22	1.5
						Wet	20	One level	35	2.4

N **25.4.3.3 Preaction Systems for CMSA Sprinklers.** Where CMSA sprinklers will be installed on a preaction sprinkler system, the designs obtained from Table 25.4.3.1 shall be based on those indicated for a dry sprinkler system.

N **25.5 In-Rack Sprinkler Protection in Combination with ESFR Ceiling-Level Sprinklers.**

N **25.5.1 Protection of Racks with Solid Shelves.**

N **25.5.1.1 General.**

N **25.5.1.1.1** The requirements of this chapter for the installation of in-rack sprinklers within open rack configurations shall apply to racks with solid shelves except as modified in this section.

N **25.5.1.1.2** ESFR ceiling-level sprinkler design criteria shall be an applicable option for open racks combined with in-rack sprinklers installed in accordance with the criteria for solid shelving.

N **25.5.1.2 Horizontal Location and Spacing of In-Rack Sprinklers in Racks with Solid Shelves.**

N **25.5.1.2.1** Where racks with solid shelves contain storage of Class I through Class IV commodities, the maximum allowable horizontal spacing of in-rack sprinklers shall be 10 ft (3.0 m).

N **25.5.1.2.2** Where racks with solid shelves contain storage of Group A plastic commodities, the maximum allowable horizontal spacing of in-rack sprinklers shall be 5 ft (1.5 m).

N **25.5.1.2.3*** Where racks with solid shelves obstruct only a portion of an open rack, in-rack sprinklers shall be extended beyond the end of the solid shelf a minimum of 4 ft (1.2 m) to the nearest flue space intersection.

N **25.5.1.3 Vertical Location and Spacing of In-Rack Sprinklers in Racks with Solid Shelves.**

N **25.5.1.3.1** Where ESFR ceiling-level sprinklers protect racks with solid shelving, in-rack sprinklers shall be installed beneath all tiers under the highest solid shelf.

N **25.5.1.3.2** Where racks with solid shelves obstruct only a portion of an open rack, in-rack sprinklers shall be installed in accordance with 25.5.1.3.1. *(See Figure A.25.5.1.2.3.)*

N **25.5.2 In-Rack Sprinkler Characteristics.**

N **25.5.2.1** The requirements of 25.1.6 for the installation of in-rack sprinklers shall apply to racks protected by ESFR ceiling-level sprinklers except as modified in this section.

N **25.5.2.2** In-rack sprinklers protecting open rack storage in combination with ESFR ceiling-level sprinklers shall be quick-response, ordinary-temperature-rated and minimum K-8.0 (K-115).

N **25.5.3 In-Rack Sprinkler Arrangements and Designs for Class I, Class II, Class III, Class IV, or Group A Plastic Commodities Protected by ESFR Ceiling-Level Sprinklers.**

N **25.5.3.1 General.** Where rack storage of encapsulated or nonencapsulated Class I through Class IV or Group A plastic commodities is protected by in-rack sprinklers, the in-rack sprinkler arrangement and design shall be selected from Figure 25.5.3.1. *(See 25.5.1 for racks with solid shelving.)*

N **25.5.3.2 Horizontal Spacing of In-Rack Sprinklers in Combination with ESFR Ceiling-Level Sprinklers.** Where rack storage of encapsulated or nonencapsulated Class I through Class IV or Group A plastic commodities is protected by ESFR ceiling-level sprinklers, the maximum allowable horizontal spacing of in-rack sprinklers shall be 5 ft (1.5 m).

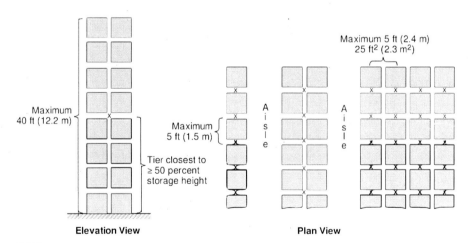

Notes:
(1) See Table 25.5.4.1 for the ESFR ceiling sprinkler design in combination with one level of in-rack sprinklers.
(2) In-rack sprinklers are ordinary-temperature-rated, quick-response, pendent or upright, K-8.0 (K-115) or K-11.2 (K-160), and designed for a minimum of eight in-rack sprinklers operating at 60 gpm (227 L/min).
(3) The symbol X represents in-rack sprinklers.
(4) Each square represents a storage cube measuring 4 ft to 5 ft (1.2 m to 1.5 m) on a side.

N **FIGURE 25.5.3.1 In-Rack Sprinkler Arrangements for Encapsulated or Nonencapsulated Class I Through Class IV and Group A Plastic Commodities Protected by ESFR Ceiling-Level Sprinklers.**

N **25.5.3.3 Design Criteria for In-Rack Sprinklers in Combination with ESFR Ceiling-Level Sprinklers.** The in-rack sprinkler system design, in terms of the number of operating sprinklers at a minimum flow from the most remote in-rack sprinkler, in combination with ESFR ceiling-level sprinklers shall be in accordance with Table 25.5.3.3.

N **25.5.4 Ceiling-Level ESFR Sprinkler Designs for Rack Storage of Class I, Class II, Class III, Class IV, and Group A Plastic Commodities in Combination with In-Rack Sprinklers.**

N **25.5.4.1** Where rack storage of encapsulated or nonencapsulated Class I, Class II, Class III, Class IV, or Group A plastic commodities will be protected by one or more levels of in-rack sprinklers, the ceiling-level sprinkler design in terms of minimum operating pressure [psi (bar)] and the number of ceiling-level sprinklers shall be in accordance with Table 25.5.4.1.

N **25.5.4.2** ESFR sprinkler systems, when supplemented with in-rack sprinklers, shall be designed such that the minimum oper-

ating pressure is not less than that indicated in Table 25.5.4.1 for type of storage, commodity, storage height, and building height involved.

N **25.5.4.3** The design area applicable to the ceiling-level design options listed in Table 25.5.4.1 shall consist of the most hydraulically demanding area of 12 sprinklers, consisting of four sprinklers on each of the three branch lines.

N **25.6 In-Rack Sprinkler Protection Options Independent of Ceiling-Level Sprinklers.**

N **25.6.1 General.**

N **25.6.1.1** Protection of closed-top Class I through Class IV and Group A plastic commodities (i.e., no open-top containers) stored on single-, double-, or multiple-row racks shall be permitted to be protected in accordance with this section.

N **Table 25.5.3.3 Design Criteria for In-Rack Sprinklers in Combination with ESFR Ceiling-Level Sprinklers**

Type of Storage	Commodity Classification	Storage Height ft (m)	Ceiling Height ft (m)	Rack Type	No. of IRAS Levels	IRAS Design, No. of IRAS @ gpm (L/min)
Storage not meeting the definition of miscellaneous	Class I, Class II, Class III	40 (12.2)	45 (13.7)	Open	1	8 @ 60 (230)
				Solid shelves	1	6 @ 30 (115)
					More than 1	10 (5 in-rack sprinklers on top 2 in-rack sprinklers levels) @ 30 (115)
	Class IV and Group A plastics	40 (12.2)	45 (13.7)	Open	1	8 @ 60 (230)
				Solid shelves	1	8 @ 30 (115)
					More than 1	14 (7 in-rack sprinklers on top 2 in-rack sprinklers levels) @ 30 (115)

N **Table 25.5.4.1 ESFR Ceiling-Level Sprinkler Design Criteria for Rack Storage of Encapsulated or Nonencapsulated Class I Through Class IV and Nonexpanded, Cartoned or Exposed, Group A Plastic Commodities Supplemented with In-Rack Sprinklers**

Storage Arrangement	Commodity Classification	Maximum Storage Height		Maximum Ceiling Height		K-Factor/ Orientation	No. of Ceiling Sprinklers in the Design	No. of Required IRAS Levels	Minimum Ceiling Sprinkler Operating Pressure	
		ft	m	ft	m				psi	bar
Single-, double-, and multiple-row racks (no open-top containers)	Class I, Class II, Class III, Class IV, and nonexpanded (cartoned and exposed) Group A plastics	40	12.2	45	13.7	14.0 (200) Pendent	12	One level	90	6.2
						16.8 (240) Pendent	12	One level	63	4.3

N **25.6.1.2** Where the storage rack will not be solely dedicated to storage requiring in-rack sprinkler protection in accordance with this section, either of the following shall apply:

(1) Extend the in-rack sprinkler protection horizontally one pallet load beyond the commodities requiring protection in accordance with this section.

(2) Install a vertical barrier to segregate the commodities requiring protection in accordance with this section from any adjacent commodities.

N **25.6.1.3** Commodities that can be protected by the ceiling-level sprinkler system shall be permitted to be stored vertically above and horizontally adjacent to the portions of the storage rack equipped as prescribed by this section.

N **25.6.2 Installation Requirements for In-Rack Sprinkler Protection Options.**

N **25.6.2.1 Sprinkler System Type.** In-rack sprinkler systems shall be wet-pipe only.

N **25.6.2.2 In-Rack Sprinkler Characteristics.** The in-rack sprinkler characteristics shall be in accordance with Table 25.6.2.2.

N **25.6.2.3 Horizontal Spacing of In-Rack Sprinklers.**

N **25.6.2.3.1** The maximum horizontal distance between in-rack sprinklers shall be in accordance with Table 25.6.2.3.1 in combination with Figure 25.6.2.3.1(a) through Figure 25.6.2.3.1(f).

N **25.6.2.3.2** The minimum horizontal distance between in-rack sprinklers shall be 27 in (700 mm).

N **25.6.2.3.3 Locating In-Rack Sprinklers Within Footprint of Rack Structure.**

N **25.6.2.3.3.1** In-rack sprinklers shall be located within the footprint of the rack structure.

N **25.6.2.3.3.2** Where the horizontal distance between a single-row rack and an adjacent full-height wall does not exceed 1 ft (0.3 m), in-rack sprinklers in Option 2a and Option 2b of Table 25.6.2.2 shall be permitted to be installed within this space as if it were a longitudinal flue of a double-row rack.

N **25.6.2.3.4** Where rack storage is protected by face sprinklers, the face sprinklers shall be located within the rack a minimum 3 in. (75 mm) from rack uprights and no more than 18 in. (450 mm) from the aisle face of storage.

N **25.6.2.4 Vertical Spacing of In-Rack Sprinklers.**

N **25.6.2.4.1** The maximum vertical spacing of in-rack sprinkler levels shall be in accordance with Table 25.6.2.4.1 in combination with Figure 25.6.2.3.1(a) through Figure 25.6.2.3.1(f).

N **Table 25.6.2.2 In-Rack Sprinkler Characteristics**

Sprinkler Type	K-factor	Coverage Type	Orientation	RTI Rating	Temperature Rating
CMDA (Option 1)	Minimum K-8.0 (K-115)	Standard-coverage	Pendent or upright	Quick-response	Ordinary-temperature
ESFR (Option 2a)	Minimum K-14.0 (K-200)	Standard-coverage	Pendent	Fast-response	Ordinary-temperature
ESFR (Option 2b)	Minimum K-22.4 (K-320)	Standard-coverage	Pendent	Fast-response	Ordinary-temperature
CMDA (Option 3)	K-25.2 (K-360)	Extended-coverage	Pendent	Fast-response	Intermediate-temperature

N **Table 25.6.2.3.1 Maximum Horizontal Spacing of In-Rack Sprinklers**

Rack Type	Option 1	Option 2a and Option 2b	Option 3
Single-row racks	5 ft (1.5 m) [See Figure 25.6.2.3.1(a).]	4.5 ft (1.4 m) [See Figure 25.6.2.3.1(b), Figure 25.6.2.3.1(c), and Figure 25.6.2.3.1(d).]	10 ft (3.0 m) [See Figure 25.6.2.3.1(e)and Figure 25.6.2.3.1(f).]
Double-row racks	5 ft (1.5 m) at each rack face 10 ft (3.0 m) within the longitudinal flue space [See Figure 25.6.2.3.1(a).]	4.5 ft (1.4 m) at each rack face* 4.5 ft (1.4 m) within the longitudinal flue space [See Figure 25.6.2.3.1(b), Figure 25.6.2.3.1(c), and Figure 25.6.2.3.1(d).]	Not required at the rack face 10 ft (3.0 m) within the longitudinal flue space [See Figure 25.6.2.3.1(e)and Figure 25.6.2.3.1(f).]
Multiple-row racks	5 ft (1.5 m) at each rack face and at each alternating rack bay 10 ft (3.0 m) between in-rack sprinkler at every other rack bay [See Figure 25.6.2.3.1(a).]	8 ft 6 in. (2.6 m) at each rack face 4.5 ft (1.4 m) in-between rack faces [See Figure 25.6.2.3.1(b), Figure 25.6.2.3.1(c), and Figure 25.6.2.3.1(d).]	10 ft (3.0 m) at each rack face 10 ft (3.0 m) in-between rack faces [See Figure 25.6.2.3.1(e) and Figure 25.6.2.3.1(f).]

Note: Option 1, Option 2a, Option 2b, and Option 3 are in reference to those listed in Table 25.6.2.2.
*The maximum horizontal distance between in-rack sprinklers is permitted to be increased to 8.5 ft (2.6 m) when the maximum distance between transverse flue spaces does not exceed 4.25 ft (1.3 m).

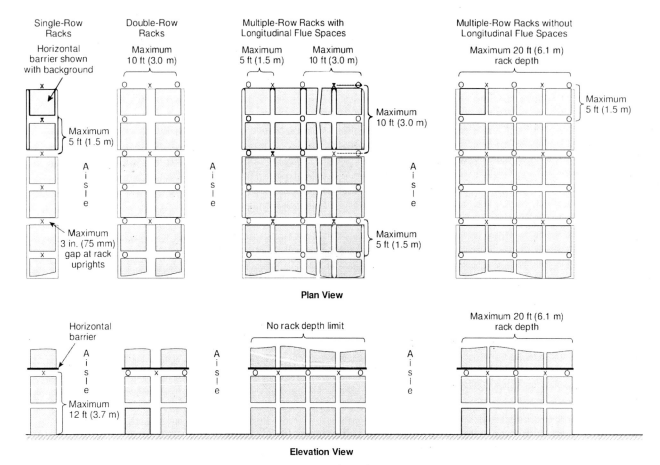

Plan View

Elevation View

Notes:
(1) In-rack sprinklers are ordinary-temperature-rated, quick-response, pendent or upright, and minimum K-8.0 (K-115). The in-rack sprinkler system is to be designed for a minimum of six in-rack sprinklers operating at 60 gpm (230 L/min) for single-row racks or a minimum of eight in-rack sprinklers operating at 60 gpm (230 L/min) for double- or multiple-row racks.
(2) The symbols X and O represent in-rack sprinklers.
(3) Each square represents a storage cube measuring 4 ft to 5 ft (1.2 m to 1.5 m) on a side. Actual load heights can vary from approximately 18 in. to 10 ft (450 mm to 3.0 m). Therefore, there could be as few as one load or as many as six loads between in-rack sprinklers that are spaced 10 ft (3.0 m) apart vertically.

N **FIGURE 25.6.2.3.1(a)   In-Rack Sprinkler Arrangements for Class I through Class IV and Group A Plastic Commodities.**

N **25.6.2.4.2** A minimum 6 in. (150 mm) vertical distance between the in-rack sprinkler deflector and the top of storage below shall be maintained.

N **25.6.2.4.3** A maximum 9 in. (225 mm) vertical distance between the in-rack sprinkler deflector and the underside of the horizontal barrier in Option 1 and Option 3 of Table 25.6.2.2 shall be maintained.

N **25.6.2.5 Horizontal Barriers.**

N **25.6.2.5.1** Where required by Table 25.6.2.4.1, horizontal barriers shall be provided in accordance with this section.

N **25.6.2.5.2** Horizontal barriers, in combination with in-rack sprinklers, shall be installed at every tier level of the dedicated storage rack where the rack is equipped with solid shelves.

N **25.6.2.5.3** Horizontal barriers shall be installed above every level of in-rack sprinklers in open frame racks in accordance with Table 25.6.2.4.1.

N **25.6.2.5.4** Horizontal barriers shall be constructed of minimum 22 gauge (0.78 mm) sheet metal or ⅜ in. (10 mm) plywood.

N **25.6.2.5.5** Horizontal barriers shall span horizontally to both faces of the racks so that all flue spaces of the rack bays are covered.

N **25.6.2.5.5.1** A maximum 3 in. (75 mm) wide gap in the horizontal barrier shall be permitted at rack uprights continuous from face of rack to face of rack.

N **25.6.2.5.5.2*** Horizontal barriers shall be fitted to within 3 in. (75 mm) of any vertical rack member or other equipment that would create an opening.

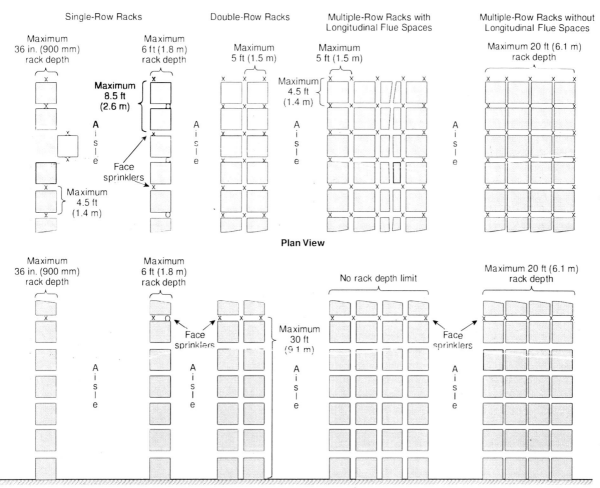

Plan View

Elevation View

Notes:
(1) In-rack sprinklers are ordinary-temperature-rated, fast-response, pendent, and minimum K-14.0 (K-200) ESFR sprinklers.
(2) Where Class I through Class IV and cartoned nonexpanded Group A plastic commodities are maintained in single-row racks having a maximum rack depth of 36 in. (900 mm), the in-rack sprinkler system is to be designed for a minimum of four in-rack sprinklers operating at 65 gpm (250 L/min).
(3) Where Class I through Class IV and cartoned (expanded and nonexpanded) Group A plastic commodities are maintained in single-row racks having a maximum rack depth of 36 in. (900 mm), the in-rack sprinkler system is to be designed for a minimum of four in-rack sprinklers operating at 100 gpm (380 L/min).
(4) Where Class I through Class IV and cartoned nonexpanded Group A plastic commodities are maintained in single-row racks having a maximum rack depth over 36 in. (900 mm) and up to and including 6 ft (1.8 m), the in-rack sprinkler system is to be designed for a minimum of five in-rack sprinklers operating at 65 gpm (250 L/min).
(5) Where Class I through Class IV and cartoned (expanded and nonexpanded) Group A plastic commodities are maintained in single-row racks having a maximum rack depth over 36 in. (900 mm) and up to and including 6 ft (1.8 m), the in-rack sprinkler system is to be designed for a minimum of five in-rack sprinklers operating at 100 gpm (380 L/min).
(6) Where Class I through Class IV and cartoned nonexpanded Group A plastic commodities are maintained in double- or multiple-row racks, the in-rack sprinkler system is to be designed for a minimum of six in-rack sprinklers operating at 65 gpm (250 L/min).
(7) Where Class I through Class IV and cartoned (expanded and nonexpanded) Group A plastic commodities are maintained in double- or multiple-row racks, the in-rack sprinkler system is to be designed for a minimum of six in-rack sprinklers operating at 100 gpm (380 L/min).
(8) The symbols X and O represent in-rack sprinklers.
(9) Each square represents a storage cube measuring 4 ft to 5 ft (1.2 m to 1.5 m) on a side. Actual load heights can vary from approximately 18 in. to 10 ft (450 mm to 3.0 m). Therefore, there could be as few as three loads or as many as 20 loads between in-rack sprinklers that are spaced 30 ft (9.1 m) apart vertically.

N **FIGURE 25.6.2.3.1(b)** **In-Rack Sprinkler Arrangements for Class I through Class IV and Cartoned Group A Plastic Commodities, Maximum 30 ft (9.1 m) Vertical Increments.**

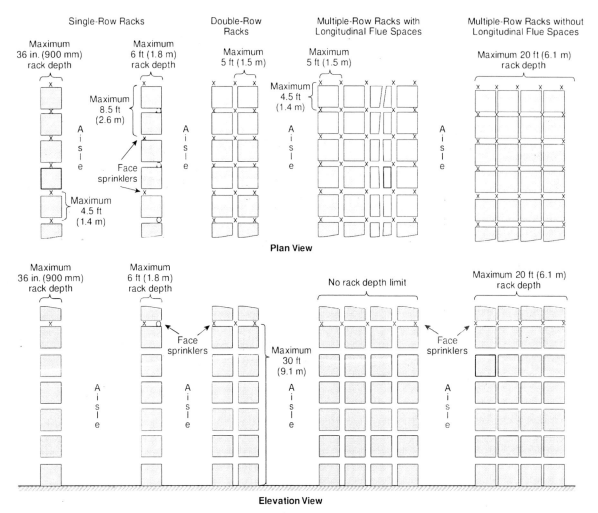

Plan View

Elevation View

Notes:
(1) In-rack sprinklers are ordinary-temperature-rated, fast-response, pendent, and minimum K-22.4 (K-320) ESFR sprinklers.
(2) Where Class I through Class IV and cartoned and exposed Group A plastic commodities are maintained in single-row racks having a maximum rack depth of 36 in. (900 mm), the in-rack sprinkler system is to be designed for a minimum of four in-rack sprinklers operating at 120 gpm (455 L/min).
(3) Where Class I through Class IV and cartoned and exposed Group A plastic commodities are maintained in single-row racks having a maximum rack depth over 3 ft (0.9 m) and up to and including 6 ft (1.8 m), the in-rack sprinkler system is to be designed for a minimum of five in-rack sprinklers operating at 120 gpm (455 L/min).
(4) Where Class I through Class IV and cartoned and exposed Group A plastic commodities are maintained in double- or multiple-row racks, the in-rack sprinkler system is to be designed for a minimum of 10 in-rack sprinklers (five in-rack sprinklers on the top level of the most remote rack as well as five in-rack sprinklers on the top level of the nearest adjacent storage rack) operating at 120 gpm (455 L/min).
(5) The symbols X and O represent in-rack sprinklers.
(6) Each square represents a storage cube measuring 4 ft to 5 ft (1.2 m to 1.5 m) on a side. Actual load heights can vary from approximately 18 in. to 10 ft (450 mm to 3.0 m). Therefore, there could be as few as three loads or as many as 20 loads between in-rack sprinklers that are spaced 30 ft (9.1 m) apart vertically.

N **FIGURE 25.6.2.3.1(c)   In-Rack Sprinkler Arrangements for Class I through Class IV and Group A Plastic Commodities, Maximum 30 ft (9.1 m) Vertical Increments.**

Shaded text = Revisions.   Δ = Text deletions and figure/table revisions.   • = Section deletions.   *N* = New material.

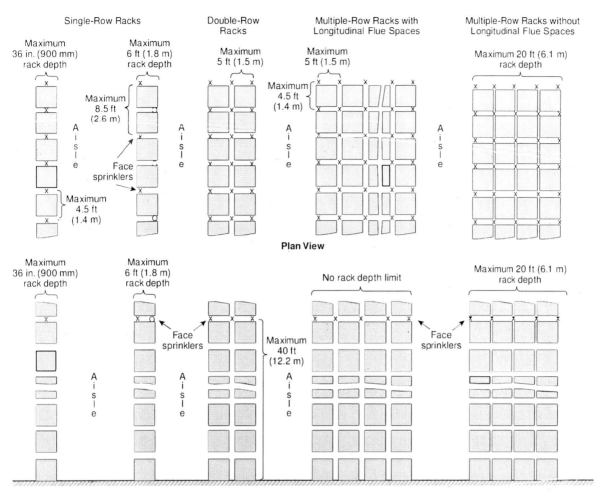

Plan View

Elevation View

Notes:
(1) In-rack sprinklers are ordinary-temperature-rated, fast-response, pendent, and minimum K-22.4 (K-320) ESFR sprinklers.
(2) Where Class I through Class IV and cartoned expanded Group A plastic commodities are maintained in single-row racks having a maximum rack depth of 36 in. (900 mm), the in-rack sprinkler system is to be designed for a minimum of four in-rack sprinklers operating at 120 gpm (455 L/min).
(3) Where Class I through Class IV and cartoned nonexpanded Group A plastic commodities are maintained in single-row racks having a maximum rack depth over 36 in. (900 mm) and up to and including 6 ft (1.8 m), the in-rack sprinkler system is to be designed for a minimum of five in-rack sprinklers operating at 120 gpm (455 L/min).
(4) Where Class I through Class IV and cartoned nonexpanded Group A plastic commodities are maintained in double- or multiple-row racks, the in-rack sprinkler system is to be designed for a minimum of six in-rack sprinklers operating at 120 gpm (455 L/min).
(5) The symbols X and O represent in-rack sprinklers.
(6) Each square represents a storage cube measuring 4 ft to 5 ft (1.2 m to 1.5 m) on a side. Actual load heights can vary from approximately 18 in. to 10 ft (450 mm to 3.0 m). Therefore, there could be as few as four loads or as many as 26 loads between in-rack sprinklers that are spaced 40 ft (12.2 m) apart vertically.

N **FIGURE 25.6.2.3.1(d)** **In-Rack Sprinkler Arrangements for Class I through Class IV and Cartoned Group A Plastic Commodities, Maximum 40 ft (12.2 m) Vertical Increments.**

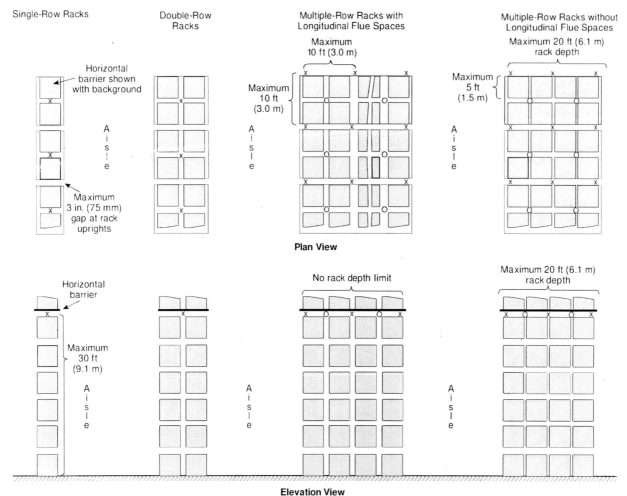

Plan View

Elevation View

Notes:
(1) In-rack sprinklers are intermediate-temperature-rated, fast-response, pendent, and minimum K-25.2 (K-360) extended-coverage CMDA sprinklers.
(2) Where Class I through Class IV and cartoned Group A plastic commodities are maintained in single- or double-row racks, the in-rack sprinkler system is to be designed for a minimum of four in-rack sprinklers operating at 138 gpm (520 L/min).
(3) Where Class I through Class IV and cartoned Group A plastic commodities are maintained in multiple-row racks, the in-rack sprinkler system is to be designed for a minimum of eight in-rack sprinklers (three at each face and two in between) operating at 138 gpm (520 L/min).
(4) The symbol X represents in-rack sprinklers.
(5) Each square represents a storage cube measuring 4 ft to 5 ft (1.2 m to 1.5 m) on a side. Actual load heights can vary from approximately 18 in. to 10 ft (450 mm to 3.0 m). Therefore, there could be as few as three loads or as many as 20 loads between in-rack sprinklers that are spaced 30 ft (9.1 m) apart vertically.

N **FIGURE 25.6.2.3.1(e)   In-Rack Sprinkler Arrangements for Class I through Class IV and Cartoned Group A Plastic Commodities, Maximum 30 ft (9.1 m) Vertical Increments.**

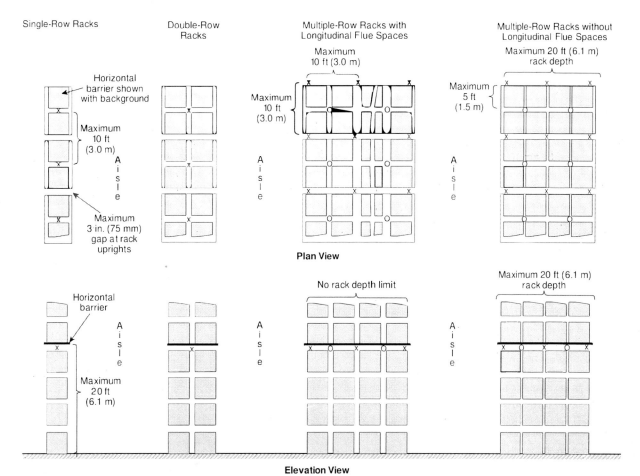

Plan View

Elevation View

Notes:
(1) In-rack sprinklers are intermediate-temperature-rated, fast-response, pendent, and minimum K-25.2 (K-360) extended-coverage CMDA sprinklers.
(2) Where Class I through Class IV and cartoned and exposed Group A plastic commodities are maintained in single- or double-row racks, the in-rack sprinkler system is to be designed for a mimimum of four in-rack sprinklers operating at 138 gpm (520 L/min).
(3) Where Class I through Class IV and cartoned and exposed Group A plastic commodities are maintained in multiple-row racks, the in-rack sprinkler system is to be designed for a minimum of eight in-rack sprinklers (three at each face and two in between) operating at 138 gpm (520 L/min).
(4) The symbol X represents in-rack sprinklers.
(5) Each square represents a storage cube measuring 4 ft to 5 ft (1.2 m to 1.5 m) on a side. Actual load heights can vary from approximately 18 in. to 10 ft (450 mm to 3.0 m). Therefore, there could be as few as two loads or as many as 13 loads between in-rack sprinklers that are spaced 20 ft (6.1 m) apart vertically.

N **FIGURE 25.6.2.3.1(f)   In-Rack Sprinkler Arrangements for Class I through Class IV and Group A Plastic Commodities, Maximum 20 ft (6.1 m) Vertical Increments.**

Shaded text = Revisions.   Δ = Text deletions and figure/table revisions.   • = Section deletions.   *N* = New material.

2022 Edition

N **Table 25.6.2.4.1 Maximum Vertical Spacing of In-Rack Sprinkler Levels**

Commodity Classification	Maximum Vertical Spacing of In-rack Sprinkler Levels			
	Option 1	Option 2a	Option 2b	Option 3
Class I through Class IV	12 ft (3.7 m) with horizontal barriers	30 ft (9.1 m)	40 ft (12.2 m)	30 ft (9.1 m) with horizontal barriers
Cartoned nonexpanded Group A plastics	12 ft (3.7 m) with horizontal barriers	30 ft (9.1 m)	40 ft (12.2 m)	30 ft (9.1 m) with horizontal barriers
Cartoned expanded Group A plastics	12 ft (3.7 m) with horizontal barriers	30 ft (9.1 m)	30 ft (9.1 m)	30 ft (9.1 m) with horizontal barriers
Exposed nonexpanded and exposed expanded Group A plastics	12 ft (3.7 m) with horizontal barriers	Not permitted	30 ft (9.1 m)	20 ft (6.1 m) with horizontal barriers

Note: Option 1, Option 2a, Option 2b, and Option 3 are in reference to those listed in Table 25.6.2.2.

N **25.6.3 Hydraulic Design Requirements for In-Rack Sprinkler Protection Options.**

N **25.6.3.1 In-Rack Sprinkler System Requirements.** Regardless of the number of in-rack sprinkler levels installed, the in-rack sprinkler system design, in terms of the number of operating sprinklers at a minimum flow from the most remote in-rack sprinkler, shall be in accordance with Table 25.6.3.1.

N **25.6.3.2 Ceiling-Level Sprinkler System Requirements.**

N **25.6.3.2.1*** Where in-rack sprinklers are in accordance with Section 25.6, the top level of in-rack sprinklers shall be considered a floor for design purposes of the ceiling sprinkler system.

N **25.6.3.2.2** The ceiling-level sprinkler system shall be in accordance with the guidelines outlined in Chapters 20, 21, 22, or 23, depending on the commodity hazard and the ceiling-level sprinkler, except as modified in Section 25.6.

N **25.6.3.3 Water Supply Requirements.**

N **25.6.3.3.1** The minimum water supply requirements for a hydraulically designed in-rack sprinkler system shall be determined by adding the hose stream allowance from Table 20.15.2.6 to the water demand for in-rack sprinklers.

N **25.6.3.3.2** The water supply requirements of 25.6.3.3.1 shall be available for a minimum duration as required in Table 20.15.2.6.

N **25.6.3.3.3*** The water supply for the in-rack sprinkler system shall be capable of providing the required in-rack sprinkler system design obtained from Section 25.6, independent of the design requirements of the ceiling sprinkler system protecting this same area.

N **25.6.3.3.4** The water supply for the ceiling-level sprinkler system shall be capable of providing the required ceiling-level sprinkler system design obtained from Chapters 21, 22, or 23, independent of the design requirements of the in-rack sprinkler system obtained from Section 25.6.

N **25.7 Evaluation or Modification of Existing Protection for Miscellaneous and Low-Piled Rack Storage Using In-Rack Sprinklers.**

N **25.7.1 Miscellaneous Rack Storage.**

N **25.7.1.1 Scope.** This section shall apply to miscellaneous rack storage up to and including 12 ft (3.7 m) in height of Class I through Class IV commodities, Group A plastic commodities and rubber tires.

N **25.7.1.2 In-Rack Sprinkler Design for Miscellaneous Storage.** Where in-rack sprinklers are installed in accordance with Section 25.3 to protect miscellaneous rack storage of Class I through Class IV commodities, Group A plastic commodities, and rubber tires up to and including 12 ft (3.7 m) in height, the in-rack sprinkler design shall be based on the hydraulically most demanding four adjacent in-rack sprinklers using a minimum flow of 22 gpm (83 L/min) from the hydraulically most remote in-rack sprinkler.

N **25.7.1.3 Horizontal Spacing of In-Rack Sprinklers for Miscellaneous Storage.** The maximum allowable horizontal spacing of in-rack sprinklers is 10 ft (3.0 m).

N **25.7.1.4 Ceiling Sprinkler Design in Combination with In-Rack Sprinklers for Miscellaneous Storage.**

N **25.7.1.4.1** Where in-rack sprinklers are installed in accordance with this chapter to protect miscellaneous rack storage of Class I through Class IV commodities, Group A plastic commodities, and rubber tires up to and including 12 ft (3.7 m) in height under a maximum 32 ft (9.8 m) high ceiling, the ceiling-level sprinkler design criteria shall be in accordance with Figure 25.7.1.4.1.

N **25.7.1.4.2** Installation criteria as permitted by this standard and design criteria and modifiers as permitted by the density/area method of Section 19.1 for ordinary hazard Group 2 occupancies shall be applicable.

N **25.7.1.4.3** The sprinkler system criteria specified in this chapter for miscellaneous storage shall not be limited to a ceiling slope of 2 in 12 (16.7 percent).

N Table 25.6.3.1 In-Rack Sprinkler System Design for Options 1, 2a, 2b, and 3

IRAS Option	Commodity Hazard	Maximum In-Rack Sprinkler Vertical Interval ft (m)	In-Rack Sprinkler K-factor	In-Rack Sprinkler System Design, No. of IRAS @ Minimum Flow, gpm (L/min)			
				Single-Row Racks up to 3 ft (0.9 m) Deep	Single-Row Racks over 3 ft (0.9 m) and up to 6 ft (1.8 m) Deep	Double-Row Racks	Multiple-Row Racks[a]
1	Class I–IV and Group A plastic (Cartoned and exposed) commodities	12 (3.7)	Minimum K-8.0 (K-115)	6 @ 60 (227)	6 @ 60 (227)	8 @ 60 (227)	8 @ 60 (227)
2a	Class I–IV and cartoned nonexpanded Group A plastics	30 (9.1)	Minimum K-14.0 (K-200) Pendent ESFR	4 @ 65 (250)	5 @ 65 (250)	6 @ 65 (250)	6 @ 65 (250)
2a	Cartoned expanded Group A plastics (Also, Class I–IV and cartoned nonexpanded Group A plastics)	30 (9.1)	Minimum K-14.0 (K-200) pendent ESFR	4 @ 100 (380)	5 @ 100 (380)	6 @ 100 (380)	6 @ 100 (380)
2b	Exposed group A plastic commodities (Also, class I–IV and cartoned Group A plastics)	30 (9.1)	Minimum K-22.4 (K-320) pendent ESFR	4 @ 120 (455)	5 @ 120 (455)	5 and 5[b] @ 120 (455)	5 and 5[b] @ 120 (455)
2b	Class I–IV and cartoned nonexpanded Group A plastics	40 (12.2)	Minimum K-22.4 (K-320) pendent ESFR	4 @ 120 (455)	5 @ 120 (455)	6 @ 120 (455)	6 @ 120 (455)
3	Class I–IV and cartoned (Nonexpanded and expanded) Group A plastic commodities	30 (9.1)	K25.2 (K-360) pendent extended coverage	4 @ 138 (520)	4 @ 138 (520)	4 @ 138 (520)	8[c] @ 138 (520)
3	Exposed group A plastic commodities (Also, Class I–IV and cartoned Group A plastics)	20 (6.1)	K25.2 (K-360) pendent extended coverage	4 @ 138 (520)	4 @ 138 (520)	4 @ 138 (520)	8[c] @ 138 (520)

Notes: Option 1, Option 2a, Option 2b, and Option 3 are in reference to those listed in Table 25.6.2.2.
[a]For maximum rack depths of 16 ft (4.9 m) for Option 2 and Option 3.
[b]This represents five sprinklers in the most remote rack as well as five sprinklers in the nearest adjacent rack.
[c]This represents three sprinklers at each rack face and the two sprinklers in-between them.

N **25.7.1.5 Hose Connections.** Hose connections shall not be required for the protection of miscellaneous storage.

N **25.7.2 Low-Piled Rack Storage.**

N **25.7.2.1 Scope.** This section shall apply to any of the following situations:

(1)   Rack storage of Class I through Class IV commodities up to and including 12 ft (3.7 m) in height
(2)* Rack storage of Group A plastic commodities up to and including 5 ft (1.5 m) in height

N **25.7.2.2 In-Rack Sprinkler Design for Low-Piled Storage.** Where in-rack sprinklers are installed in accordance with Section 25.3 to protect low-piled rack storage of Class I through Class IV commodities up to and including 12 ft (3.7 m) in height and low-piled rack storage of Group A plastic commodities up to and including 5 ft (1.5 m) in height, the in-rack sprinkler design shall be based on the hydraulically most demanding four adjacent in-rack sprinklers using a minimum

flow of 22 gpm (83 L/min) from the hydraulically most remote in-rack sprinkler.

N **25.7.2.3 Horizontal Spacing of In-Rack Sprinklers for Low-Piled Storage.** The maximum allowable horizontal spacing of in-rack sprinklers is 10 ft (3.0 m).

N **25.7.2.4 Ceiling Sprinkler Design in Combination with In-Rack Sprinklers for Low-Piled Storage.**

N **25.7.2.4.1** Where in-rack sprinklers are installed in accordance with Section 25.3 to protect low-piled rack storage of Class I through Class IV and Group A plastic commodities that does not meet the definition of miscellaneous storage, the ceiling-level design shall be in accordance with Figure 25.7.2.4.1.

N **25.7.2.4.2** The sprinkler system criteria specified in this chapter for low-piled storage shall not be limited to a ceiling slope of 2 in 12 (16.7 percent).

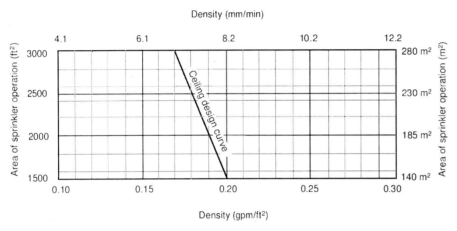

N **FIGURE 25.7.1.4.1   CMDA Ceiling-Level Sprinkler Design Criteria for Miscellaneous Storage Protected with One Level of In-Rack Sprinklers.**

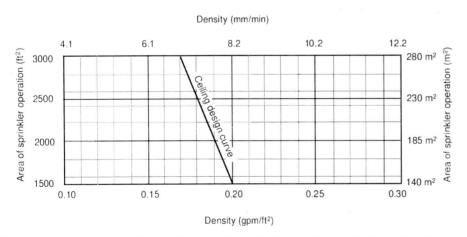

N **FIGURE 25.7.2.4.1   CMDA Ceiling-Level Sprinkler Design Criteria for Low-Piled Storage Protected with One Level of In-Rack Sprinklers.**

N **25.7.2.5 Ceiling Sprinkler Design in Combination with In-Rack Sprinklers for Low-Piled Storage with Solid Shelves.**

N **25.7.2.5.1** For low-piled rack storage with solid shelves of Class I through Class IV commodities up to and including 12 ft (3.7 m) in height that does not meet the definition of miscellaneous storage, the ceiling-level sprinkler design shall be permitted to be in accordance with Figure 25.7.2.4.1 where the in-rack sprinklers are installed in accordance with Section 20.19.

N **25.7.2.5.2** For low-piled rack storage with solid shelves of Group A plastic commodities up to and including 5 ft (1.5 m) in height that does not meet the definition of miscellaneous storage, the ceiling-level sprinkler design shall be permitted to be in accordance with Figure 25.7.2.4.1 where the in-rack sprinklers are installed in accordance with Section 20.19.

N **25.8 Evaluation or Modification of Existing CMDA Ceiling-Level Sprinkler Rack Storage Protection of Class I through Class IV Commodities Over 12 ft (3.7 m) and Up to and Including 25 ft (7.6 m) in Height Using In-Rack Sprinklers.**

N **25.8.1 General.**

N **25.8.1.1 In-Rack Sprinkler Protection in Combination with CMDA Ceiling-Level Sprinklers.**

N **25.8.1.1.1** Unless indicated otherwise, the guidelines from Section 25.1 for in-rack sprinklers shall apply to Section 25.8.

N **25.8.1.1.2** The in-rack sprinkler system design, in terms of number of operating sprinklers at a minimum flow from the most remote in-rack sprinkler, in combination with CMDA ceiling-level sprinklers shall be in accordance with Table 25.8.1.1.2.

N **25.8.1.2 CMDA Ceiling-Level Sprinkler Protection in Combination with In-Rack Sprinklers.**

N **25.8.1.2.1** Unless indicated otherwise, the guidelines from Section 25.1 for CMDA ceiling-level sprinklers shall apply to Section 25.8.

N **25.8.1.2.2** CMDA ceiling-level sprinkler design criteria, in combination with in-rack sprinklers, for rack storage over 12 ft (3.7 m) and up to and including 25 ft (7.6 m) in height of Class I through Class IV commodities shall be in accordance with the following:

(1) For the storage of exposed nonencapsulated Class I, Class II, Class III, or Class IV commodities, see 25.8.2.2

(2) For the storage of exposed encapsulated, or cartoned (nonencapsulated or encapsulated) Class I, Class II, Class III, or Class IV commodities, see 25.8.3.2.

N **25.8.1.2.3** The use of quick-response CMDA sprinklers for storage applications shall be permitted when listed for such use.

N **25.8.1.2.4** The water supply for sprinklers only shall be determined from the density/area requirements of this chapter.

N **25.8.1.2.5** The calculations shall satisfy any single point on appropriate density/area curves.

N **25.8.1.2.6** The ceiling-level sprinkler system design area shall meet the requirements of 28.2.4.2.1.

N **25.8.1.2.7** The minimum design density shall not be less than 0.15 gpm/ft^2 (6.1 mm/min) after all adjustments are made.

N **25.8.1.2.8 CMDA Ceiling-Level Sprinkler Characteristics.** CMDA Ceiling-level sprinkler characteristics in combination with in-rack sprinklers shall be in accordance with Figure 25.8.1.2.8.

N **Table 25.8.1.1.2 Design Criteria for In-Rack Sprinklers in Combination with CMDA Ceiling-Level Sprinklers for Class I through Class IV Commodities Stored Over 12 ft (3.7 m) and Up to and Including 25 ft (7.6 m)**

Commodity Classification	Rack Type	No. of IRAS Levels	IRAS Design, No. of IRAS @ gpm (L/min)
Class I, Class II or Class III	Open	1	6 @ 22 (83)
		More than 1	10 (5 in-rack sprinklers on top 2 in-rack sprinkler levels) @ 22 (83)
	Solid shelves	1	6 @ 30 (114)
		More than 1	10 (5 in-rack sprinklers on top 2 in-rack sprinkler levels) @ 30 (114)
Class IV	Open	1	8 @ 22 (83)
		More than 1	10 (5 in-rack sprinklers on top 2 in-rack sprinkler levels) @ 22 (83)
	Solid shelves	1	8 @ 30 (114)
		More than 1	14 (7 in-rack sprinklers on top 2 in-rack sprinkler levels) @ 30 (114)

Shaded text = Revisions.   Δ = Text deletions and figure/table revisions.   • = Section deletions.   *N* = New material.

2022 Edition

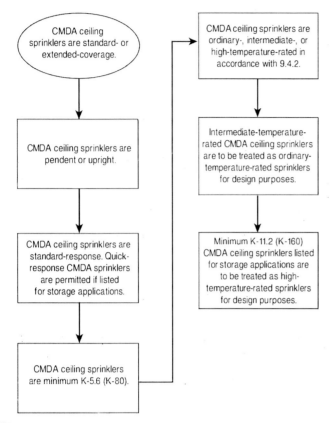

N **FIGURE 25.8.1.2.8   CMDA Ceiling-Level Sprinkler Characteristics in Combination with In-Rack Sprinklers.**

N **25.8.2 Exposed Nonencapsulated Class I, Class II, Class III, or Class IV Commodities Stored Up to and Including 25 ft (7.6 m) in Height.**

N **25.8.2.1* In-Rack Sprinkler Arrangements and Designs for Exposed Nonencapsulated Class I, Class II, Class III, or Class IV Commodities Stored Up to and Including 25 ft (7.6 m) in Height.**

N **25.8.2.1.1** Where rack storage of exposed nonencapsulated Class I through Class IV commodities stored over 12 ft (3.7 m) and up to and including 25 ft (7.6 m) in height will be protected by in-rack sprinklers, the following levels of in-rack sprinklers shall be required:

(1) One level of in-rack sprinklers where Class I through Class IV commodities are stored in single- or double-row racks up to and including 25 ft (7.6 m)
(2) One level of in-rack sprinklers where Class IV commodities are stored in multiple-row racks up to and including 20 ft (6.1 m)
(3) Two levels of in-rack sprinklers where Class IV commodities are stored in multiple-row racks over 20 ft (6.1 m) and up to and including 25 ft (7.6 m)

N **25.8.2.1.2** Where rack storage of exposed nonencapsulated Class I or Class II commodities stored over 12 ft (3.7 m) and up to and including 25 ft (7.6 m) in height will be protected by in-rack sprinklers, in-rack sprinkler arrangements and designs

shall be selected from Figure 25.8.2.1.2(a) through Figure 25.8.2.1.2(c). *(See Section 20.19 for racks with solid shelving.)*

N **25.8.2.1.3** Where rack storage of exposed nonencapsulated Class III commodities stored over 12 ft (3.7 m) and up to and including 25 ft (7.6 m) in height will be protected by in-rack sprinklers, in-rack sprinkler arrangements and designs shall be selected from Figure 25.8.2.1.3(a) through Figure 25.8.2.1.3(c). *(See Section 20.19 for racks with solid shelving.)*

N **25.8.2.1.4** Where rack storage of exposed nonencapsulated Class IV commodities stored over 12 ft (3.7 m) and up to and including 25 ft (7.6 m) in height in single- and double-row racks will be protected by in-rack sprinklers, in-rack sprinkler arrangements and designs shall be selected from Figure 25.8.2.1.4(a) through Figure 25.8.2.1.4(c). *(See Section 20.19 for racks with solid shelving.)*

N **25.8.2.1.5** Where rack storage of exposed nonencapsulated Class IV commodities stored over 12 ft (3.7 m) and up to and including 20 ft (6.1 m) in height in multiple-row racks will be protected by in-rack sprinklers, in-rack sprinkler arrangements and designs shall be selected from Figure 25.8.2.1.5(a) through Figure 25.8.2.1.5(c). *(See Section 20.19 for racks with solid shelving.)*

N **25.8.2.1.6** Where rack storage of exposed nonencapsulated Class IV commodities stored over 20 ft (6.1 m) and up to and including 25 ft (7.6 m) in height in multiple-row racks will be protected by in-rack sprinklers, in-rack sprinkler arrangements and designs shall be selected from Figure 25.8.2.1.6(a) or Figure 25.8.2.1.6(b). *(See Section 20.19 for racks with solid shelving.)*

N **25.8.2.2 CMDA Ceiling-Level Sprinkler Designs for Exposed Nonencapsulated Class I, Class II, Class III, or Class IV Commodities Stored Up to and Including 25 ft (7.6 m) in Height in Combination with In-Rack Sprinklers.**

N **25.8.2.2.1*** For single-, double-, and multiple-row rack storage of exposed nonencapsulated Class I through Class IV commodities stored over 12 ft (3.7 m) and up to and including 25 ft (7.6 m) in height, the ceiling-level sprinkler design in terms of density [gpm/ft² (mm/min)] over an area of ceiling-level sprinkler operation [ft² (186 m²)], with the provision of in-rack sprinklers, shall be determined from Table 25.8.2.2.1 and Figure 25.8.2.2.1(a) through Figure 25.8.2.2.1(d).

N **25.8.2.2.2* Ceiling-Level Sprinkler Density Adjustments.**

N **25.8.2.2.2.1*** Design densities obtained from the appropriate figure and curve specified in Table 25.8.2.2.1 for single- and double-row racks shall be selected to correspond to aisle width as follows *(See Section C.15.)*:

(1) The density given for 8 ft (2.4 m) wide aisles shall be applied to aisles wider than 8 ft (2.4 m).
(2) For aisle widths between 4 ft (1.2 m) and 8 ft (2.4 m), the rules for 4 ft (1.2 m) aisle width shall be used or direct linear interpolation between the densities shall be permitted.
(3) The density given for 4 ft (1.2 m) wide aisles shall be applied to aisles narrower than 4 ft (1.2 m) down to 3½ ft (1.1 m).
(4) Where aisles are narrower than 3½ ft (1.1 m), racks shall be considered to be multiple-row racks.

N

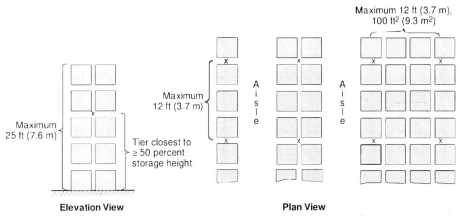

Elevation View **Plan View**

Notes:
(1) See 25.8.2.2 for the ceiling-level sprinkler design.
(2) In-rack sprinklers are ordinary-temperature-rated, quick- or standard-response, pendent or upright, minimum K-5.6 (K-80), and designed for a minimum of six (6) in-rack sprinklers operating at 22 gpm (83 L/min).
(3) The symbol X represents in-rack sprinklers.
(4) Each square represents a storage cube measuring 4 ft to 5 ft (1.2 m to 1.5 m) on a side.

N **FIGURE 25.8.2.1.2(a) In-Rack Sprinkler Arrangements for Exposed Nonencapsulated Class I or Class II Commodities Stored to a Maximum Height of 25 ft (7.6 m) with One Level of In-Rack Sprinklers.**

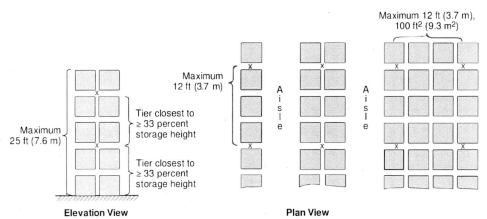

Elevation View **Plan View**

Notes:
(1) See 25.8.2.2 for the ceiling-level sprinkler design.
(2) In-rack sprinklers are ordinary-temperature-rated, quick- or standard-response, pendent or upright, minimum K-5.6 (K-80), and designed for a minimum of ten (10) in-rack sprinklers [five (5) in-rack sprinklers on the top two levels] operating at 22 gpm (83 L/min).
(3) The symbol X represents in-rack sprinklers.
(4) Each square represents a storage cube measuring 4 ft to 5 ft (1.2 m to 1.5 m) on a side.

N **FIGURE 25.8.2.1.2(b) In-Rack Sprinkler Arrangements for Exposed Nonencapsulated Class I or Class II Commodities Stored to a Maximum Height of 25 ft (7.6 m) with More Than One Level of In-Rack Sprinklers (Not at Each Tier Level).**

Shaded text = Revisions.   Δ = Text deletions and figure/table revisions.   • = Section deletions.   *N* = New material.

2022 Edition

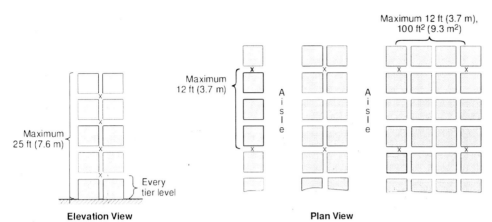

Elevation View   **Plan View**

Notes:
(1) See 25.8.2.2 for the ceiling-level sprinkler design.
(2) In-rack sprinklers are ordinary-temperature-rated, quick- or standard-response, pendent or upright, minimum
   K-5.6 (K-80), and designed for a minimum of ten (10) in-rack sprinklers [five (5) in-rack sprinklers on top two levels]
   operating at 22 gpm (83 L/min).
(3) The symbol X represents in-rack sprinklers.
(4) Each square represents a storage cube measuring 4 ft to 5 ft (1.2 m to 1.5 m) on a side.

N **FIGURE 25.8.2.1.2(c)   In-Rack Sprinkler Arrangements for Exposed Nonencapsulated Class I or Class II Commodities Stored to a Maximum Height of 25 ft (7.6 m) with In-Rack Sprinklers at Each Tier Level.**

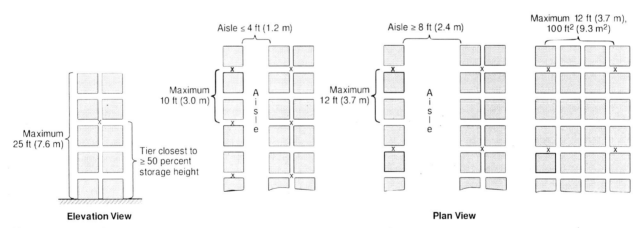

Elevation View   **Plan View**

Notes:
(1) See 25.8.2.2 for the ceiling-level sprinkler design.
(2) In-rack sprinklers are ordinary-temperature-rated, quick- or standard-response, pendent or upright, minimum
   K-5.6 (K-80), and designed for a minimum of six (6) in-rack sprinklers operating at 22 gpm (83 L/min).
(3) The symbol X represents in-rack sprinklers.
(4) Each square represents a storage cube measuring 4 ft to 5 ft (1.2 m to 1.5 m) on a side.

N **FIGURE 25.8.2.1.3(a)   In-Rack Sprinkler Arrangements for Exposed Nonencapsulated Class III Commodities Stored to a Maximum Height of 25 ft (7.6 m) with One Level of In-Rack Sprinklers.**

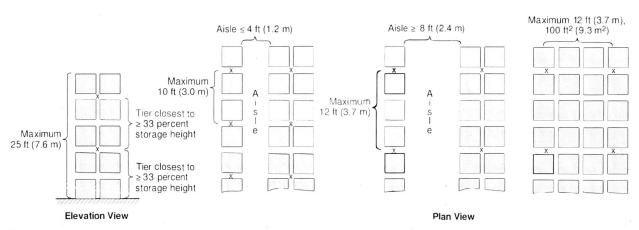

Notes:
(1) See 25.8.2.2 for the ceiling-level sprinkler design.
(2) In-rack sprinklers are ordinary-temperature-rated, quick- or standard-response, pendent or upright, minimum K-5.6 (K-80), and designed for a minimum of ten (10) in-rack sprinklers [five (5) in-rack sprinklers on top two levels] operating at 22 gpm (83 L/min).
(3) The symbol X represents in-rack sprinklers.
(4) Each square represents a storage cube measuring 4 ft to 5 ft (1.2 m to 1.5 m) on a side.

N **FIGURE 25.8.2.1.3(b)** In-Rack Sprinkler Arrangements for Exposed Nonencapsulated Class III Commodities Stored to a Maximum Height of 25 ft (7.6 m) with More Than One Level of In-Rack Sprinklers (Not at Each Tier Level).

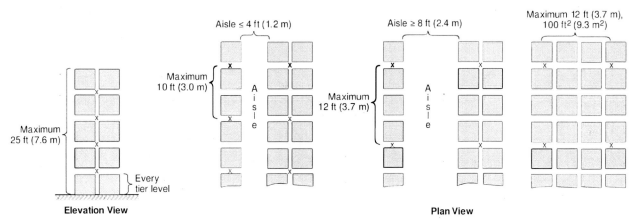

Notes:
(1) See 25.8.2.2 for the ceiling-level sprinkler design.
(2) In-rack sprinklers are ordinary-temperature-rated, quick- or standard-response, pendent or upright, minimum K-5.6 (K-80), and designed for a minimum of ten (10) in-rack sprinklers [five (5) in-rack sprinklers on top two levels] operating at 22 gpm (83 L/min).
(3) The symbol X represents in-rack sprinklers.
(4) Each square represents a storage cube measuring 4 ft to 5 ft (1.2 m to 1.5 m) on a side.

N **FIGURE 25.8.2.1.3(c)** In-Rack Sprinkler Arrangements for Exposed Nonencapsulated Class III Commodities Stored to a Maximum Height of 25 ft (7.6 m) with In-Rack Sprinklers at Each Tier Level.

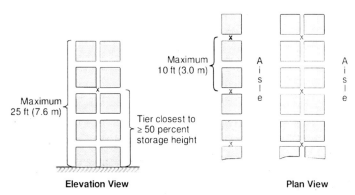

Notes:
(1) See 25.8.2.2 for the ceiling-level sprinkler design.
(2) In-rack sprinklers are ordinary-temperature-rated, quick- or standard-response, pendent or upright, minimum K-5.6 (K-80), and designed for a minimum of eight (8) in-rack sprinklers operating at 22 gpm (83 L/min).
(3) The symbol X represents in-rack sprinklers.
(4) Each square represents a storage cube measuring 4 ft to 5 ft (1.2 m to 1.5 m) on a side.

N **FIGURE 25.8.2.1.4(a)   In-Rack Sprinkler Arrangements for Exposed Nonencapsulated Class IV Commodities Stored to a Maximum Height of 25 ft (7.6 m) in Single- and Double-Row Racks with One Level of In-Rack Sprinklers.**

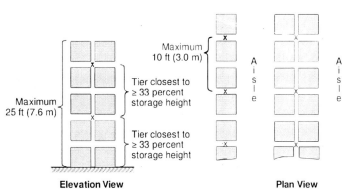

Notes:
(1) See 25.8.2.2 for the ceiling-level sprinkler design.
(2) In-rack sprinklers are ordinary-temperature-rated, quick- or standard-response, pendent or upright, minimum K-5.6 (K-80), and designed for a minimum of 14 in-rack sprinklers [seven (7) in-rack sprinklers on top two levels] operating at 22 gpm (83 L/min).
(3) The symbol X represents in-rack sprinklers.
(4) Each square represents a storage cube measuring 4 ft to 5 ft (1.2 m to 1.5 m) on a side.

N **FIGURE 25.8.2.1.4(b)   In-Rack Sprinkler Arrangements for Exposed Nonencapsulated Class IV Commodities Stored to a Maximum Height of 25 ft (7.6 m) in Single- and Double-Row Racks with More Than One Level of In-Rack Sprinklers (Not at Each Tier Level).**

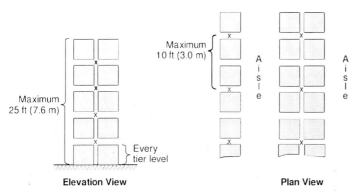

Notes:
(1) See 25.8.2.2 for the ceiling-level sprinkler design.
(2) In-rack sprinklers are ordinary-temperature-rated, quick- or standard-response, pendent or upright, minimum K-5.6 (K-80), and designed for a minimum of 14 in-rack sprinklers [seven (7) in-rack sprinklers on top two leves] operating at 22 gpm (83 L/min).
(3) The symbol X represents in-rack sprinklers.
(4) Each square represents a storage cube measuring 4 ft to 5 ft (1.2 m to 1.5 m) on a side.

N FIGURE 25.8.2.1.4(c)   In-Rack Sprinkler Arrangements for Exposed Nonencapsulated Class IV Commodities Stored to a Maximum Height of 25 ft (7.6 m) in Single- and Double-Row Racks with In-Rack Sprinklers at Each Tier Level.

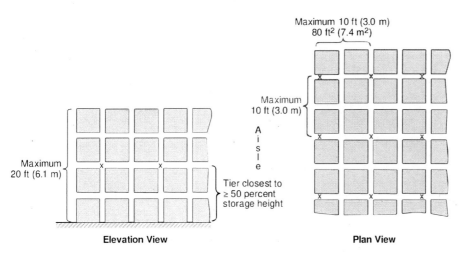

Notes:
(1) See 25.8.2.2 for the ceiling-level sprinkler design.
(2) In-rack sprinklers are ordinary-temperature-rated, quick- or standard-response, pendent or upright, minimum K-5.6 (K-80), and designed for a minimum of eight (8) in-rack sprinklers operating at 22 gpm (83 L/min).
(3) The symbol X represents in-rack sprinklers.
(4) Each square represents a storage cube measuring 4 ft to 5 ft (1.2 m to 1.5 m) on a side.

N FIGURE 25.8.2.1.5(a)   In-Rack Sprinkler Arrangements for Exposed Nonencapsulated Class IV Commodities Stored to a Maximum Height of 20 ft (6.1 m) in Multiple-Row Racks with One Level of In-Rack Sprinklers.

Shaded text = Revisions.   Δ = Text deletions and figure/table revisions.   • = Section deletions.   N = New material.

2022 Edition

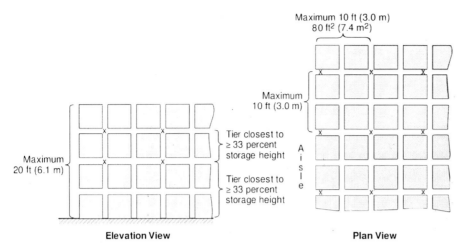

Notes:
(1) See 25.8.2.2 for the ceiling-level sprinkler design.
(2) In-rack sprinklers are ordinary-temperature-rated, quick- or standard-response, pendent or upright, minimum K-5.6 (K-80), and designed for a minimum of 14 in-rack sprinklers [seven (7) in-rack sprinklers on top two levels] operating at 22 gpm (83 L/min).
(3) The symbol X represents in-rack sprinklers.
(4) Each square represents a storage cube measuring 4 ft to 5 ft (1.2 m to 1.5 m) on a side.

N **FIGURE 25.8.2.1.5(b)   In-Rack Sprinkler Arrangements for Exposed Nonencapsulated Class IV Commodities Stored to a Maximum Height of 20 ft (6.1 m) in Multiple-Row Racks with More Than One Level of In-Rack Sprinklers.**

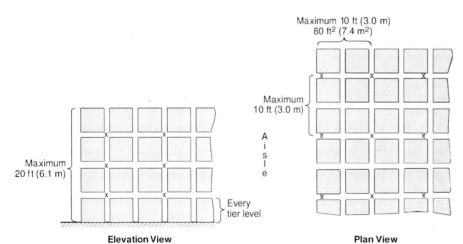

Notes:
(1) See 25.8.2.2 for the ceiling-level sprinkler design.
(2) In-rack sprinklers are ordinary-temperature-rated, quick- or standard-response, pendent or upright, minimum K-5.6 (K-80), and designed for a minimum of 14 in-rack sprinklers [seven (7) in-rack sprinklers on top two levels] operating at 22 gpm (83 L/min).
(3) The symbol X represents in-rack sprinklers.
(4) Each square represents a storage cube measuring 4 ft to 5 ft (1.2 m to 1.5 m) on a side.

N **FIGURE 25.8.2.1.5(c)   In-Rack Sprinkler Arrangements for Exposed Nonencapsulated Class IV Commodities Stored to a Maximum Height of 20 ft (6.1 m) in Multiple-Row Racks with In-Rack Sprinklers at Each Tier Level.**

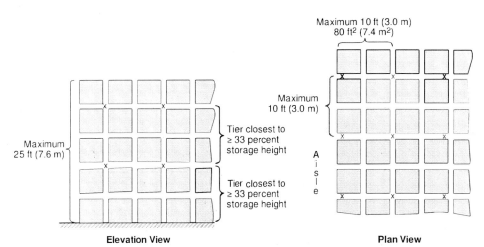

Notes:
(1) See 25.8.2.2 for the ceiling-level sprinkler design.
(2) In-rack sprinklers are ordinary-temperature-rated, quick- or standard-response, pendent or upright, minimum K-5.6 (K-80), and designed for a minimum of 14 in-rack sprinklers [seven (7) in-rack sprinklers on top two levels] operating at 22 gpm (83 L/min).
(3) The symbol X represents in-rack sprinklers.
(4) Each square represents a storage cube measuring 4 ft to 5 ft (1.2 m to 1.5 m) on a side.

N **FIGURE 25.8.2.1.6(a) In-Rack Sprinkler Arrangements for Exposed Nonencapsulated Class IV Commodities Stored Over 20 ft (6.1 m) and Up to a Maximum Height of 25 ft (7.6 m) in Multiple-Row Racks with Two Levels of In-Rack Sprinklers.**

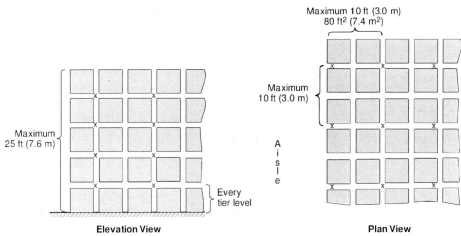

Notes:
(1) See 25.8.2.2 for the ceiling-level sprinkler design.
(2) In-rack sprinklers are ordinary-temperature-rated, quick- or standard-response, pendent or upright, minimum K-5.6 (K-80), and designed for a minimum of 14 in-rack sprinklers [seven (7) in-rack sprinklers on top two levels] operating at 22 gpm (83 L/min).
(3) The symbol X represents in-rack sprinklers.
(4) Each square represents a storage cube measuring 4 ft to 5 ft (1.2 m to 1.5 m) on a side.

N **FIGURE 25.8.2.1.6(b) In-Rack Sprinkler Arrangements for Exposed Nonencapsulated Class IV Commodities Stored Over 20 ft (6.1 m) and Up to a Maximum Height of 25 ft (7.6 m) in Multiple-Row Racks with In-Rack Sprinklers at Each Tier Level.**

N **Table 25.8.2.2.1 Determining Appropriate Ceiling-Level Protection Criteria Figure and Curve for Rack Storage of Exposed Nonencapsulated Class I through Class IV Commodities Stored Over 12 ft (3.7 m) and Up to and Including 25 ft (7.6 m)**

Commodity	Maximum Storage Height	Storage Arrangement	Aisle Width ft (m)	Minimum No. of In-Rack Sprinkler Levels Required	Appropriate Figure and Curve		
					Figure	Ceiling Sprinkler Temperature Rating	
						High	Ordinary or Intermediate
Class I	Over 12 ft (3.7 m) and up to and including 25 ft (7.6 m)	Single- and double-row racks	8 (2.4)	1 level	25.8.2.2.1(a)	A	B
			4 (1.2)			C	D
		Multiple-row racks	Any			C	D
Class II	Over 12 ft (3.7 m) and up to and including 25 ft (7.6 m)	Single- and double-row racks	8 (2.4)	1 level	25.8.2.2.1(b)	A	B
			4 (1.2)			C	D
		Multiple-row racks	Any			C	D
Class III	Over 12 ft (3.7 m) and up to and including 25 ft (7.6 m)	Single- and double-row racks	8 (2.4)	1 level	25.8.2.2.1(c)	A	B
			4 (1.2)			C	D
		Multiple-row racks	Any			C	D
Class IV	Over 12 ft (3.7 m) and up to and including 20 ft (6.1 m)	Single- and double-row racks	8 (2.4)	1 level	25.8.2.2.1(d)	A	B
			4 (1.2)			C	D
		Multiple-row racks	Any			C	D
	Over 20 ft (6.1 m) and up to and including 25 ft (7.6 m)	Single- and double-row racks	8 (2.4)	1 level	25.8.2.2.1(d)	A	B
			4 (1.2)			C	D
		Multiple-row racks	Any	2 levels		C	D

25.8.2.2.2* Density Adjustment.

N **(A)** The ceiling-level sprinkler design criteria in terms of density [gpm/ft^2 (mm/min)] and area of sprinkler operation [ft^2 (m^2) of ceiling or roof] obtained from the appropriate density/area curves of Figure 25.8.2.2.1(a) through Figure 25.8.2.2.1(d) shall be modified as appropriate by Figure 25.8.2.2.2(A) for storage height.

N **(B)** Paragraph 25.8.2.2.2(A) shall apply to portable racks arranged in the same manner as single-, double-, or multiple-row racks. *(See Section C.14.)*

N **25.8.2.2.2.3** Where in-rack sprinklers are being installed within racks of Class I through Class IV commodities stored over 12 ft (3.7 m) and up to and including 25 ft (7.6 m) in height protected with CMDA sprinklers at ceiling level along with the minimum number of required in-rack sprinkler levels, densities obtained from design curves shall be adjusted in accordance with Figure 25.8.2.2.2(A).

N **25.8.2.2.2.4** Where in-rack sprinklers are being installed within racks of Class I through Class IV commodities stored over 12 ft (3.7 m) and up to and including 25 ft (7.6 m) in height protected with CMDA sprinklers at ceiling level along with more than one level of in-rack sprinklers (not in every tier), densities obtained from design curves adjusted in accordance with Figure 25.8.2.2.2(A) shall be permitted to be reduced an additional 20 percent as indicated in Table 25.8.2.2.4.

N **25.8.2.2.2.5*** Where in-rack sprinklers are being installed within racks of Class I through Class IV commodities stored over 12 ft (3.7 m) and up to and including 25 ft (7.6 m) in height protected with CMDA sprinklers at ceiling level along with in-rack sprinklers at each tier level, densities obtained from design curves and adjusted in accordance with Figure 25.8.2.2.2(A) shall be permitted to be reduced an additional 40 percent as indicated in Table 25.8.2.2.4.

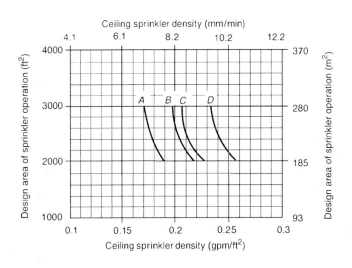

Curve   Legend

A — Single- or double-row racks with 8 ft (2.4 m) aisles with high-temperature ceiling sprinklers and ordinary-temperature in-rack sprinklers

B — Single- or double-row racks with 8 ft (2.4 m) aisles with ordinary-temperature ceiling sprinklers and ordinary-temperature in-rack sprinklers

C — Single- or double-row racks with 4 ft (1.2 m) aisles or multiple-row racks with high-temperature ceiling sprinklers and ordinary-temperature in-rack sprinklers

D — Single- or double-row racks with 4 ft (1.2 m) aisles or multiple-row racks with ordinary-temperature ceiling sprinklers and ordinary-temperature in-rack sprinklers

N **FIGURE 25.8.2.2.1(a)   CMDA Sprinkler System Design Curves — 20 ft (6.1 m) High Rack Storage — Exposed Nonencapsulated Class I Commodities — Conventional Pallets.**

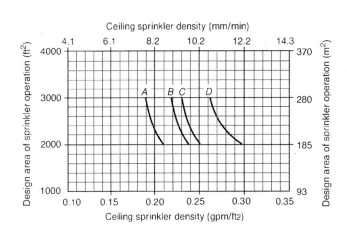

Curve   Legend

A — Single- or double-row racks with 8 ft (2.4 m) aisles with high-temperature ceiling sprinklers and ordinary-temperature in-rack sprinklers

B — Single- or double-row racks with 8 ft (2.4 m) aisles with ordinary-temperature ceiling sprinklers and ordinary-temperature in-rack sprinklers

C — Single- or double-row racks with 4 ft (1.2 m) aisles or multiple-row racks with high-temperature ceiling sprinklers and ordinary-temperature in-rack sprinklers

D — Single- or double-row racks with 4 ft (1.2 m) aisles or multiple-row racks with ordinary-temperature ceiling sprinklers and ordinary-temperature in-rack sprinklers

N **FIGURE 25.8.2.2.1(b)   CMDA Sprinkler System Design Curves — 20 ft (6.1 m) High Rack Storage — Exposed Nonencapsulated Class II Commodities — Conventional Pallets.**

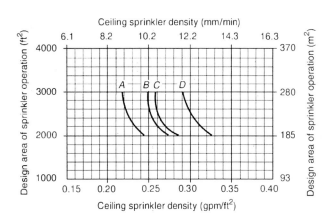

A — Single- or double-row racks with 8 ft (2.4 m) aisles with high-temperature ceiling sprinklers and ordinary-temperature in-rack sprinklers

B — Single- or double-row racks with 8 ft (2.4 m) aisles with ordinary-temperature ceiling sprinklers and ordinary-temperature in-rack sprinklers

C — Single- or double-row racks with 4 ft (1.2 m) aisles or multiple-row racks with high-temperature ceiling sprinklers and ordinary-temperature in-rack sprinklers

D — Single- or double-row racks with 4 ft (1.2 m) aisles or multiple-row racks with ordinary-temperature ceiling sprinklers and ordinary-temperature in-rack sprinklers

N FIGURE 25.8.2.2.1(c)   CMDA Sprinkler System Design Curves — 20 ft (6.1 m) High Rack Storage — Exposed Nonencapsulated Class III Commodities — Conventional Pallets.

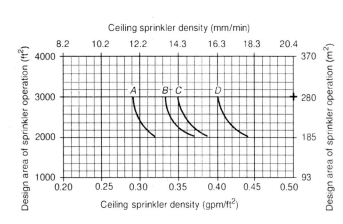

Curve   Legend

A — Single- or double-row racks with 8 ft (2.4 m) aisles with high-temperature ceiling sprinklers and ordinary-temperature in-rack sprinklers

B — Single- or double-row racks with 8 ft (2.4 m) aisles with ordinary-temperature ceiling sprinklers and ordinary-temperature in-rack sprinklers

C — Single- or double-row racks with 4 ft (1.2 m) aisles or multiple-row racks with high-temperature ceiling sprinklers and ordinary-temperature in-rack sprinklers

D — Single- or double-row racks with 4 ft (1.2 m) aisles or multiple-row racks with ordinary-temperature ceiling sprinklers and ordinary-temperature in-rack sprinklers

N FIGURE 25.8.2.2.1(d)   CMDA Sprinkler System Design Curves — 20 ft (6.1 m) High Rack Storage — Exposed Nonencapsulated Class IV Commodities — Conventional Pallets.

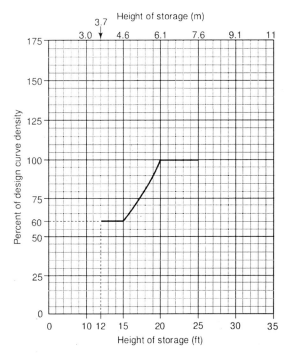

N **FIGURE 25.8.2.2.2.2(A) Allowable Adjustments to CMDA Ceiling-Level Sprinkler Densities Due to Storage Height Up to 25 ft (7.6 m).**

N **25.8.2.2.3 Excessive Clearance from Top of Storage.**

N **25.8.2.2.3.1** The ceiling-level sprinkler design obtained from the appropriate figure and curve specified in Table 25.8.2.2.1 shall be based on a maximum clearance from top of storage to ceiling of 20 ft (6.1 m).

N **25.8.2.2.3.2** Where the clearance of 25.8.2.2.3.1 exceeds 20 ft (6.1 m), one of the following two options shall be implemented:

(1) The ceiling design shall be determined from the appropriate figure and curve specified in Table 25.8.2.2.1 using a theoretical storage height that does not exceed 25 ft (7.6 m) and results in a clearance to ceiling of 20 ft (6.1 m).

(2) If not already provided, the in-rack sprinkler arrangement shall be supplemented with one level of quick-response in-rack sprinklers located directly below the top tier level of storage and at every flue space intersection.

N **25.8.3 Exposed Encapsulated or Cartoned (Nonencapsulated or Encapsulated) Class I, Class II, Class III, or Class IV Commodities Stored Up to and Including 25 ft (7.6 m) in Height.**

N **25.8.3.1* In-Rack Sprinkler Arrangements and Designs for Exposed Encapsulated or Cartoned (Nonencapsulated or Encapsulated) Class I, Class II, Class III, or Class IV Commodities Stored Up to and Including 25 ft (7.6 m) in Height.**

N **25.8.3.1.1** Where rack storage of exposed encapsulated or cartoned (nonencapsulated or encapsulated) Class I through Class IV commodities stored over 12 ft (3.7 m) and up to and including 25 ft (7.6 m) in height will be protected by in-rack sprinklers, the following levels of in-rack sprinklers shall be required:

(1) One level of in-rack sprinklers where Class I through Class IV commodities are stored in single- or double-row racks up to and including 25 ft (7.6 m)

(2) One level of in-rack sprinklers where Class IV commodities are stored in multiple-row racks up to and including 20 ft (6.1 m)

(3) Two levels of in-rack sprinklers where Class IV commodities are stored in multiple-row racks over 20 ft (6.1 m) and up to and including 25 ft (7.6 m)

N **25.8.3.1.2** Where rack storage of exposed encapsulated or cartoned (nonencapsulated or encapsulated) Class I or Class II commodities stored over 12 ft (3.7 m) and up to and including 25 ft (7.6 m) in height will be protected by in-rack sprinklers, in-rack sprinkler arrangements and designs shall be selected from Figure 25.8.3.1.2(a) through Figure 25.8.3.1.2(c). *(See Section 20.19 for racks with solid shelving.)*

N **25.8.3.1.3** Where rack storage of exposed encapsulated or cartoned (nonencapsulated or encapsulated) Class III commodities stored over 12 ft (3.7 m) and up to and including 25 ft (7.6 m) in height will be protected by in-rack sprinklers, in-rack sprinkler arrangements and designs shall be selected from 25.8.3.1.3(a) through 25.8.3.1.3(c). *(See Section 20.19 for racks with solid shelving.)*

N **25.8.3.1.4** Where rack storage of exposed encapsulated or cartoned (nonencapsulated or encapsulated) Class IV commodities stored over 12 ft (3.7 m) and up to and including 25 ft (7.6 m) in height in single- and double-row racks will be protected by in-rack sprinklers, in-rack sprinkler arrangements and designs shall be selected from Figure 25.8.3.1.4(a) through Figure 25.8.3.1.4(c). *(See Section 20.19 for racks with solid shelving.)*

N **25.8.3.1.5** Where rack storage of exposed encapsulated or cartoned (nonencapsulated or encapsulated) Class IV commodities stored over 12 ft (3.7 m) and up to and including 20 ft (6.1 m) in height in multiple-row racks will be protected by in-rack sprinklers, in-rack sprinkler arrangements and designs shall be selected from Figure 25.8.3.1.5(a) through Figure 25.8.3.1.5(c). *(See Section 20.19 for racks with solid shelving.)*

N **25.8.3.1.6** Where rack storage of exposed encapsulated or cartoned (nonencapsulated or encapsulated) Class IV commodities stored over 20 ft (6.1 m) and up to and including 25 ft (7.6 m) in height in multiple-row racks will be protected by in-rack sprinklers, in-rack sprinkler arrangements and designs shall be selected from Figure 25.8.3.1.6(a) or Figure 25.8.3.1.6(b). *(See Section 20.19 for racks with solid shelving.)*

N Table 25.8.2.2.2.4 Adjustment to Ceiling-Level Sprinkler Density Due to Storage Height and In-Rack Sprinklers

Storage Height	Apply Figure 25.8.2.2.2(A)?	In-Rack Sprinklers Levels Installed	Permitted Ceiling-Level Sprinkler Density Adjustment Due to In-Rack Sprinklers
Over 12 ft (3.7 m) and up to and including 20 ft (6.1 m)	Yes	Minimum required	None
		More than required but not at each tier level	Reduce density 20 percent from that indicated for minimum required levels of in-rack sprinklers
		Each tier level	Reduce density 40 percent from that indicated for minimum required levels of in-rack sprinklers
Over 20 ft (6.1 m) and up to and including 25 ft (7.6 m)	No	Minimum required	None
		More than required but not at each tier level	Reduce density 20 percent from that indicated for minimum required levels of in-rack sprinklers
		Each tier level	Reduce density 40 percent from that indicated for minimum required levels of in-rack sprinklers

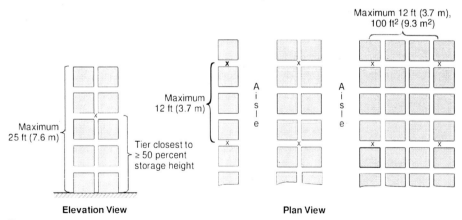

Notes:
(1) See 25.8.3.2 for the ceiling-level sprinkler design.
(2) In-rack sprinklers are ordinary-temperature-rated, quick- or standard-response, pendent or upright, minimum K-5.6 (K-80), and designed for a minimum of six (6) in-rack sprinklers operating at 22 gpm (83 L/min).
(3) The symbol X represents in-rack sprinklers.
(4) Each square represents a storage cube measuring 4 ft to 5 ft (1.2 m to 1.5 m) on a side.

N FIGURE 25.8.3.1.2(a) In-Rack Sprinkler Arrangements for Exposed Encapsulated or Cartoned (Nonencapsulated or Encapsulated) Class I or Class II Commodities Stored to a Maximum Height of 25 ft (7.6 m) with One Level of In-Rack Sprinklers.

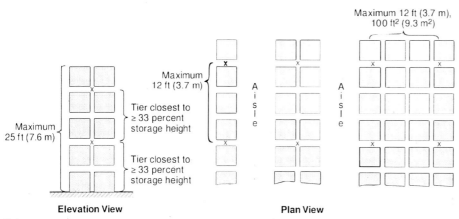

Notes:
(1) See 25.8.3.2 for the ceiling-level sprinkler design.
(2) In-rack sprinklers are ordinary-temperature-rated, quick- or standard-response, pendent or upright, minimum
    K-5.6 (K-80), and designed for a minimum of ten (10) in-rack sprinklers [five (5) in-rack sprinklers on two levels]
    operating at 22 gpm (83 L/min).
(3) The symbol X represents in-rack sprinklers.
(4) Each square represents a storage cube measuring 4 ft to 5 ft (1.2 m to 1.5 m) on a side.

N FIGURE 25.8.3.1.2(b)   In-Rack Sprinkler Arrangements for Exposed Encapsulated or Cartoned
(Nonencapsulated or Encapsulated) Class I or Class II Commodities Stored to a Maximum Height
of 25 ft (7.6 m) with More Than One Level of In-Rack Sprinklers (Not at Each Tier Level).

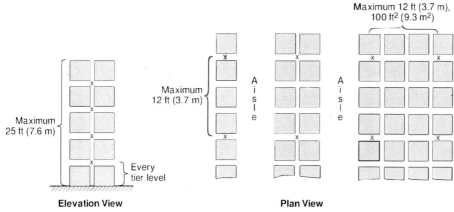

Notes:
(1) See 25.8.3.2 for the ceiling-level sprinkler design.
(2) In-rack sprinklers are ordinary-temperature-rated, quick- or standard-response, pendent or upright, minimum
    K-5.6 (K-80), and designed for a minimum of ten (10) in-rack sprinklers [five (5) in-rack sprinklers on two levels]
    operating at 22 gpm (83 L/min).
(3) The symbol X represents in-rack sprinklers.
(4) Each square represents a storage cube measuring 4 ft to 5 ft (1.2 m to 1.5 m) on a side.

N FIGURE 25.8.3.1.2(c)   In-Rack Sprinkler Arrangements for Exposed Encapsulated or Cartoned
(Nonencapsulated or Encapsulated) Class I or Class II Commodities Stored to a Maximum Height
of 25 ft (7.6 m) with In-Rack Sprinklers at Each Tier Level.

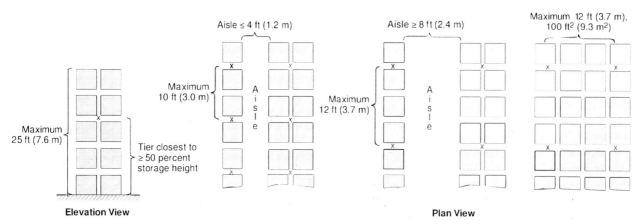

Elevation View   Plan View

Notes:
(1) See 25.8.3.2 for the ceiling-level sprinkler design.
(2) In-rack sprinklers are ordinary-temperature-rated, quick- or standard-response, pendent or upright, minimum K-5.6 (K-80), and designed for a minimum of six (6) in-rack sprinklers operating at 22 gpm (83 L/min).
(3) The symbol X represents in-rack sprinklers.
(4) Each square represents a storage cube measuring 4 ft to 5 ft (1.2 m to 1.5 m) on a side.

N FIGURE 25.8.3.1.3(a)   In-Rack Sprinkler Arrangements for Exposed Encapsulated or Cartoned (Nonencapsulated or Encapsulated) Class III Commodities Stored to a Maximum Height of 25 ft (7.6 m) with One Level of In-Rack Sprinklers.

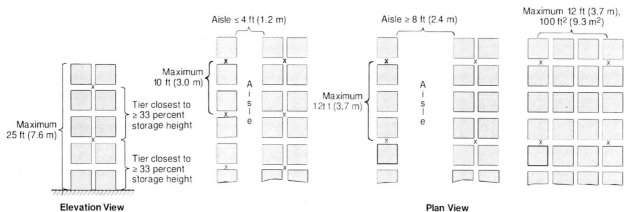

Elevation View   Plan View

Notes:
(1) See 25.8.3.2 for the ceiling-level sprinkler design.
(2) In-rack sprinklers are ordinary-temperature-rated, quick- or standard-response, pendent or upright, minimum K-5.6 (K-80), and designed for a minimum of ten (10) in-rack sprinklers [five (5) in-rack sprinklers on two levels] operating at 22 gpm (83 L/min).
(3) The symbol X represents in-rack sprinklers.
(4) Each square represents a storage cube measuring 4 ft to 5 ft (1.2 m to 1.5 m) on a side.

N FIGURE 25.8.3.1.3(b)   In-Rack Sprinkler Arrangements for Exposed Encapsulated or Cartoned (Nonencapsulated or Encapsulated) Class III Commodities Stored to a Maximum Height of 25 ft (7.6 m) with More Than One Level of In-Rack Sprinklers (Not at Each Tier Level).

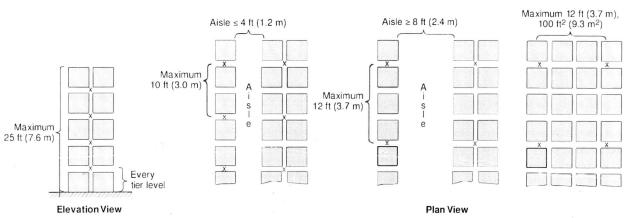

Notes:
(1) See 25.8.3.2 for the ceiling-level sprinkler design.
(2) In-rack sprinklers are ordinary-temperature-rated, quick- or standard-response, pendent or upright, minimum K-5.6 (K-80), and designed for a minimum of ten (10) in-rack sprinklers [five (5) in-rack sprinklers on two levels] operating at 22 gpm (83 L/min).
(3) The symbol X represents in-rack sprinklers.
(4) Each square represents a storage cube measuring 4 ft to 5 ft (1.2 m to 1.5 m) on a side.

N FIGURE 25.8.3.1.3(c)   In-Rack Sprinkler Arrangements for Exposed Encapsulated or Cartoned (Nonencapsulated or Encapsulated) Class III Commodities Stored to a Maximum Height of 25 ft (7.6 m) with In-Rack Sprinklers at Each Tier Level.

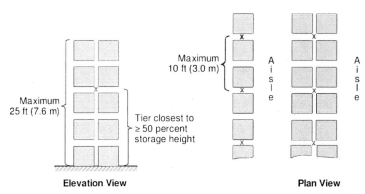

Notes:
(1) See 25.8.3.2 for the ceiling-level sprinkler design.
(2) In-rack sprinklers are ordinary-temperature-rated, quick- or standard-response, pendent or upright, minimum K-5.6 (K-80), and designed for a minimum of eight (8) in-rack sprinklers operating at 22 gpm (83 L/min).
(3) The symbol X represents in-rack sprinklers.
(4) Each square represents a storage cube measuring 4 ft to 5 ft (1.2 m to 1.5 m) on a side.

N FIGURE 25.8.3.1.4(a)   In-Rack Sprinkler Arrangements for Exposed Encapsulated or Cartoned (Nonencapsulated or Encapsulated) Class IV Commodities Stored to a Maximum Height of 25 ft (7.6 m) in Single- and Double-Row Racks with One Level of In-Rack Sprinklers.

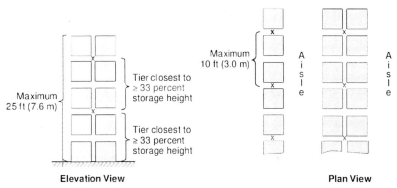

Notes:
(1) See 25.8.3.2 for the ceiling-level sprinkler design.
(2) In-rack sprinklers are ordinary-temperature-rated, quick- or standard-response, pendent or upright, minimum
    K-5.6 (K-80), and designed for a minimum of 14 in-rack [seven (7) in-rack sprinklers on top two levels]
    operating at 22 gpm (83 L/min).
(3) The symbol X represents in-rack sprinklers.
(4) Each square represents a storage cube measuring 4 ft to 5 ft (1.2 m to 1.5 m) on a side.

N **FIGURE 25.8.3.1.4(b)   In-Rack Sprinkler Arrangements for Exposed Encapsulated or Cartoned (Nonencapsulated or Encapsulated) Class IV Commodities Stored to a Maximum Height of 25 ft (7.6 m) in Single- and Double-Row Racks with More Than One Level of In-Rack Sprinklers (Not at Each Tier Level).**

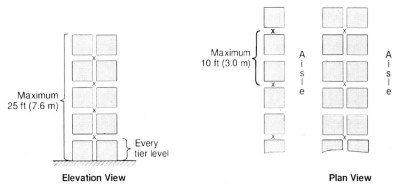

Notes:
(1) See 25.8.3.2 for the ceiling-level sprinkler design.
(2) In-rack sprinklers are ordinary-temperature-rated, quick- or standard-response, pendent or upright, minimum
    K-5.6 (K-80), and designed for a minimum of 14 in-rack [seven (7) in-rack sprinklers on top two levels]
    operating at 22 gpm (83 L/min).
(3) The symbol X represents in-rack sprinklers.
(4) Each square represents a storage cube measuring 4 ft to 5 ft (1.2 m to 1.5 m) on a side.

N **FIGURE 25.8.3.1.4(c)   In-Rack Sprinkler Arrangements for Exposed Encapsulated or Cartoned (Nonencapsulated or Encapsulated) Class IV Commodities Stored to a Maximum Height of 25 ft (7.6 m) in Single- and Double-Row Racks with In-Rack Sprinklers at Each Tier Level.**

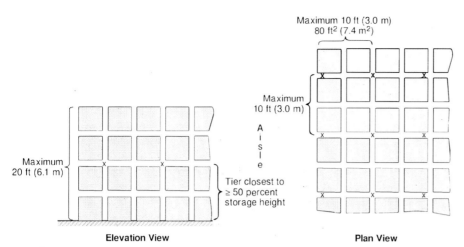

Notes:
(1) See 25.8.3.2 for the ceiling-level sprinkler design.
(2) In-rack sprinklers are ordinary-temperature-rated, quick- or standard-response, pendent or upright, minimum K-5.6 (K-80), and designed for a minimum of eight in-rack sprinklers operating at 22 gpm (83 L/min).
(3) The symbol X represents in-rack sprinklers.
(4) Each square represents a storage cube measuring 4 ft to 5 ft (1.2 m to 1.5 m) on a side.

N **FIGURE 25.8.3.1.5(a)   In-Rack Sprinkler Arrangements for Exposed Encapsulated or Cartoned (Nonencapsulated or Encapsulated) Class IV Commodities Stored to a Maximum Height of 20 ft (6.1 m) in Multiple-Row Racks with One Level of In-Rack Sprinklers.**

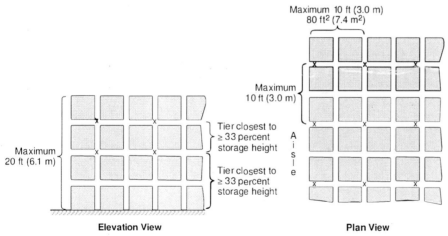

Notes:
(1) See 25.8.3.2 for the ceiling-level sprinkler design.
(2) In-rack sprinklers are ordinary-temperature-rated, quick- or standard-response, pendent or upright, minimum K-5.6 (K-80), and designed for a minimum of 14 in-rack sprinklers [seven (7) in-rack sprinklers on top two levels] operating at 22 gpm (83 L/min).
(3) The symbol X represents in-rack sprinklers.
(4) Each square represents a storage cube measuring 4 ft to 5 ft (1.2 m to 1.5 m) on a side.

N **FIGURE 25.8.3.1.5(b)   In-Rack Sprinkler Arrangements for Exposed Encapsulated or Cartoned (Nonencapsulated or Encapsulated) Class IV Commodities Stored to a Maximum Height of 20 ft (6.1 m) in Multiple-Row Racks with More Than One Level of In-Rack Sprinklers.**

Shaded text = Revisions.   Δ = Text deletions and figure/table revisions.   • = Section deletions.   *N* = New material.

2022 Edition

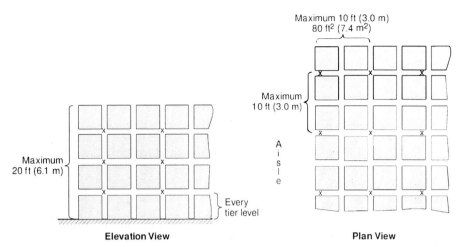

Notes:
(1) See 25.8.3.2 for the ceiling-level sprinkler design.
(2) In-rack sprinklers are ordinary-temperature-rated, quick- or standard-response, pendent or upright, minimum K-5.6 (K-80), and designed for a minimum of 14 in-rack sprinklers [seven (7) in-rack sprinklers on top two levels] operating at 22 gpm (83 L/min).
(3) The symbol X represents in-rack sprinklers.
(4) Each square represents a storage cube measuring 4 ft to 5 ft (1.2 m to 1.5 m) on a side.

N FIGURE 25.8.3.1.5(c) In-Rack Sprinkler Arrangements for Exposed Encapsulated or Cartoned (Nonencapsulated or Encapsulated) Class IV Commodities Stored to a Maximum Height of 20 ft (6.1 m) in Multiple-Row Racks with In-Rack Sprinklers at Each Tier Level.

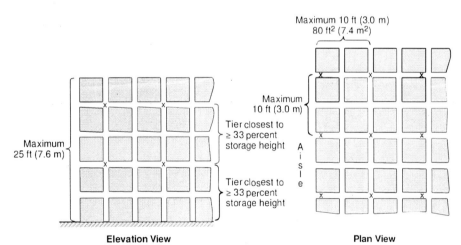

Notes:
(1) See 25.8.3.2 for the ceiling-level sprinkler design.
(2) In-rack sprinklers are ordinary-temperature-rated, quick- or standard-response, pendent or upright, minimum K-5.6 (K-80), and designed for a minimum of 14 in-rack sprinklers [seven (7) in-rack sprinklers on top two levels] operating at 22 gpm (83 L/min).
(3) The symbol X represents in-rack sprinklers.
(4) Each square represents a storage cube measuring 4 ft to 5 ft (1.2 m to 1.5 m) on a side.

N FIGURE 25.8.3.1.6(a) In-Rack Sprinkler Arrangements for Exposed Encapsulated or Cartoned (Nonencapsulated or Encapsulated) Class IV Commodities Stored Over 20 ft (6.1 m) and Up to a Maximum Height of 25 ft (7.6 m) in Multiple-Row Racks with Two Levels of In-Rack Sprinklers.

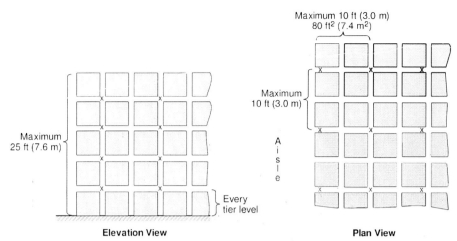

Elevation View   **Plan View**

Notes:
(1) See 25.8.3.2 for the ceiling-level sprinkler design.
(2) In-rack sprinklers are ordinary-temperature-rated, quick- or standard-response, pendent or upright, minimum K-5.6 (K-80), and designed for a minimum of 14 in-rack sprinklers [seven (7) in-rack sprinklers on top two levels] operating at 22 gpm (83 L/min).
(3) The symbol X represents in-rack sprinklers.
(4) Each square represents a storage cube measuring 4 ft to 5 ft (1.2 m to 1.5 m) on a side.

N **FIGURE 25.8.3.1.6(b)** **In-Rack Sprinkler Arrangements for Exposed Encapsulated or Cartoned (Nonencapsulated or Encapsulated) Class IV Commodities Stored Over 20 ft (6.1 m) and Up to a Maximum Height of 25 ft (7.6 m) in Multiple-Row Racks with In-Rack Sprinklers at Each Tier Level.**

N **25.8.3.2 CMDA Ceiling-Level Sprinkler Designs for Exposed Encapsulated or Cartoned (Nonencapsulated or Encapsulated) Class I, Class II, Class III, or Class IV Commodities Stored Up to and Including 25 ft (7.6 m) in Height in Combination with In-Rack Sprinklers.**

N **25.8.3.2.1*** For single-, double-, and multiple-row rack storage of exposed encapsulated or cartoned (nonencapsulated or encapsulated) Class I through Class IV commodities stored over 12 ft (3.7 m) and up to and including 25 ft (7.6 m) in height, the ceiling-level sprinkler design in terms of density [gpm/ft^2 (mm/min)] over an area of ceiling-level sprinkler operation [ft^2 (186 m^2)], with the provision of in-rack sprinklers, shall be determined from Table 25.8.3.2.1 and Figure 25.8.3.2.1(a) through Figure 25.8.3.2.1(g).

N **25.8.3.2.2* Ceiling-Level Sprinkler Density Adjustments.**

N **25.8.3.2.2.1*** Design densities obtained from the appropriate figure and curve specified in Table 25.8.3.2.1 for single- and double-row racks shall be selected to correspond to aisle width as follows *(see Section C.15.)*:

(1) The density given for 8 ft (2.4 m) wide aisles shall be applied to aisles wider than 8 ft (2.4 m).
(2) For aisle widths between 4 ft (1.2 m) and 8 ft (2.4 m), the rules for 4 ft (1.2 m) aisle width shall be used, or direct linear interpolation between the densities shall be permitted.
(3) The density given for 4 ft (1.2 m) wide aisles shall be applied to aisles narrower than 4 ft (1.2 m) down to 3½ ft (1.1 m).
(4) Where aisles are narrower than 3½ ft (1.1 m), racks shall be considered to be multiple-row racks.

N **25.8.3.2.2.2***

N **(A)** The ceiling-level sprinkler design criteria in terms of density [gpm/ft^2 (mm/min)] and area of sprinkler operation [ft^2 (m^2) of ceiling or roof] obtained from the appropriate density/area curves of Figure 25.8.3.2.1(a) through Figure 25.8.3.2.1(d) shall be modified as appropriate by Figure 25.8.3.2.2.2(A) for storage height.

N **(B)** Paragraph 25.8.3.2.2.2(A) shall apply to portable racks arranged in the same manner as single-, double- or multiple-row racks. *(See Section C.14.)*

N **25.8.3.2.2.3** Where in-rack sprinklers are being installed within racks of Class I through Class IV commodities stored over 12 ft (3.7 m) up to and including 25 ft (7.6 m) in height protected with CMDA sprinklers at ceiling level along with the minimum number of required in-rack sprinkler levels, densities obtained from design curves shall be adjusted in accordance with Figure 25.8.3.2.2.2(A) and then be multiplied by the density multiplier indicated in Table 25.8.3.2.1.

N **25.8.3.2.2.4** Where in-rack sprinklers are being installed within racks of Class I through Class IV commodities stored over 12 ft (3.7 m) and up to and including 25 ft (7.6 m) in height protected with CMDA sprinklers at ceiling level along with more than one level of in-rack sprinklers (not in every tier), densities obtained from design curves adjusted in accordance with Figure 25.8.3.2.2.2(A) and then multiplied by the density multiplier indicated in Table 25.8.3.2.1 shall be permitted to be reduced an additional 20 percent as indicated in Table 25.8.3.2.2.4.

N Table 25.8.3.2.1 Determining Appropriate Ceiling-Level Protection Criteria Figure and Curve for Rack Storage of Exposed Encapsulated or Cartoned (Nonencapsulated or Encapsulated) Class I Through Class IV Commodities Stored Over 12 ft (3.7 m) and Up to and Including 25 ft (7.6 m)

Commodity	Maximum Storage Height	Storage Arrangement	Aisle Width ft (m)	Minimum No. of In-Rack Sprinkler Levels Required	Figure	Ceiling Sprinkler Temperature Rating High	Ordinary or Intermediate	Density Multiplier
Class I	Over 12 ft (3.7 m) and up to and including 25 ft (7.6 m)	Single- and double-row racks	8 (2.4)	1 level	25.8.3.2.1(e)	A	B	1.0
			4 (1.2)			C	D	
		Multiple-row racks	Any		25.8.3.2.1(a)	C	D	1.25
Class II	Over 12 ft (3.7 m) and up to and including 25 ft (7.6 m)	Single- and double-row racks	8 (2.4)	1 level	25.8.3.2.1(e)	A	B	1.0
			4 (1.2)			C	D	
		Multiple-row racks	Any		25.8.3.2.1(b)	C	D	1.25
Class III	Over 12 ft (3.7 m) and up to and including 25 ft (7.6 m)	Single- and double-row racks	8 (2.4)	1 level	25.8.3.2.1(f)	A	B	1.0
			4 (1.2)			C	D	
		Multiple-row racks	Any		25.8.3.2.1(c)	C	D	1.25
Class IV	Over 12 ft (3.7 m) and up to and including 20 ft (6.1 m)	Single- and double-row racks	8 (2.4)	1 level	25.8.3.2.1(g)	A	B	1.0
			4 (1.2)			C	D	
		Multiple-row racks	Any		25.8.3.2.1(d)	A	B	1.5
	Over 20 ft (6.1 m) and up to and including 25 ft (7.6 m)	Single- and double-row racks	8 (2.4)	1 level	25.8.3.2.1(g)	A	B	1.0
			4 (1.2)			C	D	
		Multiple-row racks	Any	2 levels	25.8.3.2.1(d)	A	B	1.5

N **25.8.3.2.2.5*** Where in-rack sprinklers are being installed within racks of Class I through Class IV commodities stored over 12 ft (3.7 m) and up to and including 25 ft (7.6 m) in height protected with CMDA sprinklers at ceiling level along with in-rack sprinklers at each tier level, densities obtained from design curves and adjusted in accordance with Figure 25.8.3.2.2.2(A) shall be permitted to be reduced an additional 40 percent as indicated in Table 25.8.3.2.2.4.

N **25.8.3.2.3 Excessive Clearance from Top of Storage.**

N **25.8.3.2.3.1** The ceiling-level sprinkler design obtained from the appropriate figure and curve specified in Table 25.8.3.2.1 shall be based on a maximum clearance from top of storage to ceiling of 20 ft (6.1 m).

N **25.8.3.2.3.2** Where the clearance of 25.8.3.2.3.1 exceeds 20 ft (6.1 m), one of the following two options shall be implemented:

(1) The ceiling design shall be determined from the appropriate figure and curve specified in Table 25.8.3.2.1 using a theoretical storage height that does not exceed 25 ft (7.6 m) and results in a clearance to ceiling of 20 ft (6.1 m).

(2) If not already provided, the in-rack sprinkler arrangement shall be supplemented with one level of quick-response in-rack sprinklers located directly below the top tier level of storage and at every flue space intersection.

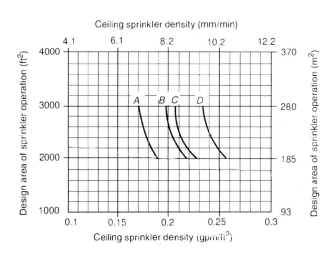

Curve   Legend

A — Single- or double-row racks with 8 ft (2.4 m) aisles with high-temperature ceiling sprinklers and ordinary-temperature in-rack sprinklers

B — Single- or double-row racks with 8 ft (2.4 m) aisles with ordinary-temperature ceiling sprinklers and ordinary-temperature in-rack sprinklers

C — Single- or double-row racks with 4 ft (1.2 m) aisles or multiple-row racks with high-temperature ceiling sprinklers and ordinary-temperature in-rack sprinklers

D — Single- or double-row racks with 4 ft (1.2 m) aisles or multiple-row racks with ordinary-temperature ceiling sprinklers and ordinary-temperature in-rack sprinklers

N FIGURE 25.8.3.2.1(a)   CMDA Sprinkler System Design Curves — 20 ft (6.1 m) High Rack Storage — Exposed Encapsulated or Cartoned (Nonencapsulated or Encapsulated) Class I Commodities in Multiple-Row Racks — Conventional Pallets.

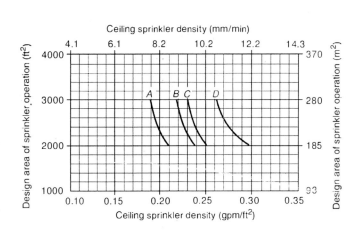

Curve   Legend

A — Single- or double-row racks with 8 ft (2.4 m) aisles with high-temperature ceiling sprinklers and ordinary-temperature in-rack sprinklers

B — Single- or double-row racks with 8 ft (2.4 m) aisles with ordinary-temperature ceiling sprinklers and ordinary-temperature in-rack sprinklers

C — Single- or double-row racks with 4 ft (1.2 m) aisles or multiple-row racks with high-temperature ceiling sprinklers and ordinary-temperature in-rack sprinklers

D — Single- or double-row racks with 4 ft (1.2 m) aisles or multiple-row racks with ordinary-temperature ceiling sprinklers and ordinary-temperature in-rack sprinklers

N FIGURE 25.8.3.2.1(b)   CMDA Sprinkler System Design Curves — 20 ft (6.1 m) High Rack Storage — Exposed Encapsulated or Cartoned (Nonencapsulated or Encapsulated) Class II Commodities in Multiple-Row Racks — Conventional Pallets.

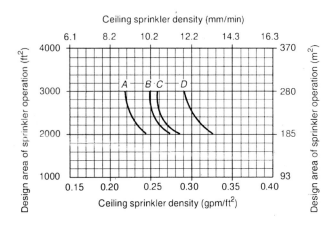

Curve   Legend

A — Single- or double-row racks with 8 ft (2.4 m) aisles with high-temperature ceiling sprinklers and ordinary-temperature in-rack sprinklers

B — Single- or double-row racks with 8 ft (2.4 m) aisles with ordinary-temperature ceiling sprinklers and ordinary-temperature in-rack sprinklers

C — Single- or double-row racks with 4 ft (1.2 m) aisles or multiple-row racks with high-temperature ceiling sprinklers and ordinary-temperature in-rack sprinklers

D — Single- or double-row racks with 4 ft (1.2 m) aisles or multiple-row racks with ordinary-temperature ceiling sprinklers and ordinary-temperature in-rack sprinklers

N   **FIGURE 25.8.3.2.1(c)   CMDA Sprinkler System Design Curves — 20 ft (6.1 m) High Rack Storage — Exposed Encapsulated or Cartoned (Nonencapsulated or Encapsulated) Class III Commodities in Multiple-Row Racks — Conventional Pallets.**

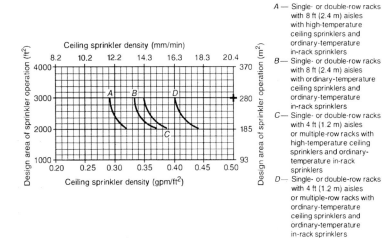

Curve   Legend

A — Single- or double-row racks with 8 ft (2.4 m) aisles with high-temperature ceiling sprinklers and ordinary-temperature in-rack sprinklers

B — Single- or double-row racks with 8 ft (2.4 m) aisles with ordinary-temperature ceiling sprinklers and ordinary-temperature in-rack sprinklers

C — Single- or double-row racks with 4 ft (1.2 m) aisles or multiple-row racks with high-temperature ceiling sprinklers and ordinary-temperature in-rack sprinklers

D — Single- or double-row racks with 4 ft (1.2 m) aisles or multiple-row racks with ordinary-temperature ceiling sprinklers and ordinary-temperature in-rack sprinklers

N   **FIGURE 25.8.3.2.1(d)   CMDA Sprinkler System Design Curves — 20 ft (6.1 m) High Rack Storage — Exposed Encapsulated or Cartoned (Nonencapsulated or Encapsulated) Class IV Commodities in Multiple-Row Racks — Conventional Pallets.**

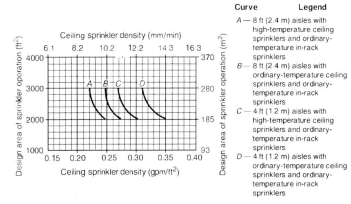

N FIGURE 25.8.3.2.1(e)   CMDA Sprinkler System Design Curves — Single- or Double-Row Racks — 20 ft (6.1 m) High Rack Storage — Exposed Encapsulated or Cartoned (Nonencapsulated or Encapsulated) Class I and Class II Commodities — Conventional Pallets.

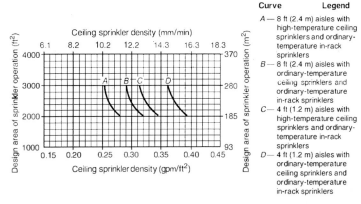

N FIGURE 25.8.3.2.1(f)   CMDA Sprinkler System Design Curves — Single- or Double-Row Racks — 20 ft (6.1 m) High Rack Storage — Exposed Encapsulated or Cartoned (Nonencapsulated or Encapsulated) Class III Commodities — Conventional Pallets.

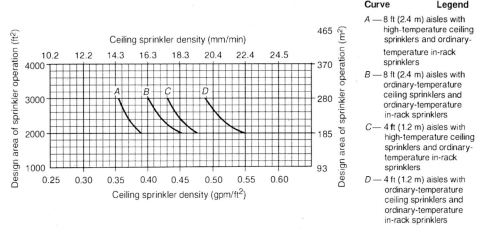

N FIGURE 25.8.3.2.1(g)   CMDA Sprinkler System Design Curves — Single- or Double-Row Racks — 20 ft (6.1 m) High Rack Storage — Exposed Encapsulated or Cartoned (Nonencapsulated or Encapsulated) Class IV Commodities — Conventional Pallets.

Shaded text = Revisions.   Δ = Text deletions and figure/table revisions.   • = Section deletions.   N = New material.

2022 Edition

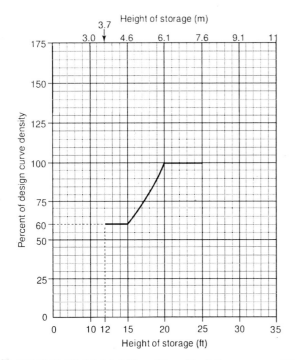

N FIGURE 25.8.3.2.2.2(A)   Allowable Adjustments to CMDA Ceiling-Level Sprinkler Densities Due to Storage Height Up to 25 ft (7.6 m).

N Table 25.8.3.2.2.4 Adjustment to Ceiling-Level Sprinkler Density Due to Storage Height and In-Rack Sprinklers

Storage Height	Apply Figure 25.8.3.2.2.2(A)?	In-Rack Sprinklers Levels Installed	Permitted Ceiling-Level Sprinkler Density Adjustment Due to In-Rack Sprinklers
Over 12 ft (3.7 m) and up to and including 20 ft (6.1 m)	Yes	Minimum required	None
		More than required but not at each tier level	Reduce density 20 percent from that indicated for minimum required levels of in-rack sprinklers
		Each tier level	Reduce density 40 percent from that indicated for minimum required levels of in-rack sprinklers
Over 20 (6.1) and up to and including 25 (7.6)	No	Minimum required	None
		More than required but not at each tier level	Reduce density 20 percent from that indicated for minimum required levels of in-rack sprinklers
		Each tier level	Reduce density 40 percent from that indicated for minimum required levels of in-rack sprinklers

N **Chapter 26 Special Designs of Storage Protection**

N **26.1* General.**

N **26.1.1*** This chapter shall cover special sprinkler system designs for storage protection.

N **26.1.2** The requirements of Chapter 20 shall apply unless modified by this chapter.

N **26.2 Plastic Motor Vehicle Components.** Group A plastic automotive components and associated packaging material shall be permitted to be protected in accordance with Table 26.2.

N **26.3* Sprinkler Design Criteria for Storage and Display of Class I Through Class IV Commodities, Cartoned Nonexpanded Group A Plastics, and Nonexpanded Exposed Group A Plastics in Retail Stores.**

N **26.3.1** A wet pipe system designed to meet two separate design points — 0.6 gpm/ft² (24.5 mm/min) density over 2000 ft² (185 m²) and 0.7 gpm/ft² (28.6 mm/min) density for the four hydraulically most demanding sprinklers with 500 gpm (1900 L/min) hose stream allowance for a 2-hour duration — shall be permitted to protect single- and double-row slatted shelf racks when the following conditions are met:

(1) An extended coverage sprinkler with a nominal K-factor of K-25.2 (360) listed for storage occupancies shall be provided.
(2) Shelves shall be either open shelving or slatted using a 2 in. (50 mm) thick by maximum 6 in. (150 mm) wide slat held in place by spacers that maintain a minimum 2 in. (50 mm) opening between each slat.
(3) There shall be no slatted shelf levels in the rack above nominal 12 ft (3.7 m) level. Wire mesh (greater than 50 percent opening) shall be permitted for shelf levels above 12 ft (3.7 m).
(4) A single level of solid shelving 3½ ft × 8 ft 3 in. (1.1 m × 2.5 m) shall be permissible at an elevation of not more than 5 ft (1.5 m).
(5) Perforated metal (open area of 40 percent or more) shall be permitted over either the open shelving or the slatted shelves up to the 5 ft (1.5 m) level.
(6) Other than what is allowed in this section, solid plywood or similar materials shall not be placed on the slatted shelves.
(7) Solid displays shall be permissible provided that all flues are maintained and only one display is installed per bay.

(8) Maximum roof height shall be 30 ft (9.1 m) in the protected area.
(9) Maximum storage height shall be 22 ft (6.7 m).
(10) Aisle widths shall be a minimum of 8 ft (2.4 m).
(11) Minimum transverse flue spaces of 3 in. every 10 ft (75 mm every 3.0 m) horizontally shall be provided.
(12) Minimum longitudinal flue spaces of 6 in. (150 mm) shall be provided for double-row racks.
(13) Storage in the aisle shall be permissible provided the aisle storage is no more than 4 ft (1.2 m) high and a minimum clear aisle of 4 ft (1.2 m) is maintained.

N **26.3.2** A wet pipe system designed to meet two separate design points — 0.425 gpm/ft² (17.3 mm/min) density over 2000 ft² (185 m²) and 0.50 gpm/ft² (20.4 mm/min) density for the four hydraulically most demanding sprinklers with 500 gpm (1900 L/min) hose stream allowance for a 2-hour duration — shall be permitted in solid steel cantilever-style retail shelving racks (gondola racks) when the following conditions are met:

(1) An extended coverage sprinkler with a nominal K-factor of K-25.2 (360) listed for storage occupancies shall be provided.
(2) Storage height shall not exceed 12 ft (3.7 m).
(3) Ceiling height shall not exceed 22 ft (6.7 m) in the protected area.
(4) Gondola rack structure shall not exceed 48 in. (1.2 m) in aggregate depth or 78 in. (1.9 m) in height.
(5) A minimum aisle of 5 ft (1.5 m) between storage shall be maintained.
(6) Rack lengths shall be no more than 70 ft (21 m).

N **26.3.3** A wet pipe system designed to meet two separate design points — 0.425 gpm/ft² (17.3 mm/min) density over 2000 ft² (185 m²) and 0.50 gpm/ft² (20.4 mm/min) density for the four hydraulically most demanding sprinklers with 500 gpm (1900 L/min) hose stream allowance for a 2-hour duration — shall be permitted in solid steel cantilever-style retail shelving racks (gondola racks) when the following conditions are met:

(1) An extended coverage sprinkler with a nominal K-factor of K-25.2 (360) listed for storage occupancies shall be provided.
(2) Storage height shall not exceed 15 ft (4.6 m).
(3) Ceiling height shall not exceed 25 ft (7.6 m) in the protected area.
(4) Gondola rack structure shall not exceed 60 in. (1.5 m) in aggregate depth or 8 ft (2.4 m) in height.

N **Table 26.2 ESFR Sprinkler Design Criteria K-25.2 (360) for Portable Racks (Closed Array) Without Solid Shelves Containing Automotive Components and Associated Packaging Material**

Maximum Storage Height		Maximum Ceiling/Roof Height		Type of System	Maximum Sprinkler Spacing[a]		Number of Design Sprinklers by Minimum Operating Pressure[b,c]		Maximum Deflector Distance Below Ceiling[d]		Hose Stream Allowance		Water Supply Duration (hours)
ft	m	ft	m		ft²	m²	psi	bar	in.	mm	gpm	L/min	
25	7.6	35	10.7	Wet	100	9.3	16 at 37 psi	16 at 2.5 bar	18	450	500	1900	2

Note: Closed array means the portable rack array is tightly nested without any flue spaces.

[a]Sprinkler spacing can exceed 100 ft² (9.3 m²) where sprinklers are listed for larger spacing.

[b]System hydraulic design is also capable of delivering a discharge density of 0.60 gpm/ft² (24.4 mm/min) over the most hydraulically remote 4000 ft² (370 m²) area.

[c]The design area consists of the hydraulically most demanding 16 sprinklers with five sprinklers on three branch lines and one sprinkler on the fourth branch line.

[d]Maximum deflector distance below ceiling is permitted to exceed 18 in. (450 mm) where sprinklers are listed for greater distances.

(5) A perforated metal deck at the 8 ft (2.4 m) level shall be permissible with storage placed on top with or without flue spaces to a maximum height from floor of 15 ft (4.6 m).

(6) Rack lengths shall not exceed 70 ft (21 m).

(7) A minimum aisle space of 6 ft (1.8 m) shall be provided.

N **26.3.4** A wet pipe system designed to meet two separate design points — 0.45 gpm/ft² (18.4 mm/min) density over 2000 ft² (185 m²) and 0.55 gpm/ft² (22.4 mm/min) density for the four hydraulically most demanding sprinklers with 500 gpm (1900 L/min) hose stream allowance for a 2-hour duration — shall be permitted without the use of in-rack sprinklers when the following conditions are met:

(1) An extended coverage sprinkler with a nominal K-factor of K-25.2 (360) listed for storage occupancies shall be provided.

(2) Storage height shall not exceed 15 ft (4.6 m).

(3) Ceiling height shall not exceed 25 ft (7.6 m).

(4) Shelving structure shall not exceed 48 in. (1.2 m) aggregate depth or 12 ft (3.7 m) in height.

(5) Shelving shall be permitted to be made of solid particleboard.

(6) A minimum aisle space of 3 ft (900 mm) shall be maintained.

(7) Shelving length shall be a maximum of 70 ft (21 m).

N **26.3.5** A wet pipe system designed to meet two separate design points — 0.38 gpm/ft² (15.5 mm/min) density over 2000 ft² (185 m²) and 0.45 gpm/ft² (18.4 mm/min) density for the four hydraulically most demanding sprinklers with 500 gpm (1900 L/min) hose stream allowance for a 2-hour duration — shall be permitted without the use of in-rack sprinklers in steel retail sales floor shelving racks where the following conditions are met:

(1) An extended coverage sprinkler with a nominal K-factor of K-25.2 (360) listed for storage occupancies shall be provided.

(2) Storage height shall not exceed 14 ft (4.3 m).

(3) Ceiling height shall not exceed 20 ft (6.1 m).

(4) Solid metal shelving shall be permissible up to the 72 in. (1.8 m) level and wire shelving shall be permissible up to the 10 ft (3.0 m) level.

(5) Solid metal shelving shall not exceed 66 in. (1.7 m) in aggregate depth with a 6 in. (150 mm) longitudinal flue between two 30 in. (750 mm) deep shelves.

(6) A minimum aisle space of 5 ft (1.5 m) shall be maintained.

(7) A minimum longitudinal flue of 6 in. (150 mm) shall be maintained.

(8) Rack length shall be a maximum of 70 ft (21 m).

N **26.3.6** A wet pipe system designed to meet two separate design points — 0.49 gpm/ft² (20 mm/min) density over 2000 ft² (185 m²) and 0.55 gpm/ft² (22.4 mm/min) density for the four hydraulically most demanding sprinklers with 500 gpm (1900 L/min) hose stream allowance for a 2-hour duration — shall be permitted without the use of in-rack sprinklers in retail solid shelved steel rack structures when the following conditions are met:

(1) An extended coverage sprinkler with a nominal K-factor of K-25.2 (360) listed for storage occupancies shall be provided.

(2) Storage height shall not exceed 16.5 ft (5.0 m).

(3) Ceiling height shall not exceed 22 ft (6.7 m).

(4) Shelving structure shall not exceed 51 in. (1.3 m) aggregate depth or 148 in. (3.7 m) in height.

(5) The intersection of perpendicular steel racks shall be permissible as long as no storage is placed within the void space at the junction of the racks.

(6) The top shelf shall be wire mesh.

(7) A minimum aisle width of 4 ft (1.2 m) shall be maintained between shelf units and other displays.

N **26.3.7** A sprinkler system with K-25.2 (360) ESFR sprinklers operating at a minimum pressure of 15 psi (1 bar) shall be permitted to protect single- and double-row racks with solid displays without the use of in-rack sprinklers in retail sales floors where the following conditions are met:

(1) Storage height shall not exceed 20 ft (6.1 m).

(2) Solid veneered particleboard/plywood displays shall be permissible, provided that all flues are maintained and only one display is installed per bay.

(3) A single display shall be permitted to have one or two solid horizontal or slanted members and a solid back.

(4) Maximum roof height shall be 30 ft (9.1 m) in the protected area.

(5) Aisle widths shall be a minimum of 6 ft (1.8 m).

(6) Minimum transverse flue spaces of 3 in. every 10 ft (75 mm every 3.0 m) horizontally shall be provided.

(7) Minimum longitudinal flue spaces of 6 in. (150 mm) shall be provided for double-row racks.

N **26.4 Special Design for Rack Storage of Class I Through Class IV Commodities and Group A Plastics Stored Up to and Including 20 ft (6.1 m) in Height.**

N **26.4.1 Slatted Shelves.**

N **26.4.1.1** Slatted rack shelves shall be considered equivalent to solid rack shelves where the shelving is not considered open rack shelving or where the requirements of 26.4.1.2 or 26.4.1.3 are not met.

N **26.4.1.2*** A wet pipe system that is designed to provide a minimum of 0.6 gpm/ft² (24.5 mm/min) density over a minimum area of 2000 ft² (185 m²) shall be permitted to protect single- and double-row racks with slatted rack shelving where all of the following conditions are met *(see Section C.20)*:

(1) Sprinklers shall be K-11.2 (160), K-14.0 (200), or K-16.8 (240) orifice spray sprinklers with a temperature rating of ordinary, intermediate, or high and shall be listed for storage occupancies.

(2) The protected commodities shall be limited to Class I through Class IV, Group B plastics, Group C plastics, cartoned (expanded and nonexpanded) Group A plastics, and exposed (nonexpanded) Group A plastics.

(3) Slats in slatted rack shelving shall be a minimum nominal 2 in. (50 mm) thick by maximum nominal 6 in. (150 mm) wide, with the slats held in place by spacers that maintain a minimum 2 in. (50 mm) opening between each slat.

(4) There shall be no slatted shelf levels in the rack above 12 ft (3.7 m) and open rack shelving using wire mesh shall be permitted for shelf levels above 12 ft (3.7 m).

(5) Transverse flue spaces at least 3 in. (75 mm) wide shall be provided at least every 10 ft (3.0 m) horizontally.

(6) Longitudinal flue spaces at least 6 in. (150 mm) wide shall be provided for double-row racks.

(7) The aisle widths shall be at least 7½ ft (2.3 m).

(8) The maximum roof height shall be 27 ft (8.2 m).

(9) The maximum storage height shall be 20 ft (6.1 m).

(10) Solid plywood or similar materials shall not be placed on the slatted shelves so that they block the 2 in. (50 mm) spaces between slats, nor shall they be placed on wire mesh shelves.

N **26.4.1.3** A wet pipe system that is designed to provide K-14.0 (200) ESFR sprinklers operating at a minimum of 50 psi (3.4 bar), K-16.8 (240) ESFR sprinklers operating at a minimum of 32 psi (2.2 bar), or K-25.2 (360) ESFR sprinklers operating at a minimum of 15 psi (1.0 bar) shall be permitted to protect single- and double-row racks with slatted rack shelving where all of the following conditions are met:

(1) The protected commodities shall be limited to Class I through Class IV, Group B plastics, Group C plastics, cartoned (expanded and nonexpanded) Group A plastics, and exposed (nonexpanded) Group A plastics.

(2) Slats in slatted rack shelving shall be a minimum nominal 2 in. (50 mm) thick by maximum nominal 6 in. (150 mm) wide with the slats held in place by spacers that maintain a minimum 2 in. (50 mm) opening between each slat.

(3) Longitudinal flue spaces shall not be required.

(4) Transverse flue spaces at least 3 in. (75 mm) wide shall be provided at least every 10 ft (3.0 m) horizontally.

(5) The aisle widths shall be at least 7½ ft (2.3 m).

(6) The maximum roof height shall be 30 ft (9.1 m).

(7) The maximum storage height shall be 20 ft (6.1 m).

(8) Solid plywood or similar materials shall not be placed on the slatted shelves so that they block the 2 in. (50 mm) spaces between slats, nor shall they be placed on the wire mesh shelves.

N **26.5* Control Mode Density/Area Sprinkler Protection Criteria for Baled Cotton Storage.**

N **26.5.1** For tiered or rack storage up to a nominal 15 ft (4.6 m) in height, sprinkler discharge densities and areas of application shall be in accordance with Table 26.5.1.

N **26.5.2** Where roof or ceiling heights would prohibit storage above a nominal 10 ft (3.0 m), the sprinkler discharge density shall be permitted to be reduced by 20 percent of that indicated in Table 26.5.1 but shall not be reduced to less than 0.15 gpm/ft² (6.1 mm/min).

N **26.6 Control Mode Density/Area Sprinkler Protection Criteria for Cartoned Records Storage with Catwalk Access.**

N **26.6.1** Cartoned records storage shall be permitted to be protected in accordance with Section 26.6. *(See Section C.25.)*

N **Table 26.5.1 Baled Cotton Storage Up to and Including 15 ft (4.6 m)**

System Type	Discharge Density per Area [gpm/ft² over ft² (mm/min over m²)]		
	Tiered Storage	Rack Storage	Untiered Storage
Wet	0.25/3000 (10.2/280)	0.33/3000 (13.5/280)	0.15/3000 (6.1/280)
Dry	0.25/3900 (10.2/360)	0.33/3900 (13.5/360)	0.15/3900 (6.1/360)

N **26.6.2** Cartoned records storage shall be permitted to be supported on shelving that is a minimum of 50 percent open from approved flue space to approved flue space.

N **26.6.2.1** Transverse flue spaces of a nominal 6 in. (150 mm) width shall be located at each rack upright.

N **26.6.2.2** Rack uprights shall be installed on a maximum of 10 ft 6 in. (3.2 m) centers.

N **26.6.2.3** Longitudinal flues shall not be required.

N **26.6.3** The storage rack structure for cartoned records storage shall consist of either of the following:

(1) A single-row rack not greater than 72 in. (1.8 m) deep

(2) Double-row racks having a total depth of not greater than 102 in. (2.6 m) aisle to aisle

N **26.6.3.1** Each storage rack shall be separated from other storage racks by aisles that are not less than 30 in. (750 mm) and not more than 36 in. (900 mm) in width.

N **26.6.3.2** Aisles used for ingress and egress shall be permitted to be up to 44 in. (1.1 m) wide when solid decking is used.

N **26.6.4** Catwalk aisles between racks shall be constructed of open metal grating that is at least 50 percent open.

N **26.6.4.1** Catwalk aisles at the ends of racks shall be permitted to be constructed of solid materials.

N **26.6.5** Catwalks shall be installed at a maximum of 12 ft (3.7 m) apart vertically.

N **26.6.6* Sprinkler Criteria.**

N **26.6.6.1** Cartoned record storage in racks with access utilizing catwalks shall be protected in accordance with this subsection.

N **26.6.6.2** The design criteria for the ceiling sprinkler system shall be in accordance with Table 26.6.6.2.

N **Table 26.6.6.2 Ceiling Sprinkler Design Criteria for Cartoned Record Storage**

	Up to 25 ft (7.6 m) High Storage		Over 25 ft (7.6 m) High Storage	
	Ordinary Temperature	High Temperature	Ordinary Temperature	High Temperature
Density				
gpm/ft²	0.33	0.29	0.3	0.4
mm/min	13.4	11.8	12.2	16.3
Area				
ft²	2000	2000	2000	2000
m²	185	185	185	185
Hose Allowance				
gpm	500	500	500	500
L/m	1900	1900	1900	1900
Duration				
hours	2	2	2	2

N **26.6.6.2.1** Ceiling sprinklers spaced to cover a maximum of 100 ft² (9.3 m²) shall be standard-response spray sprinklers with K-factors in accordance with Section 21.1.

N **26.6.6.3** Intermediate-level sprinklers shall be installed at each catwalk level in accordance with 26.6.6.3.1 through 26.6.6.3.4 and shall be quick-response, ordinary temperature, nominal K-5.6 (80), K-8.0 (115), or K-11.2 (160).

N **26.6.6.3.1** Intermediate-level sprinklers shall be installed in the center ±4 in. (100 mm) of each aisle below each catwalk level.

N **26.6.6.3.2** Intermediate-level sprinklers shall be installed a minimum 6 in. (150 mm) above the top of storage.

N **26.6.6.3.3** Sprinklers shall be supplied from the in-rack sprinkler system.

N **26.6.6.3.4** Spacing of sprinklers within the aisles shall be located to align with the transverse flues and the center of the storage unit when staggered and shall not exceed 10 ft 6 in. (3.2 m) on center.

N **26.6.6.3.5*** Sprinklers installed below each catwalk level shall be staggered vertically and horizontally. *[See Figure A.26.6.6.3.5(a) through Figure A.26.6.6.3.5(c).]*

N **26.6.6.4** Sprinklers shall be provided in transverse flue spaces in accordance with 26.6.6.4.1 and 26.6.6.4.2 and Figure 26.6.6.4.

N **26.6.6.4.1 Single-Row Racks.**

N **26.6.6.4.1.1** For single-row racks, in-rack sprinklers shall be installed in the transverse flue at each catwalk level.

N **26.6.6.4.1.2** For single-row racks, sprinklers installed in the transverse flues shall be staggered horizontally such that the sprinkler at first level is not less than 18 in. (450 mm) but not greater than 24 in. (600 mm) from the face of the rack on the catwalk side.

N **(A)** At the next level, the sprinkler in the transverse flue shall be located not less than 6 in. (150 mm) but not greater than 12 in. (300 mm) from the back face of the rack.

N **(B)** This staggering shall be repeated throughout all catwalk levels.

N **26.6.6.4.2 Double- and Multiple-Row Racks.**

N **26.6.6.4.2.1** For double- and multiple-row racks, in-rack sprinklers shall be installed in the transverse flues at each catwalk level and shall be staggered vertically.

N **26.6.6.4.2.2** For double- and multiple-row racks, sprinklers installed in the transverse flues shall be located not less than 18 in. (450 mm) but not greater than 24 in. (600 mm) from the face of the rack on the catwalk side.

N **26.6.6.4.3** In-rack sprinklers shall be installed a minimum 6 in. (150 mm) above the top of storage.

N **26.6.6.4.4** Transverse flue sprinklers shall be quick-response, ordinary temperature, nominal K-5.6 (80), K-8.0 (115), or K-11.2 (160) and installed in accordance with Figure A.26.6.6.3.5(b) and Figure A.26.6.6.3.5(c).

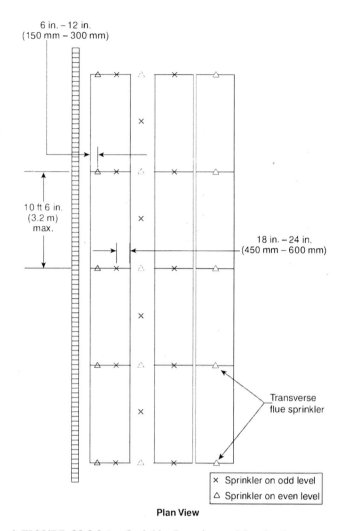

Plan View

△ **FIGURE 26.6.6.4   Sprinkler Location and Spacing in Transverse Flues.**

N **26.6.6.5 Catwalk Systems.**

N **26.6.6.5.1 Single-Level.**

N **26.6.6.5.1.1** For single-level catwalks, a minimum of six sprinklers shall be calculated with a minimum flow rate at 30 gpm (115 L/min) per sprinkler.

N **26.6.6.5.1.2** Calculated sprinklers shall be the hydraulically most demanding.

N **26.6.6.5.2 Multiple-Level.**

N **26.6.6.5.2.1** For multiple-level catwalk systems, a minimum of 10 sprinklers, five on each of the top two levels, shall be calculated with a minimum flow rate of 30 gpm (115 L/min) per sprinkler.

N **26.6.6.5.2.2** Calculated sprinklers shall be the hydraulically most demanding on each level.

N **26.6.6.5.3** The in-rack sprinkler system shall be balanced in with the ceiling system.

N **26.7 Control Mode Density/Area Protection Criteria for Compact Storage of Commodities Consisting of Paper Files, Magazines, Books, and Similar Documents in Folders and Miscellaneous Supplies with No More Than 5 Percent Plastics Up to 8 ft (2.4 m) High.**

N **26.7.1*** Compact storage modules up to 8 ft (2.4 m) high storing commodities consisting of paper files, magazines, books, and similar documents in folders and miscellaneous supplies with no more than 5 percent plastics shall be permitted to be classified as light hazard. *(See Section C.24.)*

N **26.7.2** The top of the compact storage module shall be at least 18 in. (450 mm) below the sprinkler deflector.

N **26.7.3** Sprinklers shall be ordinary temperature, quick-response, standard spray upright or pendent.

N **26.7.4** The compact storage module shall be provided with minimum solid steel 24 gauge (0.6 mm) metal longitudinal barriers installed every third carriage.

N **26.7.5*** Solid 24 gauge (0.6 mm) metal transverse barriers shall be spaced not more than 4 ft (1.2 m) apart.

N **26.7.6** Compact storage module sizes shall not exceed 250 ft² (23 m²).

N **26.7.6.1** The size of a module shall be defined as the area of compact storage bound by the length of the carriages times the distance between longitudinal barriers or to the outward edge of a fixed storage unit in the module, including the width of the aisle in the module.

N **26.7.6.2** The lengths of the carriages shall be measured to the end of the carriages enclosed by solid metal transverse panels and separated by a minimum 28 in. (700 mm) aisle to a storage unit perpendicular to the carriage.

N **26.8 Protection of High Bay Records Storage.**

N **26.8.1* Mobile High Bay Records Storage.** The requirements in this section shall be permitted to apply to ceiling-only sprinkler protection of paper products, including paper files, magazines, books, and similar paper documents in corrugated containers either closed or open top, to include corrugated totes, with no more than 5 percent plastics stored in mobile shelving units greater than 12 ft (3.7 m) and up to 34 ft (10 m) high and up to 30 shelving units (storage tiers) high, when the shelving unit structure meets all of the requirements in 26.8.3.

N **26.8.2 Fixed High Bay Records Storage.** High bay record storage shall be permitted to be fixed in place when meeting the limitations of 26.8.1 and 26.8.3.

N **26.8.3 High Bay Shelving.**

N **26.8.3.1** A wet pipe sprinkler system with nominal K-25.2 (360) ESFR sprinklers operating at a minimum of 40 psi (2.8 bar) shall be provided.

N **26.8.3.2** The shelving units shall be subject to the following limitations:

(1) Back-to-back storage shelving units, each no greater than 36 in. (900 mm) deep, separated by longitudinal flue space not less than 6 in. (150 mm) wide

(2) Solid steel shelving units not exceeding 54 in. (1.4 m) wide separated by steel barriers mechanically fastened to upright steel framing that forms a transverse flue space not less than 3 in. (75 mm) wide

(3) Upright steel framing not completely blocking transverse flue space between adjacent shelving units

(4) Noncombustible shelving backstops and side shelf supports, also referred to as side box guides, projecting not less than 3 in. (75 mm) above the shelves and that prevent stored commodities from encroaching into transverse and longitudinal flue spaces

(5) Solid steel shelving not greater than 18 in. (450 mm) on centers vertically

(6) Solid steel tops over top shelving units except at the tops of transverse and longitudinal flue spaces

(7) Open-ended, hollow tubular steel vertical (upright) shelving columns at the top of the shelving system

(8) Shelving system framing and power tracks not exceeding 3 in. (75 mm) in width and not less than 1 ft (300 mm) on centers and not less than 6 in. (150 mm) below sprinkler deflectors

(9) Minimum clearance of 36 in. (900 mm) above the top solid steel cover over the top storage shelf to the sprinkler deflector

N **26.8.3.3 Mobile Shelving Systems.**

N **26.8.3.3.1** Mobile shelving systems arranged to shift automatically shall be arranged to initiate the shifting 60 seconds after activation of ceiling-mounted smoke detectors or upon sprinkler flow, whichever is first.

N **26.8.3.3.2** Mobile shelving systems arranged to shift automatically shall form a uniform nominal 6 in. (150 mm) clearance clear space between mobile carriages supporting back-to-back shelving units.

N **26.8.3.3.3** Mobile shelving system carriage electrical motors shall be listed and integral to the mobile carriage systems for normal functions.

N **26.8.3.3.4** Mobile shelving systems carriage electrical motors shall not be required to have emergency power back-up.

N **26.9 Special Design for Palletized, Solid-Piled, Bin Box, or Shelf Storage of Class I Through Class IV Commodities.**

N **26.9.1 Bin Box and Shelf Storage.**

N **26.9.1.1** Bin box and shelf storage that is over 12 ft (3.7 m) but not in excess of the height limits of 21.2.1 and that is provided with walkways at vertical intervals of not over 12 ft (3.7 m) shall be protected with automatic sprinklers under the walkway(s).

N **26.9.1.2** Protection shall be as follows:

(1) Ceiling design density shall be based on the total height of storage within the building as provided in Chapter 21.

(2) Automatic sprinklers under walkways shall be designed to maintain a minimum discharge pressure of 15 psi (1.0 bar) for the most hydraulically demanding six sprinklers on each level. Walkway sprinkler demand shall not be required to be added to the ceiling sprinkler demand. Sprinklers under walkways shall not be spaced more than 8 ft (2.4 m) apart horizontally.

Chapter 27 Special Occupancy Requirements

27.1 General.

27.1.1 Application.

Δ **27.1.1.1** In addition to the requirements of Chapter 8 and Chapters 11 through 23, the following special occupancy reference standards and requirements shall apply for special occupancies within the scope of the referenced standards.

Δ **27.1.1.2** All provisions of design criteria in this standard, including design area increases and reductions, shall apply to the special occupancy requirements.

27.1.1.3 Where the requirements of the referenced standard differ from the requirements of this standard, the referenced standard shall take precedence.

27.1.2 Definitions. For terms not defined in Chapter 3, the definitions of the referenced standard shall apply.

27.2 Flammable and Combustible Liquids. Fire sprinkler systems for the protection of flammable and combustible liquids shall be designed and installed in accordance with this standard and NFPA 30.

27.3 Aerosol Products. Fire sprinkler systems for the protection of aerosol products shall be designed and installed in accordance with this standard and NFPA 30B.

N **27.4 Drycleaning Facilities.** Fire sprinkler systems for the protection of drycleaning facilities shall be designed and installed in accordance with this standard and NFPA 32.

27.5 Spray Applications Using Flammable or Combustible Materials. Fire sprinkler systems for the protection of spray areas used for spray applications using flammable or combustible materials shall be designed and installed in accordance with this standard and NFPA 33.

N **27.6 Dipping, Coating, and Printing Processes Using Flammable or Combustible Liquids.** Fire sprinkler systems for the protection of dipping, coating, and printing processes using flammable or combustible liquids shall be designed and installed in accordance with this standard and NFPA 34.

Δ **27.7 Solvent Extraction Plants.** Fire sprinkler systems for the protection of solvent extraction plants shall be designed and installed in accordance with this standard and NFPA 36.

Δ **27.8 Stationary Combustion Engines and Gas Turbines.** Fire sprinkler systems for the protection of stationary combustion engines and gas turbines shall be designed and installed in accordance with this standard and NFPA 37.

27.9 Cellulose Nitrate Film. Fire sprinkler systems for the protection of all cases of storage and handling of cellulose nitrate film shall be designed and installed in accordance with this standard and NFPA 40.

27.10 Laboratories Using Chemicals. Fire sprinkler systems for the protection of laboratory buildings as defined in 1.1.1 through 1.1.3 of NFPA 45 shall be designed and installed in accordance with this standard and NFPA 45.

27.11 Oxygen-Fuel Gas Systems for Welding, Cutting, and Allied Processes. Fire sprinkler systems for the protection of oxygen-fuel gas systems for welding, cutting, and allied processes as defined in 1.1.1 of NFPA 51 shall be designed and installed in accordance with this standard and NFPA 51.

27.12 Compressed Gases and Cryogenic Fluids Code. Fire sprinkler systems for the protection of compressed gases and cryogenic fluids as defined in Section 1.1 of NFPA 55 shall be designed and installed in accordance with this standard and NFPA 55.

27.13 Utility LP-Gas Plants. Fire sprinkler systems for the protection of utility LP-gas plants shall be designed and installed in accordance with this standard and NFPA 59.

27.14 Production, Storage, and Handling of Liquefied Natural Gas (LNG). Fire sprinkler systems for the protection of facilities that produce, store, and handle liquified natural gas (LNG) shall be designed and installed in accordance with this standard and NFPA 59A.

Δ **27.15 Information Technology Equipment.** Fire sprinkler systems for the protection of information technology equipment shall be designed and installed in accordance with this standard and NFPA 75.

Δ **27.16 Telecommunication Facilities.** Fire sprinkler systems for the protection of telecommunication facilities shall be designed and installed in accordance with this standard and NFPA 76.

Δ **27.17 Incinerators and Waste and Linen Handling Systems and Equipment.** Fire sprinkler systems for the protection of incinerators and waste and linen handling systems and equipment shall be designed and installed in accordance with this standard and NFPA 82.

Δ **27.18 Ovens and Furnaces.** Fire sprinkler systems for the protection of Class A, Class B, Class C, and Class D ovens, dryers, and furnaces; thermal oxidizers; and any other heated systems and related equipment used for processing of materials shall be designed and installed in accordance with this standard and NFPA 86.

27.19 Exhaust Systems for Air Conveying of Vapors, Gases, Mists, and Noncombustible Particulate Solids. Fire sprinkler systems for the protection of exhaust systems for air conveying of vapors, gases, mists, and noncombustible particulate solids shall be designed and installed in accordance with this standard and NFPA 91.

Δ **27.20 Class A Hyperbaric Chambers.** Fire sprinkler systems for the protection of Class A hyperbaric chambers shall be designed and installed in accordance with this standard and NFPA 99.

27.21 Coal Mines. Fire sprinkler systems for the protection of coal mines shall be designed and installed in accordance with this standard and NFPA 120.

27.22 Metal/Nonmetal Mining and Metal Mineral Processing Facilities. Fire sprinkler systems for the protection of metal/nonmetal mining and metal processing facilities shall be designed and installed in accordance with this standard and NFPA 122.

27.23 Fixed Guideway Transit and Passenger Rail Systems. Fire sprinkler systems for the protection of fixed guideway transit and passenger rail systems shall be designed and installed in accordance with this standard and NFPA 130.

27.24 Motion Picture and Television Production Studio Soundstages, Approved Production Facilities, and Production Locations. Fire sprinkler systems for the protection of motion picture and television production studio soundstages, approved production facilities, and production locations shall be designed and installed in accordance with this standard and NFPA 140.

27.25 Animal Housing Facilities. Fire sprinkler systems for the protection of animal housing facilities shall be designed and installed in accordance with this standard and NFPA 150.

27.26 Water Cooling Towers. Fire sprinkler systems for the protection of water cooling towers shall be designed and installed in accordance with this standard and NFPA 214.

Δ **27.27 Marine Terminals, Piers, and Wharves.** Fire sprinkler systems for the protection of marine terminals, piers, and wharves shall be designed and installed in accordance with this standard and NFPA 307.

27.28 Semiconductor Fabrication Facilities. Fire sprinkler systems for the protection of semiconductor fabrication facilities shall be designed and installed in accordance with this standard and NFPA 318.

27.29 Hazardous Materials Code. Fire sprinkler systems for the protection of hazardous materials shall be designed and installed in accordance with this standard and NFPA 400.

N **27.30 Aircraft Hangars.** Fire sprinkler systems for the protection of aircraft hangars shall be designed and installed in accordance with this standard and NFPA 409.

N **27.31 Airport Terminal Buildings, Fueling Ramp Drainage, and Loading Walkways.** Fire sprinkler systems for the protection of airport terminal buildings, fueling ramp drainage, and loading walkways shall be designed and installed in accordance with this standard and NFPA 415.

27.32 Aircraft Engine Test Facilities. Fire sprinkler systems for the protection of aircraft engine test facilities shall be designed and installed in accordance with this standard and NFPA 423.

27.33 Advanced Light Water Reactor Electric Generating Plants. Fire sprinkler systems for the protection of advanced light water reactor electric generating plants shall be designed and installed in accordance with this standard and NFPA 804.

27.34 Light Water Nuclear Power Plants. Fire sprinkler systems for the protection of light water nuclear power plants shall be designed and installed in accordance with this standard and NFPA 805.

Δ **27.35 Cultural Resource Properties — Museums, Libraries, and Places of Worship.** Fire sprinkler systems for the protection of museums, libraries, and places of worship shall be designed and installed in accordance with this standard and NFPA 909.

Chapter 28 Plans and Calculations

28.1* Working Plans.

28.1.1* Working plans shall be submitted for approval to the authority having jurisdiction before any equipment is installed or remodeled.

28.1.1.1 Working plan submittals shall include the following:

(1) Working plans of the system(s), per 28.1.3
(2) Hydraulic calculations where systems are required to be calculated
(3) Data sheets for the system components where required by the authority having jurisdiction
(4)* Signed owner's certificate

28.1.1.2 Submittals shall be permitted to be in electronic format when approved by the authority having jurisdiction.

28.1.1.3 A copy of the approved plans shall be given to the owner or owner's representative.

28.1.2 Deviation from approved plans shall require permission of the authority having jurisdiction.

Δ **28.1.3** Working plans shall be drawn to an indicated scale, on sheets of uniform size, with a plan of each floor, and shall show those items from the following list that pertain to the design of the system:

(1) Name and address of building being protected
(2) Name, telephone number, and address of installing contractor
(3) Point of compass and graphic scale indications on drawings and details as applicable
(4) Location of all partitions that extend to or are within a minimum of 18 in. (450 mm) to the finished ceiling or exposed deck above
(5) Location of all fire-rated partitions, fire barriers, draft stops, and draft curtains
(6) Identification of all rooms and spaces, regardless of occupancy or use
(7) Identification and labeling of all spaces, above and below ceilings, where sprinklers will be omitted, including appropriate citation of the section(s) of this standard for such omission(s)
(8) Location of all fixtures, diffusers, lights, and devices installed in or mounted to the ceiling structure, regardless of the ceiling type (i.e., finished or exposed to structure)
(9) Label finished or exposed ceiling heights for each space, including those that are sloped greater than 2 in 12 (16.7 percent)
(10)* Location and identification of major mechanical, plumbing, and electrical equipment installed above or below the ceiling spaces if sprinkler protection is being provided for those areas
(11)* Location and identification of all major structural members, and identification and labeling of construction types (i.e., obstructed or unobstructed) for each space or portion thereof in the building, as applicable
(12)* Location and identification of concealed spaces, regardless of combustibility, and of architectural and/or structural features not shown or easily identifiable in the floor plan or reflected ceiling plan views
(13) Water source(s) supply information, including the following:

(a) Location
(b) Type
(c) Size
(d) Dimensions
(e) Capacity
(f) Configuration
(g) Elevation
(h) Static pressure
(i) Flow rate
(j) Residual pressure
(k) Flow test locations, dates, and sources (i.e., city or private)
(l) Any adjustments from the raw data required by the engineer of record (i.e., owner's certificate) or the water authority, if applicable

(14) Information from the owner's certificate required by Section 4.2, including the edition of this standard being used
(15) Identification and labeling of design criteria for each room and/or space as shown on building plan, including the following:

(a) Hazard classification associated with each room or space
(b) Identification and location of all rooms and spaces intended for storage, including the following:

  i. Commodity classification
  ii.* Storage type and configuration
  iii. Height of storage for each dedicated room or space
  iv. Type of packaging to be used

(16) Identification and labeling of all sprinkler systems, including type and overall area protected by each system
(17) Location and labeling for the size, dimension, elevation, and type of all major sprinkler system components, including the following (*see 28.1.3.1*):

(a) Pipe, fittings, valves, and test and drain locations
(b) Sprinkler legend, per system, including the following:

  i. Orientation
  ii. Finish
  iii. Manufacturer
  iv. Model
  v. SIN number
  vi. K-factor
  vii. Temperature rating
  viii. Response type
  ix. Quantity of each
  x. If extended coverage or residential type, spacing utilized for this application

(c) Manufacturer, model, length, maximum number of bends, and minimum bend radius and corresponding K-factor applied to flexible sprinkler hose

(18) Location and labeling of all system flushing, forward flow, water flow alarm, and test and drain locations
(19) Location and labeling of sprinkler system riser(s) and, if applicable, standpipe location(s)
(20) Location and labeling of fire department connections

(21) Location and labeling of hydraulic calculation information, including the following:

   (a) Graphic indication of each area of operation, including a description of any allowed density or area modifications applied

   (b) Labeling of all node locations that correspond to each hydraulic calculation

(22) Location and labeling of seismic system components, including the following:

   (a) Zones of influence
   (b) Bracing and restraint assemblies
   (c) Flexible couplings and penetration clearances
   (d) Maximum spacing of components
   (e) Design angle category(ies)

(23) Sprinkler system details and information for other system components necessary for the complete installation, including the following:

   (a) Hanger and/or hanger assemblies intended to be used throughout

   (b) Total system volume for dry and double interlock preaction systems

   (c) Hydraulic calculation summary information, including the following:

      i. Method of calculation
      ii. Total water and pressure required
      iii. Hose demand

   (d) Special information, settings, or values required for ongoing inspection, testing, and maintenance and system use, including the following:

      i. Pressure regulating device features and means for conducting a flow test
      ii. Dry pipe, preaction, and/or deluge systems
      iii. Information regarding antifreeze solution used

N **28.1.3.1** Where a proposed new system will connect to or be installed adjacent to an existing system(s), plans shall show adequate portions of the existing system(s) pertinent to the design and installation of the new system in addition to the items listed in 28.1.3(23).

28.1.4 A signed copy of the owner's certificate and the working plan submittal shall include the manufacturer's installation instructions, for any specially listed equipment, including descriptions, applications, and limitations for any sprinklers, devices, piping, or fittings.

28.2 Hydraulic Calculation Procedures.

28.2.1* General.

28.2.1.1 A calculated system for a building, or a calculated addition to a system in an existing sprinklered building, shall supersede the rules in this standard governing pipe schedules, except that all systems shall continue to be limited by area.

28.2.1.2 Pipe sizes shall be no less than 1 in. (25 mm) nominal for black or galvanized steel piping and ¾ in. (20 mm) nominal for copper tubing or brass, stainless steel, or nonmetallic piping listed for fire sprinkler service unless permitted by Sections 30.4 and 30.6.

28.2.1.3 The size of pipe, number of sprinklers per branch line, and number of branch lines per cross main shall otherwise be limited only by the available water supply.

28.2.1.4* Unless required by other NFPA standards, the velocity of water flow shall not be limited when hydraulic calculations are performed using the Hazen–Williams or Darcy Weisbach formulas.

28.2.1.5 However, sprinkler spacing and all other rules covered in this and other applicable standards shall be observed.

28.2.1.6 Hydraulic calculations shall extend to the effective point of the water supply where the characteristics of the water supply are known.

28.2.2 Formulas.

28.2.2.1 Friction Loss Formula.

28.2.2.1.1 Pipe friction losses shall be determined on the basis of the Hazen–Williams formula, as follows:

[28.2.2.1.1]

$$p = \frac{4.52 Q^{1.85}}{C^{1.85} d^{4.87}}$$

where:
p = frictional resistance (psi/ft of pipe)
Q = flow (gpm)
C = friction loss coefficient
d = actual internal diameter of pipe (in.)

28.2.2.1.2 For SI units, the following equation shall be used:

[28.2.2.1.2]

$$p_m = 6.05 \left(\frac{Q_m^{1.85}}{C^{1.85} d_m^{4.87}} \right) 10^5$$

where:
p_m = frictional resistance (bar/m of pipe)
Q_m = flow (L/min)
C = friction loss coefficient
d_m = actual internal diameter (mm)

28.2.2.1.3 For antifreeze systems greater than 40 gal (150 L) in size, the friction loss shall also be calculated using the Darcy–Weisbach formula [use Equation 28.2.2.1.3a (US) or Equation 28.2.2.1.3b (SI)]:

[28.2.2.1.3a]

$$\Delta P = 0.000216 f \frac{l \rho Q^2}{d^5}$$

where:
ΔP = friction loss (psi)
f = friction loss factor from Moody diagram
l = length of pipe or tube (ft)
ρ = density of fluid (lb/ft³)
Q = flow in pipe or tube (gpm)
d = inside diameter of tube (in.)

N

[28.2.2.1.3b]

$$\Delta P_m = 2.252 f \frac{l \rho Q^2}{d^5}$$

where:
ΔP_m = friction loss (bar)
  f = friction loss factor from Moody diagram
  l = length of pipe or tube (m)
  ρ = density of fluid (kg/m^3)
  Q = flow in pipe or tube (L/min)
  d = inside diameter of tube (mm)

28.2.2.2 Velocity Pressure Formula. Velocity pressure shall be determined on the basis of the following formula:

[28.2.2.2]

$$P_v = \frac{0.001123Q^2}{D^4}$$

where:
P_v = velocity pressure (psi) (SI, 1 psi = 0.0689 bar)
Q = flow (gpm) (SI, 1 gal = 3.785 L)
D = inside diameter (in.) (SI, 1 in. = 25.4 mm)

28.2.2.3 Normal Pressure Formula. Normal pressure (P_n) shall be determined on the basis of the following formula:

[28.2.2.3]

$$P_n = P_t - P_v$$

where:
P_n = normal pressure
P_t = total pressure [psi (bar)]
P_v = velocity pressure [psi (bar)]

28.2.2.4 Hydraulic Junction Points.

28.2.2.4.1 Pressures at hydraulic junction points shall balance within 0.5 psi (0.03 bar).

28.2.2.4.2 The highest pressure at the junction point, and the total flows as adjusted, shall be carried into the calculations.

28.2.2.4.3 Pressure balancing shall be permitted through the use of a K-factor developed for branch lines or portions of systems using the formula in 28.2.2.5.

28.2.2.5 K-Factor Formula. K-factors, flow from an orifice, or pressure from an orifice shall be determined on the basis of the following formula:

[28.2.2.5]

$$K_n = \frac{Q}{\sqrt{P}}$$

where:
K_n = equivalent K at a node
Q = flow at the node
P = pressure at the node

28.2.3 Equivalent Pipe Lengths of Valves and Fittings.

28.2.3.1 Pipe and Fittings.

28.2.3.1.1 Table 28.2.3.1.1 shall be used to determine the equivalent length of pipe for fittings and devices unless manufacturer's test data indicate that other factors are appropriate.

28.2.3.1.2 For saddle-type fittings having friction loss greater than that shown in Table 28.2.3.1.1, the increased friction loss shall be included in hydraulic calculations.

28.2.3.1.3 Equivalent Length Modifier.

28.2.3.1.3.1 For internal pipe diameters different from Schedule 40 steel pipe [Schedule 30 for pipe diameters 8 in. (200 mm) and larger], the equivalent length shown in Table 28.2.3.1.1 shall be multiplied by a factor derived from the following formula:

[28.2.3.1.3.1]

$$\left(\frac{\text{Actual inside diameter}}{\text{Schedule 40 steel pipe inside diameter}} \right)^{4.87} = \text{Factor}$$

28.2.3.1.3.2 The factor thus obtained shall be further modified as required by Table 28.2.3.1.1. This table shall apply to other types of pipe listed in Table 28.2.3.1.1 only where modified by factors from 28.2.3.1.1 and 28.2.3.2.

28.2.3.2 C Factors. Table 28.2.3.1.1 shall be used with a Hazen–Williams C factor of 120 only.

Δ **Table 28.2.3.1.1 Equivalent Schedule 40 Steel Pipe Length Chart**

Fittings and Valves	Fittings and Valves Expressed in Equivalent Feet (Meters) of Pipe														
	½ in.	¾ in.	1 in.	1¼ in.	1½ in.	2 in.	2½ in.	3 in.	3½ in.	4 in.	5 in.	6 in.	8 in.	10 in.	12 in.
	(15 mm)	(20 mm)	(25 mm)	(32 mm)	(40 mm)	(50 mm)	(65 mm)	(80 mm)	(90 mm)	(100 mm)	(125 mm)	(150 mm)	(200 mm)	(250 mm)	(300 mm)
45° elbow	—	1 (0.3)	1 (0.3)	1 (0.3)	2 (0.6)	2 (0.6)	3 (0.9)	3 (0.9)	3 (0.9)	4 (1.2)	5 (1.5)	7 (2.1)	9 (2.7)	11 (3.3)	13 (4)
90° standard elbow	1 (0.3)	2 (0.6)	2 (0.6)	3 (0.9)	4 (1.2)	5 (1.5)	6 (1.8)	7 (2.1)	8 (2.4)	10 (3.0)	12 (3.7)	14 (4.3)	18 (5.5)	22 (6.7)	27 (8.2)
90° long-turn elbow	0.5 (0.2)	1 (0.3)	2 (0.6)	2 (0.6)	2 (0.6)	3 (0.9)	4 (1.2)	5 (1.5)	5 (1.5)	6 (1.8)	8 (2.4)	9 (2.7)	13 (4)	16 (4.9)	18 (5.5)
Tee or cross (flow turned 90°)	3 (0.9)	4 (1.2)	5 (1.5)	6 (1.8)	8 (2.4)	10 (3.0)	12 (3.7)	15 (4.6)	17 (5.2)	20 (6.1)	25 (7.6)	30 (9.1)	35 (10.7)	50 (15.2)	60 (18.3)
Butterfly valve	—	—	—	—	—	6 (1.8)	7 (2.1)	10 (3.0)	—	12 (3.7)	9 (2.7)	10 (3.0)	12 (3.7)	19 (5.8)	21 (6.4)
Gate valve	—	—	—	—	—	1 (0.3)	1 (0.3)	1 (0.3)	1 (0.3)	2 (0.6)	2 (0.6)	3 (0.9)	4 (1.2)	5 (1.5)	6 (1.8)
Vane type flow switch			6 (1.8)	9 (2.7)	10 (3.0)	14 (4.3)	17 (5.2)	22 (6.7)	—	30 (9.1)	—	16 (4.9)	22 (6.7)	29 (8.8)	36 (11)
Swing check*	—	—	5 (1.5)	7 (2.1)	9 (2.7)	11 (3.3)	14 (4.3)	16 (4.9)	19 (5.8)	22 (6.7)	27 (8.2)	32 (10)	45 (14)	55 (17)	65 (20)

Note: Information on ½ in. (15 mm) pipe is included in this table only because it is allowed under Sections 30.4 and 30.6.
*Due to the variation in design of swing check valves, the pipe equivalents indicated in this table are considered average.

28.2.3.2.1 For other values of *C*, the values in Table 28.2.3.1.1 shall be multiplied by the factors indicated in Table 28.2.3.2.1.

28.2.3.3 Valves and Components. Specific friction loss values or equivalent pipe lengths for alarm valves, dry pipe valves, deluge valves, strainers, backflow prevention devices, and other devices shall be made available to the authority having jurisdiction.

• **28.2.3.4 Differing Values.** Specific friction loss values or equivalent pipe lengths for listed fittings not in Table 7.4.1 shall be used in hydraulic calculations where these losses or equivalent pipe lengths are different from those shown in Table 28.2.3.1.1.

28.2.4* Calculation Procedure.

28.2.4.1* For all systems the design area shall be the hydraulically most demanding based on the criteria of Chapter 19, Chapter 20, or the special design approaches in accordance with the requirements of Chapter 27.

28.2.4.1.1 Room Design Method. Where the design is based on the room design method, the calculation shall be based on the room and communicating space, if any, that is hydraulically the most demanding.

28.2.4.2 Density/Area Method.

28.2.4.2.1* Where the design is based on the density/area method, the design area shall be a rectangular area having a dimension parallel to the branch lines at least 1.2 times the square root of the area of sprinkler operation *(A)* used, which shall permit the inclusion of sprinklers on both sides of the cross main.

28.2.4.2.2 Any fractional sprinkler shall be carried to the next higher whole sprinkler.

28.2.4.2.3 In systems having branch lines with an insufficient number of sprinklers to fulfill the 1.2 requirement, the design area shall be extended to include sprinklers on adjacent branch lines supplied by the same cross main.

28.2.4.2.4* Where the available floor area for a specific area/density design criteria, including any extension of area as required by 19.1.2 and Section 20.13, is less than the required minimum design area, the design area shall be permitted to only include those sprinklers within the available design area.

28.2.4.2.5* Where the total design discharge from the operating sprinklers is less than the minimum required discharge determined by multiplying the required design density times the required minimum design area, an additional flow shall be added at the point of common connection closest to the source to increase the overall demand, not including hose stream allowance, to the minimum required discharge.

N **28.2.4.2.6*** Where a sprinkler's assigned area of discharge is defined by the presence of a full-height wall assembly, the area on the opposite side of the wall of the flowing sprinkler shall not be counted towards the total design area.

Table 28.2.3.2.1 *C* Value Multiplier

Value of *C*	100	130	140	150
Multiplying factor	0.713	1.16	1.33	1.51

Note: These factors are based upon the friction loss through the fitting being independent of the *C* factor available to the piping.

28.2.4.3 CMSA Sprinkler Method.

28.2.4.3.1 For CMSA sprinklers, the design area shall be a rectangular area having a dimension parallel to the branch lines at least 1.2 times the square root of the area protected by the number of sprinklers to be included in the design area. The design area protected by the number of sprinklers to be used by the 1.2 rule shall be based on the maximum allowable area per sprinkler.

28.2.4.3.2 Any fractional sprinkler shall be carried to the next higher whole sprinkler.

28.2.4.3.3 In systems having branch lines with an insufficient number of sprinklers to fulfill the 1.2 requirement, the design area shall be extended to include sprinklers on adjacent branch lines supplied by the same cross main.

28.2.4.4 ESFR Sprinkler Method. For ESFR sprinklers, the design area shall consist of the most hydraulically demanding area of 12 sprinklers, consisting of 4 sprinklers on each of three branch lines, unless other specific numbers of design sprinklers are required in other sections of this standard.

28.2.4.5* Gridded Systems.

28.2.4.5.1 For gridded systems, the designer shall verify that the hydraulically most demanding area is being used.

28.2.4.5.2 A minimum of two additional sets of calculations shall be submitted to demonstrate peaking of demand area friction loss when compared to areas immediately adjacent on either side along the same branch lines, unless the requirements of 28.2.4.5.3 are met.

28.2.4.5.3 Computer programs that show the peaking of the demand area friction loss shall be acceptable based on a single set of calculations.

28.2.4.6 Design Densities.

28.2.4.6.1* System piping shall be hydraulically designed using design densities and areas of operation in accordance with 19.2.3.2 or Chapter 20 as required for the occupancies or hazards involved.

28.2.4.6.2* The density shall be calculated on the basis of floor area of sprinkler operation. Where sprinklers are installed under a sloped ceiling, the area used for this calculation shall be the horizontal plane below the sprinklers.

28.2.4.6.3 The area covered by any sprinkler used in hydraulic design and calculations shall be the horizontal distances measured between the sprinklers on the branch line and between the branch lines in accordance with 9.5.2.

28.2.4.6.4 Where sprinklers are installed above and below a ceiling or in a case where more than two areas are supplied from a common set of branch lines, the branch lines and supplies shall be calculated to supply the largest water demand.

28.2.4.6.5* For sloped ceiling applications, the area of sprinkler application for density calculations shall be based upon the projected horizontal area.

28.2.4.7* Design Area Sprinklers.

28.2.4.7.1 Each sprinkler in the design area and the remainder of the hydraulically designed system shall discharge at a flow rate at least equal to the stipulated minimum water application rate (density) multiplied by the area of sprinkler operation.

28.2.4.7.1.1 Where sprinklers are required to discharge a specific flow or pressure rather than a density, each sprinkler in the design area shall discharge at a flow or pressure at least equal to the minimum required.

28.2.4.7.2* Where the design area is equal to or greater than the area in Table 28.2.4.7.2 for the hazard being protected by the sprinkler system, the discharge for sprinklers protecting small compartments 55 ft² (5.1 m²) or less, such as closets, washrooms, and similar compartments that are in the design area, shall be permitted to be omitted from the hydraulic calculations.

28.2.4.7.2.1 The sprinklers in these small compartments shall be capable of discharging the minimum density appropriate for the hazard they protect in accordance with Figure 19.2.3.1.1.

28.2.4.7.2.2 The requirements of 28.2.4.7.2 shall only apply where the area of application is equal to or greater than the area shown in Table 28.2.4.7.2 for the appropriate hazard classification (including a 30 percent increase for dry pipe systems).

Δ **28.2.4.7.3*** The requirements of 28.2.4.7.1 and 28.2.4.7.1.1 to include every sprinkler in the design area shall not apply where sprinklers are provided above and below obstructions.

28.2.4.7.3.1 Sprinklers under the obstruction shall not be required to be included in the hydraulic calculation of the ceiling sprinklers.

28.2.4.7.3.2 Where the piping to sprinklers under obstructions follows the same sizing pattern as the branch lines, no additional hydraulic calculations shall be required for sprinklers under obstructions.

28.2.4.7.4 Water demand of sprinklers installed in concealed spaces shall not be required to be added to the ceiling demand.

28.2.4.7.5 Calculations shall begin at the hydraulically most remote sprinkler.

28.2.4.7.6 The calculated pressure at each sprinkler shall be used to determine the discharge flow rate for that particular sprinkler.

Table 28.2.4.7.2 Minimum Design Area

Occupancy Hazard Classification	Minimum Design Area to Omit Discharge from Sprinklers in Small Compartments in Design Area [ft² (m²)]
Light hazard–wet pipe system	1500 (140)
Light hazard–dry pipe system	1950 (180)
Ordinary hazard–wet pipe system	1500 (140)
Ordinary hazard–dry pipe system	1950 (180)
Extra hazard–wet pipe system	2500 (130)
Extra hazard–dry pipe system	3250 (300)

28.2.4.7.7 Where sprinklers are installed under a sloped ceiling, the area shall be calculated on a horizontal plane below the sprinklers.

28.2.4.8 Friction Loss.

28.2.4.8.1 Pipe friction loss shall be calculated in accordance with the Hazen–Williams formula with C values from Table 28.2.4.8.1, as follows:

(1) Pipe, fittings, and devices such as valves, meters, flow switches in pipes 2 in. (50 mm) or less in size, and strainers shall be included, and elevation changes that affect the sprinkler discharge shall be calculated.

(2) Tie-in drain piping shall not be included in the hydraulic calculations.

(3) Losses for a tee or a cross shall be calculated where flow direction change occurs based on the equivalent pipe length of the piping segment in which the fitting is included.

(4) The tee at the top of a riser nipple shall be included in the branch line, the tee at the base of a riser nipple shall be included in the riser nipple, and the tee or cross at a cross main–feed main junction shall be included in the cross main.

(5) Losses for straight-through flow in a tee or cross shall not be included.

(6) The loss of reducing elbows based on the equivalent length value of the smallest outlet shall be calculated.

(7) The equivalent length value for the standard elbow on any abrupt 90-degree turn, such as the screw-type pattern, shall be used.

(8) The equivalent length value for a fitting with a bushing shall be the same as for a similarly sized and configured reducing fitting.

(9) The equivalent length value for the long-turn elbow on any sweeping 90-degree turn, such as a flanged, welded, or mechanical joint-elbow type, shall be used. *(See Table 28.2.3.1.1.)*

(10) Losses shall be permitted to be excluded for tapered reducers.

(11) Losses shall be permitted to be excluded for a fitting with or without a bushing, directly connected to a sprinkler, except as required in 28.2.3.1.2 and 28.2.3.4.

(12) Losses through a pressure-reducing valve shall be included based on the normal inlet pressure condition, and pressure loss data from the manufacturer's literature shall be used.

(13) In new systems, an increased C value of 120 shall be permitted where nitrogen is provided in accordance with 8.2.6.9.

28.2.4.8.2* For antifreeze systems greater than 40 gal (150 L) in size, the pipe friction loss shall be calculated using the Darcy-Weisbach equation shown in 28.2.2.1.3 using a Moody diagram and ε-factors that are representative of aged pipe otherwise following the methodology presented in 28.2.4.8.1.

28.2.4.9 Orifice Plates.

28.2.4.9.1 Orifice plates shall not be used for balancing the system.

28.2.4.9.2 Unless the requirements of 28.2.4.9.3 or 28.2.4.9.4 are met, mixing of sprinklers of different K-factors by reducing the K-factor of adjacent sprinklers on the same branch line leading back to the main for the purpose of minimizing sprinkler over discharge shall not be permitted.

△ Table 28.2.4.8.1 Hazen–Williams C Values

Pipe or Tube	C Value*
Unlined cast or ductile iron	100
Black steel (dry systems including preaction)	100
Black steel (wet systems including deluge)	120
Black steel (dry system including preaction) using nitrogen[†]	120
Galvanized steel (dry systems including preaction)	100
Galvanized steel (wet systems including deluge)	120
Galvanized steel (dry systems including preaction) using nitrogen[†]	120
Plastic all (listed)	150
Cement-lined cast- or ductile iron	140
Copper tube, brass or stainless steel	150
Asbestos cement	140
Concrete	140

*The authority having jurisdiction is permitted to allow other C values.
[†]Nitrogen supply shall be installed in accordance with 8.2.6.9.

28.2.4.9.3* Sprinklers with different K-factors shall be acceptable for specific uses, such as exposure protection, small enclosures, smaller portions of a room, or directional discharge, where an adjacent sprinkler does not need to discharge as much water.

28.2.4.9.4 Extended-coverage and residential sprinklers with a different K-factor shall be acceptable for part of the protection area where installed in accordance with their listing.

28.2.4.10* Pressures.

28.2.4.10.1 When calculating flow from an orifice, the total pressure (P_t) shall be used, unless the calculation method of 28.2.4.10.2 is utilized.

28.2.4.10.2 Use of the normal pressure (P_n) calculated by subtracting the velocity pressure from the total pressure shall be permitted. Where the normal pressure is used, it shall be used on all branch lines and cross mains where applicable.

28.2.4.10.3 Flow from a sprinkler shall be calculated using the nominal K-factor except that the manufacturer's adjusted K-factors shall be utilized for dry-type sprinklers.

28.2.4.11 Minimum Operating Pressure.

28.2.4.11.1 Minimum operating pressure of any sprinkler shall be 7 psi (0.5 bar).

28.2.4.11.2 Where a higher minimum operating pressure for the desired application is specified in the listing of the sprinkler, this higher pressure shall be required.

28.2.4.12 Maximum Operating Pressure. For extra hazard occupancies, palletized, solid-piled, bin box, back-to-back shelf storage, shelf storage, or rack storage, the maximum operating pressure of any sprinkler shall be 175 psi (12 bar).

28.2.5 In-Rack Sprinklers.

28.2.5.1 Pipes to in-rack sprinklers shall be sized by hydraulic calculations.

28.2.5.2 Water demand of sprinklers installed in racks or water curtains shall be added to the ceiling sprinkler water demand at the point of connection. Demands shall be balanced to the higher pressure.

28.3 Hose Allowance. Water allowance for outside hose shall be added to the sprinkler and inside hose requirement at the connection to the city water main or a yard hydrant, whichever is closer to the system riser.

28.4 Hydraulic Calculation Forms.

28.4.1 General. Hydraulic calculations shall be prepared on form sheets that include a summary sheet, detailed worksheets, and a graph sheet. *[See Figure A.28.4.2(a), Figure A.28.4.3, and Figure A.28.4.4 for copies of typical forms.]*

28.4.2* Summary Sheet. The summary sheet shall contain the following information, where applicable:

(1) Date
(2) Location
(3) Name of owner and occupant
(4) Building number or other identification
(5) Description of hazard (for storage applications, the commodity classification, storage height, and rack configuration shall be included)
(6) Name and address of contractor or designer
(7) Name of approving agency
(8) System design requirements, as follows:

    (a) Design area of water application, ft^2 (m^2).
    (b) Minimum rate of water application (density), gpm/ft^2 (mm/min). Where sprinklers are listed with minimum water application in gpm (L/min) or pressure in psi (bar), the minimum rate of water application shall be indicated in gpm (L/min) or pressure, psi (bar).
    (c) Area per sprinkler, ft^2 (m^2).

(9) Total water requirements as calculated, including allowance for inside hose, outside hydrants, and water curtain and exposure sprinklers
(10) Allowance for in-rack sprinklers, gpm (L/min)
(11) Limitations (dimension, flow, and pressure) on extended coverage or other listed special sprinklers

28.4.3* Detailed Worksheets. Detailed worksheets or computer printout sheets shall contain the following information:

(1) Sheet number
(2) Sprinkler description and discharge constant (K)
(3) Hydraulic reference points
(4) Flow in gpm (L/min)
(5) Pipe size
(6) Pipe lengths, center-to-center of fittings
(7) Equivalent pipe lengths for fittings and devices
(8) Friction loss in psi/ft (bar/m) of pipe
(9) Total friction loss between reference points
(10) In-rack sprinkler demand balanced to ceiling demand
(11) Elevation head in psi (bar) between reference points
(12) Required pressure in psi (bar) at each reference point
(13) Velocity pressure and normal pressure if included in calculations
(14) Notes to indicate starting points or reference to other sheets or to clarify data shown
(15)* Diagram to accompany gridded system calculations to indicate flow quantities and directions for lines with sprinklers operating in the remote area

(16) Combined K-factor calculations for sprinklers on drops, armovers, or sprigs where calculations do not begin at the sprinkler

28.4.4* Graph Sheet. A graphic representation of the complete hydraulic calculation shall be plotted on semiexponential graph paper ($Q^{1.85}$) and shall include the following:

(1) Water supply curve
(2) Sprinkler system demand
(3) Hose allowance (where applicable)
(4) In-rack sprinkler demand (where applicable)

28.4.5 Hydraulic Reports.

28.4.5.1* General.

28.4.5.1.1 Hydraulic calculations shall be prepared on form sheets that include a summary sheet, a graph sheet, a water supply analysis, a node analysis, and detailed worksheets.

28.4.5.1.2 The data shall be presented in the order shown in Figure 28.4.5.1.2(a) through Figure 28.4.5.1.2(d).

28.4.5.2 Summary Sheet. The summary sheet as shown in Figure 28.4.5.1.2(a) shall contain the following information, where applicable:

(1) Project name and date
(2) Location (including street address)
(3) Owner or expected occupant of space being designed
(4) Name, address, and phone number of installing contractor
(5) Name and phone number of designer
(6) Authority having jurisdiction
(7) Standard or document system is being designed to, including the edition of the document
(8) Design area number and location
(9) Drawing or sheet number where design area is located
(10) Occupancy or commodity classification and information
(11) For storage applications (including miscellaneous), additional information including storage height, ceiling height, storage configuration, aisle width, orientation of upright or pendent, sprinkler K-factor and sprinkler temperature, and the table and or curve utilized in the design
(12) System type, including the system volume with type of protection system indicated in the notes
(13) Sprinkler type, including coverage and response type
(14) Slope of roof or ceiling within the design area
(15) System design requirements, as follows:

   (a) Design area of application, ft^2 (m^2)
   (b) Minimum rate of water application (density), gpm/ft^2 (mm/min)
   (c) Area per sprinkler, ft^2 (m^2)
   (d) Number of sprinklers calculated

(16) Total water requirements as calculated, including allowance for inside hose, outside hydrants, water curtain, and exposure sprinklers, and allowance for in-rack sprinklers, gpm (L/min)

(17) Ceiling height if used for quick response sprinkler reduction
(18) Elevation of highest calculated sprinkler
(19) Water supply information, including the following:

   (a) Date and time of test
   (b) Location of the test and flow hydrant(s)
   (c) Source of the water for the flow test
   (d) Elevation of the test hydrant relative to the finished floor
   (e) Size of fire pump, gpm @ psi (L/min @ bar)
   (f) Size of on-site water tank

(20) Notes that include peaking information for calculations performed by a computer program, type of preaction system, limitations (dimension, flow, and pressure) on extended-coverage or other listed special sprinklers, system type, including the system volume

28.4.5.3 Graph Sheet. A graphic representation of the complete hydraulic calculation shall be plotted on semiexponential graph paper ($Q^{1.85}$) as shown in Figure 28.4.5.1.2(b) and shall include the following:

(1) Water supply curve
(2) Sprinkler system demand
(3) Hose demand (where applicable)
(4) In-rack sprinkler demand (where applicable)
(5) Additional pressures supplied by a fire pump or other source (when applicable)

28.4.5.4 Supply Analysis. Information summarized from the graph sheet as shown in Figure 28.4.5.1.2(c) shall include the following:

(1) Node tag at the source
(2) Static pressure [psi (bar)] available at the source
(3) Residual pressure [psi (bar)] available at the source
(4) Total flow [gpm (L/min)] available at the source
(5) Available pressure [psi (bar)] at the source when the total calculated demand is flowing
(6) Total calculated demand [gpm (L/min)] at the source
(7) Required pressure [psi (bar)] when flowing total calculated demand

28.4.5.5 Node Analysis. Organized information as shown in Figure 28.4.5.1.2(c) regarding the node tags given to each hydraulic reference point on the system as indicated on the shop drawings shall include the following information:

(1) Node tag for each specific point on the system used in the hydraulic calculations
(2) Elevation in ft (m) of each node tag
(3) K-factor of flowing nodes (such as sprinklers)
(4) Hose allowance in gpm (L/min) requirements for the node tag
(5) Pressure in psi (bar) at the node
(6) Discharge in gpm (L/min) calculated at the node
(7) Notes that indicate any special requirements for the node

HYDRAULIC CALCULATIONS
for

Project name: _____

Location: _____

Drawing no.: _____ Date: _____

Design

   Remote area number: _____

   Remote area location: _____

   Occupancy classification: _____

   Density: _____ _____ gpm/ft^2 (mm/min)

   Area of application: _____ ft^2 (m^2)

   Coverage per sprinkler: _____ ft^2 (m^2)

   Type of sprinklers calculated: _____

   No. of sprinklers calculated: _____

   In-rack demand: _____

   Hose streams: _____

   Total water required (including hose streams): _____ gpm (mm/min) @ _____ psi (bar)

   Type of system: _____

   Volume of dry or preaction system: _____ gal (l)

Water supply information

   Date: _____

   Location: _____

   Source: _____

Name of contractor: _____

Address: _____

Phone number: _____

Name of designer: _____

Authority having jurisdiction: _____

Notes: (Include peaking information or gridded systems here.) _____

_____

_____

_____

© 2021 National Fire Protection Association   NFPA 13

Δ **FIGURE 28.4.5.1.2(a)   Summary Sheet.**

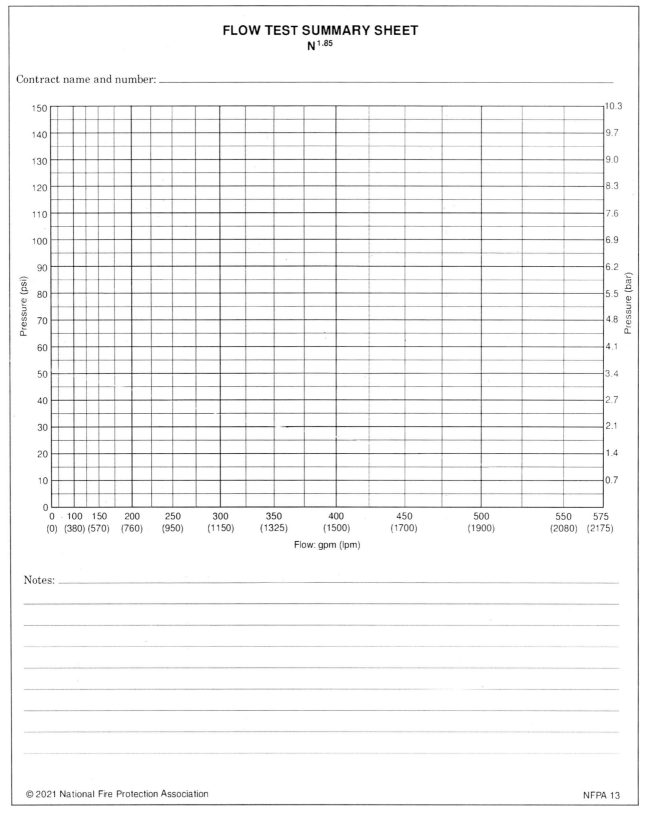

Δ **FIGURE 28.4.5.1.2(b)** **Graph Sheet.**

SUPPLY ANALYSIS

Node at Source	Static Pressure	Residual Pressure	Flow	Available Pressure	Total Demand	Required Pressure
Data	Data	Data	Data	Data	Data	Data

NODE ANALYSIS

Node Tag	Elevation	Node Type	Pressure at Node	Discharge at Node	Notes
Data	Data	Data	Data	Data	Data
Data	Data	Data	Data	Data	Data
Data	Data	Data	Data	Data	Data
Data	Data	Data	Data	Data	Data
Data	Data	Data	Data	Data	Data
Data	Data	Data	Data	Data	Data
Data	Data	Data	Data	Data	Data
Data	Data	Data	Data	Data	Data
Data	Data	Data	Data	Data	Data
Data	Data	Data	Data	Data	Data
Data	Data	Data	Data	Data	Data
Data	Data	Data	Data	Data	Data
Data	Data	Data	Data	Data	Data
Data	Data	Data	Data	Data	Data

NFPA 13

Δ **FIGURE 28.4.5.1.2(c)** **Supply and Node Analysis Sheet.**

Shaded text = Revisions. Δ = Text deletions and figure/table revisions. • = Section deletions. *N* = New material.

2022 Edition

Job name: _____   Sheet number: _____

PIPE INFORMATION

Node 1 / Node 2	Elev 1 (ft) (m)	K-Factor	Flow added — this step (q) / Total flow (Q)	Nominal ID / Actual ID	Fittings— quantity and length	L ft (m) / F ft (m) / T ft (m)	C Factor / P_f per foot (m) (psi) (bar)	total (P_t) / elev (P_e) / frict (P_f)	Notes
data 1	data 1	data 1	data 1	data	data	data	data	data 1	
					data	data	data	data	data
data 2	data 2		data	data	data	data		data	
data 1	data 1	data 1	data 1	data	data	data	data	data 1	
					data	data	data	data	data
data 2	data 2		data	data	data	data		data	
data 1	data 1	data 1	data 1	data	data	data	data	data 1	
					data	data	data	data	data
data 2	data 2		data	data	data	data		data	
data 1	data 1	data 1	data 1	data	data	data	data	data 1	
					data	data	data	data	data
data 2	data 2		data	data	data	data		data	
data 1	data 1	data 1	data 1	data	data	data	data	data 1	
					data	data	data	data	data
data 2	data 2		data	data	data	data		data	
data 1	data 1	data 1	data 1	data	data	data	data	data 1	
					data	data	data	data	data
data 2	data 2		data	data	data	data		data	
data 1	data 1	data 1	data 1	data	data	data	data	data 1	
					data	data	data	data	data
data 2	data 2		data	data	data	data		data	

NFPA 13

Δ **FIGURE 28.4.5.1.2(d)   Detailed Worksheet.**

Shaded text = Revisions.   Δ = Text deletions and figure/table revisions.   • = Section deletions.   *N* = New material.

28.4.5.6 Detailed Worksheets. Detailed worksheets as shown in Figure 28.4.5.1.2(d) or computer printout sheets shall contain the following information:

(1) Sheet number
(2) Hydraulic reference points used in each step
(3) Elevation in ft (m) at each hydraulic reference point
(4) Sprinkler description and discharge constant (K) for the flowing reference point
(5) Flow in gpm (L/min) for the flowing reference point (when applicable)
(6) Total flow in gpm (L/min) through each step
(7) Nominal pipe size in in. (mm)
(8) Actual internal diameter of pipe in in. (mm)
(9) Quantity and length in ft (m) of each type of fitting and device
(10) Pipe lengths in ft (m), center-to-center of fittings
(11) Equivalent pipe lengths in ft (m) of fittings and devices for the step
(12) Total equivalent length in ft (m) of pipes and fitting for the step
(13) C-factor used in each step
(14) Friction loss in psi/ft (bar/m) of pipe
(15) Sum of the pressures from the previous step (starting pressure at beginning)
(16) Elevation head in psi (bar) between reference points
(17) Total friction loss in psi (bar) between reference points
(18) Required pressure in psi (bar) at each reference point
(19) Notes and other information shall include the following:

   (a) Velocity pressure and normal pressure if included in calculations
   (b) In-rack sprinkler demand balanced to ceiling demand
   (c) Notes to indicate starting points or reference to other sheets or to clarify data shown
   (d) Diagram to accompany gridded system calculations to indicate flow quantities and directions for lines with sprinklers operating in the remote area
   (e) Combined K-factor calculations for sprinklers on drops, armovers, or sprigs where calculations do not begin at the sprinkler
   (f) The pressure [psi/(bar)] loss assigned the back-flow device when included on a system
   (g) Friction factor and Reynolds number when the Darcy–Weisbach equation is used

28.5 Pipe Schedules. Pipe schedules shall not be used, except in existing systems and in new systems or extensions to existing systems described in Chapter 19. Water supplies shall conform to 19.2.2.

28.5.1* General.

28.5.1.1 The pipe schedule sizing provisions shall not apply to hydraulically calculated systems.

28.5.1.2 Sprinkler systems having sprinklers with K-factors other than 5.6 nominal, listed piping material other than that covered in Table 7.3.1.1, extra hazard Group 1 and Group 2 systems, and exposure protection systems shall be hydraulically calculated.

28.5.1.3 The number of automatic sprinklers on a given pipe size on one floor shall not exceed the number given in 28.5.2, 28.5.3, or 28.5.4 for a given occupancy.

28.5.1.4* Size of Risers. Each system riser shall be sized to supply all sprinklers on the riser on any one floor as determined by the standard schedules of pipe sizes in 28.5.2, 28.5.3, or 28.5.4.

28.5.1.5 Slatted Floors, Large Floor Openings, Mezzanines, and Large Platforms. Buildings having slatted floors or large unprotected floor openings without approved stops shall be treated as one area with reference to pipe sizes, and the feed mains or risers shall be of the size required for the total number of sprinklers.

28.5.1.6 Stair Towers. Stair towers, or other construction with incomplete floors, if piped on independent risers, shall be treated as one area with reference to pipe sizes.

28.5.2 Schedule for Light Hazard Occupancies.

28.5.2.1 Branch Lines.

28.5.2.1.1 Unless permitted by 28.5.2.1.2 or 28.5.2.1.3, branch lines shall not exceed eight sprinklers on either side of a cross main.

28.5.2.1.2 Where more than eight sprinklers on a branch line are necessary, lines shall be permitted to be increased to nine sprinklers by making the two end lengths 1 in. (25 mm) and 1¼ in. (32 mm), respectively, and the sizes thereafter standard.

28.5.2.1.3 Ten sprinklers shall be permitted to be placed on a branch line, making the two end lengths 1 in. (25 mm) and 1¼ in. (32 mm), respectively, and feeding the tenth sprinkler by a 2½ in. (65 mm) pipe.

28.5.2.2 Pipe Sizes.

28.5.2.2.1 Pipe sizes shall be in accordance with Table 28.5.2.2.1.

Δ **Table 28.5.2.2.1 Light Hazard Pipe Schedules**

Steel		Copper	
1 in. (25 mm)	2 sprinklers	1 in. (25 mm)	2 sprinklers
1¼ in. (32 mm)	3 sprinklers	1¼ in. (32 mm)	3 sprinklers
1½ in. (40 mm)	5 sprinklers	1½ in. (40 mm)	5 sprinklers
2 in. (50 mm)	10 sprinklers	2 in. (50 mm)	12 sprinklers
2½ in. (65 mm)	30 sprinklers	2½ in. (65 mm)	40 sprinklers
3 in. (80 mm)	60 sprinklers	3 in. (80 mm)	65 sprinklers
3½ in. (90 mm)	100 sprinklers	3½ in. (90 mm)	115 sprinklers
4 in. (100 mm)	See Section 4.4.	4 in. (100 mm)	See Section 4.4.

28.5.2.2.2 Each area requiring more sprinklers than the number specified for 3½ in. (90 mm) pipe in Table 28.5.2.2.1 and without subdividing partitions (not necessarily fire walls) shall be supplied by mains or risers sized for ordinary hazard occupancies.

28.5.2.3 Where sprinklers are installed above and below ceilings in accordance with Figure 28.5.2.3(a) through Figure 28.5.2.3(c), and such sprinklers are supplied from a common set of branch lines or separate branch lines from a common cross main, such branch lines shall not exceed eight sprinklers above and eight sprinklers below any ceiling on either side of the cross main.

28.5.2.4 Unless the requirements of 28.5.2.5 are met, pipe sizing up to and including 2 ½ in. (65 mm) shall be as shown in Table 28.5.2.4 utilizing the greatest number of sprinklers to be found on any two adjacent levels.

28.5.2.5 Branch lines and cross mains supplying sprinklers installed entirely above or entirely below ceilings shall be sized in accordance with Table 28.5.2.2.1.

28.5.2.6* Where the total number of sprinklers above and below a ceiling exceeds the number specified in Table 28.5.2.4 for 2½ in. (65 mm) pipe, the pipe supplying such sprinklers shall be increased to 3 in. (75 mm) and sized thereafter according to the schedule shown in Table 28.5.2.2.1 for the number of sprinklers above or below a ceiling, whichever is larger.

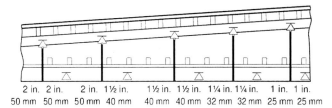

2 in.   2 in.   2 in. 1½ in.   1½ in. 1½ in. 1¼ in. 1¼ in.   1 in.   1 in.
50 mm 50 mm 50 mm 40 mm   40 mm 40 mm 32 mm 32 mm 25 mm 25 mm

FIGURE 28.5.2.3(a)   Arrangement of Branch Lines Supplying Sprinklers Above and Below Ceiling.

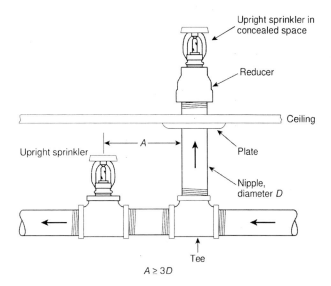

FIGURE 28.5.2.3(b)   Sprinkler on Riser Nipple from Branch Line in Lower Fire Area.

28.5.3 Schedule for Ordinary Hazard Occupancies.

28.5.3.1 Unless permitted by 28.5.3.2 or 28.5.3.3, branch lines shall not exceed eight sprinklers on either side of a cross main.

28.5.3.2 Where more than eight sprinklers on a branch line are necessary, lines shall be permitted to be increased to nine sprinklers by making the two end lengths 1 in. (25 mm) and 1¼ in. (32 mm), respectively, and the sizes thereafter standard.

28.5.3.3 Ten sprinklers shall be permitted to be placed on a branch line, making the two end lengths 1 in. (25 mm) and 1¼ in. (32 mm), respectively, and feeding the tenth sprinkler by a 2½ in. (65 mm) pipe.

28.5.3.4 Pipe sizes shall be in accordance with Table 28.5.3.4.

28.5.3.5 Where the distance between sprinklers on the branch line exceeds 12 ft (3.7 m) or the distance between the branch lines exceeds 12 ft (3.7 m), the number of sprinklers for a given pipe size shall be in accordance with Table 28.5.3.5.

28.5.3.6 Where sprinklers are installed above and below ceilings and such sprinklers are supplied from a common set of branch lines or separate branch lines supplied by a common cross main, such branch lines shall not exceed eight sprinklers above and eight sprinklers below any ceiling on either side of the cross main.

28.5.3.7 Pipe sizing up to and including 3 in. (76 mm) shall be as shown in Table 28.5.3.7 in accordance with Figure 28.5.2.3(a), Figure 28.5.2.3(b), and Figure 28.5.2.3(c) utilizing the greatest number of sprinklers to be found on any two adjacent levels.

28.5.3.8 Branch lines and cross mains supplying sprinklers installed entirely above or entirely below ceilings shall be sized in accordance with Table 28.5.3.4 or Table 28.5.3.5.

28.5.3.9* Where the total number of sprinklers above and below a ceiling exceeds the number specified in Table 28.5.3.7 for 3 in. (80 mm) pipe, the pipe supplying such sprinklers shall be increased to 3½ in. (90 mm) or larger and sized thereafter according to the schedule shown in Table 28.5.2.2.1 or Table 28.5.3.4 for the number of sprinklers above or below a ceiling, whichever is larger.

28.5.3.10 Where the distance between the sprinklers protecting the occupied area exceeds 12 ft (3.7 m) or the distance between the branch lines exceeds 12 ft (3.7 m), the branch lines shall be sized in accordance with either Table 28.5.3.5, taking into consideration the sprinklers protecting the occupied area only, or Table 28.5.3.7, whichever requires the greater size of pipe.

28.5.4* Extra Hazard Occupancies. Extra hazard occupancies shall be hydraulically calculated.

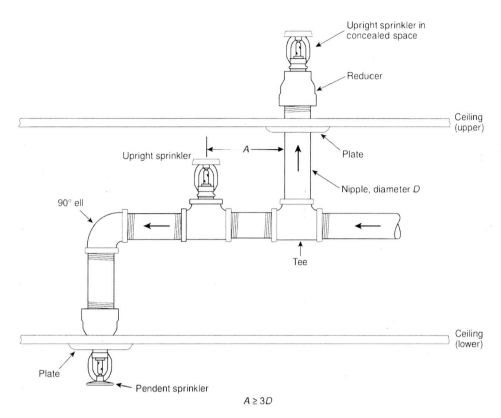

FIGURE 28.5.2.3(c)   Arrangement of Branch Lines Supplying Sprinklers Above, Between, and Below Ceilings.

Table 28.5.2.4 Number of Sprinklers Above and Below Ceiling

Steel		Copper	
1 in. (25 mm)	2 sprinklers	1 in, (25 mm)	2 sprinklers
1¼ in. (32 mm)	4 sprinklers	1¼ in. (32 mm)	4 sprinklers
1½ in. (40 mm)	7 sprinklers	1½ in. (40 mm)	7 sprinklers
2 in. (50 mm)	15 sprinklers	2 in. (50 mm)	18 sprinklers
2½ in. (65 mm)	50 sprinklers	2½ in. (65 mm)	65 sprinklers

Δ **Table 28.5.3.4 Ordinary Hazard Pipe Schedule**

Steel		Copper	
1 in. (25 mm)	2 sprinklers	1 in. (25 mm)	2 sprinklers
1¼ in. (32 mm)	3 sprinklers	1¼ in. (32 mm)	3 sprinklers
1½ in. (40 mm)	5 sprinklers	1½ in. (40 mm)	5 sprinklers
2 in. (50 mm)	10 sprinklers	2 in. (50 mm)	12 sprinklers
2½ in. (65 mm)	20 sprinklers	2½ in. (65 mm)	25 sprinklers
3 in. (80 mm)	40 sprinklers	3 in. (80 mm)	45 sprinklers
3½ in. (90 mm)	65 sprinklers	3½ in. (90 mm)	75 sprinklers
4 in. (100 mm)	100 sprinklers	4 in. (100 mm)	115 sprinklers
5 in. (125 mm)	160 sprinklers	5 in. (125 mm)	180 sprinklers
6 in. (150 mm)	275 sprinklers	6 in. (150 mm)	300 sprinklers
8 in. (200 mm)	See Section 4.4.	8 in. (200 mm)	See Section 4.4.

Shaded text = Revisions.   Δ = Text deletions and figure/table revisions.   • = Section deletions.   *N* = New material.

2022 Edition

Δ **Table 28.5.3.5 Number of Sprinklers — Greater Than 12 ft (3.7 m) Separations**

Steel		Copper	
2½ in. (65 mm)	15 sprinklers	2½ in. (65 mm)	20 sprinklers
3 in. (80 mm)	30 sprinklers	3 in. (80 mm)	35 sprinklers
3½ in. (90 mm)	60 sprinklers	3½ in. (90 mm)	65 sprinklers

Note: For other pipe and tube sizes, see Table 28.5.3.4.

Table 28.5.3.7 Number of Sprinklers Above and Below a Ceiling

Steel		Copper	
1 in. (25 mm)	2 sprinklers	1 in. (25 mm)	2 sprinklers
1¼ in. (32 mm)	4 sprinklers	1¼ in. (32 mm)	4 sprinklers
1½ in. (40 mm)	7 sprinklers	1½ in. (40 mm)	7 sprinklers
2 in. (50 mm)	15 sprinklers	2 in. (50 mm)	18 sprinklers
2½ in. (65 mm)	30 sprinklers	2½ in. (65 mm)	40 sprinklers
3 in. (80 mm)	60 sprinklers	3 in. (80 mm)	65 sprinklers

Chapter 29   Systems Acceptance

Δ **29.1* Approval of Sprinkler Systems and Private Fire Service Mains.** The installing contractor shall do the following:

(1) Notify the authority having jurisdiction and the property owner or the property owner's authorized representative of the time and date testing will be performed
(2) Perform all required acceptance tests *(see Section 29.2)*
(3) Complete and sign the appropriate contractor's material and test certificate(s) *(see Figure A.29.1)*
(4) Remove all caps and straps prior to placing the sprinkler system in service

29.2 Acceptance Requirements.

29.2.1* Hydrostatic Tests.

29.2.1.1 Unless permitted by 29.2.1.3 through 29.2.1.6, all piping and attached appurtenances subjected to system working pressure shall be hydrostatically tested at 200 psi (14 bar) and shall maintain that pressure without loss for 2 hours.

29.2.1.2 Loss shall be determined by a drop in gauge pressure or visual leakage.

29.2.1.3 Portions of systems normally subjected to system working pressures in excess of 150 psi (10 bar) shall be tested as described in 29.2.1.1, at a pressure of 50 psi (3.4 bar) in excess of system working pressure.

N **29.2.1.4** Where a fire pump is used for a system, the test pressure shall be determined using the shutoff pressure of the pump.

N **29.2.1.4.1** Where a fire pump uses a pressure limiting device or variable speed motor, the test pressure shall be calculated ignoring the settings of the pressure limiting device.

29.2.1.5 Where cold weather will not permit testing with water, an interim air test shall be permitted to be conducted as described in 29.2.2. This provision shall not remove or replace the requirement for conducting the hydrostatic test as described in 29.2.1.1.

29.2.1.6* The test pressure shall be read from a gauge located at the low elevation point of the system or portion being tested. The pressures in piping at higher elevations shall be permitted to be less than 200 psi (14 bar) when accounting for elevation losses. Systems or portions of systems that can be isolated shall be permitted to be tested separately.

29.2.1.7* Additives, corrosive chemicals such as sodium silicate, or derivatives of sodium silicate, brine, or similar acting chemicals shall not be used while hydrostatically testing systems or for stopping leaks.

29.2.1.8 Piping between the exterior fire department connection and the check valve in the fire department inlet pipe shall be hydrostatically tested in the same manner as the balance of the system. After repair or replacement work affecting the fire department connection, the piping between the exterior and the check valve in the fire department inlet pipe shall be isolated and hydrostatically tested at 150 psi (10 bar).

29.2.1.9 When systems are being hydrostatically tested, tests shall be permitted to be conducted with pendent or horizontal sidewall sprinklers or plugs installed in fittings. Any plugs shall be replaced with pendent or horizontal sidewall sprinklers after the test is completed, and a second hydrostatic test shall not be required.

29.2.1.10 When deluge systems are being hydrostatically tested, plugs shall be installed in fittings and replaced with open sprinklers after the test is completed, or the operating elements of automatic sprinklers shall be removed after the test is completed.

29.2.1.11 Provision shall be made for the proper disposal of water used for flushing or testing.

29.2.1.12* Test Blanks.

29.2.1.12.1 Test blanks shall have painted lugs protruding in such a way as to clearly indicate their presence.

29.2.1.12.2 The test blanks shall be numbered, and the installing contractor shall have a recordkeeping method ensuring their removal after work is completed.

29.2.1.13 When subject to hydrostatic test pressures, the clapper of a differential-type valve shall be held off its seat to prevent damaging the valve.

29.2.2 Dry Pipe and Double Interlock Preaction System(s) Air Test.

29.2.2.1 In addition to the standard hydrostatic test, an air pressure leakage test at 40 psi (2.8 bar) shall be conducted for 24 hours. Any leakage that results in a loss of pressure in excess of 1½ psi (0.1 bar) for the 24 hours shall be corrected.

29.2.2.2 Pipe or tube specifically investigated for suitability in dry pipe and double interlock preaction system(s) and listed for this service, shall be permitted to be tested in accordance with their listing limitations.

29.2.3 System Operational Tests.

Δ **29.2.3.1 Waterflow Devices.** Waterflow detecting devices shall be flow tested through the inspector's test connection and shall result in an audible alarm on the premises in accordance with the requirements of Section 7.7.

29.2.3.1.1 Where a fire alarm system is monitoring waterflow, an alarm signal shall activate in accordance with the requirements of the adopted fire alarm code.

29.2.3.2* Dry Pipe and Double Interlock Preaction Systems.

Δ **29.2.3.2.1** A working test shall be made by opening the inspector's test connection.

29.2.3.2.2 Where a quick opening device is present, the trip test described in 29.2.3.2.1 shall be sufficient to test the quick opening device as long as the device trips properly during the test.

Δ **29.2.3.2.3*** The test shall measure the time to trip the valve and the time for water to be discharged from the inspector's test connection.

N **29.2.3.2.3.1** All times shall be measured from the time the inspector's test connection is completely opened.

29.2.3.2.3.2* Systems calculated for water delivery in accordance with 8.2.3.6 shall be exempt from any specific delivery time requirement.

Δ **29.2.3.2.4** The results shall be recorded using the contractor's material and test certificate for aboveground piping *(see Figure A.29.1* and the general information sign *(see Figure A.29.6).*

29.2.3.3 Deluge and Preaction Systems.

29.2.3.3.1 The automatic operation of a deluge or preaction valve shall be tested in accordance with the manufacturer's instructions.

29.2.3.3.2 The manual and remote control operation, where present, shall also be tested.

29.2.3.4 Main Drain Valves.

29.2.3.4.1 The main drain valve shall be opened and remain open until the system pressure stabilizes.

29.2.3.4.2* The static and residual pressures shall be recorded on the contractor's material and test certificate *(see Figure A.29.1)* and the sprinkler system general information placard *(see Figure A.29.6).*

29.2.3.5 Operating Test for Control Valves. Each control valve shall be operated through its full range and returned to its normal position under system water pressure to ensure proper operation.

29.2.4 Pressure-Reducing Valves.

29.2.4.1 Each pressure-reducing valve shall be tested upon completion of installation to ensure proper operation under full flow and no-flow conditions.

29.2.4.2 Testing shall verify that the device properly regulates outlet pressure at both maximum and normal inlet pressure conditions.

29.2.4.3 The results of the flow test of each pressure-reducing valve shall be recorded on the contractor's material and test certificate *(see Figure A.29.1).*

29.2.4.4 The results shall include the static and residual inlet pressures, static and residual outlet pressures, and the flow rate.

29.2.5 Backflow Prevention Assemblies.

29.2.5.1 The backflow prevention assembly shall be forward flow tested to ensure proper operation.

29.2.5.2 The minimum flow rate shall be the system demand, including hose stream allowance where applicable.

29.2.6 Exposure Systems. Operating tests shall be made of exposure protection systems upon completion of the installation, where such tests do not risk water damage to the building on which they are installed or to adjacent buildings.

N **29.2.7 Automated Inspection and Testing Devices and Equipment.**

N **29.2.7.1** Automated inspection and testing devices and equipment installed on the sprinkler system shall be tested to ensure the desired result of the automated inspection or test is realized.

N **29.2.7.1.1** Automated inspection devices and equipment shall be tested to verify that the image received allows for an effective visual examination of the system or component being inspected.

N **29.2.7.1.2** Automated testing devices and equipment shall be tested to verify that they produce the same action as required by this standard to test a device.

N **29.2.7.1.2.1** The testing shall discharge water where required by this standard and NFPA 25.

N **29.2.7.2** Testing shall verify that failure of automated inspection and testing devices and equipment does not impair the operation of the system unless indicated by an audible and visual trouble signal in accordance with *NFPA 72* or other applicable fire alarm code.

N **29.2.7.3** Testing shall verify that failure of a system or component to pass automated inspection and testing devices and equipment results in an audible and visual trouble signal in accordance with *NFPA 72* or other applicable fire alarm code.

N **29.2.7.4** Testing shall verify that failure of automated inspection and testing devices and equipment results in an audible and visual trouble signal in accordance with *NFPA 72* or other applicable fire alarm code.

29.3 Instructions. The installing contractor shall provide the property owner or the property owner's authorized representative with the following:

(1) All literature and instructions provided by the manufacturer describing proper operation and maintenance of any equipment and devices installed
(2)* NFPA 25

29.4* Hydraulic Design Information Sign (Hydraulic Data Nameplate).

29.4.1 The installing contractor shall identify a hydraulically designed sprinkler system with a permanently marked weatherproof metal or rigid plastic sign secured with corrosion-resistant wire, chain, or other approved means.

29.4.2 Such signs shall be placed at every system riser, floor control assembly, alarm valve, dry pipe valve, preaction valve, or deluge valve supplying the corresponding hydraulically designed area unless the AHJ approves an alternate location.

29.4.3 The sign shall include the following information:

(1) Location of the design area or areas
(2) Size (area) of or number of sprinklers in the design area
(3) Discharge densities over the design area or areas
(4) Required flow and residual pressure demand at the base of the riser or fire pump where applicable
(5) Occupancy classification or commodity classification and maximum permitted storage height and configuration
(6) Hose stream allowance included in addition to the sprinkler demand
(7) Name of the installing contractor

N **29.5 Pipe Schedule Design Information Sign (Nameplate).**

N **29.5.1** The installing contractor shall identify a pipe scheduled sprinkler system with a permanently marked weatherproof metal or rigid plastic sign secured with corrosion-resistant wire, chain, or other approved means.

N **29.5.2** Such signs shall be placed at the corresponding system riser.

29.6* General Information Sign.

29.6.1 The installing contractor shall provide a general information sign used to determine system design basis and information relevant to the inspection, testing, and maintenance requirements required by NFPA 25.

29.6.1.1 Such general information shall be provided with a permanently marked weatherproof metal or rigid plastic sign, secured with corrosion-resistant wire, chain, or other acceptable means.

29.6.1.2 Such signs shall be placed at each system control riser, antifreeze loop, and auxiliary system control valve.

29.6.2 The sign shall include the following information:

(1) Name and location of the facility protected
(2) Occupancy classification
(3) Commodity classification
(4) Presence of high-piled and/or rack storage
(5) Maximum height of storage planned
(6) Aisle width planned
(7) Encapsulation of pallet loads
(8) Presence of solid shelving
(9) Flow test data
(10) Presence of flammable/combustible liquids
(11) Presence of hazardous materials
(12) Presence of other special storage
(13) Location of venting valve
(14) Location of auxiliary drains and low point drains on dry pipe and preaction systems
(15) Original results of main drain flow test
(16) Original results of dry pipe and double interlock preaction valve test
(17) Name of installing contractor or designer
(18) Indication of presence and location of antifreeze or other auxiliary systems
(19) Where injection systems are installed to treat MIC or corrosion, the type of chemical, concentration of the chemical, and where information can be found as to the proper disposal of the chemical
(20) Indication of presence of nitrogen where used to allow for increased C value in dry or preaction systems

29.6.3 Combination hydraulic design information and general information shall be permitted.

Chapter 30 Existing System Modifications

30.1 General.

Δ **30.1.1** In addition to the applicable requirements of this standard, the requirements of Chapter 29 shall apply where modifications or additions are made to existing systems.

N **30.1.2*** Existing systems shall be subject to the retroactivity requirements of Section 1.4.

30.1.3 Where additions or modifications are made to an existing system, enough of the existing system shall be indicated on the plans to make all conditions clear.

30.1.4 When backflow prevention devices are to be retroactively installed on existing systems, a thorough hydraulic analysis, including revised hydraulic calculations, new fire flow data, and all necessary modifications to accommodate the additional friction loss, shall be completed as a part of the installation.

30.1.5 A hydraulically calculated system for a building, or a hydraulically calculated addition to a system in an existing sprinklered building using the pipe schedule method, shall supersede the requirements in this standard governing pipe schedules, except that all systems shall continue to be limited by area.

30.1.6 Unless permitted by 30.1.6.1, when modifying existing systems protecting general storage, rack storage, rubber tire storage, roll paper storage, and baled cotton storage, using sprinklers with K-factors K-8.0 (115) or less, the requirements of 21.1.3 and 21.1.4 shall not apply.

30.1.6.1 Where applying the requirements of Table 21.5.1.1 utilizing the design criteria of 0.6 gpm/ft² per 2000 ft² (25.5 mm/min over 185 m²) to existing storage applications, standard-response spray sprinklers with a K-factor of K-11.2 (160) or larger that are listed for storage applications shall be used.

30.1.7 For modifications or additions to existing systems equipped with residential sprinklers, the listed discharge criteria less than 0.1 gpm/ft² (4.1 mm/min) shall be permitted to be used.

N **30.1.8*** When nitrogen is retroactively applied to existing dry pipe or double interlock preaction systems previously having a compressed air supply, a Hazen-Williams C-factor of 100 shall be applied.

30.1.9 Torch cutting and welding shall not be permitted as a means of modifying or repairing sprinkler systems.

30.1.10 Additives to existing systems intended for control of microbiological or other corrosion shall be listed for use within fire sprinkler systems.

30.2 Components.

30.2.1 The use of reconditioned valves and devices as replacement equipment in existing systems shall be permitted.

30.2.2 Where all or part of an inactive sprinkler system is abandoned in place, components including sprinklers, hose valves and hoses, and alarm devices shall be removed.

30.2.3 Control valves abandoned in place shall have the operating mechanisms removed.

30.2.4 Sprinkler system piping and/or valves abandoned in place shall be uniquely identified to differentiate them from active system piping and valves.

30.3 Sprinklers.

30.3.1 Reconditioned sprinklers shall not be permitted on any existing system.

30.3.2* When a threaded sprinkler is removed from a fitting or welded outlet, it shall not be reinstalled except as permitted by 30.3.2.1.

30.3.2.1 Dry sprinklers shall be permitted to be reinstalled when removed in accordance with the manufacturer's installation and maintenance instructions.

30.3.3 Where modifications or additions are made to existing light hazard systems equipped with standard response sprinklers, new standard response sprinklers shall be permitted to be used.

30.3.4 Where individual standard response sprinklers are replaced in existing light hazard systems, new standard response sprinklers shall be permitted to be used.

30.3.5 Where existing light hazard systems are converted to use quick-response or residential sprinklers, all sprinklers in a compartment shall be changed.

30.3.6 When replacing residential sprinklers manufactured prior to 2003 that are no longer available from the manufacturer and that are installed using a design density less than 0.05 gpm/ft² (2.04 mm/min), a residential sprinkler with an equivalent K-factor (±5 percent) shall be permitted to be used, provided the currently listed coverage area for the replacement sprinkler is not exceeded.

30.3.7 Where cover plates on concealed sprinklers have been painted by other than the sprinkler manufacturer, the cover plates shall be replaced.

30.4 Revamping of Pipe Schedule Systems.

30.4.1 The pipe schedule method shall be permitted as follows:

(1) Additions or modifications to existing pipe schedule systems sized according to the pipe schedules of Section 28.5
(2) Additions or modifications to existing extra hazard pipe schedule systems

30.4.2 When pipe schedule systems are revamped to accommodate added ceilings, sprinkler outlets utilized for new armover or drop nipples shall have hexagonal bushings removed when present.

30.4.3 When pipe schedule systems are revamped, a nipple not exceeding 4 in. (100 mm) in length shall be permitted to be installed in the branch line fitting.

30.4.4 All piping other than the nipple permitted in 30.4.3 and 30.4.5 shall be a minimum of 1 in. (25 mm) in diameter in accordance with Figure 30.4.4.

30.4.5 When it is necessary to pipe two new ceiling sprinklers from an existing outlet in an overhead system, the use of a nipple not exceeding 4 in. (100 mm) in length and of the same pipe thread size as the existing outlet shall be permitted in

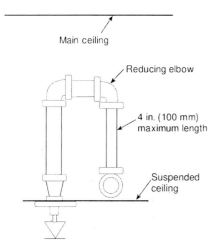

FIGURE 30.4.4   Nipple and Reducing Elbow Supplying Sprinkler Below Ceiling.

accordance with Figure 30.4.5, provided that a hydraulic calculation verifies that the design flow rate will be achieved.

30.4.6 Where an armover is attached to connect to a sprinkler, the use of pipe nipples less than 1 in. (25 mm) in diameter shall not be permitted where seismic design is required on the system.

N **30.5* Existing Systems Area/Density Curves.** Where modifications are being made to an existing system designed based on CMDA criteria differing from the single point densities identified for new systems in Chapters 19, 21, or 25, the criteria included in the respective area/density curves for existing systems shall be permitted to be applied.

30.6 Revamping of Hydraulic Design Systems.

30.6.1 When hydraulically designed systems are revamped, any existing bushing shall be removed and a nipple not exceeding 4 in. (100 mm) in length shall be permitted to be installed in the branch line fitting.

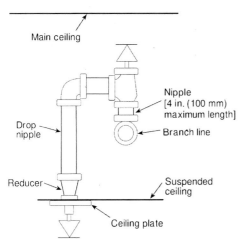

FIGURE 30.4.5   Sprinklers in Concealed Space and Below Ceiling.

30.6.2 Calculations shall be provided to verify that the system design flow rate will be achieved.

30.6.3 When it is necessary to pipe two new ceiling sprinklers from an existing outlet in an overhead system, any bushings shall be removed and the use of a nipple not exceeding 4 in. (100 mm) in length and of the same pipe thread size as the existing outlet shall be permitted, provided that a hydraulic calculation verifies that the design flow rate will be achieved.

30.6.4 Where an armover is attached to connect to a sprinkler, the use of pipe nipples less than 1 in. (25 mm) in diameter shall not be permitted where seismic design is required on the system.

30.7 System Design.

30.7.1 Where an addition or modifications are made to an existing system, enough of the existing system shall be indicated on the plans to make all conditions clear.

30.7.2 The pipe schedule method shall be permitted as follows:

(1)　For modifications or additions to existing systems equipped with residential sprinklers, the listed discharge criteria less than 0.1 gpm/ft^2 (4.1 mm/min) shall be permitted to be used.

(2)　A hydraulically calculated system for a building, or a hydraulically calculated addition to a system in an existing sprinklered building using the pipe schedule method, shall supersede the rules in this standard governing pipe schedules, except that all systems shall continue to be limited by area.

(3)　Unless permitted by 30.7.3, when modifying existing systems protecting general storage, rack storage, rubber tire storage, roll paper storage, and baled cotton storage, using sprinklers with K-factors K-8.0 (115) or less, the requirements of 30.7.2 and 30.7.3 shall not apply.

30.7.3 Where applying the requirements of Figure 25.3.2.4.1(c) and Figure 25.3.2.4.1(d) utilizing the design criteria of 0.6 gpm/ft^2 per 2000 ft^2 (25.5 mm/min over 185 m^2) to existing storage applications, standard-response spray sprinklers with a K-factor of K-11.2 (K-161) or larger that are listed for storage applications shall be used.

30.7.4 For modifications or additions to existing systems equipped with residential sprinklers, the listed discharge criteria less than 0.1 gpm/ft^2 (4.1 mm/min) shall be permitted to be used.

Δ **30.7.5** When backflow prevention devices are to be retroactively installed on existing systems, a thorough hydraulic analysis, including revised hydraulic calculations, new fire flow data, and all necessary system modifications to accommodate the additional friction loss, shall be completed as a part of the installation.

30.7.6 A hydraulically calculated system for a building, or a hydraulically calculated addition to a system in an existing sprinklered building using the pipe schedule method, shall supersede the rules in this standard governing pipe schedules, except that all systems shall continue to be limited by area.

30.7.7 Unless permitted by 30.7.3, when modifying existing systems protecting general storage, rack storage, rubber tire storage, roll paper storage, and baled cotton storage, using sprinklers with K-factors K-8.0 (115) or less, the requirements of 21.1.3 and 21.1.4 shall not apply.

N **30.7.9** A Hazen-Williams C-factor of 100 shall be used in hydraulic calculations for modifications or additions when nitrogen is retroactively applied to existing dry pipe or double interlock preaction systems previously having a compressed air supply.

30.8 Testing.

30.8.1 Modifications to existing piping systems shall require testing at system working pressure.

30.8.1.1 Where modification is made to an existing system affecting more than 20 sprinklers, the new portion shall be isolated and tested at not less than 200 psi (14 bar) for 2 hours.

30.8.1.2 Modifications that cannot be isolated, such as relocated drops, shall require testing at system working pressure.

30.8.2 Modifications to existing dry pipe or double interlock preaction systems shall be tested for air leakage using one of the following test methods:

(1) An air pressure test at 40 psi (2.7 bar) shall be performed for 2 hours as follows:

    (a) The system shall be permitted to lose up to 3 psi (0.2 bar) during the duration of the test.

    (b) Air leaks shall be addressed if the system loses more than 3 psi (0.2 bar) during this test.

(2) With the system at normal system air pressure, the air source shall be shut off for 4 hours. If the low pressure alarm goes off within this period, the leaks shall be addressed.

Chapter 31 Marine Systems

31.1 General.

31.1.1 Chapter 31 outlines the deletions, modifications, and additions that shall be required for marine application. The applicability of Chapter 31 shall be determined by the authority having jurisdiction.

31.1.2 All other requirements of this standard shall apply to merchant vessel systems except as modified by this chapter.

31.1.3* Occupancy Classifications. Marine environment classifications shall be in accordance with Section 4.3.

31.1.4* Partial Installations.

31.1.4.1 Partial installation of automatic sprinklers shall not be permitted, unless the requirements of 31.1.4.2 or 31.1.4.3 are met.

31.1.4.2 Spaces shall be permitted to be protected with an alternative, approved fire suppression system where such areas are separated from the sprinklered areas with a 1-hour-rated assembly.

31.1.4.3 The requirements of 31.1.4.1 shall not apply where specific sections of this standard permit the omission of sprinklers.

31.2 System Components, Hardware, and Use.

31.2.1* Sprinklers shall have a K-factor of K-2.8 (40) or greater.

31.2.2* Sprinkler piping penetrations shall be designed to preserve the fire integrity of the ceiling or bulkhead penetrated.

31.2.3 Spare Sprinklers.

31.2.3.1 The required stock of spare sprinklers shall be carried for each type of sprinkler installed onboard the vessel.

31.2.3.2 Where fewer than six sprinklers of a particular type are installed, 100 percent spares shall be kept in stock.

31.2.3.3 Where applicable, at least one elastometric gasket shall be kept in the cabinet for each fire department connection that is installed onboard the vessel.

31.2.3.4 The cabinet containing spare sprinklers, special wrenches, and elastometric gaskets shall be located in the same central safety station that contains the alarm annunciator panel(s) and supervisory indicators.

31.2.4 System Pipe and Fittings.

31.2.4.1* When ferrous materials are used for piping between the sea chest and zone control valves, these materials shall be protected against corrosion by hot dip galvanizing or by the use of Schedule 80 piping.

31.2.4.2 Maximum design pressure for copper and brass pipe shall not exceed 250 psi (17.2 bar).

31.2.5 Pipe Support.

31.2.5.1* Pipe supports shall comply with the following:

(1) Pipe supports shall be designed to provide adequate lateral, longitudinal, and vertical sway bracing.

(2) The design shall account for the degree of bracing, which varies with the route and operation of the vessel.

(3) Bracing shall be designed to ensure the following:

 (a) Slamming, heaving, and rolling will not shift sprinkler piping, potentially moving sprinklers above ceilings, bulkheads, or other obstructions.

 (b) Piping and sprinklers will remain in place at a steady heel angle at least equal to the maximum required damaged survival angle.

(4) Pipe supports shall be welded to the structure.

(5) Hangers that can loosen during ship motion or vibration, such as screw-down-type hangers, shall not be permitted.

(6) Hangers that are listed for seismic use shall be permitted to be used in accordance with their listing.

31.2.5.2 Sprinkler piping shall be supported by the primary structural members of the vessel such as beams, girders, and stiffeners.

31.2.5.3* The components of hanger assemblies that are welded directly to the ship structure shall not be required to be listed.

31.2.5.4* U-hook sizes shall be no less than that specified in Table 17.2.1.4.

31.2.6 Valves.

31.2.6.1* All indicating, supply, and zone control valves shall be supervised open from a central safety station.

31.2.6.2 Drain and test valves shall meet the applicable requirements of 46 CFR 56.20 and 56.60.

31.2.6.3 Valve markings shall include the information required by 46 CFR 56.20-5(a).

31.2.7 Fire Department Connections and International Shore Connections.

31.2.7.1* A fire department connection and an International Shore Connection shall be installed.

31.2.7.2 The requirements for a fire department connection in 31.2.7.1 shall not apply to vessels that operate primarily on international voyages.

31.2.7.3 Connections shall be located near the gangway or other shore access point so that they are accessible to the land-based fire department.

31.2.7.4 Fire department and International Shore Connections shall be colored and marked so that the connections are easily located from the shore access point (i.e., gangway location) and will not be confused with a firemain connection.

31.2.7.5 An 18 in. × 18 in. (450 mm × 450 mm) sign displaying the symbol for fire department connection as shown in Table 5.2 of NFPA 170 shall be placed at the connection so that it is in plain sight from the shore access point.

31.2.7.6 Connections on both sides of the vessel shall be provided where shore access arrangements make it necessary.

31.2.7.7* Fire department connection thread type shall be compatible with fire department equipment.

31.2.7.8 International shore connections shall comply with ASTM F1121, *Standard Specification for International Shore Connections for Marine Fire Applications.*

31.3 System Requirements.

31.3.1* Relief Valves. Relief valves shall be provided on all wet pipe systems.

31.3.2 Spare Detection Devices. The number of spare detection devices or fusible elements used for protection systems that shall be carried per temperature rating is as follows:

(1) Vessels shall have two spare detection devices or fusible elements when operating voyages are normally less than 24 hours.
(2) Vessels shall have four spare detection devices or fusible elements when operating voyages are normally more than 24 hours.

31.3.3 System Piping Supervision. All preaction sprinkler systems shall be supervised regardless of the number of sprinklers supplied.

31.3.4 Circulating Closed Loop Systems. Circulating closed loop systems shall not be permitted.

31.4 Installation Requirements.

31.4.1 Temperature Zones. Intermediate-temperature-rated sprinklers shall be installed under a noninsulated steel deck that is exposed to sunlight.

31.4.2* Residential Sprinklers. Residential sprinklers shall be permitted for use only in sleeping accommodation areas.

31.4.3 Window Protection. Where required, windows shall be protected by sprinklers installed at a distance not exceeding 1 ft (300 mm) from the glazing at a spacing not exceeding 6 ft (1.8 m) such that the entire glazing surface is wetted at a linear density not less than 6 gpm/ft (75 mm/min), unless listed window sprinkler protection systems are installed in accordance with their installation and testing criteria.

31.4.4* Concealed Spaces.

31.4.4.1 Concealed spaces that are constructed of combustible materials, or materials with combustible finishes or that contain combustible materials, shall be sprinklered.

31.4.4.2 The requirements of 31.4.4.1 shall not apply to concealed spaces that contain only nonmetallic piping that is continuously filled with water.

31.4.5 Vertical Shafts.

31.4.5.1 Sprinklers shall not be required in vertical shafts used as duct, electrical, or pipe shafts that are nonaccessible, noncombustible, and enclosed in an A-Class-rated assembly.

31.4.5.2 Stairway enclosures shall be fully sprinklered.

31.4.6 Bath Modules. Sprinklers shall be installed in bath modules (full room modules) constructed with combustible materials, regardless of room fire load.

31.4.7 Ceiling Types. Drop-out ceilings shall not be used in conjunction with sprinklers.

31.4.8 Return Bends.

31.4.8.1 To prevent sediment buildup, return bends shall be installed in all shipboard sprinkler systems where pendent-type or dry pendent-type sprinklers are used in wet systems *(see Figure 16.3.11.2)*.

31.4.8.2 Consideration shall be given concerning the intrusion of saltwater into the system.

31.4.8.3 Specifically, sprinklers shall not be rendered ineffective by corrosion related to saltwater entrapment within the return bend.

31.4.9 Hose Connections. Sprinkler system piping shall not be used to supply hose connections or hose connections for fire department use.

31.4.10 Heat-Sensitive Piping Materials.

31.4.10.1 Portions of the piping system constructed with a heat-sensitive material shall be subject to the following restrictions:

(1) Piping shall be of non–heat-sensitive type from the sea suction up through the penetration of the last A-Class barrier enclosing the space(s) in which the heat-sensitive piping is installed.
(2) B-Class draft stops shall be fitted not more than 45 ft (14 m) apart between the marine thermal barrier *(see definitions in Chapter 3 and 31.1.3)* and the deck or shell.
(3) Portions of a system that are constructed from heat-sensitive materials shall be installed behind a marine thermal barrier, unless the provisions of item (4) are met.
(4)* Piping materials with brazed joints shall not be required to be installed behind a marine thermal barrier, provided the following conditions are met:

    (a) The system is of the wet pipe type.
    (b) The piping is not located in spaces containing boilers, internal combustion engines, or piping containing flammable or combustible liquids or gases under pressure, cargo holds, or vehicle decks.
    (c) A relief valve in compliance with 8.1.2 is installed in each section of piping that is capable of being isolated by a valve(s).
    (d) A valve(s) isolating the section of piping from the remainder of the system is installed in accordance with 31.4.10.2 and 31.4.10.3.

31.4.10.2 Each zone in which heat-sensitive piping is installed shall be fitted with a valve capable of segregating that zone from the remainder of the system.

31.4.10.3 The valve shall be supervised and located outside of the zone controlled and within an accessible compartment having A-Class boundaries or within a Type 1 stair.

31.4.11 Discharge of Drain Lines.

31.4.11.1 Drain lines shall not be connected to housekeeping, sewage, or deck drains. Drains shall be permitted to be discharged to bilges.

31.4.11.2 Overboard discharges shall meet the requirements of 46 CFR 56.50-95 and shall be corrosion resistant in accordance with 46 CFR 56.60.

31.4.11.3 Systems that contain water additives that are not permitted to be discharged into the environment shall be specially designed to prevent such discharge.

31.4.11.4 Discharges shall be provided with a down-turned elbow.

31.4.12 Alarm Signals and Devices.

31.4.12.1* A visual and audible alarm signal shall be given at the central safety station to indicate when the system is in operation or when a condition that would impair the satisfactory operation of the system exists.

31.4.12.2 Alarm signals shall be provided for, but not limited to, each of the following: monitoring position of control valves, fire pump power supplies and operating condition, water tank levels and temperatures, zone waterflow alarms, pressure of tanks, and air pressure on dry pipe valves.

31.4.12.3 Alarms shall give a distinct indication for each individual system component that is monitored.

31.4.12.4 An audible alarm shall be given at the central safety station within 30 seconds of waterflow.

31.4.12.5 Waterflow alarms shall be installed for every zone of the sprinkler system.

31.4.12.6 Sprinkler zones shall not encompass more than two adjacent decks or encompass more than one main vertical zone.

31.4.12.7 Electrically operated alarm attachments shall comply with, meet, and be installed in accordance with the requirements of 46 CFR, Subchapter J, "Electrical Engineering."

31.4.12.8 All wiring shall be chosen and installed in accordance with IEEE 45, *Recommended Practice for Electrical Installations on Shipboard.*

31.4.13 Test Connections. Where test connections are below the bulkhead deck, they shall comply with the overboard discharge arrangements of 46 CFR 56.50-95.

31.4.14 Protection of Copper Tubing. Copper tubing materials shall be protected against physical damage in areas where vehicles and stores handling equipment operate.

31.5 Design Approaches.

31.5.1 Design Options.

31.5.1.1 Marine sprinkler systems shall be designed using the hydraulic calculation procedure of Chapter 23.

31.5.1.2 The pipe schedule method shall not be used to determine the water demand requirements.

31.5.2* Window Protection. Minimum water demand requirements shall include sprinklers that are installed for the protection of windows as described in 31.4.3.

31.5.3* Hose Stream Allowance. No allowance for hose stream use shall be required.

31.6 Plans and Calculations.

31.6.1 Additional Information. The pressure tank size, high-pressure relief setting, high- and low-water alarm settings, low-pressure alarm setting, and pump start pressure shall be provided.

31.6.2 Sprinklers specifically installed for the protection of windows under 31.4.3 shall be permitted to be of a different size from those protecting the remainder of the occupancy classification.

31.6.3 All of the window sprinklers, however, shall be of the same size.

31.6.4* Marine sprinkler systems shall be designed and installed to be fully operational without a reduction in system performance when the vessel is upright and inclined at the angles of inclination specified in 46 CFR 58.01-40.

31.7 Water Supplies.

31.7.1 General. The water supply requirements for marine applications shall be in accordance with Section 31.7.

31.7.2 Pressure Tank.

31.7.2.1 Unless the requirements of 31.7.2.2 are met, a pressure tank shall be provided. The pressure tank shall be sized and constructed so that the following occurs:

(1) The tank shall contain a standing charge of freshwater equal to that specified by Table 31.7.2.1.
(2) The pressure tank shall be sized in accordance with 5.2.4.
(3) A glass gauge shall be provided to indicate the correct level of water within the pressure tank.
(4) Arrangements shall be provided for maintaining an air pressure in the tank such that, while the standing charge of water is being expended, the pressure will not be less than that necessary to provide the design pressure and flow of the hydraulically most remote design area.
(5) Suitable means of replenishing the air under pressure and the freshwater standing charge in the tank shall be provided.
(6) Tank construction shall be in accordance with the applicable requirements of 46 CFR, Subchapter F, "Marine Engineering."

Table 31.7.2.1 Required Water Supply

System Type	Additional Water Volume
Wet pipe system	Flow requirement of the hydraulically most remote system demand for 1 minute
Preaction system Deluge system Dry pipe system	Flow requirement of the hydraulically most remote system demand for 1 minute of system demand plus the volume needed to fill all dry piping

31.7.2.2 Pressure Tank Alternative. In lieu of a pressure tank, a dedicated pump connected to a freshwater tank shall be permitted to be used, provided the following conditions are met:

(1) The pump is listed for marine use and is sized to meet the required system demand.
(2) The suction for the fire pump is located below the suction for the freshwater system so that there shall be a minimum water supply of at least 1 minute for the required system demand.
(3) Pressure switches are provided in the system and the controller for the pump that automatically start the pump within 10 seconds after detection of a pressure drop of more than 5 percent.
(4) There shall be a reduced pressure zone backflow preventer to prevent contamination of the potable water system by saltwater.

(5) This pump has at least two sources of power. Where the sources of power are electrical, these shall be a main generator and an emergency source of power. One supply shall be taken from the main switchboard, by separate feeder reserved solely for that purpose. This feeder shall be run to an automatic changeover switch situated near the sprinkler unit, and the switch shall normally be kept closed to the feeder from the emergency switchboard. The changeover switch shall be clearly labeled, and no other switch shall be permitted in these feeders.

31.7.2.3 Relief Valves.

31.7.2.3.1 Relief valves shall be installed on the tank to avoid overpressurization and false actuation of any dry pipe valve.

31.7.2.3.2 Relief valves shall comply with 46 CFR 54.15-10.

31.7.2.4 Power Source.

31.7.2.4.1 There shall be not less than two sources of power for the compressors that supply air to the pressure tank.

31.7.2.4.2 Where the sources of power are electrical, these shall be a main generator and an emergency source of power.

31.7.2.4.3 One supply shall be taken from the main switchboard, by separate feeders reserved solely for that purpose.

31.7.2.4.4 Such feeders shall be run to a changeover switch situated near the air compressor, and the switch normally shall be kept closed to the feeder from the emergency switchboard.

31.7.2.4.5 The changeover switch shall be clearly labeled, and no other switch shall be permitted in these feeders.

31.7.2.5 Multiple Tanks.

31.7.2.5.1 More than one pressure tank can be installed, provided that each is treated as a single water source when determining valve arrangements.

31.7.2.5.2 Check valves shall be installed to prohibit flow from tank to tank or from pump to tank, unless the tank is designed to hold only pressurized air.

31.7.2.6 In systems subject to use with saltwater, valves shall be so arranged as to prohibit contamination of the pressure tank with saltwater.

31.7.2.7* Where applicable, a means shall be provided to restrict the amount of air that can enter the pressure tank from the air supply system. A means shall also be provided to prevent water from backflowing into the air supply system.

31.7.3 Fire Pump.

31.7.3.1 A dedicated, automatically controlled pump that is listed for marine service, which takes suction from the sea, shall be provided to supply the sprinkler system.

31.7.3.2 Where two pumps are required to ensure the reliability of the water supply, the pump that supplies the fire main shall be allowed to serve as the second fire pump.

31.7.3.3* The pump shall be sized to meet the water demand of the hydraulically most demanding area.

31.7.3.4 Pumps shall be designed to not exceed 120 percent of the rated capacity of the pump.

31.7.3.5 The system shall be designed so that, before the supply falls below the design criteria, the fire pump shall be automatically started and shall supply water to the system until manually shut off.

31.7.3.6 Where pump and freshwater tank arrangement is used in lieu of the pressure tank, there must be a pressure switch that senses a system pressure drop of 25 percent, and the controller must automatically start the fire pump(s) if pressure is not restored within 20 seconds.

31.7.3.7 There shall be not less than two sources of power supply for the fire pumps. Where the sources of power are electrical, these shall be a main generator and an emergency source of power.

31.7.3.8 One supply shall be taken from the main switchboard by separate feeders reserved solely for that purpose.

31.7.3.9 Such feeders shall be run to a changeover switch situated near to the sprinkler unit, and the switch normally shall be kept closed to the feeder from the emergency switchboard.

31.7.3.10 The changeover switch shall be clearly labeled, and no other switch shall be permitted in these feeders.

31.7.3.11 Test Valves.

31.7.3.11.1 A test valve(s) shall be installed on the discharge side of the pump with a short open-ended discharge pipe.

31.7.3.11.2 The area of the pipe shall be adequate to permit the release of the required water output to supply the demand of the hydraulically most remote area.

31.7.3.12 Multiple Pumps.

31.7.3.12.1 Where two fire pumps are required to ensure the reliability of the water supply, each fire pump shall meet the requirements of 31.7.3.1 through 31.7.3.4.

31.7.3.12.2 In addition, a system that is required to have more than one pump shall be designed to accommodate the following features:

(1)* Pump controls and system sensors shall be arranged such that the secondary pump will automatically operate if the primary pump fails to operate or deliver the required water pressure and flow. *[Figure A.31.7.3.12.2(1) is an example of an acceptable dual pump arrangement.]*

(2) Both pumps shall be served from normal and emergency power sources. However, where approved by the authority having jurisdiction, the secondary pump shall be permitted to be nonelectrically driven.

(3) Pump failure or operation shall be indicated at the central safety station.

31.7.3.13* If not specifically prohibited, the fire pump that supplies the fire main shall be permitted to be used as the second pump, provided the following conditions are met:

(1) The pump is adequately sized to meet the required fire hose and sprinkler system pressure and flow demands simultaneously.

(2) The fire main system is segregated from the sprinkler system by a normally closed valve that is designed to automatically open upon failure of the designated fire pump.

(3) The fire pump that supplies the fire main is automatically started in the event of dedicated fire pump failure or loss of pressure in the sprinkler main. *(See Figure A.31.7.3.13.)*

31.7.4 Water Supply Configurations.

31.7.4.1 The pressure tank and fire pump shall be located in a position reasonably remote from any machinery space of Category A.

31.7.4.2 All valves within the water supply piping system shall be supervised.

31.7.4.3 Only freshwater shall be used as the initial charge within the piping network.

31.7.4.4 The sprinkler system shall be cross-connected with the ship's fire main system and fitted with a lockable screwdown nonreturn valve such that backflow from the sprinkler system to the fire main is prevented.

31.7.4.5 The piping, tanks, and pumps that make up the water supply shall be installed in accordance with the applicable requirements of 46 CFR, Subchapter F, "Marine Engineering."

31.7.4.6* When a shorewater supply is to be used during extended dockside periods, the water supply shall be qualified in the manner described in 5.2.2.

31.7.4.7 Tests shall be conducted in accordance with the requirements of the local shore-based authority having jurisdiction.

31.7.4.8 The water supply information listed in Section 4.5 shall then be provided to the authority having jurisdiction.

31.8 System Acceptance.

31.8.1 Hydrostatic Tests. In addition to the interior piping, the test required by 29.2.1.8 shall also be conducted on all external water supply connections including international shore and fireboat connections.

31.8.2 Alarm Test. A waterflow test shall result in an alarm at the central safety station within 30 seconds after flow through the test connection begins.

31.8.3 Operational Tests.

31.8.3.1 Pressure tank and pump operation, valve actuation, and waterflow shall also be tested.

31.8.3.2 Pump operation and performance shall be tested in accordance with Chapter 14 of NFPA 20.

31.9 System Instructions and Maintenance.

31.9.1 Instructions for operation, inspection, maintenance, and testing shall be kept on the vessel.

31.9.2 Records of inspections, tests, and maintenance required by NFPA 25 shall also be kept on the vessel.

Chapter 32 System Inspection, Testing, and Maintenance

Δ **32.1* General.** A sprinkler system installed in accordance with this standard shall be inspected, tested, and maintained by the property owner or their authorized representative in accordance with NFPA 25 to ensure the system continues to provide a reasonable degree of protection for life and property from fire.

Annex A Explanatory Material

Annex A is not a part of the requirements of this NFPA document but is included for informational purposes only. This annex contains explanatory material, numbered to correspond with the applicable text paragraphs.

A.1.1 This standard provides a range of sprinkler system approaches, design development alternatives, and component options that are all acceptable. Building owners and their designated representatives are advised to carefully evaluate proposed selections for appropriateness and preference.

A.1.1.2 Various codes and standards allow exceptions and reductions in building fire protection and other construction features where fire sprinkler systems are installed in accordance with NFPA standards. Only after appropriate analysis and evaluation of a tested mist system has been performed for the intended installation, and taking into consideration criteria other than solely fire-fighting performance (visibility, pressure ratings of backup systems, etc.) should exceptions and reductions in building fire protection and other construction features be allowed by the authority having jurisdiction. These systems are adequately described in NFPA 750.

A.1.1.3 This standard also provides guidance for the installation of systems for exterior protection and specific hazards. Where these systems are installed, they are also designed for protection of a fire from a single ignition source.

Δ **A.1.2** Since its inception, this document has been developed on the basis of standardized materials, devices, and design practices. However, Sections 1.2 and 15.2 allow the use of materials and devices not specifically designated by this standard, provided such use is within parameters established by a listing organization. In using such materials or devices, it is important that all conditions, requirements, and limitations of the listing be fully understood and accepted and that the installation be in complete accord with such listing requirements.

A.1.6.1.4 Where both units of measure are presented (SI and Imperial), users of this standard should apply one set of units consistently and should not alternate between units.

A.1.6.3 Some dimensions used in this standard require a tight precision and others do not. For example, when performing hydraulic calculations more precision is required than when specifying a nominal dimension. An example is pipe sizes, where we typically refer to a nominal diameter rather than the exact diameter. The metric equivalents also have a set of generally accepted nominal measurements, and they are not a precise conversion from the "English Unit" nominal dimension. Throughout the standard the generally accepted nominal pipe sizes have been used. For example, 1 in. pipe = 25 mm, 1¼ in. pipe = 32 mm, 1½ in. pipe = 40 mm, and so forth. In other cases, rounding is used and the number of significant digits taken into account. For example, a 30 ft ceiling would be 9.144 m. This implies a level of precision that is higher than used for the original dimension, and a conversion to 9.1 m or even 9 m is more appropriate. Another example is that in the standard, 1 in. has been converted to 25 mm and not 25.4 mm, 2 in. to 50 mm, 6 in. to 150 mm, and so forth. Finally, locally available material can have different characteristics in countries that use metric units than are typically found in the United States. Examples are things like standard door or window sizes, rack dimensions, and so forth. In these cases an approximate conversion can also be used. Where approximate conversions have been used, it is acceptable for a designer or installer to use an exact conversion rather than the approximate conversion used in the standard.

A.3.2.1 Approved. The National Fire Protection Association does not approve, inspect, or certify any installations, procedures, equipment, or materials; nor does it approve or evaluate testing laboratories. In determining the acceptability of installations, procedures, equipment, or materials, the authority having jurisdiction may base acceptance on compliance with NFPA or other appropriate standards. In the absence of such standards, said authority may require evidence of proper installation, procedure, or use. The authority having jurisdiction may also refer to the listings or labeling practices of an organization that is concerned with product evaluations and is thus in a position to determine compliance with appropriate standards for the current production of listed items.

A.3.2.2 Authority Having Jurisdiction (AHJ). The phrase "authority having jurisdiction," or its acronym AHJ, is used in NFPA documents in a broad manner, since jurisdictions and approval agencies vary, as do their responsibilities. Where public safety is primary, the authority having jurisdiction may be a federal, state, local, or other regional department or individual such as a fire chief; fire marshal; chief of a fire prevention bureau, labor department, or health department; building official; electrical inspector; or others having statutory authority. For insurance purposes, an insurance inspection department, rating bureau, or other insurance company representative may be the authority having jurisdiction. In many circumstances, the property owner or his or her designated agent assumes the role of the authority having jurisdiction; at government installations, the commanding officer or departmental official may be the authority having jurisdiction.

A.3.2.3 Listed. The means for identifying listed equipment may vary for each organization concerned with product evaluation; some organizations do not recognize equipment as listed unless it is also labeled. The authority having jurisdiction should utilize the system employed by the listing organization to identify a listed product.

A.3.3.4 Aisle Width. See Figure A.3.3.4. (AUT-SSD)

A.3.3.8.3 Open Array (Palletized, Solid-Piled, Bin Box, and Shelf Storage). Fire tests conducted to represent a closed array utilized 6 in. (150 mm) longitudinal flues and no transverse flues. Fire tests conducted to represent an open array utilized 12 in. (300 mm) longitudinal flues. (AUT-SSD)

A.3.3.8.5 Standard Array (Rolled Paper). The occasional presence of partially used rolls on top of columns of otherwise uniform diameter rolls does not appreciably affect the burning characteristics. (AUT-SSD)

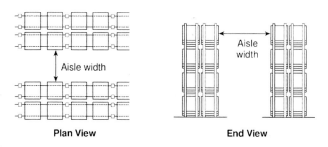

Plan View   **End View**

FIGURE A.3.3.4   Illustration of Aisle Width.

A.3.3.13 Back-to-Back Shelf Storage. The requirement for the lack of a longitudinal flue space does not prohibit a small gap between the units or a small gap between the shelves and the vertical barrier. See Figure A.3.3.13. (AUT-SSD)

A.3.3.14 Baled Cotton. "Linter" is another name for lint removed from cotton seed; "mote" is another name for residual materials from the ginning process.

See Table A.3.3.14. (AUT-SSD)

A.3.3.17 Bathroom. A room is still considered a bathroom if it contains just a toilet. Additionally, two bathrooms can be adjacent to each other and are considered separate rooms, provided they are enclosed with the required level of construction. A compartment containing only a toilet, regardless of its intended use, is considered a bathroom. (AUT-SSI)

A.3.3.23 Carton Records Storage. Carton records storage is a Class III commodity when it is within the definition of 20.4.3 and is permitted to contain a limited amount (5 percent by weight or volume or less) of Group A or Group B plastics. Materials stored include Class I and II commodities, paper business records, books, magazines, stationery, newspapers, cardboard dividers, and cartons. See Table A.20.4.3. (AUT-SSD)

A.3.3.27 Ceiling Pocket. It is not the intent of this definition to be applied to structural and/or framing members otherwise used to define obstructed or unobstructed construction. Ceiling pockets can be protected or unprotected. A ceiling pocket where the upper ceiling is within the allowable vertical distance from the sprinkler deflector should be considered a protected ceiling pocket. Buildings with protected ceiling pockets are permitted to use the quick-response reduction of 19.2.3.2.3. Buildings with unprotected ceiling pockets greater than 32 ft² (3.0 m²) are not allowed to use the quick-response reduction of 19.2.3.2.3.

Where a sprinkler(s) in the upper ceiling level is obstructed or where placing sprinklers in the lower ceiling (only) would

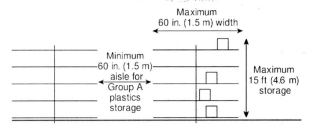

FIGURE A.3.3.13   Back-to-Back Shelf Storage.

violate the allowable deflector distance from the upper level ceiling, additional sprinklers would be necessary. (AUT-SSI)

A.3.3.41 Compartmented. Cartons used in most of the FM Global–sponsored plastic tests involved an ordinary 200 lb (91 kg) test of outside corrugated cartons with five layers of vertical pieces of corrugated carton used as dividers on the inside. There were also single horizontal pieces of corrugated carton between each layer.

Other tests sponsored by the Society of Plastics Industry, Industrial Risk Insurers, FM Global, and Kemper used two vertical pieces of carton (not corrugated) to form an "X" in the carton for separation of product. This arrangement was not considered compartmented, as the pieces of carton used for separations were flexible (not rigid), and only two pieces were used in each carton. (AUT-SSD)

A.3.3.43.1 Obstructed Construction. The following examples of obstructed construction are provided to assist the user in determining the type of construction feature:

(1) *Beam and Girder Construction.* The term *beam and girder construction* as used in this standard includes noncombustible and combustible roof or floor decks supported by wood beams of 4 in. (100 mm) or greater nominal thickness or concrete or steel beams spaced 3 ft to 7½ ft (900 mm to 2.3 m) on center and either supported on or framed into girders. [Where supporting a wood plank deck, this includes semi-mill and panel construction, and where supporting (with steel framing) gypsum plank, steel deck, concrete, tile, or similar material, this includes much of the so-called noncombustible construction.]

(2) *Concrete Tee Construction.* The term *concrete tee construction* as it is used in this standard refers to solid concrete members with stems (legs) having a nominal thickness less than the nominal height. [*See Figure A.3.3.43.1(a) for examples of concrete tee construction.*]

(3) *Composite Wood Joist Construction.* The term *composite wood joist construction* refers to wood beams of "I" cross section constructed of wood flanges and solid wood web, supporting a floor or roof deck. Composite wood joists can vary in depth up to 48 in. (1.2 m), can be spaced up to 48 in. (1.2 m) on centers, and can span up to 60 ft (18 m) between supports. Joist channels should be fire-stopped to the full depth of the joists with material equivalent to the web construction so that individual channel areas do not exceed 300 ft² (28 m²). [*See Figure A.3.3.43.1(b) for an example of composite wood joist construction.*]

Δ **Table A.3.3.14 Typical Cotton Bale Types and Approximate Sizes**

	Dimensions		Average Weight		Volume		Density	
Bale Type	in.	mm	lb	kg	ft³	m³	lb/ft³	kg/m³
Compressed, standard	57 × 29 × 23	1425 × 725 × 575	500	225	22.0	0.62	22.7	365
Gin, standard	55 × 31 × 21	1325 × 775 × 525	500	225	20.7	0.59	24.2	390
Compressed, universal	58 × 25 × 21	1450 × 625 × 525	500	225	17.6	0.50	28.4	455
Gin, universal	55 × 26 × 21	1375 × 650 × 525	500	225	17.4	0.49	28.7	460
Compressed, high density	58 × 22 × 21	1450 × 550 × 525	500	225	15.5	0.44	32.2	515
Densely packed baled cotton	55 × 21 × 27.6 to 35.4	1375 × 525 × 690 to 885	500	225	21.1	0.60	22.0	350

(4) *Panel Construction.* The term *panel construction* as used in this standard includes ceiling panels formed by members capable of trapping heat to aid the operation of sprinklers and limited to a maximum of 300 ft² (28 m²) in area. There should be no unfilled penetrations in the cross-sectional area of the bounding structural members including the interface at the roof. Beams spaced more than 7½ ft (2.3 m) apart and framed into girders qualify as panel construction, provided the 300 ft² (28 m²) area limitation is met.

(5) *Semi-Mill Construction.* The term *semi-mill construction* as used in this standard refers to a modified standard mill construction, where greater column spacing is used and beams rest on girders.

(6) *Wood Joist Construction.* The term *wood joist construction* refers to solid wood members of rectangular cross section, which can vary from 2 in. to 4 in. (50 mm to 100 mm) nominal width and can be up to 14 in. (350 mm) nominal depth, spaced up to 3 ft (900 mm) on centers, and can span up to 40 ft (12 m) between supports, supporting a floor or roof deck. Solid wood members less than 4 in. (100 mm) nominal width and up to 14 in. (350 mm) nominal depth, spaced more than 3 ft (900 mm) on centers, are also considered as wood joist construction. Wood joists can exceed 14 in. (350 mm) in nominal depth.

(7) *Bar Joist Construction with Fireproofing.* In order to meet building codes, bar joists are often covered with fireproofing materials. In such an event, if greater than 30 percent of the area of the joist is obstructed, it should be considered obstructed construction.

(8) *Steel Purlin Construction.* This term refers to clear span or multiple span buildings with straight or tapered columns and frames supporting C- or Z-type purlins greater than 4 in. (100 mm) in depth spaced up to 7½ ft (2.3 m) on center.

(9) *Truss Construction (Wood or Steel).* The term *truss construction* refers to parallel or pitched chord members connected by open web members supporting a roof or floor deck with top and bottom members greater than 4 in. (100 mm) in depth. [See Figure A.3.3.43.1(c).]

(10) *Bar Joist Construction (Wood or Steel).* The term *bar joist construction* refers to construction employing joists consisting of steel truss-shaped members. Wood truss-shaped members, which consist of wood top and bottom chord members with steel tube or bar webs, are also defined as bar joists. Bar joists include noncombustible or combustible roof or floor decks on bar joist construction with top and bottom chord members greater than 4 in. (100 mm) in depth. [See Figure A.3.3.43.2(a) and Figure A.3.3.43.2(b) for examples of bar joist construction.] (AUT-SSI)

A.3.3.43.2 Unobstructed Construction. The following examples of unobstructed construction are provided to assist the user in determining the type of construction feature:

(1) *Bar Joist Construction.* The term *bar joist construction* refers to construction employing joists consisting of steel truss-shaped members. Wood truss-shaped members, which consist of wood top and bottom chord members with steel tube or bar webs, are also defined as bar joists. Bar joists include noncombustible or combustible roof or floor decks on bar joist construction with top and bottom chord members not exceeding 4 in. (100 mm) in depth.

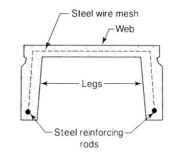

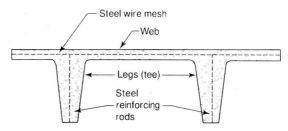

FIGURE A.3.3.43.1(a)   Typical Concrete Tee Construction.

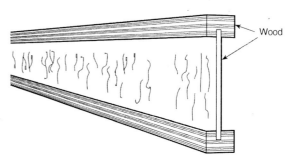

FIGURE A.3.3.43.1(b)   Typical Composite Wood Joist Construction.

[See Figure A.3.3.43.2(a) and Figure A.3.3.43.2(b) for examples of bar joist construction.]

(2) *Open-Grid Ceilings.* The term *open-grid ceilings* as used in this standard refers to ceilings in which the openings are ¼ in. (6 mm) or larger in the least dimension, the thickness of the ceiling material does not exceed the least dimension of the openings, and the openings constitute at least 70 percent of the ceiling area.

(3) *Smooth Ceiling Construction.* The term *smooth ceiling construction* as used in this standard includes the following:

(a) Flat slab, pan-type reinforced concrete

(b) Continuous smooth bays formed by wood, concrete, or steel beams spaced more than 7½ ft (2.3 m) on centers — beams supported by columns, girders, or trusses

(c) Smooth roof or floor decks supported directly on girders or trusses spaced more than 7½ ft (2.3 m) on center

(d) Smooth monolithic ceilings of at least ¾ in. (19 mm) of plaster on metal lath or a combination of materials of equivalent fire-resistive rating attached to the underside of wood joists, wood trusses, and bar joists

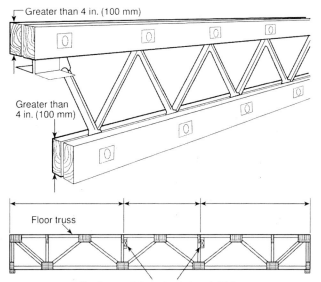

△ FIGURE A.3.3.43.1(c)   Wood Truss Construction.

(e)   Open-web-type steel beams, regardless of spacing
(f)   Smooth shell-type roofs, such as folded plates, hyperbolic paraboloids, saddles, domes, and long barrel shells
(g)   Suspended ceilings of combustible or noncombustible construction
(h)   Smooth monolithic ceilings with fire resistance less than that specified under item A.3.3.43.2(3)(d) and attached to the underside of wood joists, wood trusses, and bar joists

Combustible or noncombustible floor decks are permitted in the construction specified in A.3.3.43.2(3)(b) through A.3.3.43.2(3)(f). A.3.3.43.2(3)(b) would include standard mill construction.

(4)   *Standard Mill Construction.* The term *standard mill construction* as used in this standard refers to heavy timber construction as defined in NFPA 220.

(5)   *Truss Construction (Wood or Steel).* The term *truss construction* refers to parallel or pitched chord members connected by open web members supporting a roof or floor deck with top and bottom members not exceeding 4 in. (100 mm) in depth. *[See Figure A.3.3.43.2(c).]* (AUT-SSI)

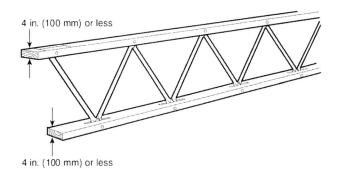

FIGURE A.3.3.43.2(a)   Wood Bar Joist Construction.

A.3.3.44 Container (Shipping, Master, or Outer Container). The term *container* includes items such as cartons and wrappings. Fire-retardant containers or tote boxes do not by themselves create a need for automatic sprinklers unless coated with oil or grease. Containers can lose their fire-retardant properties if washed. For obvious reasons, they should not be exposed to rainfall. (AUT-SSD)

A.3.3.59 Draft Curtain. Additional information about the size and installation of draft curtains can be found in NFPA 204. (AUT-SSD)

A.3.3.68 Encapsulation. Totally noncombustible commodities on wood pallets enclosed only by a plastic sheet as described are not covered under this definition. Banding (i.e., stretch-wrapping around the sides only of a pallet load) is not considered to be encapsulation. Where there are holes or voids in the plastic or waterproof cover on the top of the carton that exceed more than half of the area of the cover, the term *encapsulated* does not apply. The term *encapsulated* does not apply to plastic-enclosed products or packages inside a large, nonplastic, enclosed container. (AUT-SSD)

A.3.3.76 Face Sprinklers. All face sprinklers should be located within the rack structure. The flue spaces are generally created

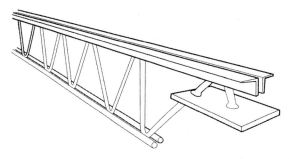

FIGURE A.3.3.43.2(b)   Open-Web Bar Joist Construction.

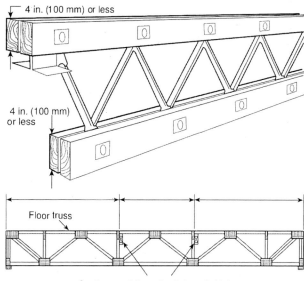

△ FIGURE A.3.3.43.2(c)   Examples of Wood Truss Construction.

by the arrangement of the racks, and "walkways" should not be considered flue spaces. (AUT-SSD)

A.3.3.88 Four-Way Bracing. A sway brace assembly could include a lateral and longitudinal brace in combination. (AUT-HBS)

N **A.3.3.89 Free-Flowing Plastic Materials.** Examples of free-flowing plastic materials include powder, pellets, flakes, or random-packed small objects [e.g., razor blade dispensers, 1 oz to 2 oz (28 g to 57 g) bottles]. (AUT-SSD)

N **A.3.3.100 High-Piled Storage.** The definition of the term *high-piled storage* is meant to be applied only in this standard to sprinkler system design and installation requirements, and does not define the same term in other codes and standards. Stockpiles in retail stores and similar locations should not be considered high-piled storage. In addition, high-piled storage requirements are intended to be limited to storage occupancies protected in accordance with Chapters 20 through 25. (AUT-SSD)

Δ **A.3.3.120 Limited-Combustible Material.** Material subject to increase in combustibility or flame spread index beyond the limits herein established through the effects of age, moisture, or other atmospheric condition is considered combustible. See NFPA 259 and NFPA 220.

A.3.3.122 Longitudinal Flue Space. See Figure A.3.3.122. (AUT-SSD)

A.3.3.124 Low-Piled Storage. This definition is not intended to address allowable design approaches and protection schemes. See A.3.3.100. (AUT-SSD)

A.3.3.125.4 Heat-Sensitive Material. The backbone of the fire protection philosophy for U.S. flagged vessels and passenger vessels that trade internationally is limiting a fire to the compartment of origin by passive means. Materials that do not withstand a 1-hour fire exposure when tested in accordance with ASTM E119, *Standard Test Methods for Fire Tests of Building Construction and Materials,* or ANSI/UL 263, *Fire Tests of Building Construction Materials,* are considered "heat sensitive." (AUT-SSI)

A.3.3.125.7 International Shore Connection. See Figure A.3.3.125.7. (AUT-SSI)

Δ **A.3.3.125.8 Marine System.** Some types of sprinkler systems can closely resemble marine systems, such as a system installed on a floating structure that has a permanent water supply connection to a public main. For these types of systems, judgment should be used in determining if certain aspects of Chapter 26 are applicable. (AUT-SSI)

A.3.3.125.9 Marine Thermal Barrier. A marine thermal barrier is typically referred to as a B-15 boundary. (AUT-SSI)

Δ **A.3.3.130 Miscellaneous Storage.** The sprinkler system design criteria for miscellaneous storage are covered in 4.3.1.7 and 4.3.1.4. (AUT-SSD)

A.3.3.131 Miscellaneous Tire Storage. The limitations on the type and size of storage are intended to identify those situations where tire storage is present in limited quantities and incidental to the main use of the building. Occupancies such as aircraft hangars, automobile dealers, repair garages, retail storage facilities, automotive and truck assembly plants, and mobile home assembly plants are types of facilities where miscellaneous storage could be present. (AUT-SSD)

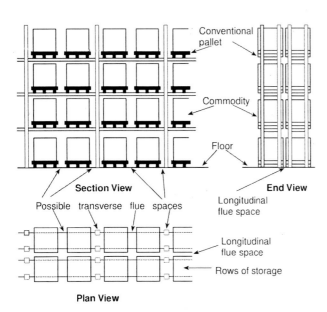

FIGURE A.3.3.122   Typical Double-Row (Back-to-Back) Rack Arrangement.

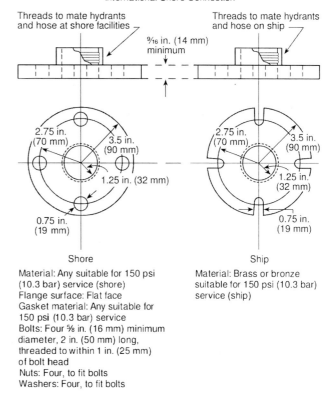

Δ **FIGURE A.3.3.125.7   International Shore Fire Connection.**

A.3.3.149 Open-Top Container. Open-top containers can prevent water from running across the top to storage and down the flues and can also collect water. The container will prevent water penetration to a fire in lower levels where it is needed. Rack or flue collapse can also occur if too much water is collected. Consideration should be given to the potential degree of water collection possible within the container when applying the definition of an open-top container. The following conditions should be considered:

(1) Small openings at the top of containers containing such items as fresh produce are quite common and should not be considered as an open-top container.
(2) Arrangements that include open-top containers that are all located on the bottom tier of rack storage do not prevent penetration of water and should not be considered an open-top container.
(3) Containers having either wire mesh siding or large uniform openings along the bottom perimeter of each container, such that water enters the container at the same flow rate and discharge evenly into the flue spaces should not be considered as an open-top container provided the contents of the container are not water absorbent and are not capable of blocking such container openings.
(4) Open-top containers that are stored in fixed location on racks equipped with flat or domed-shaped fixed-in-place lids that are provided directly above the open-top containers and prevent water from entering the open-top container, as well as distribute water equally into all flue spaces should not be considered an open-top container. (AUT-SSD)

A.3.3.154.1 Conventional Pallet. See Figure A.3.3.154.1. (AUT-SSD)

A.3.3.154.3 Reinforced Plastic Pallet. See Figure A.3.3.154.3(a) and Figure A.3.3.154.3(b). (AUT-SSD)

A.3.3.159 Pile Stability, Stable Piles. Pile stability performance has been shown to be a difficult factor to judge prior to a pile being subjected to an actual fire. In the test work comple-

Conventional pallet

Solid flat bottom
wood pallet (slave pallet)

FIGURE A.3.3.154.1   Typical Pallets.

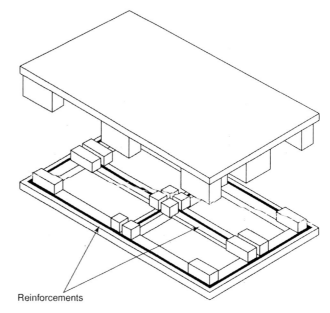

Reinforcements

FIGURE A.3.3.154.3(a)   Cut-Away Reinforced Plastic Pallet.

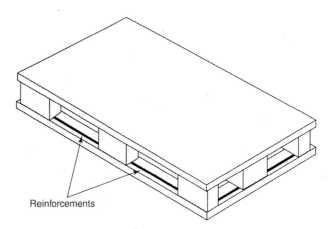

Reinforcements

FIGURE A.3.3.154.3(b)   Assembled Reinforced Plastic Pallet.

ted, compartmented cartons *(see A.3.3.41, Compartmented)* have been shown to be stable under fire conditions. Tests also indicated cartons that were not compartmented tended to be unstable under fire conditions.

Storage on pallets, compartmented storage, and plastic components that are held in place by materials that do not deform readily under fire conditions are examples of stable storage. (AUT-SSD)

A.3.3.160 Pile Stability, Unstable Piles. Leaning stacks, crushed bottom cartons, and reliance on combustible bands for stability are examples of potential pile instability under a fire condition. An increase in pile height tends to increase instability. (AUT-SSD)

A.3.3.165 Post-Installed Anchors. Examples of these are wedge or undercut anchors, or powder-driven studs. (AUT-HBS)

A.3.3.170 Private Fire Service Main. See Figure A.3.3.170.

A.3.3.171 Prying Factor. Prying factors in NFPA 13 are utilized to determine the design loads for attachments to concrete. Prying is a particular concern for anchorage to concrete because the anchor could fail in a brittle fashion. (AUT-HBS)

A.3.3.177 Rack. Shelving can be solid, slatted, or open. Racks can be fixed, portable, or movable. Loading can be either manual, using lift trucks, stacker cranes, or hand placement, or automatic, using machine-controlled storage and retrieval systems.

Rack storage as referred to in this standard contemplates commodities in a rack structure, usually steel. Many variations

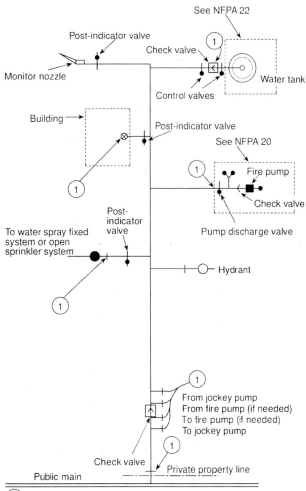

① End of private fire service main

Note: The piping (aboveground or buried) shown is specific as to the end of the private fire service main and schematic only for illustrative purposes beyond. Details of valves and their location requirements are covered in the specific standard involved.

FIGURE A.3.3.170   Typical Private Fire Service Main.

of dimensions are found. Racks can be single-, double-, or multiple-row, with or without solid shelving. The standard commodity used in most of the tests was 42 in. (1.1 m) on a side. Examples of the types of racks covered in this standard are as follows:

(1) *Double-Row Racks.* Pallets rest on two beams parallel to the aisle. Any number of pallets can be supported by one pair of beams. *[See Figure A.3.3.177(a) through Figure A.3.3.177(d).]*

(2) *Automatic Storage-Type Rack.* The pallet is supported by two rails running perpendicular to the aisle. *[See Figure A.3.3.177(e).]*

(3) *Multiple-Row Racks More Than Two Pallets Deep, Measured Aisle to Aisle.* These racks include drive-in racks, drive-through racks, flow-through racks, portable racks arranged in the same manner, and conventional or automatic racks with aisles less than 42 in. (1.1 m) wide. *[See Figure A.3.3.177(f) through Figure A.3.3.177(i).]*

(4) *Movable Racks.* Movable racks are racks on fixed rails or guides. They can be moved back and forth only in a horizontal, two-dimensional plane. A moving aisle is created as abutting racks are either loaded or unloaded, then moved across the aisle to abut other racks. *[See Figure A.3.3.177(k).]*

(5) *Cantilever Rack.* The load is supported on arms that extend horizontally from columns. The load can rest on the arms or on shelves supported by the arms. *[See Figure A.3.3.177(j).]*

Load depth in conventional or automatic racks should be considered a nominal 4 ft (1.2 m). *[See Figure A.3.3.177(b).]*

When catwalks are installed between racks, these areas are not to be considered flue spaces. (AUT-SSD)

A.3.3.180 Raw Water Source. Examples of raw water sources are mill ponds, lakes, streams, open-top reservoirs, and so forth. Examples of non-raw water sources can include city water supplies, cisterns, pressure tanks, gravity tanks, break tanks, aquifers, and so forth. Water sources that are closed or protected from direct contact with the environment should not be considered raw. (AUT-SSD)

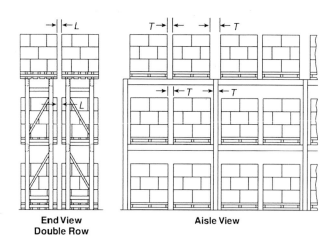

L Longitudinal flue space
T Transverse flue space

FIGURE A.3.3.177(a)   Conventional Pallet Rack.

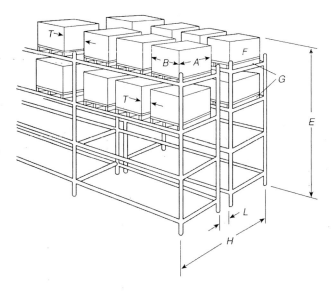

A Load depth   G Pallet
B Load width   H Rack depth
E Storage height   L Longitudinal flue space
F Commodity   T Transverse flue space

FIGURE A.3.3.177(b)   Double-Row Racks Without Solid or Slatted Shelves.

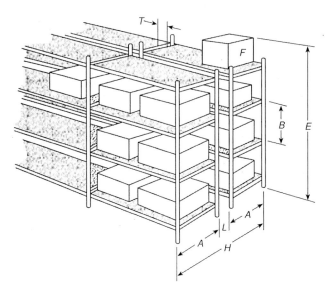

A Shelf depth   H Rack depth
B Shelf height   L Longitudinal flue space
E Storage height   T Transverse flue space
F Commodity

FIGURE A.3.3.177(c)   Double-Row Racks with Solid Shelves.

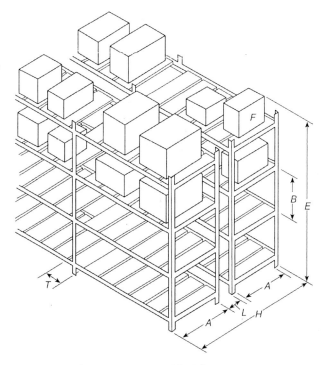

A Shelf depth   H Rack depth
B Shelf height   L Longitudinal flue space
E Storage height   T Transverse flue space
F Commodity

FIGURE A.3.3.177(d)   Double-Row Racks with Slatted Shelves.

A.3.3.188.3 Roll Paper Storage Height. The size of rolls and limitations of mechanical handling equipment should be considered in determining maximum storage height. (AUT-SSD)

A.3.3.188.5 Wrapped Roll Paper Storage. Rolls that are completely protected with a heavyweight kraft wrapper on both sides and ends are subject to a reduced degree of fire hazard. Standard methods for wrapping and capping rolls are outlined in Figure A.3.3.188.5.

In some cases, rolls are protected with laminated wrappers, using two sheets of heavy kraft with a high-temperature wax laminate between the sheets. Where using this method, the overall weight of wax-laminated wrappers should be based on the basis weight per 1000 ft^2 (93 m^2) of the outer sheet only, rather than on the combined basis weight of the outer and inner laminated wrapper sheets. A properly applied wrapper can have the effect of changing the class of a given paper to essentially that of the wrapper material. The effect of applying a wrapper to tissue has not been determined by test. (AUT-SSD)

A.3.3.191 Rubber Tire Rack Illustrations. Figure A.3.3.191(a) through Figure A.3.3.191(g) do not necessarily cover all possible rubber tire storage configurations.

A.3.3.194 Seismic Separation Assembly. Seismic separation assemblies include traditional assemblies as shown in Figure A.18.3(a) and seismic loops as shown in Figure A.18.3(b). (AUT-HBS)

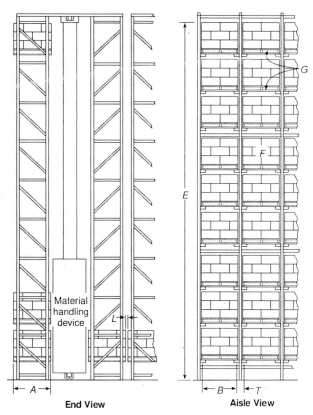

A Load depth   G Pallet
B Load width   L Longitudinal flue space
E Storage height   T Transverse flue space
F Commodity

FIGURE A.3.3.177(e)   Automatic Storage-Type Rack.

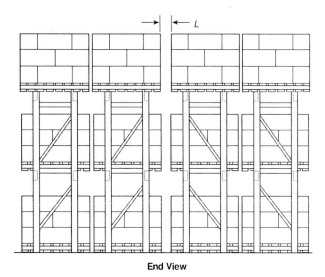

L Longitudinal flue space

FIGURE A.3.3.177(f)   Multiple-Row Rack Served by Reach Truck.

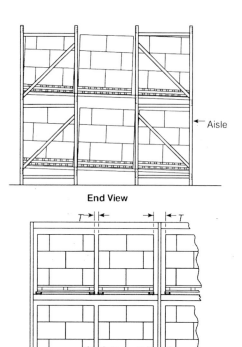

T Transverse flue space

FIGURE A.3.3.177(g)   Flow-Through Pallet Rack.

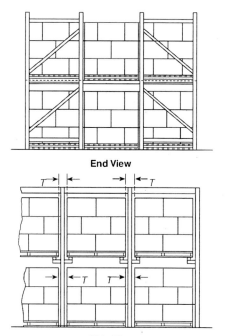

T Transverse flue space

FIGURE A.3.3.177(h)   Drive-In Rack — Two or More Pallets Deep (Fork Truck Drives into Rack to Deposit and Withdraw Loads in Depth of Rack).

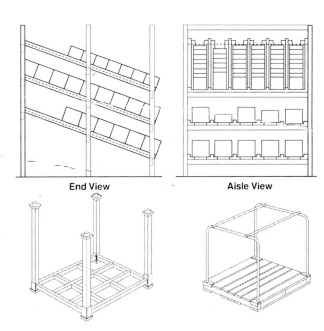

End View   **Aisle View**

FIGURE A.3.3.177(i)   Flow-Through Racks (Top) and Portable Racks (Bottom).

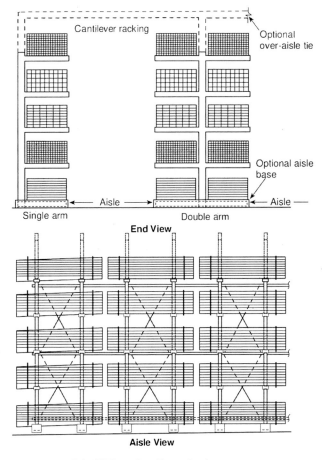

Cantilever racking

Optional over-aisle tie

Optional aisle base

Single arm   Double arm

Aisle   Aisle

End View

Aisle View

FIGURE A.3.3.177(j)   Cantilever Rack.

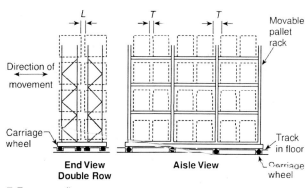

Direction of movement

Carriage wheel

Movable pallet rack

Track in floor

Carriage wheel

End View Double Row   **Aisle View**

T Transverse flue space
L Longitudinal flue space

FIGURE A.3.3.177(k)   Movable Rack.

Wrapper

Exterior wrapper	General term for protective wrapping of sides and ends on roll.
Body wrapper	

Body wrap

Sleeve wrap	Wrapper placed around circumference of roll. No heads or caps needed.
Wrap — do not cap	

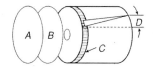

Heads

Headers	Protection applied to the ends of the rolls (A and B). Heads do not lap over the end of the roll.
Inside heads	Protection applied to the ends of the rolls next to the roll itself (B). The wrapper of the rolls is crimped down over these heads.
Outside heads	Protection applied to the ends of the rolls on the outside (A). This head is applied after the wrapper is crimped.

Edge protectors

Edge bands	Refers to extra padding to prevent damage to roll edges (C).
Overwrap	The distance the body wrap or wrapper overlaps itself (D).
Roll cap	A protective cover placed over the end of a roll. Edges of cap lap over the end of the roll and are secured to the sides of the roll.

FIGURE A.3.3.188.5   Wrapping and Capping Terms and Methods.

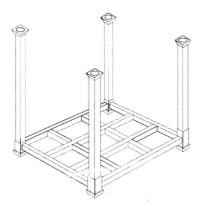

FIGURE A.3.3.191(a) **Typical Open Portable Tire Rack Unit.**

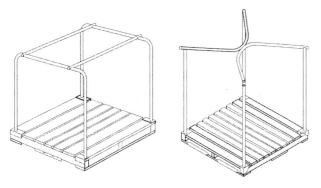

FIGURE A.3.3.191(b) **Typical Palletized Portable Tire Rack Units.**

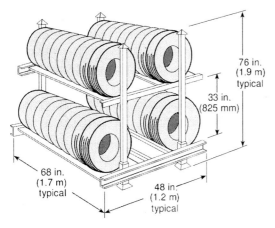

Δ FIGURE A.3.3.191(c) **Open Portable Tire Rack.**

N **A.3.3.195 Shadow Area.** Water is not required to fall on every square inch of floor space of the occupancy. This definition establishes a term that will be used to address the rules for acceptable *dry spaces* that occur when walls interfere with the residential sprinkler's spray pattern. Angled walls, wing walls, and slightly indented walls can disrupt water discharging from a sprinkler, which does not travel only in an absolute straight line, as if it were beams of light. Where small (typically triangular) shadowed areas are formed on the floor adjacent to the

wall, these shadowed areas are purely on paper and do not take into account the dynamic variables of sprinkler discharge. In order to be acceptable, the shadow area needs to be within the coverage area of a sprinkler, meaning that water would discharge to the space directly if the structural or architectural feature was not there. The purpose of allowing the shadow area is not to replace any existing obstruction requirements. Instead, the shadow area concept has been added to the standard to provide clarity to specific situations in which walls form non-rectangular-shaped rooms, as shown in Figure A.9.1.1(3)(a) and Figure A.9.1.1(3)(b).

A.3.3.196 Shelf Storage. Shelves are usually 2 ft (600 mm) apart vertically. (AUT-SSD)

A.3.3.200 Single-Row Racks. When a narrow rack with a depth up to 6 ft (1.8 m) is located within 24 in. (600 mm) of a wall, it is considered to have a longitudinal flue and is treated as a double-row rack. (AUT-SSD)

A.3.3.205 Small Openings. A return air diffuser can be 4 ft by 2 ft (1.2 m by 600 mm) and meet the definition of a small opening. A linear diffuser can be longer than 4 ft (1.2 m) but is then limited to 8 in. (200 mm) in width (or least dimension). Spaces between ceiling panels of architectural features that create a concealed space must meet the same criteria. (AUT-SSI)

A.3.3.209 Solid Shelving. The placement of loads affects the calculated area of the shelf. It is the intent to apply this definition to loads on the rack where 6 in. (150 mm) nominal flues are not provided on all four sides, regardless of whether shelving materials are present. See 20.5.3.1.2 for additional allowances for double-row racks up 25 ft (7.6 m) and for multiple-row racks of any height without a longitudinal flue space. (AUT-SSD)

A.3.3.215.2 General Sprinkler Characteristics. The response time index (RTI) is a measure of the sensitivity of the sprinkler's thermal element as installed in a specific sprinkler. It is usually determined by plunging a sprinkler into a heated laminar airflow within a test oven. The plunge test is not currently applicable to certain sprinklers.

The RTI is calculated using the following:

(1) The operating time of the sprinkler
(2) The operating temperature of the sprinkler's heat-responsive element (as determined in a bath test)
(3) The air temperature of the test oven
(4) The air velocity of the test oven
(5) The sprinkler's conductivity (*c*) factor, which is the measure of conductance between the sprinkler's heat-responsive element and the sprinkler oven mount

Other factors affecting response include the temperature rating, sprinkler position, fire exposure, and radiation.

ISO 6182-1, *Fire protection — Automatic sprinkler systems — Part 1: Requirements and test methods for sprinklers*, currently recognizes the RTI range of greater than 50 (meters-seconds)$^{1/2}$ and less than 80 (meters-seconds)$^{1/2}$ as special response. Such sprinklers can be recognized as special sprinklers under 15.2.1.

It should be recognized that the term *fast response* (like the term *quick response* used to define a particular type of sprinkler) refers to the thermal sensitivity within the operating element of a sprinkler, not the time of operation in a particular installation. Many other factors, such as ceiling height, spacing, ambi-

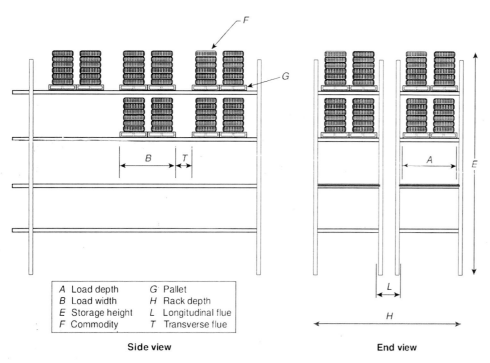

A Load depth   G Pallet
B Load width   H Rack depth
E Storage height   L Longitudinal flue
F Commodity   T Transverse flue

Side view   End view

FIGURE A.3.3.191(d)   Double-Row Fixed Tire Rack Storage.

ent room temperature, and distance below ceiling, affect the time of response of sprinklers. In most fire scenarios, sprinkler activation times will be shortest where the thermal elements are located 1 in. (25 mm) to 3 in. (75 mm) below the ceiling. A fast-response sprinkler is expected to operate quicker than a standard-response sprinkler in the same installation orientation. For modeling purposes, concealed sprinklers can be considered equivalent to pendent sprinklers having a similar thermal response sensitivity installed 12 in. (300 mm) below smooth unobstructed ceilings, and recessed sprinklers can be considered equivalent to pendent sprinklers having a similar thermal response sensitivity installed 8 in. (200 mm) below smooth unobstructed ceilings. (AUT-SSI)

A.3.3.215.4.1 Control Mode Density/Area (CMDA) Sprinkler. This definition is focused on the storage application since the term CMDA is used in the storage chapters. As indicated in Chapter 20, spray sprinklers intended for storage applications requiring a design density greater than 0.34 gpm/ft (13.9 mm/min) should have a nominal K-factor of K-11.2 (K-160) or larger and be listed for storage applications. Spray sprinklers having a nominal K-factor of K-5.6 (K-80) or K-8.0 (K-115) are permitted to be used for storage applications as a CMDA sprinkler within certain design densities as described in Chapter 20.

Spray type sprinklers intended for use in accordance with the occupancy hazard density/area curves could also be considered CMDA sprinklers. However, the CMDA terminology is generally not referenced in the non-storage chapters, and this term is not used to describe these sprinklers in the product listings. (AUT-SSI)

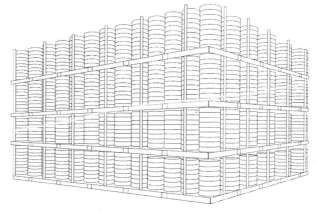

FIGURE A.3.3.191(e)   Palletized Portable Tire Rack, On-Side Storage Arrangement (Banded or Unbanded).

FIGURE A.3.3.191(f)   On-Floor Storage; On-Tread, Normally Banded.

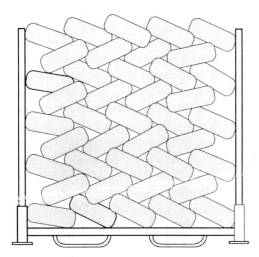

FIGURE A.3.3.191(g)   Typical Laced Tire Storage.

A.3.3.215.4.2 Control Mode Specific Application (CMSA) Sprinkler. A large drop sprinkler is a type of CMSA sprinkler that is capable of producing characteristic large water droplets and that is listed for its capability to provide fire control of specific high-challenge fire hazards. (AUT-SSI)

A.3.3.215.4.4 Dry Sprinkler. Under certain ambient conditions, wet pipe systems having dry pendent (or upright) sprinklers can freeze due to heat loss by conduction. Therefore, due consideration should be given to the amount of heat maintained in the heated space, the length of the nipple in the heated space, and other relevant factors.

Dry sprinklers are intended to extend into an unheated area from a wet pipe system or to be used on a dry pipe system. (AUT-SSI)

A.3.3.215.4.5 Early Suppression Fast-Response (ESFR) Sprinkler. It is important to realize that the effectiveness of these highly tested and engineered sprinklers depends on the combination of fast response and the quality and uniformity of the sprinkler discharge. It should also be realized that ESFR sprinklers cannot be relied upon to provide fire control, let alone suppression, if they are used outside the guidelines specified in Chapter 20. (AUT-SSI)

A.3.3.215.4.16 Quick-Response (QR) Sprinkler. Quick response is a listing for sprinklers that combines the deflector, frame, and body of a spray sprinkler with a fast-response element [see 3.3.215.2(1)(a)] to create a technology that will respond quickly in the event of a fire and deliver water in the same fashion as other types of spray sprinklers. (AUT-SSI)

A.3.3.216 Sprinkler System. As applied to the definition of a sprinkler system, each system riser serving a portion of a single floor of a facility or where individual floor control valves are used in a multistory building should be considered a separate sprinkler system. Multiple sprinkler systems can be supplied by a common supply main. (AUT-SSI)

A.3.3.216.5 Gridded Sprinkler System. See Figure A.3.3.216.5. (AUT-SSD)

A.3.3.216.6 Looped Sprinkler System. See Figure A.3.3.216.6. (AUT-SSD)

A.3.3.216.9 Preaction Sprinkler System. The actuating means of the valve are described in 8.3.2.1. Actuation of the detection system and sprinklers in the case of double-interlocked systems opens a valve that permits water to flow into the sprinkler piping system and to be discharged from any sprinklers that are open. (AUT-SSI)

A.3.3.229 Tiered Storage (Baled Cotton). Untiered storage limits storage to the height of one bale, on side or on end. Sprinkler protection designed on this basis would likely prohibit future tiering without redesign of the sprinkler system. (AUT-SSD)

A.3.3.235.2 Control Valve. Control valves do not include hose valves, inspector's test valves, drain valves, trim valves for dry pipe, preaction and deluge valves, check valves, or relief valves. (AUT-SSI)

A.3.3.235.3 Indicating Valve. Examples are outside screw and yoke (OS&Y) gate valves, butterfly valves, and underground gate valves with indicator posts.

N **A.3.3.235.4 Water Control Valve.** Water control valves include dry pipe, preaction, and deluge valves. (AUT-SSI)

Δ **A.4.2** A building constructed where the expected occupancy hazard and commodity classification of tenant uses are unknown at the time of the sprinkler system's design and installation presents special problems due to unknown factors. The design of sprinkler systems for such buildings should be carefully reviewed with the owners, builders, leasing agents, and local authorities having jurisdiction prior to the selection of design criteria and installation of the system. Consideration should be given to the available height for storage, as well as

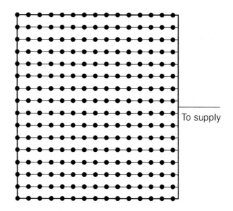

FIGURE A.3.3.216.5   Gridded System.

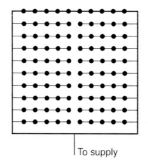

FIGURE A.3.3.216.6   Looped System.

the occupancy hazards of potential tenants and their likely storage needs.

The short period response parameter, S_s is defined in 3.3.198. Additional information about S_s is provided in 18.5.9.

The intent of Section 4.2 is to provide the owner's certificate for all new systems and where there is a change of occupancy and/or building use. [See Figure A.28.1(b).]

A.4.2(4) Recycled or reclaimed water used in a sprinkler system should not have contaminants in the water that are combustible or that will have a detrimental effect on the sprinkler system performance or the life of the sprinkler system.

A.4.3 Occupancy examples in the listings as shown in the various hazard classifications are intended to represent the norm for those occupancy types. Unusual or abnormal fuel loadings or combustible characteristics and susceptibility for changes in these characteristics, for a particular occupancy, are considerations that should be weighed in the selection and classification.

The light hazard classification is intended to encompass residential occupancies; however, this is not intended to preclude the use of listed residential sprinklers in residential occupancies or residential portions of other occupancies.

A.4.3.1.4 Miscellaneous storage is intended to be storage that is ancillary to the primary function of the building. One example is a manufacturing facility where storage on the manufacturing floor is limited.

A.4.3.2 Light hazard occupancies include occupancies having uses and conditions similar to the following:

(1) Animal shelters
(2) Churches
(3) Clubs
(4) Eaves and overhangs, if of combustible construction with no combustibles beneath
(5) Educational
(6) Hospitals, including animal hospitals and veterinary facilities
(7) Institutional
(8) Kennels
(9) Libraries, except large stack rooms
(10) Museums
(11) Nursing or convalescent homes
(12) Offices, including data processing
(13) Residential
(14) Restaurant seating areas
(15) Theaters and auditoriums, excluding stages and prosceniums
(16) Unused attics

Note that it is not the committee's intent to automatically equate library bookshelves with ordinary hazard occupancies or with library stacks. Typical library bookshelves of approximately 8 ft (2.4 m) in height, containing books stored vertically on end, held in place in close association with each other, with aisles wider than 30 in. (750 mm) can be considered to be light hazard occupancies. Similarly, library stack areas, which are more akin to shelf storage or record storage, as defined in NFPA 232, should be considered to be ordinary hazard occupancies.

N **A.4.3.3** Class I, Class II, Class III, and Class IV commodities are considered to have moderate rates of heat release, while Group A plastics are considered to have high rates of heat release.

Stockpiles are considered to include display merchandise (e.g., mercantile stockpiles) and arrangements of combustibles ancillary to operations within the occupancy as opposed to dedicated storage areas where the fire loading is generally more severe.

Δ **A.4.3.3.1** Ordinary hazard (Group 1) occupancies include occupancies having uses and conditions similar to the following:

(1) Automobile showrooms
(2) Bakeries
(3) Beverage manufacturing
(4) Canneries
(5) Dairy products manufacturing and processing
(6) Electronic plants
(7) Glass and glass products manufacturing
(8) Laundries
(9) Restaurant service areas
(10) Porte cocheres
(11) Mechanical rooms

Δ **A.4.3.3.2** Ordinary hazard (Group 2) occupancies include occupancies having uses and conditions similar to the following:

(1) Agricultural facilities
(2) Automobile parking garages
(3) Barns and stables
(4) Cereal mills
(5) Chemical plants — ordinary
(6) Confectionery products
(7) Distilleries
(8) Dry cleaners
(9) Exterior loading docks (Note that exterior loading docks only used for loading and unloading of ordinary combustibles should be classified as OH2. For the handling of flammable and combustible liquidsor hazardous materials, or where utilized for storage, exterior and interior loading docks should be protected based upon the actual occupancy and the materials handled on the dock, as if the materials were actually stored in that configuration.)
(10) Feed mills
(11) Horse stables
(12) Leather goods manufacturing
(13) Libraries — large stack room areas
(14) Machine shops
(15) Metal working
(16) Mercantile
(17) Paper and pulp mills
(18) Paper process plants
(19) Piers and wharves
(20) Plastics fabrication, including blow molding, extruding, and machining; excluding operations using combustible hydraulic fluids
(21) Post offices
(22) Printing and publishing
(23) Racetrack stable/kennel areas, including those stable/kennel areas, barns, and associated buildings at state, county, and local fairgrounds
(24) Repair garages
(25) Resin application area
(26) Stages
(27) Textile manufacturing
(28) Tire manufacturing
(29) Tobacco products manufacturing

(30) Wood machining
(31) Wood product assembly

A.4.3.4 Extra hazard (Group 1) occupancies include occupancies having uses and conditions similar to the following:

(1) Aircraft hangars (except as governed by NFPA 409)
(2) Combustible hydraulic fluid use areas
(3) Die casting
(4) Metal extruding
(5) Plywood and particleboard manufacturing
(6) Printing [using inks having flash points below 100°F (38°C)]
(7) Rubber reclaiming, compounding, drying, milling, vulcanizing
(8) Saw mills
(9) Textile picking, opening, blending, garnetting, or carding, combining of cotton, synthetics, wool shoddy, or burlap
(10) Upholstering with plastic foams

A.4.3.5 Extra hazard (Group 2) occupancies include occupancies having uses and conditions similar to the following:

(1) Asphalt saturating
(2) Flammable liquids spraying
(3) Flow coating
(4) Manufactured home or modular building assemblies (where finished enclosure is present and has combustible interiors)
(5) Open oil quenching
(6) Plastics manufacturing
(7) Solvent cleaning
(8) Varnish and paint dipping
(9) Car stackers and car lift systems with 2 cars stacked vertically

Δ **A.4.3.7** Other NFPA standards contain design criteria for fire control or fire suppression (see 4.3.7 and Chapter 2). While these can form the basis of design criteria, this standard describes the design, installation, fabrication, calculation, and evaluation methods of water supplies that should be used for the specific design of the system.

Other NFPA standards contain sprinkler system design criteria for fire control or suppression of specific hazards. These other standards are referenced in Chapter 27.

A.4.4.1(3) Pipe schedule — 25,000 ft² (2320 m²).

A.4.4.6 Buildings adjacent to a primary structure can be protected by extending the fire sprinkler system from the primary structure. This eliminates the need to provide a separate fire sprinkler system for small auxiliary buildings. Items that should be considered before finalizing fire sprinkler design should include the following:

(1) Actual physical distance between adjacent structures
(2) Potential for the property to be split into separate parcels and sold separately
(3) Square footage of both the primary and auxiliary structures
(4) Difficulties in providing a separate water supply to the auxiliary structure
(5) Occupancy/hazard of the auxiliary structure
(6) Ability of emergency response personnel to easily identify the structure from which waterflow is originating

A.4.5.1.1 Alternative means of determining available water supplies should be considered where drought or other concerns are present.

A.4.6 Bacterial inhibitors and other chemicals that are listed and used for the prevention and mitigation of MIC and that do not adversely affect the fire-fighting properties of the water or the performance of the fire sprinkler system components are not prohibited.

A.4.8 Non-system components can adversely affect the operation and longevity of the fire sprinkler system. Objects connected to the sprinkler system can displace sprinkler system piping, causing obstruction to the spray pattern of sprinklers, delay the activation of a sprinkler, or cause chemical compatibility problems that can cause the failure of sprinkler system components.

A.4.9.1 The provisions of 4.9.1 do not require inherently noncombustible materials to be tested in order to be classified as noncombustible materials. [5000:A.7.1.4.1]

A.4.9.1.1(1) Examples of such materials include steel, concrete, masonry and glass. [5000:A.7.1.4.1.1(1)]

A.4.9.2 Material subject to increase in combustibility or flame spread index beyond the limits herein established through the effects of age, moisture, or other atmospheric condition is considered combustible. (See NFPA 259 and NFPA 220.) [5000:A.7.1.4.2]

A.5.1.3 For typical combined domestic/fire sprinkler demands, systems with 4 in. (100 mm) pipe or larger typically do not need to include the domestic demand in the calculations because it is such a small fraction of the total flow that it does not make a significant difference in the results. But for situations where 4 in. (100 mm) pipe is used for the combined domestic/fire sprinkler systems and the domestic demand is considerable, then the domestic demand should be included in the calculations. Generally, pipe that is 6 in. (150 mm) or larger can carry combined domestic/fire protection demand without any consideration for domestic demand being necessary.

A.5.1.4 Evaluation of the water supply and environmental conditions does not necessarily require a water sample analysis by a laboratory. Instead, general knowledge of the long-term condition of sprinkler systems with similar piping materials in similar environments on the same water supply can be a sufficient evaluation.

There are several options to address the effects of MIC on sprinkler systems. Some types of sprinkler pipe such as CPVC have not shown to be affected by MIC. Other types of pipe are being manufactured with a biofilm that resists the effects of MIC.

Where water supplies are treated with bacterial inhibitors, evaluation of the effects of the bacterial inhibitor on sprinkler system components (pipe, fittings, sprinklers, gaskets, valves, and seals) is just as important as evaluating the effect the bacterial inhibitor has on the organisms. Where water treatment is selected as the method to deal with MIC, all water entering the system during testing or flushing needs to be treated so that the organisms do not get a chance to establish themselves.

Since all of the conditions that can affect the growth of MIC are unknown, a plan to sample randomly selected interior positions in the system can be effective. The frequency and location of the interior inspections will depend on the extent of the known MIC problem with the same water supply and similar environmental conditions.

A.5.1.5.2 Where the system riser is close to an outside wall, underground fittings of proper length should be used in order to avoid pipe joints located in or under the wall. Where the connection passes through the foundation wall below grade, a 1 in. to 3 in. (25 mm to 75 mm) clearance should be provided around the pipe and the clear space filled with asphalt mastic or similar flexible waterproofing material.

A.5.1.6 Where water meters are in the supply lines to a sprinkler system, they should be rated to deliver the proper system demand. The amount of water supplied through a water meter varies with its size and type and might not provide the required demand, regardless of the water supply available.

A.5.1.7 Where connections are made from public waterworks systems, such systems should be guarded against possible contamination as follows *(see AWWA M14, Recommended Practice for Backflow Prevention and Cross-Connection Control)*:

(1) For private fire service mains with direct connections from public waterworks mains only or with booster pumps installed in the connections from the street mains, no tanks or reservoirs, no physical connection from other water supplies, no antifreeze or other additives of any kind, and with all drains discharging to atmosphere, dry well, or other safe outlets, no backflow protection is recommended at the service connection.

(2) For private fire service mains with direct connection from the public water supply main plus one or more of the following: elevated storage tanks or fire pumps taking suction from aboveground covered reservoirs or tanks (all storage facilities are filled or connected to public water only and the water in the tanks is to be maintained in a potable condition), an approved double check valve assembly is recommended.

(3) For private fire service mains directly supplied from public mains with an auxiliary water supply such as a pond or river on or available to the premises and dedicated to fire department use; or for systems supplied from public mains and interconnected with auxiliary supplies, such as pumps taking suction from reservoirs exposed to contamination or rivers and ponds; driven wells, mills, or other industrial water systems; or for systems or portions of systems where antifreeze or other solutions are used, an approved reduced pressure zone-type backflow preventer is recommended.

Where connections are made from public waterworks systems, it might be necessary to guard against possible contamination of the public supply.

A.5.2.1 Acceptable water supplies for fire sprinkler systems must provide sufficient flow and pressure for the required duration. Many water supply sources contain sufficient flow and volume but do not possess sufficient pressure. Some acceptable water supplies, such as storage tanks located at or below grade, rivers, lakes, and reservoirs, will almost always require combination with a pump to provide the needed pressure. Fire pumps are used with other supplies such as waterworks or gravity tanks to provide additional pressure needed to meet the system demand.

A.5.2.1(7) In an effort to help comply with efforts for sustainable and renewable building construction, some engineers and architects have suggested the use of reclaimed or recycled water to use in fire sprinkler systems rather than the potable water typically used from the public water supply. While this effort has some merit, there is a concern about the quality of the water from these recycled and reclaimed systems. The capture of rainwater is generally not considered a problem since NFPA 13 has long allowed the use of open lakes, rivers, and ponds, which are nothing more than open collections of rainwater and melted snow. But other systems that are recycling water that has been used in some industrial or other process might have contaminants that are combustible, or they might be detrimental to the sprinkler system by preventing it from working properly or accelerating corrosion. Recycled or reclaimed water should never be used in a sprinkler system until an analysis of what contaminants might be in the water has determined that nothing will be detrimental to sprinkler system performance or the expected reasonable life of the sprinkler system. When such an analysis is completed successfully, the information should be transmitted to the sprinkler contractor through the use of the Owner's Certificate required by Section 4.2.

A.5.2.2 Care should be taken in making water tests to be used in designing or evaluating the capability of sprinkler systems. The water supply tested should be representative of the supply that might be available at the time of a fire. For example, testing of public water supplies should be done at times of normal demand on the system. Public water supplies are likely to fluctuate widely from season to season and even within a 24-hour period. Allowance should be made for seasonal or daily fluctuations, for drought conditions, for possibility of interruption by flood, or for ice conditions in winter. Testing of water supplies also normally used for industrial use should be done while water is being drawn for industrial use. The range of industrial-use demand should be taken into account. In special situations where the domestic water demand could significantly reduce the sprinkler water supply, an increase in the size of the pipe supplying both the domestic and sprinkler water can be justified.

Future changes in water supplies should be considered. For example, a large, established, urban supply is not likely to change greatly within a few years. However, the supply in a growing suburban industrial park might deteriorate quite rapidly as greater numbers of plants draw more water.

Dead-end mains should be avoided, if possible, by arranging for mains supplied from both directions. When private fire service mains are connected to dead-end public mains, each situation should be examined to determine if it is practical to request the water utility to loop the mains in order to obtain a more reliable supply.

Testing of Water Supply. To determine the value of public water as a supply for automatic sprinkler systems, it is generally necessary to make a flow test to determine how much water can be discharged at a residual pressure at a rate sufficient to give the required residual pressure under the roof (with the volume flow hydraulically translated to the base of the riser) — that is, a pressure head represented by the height of the building plus the required residual pressure.

The proper method of conducting this test is to use two hydrants in the vicinity of the property. The static pressure should be measured on the hydrant in front of or nearest to the property and the water allowed to flow from the hydrant next nearest the property, preferably the one farthest from the source of supply if the main is fed only one way. The residual pressure will be that indicated at the hydrant where water is not flowing.

Referring to Figure A.5.2.2, the method of conducting the flow tests is as follows:

(1) Attach the gauge to the hydrant *(A)* and obtain static pressure.
(2) Either attach a second gauge to the hydrant *(B)* or use the pitot tube at the outlet. Have hydrant *(B)* opened wide and read pressure at both hydrants.
(3) Use the pressure at *(B)* to compute the gallons flowing and read the gauge on *(A)* to determine the residual pressure or that which will be available on the top line of sprinklers in the property.

Water pressure in pounds per square inch for a given height in feet equals height multiplied by 0.433.

In making flow tests, whether from hydrants or from nozzles attached to hose, always measure the size of the orifice. While hydrant outlets are usually 2½ in. (65 mm), they are sometimes smaller and occasionally larger. Underwriters Laboratories play pipe is 1⅛ in. (28.6 mm) and 1¾ in. (44.5 mm) with the tip removed, but occasionally nozzles will be 1 in. (25.4 mm) or 1¼ in. (31.8 mm), and with the tip removed the opening can be only 1½ in. (38.1 mm).

The pitot tube should be held approximately one-half the diameter of the hydrant or nozzle opening away from the opening. It should be held in the center of the stream, except that in using hydrant outlets the stream should be explored to ascertain the average pressure.

For further information on water supply testing, see NFPA 291.

A.5.2.2.2 An adjustment to the waterflow test data to account for daily and seasonal fluctuations, possible interruption by flood or ice conditions, large simultaneous industrial use, future demand on the water supply system, or any other condition that could affect the water supply should be made as appropriate.

A.5.2.3 An automatically controlled vertical turbine pump taking suction from a reservoir, pond, lake, river, cistern, or well or a centrifugal pump supplied from a waterworks system connection, or tank, complies with 5.2.3.

See sections dealing with sprinkler equipment supervisory and waterflow alarm services in *NFPA 72* or other approved fire alarm code.

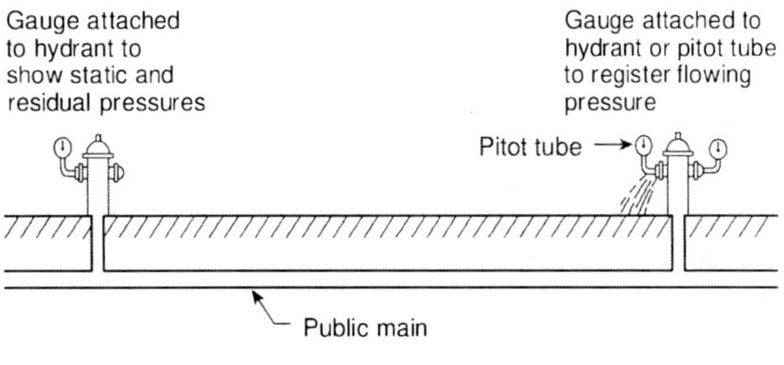

FIGURE A.5.2.2   Method of Conducting Flow Tests.

A.5.2.4.3 For pipe schedule systems, the air pressure to be carried and the proper proportion of air in the tank can be determined from the following formulas where:

P = air pressure carried in pressure tank

A = proportion of air in tank

H = height of highest sprinkler above tank bottom

When the tank is placed above the highest sprinkler, use the following formula:

[A.5.2.4.3a]

$$P = \frac{30}{A} - 15$$

If $A = ⅓$, then $P = 90 - 15 = 75$ psi (5.2 bar)

If $A = ½$, then $P = 60 - 15 = 45$ psi (3.1 bar)

If $A = ⅔$, then $P = 45 - 15 = 30$ psi (2.1 bar)

When the tank is below the level of the highest sprinkler, use the following formula:

[A.5.2.4.3b]

$$P = \frac{30}{A} - 15 + \frac{0.434H}{A}$$

If $A = ⅓$, then $P = 75 + 1.30H$

If $A = ½$, then $P = 45 + 0.87H$

If $A = ⅔$, then $P = 30 + 0.65H$

The preceding respective air pressures are calculated to ensure that the last water will leave the tank at a pressure of 15 psi (1 bar) when the base of the tank is on a level with the highest sprinkler or at such additional pressure as is equivalent to a head corresponding to the distance between the base of the tank and the highest sprinkler when the latter is above the tank.

For hydraulically calculated systems, the following formula should be used to determine the tank pressure and ratio of air to water:

[A.5.2.4.3c]

$$P_i = \frac{P_f + 15}{A} - 15$$

where:
P_i = tank pressure
P_f = pressure required from hydraulic calculations
A = proportion of air

Example: Hydraulic calculations indicate 75 psi (5.2 bar) is required to supply the system. What tank pressure will be required?

[A.5.2.4.3d]

$$P_i = \frac{75 + 15}{0.5} - 15$$

$$P_i = 180 - 15 = 165 \text{ psi}$$

For SI units, 1 ft = 0.3 m; 1 psi = 0.07 bar.

In this case, the tank would be filled with 50 percent air and 50 percent water, and the tank pressure would be 165 psi (11.4 bar). If the pressure is too high, the amount of air carried in the tank will have to be increased.

Pressure tanks should be located above the top level of sprinklers but can be located in the basement or elsewhere.

A.6.1 Copper tubing (Type K) with brazed joints conforming to Table 6.1.1.1 and Table 6.2.1.1 is acceptable for underground service.

(1) *Listing and labeling.* Certification organizations list or label the following:

    (a) Cast iron and ductile iron pipe (cement-lined and unlined, coated and uncoated)
    (b) Steel pipe
    (c) Copper pipe
    (d) Fiberglass filament-wound epoxy pipe and couplings
    (e) Polyethylene pipe
    (f) Polyvinyl chloride (PVC) pipe and couplings
    (g) Reinforced concrete pipe (cylinder pipe, nonprestressed and prestressed)

[**24**:A.10.1]

A.6.1.1 The type and class of pipe for a particular underground installation should be determined through consideration of the following factors:

(1) Maximum system working pressure
(2) Maximum pressure from pressure surges and anticipated frequency of surges
(3) Depth at which the pipe is to be installed
(4) Soil conditions
(5) Corrosion
(6) Susceptibility of pipe to external loads, including earth loads, installation beneath buildings, and traffic or vehicle loads

The following pipe design manuals and standards can be used as guides:

(1) AWWA C150/A21.50, *Thickness Design of Ductile-Iron Pipe*
(2) AWWA M23, *PVC Pipe — Design and Installation*
(3) AWWA M55, *PE Pipe — Design and Installation*
(4) AWWA M41, *Ductile-Iron Pipe and Fittings*
(5) *Concrete Pipe Handbook*, American Concrete Pipe Association

[**24**:A.10.1.1]

A.6.1.2 For underground system components, a minimum system pressure rating of 150 psi (10 bar) is specified in 6.1.2, based on satisfactory historical performance. Also, this pressure rating reflects that of the components typically used underground, such as piping, valves, and fittings. Where system pressures are expected to exceed pressures of 150 psi (10 bar), system components and materials manufactured and listed for higher pressures should be used. Systems that do not incorporate a fire pump or are not part of a combined standpipe system do not typically experience pressures exceeding 150 psi (10 bar) in underground piping. However, each system should be evaluated on an individual basis. It is not the intent of this section to include the pressures generated through fire department connections as part of the maximum working pressure. [**24**:A.10.1.2]

A.6.1.3 See Table A.6.1.3. [**24**:A.10.1.3]

A.6.1.4 Where nonmetallic underground piping is provided above grade or inside a building, the following should be considered:

(1) Exposure from direct rays of sunlight
(2) Compatibility with chemicals such as floor coatings and termiticides/insecticides
(3) Support of piping and appurtenances attached thereto (e.g., sprinkler risers, backflow preventers)

[**24**:A.10.1.4]

A.6.3.1 The following standards apply to joints used with the various types of pipe:

(1) ASME B16.1, *Gray Iron Pipe Flanges and Flanged Fittings Classes 25, 125, and 250*
(2) AWWA C111/A21.11, *Rubber-Gasket Joints for Ductile-Iron Pressure Pipe and Fittings*
(3) AWWA C115/A21.15, *Flanged Ductile-Iron Pipe with Ductile-Iron or Gray-Iron Threaded Flanges*
(4) AWWA C206, *Field Welding of Steel Water Pipe*
(5) AWWA C606, *Grooved and Shouldered Joints*

[**24**:A.10.3.1]

A.6.3.5.3 Fittings and couplings are listed for specific pipe materials that can be installed underground. Fittings and couplings do not necessarily indicate that they are listed specifically for underground use. [**24**:A.10.3.5.3]

A.6.4.1.3 Gray cast iron is not considered galvanically dissimilar to ductile iron. Rubber gasket joints (unrestrained push-on or mechanical joints) are not considered connected electrically. Metal thickness should not be considered a protection against corrosive environments. In the case of cast iron or ductile iron pipe for soil evaluation and external protection systems, see Appendix A of AWWA C105/A21.5, *Polyethylene Encasement for Ductile-Iron Pipe Systems.* [**24**:A.10.4.1.3]

Δ **A.6.4.2** As there is normally no circulation of water in private fire service mains, they require greater depth of covering than do public mains. Greater depth is required in a loose gravelly soil (or in rock) than in compact soil containing large quantities of clay. The recommended depth of cover above the top of underground yard mains is shown in Figure A.6.4.2.

In determining the need to protect aboveground piping from freezing, the lowest mean temperature should be considered. [**24**:A.10.4.2]

A.6.4.2.1.1 Consideration should be given to the type of soil and the possibility of settling. Also, many times the inspection of the piping might occur before final grading and fill of the installation is complete. The final grade should be verified. [**24**:A.10.4.2.1.1]

A.6.4.3.1 The intent of this section is to limit the total length of horizontal pipe beneath the building to not more than 10 ft (3 m). See Figure A.6.4.3.1. [**24**:A.10.4.3.1]

Δ **A.6.4.3.1.1** The individual piping standards should be followed for load and bury depth, accounting for the load and stresses imposed by the building foundation. [**24**:A.10.4.3.1.1]

Δ **A.6.4.3.1.2** Sufficient clearance should be provided when piping passes beneath foundations or footers. [**24**:A.10.4.3.1.2]

Table A.6.1.3 Internal Diameters (IDs) for Cement-Lined Ductile Iron Pipe

Pipe Size [in. (mm)]	OD [in. (mm)]	Pressure Class	Thickness Class	Wall Thickness		Minimum Lining Thickness* [in. (mm)]	ID with Lining	
				in.	mm		in.	mm
3 in. (80 mm)	3.96 in. (100 mm)	350	51	0.25	6	1/16 in. (1.6 mm)	3.34	84
3 in. (80 mm)	3.96 in. (100 mm)	350	52	0.28	7	1/16 in. (1.6 mm)	3.28	82
3 in. (80 mm)	3.96 in. (100 mm)	350	53	0.31	8	1/16 in. (1.6 mm)	3.22	81
3 in. (80 mm)	3.96 in. (100 mm)	350	54	0.34	9	1/16 in. (1.6 mm)	3.16	79
3 in. (80 mm)	3.96 in. (100 mm)	350	55	0.37	9	1/16 in. (1.6 mm)	3.1	78
3 in. (80 mm)	3.96 in. (100 mm)	350	56	0.4	10	1/16 in. (1.6 mm)	3.04	76
4 in. (100 mm)	4.8 in. (120 mm)	350		0.25	6	1/16 in. (1.6 mm)	4.18	105
4 in. (100 mm)	4.8 in. (120 mm)	350	51	0.26	7	1/16 in. (1.6 mm)	4.16	104
4 in. (100 mm)	4.8 in. (120 mm)	350	52	0.29	7	1/16 in. (1.6 mm)	4.1	103
4 in. (100 mm)	4.8 in. (120 mm)	350	53	0.32	8	1/16 in. (1.6 mm)	4.04	101
4 in. (100 mm)	4.8 in. (120 mm)	350	54	0.35	9	1/16 in. (1.6 mm)	3.98	100
4 in. (100 mm)	4.8 in. (120 mm)	350	55	0.38	10	1/16 in. (1.6 mm)	3.92	98
4 in. (100 mm)	4.8 in. (120 mm)	350	56	0.41	10	1/16 in. (1.6 mm)	3.86	97
6 in. (150 mm)	6.90 in. (175 mm)	350		0.25	6	1/16 in. (1.6 mm)	6.28	157
6 in. (150 mm)	6.90 in. (175 mm)	350	50	0.25	6	1/16 in. (1.6 mm)	6.28	157
6 in. (150 mm)	6.90 in. (175 mm)	350	51	0.28	7	1/16 in. (1.6 mm)	6.22	156
6 in. (150 mm)	6.90 in. (175 mm)	350	52	0.31	8	1/16 in. (1.6 mm)	6.16	154
6 in. (150 mm)	6.90 in. (175 mm)	350	53	0.34	9	1/16 in. (1.6 mm)	6.1	153
6 in. (150 mm)	6.90 in. (175 mm)	350	54	0.37	9	1/16 in. (1.6 mm)	6.04	151
6 in. (150 mm)	6.90 in. (175 mm)	350	55	0.4	10	1/16 in. (1.6 mm)	5.98	150
6 in. (150 mm)	6.90 in. (175 mm)	350	56	0.43	11	1/16 in. (1.6 mm)	5.92	148
8 in. (200 mm)	9.05 in. (225 mm)	350		0.25	6	1/16 in. (1.6 mm)	8.43	211
8 in. (200 mm)	9.05 in. (225 mm)	350	50	0.27	7	1/16 in. (1.6 mm)	8.39	210
8 in. (200 mm)	9.05 in. (225 mm)	350	51	0.3	8	1/16 in. (1.6 mm)	8.33	208
8 in. (200 mm)	9.05 in. (225 mm)	350	52	0.33	8	1/16 in. (1.6 mm)	8.27	207
8 in. (200 mm)	9.05 in. (225 mm)	350	53	0.36	9	1/16 in. (1.6 mm)	8.21	205
8 in. (200 mm)	9.05 in. (225 mm)	350	54	0.39	10	1/16 in. (1.6 mm)	8.15	204
8 in. (200 mm)	9.05 in. (225 mm)	350	55	0.42	11	1/16 in. (1.6 mm)	8.09	202
8 in. (200 mm)	9.05 in. (225 mm)	350	56	0.45	11	1/16 in. (1.6 mm)	8.03	201
10 in. (250 mm)	11.1 in. (280 mm)	350		0.26	7	1/16 in. (1.6 mm)	10.46	262
10 in. (250 mm)	11.1 in. (280 mm)	350	50	0.29	7	1/16 in. (1.6 mm)	10.4	260
10 in. (250 mm)	11.1 in. (280 mm)	350	51	0.32	8	1/16 in. (1.6 mm)	10.34	259
10 in. (250 mm)	11.1 in. (280 mm)	350	52	0.35	9	1/16 in. (1.6 mm)	10.28	257
10 in. (250 mm)	11.1 in. (280 mm)	350	53	0.38	10	1/16 in. (1.6 mm)	10.22	256
10 in. (250 mm)	11.1 in. (280 mm)	350	54	0.41	10	1/16 in. (1.6 mm)	10.16	254
10 in. (250 mm)	11.1 in. (280 mm)	350	55	0.44	11	1/16 in. (1.6 mm)	10.1	253
10 in. (250 mm)	11.1 in. (280 mm)	350	56	0.47	12	1/16 in. (1.6 mm)	10.04	251
12 in. (300 mm)	13.2 in. (330 mm)	350		0.28	7	1/16 in. (1.6 mm)	12.52	313
12 in. (300 mm)	13.2 in. (330 mm)	350	50	0.31	8	1/16 in. (1.6 mm)	12.46	312
12 in. (300 mm)	13.2 in. (330 mm)	350	51	0.34	9	1/16 in. (1.6 mm)	12.4	310
12 in. (300 mm)	13.2 in. (330 mm)	350	52	0.37	9	1/16 in. (1.6 mm)	12.34	309
12 in. (300 mm)	13.2 in. (330 mm)	350	53	0.4	10	1/16 in. (1.6 mm)	12.28	307
12 in. (300 mm)	13.2 in. (330 mm)	350	54	0.43	11	1/16 in. (1.6 mm)	12.22	306
12 in. (300 mm)	13.2 in. (330 mm)	350	55	0.46	12	1/16 in. (1.6 mm)	12.16	304
12 in. (300 mm)	13.2 in. (330 mm)	350	56	0.49	12	1/16 in. (1.6 mm)	12.1	303
14 in. (350 mm)	15.3 in. (385 mm)	250		0.28	7	3/32 in. (2 mm)	14.55	364
14 in. (350 mm)	15.3 in. (385 mm)	300		0.3	8	3/32 in. (2 mm)	14.51	363
14 in. (350 mm)	15.3 in. (385 mm)	350		0.31	8	3/32 in. (2 mm)	14.49	362
14 in. (350 mm)	15.3 in. (385 mm)		50	0.33	8	3/32 in. (2 mm)	14.45	361
14 in. (350 mm)	15.3 in. (385 mm)		51	0.36	9	3/32 in. (2 mm)	14.39	360
14 in. (350 mm)	15.3 in. (385 mm)		52	0.39	10	3/32 in. (2 mm)	14.33	358
14 in. (350 mm)	15.3 in. (385 mm)		53	0.42	11	3/32 in. (2 mm)	14.27	357
14 in. (350 mm)	15.3 in. (385 mm)		54	0.45	11	3/32 in. (2 mm)	14.21	355
14 in. (350 mm)	15.3 in. (385 mm)		55	0.48	12	3/32 in. (2 mm)	14.15	354
14 in. (350 mm)	15.3 in. (385 mm)		56	0.51	13	3/32 in. (2 mm)	14.09	352
16 in. (400 mm)	17.4 in. (435 mm)	250		0.3	8	3/32 in. (2 mm)	16.61	415
16 in. (400 mm)	17.4 in. (435 mm)	300		0.32	8	3/32 in. (2 mm)	16.57	414

(continues)

Table A.6.1.3 *Continued*

Pipe Size [in. (mm)]	OD [in. (mm)]	Pressure Class	Thickness Class	Wall Thickness		Minimum Lining Thickness* [in. (mm)]	ID with Lining	
				in.	mm		in.	mm
16 in. (400 mm)	17.4 in. (435 mm)	350		0.34	9	3⁄32 in. (2 mm)	16.53	413
16 in. (400 mm)	17.4 in. (435 mm)		50	0.34	9	3⁄32 in. (2 mm)	16.53	413
16 in. (400 mm)	17.4 in. (435 mm)		51	0.37	9	3⁄32 in. (2 mm)	16.47	412
16 in. (400 mm)	17.4 in. (435 mm)		52	0.4	10	3⁄32 in. (2 mm)	16.41	410
16 in. (400 mm)	17.4 in. (435 mm)		53	0.43	11	3⁄32 in. (2 mm)	16.35	409
16 in. (400 mm)	17.4 in. (435 mm)		54	0.46	12	3⁄32 in. (2 mm)	16.29	407
16 in. (400 mm)	17.4 in. (435 mm)		55	0.49	12	3⁄32 in. (2 mm)	16.23	406
16 in. (400 mm)	17.4 in. (435 mm)		56	0.52	13	3⁄32 in. (2 mm)	16.17	404
18 in. (450 mm)	19.5 in. (488 mm)	250		0.31	8	3⁄32 in. (2 mm)	18.69	467
18 in. (450 mm)	19.5 in. (488 mm)	300		0.34	9	3⁄32 in. (2 mm)	18.63	466
18 in. (450 mm)	19.5 in. (488 mm)	350		0.36	9	3⁄32 in. (2 mm)	18.59	465
18 in. (450 mm)	19.5 in. (488 mm)		50	0.35	9	3⁄32 in. (2 mm)	18.61	465
18 in. (450 mm)	19.5 in. (488 mm)		51	0.35	9	3⁄32 in. (2 mm)	18.61	465
18 in. (450 mm)	19.5 in. (488 mm)		52	0.41	10	3⁄32 in. (2 mm)	18.49	462
18 in. (450 mm)	19.5 in. (488 mm)		53	0.44	11	3⁄32 in. (2 mm)	18.43	461
18 in. (450 mm)	19.5 in. (488 mm)		54	0.47	12	3⁄32 in. (2 mm)	18.37	459
18 in. (450 mm)	19.5 in. (488 mm)		55	0.5	13	3⁄32 in. (2 mm)	18.31	458
18 in. (450 mm)	19.5 in. (488 mm)		56	0.53	13	3⁄32 in. (2 mm)	18.25	456
20 in. (500 mm)	21.6 in. (540 mm)	250		0.33	8	3⁄32 in. (2 mm)	20.75	519
20 in. (500 mm)	21.6 in. (540 mm)	300		0.36	9	3⁄32 in. (2 mm)	20.69	517
20 in. (500 mm)	21.6 in. (540 mm)	350		0.38	10	3⁄32 in. (2 mm)	20.65	516
20 in. (500 mm)	21.6 in. (540 mm)		50	0.36	9	3⁄32 in. (2 mm)	20.69	517
20 in. (500 mm)	21.6 in. (540 mm)		51	0.39	10	3⁄32 in. (2 mm)	20.63	516
20 in. (500 mm)	21.6 in. (540 mm)		52	0.42	11	3⁄32 in. (2 mm)	20.57	514
20 in. (500 mm)	21.6 in. (540 mm)		53	0.45	11	3⁄32 in. (2 mm)	20.51	513
20 in. (500 mm)	21.6 in. (540 mm)		54	0.48	12	3⁄32 in. (2 mm)	20.45	511
20 in. (500 mm)	21.6 in. (540 mm)		55	0.51	13	3⁄32 in. (2 mm)	20.39	510
20 in. (500 mm)	21.6 in. (540 mm)		56	0.54	14	3⁄32 in. (2 mm)	20.33	508
24 in. (600 mm)	25.8 in. (645 mm)	200		0.33	8	3⁄32 in. (2 mm)	24.95	624
24 in. (600 mm)	25.8 in. (645 mm)	250		0.37	9	3⁄32 in. (2 mm)	24.87	622
24 in. (600 mm)	25.8 in. (645 mm)	300		0.4	10	3⁄32 in. (2 mm)	24.81	620
24 in. (600 mm)	25.8 in. (645 mm)	350		0.43	11	3⁄32 in. (2 mm)	24.75	619
24 in. (600 mm)	25.8 in. (645 mm)		50	0.38	10	3⁄32 in. (2 mm)	24.85	621
24 in. (600 mm)	25.8 in. (645 mm)		51	0.41	10	3⁄32 in. (2 mm)	24.79	620
24 in. (600 mm)	25.8 in. (645 mm)		52	0.44	11	3⁄32 in. (2 mm)	24.73	618
24 in. (600 mm)	25.8 in. (645 mm)		53	0.47	12	3⁄32 in. (2 mm)	24.67	617
24 in. (600 mm)	25.8 in. (645 mm)		54	0.5	13	3⁄32 in. (2 mm)	24.61	615
24 in. (600 mm)	25.8 in. (645 mm)		55	0.53	13	3⁄32 in. (2 mm)	24.55	614
24 in. (600 mm)	25.8 in. (645 mm)		56	0.56	14	3⁄32 in. (2 mm)	24.49	612

ID: internal diameter; OD: outside diameter.

*This table is appropriate for single lining thickness only. The actual lining thickness should be obtained from the manufacturer.

[**24**:Table A.10.1.3]

A.6.4.3.2 The design concepts in 6.4.3.2.1 through 6.4.3.2.1.3 should apply to both new installations and existing private fire service mains approved to remain under new buildings. [**24**:A.10.4.3.2]

N **A.6.4.3.2.1** See Figure A.6.4.3.2.1. [**24**:A.10.4.3.2.1]

A.6.4.3.2.1.1 A grate or steel plate are common methods of accessing the trench. [**24**:A.10.4.3.2.1.1]

A.6.4.3.2.1.4 The intent of this requirement is to prevent the piping from being exposed to standing water. Draining can be accomplished by providing a floor drain, sloping the trench, or other approved method. [**24**:A.10.4.3.2.1.4]

A.6.4.3.2.3 It is the intent of this section to require a valve at each point where the pipe enters the trench when the trench traverses the entire building. Generally, if the piping terminates at a point within the building, a valve is usually provided at a riser, allowing the isolation of the pipe section in the trench. [**24**:A.10.4.3.2.3]

A.6.5.1 Where lightning protection is provided for a structure, Section 4.14 of NFPA 780 requires that all grounding media, including underground metallic piping systems, be interconnected to provide common ground potential. These underground piping systems are not permitted to be substituted for grounding electrodes but must be bonded to the lightning protection grounding system. Where galvanic corrosion is of concern, this bond can be made via a spark gap or gas discharge tube. [**24**:A.10.5.1]

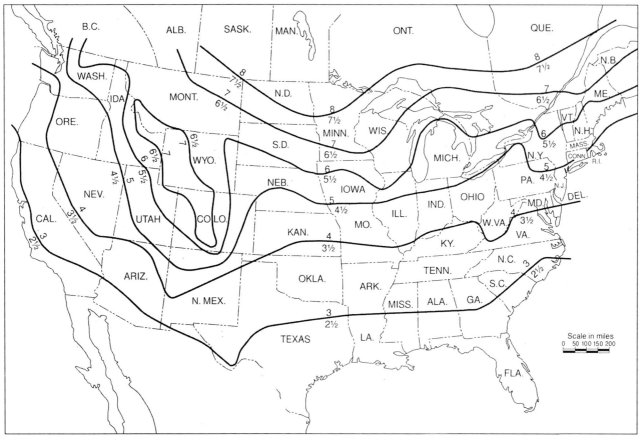

Notes:
1. For SI Units, 1 in. = 25.4 mm; 1 ft = 0.304 m.
2. Where frost penetration is a factor, the depth of cover shown averages 6 in. greater than that usually provided by the municipal waterworks. Greater depth is needed because of the absence of flow in yard mains.

Δ **FIGURE A.6.4.2   Recommended Depth of Cover (in feet) Above Top of Underground Yard Mains. [24:Figure A.10.4.2]**

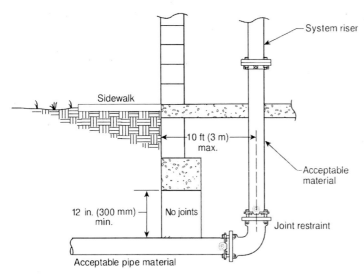

Δ **FIGURE A.6.4.3.1   Riser Entrance Location and Clearance. [24:Figure A.10.4.3.1]**

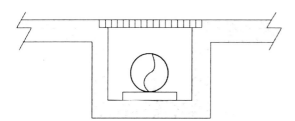

N **FIGURE A.6.4.3.2.1 Private Service Main in a Covered Trench. [24:Figure A.10.4.3.2.1]**

A.6.5.1.1 While the use of the underground fire protection piping as the grounding electrode for the building is prohibited, *NFPA 70* requires that all metallic piping systems be bonded and grounded to disperse stray electrical currents. Therefore, the fire protection piping will be bonded to other metallic systems and grounded, but the electrical system will need an additional ground for its operation. [24:A.10.5.1.1]

A.6.6 It is a fundamental design principle of fluid mechanics that dynamic and static pressures, acting at changes in size or direction of a pipe, produce unbalanced thrust forces at locations such as bends, tees, wyes, dead ends, and reducer offsets. This design principle includes consideration of lateral soil pressure and pipe/soil friction, variables that can be reliably determined using current soil engineering knowledge. Refer to A.6.6.2 for a list of references for use in calculating and determining joint restraint systems.

Section 6.6 does not mandate which method of restraint should be used. This decision is left to the design professional or the owner.

Except for the case of welded joints and approved special restrained joints, such as is provided by approved mechanical joint retainer glands or locked mechanical and push-on joints, the usual joints for underground pipe are expected to be held in place by the soil in which the pipe is buried. Gasketed push-on and mechanical joints without special locking devices have limited ability to resist separation due to movement of the pipe. [24:A.10.6]

A.6.6.1 The use of concrete thrust blocks is one method of restraint, provided that stable soil conditions prevail and space requirements permit placement. Successful blocking is dependent on factors such as location, availability and placement of concrete, and possibility of disturbance by future excavations.

Resistance is provided by transferring the thrust force to the soil through the larger bearing area of the block so that the resultant pressure against the soil does not exceed the horizontal bearing strength of the soil. The design of thrust blocks consists of determining the appropriate bearing area of the block for a particular set of conditions. The parameters involved in the design include pipe size, design pressure, angle of the bend (or configuration of the fitting involved), and the horizontal bearing strength of the soil.

Table A.6.6.1(a) gives the nominal thrust at fittings for various sizes of ductile-iron and PVC piping. Figure A.6.6.1(a) shows an example of how thrust forces act on a piping bend.

Thrust blocks are generally categorized into two groups — bearing and gravity blocks. Figure A.6.6.1(b) depicts a typical bearing thrust block on a horizontal bend. [24:A.10.6.1]

The following are general criteria for bearing block design:

(1) The bearing surface should, where possible, be placed against undisturbed soil.
(2) Where it is not possible to place the bearing surface against undisturbed soil, the fill between the bearing surface and undisturbed soil must be compacted to at least 90 percent Standard Proctor density.
(3) Block height (*h*) should be equal to or less than one-half the total depth to the bottom of the block (H_t) but not less than the pipe diameter (*D*).
(4) Block height (*h*) should be chosen such that the calculated block width (*b*) varies between one and two times the height.
(5) Gravity thrust blocks can be used to resist thrust at vertical down bends. In a gravity thrust block, the weight of the block is the force providing equilibrium with the thrust force. The design problem is then to calculate the required volume of the thrust block of a known density. The vertical component of the thrust force in Figure A.6.6.1(c) is balanced by the weight of the block. For required horizontal bearing block areas, see Table A.6.6.1(b).

The required block area (A_b) is as follows:

[A.6.6.1a]

$$A_b = (h)(b) = \frac{T(S_f)}{S_b}$$

where:
A_b = required block area (ft²)
h = block height (ft)
b = calculated block width (ft)
T = thrust force (lbf)
S_f = safety factor (usually 1.5)
S_b = bearing strength (lb/ft²)

Then, for a horizontal bend, the following formula is used:

[A.6.6.1b]

$$b = \frac{2(S_f)(P)(A)\sin\frac{\theta}{2}}{(h)(S_b)}$$

where:
b = calculated block width (ft)
S_f = safety factor (usually 1.5 for thrust block design)
P = water pressure (lb/in.²)
A = cross-sectional area of the pipe based on outside diameter
h = block height (ft)
S_b = horizontal bearing strength of soil (lb/ft²) (in.²)

A similar approach can be used to design bearing blocks to resist the thrust forces at locations such as tees and dead ends. Typical values for conservative horizontal bearing strengths of various soil types are listed in Table A.6.6.1(c). [24:A.10.6.1]

In lieu of the values for soil bearing strength shown in Table A.6.6.1(c), a designer might choose to use calculated Rankine passive pressure (P_p) or other determination of soil-bearing strength based on actual soil properties.

It can be easily shown that $T_y = PA \sin \theta$. The required volume of the block is as follows:

[A.6.6.1c]

$$V_g = \frac{S_f PA \sin \theta}{W_m}$$

where:
V_g = block volume (ft³)
S_f = safety factor
P = water pressure (psi)
A = cross-sectional area of pipe interior
W_m = density of block material (lb/ft³)

In a case such as the one shown, the horizontal component of thrust force is calculated as follows:

[A.6.6.1d]

$$T_x = PA(1 - \cos \theta)$$

where:
T_x = horizontal component of thrust force
P = water pressure (psi)
A = cross-sectional area of pipe interior

The horizontal component of thrust force must be resisted by the bearing of the right side of the block against the soil. Analysis of this aspect follows the same principles as the previous section on bearing blocks.
[24:A.10.6.1]

A.6.6.2 A method for providing thrust restraint is the use of restrained joints. A restrained joint is a special type of joint that is designed to provide longitudinal restraint. Restrained joint systems function in a manner similar to thrust blocks, insofar as the reaction of the entire restrained unit of piping with the soil balances the thrust forces.

The objective in designing a restrained joint thrust restraint system is to determine the length of pipe that must be restrained on each side of the focus of the thrust force, which occurs at a change in direction. This will be a function of the pipe size, the internal pressure, the depth of cover, and the characteristics of the solid surrounding the pipe. The manufacturer's installation instructions should be referenced to determine the distance from each change in direction that joints should be restrained.

The following documents apply to the design, calculation, and determination of restrained joint systems:

(1) *Thrust Restraint Design for Ductile Iron Pipe*, Ductile-Iron Pipe Research Association
(2) AWWA M41, *Ductile-Iron Pipe and Fittings*
(3) AWWA M9, *Concrete Pressure Pipe*
(4) AWWA M11, *Steel Pipe — A Guide for Design and Installation*
(5) *Thrust Restraint Design Equations and Tables for Ductile Iron and PVC Pipe*, EBAA Iron, Inc.

Figure A.6.6.2 shows an example of a typical connection to a fire protection system riser utilizing restrained joint pipe. [24:A.10.6.2]

Table A.6.6.1(a) Thrust at Fittings at 100 psi (6.9 bar) Water Pressure for Ductile Iron and PVC Pipe

Nominal Pipe Diameter [in. (mm)]	Total Pounds (Newtons)											
	Dead End		90 Degree		45 Degree		22½ Degree		11¼ Degree		5⅛ Degree	
	lbf	N	lbf	N	lbf	N	lbf	N	lbf	N	lbf	N
4 (100)	1,810	8,051	2,559	11,383	1,385	6,161	706	3,140	355	1,579	162	721
6 (150)	3,739	16,632	5,288	23,522	2,862	12,731	1,459	6,490	733	3,261	334	1,486
8 (200)	6,433	28,615	9,097	40,465	4,923	21,899	2,510	11,165	1,261	5,609	575	2,558
10 (250)	9,677	43,045	13,685	60,874	7,406	32,944	3,776	16,796	1,897	8,438	865	3,848
12 (300)	13,685	60,874	19,353	86,086	10,474	46,591	5,340	23,753	2,683	11,935	1,224	5,445
14 (350)	18,385	81,781	26,001	115,658	14,072	62,595	7,174	31,912	3,604	16,031	1,644	7,313
16 (400)	23,779	105,774	33,628	149,585	18,199	80,953	9,278	41,271	4,661	20,733	2,126	9,457
18 (450)	29,865	132,846	42,235	187,871	22,858	101,677	11,653	51,835	5,855	26,044	2,670	11,877
20 (500)	36,644	163,001	51,822	230,516	28,046	124,755	14,298	63,601	7,183	31,952	3,277	14,577
24 (600)	52,279	232,548	73,934	328,875	40,013	177,987	20,398	90,735	10,249	45,590	4,675	20,795
30 (750)	80,425	357,748	113,738	505,932	61,554	273,806	31,380	139,585	15,766	70,131	7,191	31,987
36 (900)	115,209	512,475	162,931	724,753	88,177	392,231	44,952	199,956	22,585	100,463	10,302	45,826
42 (1,050)	155,528	691,823	219,950	978,386	119,036	529,498	60,684	269,936	30,489	135,622	13,907	61,861
48 (1,200)	202,683	901,579	286,637	1,275,024	155,127	690,039	79,083	351,779	39,733	176,741	18,124	80,620

Notes:
(1) For SI units, 1 lb = 0.454 kg; 1 in. = 25 mm.
(2) To determine thrust at pressure other than 100 psi (6.9 bar), multiply the thrust obtained in the table by the ratio of the pressure to 100 psi (6.9 bar). For example, the thrust on a 12 in. (305 mm), 90-degree bend at 125 psi (8.6 bar) is 19,353 × 125/100 = 24,191 lb (10,973 kg).
[24:Table A.10.6.1(a)]

Δ **Table A.6.6.1(b) Required Horizontal Bearing Block Area**

Nominal Pipe Diameter [in. (mm)]	Bearing Block Area [ft² (m²)]	Nominal Pipe Diameter [in. (mm)]	Bearing Block Area [ft² (m²)]	Nominal Pipe Diameter [in. (mm)]	Bearing Block Area [ft² (m²)]
3 (80)	2.6 (0.24)	12 (300)	29.0 (2.7)	24 (600)	110.9 (10.3)
4 (100)	3.8 (0.35)	14 (350)	39.0 (3.6)	30 (750)	170.6 (15.8)
6 (150)	7.9 (0.73)	16 (400)	50.4 (4.7)	36 (900)	244.4 (22.7)
8 (200)	13.6 (1.3)	18 (450)	63.3 (5.9)	42 (1050)	329.9 (30.6)
10 (250)	20.5 (2)	20 (500)	77.7 (7.2)	48 (1200)	430.0 (39.9)

Notes:
(1) Although the bearing strength values in this table have been used successfully in the design of thrust blocks and are considered to be conservative, their accuracy is totally dependent on accurate soil identification and evaluation. The ultimate responsibility for selecting the proper bearing strength of a particular soil type must rest with the design engineer.
(2) Values listed are based on a 90-degree horizontal bend, an internal pressure of 100 psi (6.9 bar), a soil horizontal bearing strength of 1000 lb/ft² (47.9 kN/m²), a safety factor of 1.5, and ductile iron pipe outside diameters.
(a) For other horizontal bends, multiply by the following coefficients: for 45 degrees, 0.541; for 22½ degrees, 0.276; for 11¼ degrees, 0.139.
(b) For other internal pressures, multiply by ratio to 100 psi (69 bar).
(c) For other soil horizontal bearing strengths, divide by ratio to 1000 lb/ft² (47.9 kN/m²).
(d) For other safety factors, multiply by ratio to 1.5.
Example: Using Table A.6.6.1(b), find the horizontal bearing block area for a 6 in. (150 mm) diameter, 45-degree bend with an internal pressure of 150 psi (10 bar). The soil bearing strength is 3000 lb/ft² (145 kN/m²), and the safety factor is 1.5.
From Table A.6.6.1(b), the required bearing block area for a 6 in. (150 mm) diameter, 90-degree bend with an internal pressure of 100 psi (6.9 bar) and a soil horizontal bearing strength of 1000 psi (70 bar) is 7.9 ft² (0.73 m²).
For example:

$$Area = \frac{7.9 \text{ ft}^2 (0.541)\frac{150}{100}}{\frac{3000}{1000}} = 2.1 \text{ ft}^2$$

[24:Table A.10.6.1(b)]

Δ **A.6.6.2.1** Examples of materials and the standards covering these materials are as follows:

(1) Clamps, steel
(2) Rods, steel
(3) Bolts, steel (ASTM A307, *Standard Specification for Carbon Steel Bolts, Studs, Threaded Rod 60,000 psi Tensile Strength*)
(4) Washers, steel, cast iron (Class A cast iron as defined by ASTM A126, *Standard Specification for Gray Iron Castings for Valves, Flanges and Pipe Fittings*)
(5) Anchor straps, plug straps, steel
(6) Rod couplings, turnbuckles, malleable iron (ASTM A197/A197M, *Standard Specification for Cupola Malleable Iron*)
[24:A.10.6.2.1]

A.6.6.3 Solvent-cemented and heat-fused joints such as those used with CPVC piping and fittings are considered restrained. They do not require thrust blocks. [24:A.10.6.3]

Table A.6.6.1(c) Horizontal Bearing Strengths

Soil	Bearing Strength, S_b	
	lb/ft²	kN/m²
Muck	0	0
Soft clay	1000	47.9
Silt	1500	71.8
Sandy silt	3000	143.6
Sand	4000	191.5
Sandy clay	6000	287.3
Hard clay	9000	430.9

Note: Although the bearing strength values in this table have been used successfully in the design of thrust blocks and are considered to be conservative, their accuracy is totally dependent on accurate soil identification and evaluation. The ultimate responsibility for selecting the proper bearing strength of a particular soil type must rest with the design engineer.
[24:Table A.10.6.1(c)]

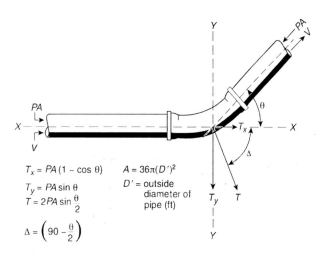

$T_x = PA\,(1 - \cos\theta)$ $A = 36\pi(D')^2$

$T_y = PA\sin\theta$ $D' = $ outside diameter of pipe (ft)

$T = 2PA\sin\dfrac{\theta}{2}$

$\Delta = \left(90 - \dfrac{\theta}{2}\right)$

T = thrust force resulting from change in direction of flow (lbf)

T_x = component of thrust force acting parallel to original direction of flow (lbf)

T_y = component of thrust force acting perpendicular to original direction of flow (lbf)

P = water pressure (psi²)

A = cross-sectional area of pipe based on outside diameter. (in.²)

V = velocity in direction of flow

FIGURE A.6.6.1(a)   Thrust Forces Acting on Bend.
[24:Figure A.10.6.1(a)]

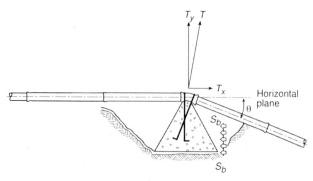

T = thrust force resulting from change of direction of flow

T_x = horizontal component of thrust force

T_y = vertical component of thrust force

S_b = horizontal bearing strength of soil

FIGURE A.6.6.1(c)   Gravity Thrust Block. [24:Figure A.10.6.1(c)]

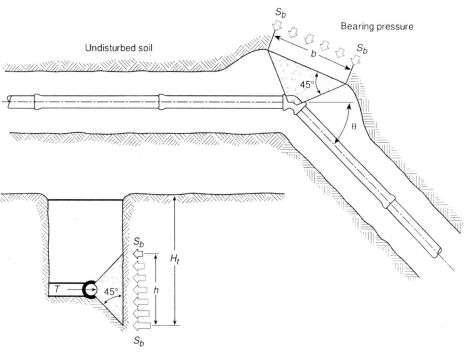

T = thrust force resulting from change in direction of flow

S_b = horizontal bearing strength of soil

h = block height

H_t = total depth to bottom of block

FIGURE A.6.6.1(b)   Bearing Thrust Block. [24:Figure A.10.6.1(b)]

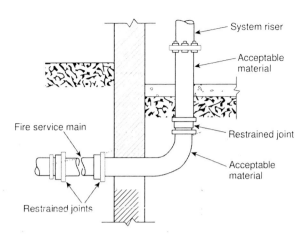

FIGURE A.6.6.2   Typical Connection to a Fire Protection System Riser Illustrating Restrained Joints. [24:Figure A.10.6.2]

A.6.9.3 The maximum particle size allowed next to most types of pipe can be found in ASTM C136/136M, *Standard Test Method for Sieve Analysis of Fine and Coarse Aggregates,* ASTM D2487, *Standard Practice for Classification of Soils for Engineering Purposes (Unified Soil Classification System),* AWWA M55, *PE Pipe — Design and Installation,* AWWA M23, *PVC Pipe — Design and Installation,* trade association handbooks, or manufacturers' literature. These publications typically recommend one maximum allowable particle size that applies to the bedding, embedment, and backfill, which might be different materials. The maximum particle size might be dependent on the pipe diameter. [24:A.10.9.3]

A.6.10.2.1 Underground mains and lead-in connections to system risers should be flushed through hydrants at dead ends of the system or through accessible aboveground flushing outlets allowing the water to run until clear. Figure A.6.10.2.1 shows acceptable examples of flushing the system. If water is supplied from more than one source or from a looped system, divisional valves should be closed to produce a high-velocity flow through each single line. The flows specified in Table 6.10.2.1.3 will produce a velocity of at least 10 ft/sec (3.0 m/sec), which is necessary for cleaning the pipe and for lifting foreign material to an aboveground flushing outlet. [24:A.10.10.2.1]

A.6.10.2.1.3 The velocity of approximately 10 ft/sec (3.0 m/sec) was used to develop Table 6.10.2.1.3 because this velocity has been shown to be sufficient for moving obstructive material out of the pipes. It is not important that the velocity equal exactly 10 ft/sec (3.0 m/sec), so there is no reason to increase the flow during the test for slightly different internal pipe dimensions. Note that where underground pipe serves as suction pipe for a fire pump, NFPA 20 requires greater flows for flushing the pipe. [24:A.10.10.2.1.3]

N **A.6.10.2.1.4** An example of a swab would be polyurethane foam. The manufacturer's recommended procedure should be followed when swabbing is used. [24:A.10.10.2.1.4]

A.6.10.2.2.1 For example, consider a sprinkler system with a connection to a public water service main for its water supply. A 100 psi (6.9 bar) rated pump is installed in the connection. With a maximum normal public water supply of 70 psi (4.8

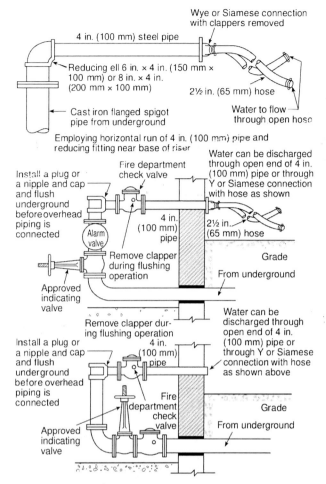

Employing fire department connections

Δ FIGURE A.6.10.2.1   Methods of Flushing Water Supply Connections. [24:Figure A.10.10.2.1]

bar) at the low elevation point of the individual system or portion of the system being tested and a 120 psi (8.3 bar) pump (churn) pressure, the hydrostatic test pressure is 70 psi (4.8 bar), 120 psi (8.3 bar), 50 psi (3.5 bar), or 240 psi (16.5 bar).

To reduce the possibility of serious water damage in case of a break, pressure can be introduced by a small pump, the main controlling gate meanwhile being kept shut during the test.

Polybutylene pipe will undergo expansion during initial pressurization. In this case, a reduction in gauge pressure might not necessarily indicate a leak. The pressure reduction should not exceed the manufacturer's specifications and listing criteria.

When systems having rigid thermoplastic piping such as CPVC are pressure tested, the sprinkler system should be filled with water. The air should be bled from the highest and farthest sprinklers. Compressed air or compressed gas should never be used to test systems with rigid thermoplastic pipe.

A recommended test procedure is as follows: The water pressure is to be increased in 50 psi (3.5 bar) increments until the test pressure described in 6.10.2.2.1 is attained. After each increase in pressure, observations are to be made of the stability of the joints. These observations are to include such items as protrusion or extrusion of the gasket, leakage, or other factors likely to affect the continued use of a pipe in service. During the test, the pressure is not to be increased by the next increment until the joint has become stable. This applies particularly to movement of the gasket. After the pressure has been increased to the required maximum value, it is held for 2 hours while observations are made for leakage and the pressure readings are checked. [**24**:A.10.10.2.2.1]

A.6.10.2.2.4 Hydrostatic tests should be made before the joints are covered, so that any leaks can be detected. Thrust blocks should be sufficiently hardened before hydrostatic testing is begun. If the joints are covered with backfill prior to testing, the contractor remains responsible for locating and correcting any leakage in excess of that permitted. [**24**:A.10.10.2.2.4]

A.6.10.2.2.6 One acceptable means of completing this test is to utilize a pressure pump that draws its water supply from a full container. At the completion of the 2-hour test, the amount of water to refill the container can be measured to determine the amount of makeup water. In order to minimize pressure loss, the piping should be flushed to remove any trapped air. Additionally, the piping could be pressurized prior to the hydrostatic test to account for expansion, absorption, entrapped air, and so on.

The use of a blind flange or skillet is preferred for hydrostatically testing segments of new work. Metal-seated valves are susceptible to developing slight imperfections during transport, installation, and operation and thus can be likely to leak more than 1 fl oz/in. (1.2 mL/mm) of valve diameter per hour. For this reason, the blind flange should be used when hydrostatically testing. [**24**:A.10.10.2.2.6]

A.6.10.2.3 As an example, the following standards contain test requirements AWWA C600, *Installation of Ductile Iron Water Mains and Their Appurtenances*, AWWA C602, *Cement-Mortar Lining of Water Pipe Lines in Place, 4 in. (100 mm) and Larger*, AWWA C900, *Polyvinyl Chloride (PVC) Pressure Pipe and Fabricated Fittings, 4 in. Through 60 in (100 mm Through 1,500 mm)*, or ASTM F2164, *Standard Practice for Field Leak Testing of Polyethylene (PE) and Crosslinked Polyethylene (PEX) Pressure Piping Systems Using Hydrostatic Pressure*. [**24**:A.10.10.2.3]

N **A.6.10.2.3.1** Examples include cut-in tees, repair sleeves, or hot taps. [**24**:A.10.10.2.3.1]

A.7.1.1 Included among items requiring listing are sprinklers, some pipe and some fittings, hangers, alarm devices, valves controlling flow of water to sprinklers, supervisory switches, and electrically operated solenoid valves. Products are typically investigated in accordance with published standards. Examples of standards used to investigate several products installed in sprinkler systems are referenced in Table A.7.1.1. This table does not include a comprehensive list of all product standards used to investigate products installed in sprinkler systems.

Δ **Table A.7.1.1 Examples of Standards for Sprinkler System Products**

Category	Standard
Sprinklers	UL 199, *Automatic Sprinklers for Fire Protection Service*
	FM 2000, *Automatic Control Mode Sprinklers for Fire Protection*
	FM 2030, *Residential Automatic Sprinklers*
	FM 2008, *Suppression Mode ESFR Automatic Sprinklers*
	FM 1632, *Telescoping Sprinkler Assemblies for Use in Fire Protection Systems for Anechoic Chambers*
Antifreeze and Corrosion Control	UL 2901, *Antifreeze Solutions for Use in Fire Sprinkler Systems*
	UL 2901A, *Outline for Corrosion Control Additives for Use in Fire Sprinkler Systems*
Valves	UL 193, *Alarm Valves for Fire Protection Service*
	FM 1041, *Alarm Check Valves*
	UL 260, *Dry Pipe and Deluge Valves for Fire Protection Service*
	FM 1021, *Dry Pipe Valves*
	FM 1020, *Automatic Water Control Valves*
	UL 262, *Gate Valves for Fire Protection Service*
	FM 1120, 1130, *Fire Service Water Control Valves (OS & Y and NRS Type Gate Valves)*
	UL 312, *Check Valves for Fire Protection Service*
	FM 1210, *Swing Check Valves*
	UL 1091, *Butterfly Valves for Fire Protection Service*
	FM 1112, *Indicating Valves (Butterfly or Ball Type)*
	UL 1468, *Direct Acting Pressure Reducing and Pressure Restricting Valves*
	UL 1739, *Pilot-Operated Pressure-Control Valves for Fire Protection Service*
	FM 1362, *Pressure Reducing Valves*
	FM 1011/1012/1013, *Deluge and Preaction Sprinkler Systems*
	FM 1031, *Quick Opening Devices (Accelerators and Exhausters) for Dry Pipe Valves*
	UL 1486, *Quick Opening Devices for Dry Pipe Valves for Fire Protection Service*
	UL 346, *Waterflow Indicators for Fire Protective Signaling Systems*
	FM 1042, *Waterflow Alarm Indicators (Vane Type)*
	FM 1045, *Waterflow Detector Check Valves*
	FM 1140, *Quick Opening Valves ¼ Inch Through 2 Inch Nominal Size*
Hangers	UL 203, *Pipe Hanger Equipment for Fire Protection Service*
	FM 1951, 1952, 1953, *Pipe Hanger Components for Automatic Sprinkler Systems*
	FM 1950, *Seismic Sway Brace Components for Automatic Sprinkler Systems*
	UL 203A, *Sway Brace Devices for Sprinkler System Piping*

(continues)

Shaded text = Revisions. Δ = Text deletions and figure/table revisions. • = Section deletions. *N* = New material.

Δ **Table A.7.1.1**   *Continued*

Category	Standard
Fittings	UL 213, *Rubber Gasketed Fittings for Fire Protection Service* FM 1920, *Pipe Couplings and Fittings for Fire Protection Systems* UL 1474, *Adjustable Drop Nipples for Sprinkler Systems* FM 1631, *Adjustable and Fixed Sprinkler Fittings ½ Inch through 1 Inch Nominal Size* UL 2443, *Flexible Sprinkler Hose with Fittings for Fire Protection Service* FM 1637, *Flexible Sprinkler Hose with Fittings*
Pipe — Aboveground	UL 852, *Metallic Sprinkler Pipe for Fire Protection Service* FM 1630, *Steel Pipe for Automatic Fire Sprinkler Systems* UL 1821, *Thermoplastic Sprinkler Pipe and Fittings for Fire Protection Service* FM 1635, *Plastic Pipe & Fittings for Automatic Sprinkler Systems* FM 1636, *Fire Resistant Barriers for Use with CPVC Pipe and Fittings in Light Hazard Occupancies*
Pipe — Underground	UL 1285, *Polyvinyl Chloride (PVC) Pipe and Couplings for Underground Fire Service* FM 1612, *Polyvinyl Chloride (PVC) Pipe and Fittings for Underground Fire Protection Service* FM 1613, *Polyethylene (PE) Pipe and Fittings for Underground Fire Protection Service* FM 1610, *Ductile Iron Pipe and Fittings, Flexible Fittings and Couplings* UL 194, *Gasketed Joints for Ductile-Iron Pipe and Fittings for Fire Protection Service* FM 1620, *Pipe Joints and Anchor Fittings for Underground Fire Service Mains*

A.7.1.1.5 Certain components installed in sprinkler systems are not required to be listed as their improper operation will not detrimentally affect the automatic system performance. Examples include but are not limited to drain valves, drain piping, signs, gauges, automated inspection and test devices, distance monitoring devices, fire department connections that do not use threadless couplings, and so forth.

Certain devices and equipment that could be used to perform inspection and testing procedures from a distant location are not integral to the system and do not affect system performance. Automated inspection and testing devices and equipment, such as a digital camera, might be in the riser room or attached to the system externally but are not an integral part of the system. Such devices do not need to be listed.

Certain devices and equipment that could be used to monitor system or component status from a distance are not integral to the system and do not affect system performance. Distance monitoring devices, such as an external thermometer, might be attached to the system externally and therefore are not subjected to system pressure. Such devices do not need to be listed.

A.7.2.1 The four- to six-character sprinkler identification number, with no intervening spaces, is intended to identify the sprinkler operating characteristics in lieu of the traditional laboratory approval marking (e.g., SSU, SSP, EC, QR, etc.). The number, marked on the deflector of most sprinklers and elsewhere on decorative ceiling sprinklers, consists of one or two characters identifying the manufacturer, followed by three or four digits.

Sprinkler manufacturers have identified their manufacturer designations for the listing organizations. In order to identify a manufacturer based on the Sprinkler Identification Number, see the listing at www.firesprinkler.global. Each change in K-factor, response characteristics, or deflector (distribution) characteristics results in a new sprinkler identification number. The numbers do not identify specific characteristics of sprinklers but can be referenced in the database information compiled by the listing organizations. At the plan review stage, the sprinkler identification number should be checked against such a database or the manufacturer's literature to ensure that sprinklers are being used properly and within the limitations of their listings. Field inspections can include spot checks to ensure that the model numbers on the plans are those actually installed.

A.7.2.2.1 See Table A.7.2.2.1.

A.7.2.4 Information regarding the highest temperature that can be encountered in any location in a particular installation can be obtained by use of a thermometer that will register the highest temperature encountered; it should be hung for several days in the location in question, with equipment in operation that produces heat.

N **A.7.2.4.1** Table 7.2.4.1(a) and Table 7.2.4.1(b) should not be used to determine where sprinklers with specific temperature ratings are to be installed but only to classify sprinklers according to their temperature ratings. See 9.4.2 for specific temperature rating requirements.

A.7.2.5.1 Examples of such locations include the following:

(1) Paper mills
(2) Packing houses
(3) Tanneries
(4) Alkali plants
(5) Organic fertilizer plants
(6) Foundries

Δ **Table A.7.2.2.1 Nominal Sprinkler Orifice Sizes**

Nominal K-Factor		Nominal Orifice Size	
U.S. [gpm/(psi)$^{1/2}$]	Metric [L/min/(bar)$^{1/2}$]	in.	mm
1.4	20	¼	6.4
1.9	27	5/16	8.0
2.8	40	⅜	10
4.2	60	7/16	11
5.6	80	½	13
8.0	115	17/32	13
11.2	160	⅝	16
14.0	200	¾	20
16.8	240	—	—
19.6	280	—	—
22.4	320	—	—
25.2	360	—	—
28.0	400	—	—
33.6	480	—	—

(7) Forge shops
(8) Fumigation, pickle, and vinegar works
(9) Stables
(10) Storage battery rooms
(11) Electroplating rooms
(12) Galvanizing rooms
(13) Steam rooms of all descriptions, including moist vapor dry kilns
(14) Salt storage rooms
(15) Locomotive sheds or houses
(16) Driveways
(17) Areas exposed to outside weather, such as piers and wharves exposed to salt air
(18) Areas under sidewalks
(19) Areas around bleaching equipment in flour mills
(20) All portions of cold storage buildings where a direct ammonia expansion system is used
(21) Portions of any plant where corrosive vapors prevail
(22) Area over and around swimming pools, chlorine storage rooms, and pool pump rooms

A.7.2.5.2 Painting of sprinklers can retard the thermal response of the heat-responsive element, can interfere with the free movement of parts, and can render the sprinkler inoperative. Moreover, painting can invite the application of subsequent coatings, thus increasing the possibility of a malfunction of the sprinkler.

A.7.2.6.2 The use of the wrong type of escutcheon with recessed or flush-type sprinklers can result in severe disruption of the spray pattern, which can destroy the effectiveness of the sprinkler.

A.7.3.2 CPVC is a plastic material, and consideration is necessary when other materials or chemicals come in contact with CPVC that can cause degradation of performance of the pipe due to interaction of materials. Other construction materials include but are not limited to materials used in fabrication of the sprinkler system, additives to water supplies, cable, and wiring, and certain insecticides and fungicides. Compliance with 7.3.2 combined with following the manufacturer's guidance on installation and compatible materials will help prevent premature performance degradation of non-metallic piping. Mechanical stress caused by hanging methods or bending on non-metallic piping beyond the manufacturers recommended limitations can cause stress failure over time and should be avoided.

Other types of pipe and tube that have been investigated and listed for sprinkler applications include thermoplastic pipe and fittings. While these products can offer advantages, such as ease of handling and installation, cost-effectiveness, reduction of friction losses, and improved corrosion resistance, it is important to recognize that they also have limitations that are to be considered by those contemplating their use or acceptance.

With respect to thermoplastic pipe and fittings, exposure of such piping to elevated temperatures in excess of that for which it has been listed can result in distortion or failure. Accordingly, care must be exercised when locating such systems to ensure that the ambient temperature, including seasonal variations, does not exceed the rated value.

The upper service temperature limit of currently listed CPVC sprinkler pipe is 150°F (65.5°C) at 175 psi (12.1 bar).

Not all pipe or tube made to ASTM F442, *Standard Specification for Chlorinated Poly (Vinyl Chloride) (CPVC) Plastic Pipe (SDR-PR)*, is listed for fire sprinkler service. Listed pipe is identified by the logo of the listing agency.

Not all fittings made to ASTM F437, *Standard Specification for Threaded Chlorinated Poly (Vinyl Chloride) (CPVC) Plastic Pipe Fittings, Schedule 80*, ASTM F438, *Standard Specification for Socket-Type Chlorinated Poly (Vinyl Chloride) (CPVC) Plastic Pipe Fittings, Schedule 40*, and ASTM F439, *Standard Specification for Socket-Type Chlorinated Poly (Vinyl Chloride) (CPVC) Plastic Pipe Fittings, Schedule 80*, as described in 7.4.4, are listed for fire sprinkler service. Listed fittings are identified by the logo of the listing agency.

Consideration must also be given to the possibility of exposure of the piping to elevated temperatures during a fire. The survival of thermoplastic piping under fire conditions is primarily due to the cooling effect of the discharge from the sprinklers it serves. As this discharge might not occur simultaneously with the rise in ambient temperature and, under some circumstances, can be delayed for periods beyond the tolerance of the piping, protection in the form of a fire-resistant membrane is generally required. (Some listings do provide for the use of exposed piping in conjunction with residential or quick-response sprinklers, but only under specific, limited installation criteria.)

Where protection is required, it is described in the listing information for each individual product, and the requirements given must be followed. It is equally important that such protection must be maintained. Removal of, for example, one or more panels in a lay-in ceiling can expose piping in the concealed space to the possibility of failure in the event of a fire. Similarly, the relocation of openings through protective ceilings that expose the pipe to heat, inconsistent with the listing, would place the system in jeopardy. The potential for loss of the protective membrane under earthquake conditions should also be considered.

While the listings of thermoplastic piping do not prohibit its installation in combustible concealed spaces where the provision of sprinkler protection is not required, and while the statistical record of fire originating in such spaces is low, it should be recognized that the occurrence of a fire in such a space could result in failure of the piping system. The investigation of pipe and tube other than described in Table 7.3.1.1 should involve consideration of many factors, including the following:

(1) Pressure rating
(2) Beam strength (hangers)
(3) Unsupported vertical stability
(4) Movement during sprinkler operation (affecting water distribution)
(5) Corrosion (internal and external), chemical and electrolytic
(6) Resistance to failure when exposed to elevated temperatures
(7) Methods of joining (strength, permanence, fire hazard)
(8) Physical characteristics related to integrity during earthquakes

A.7.3.3 Other types of pipe and tube that have been investigated and listed for sprinkler applications include lightweight steel pipe. While these products can offer advantages, such as ease of handling and installation, cost effectiveness, and reduction of friction losses, it is important to recognize that they also have limitations that are to be considered by those contemplating their use or acceptance.

Corrosion studies have shown that, in comparison to Schedule 40 pipe, the effective life of lightweight steel pipe can be reduced, the level of reduction being related to its wall thickness. Further information with respect to corrosion resistance is contained in the individual listings for such pipe.

A.7.3.4.1 Where approved, the pipe identification can be covered with paint or other protective coatings before installation.

A.7.4.4 Rubber-gasketed pipe fittings and couplings should not be installed where ambient temperatures can be expected to exceed 150°F (66°C) unless listed for this service. If the manufacturer further limits a given gasket compound, those recommendations should be followed.

Other construction materials include but are not limited to materials used in fabrication of the sprinkler system, additives to water supplies, cable and wiring, and certain insecticides and fungicides.

A.7.5.1.2 Some steel piping material having lesser wall thickness than specified in 7.5.1.2 has been listed for use in sprinkler systems where joined with threaded connections. The service life of such products can be significantly less than that of Schedule 40 steel pipe, and it should be determined if this service life will be sufficient for the application intended.

All such threads should be checked by the installer using working ring gauges conforming to the "Basic Dimensions of Ring Gauges for USA (American) Standard Taper Pipe Threads, NPT," as per Table 8 of ASME B1.20.1, *Pipe Threads, General Purpose (Inch).*

A.7.5.2.2 Cutting and welding operations account for 4 percent of fires each year in nonresidential properties and 8 percent in industrial and manufacturing properties. In-place welding of sprinkler piping introduces a significant hazard that can normally be avoided by shop-welding the piping and installing the welded sections with mechanical fittings. As a result, the standard requires that all piping be shop-welded. When such situations cannot be avoided, the exceptions outline procedures and practices that minimize the increase in hazard.

A.7.5.2.3.1 Listed, shaped, and contoured nipples meet the definition of fabricated fittings.

A.7.5.2.4.1 Partial penetration welds on outlet fitting connections are considered adequate, since there is no significant load on the joint other than that caused by pressure internal to the pipe *(see Figure A.7.5.2.4.1).*

A.7.5.2.4.2 The load due to the internal pressure can be accommodated with a weld that has a conservative weld throat thickness that can be calculated as follows:

$$[A.7.5.2.4.2]$$
$$\text{Weld throat thickness (in.)} = PD \times 0.000035$$

where:
P = rated system gauge pressure (psi)
D = outside diameter (OD) of fitting (in.)

For example, if you assume a gauge pressure of 300 psi (21 bar) and the OD of the outlet fitting of 3 in. (75 mm), the result of the thickness calculation is 0.0315 in. (0.8 mm). When compared to the minimum throat thickness of ³⁄₁₆ in. (5 mm), there is a factor of more than 5 times the calculated thickness value.

A.7.5.2.4.3 The preparation of mating surfaces is important to the proper fabrication of a weld joint. To accomplish this, the mating surfaces for a circumferential weld butt joint should be prepared and configured so that a full penetration weld is achievable, but a partial penetration weld is acceptable. *(See Figure A.7.5.2.4.3.)*

N **A.7.5.2.4.8** Loose welding slag or residue should be removed from piping, but a small amount should be acceptable as it is impossible to remove all the slag especially in long runs of pipe.

A.7.5.3.1 It is not the intent to require specific listing of every combination of grooved coupling, pipe, fitting, valve, and device, provided the standard groove dimensions as specified in ANSI/UL 213, *Rubber Gasketed Fittings for Fire Protection Service,* are used. Material strength and pressure rating of the fitting, valve, or device used with the grooved couplings should be considered when determining the appropriate application of a coupling when joining these components.

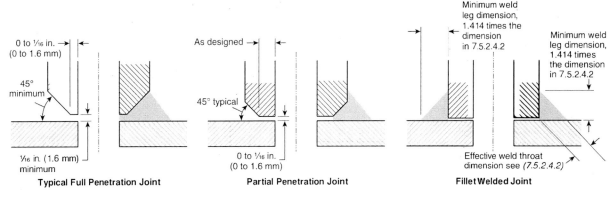

Δ **FIGURE A.7.5.2.4.1** Weld Descriptions.

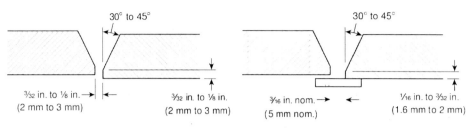

△ FIGURE A.7.5.2.4.3   Weld Diagram.

A.7.5.3.1.1 Standardized groove specifications pertain to the grooved couplings that comply with and the groove dimensions described in ANSI/UL 213, *Rubber Gasketed Fittings for Fire-Protection Service*. The standard dimensions are specified in ANSI/UL 213.

A.7.5.4 The fire hazard of the brazing and soldering processes should be suitably safeguarded.

A.7.5.4.5 Soldering fluxes manufactured to the specifications required by Table 7.3.1.1 are unlikely to cause damage to the seats of sprinklers. When brazing flux is used, it must be of a type not likely to damage the seats of sprinklers.

N **A.7.7.1** The intent of the 5 minute allowance is to accommodate fluctuations in water flow in large systems.

N **A.7.7.2** Where buildings are equipped with fire alarm systems, the requirements of the applicable fire alarm code should prevail. It is the intent of this section to also apply to electrically activated local alarm bells. The 100 second allowance is to meet the requirement of 90 second plus 10 second delay in responding to the signal from the initiating device (i.e. flow or pressure switch).

A.8.1.1.2 Pressure gauges installed on both sides of a check valve are necessary for several reasons. They can quickly indicate an abnormal condition such as a closed valve or an inoperable check valve. If the pressure on the downstream side of a check valve is less than the pressure on the upstream side, either the pressure gauges are faulty or the check valve is inoperable. If the pressure on the upstream side of a check valve is less than the pressure on the downstream side, the pressure is trapped indicating a higher than normal pressure. This erroneous pressure will then be part of a main drain test. If a pressure gauge is installed only on the downstream side of the check valve a pressure would be indicated but the pressure on the upstream side could be 0.0 psi indicating a severe problem.

A.8.2 A dry pipe system should be installed only where heat is not adequate to prevent freezing of water in all parts of, or in sections of, the system. Dry pipe systems should be converted to wet pipe systems when they become unnecessary because adequate heat is provided. Sprinklers should not be shut off in cold weather.

Where two or more dry pipe valves are used, systems preferably should be divided horizontally to prevent simultaneous operation of more than one system and the resultant increased time delay in filling systems and discharging water and to prevent receipt of more than one waterflow alarm signal.

Where adequate heat is present in sections of the dry pipe system, consideration should be given to dividing the system into a separate wet pipe system and dry pipe system. Minimized use of dry pipe systems is desirable where speed of operation is of particular concern.

A.8.2.2.2(2) Installation limitations of listed dry pendent sprinklers can vary with different products. Limitations should be included in product installation instructions to warn the user of the potential accumulation of water, scale, and sediment from collecting at the sprinkler.

A.8.2.3 The capacities of the various sizes of pipe given in Table A.8.2.3 are for convenience in calculating the capacity of a system.

A.8.2.3.1 The 60-second limit does not apply to dry systems with capacities of 500 gal (1900 L) or less, nor to dry systems with capacities of 750 gal (2850 L) or less if equipped with a quick-opening device.

A.8.2.3.7 See Figure A.8.2.3.7.

A.8.2.5 The dry pipe valve should be located in an accessible place near the sprinkler system it controls. Where exposed to cold, the dry pipe valve should be located in a valve room or enclosure of adequate size to properly service equipment.

A.8.2.5.1 The dry pipe valve and supply piping should be in an area maintained at or above 40°F (4°C). It is the intent of the committee to protect the valves from freezing. The occasional exposure of valves to short exposures of air temperatures below 40°F (4°C) that would not cause the valves to freeze does not justify the construction of a valve room.

A.8.2.6.3 The compressor should draw its air supply from within the operating criteria allowed by the manufacturer of the compressor. Air piping should not be attached to the intake of the compressor unless acceptable to the compressor manufacturer and installed in accordance with 8.8.2.7. Damage, air reduction, or reduced life expectancy can result if guidelines are not followed.

A.8.2.6.3.2 When a single compressor serves multiple dry pipe systems, the 30-minute fill time is based on the single largest system.

A.8.2.6.4.1 The connection from an air compressor to the dry pipe valve should be of a type recommended by the manufacturer and approved by the authority having jurisdiction, taking into consideration the pressures, temperatures, and vibrations that the connection and adjacent equipment will endure. Flexi-

Table A.8.2.3 Capacity of 1 ft of Pipe (Based on Actual Internal Pipe Diameter)

Nominal Pipe Diameter		Pipe		Nominal Pipe Diameter		Pipe	
in.	mm	Schedule 40 [gal (L)]	Schedule 10 [gal (L)]	in.	mm	Schedule 40 [gal (L)]	Schedule 10 [gal (L)]
¾	20	0.028 (0.11)		3	80	0.383 (1.45)	0.433 (1.64)
1	25	0.045 (0.17)	0.049 (0.19)	3½	90	0.513 (1.94)	0.576 (2.18)
1¼	32	0.078 (0.30)	0.085 (0.32)	4	100	0.660 (2.50)	0.740 (2.80)
1½	40	0.106 (0.40)	0.115 (0.43)	5	125	1.040 (3.94)	1.144 (4.33)
2	50	0.174 (0.66)	0.190 (0.72)	6	150	1.501 (5.68)	1.649[b] (6.24)
2½	65	0.248 (0.94)	0.283 (1.07)	8	200	2.66[a] (10.1)	2.776[c] (10.5)

[a]Schedule 30.
[b]0.134 wall pipe.
[c]0.188 wall pipe.

ble hose should be considered suitable when capable of withstanding expected vibration, a maximum pressure of 175 psi (12 bar) or greater, and a maximum temperature of 150°F (66°C) or greater.

A.8.2.6.6.1 Air maintenance devices are unique components within the air supply and need to be listed for use. Compressors are not air maintenance devices and this section does not require air compressors to be listed.

A.8.2.6.8.1 The nitrogen or other approved gas can be either generated on site or from storage containers, sized to provide a reliable supply for at least 6 months of expected maintenance use.

A.8.2.6.8.4 When a single nitrogen or other approved gas source serves multiple dry pipe systems, the 30-minute fill time is based on the single largest system.

N A.8.2.6.9 Nitrogen systems are equipped with an air compressor capable of restoring system air pressure within 30 or 60 minutes. It is not the intent of this section to require a 98 percent concentration of nitrogen within the 30 or 60 minutes as required in 8.2.6.8.

A.8.3.1 Conditions of occupancy or special hazards might require quick application of large quantities of water, and, in such cases, deluge systems might be needed.

Fire detection devices should be selected to ensure operation yet guard against premature operation of sprinklers based on normal room temperatures and draft conditions.

In locations where ambient temperature at the ceiling is high from heat sources other than fire conditions, heat-responsive devices that operate at higher than ordinary temperature and that are capable of withstanding the normal high temperature for long periods of time should be selected.

Where corrosive conditions exist, materials or protective coatings that resist corrosion should be used.

To help avoid ice formation in piping due to accidental tripping of dry pipe valves in cold storage rooms, a deluge automatic water control valve can be used on the supply side of the dry pipe valve. Where this method is employed, the following also apply:

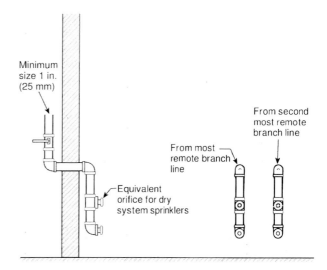

FIGURE A.8.2.3.7 Example Manifold Arrangement (Four Sprinklers).

(1) Dry systems can be manifolded to a deluge valve, with the protected area not exceeding 40,000 ft² (3720 m²).
(2) Where a dry system is manifolded to a deluge valve, the distance between valves should be as short as possible to minimize water hammer.
(3) The dry pipe valves should be pressurized to 50 psi (3.4 bar) to reduce the possibility of dry pipe valve operation from water hammer.

A.8.3.1.1 When using electrical operating methods to actuate preaction systems and deluge systems, care should be observed in selecting the solenoid valve. This valve must be compatible with the fire detection system, including its control panel, and the preaction or deluge valve. This often involves listing with both the preaction or deluge valve manufacturer and the fire detection system manufacturer. Information regarding solenoid compatibility is included in the releasing device (panel) installation instructions.

Small preaction and deluge systems with and without separate electrical-based detection and control panels have been installed prior to the introduction of the detection system requirements of *NFPA 72* or other approved fire alarm code. Pneumatic-based actuation using heat-actuated devices (HADs), pneumatic line–type detection, and pilot sprinklers are examples of non-electric-based detectors and control devices. NFPA 13 recognizes the use and installation of these types of systems and provides guidance in producing a reliable detection and suppression system combination. Remote manual operation of combined dry pipe and preaction systems is needed because of the often very long length dimension of such systems and the long travel time to reach the control valves. Such remote manual operation speeds water into the piping network.

A.8.3.1.7.4 Preaction and deluge valves should be fully trip tested wherever possible. Providing a functional trip test without waterflow does not reveal other potential problems such as obstructions and/or misaligned nozzles.

A.8.3.2.3.1.4 Although the time criterion for calculated systems is not required, a test is still required to document the initial water delivery for comparison to future inspection test requirements. If the time of a single sprinkler test outlet exceeds 70 seconds, evaluation of the calculations and the system installation might be necessary.

A.8.3.2.4 Supervision, either electrical or mechanical, as used in 8.3.2.4 refers to constant monitoring of piping and detection equipment to ensure the integrity of the system. Detection devices of listed flow cycling assemblies that cause an alarm during a single open or a single ground fault condition should be considered to satisfy the supervision requirement.

A.8.3.2.6(2) See A.8.2.2.2(2).

A.8.3.3 Where 8 in. (200 mm) piping is employed to reduce friction losses in a system operated by fire detection devices, a 6 in. (150 mm) preaction or deluge valve and a 6 in. (150 mm) gate valve between tapered reducers should be permitted.

A.8.4.2 Systems described by Section 8.4 are special types of noninterlocking preaction systems intended for use in, but not limited to, structures where a number of dry pipe valves would be required if a dry pipe system were installed. These systems are primarily used in piers and wharves.

A.8.4.2.1 See Figure A.8.4.2.1.

A.8.4.2.4(2) See A.8.2.2.2(2).

A.8.4.3.2 Figure A.8.4.3.2 is a depiction of a valve arrangement complying with 8.4.3.2.

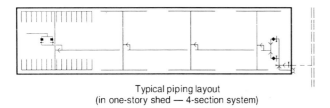

Typical piping layout
(in one-story shed — 4-section system)

FIGURE A.8.4.2.1 Typical Piping Layout for Combined Dry Pipe and Preaction Sprinkler System.

A.8.6 In cold climates and areas where the potential for freezing of pipes is a concern, options other than antifreeze are available. Such options include installing the pipe in warm spaces, tenting insulation over the piping [as illustrated in Figure A.9.9.1(a) through Figure A.9.9.1(f) of NFPA 13D], listed heat tracing, and the use of dry pipe systems and preaction systems.

A.8.6.1 The definition of an antifreeze system states that water will discharge after the antifreeze leaves the pipes. Systems that are all antifreeze, including tanks of antifreeze solution that will not discharge plain water, are not true antifreeze systems. Such systems should not be used without consideration to issues such as the combustibility of the antifreeze solution and the friction loss in the piping during cold conditions. Any listing associated with an antifreeze sprinkler system should address the inability for the specific antifreeze solution tested to ignite when discharged from specific sprinklers.

N **A.8.6.1.3** Drops connecting pendent sprinklers to branchlines can be removed and replaced in order to remove water. Additional hydrostatic testing is not required.

A.8.6.2 Listed nonmetallic sprinkler pipe and fittings should be protected from freezing with compatible listed solutions only. In addition, due to antifreeze solution limitations, other methods of freeze protection such as electric heat tracing or insulated coverings, which are approved for use on nonmetallic piping, can be used to protect nonmetallic pipes from freezing.

The following is a list of research reports that have been issued by the Fire Protection Research Foundation (FPRF) related to the use of antifreeze in sprinkler systems:

(1) *Antifreeze Systems in Home Fire Sprinkler Systems — Literature Review and Research Plan*, Fire Protection Research Foundation, June 2010
(2) *Antifreeze Systems in Home Fire Sprinkler Systems — Phase II Final Report*, Fire Protection Research Foundation, December 2010
(3) *Antifreeze Solutions Supplied through Spray Sprinklers — Interim Report*, Fire Protection Research Foundation, February 2012

Table A.8.6.2 provides a summarized overview of the testing.

A.8.6.2.1 Where existing antifreeze systems have been analyzed and approved to remain in service, antifreeze solutions should be limited to premixed antifreeze solutions of glycerine (chemically pure or United States Pharmacopoeia 96.5 percent) at a maximum concentration of 48 percent by volume, or propylene glycol at a maximum concentration of 38 percent by volume. The use of antifreeze solutions in all new sprinkler systems should be restricted to listed antifreeze solutions only. Where existing antifreeze systems are in service, the solution concentration should be limited to those noted in A.8.6.2, and the system requires an analysis and approval of the authority having jurisdiction to remain in service. Antifreeze that is "UL certified" meets the definition of *listed* in accordance with this standard.

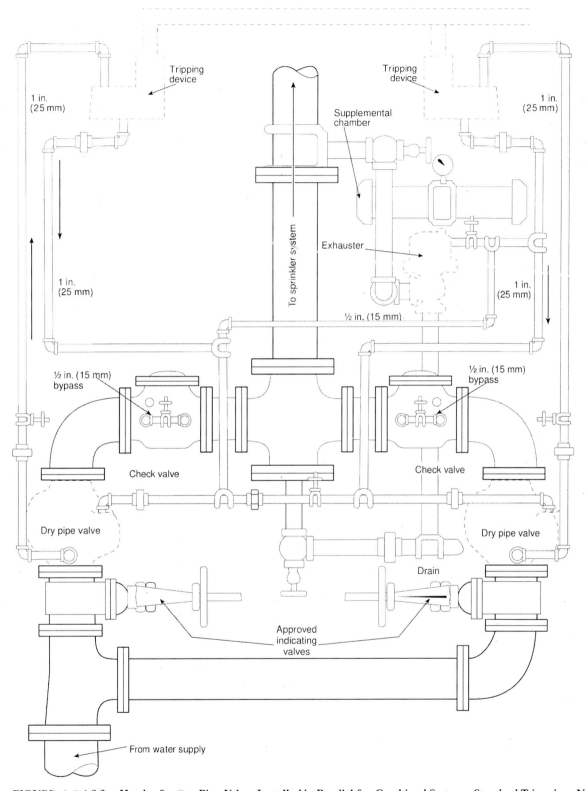

Tubing or wiring to fire detection system

FIGURE A.8.4.3.2   Header for Dry Pipe Valves Installed in Parallel for Combined Systems; Standard Trimmings Not Shown. Arrows Indicate Direction of Fluid Flow.

Table A.8.6.2 FPRF Antifreeze Testing Summary

Topic	Information
Scope of sprinklers tested	The following sprinklers were used during the residential sprinkler research program described in the report dated December 2010: (1) Residential pendent style having nominal K-factors of 3.1, 4.9, and 7.4 gpm/psi$^{1/2}$ (45, 71, and 106 lpm/bar$^{1/2}$) (2) Residential concealed pendent style having a nominal K-factor of 4.9 gpm/psi$^{1/2}$ (71 lpm/bar$^{1/2}$) (3) Residential sidewall style having nominal K-factors of 4.2 and 5.5 gpm/psi$^{1/2}$ (60 and 79 lpm/bar$^{1/2}$) The following sprinklers were used during the spray sprinkler research program described in the report dated February 2012: (1) Residential pendent style having a nominal K-factor of 3.1 gpm/psi$^{1/2}$ (45 lpm/bar$^{1/2}$) (2) Standard spray pendent style having nominal K-factors of 2.8, 4.2, 5.6, and 8.0 gpm/psi$^{1/2}$ (40, 60, 80, and 115 lpm/bar$^{1/2}$) (3) Standard spray concealed pendent style having a nominal K-factor of 5.6 gpm/psi$^{1/2}$ (80 lpm/bar$^{1/2}$) (4) Standard spray upright style having a nominal K-factor of 5.6 gpm/psi$^{1/2}$ (80 lpm/bar$^{1/2}$) (5) Standard spray extended coverage pendent style having a nominal K-factor of 5.6 gpm/psi$^{1/2}$ (80 lpm/bar$^{1/2}$)
Antifreeze solution concentration	<50% glycerine and <40% propylene glycol antifreeze solutions: Solutions were not tested. 50% glycerine and 40% propylene glycol antifreeze solutions: Large-scale ignition of the sprinkler spray did not occur in tests with sprinkler discharge onto a fire having a nominal heat release rate (HRR) of 1.4 megawatts (MW). Large-scale ignition of sprinkler spray occurred in multiple tests with sprinkler discharge onto a fire having a nominal HRR of 3.0 MW. 55% glycerine and 45% propylene glycol antifreeze solutions: Large-scale ignition of the sprinkler spray occurred in tests with sprinkler discharge onto a fire having a nominal HRR of 1.4 MW. > 55% glycerine and > 45% propylene glycol antifreeze solutions: Large-scale ignition of the sprinkler spray occurred in tests with sprinkler discharge onto a fire having an HRR of less than 500 kW. 70% glycerine and 60% propylene glycol antifreeze solutions: Maximum antifreeze solution concentrations tested.
Sprinkler inlet pressure	Large-scale ignition of the sprinkler discharge spray was not observed when the sprinkler inlet pressure was 50 psi or less for tests using 50% glycerine or 40% propylene glycol.
Ceiling height	When discharging 50% glycerine and 40% propylene glycol antifreeze solutions onto fires having an HRR of 1.4 MW, no large-scale ignition of the sprinkler spray was observed with ceiling heights up to 20 ft (6.1 m). When discharging 50% glycerine and 40% propylene glycol antifreeze solutions onto fires having a HRR of 3.0 MW, large-scale ignition of the sprinkler spray was observed at a ceiling height of 20 ft (6.1 m).
Fire control	The test results described in the test reports dated December 2010 and February 2012 indicated that discharging glycerine and propylene glycol antifreeze solutions onto a fire can temporarily increase the fire size until water is discharged. As a part of the residential sprinkler research described in the report dated December 2010, tests were conducted to evaluate the effectiveness of residential sprinklers to control fires involving furniture and simulated furniture. The results of these tests indicated that 50% glycerine and 40% propylene glycol antifreeze solutions demonstrated the ability to control the furniture type fires in a manner similar to water. For standard spray type sprinklers, no tests were conducted to investigate the ability of these sprinklers to control the types and sizes of fires that these sprinklers are intended to protect.

A.8.6.3.2 One formula for sizing the chamber is as follows. Other methods also exist.

$$\Delta L = S_V \left(\frac{D_L}{D_H} - 1 \right) \qquad \text{[A.8.6.3.2a]}$$

where:
ΔL = change in antifreeze solution volume (gal) due to thermal expansion
S_V = volume (gal) of antifreeze system, not including the expansion chamber
D_L = density (gm/mL) of antifreeze solution at lowest expected temperature
D_H = density (gm/mL) of antifreeze solution at highest expected temperature

This method is based on the following information:

$$\frac{P_0 \cdot V_0}{T_0} = \frac{P_1 \cdot V_1}{T_1} = \frac{P_2 \cdot V_2}{T_2} \qquad \text{[A.8.6.3.2b]}$$

where:
V_{EC} = minimum required volume (gal) of expansion chamber
V_0 = air volume (gal) in expansion chamber at precharge (before installation)
V_1 = air volume (gal) in expansion chamber at normal static pressure.
V_2 = air volume (gal) in expansion chamber at post-expansion pressure (antifreeze at high temperature)
P_0 = absolute precharge pressure (psia) on expansion chamber before installation
P_1 = absolute static pressure (psi) on water (supply) side of backflow preventer
P_2 = absolute maximum allowable working pressure (psi) for antifreeze system
T_0 = temperature (°R) of air in expansion chamber at precharge
T_1 = temperature (°R) of air in expansion chamber when antifreeze system piping is at lowest expected temperature
T_2 = temperature (°R) of air in expansion chamber when antifreeze system piping is at highest expected temperature

This equation is one formulation of the ideal gas law from basic chemistry. The amount of air in the expansion chamber will not change over time. The pressure, temperature, and volume of the air at different times will be related in accordance with this formula:

$$V_2 = V_1 - \Delta L \qquad \text{[A.8.6.3.2c]}$$

The antifreeze in the system is essentially incompressible, so the air volume in the expansion chamber will decrease by an amount equal to the expansion of the antifreeze.

It is assumed that there is no trapped air in the system piping, so the only air in the system is in the expansion chamber. This is a conservative assumption, since more air is better. In reality, there will be at least some trapped air. However, only the air in the expansion chamber can be relied upon to be available when needed.

$$V_{EC} = V_0 \qquad \text{[A.8.6.3.2d]}$$

At precharge, the chamber will be completely full of air.

$$V_{EC} = \frac{P_1 \cdot T_0 \cdot P_2 \cdot \Delta L \cdot T_1}{P_0 \cdot T_1 \left(P_2 \cdot T_1 - P_1 \cdot T_2 \right)} \qquad \text{[A.8.6.3.2e]}$$

In cases where the normal static pressure on the sprinkler system is close to the maximum working pressure, antifreeze systems are not advisable if the connection to the wet pipe system will incorporate a backflow device. In these cases, expansion of the antifreeze solution during warm weather will cause the antifreeze system to exceed the maximum working pressure, regardless of the size of the expansion chamber. The normal static pressure is too close to the maximum working pressure if the preceding formula for V_{EC} yields a negative result. If this occurs, use a dry pipe system instead or install a pressure-reducing valve before the backflow preventer.

A.8.6.3.3 The expansion chamber should be appropriately sized and precharged with air pressure.

A.8.6.3.6 Systems are required by NFPA 25 to have the concentration levels checked at the supply inlet to the antifreeze system and at a remote point of the system.

A.8.7.4.2.1 See Figure A.8.7.4.2.1.

A.8.7.4.2.3 See Figure A.8.7.4.2.3.

A.8.7.9 In the design of an exposure protection system, the flow rate from window and cornice sprinklers is shown in Table 8.7.9.1. The flow rates are based on the guide numbers selected from Table 4.3.7.3 of NFPA 80A, which can be utilized as the basis for determining whether exposure protection is needed.

A.8.8 Careful installation and maintenance, and some special arrangements of piping and devices as outlined in this section, are needed to avoid the formation of ice and frost inside piping in cold storage rooms that will be maintained at or

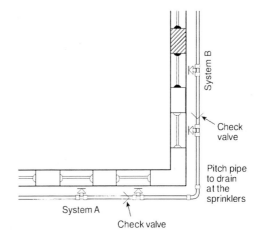

FIGURE A.8.7.4.2.1   Typical Arrangement of Check Valves.

below 32°F (0°C). Conditions are particularly favorable to condensation where pipes enter cold rooms from rooms having temperatures above freezing.

Whenever the opportunity offers, fittings such as those specified in 8.8.2.1, as well as flushing connections, should be provided in existing systems.

Where possible, risers should be located in stair towers or other locations outside of refrigerated areas, which would reduce the probabilities of ice or frost formation within the riser (supply) pipe.

Cross mains should be connected to risers or feed mains with flanges. In general, flanged fittings should be installed at points that would allow easy dismantling of the system. Split ring or other easily removable types of hangers will facilitate the dismantling.

Because it is not practical to allow water to flow into sprinkler piping in spaces that might be constantly subject to freezing, or where temperatures must be maintained at or below 40°F (4.4°C), it is important that means be provided at the time of system installation to conduct trip tests on dry pipe valves that service such systems. NFPA 25 contains requirements in this matter.

A.8.8.2 The requirements in 8.8.2 are intended to minimize the chances of ice plug formation inside sprinkler system piping protecting freezers.

A.8.8.2.1.1 It is not the intent of this section to apply to a dry sprinkler. An additional pipe is not needed when a dry sprinkler penetrates a refrigerated space.

A.8.8.2.4 A higher degree of preventing the formation of ice blocks can be achieved by lowering the moisture of the air supply entering the refrigerated space to a pressure dew point no greater than 20°F (−6.6°C) below the lowest nominal temperature of the refrigerated space. The pressure dew point of the air supply can cause moisture to condense and freeze in sprinkler pipe even when the air supply is from the freezer. One method of reducing the moisture content of the air by use of air drying systems is illustrated in Figure A.8.8.2.4.

When compressors and dryers are used for an air supply, consideration should be given to pressure requirements of the regenerative dryers, compressor size, air pressure regulator

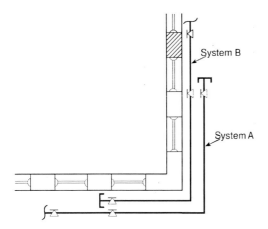

FIGURE A.8.7.4.2.3   Alternate Arrangement of Check Valves.

capacity, and air fill rate. Application of these factors could necessitate the use of increased air pressures and a larger air compressor.

The compressed air supply should be properly prepared prior to entering a regenerative-type air dryer, such as minimum air pressure, maximum inlet air temperature, and proper filtration of compressed air.

A.8.8.2.5 A major factor contributing to the introduction of moisture into the system piping is excessive air compressor operation caused by system leakage. Where excessive compressor operation is noted or ice accumulates in the air supply piping, the system should be checked for leakage and appropriate corrective action should be taken.

A.8.8.2.6 The purpose of the check valve is to prevent evaporation of priming water into the system piping.

A.8.8.2.7.1 The dual lines feeding the system air entering the cold area are intended to facilitate continued service of the system when one line is removed for inspection. It should be noted that, when using a system as described in Figure A.8.8.2.4, differences in the pressures at gauge P1 and gauge P2 indicate blockage in the air supply line or other malfunctions.

A.8.8.2.8.1.1 While it is the intent to require the detection system to operate prior to sprinklers, it is possible that in some fire scenarios the sprinklers could operate prior to the detection system. In general, the detection system, at its installed location and spacing, should be more sensitive to fire than the sprinklers.

A.8.9.2 See Figure A.8.9.2.

Δ **A.9.1** The installation requirements are specific for the normal arrangement of structural members. There will be arrangements of structural members not specifically detailed by the requirements. By applying the basic principles, layouts for such construction can vary from specific illustrations, provided the maximums specified for the spacing and location of sprinklers are not exceeded.

Where buildings or portions of buildings are of combustible construction or contain combustible material, standard fire barriers should be provided to separate the areas that are sprinkler protected from adjoining unsprinklered areas. All openings should be protected in accordance with applicable standards, and no sprinkler piping should be placed in an unsprinklered area unless the area is permitted to be unsprinklered by this standard.

Water supplies for partial systems should be designed with consideration to the fact that in a partial system more sprinklers might be opened in a fire that originates in an unprotected area and spreads to the sprinklered area than would be the case in a completely protected building. Fire originating in a nonsprinklered area might overpower the partial sprinkler system.

A.9.1.1 This standard contemplates full sprinkler protection for all areas including walk-in coolers, freezers, bank vaults, and similar areas. Other NFPA standards that mandate sprinkler installation might not require sprinklers in certain areas. Based upon experience and testing, sprinklers have been found to be effective and necessary at heights in excess of 50 ft (15 m). For a building to meet the intended level of protection afforded by NFPA 13, sprinklers must not be omitted from such high ceiling spaces. The requirements of this standard should be used

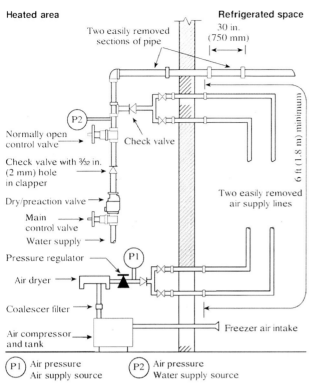

Notes:
1. If pressure gauge PI and P2 do not indicate equal pressures, it could mean the air line is blocked or the air supply is malfunctioning.
2. Air dryer and coalescer filter not required when system piping capacity is less than 250 gal (946 l).

Δ **FIGURE A.8.8.2.4   Refrigerator Area Sprinkler Systems Used to Minimize Chances of Developing Ice Plugs.**

insofar as they are applicable. The authority having jurisdiction should be consulted in each case. A building is considered sprinklered throughout when protected in accordance with the requirements of this standard.

In situations such as computer rooms where a gas system is installed, the sprinkler protection should not be eliminated. Many gas systems do not have the same duration requirements of a fire sprinkler system, and if the fire is not extinguished with the initial discharge, the fire could grow large enough to overpower the sprinkler system.

Δ **A.9.1.1(3)** Notwithstanding the obstruction rules provided in Chapters 9 through 14, it is not intended or expected that water will fall on the entire floor space of the occupancy.

When obstructions or architectural features interfere with the sprinkler's spray pattern, such as columns, angled walls, wing walls, slightly indented walls, and various soffit configurations, shadowed areas can occur. Where small shadowed areas are formed on the floor adjacent to their referenced architectural features, these shadowed areas are purely on paper and do not take into account the dynamic variables of sprinkler discharge. Examples of shadow areas are shown in Figure A.9.1.1(3)(a) and Figure A.9.1.1(3)(b).

A.9.2.1 Paragraphs 9.2.1.3, 9.2.1.4, and 9.2.1.5 do not require sprinkler protection because it is not physically practical to install sprinklers in the types of concealed spaces discussed in these three exceptions. To reduce the possibility of uncontrolled fire spread, consideration should be given in these unsprinklered concealed space situations to using 9.2.1.7, 9.2.1.12, and 9.2.1.14. Omitting sprinklers from combustible concealed spaces will require further evaluation of the sprinkler system design area in accordance with 19.2.3.1.5.

A.9.2.1.1 Minor quantities of combustible materials such as, but not limited to, cabling, nonmetallic plumbing piping, nonstructural wood, and so forth can be present in concealed spaces constructed of limited or noncombustible materials but should not typically be viewed as requiring sprinklers (see 9.3.17.1). For example, it is not the intent of this section to require sprinklers, which would not otherwise be required, in the interstitial space of a typical office building solely due to the presence of the usual amount of cabling within the space. The use of acoustical tile ceilings does not negate that the space above the tile is a concealed space because a tile could be removed. The threshold value at which sprinklers become necessary in the concealed space is not defined.

N **A.9.2.1.1.2** Noncombustible spaces with non-fuel-fired equipment and access panels should be considered a concealed space and should not require sprinkler protection.

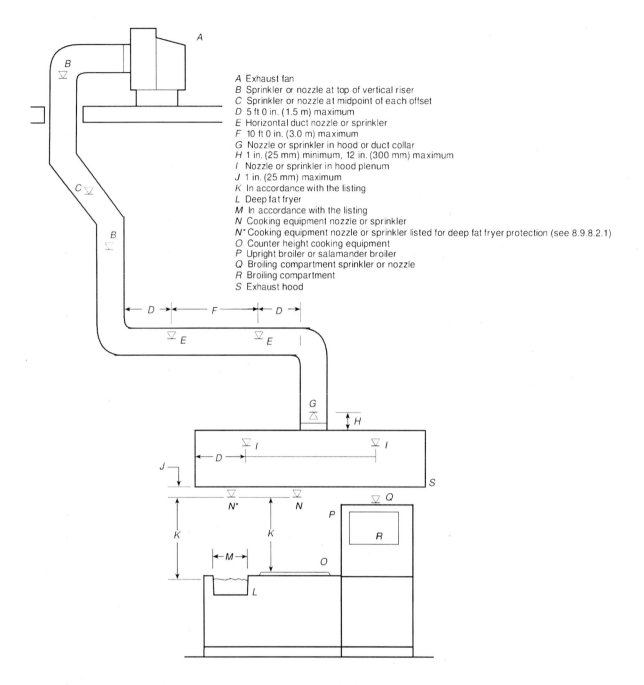

A Exhaust fan
B Sprinkler or nozzle at top of vertical riser
C Sprinkler or nozzle at midpoint of each offset
D 5 ft 0 in. (1.5 m) maximum
E Horizontal duct nozzle or sprinkler
F 10 ft 0 in. (3.0 m) maximum
G Nozzle or sprinkler in hood or duct collar
H 1 in. (25 mm) minimum, 12 in. (300 mm) maximum
I Nozzle or sprinkler in hood plenum
J 1 in. (25 mm) maximum
K In accordance with the listing
L Deep fat fryer
M In accordance with the listing
N Cooking equipment nozzle or sprinkler
N* Cooking equipment nozzle or sprinkler listed for deep fat fryer protection (see 8.9.8.2.1)
O Counter height cooking equipment
P Upright broiler or salamander broiler
Q Broiling compartment sprinkler or nozzle
R Broiling compartment
S Exhaust hood

Δ **FIGURE A.8.9.2** **Typical Installation Showing Automatic Sprinklers or Automatic Nozzles Being Used for Protection of Commercial Cooking Equipment and Ventilation Systems.**

N **A.9.2.1.2.2** Noncombustible and limited-combustible spaces with non-fuel-fired equipment and access panels should be considered a concealed space and should not require sprinkler protection.

A.9.2.1.5 Solid metal purlin construction with a wood deck is one example of similar solid member construction.

A.9.2.1.6 The 3½ in. (90 mm) of insulation is only required when the ceiling is not directly attached to the joist. The 160 ft³

(4.5 m³) is the volume of the individual channel excluding the portion occupied by insulation. (*See Figure A.9.2.1.6.*)

N **A.9.2.1.11** Sprinklers are allowed to be omitted from horizontal chases and soffits that have noncombustible or limited combustible finishes that can contain mechanical and or plumbing equipment, ductwork, or electrical components. The 160 ft³ (4.5 m³) limitation is intended to limit the movement of fire within the chase or soffit. It is not the intent of this volume limitation to require dampers or other mechanical separations

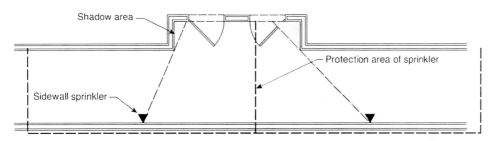

△ FIGURE A.9.1.1(3)(a)   Shadow Area in Corridor.

within ductwork, or other equipment that are not otherwise required. See Figure A.9.2.1.11.

A.9.2.1.13 The allowance to omit sprinklers for fire retardant–treated wood requires a pressure-treated application. It does not apply to coated applications.

A.9.2.1.18 See Figure A.9.2.1.18 for one example.

A.9.2.1.19 See Figure A.9.2.1.19.

A.9.2.3 Exterior projections include, but are not limited to, exterior roofs, canopies, porte-cocheres, balconies, decks, or similar projections. Sprinklers should not be required beneath trellis overhangs or similar construction not capable of collecting heat to aid in the operation of the sprinkler.

A.9.2.3.1 Vehicles that are temporarily parked are not considered storage. Areas located at drive-in bank windows or porte-cocheres at hotels and motels normally do not require sprinklers where there is no occupancy above, where the area is entirely constructed of noncombustible or limited-combustible materials or fire retardant–treated lumber, and where the area is not the only means of egress.

A.9.2.4.1.1 A door is not required in order to omit sprinklers as long as the bathroom complies with the definition for compartment.

A.9.2.5.2 This exception is limited to hospitals as nursing homes, and many limited-care facilities can have more combustibles within the closets. The limited amount of clothing found in the small clothes closets in hospital patient rooms is typically far less than the amount of combustibles in casework cabinets that do not require sprinkler protection, such as nurse servers. In many hospitals, especially new hospitals, it is difficult to make a distinction between clothes closets and cabinet work. The exception is far more restrictive than similar exceptions for hotels and apartment buildings. NFPA 13 already permits the omission of sprinklers in wardrobes *[see 9.2.9]*. It is not the intent of this paragraph to affect the wardrobe provisions of NFPA 13. It is the intent that the sprinkler protection in the room covers the closet as if there was no door on the closet *(see 9.5.3.2)*.

△ **A.9.2.6** Sprinklers and sprinkler piping is permitted in and is permitted to pass through an electrical room as long as the piping is not within the "dedicated electrical space" as defined by *NFPA 70*.

In 110.26(E)(1)(a) of *NFPA 70*, a dedicated electrical space is defined as the space equal to the width and the depth of the equipment extending from the floor to a height of 6 ft (1.8 m) above the equipment or the structural ceiling, whichever is lower. This section further states that no foreign systems are

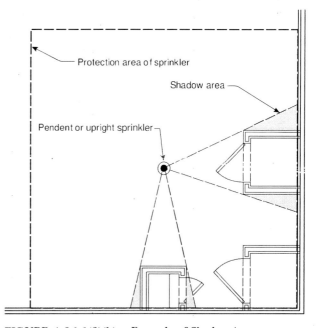

FIGURE A.9.1.1(3)(b)   Example of Shadow Area.

allowed in this zone. So, as long as the sprinkler piping does not run through this dedicated electrical space, it can go in and out of the electric room without issue. Paragraph 110.26(E)(1)(b) of *NFPA 70* allows foreign systems in the area above the dedicated electrical space as long as the electrical equipment is properly protected against leaks or breaks in the foreign system. So the sprinkler piping can run above the dedicated electrical space [6 ft (1.8 m) above equipment] as long as the equipment below is protected from leaks. Additionally, sprinklers and sprinkler piping are not permitted to be located directly within the working space for the equipment as defined by *NFPA 70*. See Figure A.9.2.6.

A.9.2.7.1 An opening in the ceiling can be located along a wall or can occur between panels to give an architectural effect such as a floating ceiling. Fire modeling results have shown that there will be heat loss to the space above the ceiling when the openings are too large. The modeling results indicate that sprinklers should activate on the lower ceiling level when the opening dimension is no greater than 1 in. per ft (8 mm/m) of elevation above the floor. When an opening between ceiling panels, or a ceiling panel and a wall, are any larger, the space above the ceiling panels should not be considered a concealed space. Figure A.9.2.7.1 shows plan and elevation views of a cloud ceiling installation.

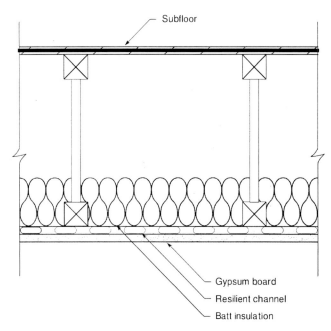

FIGURE A.9.2.1.6   Combustible Concealed Space Cross Section.

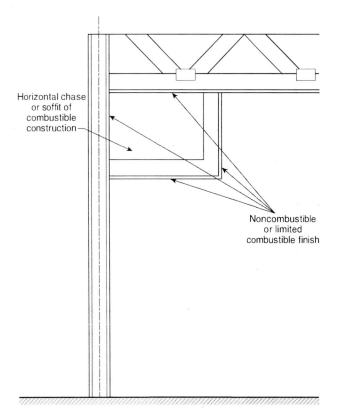

N   **FIGURE A.9.2.1.11   Horizontal Chase or Soffit of Combustible Construction.**

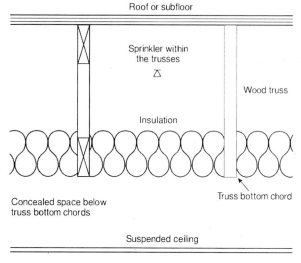

FIGURE A.9.2.1.18   One Acceptable Arrangement of Concealed Space in Truss Construction Not Requiring Sprinklers.

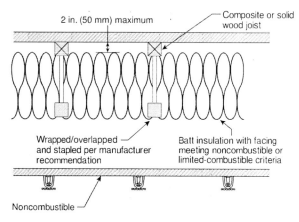

FIGURE A.9.2.1.19   Acceptable Arrangement of Concealed Space Not Requiring Sprinklers.

A.9.2.7.1(1) To determine the maximum allowed gap distance for omission of sprinklers above cloud ceilings, the following formula can be used:

$$A / B = X \qquad \text{[A.9.2.7.1(1)]}$$

where:
A = inches of gap between clouds or between a cloud and a wall
B = ceiling height
X = maximum inches of gap

Example:

A = 9 in. (225 mm) maximum gap dimension

B = 14 ft (4.3 m) ceiling height

X = 0.64 in. (16 mm) of gap/ft of ceiling height

Shaded text = Revisions.   Δ = Text deletions and figure/table revisions.   • = Section deletions.   *N* = New material.

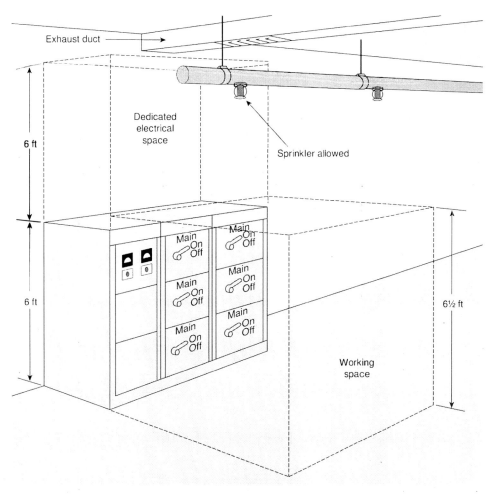

FIGURE A.9.2.6   The Working Space and the Dedicated Electrical Space.

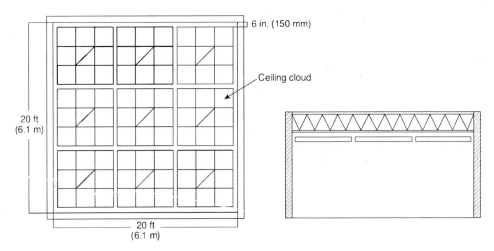

Δ FIGURE A.9.2.7.1   Cloud Ceiling Openings.

Therefore, ≤0.75 in. (19 mm) of gap/ft of ceiling height spacing used.

A.9.2.7.2.5 The research testing and modeling used to determine the base data used for Table 9.2.7.1 is based on rectangular and equally spaced cloud configurations. Nonrectangular shapes are allowed to be considered with this section; however, the minimum width of the cloud and maximum width of the gap should be used to determine the worst geometric shape creating a conservative approach. Figure A.9.2.7.2.5 provides an example of an irregular cloud.

N **A.9.2.9** Furniture includes such items as portable wardrobe units, lockers, cabinets, or trophy cases.

Portable wardrobe units, such as those typically used in nursing homes and mounted to the wall, do not require sprinklers to be installed in them. Although the units are attached to the finished structure, this standard views these units as pieces of furniture rather than as a part of the structure; thus, sprinklers are not required.

N **A.9.2.10.1** These isolated spaces are similar to hearing testing booths, lactation rooms, phone booths, or pods and are not used for storage. Miscellaneous furniture, wastebaskets, and other nonstorage items are allowed in the space. *Isolated* is intended to mean that units should not be located adjacent to each other and are physically separated.

A.9.2.11 Equipment having access for routine maintenance should not be considered as intended for occupancy.

A.9.3.3.2 Where practicable, sprinklers should be staggered at the alternate floor levels, particularly where only one sprinkler is installed at each floor level.

A.9.3.4.1.2 Sprinklers at each floor level landing should be positioned to protect both the floor level landing and any intermediate landing.

N **A.9.3.4.2.3.1** There are several methods of preventing storage under the bottom landing/riser of stairs. These can be permanent walls separating the space or railings installed to prevent storage. Simply placing a sign indicating no storage allowed is insufficient.

A.9.3.4.3 See Figure A.9.3.4.3(a) and Figure A.9.3.4.3(b). Sprinklers would be required in the case shown in Figure A.9.3.4.3(a) but not in the case shown in Figure A.9.3.4.3(b).

A.9.3.5 Where sprinklers in the normal ceiling pattern are closer than 6 ft (1.8 m) from the water curtain, it might be preferable to locate the water curtain sprinklers in recessed baffle pockets. (*See Figure A.9.3.5.*)

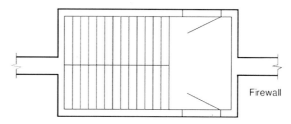

FIGURE A.9.3.4.3(a)   Noncombustible Stair Shaft Serving Two Sides of Fire Wall.

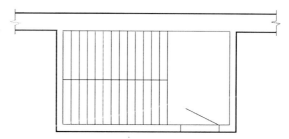

FIGURE A.9.3.4.3(b)   Noncombustible Stair Shaft Serving One Side of Fire Wall.

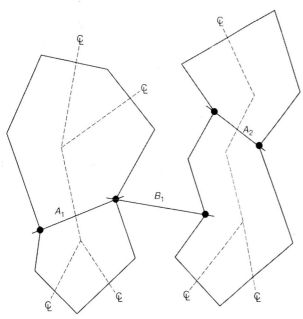

A = Minimum cloud width   *B* = Maximum open width

Δ **FIGURE A.9.2.7.2.5   Irregular Shaped Cloud Dimensioning.**

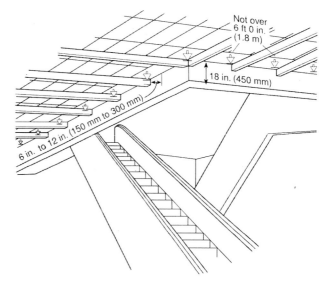

FIGURE A.9.3.5   Sprinklers Around Escalators.

A.9.3.5.1 It is the intent of this section to require closely spaced sprinklers and draft curtains to openings where protection or enclosure is required by building and life safety codes.

N **A.9.3.6.1** The sprinklers in the pit are intended to protect against fires caused by debris, which can accumulate over time. Ideally, the sprinklers should be located near the side of the pit below the elevator doors, where most debris accumulates. However, care should be taken that the sprinkler location does not interfere with the elevator toe guard, which extends below the face of the door opening.

A.9.3.6.4 ASME A17.1, *Safety Code for Elevators and Escalators,* requires the shutdown of power to the elevator upon or prior to the application of water in elevator machine rooms or hoistways. This shutdown can be accomplished by a detection system with sufficient sensitivity that operates prior to the activation of the sprinklers *(see also NFPA 72 or other approved fire alarm code).* As an alternative, the system can be arranged using devices or sprinklers capable of effecting power shutdown immediately upon sprinkler activation, such as a waterflow switch without a time delay. This alternative arrangement is intended to interrupt power before significant sprinkler discharge.

A.9.3.6.6 Passenger elevator cars that have been constructed in accordance with ASME A17.1, *Safety Code for Elevators and Escalators,* Rule 204.2a (under A17.1a-1985 and later editions of the code) have limited combustibility. Materials exposed to the interior of the car and the hoistway, in their end-use composition, are limited to a flame spread index of 0 to 75 and a smoke-developed index of 0 to 450, when tested in accordance with ASTM E84, *Standard Test Method of Surface Burning Characteristics of Building Materials.*

A.9.3.7 Library stacks are high-density book storage areas and should not be confused with the typical library bookshelves and aisles in the general browsing areas. Examples of record storage include medical or paper records.

A.9.3.8 The combustible materials present inside industrial ovens and furnaces can be protected by automatic sprinklers. Wet sprinkler systems are preferred. However, water-filled piping exposed to heat within an oven or furnace can incur deposition and buildup of minerals within the pipe. If the oven or furnace could be exposed to freezing temperatures, dry pendent sprinklers are an alternative to wet pipe systems. Another option is to use a dry pipe system.

The preferred arrangement for piping is outside of the oven; the sprinkler should be installed in the pendent position. The sprinkler temperature rating should be at least 50°F (10°C) greater than the high-temperature limit setting of the oven or applicable zone. As a minimum, the sprinkler system inside the oven or furnace should be designed to provide 15 psi (1 bar) with all sprinklers operating inside the oven/furnace. Sprinkler spacing on each branch line should not exceed 12 ft (3.7 m).

A.9.3.10 The installation of open-grid egg crate, louver, or honeycomb ceilings beneath sprinklers restricts the sideways travel of the sprinkler discharge and can change the character of discharge.

A.9.3.11.1 There are ceiling panels and ceiling materials that have been investigated as a ceiling material in accordance with UL Subject 723S, *Outline of Investigation for Drop-Out Ceilings Installed Beneath Automatic Sprinklers,* or as FM Class Number 4651, *Plastic Suspended Ceiling Panels.* Such ceiling panels and ceiling materials are designed such that the activation of the

sprinkler and the ability of the sprinkler discharge to reach the hazard being protected are not adversely impacted.

A.9.3.11.4 Drop-out ceilings do not provide the required protection for soft-soldered copper joints or other piping that requires protection.

A.9.3.11.5 The ceiling tiles might drop before sprinkler operation. Delayed operation might occur because heat must then bank down from the deck above before sprinklers will operate.

A.9.3.12 For tests of sprinkler performance in fur vaults, see "Fact Finding Report on Automatic Sprinkler Protection for Fur Storage Vaults" of Underwriters Laboratories Inc., dated November 25, 1947.

Sprinklers should be listed old-style with orifice sizes selected to provide a flow rate as close as possible to, but not less than, 20 gpm (75 L/min) per sprinkler, for four sprinklers, based on the water pressure available.

Sprinklers in fur storage vaults should be located centrally over the aisles between racks and should be spaced not over 5 ft (1.5 m) apart along the aisles.

Where sprinklers are spaced 5 ft (1.5 m) apart along the sprinkler branch lines, pipe sizes should be in accordance with the following schedule:

1 in. (25 mm) — 4 sprinklers

1¼ in. (32 mm) — 6 sprinklers

1½ in. (40 mm) — 10 sprinklers

2 in. (50 mm) — 20 sprinklers

2½ in. (65 mm) — 40 sprinklers

3 in. (80 mm) — 80 sprinklers

A.9.3.14.3 See Figure A.9.3.14.3.

Δ **A.9.3.15** It is not the intent of this section to apply to sprinkler protection of glass atrium enclosures and pedestrian walkways that are permitted by NFPA *101* or to apply to model building codes protected by standard spray sprinklers that are installed in accordance with the special provisions set forth in those codes for atrium construction. In some cases, sprinkler protected assemblies as an alternative to a required fire-rated wall or window assembly could require the approval of the building official.

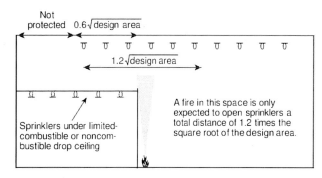

FIGURE A.9.3.14.3   Extension of Sprinkler System Above Drop Ceiling.

A.9.3.17.1.1 Utilities and other building services can be located within the concealed spaces.

A.9.3.19.1 Sprinkler protection under exterior projections should not be required to spray beyond the support beam on the exterior edge of the exterior projection as long as the maximum distance from the interior edge of support beam to the exterior edge of the projection does not exceed 4 ft (1.2 m). An additional line of sprinklers on the exterior edge is not required due to obstruction rules. This is considered a reasonable level of protection because sprinklers are located between the structure and the exterior edge. See Figure A.9.3.19.1.

A.9.3.19.2 Short-term transient storage, such as that for delivered packages, and the presence of planters, newspaper machines, and so forth, should not be considered for storage or handling of combustibles. The presence of combustible furniture on balconies for occupant use should not require sprinkler protection.

N **A.9.3.20** This requirement to install sprinklers on exterior balconies, attached exterior decks, and ground floor patios serving dwelling units is consistent with the requirements in the *International Building Code* and NFPA 13R.

N **A.9.3.20.1** Type V construction generally refers to buildings constructed with structural elements entirely or partially wood or other similar combustible material.

A.9.4.1.1 Whenever possible, sprinklers should be installed in piping after the piping is placed in its final position and secured by hangers in accordance with this standard.

A.9.4.1.3 The purpose of this requirement is to minimize the obstruction of the discharge pattern.

A.9.4.1.5.1 Protective caps and straps are intended to provide temporary protection for sprinklers during shipping and installation.

A.9.4.1.5.2 Protective caps and straps can be removed from upright sprinklers, from sprinklers that are fitted with sprinkler guards, and from sprinklers that are not likely to be subject to damage due to construction activities or other events. In general, protective caps and straps should not be removed until construction activities or other events have progressed to the point where the sprinklers will not be subjected to conditions that could cause them to be damaged. Consideration should be given to leaving the protective caps and straps in place where other construction work is expected to take place, adjacent to the sprinklers following their installation, until that activity is complete. Protective caps and straps on sidewall and pendent sprinklers, for example, should be left in place pending installation of the wall and ceiling systems and then removed as finish escutcheons are being installed. In retrofit applications, with minimal follow-on trade construction activity, and with upright sprinklers, it would be reasonable to remove the caps and straps immediately following the installation on the sprinkler piping.

A.9.4.2.1 It is acceptable to install ordinary-temperature sprinklers throughout a building, intermediate-temperature sprinklers throughout a building, or a mix of ordinary- and intermediate-temperature sprinklers throughout a building.

A.9.4.2.5 A diffuser in ceiling sheathing labeled by the manufacturer as "horizontal discharge" has directional vanes to move air further along the ceiling, and sprinklers located within the 2 ft 6 in. (750 mm) radius should have an intermediate-temperature rating. See Figure A.9.4.2.5(a) through Figure A.9.4.2.5(d).

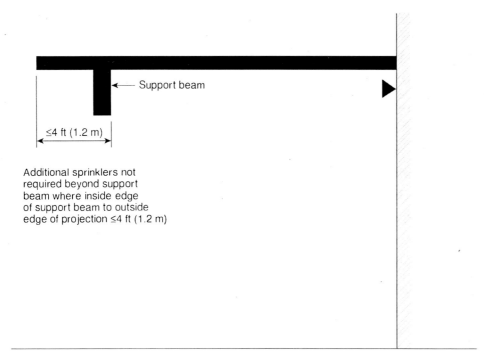

FIGURE A.9.3.19.1   Exterior Projection with Sprinklers.

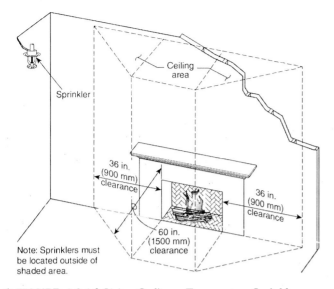

Note: Sprinklers must be located outside of shaded area.

Δ **FIGURE A.9.4.2.5(a)** Ordinary-Temperature Sprinkler over Recessed Fireplace.

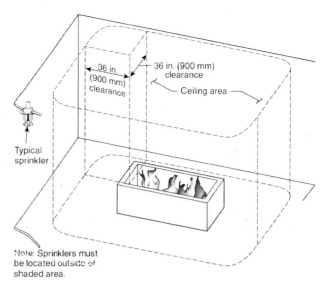

Note: Sprinklers must be located outside of shaded area.

FIGURE A.9.4.2.5(c) Ordinary-Temperature Sprinkler over Open Fireplace.

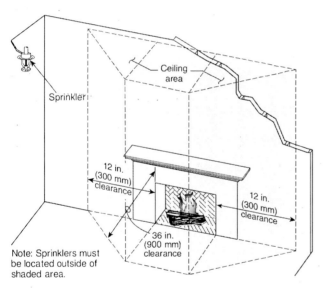

Note: Sprinklers must be located outside of shaded area.

Δ **FIGURE A.9.4.2.5(b)** Intermediate-Temperature Sprinkler over Recessed Fireplace.

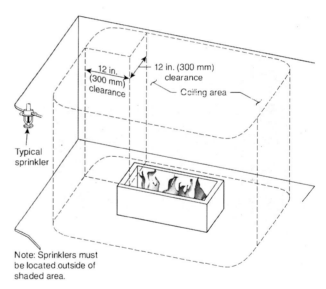

Note: Sprinklers must be located outside of shaded area.

FIGURE A.9.4.2.5(d) Intermediate-Temperature Sprinkler over Open Fireplace.

Shaded text = Revisions. Δ = Text deletions and figure/table revisions. • = Section deletions. *N* = New material.

2022 Edition

A.9.4.2.5(1) Areas used for hot yoga facilities, steam rooms, saunas, indoor areas containing hot tubs, and similar heated areas should be evaluated to determine the potential maximum ambient temperature before selection of sprinkler temperature rating to be installed in the space.

A.9.4.2.7 Where high temperature–rated sprinklers are installed at the ceiling, high temperature–rated sprinklers also should extend beyond storage in accordance with Table A.9.4.2.7.

Table A.9.4.2.7 Distance Beyond Perimeter of Storage for High Hazard Occupancies Protected with High Temperature–Rated Sprinklers

Design Area		Distance	
ft²	m²	ft	m
2000	185	30	9.1
3000	280	40	12
4000	370	45	14
5000	465	50	15
6000	555	55	17

N **A.9.5.1.3** Small areas created by architectural features include items such as planter box windows, wing walls, and similar features.

N **A.9.5.3.2.3** Furniture includes such items as portable wardrobe units, lockers, cabinets, and trophy cases.

A.9.5.4.1 Batt insulation creates an effective thermal barrier and can be considered the ceiling/roof deck when determining distances between deflector and ceiling. The insulation needs to be installed in each pocket (not just above the sprinkler) and attached to the ceiling/roof in such a manner that it will not fall out during a fire prior to sprinkler activation.

A.9.5.4.1.4 The rules describing the maximum distance permitted for sprinklers below ceilings must be followed. The concept of placing a small "heat collector" above a sprinkler to assist in activation is not appropriate, nor is it contemplated in this standard. There is evidence that objects above a sprinkler will delay the activation of the sprinkler where fires are not directly below the sprinkler (but are still in the coverage area of the sprinkler). One of the objectives of the standard is to cool the ceiling near the structural members with spray from a nearby sprinkler, which is not accomplished by a sprinkler far down from the ceiling, and a heat collector will not help this situation.

Δ **A.9.5.5.1** See Figure A.9.5.5.1 for a representation of a typical spray sprinkler pattern.

NFPA 13 strives to minimize the effect of obstructions through the use of specific criteria in 9.5.5, 10.2.7, 10.3.6, 11.2.5, 11.3.6, 12.1.10, 12.1.11, 13.2.8, and 14.2.11. The obstruction criteria for storage sprinklers in 13.2.8 and 14.2.11 is the most stringent. For other types of sprinklers, dry spaces caused be obstructions such as columns and wall configurations will occur and can comply with the standard. The general rules known as the Three Times Rule and the Four Times Rule define *shadow areas* that are acceptable behind obstructions like columns and walls. Tests have shown that the larger the column, the larger the shadow area behind the column will be and the longer it will take for sprinklers on the other side of

the column to react to the fire behind the column. In a very large compartment, the delay could become unacceptable. The delay in sprinkler response can be minimized with smaller columns, with smaller compartments, or by putting sprinklers on the other side of the column.

Where offset walls create shadowed areas, the sprinkler does not appear to be significantly delayed in activation. Tests have shown that once the sprinkler activates, water will not cover all areas behind the obstructions.

Δ **A.9.5.5.2** Where of a depth that will obstruct the spray discharge pattern, girders, beams, or trusses forming narrow pockets of combustible construction along walls can require additional sprinklers.

Where the obstruction criteria established by this standard are followed, sprinkler spray patterns will not necessarily get water to every square foot of space within a room.

A.9.5.5.3 Frequently, additional sprinkler equipment can be avoided by reducing the width of decks or galleries and providing proper clearances. Slatting of decks or walkways or the use of open grating as a substitute for automatic sprinklers thereunder is not acceptable. The use of cloth or paper dust tops for rooms forms obstruction to water distribution. If dust tops are used, the area below should be sprinklered.

A.9.5.5.3.1 When obstructions are located more than 18 in. (450 mm) below the sprinkler deflector, an adequate spray pattern develops and obstructions up to and including 4 ft (1.2 m) wide do not require additional protection underneath. Examples are ducts, decks, open grate flooring, catwalks, cutting tables, overhead doors, soffits, ceiling panels, and other similar obstructions.

A.9.5.5.3.1.1 Where multiple levels of ducts, pipes, or other similar horizontal obstructions that are over 4 ft (1.2 m) wide are stacked vertically, additional levels of sprinkler protection between the vertical levels are not required. A single level of sprinklers beneath the lowest level of the obstruction is adequate, provided that the obstructions are noncombustible

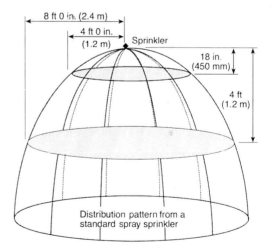

FIGURE A.9.5.5.1 **Obstructions to Sprinkler Discharge Pattern Development for Standard Upright or Pendent Spray Sprinklers.**

and that combustible materials are not stored between the levels.

A.9.5.5.3.1.2 See Figure A.9.5.5.3.1.2(a) and Figure A.9.5.5.3.1.2(b).

A.9.5.5.3.2 A conference table is an example of an obstruction that is not fixed in place.

A.9.5.5.3.4 Sprinklers under open gratings should be provided with shields. Shields over automatic sprinklers should not be less, in least dimension, than four times the distance between the shield and fusible element, except special sprinklers incorporating a built-in shield need not comply with this recommendation if listed for the particular application.

A.10.2.4.2.1 When the spacing between sprinklers perpendicular to the slope exceeds 8 ft (2.4 m), it is necessary to increase the minimum density or sprinkler operating pressure as noted in Table 10.2.4.2.1(a) and in 10.2.6.1.4. Time to sprinkler activation and water distribution can be affected within combustible concealed spaces with sloped roofs or ceilings in these combustible concealed spaces, especially where wood joist rafters or wood truss construction is used. To reduce the proba-

bility of fires in these combustible concealed spaces involving the combustible roof or ceiling construction above standard spray sprinklers, more stringent spacing and installation guidelines apply.

A.10.2.5.2.2 The example in Figure A.10.2.5.2.2 is for a light hazard occupancy. However, the irregular-shaped room allowance also applies to ordinary and extra hazard occupancies.

A.10.2.5.2.3 Examples of sprinklers in small rooms are shown in Figure A.10.2.5.2.3(a), Figure A.10.2.5.2.3(b), Figure A.10.2.5.2.3(c), and Figure A.10.2.5.2.3(d).

A.10.2.6.1.2(5) For concrete joists spaced less than 3 ft (900 mm) on center, the rules for obstructed construction shown in 10.2.6.1.2 apply. For concrete tee construction with stems spaced less than 7 ft 6 in. (2.3 m) on center, the sprinkler deflector can be located at or above a horizontal plane 1 in. (25 mm) below the bottom of the stems of the tees. This includes sprinklers located between the stems. *[See Figure A.10.2.6.1.2(5).]*

A.10.2.6.1.3.2 Saw-toothed roofs have regularly spaced monitors of saw tooth shape, with the nearly vertical side glazed and usually arranged for venting. Sprinkler placement is limited to

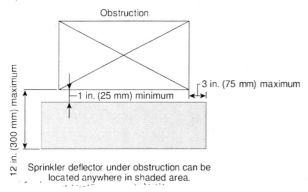

FIGURE A.9.5.5.3.1.2(a) Sprinkler Location Below Obstruction.

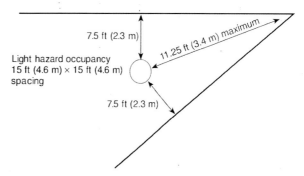

FIGURE A.10.2.5.2.2 Maximum Distance from Walls.

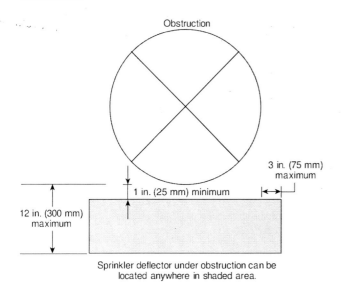

N FIGURE A.9.5.5.3.1.2(b) Sprinkler Location Below Circular Obstruction.

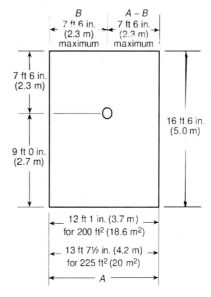

Δ FIGURE A.10.2.5.2.3(a) Small Room Provision — One Sprinkler.

Shaded text = Revisions. Δ = Text deletions and figure/table revisions. • = Section deletions. N = New material.

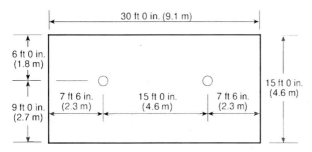

FIGURE A.10.2.5.2.3(b)   Small Room Provision — Two Sprinklers Centered Between Sidewalls.

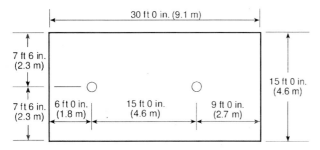

FIGURE A.10.2.5.2.3(c)   Small Room Provision — Two Sprinklers Centered Between Top and Bottom Walls.

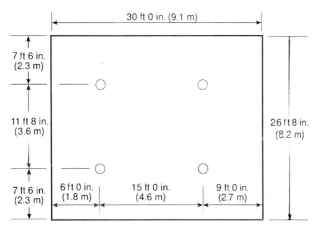

FIGURE A.10.2.5.2.3(d)   Small Room Provision — Four Sprinklers.

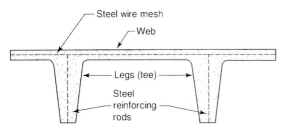

FIGURE A.10.2.6.1.2(5)   Typical Concrete Joist Construction.

a maximum of 3 ft (900 mm) down the slope from the peak because of the effect of venting on sprinkler sensitivity.

A.10.2.6.1.3.3 Generally, where applying the requirements of this section, a surface having a slope greater than or equal to 18 in 12 is needed.

A.10.2.6.1.4.3 Attic width and sprinkler spacing should be measured from the point of intersection between the bottom of the top cord of the roof joist or truss and the top of the ceiling joist or noncombustible insulation. *(See Figure A.10.2.6.1.4.3.)*

A.10.2.6.1.4.4 See Figure A.10.2.6.1.4.4.

A.10.2.6.1.4.5 See Figure A.10.2.6.1.4.5.

A.10.2.7.2 The intent of 10.2.7.2(3) is to apply to soffits that are located within the 18 in. (450 mm) plane from the sprinkler deflector. A soffit or other obstruction (i.e., shelf) located against a wall that is located entirely below the 18 in. (450 mm) plane from the sprinkler deflector should be in accordance with 10.2.7.4.2. *(See Figure A.10.2.7.2.)*

The sprinkler should be located at least 4 in. (100 mm) away from the face of the soffit as if it were a wall.

Δ **A.10.2.7.3.1.3** The rules of 10.2.7.3.1.3 (known as the Three Times Rule) have been written to apply to obstructions where the sprinkler can be expected to get water to both sides of the obstruction without allowing a significant shadow area on the other side of the obstruction. This works for small noncontinuous obstructions and for continuous obstructions where the sprinkler can throw water over and under the obstruction, such as the bottom chord of an open truss or joist. For solid continuous obstructions, such as a beam, the Three Times Rule is ineffective since the sprinkler cannot throw water over and under the obstruction. Sufficient water must be thrown under the obstruction to adequately cover the floor area on the other side of the obstruction. To ensure this, compliance with the rules of 10.2.7.2 is necessary.

A.10.2.7.3.1.4 It is the intent of this section to exempt nonstructural elements in light and ordinary hazard occupancies from the obstruction criteria commonly called the "Three Times Rule." However, the other obstruction rules, including the "Beam Rule" *(see 10.2.7.2)* and the "Wide Obstruction Rule" *(see 10.2.7.4.2)*, still apply. If an obstruction is so close to a sprinkler that water cannot spray on both sides, it is effectively a continuous obstruction as far as the sprinkler is concerned and the Beam Rule should be applied.

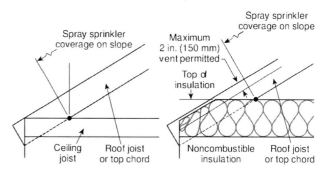

FIGURE A.10.2.6.1.4.3   Attic Width and Sprinkler Spacing Measurements.

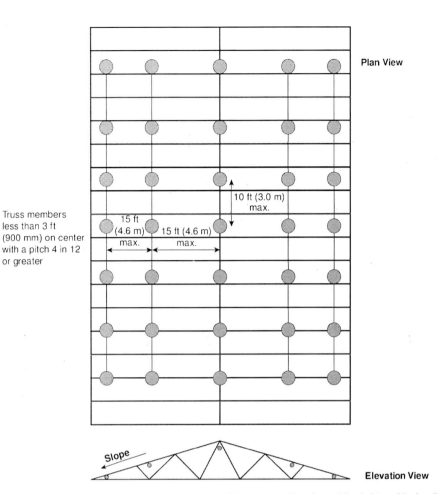

FIGURE A.10.2.6.1.4.4   Protection Area and Maximum Spacing of Sprinklers Under Sloped Roof.

It is not the intent of this section to permit the use of fixtures and architectural features or treatments to conceal, obscure, or otherwise obstruct sprinkler discharge. The requirement should be applied in accordance with the performance objectives in 10.2.7.1.

A.10.2.7.3.1.10 The housing unit of the ceiling fan is expected to be addressed by the Three Times Rule.

A.10.2.7.3.2.2 Testing has shown that privacy curtains supported from the ceiling by mesh fabric do not obstruct the distribution pattern in a negative way as long as the mesh is 70 percent or more open and extends from the ceiling a minimum of 22 in. (550 mm).

A.10.2.7.4 See A.9.5.5.3.

A.10.2.7.4.2 When obstructions are located more than 18 in. (450 mm) below the sprinkler deflector, an adequate spray pattern develops and obstructions up to and including 4 ft (1.2 m) wide do not require additional protection underneath. Examples are ducts, decks, open grate flooring, catwalks, cutting tables, overhead doors, soffits, ceiling panels, and other similar obstructions.

The width of an object is the lesser of the two horizontal dimensions (with the length being the longer horizontal dimension). Sprinkler protection is not required under objects where the length is greater than 4 ft (1.2 m) and the width is 4 ft (1.2 m) or less.

Δ **A.10.2.8.1** The 18 in. (450 mm) clearance is not intended to apply to vehicles in parking structures.

A.10.2.9.1 Ceiling features in unobstructed construction that are protected by sprinklers in the lower ceiling elevation when the higher ceiling elevation is within 12 in. (300 mm) of the deflectors or greater for sprinklers with greater listed distances from the higher ceiling should not be considered unprotected ceiling pockets.

A.10.2.9.2(4) It is the intent of this section to allow compartments with multiple pockets, where the cumulative volume of the pockets exceeds 1000 ft³ (28 m³) and separated from each other by 10 ft (3.05 m) or more and still be permitted to be unprotected because with these values, a sprinkler would be required between such pockets. For smaller pockets where the cumulative volume does not exceed 1000 ft³ (28 m³), there is no reason to separate the pockets by any specific distance because they are not worse than a single pocket that is 1000 ft³ (28 m³).

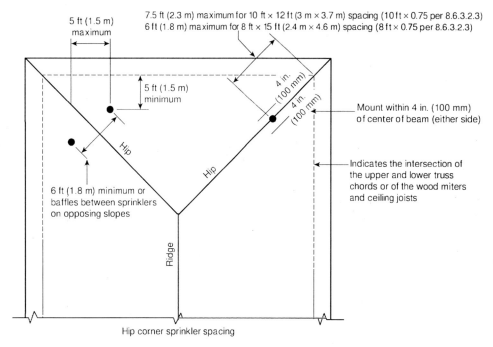

△ **FIGURE A.10.2.6.1.4.5   Hip Roof Installations.**

N **A.10.3.2(9)** Where sprinkler protection is provided under each level of cars, the ceiling sprinklers should be designed based upon the occupancy classification of parking garages. Not all car stackers or car lift systems will be able to have a sidewall sprinkler installed due to car stacker design or operation. The sidewall sprinklers must be installed meeting the requirements in the body of the standard including 9.5.5.3.1.2. A performance-based design is allowed with proper documentation to show equivalent protection. If the car stacker or car lift system design and/or operation prohibits the coverage under the cars, then the overhead system would be required to be designed to Extra Hazard Group 2 occupancy classification *[see A.4.3.5(9)]*.

A.10.3.5.1.2.1 The 6 in. (150 mm) as referenced is measured from the wall to the vertical plane representing the surface of attachment of the deflector. See Figure A.10.3.5.1.2.1.

A.10.3.5.1.3.2 See Figure A.10.3.5.1.3.2.

A.10.3.5.1.3.3 See Figure A.10.3.5.1.3.3.

A.10.3.5.1.4 The requirements in 10.3.5.1.4 were developed from years of experience with NFPA 13 obstruction requirements and an additional test series conducted by the National Fire Sprinkler Association with the help of Tyco International (Valentine and Isman, *Kitchen Cabinets and Residential Sprinklers*, National Fire Sprinkler Association, November 2005), which included fire modeling, distribution tests, and full-scale fire tests. The test series showed that pendent sprinklers definitely provide protection for kitchens, even for fires that start under the cabinets. The information in the series was less than definitive for sidewall sprinklers, but distribution data show that sprinklers in the positions in this standard provide adequate water distribution in front of the cabinets and that sidewall sprinklers should be able to control a fire that starts under the cabinets. When protecting kitchens or similar rooms

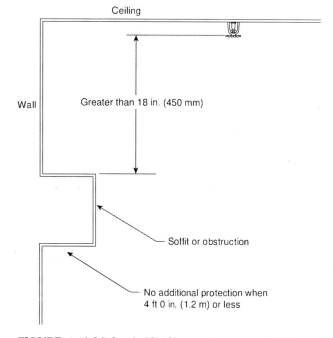

FIGURE A.10.2.7.2   Soffit/Obstruction Against Wall Greater Than 18 in. (450 mm) Below Deflector.

with cabinets, the pendent sprinkler should be the first option. If pendent sprinklers cannot be installed, the next best option is a sidewall sprinkler on the opposite wall from the cabinets, spraying in the direction of the cabinets. The third best option is the sidewall sprinkler on the same wall as the cabinets, on a soffit flush with the face of the cabinet. The last option should

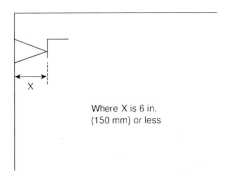

FIGURE A.10.3.5.1.2.1   Sidewall Sprinkler Deflector Measurement From Walls.

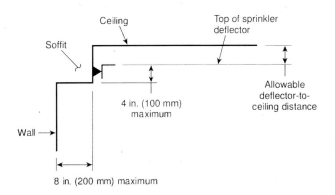

FIGURE A.10.3.5.1.3.2   Location Sidewalls with Respect to Soffits — Sidewall in Soffit.

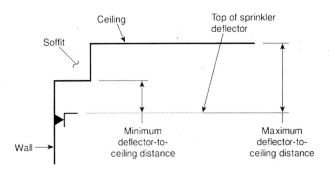

FIGURE A.10.3.5.1.3.3   Location Sidewalls with Respect to Soffits — Sidewall Under Soffit.

be putting sprinklers on the wall back behind the face of the cabinet because this location is subject to being blocked by items placed on top of the cabinets. It is not the intent of the committee to require sprinklers under kitchen cabinets.

Δ **A.10.3.6.2.1.3** The rules of 10.3.6.2.1.3 (known as the Three Times Rule) have been written to apply to obstructions where the sprinkler can be expected to get water to both sides of the obstruction without allowing a significant shadow area on the other side of the obstruction. This works for small noncontinuous obstructions and for continuous obstructions where the sprinkler can throw water over and under the obstruction, such as the bottom chord of an open truss or joist. For solid continuous obstructions, such as a beam, the Three Times Rule is inef-

fective since the sprinkler cannot throw water over and under the obstruction. Sufficient water must be thrown under the obstruction to adequately cover the floor area on the other side of the obstruction. To ensure this, compliance with the rules of 10.3.6.1.2 is necessary.

A.10.3.6.2.1.6 The housing unit of the ceiling fan is expected to be addressed by the Three Times Rule.

A.10.3.6.2.2.1 Testing has shown that privacy curtains supported from the ceiling by mesh fabric do not obstruct the distribution pattern in a negative way as long as the mesh is 70 percent or more open and extends from the ceiling a minimum of 22 in. (550 mm).

A.10.3.6.3 See A.9.5.5.3.

A.10.3.6.3.2 When obstructions are located more than 18 in. (450 mm) below the sprinkler deflector, an adequate spray pattern develops and obstructions up to and including 4 ft (1200 mm) wide do not require additional protection underneath. Examples are ducts, stairs, landings, and other similar obstructions.

A.10.3.7 See 10.2.8.4.

A.11.2.2.1 The protection area for extended coverage upright and pendent sprinklers is defined in the listing of the sprinkler as a maximum square area. Listing information is presented in even 2 ft (0.6 m) increments up to 20 ft (6.1 m). When a sprinkler is selected for an application, its area of coverage must be equal to or greater than both the length and width of the hazard area. For example, if the hazard to be protected is a room 13 ft 6 in. (4.1 m) wide and 17 ft 6 in. (5.3 m) long as indicated in Figure A.11.2.2.1, a sprinkler that is listed to protect an area of 18 ft × 18 ft (5.5 m × 5.5 m) must be selected. The flow used in the calculations is then selected as the flow required by the listing for the selected coverage.

A.11.2.2.2.1 Testing has shown that privacy curtains supported from the ceiling by mesh fabric do not obstruct the distribution pattern in a negative way as long as the mesh is 70 percent or more open and extends from the ceiling a minimum of 22 in. (550 mm).

A.11.2.4.1.1.4(A) See Figure A.11.2.4.1.1.4(A).

A.11.2.4.1.1.4(B) See Figure A.11.2.4.1.1.4(B).

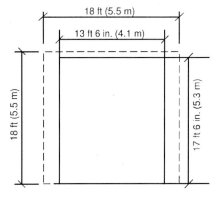

FIGURE A.11.2.2.1   Determination of Protection Area of Coverage for Extended Coverage Upright and Pendent Sprinklers.

A.11.2.4.1.3 Saw-toothed roofs have regularly spaced monitors of saw tooth shape, with the nearly vertical side glazed and usually arranged for venting. Sprinkler placement is limited to a maximum of 3 ft (900 mm) down the slope from the peak because of the effect of venting on sprinkler sensitivity.

A.11.2.5.1.2 The intent of 11.2.5.1.2(3) is to apply to soffits that are located within the 18 in. (450 mm) plane from the sprinkler deflector. A soffit or other obstruction (i.e., shelf) located against a wall that is located entirely below the 18 in. (450 mm) plane from the sprinkler deflector should be in accordance with 11.2.5.3.2. *(See Figure A.11.2.5.1.2.)*

Δ **A.11.2.5.2.1.3** The rules of 11.2.5.2.1.3 (known as the Four Times Rule) have been written to apply to obstructions where the sprinkler can be expected to get water to both sides of the obstruction without allowing a significant shadow area on the other side of the obstruction. This works for small noncontinuous obstructions and for continuous obstructions where the sprinkler can throw water over and under the obstruction, such as the bottom chord of an open truss or joist. For solid continuous obstructions, such as a beam, the Four Times Rule is ineffective since the sprinkler cannot throw water over and under the obstruction. Sufficient water must be thrown under the obstruction to adequately cover the floor area on the other side

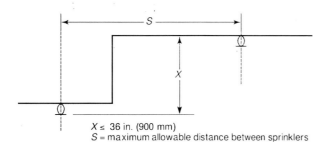

$X \leq 36$ in. (900 mm)
S = maximum allowable distance between sprinklers

FIGURE A.11.2.4.1.1.4(A) Vertical Change in Ceiling Elevation Less Than or Equal to 36 in. (900 mm).

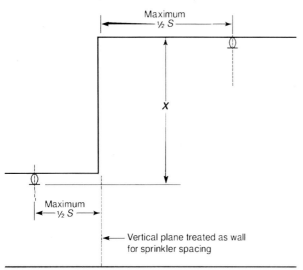

Maximum ½ S

Maximum ½ S

Vertical plane treated as wall for sprinkler spacing

$X > 36$ in. (900 mm)
S = maximum allowable distance between sprinklers

FIGURE A.11.2.4.1.1.4(B) Vertical Change in Ceiling Elevation Greater Than 36 in. (900 mm).

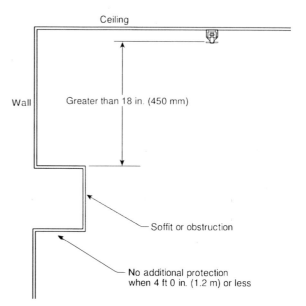

Ceiling

Wall

Greater than 18 in. (450 mm)

Soffit or obstruction

No additional protection when 4 ft 0 in. (1.2 m) or less

FIGURE A.11.2.5.1.2 Soffit/Obstruction Against Wall Greater Than 18 in. (450 mm) Below Deflector.

of the obstruction. To ensure this, compliance with the rules of 11.2.5.1.2 is necessary.

A.11.2.5.2.1.9 The housing unit of the ceiling fan is expected to be addressed by the Four Times Rule.

A.11.2.5.3 See A.9.5.5.3.

A.11.2.5.3.2 When obstructions are located more than 18 in. (450 mm) below the sprinkler deflector, an adequate spray pattern develops and obstructions up to and including 4 ft (1200 mm) wide do not require additional protection underneath. Examples are ducts, stairs, landings, and other similar obstructions.

N **A.11.2.6.1** The 18 in. (450 mm) does not apply to vehicles in parking structures.

A.11.2.7.1 Ceiling features in unobstructed construction that are protected by sprinklers in the lower ceiling elevation when the higher ceiling elevation is within 12 in. (300 mm) of the deflectors or greater for sprinklers with greater listed distances from the higher ceiling should not be considered unprotected ceiling pockets.

A.11.2.7.2(4) It is the intent of this section to allow compartments with multiple pockets, where the cumulative volume of the pockets exceeds 1000 ft^3 (28 m^3) and separated from each other by 10 ft (3 m) or more and still be permitted to be unprotected because with these values, a sprinkler would be required between such pockets. For smaller pockets where the cumulative volume does not exceed 1000 ft^3 (28 m^3), there is no reason to separate the pockets by any specific distance because they are not worse than a single pocket that is 1000 ft^3 (28 m^3).

A.11.3 See 10.2.8.2.

A.11.3.3.1 The protection area for extended coverage sidewall spray sprinklers is defined in the listing of the sprinkler as a maximum square or rectangular area. Listing information is presented in even 2 ft (0.6 m) increments up to 28 ft (9 m) for extended coverage sidewall spray sprinklers. When a sprinkler is selected for an application, its area of coverage must be equal to or greater than both the length and width of the hazard area. For example, if the hazard to be protected is a room 14 ft 6 in. (4.4 m) wide and 20 ft 8 in. (6.3 m) long as indicated in Figure A.11.3.3.1, a sprinkler that is listed to protect an area of 16 ft × 22 ft (4.9 m × 6.7 m) must be selected. The flow used in the calculations is then selected as the flow required by the listing for the selected coverage.

A.11.3.5.1.2.1 See A.10.3.5.1.2.1.

A.11.3.5.1.3.1 See Figure A.11.3.5.1.3.1.

A.11.3.5.1.3.2 See Figure A.11.3.5.1.3.2.

A.11.3.5.1.4 The requirements in 11.3.5.1.4 were developed from years of experience with NFPA 13 obstruction requirements and an additional test series conducted by the National Fire Sprinkler Association with the help of Tyco International (Valentine and Isman, *Kitchen Cabinets and Residential Sprinklers*, National Fire Sprinkler Association, November 2005), which included fire modeling, distribution tests, and full-scale fire tests. The test series showed that pendent sprinklers definitely provide protection for kitchens, even for fires that start under the cabinets. The information in the series was less than definitive for sidewall sprinklers, but distribution data show that sprinklers in the positions in this standard provide adequate

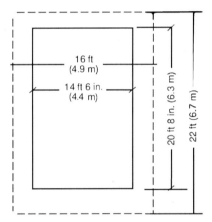

FIGURE A.11.3.3.1 **Determination of Protection Area of Coverage for Extended Coverage Sidewall Sprinklers.**

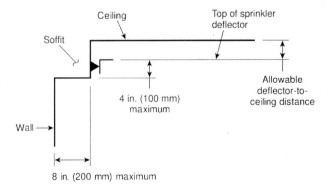

FIGURE A.11.3.5.1.3.1 **Location of Extended Coverage Sidewalls with Respect to Soffits — Sidewall in Soffit.**

water distribution in front of the cabinets and that sidewall sprinklers should be able to control a fire that starts under the cabinets. When protecting kitchens or similar rooms with cabinets, the pendent sprinkler should be the first option. If pendent sprinklers cannot be installed, the next best option is a sidewall sprinkler on the opposite wall from the cabinets, spraying in the direction of the cabinets. The third best option is the sidewall sprinkler on the same wall as the cabinets, on a soffit flush with the face of the cabinet. The last option should be putting sprinklers on the wall back behind the face of the cabinet because this location is subject to being blocked by items placed on top of the cabinets. It is not the intent of the committee to require sprinklers under kitchen cabinets.

Δ **A.11.3.6.2.1.3** The rules of 11.3.6.2.1.3 (known as the Four Times Rule) have been written to apply to obstructions where the sprinkler can be expected to get water to both sides of the obstruction without allowing a significant shadow area on the other side of the obstruction. This works for small noncontinuous obstructions and for continuous obstructions where the sprinkler can throw water over and under the obstruction, such as the bottom chord of an open truss or joist. For solid continuous obstructions, such as a beam, the Four Times Rule is ineffective since the sprinkler cannot throw water over and under the obstruction. Sufficient water must be thrown under the obstruction to adequately cover the floor area on the other side of the obstruction. To ensure this, compliance with the rules of 11.3.6.1.2 is necessary.

A.11.3.6.2.1.6 The housing unit of the ceiling fan is expected to be addressed by the Four Times Rule.

A.11.3.6.2.2.1 Testing has shown that privacy curtains supported from the ceiling by mesh fabric do not obstruct the distribution pattern in a negative way as long as the mesh is 70 percent or more open and extends from the ceiling a minimum of 22 in. (550 mm).

A.11.3.6.3 When obstructions are located more than 18 in. (450 mm) below the sprinkler deflector, an adequate spray pattern develops and obstructions up to and including 4 ft (1200 mm) wide do not require additional protection underneath. Examples are ducts, decks, open grate flooring, catwalks, cutting tables, overhead doors, soffits, ceiling panels, and other similar obstructions.

A.11.3.6.3.2 When obstructions are located more than 18 in. (450 mm) below the sprinkler deflector, an adequate spray pattern develops and obstructions up to and including 4 ft (1200 mm) wide do not require additional protection under-

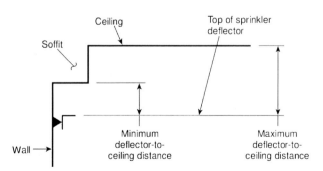

FIGURE A.11.3.5.1.3.2 **Location of Extended Coverage Sidewalls with Respect to Soffits — Sidewall Under Soffit.**

neath. Examples are ducts, stairs, landings, and other similar obstructions.

Δ **A.12.1.1** The response and water distribution pattern of listed residential sprinklers have been shown by extensive fire testing to provide better control than spray sprinklers in residential occupancies. These sprinklers are intended to prevent flashover in the room of fire origin, thus improving the chance for occupants to escape or be evacuated.

The protection area for residential sprinklers is defined in the listing of the sprinkler as a maximum square or rectangular area. Listing information is presented in even increments from 12 ft to 20 ft (3.7 m to 6.1 m). When a sprinkler is selected for an application, its area of coverage must be equal to or greater than both the length and width of the hazard area. For example, if the hazard to be protected is a room 13 ft 6 in. (4.1 m) wide and 17 ft 6 in. (5.3 m) long, a sprinkler that is listed to protect a rectangular area of 14 ft × 18 ft (4.3 m × 5.5 m) or a square area of 18 ft × 18 ft (5.5 m × 5.5 m) must be selected. The flow used in the calculations is then selected as the flow required by the listing for the selected coverage.

Residential sprinklers can be used in corridors that lead to dwelling units. However, the corridors that lead to dwelling units can also lead to other hazards that are not dwelling units and can still be protected with residential sprinklers. An example would be in a hotel occupancy where the corridor immediately leading to the guest rooms also has doors to rooms such as conference rooms, housekeeping closets, laundry rooms, back of house offices, and so forth.

A.12.1.6 Residential sprinklers should be used in compliance with their listing limits. Where there are no listed residential sprinklers for a particular arrangement, other design approaches from NFPA 13 should be utilized, such as using quick-response sprinklers.

Δ **A.12.1.10.2.1.3** The rules of 12.1.10.2.1.3 (known as the Four Times Rule) have been written to apply to obstructions where the sprinkler can be expected to get water to both sides of the obstruction without allowing a significant shadow area on the other side of the obstruction. This works for small noncontinuous obstructions and for continuous obstructions where the sprinkler can throw water over and under the obstruction, such as the bottom chord of an open truss or joist. For solid continuous obstructions, such as a beam, the Four Times Rule is ineffective since the sprinkler cannot throw water over and under the obstruction. Sufficient water must be thrown under the obstruction to adequately cover the floor area on the other side of the obstruction. To ensure this, compliance with the rules of 12.1.10.1.2 is necessary.

A.12.1.10.2.1.9 The housing unit of the ceiling fan is expected to be addressed by the Three Times Rule or the Four Times Rule.

A.12.1.10.2.3 See A.9.1.1(3), Figure A.9.1.1(3)(a), and Figure A.9.1.1(3)(b).

A.12.1.10.3 See A.9.5.5.3.

A.12.1.11.1.5 The requirements in 12.1.11.1.5 were developed from years of experience with NFPA 13 obstruction requirements and an additional test series conducted by the National Fire Sprinkler Association with the help of Tyco International (Valentine and Isman, *Kitchen Cabinets and Residential Sprinklers,* National Fire Sprinkler Association, November 2005), which

included fire modeling, distribution tests, and full-scale fire tests. The test series showed that pendent sprinklers definitely provide protection for kitchens, even for fires that start under the cabinets. The information in the series was less than definitive for sidewall sprinklers, but distribution data shows that sprinklers in the positions in this standard provide adequate water distribution in front of the cabinets and that sidewall sprinklers should be able to control a fire that starts under the cabinets. When protecting kitchens or similar rooms with cabinets, the pendent sprinkler should be the first option. If pendent sprinklers cannot be installed, the next best option is a sidewall sprinkler on the opposite wall from the cabinets, spraying in the direction of the cabinets. The third best option is the sidewall sprinkler on the same wall as the cabinets on a soffit flush with the face of the cabinet. The last option should be putting sprinklers on the wall back behind the face of the cabinet because this location is subject to being blocked by items placed on top of the cabinets. It is not the intent of the committee to require sprinklers under kitchen cabinets.

Δ **A.12.1.11.2.1.3** The rules of 12.1.11.2.1.3 (known as the Four Times Rule) have been written to apply to obstructions where the sprinkler can be expected to get water to both sides of the obstruction without allowing a significant shadow area on the other side of the obstruction. This works for small noncontinuous obstructions and for continuous obstructions where the sprinkler can throw water over and under the obstruction, such as the bottom chord of an open truss or joist. For solid continuous obstructions, such as a beam, the Four Times Rule is ineffective since the sprinkler cannot throw water over and under the obstruction. Sufficient water must be thrown under the obstruction to adequately cover the floor area on the other side of the obstruction. To ensure this, compliance with the rules of 12.1.10.1.2 is necessary.

A.12.1.11.2.1.7 The housing unit of the ceiling fan is expected to be addressed by the Four Times Rule.

A.12.1.11.2.2 Floor-mounted obstructions can be parallel or perpendicular to the wall with the sidewall sprinkler.

A.12.1.11.3 See A.9.5.5.3.

A.12.1.11.3.2 When obstructions are located more than 18 in. (450 mm) below the sprinkler deflector, an adequate spray pattern develops and obstructions up to and including 4 ft (1.2 m) wide do not require additional protection underneath. Examples are ducts, stairs, landings, and other similar obstructions.

A.13.2.5 Tests involving areas of coverage over 100 ft^2 (9 m^2) for CMSA sprinklers are limited in number, and use of areas of coverage over 100 ft^2 (9 m^2) should be carefully considered.

A.13.2.6.1 It is important that sprinklers in the immediate vicinity of the fire center not skip, and this requirement imposes certain restrictions on the spacing.

A.13.2.7.1 If all other factors are held constant, the operating time of the first sprinkler will vary exponentially with the distance between the ceiling and deflector. At distances greater than 7 in. (175 mm), for other than open wood joist construction, the delayed operating time will permit the fire to gain headway, with the result that substantially more sprinklers operate. At distances less than 7 in. (175 mm), other effects occur. Changes in distribution, penetration, and cooling nullify the advantage gained by faster operation. The net result again is increased fire damage accompanied by an increase in the number of sprinklers operated. The optimum clearance between deflectors and ceiling is therefore 7 in. (175 mm). For open wood joist construction, the optimum clearance between deflectors and the bottom of joists is 3½ in. (90 mm).

A.13.2.8 To a great extent, CMSA sprinklers rely on direct attack to gain rapid control of both the burning fuel and ceiling temperatures. Therefore, interference with the discharge pattern and obstructions to the distribution should be avoided.

Δ **A.13.2.8.2.1.3** The rules of 13.2.8.2.1.3 (known as the Three Times Rule) have been written to apply to obstructions where the sprinkler can be expected to get water to both sides of the obstruction without allowing a significant shadow area on the other side of the obstruction. This works for small noncontinuous obstructions and for continuous obstructions where the sprinkler can throw water over and under the obstruction, such as the bottom chord of an open truss or joist. For solid continuous obstructions, such as a beam, the Three Times Rule is ineffective since the sprinkler cannot throw water over and under the obstruction. Sufficient water must be thrown under the obstruction to adequately cover the floor area on the other side of the obstruction. To ensure this, compliance with the rules of 13.2.8.1.2 is necessary.

A.13.2.8.3 See A.9.5.5.3.

A.14.2.4 Storage in single-story or multistory buildings can be permitted, provided the maximum ceiling/roof height as specified in Table 14.2.8.2.1 is satisfied for each storage area.

N **A.14.2.7** It is not the intent of this section to allow ESFR sprinklers to be adjusted to light or ordinary spacing criteria. However, it does allow flexibility for spacing to walls, when walls are added to create light or ordinary hazard areas to existing ESFR systems.

A.14.2.8.2.3 See Figure A.14.2.8.2.3.

N **A.14.2.8.3.1** Examples of solid structural members are beams, stem, and so forth.

A.14.2.9.1(3) See Figure A.14.2.8.2.3.

N **A.14.2.9.4.1** Examples of solid structural members are beams, stem, and so forth.

A.14.2.11 The obstruction rules of 14.2.11 have been primarily written to address horizontal obstructions like ducts and lights where the sprinkler needs to spray under the obstruction or get water both over and under the obstruction. For vertical obstruction situations like columns where the water needs to get to two sides of the obstruction, the guidance in 14.2.11 to keep the sprinklers at least 12 in. (300 mm) from obstructions up to 12 in. (300 mm) wide and to keep the sprinkler 24 in. (600 mm) from obstructions over 12 in. (300 mm) to 24 in. (600 mm) wide can be used. For obstructions like columns that are more than 24 in. (600 mm) wide, a sprinkler should be placed on the opposite side of the obstruction while following the minimum and maximum spacing requirements of 14.2.8.

A.14.2.11.2 Isolated obstructions that block adjacent sprinklers in a similar manner should be treated as a continuous obstruction. High-volume, low-speed fans with large diameters [(20 ft (6.1 m)] represent potential obstructions for ESFR sprinklers and should be positioned in accordance with the provisions of 14.2.11.2 with regard to both the fan motor unit and the blades.

Examples include obstructions such as light fixtures and unit heaters.

N **A.14.2.11.2(8)** Examples of high-piled storage are rack structures and solid-piled storage.

A.14.2.11.3.4 For example, a 1 in. (25 mm) diameter conduit would need to be 3 in. (75 mm) from the nearest pipe or conduit to be considered as an individual obstruction. Otherwise, the pipes and/or conduits would be considered as a group when applying the obstruction criteria in 14.2.11.3.1.

A.15.3.1 Dry sprinklers must be of sufficient length to avoid freezing of the water-filled pipes due to conduction along the barrel. The values of exposed barrel length in Table 15.3.1(a) and Table 15.3.1(b) have been developed using an assumption of a properly sealed penetration and an assumed maximum wind velocity on the exposed sprinkler of 30 mph (48 km/h). Where higher wind velocity is expected, longer exposed barrel lengths will help avoid freezing of the wet piping. The total length of the barrel of the dry sprinkler must be longer than the values shown in Table 15.3.1(a) and Table 15.3.1(b) because the length shown in the tables is the minimum length of the barrel that needs to be exposed to the warmer ambient temperature in the heated space. See Figure A.15.3.1(a), Figure A.15.3.1(c), and Figure A.15.3.1(e) for examples of where to measure the exposed barrel length for a sidewall sprinkler penetrating an exterior wall and Figure A.15.3.1(b) and Figure A.15.3.1(d) for examples of where to measure the exposed barrel length for a pendent sprinkler penetrating a ceiling or top of a freezer.

A.15.3.3 The clearance space around the sprinkler barrel should be sealed to avoid leakage of air into the freezing area that could result in the formation of condensate around the sprinkler frame that could inhibit or cause premature operation. See Figure A.15.3.3(a) and Figure A.15.3.3(b).

A.15.3.4 Generally dry sprinklers are installed in tees. Dry sprinklers should never be installed in 90-degree elbows. Some manufacturers allow installation of dry sprinklers in couplings, CPVC adapters, and so forth.

A.16.1.1 The components need not be open or exposed. Doors, removable panels, or valve pits can satisfy this need. Such equipment should not be obstructed by such permanent features as walls, ducts, columns, or direct burial.

A.16.2.1.1 Sprinklers should be permitted to be reinstalled when the sprinkler being removed from the system remains attached to the original fitting or welded outlet or can be removed by a grooved connection, provided care has been taken to ensure the sprinkler has not been damaged. Flexible hose connections are considered a fitting.

In new installations, where sprinklers are installed on pendent drop nipples or sidewall sprinklers prior to final cut-back, protective caps and/or straps should remain in place until after the drop nipple has been cut to fit to the final ceiling elevation.

A.16.2.2.1.1 Care should be taken in the handling and installation of wax-coated or similar sprinklers to avoid damaging the coating.

A.16.2.4.2 Plastic bags should not be used for this purpose due to the fact that shrinkage prior to development of temperatures needed to ensure sprinkler activation can interfere with proper sprinkler operation and development of spray patterns. The prohibition against plastic bags should include polypropy-

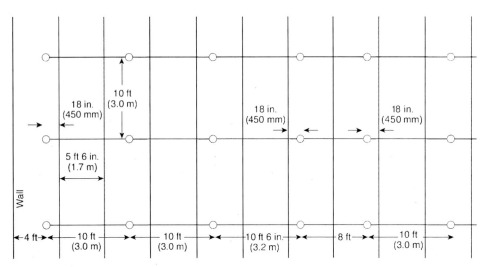

Example 1 of ESFR "Shift" Rule (bar joists or trusses 5 ft 6 in. (1.7 m) o.c.)
Measurement shown is from centerline for ease of illustration; actual
measurement to obstruction is to near edge of structural member.

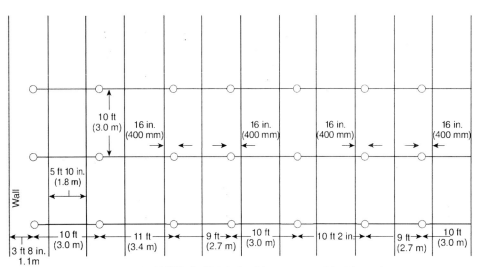

Example 2 of ESFR "Shift" Rule (bar joists or trusses 5 ft 10 in. o.c.)
Measurement shown is from centerline for ease of illustration; actual
measurement to obstruction is to near edge of structural member.

FIGURE A.14.2.8.2.3   ESFR Sprinkler Spacing Within Trusses and Bar Joists.

lene bags commonly marketed as "cello" bags. True cellophane
degrades rather than melts and, like paper, does not display
shrinkage.

A.16.2.5.2 The use of the wrong type of escutcheon with
recessed or flush-type sprinklers can result in severe disruption
of the spray pattern, which can destroy the effectiveness of the
sprinkler.

A.16.2.7.1 It is the intent of this section to require spare sprin‐
klers and associated manufacturer's sprinkler wrenches based
on the facility as opposed to individual buildings or systems.
Spare sprinklers for campus arrangements such as schools,
hospitals, or multifamily complexes should be located under
the owner's control and are not necessarily required to be
provided at each building or riser location.

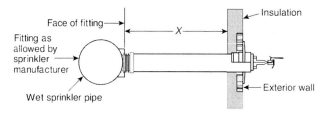

X = Minimum exposed barrel length

X is measured from the face of the sprinkler fitting
to the inside surface of the exterior wall or insulation —
whichever is closer to the fitting.

Δ FIGURE A.15.3.1(a)   Dry Sidewall Sprinkler Through Wall.

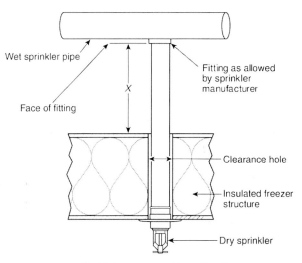

X = Minimum exposed barrel length

X is measured from the face of the sprinkler fitting
to the inside surface of the exterior wall or insulation —
whichever is closer to the fitting.

Δ **FIGURE A.15.3.1(b) Dry Pendent Sprinkler Through Ceiling or Top of Freezer.**

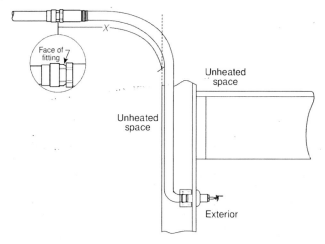

Δ **FIGURE A.15.3.1(c) Dry Sidewall Sprinkler Through Wall**

N A.16.2.7.2 It is not the intent to provide a spare sprinkler box for each building in the one location. A sufficiently sized cabinet(s) capable of meeting the requirements for a single building is adequate. The box should contain all the various types found on the property in the quantities prescribed in Chapter 16. A prime example is an apartment complex.

A.16.2.7.6 One sprinkler wrench design can be appropriate for many types of sprinklers and should not require multiple wrenches of the same design.

A.16.2.7.7.1 The minimum information in the list contained in the spare sprinkler cabinet should be marked with the sprinkler identification described in 7.2.1; a general description of the sprinkler, including upright, pendent, residential, ESFR,

and so forth; and the quantity of sprinklers that is to be maintained in the spare sprinkler cabinet.

An example of the list is shown in Figure A.16.2.7.7.1.

A.16.3.2 See Table A.16.3.2.

N A.16.3.5 See Table A.16.3.5.

A.16.3.9.4 When fabricating steel pipe for a combination (CPVC–steel) system, the cutting oil and lubricants can cause performance degradation of the CPVC piping. Cutting oils and lubricants found to be compatible are available and should be used.

A.16.3.12.1 Outlets meeting the requirements of this standard should be provided in anticipation of the final finished area.

A.16.3.12.2 Providing 1 in. (25 mm) minimum outlets with bushings can provide for future changes in building uses or occupancies.

A.16.4.1.1 Water-filled piping can be run in spaces above heated room, such as attics, even if the space above the room is not heated itself. Insulation can be located above the pipe to trap the heat from below and prevent the pipe from freezing. It is important not to bury the piping in the insulation because if too much insulation ends up between the pipe and the heated space, the insulation will prevent the heat from getting to the pipe. This method of protecting the pipe is acceptable to this standard.

N A.16.4.1.4 Requirements for heat tracing and associated controls intended for the fire protection application can be found in UL 515A, *Outline of Investigation for Electrical Resistance Trace Heating and Associated Controls for Use in Sprinkler and Standpipe Systems*. Also, since heat tracing has the potential to overheat sprinklers and system piping as well as adversely impact the sprinkler discharge characteristics, heating tracing use for branch lines is required to be specifically listed for this use.

A.16.4.2 Where approved, the pipe identification can be covered with paint or other protective coatings before installation.

A.16.4.2.1 Being exposed to the outside atmosphere is not necessarily a corrosive environment. Types of locations where corrosive conditions can exist include bleacheries, dye houses, metal plating processes, animal pens, and certain chemical plants. If corrosive conditions are not of great intensity and humidity is not abnormally high, good results can be obtained by using a good grade of commercial acid-resisting paint. The paint manufacturer's instructions should be followed in the preparation of the surface and in the method of application.

Where moisture conditions are severe but corrosive conditions are not of great intensity, copper tube or galvanized steel pipe, fittings, and hangers might be suitable. The exposed threads of steel pipe should be painted.

In instances where the piping is not accessible and where the exposure to corrosive fumes is severe, either a protective coating of high quality can be employed or some form of corrosion-resistant material used.

A.16.4.3 Protection should be provided in any area of a structure or building that poses a degree of hazard greater than that normal to the general occupancy of the building or structure. These areas include areas for the storage or use of combusti-

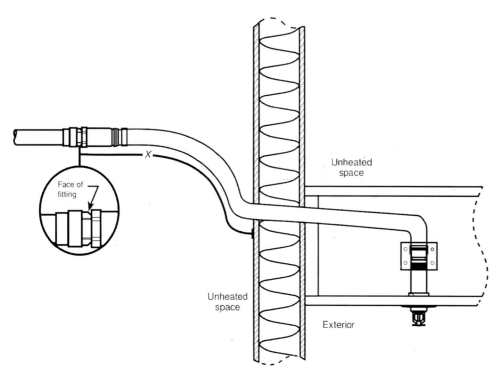

△ FIGURE A.15.3.1(d)   Dry Pendent Sprinkler Through Ceiling

bles or flammables; toxic, noxious, or corrosive materials; and heat-producing appliances.

A.16.7 A manual or automatic air venting valve can be a reasonable approach on wet pipe sprinkler systems to reduce corrosion activity. The purpose of the air venting valve is to exhaust as much trapped air as possible from a single location every time the system is filled. The objective of venting is to reduce the amount of oxygen trapped in the system that will fuel corrosion and microbial activity. It is neither the intent nor practical to exhaust all trapped air from a single location on a wet pipe sprinkler system; however, more than one vent can be used on a system at the designer's discretion. Interconnection of branch line piping for venting purposes is not necessary. An inspector's test valve can serve this purpose.

The air venting valve should be located where it will be most effective. System piping layout will guide the designer in choosing an effective location for venting. In order to effectively accomplish venting, it is necessary to choose a location where the greatest volume of trapped air is vented during the first fill and each subsequent drain and fill event. The vent connection to the system should be located off the top of horizontal piping at a high point in the system; however, the vent connection can also be effectively located off the side of a riser or riser nipple at a high point in the system.

Manual air venting valves should be accessible. The manual air venting valve should be located at an accessible point and preferably not over 7 ft (2.1 m) above the floor. Automatic air valves are not required to comply with the accessibility requirement of manual air venting valves; however, it is recommended the designer locate automatic air vents over areas without ceilings, above a lay-in ceiling, or above an access panel.

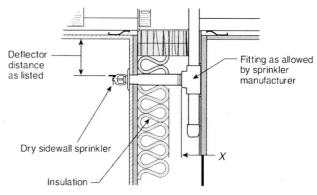

X = Minimum exposed barrel length

X is measured from the face of the sprinkler fitting to the inside surface of the exterior wall or insulation — whichever is closer to the fitting.

N FIGURE A.15.3.1(e)   Dry Sidewall Sprinkler Through Wall.

Each wet pipe sprinkler system should be vented every time the system is filled.

A.16.8.2.1 CPVC is a plastic material and consideration is necessary when other materials or chemicals come in contact with CPVC that can cause degradation of performance of the fitting due to interaction of materials. Compliance with 7.4.3 combined with following manufacturer's guidance on installation and compatible materials will help prevent premature performance degradation of non-metallic fittings. Mechanical stress caused by hanging methods or bending on non-metallic piping beyond the manufacturer's recommended limitations can cause stress failure over time and should be avoided.

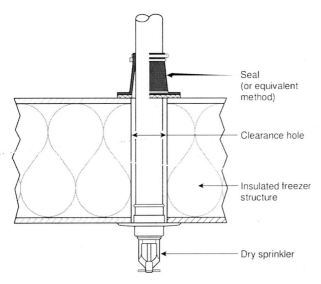

FIGURE A.15.3.3(a)   Dry Sprinkler Seal Arrangement — Seal on Exterior of Freezer Structure.

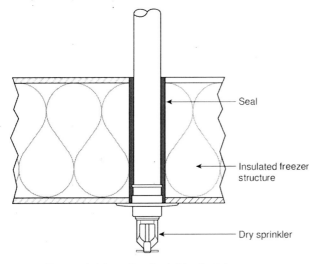

FIGURE A.15.3.3(b)   Dry Sprinkler Seal Arrangement — Seal Within Freezer Structure.

Sprinklers Contained in this Cabinet			
Sprinkler Identification, SIN	General Description	Temperature Rating, °F	Sprinkler Quantity Maintained
TY9128	Extended Coverage, K-25, upright	165	6
VK494	Residential concealed pendent	155	6
Issued: 8/31/19	Revised:		

Δ **FIGURE A.16.2.7.7.1   Sample List.**

A.16.8.2.2 When fabricating steel pipe for a system using non-metallic and steel pipe, the cutting oil and lubricants can cause performance degradation of the non-metallic fitting.

A.16.8.3 The rupture strength of cast-iron fittings 2 in. (50 mm) in size and smaller and malleable iron fittings 6 in. (150 mm) in size and smaller is sufficient to provide an adequate factor of safety.

A.16.8.4 Listed flexible connections are permissible and encouraged for sprinkler installations in racks to reduce the possibility of physical damage. Where flexible tubing is used, it should be located so that it will be protected against mechanical injury.

A.16.9.3 See Figure A.16.9.3.

A.16.9.3.1 A water supply connection should not extend into a building or through a building wall unless such connection is under the control of an outside listed indicating valve or an inside listed indicating valve located near the outside wall of the building.

All valves controlling water supplies for sprinkler systems or portions thereof, including floor control valves, should be accessible to authorized persons during emergencies. Permanent ladders, clamped treads on risers, chain-operated hand wheels, or other accepted means should be provided where necessary.

Outside control valves are suggested in the following order of preference:

(1) Listed indicating valves at each connection into the building at least 40 ft (12 m) from buildings if space permits
(2) Control valves installed in a cutoff stair tower or valve room accessible from outside
(3) Valves located in risers with indicating posts arranged for outside operation
(4) Key-operated valves in each connection into the building

A.16.9.3.3 The management is responsible for the supervision of valves controlling water supply for fire protection and should exert every effort to see that the valves are maintained in the normally open position. This effort includes special precautions to ensure that protection is promptly restored by completely opening valves that are necessarily closed during repairs or alterations. The precautions apply equally to valves controlling sprinklers and other fixed water-based fire suppression systems, hydrants, tanks, standpipes, pumps, street connections, and sectional valves.

Either one or a combination of the methods of valve supervision described in the following list is considered essential to ensure that the valves controlling fire protection systems are in the normally open position. The methods described are intended as an aid to the person responsible for developing a systematic method of determining that the valves controlling sprinkler systems and other fire protection devices are open.

Continual vigilance is necessary if valves are to be kept in the open position. Responsible day and night employees should be familiar with the location of all valves and their proper use.

Δ **Table A.16.3.2 Steel Pipe Dimensions**

Nominal Pipe Size		Outside Diameter		Schedule 5				Schedule 10ᵃ				Schedule 30				Schedule 40			
				Inside Diameter		Wall Thickness		Inside Diameter		Wall Thickness		Inside Diameter		Wall Thickness		Inside Diameter		Wall Thickness	
in.	mm	in.	mm	in.	mm	in.	mm	in.	mm	in.	mm	in.	mm	in.	mm	in.	mm	in.	mm
½ᵇ	15	0.840	21.3	—	—	—	—	0.674	17.1	0.083	2.1	—	—	—	—	0.622	15.8	0.109	2.77
¾ᵇ	20	1.050	26.7	—	—	—	—	0.884	22.4	0.083	2.1	—	—	—	—	0.824	21.0	0.113	2.87
1	25	1.315	33.4	1.185	30.1	0.065	1.7	1.097	27.9	0.109	2.8	—	—	—	—	1.049	26.6	0.133	3.37
1¼	32	1.660	42.2	1.530	38.9	0.065	1.7	1.442	36.6	0.109	2.8	—	—	—	—	1.380	35.1	0.140	3.56
1½	40	1.900	48.3	1.770	45.0	0.065	1.7	1.682	42.7	0.109	2.8	—	—	—	—	1.610	40.9	0.145	3.68
2	50	2.375	60.3	2.245	57.0	0.065	1.7	2.157	54.8	0.109	2.8	—	—	—	—	2.067	52.5	0.154	3.91
2½	65	2.875	73.0	2.709	68.8	0.083	2.1	2.635	66.9	0.120	3.0	—	—	—	—	2.469	62.7	0.203	5.16
3	80	3.500	88.9	3.334	84.7	0.083	2.1	3.260	82.8	0.120	3.0	—	—	—	—	3.068	77.9	0.216	5.49
3½	90	4.000	101.6	3.834	97.4	0.083	2.1	3.760	95.5	0.120	3.0	—	—	—	—	3.548	90.1	0.226	5.74
4	100	4.500	114.3	4.334	110.1	0.083	2.1	4.260	108.2	0.120	3.0	—	—	—	—	4.026	102.3	0.237	6.02
5	125	5.563	141.3	—	—	—	—	5.295	134.5	0.134	3.4	—	—	—	—	5.047	128.2	0.258	6.55
6	150	6.625	168.3	6.407	162.7	0.109	2.8	6.357	161.5	0.134ᶜ	3.4	—	—	—	—	6.065	154.1	0.280	7.11
8	200	8.625	219.1	—	—	—	—	8.249	209.5	0.188ᶜ	4.8	8.071	205.0	0.277ᵈ	7.0	7.981	—	0.322	—
10	250	10.750	273.1	—	—	—	—	10.370	263.4	0.188ᶜ	4.8	10.140	257.6	0.307ᵈ	7.8	10.020	—	0.365	—
12	300	12.750	—	—	—	—	—	—	—	—	—	12.090	—	0.330ᶜ	—	11.938	—	0.406	—

ᵃSchedule 10 defined to 5 in. (127 mm) nominal pipe size by ASTM A135, *Standard Specification for Electric-Resistance-Welded Steel Pipe.*
ᵇThese values applicable when used in conjunction with Section 30.4 and Section 30.6.
ᶜWall thickness specified in 16.3.2.
ᵈWall thickness specified in 16.3.3.

N **Table A.16.3.5 Copper Tube Dimensions**

Nominal Tube Size		Outside Diameter		Type K				Type L				Type M			
				Inside Diameter		Wall Thickness		Inside Diameter		Wall Thickness		Inside Diameter		Wall Thickness	
in.	mm	in.	mm	in.	mm	in.	mm	in.	mm	in.	mm	in.	mm	in.	mm
¾	20	0.875	22.2	0.745	18.9	0.065	1.7	0.785	19.9	0.045	1.1	0.811	20.6	0.032	0.8
1	25	1.125	28.6	0.995	25.3	0.065	1.7	1.025	26.0	0.050	1.3	1.055	26.8	0.035	0.9
1¼	32	1.375	34.9	1.245	31.6	0.065	1.7	1.265	32.1	0.055	1.4	1.291	32.8	0.042	1.1
1½	40	1.625	41.3	1.481	37.6	0.072	1.8	1.505	38.2	0.060	1.5	1.527	38.8	0.049	1.2
2	50	2.125	54.0	1.959	49.8	0.083	2.1	1.985	50.4	0.070	1.8	2.009	51.0	0.058	1.5
2½	65	2.625	66.7	2.435	61.8	0.095	2.4	2.465	62.6	0.080	2.0	2.495	63.4	0.065	1.7
3	80	3.125	79.4	2.907	73.8	0.109	2.8	2.945	74.8	0.090	2.3	2.981	75.7	0.072	1.8
3½	90	3.625	92.1	3.385	86.0	0.120	3.0	3.425	87.0	0.100	2.5	3.459	87.9	0.083	2.1
4	100	4.125	104.8	3.857	98.0	0.134	3.4	3.905	99.2	0.110	2.8	3.935	99.9	0.095	2.4
5	125	5.125	130.2	4.805	122.0	0.160	4.1	4.875	123.8	0.125	3.2	4.907	124.6	0.109	2.8
6	150	6.125	155.6	5.741	145.8	0.192	4.9	5.845	148.5	0.140	3.6	5.881	149.4	0.122	3.1
8	200	8.125	206.4	7.583	192.6	0.271	6.9	7.725	196.2	0.200	5.1	7.785	197.7	0.170	4.3
10	250	10.130	257.3	9.449	240.0	0.338	8.6	9.625	244.5	0.250	6.4	9.701	246.4	0.212	5.4

The authority having jurisdiction should be consulted as to the type of valve supervision required. Contracts for equipment should specify that all details are to be subject to the approval of the authority having jurisdiction.

(1) *Central Station Supervisory Service.* Central station supervisory service systems involve complete, constant, and automatic supervision of valves by electrically operated devices and circuits continually under test and operating through an approved outside central station, in compliance with *NFPA 72* or other approved fire alarm code. It is understood that only such portions of *NFPA 72* or other approved fire alarm code that relate to valve supervision should apply.

(2) *Proprietary Supervisory Service Systems.* Proprietary supervisory service systems include systems where the operation of a valve produces some form of signal and record at a common point by electrically operated devices and circuits continually under test and operating through a central supervising station at the property protected, all in compliance with the standards for the installation, maintenance, and use of local protective, auxiliary protective, remote station protective, and proprietary signaling systems. It is understood that only portions of the standards that relate to valve supervision should apply.

The standard method of locking, sealing, and tagging valves to prevent, so far as possible, their unnecessary closing, to obtain notification of such closing, and to aid in restoring the valve to normal condition is a satisfactory alternative to valve supervision. The authority having jurisdiction should be consulted regarding details for specific cases.

Where electrical supervision is not provided, locks or seals should be provided on all valves and should be of a type acceptable to the authority having jurisdiction.

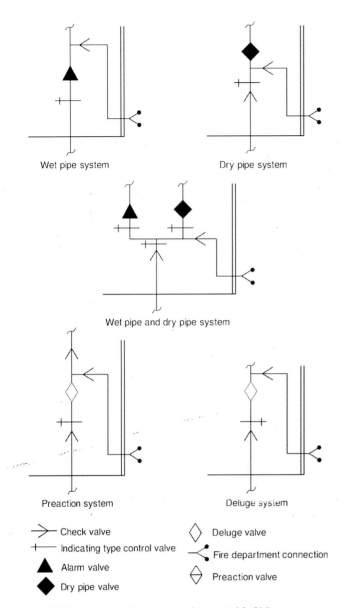

Wet pipe system   Dry pipe system

Wet pipe and dry pipe system

Preaction system   Deluge system

→ Check valve

+ Indicating type control valve

▲ Alarm valve

◆ Dry pipe valve

◇ Deluge valve

< Fire department connection

◇ Preaction valve

FIGURE A.16.9.3   Examples of Acceptable Valve Arrangements.

Seals can be marked to indicate the organization under whose jurisdiction the sealing is conducted. All seals should be attached to the valve in such a manner that the valves cannot be operated without breaking the seals. Seals should be of a character to prevent injury in handling and to prevent reassembly when broken. When seals are used, valves should be inspected weekly. The authority having jurisdiction can require a valve tag to be used in conjunction with the sealing.

A padlock, with a chain where necessary, is especially desirable to prevent unauthorized closing of valves in areas where valves are subject to tampering. When such locks are employed, valves should be inspected monthly.

If valves are locked, any distribution of keys should be restricted to only those directly responsible for the fire protec-

tion system. Multiple valves should not be locked together; they should be individually locked.

The individual performing the inspections should determine that each valve is in the normal position, properly locked or sealed, and so note on an appropriate record form while still at the valve. The authority having jurisdiction should be consulted for assistance in preparing a suitable report form for this activity.

Identification signs should be provided at each valve to indicate its function and what it controls.

The position of the spindle of OS&Y valves or the target on the indicator valves cannot be accepted as conclusive proof that the valve is fully open. The opening of the valve should be followed by a test to determine that the operating parts have functioned properly.

The test consists of opening the main drain valve and permitting free flow of water until the gauge reading becomes stationary. If the pressure drop is excessive for the water supply involved, the cause should be determined immediately and the proper remedies taken. When sectional valves or other special conditions are encountered, other methods of testing should be used.

If it becomes necessary to break a seal for emergency reasons, the valve, following the emergency, should be opened by the person responsible for the fire protection of the plant, or his or her designated representative, and this person should apply a seal at the time of the valve opening. This seal should be maintained in place until such time as the authority having jurisdiction can replace it with one of its own.

Seals or locks should not be applied to valves reopened after closure until such time as the inspection procedure is carried out.

Where water is shut off to the sprinkler or other fixed water-based fire suppression systems, a guard or other qualified person should be placed on duty and required to continuously patrol the affected sections of the premises until such time as protection is restored.

During specific critical situations, a person should be stationed at the valve so that the valve can be reopened promptly if necessary. It is the intent of this section that the person remain within sight of the valve and have no other duties beyond this responsibility. This procedure is considered imperative when fire protection is shut off immediately following a fire.

An inspection of all other fire protection equipment should be made prior to shutting off water in order to make sure it is in operative condition.

In case of changes to fire protection equipment, all possible work should be done in advance of shutting off the water so that final connections can be made quickly and protection restored promptly. Many times it will be found that by careful planning open outlets can be plugged and protection restored on a portion of the equipment while the alterations are being made.

Where changes are being made in underground piping, all possible piping should be laid before shutting off the water for final connections. Where possible, temporary feed lines, such as temporary piping for reconnection of risers by hose lines, and so forth, should be used to afford maximum protection. The plant, public fire department, and other authorities having jurisdiction should be notified of all impairments to fire protection equipment.

A.16.9.3.4 It might be necessary to provide valves located in pits with an indicator post extending above grade or other means so that the valve can be operated without entering the pit.

A.16.9.4 Where check valves are buried, they should be made accessible for maintenance. This can be accomplished by a valve pit or any means that renders the valve accessible. See Figure A.16.9.5.

A.16.9.4.5 Where a system having only one dry pipe valve is supplied with city water and a fire department connection, it will be satisfactory to install the main check valve in the water supply connection immediately inside of the building. In instances where there is no outside control valve, the system indicating valve should be placed at the service flange, on the supply side of all fittings.

A.16.9.5 See Figure A.16.9.5. For additional information on controlling valves, see NFPA 22.

A.16.9.5.5 For additional information on controlling valves, see NFPA 22.

A.16.9.6 Check valves on tank or pump connections, when located underground, can be placed inside of buildings and at a safe distance from the tank riser or pump, except in cases where the building is entirely of one fire area, when it is ordinarily considered satisfactory to locate the check valve overhead in the lowest level.

A.16.9.7.3 Where the relief valve operation would result in water being discharged onto interior walking or working surfaces, consideration should be given to piping the discharge from the valve to a drain connection or other safe location.

N **A.16.9.7.5.2** Hose connections on a standpipe or on a fire pump test header can be utilized for the full flow test.

N **A.16.9.7.5.3** Providing another means is at the discretion of the designer in consultation with the owner or developer. Any number of arrangements would be acceptable as long as the flow through the pressure-reducing valve can be measured to verify it is equal to or greater than the system demand. One example is the use of the fire department connection as long as it will accommodate the required flow and the check valve has a bypass with a shut-off valve provided for this purpose.

A.16.9.8 Outside control valves are suggested in the following order of preference:

(1) Listed indicating valves at each connection into the building at least 40 ft (12 m) from buildings if space permits
(2) Control valves installed in a cutoff stair tower or valve room accessible from outside
(3) Valves located in risers with indicating posts arranged for outside operation
(4) Key-operated valves in each connection into the building

   Post-indicator valves should be located not less than 40 ft (12 m) from buildings. When post-indicator valves cannot be placed at this distance, they are permitted to be located closer, or wall post-indicator valves can be used, provided they are set in locations by blank walls where the possibility of injury by falling walls is unlikely and from which people are not likely to be driven by smoke or heat. Usually, in crowded plant yards, they can be placed beside low buildings, near brick stair towers, or at angles formed by substantial brick walls that are not likely to fall.

A.16.9.9.2 A valve wrench with a long handle should be provided at a convenient location on the premises.

• **A.16.9.11** The intent of 16.9.11 is to provide assistance in determining the area of a building served by a particular control valve.

A.16.9.11.3.1 Care should be taken to ensure that all water supplies are isolated before work begins. Work on systems by shutting one valve and not knowing about another valve could result in unexpected water discharge.

N **A.16.10.1** All piping should be arranged where practicable to drain to the main drain valve.

Δ **A.16.10.4** Figure A.16.10.4(a) is an example of an unacceptable arrangement. Because it will not give a true residual reading, it will indicate an excessive pressure drop. Figure A.16.10.4(b) is an example of an acceptable drain connection for a system riser.

N **A.16.10.4.2** Sizing the main drain connection so that it can flow the sprinkler system demand flow rate provides a practical means for performing the forward flow test of the backflow device as required by 16.14.5.1.

A.16.10.5.2.1 An example of an accessible location would be a valve located approximately 7 ft (2.1 m) above the floor level to

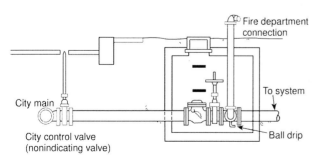

FIGURE A.16.9.5   Pit for Gate Valve, Check Valve, and Fire Department Connection.

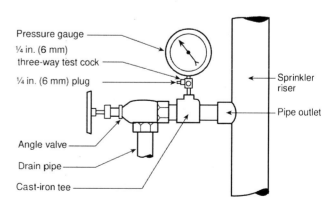

FIGURE A.16.10.4(a)   Unacceptable Pressure Gauge Location.

which a hose could be connected to discharge the water in an acceptable manner.

N **A.16.10.5.3.4** The requirements of 16.10.5.3.4 should not apply since there is no water condensate to collect in the barrel of a dry sprinkler. Moisture inside the pipe will freeze when located in areas that maintain a freezing temperature.

N **A.16.10.6.1** Where possible, the main sprinkler riser drain should discharge outside the building at a point free from the possibility of causing water damage. Where it is not possible to discharge outside the building wall, the drain should be piped to a sump, which in turn should discharge by gravity or be pumped to a wastewater drain or sewer. The main sprinkler riser drain connection should be of a size sufficient to carry off water from the fully open drain valve while it is discharging under normal water system pressures. Where this is not possible, a supplementary drain of equal size should be provided for test purposes with free discharge, located at or above grade.

A.16.11.1.1 Audible alarms are normally located on the outside of the building. Listed electric gongs, bells, horns, or sirens inside the building, or a combination of such used inside and outside, are sometimes advisable.

Outside alarms might not be necessary where the sprinkler system is used as part of a central station, auxiliary, remote station, or proprietary signaling fire alarm system, utilizing listed audible inside alarm devices.

A.16.11.1.2 All alarm apparatus should be so located and installed that all parts are accessible for inspection, removal, and repair, and such apparatus should be substantially supported.

A water motor-operated gong bell mechanism should be protected from weather-related elements such as rain, snow, or ice. To the extent practicable, it should also be protected from other influencing factors such as birds or other small animals that might attempt to nest in such a device.

A.16.11.2 Central station, auxiliary, remote station, or proprietary protective signaling systems are a highly desirable supplement to local alarms, especially from a safety to life standpoint. *(See 16.11.10.)*

Approved identification signs, as shown in Figure A.16.11.2, should be provided for outside alarm devices. The sign should be located near the device in a conspicuous position and should be worded as follows:

SPRINKLER FIRE ALARM — WHEN BELL RINGS

CALL FIRE DEPARTMENT OR POLICE.

A.16.11.3.4 The surge of water that occurs when the valve trips can seriously damage the device. Paddle-type waterflow devices are also permitted to be installed on wet systems that supply auxiliary dry pipe and/or preaction systems.

A.16.11.7 Switches that will silence electric alarm-sounding devices by interruption of electric current are not desirable; however, if such means are provided, then the electric alarm-sounding device circuit should be arranged so that, when the sounding device is electrically silenced, that fact should be indicated by means of a conspicuous light located in the vicinity of the riser or alarm control panel. This light should remain in operation during the entire period of the electric circuit interruption.

A.16.11.8 Water motor-operated devices should be located as near as practicable to the alarm valve, dry pipe valve, or other waterflow detection device. The total length of the pipe to these devices should not exceed 75 ft (23 m), nor should the water motor-operated device be located over 20 ft (6.1 m) above the alarm device or dry pipe valve.

A.16.11.10 Monitoring should include but not be limited to control valves, building temperatures, fire pump power supplies and running conditions, and water tank levels and temperatures. Pressure supervision should also be provided on pressure tanks.

Check valves can be required to prevent false waterflow signals on floors where sprinklers have not activated — for example, floor systems interconnected to two supply risers.

A.16.12 The fire department connection should be located not less than 18 in. (500 mm) and not more than 4 ft (1.2 m) above the level of the adjacent grade or access level. Typical fire department connections are shown in Figure A.16.12. See NFPA 13E.

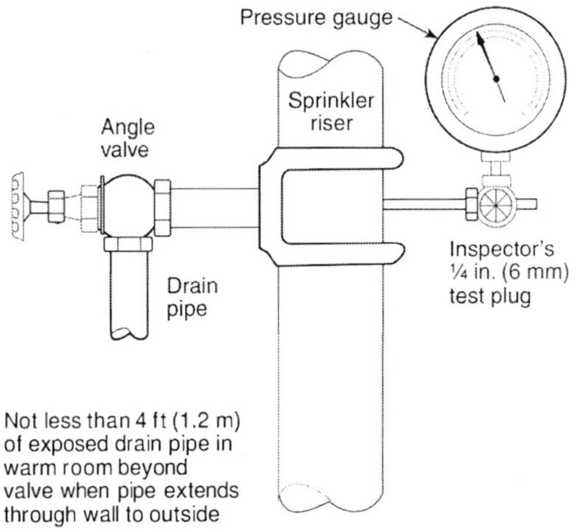

FIGURE A.16.10.4(b)   Drain Connection for System Riser.

FIGURE A.16.11.2   Identification Sign.

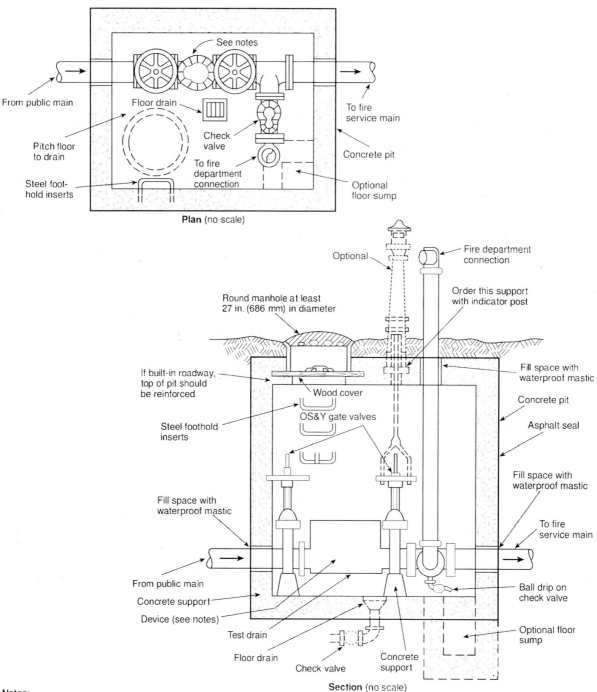

Notes:
1. Various backflow prevention regulations accept different devices at the connection between public water mains and private fire service mains.
2. The device shown in the pit could be any or a combination of the following:
   (a) Gravity check valve
   (b) Detector check valve
   (c) Double check valve assembly
   (d) Reduced pressure zone (RPZ) device
   (e) Vacuum breaker
3. Some backflow prevention regulations prohibit these devices from being installed in a pit.
4. In all cases, the device(s) in the pit should be approved or listed as necessary. The requirements of the local or municipal water department should be reviewed prior to design or installation of the connection.
5. Pressure drop should be considered prior to the installation of any backflow prevention devices.

FIGURE A.16.12   Typical City Water Pit — Valve Arrangement.

A.16.12.1 Fire department connections should be located and arranged so that hose lines can be readily and conveniently attached without interference from nearby objects, including buildings, fences, posts, or other fire department connections. Where a hydrant is not available, other water supply sources such as a natural body of water, a tank, or a reservoir should be utilized. The water authority should be consulted when a nonpotable water supply is proposed as a suction source for the fire department.

A.16.12.3.1 The purpose of the fire department connection is to supplement the water supply but not necessarily provide the entire sprinkler system demand. Fire department connections are not intended to deliver a specific volume of water.

A.16.12.4 The purpose of a fire department connection is to supplement the pressure to an automatic fire sprinkler system. It is not the intent to size the fire department connection piping based on system demand. For multiple system risers supplied by a manifold, the fire department connection need not be larger than that for an individual system.

A.16.12.5 The check valve should be located to maximize accessibility and minimize freezing potential. It is recommended that the check valve be located to reduce the length of nonpressurized pipe in the fire department connection supply line.

A.16.12.5.1 The fire department connection should be connected to the system riser. For single systems, it is an acceptable arrangement to attach the fire department connection to any point in the system, provided the pipe size meets the requirements of 16.12.4.

A.16.12.5.5 Figure A.16.12.5.5(a) and Figure A.16.12.5.5(b) depict fire department connections to the underground pipe.

A.16.12.5.7 Obstructions to fire department connections include but are not limited to buildings, fences, posts, shrubbery, other fire department connections, gas meters, and electrical equipment.

A.16.12.7 In cases where water in the piping between the system side and the fire department connection check valve would be trapped, an auxiliary drain is required.

A.16.14.1 The purpose of this alarm test connection is to make sure the alarm device is sensitive enough to determine the flow from a single sprinkler and sound an alarm. The

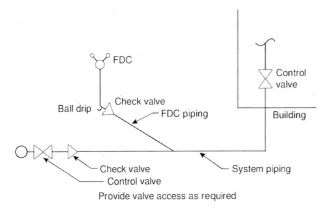

FIGURE A.16.12.5.5(a)   Fire Department Connection to Underground Piping for a Single System.

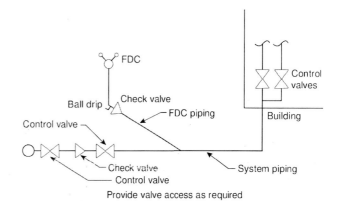

FIGURE A.16.12.5.5(b)   Fire Department Connection to Underground Piping for Multiple Systems.

purpose of this test connection is not to ensure that water will flow through the entire system. When this test connection is installed on the upper story, and at the end of the most remote branch line, the user is able to tell that there is water flowing in one path through the system, but there is no assurance that water will flow to other branch lines. Putting the test connection at the most remote portion of the system causes the introduction of fresh oxygen into a large part of the system each time the alarm is tested and increases the corrosion that will occur in the piping. The discharge should be at a point where it can be readily observed. In locations where it is not practical to terminate the test connection outside the building, the test connection is permitted to terminate into a drain capable of accepting full flow under system pressure. In this event, the test connection should be made using an approved sight test connection containing a smooth bore corrosion-resistant orifice giving a flow equivalent to one sprinkler simulating the least flow from an individual sprinkler in the system. *[See Figure A.16.14.1(a) and Figure A.16.14.1(b).]* The test valve should be located at an accessible point and preferably not over 7 ft (2.1 m) above the floor. The control valve on the test connection should be located at a point not exposed to freezing.

A.16.14.2 See Figure A.16.14.2 and Figure A.8.2.3.7.

A.16.14.5 Where backflow prevention devices are installed, they should be in an accessible location to provide for inspection, testing, service, and maintenance. When a backflow prevention device is retroactively installed on a pipe schedule system, the revised hydraulic calculation still follows the pipe schedule method of 19.3.2 with the inclusion of friction loss for the device.

Δ **A.16.14.5.1** System demand refers to flow rate and pressure. This test is only concerned with testing at the proper flow rate.

N **A.16.14.5.1.2** Hose connections on a standpipe or on a fire pump test header can be utilized for the full flow test.

N **A.16.14.5.1.3** Providing another means is at the discretion of the designer in consultation with the owner or developer. Any number of arrangements would be acceptable as long as the flow through the backflow prevention valve can be measured to verify it is equal to or greater than the system demand. One example is the use of the fire department connection as long as it will accommodate the required flow and the check valve has a bypass with a shut-off valve provided for this purpose.

A.16.15.1.1 One and one-half inch (40 mm) fire hose packs are not required unless designated by the authority having jurisdiction, as it is not likely that such hoses will be adequately maintained for safe use by first responders. Civilian workers who are not properly trained in fire-fighting techniques are expected to evacuate the building in the event of a fire.

A.16.15.1.4 This standard covers 1½ in. (40 mm) hose connections for use in storage occupancies and other locations where standpipe systems are not required. Where Class II standpipe systems are required, see the appropriate provisions of NFPA 14 with respect to hose stations and water supply for hose connections from sprinkler systems.

A.16.15.2.2 See Figure A.16.15.2.2(a), Figure A.16.15.2.2(b), and Figure A.16.15.2.2(c).

A.16.16.2 While the use of the sprinkler system piping as the grounding electrode for the building is prohibited, *NFPA 70* requires that all metallic piping systems be bonded to disperse

stray electrical currents. Therefore, the sprinkler system piping might be bonded to other metallic systems.

A.16.17 Table A.16.17 is a summary of the requirements for signs in NFPA 13.

Δ **A.17.1** Throughout Chapter 17, metric units have been included where practicable. There are subjects, (e.g., section modulus) where a metric conversion might not be useful. In such situations, it is recommended to consult local requirements and products to determine whether support components are adequate for the loads, including appropriate safety factors.

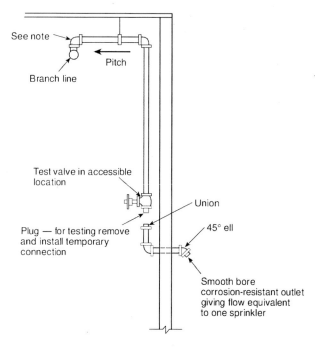

Note: To minimize condensation of water in the drop to the test connection, provide a nipple-up off of the branch line.

FIGURE A.16.14.2 System Test Connection on Dry Pipe System.

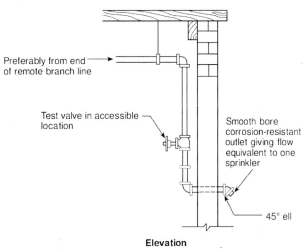

Elevation

Note: Not less than 4 ft (1.2 m) of exposed test pipe in warm room beyond valve where pipe extends through wall to outside.

FIGURE A.16.14.1(a) System Test Connection on Wet Pipe System.

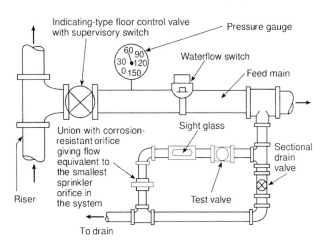

FIGURE A.16.14.1(b) Zone Control Station System Test Connection on Wet Pipe System.

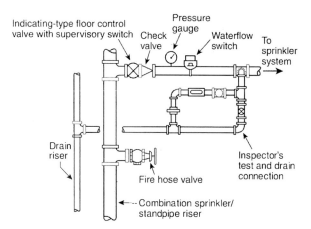

FIGURE A.16.15.2.2(a) Acceptable Piping Arrangement for Combined Sprinkler/Standpipe System. [14:Figure A.6.3.5(a)]

See Figure A.17.1. As an alternative to the conventional method of hanging pipe from the structure using attachments and rod, the piping can be simply laid on the structural member, provided the structure can adequately support the added load in accordance with 17.4.1.3.1 and the maximum distance between supports required by Chapter 17 is not exceeded. Listed pipe should still be installed and supported in accordance with its listing limitations.

To prevent movement, the pipe should be secured with an approved device to the structure and located such that the system piping remains in its original location and position.

A.17.1.3.1 The rules covering the hanging of sprinkler piping take into consideration the weight of water-filled pipe plus a safety factor. No allowance has been made for the hanging of non-system components from sprinkler piping. NFPA 13

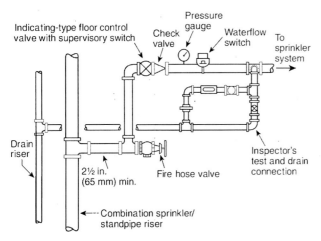

FIGURE A.16.15.2.2(b)   Acceptable Piping Arrangement for Combined Sprinkler/Standpipe System. [14:Figure A.6.3.5(b)]

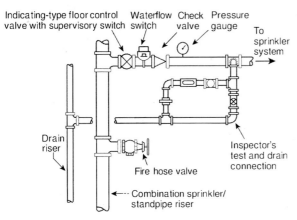

N **FIGURE A.16.15.2.2(c)   Acceptable Piping Arrangement for Combined Sprinkler/Standpipe System.**

provides the option to support sprinkler piping from other sprinkler piping where the requirements of 17.1.2 are met.

A.17.1.4.1 A shared support assembly can be in the form of a pipe rack structure, a trapeze assembly, pipe stand, or other similar assembly. It is not the intent of this section for a building structure to be considered a shared support assembly. Storage racks are not intended to be considered a shared support assembly.

A.17.1.4.1.4 It is not the intent of 17.1.4.1 to apply to flexible sprinkler hose fittings or ceiling systems.

A.17.1.6.1 The listing requirements for water-based fire protection system hanger components include five times the weight of water-filled piping plus 250 lb (115 kg). However, once the listing is achieved, manufacturers often present their data in simple terms of what size pipe can be supported. The published loads in technical data sheets often represent one times the load of the piping that can be supported at maximum hanger spacing. If the product has been listed for use with fire protection systems, it has been shown to accommodate five times the weight of the water-filled pipe plus 250 lb (115 kg).

A.17.1.6.2 Generic items utilized with hanger rods and fasteners are not required to be listed. These include items such as bolts, screws, washers, nuts, and lock nuts.

A.17.1.6.3 Generic items utilized with hanger rods and fasteners are not required to be listed. These include items such as bolts, screws, washers, nuts, and lock nuts.

A.17.2.1.3(1) Hanger rods are intended only to be loaded axially (along the rod). Lateral loads can result in bending, weakening, and even breaking of the rod. Additional hangers or restraints could be necessary to minimize nonaxial loads that could induce bending or deflection of the rods. See Figure A.17.2.1.3(1) for an example of additional hangers utilized to minimize nonaxial loads.

A.17.2.2 In areas that are subject to provisions for earthquake protection, the fasteners in concrete will need to be prequalified. See 18.7.8 for information.

A.17.2.2.9.3 The ability of concrete to hold the studs varies widely according to type of aggregate, quality of concrete, and proper installation.

For existing structures with concrete tested to the appropriate testing standards at the time of construction, the compressive strength of the concrete should be tested and deemed adequate. The structural capacity of existing concrete might not be known. In such cases, such capacity should be confirmed prior to relying on the structure to properly accommodate the intended load of sprinkler system attachments.

A.17.2.3.1 Powder-driven studs should not be used in steel of less than $\frac{3}{16}$ in. (5 mm) total thickness.

Δ **Table A.16.17 Sprinkler System Signage Summary**

Section	Sign Location	Sign Information/Requirements
16.9.11	Control valves Drain valves Test connection valves	Identification sign Sign must be made of weatherproof metal or rigid plastic and attached with corrosion-resistant wire or chain

8.6.1.4 and 8.6.1.5	Antifreeze system main valve	Indicate the following:
		    Antifreeze manufacturer
		    Antifreeze type
		    Antifreeze concentration

16.9.3.5	Control valves	Indicate valve function Indicate system being controlled
16.10.5.3.7	Dry valve Preaction valve	Number of low point drains Location of each drain
16.12.5.6	Fire department connections not serving the whole building	Indicate portion of the building served by the fire department connection
16.12.5.8	All fire department connections	Indicate systems served by the fire department connection Indicate system pressure demand [for systems requiring more than 150 psi (10 bar)] Letters must be 1 in. (25 mm) in height

29.4	Alarm valve
	Dry pipe valve
	Preaction valve
	Deluge valve
		Indicate the following:
		    Location of the design area or areas
		    Size (area) of or number of sprinklers in the design area
		    Discharge densities over the design area or areas
		    Required flow and residual pressure demand at the base of the riser
		    Occupancy classification or commodity classification and maximum permitted storage height and configuration
		    Hose stream allowance
		    The installing contractor
		    Sign must be made of weatherproof metal or rigid plastic and attached with corrosion-resistant wire or chain

29.6	System control riser
	Antifreeze loops
	Auxiliary systems
	Control valves
		Indicate the following:
		    Name and location of the facility protected
		    Occupancy classification
		    Commodity classification
		    Presence of high-piled and/or rack storage
		    Maximum height of storage planned
		    Aisle width planned
		    Encapsulation of pallet loads
		    Presence of solid shelving
		    Flow test data
		    Presence of flammable/combustible liquids
		    Presence of hazardous materials
		    Presence of other special storage
		    Location of venting valve
		    Location of auxiliary drains and low point drains on dry pipe and preaction systems
		    Sign must be made of weatherproof metal or rigid plastic and attached with corrosion-resistant wire or chain

31.2.7.5	Fire department connection (FDC)	18 in. × 18 in. (450 mm × 450 mm) sign FDC symbol from NFPA 170 Located at connection in plain sight from shore access point

A.16.11.2	Central station, auxiliary, remote station, or proprietary protective signaling systems	Recommended:
		    Located near the device
		    Direct people to call police or fire department when bell rings

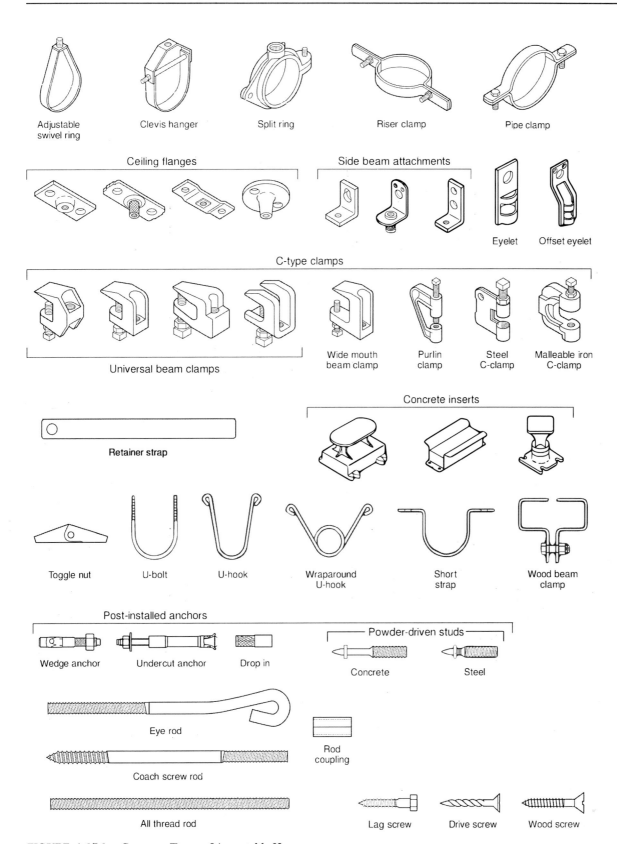

FIGURE A.17.1   Common Types of Acceptable Hangers.

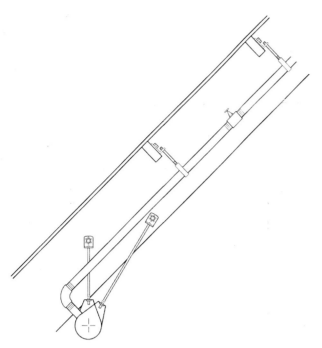

FIGURE A.17.2.1.3(1)   Example of Additional Hangers Utilized to Minimize Nonaxial Loads.

A.17.3 Table 17.3.1(a) assumes that the load from 15 ft (5 m) of water-filled pipe, plus 250 lb (115 kg), is located at the midpoint of the span of the trapeze member, with a maximum allowable bending stress of 15 ksi (103 MPa). If the load is applied at other than the midpoint, for the purpose of sizing the trapeze member, an equivalent length of trapeze can be used, derived from the following formula:

[A.17.3]

$$L = \frac{4ab}{a+b}$$

where:
L = equivalent length
a = distance from one support to the load
b = distance from the other support to the load

Where multiple mains are to be supported or multiple trapeze hangers are provided in parallel, the required or available section modulus can be added. The table values are based on the trapeze being a single continuous member.

A.17.3.5 Hanger components are sized based upon an ultimate strength limit of 5 times the weight of water-filled pipe plus 250 lb (115 kg). The section moduli used to size the trapeze member are based on a maximum bending stress, which provides an acceptable level of safety that is comparable to that of the other hanger components.

A.17.4 To enhance permanence, proper hanger installation is important. Installation procedures should meet industry standards of practice and craftsmanship. For example, hanger assemblies are straight, perpendicular to the pipe, uniformly located, and snug to the structure with fasteners fully engaged.

A.17.4.1.1.1 Fasteners used to support sprinkler system piping should not be attached to ceilings of gypsum or other similar soft material.

A.17.4.1.3 The method used to attach the hanger to the structure and the load placed on the hanger should take into account any limits imposed by the structure. Design manual information for pre-engineered structures or other specialty construction materials should be consulted, if appropriate.

System mains hung to a single beam, truss, or purlin can affect the structural integrity of the building by introducing excessive loads not anticipated in the building design. Also, special conditions such as collateral and concentrated load limits, type or method of attachment to the structural components, or location of attachment to the structural components might need to be observed when hanging system piping in pre-engineered metal buildings or buildings using other specialty structural components such as composite wood joists or combination wood and tubular metal joists.

The building structure is only required to handle the weight of the water-filled pipe and components, while the hangers are required to handle 5 times the weight of the water-filled pipe. In addition, a safety factor load of 250 lb (115 kg) is added in both cases. The difference in requirements has to do with the different ways that loads are calculated and safety factors are applied.

When sprinkler system loads are given to structural engineers for calculation of the structural elements in the building, they apply their own safety factors in order to determine what structural members and hanging locations will be acceptable.

In contrast, when sprinkler system loads are calculated for the hangers themselves, there is no explicit safety factor, so NFPA 13 mandates a safety factor of 5 times the weight of the pipe.

A.17.4.1.3.3 Examples of areas of use include cleanrooms, suspended ceilings, and exhaust ducts.

Δ **A.17.4.1.3.3.3** The committee evaluation of flexible sprinkler hose fittings supported by suspended ceilings was based on information provided to the committee showed that the maximum load shed to the suspended ceiling by the flexible hose fitting was approximately 6 lb (2.7 kg) and that a suspended ceiling meeting ASTM C635/C635M, *Standard Specification for Manufacture, Performance, and Testing of Metal Suspension Systems for Acoustical Tile and Lay-In Panel Ceilings,* and installed in accordance with ASTM C636/C636M, *Standard Practice for Installation of Metal Ceiling Suspension Systems for Acoustical Tile and Lay-In Panels,* can substantially support that load. In addition, the supporting material showed that the flexible hose connection can be attached to the suspended ceilings because it allows the necessary deflections under seismic conditions.

A.17.4.1.3.3.4 An example of language for the label is as follows:

CAUTION: DO NOT REMOVE THIS LABEL.

Relocation of this device should only be performed by qualified and/or licensed individuals that are aware of the original system design criteria, hydraulic criteria, sprinkler listing parameters, and knowledge of the state and local codes including NFPA 13 installation standards. Relocation of the device without this knowledge could adversely affect the performance of this fire protection and life safety system.

A.17.4.1.4.1 Piping in excess of 1 in. (25 mm) shall be permitted to be supported from a metal deck if the method of attachment and ability of the deck to support loads as specified in 17.4.1.3.1 are approved by a registered professional engineer.

A.17.4.2 Where copper tube is to be installed in moist areas or other environments conducive to galvanic corrosion, copper hangers or ferrous hangers with an insulating material should be used.

A.17.4.3.2 The hangers required by Chapter 9 are intended to accommodate general loading such as check valves, control valves, or dry or deluge valves. Where additional equipment such as backflow prevention assemblies and other devices with substantial loads are added, additional hangers should be considered.

A.17.4.3.2.2 See Figure A.17.4.3.2.2.

A.17.4.3.2.4 The "starter length" is the first piece of pipe on a branch line between the main, riser nipple, or drop and the first sprinkler. Starter pieces that are less than 6 ft (1.8 m) in length do not need a hanger of their own because they are supported by the main. However, if the intermediate hanger on the main is omitted, the starter piece needs to have a hanger because the main is going to be supported from the branch lines. The starter lengths can also apply to other piping, such as drains and test connections.

A.17.4.3.2.5 When a branchline contains offsets, sections of pipe are considered adequately supported by the hangers on the adjacent pipe sections when the overall distance between hangers does not exceed the requirements in Table 17.4.2.1(a) and Table 17.4.2.1(b). The cumulative distance includes

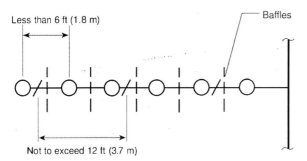

FIGURE A.17.4.3.2.2   **Distance Between Hangers.**

changes in horizontal direction. Multiple consecutive sections of pipe should be permitted to omit hangers.

A.17.4.3.4 Sprinkler piping should be adequately secured to restrict the movement of piping upon sprinkler operation. The reaction forces caused by the flow of water through the sprinkler could result in displacement of the sprinkler, thereby adversely affecting sprinkler discharge. Listed CPVC pipe has specific requirements for piping support to include additional pipe bracing of sprinklers. *(See Figure A.17.4.3.4.)*

A.17.4.3.4.4 See Figure A.17.4.3.4.4(a) and Figure A.17.4.3.4.4(b).

A.17.4.3.5 See Figure A.17.4.3.5.

A.17.4.3.5.2 See Figure A.17.4.3.5.2.

A.17.4.3.6 The movement that is being restrained is to keep the sidewall sprinkler in its intended location during and post-operation. This should not be confused with the loads applicable to seismic restraints.

A.17.4.4.8 When a main contains offsets, sections of pipe are considered adequately supported by the hangers on the adjacent pipe sections when the overall distance between hangers does not exceed the requirements in Table 17.4.2.1(a) and Table 17.4.2.1(b). The cumulative distance includes changes in horizontal direction. Multiple consecutive sections of pipe should be permitted to omit hangers.

A.17.4.5.3 This arrangement is acceptable to establish and secure the riser's lateral position but not to support the riser's vertical load.

A.17.4.5.4.2 The restraint required by 17.4.5.4.2 is needed to prevent accumulated vertical movement when the riser is pressurized. Restraint is generally provided by use of a riser clamp at the underside of a floor slab.

A.17.5 Where applicable, the design of pipe stands should consider additional loading from other sources. Environmental impacts, including water accumulation at the base, corrosion, and wind, should also be taken into account as appropriate.

The performance of piping support systems should allow for expansion and contraction due to temperature change, expansion due to internal water pressure (thrust), restrained and/or unrestrained joints or pipe runs, heavy point loads (e.g., valves), and pipe deflection (span/support spacing). Manufac-

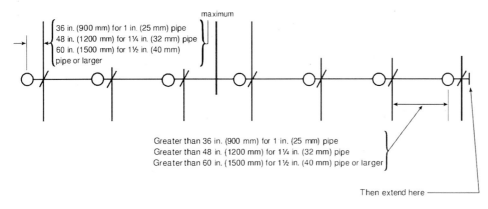

△ FIGURE A.17.4.3.4   **Distance from Sprinkler to Hanger.**

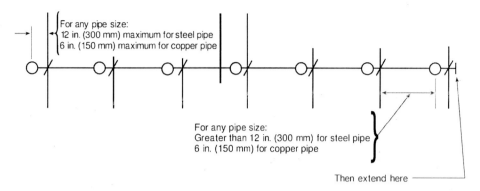

△ FIGURE A.17.4.3.4.4(a) Distance from Sprinkler to Hanger Where Maximum Pressure Exceeds 100 psi (6.9 bar) and Branch Line Above Ceiling Supplies Pendent Sprinklers Below Ceiling.

turer's installation instructions and engineering design guides should be consulted when available.

Examples of common applications include headers and horizontal runs of pipe that need support from the floor.

A.17.5.3.1 When a pipe stand does not resist lateral (e.g., earthquake or wind) forces, its maximum height and the weight of pipe it can support are based primarily on a limiting slenderness ratio (Kl/r), and on the axial and bending stresses caused by the vertical load applied at a specified eccentricity.

The pipe stand heights presented in Table 17.5.3.1(a) and Table 17.5.3.1(b) have been calculated using a "K" of 2.1 (i.e., assuming the pipe stand is an individual cantilever column) and a slenderness ratio limit of 300, except where combined axial and bending stresses caused by the vertical load at an eccentricity of 12 in. (300 mm) controls the design. In these cases, the pipe stand height is reduced such that the allowable axial stress (F_a) is sufficient to limit the combined axial stress ratio (f_a/F_a, i.e., actual axial stress divided by allowable axial stress) plus the bending stress ratio (f_b/F_b, i.e., actual bending stress divided by allowable bending stress) to 1.0. Two cases are considered: a vertical load at a 12 in. (300 mm) eccentricity equals a) 5 times the weight of the water-filled pipe plus 250 lb (115 kg) using a bending stress allowable of 28,000 psi (193 MPa), and b) the weight of the water-filled pipe plus 250 lb (115 kg) using a bending stress allowable of 15,000 psi (103 MPa). No drift limit was imposed.

When an engineering analysis is conducted, different pipe stand heights could be calculated if other assumptions are warranted based on actual conditions. For example, K=1.0 can be used if the pipe at the top of the pipe stand is braced in both horizontal directions, or a shorter cantilever column could be used to limit drift.

Pipe stands are intended to be a single piece of pipe. For lengths that require joining pipes, the pipes should be welded to ensure that strength is maintained. A single threaded fitting at the top of the pipe stand should be allowed for height adjustment in the field. *(See Figure A.17.5.3.1.)*

A.17.5.3.2 These short pipe stands commonly support items such as backflow preventers, header piping, and other appurtenances.

A.17.5.3.2(2) The allowances for these short pipe stands do not account for eccentric loadings. See Figure A.17.5.3.2(2).

A.17.5.4.2 Where welded steel flanges are used for the base plate, the entire circumference of the flange should be welded.

A.17.5.4.3 Examples of acceptable anchors can be listed inserts set in concrete, listed post-installed anchors, bolts for concrete, or cast-in-place J hooks.

A.17.5.5.3 See Figure A.17.5.5.3.

A.17.5.6.1 The support and restraint are needed in order to maintain system performance and integrity. Water surges could be from filling the system, from system operation, or water supply related.

A.17.5.6.2 Traditionally, pipe saddles have been used, which creates a "U" for the pipe to rest in. However, thrust forces in some applications can be large enough to move the pipe off the saddle. Therefore, a pipe ring or clamps should be around the system piping to keep it in place.

△ A.18.1 Sprinkler systems are protected against earthquake damage by means of the following:

(1) Stresses that would develop in the piping due to differential building movement are minimized using flexible joints or clearances.
(2) Bracing is used to keep the piping fairly rigid when supported from a building component expected to move as a unit, such as a ceiling.

Areas known to have earthquake potential have been identified in building codes and insurance maps. Based on the project location, local codes and requirements will be applied. For projects using metric units, it is likely that the enforced codes, standards, and guidelines will vary compared to those used to create the simplified approaches to seismic protection in Chapter 18. These variations could include strength design of components instead of the allowable stress design (ASD) of components, such as concrete anchors, tested by way of methods other than those listed in ACI 355.2, *Qualification of Post-Installed Mechanical Anchors in Concrete and Commentary.* Therefore, metric units have been included where practicable. In such situations, it is recommended to consult local requirements, authorities, and products to determine whether components are adequate for the seismic loads, including appropriate safety factors.

Displacement due to story drift is addressed in Sections 18.2 through 18.4.

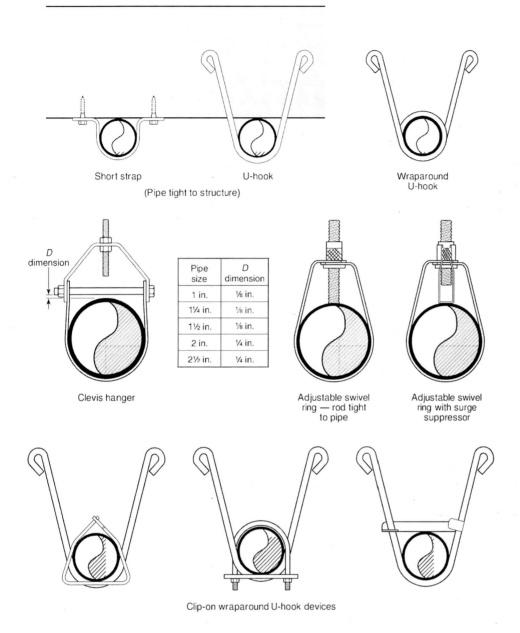

Short strap   U-hook

(Pipe tight to structure)

Wraparound
U-hook

Pipe size	D dimension
1 in.	⅛ in.
1¼ in.	⅛ in.
1½ in.	⅛ in.
2 in.	¼ in.
2½ in.	¼ in.

Clevis hanger

Adjustable swivel
ring — rod tight
to pipe

Adjustable swivel
ring with surge
suppressor

Clip-on wraparound U-hook devices

For SI units, 1 in. = 25.4 mm.

Δ **FIGURE A.17.4.3.4.4(b)**   **Examples of Acceptable Hangers for End-of-Line (or Armover) Pendent Sprinklers.**

Piping in racks needs to be treated like other sprinkler piping and protected in accordance with the proper rules. Piping to which in-rack sprinklers are directly attached should be treated as branch line piping. Piping that connects branch lines in the racks should be treated as mains. The bracing, restraint, flexibility, and requirements for flexible couplings are the same in the rack structures as at the ceiling.

Cloud ceilings can cause challenges for a sprinkler system in an earthquake where sprinklers are installed below the clouds to protect the floor below. Depending on the support structure of the cloud and the construction material of the cloud, differ-

ential movement could damage a sprinkler that is not installed in a fashion to accommodate the movement. Currently, there are no structural requirements in ASCE/SEI 7, *Minimum Design Loads for Buildings and Other Structures,* for the clouds to be seismically braced. Unbraced cloud ceilings in higher seismic areas could easily displace during design earthquakes half the suspension length or more. One solution might be to use flexible sprinkler hose with the bracket connected to the cloud so that the sprinkler will move with the cloud during seismic motion, provided the ceiling system is constructed per ASTM C635/C635M, *Standard Specification for Manufacture, Performance, and Testing of Metal Suspension Systems for Acoustical Tile and Lay-*

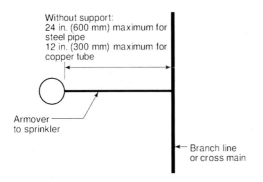

△ FIGURE A.17.4.3.5   Maximum Length for Unsupported Armover.

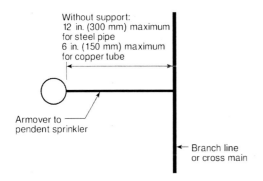

Note: The pendent sprinkler can be installed either directly in the fitting at the end of the armover or in a fitting at the bottom of a drop nipple.

△ FIGURE A.17.4.3.5.2   Maximum Length of Unsupported Armover Where Maximum Pressure Exceeds 100 psi (6.9 bar) and Branch Line Above Ceiling Supplies Pendent Sprinklers Below Ceiling.

In Panel Ceilings, and ASTM C636/C636M, *Standard Practice for Installation of Metal Ceiling Suspension Systems for Acoustical Tile and Lay-In Panels*. When a sprinkler is rigidly piped to the cloud, appropriate flexibility and clearances should be maintained to handle the anticipated movement.

A.18.2 Strains on sprinkler piping can be greatly lessened and, in many cases, damage prevented by increasing the flexibility between major parts of the sprinkler system. One part of the piping should never be held rigidly and another part allowed to move freely without provision for relieving the strain. Flexibility can be provided by using listed flexible couplings, by joining grooved end pipe at critical points, and by allowing clearances at walls and floors.

Tank or pump risers should be treated the same as sprinkler risers for their portion within a building. The discharge pipe of tanks on buildings should have a control valve above the roof line so any pipe break within the building can be controlled.

Piping 2 in. (50 mm) or smaller in size is pliable enough so that flexible couplings are not usually necessary. "Rigid-type" couplings that permit less than 1 degree of angular movement at the grooved connections are not considered to be flexible couplings. *[See Figure A.18.2(a) and Figure A.18.2(b).]*

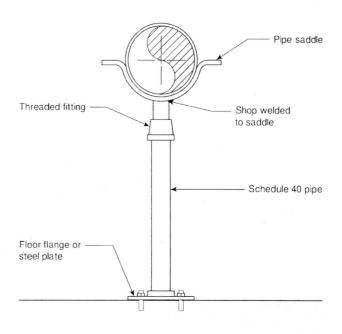

N FIGURE A.17.5.3.1   Pipe Stand.

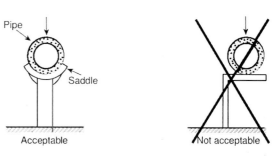

FIGURE A.17.5.3.2(2)   Acceptable Axial Loading and Unacceptable Loading.

A.18.2.3.1(1) Risers do not include riser nipples as defined in 3.3.186.

A.18.2.3.1(2)(a) See Figure A.18.2.3.1(2)(a).

A.18.2.3.1(4) A building expansion joint is usually a bituminous fiber strip used to separate blocks or units of concrete to prevent cracking due to expansion as a result of temperature changes. Where building expansion joints are used, the flexible coupling is required on one side of the joint by 18.2.3.1(4).

For seismic separation joints, considerably more flexibility is needed, particularly for piping above the first floor. Figure A.18.3(a) shows a method of providing additional flexibility through the use of swing joints.

A.18.2.3.2(1) See Figure A.18.2.3.2(1).

A.18.2.3.2(2) The flexible coupling should be at the same elevation as the flexible coupling on the main riser. *[See Figure A.18.2.3.2(2).]*

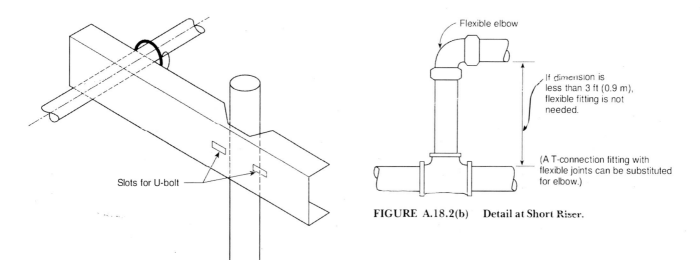

Slots for U-bolt

Flexible elbow

If dimension is less than 3 ft (0.9 m), flexible fitting is not needed.

(A T-connection fitting with flexible joints can be substituted for elbow.)

FIGURE A.18.2(b)   Detail at Short Riser.

FIGURE A.17.5.5.3   Example of a Horizontal Bracket Attached to a Pipe Stand.

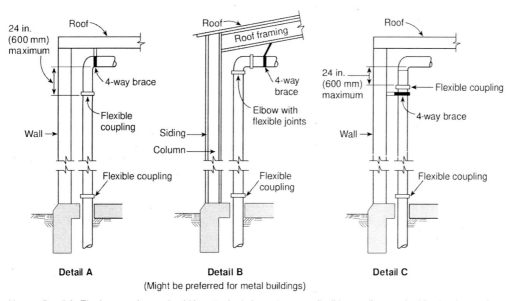

24 in. (600 mm) maximum

Roof

4-way brace

Flexible coupling

Wall

Flexible coupling

Detail A

Roof

Roof framing

4-way brace

Elbow with flexible joints

Siding

Column

Flexible coupling

Detail B

(Might be preferred for metal buildings)

Roof

24 in. (600 mm) maximum

Flexible coupling

4-way brace

Wall

Flexible coupling

Detail C

Note to Detail A: The four-way brace should be attached above the upper flexible coupling required for the riser and preferably to the roof structure if suitable. The brace should not be attached directly to a plywood or metal deck.

Δ **FIGURE A.18.2(a)   Riser Details.**

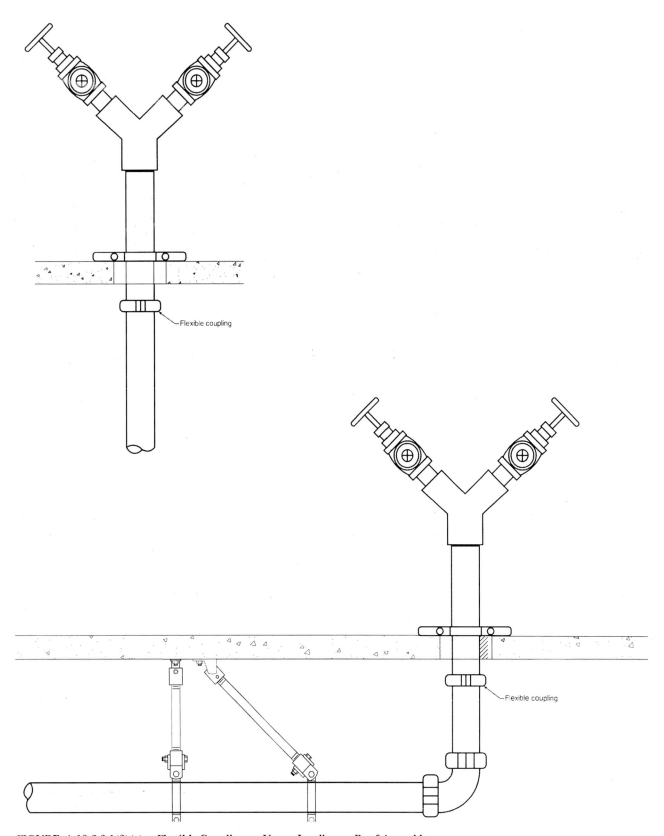

FIGURE A.18.2.3.1(2)(a)   Flexible Coupling on Upper Landing or Roof Assembly.

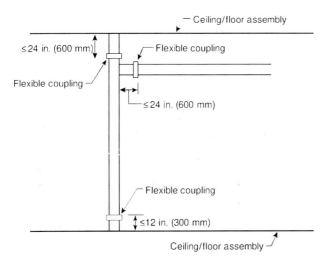

△ FIGURE A.18.2.3.2(1)   Flexible Coupling on Horizontal Portion of Tie-In.

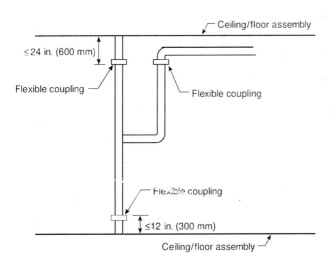

△ FIGURE A.18.2.3.2(2)   Flexible Coupling on Vertical Portion of Tie-In.

A.18.2.4 See Figure A.18.2.4. Drops that extend into free-standing storage racks or other similar structures should be designed to accommodate a horizontal relative displacement between the storage rack and the overhead supply piping. Free standing structures include but are not limited to freezers, coolers, spray booths, and offices.

The horizontal relative displacement should be determined using the least value from one of the following formulas and be taken as the height of the top point of attachment to the storage rack above its base or the highest point of potential contact between the rack structure and the piping above its base, whichever is higher. The design should account for the differential movement value as determined from one of the two formulas, not both, and the lesser of the two values is acceptable. It should be determined how to account for the differential movement using flexible couplings or other approved means.

[A.18.2.4]
$$D = H * 0.06 * S_1 * F_v$$
$$\text{or}$$
$$D = H * 0.05$$

where:
D = differential movement between the rack and the roof [ft (m)]
H = height of the top point of attachment to the rack [ft (m)]
S_1 = one second period spectral acceleration per USGS 2010 Seismic Design Maps (see ASCE/SEI 7)
F_v = one second period site coefficient (Site Class D)

F_v is a function of S_1 and is determined as follows:

S_1	F_v
≤0.1	2.4
=0.2	2.0
=0.3	1.8
=0.4	1.6
≥0.5	1.5

Note: Use straight-line interpolation for intermediate values of S_1.

A.18.3 Plan and elevation views of a seismic separation assembly configured with flexible elbows are shown in Figure A.18.3(a) or Figure A.18.3(b).

The extent of permitted movement should be sufficient to accommodate calculated differential motions during earthquakes. In lieu of calculations, permitted movement can be made at least twice the actual separations, at right angles to the separation as well as parallel to it.

A.18.3.3 Each four-way brace should be attached to the building structure on opposite sides of the seismic separation joint.

A.18.4 While clearances are necessary around the sprinkler piping to prevent breakage due to building movement, suitable provision should also be made to prevent passage of water, smoke, or fire.

Drains, fire department connections, and other auxiliary piping connected to risers should not be cemented into walls or floors; similarly, pipes that pass horizontally through walls or foundations should not be cemented solidly, or strains will accumulate at such points.

Where risers or lengths of pipe extend through suspended ceilings, they should not be fastened to the ceiling framing members.

In areas that use suspended ceilings and are a seismic design category of D, E, or F, a larger clearance could be necessary around the sprinkler unless the suspended ceiling is rigidly braced or flexible sprinkler hose fitting are used as noted in ASTM E580/E580M, *Standard Practice for Installation of Ceiling Suspension Systems for Acoustical Tile and Lay-in Panels in Areas Subject to Earthquake Ground Motions.*

A.18.4.1 Penetrations with or without clearance for seismic protection also need to meet building code requirements for fire resistance ratings as applicable.

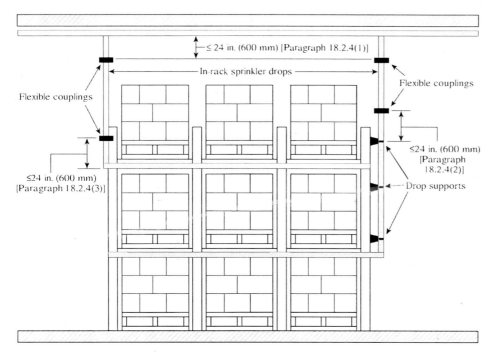

Δ **FIGURE A.18.2.4   Flexible Couplings for Drops.**

A.18.4.10 Figure A.18.4.10 is an example of piping supported by structure where there is no clearance required at the point of contact between the piping and structure.

A.18.4.11 Structural elements include, but are not limited to, beams, girders, and trusses. Frangible ceilings should not be considered structural elements for this purpose.

A.18.5 Figure A.18.5(a) and Figure A.18.5(b) are examples of forms used to aid in the preparation of bracing calculations.

A.18.5.1.3 All horizontal loads given in this document are at allowable stress design levels. When performing a more advanced analysis procedure, as described in 18.1.2, care should be taken to ensure that the correct load factors (strength design or allowable stress design) are used.

A.18.5.1.4 A shared support assembly can be used to provide both support as defined in 17.1.4.1 and provide resistance to seismic forces. When a shared support assembly is used for both support and seismic forces, the shared support assembly should be designed to resist the seismic force for all of the distribution system. The shared support assembly should be designed for a load in which the zone of influence includes the water-filled sprinkler pipe and all other distribution systems attached to the shared support assembly.

A.18.5.1.5 It is the intent of this section to avoid any incompatibility of displacements between the shared support assembly and the sprinkler seismic bracing, as might occur if the supports are located on separate adjacent structures.

A.18.5.2.3 The listed load rating should include a minimum safety factor of 2.2 against the ultimate break strength of the brace components and then be further reduced according to the brace angles.

A.18.5.2.3.1 Depending on the configuration of bracing fittings and connections, it is not always the case that the weakest component of a brace assembly tested at a brace angle of 90 degrees will be the same or will fail in the same way as the weakest component when tested at other brace angles. Therefore, determining an allowable horizontal load using the factors in Table 18.5.2.3 and a listed load rating established solely by testing along the brace assembly at 90 degrees might not be conservative. In most cases, a single listed load rating can be determined by testing the brace assembly at angles of 30, 45, 60, and 90 degrees, reducing the horizontal force at failure found for each of these angles by an appropriate safety factor and then resolving the resulting maximum allowable horizontal loads to a direction along the brace, and finally taking the minimum of these values along the brace assembly as the listed load rating. By taking the minimum value so determined as the listed load rating, allowable horizontal loads determined using Table 18.5.2.3 will be conservative. In some cases, and where justified by engineering judgment, fewer or additional tests might be needed to establish a listed load rating.

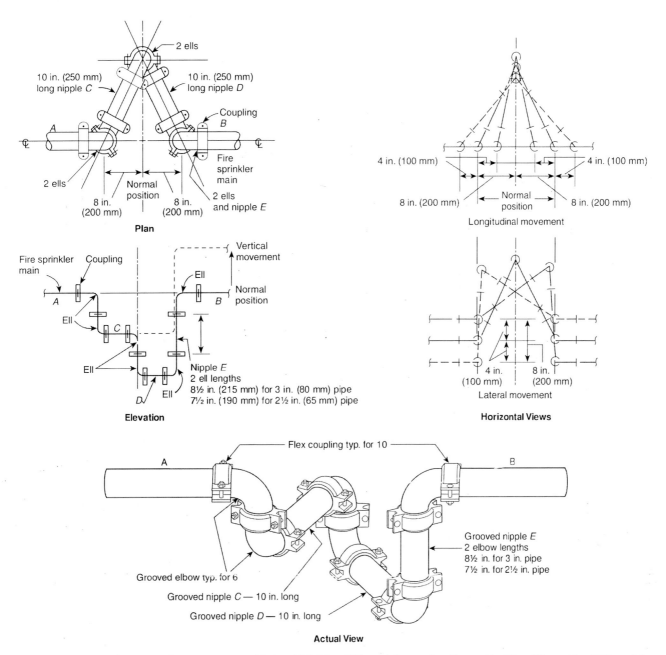

Plan

Elevation

Nipple *E*
2 ell lengths
8½ in. (215 mm) for 3 in. (80 mm) pipe
7½ in. (190 mm) for 2½ in. (65 mm) pipe

Longitudinal movement

Lateral movement

Horizontal Views

Actual View

Flex coupling typ. for 10

Grooved nipple *E*
2 elbow lengths
8½ in. for 3 in. pipe
7½ in. for 2½ in. pipe

Grooved elbow typ. for 6

Grooved nipple *C* — 10 in. long

Grooved nipple *D* — 10 in. long

Δ **FIGURE A.18.3(a)** **Seismic Separation Assembly in which 8 in. (200 mm) Separation Crossed by Pipes Up to 4 in. (100 mm) in Nominal Diameter. (For other separation distances and pipe sizes, lengths and distances should be modified proportionally.)**

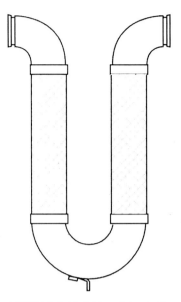

FIGURE A.18.3(b)   Seismic Separation Assembly Incorporating Flexible Piping.

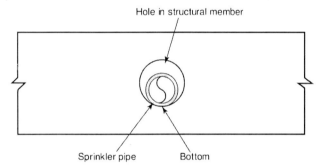

FIGURE A.18.4.10   Pipe with Zero Clearance.

A.18.5.4.2 The investigation of tension-only bracing using materials, connection methods, or both, other than those described in Table 18.5.11.8(a) through Table 18.5.11.8(f), should involve consideration of the following:

(1) Corrosion resistance.
(2) Prestretching to eliminate permanent construction stretch and to obtain a verifiable modulus of elasticity.
(3) Color coding or other verifiable marking of each different size cable for field verification.
(4) The capacity of all components of the brace assemblies, including the field connections, to maintain the manufacturer's minimum certified break strength.
(5) Manufacturer's published design data sheets/manual showing product design guidelines, including connection details, load calculation procedures for sizing of braces, and the maximum recommended horizontal load-carrying capacity of the brace assemblies including the associated fasteners as described in Figure 18.5.12.1. The maximum allowable horizontal loads must not exceed the manufacturer's minimum certified break strength of the

brace assemblies, excluding fasteners, after taking a safety factor of 2.2 and then adjusting for the brace angle.
(6) Bracing product shipments accompanied by the manufacturer's certification of the minimum break strength and prestretching and installation instructions.
(7) The manufacturer's literature, including any special tools or precautions required to ensure proper installation.
(8) A means to prevent vertical motion due to seismic forces when required.

Table A.18.5.4.2 identifies standards for specially listed tension-only bracing systems.

A.18.5.5.1 A brace assembly includes the brace member, the attachment components to pipe and building, and their fasteners. There are primarily two considerations in determining the spacing of lateral earthquake braces in straight runs of pipe: (1) deflection and (2) stress. Both deflection and stress tend to increase with the spacing of the braces. The larger the midspan deflection, the greater the chance of impact with adjacent structural/nonstructural components. The higher the stress in the pipe, the greater the chance of rupture in the pipe or coupling. Braces are spaced to limit the stresses in the pipe and fittings to the levels permitted in modern building codes, with an upper limit of 40 ft (12.2 m). The braces also serve to control deflection of the pipe under earthquake loads. In the longitudinal direction, there is no deflection consideration, but the pipe must transfer the load to the longitudinal braces without inducing large axial stresses in the pipe and the couplings.

A.18.5.5.2 The sway brace spacings in Table 18.5.5.2(a) through Table 18.5.5.2(m) were developed to allow designers to continue to use familiar concepts, such as zone of influence, to lay out and proportion braces while ensuring compatibility with modern seismic requirements. The spacing of braces was determined using the provisions of ASCE/SEI 7, *Minimum Design Loads for Buildings and Other Structures*, assuming steel pipe with threaded or grooved connections for Table 18.5.5.2(a) through Table 18.5.5.2(f). The tabulated values are based on conservative simplifying assumptions. A detailed engineering analysis, taking into account the properties of the specific system, might provide greater spacing. However, in order to control deflections, in no case should the lateral sway brace spacing exceed 40 ft (12.2 m).

A.18.5.5.10 This does not apply to piping supported by or suspended from trapeze hangers.

A.18.5.5.10.1(1) Figure A.18.5.5.10.1(1)(a) and Figure A.18.5.5.10.1(1)(b) are examples of how to measure the distance between the top of pipe and the point of attachment.

A.18.5.5.10.2(1) See Figure A.18.5.5.10.1(1)(a) and Figure A.18.5.5.10.1(1)(b).

A.18.5.7.2 See Figure A.18.5.7.2.

A.18.5.8.1 The four-way brace provided at the riser can also provide longitudinal and lateral bracing for adjacent mains. This section is not intended to require four-way bracing on a sprig or on a drop to a single sprinkler.

A.18.5.8.1.1 See Figure A.18.2.3.1(2)(a).

Seismic Bracing Calculations

Sheet _____ of _____

Project: _____   Contractor: _____

Address: _____   Address: _____

_____   _____

Telephone: _____

Fax: _____

Brace Information	**Seismic Brace Attachments**
Length of brace: _____	Structure attachment fitting or tension-only bracing system:
Diameter of brace: _____	Make: _____ Model: _____
Type of brace: _____	Transition attachment fitting (where applicable):
Angle of brace: _____	Make: _____ Model: _____
Least radius of gyration:* _____	Listed load rating: _____ Adjusted load rating per 18.5.2.3: _____
l/r value:* _____	Sway brace (pipe attachment) fitting:
Maximum horizontal load: _____	Make: _____ Model: _____
	Listed load rating: _____ Adjusted load rating per 18.5.2.3: _____

Fastener Information	**Seismic Brace Assembly Detail** (Provide detail on plans)
Orientation of connecting surface: _____	
Fastener:	
Type: _____	
Diameter: _____	
Length (in wood): _____	
Maximum load: _____	Brace identification no. (to be used on plans) _____

☐ Lateral brace   ☐ Longitudinal brace   ☐ 4-way brace

Sprinkler System Load Calculation ($F_{pw} = C_p W_p$)

$C_p =$ _____

Diameter	Type	Length (ft)	Total (ft)	Weight per ft	Weight
				lb/ft	lb
				lb/ft	lb
				lb/ft	lb
				lb/ft	lb
				lb/ft	lb
				Subtotal weight	lb
				W_p (incl. 15%)	lb
Main Size Type\Sch. Spacing (ft)				Total (F_{pw})	lb
			Maximum F_{pw} per 18.5.5.2 (if applicable)		

* Excludes tension-only bracing systems
© 2021 National Fire Protection Association   NFPA 13

Δ **FIGURE A.18.5(a)   Seismic Bracing Calculation Form.**

Seismic Bracing Calculations

Sheet _____ of _____

Project: Acme Warehouse	Contractor: Smith Sprinkler Company
Address: 321 First Street	Address: 123 Main Street
Any City, Any State	Any City, Any State
	Telephone: (555) 555-1234
	Fax: (555) 555-4321

Brace Information

Length of brace:	3 ft 6 in.
Diameter of brace:	1 in.
Type of brace:	Schedule 40
Angle of brace:	45ϒ to 59ϒ
Least radius of gyration:*	0.421
l/r value:*	100
Maximum horizontal load:	4455 lb

Seismic Brace Attachments

Structure attachment fitting or tension-only bracing system:

Make: Bolt   Model: Bolt

Listed load rating: _ _ _ _ Adjusted load rating per 18.5.2.3: - - -

Transition attachment fitting (where applicable):

Make: Acme   Model: 123

Listed load rating: 1000   Adjusted load rating per 18.5.2.3: 707

Sway brace (pipe attachment) fitting:

Make: Acme   Model: 321

Listed load rating: 1200   Adjusted load rating per 18.5.2.3: 849

Fastener Information

Orientation of connecting surface: "E"

Fastener:

Type:	Through bolt
Diameter:	¾ in.
Length (in wood):	5 ½ in.
Maximum load:	620 lb

Seismic Brace Assembly Detail
(Provide detail on plans)

¾ in. x 6 in. through bolt with nut and washer
Acme 123
½ beam depth minimum
Nominal 6 in. x 12 in. beam
50ϒ
1 in. Schedule 40
Acme 321
4 in. Sch. 10

Brace identification no. (to be used on plans)	SB-1

☒ Lateral brace   ☐ Longitudinal brace   ☐ 4-way brace

Sprinkler System Load Calculation ($F_{pw} = C_p W_p$)

$$C_p = \underline{\quad 0.40 \quad}$$

Diameter	Type	Length (ft)	Total (ft)	Weight per ft		Weight	
1 in.	Sch. 40	15 ft + 25 ft + 8 ft + 22 ft	70 ft	2.05	lb/ft	143.5	lb
1¼ in.	Sch. 40	25 ft + 33 ft + 18 ft	76 ft	2.93	lb/ft	222.7	lb
1½ in.	Sch. 40	8 ft + 8 ft + 10 ft + 10 ft	36 ft	3.61	lb/ft	130.0	lb
2 in.	Sch. 40	20 ft	20 ft	5.13	lb/ft	102.6	lb
4 in.	Sch. 10	20 ft	20 ft	11.78	lb/ft	235.6	lb
				Subtotal weight		834.4	lb
				W_p (incl. 15%)		959.6	lb
Main Size	Type\Sch.	Spacing (ft)		Total (F_{pw})		383.8	lb
4 in.	Sch. 10	20 ft		Maximum F_{pw} per 18.5.5.2 (if applicable)		1634	

* Excludes tension-only bracing systems

© 2021 National Fire Protection Association

NFPA 13

Δ **FIGURE A.18.5(b)**   Sample Seismic Bracing Calculation Form.

Δ **Table A.18.5.4.2 Specially Listed Tension-Only Seismic Bracing**

Materials and Dimensions	Standard (or Document)
Structural application of steel cables	ASCE 19
Wire rope	*Wire Rope Users Manual*
Mechanical strength	ASTM A603
Small diameter steel cable for bracing	ASTM A1023/A1023M
Breaking strength failure test	ASTM E8/E8M

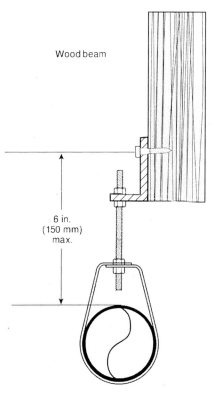

Δ **FIGURE A.18.5.5.10.1(1)(b) Measurement for Distance Between Top of Pipe and Point of Attachment (Example 2).**

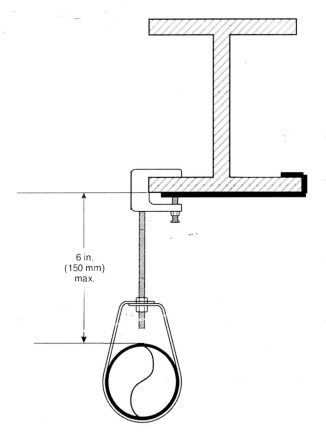

Δ **FIGURE A.18.5.5.10.1(1)(a) Measurement for Distance Between Top of Pipe and Point of Attachment (Example 1).**

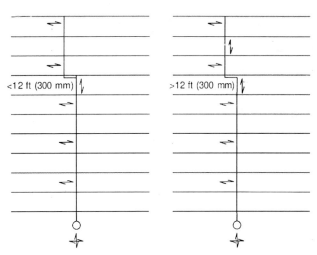

Δ **FIGURE A.18.5.7.2 Examples of Brace Locations for Change in Direction of Pipe.**

A.18.5.9 *Location of Sway Bracing.* Two-way braces are either longitudinal or lateral, depending on their orientation with the axis of the piping. *[See Figure A.18.5.9(a), Figure A.18.5.9(b), Figure A.18.5.9(c), and Figure A.18.5.9(d).]* The simplest form of two-way brace is a piece of steel pipe or angle. Because the brace must act in both compression and tension, it is necessary to size the brace to prevent buckling.

An important aspect of sway bracing is its location. In Building 1 of Figure A.18.5.9(a), the relatively heavy main will pull on the branch lines when shaking occurs. If the branch lines are held rigidly to the roof or floor above, the fittings can fracture due to the induced stresses. In selecting brace locations, one must consider both the design load on the brace, as well as the ability of the pipe to span between brace locations.

Bracing should be on the main as indicated at Location B of Figure A.18.5.9(a). With shaking in the direction of the arrows, the light branch lines will be held at the fittings. Where necessary, a lateral brace or other restraint should be installed to prevent a branch line from striking against building components or equipment.

A four-way brace is indicated at Location A of Figure A.18.5.9(a). This keeps the riser and main lined up and also prevents the main from shifting.

In Building 1 of Figure A.18.5.9(a), the branch lines are flexible in a direction parallel to the main, regardless of building movement. The heavy main cannot shift under the roof or floor, and it also steadies the branch lines. While the main is braced, the flexible couplings on the riser allow the sprinkler system to move with the floor or roof above, relative to the floor below.

Figure A.18.5.9(b), Figure A.18.5.9(c), and Figure A.18.5.9(d) show typical locations of sway bracing.

For all threaded connections, sight holes or other means should be provided to permit indication that sufficient thread is engaged.

To properly size and space braces, it is necessary to employ the following steps:

(1) Determine the seismic coefficient, C_p, using the procedures in 18.5.9.3 or 18.5.9.4. This is needed by the designer to verify that the piping can span between brace points. For the purposes of this example, assume that $C_p = 0.5$.

(2) Based on the distance of system piping from the structural members that will support the braces, choose brace shapes and sizes from Table 18.5.11.8(a) through Table 18.5.11.8(f) such that the maximum slenderness ratios, l/r, do not exceed 300. The angle of the braces from the vertical should be at least 30 degrees and preferably 45 degrees or more.

(3) Tentatively space lateral braces at 40 ft (12 m) maximum distances along system piping, and tentatively space longitudinal braces at 80 ft (24 m) maximum distances along system piping. Lateral braces should meet the piping at right angles, and longitudinal braces should be aligned with the piping.

(4) Determine the total load tentatively applied to each brace in accordance with the examples shown in Figure A.18.5.9(e) and the following:

  (a) For the loads on lateral braces on cross mains, add C_p times the weight of the branch line to C_p times the weight of the portion of the cross main within the zone of influence of the brace. *[See examples 1, 3, 6, and 7 in Figure A.18.5.9(e).]*

  (b) For the loads on longitudinal braces on cross mains, consider only C_p times the weight of the cross mains and feed mains within the zone of influence. Branch lines need not be included. *[See examples 2, 4, 5, 7, and 8 in Figure A.18.5.9(e).]*

  (c) For the four-way brace at the riser, add the longitudinal and lateral loads within the zone of influence of the brace *[see examples 2, 3, and 5 in Figure A.18.5.9(e)]*. For the four-way bracing at the top of the riser, C_p times the weight of the riser should be assigned to both the lateral and longitudinal loads as they are separately considered.

  (d) When a single brace has a combined load from both lateral and longitudinal forces (such as a lateral brace at the end of a main that turns 90 degrees), only the lateral should be considered for comparison with the load tables in 18.5.5.2.

(5) If the total expected loads are less than the maximums permitted in Table 18.5.11.8(a) through Table 18.5.11.8(f) for the particular brace and orientation, and the maximum loads in the zone of influence of each lateral sway brace are less than the maximum values in Table 18.5.5.2(a) or Table 18.5.5.2(c), go on to A.18.5.9(6). If not, add additional braces to reduce the zones of influence of overloaded braces.

(6) Check that fasteners connecting the braces to structural supporting members are adequate to support the expected loads on the braces in accordance with Figure 18.5.12.1. If not, again add additional braces or additional means of support. Plates using multiple fasteners in seismic assemblies should follow the plate manufacturer guidelines regarding the applied loads.

Use the information on weights of water-filled piping contained within Table A.18.5.9. The factor of 1.15 is intended to approximate the additional weight of all the valves, fittings, and other devices attached to the system.

A.18.5.9.1 The factors used in the computation of the horizontal seismic load should be available from several sources, including the project architect or structural engineer or the authority having jurisdiction. In addition, the ground motion parameter S_s is available using maps or software developed by the U.S. Geological Survey. The approach presented in NFPA 13 is compatible with the requirements of ASCE/SEI 7, *Minimum Design Loads for Buildings and Other Structures*, which provides the seismic requirements for model building codes. Sprinkler systems are emergency systems and as such should be designed for an importance factor (I_p) of 1.5. Seismic load equations allow the reduction of the seismic force by a component response modification factor (R_p) that reflects the ductility of the system; systems where braced piping is primarily joined by threaded fittings should be considered less ductile than systems where braced piping is joined by welded or mechanical-type fittings. In addition, a factor, a_p, is used to account for dynamic amplification of nonstructural systems supported by structures. Currently, steel piping systems typically used for fire sprinklers are assigned an R_p factor of 4.5 and an a_p factor of 2.5.

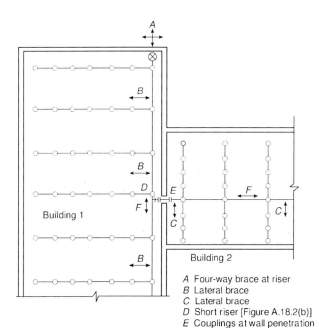

A Four-way brace at riser
B Lateral brace
C Lateral brace
D Short riser [Figure A.18.2(b)]
E Couplings at wall penetration
F Longitudinal brace

Δ FIGURE A.18.5.9(a) Typical Earthquake Protection for Sprinkler Main Piping.

Table A.18.5.9 Piping Weights for Determining Horizontal Load

Nominal Dimensions		Weight of Water-Filled Pipe	
in.	mm	lb/ft	kg/m
Schedule 40 Pipe			
1	25	2.05	3.05
1¼	32	2.93	4.36
1½	40	3.61	5.37
2	50	5.13	7.63
2½	65	7.89	11.74
3	80	10.82	16.10
3½	90	13.48	20.06
4	100	16.40	24.40
5	125	23.47	34.92
6	150	31.69	47.15
8*	200	47.70	70.98
Schedule 10 Pipe			
1	25	1.81	2.69
1¼	32	2.52	3.75
1½	40	3.04	4.52
2	50	4.22	6.28
2½	65	5.89	8.76
3	80	7.94	11.81
3½	90	9.78	14.55
4	100	11.78	17.53
5	125	17.30	25.74
6	150	23.03	34.27
8	200	40.08	59.64

*Schedule 30.

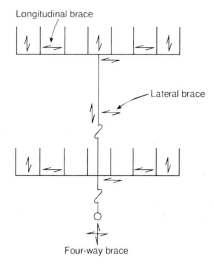

FIGURE A.18.5.9(b) Typical Location of Bracing on Mains on Tree System.

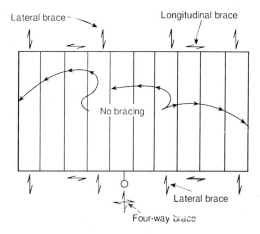

FIGURE A.18.5.9(c) Typical Location of Bracing on Mains on Gridded System.

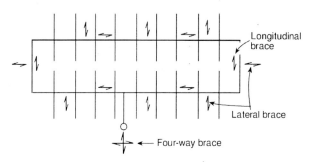

FIGURE A.18.5.9(d) Typical Location of Bracing on Mains on Looped System.

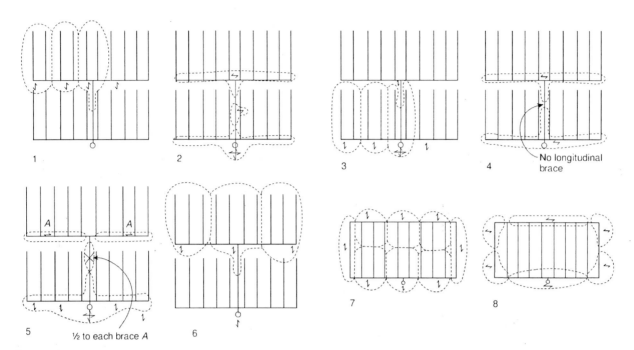

FIGURE A.18.5.9(e)　Examples of Load Distribution to Bracing.

N **A.18.5.9.3.2.1** The authority having jurisdiction for the site class determination of the building can be someone other than the authority having jurisdiction for the sprinkler system.

N **A.18.5.9.3.2.2** When a structure is built on a site class E or F, the building design might incorporate features apart from the assumptions used in this standard for how a building will move when subjected to seismic forces. In these situations, the approaches used to protect mechanical systems should be confirmed.

A.18.5.9.3.3 As linear interpolation of Table 18.5.9.3 is permitted, the following equation can be used to achieve the interpolated values:

$$\text{[A.18.5.9.3.3]}$$

$$C_p = C_{p-\text{low}} + \frac{C_{p-\text{high}} - C_{p-\text{low}}}{S_{s-\text{high}} - S_{s-\text{low}}}\left(S_s - S_{s-\text{low}}\right)$$

where:
　　C_p = seismic coefficient value being sought
　　$C_{p\text{-low}}$ = next lower seismic coefficient value from Table 18.5.9.3
　　$C_{p\text{-high}}$ = next higher seismic coefficient value from Table 18.5.9.3
　　S_s = spectral response as defined in 3.3.207
　　$S_{s\text{-low}}$ = next lower S_s value from Table 18.5.9.3
　　$S_{s\text{-high}}$ = next higher S_s value from Table 18.5.9.3

N **A.18.5.9.3.4** See Figure A.18.5.9.3.4.

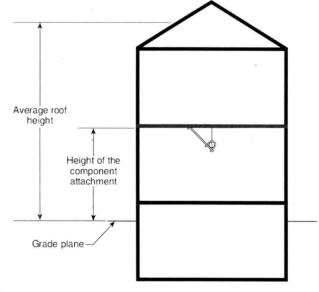

N **FIGURE A.18.5.9.3.4　Typical Example of the Component Attachment to the Structure Relative to the Average Roof Height and Ceiling Height.**

Δ **Table A.18.5.9.6.1 Required Yield Strength Calculation Based on Riser Nipple Length on C_p**

Riser Nipple Length	Seismic Coefficient			
	$C_p \le 0.50$	$C_p \le 0.67$	$C_p < 1.0$	$C_p > 1.0$
>4 ft (>1.2 m)	X	X	X	X
≤4 ft (≤1.2 m)		X	X	X
≤3 ft (≤915 mm)			X	X
≤2 ft (≤610 mm)				X

Note: Conditions marked X are required to satisfy the equation provided in 18.5.9.6.2.

A.18.5.9.4 NFPA 13 has traditionally used the allowable stress design (ASD) method for calculations. The building codes typically use an ultimate strength design. The 0.7 referred to in this section is a conversion value to accommodate the different calculation methods. (*See also Annex E.*)

A.18.5.9.5 S_s is a measure of earthquake shaking intensity. S_s shall be taken as the maximum considered earthquake ground motion for 0.2-second spectral response acceleration (5 percent of critical damping), Site Class B. The data are available from the authority having jurisdiction or, in the United States, from maps developed by the U.S. Geological Survey. All that is required to get S_s is the latitude and longitude of the project site.

The horizontal force factor was given as F_p in earlier editions of NFPA 13. It has been changed to F_{pw} to clearly indicate that it is a working, not an ultimate, load. In model building codes, F_p is used to denote the strength design level load.

It is not the intent of this section to default to the C_p value of 0.5 before attempts to determine the value of S_s and related coefficient value for C_p are made, such as on-line information provided by the U.S. Geological Survey website.

A.18.5.9.6 The zones of influence do not have to be symmetrically based on brace spacing. It is the intent of NFPA 13 that the chosen zone of influence be the worst-case load scenario.

Δ **A.18.5.9.6.1** Where the C_p is 1.0 or greater, the calculation should be done for any riser nipple length. The loads in this condition can rapidly exceed the yield strength. Where Schedule 10 and Schedule 40 steel pipe are used, the section modulus can be found in Table 17.3.1(c) or Table 17.3.1(d). Table A.18.5.9.6.1 illustrates when the required yield strength calculation based on riser nipple length is necessary.

A.18.5.11 Sway brace members should be continuous. Where necessary, splices in sway bracing members should be designed and constructed to ensure that brace integrity is maintained.

A.18.5.11.1 Sway brace design and installation is critical to performance and requires attention to detail. Sway brace design parameters are dynamic and interdependent. Accordingly, seismic force is influenced by geography, brace location is impacted by system design, and brace geometry is relative to the building structure.

To enhance system durability and performance, sway brace installation should show evidence of good craftsmanship in conformance to approved drawings, correctly assembled and mounted at proper angles on a plane that corresponds to the parallel and perpendicular axis of the system pipe.

A.18.5.11.9 Maximum allowable horizontal loads for steel sway braces shown in Table 18.5.11.8(a) through Table 18.5.11.8(f) are applicable when the system is designed using allowable stress design methods. The maximum allowable loads have been derived for the controlling condition (braces in compression) using allowable stress design provisions of American Institute of Steel Construction (AISC) 360, *Specification for Structural Steel Buildings*.

In determining allowable horizontal loads in the tables, a modulus of elasticity (*E*) of 29,000 ksi, a yield stress (*F_y*) of 36 ksi, and an effective length factor (*K*) of 1.0 were assumed, since these are common. If these values are different in a specific situation, table values might need to be adjusted. Gross section properties are used for all shapes except for all-thread rods. For all-thread rods, area and radius of gyration are based on the minimum area of the threaded rod based on the radius at the root of the threads.

Δ **A.18.5.12** Concrete anchors can be cast-in-place [installed before the concrete is placed — see Figure A.18.5.12(a) and Figure A.18.5.12(b)] or post-installed [installed in hardened concrete — see Figure A.18.5.12(c)]. Examples of cast-in-place concrete anchors are embedded steel bolts or concrete inserts. There are several types of post-installed anchors, including expansion anchors, chemical or adhesive anchors, and undercut anchors. The criteria in Table 18.5.12.2(a) through Table 18.5.12.2(j) are based on the use of listed cast-in-place concrete inserts and listed post-installed wedge expansion anchors. The values for "effective embedment" for cast-in-place anchors and "nominal embedment" for post-installed anchors as shown in the tables represent the majority of commonly available anchors on the market at the time of publishing. Use of other anchors in concrete should be in accordance with the listing provisions of the anchor. Anchorage designs are usable under allowable stress design (ASD) methods.

Values in Table 18.5.12.2(a) through Table 18.5.12.2(j) are based on ultimate strength design values obtained using the procedures in Chapter 17 of ACI 318, *Building Code Requirements for Structural Concrete and Commentary*, which are then adjusted for ASD. Concrete inserts are installed into wood forms for concrete members using fasteners prior to the casting of concrete, inserted into wood forms for concrete members using fasteners prior to the casting of concrete, or inserted into a hole cut in steel deck that will be filled with concrete topping slab. A bolt or rod can be installed into the internally threaded concrete insert after the wood form is removed from the concrete or from the underside of the steel deck after it is filled with concrete topping slab. Wedge anchors are torque-controlled expansion anchors that are set by applying a torque

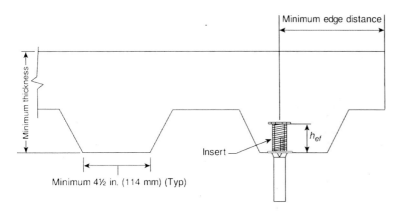

Note: h_{ef} is the effective embedment depth per Table 18.5.12.2(f).

Δ **FIGURE A.18.5.12(a)   Metal Deck Insert.**

to the anchor's nut, which causes the anchor to rise while the wedge stays in place. This causes the wedge to be pulled onto a coned section of the anchor and presses the wedge against the wall of the hole. Undercut anchors might or might not be torque-controlled. Typically, the main hole is drilled, a special second drill bit is inserted into the hole, and flare is drilled at the base of the main hole. Some anchors are self-drilling and do not require a second drill bit. The anchor is then inserted into the hole and, when torque is applied, the bottom of the anchor flares out into the flared hole and a mechanical lock is obtained. Consideration should be given with respect to the position near the edge of a slab and the spacing of anchors. For full capacity in Table 18.5.12.2(a) through Table 18.5.12.2(j), the edge distance spacing between anchors and the thickness of concrete should conform to the anchor manufacturer's recommendations.

Calculation of ASD shear and tension values to be used in A.18.5.12.2 calculations should be performed in accordance with formulas in Chapter 17 of ACI 318 using the variables and recommendations obtained from the approved evaluation service reports (such as ICC-ES reports) for a particular anchor, which should then be adjusted to ASD values. All post-installed concrete anchors must be prequalified in accordance with ACI 355.2, *Qualification of Post-Installed Mechanical Anchors in Concrete and Commentary*, or other approved qualification procedures (Section 13.4.2.3 of ASCE/SEI 7, *Minimum Design Loads for Buildings and Other Structures*). This information is usually available from the anchor manufacturer.

The following variables are among those contained in the approved evaluation reports for use in calculations according to Chapter 17 of ACI 318. These variables do not include the allowable tension and shear capacities but do provide the information needed to calculate them. The strength design capacities must be calculated using the appropriate procedures in Chapter 17 of ACI 318 and then converted to allowable stress design capacities.

D_a = anchor diameter

L_{anch} = total anchor length

h_{nom} = nominal embedment

h_{ef} = effective embedment

h_{min} = minimum concrete thickness

C_{ac} = critical edge distance

N_{sa} = steel strength in tension

l_e = length of anchor in shear

$N_{p,cr}$ = pull-out strength cracked concrete

K_{cp} = coefficient for pryout strength

$V_{sa,eq}$ = shear strength single anchor seismic loads

$V_{sl,deck,eq}$ = shear strength single anchor seismic loads installed through the soffit of the metal deck

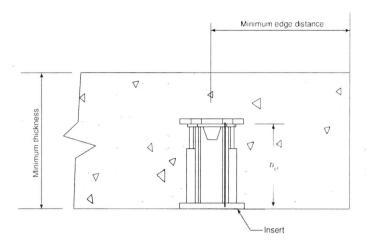

Note: h_{ef} is the effective embedment depth given in Tables 18.5.12.2(g) through (j)

Δ FIGURE A.18.5.12(b)   Wood Form Insert.

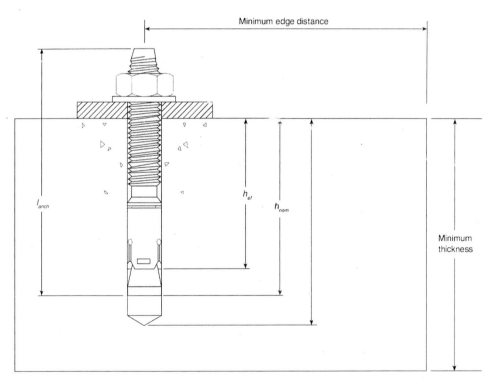

Note: h_{nom} is the nominal embedment depth given in Tables 18.5.12.2(a) through (e).

FIGURE A.18.5.12(c)   Wedge Anchor.

A.18.5.12.2 The values for the concrete insert and wedge anchor tables have been developed using the following formula:

[A.18.5.12.2a]

$$\left(\frac{T}{T_{allow}}\right)+\left(\frac{V}{V_{allow}}\right)\leq 1.2$$

where:

T = applied service tension load, including the effect of prying ($F_{pw}\times Pr$)

F_{pw} = horizontal earthquake load

Pr = prying factor based on fitting geometry and brace angle from vertical

T_{allow} = allowable service tension load

V = applied service shear load

V_{allow} = allowable service shear load

T/T_{allow} = shall not be greater than 1.0.

V/V_{allow} = shall not be greater than 1.0.

The allowable tension and shear loads come from the anchor manufacturer's published data. The design loads have been amplified by an overstrength factor of 2.0, and the allowable strength of the anchors has been increased by a factor of 1.2. The effect of prying on the tension applied to the anchor is considered when developing appropriate capacity values. The applied tension equation includes the prying effect, which varies with the orientation of the fastener in relationship to the brace necessary at various brace angles. The letters A through D in the following equations are dimensions of the attachment geometry as indicated in Figure A.18.5.12.2(a) through Figure A.18.5.12.2(c).

where:

Cr = critical angle at which prying flips to the toe or the heel of the structure attachment fitting

Pr = prying factor for service tension load effect of prying

$Tan\theta$ = tangent of brace angle from vertical

$Sin\theta$ = sine of brace angle from vertical

The greater Pr value calculated in tension or compression applies.

The Pr value cannot be less than $1.000/Tan\theta$ for designated angle category A, B, and C; 1.000 for designated angle category D, E, and F; or 0.000 for designated angle category G, H, and I.

For designated angle category A, B, and C, the applied tension, including the effect of prying (Pr), is as follows:

[A.18.5.12.2b]

$$Cr = Tan^{-1}\left(\frac{C}{D}\right)$$

For braces acting in **TENSION**

If Cr > brace angle from vertical:

[A.18.5.12.2c]

$$Pr = \frac{\left(\frac{C+A}{Tan\theta}\right)-D}{A}$$

If Cr < brace angle from vertical:

[A.18.5.12.2d]

$$Pr = \frac{D-\left(\frac{C-B}{Tan\theta}\right)}{B}$$

For braces acting in **COMPRESSION**

If Cr > brace angle from vertical:

[A.18.5.12.2e]

$$Pr = \frac{\left(\frac{C-B}{Tan\theta}\right)-D}{B}$$

If Cr < brace angle from vertical:

[A.18.5.12.2f]

$$Pr = \frac{D-\left(\frac{C+A}{Tan\theta}\right)}{A}$$

For designated angle category D, E, and F, the applied tension, including the effect of prying (Pr), is as follows:

[A.18.5.12.2g]

$$Cr = Tan^{-1}\left(\frac{D}{C}\right)$$

For braces acting in **TENSION**

If Cr > brace angle from vertical:

[A.18.5.12.2h]

$$Pr = \frac{\left(\frac{D}{Tan\theta}\right)-(C-B)}{B}$$

If Cr < brace angle from vertical:

[A.18.5.12.2i]

$$Pr = \frac{(C+A)-\left(\frac{D}{Tan\theta}\right)}{A}$$

For braces acting in **COMPRESSION**

If $Cr >$ brace angle from vertical:

[A.18.5.12.2j]

$$Pr = \frac{\left(\dfrac{D}{Tan\theta}\right) - (C + A)}{A}$$

If $Cr <$ brace angle from vertical:

[A.18.5.12.2k]

$$Pr = \frac{(C - B) - \left(\dfrac{D}{Tan\theta}\right)}{B}$$

For designated angle category G, H, and I the applied tension, including the effect of prying (Pr), is as follows:

For braces acting in **TENSION**

[A.18.5.12.2l]

$$Pr = \frac{\left(\dfrac{D}{B}\right)}{Sin\theta}$$

For braces acting in **COMPRESSION**

[A.18.5.12.2m]

$$Pr = \frac{\left(\dfrac{D}{A}\right)}{Sin\theta}$$

The lightweight concrete anchor tables, Table 18.5.12.2(a) through Table 18.5.12.2(c) were based on sand lightweight concrete, which represents a conservative assumption for the strength of the material. For seismic applications, cracked concrete was assumed.

A.18.5.12.3 Listed devices might have accompanying software that performs the calculations to determine the allowable load.

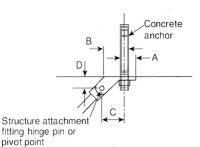

FIGURE A.18.5.12.2(a)   Dimensions of Concrete Anchor for Orientations A, B, and C.

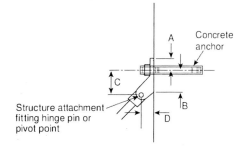

FIGURE A.18.5.12.2(b)   Dimensions of Concrete Anchor for Orientations D, E, and F.

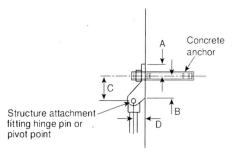

FIGURE A.18.5.12.2(c)   Dimensions of Concrete Anchor for Orientations G, H, and I.

A.18.5.12.4 Through-bolt as described in 18.5.12.4 is intended to describe a method of bolting and attachment. It is the intent of the committee that a "through-bolt" could consist of threaded rod with a flat washer and nut on each end.

N A.18.5.12.7 The requirements for concrete anchor and concrete insert capacities in 18.5.12.7.1 through 18.5.12.7.5 are based on calculations performed in accordance with ACI 318, *Building Code Requirements for Structural Concrete and Commentary*, adjusted for allowable stress design (ASD), and using imperial units for anchors and inserts that have been seismically prequalified in accordance with ACI 355.2, *Qualification of Post-Installed Mechanical Anchors in Concrete and Commentary*. In jurisdictions that are working in metric units, it is likely that ASD is not the standardized method of calculation for these components. For example, in some areas of the world, it is commonly required that concrete anchor and insert calculations are determined in accordance with the procedures for load and resistance factor design (LRFD), and metric-sized anchors and inserts complying with standards other than those cited within this standard are used. In those instances, the calculation procedures, along with the required concrete anchors and inserts acceptable to the authority having jurisdiction, should be used.

A.18.5.12.7.1 Concrete anchors included in current evaluation service reports conforming to the requirements of acceptance criteria AC193 as issued by ICC Evaluation Service, Inc. should be considered to meet ACI 355.2, *Qualification of Post-Installed Mechanical Anchors in Concrete and Commentary*.

Δ A.18.5.12.7.3.4 The values from Chapter 17 of ACI 318, *Building Code Requirements for Structural Concrete and Commentary*, are load and resistance factor design (LRFD) values that must be divided by 1.4 in order to convert them to allowable stress design (ASD) values. The factor of 0.43 was created to simplify the steps needed to account for the strength capacities and the ASD method of calculation. The 0.43 is a rounded value determined by 1.2 (allowable stress increase), divided by the quantity of 2.0 multiplied by 1.4 [i.e., $0.4286 = 1.2/(2.0 \times 1.4)$].

A.18.6.1 Wires used for piping restraints should be attached to the branch line with two tight turns around the pipe and fastened with four tight turns within 1½ in. (38 mm) and should be attached to the structure in accordance with the details shown in Figure A.18.6.1(a) through Figure A.18.6.1(d) or other approved method.

A.18.6.1(5) See Figure A.18.6.1(5)(a) and Figure A.18.6.1(5)(b). When hangers are installed on both sides of the pipe, the l/r is not restricted.

A.18.6.4 Modern seismic codes require branch lines to be restrained, both to limit interaction of the pipe with other portions of the structure and to limit stresses in the pipes to permissible limits. The maximum spacing between restraints is dependent on the seismic coefficient, C_p, as shown in Table 18.6.4(a). Table 18.6.4(a) has been limited to 2 in. (50 mm) lines and smaller, because branch lines 2½ in. (65 mm) or larger are required to be seismically braced.

It is not the intent of this section to require restraint of piping associated with valve trim, water motor gong piping, air or nitrogen supply piping, or other piping that is not essential to the operation of the sprinkler system. Essential piping such as fire pump sensing lines and diesel fuel lines are some examples of small piping that should be restrained.

A.18.6.6 Such restraint can be provided by using the restraining wire discussed in 18.6.1. For the purposes of determining the need for restraint, the length of the sprig is determined by measuring the length of the exposed pipe and does not include the fittings and sprinkler.

A.18.7.8 Concrete anchors included in current Evaluation Service Reports conforming to the requirements of acceptance criteria AC193 or AC308 as issued by ICC Evaluation Service,

Inc. should be considered to meet ACI 355.2, *Qualification of Post-Installed Mechanical Anchors in Concrete and Commentary*.

A.18.8 When using a pipestand to support the gravity load of a water-based fire protection system in an earthquake area, care should be taken in planning the seismic protection. This includes close attention to the differential movement between the system and the building or other components.

N **A.19.1.1** More than one design approach can be selected for a single building or system. It is the designer's discretion as to which design approaches or methods to utilize; prior approval by the authority having jurisdiction is not required.

A.19.1.2 The situation frequently arises where a small area of a higher hazard is surrounded by a lesser hazard. For example, consider a 600 ft² (56 m²) area consisting of 10 ft (3 m) high on-floor storage of cartoned nonexpanded plastic commodities surrounded by a plastic extruding operation in a 15 ft (4.6 m) high building. In accordance with Chapter 20, the density required for the plastic storage must meet the requirements for extra hazard (Group 1) occupancies. The plastic extruding operation should be considered an ordinary hazard (Group 2) occupancy. In accordance with Chapter 19, the corresponding discharge densities should be 0.3 gpm/ft² (12.2 mm/min) over 2500 ft² (230 m²) for the storage and 0.2 gpm/ft² (8.1 mm/min) over 1500 ft² (140 m²) for the remainder of the area. *(Also see Chapter 19 for the required minimum areas of operation.)*

If the storage area is not separated from the surrounding area by a wall or partition *(see 19.1.2)*, the size of the operating area is determined by the higher hazard storage.

For example, the operating area is 2500 ft² (230 m²). The system must be able to provide the 0.3 gpm/ft² (12.2 mm/min) density over the storage area and 15 ft (4.6 m) beyond. If part of the remote area is outside the 600 ft² (56 m²) plus the 15 ft (4.6 m) overlap, only 0.2 gpm/ft² (8.1 mm/min) is needed for that portion.

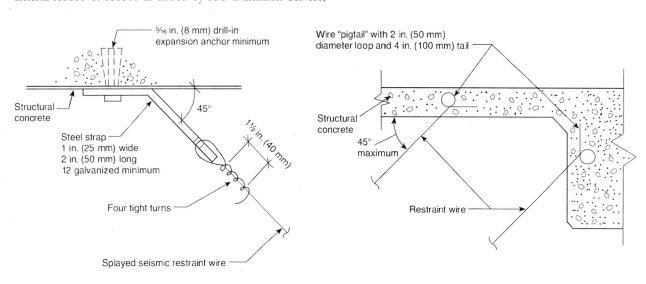

Detail A — Splayed seismic restraint wire attachment

Detail B

Δ **FIGURE A.18.6.1(a)** **Wire Attachment to Cast-in-Place Concrete.**

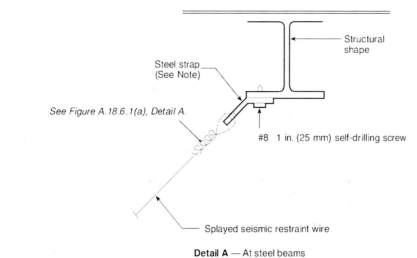

Detail A — At steel beams
[Note: See Figure A.18.6.1(a), Detail A.]

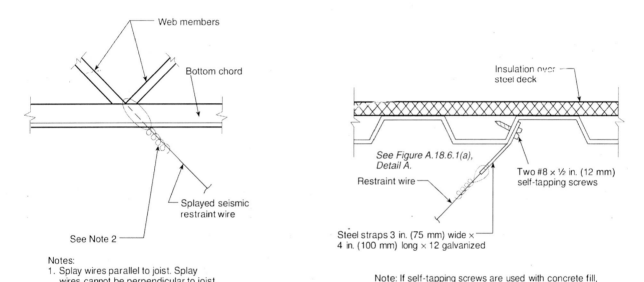

Notes:
1. Splay wires parallel to joist. Splay wires cannot be perpendicular to joist.
2. See Figure A.18.6.1(a), Detail A.

Detail B — At open web steel joist

Note: If self-tapping screws are used with concrete fill, set screws before placing concrete.

Detail C — At steel roof deck

Δ **FIGURE A.18.6.1(b)   Acceptable Details — Wire Connections to Steel Framing.**

If the storage is separated from the surrounding area by a floor-to-ceiling/roof partition that is capable of preventing heat from a fire on one side from fusing sprinklers on the other side, the size of the operating area is determined by the occupancy of the surrounding area. In this example, the design area is 1500 ft² (140 m²). A 0.3 gpm/ft² (12.2 mm/min) density is needed within the separated area with 0.2 gpm/ft² (8.1 mm/min) in the remainder of the remote area.

When the small higher hazard area is larger than the required minimum area dictated by the surrounding occupancy, even when separated by partitions capable of stopping heat, the size of the operating area is determined by the higher hazard storage.

A.19.1.4.1 See A.4.2.

A.19.1.4.2 Appropriate area/density, other design criteria, and water supply requirements should be based on scientifically based engineering analyses that can include submitted fire testing, calculations, or results from appropriate computational models.

Recommended water supplies anticipate successful sprinkler operation. Because of the small but still significant number of uncontrolled fires in sprinklered properties, which have various causes, there should be an adequate water supply available for fire department use.

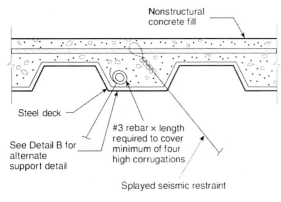

Detail A — At steel deck with insulating fill

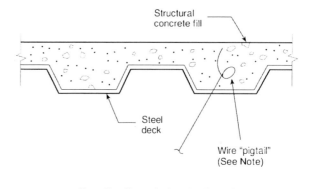

Note: See Figure A.18.6.1(a), Detail B.
Detail B — At steel deck with concrete fill

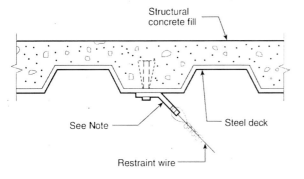

Note: See Figure A.18.6.1(a), Detail A.
Detail C — At steel deck with concrete fill

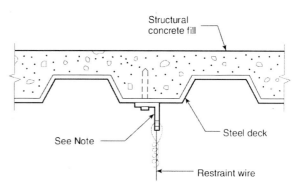

Note: See Figure A.18.6.1(a), Detail A.
Detail D — At steel deck with concrete fill

For SI units, 1 in. = 25.4 mm.
Note: If self-tapping screws are used with concrete fill, set screws before placing concrete.

Δ **FIGURE A.18.6.1(c)   Acceptable Details — Wire Connections to Steel Decking with Fill.**

The hose stream demand required by this standard is intended to provide the fire department with the extra flow they need to conduct mop-up operations and final extinguishment of a fire at a sprinklered property. This is not the fire department manual fire flow, which is determined by other codes or standards. However, it is not the intent of this standard to require that the sprinkler demand be added to the manual fire flow demand required by other codes and standards. While the other codes and standards can factor in the presence of a sprinkler system in the determination of the manual fire flow requirement, the sprinkler system water demand and manual fire flow demand are intended to be separate stand-alone calculations. NFPA 1 emphasizes this fact by the statement in A.18.4.1 that "It is not the intent to add the minimum fire protection water supplies, such as for a sprinkler system, to the minimum fire flow for manual fire suppression purposes required by this section."

A.19.1.5.2 Where tanks serve sprinklers only, they can be sized to provide the duration required for the sprinkler system, ignoring any hose stream demands. Where tanks serve some combination of sprinklers, inside hose stations, outside hose stations, or domestic/process use, the tank needs to be capable of providing the duration for the equipment that is fed from the tank, but the demands of equipment not connected to the tank can be ignored. Where a tank is used for both domestic/process water and fire protection, the entire duration demand of the domestic/process water does not need to be included in the tank if provisions are made to segregate the tank so that adequate fire protection water is always present or if provisions are made to automatically cut off the simultaneous use in the event of fire.

A.19.1.5.3 Where pumps serve sprinklers only, they can be sized to provide the flow required for the sprinkler system, ignoring any hose stream demands. Where pumps serve some combination of sprinklers, inside hose stations, or outside hose stations, the pump needs to be capable of providing the flow for the equipment that is fed from the pump, but the demands of equipment not connected to the pump can be ignored except for evaluating their impact on the available water supply to the pump.

A.19.1.6.1(3) When a light hazard occupancy, such as a school, contains separate ordinary hazard rooms no more than 400 ft² (37 m²), the hose stream allowance and water supply duration would be that required for a light hazard occupancy.

A.19.1.6.2 When the hose demand is provided by a separate water supply, the sprinkler calculation does not include the outside hose demand.

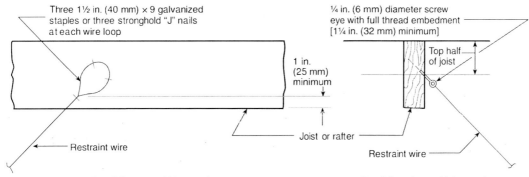

Three 1½ in. (40 mm) × 9 galvanized staples or three stronghold "J" nails at each wire loop

1 in. (25 mm) minimum

Joist or rafter

Restraint wire

Detail A — Wood joist or rafter

¼ in. (6 mm) diameter screw eye with full thread embedment [1¼ in. (32 mm) minimum]

Top half of joist

Restraint wire

Detail B — At wood joist or rafter

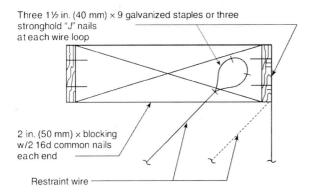

Three 1½ in. (40 mm) × 9 galvanized staples or three stronghold "J" nails at each wire loop

2 in. (50 mm) × blocking w/2 16d common nails each end

Restraint wire

Detail C — At wood joist or block

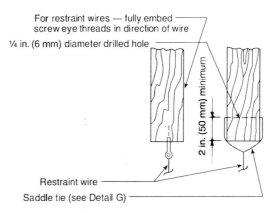

For restraint wires — fully embed screw eye threads in direction of wire

¼ in. (6 mm) diameter drilled hole

2 in. (50 mm) minimum

Restraint wire

Saddle tie (see Detail G)

Detail D — To bottom of joist

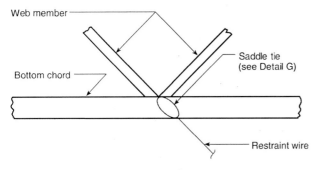

Web member

Bottom chord

Saddle tie (see Detail G)

Restraint wire

Detail E — Restraint wire parallel to wood truss

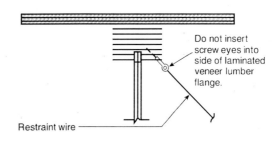

Do not insert screw eyes into side of laminated veneer lumber flange.

Restraint wire

Detail F — Laminated veneer lumber upper flange

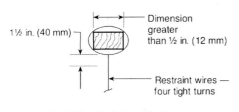

1½ in. (40 mm)

Dimension greater than ½ in. (12 mm)

Restraint wires — four tight turns

Detail G — Typical saddle tie

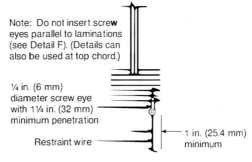

Note: Do not insert screw eyes parallel to laminations (see Detail F). (Details can also be used at top chord.)

¼ in. (6 mm) diameter screw eye with 1¼ in. (32 mm) minimum penetration

Restraint wire

1 in. (25.4 mm) minimum

Detail H — Laminated veneer lumber lower flange

Δ **FIGURE A.18.6.1(d)   Acceptable Details — Wire Connections to Wood Framing.**

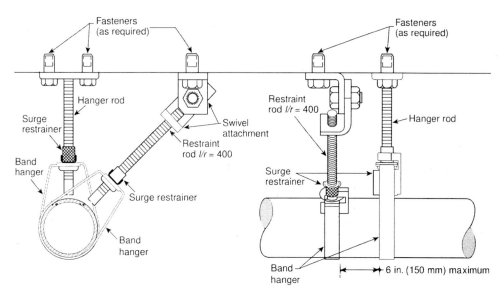

Δ **FIGURE A.18.6.1(5)(a)   Hangers, with Surge Clips, Used in Combination for Restraint of Branch Lines.**

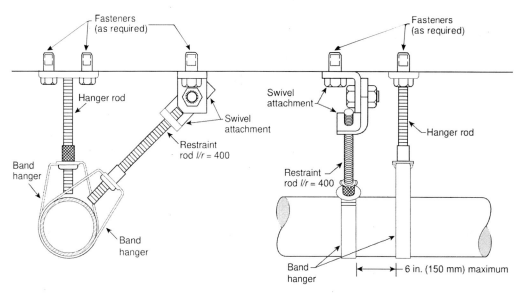

Δ **FIGURE A.18.6.1(5)(b)   Hangers, with Threaded Rod Extended to Pipe, Used in Combination for Restraint of Branch Lines.**

A.19.1.6.4 For fully sprinklered buildings, if hose valves or stations are provided on a combination sprinkler riser and standpipe for fire department use in accordance with NFPA 14, the hydraulic calculation for the sprinkler system is not required to include the standpipe allowance.

A.19.1.7 A series of 10 full-scale fire tests and limited-scale testing were conducted to determine the impact of HVLS fan operation on the performance of sprinkler systems. The project, sponsored by the Property Insurance Research Group (PIRG) and other industry groups, was coordinated by the Fire Protection Research Foundation (FPRF). The complete test report, *High Volume/Low Speed Fan and Sprinkler Operation — Ph. 2 Final Report (2011)*, is available from the FPRF. Both control mode density area and early suppression fast response sprinklers were tested. Successful results were obtained when the HVLS fan was shut down upon the activation of the first sprinkler followed by a 90-second delay. Other methods of fan shutdown were also tested including shutdown by activation of air sampling–type detection and ionization-type smoke detectors. Earlier fan shutdown resulted in less commodity damage.

A.19.2.1.1 This approach is based on a general occupancy classification applied to the building or a portion of the building.

A.19.2.2.5 The additional pressure that is needed at the level of the water supply to account for sprinkler elevation is 0.433 psi/ft (0.098 bar/m) of elevation above the water supply.

A.19.2.3.1.4(1) The area of sprinkler operation typically encompasses enough of the floor area to make-up the minimum allowed size of the remote area up to the entire area of a single floor of the building.

A.19.2.3.1.5.1 This section is included to compensate for possible delay in operation of sprinklers from fires in combustible concealed spaces found in wood frame, brick veneer, and ordinary construction.

In order for the minimum 3000 ft^2 (280 m^2) requirement for the size of the remote area to not be extended to the adjacent area, the qualifying concealed space must be separated by the entire fire-rated assembly. Such assemblies often have combustible structural members separating the exterior membranes that can create a concealed combustible space that can qualify for omitting sprinkler protection. If the fire-rated assembly is the qualifying concealed space, an interior fire would greatly reduce the assigned fire-rated duration.

A.19.2.3.1.5.2(4) Composite wood joists are not considered solid wood joists for the purposes of this section. Their web members are too thin and easily penetrated to adequately compartment a fire in an unsprinklered space. Application of this item is not affected by the depth of the joist channel except in determining the volume. The concealed space above the insulation can be an attic, roof space, or floor space within a floor assembly.

A.19.2.3.1.5.2(10) The gypsum board (or equivalent material) used as the firestopping will compartment the concealed space and restrict the ability for fire to spread beyond 160 ft^3 (4.5 m^3) zones covering multiple joist channels.

A.19.2.3.2.5 Where extended coverage sprinklers are used and the design area (after appropriate increases) is satisfied by five sprinklers, no additional increase is required. With regard to preaction systems, the discharge criteria of Chapter 11 are written based upon the assumption that the release system will activate before the sprinkler system. It is generally accepted that smoke detectors and rate-of-rise detectors are more sensitive than sprinklers and that fixed-temperature release devices with RTIs lower than sprinklers will react faster than sprinklers at similar spacings and locations.

A.19.2.3.2.8 *Example 1.* A dry pipe sprinkler system (OH2) in a building with a ceiling slope exceeding 2 in 12 (16.7 percent). The initial area must be increased 30 percent for the dry pipe system and the resulting area an additional 30 percent for the roof slope. If the point 0.2 gpm/ft^2 (8.2 mm/min) over 1500 ft^2 (140 m^2) is chosen from Figure 19.2.3.1.1, the 1500 ft^2 (140 m^2) area is increased 450 ft^2 (42 m^2) to 1950 ft^2 (180 m^2), which is then further increased 585 ft^2 (54 m^2). The final discharge criterion is then 0.2 gpm/ft^2 (8.2 mm/min) over 2535 ft^2 (235 m^2).

Example 2. A wet pipe sprinkler system (light hazard) in a building with a 16 ft 8 in. (5.1 m) ceiling and a slope exceeding 2 in 12 (16.7 percent) employs quick-response sprinklers qualifying for a 30 percent reduction as permitted by 19.2.3.2.3. The initial area must be increased 30 percent for the ceiling slope and the resulting area decreased 30 percent for quick-response sprinklers. It does not matter whether the reduction is applied first. If a discharge density of 0.1 gpm/ft^2 (4.1 mm/min) over 1500 ft^2 (140 m^2) is chosen from Figure 19.2.3.1.1, the 1500 ft^2 (140 m^2) is increased 450 ft^2 (42 m^2), resulting in 1950 ft^2 (180 m^2), which is then decreased 585 ft^2 (54 m^2). The final design is 0.1 gpm/ft^2 (4.1 mm/min) over 1365 ft^2 (125 m^2).

A.19.2.3.3.1 This subsection allows for calculation of the sprinklers in the largest room, so long as the calculation produces the greatest hydraulic demand among selection of rooms and communicating spaces. For example, in a case where the largest room has four sprinklers and a smaller room has two sprinklers but communicates through unprotected openings with three other rooms, each having two sprinklers, the smaller room and group of communicating spaces should also be calculated.

Corridors are rooms and should be considered as such.

Walls can terminate at a substantial suspended ceiling and need not be extended to a rated floor slab above for this section to be applied.

A.19.2.3.4.2 This section is intended to apply to all types of systems including dry pipe and preaction systems.

A.19.3.1.1 In Figure A.19.3.1.1(a), calculate the area indicated by the heavy outline and X. The circle indicates sprinklers.

The protection area for residential sprinklers with extended coverage areas is defined in the listing of the sprinkler as a maximum square area for pendent sprinklers or a square or rectangular area. Listing information is presented in even 2 ft (600 mm) increments for residential sprinklers. When a sprinkler is selected for an application, its area of coverage must be equal to or greater than both the length and width of the hazard area. For example, if the hazard to be protected is a room 14 ft 6 in. (4.4 m) wide and 20 ft 8 in. (6.3 m) long, a sprinkler that is listed to protect an area of 16 ft × 22 ft (4.9 m × 6.7 m) must be selected. The flow used in the calculations is then selected as the flow required by the listing for the selected coverage. *[See Figure A.19.3.1.1(b).]*

When a single compartment has a branch line with four or more sprinklers, the calculation should include all four sprinklers on the one branch line. When the remote area consists of eight sprinklers in compliance with 19.3.1.2.1, it is not necessary to include all eight sprinklers on the one branch line. One should include sprinklers that are adjacent when viewed as a group and not simply viewed as being next to one downstream sprinkler.

A.19.3.1.2 It should be noted that the provisions of Section 19.2 do not normally apply to the residential sprinkler design approach. The reference to 19.2.3.1.5.2 is merely to provide a consistent approach between the occupancy hazard fire control approach and the residential sprinkler design approach with respect to unsprinklered combustible concealed spaces.

A.19.3.1.2.1 In order for the minimum eight sprinkler requirement for the size of the remote area to not be extended to the adjacent area, the qualifying concealed space must be separated by the entire fire-rated assembly. Such assemblies often have combustible structural members separating the exterior membranes that can create a concealed combustible space that can qualify for omitting sprinkler protection. If the fire-rated assembly is the qualifying concealed space, an interior fire would greatly reduce the assigned fire-rated duration.

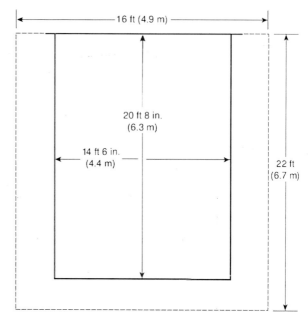

FIGURE A.19.3.1.1(b)   Determination of Protection Area of Coverage for Residential Sprinklers.

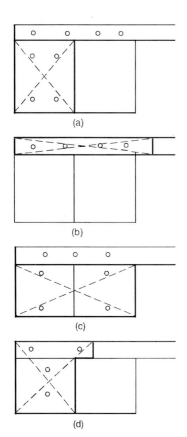

FIGURE A.19.3.1.1(a)   Examples of Design Area for Dwelling Units.

A.19.3.2.1 If the system is a deluge type, all the sprinklers need to be calculated even if they are located on different building faces.

A.20.2.1 Information for the protection of Classes I, II, III, and IV commodities was extrapolated from full-scale fire tests that were performed at different times than the tests that were used to develop the protection for plastic commodities. It is possible that, by selecting certain points from the tables (and after applying the appropriate modifications), the protection specified by 21.4.1.7 exceeds the requirements of Section 21.5. In such situations, the protection specified for plastics, although less than that required by the tables, can adequately protect Class I, II, III, and IV commodities.

This section also allows storage areas that are designed to protect plastics to store Class I, II, III, and IV commodities without a re-evaluation of fire protection systems.

A.20.2.3(3) When a light hazard occupancy, such as a school, contains separate ordinary hazard rooms no more than 400 ft² (37 m²), the hose stream allowance and water supply duration would be that required for a light hazard occupancy.

A.20.3 Commodity classification is governed by the types and amounts of materials (e.g., metal, paper, wood, plastics) that are a part of a product and its primary packaging. Consideration of all characteristics of the individual storage units, not just the product, is critical to identify the appropriate commodity classification. Refer to Table A.20.3 for general guidance for classifying commodities. For situations where it is difficult to determine the appropriate classification, testing should be considered to appropriately characterize the commodity.

A.20.3.1 Unit loads and pallet loads are examples of individual storage units.

Table A.20.3 General Guide to Identifying the Commodity Class for Solid Combustibles

Characteristics of Unit Load			
Material Used to Construct Product	**Packaging Material**	**Pallet Material**	**Commodity Class**
Noncombustible Product			
Entirely noncombustible	None or single-layer corrugated cartons	None, metal, or wood	Class I
Entirely noncombustible	None or single-layer corrugated cartons	Plastic	Class I, II, or III; see 20.3.2
Entirely noncombustible	Multiple-layered corrugated cartons, wooden crates, or wood boxes	None, metal, or wood	Class II
Entirely noncombustible	Multiple-layered corrugated cartons, wooden crates, or wood boxes	Plastic	Class II, III, or IV; see 20.3.2
Entirely noncombustible	Corrugated cartons, wooden crates, or wood boxes, with internal plastic packaging	None, metal, or wood	See Figure 20.4.3.3(a)
Entirely noncombustible	Corrugated cartons, wooden crates, or wooden boxes, with internal plastic packaging	Plastic	See 20.3.2 and Figure 20.4.3.3(a)
Wood, Paper, Natural Fibers, or Group C Plastics			
Entirely wood, paper, natural fibers, or Group C plastics, or a mix of these with noncombustible materials	None, corrugated cartons, wooden crates, or wood boxes	None, metal, or wood	Class III
Entirely wood, paper, natural fibers, or Group C plastics, or a mix of these with noncombustible materials	Corrugated cartons, wooden crates, or wood boxes, with internal plastic packaging	None, metal, or wood	See Figure 20.4.3.3(a)
Entirely wood, paper, natural fibers, or Group C plastics, or a mix of these with noncombustible materials	None, corrugated cartons, wooden crates, or wood boxes	Plastic	Class III or IV or cartoned nonexpanded Group A plastic; see 20.3.2
Entirely wood, paper, natural fibers, or Group C plastics, or a mix of these with noncombustible materials	Corrugated cartons, wooden crates, or wood boxes, with internal plastic packaging	Plastic	See 20.3.2 and Figure 20.4.3.3(a)
Group B Plastics			
Entirely Group B plastics, or a mix of these with noncombustible, wood, paper, natural fibers, or Group C plastics materials	None, corrugated cartons, wooden crates, or wood boxes	None, metal, or wood	Class IV
Entirely Group B plastics, or a mix of these with noncombustible, wood, paper, natural fibers, or Group C plastics materials	Corrugated cartons, wooden crates, or wood boxes	Plastic	Class IV or cartoned nonexpanded Group A plastic; see 20.3.2
Entirely Group B plastics, or a mix of these with noncombustible, wood, paper, natural fibers, or Group C plastics materials	None	Plastic	Class IV or cartoned nonexpanded Group A plastic; see 20.3.2
Entirely Group B plastics, or a mix of these with noncombustible, wood, paper, natural fibers, or Group C plastics materials	Corrugated cartons, wooden crates, or wood boxes, with plastic internal packaging	None, metal, or wood	See Figure 20.4.3.3(a)
Entirely Group B plastics, or a mix of these with noncombustible, wood, paper, natural fibers, or Group C plastics materials	Corrugated cartons, wooden crates, or wood boxes, with plastic internal packaging	Plastic	See 20.3.2 and Figure 20.4.3.3(a)

(continues)

Table A.20.3 *Continued*

Characteristics of Unit Load			
Material Used to Construct Product	Packaging Material	Pallet Material	Conunodity Class
Group A Plastics			
Free-flowing Group A plastic materials	Corrugated cartons, wooden crates, wood boxes, or bagged	None, metal, wood	Class IV
Free-flowing Group A plastic materials	Corrugated cartons, wooden crates, wood boxes, or bagged	Plastic	Class IV or cartoned nonexpanded Group A plastic; see 20.3.2
Entirely nonexpanded Group A plastic	Corrugated cartons, wooden crates, or wood boxes	None, metal, wood, or plastic	Cartoned nonexpanded Group A plastic
Entirely nonexpanded Group A plastic	None	None, metal, wood, or plastic	Exposed nonexpanded Group A plastic
Entirely nonexpanded Group A plastic	Corrugated cartons, wooden crates, or wood boxes, with internal plastic packaging	None, metal, wood, or plastic	See Figure 20.4.3.3(a)
Entirely expanded Group A plastic	Corrugated cartons, wooden crates, or wood boxes, with or without internal plastic packaging	None, metal, wood, or plastic	Cartoned expanded Group A plastic
Entirely expanded Group A plastic	None	None, metal, wood, or plastic	Exposed expanded Group A plastic
Mix of Group A plastics, noncombustible, wood, paper, natural fibers, Group B or C plastics materials	Corrugated cartons, wooden crates, or wood boxes, with or without internal plastic packaging	None, metal, or wood	See Figure 20.4.3.3(a)
Mix of Group A plastics, noncombustible, wood, paper, natural fibers, Group B or C plastics materials	Corrugated cartons, wooden crates, or wood boxes	Plastic	See 20.3.2 and Figure 20.4.3.3(a)
Mix of Group A plastics, noncombustible, wood, paper, natural fibers, Group B or C plastics materials	None	None, metal, or wood	See Figure 20.4.3.3(b)
Mix of Group A plastics, noncombustible, wood, paper, natural fibers, Group B or C plastics materials	None	Plastic	See 20.3.2 and Figure 20.4.3.3(b)

Note: This table provides guidance for the general characteristics to be considered in classifying a commodity. The additional commodity classification information included in this standard as well as any relevant test data that is available should be considered in identifying the appropriate classification.

A.20.3.2.2.1 For example, Class III will become Class IV, and Class IV will become a cartoned nonexpanded Group A plastic commodity.

A.20.3.2.2.2.1 For example, Class II will become Class IV, and Class III and Class IV will become a cartoned nonexpanded Group A plastic commodity.

A.20.4 Specification of the type, amount, and arrangement of combustibles for any commodity classification is essentially an attempt to define the potential fire severity, based on its burning characteristics, so the fire can be successfully controlled by the prescribed sprinkler protection for the commodity class. In actual storage situations, however, many storage arrays do not fit precisely into one of the fundamental classifications; therefore, the user needs to make judgments after comparing each classification to the existing storage conditions. Storage arrays consist of thousands of products, which makes it impossible to specify all the acceptable variations for any class. As an alternative, a variety of common products are classified in this annex based on judgment, loss experience, and fire test results.

Table A.20.4(a) provides examples of commodities not addressed by the classifications in Section 20.4. The commodities listed in Table A.20.4(a) are outside the scope of NFPA 13 protection.

Table A.20.4(a) includes lithium ion batteries. Lithium ion batteries have been a research project within the NFPA Research Foundation. As a result, the following reports have been published:

(1) *Lithium Ion Batteries Hazard and Use Assessment*, published July 2011 and available at the NFPA Research Foundation web site.
(2) *Flammability Characterization of Lithium-ion Batteries in Bulk Storage*, published March 2013 and available at www.fmglobal.com/researchreports.

(3) *Lithium Ion Batteries Hazard and Use Assessment Phase IIB, Flammability Characterization of Li-ion Batteries for Storage Protection,* published April 2013 and available at the NFPA Research Foundation web site.

(4) *Lithium Ion Batteries Hazard and Use Assessment — Phase III,* published November 2016 and available at the NFPA Research Foundation web site.

Table A.20.4(b) is an alphabetized list of commodities with corresponding classifications.

Table A.20.4.1, Table A.20.4.2, Table A.20.4.3, Table A.20.4.4, and Table A.20.4.5.1 provide examples of commodities within a specific class.

A.20.4.1 See Table A.20.4.1.

A.20.4.2 See Table A.20.4.2.

A.20.4.3 See Table A.20.4.3.

A.20.4.4 Cartons containing Group A plastic materials can be treated as Class IV commodities when the plastic materials are surrounded by noncombustible material or a sufficient layer(s) of cardboard to significantly delay fire involvement. For more information on the total range of materials that can be treated as Class IV commodity, see Table A.20.4.4.

A.20.4.5 The categories listed in 20.4.5.1, 20.4.6, and 20.4.7 are based on unmodified plastic materials. The use of fire- or flame-retarding modifiers or the physical form of the material could change the classification.

The addition of fire retardants to plastic should not be relied upon as the sole basis for a reduction in classification given the unknown performance of the fire retardant under a storage scenario. It is expected that full-scale or commodity classification type testing would be necessary to justify any such reduction in classification. No reduction in classification should be given for plastics simply because they contain a fire retardant.

Plastic materials not specifically classified in 20.4.5 should be protected as Group A plastics unless full-scale or commodity classification type testing demonstrates otherwise. It is not possible to classify full-scale fire performance of plastics by looking solely at heat of combustion. Plastic materials should not be categorized into a Group (A, B, or C) based upon comparing heat of combustion with values for plastics already classified in NFPA 13.

A.20.4.5.1 See Table A.20.4.5.1.

A.20.4.5.2 Generally, expanded plastics are low-density materials and commonly referred to as "foam plastics."

A.20.4.8 All arrangements of exposed plastics cannot be protected with all types of sprinklers. Only certain combinations of ceiling sprinklers and in-rack sprinklers have been found to provide acceptable protection. No full-scale fire testing has been performed that has determined acceptable criteria for exposed expanded plastics. Factory Mutual has published criteria in its data sheets to protect exposed expanded plastics based on a risk analysis and small/intermediate-scale test data. Some authorities having jurisdiction accept that criteria as an alternative to the intent of NFPA 13.

Table A.20.4(a) Examples of Commodities Not Addressed by Classifications in Section 20.4

Ammunition Components
  - Bulk primers and powder
Batteries
  - Lithium and other similar exotic metals
  - Lithium-ion and other rechargeable batteries that contain combustible electrolyte
Boat Storage
  - Stored on racks
Boxes, Crates
  - Empty, wood slatted*
Carpet Rolls
Combustible Metals — unless specifically identified otherwise
Compressed or Liquefied Flammable Gases (i.e., filled propane cylinders) — unless specifically identified otherwise
Explosives
  - Blasting primers and similar items
Fertilizers (nitrates)
Fireworks
  - Consumer and display
Flammable and Combustible Liquids — unless specifically identified otherwise
  - Liquids that contain greater than 20 percent alcohol
Hanging Garments, Bulk Storage
Lighters (butane)
  - Loose in large containers (Level 3 aerosol)
Storage Container
  - Large container storage of household goods

*Should be treated as idle pallets.

Δ **Table A.20.4(b) Alphabetical Listing of Commodity Classes**

Product Heading	Product	NFPA 13
Batteries	Dry cells (excludes lithium, lithium-ion, and other similar exotic metals or combustible electrolyte); without blister packing (if blister packed refer to commodity classification definitions)	Class I
	Vehicle; any size (e.g., automobile or truck); empty plastic casing	Group A Nonexpanded
	Vehicle; large (e.g., truck or larger); dry or wet (excludes lithium-ion and other cells containing combustible electrolyte) cells	Group A Nonexpanded
	Vehicle; small (e.g., automobile); wet (excludes lithium-ion and other cells containing combustible electrolyte) cells	Class I
Empty Containers	Noncombustible	Class I
	PET, bottles or jars	Class IV
	Rigid plastic (not including PET), up to 32 oz. (1 L)	Group A Nonexpanded
	Rigid plastic (not including PET), greater than 32 oz. (1 L)	Group A Expanded
	Wood; solid sided (e.g., crates, boxes)	Class II
Film Rolls, Including Photographic	Film (polypropylene, polyester, polyethylene); rolled on any reel type	Group A Nonexpanded
	Film; 35 mm metal film cartridges in polyethylene cans; cartoned	Class III
	Film; motion picture or bulk rolls in polycarbonate, polyethylene or in metal cans; polyethylene bagged; cartoned	Class II
	Film; rolls in polycarbonate plastic cassettes; cartoned	Class IV
	Photographic paper; sheets; bagged in polyethylene; cartoned	Class III
Flammable/Combustible Liquids	Aerosol; Level 1	Class III
	Lighters; butane; blister-packed; cartoned	Group A Nonexpanded
	Liquids; up to 20 percent alcohol (e.g. alcoholic beverages, flavoring extracts); greater than 5 gal (20 L) plastic containers with wall thickness greater than ¼ in. (6 mm)	Group A Nonexpanded
	Liquids; up to 20 percent alcohol (e.g., alcoholic beverages, flavoring extracts); metal, glass or ceramic containers	Class I
	Liquids; up to 20 percent alcohol (e.g., alcoholic beverages, flavoring extracts); plastic containers greater than 5 gal (20 L) and wall thickness up to ¼ in. (6 mm)	Class II
	Liquids; up to 20 percent alcohol (e.g., alcoholic beverages, flavoring extracts); up to 5 gal (20 L) plastic bottles or jars	Class I
	Liquids; up to 20 percent alcohol (e.g., alcoholic beverages, flavoring extracts); wood containers	Class II
Food Products — Frozen	Frozen foods; nonwaxed or nonplastic packaging	Class I
	Frozen foods; plastic trays	Class III
	Frozen foods; waxed or plastic-coated paper packaging	Class II
Food Products — Non-Frozen	Butter (stick or whipped spread) or margarine (up to 50 percent oil)	Class III
	Dry foods (such as baked goods, candy, cereals, cheese, chocolate, cocoa, coffee, grains, granular sugar, nuts, etc.); bagged or cartoned	Class III
	Foods (e.g., coffee, fish products, fruit, meat products, nuts, poultry, etc.); metal cans	Class I
	Fruits and vegetables (noncombustible semi-liquids); crushed; plastic containers up to 5 gal (20 L)	Class I
	Fruits and vegetables; fresh; wood spacers, non-plastic trays or containers	Class I
	Margarine; over 50 and up to 80 percent oil	Group A Nonexpanded
	Meat; fresh; no plastic packaging; exposed	Class I
	Meat; fresh; no plastic packaging; cartoned	Class II
	Meat; fresh; plastic trays	Class III
	Milk; any container; stored in solid plastic crates	Group A Nonexpanded

(continues)

Δ **Table A.20.4(b)**   *Continued*

Product Heading	Product	NFPA 13
	Milk; paper containers, or plastic bottles or jars up to 5 gal (20 L) plastic bottles or jars	Class I
	Salt; bagged	Class I
	Salt; cartoned	Class II
	Snack foods (e.g., potato chips); plasticized aluminum bags; cartoned	Group A Nonexpanded
	Syrup; wooden container	Class II
Furniture and Bedding	Furniture and bedding; with foam cushioning	Group A Expanded
	Furniture; metal (e.g., file cabinets or desks with plastic trim); cartoned	Class I
	Furniture; wood (e.g., doors, windows, cabinets, etc.); no plastic coverings or foam cushioning	Class III
	Furniture; wood; plastic coverings nonexpanded plastic trim	Class IV
	Box spring; standard (minimal plastic materials)	Class III
	Box spring; wrapped in plastic cover	Class IV
	Mattress; foam (in finished form)	Group A Expanded
Housing Materials/ Appliances	Appliances; major (e.g., stoves, refrigerators); no appreciable plastic interior or exterior trim; cartoned	Class II
	Appliances; major (e.g., stoves, refrigerators); no appreciable plastic interior or exterior trim; exposed	Class I
	Appliances; no appreciable plastic exterior trim (interior of unit can have appreciable plastic)	Class III
	Carpet tiles; cartoned	Group A Nonexpanded
	Fiberglass insulation; paper-backed rolls; bagged or unbagged	Class IV
	Floor coverings; vinyl, stacked tiles	Class IV
	Floor coverings; vinyl; rolled	Group A Nonexpanded
	Gypsum board	Class I
	Housing materials (such as sinks, countertops, etc.); noncombustible, cartoned or crated	Class II
	Paint; oil-based; friction-top metal containers; cartoned	Class IV
	Paint; water-based (latex); friction-top metal containers; cartoned	Class I
	Roofing shingles; asphalt-coated fiberglass	Class III
	Roofing shingles; asphalt-impregnated felt	Class IV
Miscellaneous	Ammunition; small arms and shotgun; cartoned	Class IV
	Charcoal; mineral spirit impregnated; bagged	Group A Expanded
	Charcoal; standard (non-mineral spirit impregnated); bagged	Class III
	Leather hides; baled	Class II
	Leather; finished products (e.g., shoes, jackets, gloves, bags, luggage, belts)	Class III
	Motors; electric	Class I
	Shock absorbers; metal dust cover	Class II
	Shock absorbers; plastic dust cover	Class III
	Skis; composite materials (plastic, fiberglass, foam, etc.)	Class IV
	Tobacco products; cartoned	Class III
	Toys; stuffed; foam or synthetic	Group A Expanded
	Transformer; dry or empty (i.e., void of oil)-filled	Class I
Noncombustible Liquids	Liquids or semi-liquids; PET containers greater than 5 gal (20 L) having a nominal wall thickness greater than 0.25 in. (6 mm)	Class IV

(continues)

Shaded text = Revisions.   Δ = Text deletions and figure/table revisions.   • = Section deletions.   *N* = New material.

Δ Table A.20.4(b)   *Continued*

Product Heading	Product	NFPA 13
	Liquids or semi-liquids; PET containers up to 5 gal (20 L) or greater than 5 gal (20 L) having a nominal wall thickness up to 0.25 in. (6 mm)	Class I
	Liquids or semi-liquids (e.g., crushed fruits and vegetables); plastic containers up to 5 gal (18.9 L) capacity	Class I
	Liquids or semi-liquids; plastic (except PET) containers greater than 5 gal (20 L) capacity having a nominal wall thickness greater than 0.25 in. (6 mm)	Group A Nonexpanded
	Liquids or semi-liquids; plastic (except PET) containers greater than 5 gal (20 L) capacity having a nominal wall thickness up to 0.25 in. (6 mm)	Class II
	Liquids; cardboard drink boxes, plastic-coated, wax-coated, and/or aluminum-lined; exposed or on corrugated carton trays with plastic sheeting.	Class I
	Liquids; cardboard drink boxes, plastic-coated, wax-coated, and/or aluminum-lined; stored in plastic containers	Group A Nonexpanded
	Liquids; glass bottles or jars; cartoned	Class I
	Liquids; pharmaceuticals (nonflammable); glass bottles or jars; cartoned	Class II
	Liquids; plastic bottles or jars; stored in open or solid plastic crates	Group A Nonexpanded
Paper Products	Book signatures (paper part of book without hard cover)	Class II
	Cartons (i.e., cardboard flats); corrugated; partially assembled	Class IV
	Cartons (i.e., cardboard flats); corrugated; unassembled in neat piles	Class III
	Cartons; wax-coated, single-walled corrugated	Group A Nonexpanded
	Cellulosic paper products; nonwax-coated (e.g., books, cardboard games, cartoned tissue products, magazines, newspapers, paper cups, paper plates, paper towels, plastic-coated paper food containers, stationery)	Class III
	Cellulosic paper products; wax-coated (e.g., paper plates, cups); loosely packed; cartoned	Group A Nonexpanded
	Cellulosic paper products; wax-coated (e.g., paper plates, cups.); nested; cartoned	Class IV
	Matches; paper-type; cartoned	Class IV
	Matches; wooden; cartoned	Group A Nonexpanded
	Rolled; lightweight; in storage racks	Class IV
	Rolled; medium or heavyweight; in storage racks or on-side	Class III
	Tissue products; plastic-wrapped; cartoned	Class III
	Tissue products; plastic-wrapped; exposed	Group A Nonexpanded
Plastic/Rubber	ABS (Acrylonitrile-butadiene-styrene copolymer)	Group A Nonexpanded
	Acetal (polyformaldehyde)	Group A Nonexpanded
	Acrylic (polymethyl methacrylate)	Group A Nonexpanded
	Automobile bumpers and dashboards	Group A Expanded
	Butyl rubber	Group A Nonexpanded
	Cellulose Acetate	Class IV
	Cellulose Acetate Butyrate	Group A Nonexpanded
	Chloroprene rubber	Class IV
	Containers; nonexpanded plastic gridded or solid; collapsed or nested with no air spaces	Group A Nonexpanded
	ECTFE (ethylene-chlorotrifluoro-ethylene copolymer)	Class IV
	EPDM (ethylene-propylene rubber)	Group A Nonexpanded
	ETFE (ethylene-tetrafluoroethylene copolymer)	Class IV
	Ethyl Cellulose	Group A Nonexpanded
	FEP (fluorinated ethylene-propylene copolymer)	Class IV
	FRP (fiberglass-reinforced polyester)	Group A Nonexpanded

(continues)

Shaded text = Revisions.   Δ = Text deletions and figure/table revisions.   • = Section deletions.   *N* = New material.

Δ **Table A.20.4(b)**   *Continued*

Product Heading	Product	NFPA 13
	Melamine (melamine formaldehyde)	Class III
	Nitrile Rubber (acrylonitrile-butadiene rubber)	Group A Nonexpanded
	Nylon (nylon 6, nylon 6/6)	Group A Nonexpanded
	PCTFE (polychlorotrifluoroethylene)	Class III
	PET (Polyethylene Terephthalate — thermoplastic polyester)	Group A Nonexpanded
	Phenolic	Class III
	Plastics; stored in fully closed and solid (no openings), metal containers	Class I
	Polybutadiene	Group A Nonexpanded
	Polycarbonate	Group A Nonexpanded
	Polyester elastomer	Group A Nonexpanded
	Polyethylene	Group A Nonexpanded
	Polypropylene	Group A Nonexpanded
	Polystyrene; foam products (plates, cups, etc.)	Group A Expanded
	Polystyrene; rigid products	Group A Nonexpanded
	Polyurethane	Group A Expanded
	PTFE (polytetrafluoroethylene)	Class III
	PVC (polyvinyl chloride) products, up to 20 percent plasticizer	Class III
	PVC (polyvinyl chloride) products, greater than 20 percent plasticizer	Group A Nonexpanded
	PVC resins; bagged	Class III
	PVDC (polyvinylidene chloride)	Class III
	PVDF (polyvinylidene fluoride)	Class III
	PVF (polyvinyl fluoride)	Group A Nonexpanded
	Rubber; natural in blocks; cartoned	Group A Nonexpanded
	Rubber; natural; expanded	Group A Expanded
	Rubber; natural; nonexpanded	Group A Nonexpanded
	Rubber; synthetic (santoprene)	Group A Nonexpanded
	SAN (styrene acrylonitrile)	Group A Nonexpanded
	SBR (styrene-butadiene rubber)	Group A Nonexpanded
	Silicone rubber	Class IV
	Urea (urea formaldehyde)	Class III
Plastic Containers	Bottles or jars (except PET) greater than 1 gal (4 L) containing noncombustible solids	Group A Nonexpanded
	Bottles or jars (except PET) up to 1 gal (4 L) containing noncombustible solids	Group A, cartoned (treat as cartoned even if exposed) Nonexpanded
Powders/Pills	Pharmaceutical pills; glass bottles or jars; cartoned	Class II
	Pharmaceuticals pills; plastic bottles or jars; cartoned	Class IV
	Polyvinyl Alcohol (PVA) resins; bagged	Class IV
	Powders; combustible (ordinary such as sugar or flour); free-flowing; bagged	Class II
	Powders; noncombustible free-flowing powdered or granular materials (cement, calcium chloride, clay, iron oxide, sodium chloride, sodium silicate, etc.)	Class I
	Powders; noncombustible; glass bottles or jars; cartoned	Class I
	Powders; noncombustible; PET bottles or jars	Class II
	Powders; noncombustible; plastic (other than PET) bottles or jars; exposed	Group A Nonexpanded

(continues)

Δ Table A.20.4(b)   *Continued*

Product Heading	Product	NFPA 13
	Powders; noncombustible; plastic bottles or jars greater than 1 gal (4 L) capacity	Group A Nonexpanded
	Powders; noncombustible; plastic bottles or jars up to 1 gal (4 L) capacity; cartoned	Class IV
Textile Materials/Products	Cloth; natural fibers; baled	Class III
	Cloth; synthetic cloth	Group A Nonexpanded
	Clothing; natural fibers (e.g., wool, cotton) and viscose	Class III
	Cotton; cartoned	Class III
	Diapers; cotton or linen	Class III
	Diapers; plastic or nonwoven fabric; cartoned	Class IV
	Diapers; plastic or nonwoven fabric; plastic-wrapped; exposed	Group A Nonexpanded
	Fabric; rayon and nylon	Group A Nonexpanded
	Fabric; synthetic (except rayon and nylon); greater than 50/50 blend	Group A Nonexpanded
	Fabric; synthetic (except rayon and nylon); up to 50/50 blend	Group A Nonexpanded
	Fabric; vinyl-coated (e.g., tablecloth); cartoned	Group A Nonexpanded
	Fibers; rayon and nylon; baled	Class IV
	Fibers; synthetic (except rayon and nylon); baled	Group A Nonexpanded
	Thread or yarn; rayon and nylon; wood or paper spools	Class IV
	Thread or yarn; rayon or nylon; plastic spools	Group A Nonexpanded
	Thread or yarn; synthetic (except rayon and nylon); greater than 50/50 blend; paper or wood spools	Group A Nonexpanded Plastic
	Thread or yarn; synthetic (except rayon and nylon); greater than 50/50 blend; plastic spools	Group A Nonexpanded
	Thread or yarn; synthetic (except rayon and nylon); up to 50/50 blend; plastic spools	Group A Nonexpanded
	Thread or yarn; synthetic (except rayon and nylon); up to 50/50 blend; wood or paper spools	Group A Nonexpanded Plastic
Wax Products	Candles Paraffin or petroleum wax; blocks	Group A Expanded Group A Expanded
Wire/Cable/Spools	Spools; plastic; empty	Group A Nonexpanded
	Spools; wood; empty	Class III
	Wire or cable; PVC insulated; metal or wood spools	Class II
	Wire or cable; PVC insulated; plastic spools	Class IV
	Wire; bare; metal spools, exposed	Class I
	Wire; bare; metal spools; cartoned	Class II
	Wire; bare; plastic spools; cartoned	Class IV
	Wire; bare; plastic spools; exposed	Group A Nonexpanded
	Wire; bare; wood or cardboard spools	Class II
Wood Products	Wood patterns	Class IV
	Wood products (e.g., fiberboard, lumber, particle board, plywood, pressboard with smooth ends and edges); bundled solid blocks	Class II
	Wood products (e.g., fiberboard, lumber, particle board, plywood, pressboard with smooth ends and edges); unbundled or non-solid blocks	Class III
	Wood products (e.g., toothpicks, clothespins and hangers)	Class III

Table A.20.4.1 Examples of Class I Commodities

Product Heading	Product
Batteries	Dry cells (excludes lithium, lithium-ion, and other similar exotic metals or combustible electrolyte); without blister packing (if blister packed refer to commodity classification definitions)
	Vehicle; small (e.g., automobile); wet (excludes lithium-ion and other cells containing combustible electrolyte) cells
Empty Containers	Noncombustible
Flammable/Combustible Liquids	Liquids; up to 20 percent alcohol (e.g., alcoholic beverages, flavoring extracts); metal, glass or ceramic containers
	Liquids; up to 20 percent alcohol (e.g., alcoholic beverages, flavoring extracts); up to 5 gal (20 L) plastic bottles or jars
Food Products — Frozen	Frozen foods; nonwaxed or nonplastic packaging
Food Products — Non-Frozen	Foods (coffee, fish products, fruit, meat products, nuts, poultry, etc.); metal cans
	Fruits and vegetables (noncombustible semi-liquids); crushed; plastic containers up to 5 gal (20 L)
	Fruits and vegetables; fresh; wood spacers, non-plastic trays or containers
	Meat; fresh; no plastic packaging; exposed
	Milk; paper containers, or plastic bottles or jars up to 5 gal (20 L) plastic bottles or jars
	Salt; bagged
Furniture and Bedding	Furniture; metal (e.g., file cabinets or desks with plastic trim); cartoned
Housing Materials/Appliances	Appliances; major (e.g., stoves, refrigerators); no appreciable plastic interior or exterior trim; cartoned
	Gypsum board
	Paint; water-based (latex); friction-top metal containers; cartoned
Miscellaneous	Motors; electric
	Transformer; dry or empty (i.e., void of oil)
Noncombustible Liquids	Liquids or semi liquids; PET containers greater than 5 gal (20 L) having a nominal wall thickness greater than 0.25 in. (6 mm)
	Liquids or semi-liquids (e.g., crushed fruits and vegetables); plastic containers up to 5 gal (20 L) capacity
	Liquids; cardboard drink boxes, plastic-coated, wax-coated, and/or aluminum-lined; exposed or on corrugated carton trays with plastic sheeting
	Liquids; glass bottles or jars; cartoned
Plastic/Rubber	Plastics; stored in fully closed and solid (no openings), metal containers
Powders/Pills	Powders; noncombustible free-flowing powdered or granular materials (cement, calcium chloride, clay, iron oxide, sodium chloride, sodium silicate, etc.); bagged
	Powders; noncombustible; glass bottles or jars; cartoned
Wire/Cable/Spools	Wire; bare; metal spools, exposed

Table A.20.4.2 Examples of Class II Commodities

Product Heading	Product
Empty Containers	Wood; solid sided (e.g., crates, boxes)
Film Rolls, Including Photographic	Film; motion picture or bulk rolls in polycarbonate, polyethylene or in metal cans; polyethylene bagged; cartoned
Flammable/Combustible Liquids	Liquids; up to 20 percent alcohol (e.g., alcoholic beverages, flavoring extracts); plastic containers greater than 5 gal (20 L) and wall thickness up to ¼ in. (6 mm)
	Liquids; up to 20 percent alcohol (e.g., alcoholic beverages, flavoring extracts); wood containers
Food Products — Frozen	Frozen foods; waxed or plastic-coated paper packaging
Food Products — Non-Frozen	Meat; fresh; no plastic packaging; cartoned
	Salt; cartoned
	Syrup; wooden container
Housing Materials/Appliances	Appliances; major (e.g., stoves, refrigerators); no appreciable plastic interior or exterior trim; cartoned
	Housing materials (such as sinks, countertops, etc.); noncombustible, cartoned or crated
Miscellaneous	Leather hides; baled
	Shock absorbers; metal dust cover
Noncombustible Liquids	Liquids or semi-liquids; plastic (except PET) containers greater than 5 gal (20 L) capacity having a nominal wall thickness up to 0.25 in. (6 mm)
	Liquids; pharmaceuticals (nonflammable); glass bottles or jars; cartoned
Paper Products	Book signatures (paper part of book without hard cover)
Powders/Pills	Pharmaceutical pills; glass bottles or jars; cartoned
	Powders; combustible (ordinary such as sugar or flour); free-flowing; bagged
	Powders; noncombustible; PET bottles or jars
Wire/Cable/Spools	Wire or cable; PVC insulated; metal or wood spools
	Wire; bare; metal spools; cartoned
	Wire; bare; wood or cardboard spools
Wood Products	Wood products (e.g., fiberboard, lumber, particle board, plywood, pressboard with smooth ends and edges); bundled solid blocks

Table A.20.4.3 Examples of Class III Commodities

Product Heading	Product
Film Rolls, Including Photographic	Film; 35 mm metal film cartridges in polyethylene cans; cartoned
	Photographic paper; sheets; bagged in polyethylene; cartoned
Flammable/Combustible Liquids	Aerosol; Level 1
Food Products — Frozen	Frozen foods; plastic trays
Food Products — Non-Frozen	Butter (stick or whipped spread) or margarine (up to 50 percent oil)
	Dry foods (such as baked goods, candy, cereals, cheese, chocolate, cocoa, coffee, grains, granular sugar, nuts, etc.); bagged or cartoned
	Meat; fresh; plastic trays
Furniture and Bedding	Furniture; wood (doors, windows, cabinets, etc.); no plastic coverings or foam cushioning
	Box spring; standard (minimal plastic materials)
Housing Materials/Appliances	Appliances; no appreciable plastic exterior trim (interior of unit can have appreciable plastic)
	Roofing shingles; asphalt-coated fiberglass
Miscellaneous	Charcoal; standard (non-mineral spirit impregnated); bagged
	Leather; finished products (e.g., shoes, jackets, gloves, bags, luggage, belts)
	Shock absorbers; plastic dust cover
	Tobacco products; cartoned
Paper Products	Cartons (i.e., cardboard flats); corrugated; unassembled in neat piles
	Cellulosic paper products; nonwax-coated (e.g., books, cardboard games, cartoned tissue products, magazines, newspapers, paper cups, paper plates, paper towels, plastic-coated paper food containers, stationery)
	Rolled; medium or heavyweight; in storage racks or on-side
	Tissue products; plastic-wrapped; cartoned
Plastic/Rubber	Melamine (melamine formaldehyde)
	PCTFE (polychlorotrifluoroethylene)
	Phenolic
	PTFE (polytetrafluoroethylene)
	PVC (polyvinyl chloride) products, up to 20 percent plasticizer
	PVC resins; bagged
	PVDC (polyvinylidene chloride)
	PVDF (polyvinylidene fluoride)
	Urea (urea formaldehyde)
Textile Materials/Products	Cloth; natural fibers; baled
	Clothing; natural fibers (e.g., wool, cotton) and viscose
	Cotton; cartoned
	Diapers; cotton or linen
	Fabric; synthetic (except rayon and nylon); up to 50/50 blend
	Thread or yarn; synthetic (except rayon and nylon); up to 50/50 blend; wood or paper spools
Wire/Cable/Spools	Spools; wood; empty
Wood Products	Wood products (e.g., fiberboard, lumber, particle board, plywood, pressboard with smooth ends and edges); unbundled or non-solid blocks
	Wood products (e.g., toothpicks, clothespins and hangers)

Δ **Table A.20.4.4 Examples of Class IV Commodities**

Product Heading	Product
Empty containers	PET, bottles or jars
Film rolls, including photographic	Film; rolls in polycarbonate plastic cassettes; cartoned
Furniture and bedding	Furniture; wood; plastic coverings; nonexpanded plastic trim
	Box spring; wrapped in plastic cover
Housing materials/ appliances	Fiberglass insulation; paper-backed rolls; bagged or unbagged
	Floor coverings; vinyl, stacked tiles
	Paint; oil-based; friction-top metal containers; cartoned
	Roofing shingles; asphalt-impregnated felt
Miscellaneous	Ammunition; small arms and shotgun; cartoned
	Skis; composite materials (e.g., plastic, fiberglass, foam)
Noncombustible liquids	Liquids or semi-liquids; PET containers greater than 5 gal (20 L) having a nominal wall thickness greater than 0.25 in. (6 mm)
Paper products	Cartons (i.e., cardboard flats); corrugated; partially assembled
	Cellulosic paper products; wax-coated (e.g., paper plates, paper cups); nested; cartoned
	Matches; paper-type; cartoned
	Rolled; lightweight; in storage racks
Plastic/rubber	Cellulose acetate
	Chloroprene rubber
	Ethylene-chlorotrifluoro-ethylene copolymer (ECTFE)
	Ethylene-tetrafluoroethylene copolymer (ETFE)
	Fluorinated ethylene-propylene copolymer (FEP)
	Silicone rubber
Powders/pills	Pharmaceuticals pills; plastic bottles or jars; cartoned
	Polyvinyl alcohol (PVA) resins; bagged
	Powders; noncombustible; plastic bottles or jars up to 1 gal (4 L) capacity; cartoned
Textile materials/products	Cloth; synthetic cloth
	Diapers; plastic or nonwoven fabric; cartoned
	Fabric; rayon and nylon
	Fibers; rayon and nylon; baled
	Thread or yarn; rayon and nylon; wood or paper spools
	Thread or yarn; synthetic (except rayon and nylon); greater than 50/50 blend; paper or wood spools
Wire/cable/spools	Wire or cable; PVC insulated; plastic spools
	Wire; bare; plastic spools; cartoned
Wood products	Wood patterns

Table A.20.4.5.1 Examples of Group A Plastic Commodities

Product Heading	Product	Expanded/ Nonexpanded
Batteries	Vehicle; any size (e.g., automobile or truck); empty plastic casing	Nonexpanded
	Vehicle; large (e.g. truck or larger); dry or wet (excludes lithium-ion and other cells containing combustible electrolyte) cells	Nonexpanded
Empty Containers	Rigid plastic (not including PET), up to 32 oz (1 L)	Nonexpanded
	Rigid plastic (not including PET), greater than 32 oz (1 L)	Expanded
Film Rolls, Including Photographic	Film (polypropylene, polyester, polyethylene); rolled on any reel type	Nonexpanded
Flammable/Combustible Liquids	Lighters; butane; blister-packed; cartoned	Nonexpanded
	Liquids; up to 20 percent alcohol (e.g. alcoholic beverages, flavoring extracts); greater than 5 gal (20 L) plastic containers with wall thickness greater than $\frac{1}{4}$ in. (6 mm)	Nonexpanded
Food Products — Non-Frozen	Margarine; over 50 and up to 80 percent oil	Nonexpanded
	Milk; any container; stored in solid plastic crates	Nonexpanded
	Snack foods (e.g., potato chips); plasticized aluminum bags; cartoned	Nonexpanded
Furniture and Bedding	Furniture and bedding; with foam cushioning	Expanded
	Mattress; foam (in finished form)	Expanded
Housing Materials/Appliances	Carpet tiles; cartoned	Nonexpanded
	Floor coverings; vinyl; rolled	Nonexpanded
Miscellaneous	Charcoal; mineral spirit impregnated; bagged	Expanded
	Toys; stuffed; foam or synthetic	Expanded
Noncombustible Liquids	Liquids or semi-liquids; plastic (except PET) containers greater than 5 gal (20 L) capacity having a nominal wall thickness greater than $\frac{1}{4}$ in. (6 mm)	Nonexpanded
	Liquids; cardboard drink boxes, plastic-coated, wax-coated, and/or aluminum-lined; stored in plastic containers	Nonexpanded
	Liquids; plastic bottles or jars; stored in open or solid plastic crates	Nonexpanded
Paper Products	Cartons; wax-coated, single-walled corrugated	Nonexpanded
	Cellulosic paper products; wax-coated (paper plates, cups, etc.); loosely packed; cartoned	Nonexpanded
	Matches; wooden; cartoned	Nonexpanded
	Tissue products; plastic-wrapped; exposed	Nonexpanded
Plastic/Rubber	ABS (Acrylonitrile-butadiene-styrene copolymer)	Nonexpanded
	Acetal (polyformaldehyde)	Nonexpanded
	Acrylic (polymethyl methacrylate)	Nonexpanded
	Automobile bumpers and dashboards	Expanded
	Butyl rubber	Nonexpanded
	Cellulose Acetate Butyrate	Nonexpanded
	Containers; nonexpanded plastic gridded or solid; collapsed or nested with no air spaces	Nonexpanded
	EPDM (ethylene-propylene rubber)	Nonexpanded
	Ethyl Cellulose	Nonexpanded
	FRP (fiberglass-reinforced polyester)	Nonexpanded

(continues)

Table A.20.4.5.1 *Continued*

Product Heading	Product	Expanded/Nonexpanded
	Nitrile Rubber (acrylonitrile-butadiene rubber)	Nonexpanded
	Nylon (nylon 6, nylon 6/6)	Nonexpanded
	PET (Polyethylene Terephthalate - thermoplastic polyester)	Nonexpanded
	Polybutadiene	Nonexpanded
	Polycarbonate	Nonexpanded
	Polyester elastomer	Nonexpanded
	Polyethylene	Nonexpanded
	Polypropylene	Nonexpanded
	Polystyrene; foam products (e.g., plates, cups, etc.)	Expanded
	Polystyrene; rigid products	Nonexpanded
	Polyurethane	Expanded
	PVC (polyvinyl chloride) products, greater than 20 percent plasticizer	Nonexpanded
	PVF (polyvinyl fluoride)	Nonexpanded
	Rubber; natural in blocks; cartoned	Nonexpanded
	Rubber; natural; expanded	Expanded
	Rubber; natural; nonexpanded	Nonexpanded
	Rubber; synthetic (santoprene)	Nonexpanded
	SAN (styrene acrylonitrile)	Nonexpanded
	SBR (styrene-butadiene rubber)	Nonexpanded
Plastic Containers	Bottles or jars (except PET) greater than 1 gal (4 L) containing noncombustible solids	Nonexpanded
	Bottles or jars (except PET) up to 1 gal (4 L) containing noncombustible solids (Group A, cartoned (treat as cartoned even if exposed)	Nonexpanded
Powders/Pills	Powders; noncombustible; plastic (other than PET) bottles or jars; exposed	Nonexpanded
	Powders; noncombustible; plastic bottles or jars greater than 1 gal (4 L) capacity	Nonexpanded
Textile Materials/Products	Diapers; plastic or nonwoven fabric; plastic-wrapped; exposed	Nonexpanded
	Fabric; vinyl-coated (e.g., tablecloth); cartoned	Nonexpanded
	Fabric; synthetic (except rayon and nylon; greater than 50/50 blend	Nonexpanded
	Fibers; synthetic (except rayon and nylon); baled	Nonexpanded
	Thread or yarn; rayon or nylon; plastic spools	Nonexpanded
	Thread or yarn; synthetic (except rayon and nylon); greater than 50/50 blend; plastic spools	Nonexpanded
	Thread or yarn; synthetic (except rayon and nylon); up to 50/50 blend; plastic spools	Nonexpanded
Wax Products	Candles	Expanded
	Paraffin or petroleum wax; blocks	Expanded
Wire/Cable/Spools	Spools; plastic; empty	Nonexpanded
	Wire; bare; plastic spools; exposed	Nonexpanded

Table A.20.4.10 Paper Classification

Heavyweight	Mediumweight	Lightweight	Tissue
Linerboards	Bond and reproduction	Carbonizing tissue	Toilet tissue
Medium	Vellum	Cigarette	Towel tissue
Kraft roll wrappers	Offset	Fruit wrap	
Milk carton board	Tablet	Onion skin	
Folding carton board	Computer		
Bristol board	Envelope		
Tag	Book		
Vellum bristol board	Label		
Index	Magazine		
Cupstock	Butcher		
Pulp board	Bag		
	Newsprint (unwrapped)		

A.20.4.10 *Paper Classification.* These classifications were derived from a series of large-scale and laboratory-type small-scale fire tests. It is recognized that not all paper in a class burns with exactly the same characteristics.

Paper can be soft or hard, thick or thin, or heavy or light and can also be coated with various materials. The broad range of papers can be classified according to various properties. One important property is basis weight, which is defined as the weight of a sheet of paper of a specified area. Two broad categories are recognized by industry — paper and paperboard. Paperboard normally has a basis weight of 20 lb (100 g/m^2) or greater measured on a 1000 ft^2 (93 m^2) sheet. Stock with a basis weight less than 20 lb/1000 ft^2 (100 g/m^2) is normally categorized as paper. The basis weight of paper is usually measured on a 3000 ft^2 (280 m^2) sheet. The basis weight of paper can also be measured on the total area of a ream of paper, which is normally the case for the following types of printing and writing papers:

(1) *Bond paper* — 500 sheets, 17 in. × 22 in. (425 mm × 550 mm) = 1300 ft^2 (120 m^2) per ream
(2) *Book paper* — 500 sheets, 25 in. × 38 in. (625 mm × 950 mm) = 3300 ft^2 (305 m^2) per ream
(3) *Index paper* — 500 sheets, 25½ in. × 30½ in. (640 mm × 765 mm) = 2700 ft^2 (250 m^2) per ream
(4) *Bristol paper* — 500 sheets, 22½ in. × 35 in. (565 mm × 890 mm) = 2734 ft^2 (255 m^2) per ream
(5) *Tag paper* — 500 sheets, 24 in. × 36 in. (600 mm × 900 mm) = 3000 ft^2 (280 m^2) per ream

For the purposes of this standard, all basis weights are expressed in lb/1000 ft^2 (kg/93 m^2) of paper. To determine the basis weight per 1000 ft^2 (93 m^2) for papers measured on a sheet of different area, the following formula should be applied:

$$\frac{\text{Base weight}}{1000 \text{ ft}^2} = \text{basis weight} \times 1000 \text{ measured area} \quad \text{[A.20.4.10a]}$$

Example: To determine the basis weight per 1000 ft^2 (93 m^2) of 16 lb (7.3 kg) bond paper:

$$\left(\frac{16 \text{ lb}}{1300 \text{ ft}^2}\right)1000 = \frac{12.3 \text{ lb}}{1000 \text{ ft}^2} \quad \text{[A.20.4.10b]}$$

Large- and small-scale fire tests indicate that the burning rate of paper varies with the basis weight. Heavyweight paper burns more slowly than lightweight paper. Full-scale roll paper fire tests were conducted with the following types of paper:

(1) *Linerboard* — 42 lb/1000 ft^2 (0.2 kg/m^2) nominal basis weight
(2) *Newsprint* — 10 lb/1000 ft^2 (50 g/m^2) nominal basis weight
(3) *Tissue* — 5 lb/1000 ft^2 (20 g/m^2) nominal basis weight

The rate of firespread over the surface of the tissue rolls was extremely rapid in the full-scale fire tests. The rate of firespread over the surface of the linerboard rolls was slower. Based on the overall results of these full-scale tests, along with additional data from small-scale testing of various paper grades, the broad range of papers has been classified into three major categories as follows:

(1) *Heavyweight* — Basis weight of 20 lb/1000 ft^2 (100 g/m^2) or greater
(2) *Mediumweight* — Basis weight of 10 lb to 20 lb/1000 ft^2 (100 g/m^2)
(3) *Lightweight* — Basis weight of less than 10 lb/1000 ft^2 (50 g/m^2) and tissues regardless of basis weight

The following SI units were used for conversion of U.S. customary units:

1 lb = 0.45 kg

1 in. = 25 mm

1 ft = 0.3 m

1 ft^2 = 0.09 m^2

The various types of papers normally found in each of the four major categories are provided in Table A.20.4.10.

A.20.5.3 Many factors affect the protection of rack storage. Section 20.5.3 defined the variables that limit or change the available protection criteria found in Chapters 21 through 25. Paragraphs 20.5.3.1 through 20.5.3.4 identify the general terms of rack storage that identify which type of rack and shelving criteria is to be used in Chapters 21 through 25.

A.20.5.3.2 Slatting of decks or walkways or the use of open grating as a substitute for automatic sprinkler thereunder is not acceptable.

In addition, where shelving of any type is employed, it is for the basic purpose of providing an intermediate support between the structural members of the rack. As a result, it becomes almost impossible to define and maintain transverse flue spaces across the rack as required.

A.20.7 Exposed, expanded Group A plastic dunnage, instrument panels, and plastic bumper facia were the automotive components with their related packaging that were utilized in the fire tests. This test commodity used in the large-scale sprinklered fire test proved to be the worst challenge per the large-scale calorimeter tests of available components. See *Technical Report of Fire Testing of Automotive Parts in Portable Storage Racking*, prepared by Underwriters Laboratories, Project 99NK29106, NC4004, January 5, 2001, and *Commodity Hazard Comparison of Expanded Plastic in Portable Bins and Racking*, Project 99NK29106, NC4004, September 8, 2000.

A.20.8 A series of 10 full-scale fire tests and limited-scale testing were conducted to determine the impact of HVLS fan operation on the performance of sprinkler systems. The project, sponsored by the Property Insurance Research Group (PIRG) and other industry groups, was coordinated by the Fire Protection Research Foundation (FPRF). The complete test report, *High Volume/Low Speed Fan and Sprinkler Operation — Ph. 2 Final Report (2011)*, is available from the FPRF. Both control mode density area and early suppression fast response sprinklers were tested. Successful results were obtained when the HVLS fan was shut down upon the activation of the first sprinkler followed by a 90-second delay. Other methods of fan shutdown were also tested including shutdown by activation of air sampling–type detection and ionization-type smoke detectors. Earlier fan shutdown resulted in less commodity damage.

A.20.9.2 The fire protection system design should consider the maximum storage height. For new sprinkler installations, maximum storage height is the usable height at which commodities can be stored above the floor while the minimum required unobstructed space below sprinklers is maintained. Where evaluating existing situations, maximum storage height is the maximum existing storage height if space between the sprinklers and storage is equal to or greater than that required.

Building heights where baled cotton is stored should allow for proper clearance between the pile height and sprinkler deflectors. Fire tests of high-piled storage have shown that sprinklers are generally more effective if located 1½ ft to 4½ ft (450 mm to 1.4 m) above the storage height.

A.20.9.2.5 In the example shown in Figure A.20.9.2.5, the maximum ceiling height shown is 30 ft (9.1 m). Sprinkler protection under the highest part of the ceiling must be designed for that height to a point at least 15 ft (4.6 m) beyond where the ceiling height drops to 25 ft (7.6 m). Sprinkler protection beyond that point can be designed for a 25 ft (7.6 m) ceiling.

A.20.9.4.1 Batt insulation creates an effective thermal barrier and can be considered the ceiling/roof deck when determin-

ing the clearance to ceiling. The insulation needs to be installed in each pocket (not just above the sprinkler) and attached to the ceiling/roof in such a manner that it will not fall out during a fire prior to sprinkler activation.

A.20.9.5.1 Sprinkler protection criteria are based on the assumption that roof vents and draft curtains are not being used. *(See Section C.6.)*

A.20.9.5.3 Draft curtains have been shown to have a negative effect on sprinkler effectiveness. If they are mandated, extreme care needs to be taken to minimize any potential impacts.

A.20.10.1 In order for the minimum 3000 ft² (280 m²) requirement for the size of the remote area to not be extended to the adjacent area, the qualifying concealed space must be separated by the entire fire-rated assembly. Such assemblies often have combustible structural members separating the exterior membranes that can create a concealed combustible space that can qualify for omitting sprinkler protection. If the fire-rated assembly is the qualifying concealed space, an interior fire would greatly reduce the assigned fire-rated duration.

A.20.11.1 This subsection allows for calculation of the sprinklers in the largest room, so long as the calculation produces the greatest hydraulic demand among selection of rooms and communicating spaces. For example, in a case where the largest room has four sprinklers and a smaller room has two sprinklers but communicates through unprotected openings with three other rooms, each having two sprinklers, the smaller room and group of communicating spaces should also be calculated.

Corridors are rooms and should be considered as such.

Walls can terminate at a substantial suspended ceiling and need not be extended to a rated floor slab above for this section to be applied.

N **A.20.11.3** This section is not intended to limit the use of the room design method to density/area sprinkler design. The room design method can be used with any type of ceiling sprinklers if the room enclosure requirements are met.

A.20.12 Detection systems, concentrate pumps, generators, and other system components that are essential to the opera-

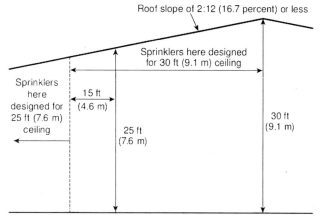

△ **FIGURE A.20.9.2.5   Extended Sprinkler Coverage Under Sloped Ceilings.**

tion of the system should have an approved standby power source.

Where high-expansion foam is contemplated as the protection media, consideration should be given to possible damage to the commodity from soaking and corrosion. Consideration also should be given to the problems associated with the removal of the foam after discharge.

A.20.13 The situation frequently arises where a small area of a higher hazard is surrounded by a lesser hazard. For example, consider a 600 ft² (56 m²) area consisting of 10 ft (3 m) high on-floor storage of cartoned nonexpanded plastic commodities surrounded by a plastic extruding operation in a 15 ft (4.6 m) high building. In accordance with Chapter 12, the density required for the plastic storage must meet the requirements for extra hazard (Group 1) occupancies. The plastic extruding operation should be considered an ordinary hazard (Group 2) occupancy. In accordance with Chapter 11, the corresponding discharge densities should be 0.3 gpm/ft² (12.2 mm/min) over 2500 ft² (230 m²) for the storage and 0.2 gpm/ft² (8.1 mm/min) over 1500 ft² (140 m²) for the remainder of the area. *(Also see Chapter 11 for the required minimum areas of operation.)*

If the storage area is not separated from the surrounding area by a wall or partition *(see 19.1.2)*, the size of the operating area is determined by the higher hazard storage.

For example, the operating area is 2500 ft² (230 m²). The system must be able to provide the 0.3 gpm/ft² (12.2 mm/min) density over the storage area and 15 ft (4.6 m) beyond. If part of the remote area is outside the 600 ft² (56 m²) plus the 15 ft (4.6 m) overlap, only 0.2 gpm/ft² (8.1 mm/min) is needed for that portion.

If the storage is separated from the surrounding area by a floor-to-ceiling/roof partition that is capable of delaying heat from a fire on one side from fusing sprinklers on the other side, the size of the operating area is determined by the occupancy of the surrounding area. In this example, the design area is 1500 ft² (140 m²). A 0.3 gpm/ft² (12.2 mm/min) density is needed within the separated area with 0.2 gpm/ft² (8.1 mm/min) in the remainder of the remote area.

Where high temperature–rated sprinklers are installed at the ceiling, high temperature–rated sprinklers also should extend beyond storage in accordance with Table A.20.13.

When the small higher hazard area is larger than the required minimum area dictated by the surrounding occupancy, even when separated by draft curtains, barriers, or partitions capable of delaying heat, the size of the operating area is determined by the higher hazard storage.

A.20.14 Authorities having jurisdiction have varying requirements for plant first-aid and fire-fighting operations. Examples include no hose stations, hose stations with hose line and nozzles, and hose stations with no hose line or nozzles.

A.20.15.2.1 Where tanks serve sprinklers only, they can be sized to provide the duration required for the sprinkler system, ignoring any hose stream demands. Where tanks serve some combination of sprinklers, inside hose stations, outside hose stations, or domestic/process use, the tank needs to be capable of providing the duration for the equipment that is fed from the tank, but the demands of equipment not connected to the tank can be ignored. Where a tank is used for both domestic/process water and fire protection, the entire duration demand

of the domestic/process water does not need to be included in the tank if provisions are made to segregate the tank so that adequate fire protection water is always present or if provisions are made to automatically cut off the simultaneous use in the event of fire.

A.20.15.2.2 Where pumps serve sprinklers only, they can be sized to provide the flow required for the sprinkler system, ignoring any hose stream demands. Where pumps serve some combination of sprinklers, inside hose stations, or outside hose stations, the pump needs to be capable of providing the flow for the equipment that is fed from the pump, but the demands of equipment not connected to the pump can be ignored.

A.20.16.2 Wet systems are recommended for storage occupancies. Dry pipe systems should be permitted only where it is impractical to provide heat.

A.20.16.2.2 Wet systems are recommended for rack storage occupancies. Dry systems are permitted only where it is impractical to provide heat. Preaction systems should be considered for rack storage occupancies that are unheated, particularly where in-rack sprinklers are installed or for those occupancies that are highly susceptible to water damage.

A.20.17 Idle pallet storage introduces a severe fire condition. Stacking idle pallets in piles is the best arrangement of combustibles to promote rapid spread of fire, heat release, and complete combustion. After pallets are used for a short time in warehouses, they dry out and edges become frayed and splintered. In this condition, they are subject to easy ignition from a small ignition source. Again, high piling increases considerably both the challenge to sprinklers and the probability of involving a large number of pallets when fire occurs. Therefore, it is preferable to store pallets outdoors where possible.

A fire in stacks of idle plastic or wood pallets is one of the greatest challenges to sprinklers. The undersides of the pallets create a shadow area on which a fire can grow and expand to other dry or partially wet areas. This process of jumping to other dry, closely located, parallel, combustible surfaces continues until the fire bursts through the top of the stack. Once this happens, very little water is able to reach the base of the fire. The only practical method of stopping a fire in a large concentration of pallets with ceiling sprinklers is by means of prewetting. In high stacks, this cannot be done without abnormally high water supplies. The storage of empty wood pallets should not be permitted in an unsprinklered warehouse containing other storage.

Table A.20.13 Extension of Installation of High-Temperature Sprinklers over Storage

Design Area for High Temperature–Rated Sprinklers		Distance Beyond Perimeter of High Hazard Occupancy for High Temperature–Rated Sprinklers	
ft²	m²	ft	m
2000	185	30	9.1
3000	280	40	12
4000	370	45	14
5000	465	50	15
6000	555	55	17

A series of seven large-scale fire tests involving idle wood pallets stored on the floor was conducted at Underwriters Laboratories in 2009 and 2010. This testing was conducted to investigate the performance of an upright sprinkler having a nominal K-factor of 11.2 (160) when installed to protect a 8 ft (2.4 m) high array of new 4-way entry, softwood pallets under a 30 ft (9.1 m) ceiling. The pallets used for this test series were supplied by CHEP USA. The impact of the sprinkler temperature rating on fire control performance was the key variable investigated during this test series. Except for the temperature rating of the sprinkler's heat responsive element, the same sprinkler design was used for all seven tests. Three tests were conducted using 286°F (141°C) temperature-rated sprinklers,

two tests were conducted using 200°F (93°C) temperature-rated sprinklers, and two tests conducted using 155°F (68°C) temperature-rated sprinklers. The ignition location for all tests was centered between four sprinklers. To enhance test repeatability, the four sprinklers nearest the ignition location were arranged to discharge water when the first sprinkler operated. The results of this test series are summarized in Table A.20.17.

The results of this large-scale fire test series indicated that sprinklers in the 155°F (68°C) and 200°F (93°C) temperature ratings performed significantly better than the 286°F (141°C) temperature-rated sprinklers as evidenced by a reduced number of operated sprinklers and lower steel temperatures.

Table A.20.17 Summary of Fire Test Data for Idle Pallets (4-Way Entry Softwood) Stored on Floor

Test Date	Test Array	Nominal Storage Height ft (m)	Ceiling Height ft (m)	Sprinkler Information	Number of Operated Sprinklers	Time of First Sprinkler Operation (min:sec)	Time of Last Sprinkler Operation (min:sec)	Max. 1 Min. Ave. Steel Temp. °F (°C)
9/1/2009	2 × 3 with 6 in. (150 mm) longitudinal flue main array 2 × 1 target pallets on each end with 6 in. (150 mm) longitudinal and transverse flues	8 (2.4)	30 (9.1)	286°F, K-11.2, 0.45 gpm/ft² (141°C, K-160, 18.3 mm/min)	12	5:00	23:03	220 (104)
9/10/2009	2 × 3 with 6 in. (150 mm) longitudinal flue main array 2 × 1 target pallets on each end with 6 in. (150 mm) longitudinal and transverse flues	8 (2.4)	30 (9.1)	286°F, K-11.2, 0.45 gpm/ft² (141°C, K-160, 18.3 mm/min)	13	5:05	19:10	208 (98)
9/11/2009	2 × 3 with 6 in. (150 mm) longitudinal flue main array 2 × 1 target pallets on each end with 6 in. (150 mm) longitudinal and transverse flues	8 (2.4)	30 (9.1)	286°F, K-11.2, 0.45 gpm/ft² (141°C, K-160, 18.3 mm/min)	16	5:48	19:04	228 (109)
6/21/2010	2 × 3 with 6 in. (150 mm) longitudinal flue main array 2 × 1 target pallets on each end with 6 in. (150 mm) longitudinal and transverse flues	8 (2.4)	30 (9.1)	200°F, K-11.2, 0.45 gpm/ft² (93°C, K-160, 18.3 mm/min)	4	4:10	4:10	134 (57)
6/22/2010	2 × 3 with 6 in. (150 mm) longitudinal flue main array 2 × 1 target pallets on each end with 6 in. (150 mm) longitudinal and transverse flues	8 (2.4)	30 (9.1)	200°F, K-11.2, 0.45 gpm/ft² (93°C, K-160, 18.3 mm/min)	4	3:34	3:34	135 (57)
6/23/2010	2 × 3 with 6 in. (150 mm) longitudinal flue main array 2 × 1 target pallets on each end with 6 in. (150 mm) longitudinal and transverse flues	8 (2.4)	30 (9.1)	155°F, K-11.2, 0.45 gpm/ft² (68°C, K-160, 18.3 mm/min)	4	3:46	3:46	115 (46)
6/23/2010	2 × 3 with 6 in. (150 mm) longitudinal flue main array 2 × 1 target pallets on each end with 6 in. (150 mm) longitudinal and transverse flues	8 (2.4)	30 (9.1)	155°F, K-11.2, 0.45 gpm/ft² (68°C, K-160, 18.3 mm/min)	4	3:09	3:09	113 (45)

Table A.20.17.1.1(a) Control Mode Density/Area Sprinkler Protection for Indoor Storage of Idle Wood Pallets

Type of Sprinkler	Location of Storage	Nominal K-Factor	Maximum Storage Height		Maximum Ceiling/ Roof Height		Sprinkler Density		Area of Operation		Hose Stream Allowance		Water Supply Duration (hours)
			ft	m	ft	m	gpm/ft²	mm/min	ft²	m²	gpm	L/min	
Control mode density/area	On floor	8 (115) or larger	Up to 6	Up to 1.8	20	6.1	0.2	8.2	3000*	280*	500	1900	1½
	On floor	11.2 (160) or larger	Up to 8	Up to 2.4	30	9.1	0.45	18.3	2500	230	500	1900	1½
	On floor or rack without solid shelves	11.2 (160) or larger	>8 to 12	>2.4 to 3.7	30	9.1	0.6	24.5	3500	325	500	1900	1½
			>12 to 20	>3.7 to 6.1	30	9.1	0.6	24.5	4500	420	500	1900	1½
	On floor	16.8 (240) or larger	Up to 20	Up to 6.1	30	9.1	0.6	24.5	2000	185	500	1900	1½

*The area of sprinkler operation can be permitted to be reduced to 2000 ft² (185 m²) when sprinklers having a nominal K-factor of 11.2 (160) or larger are used, or if high temperature–rated sprinklers having a nominal K-factor of 8.0 (115) are used.

Table A.20.17.1.1(b) Reconnnended Clearance Between Outside Idle Wood Pallet Storage and Building

Wall Construction		Minimum Distance Between Wall and Storage					
		Under 50 Pallets		50 to 200 Pallets		Over 200 Pallets	
Wall Type	Openings	ft	m	ft	m	ft	m
Masonry	None	0	0	0	0	0	0
	Wired glass with outside sprinklers and 1-hour doors	0	0	10	3.0	20	6.1
	Wired or plain glass with outside sprinklers and ¾-hour doors	10	3.0	20	6.1	30	9.1
Wood or metal with outside sprinklers		10	3.0	20	6.1	30	9.1
Wood, metal, or other		20	6.1	30	9.1	50	15

Notes:
(1) Fire-resistive protection comparable to that of the wall also should be provided for combustible eaves lines, vent openings, and so forth.
(2) Where pallets are stored close to a building, the height of storage should be restricted to prevent burning pallets from falling on the building.
(3) Manual outside open sprinklers generally are not a reliable means of protection unless property is attended to at all times by plant emergency personnel.
(4) Open sprinklers controlled by a deluge valve are preferred.

A.20.17.1.1 Table A.20.17.1.1(a) gives recommended clearances between outside idle wood pallet storage and a building. If plastic pallets are stored outdoors, consideration should be given to the anticipated radiated heat produced by the materials used to construct the pallet to establish the appropriate separation distance. [See Table A.20.17.1.1(b).]

A.20.18.1 Columns at the ends of racks or in the aisles need to be protected from the heat of a fire in the racks if they are near the racks. Columns within the flue spaces are already within the footprint of the racks and need protection. In Figure A.20.18.1, Column 1 is within the flue space and needs protection. Column 2 is within 12 in. (300 m) of the rack and needs protection. Column 3 is more than 12 in. (300 m) away from the rack and does not need protection even though it is in an aisle. A portion of Column 4 is within 12 in. (300 m) of the rack and therefore requires sprinkler protection.

A.21.1.2 The reasons for using larger orifice sprinklers in storage situations are based on a number of fire tests in recent years that continue to show an advantage of the larger orifice [K-11.2 (K-160) and K-16.8 (K-240)] sprinklers over the K-5.6 (K-80) and even the K-8.0 (K-115) orifice sprinklers. Following are four sets of fire test comparisons using constant densities [see Table A.21.1.2(a) and Table A.21.1.2(b)]:

(1) K-5.6 (K-80) vs. K-11.2 (K-160)

   (a) Commodity — idle wood two-way pallets
   (b) 2 stacks × 3 stacks × 8 ft (2.4 m) high
   (c) Ceiling height — 30 ft (9.1 m)
   (d) Density — constant 0.30 gpm/ft² (12.2 mm/min)
   (e) Test #1 — 165°F (74°C) rated, K-11.2 (K-160) sprinklers
   (f) Test #2 — 165°F (74°C) rated, K-5.6 (K-80) sprinklers
   (g) Test #1 results — 4 A.S. operated

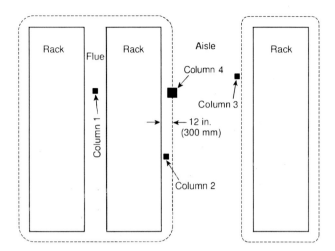

△ FIGURE A.20.18.1   Protection of Columns Within and Adjacent to Rack Structure.

(h) Test #2 results — 29 A.S. operated, less fire control and greater temperatures

(2) K-8.0 (K-115) vs. K-11.2 (K-160) vs. K-16.8 (K-240)

  (a) Commodity — idle wood four-way pallets
  (b) Two stacks × three stacks × 12 ft high (3.7 m)
  (c) Ceiling height — 30 ft (9.1 m)
  (d) Density — constant 0.6 gpm/ft² (24.5 mm/min)
  (e) Test #1 — 286°F (141°C) rated, K-8.0 (K-115) sprinklers
  (f) Test #2 — 165°F (74°C) rated, K-11.2 (K-160) sprinklers
  (g) Test #3 — 165°F (74°C) rated, K-16.8 (K-240) sprinklers
  (h) Test #1 results — 10 A.S. operated, 1215°F (658°C) maximum steel temperature, fire spread to all sides
  (i) Test #2 results — 13 A.S. operated, 200°F (94°C) maximum steel temperature, fire spread to three sides
  (j) Test #3 results — 6 A.S. operated, 129°F (54°C) maximum steel temperature, fire spread (just reached) one side

(3) K-5.6 (K-80) vs. K-16.8 (K-240)

  (a) Commodity — FMRC standard plastic commodity rack style 9 ft (2.7 m) high
  (b) Ceiling height — 30 ft (9.1 m)
  (c) Density — 0.45 gpm/ft² (18.3 mm/min)
  (d) Test #1 — K-5.6 (K-80) orifice sprinklers
  (e) Test #2 — K-16.8 (K-240) orifice sprinklers
  (f) Test #1 results — 29 A.S. operated, 14 pallet loads consumed
  (g) Test #2 results — 5 A.S. operated, 2 pallet loads consumed

(4) K-8.0 (K-115) vs. K-16.8 (K-240)

  (a) Commodity — FMRC standard plastic commodity rack stage 14 ft (4.3 m) high
  (b) Ceiling height — 25 ft (7.6 m)
  (c) Density — 0.60 gpm/ft² (24.5 mm/min)
  (d) Test #1 — K-8.0 (K-115) sprinklers
  (e) Test #2 — K-16.8 (K-240) sprinklers

  (f) Test #1 results — 29 A.S. operated, 25 pallet loads consumed
  (g) Test #2 results — 7 A.S. operated, 4 pallet loads consumed

On an equal density basis, the fire test comparisons show the advantage of the larger orifices. A possibly even bigger advantage can be seen when investigating the performance of larger orifice sprinklers in the real world condition of high initial operating pressures.

The volume of water discharged through the larger K-factor for the initial sprinklers has three significant effects:

(1) First, the increase in sheer volume flowing through the larger orifice enhances performance. For example, a 165 psi (11 bar) initial operating pressure would provide 102.8 gpm (390 L/min) from a K-8.0 (K-115), while the K-16.8 (K-240) will discharge 215.8 gpm (815 L/min).
(2) Second, fire testing at high pressures [100+ psi (6.9 bar)] with K-5.6 (K-80) and K-8.0(K-115) (when high fire updrafts occur) has shown less water penetration and more sprinkler skipping. When fire testing the K-11.2(K-160) and K-16.8 (K-240) sprinklers at 100+ psi (6.9 bar), more water penetration is evident and little or no sprinkler skipping has occurred.
(3) Third, with such high initial discharge rates among K-16.8 (K-240) sprinklers, the friction loss in the supply pipes would be greater. This would result in lower initial pressures than a K-8.0(K-115) as well as being farther down the water supply curve with greater flows resulting in lower initial operating pressures.

Figure A.21.1.2 highlights the differences between the K-8.0(K-115) and K-16.8 (K-240) initial operating pressures.

The higher flow rate of the K-16.8 (K-240) sprinkler results in greater friction losses in the initial operating heads as compared to the K-8.0(K-115) sprinkler. Combined with the lower pressure available on the water supply curve, the end result is a self-regulating K-factor allowing greater initial pressures without a negative impact.

Table A.21.1.2(c) summarizes the paper product testing.

The results. The tests indicated that even at a high temperature of 286°F (141°C), the K-8.0 (K-115) sprinklers operating at higher pressures were not effective in controlling the fire. Conversely, the K-16.8 (K-240) sprinkler was able to control the fire at the lower temperature [155°F (68°C)], by operating sooner, and at lower, self-regulating flowing pressures.

Conclusions. The larger K-factor of the K-16.8 (K-240) sprinkler is not affected by high initial operating pressures. In fact, the protection is enhanced, providing better fire protection.

The ability to use lower-rated temperatures, such as 155°F (68°C) in lieu of 286°F (141°C), shows that the performance of the initial operating sprinklers is effective in controlling the fire. Therefore, using high-temperature sprinklers to reduce the number of surrounding rings of sprinklers to open is not necessary when using the K-16.8 (K-240) technology.

In short, the K-16.8 (K-240) sprinkler proved highly effective when subjected to high initial operating pressures.

A.21.1.5 Modification of an existing system includes extending sprinkler protection into adjacent areas.

Table A.21.1.2(a) Ceiling Type

Fire Type	Ceiling Type	Sprinkler Distance Below Ceiling [in. (mm)]	Time to Activation (seconds)	Size of Fire at Activation [Btu/s (kW)]
Fast-growing fire	Insulated deck	1 (25)	76	450 (475)
	Steel	1 (25)	97	580 (612)
	Wood	1 (25)	71	420 (443)
	Insulated deck	12 (300)	173	1880 (1985)
	Steel	12 (300)	176	1930 (2035)
	Wood	12 (300)	172	1900 (475)
Slow-growing fire	Insulated deck	1 (25)	281	220 (232)
	Steel	1 (25)	375	390 (411)
	Wood	1 (25)	268	200 (211)
	Insulated deck	12 (300)	476	630 (665)
	Steel	12 (300)	492	675 (712)
	Wood	12 (300)	473	620 (654)

Table A.21.1.2(b) Ceiling Arrangement

Situation	Fire	Time to Activate Sprinkler (seconds)	Fire Size at Time of Activation [Btu/s (kW)]
Ceiling with pocket	Fast	86 to 113	585 (617)
Sprinkler 12 in. below ceiling	Fast	172 to 176	1880 to 1900 (1985 to 2005)
Ceiling with pocket	Slow	288 to 395	490 (517)
Sprinkler 12 in. below ceiling	Slow	473 to 492	620 to 675 (654 to 712)

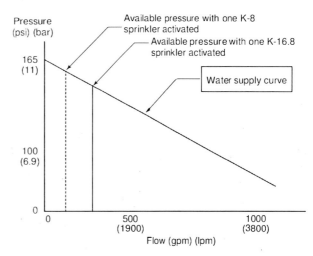

△ FIGURE A.21.1.2   Available Pressure Comparison.

A.21.2 The following procedure should be followed in determining the proper density and area as specified in Chapter 12:

(1) Determine the commodity class
(2) Select the density and area of application
(3) Adjust the required density for storage height
(4) Increase the operating area by 30 percent where a dry pipe system is used
(5) Satisfy the minimum densities and areas *Example:* Storage — greeting cards in boxes in cartons on pallets Height — 22 ft (6.7 m) Clearance to ceiling — 6 ft (1.8 m) Sprinklers — ordinary temperature System type — dry

(a) Classification — Class III
(b) Selection of density/area — 0.225 gpm/ft^2 (9.2 mm/min) over 3000 ft^2 (280 m^2)
(c) Adjustment for height of storage — 1.15 × 0.225 gpm/ft^2 (9.2 mm/min) = 0.259 gpm/ft^2 (10.553 mm/min), rounded up to 0.26 gpm/ft^2 (10.6 mm/min)
(d) Adjustment of area of operation for dry system — 1.3 × 3000 ft^2 (280 m^2) = 3900 ft^2 (360 m^2)
(e) Confirmation that minimum densities and areas have been achieved

△ Table A.21.1.2(c) Paper Product Testing Results

Test Parameters	Test Date			
	3/25/98	3/18/98*	4/4/98	6/4/98†
Sprinklers	K-8.0 (K-115)	K-8.0 (K-115)	K-11.2 (K-160)	K-16.8 (K-240)
Temperature	286°F (141°C)	286°F (141°C)	165°F (74°C)	155°F (68°C)
Storage Type	4 tier pyramid	5 tier pyramid	4 tier pyramid	5 tier pyramid
Storage Height	16 ft (4.9 m)	22 ft (6.7 m)	16 ft (4.9 m)	22 ft (6.7 m)
Ceiling Height	30 ft (9.1 m)	31 ft (9.1 m)	30 ft (9.1 m)	31 ft (9.1 m)
Sprinkler Flow Pressure	22.6 psi (1.6 bar)	175 psi (12.1 bar)	11.9 psi (0.82 bar)	130 psi (9.0 bar)
Number of Operated Sprinklers	15	2	10	2
Peak Gas Temperature	—	868°F (464°C)	—	424°F (217°C)
Peak Steel Temperature	—	421°F (216°C)	—	113°F (45°C)
Fire Spread Across Aisle (30 in.)	N/A	Yes	N/A	No

*This test was run with a fire brigade response of 20:00 minutes.
†This test was run with a fire brigade response of 7:00 minutes.

Shaded text = Revisions.   △ = Text deletions and figure/table revisions.   • = Section deletions.   *N* = New material.

The minimum design density for a dry sprinkler system is 0.15 gpm/ft² over 2600 ft² (6.1 mm/min over 240 m²) for Class III.

The corresponding minimum density at 3000 ft² (280 m²) is 0.17 gpm/ft² (7 mm/min) (satisfied); 1.3 × 3000 ft² (280 m²) = 3900 ft² (363 m²), 0.17 gpm/ft² over 3900 ft² (7 mm/min over 360 m²).

The design density and area of application equals 0.26 gpm/ft² over 3900 ft² (10.6 mm/min over 360 m²).

A.21.2.1(3) Full-scale tests show no appreciable difference in the number of sprinklers that open for either nonencapsulated or encapsulated products up to 15 ft (4.6 m) high. Test data are not available for encapsulated products stored higher than 15 ft (4.6 m). However, in rack storage tests involving encapsulated storage 20 ft (6.1 m) high, increased protection was needed over that for nonencapsulated storage.

The protection specified contemplates a maximum of 10 ft (3.0 m) clearances from top of storage to sprinkler deflectors for storage heights of 15 ft (4.6 m) and higher.

A.21.3.2 There are few storage facilities in which the commodity mix or storage arrangement remains constant, and a designer should be aware that the introduction of different materials can change protection requirements considerably. Design should be based on higher densities and areas of application, and the various reductions allowed should be applied cautiously. For evaluation of existing situations, however, the allowances can be quite helpful.

A.21.3.3 Test data are not available for all combinations of commodities, storage heights, and clearances to ceiling. Some of the protection criteria in this standard are based on extrapolations of test data for other commodities and storage configurations, as well as available loss data.

For example, there are very limited test data for storage of expanded plastics higher than 20 ft (6.1 m). The protection criteria in this standard for expanded plastics higher than 20 ft (6.1 m) are extrapolated from test data for expanded plastics storage 20 ft (6.1 m) and less in height and test data for nonexpanded plastics above 20 ft (6.1 m).

Further examples can be found in the protection criteria for clearance to ceiling up to 15 ft (4.6 m). Test data are limited for clearance to ceiling greater than 10 ft (3.0 m). It should be assumed that, if protection is adequate for a given storage height in a building of a given height, the same protection will protect storage of any lesser height in the same building. For example, protection adequate for 20 ft (6.1 m) storage in a 30 ft (9.1 m) building [10 ft (3.0 m) clearance to ceiling] would also protect 15 ft (4.6 m) storage in a 30 ft (9.1 m) building [15 ft (4.6 m) clearance to ceiling]. Therefore, the protection criteria in Table 21.3.3(a) for 15 ft (4.6 m) clearance to ceiling are based on the protection criteria for storage 5 ft (1.5 m) higher than the indicated height with 10 ft (3.0 m) clearance to ceiling.

Table 21.3.3(a) is based on tests that were conducted primarily with high temperature–rated, K-8 orifice sprinklers. Other tests have demonstrated that, where sprinklers are used with orifices greater than K-8, ordinary-temperature sprinklers are acceptable.

A.21.3.3.1 Two direct comparisons between ordinary temperature– and high temperature–rated sprinklers are possible, as follows:

(1) With nonexpanded polyethylene 1 gal (3.8 L) bottles in corrugated cartons, a 3 ft (0.9 m) clearance, and the same density, approximately the same number of sprinklers operated (nine at high temperature versus seven at ordinary temperature)
(2) With exposed, expanded polystyrene meat trays, a 9.5 ft (1.9 m) clearance, and the same density, three times as many ordinary temperature–rated sprinklers operated as did high temperature–rated sprinklers (11 at high temperature versus 33 at ordinary temperature)

A.21.3.3.2 The "up to" in Table 21.3.3(a) and Table 21.3.3(b) is intended to aid in the interpolation of densities between storage heights.

A.21.4.1.1 Bulkheads are not a substitute for sprinklers in racks. Their installation does not justify reduction in sprinkler densities or design operating areas as specified in the design curves.

A.21.4.1.2.2.1 Data indicate that the sprinkler protection criteria in Figure 21.4.1.2.2.1(a) through Figure 21.4.1.2.2.1(e) are ineffective, by themselves, for rack storage with solid shelves, if the required flue spaces are not maintained. Use of Figure 21.4.1.2.2.1(a) through Figure 21.4.1.2.2.1(e), along with the additional provisions that are required by this standard, can provide acceptable protection.

A.21.4.1.2.3 The aisle width and the depth of racks are determined by material-handling methods. The widths of aisles should be considered in the design of the protection system. Storage in aisles can render protection ineffective and should be discouraged.

A.21.4.2.1 Water demand for storage height over 25 ft (7.6 m) on racks separated by aisles at least 4 ft (1.2 m) wide and with more than 10 ft (3.0 m) between the top of storage and the sprinklers should be based on sprinklers in a 2000 ft² (185 m²) operating area for double-row racks and a 3000 ft² (280 m²) operating area for multiple-row racks discharging a minimum of 0.18 gpm/ft² (7.3 mm/min) for Class I commodities, 0.21 gpm/ft² (8.5 mm/min) for Class II and Class III commodities, and 0.25 gpm/ft² (10.2 mm/min) for Class IV commodities for ordinary temperature–rated sprinklers or a minimum of 0.25 gpm/ft² (10.2 mm/min) for Class I commodities, 0.28 gpm/ft² (11.4 mm/min) for Class II and Class III commodities, and 0.32 gpm/ft² (13 mm/min) for Class IV commodities for high temperature–rated sprinklers. (*See 25.3.3.1.1.1 through 25.3.3.1.1.3 and 25.3.3.2.1.1 through 25.3.3.2.1.3.*)

Where such storage is encapsulated, ceiling sprinkler density should be 25 percent greater than for nonencapsulated storage.

Data indicate that the sprinkler protection criteria in 21.4.2.1 are ineffective, by themselves, for rack storage with solid shelves if the required flue spaces are not maintained. Use of 21.4.2.1, along with the additional provisions that are required by this standard, can provide acceptable protection.

A.21.7 The protection criteria in Table 21.7.1(a) and Table 21.7.1(b) have been developed from fire test data. Protection requirements for other storage methods are beyond the scope of this standard at the present time. From fire testing with densities of 0.45 gpm/ft² (18.3 mm/min) and higher, there have been indications that large orifice sprinklers at greater than 50 ft² (4.6 m²) spacing produce better results than the ½ in. (15 mm) orifice sprinklers at 50 ft² (4.6 m²) spacing.

Table 21.7.1(a) is based on operation of standard sprinklers. Use of quick-response or other special sprinklers should be based on appropriate tests as approved by the authority having jurisdiction.

The current changes to Table 21.7.1(a) and Table 21.7.1(b) represent test results from rubber tire fire tests performed at the Factory Mutual Research Center.

Storage heights and configurations, or both [e.g., automated material-handling systems above 30 ft (9.1 m)], beyond those indicated in the table have not had sufficient test data developed to establish recommended criteria. Detailed engineering reviews of the protection should be conducted and approved by the authority having jurisdiction.

A.21.8.4 Generally, more sprinklers open in fires involving roll paper storage protected by sprinklers rated below the high-temperature range. An increase of 67 percent in the design area should be considered.

A.22.1.5.4 An evaluation for each field situation should be made to determine the worst applicable height–clearance to ceiling relationship that can be expected to appear in a particular case. Fire tests have shown that considerably greater demands occur where the clearance to ceiling is 10 ft (3.0 m) as compared to 3 ft (900 mm) and where a pile is stable as compared to an unstable pile. Since a system is designed for a particular clearance to ceiling, the system could be inadequate when significant areas do not have piling to the design height and larger clearances to ceiling. This can also be true where the packaging or arrangement is changed so that stable piling is created where unstable piling existed. Recognition of these conditions is essential to avoid installation of protection that is inadequate or becomes inadequate because of changes.

No tests were conducted simulating a peaked roof configuration. However, it is expected that the principles of Chapter 20 still apply. The worst applicable height–clearance to ceiling relationship that can be expected to occur should be found, and protection should be designed for it. If storage is all at the same height, the worst height–clearance to ceiling relationship creating the greatest water demand would occur under the peak. If commodities are stored higher under the peak, the various height–clearance to ceiling relationships should be tried and the one creating the greatest water demand used for designing protection.

A.22.1.6 Solid shelf racks as defined in 3.3.208 or obstructions resulting in solid shelf requirements could require additional in-rack sprinklers that could affect the ceiling design requirements.

Δ **A.23.4** The Fire Protection Research Foundation conducted a series of full-scale fire tests at Underwriters Laboratories to develop protection criteria for the rack storage of exposed expanded Group A plastic commodities. The tests are documented in the report, *Protection of Rack Stored Exposed Expanded Group A Plastics with ESFR Sprinklers and Vertical Barriers.* The criteria for exposed expanded plastics are based on Tests 2, 3, 7, and 8 of the series, which investigated a 40 ft (12.2 m) ceiling with a range of storage heights. The tests used K-25.2 intermediate-temperature ESFR sprinklers with vertical barriers attached to the rack uprights at nominal 16 ft (4.9 m) apart. Vertical barriers of sheet metal and ⅜ in. plywood were both investigated. In Tests 1 through 6, transverse flue spaces between commodities were blocked. Comparing the results of Test 6, with blocked transverse flue spaces, and Test 7, with no blocking of transverse flue spaces, revealed the number of operated sprinklers decreased from 11 to 7 and improved suppression of the fire. The criteria for exposed expanded plastics are based on Tests 9 and 10 of the series, which investigated a 30 ft (9.1 m) ceiling with a range of storage heights. The tests used K-25.2 intermediate-temperature ESFR sprinklers with vertical barriers attached to the rack uprights at 16 ft (4.9 m) (nominal) apart. Vertical barriers of ⅜ in. plywood was investigated.

The area limitation between the vertical barriers and aisles indicated in 23.4.7.2 will limit the depth of a multiple-row rack arrangement. The hose stream allowance and water supply duration requirements considered the burning characteristics of the exposed expanded plastic commodity, which generates a high rate of heat release very quickly. However, the commodity involved in the combustion process is quickly consumed after fire suppression or control is achieved.

A.24.1 The intent of this chapter is to provide protection options for the commodity hazards and storage arrangements outlined in Chapters 20 through 25 based on the characteristics of the sprinkler, such as K-factor, orientation, RTI rating, sprinkler spacing type and temperature rating, and using a design format of number of sprinklers at a minimum operating pressure. The protection options offered in this chapter will be based on the results of full-scale fire testing, as outlined in A.24.2 or A.24.3, while incorporating a minimum 50 percent safety factor into the number of sprinklers provided in the design. The intent of this chapter is to offer protection options using sprinklers having a nominal K-factor of 11.2 (160) or higher.

A.24.2 The protection options offered in Section 24.2 are intended to be based on the results of full-scale fire tests conducted at a recognized testing laboratory using the standardized testing methods established by the testing laboratory and supplemented within this chapter.

Protection options for this chapter can be based on storage arrangements other than palletized, solid piled, bin box, shelf storage, or back-to-back shelf storage, provided that the tested storage arrangement (such as rack storage) is deemed more hazardous than the storage arrangements outlined for this chapter.

Ceiling-level sprinkler system designs for this chapter should include a series of tests to evaluate the ability of the sprinkler to control or suppress a fire under a range of test variables for the commodity to be protected when maintained in a storage arrangement applicable to Section 24.2. The sprinkler standards referenced in Table A.7.1.1 provide detailed information regarding representative test commodities, measurement of steel temperatures, and the construction of igniters used to initiate the fire.

Test parameters to be held constant during the test series should include at least the following:

(1) Minimum operating pressure of the sprinklers
(2) Highest commodity hazard that will apply to the protection option
(3) Storage arrangement type

Test parameters that can vary during the test series should include at least the following:

(1) Ignition locations relative to the overhead sprinklers including the following:

  (a) Under one sprinkler
  (b) Between two sprinklers on the same branch line
  (c) Between four sprinklers
  (d) ADD analysis can be used to choose either A.24.2(1)(b) or A.24.2(1)(c)

(2) Maximum ceiling height *(see Table A.24.2 for ceiling height variance)*; representative tests at each ceiling height limitation that has a discrete minimum operating pressure or number of sprinklers required to be included in the hydraulic calculation

(3) Storage heights that are based on the following clearances between the deflector of the ceiling-level sprinkler and the top of storage:

  (a) Minimum clearance, which is typically 3 ft (900 mm)
  (b) Nominal 10 ft (3.0 m) clearance
  (c) Nominal 20 ft (6.1 m) clearance for maximum ceiling heights of 40 ft (12.2 m) or higher

(4) Minimum and maximum temperature ratings
(5) Minimum and maximum sprinkler spacing
(6) Maximum sprinkler distance below the ceiling when greater than 12 in. (300 mm).

See Figure A.24.2 for an example of a nominal 25 ft (7.6 m) high palletized storage fire test arrangement. See Table A.24.2 for a typical large-scale fire test series to investigate the performance of a sprinkler covered by this chapter having a standard coverage area and a discrete minimum operating pressure for a 30 ft (9.1 m) ceiling height.

In addition to determining the number of operated sprinklers, the maximum 1 minute average steel temperature measured above the fire should not exceed 1000°F (538°C), and there should be no sustained combustion at the far end of the main test array and at the outer edges of the target arrays during each test. In addition, no sprinklers should operate at the outer edges of the installed sprinkler system.

The number of sprinklers to be used in the sprinkler system design will be based on the worst-case result obtained from the full-scale fire test series increased by a minimum 50 percent. Regardless of the number of sprinklers that operated during the worst-case full-scale fire test, the number in the sprinkler system demand will be no less than 12 sprinklers for standard coverage sprinklers or six sprinklers for extended coverage sprinklers.

A.24.3 The protection options offered in Section 24.3 are intended to be based on the results of full-scale fire tests conducted at a recognized testing laboratory using the standardized testing methods established by the testing laboratory and supplemented within this chapter.

Ceiling-level sprinkler system designs for this chapter should include a series of tests to evaluate the ability of the sprinkler to control or suppress a fire under a range of test variables for the commodity to be protected when maintained in a storage arrangement applicable to Section 24.3. The sprinkler standards referenced in Table A.7.1.1 provide detailed information regarding representative test commodities, measurement of steel temperatures, and the construction of igniters used to initiate the fire.

Table A.24.2 Typical Example of 25 ft (7.6 m) Palletized Storage Under 30 ft (9.1 m) Ceiling Full-Scale Fire Test Series on Simulated Wet-Type Sprinkler System (considers ADD results)

Parameter	Test 1	Test 2	Test 3	Test 4
Storage type	Palletized	Palletized	Palletized	Palletized
Nominal storage height, ft (m)	20 (6.1)	25 (7.6)	20 (6.1)	20 (6.1)
Nominal ceiling height, ft (m)	30 (9.1)	Adjusted to achieve minimum sprinkler deflector to commodity clearance	30 (9.1)	30 (9.1)
Sprinkler temperature rating	Minimum temperature rating	Maximum temperature rating	Minimum temperature rating	Minimum temperature rating
Nominal deflector to ceiling distance, in. (cm)	Maximum specified by manufacturer	Maximum specified by manufacturer	Maximum specified by manufacturer	Maximum specified by manufacturer
Sprinkler spacing	Maximum permitted by NFPA 13	Maximum permitted by NFPA 13	Minimum permitted by NFPA 13	Maximum permitted by NFPA 13
Nominal discharge pressure, psig (kPa)	Minimum operating	Minimum operating	Minimum operating	Minimum operating
Ignition location	Under one	Between two on same branch line or between four	Under one	Between two on same branch line or between four
Test duration, minutes	30	30	30	30

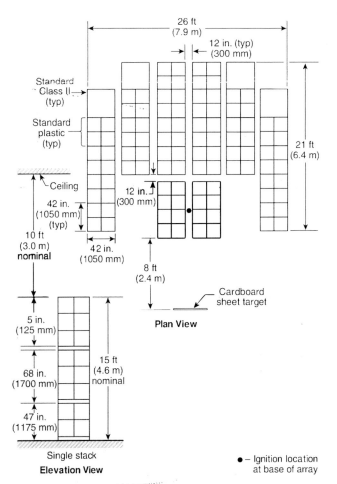

Standard Class II (typ)
Standard plastic (typ)
Ceiling
42 in. (1050 mm) (typ)
10 ft (3.0 m) nominal
42 in. (1050 mm)
26 ft (7.9 m)
12 in. (typ) (300 mm)
21 ft (6.4 m)
12 in. (300 mm)
8 ft (2.4 m)
Cardboard sheet target

Plan View

5 in. (125 mm)
68 in. (1700 mm)
47 in. (1175 mm)
15 ft (4.6 m) nominal

Single stack
Elevation View

● – Ignition location at base of array

Δ **FIGURE A.24.2   Typical Example of 15 ft (4.6 m) Palletized Storage Full-Scale Fire Test Arrangement.**

Test parameters to be held constant during the test series should include at least the following:

(1) Minimum operating pressure of the ceiling-level sprinklers
(2) Highest commodity hazard that will apply to the protection option
(3) Storage arrangement type
(4) Minimum aisle width

Test parameters that can vary during the test series should include at least the following:

(1) Ignition locations relative to the overhead sprinklers including the following:

    (a) Under one sprinkler
    (b) Between two sprinklers on the same branch line
    (c) Between four sprinklers
    (d) ADD analysis can be used to choose either A.24.3(1)(b) or A.24.3(1)(c)

(2) Maximum ceiling height *(see Table A.24.2 for ceiling height variance)*; representative tests at each ceiling height limitation that has a discrete minimum operating pressure or number of sprinklers required to be included in the hydraulic calculation

(3) Storage heights that are based on the following clearances between the deflector of the ceiling-level sprinkler and the top of storage:

    (a) Minimum clearance, which is typically 3 ft (900 mm)
    (b) Nominal 10 ft (3.0 m) clearance
    (c) Nominal 20 ft (6.1 m) clearance for maximum ceiling heights of 40 ft (12.2 m) or higher

(4) Minimum and maximum temperature ratings
(5) Minimum and maximum sprinkler spacing
(6) Maximum sprinkler distance below the ceiling when greater than 12 in. (300 mm)

Historical testing has indicated that a double-row rack storage arrangement is considered representative of single- and multiple-row rack storage. The ignition location relative to the sprinkler has been demonstrated to be a key variable associated with full-scale fire tests. The critical ignition scenarios include locating (1) one of the sprinklers directly above the center of the main storage array, (2) two of the sprinklers on the same branch line such that the midpoint between the two sprinklers is directly above the center of the storage array, and (3) four sprinklers (two each on adjacent branch lines) such that the geometric center point between the four sprinklers is located directly above the center of the main storage array. The igniters for this testing should be placed at the base of the storage array and offset from the center of the main array in the transverse flue space as illustrated in Figure A.24.3. Previous testing has demonstrated that an offset ignition location represents a challenging test scenario.

A double-rack storage array should be a nominal 32 ft (9.8 m) long with single-row target arrays located on each side of the main array. The sprinkler branch lines should be installed in a direction that is perpendicular to the longitudinal flue spacing of the storage arrangement, and the branch lines over the test array should be sized such that they represent the largest obstruction for upright-style sprinklers. See Figure A.24.3 for an example of a nominal 30 ft (9.1 m) high double-row rack storage fire test arrangement. See Table A.24.3(a) and Table A.24.3(b) for a typical full-scale fire test series to investigate the performance of a sprinkler covered by this chapter having a standard coverage area and a discrete minimum operating pressure for a 40 ft (12.2 m) ceiling height.

In addition to determining the number of operated sprinklers, the maximum 1 minute average steel temperature measured above the fire should not exceed 1000°F (538°C), and there should be no sustained combustion at the far end of the main test array and at the outer edges of the target arrays during each test. In addition, no sprinklers should operate at the outer edges of the installed sprinkler system.

The number of sprinklers to be used in the sprinkler system design will be based on the worst-case result obtained from the full-scale fire test series increased by a minimum 50 percent. Regardless of the number of sprinklers that operated during the worst-case full-scale fire test, the number in the sprinkler system demand will be no less than 12 sprinklers for standard coverage sprinklers or six sprinklers for extended coverage sprinklers.

Once the number of sprinklers for a demand area has been established, the minimum operating area, based on the proposed sprinkler spacing, cannot be less than 768 ft² (71 m²).

Δ **Table A.24.3(a) Typical Example of a 35 ft (10.7 m) Rack Storage Under a 40 ft (12.2 m) Ceiling Full-Scale Fire Test Series on a Simulated Wet-Type Sprinkler System (considers ADD results)**

Parameter	Test 1	Test 2	Test 3	Test 4
Storage type	Double-row rack	Double-row rack	Double-row rack	Double-row rack
Nominal storage height, ft (m)	30 (9.1)	35 (10.7)	30 (9.1)	20 (6.1)
Nominal ceiling height, ft (m)	40 (12.2)	Adjusted to achieve minimum sprinkler deflector to commodity clearance	40 (12.2)	40 (12.2)
Sprinkler temperature rating	Minimum temperature rating	Maximum temperature rating	Minimum temperature rating	Minimum temperature rating
Nominal deflector to ceiling distance, in. (mm)	Maximum specified by manufacturer	Maximum specified by manufacturer	Maximum specified by manufacturer	Maximum specified by manufacturer
Sprinkler spacing	Maximum permitted by NFPA 13	Maximum permitted by NFPA 13	Minimum permitted by NFPA 13	Maximum permitted by NFPA 13
Nominal discharge pressure, psig (kPa)	Minimum operating	Minimum operating	Minimum operating	Minimum operating
Ignition location	Under one	Between two on same branch line or between four	Under one	Between two on same branch line or between four
Test duration, minutes	30	30	30	30

Δ **Table A.24.3(b) Typical Example of 35 ft (10.7 m) Rack Storage Under 40 ft (12.2 m) Ceiling Full-Scale Fire Test Series on a Simulated Wet-Type Sprinkler System**

Parameter	Test 1	Test 2	Test 3	Test 4
Storage type	Double-row rack	Double-row rack	Double-row rack	Double-row rack
Nominal storage height, ft (m)	30 (9.1)	35 (10.7)	30 (9.1)	20 (6.1)
Nominal ceiling height, ft (m)	40 (12.2)	Adjusted to achieve minimum sprinkler deflector to commodity clearance	40 (12.2)	40 (12.2)
Sprinkler temperature rating	Minimum temperature rating	Maximum temperature rating	Minimum temperature rating	Minimum temperature rating
Nominal deflector to ceiling distance, in. (mm)	Within 12 (300)	Maximum specified by manufacturer	Maximum specified by manufacturer	Maximum specified by manufacturer
Sprinkler spacing	10 × 10 (3.0 × 3.0)	10 × 10 (3.0 × 3.0)	10 × 10 (3.0 × 3.0)	10 × 10 (3.0 × 3.0)
Nominal discharge pressure, psig (kPa)	Minimum operating	Minimum operating	Minimum operating	Minimum operating
Ignition location	Under one	Between four	Between two on same branch line	Between two on same branch line
Test duration, minutes	30	30	30	30

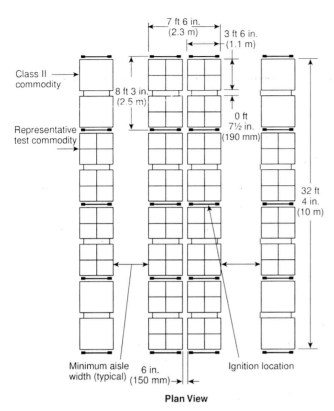

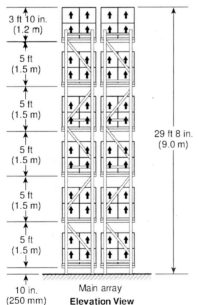

Δ **FIGURE A.24.3   Typical Example of 30 ft (9.1 m) Double-Row Rack Storage Fire Test Arrangement.**

N **A.25.1.1.1** The following information should be obtained prior to using Chapter 25 to assist in determining the proper protection options provided in the chapter:

(1) Commodity classification of the storage, using Chapter 20
(2) If Class I through Class IV, whether the commodity is exposed and nonencapsulated, exposed and encapsulated, or cartoned
(3) The maximum storage height and ceiling height for the storage area
(4) Rack type (i.e., fixed-in-place, portable, or moveable) in which the storage will be maintained
(5) Aisle width between storage racks
(6) Depth of the storage racks
(7) Rack arrangements (i.e., single-, double-, or multiple-row racks) in which the storage will be maintained
(8) Whether solid shelves will be present and, if applicable, shelf size

N **A.25.1.4.2** In-rack sprinklers and ceiling sprinklers selected for protection should be controlled by at least two separate indicating valves and drains. In higher rack arrangements, consideration should be given to providing more than one in-rack control valve in order to limit the extent of any single impairment.

N **A.25.1.4.3** See A.16.11.2 and Section C.4.

N **A.25.1.5** Solid shelf racks as defined in 3.3.208 or obstructions resulting in solid shelf requirements could require additional in-rack sprinklers that could affect the ceiling design requirements.

N **A.25.1.7.3** In-rack sprinklers have proven to be the most effective way to fight fires in rack storage. To accomplish this, however, in-rack sprinklers must be located where they will operate early in a fire and direct water where it will do the most good. Simply maintaining a minimum horizontal spacing between sprinklers does not achieve this goal because fires in rack storage develop and grow in transverse and longitudinal flues, and in-rack sprinklers do not operate until flames actually impinge on them. To ensure early operation and effective discharge, in-rack sprinklers in the longitudinal flue of open-frame racks need to be located at transverse flue intersections.

N **A.25.1.7.8** Where rack storage is up to and including 25 ft (7.6 m) in height, in-rack sprinklers should be a minimum 3 in. (75 mm) radially from the side of rack uprights.

N **A.25.1.7.10.2** See Figure A.25.1.7.10.2 for an example of in-rack sprinklers being installed between a single-row rack and an adjacent full-height wall.

N **A.25.1.8.1** Where one level of in-rack sprinklers is required by the guidelines in Chapter 25, in-rack sprinklers for multiple-row rack storage up to and including 25 ft (7.6 m) of Class I through Class IV commodities should be installed at the first tier level nearest one-half to two-thirds of the highest expected storage height.

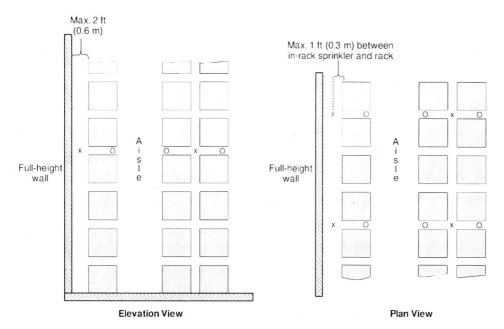

N FIGURE A.25.1.7.10.2   Example of In-Rack Sprinklers Installed Between a Single-Row Rack and an Adjacent Full-Height Wall.

N **A.25.1.8.3.1** Where storage tiers in a double-row rack are not the same size on each side of the longitudinal flue, one side of the flue should be protected with sprinklers at the proper elevation above the load. The next level of sprinklers should protect the other side of the flue with the sprinklers at the proper elevation above that load as indicated in Figure A.25.1.8.3.1. The vertical spacing requirements for in-rack sprinklers, as specified in the appropriate section for the commodity and storage height, should be followed.

N **A.25.1.8.3.2** Where possible, it is recommended that in-rack sprinkler deflectors be located at least 6 in. (150 mm) vertically above the top of storage located below them.

N **A.25.1.9.1** Barriers should be of sufficient strength to avoid sagging that interferes with loading and unloading operations.

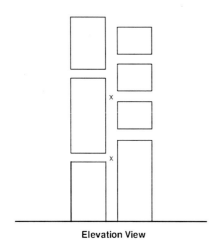

N FIGURE A.25.1.8.3.1   Placement of In-Rack Sprinklers Where Rack Levels Have Varying Heights.

N **A.25.1.12** Information for the protection of Class I through Class IV commodities was extrapolated from full-scale fire tests that were performed at different times than the tests that were used to develop the protection for Group A plastic commodities. It is possible that, by selecting certain points from the tables, and after applying the appropriate modifications, the protection specified by 25.3.2.1 or 25.3.2.2 for Class I through Class IV commodities exceeds the requirements for Group A plastic commodities. In such situations, the protection specified for Group A plastic commodities, although less than that required by the tables, can adequately protect Class I through Class IV commodities. This section also allows storage areas that are designed to protect Group A plastic commodities to store Class I through Class IV commodities without a re-evaluation of the fire protection systems.

N **A.25.2.2.1(2)** All rack fire tests of Group A plastic commodities were run with an approximate 10 ft (3.0 m) maximum clearance to ceiling.

N **A.25.3.2.1.1** Spacing of sprinklers on branchlines in racks in the various tests demonstrates that maximum spacing as specified is proper.

N **A.25.3.2.1.2.1** Bulkheads are not a substitute for sprinklers in racks. Their installation does not justify reduction in sprinkler densities or design operating areas as specified in the design curves. Data indicate that the sprinkler protection criteria in Table 25.3.2.1.2.1(A)(a) through Table 25.3.2.1.2.1(A)(d) are ineffective, by themselves, for rack storage with solid shelves if the required flue spaces are not maintained. Use of Table 25.3.2.1.2.1(A)(a) through Table 25.3.2.1.2.1(A)(d), along with the additional provisions that are required by this standard, can provide acceptable protection. It is not the intent that an in-rack sprinkler be installed above the top-tier of storage when utilizing in-rack sprinklers at each tier level.

N **A.25.3.2.1.2.1(B)** The aisle width and the depth of racks are determined by material-handling methods. The widths of aisles should be considered in the design of the protection system. Storage in aisles can render protection ineffective and should be discouraged.

N **A.25.3.2.2.1** Spacing of sprinklers on branchlines in racks in the various tests demonstrates that maximum spacing as specified is proper.

N **A.25.3.2.2.2.1** Bulkheads are not a substitute for sprinklers in racks. Their installation does not justify reduction in sprinkler densities or design operating areas as specified in the design curves. Data indicate that the sprinkler protection criteria in Table 25.3.2.2.2.1(A)(a) through Table 25.3.2.2.2.1(A)(d) are ineffective, by themselves, for rack storage with solid shelves if the required flue spaces are not maintained. Use of Table 25.3.2.2.2.1(A)(a) through Table 25.3.2.2.2.1(A)(d), along with the additional provisions that are required by this standard, can provide acceptable protection. It is not the intent that an in-rack sprinkler be installed above the top-tier of storage when utilizing in-rack sprinklers at each tier level.

N **A.25.3.2.2.2.1(B)** Bulkheads are not a substitute for sprinklers in racks. Their installation does not justify reduction in sprinkler densities or design operating areas as specified in the design curves. Data indicate that the sprinkler protection criteria in Table 25.3.2.1.2.1(A)(a) through Table 25.3.2.1.2.1(A)(d) are ineffective, by themselves, for rack storage with solid shelves if the required flue spaces are not maintained. Use of Table 25.3.2.1.2.1(A)(a) through Table 25.3.2.1.2.1(A)(d), along with the additional provisions that are required by this standard, can provide acceptable protection. It is not the intent that an in-rack sprinkler be installed above the top-tier of storage when utilizing in-rack sprinklers at each tier level.

N **A.25.3.2.3.1.2** In most of the figures listed in 25.3.2.3.1.1, the designer is presented with multiple options from which to choose. The single column of boxes in the elevation view represents single-row rack storage, the double column of boxes in the elevation view represents double-row rack storage, and the options with three or four columns of boxes represent different arrangements of multiple-row rack storage. The symbols *X* and *O* in the elevation and plan views represent different rows of in-rack sprinklers: the symbols in the elevation view show the vertical spacing of the in-rack sprinklers, while the symbols in the plan view show the horizontal spacing of in-rack sprinklers. Different symbols are used so that the upper and lower levels of in-rack sprinklers can be determined when looking at the plan view.

N **A.25.3.2.4.1** Each of the figures listed in 25.3.2.4.1 shows a variety of different potential rack arrangements. The first single-row rack (SRR) to the left in each figure shows a single-row rack with aisles on each side. The double-row rack (DRR) is in the center of the figure. The multiple-row rack (MRR) on the right shows rack structures where the in-rack sprinkler pattern can be repeated.

N **A.25.3.3.1.1.6(A)** Where the clearance to ceiling exceeds 10 ft (3.0 m) with CMDA ceiling-level sprinklers protecting exposed nonencapsulated Class I, Class II, Class III, or Class IV commodities, a horizontal barrier should be installed above storage with one level of in-rack sprinklers under the barrier.

N **A.25.3.3.1.2** Data indicate that the sprinkler protection criteria in 25.3.3.1.2 are ineffective, by themselves, for rack storage

with solid shelves if the required flue spaces are not maintained. Use of 25.3.3.1.2, along with the additional provisions that are required by this standard, can provide acceptable protection.

N **A.25.3.3.2.1.6(A)** Where the clearance to ceiling exceeds 10 ft (3.0 m) with CMDA ceiling-level sprinklers protecting exposed encapsulated, or cartoned (nonencapsulated or encapsulated) Class I, Class II, Class III, or Class IV commodities, a horizontal barrier should be installed above storage with one level of in-rack sprinklers under the barrier.

N **A.25.3.3.2.2** Data indicate that the sprinkler protection criteria in 25.3.3.2.2 are ineffective, by themselves, for rack storage with solid shelves if the required flue spaces are not maintained. Use of 25.3.3.2.2, along with the additional provisions that are required by this standard, can provide acceptable protection.

N **A.25.3.3.3.2** Ordinary-, intermediate-, or high-temperature ceiling-level sprinklers can be used in this application. There are no data to support temperature rating restrictions for this section.

N **A.25.3.3.4.2** Ordinary-, intermediate-, or high-temperature ceiling-level sprinklers can be used in this application. There are no data to support temperature rating restrictions for this section.

N **A.25.4.1.2.3** See Figure A.25.4.1.2.3 for an example showing the installation of in-rack sprinklers within racks having solid shelves that obstruct only a portion of an open rack protected by CMSA ceiling-level sprinklers.

N **A.25.4.3.1** There are currently no situations where in-rack sprinklers are required to be used to protect Group A plastic commodities stored over 25 ft (7.6 m) in height where CMSA sprinklers are used at the ceiling.

N **A.25.5.1.2.3** See Figure A.25.5.1.2.3 for an example showing the installation of in-rack sprinklers within racks having solid shelves that obstruct only a portion of an open rack protected by ESFR ceiling-level sprinklers.

N **A.25.6.2.5.5.2** An example of equipment that might create an opening is a pipe drop.

A.25.6.3.2.1 The design for the ceiling sprinkler system can treat the top level of in-rack sprinklers as a floor, thus allowing for storage heights above the top in-rack sprinkler level that exceed 10 ft (3.0 m). For example, if open rack storage of cartoned Group A plastics was stored to 70 ft (21.3 m) high under an 80 ft (24.4 m) ceiling and one level of in-rack sprinklers was installed in accordance with Option 2 of Table 25.6.2.2 at the 40 ft (12.2 m) level, then the ceiling level sprinkler system could be designed based on 30 ft (9.1 m) high storage being maintained under a 40 ft (12.2 m) high ceiling.

N **A.25.6.3.3.3** Hydraulic balancing with the ceiling sprinkler system is not required.

N **A.25.7.2.1(2)** All rack fire tests of Group A plastic commodities were run with an approximate 10 ft (3.0 m) maximum clearance to ceiling.

N **A.25.8.2.1** Spacing of sprinklers on branchlines in racks in the various tests demonstrates that maximum spacing as specified is proper.

N **A.25.8.2.2.1** Bulkheads are not a substitute for sprinklers in racks. Their installation does not justify reduction in sprinkler densities or design operating areas as specified in the design curves. Data indicate that the sprinkler protection criteria in Table 25.8.2.2.1 are ineffective, by themselves, for rack storage with solid shelves if the required flue spaces are not maintained. Use of Table 25.8.2.2.1, along with the additional provisions that are required by this standard, can provide acceptable protection. It is not the intent that an in-rack sprinkler be installed above the top-tier of storage when utilizing in-rack sprinklers at each tier level.

N **A.25.8.2.2.2** The adjustments in 25.8.2.2.2 apply to solid shelves where the minimum required level of in-rack sprinklers from an open rack option is exceeded.

N **A.25.8.2.2.2.1** The aisle width and the depth of racks are determined by material-handling methods. The widths of aisles should be considered in the design of the protection system. Storage in aisles can render protection ineffective and should be discouraged.

N **A.25.8.2.2.2.2** Data indicate that the sprinkler protection criteria in Figure 25.8.2.2.1(a) through Figure 25.8.2.2.1(d) are ineffective, by themselves, for rack storage with solid shelves if the required flue spaces are not maintained. Use of Figure 25.8.2.2.1(a) through Figure 25.8.2.2.1(d), as specified by Table 25.8.2.2.1, along with the additional provisions that are required by this standard can provide acceptable protection.

N **A.25.8.2.2.2.5** It is not the intent that an in-rack sprinkler be installed above the top-tier of storage when utilizing in-rack sprinklers at each tier level.

N **A.25.8.3.1** Spacing of sprinklers on branchlines in racks in the various tests demonstrates that maximum spacing as specified is proper.

N **A.25.8.3.2.1** Bulkheads are not a substitute for sprinklers in racks. Their installation does not justify reduction in sprinkler densities or design operating areas as specified in the design curves. Data indicate that the sprinkler protection criteria obtained from Table 25.8.3.2.1 are ineffective, by themselves, for rack storage with solid shelves if the required flue spaces are not maintained. Use of Table 25.8.3.2.1, along with the additional provisions that are required by this standard, can provide acceptable protection. It is not the intent that an in-rack sprinkler be installed above the top-tier of storage when utilizing "in-rack sprinklers at each tier level."

N **A.25.8.3.2.2** The adjustments in 25.8.3.2.2 apply to solid shelves where the minimum required level of in-rack sprinklers from an open rack option is exceeded.

N **A.25.8.3.2.2.1** The aisle width and the depth of racks are determined by material-handling methods. The widths of aisles should be considered in the design of the protection system. Storage in aisles can render protection ineffective and should be discouraged.

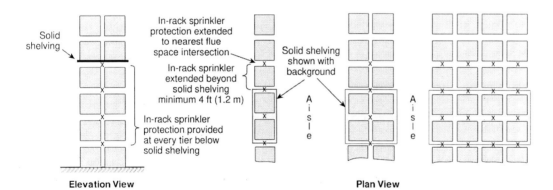

N **FIGURE A.25.4.1.2.3**   Example of Horizontal and Vertical In-Rack Sprinkler Installation When Only a Portion of an Open Rack, Protected by CMSA Ceiling-Level Sprinklers, is Obstructed by Solid Shelving.

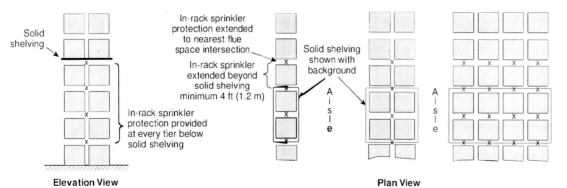

N **FIGURE A.25.5.1.2.3**   Example of Horizontal and Vertical In-Rack Sprinkler Installation When Only a Portion of an Open Rack, Protected by ESFR Ceiling-Level Sprinklers, is Obstructed by Solid Shelving.

N **A.25.8.3.2.2.2** Data indicate that the sprinkler protection criteria in Figure 25.8.3.2.1(a) through Figure 25.8.3.2.1(d) are ineffective, by themselves, for rack storage with solid shelves, if the required flue spaces are not maintained. Use of Figure 25.8.2.2.1(a) through Figure 25.8.2.2.1(d), as specified by Table 25.8.3.2.1, along with the additional provisions that are required by this standard, can provide acceptable protection.

N **A.25.8.3.2.2.5** It is not the intent that an in-rack sprinkler be installed above the top-tier of storage when utilizing in-rack sprinklers at each tier level.

N **A.26.1** Compliance with these provisions requires the storage arrangements and the sprinkler system design to comply with all limitations in the option that is selected. The use of a designation associated with a specific industry usage, such as retail, automotive, or records storage, is not intended to mandate the use of such protection criteria to only that applicable to such industries, nor is it intended to limit the use of the specified criteria to only such industries, provided the storage arrangement and protected commodities fall within the bounds of permitted protection.

N **A.26.1.1** These storage configurations do not conform precisely with the storage arrangements detailed in Chapters 20 through 25. The designs are the result of specific research and test data that have been provided to support the specific protection requirements for the unique storage arrangements. The special sprinkler system designs for storage protection of Chapter 26 are options to general storage requirements.

A.26.3 These special designs are based on fire heat release calorimeter tests and 11 full-scale tests conducted by the Retail Fire Research Coalition at Underwriters Laboratories in 2000 and 2007. *[See Figure A.26.3(a) through Figure A.26.3(f).]*

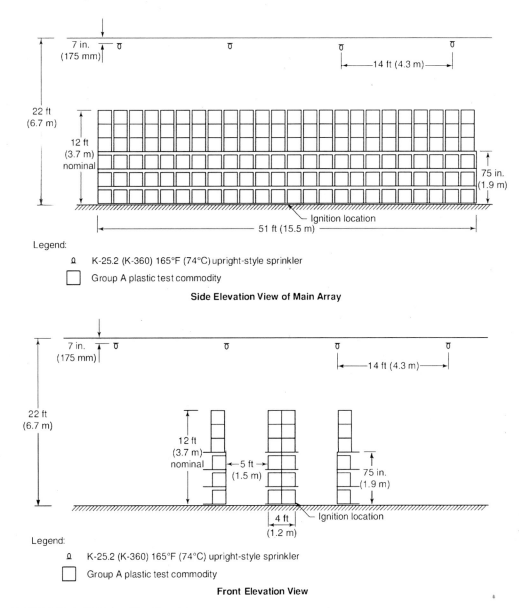

Side Elevation View of Main Array

Legend:

Ω   K-25.2 (K-360) 165°F (74°C) upright-style sprinkler

☐   Group A plastic test commodity

Front Elevation View

Δ **FIGURE A.26.3(a)   Fire Test A1.**

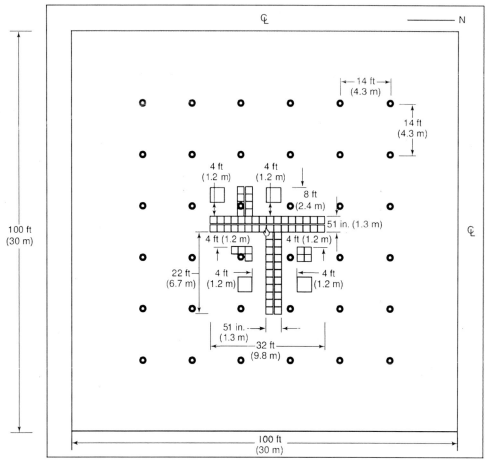

Shelving suspended on wire uprights at 24 in. (600 mm), 48 in. (1200 mm), 72 in. (1800 mm), 96 in. (2400 mm), and 120 in. (3000 mm) with a wire shelf at 148 in. (3.7 m)

Legend:

○   K-25.2 (K-360) upright-style sprinkler 165°F (74°C) QR, 0.55 gpm/ft² (22.4 mm/min/m²) water density for first four sprinkler operations, then 0.49 gpm/ft² (20 mm/min/m²) for all additional operations

▫   Group A plastic test commodity

▫   Class II target commodity

⬧   Ignition location

Plan View

Δ **FIGURE A.26.3(b)   Fire Test A2.**

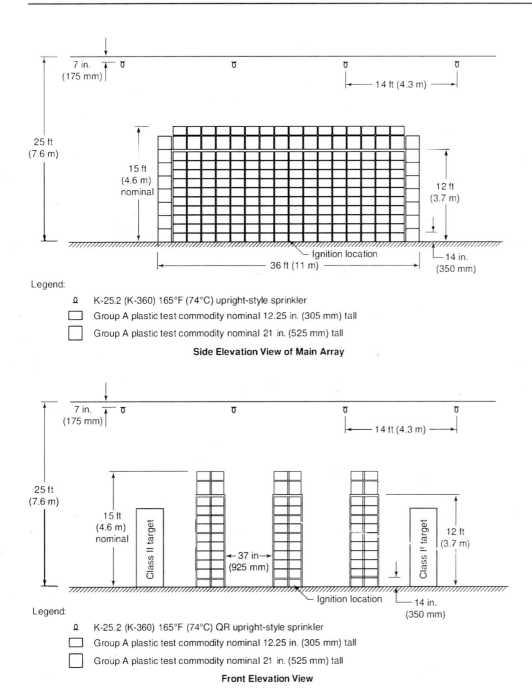

Legend:

Ω   K-25.2 (K-360) 165°F (74°C) upright-style sprinkler

☐   Group A plastic test commodity nominal 12.25 in. (305 mm) tall

☐   Group A plastic test commodity nominal 21 in. (525 mm) tall

Side Elevation View of Main Array

Legend:

Ω   K-25.2 (K-360) 165°F (74°C) QR upright-style sprinkler

☐   Group A plastic test commodity nominal 12.25 in. (305 mm) tall

☐   Group A plastic test commodity nominal 21 in. (525 mm) tall

Front Elevation View

Δ **FIGURE A.26.3(c)   Fire Test A3.**

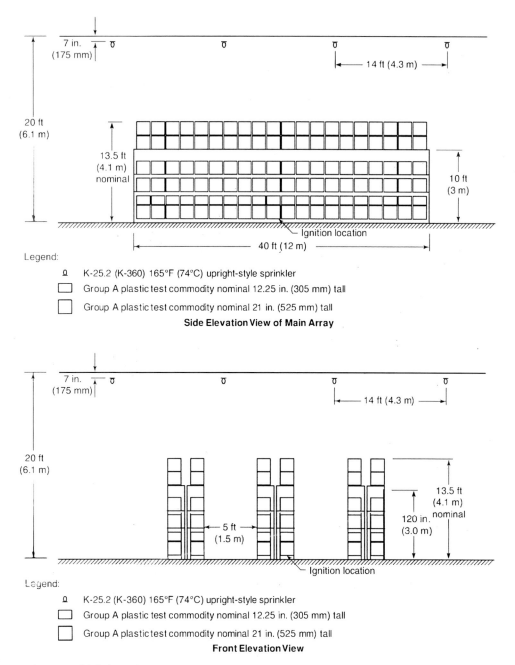

Side Elevation View of Main Array

Front Elevation View

Δ FIGURE A.26.3(d)   Fire Test A4.

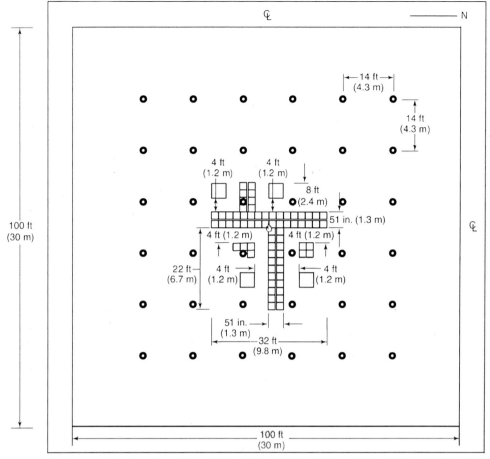

Shelving suspended on wire uprights at 24 in. (600 mm), 48 in. (1200 mm), 72 in. (1800 mm), 96 in. (2400 mm), and 120 in. (3000 mm) with a wire shelf at 148 in. (3700 mm)

Legend:

⊙   K-25.2 (K-360) upright-style sprinkler 165°F (74°C) QR, 0.55 gpm/ft² (22.4 mm/min/m²) water density for first four sprinkler operations, then 0.49 gpm/ft² (20 mm/min/m²) for all additional operations

▢   Group A plastic test commodity

▢   Class II target commodity

⚶   Ignition location

Plan View

Δ **FIGURE A.26.3(e)**   **Fire Test A6 — Plan View.**

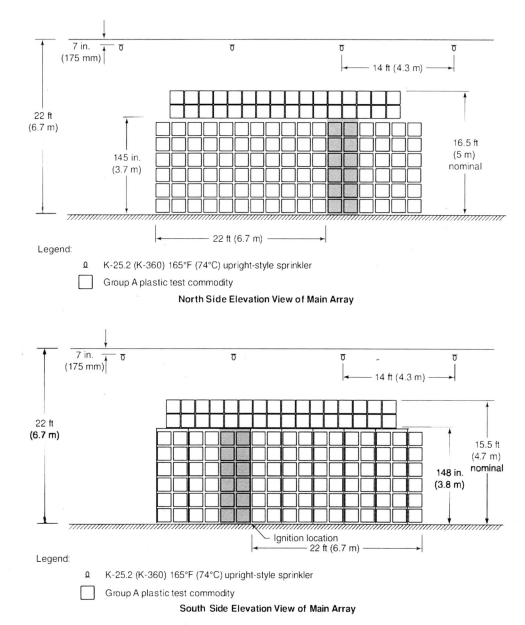

Legend:

Ω   K-25.2 (K-360) 165°F (74°C) upright-style sprinkler

☐   Group A plastic test commodity

North Side Elevation View of Main Array

Legend:

Ω   K-25.2 (K-360) 165°F (74°C) upright-style sprinkler

☐   Group A plastic test commodity

South Side Elevation View of Main Array

Δ **FIGURE A.26.3(f)   Fire Test A6 — Main Array (North/South).**

N **A.26.4.1.2** *(See Section C.20.)*

A.26.5 For the protection of baled cotton, fire tests and actual fire experience indicate an initial low heat release; thus, sprinklers in the ordinary-temperature range should offer some advantage by opening faster than those of intermediate- or high-temperature classifications under similar conditions.

N **A.26.6.6** See Section C.25.

A.26.6.6.3.5 Figure A.26.6.6.3.5(a) through Figure A.26.6.6.3.5(c) illustrate a typical rack layout for cartoned record storage showing the design and installation of in-rack sprinklers underneath the catwalks and in the transverse flues.

A.26.7.1 NFPA 13 contains protection criteria for limited configurations of compact mobile storage units and materials stored. Storage arrangements not specifically addressed in NFPA 13 are outside the scope of the standard (i.e., protection for commodities other than paper files, magazines, or books in compact mobile storage units does not simply follow high-piled storage protection criteria for shelves or racks). Where compact mobile storage configurations outside the scope of NFPA 13 are to be utilized, they must be addressed on a case-by-case basis with consideration given to the fact that no known sprinkler protection criteria is currently available. Additional protection features, such as rated construction, barriers within the storage, consideration for safe locating away from vulnerable areas, and methods for control or exhausting of the smoke, should be considered.

A.26.7.5 Steel barriers that are shown to have equivalent resistance to passage of flames and heat transfer in fire tests as solid 24 gauge (0.6 mm) steel barriers are permitted.

A.26.8.1 See Figure A.26.8.1.

Δ FIGURE A.26.6.6.3.5(a)   Typical Cartoned Record Storage Sprinkler Installation.

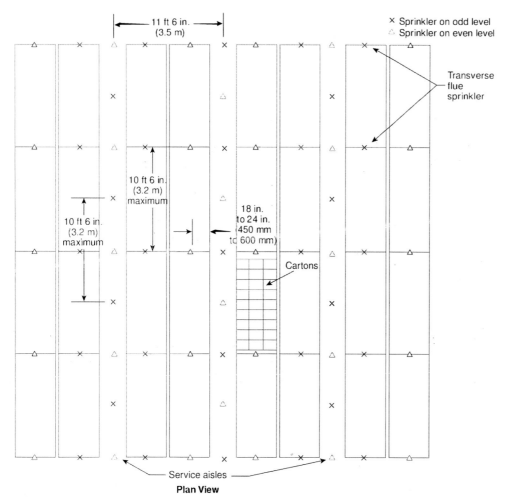

△ FIGURE A.26.6.6.3.5(b)   Plan View of Sprinkler Locations in Cartoned Record Storage.

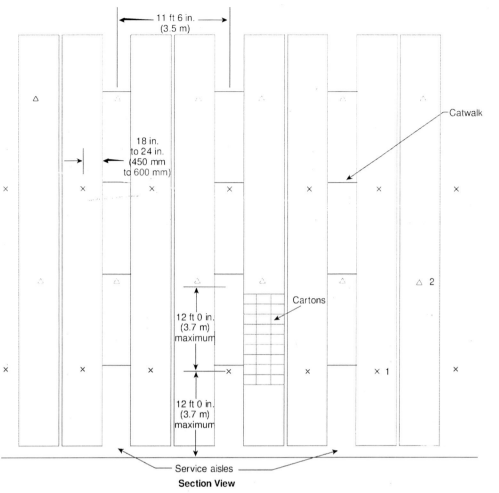

Notes:
(1) Sprinkler labeled 1 located at odd levels 1, 3, 5, 7, etc.
(2) Sprinkler labeled 2 located at even levels 2, 4, 6, 8, etc.
(3) For storage higher than represented, the cycle defined by Notes 1 and 2 is repeated, with stagger as indicated.
(4) Symbols △ and × indicate sprinkler on vertical horizontal stagger.
(5) Each rack level has maximum 81 cartons, which represents a single load.
(6) Transverse flues at rack uprights.
(7) 0 in. to 2 in. (0 mm to 50 mm) service space between back-to-back units.
(8) Transverse flue and aisle sprinklers upright with deflector minimum 6 in. (150 mm) above storage.

△ FIGURE A.26.6.6.3.5(c)   Section View of Sprinkler Locations in Cartoned Record Storage.

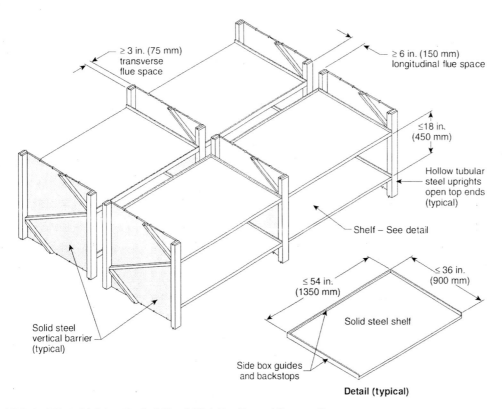

△ FIGURE A.26.8.1   Typical Fixed High Bay Record Storage Structure.

△ **A.28.1** Preliminary plans should be submitted for review to the authority having jurisdiction prior to the development of working plans *[see Figure A.28.1(a)]*. The preliminary plans can be part of the construction documents submitted in order to obtain a building permit. However, working drawings in accordance with Section 28.1 should be submitted and approved prior to the installation of system equipment. Preliminary plans should include as much information as is required to provide a clear representation of the hazard to be protected, the system design concept, the proposed water supply configuration, and the building construction information pertinent to the system layout and detailing.

The owner's information certificate, shown in Figure A.28.1(b), should be used to obtain a declaration of the intended use of the occupancy to be protected.

Drawings that accompany the certificate should include the following:

(1) Name of owner and occupant
(2) Location, including street address
(3) Point of compass
(4) Construction and occupancy of each building
(5) Building height in feet
(6) Waterflow test information and, if a waterflow test of the city main is available, indicate the following:

  (a) Date and time of the test
  (b) Name of party that conducted the test
  (c) Location of the hydrants where the flow was taken and where static and residual pressure readings were recorded *(see A.5.2.2)*

  (d) Size and configuration of mains supplying the hydrants
  (e) Size and number of open hydrant butts that flood
  (f) Results of the test
(7) Building features such as combustible concealed spaces, floor openings, areas subject to freezing, and areas from which it is intended to omit sprinkler protection
(8) Proposed location and approximate size, if a water supply employing pumps or tanks is contemplated
(9) Name and address of party submitting the preliminary plans
(10) Tentative location of major piping, including mains underground, risers, overhead mains, and fire department connections

A.28.1.1 See Figure A.28.1.1.

A.28.1.1.1(4) It is the intent to provide the owner's certificate for all new systems and where there is a change of occupancy and/or building use.

N **A.28.1.3(10)** Examples of such major mechanical, plumbing, and electrical equipment include, but are not limited to, ducts, piping, cable trays, and air handling and heating units.

N **A.28.1.3(11)** Examples of such major structural members include, but are not limited to, beams, joists, and ceiling and roof deck types.

N **A.28.1.3(12)** Examples of such major structural members include, but are not limited to, walls, floors, ceilings, and roof systems.

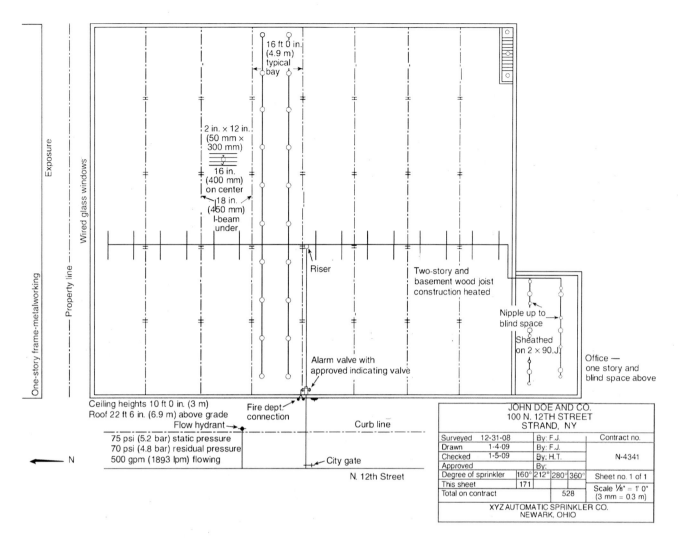

OWNER'S INFORMATION CERTIFICATE

Name/address of property to be protected with sprinkler protection:

_____

_____

Name of owner: _____

Existing or planned construction is:

❏ Fire resistive or noncombustible

❏ Wood frame or ordinary (masonry walls with wood beams)

❏ Unknown

Describe the intended use of the building: _____

_____

_____

Note regarding speculative buildings: The design and installation of the fire sprinkler system is dependent on an accurate description of the likely use of the building. Without specific information, assumptions will need to be made that will limit the actual use of the building. Make sure that you communicate any and all use considerations to the fire sprinkler contractor in this form and that you abide by all limitations regarding the use of the building based on the limitations of the fire sprinkler system that is eventually designed and installed.

Is the system installation intended for one of the following special occupancies:

Aircraft hangar	❏ Yes	❏ No
Fixed guideway transit system	❏ Yes	❏ No
Race track stable	❏ Yes	❏ No
Marine terminal, pier, or wharf	❏ Yes	❏ No
Airport terminal	❏ Yes	❏ No
Aircraft engine test facility	❏ Yes	❏ No
Power plant	❏ Yes	❏ No
Water-cooling tower	❏ Yes	❏ No

If the answer to any of the above is "yes," the appropriate NFPA standard should be referenced for sprinkler density/area criteria.

Indicate whether any of the following special materials are intended to be present:

Flammable or combustible liquids	❏ Yes	❏ No
Aerosol products	❏ Yes	❏ No
Nitrate film	❏ Yes	❏ No
Pyroxylin plastic	❏ Yes	❏ No
Compressed or liquefied gas cylinders	❏ Yes	❏ No
Liquid or solid oxidizers	❏ Yes	❏ No
Organic peroxide formulations	❏ Yes	❏ No
Idle pallets	❏ Yes	❏ No

If the answer to any of the above is "yes," describe type, location, arrangement, and intended maximum quantities.

_____

_____

© 2021 National Fire Protection Association   NFPA 13 (p. 1 of 2)

Δ **FIGURE A.28.1(b)   Owner's Information Certificate.**

Indicate whether the protection is intended for one of the following specialized occupancies or areas:

Spray area or mixing room	❏ Yes	❏ No
Solvent extraction	❏ Yes	❏ No
Laboratory using chemicals	❏ Yes	❏ No
Oxygen-fuel gas system for welding or cutting	❏ Yes	❏ No
Acetylene cylinder charging	❏ Yes	❏ No
Production or use of compressed or liquefied gases	❏ Yes	❏ No
Commercial cooking operation	❏ Yes	❏ No
Class A hyperbaric chamber	❏ Yes	❏ No
Cleanroom	❏ Yes	❏ No
Incinerator or waste handling system	❏ Yes	❏ No
Linen handling system	❏ Yes	❏ No
Industrial furnace	❏ Yes	❏ No
Water-cooling tower	❏ Yes	❏ No

If the answer to any of the above is "yes," describe type, location, arrangement, and intended maximum quantities.

_____

_____

Will there be any storage of products over 12 ft (3.7 m) in height?   ❏ Yes   ❏ No

If the answer is "yes," describe product, intended storage arrangement, and height.

_____

_____

Will there be any storage of plastic, rubber, or similar products over 5 ft (1.5 m) high except as described above?
❏ Yes   ❏ No

If the answer is "yes," describe product, intended storage arrangement, and height.

_____

_____

Is there any special information concerning the water supply?   ❏ Yes   ❏ No

If the answer is "yes," provide the information, including known environmental conditions that might be responsible for corrosion, including microbiologically influenced corrosion (MIC).

Provide water supply data for the project: _____

_____

Is seismic protection required?   ❏ Yes   ❏ No
Provide short-period spectral response parameter: _____

_____

I certify that I have knowledge of the intended use of the property and that the above information is correct.

Signature of owner's representative or agent: _____   Date:_____

Name of owner's representative or agent completing certificate (print): _____

Relationship and firm of agent (print): _____

NFPA 13 (p. 2 of 2)

Δ **FIGURE A.28.1(b)**   *Continued*

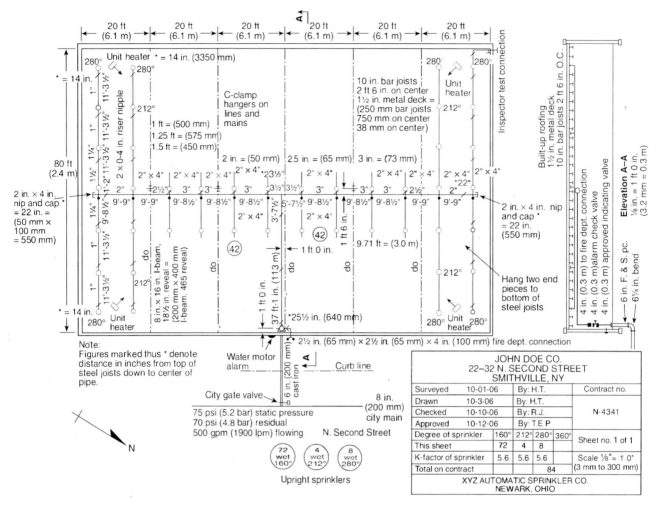

FIGURE A.28.1.1   Typical Working Plans.

N **A.28.1.3(15)(b)(ii)** Examples of such configurations include, but are not limited to, solid piled, rack, shelf, and palletized.

A.28.2.1 When additional sprinkler piping is added to an existing system, the existing piping does not have to be increased in size to compensate for the additional sprinklers, provided the new work is calculated and the calculations include that portion of the existing system that can be required to carry water to the new work.

A.28.2.1.4 NFPA 13 does not provide a specific velocity limitation for the use of the Hazen-Williams formula. This is, in part, due to an expectation that excessive friction loss values will result in increasing pipe sizes, thereby serving as an inherent limit on velocity. However, the fact that NFPA 13 does not provide a specific limit should not be taken as an endorsement that the formula can be used for any velocity of water flow. The formula was empirically determined using "normal" conditions. When the velocity in the pipe exceeds that which was used to determine the formula, the formula might no longer be valid. There has been some research performed (Huggins 1996) in which results using the Hazen-Williams formula and the Darcy-Weisbach formula were compared, and the conclusion was that

a specific velocity limit applied to all pipe sizes is not appropriate.

A.28.2.4 See Figure A.28.2.4.

A.28.2.4.1 See Figure A.28.2.4.1(a), Figure A.28.2.4.1(b), and Figure A.28.2.4.1(c).

A.28.2.4.2.1 The word "rectangular" in this section is not meant to imply that the design area always has to be a rectangle. Instead, the intent is to require a design area with sides that meet at right angles and the longer side parallel to the branch lines. In many cases, this will be a perfect rectangle with four sides. However, in some cases with multiple sprinklers on multiple branch lines within the design area, the design area can be satisfied with fewer sprinklers on the last branch line than on the first, resulting in a design area that is a rectangle with the corner cut out as shown in Figure A.28.2.4.2.1.

A.28.2.4.2.4 The following steps outline the procedure for calculation in accordance with 28.2.4.2.4:

(1) Calculate the hydraulic design discharge including those sprinklers within the available floor area.

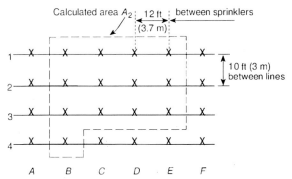

Notes:

1. For gridded systems, the extra sprinkler (or sprinklers) on branch line 4 can be placed in any adjacent location from *B* to *E* at the designer's option.

2. For tree and looped systems, the extra sprinkler on line 4 should be placed closest to the cross main.

Assume a remote area of 1500 ft^2 (139 m^2) with sprinkler coverage of 120 ft^2 (11.1 m^2)

$$\text{Total sprinklers to calculate} = \frac{\text{Design area}}{\text{Area per sprinkler}}$$

$$= \frac{1500\ (139\ \text{m}^2)}{120\ (11.1\ \text{m}^2)} = 12.5,\ \text{calculate } 13$$

$$\text{Number of sprinklers on branch line} = \frac{1.2\sqrt{A}}{S}$$

Where:
A = design area
S = distance between sprinklers on branch line

$$\text{Number of sprinklers on branch line} = \frac{1.2\sqrt{1500}}{12} = 3.87$$

For SI units, 1 ft = 0.3048 m; 1 ft^2 = 0.0929 m^2.

FIGURE A.28.2.4   Example of Determining the Number of Sprinklers to Be Calculated.

(2) Calculate the minimum required discharge by multiplying the required design density times the required minimum design area.

(3) Subtract the discharge calculated in Step 1 from the discharge calculate in Step 2.

(4) Where the discharge calculated in Step 3 is greater than 0, the hydraulic design discharge is recalculated including an additional flow equal to that calculated in Step 3. The additional flow is added at the point of connection of the branch line to the cross main furthest from the source.

(5) Where the discharge calculated in Step 3 is less than or equal to 0, the hydraulic design discharge is as calculated in Step 1.

N **A.28.2.4.2.5** See Figure A.28.2.4.2.5.

N **A.28.2.4.2.6** When determining the hydraulic design area, walls and physical barriers that can impact water distribution, as well as fire load, and growth of radiant heat need to be considered. Extending the hydraulic design area beyond a wall should not be done and spacing directly between sprinklers should not be used for hydraulic advantage.▨ All areas of operation should represent the most demanding area of operation

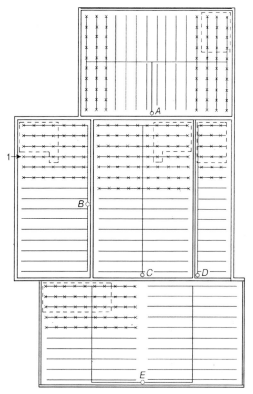

1 This sprinkler is not in the selected area of operation.

FIGURE A.28.2.4.1(a)   Example of Hydraulically Most Demanding Area.

based on the actual piping configuration and consideration for the use of the building.

A.28.2.4.5 See Figure A.28.2.4.5.

A.28.2.4.6.1 When listed with antifreeze solution, sprinklers should be hydraulically calculated in accordance with the listing and manufacturer's instructions.

A.28.2.4.6.2 See Figure A.28.2.4.6.2.

A.28.2.4.6.5 Where the slope is parallel with the branch lines, the area per sprinkler for hydraulic calculation purposes would be found as

[A.28.2.4.6.5]
$$A_s = S' \times L$$

where:
$S' = (\cos\theta)S$
θ = angle of slope
S = distance between sprinklers on branch line per 9.5.2.1.2

See Figure A.28.2.4.6.5.

A.28.2.4.7 When it is not obvious by comparison that the design selected is the hydraulically most remote, additional calculations should be submitted. The most distant area is not necessarily the hydraulically most remote.

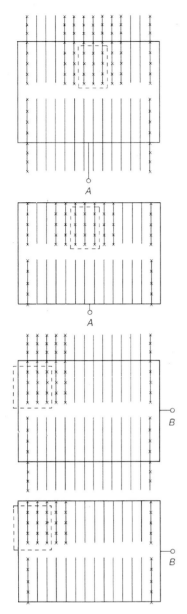

FIGURE A.28.2.4.1(b)   Example of Hydraulically Most Demanding Area for Various Piping Arrangements.

A.28.2.4.7.2 The intent of this section is not to allow the omission of discharge from sprinklers in small compartments where the design area has been reduced below the values in Table 28.2.4.7.2 for situations such as quick-response sprinklers. Where quick-response sprinklers are used, the discharge from sprinklers in small compartments in the design area can be omitted as long as the design area meets the size required by Table 28.2.4.7.2.

N **A.28.2.4.7.3** Examples of obstructions are wide ducts or tables.

A.28.2.4.8.2 See Figure A.28.2.4.8.2 for a Moody diagram and Table A.28.2.4.8.2 for ε-factors that correspond to Hazen–Williams *C* factors. The corresponding Hazen-Williams *C* factor

should be used for the calculation of equivalent pipe length in accordance with 28.2.3.

A.28.2.4.9.3 The use of sprinklers with differing K-factors in situations where different protection areas are needed is not considered balancing. An example would be a room that could be protected with sprinklers having different K-factors in closets, foyers, and room areas. However, this procedure introduces difficulties when restoring a system to service after operation since it is not always clear which sprinklers go where.

A.28.2.4.10 Where the normal pressure (P_n) is used to calculate the flow from an orifice, the following assumptions should be used:

(1) At any flowing outlet along a pipe, except the end outlet, only the normal pressure (P_n) can act on the outlet. At the end outlet, the total pressure (P_t) can act. The following should be considered end outlets:

    (a) The last flowing sprinkler on a dead-end branch line

    (b) The last flowing branch line on a dead-end cross main

    (c) Any sprinkler where a flow split occurs on a gridded branch line

    (d) Any branch line where a flow split occurs on a looped system

(2) At any flowing outlet along a pipe, except the end outlet, the pressure acting to cause flow from the outlet is equal to the total pressure (P_t) minus the velocity pressure (P_v) on the upstream (supply) side.

(3) To find the normal pressure (P_n) at any flowing outlet, except the end outlet, assume a flow from the outlet in question and determine the velocity pressure (P_v) for the total flow on the upstream side. Because normal pressure (P_n) equals total pressure (P_t) minus velocity pressure (P_v), the value of the normal pressure (P_n) so found should result in an outlet flow approximately equal to the assumed flow; if not, a new value should be assumed, and the calculations should be repeated.

A.28.4.2 See Figure A.28.4.2(a) through Figure A.28.4.2(d).

A.28.4.3 See Figure A.28.4.3.

A.28.4.3(15) See Figure A.28.4.3(15).

A.28.4.4 See Figure A.28.4.4.

A.28.4.5.1 Additional data can be added to any of the forms, provided that the format and order of the original information shown in Figure 28.4.5.1.2(a), Figure 28.4.5.1.2(b), Figure 28.4.5.1.2(c), and Figure 28.4.5.1.2(d) is followed.

A.28.5.1 The demonstrated effectiveness of pipe schedule systems is limited to their use with ½ in. (15 mm) orifice sprinklers. The use of other size orifices can require hydraulic calculations to prove their ability to deliver the required amount of water within the available water supply.

A.28.5.1.4 Where the construction or conditions introduce unusually long runs of pipe or many angles in risers or feed or cross mains, an increase in pipe size over that called for in the schedules can be required to compensate for increased friction losses.

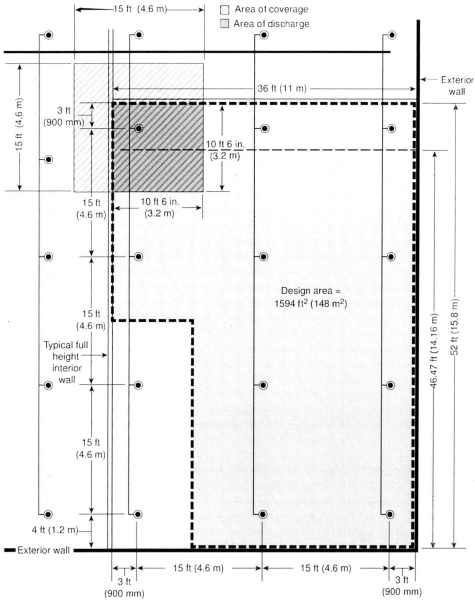

Notes:
(1) Full height walls impact the design area boundaries.
(2) Sprinkler spacing: 15 ft × 15 ft (4.6 m × 4.6 m)
   Mimimum area of operations: 1500 ft² (140 m²)
(3) Number of sprinklers on a branch line: $(1.2\sqrt{1500})/15 = 3.09$ (calculate 4)
   Mimimum length of design area (parallel to branch lines): $1.2\sqrt{1500} = 46.47$ ft (14.16 m)

N FIGURE A.28.2.4.1(c)   Example of Hydraulically Most Demanding Area Boundary When Interior Walls are Present.

Shaded text = Revisions.   Δ = Text deletions and figure/table revisions.   • = Section deletions.   N = New material.

2022 Edition

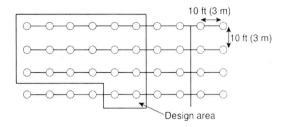

Discharge criteria: 0.45 gpm²/2000 ft² (18.3 mm/min/m²)/185 m²
20 sprinklers in design area 1.2(2000)0.5/10 (185 m²) = 5.3 rounded
up to 6 sprinklers per branch line.
Note that the design area is not a perfect rectangle.
The 2000 ft² (185 m²) requirement can be met with fewer sprinklers on the
fourth branch line back, so there is no need to include the additional four
sprinklers on the fourth branch line.

Δ FIGURE A.28.2.4.2.1   Example of Nonsymmetrical Hydraulically Most Demanding Area.

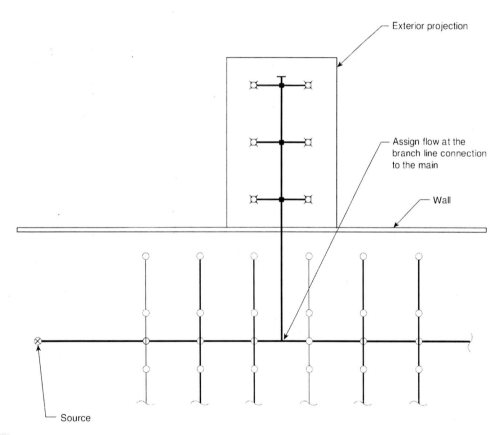

N FIGURE A.28.2.4.2.5   Point of Connection for Additional Flow.

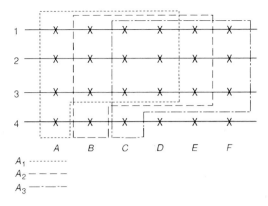

FIGURE A.28.2.4.5   Example of Determining the Most Remote Area for Gridded System.

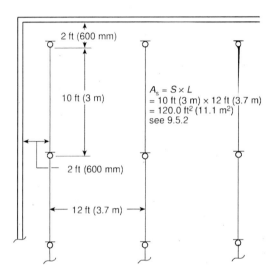

$A_s = S \times L$
$= 10 \text{ ft } (3 \text{ m}) \times 12 \text{ ft } (3.7 \text{ m})$
$= 120.0 \text{ ft}^2 (11.1 \text{ m}^2)$
see 9.5.2

△ **FIGURE A.28.2.4.6.2   Sprinkler Spacing.**

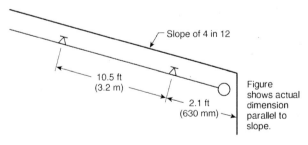

Calculation floor area = 10 ft × 12 ft (3.0 m × 3.7 m) *(see Figure A.27.2.4.6.2)*

△ **FIGURE A.28.2.4.6.5   Determination of Floor Area Under Sloped Ceiling/Roof.**

Table A.28.2.4.8.2 Suggested Ɛ-Factor for Aged Pipe

Pipe	Hazen–Williams C Factor	Ɛ-Factor [in. (mm)]
Steel (new)	143	0.0018 (0.045)
Steel	120	0.004 (0.100)
Steel	100	0.015 (0.375)
Copper	150	0.000084 (0.0021)
Plastic	150	0.000084 (0.0021)

For SI units, 1 in. = 25 mm.

A.28.5.2.6 For example, a 2½ in. (65 mm) steel pipe, which is permitted to supply 30 sprinklers, can supply a total of 50 sprinklers where not more than 30 sprinklers are above or below a ceiling.

A.28.5.3.9 For example, a 3 in. (80 mm) steel pipe, which is permitted to supply 40 sprinklers in an ordinary hazard area, can supply a total of 60 sprinklers where not more than 40 sprinklers protect the occupied space below the ceiling.

A.28.5.4 The piping schedule shown in Table A.28.5.4 is reprinted only as a guide for existing systems. New systems for extra hazard occupancies should be hydraulically calculated as required in 28.5.4.

N **A.29.1** See Figure A.29.1.

A.29.2.1 The use of noncombustible compressed gas to increase the pressure in a water-filled system is an acceptable test procedure.

A.29.2.1.6 As an example, in a system that had piping at an elevation that was 25 ft (7.6 m) higher than the test gauge, an acceptable pressure during the hydrostatic test is 189 psi (13 bar) at the top of the system due to the loss of 11 psi (0.8 bar) in elevation pressure [25 ft × 0.433 psi/ft = 11 psi (0.8 bar)].

A.29.2.1.7 Bacterial inhibitors and other chemicals that are approved and used for the prevention and mitigation of MIC and that do not adversely affect the fire-fighting properties of the water or the performance of the fire sprinkler system components are not prohibited.

A.29.2.1.12 Valves isolating the section to be tested might not be "drop-tight." When such leakage is suspected, test blanks of the type required in 29.2.1.12 should be used in a manner that includes the valve in the section being tested.

A.29.2.3.2 When the acceptance test is being performed during freezing conditions, a partial flow trip test should be conducted at that time and the full flow trip test specified should be conducted as soon as conditions permit.

A.29.2.3.2.3 The test criteria are based on the first evidence of waterflow to the inspector's test. Air can be mixed with the water for several minutes until the air is completely flushed from the system.

A.29.2.3.2.3.2 Although the time criteria for calculated systems is not required to be verified, a test is still required to document the initial water delivery for comparison to future inspection test requirements. If the time of a single sprinkler test outlet exceeds 70 seconds, evaluation of the calculations and the system installation might be necessary.

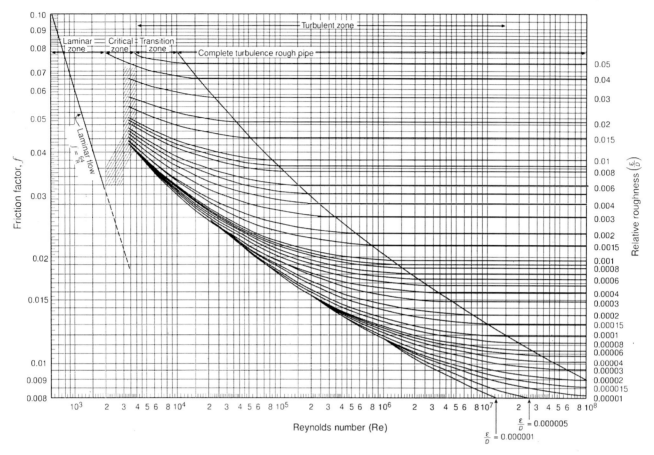

FIGURE A.28.2.4.8.2   Moody Diagram.

A.29.2.3.4.2 Measuring the flow during a main drain test is not required.

A.29.3(2) A copy of NFPA 25 is not required for system alterations or additions.

A.29.4 See Figure A.29.4.

A.29.6 While the information on this sign is useful during an inspection, such use should not be considered a hazard assessment based on the requirements of this standard. *(See Figure A.29.6.)*

N **A.30.1.2** This chapter is intended to apply to evaluations, modifications, or additions to existing systems. As provided by the retroactivity provisions of Section 1.4, the provisions of the standard are generally not intended to apply to existing systems unless otherwise specified herein as being retroactive or where the authority having jurisdiction has determined that the existing condition represents an unacceptable risk.

The development of the standard reflects an ever-changing consensus of what is considered as being an acceptable degree of protection. Evaluation of existing system installations should be based on the provisions of the edition of the standard and approval of the authority having jurisdiction at the time of installation (standard of record), if known. Additional consideration might be given to an evaluation of the level of risk associated with maintaining existing installations evaluated under the standard of record.

N **A.30.1.8** Nitrogen is often added to existing dry pipe and preaction sprinkler systems already identified as having corrosion damage with the intent of extending the life of these systems. The addition of nitrogen will not remediate the corrosion damage already incurred to the sprinkler system piping. It is recommended to assess existing piping to determine where replacement is necessary and where acceptable for continued use. The addition of nitrogen will remove the oxygen from the corrosion process, which will minimize continued corrosion but will not remove any previous damage.

The use of compressed air is not always damaging to dry pipe or preaction sprinkler system piping. It has been used as a supervisory gas for nearly a century without catastrophic effects. Dry air has been found to provide an effective means of limiting corrosion. However, corrosion has been observed in systems having compressed air supplies without dry air. Problems have been observed in hot and humid areas and when compressors generate heating after being run for long periods. Water condensation caused by this process has been identified as a contributing factor to corrosion in dry pipe and preaction sprinkler systems.

N **A.30.3.2** See A.16.2.1.1.

```
┌─────────────────────────────────────────────┐
│                                               │
│           Hydraulic Calculations              │
│                     for                       │
│     ABC Company, employee garage              │
│                                               │
│     7499 Franklin Road                        │
│                                               │
│     Charleston, SC                            │
│                                               │
│                                               │
│          Contract No. ____4001____            │
│                                               │
│          Date____1 – 7 – 08____               │
│                                               │
│                                               │
│  Design data:                                 │
│                                               │
│    Occupancy classification ___ORD. GR. 1___  │
│    Density _0.15_ gpm/ft² (6.1 mm/min/m²)     │
│    Area of application _1500_ ft² (139 m²)    │
│    Coverage per sprinkler _130_ ft² (12.1 m²) │
│    Special sprinklers _____  │
│    No. of sprinklers calculated ____12____    │
│    In-rack demand _____  │
│    Hose streams _250 gpm (950 lpm)_           │
│    Total water required ___510.4___ gpm       │
│    (1930 lpm)                                 │
│    including hose streams                     │
│                                               │
│                                               │
│  Name of contractor _____ │
│                                               │
│  Name of designer _____ │
│                                               │
│  Address _____ │
│                                               │
│  Authority having jurisdiction _____ │
│                                               │
└─────────────────────────────────────────────┘
```

FIGURE A.28.4.2(a)   Summary Sheet.

N A.30.5 The density/area curves have been maintained in the standard for use with existing systems. This includes the allowance for the use of the density/area curves for re-evaluation of existing sprinkler systems when changes in use or occupancy occur. This also allows the use of the density/area curves when modifications to existing systems are made.

A.31.1.3 In addition to the examples provided in A.4.3, Table A.31.1.3 provides additional examples of occupancy definitions of typical shipboard spaces.

A.31.1.4 Experience has shown that structures that are partially sprinklered can be overrun by well-developed fires originating in unsprinklered areas. Therefore, the entire vessel should be sprinklered whenever sprinkler systems are considered.

A.31.2.1 Sprinklers with a nominal K-factor of 2.8 (40) or less coupled with a system strainer minimize the potential for clogging.

A.31.2.2 Where a marine thermal barrier is penetrated, limiting the opening around the sprinkler pipe to $\frac{1}{16}$ in. (1 mm) is considered as meeting this requirement.

A.31.2.4.1 When nonferrous materials are used, consideration should be given to protecting against galvanic corrosion where the nonferrous materials connect to steel pipe. Consideration

should also be given to protection against galvanic corrosion from pipe hangers in areas of high humidity.

The piping between the sea chest and the sprinkler zone valves are likely to see the frequent flow of saltwater when testing. Sprinkler zone piping will rarely, if ever, be exposed to saltwater. In such an event, NFPA 25 requires flushing of the piping. Even if the piping is not flushed, the saltwater will not be replenished and will lose oxygen content in fairly short order.

Even if galvanized, the failure from corrosion from the interior of the pipe is likely to be at all threaded connections, welded assembly connections, and where brass sprinklers thread into ferrous pipe. Only hot dipped galvanized after fabrication of assembly (as opposed to simply hot dipped galvanized pipe and fittings) will protect against some of those failures. Hot dipped galvanized after fabrication of assembly is practical from the sea chest to the sprinkler manifold where spaces are open and pipe is relatively large and uses flanged takedown joints instead of threaded unions. Hot dipped galvanized after fabrication of assembly is not practical in the sprinkler zone pipe where it is mainly field fit.

A.31.2.5.1 When designing supports, the selection and spacing of pipe supports should take into account the pipe dimensions, mechanical and physical properties of piping materials and supports, operating temperature, thermal expansion effects, external loads, thrust forces, vibration, maximum accelerations, differential motions to which the system might be subjected, and the type of support.

The route of the vessel is intended to be descriptive of its usual operating area. For example, expected motion of the system on an ocean vessel is expected to be considerably greater than the motion of a vessel that operates on a river. A vessel that operates within the confines of any of the Great Lakes is expected to subject the system pipe to greater motion than would a vessel that operates on a lake such as Lake Tahoe.

It is recommended that the designer review the requirements for automatic sprinkler systems that are subject to earthquakes. While it is obvious that shipboard motions and accelerations differ from those that occur during an earthquake, the general principle of protecting the piping system against damage applies. Individual hanger design, however, will be very similar.

Earthquake protection does not apply to ships; however, motions are similar to those that a ship will experience in a seaway. The design principles discussed in this section should be used as a guide for shipboard system design.

A.31.2.5.3 Use of heat-sensitive materials for pipe hangers and supports might be desirable in some cases. Where heat-sensitive materials are used, the hangers and supports should be adequately protected by either the direct application of insulation or installation behind a marine thermal barrier. Insulation materials applied directly to hangers should be insulated in accordance with the method provided in Society of Naval Architects and Marine Engineers Technical Research Bulletin 2-21, "Aluminum Fire Protection Guidelines."

A.31.2.5.4 Consideration should be given to increasing the size of rods and U-hooks as necessary, to account for service and operational loading, including ship motion and vibrations.

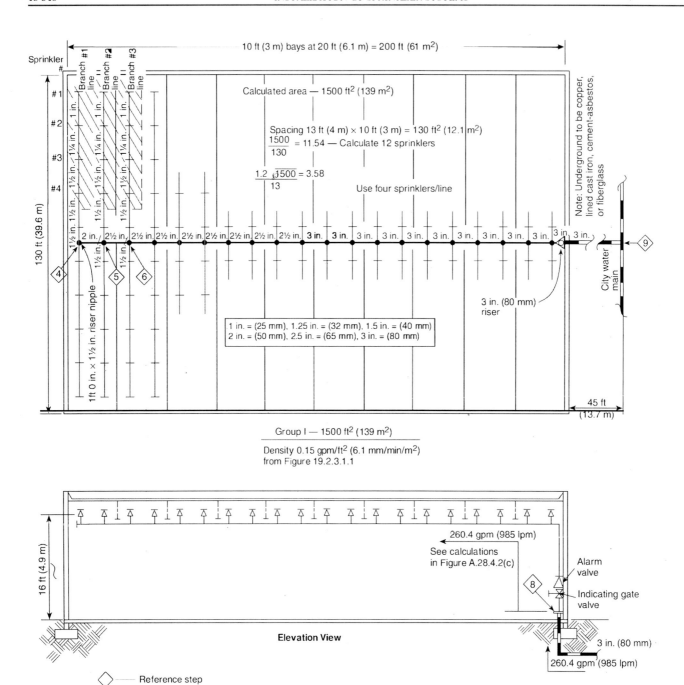

△ FIGURE A.28.4.2(b)   Hydraulic Calculation Example (Plan View and Elevation View).

Contract Name __GROUP I 1500 ft² (139 m²)__   Sheet __2__ Of __3__

Step No.	#	Nozzle Ident. and Location	Flow in gpm (lpm)	(mm) Pipe Size	Pipe Fittings and Devices	Equiv. Pipe Length (m)	Friction Loss psi Foot	(bar) Pressure Summary	Normal Pressure	$D = 0.15\ gpm/ft^2$ Notes $K = 5.6$	Ref. Step
1	1	BL-1	q Q 19.5 (74)	1 in. (25 mm)		L 13 ft (4 m) F T 13 ft (4 m)	C=120 0.124	P_t 12.1 P_e P_f 1.6	P_t P_v P_n	$Q = 130 \times 0.15 = 19.5$ (74 lpm) $P = (19.5/5.6)^2 = 12.1$ psi (0.83 bar)	
2	2		q 20.7 (78.4) Q 40.2 (152.2)	1¼ in. (32 mm)		L 13 ft (4 m) F T 13 ft (4 m)	0.125	P_t 13.7 P_e P_f 1.6	P_t P_v P_n	$q = 5.6\ \sqrt{13.7}$	
3	3		q 21.9 (83) Q 62.1 (235.1)	1½ in. (40 mm)		L 13 ft (4 m) F T 13 ft (4 m)	0.131	P_t 15.3 P_e P_f 1.7	P_t P_v P_n	$q = 5.6\ \sqrt{15.3}$	4
4	4	DN RN	q 23.1 (87.4) Q 85.2 (322.5)	1½ in. (40 mm)	2T-16	L 20.5 ft (6.2 m) F 16 ft (4.8 m) T 36.5 ft (11 m)	0.236	P_t 17.0 P_e 0.4 P_f 8.6	P_t P_v P_n	$q = 5.6\ \sqrt{17}$ $P_e = 1 \times 0.433$	5
5		CM TO BL-2	q Q 85.2 (322.5)	2 in. (50 mm)		L 10 ft (3 m) F T 10 ft (3 m)	0.07	P_t 26.0 P_e P_f 0.7	P_t P_v P_n	$K = \dfrac{85.2}{\sqrt{26}}$ $K = 16.71$	
6		BL-2 CM TO BL-3	q 86.3 (326.7) Q 171.5 (549.2)	2½ in. (65 mm)		L 10 ft (3 m) F T 10 ft (3 m)	0.107	P_t 26.7 P_e P_f 1.1	P_t P_v P_n	$q = 16.71\ \sqrt{26.7}$	6
7		BL-3 CM	q 88.1 (333.5) Q 259.6 (982.7)	2½ in. (65 mm)		L 70 ft (21 m) F T 70 ft (21 m)	0.231	P_t 27.8 P_e P_f 16.2	P_t P_v P_n	$q = 16.7\ \sqrt{27.8}$	
8		CM TO FIS	q Q 259.6 (982.7)	3 in. (80 mm)	E5 AV15 GV1	L 119 ft (36 m) F 21 ft (6.4 m) T 140 ft (43 m)	0.081	P_t 44.0 P_e 6.5 P_f 11.2	P_t P_v P_n	$P_e = 15 \times 0.433$	8
9		THROUGH UNDER-GROUND TO CITY MAIN	q Q 259.6 (982.7)	3 in. (80 mm)	E5 GV1 T15	L 50 ft (15 m) F 27.6 ft (8.4 m) T 77.6 ft (24 m)	C=150 TYPE 'M' 0.061	P_t 61.7 P_e P_f 4.7	P_t P_v P_n	$F = F_{40} \times 1.51 \times F_c$ $F_c = [2.981/3.068]^{4.87} = 0.869$ $F = 21 \times 1.51 \times 0.869$ $F = 27.6$	9
			q Q			L F T		P_t 66.4 P_e P_f	P_t P_v P_n		
			q Q			L F T		P_t P_e P_f P_t	P_t P_v P_n		

FIGURE A.28.4.2(c) **Hydraulic Calculations.**

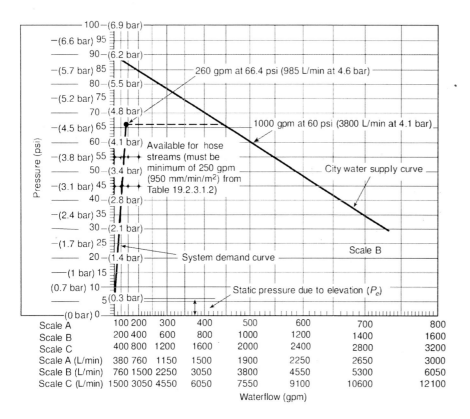

△ **FIGURE A.28.4.2(d)   Hydraulic Graph.**

A.31.2.6.1 Shipboard installations will normally require more than one valve per water supply. Locking valves in the open position is not an acceptable substitute for the requirement of 31.2.6.1 but can be done in addition to the supervision requirement.

A.31.2.7.1 International Shore Connections are portable universal couplings that permit connections of shipboard sprinkler or firemain systems between one ship and another or between a shore facility and a ship. Both the ship and the shore facility are expected to have an international shore connection fitting such that in an emergency they can be attached to their respective fire hoses and bolted together to permit charging the ship's system. It must be portable to accommodate hose-to-hose connection and allow assistance from any position.

Installation of an additional fire boat connection might be required on-board vessels whose route is such that regular access to fire boats is possible. An additional fire boat connection might not be necessary where fire boats are equipped to connect to the regular fire department connection. *(See A.31.2.7.7.)*

A.31.2.7.7 Selection of the pipe thread for the fire department connection should be done very carefully. It is recommended that a 2½ in. (63 mm) siamese connection with National Standard Hose Thread be used since a majority of fire department hose lines will be compatible with this thread. However, it must be noted that some fire jurisdictions might not be compatible with a connection of this type. Serious consideration should be given to the vessel's typical operating

area. Precautions and planning should avert the possibility of the vessel being forced ashore by fire at a location where the fire department equipment is not compatible with this connection. Carriage of extra fittings and pre-voyage arrangements with all applicable jurisdictions should be considered. The international shore connection is required to ensure that all vessels fitted with sprinkler systems have at least one type of common connection.

A.31.3.1 Special consideration should be given to the installation of relief valves in all wet pipe systems. Ambient ship temperatures can vary greatly depending on operating environment, duration of voyage, and failure of climate control systems.

A.31.4.2 Areas fitted primarily with multiple staterooms and corridors should be considered sleeping accommodation areas.

A.31.4.4 If combustibles are present such that they constitute a threat, the space should be sprinklered. One example would be the presence of large bundles of unsheathed computer or electrical cable. Typical amounts of lighting or control cabling should not be considered to constitute a fire threat.

A.31.4.10.1(4) Because of its melting point, brazing would be considered heat sensitive. The criterion of this paragraph is intended to permit brazed joints without requiring that they be installed behind a marine thermal barrier, while maintaining the fire resistance as stated in 31.4.10.1 under reasonably foreseeable failure modes.

Contract no. _____   Sheet no. _____ of _____

Name and location _____

Reference	Nozzle type and location	Flow in gpm (L/min)	Pipe size (in.)	Fitting and devices	Pipe equivalent length		Friction loss psi/ft (bar/m)	Required psi (bar)	Normal Pressure	Notes
	q				length			P_t	P_t	
					fitting			P_f	P_v	
	Q				total			P_e	P_n	
	q				length			P_t	P_t	
					fitting			P_f	P_v	
	Q				total			P_e	P_n	
	q				length			P_t	P_t	
					fitting			P_f	P_v	
	Q				total			P_e	P_n	
	q				length			P_t	P_t	
					fitting			P_f	P_v	
	Q				total			P_e	P_n	
	q				length			P_t	P_t	
					fitting			P_f	P_v	
	Q				total			P_e	P_n	
	q				length			P_t	P_t	
					fitting			P_f	P_v	
	Q				total			P_e	P_n	
	q				length			P_t	P_t	
					fitting			P_f	P_v	
	Q				total			P_e	P_n	
	q				length			P_t	P_t	
					fitting			P_f	P_v	
	Q				total			P_e	P_n	
	q				length			P_t	P_t	
					fitting			P_f	P_v	
	Q				total			P_e	P_n	
	q				length			P_t	P_t	
					fitting			P_f	P_v	
	Q				total			P_e	P_n	
	q				length			P_t	P_t	
					fitting			P_f	P_v	
	Q				total			P_e	P_n	
	q				length			P_t	P_t	
					fitting			P_f	P_v	
	Q				total			P_e	P_n	
	q				length			P_t	P_t	
					fitting			P_f	P_v	
	Q				total			P_e	P_n	
	q				length			P_t	P_t	
					fitting			P_f	P_v	
	Q				total			P_e	P_n	
	q				length			P_t	P_t	
					fitting			P_f	P_v	
	Q				total			P_e	P_n	
	q				length			P_t	P_t	
					fitting			P_f	P_v	
	Q				total			P_e	P_n	
	q				length			P_t	P_t	
					fitting			P_f	P_v	
	Q				total			P_e	P_n	
	q				length			P_t	P_t	
					fitting			P_f	P_v	
	Q				total			P_e	P_n	

P_t: total pressure. P_f: friction loss pressure. P_v: velocity pressure. P_e: elevation pressure.

© 2021 National Fire Protection Association

NFPA 13

Δ **FIGURE A.28.4.3   Sample Worksheet.**

Shaded text = Revisions.   Δ = Text deletions and figure/table revisions.   • = Section deletions.   *N* = New material.

2022 Edition

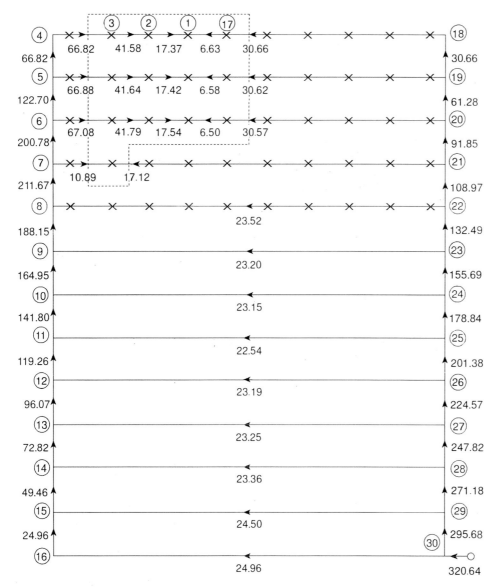

FIGURE A.28.4.3(15)   Example of Hydraulically Remote Area — Grid System.

A.31.4.12.1 While not required, a dual annunciator alarm panel system is recommended. One panel should show the piping system layout and indicate status of zone valves, tank pressures, water supply valves, pump operation, and so forth. The second panel should show the vessel's general arrangement and indicate status of waterflow (i.e., fire location) alarms.

A.31.5.2 For example, a design area of 1500 ft² (140 m²) is used to design a sprinkler system for an unobstructed light hazard occupancy. In this case, the system must supply at least seven sprinklers that are installed within that area. If eight sprinklers are installed to protect windows within this design area, the water demand of these sprinklers is added to the total water demand. Thus, 15 sprinklers must be supplied by this system.

A.31.5.3 Hose stream flow need not be added to the water demand. The water supply for fire streams is supplied by separate fire pump(s) that supply the vessel's fire main.

A.31.6.4 In vessels, the elevation of sprinklers with respect to the water supply varies as the vessel heels to either side or trims by the bow or stern. The water demand requirements can be increased or decreased under these conditions. This requirement aligns the operational parameters of this safety system with that required for other machinery vital to the safety of the vessel.

A.31.7.2.7 The purpose of this requirement is to ensure that the pressure tank air supply will not keep the tank "fully" pressurized while water is expelled, thus preventing pump actuation.

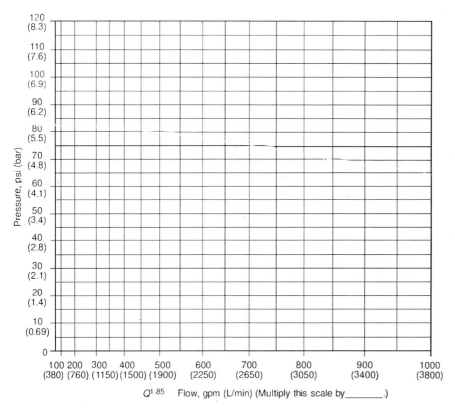

FIGURE A.28.4.4   Sample Graph Sheet.

Table A.28.5.4 Extra Hazard Pipe Schedule

Steel		Copper	
Size [in. (mm)]	Number of Sprinklers	Size [in. (mm)]	Number of Sprinklers
1 (25)	1	1 (25)	1
1¼ (32)	2	1¼ (32)	2
1½ (40)	5	1½ (40)	5
2 (50)	8	2 (50)	8
2½ (65)	15	2½ (65)	20
3 (80)	27	3 (80)	30
3½ (90)	40	3½ (90)	45
4 (100)	55	4 (100)	65
5 (125)	90	5 (125)	100
6 (150)	150	6 (150)	170

For SI units, 1 in. = 25.4 mm.

Contractor's Material and Test Certificate for Aboveground Piping

PROCEDURE
Upon completion of work, inspection and tests shall be made by the contractor's representative and witnessed by the property owner or their authorized agent. All defects shall be corrected and system left in service before contractor's personnel finally leave the job.

A certificate shall be filled out and signed by both representatives. Copies shall be prepared for approving authorities, owners, and contractor. It is understood the owner's representative's signature in no way prejudices any claim against contractor for faulty material, poor workmanship, or failure to comply with approving authority's requirements or local ordinances.

Property name		Date

Property address		
New installation?	☐ Yes	☐ No
Modification? If yes, complete applicable portions of the form.	☐ Yes	☐ No
Provide a description of the scope of work on page 3.		

Plans	Accepted by approving authorities (names)		
	Address		
	Installation conforms to accepted plans	☐ Yes	☐ No
	Equipment used is approved	☐ Yes	☐ No
	If no, explain deviations		

Instructions	Has person in charge of fire equipment been instructed as to location of control valves and care and maintenance of this new equipment? If no, explain	☐ Yes	☐ No
	Have copies of the following been left on the premises?	☐ Yes	☐ No
	1. System components instructions	☐ Yes	☐ No
	2. Care and maintenance instructions	☐ Yes	☐ No
	3. NFPA 25	☐ Yes	☐ No

Location of system	Supplies buildings

Sprinklers	Make	Model	Year of manufacture	Orifice size	Quantity	Temperature rating

Pipe and fittings	Type of pipe _____
	Type of fittings _____

Alarm valve or flow indicator		Alarm device		Maximum time to operate through test connection	
	Type	Make	Model	Minutes	Seconds

Dry pipe and double-interlock preaction operating test		Dry valve			Q. O. D.		
		Make	Model	Serial no.	Make	Model	Serial no.

		Time to trip through test connection[a,b]		Water pressure	Air pressure	Trip point air pressure	Time water reached test outlet[a,b]		Alarm operated properly	
		Minutes	Seconds	psi	psi	psi	Minutes	Seconds	Yes	No
	Without Q.O.D.									
	With Q.O.D.									
	If no, explain									

© 2021 National Fire Protection Association   NFPA 13 (p. 1 of 3)

[a] Measured from time inspector's test connection is opened.
[b] NFPA 13 only requires the 60-second limitation in specific sections.

N **FIGURE A.29.1   Contractor's Material and Test Certificate for Aboveground Piping.**

Deluge and preaction valves	Operation	☐ Pneumatic		☐ Electric		☐ Hydraulics			
	Piping supervised	☐ Yes ☐ No		Detecting media supervised				☐ Yes	☐ No
	Does valve operate from the manual trip, remote, or both control stations?							☐ Yes	☐ No
	Is there an accessible facility in each circuit for testing? ☐ Yes ☐ No				If no, explain				

	Make	Model	Does each circuit operate supervision loss alarm?		Does each circuit operate valve release?		Maximum time to operate release	
			Yes	No	Yes	No	Minutes	Seconds

Pressure-reducing valve test	Location and floor	Make and model	Setting	Static pressure		Residual pressure (flowing)		Flow rate
				Inlet (psi)	Outlet (psi)	Inlet (psi)	Outlet (psi)	Flow (gpm)

Backflow device forward flow test	Indicate means used for forward flow test of backflow device: _____ When means to test device was opened, was system flow demand created? ☐ Yes ☐ No ☐ N/A

Test description	Hydrostatic: Hydrostatic tests shall be made at not less than 200 psi (13.8 bar) for 2 hours or 50 psi (3.4 bar) above static pressure in excess of 150 psi (10.3 bar) for 2 hours. Differential dry pipe valve clappers shall be left open during the test to prevent damage. All aboveground piping leakage shall be stopped. Pneumatic: Establish 40 psi (2.7 bar) air pressure and measure drop, which shall not exceed 1½ psi (0.1 bar) in 24 hours. Test pressure tanks at normal water level and air pressure and measure air pressure drop, which shall not exceed 1½ psi (0.1 bar) in 24 hours.

Tests	All piping hydrostatically tested at ____ psi (____ bar) for ____ hours Dry piping pneumatically tested ☐ Yes ☐ No Equipment operates properly ☐ Yes ☐ No	If no, state reason
	Do you certify as the sprinkler contractor that additives and corrosive chemicals, sodium silicate or derivatives of sodium silicate, brine, or other corrosive chemicals were not used for testing systems or stopping leaks? ☐ Yes ☐ No	
	Drain test	Reading of gauge located near water supply test connection: ____ psi (____ bar)	Residual pressure with valve in test connection open wide: ____ psi (____ bar)
	Underground mains and lead-in connections to system risers flushed before connection made to sprinkler piping Verified by copy of the Contractor's Material and Test Certificate for Underground Piping. ☐ Yes ☐ No Other Explain Flushed by installer of underground sprinkler piping ☐ Yes ☐ No	
	If powder-driven fasteners are used in concrete, has representative sample testing been satisfactorily completed? ☐ Yes ☐ No If no, explain	

Blank testing gaskets	Number used	Locations	Number removed

Welding	Welding piping ☐ Yes ☐ No	
	If yes . . .	
	Do you certify as the sprinkler contractor that welding procedures used complied with the minimum requirements of AWS B2.1, ASME Section IX *Welding and Brazing Qualifications*, or other applicable qualification standard as required by the AHJ?	☐ Yes ☐ No
	Do you certify that all welding was performed by welders or welding operators qualified in accordance with the minimum requirements of AWS B2.1, ASME Section IX *Welding and Brazing Qualifications*, or other applicable qualification standard as required by the AHJ?	☐ Yes ☐ No
	Do you certify that the welding was conducted in compliance with a documented quality control procedure to ensure that (1) all discs are retrieved; (2) that openings in piping are smooth, that slag and other welding residue are removed; (3) the internal diameters of piping are not penetrated; (4) completed welds are free from cracks, incomplete fusion, surface porosity greater than 1/16 in. (1.6 mm) diameter, undercut deeper than the lesser of 25% of the wall thickness or 1/32 in. (0.8 mm); and (5) completed circumferential butt weld reinforcement does not exceed 3/32 in. (2.4 mm)?	☐ Yes ☐ No

© 2021 National Fire Protection Association

NFPA 13 (p. 2 of 3)

N **FIGURE A.29.1** *Continued*

Shaded text = Revisions. Δ = Text deletions and figure/table revisions. • = Section deletions. N = New material.

2022 Edition

Cutouts (discs)	Do you certify that you have a control feature to ensure that all cutouts (discs) are retrieved?		☐ Yes ☐ No
Hydraulic data nameplate	Nameplate provided ☐ Yes ☐ No	If no, explain	
Sprinkler contractor removed all caps and straps? ☐ Yes ☐ No			
Remarks	Date left in service with all control valves open		

Signatures

Name of sprinkler contractor

Tests witnessed by

The property owner or their authorized agent (signed)	Title	Date
For sprinkler contractor (signed)	Title	Date

Additional explanations and notes

NFPA 13 (p. 3 of 3)

N **FIGURE A.29.1** *Continued*

Shaded text = Revisions. Δ = Text deletions and figure/table revisions. • = Section deletions. *N* = New material.

```
This system as shown on . . . . . . . . . . . . . . . . . . . . company

print no . . . . . . . . . . . . . . . . . . . . . . . . . dated . . . . . . . . . . . . . .

for . . . . . . . . . . . . . . . . . . . . . . . . . . . . . . . . . . . . . . . . . . . . . . . .

at . . . . . . . . . . . . . . . . . . . . . . . . . . . . . contract no . . . . . . . .

is designed to discharge at a rate of . . . . . . . . . . . . . gpm/ft²

(L/min/m²) of floor area over a maximum area of . . . . . . . . .

ft² (m²) when supplied with water at a rate of . . . . . . . . . . . . .

gpm (L/min) at . . . . . . . . . . . psi (bar) at the base of the riser.

Hose stream allowance of  . . . . . . . . . . . . . . . . . . gpm (L/min)

is included in the above.

Occupancy classification . . . . . . . . . . . . . . . . . . . . . . . . . . . . .

Commodity classification . . . . . . . . . . . . . . . . . . . . . . . . . . . . .

Maximum storage height . . . . . . . . . . . . . . . . . . . . . . . . . . . . .
```

FIGURE A.29.4   Sample Hydraulic Design Information Sign.

A.31.7.3.3 NFPA 20 requires that fire pumps furnish not less than 150 percent of their rated capacity at not less than 65 percent of their rated heat. The intention of the requirement of 31.7.3.3 is to limit designers to 120 percent of the rated capacity of the pump to provide an additional factor of safety for marine systems.

A.31.7.3.12.2(1) Pumps should not be located within the same compartment. However, where this is not reasonable or practical, special attention should be given to protecting pumps such that a single failure will not render the sprinkler system inoperative. *[See Figure A.31.7.3.12.2(1).]*

A.31.7.3.13 See Figure A.31.7.3.13.

A.31.7.4.6 This procedure should be used to qualify each water supply to which the vessel is to be attached. For example, this might require testing of multiple hydrants or connections in the same mooring area. The pressure loss effect of the hose or piping leading from the water supply to the ship should also be considered when qualifying each hydrant.

A.32.1 *Impairments.* Before shutting off a section of the fire service system to make sprinkler system connections, notify the authority having jurisdiction, plan the work carefully, and assemble all materials to enable completion in the shortest possible time. Work started on connections should be completed without interruption, and protection should be restored as promptly as possible. During the impairment, provide emergency hose lines and extinguishers and maintain extra watch service in the areas affected.

When changes involve shutting off water from any considerable number of sprinklers for more than a few hours, temporary water supply connections should be made to sprinkler systems so that reasonable protection can be maintained. In adding to old systems or revamping them, protection should be restored each night so far as possible. The members of the private fire brigade as well as public fire departments should be notified as to conditions.

Maintenance Schedule. The items shown in Table A.32.1 should be checked on a routine basis.

SPRINKLER SYSTEM — GENERAL INFORMATION
for

_____

_____

_____

Pipe schedule system   ❑ Yes   ❑ No   **Date:** _____

High-piled storage   ❑ Yes   ❑ No

Rack storage: ❑ Yes   ❑ No   **Flow test data:**

Commodity class: _____   Static: _____ psi   bar

Max. storage height _____ ft   m   Resid: _____ psi   bar

Aisle width (min.) _____ ft   m   Flow: _____ gpm   lpm

Encapsulation   ❑ Yes   ❑ No   **Pitot:** _____ psi   bar

Solid shelving: ❑ Yes   ❑ No   **Date:** _____

Flammable/
combustible liquids: ❑ Yes   ❑ No   **Location:** _____

Other storage: ❑ Yes   ❑ No   Location of aux/low point drains:

_____

Hazardous materials: ❑ Yes   ❑ No

Idle pallets: ❑ Yes   ❑ No   _____

Antifreeze systems   ❑ Yes   ❑ No   Dry pipe/double interlock preaction valve
   Location: _____   test results

Dry or aux systems   ❑ Yes   ❑ No   **Original main drain test results:**
   Location: _____   Static: _____ psi   bar

     Residual: _____ psi   bar

     Venting valve location: _____

Where injection systems are used to treat MIC or corrosion:

Type of chemical: _____ Concentration: _____ For proper disposal, see:

_____

Name of contractor or designer: _____

Address: _____

Phone: _____

FIGURE A.29.6   Sprinkler System General Information.

Δ Table A.31.1.3 Examples of Shipboard Space Occupancy Classification

| Occupancy Type | Space Types Included | | Examples |
	CFR[a]	SOLAS[b]	
Light hazard	1[c], 2, 3, 4, 5, 6, 7, 8[d], 13	1[c], 2, 3, 4, 5, 6, 7, 8, 9	Accommodation spaces Small pantries
Ordinary hazard (Group 1)	8[d], 9[d]	12, 13[d]	Galleys Storage areas Sales shops Laundries Pantries with significant storage
Ordinary hazard (Group 2)	9[d], 11[d]	12[d], 13[d]	Sales shops Storage areas Stages (with sets) Machine shops
Extra hazard (Group 1)	1, 9[d], 10, 11[d]	1, 12[d], 13[d]	Auxiliary machinery — limited-combustible liquids[e] Steering rooms — combustible hydraulic fluid in use[e]
Extra hazard (Group 2)	1, 9[d], 10, 11[d]	1, 12[d], 13[d]	Auxiliary machinery — with combustible liquids[e] Machinery spaces[e]

[a]Space-type designations are given in 46 CFR 72.05-5.

[b]Space-type designations are given in the *International Convention for the Safety of Life at Sea*, 1974 (SOLAS 74), as amended, regulations II-2/3 and II-2/26.

[c]Primarily for accommodation-type control stations, such as the wheel house, which would not include generator rooms or similar-type spaces.

[d]Depends on storage type, quantity, and height and distance below sprinkler.

[e]Automatic sprinklers typically will not be the primary means of protection in these areas; total flooding systems are usually used.

The classifications in Table A.31.1.3 are not meant to be applied without giving consideration to the definition of each occupancy hazard given in the standard. Table A.31.1.3 is general guidance for classification of typical spaces. Where a space is outfitted such that the occupancy definitions indicate that another classification would be more appropriate, the most representative and most demanding occupancy classification should be used. For example, it would certainly be possible to outfit a stateroom to require upgrading the occupancy to ordinary hazard, Group 1.

When a vessel undergoes modifications, alterations, or service changes that significantly affect the fire risk of the occupancy of one or more compartments, the occupancy classification should be reevaluated to determine if it has changed.

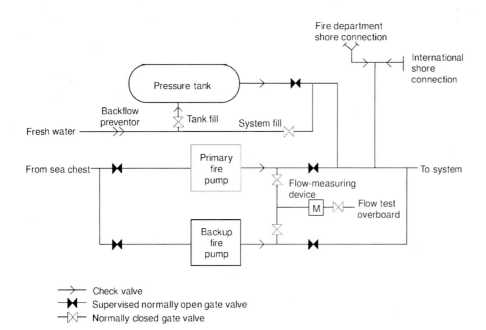

Check valve
Supervised normally open gate valve
Normally closed gate valve

FIGURE A.31.7.3.12.2(1) Abbreviated Example of Dual Fire Pump Water Supply.

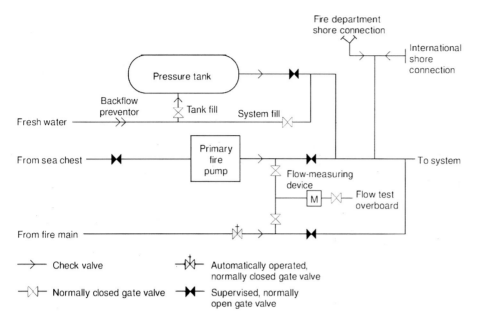

FIGURE A.31.7.3.13   Abbreviated Example of Water Supply with Fire Pump Backup.

Table A.32.1 Maintenance Schedule

Parts	Activity	Frequency
Flushing piping	Test	5 years
Fire department connections	Inspection	Monthly
Control valves	Inspection	Weekly — sealed
	Inspection	Monthly — locked
	Inspection	Monthly — tamper switch
	Maintenance	Yearly
Main drain	Flow test	Quarterly — annual
Open sprinklers	Test	Annually
Pressure gauge	Calibration test	
Sprinklers	Test	50 years
Sprinklers — high-temperature	Test	5 years
Sprinklers — residential	Test	20 years
Waterflow alarms	Test	Quarterly
Preaction/deluge detection system	Test	Semiannually
Preaction/deluge systems	Test	Annually
Antifreeze solution	Test	Annually
Cold weather valves	Open and close valves	Fall, close; spring, open
Dry/preaction/deluge systems		
Air pressure and water pressure	Inspection	Weekly
Enclosure	Inspection	Daily — cold weather
Priming water level	Inspection	Quarterly
Low-point drains	Test	Fall
Dry pipe valves	Trip test	Annually — spring
Dry pipe valves	Full flow trip	3 years — spring
Quick-opening devices	Test	Semiannually

Annex B   Miscellaneous Topics

This annex is not a part of the requirements of this NFPA document but is included for informational purposes only.

B.1 Figure B.1 shows acceptable methods for interconnection of the fire protection and domestic water supply.

B.2 Sprinkler System Performance Criteria.

B.2.1 Sprinkler system performance criteria have been based on test data. The factors of safety are generally small, are not definitive, and can depend on expected (but not guaranteed) inherent characteristics of the sprinkler systems involved. These inherent factors of safety consist of the following:

(1) The flow-declining pressure characteristic of sprinkler systems whereby the initial operating sprinklers discharge at a higher flow than with all sprinklers operating within the designated area.
(2) The flow-declining pressure characteristic of water supplies, which is particularly steep where fire pumps are the water source. This characteristic similarly produces higher than design discharge at the initially operating sprinklers.

The user of these standards can elect an additional factor of safety if the inherent factors are not considered adequate.

B.2.1.1 Performance-specified sprinkler systems, as opposed to scheduled systems, can be designed to take advantage of multiple loops or gridded configurations. Such configurations result in minimum line losses at expanded sprinkler spacing, in contrast to the older tree-type configurations, where advantage cannot be taken of multiple path flows.

Where the water supply characteristics are relatively flat with pressures being only slightly above the required sprinkler pressure at the spacing selected, gridded systems with piping designed for minimal economic line losses can all but eliminate the inherent flow-declining pressure characteristic generally assumed to exist in sprinkler systems. In contrast, the economic design of a tree-type system would likely favor a system design with closer sprinkler spacing and greater line

losses, demonstrating the inherent flow-declining pressure characteristic of the piping system.

Elements that enter into the design of sprinkler systems include the following:

(1) Selection of density and area of application
(2) Geometry of the area of application (remote area)
(3) Permitted pressure range at sprinklers
(4) Determination of the water supply available
(5) Ability to predict expected performance from calculated performance
(6) Future upgrading of system performance
(7) Size of sprinkler systems

In developing sprinkler specifications, each of these elements needs to be considered individually. The most conservative design should be based on the application of the most stringent conditions for each of the elements.

B.2.1.2 Selection of Density and Area of Application. Specifications for density and area of application are developed from NFPA standards and other standards. It is desirable to specify densities rounded upward to the nearest 0.005 gpm/ft² (0.2 mm/min).

Prudent design should consider reasonable-to-expect variations in occupancy. This design would include not only variations in type of occupancy but also, in the case of warehousing, the anticipated future range of materials to be stored, clearance to ceiling, types of arrays, packaging, pile height, and pile stability, as well as other factors.

Design should also consider some degree of adversity at the time of a fire. To take this into account, the density and/or area of application can be increased. Another way is to use a dual-performance specification where, in addition to the normal primary specifications, a secondary density and area of application are specified. The objective of such a selection is to control the declining pressure-flow characteristic of the sprinkler system beyond the primary design flow.

A case can be made for designing feed and cross mains to lower velocities than branch lines to achieve the same result as specifying a second density and area of application.

B.2.1.3 Geometry of Area of Application (Remote Area). It is expected that, over any portion of the sprinkler system equivalent in size to the area of application, the system will achieve the minimum specified density for each sprinkler within that area.

Where a system is computer-designed, ideally the program should verify the entire system by shifting the area of application the equivalent of one sprinkler at a time so as to cover all portions of the system. Such a complete computer verification of performance of the system is most desirable, but unfortunately not all available computer verification programs currently do this.

This selection of the proper Hazen–Williams coefficient is important. New unlined steel pipe has a Hazen–Williams coefficient close to 140. However, it quickly deteriorates to 130 and, after a few years of use, to 120. Hence, the basis for normal design is a Hazen–Williams coefficient of 120 for steel-piped wet systems. A Hazen–Williams coefficient of 100 is generally used for dry pipe systems because of the increased tendency for deposits and corrosion in these systems. However, it should be

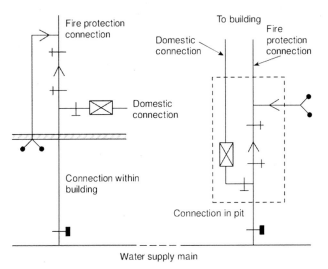

FIGURE B.1   Permitted Arrangements Between Fire Protection Water Supply and Domestic Water Supply.

Shaded text = Revisions.   Δ = Text deletions and figure/table revisions.   • = Section deletions.   *N* = New material.

2022 Edition

realized that a new system will have fewer line losses than calculated, and the distribution pattern will be affected accordingly.

Conservatism can also be built into systems by intentionally designing to a lower Hazen–Williams coefficient than that indicated.

B.2.1.4 Ability to Predict Expected Performance from Calculated Performance. Ability to accurately predict the performance of a complex array of sprinklers on piping is basically a function of the pipe line velocity. The greater the velocity, the greater is the impact on difficult-to-assess pressure losses. These pressure losses are presently determined by empirical means that lose validity as velocities increase. This is especially true for fittings with unequal and more than two flowing ports.

The inclusion of velocity pressures in hydraulic calculations improves the predictability of the actual sprinkler system performance. Calculations should come as close as practicable to predicting actual performance. Conservatism in design should be arrived at intentionally by known and deliberate means. It should not be left to chance.

B.2.1.5 Future Upgrading of System Performance. It is desirable in some cases to build into the system the capability to achieve a higher level of sprinkler performance than needed at present. If this is to be a consideration in conservatism, consideration needs to be given to maintaining sprinkler operating pressures on the lower side of the optimum operating range and/or designing for low pipeline velocities, particularly on feed and cross mains, to facilitate future reinforcement.

B.3 Effect of Clearance to Ceiling on Sprinkler Performance. The problems with large clearances to ceiling were well recognized by the 1970s in terms of the effect both on delayed sprinkler activation and on the effect on droplet penetration through the fire plume. The work of Alpert (1972, 1975), Heskestad and Delichatsios (1979), and Beyler (1984) clearly identified the effect of clearance to ceiling on detection and activation of sprinklers. This was supplemented by the work of Heskestad and Smith (1976) in which the thermal responsiveness of sprinklers was studied and modeled. Similarly, the effect of the strong plumes resulting from large clearances to ceiling and highly challenging fires was recognized in the 1970s through the work of Yao and Kalelkar (1970), Yao (1976), and Yao (1980). This understanding was reflected in the development of large drop sprinklers in the 1970s [Yao (1997)]. The inability of ½ in. and $^{17}\!/_{32}$ in. (12.7 mm and 13 mm) standard sprinklers to penetrate high-challenging fires was well understood and demonstrated in the 1970s [Yao (1976)]. The effect of excessive clearance to ceiling was also demonstrated in the testing summarized in Annex C.

This understanding of the role of clearance to ceiling on fire performance had a strong effect on the development of advanced sprinkler technologies.

References:

Alpert, R. (1972), "Calculation of Response Time of Ceiling-mounted Fire Detectors," *Fire Technology* 8, pp. 181–195.

Alpert, R. (1975), "Turbulent Ceiling Jet Induced by Large Scale Fire," *Combustion Science and Technology* 11, pp. 197–213.

Beyler, C.L. (1984), "A Design Method for Flaming Fire Detection," *Fire Technology* 20, No. 4, 1984, p. 5.

Heskestad, G., and Smith, H. (1976), "Investigation of a New Sprinkler Sensitivity Approval Test: The Plunge Test," FMRC Serial No. 22485, Factory Mutual Research Corporation, Norwood, MA, December 1976.

Heskestad, G., and Delichatsios, M. (1979), "The Initial Convective Flow in Fire," Seventeenth Symposium (International) on Combustion, The Combustion Institute, Pittsburgh, PA, pp. 1113–1123.

Yao, C., and Kalelkar, A. (1970), "Effect of Drop Size on Sprinkler Performance," *Fire Technology* 6, 1970.

Yao, C. (1976), "Development of Large-Drop Sprinklers," FMRC Serial 22476, RC76-T-18, Factory Mutual Research Corporation, Norwood, MA.

Yao, C. (1980), "Application of Sprinkler Technology," Engineering Applications of Fire Technology, National Bureau of Standards, Gaithersburg MD, and FMRC RC80-TP-34.

Yao, C. (1997), "Overview of Sprinkler Technology Research," Fire Safety Science-Proceedings of the Fifth International Symposium, Y. Hasemi (Ed.), International Association for Fire Safety Science, Boston, MA, pp. 93–110.

Annex C   Explanation of Test Data and Procedures for Rack Storage

This annex is not a part of the requirements of this NFPA document but is included for informational purposes only.

C.1 Annex C provides an explanation of the test data and procedures that led to the development of sprinkler system discharge criteria for rack storage applications. Numbers in brackets refer to paragraphs in the text.

C.2 [20.3] A review of full-scale fire tests run on the standard commodity (double tri-wall carton with metal liner), of Hallmark products and 3M products (e.g., abrasives, pressure-sensitive tapes of plastic fiber, and paper), and of the considerable number of commodity tests conducted provides a guide for commodity classifications. Such guidance is not related to any other method of classification of materials; therefore, sound engineering judgment and analysis of the commodity and the packaging should be used when selecting a commodity classification.

C.3 [25.1.6.4] Tests 71, 73, 81, 83, 91, 92, 95, and 100 in the 20 ft (6.1 m) high array involving a single level of in-rack sprinklers were conducted without heat or water shields. Results were satisfactory.

Test 115 was conducted with two levels of sprinklers in racks with shields. Test 116, identical to Test 115 but without water shields, produced a lack of control. Visual observation of lower level in-rack sprinklers that did not operate although they were in the fire area indicated a need for water shields.

Tests 115 and 116 were conducted to investigate the necessity for water shields where multiple levels of in-rack sprinklers are installed. Where water shields were not installed in Test 116, the fire jumped the aisle, and approximately 76 boxes were damaged. In Test 115 with water shields, the fire did not jump the aisle, and only 32 boxes were damaged. Water shields are, therefore, suggested wherever multiple levels of in-rack sprinklers are installed, except for installations with horizontal barriers or shelves that serve as water shields.

C.4 [A.25.1.4.3] The time of operation of the first sprinkler varied from 52 seconds to 3 minutes and 55 seconds, with most tests under 3 minutes, except in Test 64 (Class III), where the first sprinkler operated in 7 minutes and 44 seconds. Fire detection more sensitive than waterflow is, therefore, considered necessary only in exceptional cases.

C.5 [16.15.1 and 20.14.1] In most tests conducted, it was necessary to use small hose for mop-up operations. Small hose was not used in the high-expansion foam test.

Test 97 was conducted to evaluate the effect of dry pipe sprinkler operation. Test results were approximately the same as the base test with a wet pipe system. A study of NFPA records, however, indicates an increase in area of operation of 30 percent to be in order for dry pipe systems as compared with wet pipe systems.

C.6 [20.9.5] Tests were conducted as a part of this program with eave line windows or louvers open to simulate smoke and heat venting. These tests opened 87.5 percent and 91 percent more sprinklers than did comparative tests without windows or louvers open. Venting tests that have been conducted in other programs were without the benefit of sprinkler protection and, as such, are not considered in this report, which covers only buildings protected by sprinklers. The design curves are based upon the absence of roof vents or draft curtains in the building. During mop-up operations, ventilating systems, where installed, should be capable of manual exhaust operations.

C.7 [20.17.1.3] No tests were conducted with idle pallets in racks using standard spray sprinklers. However, tests were conducted using ESFR and large drop sprinklers. Such storage conceivably would introduce fire severity in excess of that contemplated by protection criteria for an individual commodity classification.

C.8 [20.19] In all valid tests with double-row racks, sprinkler water supplies were shut off at approximately 60 minutes. In only one test did the last sprinkler operate in excess of 30 minutes after ignition; the last sprinkler operated in excess of 25 minutes in three tests, with the majority of tests involving the last sprinkler operating within 20 minutes.

Δ **C.9 [25.1.1.2]** The discharge criteria of Section 20.13 uses as a basis the large-scale fire test series conducted at the Factory Mutual Research Center, West Glocester, Rhode Island.

The test building is approximately 200 ft × 250 ft (61 m × 76 m) [50,000 ft² (4650 m²) in area], of fire-resistive construction, and contains a volume of approximately 2.25 million ft³ (63,713 m³), the equivalent of a 100,000 ft² (9230 m²) building that is 22.5 ft (6.9 m) high. The test building has two primary heights beneath a single large ceiling. The east section is 30 ft (9.1 m) high, and the west section is 60 ft (18 m) high.

The test series for storage height of 20 ft (6.1 m) was conducted in the 30 ft (9.1 m) section with clearances from the top of storage to the ceiling nominally 10 ft (3.0 m).

Doors at the lower and intermediate levels and ventilation louvers at the tops of walls were kept closed during the majority of the fire tests, which minimized the effect of exterior conditions.

The entire test series was fully instrumented with thermocouples attached to rack members, simulated building columns, bar joists, and the ceiling.

Racks were constructed of steel vertical and horizontal members designed for 4000 lb (1815 kg) loads. Vertical members were 8 ft (2.4 m) on center for conventional racks and 4 ft (1.2 m) on center for simulated automated racks. Racks were 3½ ft (1 m) wide with 6 in. (150 mm) longitudinal flue space for an overall width of 7½ ft (2.3 m). Simulated automated racks and slave pallets were used in the main central rack in the 4 ft (1.2 m) aisle tests. Conventional racks and conventional pallets were used in the main central rack in the 8 ft (2.4 m) aisle tests. The majority of the tests were conducted with 100 ft² (9.3 m²) sprinkler spacing.

The test configuration for storage heights of 15 ft (4.6 m), 20 ft (6.1 m), and 25 ft (7.6 m) covered an 1800 ft² (167.2 m²) floor area, including aisles between racks. Tests that were used in producing this standard limited fire damage to this area. The maximum water damage area anticipated in the standard is 6000 ft² (555 m²), the upper limit of the design curves.

The test data show that, as density is increased, both the extent of fire damage and sprinkler operation are reduced. The data also indicate that, with sprinklers installed in the racks, a reduction is gained in the area of fire damage and sprinkler operations (e.g., water damage).

Table C.9 illustrates these points. The information shown in the table is taken from the test series for storage height of 20 ft (6.1 m) using the standard commodity.

The fact that there is a reduction in both fire damage and area of water application as sprinkler densities are increased or where sprinklers are installed in racks should be considered carefully by those responsible for applying this standard to the rack storage situation.

In the test for storage height of 25 ft (7.6 m), a density of 0.55 gpm/ft² (22.4 mm/min) produced 42 percent, or 756 ft² (70 m²), fire damage in the test array and a sprinkler-wetted area of 1400 ft² (130 m²). Lesser densities would not be expected to achieve the same limited degree of control. Therefore, if the goal of smaller areas of fire damage is to be achieved, sprinklers in racks should be considered.

The test series for storage height over 25 ft (7.6 m) was conducted in the 60 ft (18 m) section of the test building with nominal clearances from the top of storage to the ceiling of either 30 ft (9.1 m) or 10 ft (3.0 m).

Doors at the lower and intermediate levels and ventilation louvers at the top of walls were kept closed during the fire tests, which minimized the effect of exterior wind conditions.

The purpose of the tests for storage height over 25 ft (7.6 m) was to accomplish the following:

(1) Determine the arrangement of in-rack sprinklers that can be repeated as pile height increases and that provide control of the fire
(2) Determine other protective arrangements, such as high-expansion foam, that provide control of the fire

Control was considered to have been accomplished if the fire was unlikely to spread from the rack of origin to adjacent racks or spread beyond the length of the 25 ft (7.6 m) test rack. To aid in this judgment, control was considered to have been achieved if the fire failed to exhibit the following characteristics:

(1) Jump the 4 ft (1.2 m) aisles to adjoining racks
(2) Reach the end face of the end stacks (north or south ends) of the main rack

Control is defined as holding the fire in check through the extinguishing system until the commodities initially involved are consumed or until the fire is extinguished by the extinguishing system or manual aid.

The standard commodity as selected in the 20 ft (6.1 m) test series was used in the majority of tests for storage over 25 ft (7.6 m). Hallmark products and 3M products described in the 20 ft (6.1 m) test series report also were used as representative of Class III or Class IV commodities, or both, in several tests. The results of privately sponsored tests on Hallmark products and plastic encapsulated standard commodities also were made available to the committee.

A 25 ft (7.6 m) long test array was used for the majority of the tests for storage over 25 ft (7.6 m). The decision to use such an array was made because it was believed that a fire in racks over 25 ft (7.6 m) high that extended the full length of a 50 ft (15 m) long rack could not be considered controlled, particularly as storage heights increased.

One of the purposes of the tests was to determine arrangements of in-rack sprinklers that can be repeated as pile height

increases and that provide control of the fire. The tests for storage height of 30 ft (9.1 m) explored the effect of such arrays. Many of these tests, however, produced appreciable fire spread in storage in tiers above the top level of protection within the racks. (In some cases, a total burnout of the top tiers of both the main rack and the target rack occurred.) In the case of the 30 ft (9.1 m) Hallmark Test 134 on the 60 ft (18 m) site, the material in the top tiers of storage burned vigorously, and the fire jumped the aisle above the fourth tier. The fire then burned downward into the south end of the fourth tier. In the test on the floor, a nominal 30 ft (9.1 m) clearance occurred between the top of storage and the ceiling sprinklers, whereas on the platform this clearance was reduced to nominal 10 ft (3.0 m). In most cases, the in-rack sprinklers were effective in controlling fire below the top level of protection within the racks. It has been assumed by the Test Planning Committee that in an actual case with a clearance of 10 ft (3.0 m) or less above storage, ceiling sprinklers would be expected to control damage above the top level of protection within the racks. Tests have been planned to investigate lesser clearances.

Tests 114 and 128 explore the effect of changing the ignition point from the in-rack standard ignition point to a face ignition location. It should be noted, however, that both of these tests were conducted with 30 ft (9.1 m) clearance from the ceiling sprinklers to the top of storage and, as such, ceiling sprinklers had little effect on the fire in the top two tiers of storage. Firespread in the three lower tiers is essentially the same. A similar change in the firespread where the ignition point is changed was noted in Tests 126 and 127. Once again, 30 ft (9.1 m) clearance occurred between the top of storage and the ceiling sprinklers, and, as such, the ceiling sprinklers had little effect on the face fire. Comparisons of Tests 129, 130, and 131 in the test series for storage height of 50 ft (15 m) indicate little effect of point of ignition in the particular configuration tested.

Test 125, when compared with Test 133, indicates no significant difference in result between approved low-profile sprinklers and standard sprinklers in the racks.

C.10 [20.18.1] Temperatures in the test column were maintained below 1000°F (538°C) with densities, of roof ceiling sprinklers only, of 0.375 gpm/ft² (15.3 mm/min) with 8 ft (2.4 m) aisles and 0.45 gpm/ft² (18.3 mm/min) with 4 ft (1.2 m) aisles using the standard commodity.

C.11 [20.19.3.1] Test 98 with solid shelves 24 ft (7.3 m) long and 7½ ft (2.3 m) deep at each level produced total destruction of the commodity in the main rack and jumped the aisle. Density was 0.3 gpm/ft² (12.2 mm/min) from the ceiling sprinklers only. Test 108 with shelves 24 ft (7.3 m) long and 3½ ft (1.0 m) deep and with a 6 in. (150 mm) longitudinal flue space and one level of sprinklers in the rack resulted in damage to most of the commodity in the main rack but did not jump the aisle. Density from ceiling sprinklers was 0.375 gpm/ft² (15.3 mm/min), and rack sprinklers discharged at 15 psi (1.0 bar).

These tests did not yield sufficient information to develop a comprehensive protection standard for solid shelf racks. Items such as increased ceiling density, use of bulkheads, other configurations of sprinklers in racks, and limitation of shelf length and depth should be considered.

Δ **Table C.9 Summary of Relationship Between Sprinkler Discharge Density and the Extent of Fire Damage and Sprinkler Operation**

Density [gpm/ft² (mm/min)]	Fire Damage in Test Array		Sprinkler Operation [165°F (74°C)] Area [ft² (m²)]
	%	ft² (m²)	
0.30 (12.2) (ceiling only)	22	395 (37)	4500–4800 (420–445)
0.375 (15.3) (ceiling only)	17	306 (24)	1800 (165)
0.45 (18.3) (ceiling only)	9	162 (15)	700 (65)
0.20 (8.2) (ceiling only)	28–36	504–648 (46–60)	13,100–14,000 (1215–1300)
0.20 (8.2) (sprinklers at ceiling and in racks)	8	144 (13)	4100 (380)
0.30 (12.2) (sprinklers at ceiling and in racks)	7	126 (12)	700 (65)

For SI units. 1 ft = 0.3048 m; °C = ⅝ (°F − 32); 1 gpm/ft² = 40.746 mm/min.

Where such rack installations exist or are contemplated, the damage potential should be considered, and sound engineering judgment should be used in designing the protection system.

Test 98, with solid shelving obstructing both the longitudinal and transverse flue space, produced unsatisfactory results and indicates a need for sprinklers at each level in such a rack structure.

Test 147 was conducted with ceiling sprinklers only. Density was 0.45 gpm/ft² (18.3 mm/min) with a sprinkler spacing of 100 ft² (9 m²). A total of 47 sprinklers opened, and 83 percent of the commodity was consumed. The fire jumped both aisles and spread to both ends of the main and target racks. The test was considered unsuccessful.

Test 148 was conducted with ceiling sprinklers and in-rack sprinklers. In-rack sprinklers were provided at each level (top of first, second, and third tiers) and were located in the longitudinal flue. They were directly above each other and 24 ft (7.3 m) on center or 22 ft (6.7 m) on each side of the ignition flue. Ceiling sprinkler discharge density was 0.375 gpm/ft² (15.3 mm/min). In-rack sprinkler discharge pressure was 30 psi (2.1 bar). A total of 46 ceiling sprinklers and three in-rack sprinklers opened, and 34 percent of the commodity was consumed. The fire consumed most of the material between the in-rack sprinklers and jumped both aisles.

C.12 [20.3.3] Fire tests with open-top containers in the upper tier of storage and a portion of the third tier of storage produced an increase in sprinkler operation from 36 to 41 sprinklers and a more pronounced aisle jump and increase in firespread in the main array. The smooth underside of the containers closely approximates fire behavior of slave pallets.

C.13 [20.5.3.4.1.1] Test 80 was conducted to determine the effect of closing back-to-back longitudinal 6 in. (150 mm) flue spaces in conventional pallet racks. Test results indicated fewer sprinklers operating than with the flue space open, and, as such, no minimum back-to-back clearance is necessary if the transverse flue space is kept open.

Tests 145 and 146 were conducted to investigate the influence of longitudinal and transverse flue dimensions in double-row racks without solid shelves. Results were compared with Tests 65 and 66. Flue dimensions in Tests 65, 66, 145, and 146 were 6 in. (150 mm), 6 in. (150 mm), 3 in. (75 mm), and 12 in. (300 mm), respectively. All other conditions were the same.

In Tests 65, 66, 45, and 48, sprinklers operated compared with Tests 59 and 58 for Tests 145 and 146, respectively. Fire damage in Tests 145 and 146 was somewhat less than in Tests 65

and 66; 2100 ft³ (59 m³) and 1800 ft³ (51 m³) in Tests 145 and 146, respectively, versus 2300 ft³ (65 m³) and 2300 ft³ (65 m³) in Tests 65 and 66, respectively, of combustible material were consumed.

Test results indicate narrow flue spaces of about 3 in. (75 mm) allow reasonable passage of sprinkler water down through the racks.

Tests 96 and 107, on multiple-row racks, used 6 in. (150 mm) transverse flue spaces. The water demand recommended in the standard is limited to those cases with nominal 6 in. (150 mm) transverse flues in vertical alignment.

C.14 [21.4.1.1.1, 21.4.1.1.2, 25.8.2.2.2.2(B), and 25.8.3.2.2.2(B)] Tests 65 and 66, compared with Test 69, and Test 93, compared with Test 94, indicated a reduction in areas of application of 44.5 percent and 45.5 percent, respectively, with high-temperature-rated sprinklers as compared with ordinary-temperature-rated sprinklers. Other extensive Factory Mutual tests produced an average reduction of 40 percent. Design curves are based on this area reduction. In constructing the design curves, the high-temperature curves above 3600 ft² (335 m²) of application, therefore, represent 40 percent reductions in area of application of the ordinary-temperature curves in the 6000 ft² to 10,000 ft² (555 m² to 930 m²) range.

Test 84 indicated the number of intermediate-temperature-rated sprinklers operating is essentially the same as ordinary-temperature-rated sprinklers.

C.15 [21.4.1.2.3, 25.3.2.2.2.1(B), 25.8.2.2.2.1, and 25.8.3.2.2.1] Tests were not conducted with aisles wider than 8 ft (2.4 m) or narrower than 4 ft (1.2 m). It is, therefore, not possible to determine whether lower ceiling densities should be used for aisle widths greater than 8 ft (2.4 m) or if higher densities should be used for aisle widths less than 4 ft (1.2 m).

C.16 [25.1.8.3.2] In one 20 ft (6.1 m) high test, sprinklers were buried in the flue space 1 ft (300 mm) above the bottom of the pallet load, and results were satisfactory. Coverage of aisles by in-rack sprinklers is, therefore, not necessary, and distribution across the tops of pallet loads at any level is not necessary for the occupancy classes tested.

C.17 [25.1.7.7] In all tests with in-rack sprinklers, obstructions measuring 3 in. × 3 ft (75 mm × 900 mm) were introduced on each side of the sprinkler approximately 3 in. (75 mm) from the sprinkler to simulate rack structure member obstruction. This obstruction had no effect on sprinkler performance in the 20 ft (6.1 m) high tests.

Tests 103, 104, 105, and 109 in the 30 ft (9.1 m) high test with in-rack sprinklers obstructed by rack uprights produced unsatisfactory results. Tests 113, 114, 115, 117, 118, and 120 in the 30 ft (9.1 m) high test series with in-rack sprinklers located a minimum of 2 ft (600 mm) from rack uprights produced improved results.

C.18 [25.3.1.1] In all except one case, using the standard commodity with one line of sprinklers installed in racks, only two sprinklers opened. In the one exception, two sprinklers opened in the main rack, and two sprinklers opened in the target rack.

C.19 [25.3.1.1] Operating pressures were 15 psi (1.0 bar) on all tests of sprinklers in racks with storage 20 ft (6.1 m) high and 30 psi (2.1 bar) for storage 30 ft (9.1 m) and 50 ft (15 m) high.

Tests 112 and 124 were conducted to compare the effect of increasing sprinkler discharge pressure at in-rack sprinklers from 30 psi to 75 psi (2.1 bar to 5.2 bar). With the higher discharge pressure, the fire did not jump the aisle, and damage below the top level of protection within the racks was somewhat better controlled by the higher discharge pressure of the in-rack sprinklers. A pressure of 15 psi (1 bar) was maintained on in-rack sprinklers in the first 30 ft (9.1 m) high tests (Tests 103 and 104). Pressure on in-rack sprinklers in subsequent tests was 30 psi (2.1 bar), except in Test 124, where it was 75 psi (5.2 bar).

Δ **C.20 [20.5.3.2]** A full-scale test program was conducted with various double-row rack storage arrangements of a cartoned Group A nonexpanded plastic commodity at the Factory Mutual Research Corporation (FMRC) test facility. The series of nine tests included several variations, one of which involved the use of the following four distinct shelving arrangements: slatted wood, solid wood, wire mesh, and no shelving. The results of the testing program, specifically Tests 1, 2, 3, and 5, clearly demonstrate the acceptable performance of sprinkler systems protecting storage configurations that involve the use of slated shelving as described in 26.4.1. As a result of the test program, Factory Mutual has amended FM Loss Prevention Data Sheet 8-9 to allow slatted shelving to be protected in the same manner as an open rack arrangement.

Complete details of the test program are documented in the FMRC technical report FMRC J. I. 0X1R0.RR, "Large-Scale Fire Tests of Rack Storage Group A Plastics in Retail Operation Scenarios Protected by Extra Large Orifice (ELO) Sprinklers."

C.21 [20.4.8 and 21.5.1] In the RSP rack storage test series as well as the stored plastics program palletized test series, compartmented 16 oz (1.1 bar) polystyrene jars were found to produce significantly higher protection requirements than the same commodity in a nested configuration. Polystyrene glasses and expanded polystyrene plates were comparable to the nested jars.

Different storage configurations within cartons or different products of the same basic plastic might, therefore, require reduced protection requirements.

In Test RSP-7, with nominal 15 ft (4.6 m) high storage with compartment jars, a 0.6 gpm/ft^2 (24.5 mm/min) density, 8 ft (2.4 m) aisles, and a 10 ft (3.0 m) clearance to ceiling, 29 sprinklers opened. In Tests RSP-4 with polystyrene glasses, RSP-5 with expanded polystyrene plates, and RSP-16 with nested polystyrene jars all stored at nominal 15 ft (4.6 m) height, 10 ft

(3.1 m) clearance to ceiling, 8 ft (2.4 m) aisles, and 0.6 gpm/ft^2 (24.5 mm/min) density, only four sprinklers opened.

However, Test RSP-11, with expanded polystyrene plates and 6 ft (1.8 m) aisles, demonstrated an increase in the number of operating sprinklers to 29. Test RSP-10 with expanded polystyrene plates, nominally 15 ft (4.6 m) high with a 10 ft (3.1 m) clearance and 8 ft (2.4 m) aisles, but protected only by 0.45 gpm/ft^2 (18.3 mm/min) density, opened 46 sprinklers and burned 100 percent of the plastic commodity.

At a nominal 20 ft (6.1 m) storage height with 8 ft (2.4 m) aisles, a 3 ft (900 mm) clearance to ceiling, and a 0.6 gpm/ft^2 (24.5 mm/min) density opened four sprinklers with polystyrene glasses in Test RSP-2 and 11 sprinklers with expanded polystyrene plates in Test RSP-6. In Test RSP-8, however, with the clearance to ceiling increased to 10 ft (3.1 m) and other variables held constant, 51 sprinklers opened, and 100 percent of the plastic commodity burned.

Test RSP-3, with polystyrene glasses at a nominal height of 25 ft (7.6 m) with a 3 ft (900 mm) clearance to ceiling, 8 ft (2.4 m) aisles, and 0.6 gpm/ft^2 (24.5 mm/min) ceiling sprinkler density in combination with one level of in-rack sprinklers, resulted in four ceiling sprinklers and two in-rack sprinklers operating. Test RSP-9, with the same configuration but with polystyrene plates, opened 12 ceiling sprinklers and three in-rack sprinklers.

No tests were conducted with compartmented polystyrene jars at storage heights in excess of a nominal 15 ft (4.6 m) as a part of this program.

C.22 [21.5.1.1] The protection of Group A plastics by extra large orifice (ELO) sprinklers designed to provide 0.6 gpm/ft^2/2000 ft^2 (24.5 mm/min/185 m^2) or 0.45 gpm/ft^2/2000 ft^2 (18.3 mm/min/186 m^2) without the installation of in-rack sprinklers was developed from full-scale testing conducted with various double-row rack storage arrangements of a cartoned Group A nonexpanded plastic commodity at the Factory Mutual Research Corporation (FMRC) test facility. The results of this test program are documented in the FMRC technical report, FMRC J.I. 0X1R0.RR, "Large-Scale Fire Tests of Rack Stored Group A Plastics in Retail Operation Scenarios Protected by Extra Large Orifice (ELO) Sprinklers." The test program was initiated to address the fire protection issues presented by warehouse-type retail stores with regard to the display and storage of Group A plastic commodities including, but not limited to, acrylonitrile-butadiene-styrene copolymer (ABS) piping, polyvinyl chloride (PVC) hose and hose racks, tool boxes, polypropylene trash and storage containers, and patio furniture. Tests 1 and 2 of this series included protection of the Group A plastic commodity stored to 20 ft (6.1 m) under a 27 ft (8.2 m) ceiling by a design density of 0.6 gpm/ft^2 (24.5 mm/min) utilizing ELO sprinklers. The results of the testing program clearly demonstrate the acceptable performance of sprinkler systems that protect storage configurations involving Group A plastics up to 20 ft (6.1 m) in height under a 27 ft (8.2 m) ceiling where using ELO sprinklers to deliver a design density of 0.6 gpm/ft^2 (24.5 mm/min) and Group A plastics up to 14 ft (4.2 m) in height under a 22 ft (6.7 m) ceiling where using ELO sprinklers to deliver a design density of 0.45 gpm/ft^2 (18.3 mm/min). The tabulation of the pertinent tests shown in Table C.22 demonstrates acceptable performance.

Table C.22 Summary of Test Results for Plastic Commodities Using ⅝ in. (15.9 mm) Orifice Sprinklers

Test Parameters	Date of Test						
	8/20/93	8/25/93	9/2/93	10/7/93	2/17/94	2/25/94	4/27/94
Type of shelving	Slatted wood	Slatted wood	Slatted wood	Slatted wood	Slatted wood	Slatted wood	Wire mesh
Other conditions/inclusions	—	—	—	—	Draft curtains	Draft curtains	—
Storage height (ft-in.)	19-11	19-11	15-4	15-4	19-11	19-11	13-11
Number of tiers	6[a]	6[a]	5[b]	5[b]	6[a]	6[b]	3
Clearance to ceiling/ sprinklers (ft-in.)	6-10/6-3	6-10/6-3	11-5/10-10	11-5/10-10	6-10/6-3	6-10/6-3	8-4/7-9
Longitudinal/transverse flues (in.)	6/6 to 7½	6/6 to 7½	6/6 to 7	6/6 to 7½	6/6 to 7½	6/6 to 7½	6/3[c]
Aisle width (ft)	7½	7½	7½	7½	7½	7½	7½
Ignition centered below (number of sprinklers)	2	2	1	1	2	2	1
Sprinkler orifice size (in.)	0.64	0.64	0.64	0.64	0.64	0.64	0.64
Sprinkler temperature rating (°F)	165	286	286	165	165	286	286
Sprinkler RTI (ft-sec)$^{1/2}$	300	300	300	300	300	300	300
Sprinkler spacing (ft × ft)	8 × 10	8 × 10	8 × 10	8 × 10	8 × 10	8 × 10	10 × 10
Sprinkler identification	ELO-231	ELO-231	ELO-231	ELO-231	ELO-231	ELO-231	ELO-231
Constant water pressure (psi)	19	19	19	19	19	19	15.5
Minimum density (gpm/ft²)	0.6	0.6	0.6	0.6	0.6	0.6	0.45
Test Results							
First sprinkler operation (min:sec)	2:03	2:25	1:12	0:44	1:25	0:52	0:49
Last sprinkler operation (min:sec)	2:12	15:19	6:34	7:34	15:54	14:08	10:58
Total sprinklers opened	4	9	7	13	35	18	12
Total sprinkler discharge (gpm)	205	450	363	613	1651	945	600
Average discharge per sprinkler (gpm)	51	50	52	47	47	52	50
Peak/maximum 1-min average gas temperature (°F)	1107/566	1412/868	965/308	662/184	1575/883	1162/767	1464/895
Peak/maximum 1-min average steel temperature (°F)	185/172	197/196	233/232	146/145	226/225	255/254	502/500
Peak/maximum 1-min average plume velocity (ft/sec)	27/15	25/18	18/15[d]	14/10[d]	26/23	20/18[d]	33/20
Peak/maximum 1-min heat flux (Btu/ft²/sec)	0.6/0.5	2.0/1.9	2.8/2.5	1.1/0.8	1.0/0.9	4.8/3.0	1.6/1.4
Aisle jump, east/west target ignition (min:sec)	None	8:24/None	5:35/10:10	None	None	[e]/8:18	[e]/None
Equivalent number of pallet loads consumed	3	9	6	5	12	13	12
Test duration (min)	30	30	30	30	30	30	30
Results acceptable	Yes	Yes	Yes	Yes	No[f]	No[g]	Yes

For SI units, 1 ft = 0.305 m; 1 in. = 25.4 mm; °F = (1.8 ×°C) + 32; °C = (°F − 32)/1.8; 1 psi = 0.069 bar; 1 gpm = 3.8 L/min; 1 ft/sec = 0.31 m/sec; 1 gpm/ft² = 40.746 mm/min.

[a]Main (ignition) racks divided into five or six tiers; bottom tiers each approximately 2 ft (600 mm) high and upper tiers each about 5 ft (1.5 m) high; wood shelving below commodity at second through fifth tiers.

[b]Main (ignition) racks divided into five or six tiers; bottom tiers each approximately 2 ft (600 mm) high and upper tiers each about 5 ft (1.5 m) high; wood shelving below commodity at second through fifth tiers; wire mesh shelving below commodity at sixth tier or below fifth (top) tier commodity.

[c]Transverse flues spaced 8 ft (2.4 m) apart [versus 3½ ft (1.1 m) apart in all other tests].

[d]Instrumentation located 5 ft (1.5 m) north of ignition.

[e]Minor surface damage to cartons.

[f]High water demand.

[g]Excessive firespread; marginally high water demand.

C.23 [25.3.3.1.1.1 and 25.3.3.2.1.1] The recommended use of ordinary-temperature-rated sprinklers at ceiling for storage higher than 25 ft (7.6 m) was determined by the results of fire test data. A test with high-temperature-rated sprinklers and 0.45 gpm/ft² (18.3 mm/min) density resulted in fire damage in the two top tiers just within acceptable limits, with three ceiling sprinklers operating. A test with 0.45 gpm/ft² (18.3 mm/min) density and ordinary-temperature-rated sprinklers produced a dramatic reduction in fire damage with four ceiling sprinklers operating.

The four ordinary-temperature-rated ceiling sprinklers operated before the first of the three high-temperature-rated ceiling sprinklers. In both tests, two in-rack sprinklers at two levels operated at approximately the same time. The high-temperature-rated sprinklers were at all times fighting a larger fire with less water than the ordinary-temperature-rated ceiling sprinklers.

Tests 115 and 119 compare ceiling sprinkler density of 0.3 gpm/ft² (12.2 mm/min) with 0.45 gpm/ft² (18.3 mm/min). Damage patterns coupled with the number of boxes damaged in the main rack suggest that the increase in density produces improved control, particularly in the area above the top tier of in-rack sprinklers.

Tests 119 and 122 compare ceiling sprinkler temperature ratings of 286°F (141°C) and 165°F (74°C). A review of the number of boxes damaged and the firespread patterns indicates that the use of ordinary-temperature-rated ceiling sprinklers on a rack configuration that incorporates in-rack sprinklers dramatically reduces the amount of firespread. Considering that in-rack sprinklers in the tests for storage over 25 ft (7.6 m) operated prior to ceiling sprinklers, it would seem that the installation of in-rack sprinklers converts an otherwise rapidly developing fire, from the standpoint of ceiling sprinklers, to a slower developing fire with a lower rate of heat release.

In the 20 ft (6.1 m) high test series, ceiling sprinklers operated before in-rack sprinklers. In the 30 ft (9.1 m) high series, ceiling sprinklers operated after in-rack sprinklers. The 50 ft (15 m) high test did not operate ceiling sprinklers. Ceiling sprinklers would, however, be needed if fire occurred in upper levels.

The results of these tests indicate the effect of in-rack sprinklers on storage higher than 25 ft (7.6 m). From the ceiling sprinkler operation standpoint, a fire with an expected high heat release rate was converted to a fire with a much lower heat release rate.

Since the fires developed slowly and opened sprinklers at two levels in the racks, only a few ceiling sprinklers were needed to establish control. Thus, the sprinkler operating area does not vary with height for storage over 25 ft (7.6 m) or for changes in sprinkler temperature rating and density.

All tests with sprinklers in racks were conducted using nominal ½ in. (15 mm) orifice size sprinklers of ordinary temperature.

C.24 [26.7] A series of fire tests were conducted by Spacesaver Corporation that indicated control was achieved with light hazard sprinkler spacing and design. The tests used quick-response, ordinary-temperature sprinklers on 15 ft × 15 ft (4.6 m × 4.6 m) spacing with an 8 ft (2.4 m) high compact storage unit located in the middle of the sprinkler array. Results

indicated a classic definition of control, the fire was held in check within the compact storage module and the fire did not jump the aisle or ignite any of the target arrays.

Δ **C.25 [26.6]** In July and August of 2007, a series of three large-scale fire tests were conducted at Southwest Research Institute to investigate the effectiveness of a specific ceiling and in-rack sprinkler protection scheme dedicated for the protection of paper files in 12 in. (300 mm) wide and 16 in. (400 mm) and 10 in. (250 mm) high corrugated cardboard boxes (containers) maintained in multiple-row racks to a nominal height of 37 ft (11 m).

The storage rack for the main array in all three tests consisted of two 50 in. (1250 mm) deep racks placed back-to-back and separated by a 2 in. (50 mm) gap. The storage rack for the target array in all three tests consisted of a single 50 in. (1250 mm) deep rack separated on both sides of the main array by a 30 in. (750 mm) wide aisle. Rack uprights were a nominal 3 in. (75 mm) wide. Rack bays were 120 in. (3000 mm) wide, 38 in. (950 mm) high, and equipped with perforated metal decking having a minimum of 50 percent openings. Each storage bay was provided with nine containers between uprights that was three containers deep and three containers high for a total of 81 containers per rack bay. Nominal 6 in. (150 mm) wide transverse flue spaces were provided at each rack upright. Both the main array and the target array were four bays long for an overall length of 41 ft 3 in. (13 m).

Open-grated (expanded) catwalks were provided in both storage aisles at the top of the third [9 ft 8 in. (2.9 m)], sixth [19 ft 2 in. (5.8 m)], and ninth [28 ft 8 in. (8.7 m)] tier levels.

The ceiling sprinkler system consisted of K-8.0 (K-115), 165°F (74°C) nominally rated, standard-response pendent automatic sprinklers installed on 10 ft × 10 ft (3.0 m × 3.0 m) spacing arranged to provide a constant 0.30 gpm/ft² (12.2 mm/min) density. A nominal 3 ft (900 mm) clearance was provided between the top of storage and the ceiling sprinklers.

The in-rack sprinkler system consisted of K-8.0 (K-115), 165°F (74°C) nominally rated, quick-response upright automatic sprinklers that were equipped with water shields and arranged to provide a constant 30 gpm (115 L/min) flow from each operating in-rack sprinkler. In-rack sprinklers were provided within the transverse flue spaces of the main array, 2 ft (600 mm) horizontally from the face of the rack, at the top of the third and ninth tier levels on one side of the main array and at the top of the sixth tier level on the other side of the main array. A minimum 6 in. (150 mm) vertical clearance was provided between the in-rack sprinkler and the top of storage within the storage rack.

The same type of sprinklers installed within the storage racks were also installed under each catwalk and designed to provide a constant 30 gpm (115 L/min) flow from each operating sprinkler. These sprinklers were centered within the aisles and installed 10 ft 3 in. (3.1 m) on line. They were arranged to be aligned with the adjacent transverse flue space when the flue space was not equipped with an in-rack sprinkler; they were positioned halfway between transverse flue spaces when the adjacent flue spaces were equipped with in-rack sprinklers.

In Test No. 1, ignition was at grade level at the face of the rack and centered between rack uprights. The in-rack sprinklers within the transverse flue spaces nearest to the ignition location were at the top of the sixth tier level; the sprinkler under the catwalk at the top of the sixth tier level was located a horizontal distance of 15 in. (375 mm) away from the ignition location. The sprinkler under the catwalk at the top of the sixth tier level was the first sprinkler to operate at a time 2 minutes and 49 seconds after ignition. A total of 3 in-rack sprinklers and 1 catwalk sprinkler operated during this test; no ceiling-level sprinklers operated. The results of the test were considered acceptable.

In Test No. 2, ignition was at grade level at a rack upright, 2 ft (600 mm) horizontally from the rack face. The in-rack sprinkler within the transverse flue space of fire origin was at the top of the sixth tier level. The in-rack sprinkler directly over the ignition location was the first sprinkler to operate at a time 2 minutes and 9 seconds after ignition. A total of 2 in-rack sprinklers operated during this test; no ceiling-level sprinklers operated. The results of the test were considered acceptable.

In Test No. 3, ignition was at grade level, centered between rack uprights within the 2 in. (50 mm) gap. To allow vertical fire growth directly above the point of ignition, the gap was maintained open throughout the height of the storage rack. A total of four in-rack sprinklers and one sprinkler under a catwalk operated during the test; no ceiling-level sprinklers operated. The first in-rack sprinkler to operate was located at the top of the sixth tier level at a time 3 minutes and 1 second after ignition. The second in-rack sprinkler to operate was also at the top of the sixth tier level. The last two in-rack sprinklers to operate were both located at the top of the third tier level. The fifth and final sprinkler to operate was a sprinkler located under a catwalk at the top of the third tier level. The results of the test were considered acceptable.

All three tests were considered successful and confirmed that the ceiling and in-rack sprinkler protection scheme outlined in this standard for the protection of cartoned records storage maintained in multiple-row racks with catwalk access is acceptable.

C.26 [20.5.3.4.2.2] During full-scale fire tests, flue space width and alignment are typically set with care for test consistency and repeatability. Some full-scale fire tests and fire experience have shown sprinkler protection designed and installed in accordance with this standard are able to tolerate random variations in flue width and vertical flue alignment. For example, see Test 7 in the National Quick Response Sprinkler Research Project: *Large-Scale Test Evaluation of Early Suppression Fast-Response (ESFR) Automatic Sprinklers* (report available from the NFPA Research Foundation website). For Test 7, transverse flue variations were substantial such that some flues at various tiers were completely closed (i.e., pallet loads placed immediately adjacent to each other), and the vertical alignment of one transverse flue was completely disrupted. The result was the operation of eight K-14 (K-200) ESFR sprinklers as well as minor aisle jump to both target racks. Reported damage was 2½ pallet loads in the main rack array and ¼ pallet load in the large racks. Findings such as Test 7 support the toleration of flue variations in the real world. However, ideally pallet loads should be positioned in racks with care to reduce the challenge faced by sprinklers should a fire occur.

Δ **Annex D Sprinkler System Information from the 2021 Edition of the *Life Safety Code***

This annex is not a part of the requirements of this NFPA document but is included for informational purposes only.

D.1 Introduction. This annex is provided as an aid to the user of NFPA 13 by identifying those portions of the 2021 edition of NFPA *101* that pertain to sprinkler system design and installation. It is not intended that this annex provide complete information regarding all aspects of fire protection addressed by NFPA *101*. It is important to note that this information was copied from NFPA *101* but did not use NFPA's extract policy and is not intended to be a part of the requirements of NFPA 13.

D.1.1 The following sections cover situations where NFPA *101* provides different guidance on the design or installation of a fire sprinkler system from NFPA 13. In some cases, this different guidance is based on descriptions of unique situations handled by NFPA *101*. In other cases, this different guidance stems from the different objective for NFPA *101*, life safety of the occupant, rather than the property protection afforded by NFPA 13.

D.1.1.1 Features of Fire Protection.

Δ **D.1.1.1.1 Atriums.** Glass walls and inoperable windows shall be permitted in lieu of the fire barriers where all the following are met:

(1) Automatic sprinklers are spaced along both sides of the glass wall and the inoperable windows at intervals not to exceed 6 ft (1.8 m).
(2) The automatic sprinklers specified in 8.6.7(1)(c)(i) of NFPA *101* are located at a distance from the glass wall not to exceed 12 in. (300 mm) and arranged so that the entire surface of the glass is wet upon operation of the sprinklers.
(3) The glass wall is of tempered, wired, laminated, or ceramic glass held in place by a retention system that allows the glass framing system to deflect without breaking (loading) the glass before the sprinklers operate.
(4) The automatic sprinklers required by 8.6.7(1)(c)(i) of NFPA *101* are not required on the atrium side of the glass wall and the inoperable window where there is no walkway or other floor area on the atrium side above the main floor level.
[*101*:8.6.7(1)(c)]

D.1.1.2 Special Structures and High-Rise Buildings. High-rise buildings shall be protected throughout by an approved, supervised automatic sprinkler system in accordance with NFPA *101*, Section 9.7. A sprinkler control valve and a waterflow device shall be provided for each floor. [*101*:11.8.3.1]

D.1.1.3 Lodging or Rooming Houses.

Δ **D.1.1.3.1** In buildings sprinklered in accordance with NFPA 13 closets that contain equipment such as washers, dryers, furnaces, or water heaters shall be sprinklered, regardless of size. [*101*:26.3.6.2.5]

D.1.1.3.2 In existing lodging or rooming houses, sprinkler installations shall not be required in closets not exceeding 24 ft² (2.2 m²) and in bathrooms not exceeding 55 ft² (5.1 m²). [*101*:26.3.6.2.6]

D.1.1.4 New Hotels and Dormitories. The provisions for draft stops and closely spaced sprinklers in NFPA 13 shall not be required for openings complying with 8.6.9.1of NFPA 101where the opening is within the guest room or guest suite. [*101*:28.3.5.4]

D.1.1.5 Existing Hotels and Dormitories. In guest rooms and in guest room suites, sprinkler installations shall not be required in closets not exceeding 24 ft² (2.2 m²) and in bathrooms not exceeding 55 ft² (5.1 m²). [*101*:29.3.5.5]

D.1.1.6 New Apartment Buildings.

D.1.1.6.1 Closets. In buildings sprinklered in accordance with NFPA 13, closets shall meet the following requirements:

(1) Closets less than 12 ft² (1.1 m²) in individual dwelling units shall not be required to be sprinklered.
(2) Closets that contain equipment such as washers, dryers, furnaces, or water heaters shall be sprinklered, regardless of size.
[*101*:30.3.5.3]

D.1.1.6.2 Convenience Openings. The draft stop and closely spaced sprinkler requirements of NFPA 13 shall not be required for convenience openings complying with 8.6.9.1 of NFPA *101* where the convenience opening is within the dwelling unit. [*101*:30.3.5.4]

D.1.1.7 Existing Apartment Buildings.

D.1.1.7.1 In individual dwelling units, sprinkler installation shall not be required in closets not exceeding 24 ft² (2.2 m²) and in bathrooms not exceeding 55 ft² (5.1 m²). Closets that contain equipment such as washers, dryers, furnaces, or water heaters shall be sprinklered, regardless of size. [*101*:31.3.5.3]

Δ **D.1.1.7.2** In buildings sprinklered in accordance with NFPA 13 bathrooms not greater than 55 ft² (5.1 m²) in individual dwelling units shall not be required to be sprinklered. [*101*:31.3.5.4]

D.1.1.7.3 The draft stop and closely spaced sprinkler requirements of NFPA 13 shall not be required for convenience openings complying with 8.6.9.1 of NFPA *101* where the convenience opening is within the dwelling unit. [*101*:31.3.5.5]

D.1.1.8 Existing Residential Board and Care Occupancies.

D.1.1.8.1 Standard-response sprinklers shall be permitted for use in hazardous areas in accordance with 33.2.3.2 of NFPA *101*. [*101*:33.2.2.2.4]

D.1.1.8.2 Where an automatic sprinkler system is installed, for either total or partial building coverage, all of the following requirements shall be met:

(1) The system shall be in accordance with Section 9.7 of NFPA *101* and shall initiate the fire alarm system in accordance with 33.2.3.4.1, as modified by 33.2.3.5.3.1 through 33.2.3.5.3.6 of NFPA *101*.
(2) The adequacy of the water supply shall be documented to the authority having jurisdiction.
[*101*:33.2.3.5.3]

D.1.1.8.2.1 In prompt evacuation capability facilities, all of the following shall apply:

(1) An automatic sprinkler system in accordance with NFPA 13D shall be permitted.

Shaded text = Revisions. Δ = Text deletions and figure/table revisions. • = Section deletions. *N* = New material.

(2) Automatic sprinklers shall not be required in closets not exceeding 24 ft² (2.2 m²) and in bathrooms not exceeding 55 ft² (5.1 m²), provided that such spaces are finished with lath and plaster or materials providing a 15-minute thermal barrier.
[*101*:33.2.3.5.3.1]

D.1.1.8.2.2 In slow and impractical evacuation capability facilities, all of the following shall apply:

(1) An automatic sprinkler system in accordance with NFPA 13D with a 30-minute water supply, shall be permitted.
(2) All habitable areas and closets shall be sprinklered.
(3) Automatic sprinklers shall not be required in bathrooms not exceeding 55 ft² (5.1 m²), provided that such spaces are finished with lath and plaster or materials providing a 15-minute thermal barrier.
[*101*:33.2.3.5.3.2]

Δ **D.1.1.8.2.3** In prompt and slow evacuation capability facilities, where an automatic sprinkler system is in accordance with NFPA 13 sprinklers shall not be required in closets not exceeding 24 ft² (2.2 m²) and in bathrooms not exceeding 55 ft² (5.1 m²), provided that such spaces are finished with lath and plaster or materials providing a 15-minute thermal barrier.
[*101*:33.2.3.5.3.3]

D.1.1.8.2.4 In prompt and slow evacuation capability facilities in buildings four or fewer stories above grade plane, systems in accordance with NFPA 13R shall be permitted.
[*101*:33.2.3.5.3.4]

D.1.1.8.2.5 In impractical evacuation capability facilities in buildings four or fewer stories above grade plane, systems in accordance with NFPA 13R shall be permitted. All habitable areas and closets shall be sprinklered. Automatic sprinklers shall not be required in bathrooms not exceeding 55 ft² (5.1 m²), provided that such spaces are finished with lath and plaster or materials providing a 15-minute thermal barrier.
[*101*:33.2.3.5.3.5]

D.1.1.8.2.6 Initiation of the fire alarm system shall not be required for existing installations in accordance with 33.2.3.5.6 of NFPA *101*. [*101*:33.2.3.5.3.6]

D.1.1.8.2.7 All impractical evacuation capability facilities shall be protected throughout by an approved, supervised automatic sprinkler system in accordance with 33.2.3.5.3 of NFPA *101*.
[*101*:33.2.3.5.3.7]

D.1.1.9 New Mercantile Occupancies.

Δ **D.1.1.9.1 Protection of Vertical Openings.** Any vertical opening shall be protected in accordance with Section 8.6 of NFPA *101*, except under the following conditions:

(1) In Class A or Class B mercantile occupancies protected throughout by an approved, supervised automatic sprinkler system in accordance with 9.7.1.1(1) of NFPA *101*, unprotected vertical openings shall be permitted at one of the following locations:
  (a) Between any two floors
  (b) Among the street floor, the first adjacent floor below, and the adjacent floor (or mezzanine) above
(2) In Class C mercantile occupancies, unprotected openings shall be permitted between the street floor and the mezzanine.

(3) The draft stop and closely spaced sprinkler requirements of NFPA 13 shall not be required for unenclosed vertical openings permitted in 36.3.1(1) and 37.3.1(2) of NFPA *101*.
[*101*:36.3.1]

Δ **D.1.1.9.2** Rooms housing building service equipment, janitor closets, and service elevators shall be permitted to open directly onto exit passageways, provided that all of the following criteria are met:

(1) The required fire resistance rating between such rooms or areas and the exit passageway shall be maintained in accordance with 7.1.3.2 of NFPA *101*.
(2) Such rooms or areas shall be protected by an approved, supervised automatic sprinkler system in accordance with 9.7.1.1(1) of NFPA *101*, but the exceptions in NFPA 13 allowing the omission of sprinklers from such rooms shall not be permitted.
[*101*:36.4.4.9.2]

D.1.1.10 Existing Mercantile Occupancies.

Δ **D.1.1.10.1 Protection of Vertical Openings.** Any vertical opening shall be protected in accordance with Section 8.6 of NFPA *101*, except under any of the following conditions:

(1) In Class A or Class B mercantile occupancies protected throughout by an approved, supervised automatic sprinkler system in accordance with 9.7.1.1(1) of NFPA *101*, unprotected vertical openings shall be permitted at one of the following locations:
  (a) Between any two floors
  (b) Among the street floor, the first adjacent floor below, and the adjacent floor (or mezzanine) above
(2) In Class C mercantile occupancies, unprotected openings shall be permitted between the street floor and the mezzanine.
(3) The draft stop and closely spaced sprinkler requirements of NFPA 13 shall not be required for unenclosed vertical openings permitted in 36.3.1(1) and 36.3.1(2) of NFPA *101*.
[*101*:37.3.1]

Δ **D.1.1.10.2** Rooms housing building service equipment, janitor closets, and service elevators shall be permitted to open directly onto exit passageways, provided that all of the following criteria are met:

(1) The required fire resistance rating between such rooms or areas and the exit passageway shall be maintained in accordance with 7.1.3.2 of NFPA *101*.
(2) Such rooms or areas shall be protected by an approved automatic sprinkler system in accordance with 9.7.1.1(1) of NFPA *101*, but the exceptions in NFPA 13 allowing the omission of sprinklers from such rooms shall not be permitted.
[*101*:37.4.4.9.2]

D.1.1.11 Industrial Occupancies.

Δ **D.1.1.11.1 Special Provisions — High-Rise Buildings.** The provisions of 11.8.5.3.4(1) of NFPA *101* for jockey pumps and 11.8.5.3.4(2) of NFPA *101* for air compressors serving dry-pipe and preaction systems shall not apply to special-purpose industrial occupancies. [*101*:40.4.2.4]

D.2 Life Safety Code.

D.2.1 Features of Fire Protection.

D.2.1.1 Design Requirements. (Reserved)

D.2.1.2 Installation Requirements.

Δ **D.2.1.2.1 Atriums.** Glass walls and inoperable windows shall be permitted in lieu of the fire barriers where all the following are met:

(1) Automatic sprinklers are spaced along both sides of the glass wall and the inoperable windows at intervals not to exceed 6 ft (1.8 m).
(2) The automatic sprinklers specified in 8.6.7(1)(c)(i) of NFPA *101* are located at a distance from the glass wall not to exceed 12 in. (300 mm) and arranged so that the entire surface of the glass is wet upon operation of the sprinklers.
(3) The glass wall is of tempered, wired, laminated, or ceramic glass held in place by a retention system that allows the glass framing system to deflect without breaking (loading) the glass before the sprinklers operate.
(4) The automatic sprinklers required by 8.6.7(1)(c)(i) of NFPA *101* are not required on the atrium side of the glass wall and the inoperable window where there is no walkway or other floor area on the atrium side above the main floor level.

[*101*:8.6.7(1)(c)]

D.2.2 Special Structures and High-Rise Buildings.

D.2.2.1 Design Criteria. High-rise buildings shall be protected throughout by an approved, supervised automatic sprinkler system in accordance with Section 9.7 of NFPA *101*. A sprinkler control valve and a waterflow device shall be provided for each floor. [*101*:11.8.3.1]

D.2.3 New Assembly Occupancies.

D.2.3.1 Design Criteria.

D.2.3.1.1 Protection of Vertical Openings. Any vertical opening shall be enclosed or protected in accordance with Section 8.6 of NFPA *101*, unless otherwise permitted by one of the following:

(1) Stairs or ramps shall be permitted to be unenclosed between balconies or mezzanines and main assembly areas located below, provided that the balcony or mezzanine is open to the main assembly area.
(2) Exit access stairs from lighting and access catwalks, galleries, and gridirons shall not be required to be enclosed.
(3) Assembly occupancies protected by an approved, supervised automatic sprinkler system in accordance with Section 9.7 of NFPA *101* shall be permitted to have unprotected vertical openings between any two adjacent floors, provided that such openings are separated from unprotected vertical openings serving other floors by a barrier complying with 8.6.5 of NFPA *101*.
(4) Assembly occupancies protected by an approved, supervised automatic sprinkler system in accordance with Section 9.7 of NFPA *101* shall be permitted to have convenience stair openings in accordance with 8.6.9.2 of NFPA *101*.

[*101*:12.3.1]

D.2.3.2 Installation Requirements. (Reserved)

D.2.4 Existing Assembly Occupancies.

D.2.4.1 Design Criteria.

Δ **D.2.4.1.1 Protection of Vertical Openings.** Any vertical opening shall be enclosed or protected in accordance with Section 8.6 of NFPA *101*, unless otherwise permitted by one of the following:

(1) Stairs or ramps shall be permitted to be unenclosed between balconies or mezzanines and main assembly areas located below, provided that the balcony or mezzanine is open to the main assembly area.
(2) Exit access stairs from lighting and access catwalks, galleries, and gridirons shall not be required to be enclosed.
(3) Assembly occupancies protected by an approved, supervised automatic sprinkler system in accordance with Section 9.7 of NFPA *101* shall be permitted to have unprotected vertical openings between any two adjacent floors, provided that such openings are separated from unprotected vertical openings serving other floors by a barrier complying with 8.6.5 of NFPA *101*.
(4) Assembly occupancies protected by an approved, supervised automatic sprinkler system in accordance with Section 9.7 of NFPA *101* shall be permitted to have convenience stair openings in accordance with 8.6.9.2 of NFPA *101*.

[*101*:13.3.1]

D.2.4.2 Installation Requirements. (Reserved)

D.2.5 New Educational Occupancies. (Reserved)

D.2.6 Existing Educational Occupancies. (Reserved)

D.2.7 New Day-Care Occupancies. (Reserved)

D.2.8 Existing Day-Care Occupancies. (Reserved)

D.2.9 New Health Care Occupancies. (Reserved)

D.2.10 Existing Health Care Occupancies. (Reserved)

D.2.11 New Ambulatory Health Care Occupancies. (Reserved)

D.2.12 Existing Ambulatory Health Care Occupancies. (Reserved)

D.2.13 New Detention and Correctional Occupancies. (Reserved)

D.2.14 Existing Detention and Correctional Occupancies. (Reserved)

D.2.15 One- and Two-Family Dwellings. (Reserved)

D.2.16 Lodging or Rooming Houses.

D.2.16.1 Design Requirements. (Reserved)

D.2.16.2 Installation Requirements.

D.2.16.2.1 In buildings sprinklered in accordance with NFPA 13 closets that contain equipment such as washers, dryers, furnaces, or water heaters shall be sprinklered, regardless of size. [*101*:26.3.6.2.5]

D.2.16.2.2 In existing lodging or rooming houses, sprinkler installations shall not be required in closets not exceeding 24 ft² (2.2 m²) and in bathrooms not exceeding 55 ft² (5.1 m²). [*101*:26.3.6.2.6]

D.2.17 New Hotels and Dormitories.

D.2.17.1 Design Requirements. (Reserved)

D.2.17.2 Installation Requirements. The provisions for draft stops and closely spaced sprinklers in NFPA 13 shall not be required for openings complying with 8.6.9.1 of NFPA *101* where the opening is within the guest room or guest suite. [*101*:28.3.5.4]

D.2.18 Existing Hotels and Dormitories.

D.2.18.1 Design Requirements. (Reserved)

D.2.18.2 Installation Requirements. In guest rooms and in guest room suites, sprinkler installations shall not be required in closets not exceeding 24 ft² (2.2 m²) and in bathrooms not exceeding 55 ft² (5.1 m²). [*101*:29.3.5.5]

D.2.19 New Apartment Buildings.

D.2.19.1 Design Requirements. (Reserved)

D.2.19.2 Installation Requirements.

D.2.19.2.1 Closets. In buildings sprinklered in accordance with NFPA 13:

(1) Closets less than 12 ft² (1.1 m²) in individual dwelling units shall not be required to be sprinklered.
(2) Closets that contain equipment such as washers, dryers, furnaces, or water heaters shall be sprinklered, regardless of size.

[*101*:30.3.5.3]

D.2.19.2.2 Convenience Openings. The draft stop and closely spaced sprinkler requirements of NFPA 13 shall not be required for convenience openings complying with 8.6.9.1 of NFPA *101* where the convenience opening is within the dwelling unit. [*101*:30.3.5.4]

D.2.20 Existing Apartment Buildings.

D.2.20.1 Design Requirements. (Reserved)

D.2.20.2 Installation Requirements.

D.2.20.2.1 In individual dwelling units, sprinkler installation shall not be required in closets not exceeding 24 ft² (2.2 m²) and in bathrooms not exceeding 55 ft² (5.1 m²). Closets that contain equipment such as washers, dryers, furnaces, or water heaters shall be sprinklered, regardless of size. [*101*:31.3.5.3]

D.2.20.2.2 The draft stop and closely spaced sprinkler requirements of NFPA 13 shall not be required for convenience openings complying with 8.6.9.1 of NFPA *101* where the convenience opening is within the dwelling unit. [*101*:31.3.5.5]

D.2.21 New Residential Board and Care Occupancies. (Reserved)

D.2.22 Existing Residential Board and Care Occupancies.

D.2.22.1 Design Requirements. (Reserved)

D.2.22.2 Installation Requirements.

D.2.22.2.1 Standard-response sprinklers shall be permitted for use in hazardous areas in accordance with 33.2.3.2 of NFPA *101*. [*101*:33.2.2.2.4]

D.2.22.2.2 In prompt and slow evacuation facilities, where an automatic sprinkler system is in accordance with NFPA 13 sprinklers shall not be required in closets not exceeding 24 ft² (2.2 m²) and in bathrooms not exceeding 55 ft² (5.1 m²), provided that such spaces are finished with lath and plaster or materials providing a 15-minute thermal barrier. [*101*:33.2.3.5.3.3]

D.2.23 New Mercantile Occupancies.

D.2.23.1 Design Requirements. (Reserved)

D.2.23.2 Installation Requirements.

Δ **D.2.23.2.1 Protection of Vertical Openings.** Any vertical opening shall be protected in accordance with Section 8.6 of NFPA *101*, except under any of the following conditions:

(1) In Class A or Class B mercantile occupancies protected throughout by an approved, supervised automatic sprinkler system in accordance with 9.7.1.1(1) of NFPA *101*, unprotected vertical openings shall be permitted at one of the following locations:

    (a) Between any two floors
    (b) Among the street floor, the first adjacent floor below, and the adjacent floor (or mezzanine) above

(2) In Class C mercantile occupancies, unprotected openings shall be permitted between the street floor and the mezzanine.

(3) The draft stop and closely spaced sprinkler requirements of NFPA 13 shall not be required for unenclosed vertical openings permitted in 36.3.1(1) and 36.3.1(2) of NFPA *101*.

[*101*:36.3.1]

Δ **D.2.23.2.2** Rooms housing building service equipment, janitor closets, and service elevators shall be permitted to open directly onto exit passageways, provided that all of the following criteria are met:

(1) The required fire resistance rating between such rooms or areas and the exit passageway shall be maintained in accordance with 7.1.3.2 of NFPA *101*.

(2) Such rooms or areas shall be protected by an approved, supervised automatic sprinkler system in accordance with 9.7.1.1(1) of NFPA *101*, but the exceptions in NFPA 13 allowing the omission of sprinklers from such rooms shall not be permitted.

[*101*:36.4.4.9.2]

D.2.24 Existing Mercantile Occupancies.

D.2.24.1 Design Requirements. (Reserved)

D.2.24.2 Installation Requirements.

Δ **D.2.24.2.1 Protection of Vertical Openings.** Any vertical opening shall be protected in accordance with Section 8.6 of NFPA *101*, except under any of the following conditions:

(1) In Class A or Class B mercantile occupancies protected throughout by an approved, supervised automatic sprinkler system in accordance with 9.7.1.1(1) of NFPA *101*, unprotected vertical openings shall be permitted at one of the following locations:

    (a) Between any two floors
    (b) Among the street floor, the first adjacent floor below, and the adjacent floor (or mezzanine) above

(2) In Class C mercantile occupancies, unprotected openings shall be permitted between the street floor and the mezzanine.

(3) The draft stop and closely spaced sprinkler requirements of NFPA 13 shall not be required for unenclosed vertical openings permitted in 36.3.1(1) and 37.3.1(2) of NFPA *101*.
[*101*:37.3.1]

Δ **D.2.24.2.2** Rooms housing building service equipment, janitor closets, and service elevators shall be permitted to open directly onto exit passageways, provided that all of the following criteria are met:

(1) The required fire resistance rating between such rooms or areas and the exit passageway shall be maintained in accordance with 7.1.3.2 of NFPA *101*.

(2) Such rooms or areas shall be protected by an approved automatic sprinkler system in accordance with 9.7.1.1(1) of NFPA *101*, but the exceptions in NFPA 13 allowing the omission of sprinklers from such rooms shall not be permitted.
[*101*:37.4.4.9.2]

D.2.25 New Business Occupancies.

D.2.25.1 Design Requirements. (Reserved)

D.2.25.2 Installation Requirements. (Reserved)

D.2.26 Existing Business Occupancies.

D.2.26.1 Design Requirements. (Reserved)

D.2.26.2 Installation Requirements. (Reserved)

D.2.27 Industrial Occupancies. (Reserved)

D.2.27.1 Design Criteria.

Δ **D.2.27.1.1 Special Provisions — High-Rise Buildings.** The provisions of 11.8.5.3.4(1) of NFPA *101* for jockey pumps and 11.8.5.3.4(2) of NFPA *101* for air compressors serving dry-pipe and preaction systems shall not apply to special-purpose industrial occupancies. [*101*:40.4.2.4]

D.2.28 Storage Occupancies. (Reserved)

Annex E Development of the Design Approach to Conform with ASCE/SEI 7 and Suggested Conversion Factor Adjustments for Locations Outside the United States

This annex is not a part of the requirements of this NFPA document but is included for informational purposes only.

Δ **E.1 General.** Seismic design of nonstructural components is governed by the provisions of Chapter 13 of ASCE/SEI 7, *Minimum Design Loads and Associated Criteria for Buildings and Other Structures.* In ASCE/SEI 7, fire sprinkler piping is classified as a "Designated Seismic System," due to its critical safety function. Design earthquake forces are multiplied by an importance factor, $I_p = 1.5$, and both the bracing and the piping itself must be designed for seismic forces. The seismic design requirements for the hanging and bracing of sprinkler piping systems provided in Chapter 18 of NFPA 13 presume that sprinkler piping is being constructed in the United States or in a country or jurisdictions where the seismic requirements are those specified in ASCE/SEI 7. There are locations outside the United States that wish to use the seismic design requirements of Chapter 18 of NFPA 13. In Section E.3, suggested conversion factor adjustments are provided to adjust country building code design ground motion criteria to those in ASCE/SEI 7 so the procedures of Chapter 18 of NFPA 13 can be used.

The lateral sway bracing provisions of 18.5.5 were developed to allow the use of the concept of zone of influence (ZOI), while providing designs that comply with ASCE/SEI 7. One of the main changes between the current seismic sway bracing design approach adopted in NFPA 13 and the approach used in early editions of NFPA 13 is that the spacing of the sway braces can be constrained by the flexural capacity of the pipe, as well as the capacity of the brace assembly or the capacity of the connection between the brace assembly and the supporting structure. NFPA 13 provides a design that complies with the seismic design requirements of ASCE/SEI 7 for the pipe itself.

The ZOI approach yields the force demand on the bracing element and connections to the structure. Another way to look at a ZOI force is as a reaction in a system of continuous beams (i.e., the multiple spans of a piping system). By using conservative simplifying assumptions, a maximum ZOI force limited by the flexural capacity of the pipe can be developed for a given pipe size and span (spacing between horizontal sway braces). The method used to develop these maximum ZOI forces is described in the following paragraphs, along with a discussion of the assumptions on the geometry of the piping system, the determination of the seismic design force coefficients, and the flexural capacity of the pipe.

In the discussion that follows, the term "main" can be taken to mean a sprinkler main, either a feed main or a cross-main, that requires sway bracing.

E.2 Assumptions on System Geometry. While every fire sprinkler system is uniquely designed for a particular structure, there are general similarities in the layout and geometry that can be used to simplify the design approach for earthquake protection. These similarities were used to develop assumptions on the effects of piping system continuity on the distribution of bending and shear forces in the pipe, and assumptions on spacing of branch lines between sway brace locations.

E.2.1 Continuity in Piping Systems. For lateral brace design purposes, piping systems can be idealized as a system of continuous beams. The bending moments in the sprinkler mains (the beams) were computed assuming three continuous spans, which generates the largest bending moment in any system of continuous beams. The loads generated by the branch lines are idealized as point loads. The tributary mass of the main is lumped along with the mass of the branch lines as point loads at the assumed branch line locations.

E.2.2 Branch Line Locations. In many sprinkler system installations, the branch lines constitute a substantial portion of the seismic mass. While there are significant variations in the spacing of the branch lines, their geometry is constrained by the need to provide adequate water coverage, which imposes limits on the spacing of the branches. Defining a "span" of the main as the distance between lateral sway braces, the seismic provisions make the following assumptions:

(1) There is a branch located at the center of the sprinkler main for spans of 25 ft (7.6 m) or less.
(2) There are branches at third-points of the sprinkler main for spans greater than 25 ft (7.6 m) and less than 40 ft (12 m).
(3) There are branches at quarter-points of the sprinkler main for spans of 40 ft (12 m).

It was further assumed that there is a branch line located in close proximity to each sway brace.

The layout of branch lines, maximum bending moment M_{max} in the pipe, and reaction R_{max} (horizontal loads at sway brace locations) for sprinkler mains with spans less than 25 ft (7.6 m) is illustrated in Figure E.2.2(a). Maximum demands for spans greater than 25 ft (7.6 m) and less than 40 ft (12 m) are given in Figure E.2.2(b), and for spans of 40 ft (12 m) in Figure E.2.2(c).

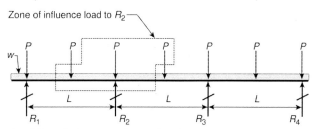

Zone of influence load to R_2

L = distance between sway braces (span)
P = branch line lateral load + tributary lateral load from main
w = lateral load of the main (included in P)
R_1, R_2, R_3, R_4 = zone of influence load (reactions)

$$M_{max} = 0.175PL$$
$$R_{max} \approx 2P$$

FIGURE E.2.2(a) Maximum Demands for Spans Less Than 25 ft (7.6 m).

Δ **E.3 Computing the Seismic Demand on Piping Systems.** In ASCE/SEI 7, seismic demands on nonstructural components and systems are a function of the ground shaking intensity, the ductility and dynamic properties of the component(s) or system, and the height of attachment of the component(s) in the structure. Seismic forces are determined at strength design (SD) levels. The horizontal seismic design force is given by Equation E.3a:

[E.3a]

$$F_p = \frac{0.4 a_p S_{DS} W_p}{\left(\dfrac{R_p}{I_p}\right)} \left(1 + 2\frac{z}{h}\right)$$

where:

F_p = seismic design force

a_p = component amplification factor, taken as 2.5 for piping systems

S_{DS} = short-period spectral acceleration, which takes into account soil conditions at the site

W_p = component operating weight

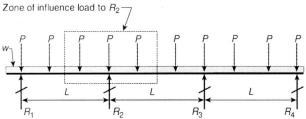

Zone of influence load to R_2

L = distance between sway braces (span)
P = branch line lateral load + tributary lateral load from main
w = lateral load of the main (included in P)
R_1, R_2, R_3, R_4 = zone of influence load (reactions)

$$M_{max} = 0.267PL$$
$$R_{max} \approx 3P$$

FIGURE E.2.2(b) **Maximum Demands for Spans Greater Than 25 ft (7.6 m) and Less Than 40 ft (12.2 m).**

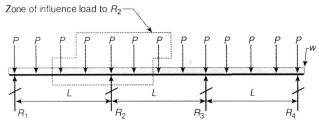

Zone of influence load to R_2

L = distance between sway braces (span)
P = branch line lateral load + tributary lateral load from main
w = lateral load of the main (included in P)
R_1, R_2, R_3, R_4 = zone of influence load (reactions)

$$M_{max} = 0.372PL$$
$$R_{max} \approx 4P$$

FIGURE E.2.2(c) **Maximum Demands for Spans of 40 ft (12 m).**

R_p = component response modification factor as follows: (1) 9 for high-deformability piping with joints made by welding or brazing; (2) 4.5 for high- or limited-deformability piping with joints made by threading, bonding, compression couplings, or grooved couplings; or (3) 1.5 for low-deformability piping such as cast iron and nonductile plastics

I_p = component importance factor, taken as 1.5 for fire sprinkler systems

z = height of the component attachment to the structure with respect to the grade plane

h = average roof height of the structure with respect to the grade plane

F_p need not be greater than $1.6\ S_{DS} I_p W_p$, and cannot be less than $0.30\ S_{DS} I_p W_p$.

As illustrated in Figure E.3(a), NFPA 13 uses a default seismic factor, C_p, which combines ground shaking, S_{DS}; dynamic amplification, a_p; component response, R_p/I_p; and location in the building, (z/h), into a single variable. Conservative assumptions are made for each variable so that the only information needed to find C_p is the short-period mapped spectral acceleration for the maximum considered earthquake (MCE), S_s.

The importance factor, I_p, for fire sprinkler systems is specified in ASCE/SEI 7 as 1.5. The amplification factor, a_p, for piping systems is specified as 2.5. Piping systems (even when seismically braced) are considered flexible, since the fundamental period of vibration for the system is greater than 0.06 seconds. A component response factor, R_p, of 4.5 was assumed for all piping. Finally, it was assumed that the system is installed at the roof level, h.

Assume the system is laterally braced at the roof, $z = h$, and substitute these values into the lateral force Equation E.3b as follows:

[E.3b]

$$F_p = \frac{0.4 a_p S_{DS} W_p}{\left(\dfrac{R_p}{I_p}\right)}\left(1 + 2\frac{z}{h}\right) = \frac{0.4(2.5) S_{DS} W_p}{\left(\dfrac{4.5}{1.5}\right)}\left(1 + 2\frac{h}{h}\right) = (1.0) S_{DS} W_p$$

ASCE/SEI 7 forces are determined at the SD level. NFPA 13 is based on allowable stress design (ASD). To convert F_p to an ASD load, F_{pw}, the load from ASCE/SEI 7 is multiplied by a 0.7 load factor as follows in Equation E.3c:

[E.3c]

$$F_{pw} = 0.7 F_p = 0.7 S_{DS} W_p = C_p W_p$$

Solve for C_p as follows in Equation E.3d:

[E.3d]

$$C_p = 0.7 S_{DS}$$

The short-period spectral acceleration, S_{DS}, is obtained by modifying the mapped short-period spectral acceleration, S_S, for the effects of the local soil conditions. In the United States, values for S_S are obtained from seismic hazard maps published by the U.S. Geological Survey (USGS). Web-based tools available from USGS will generate values for S_S based on the latitude and longitude of the project site. Most countries do not base their seismic hazard maps on the ground motion criteria that USGS uses to determine the S_S values specified in ASCE/SEI 7. Instead, they might use seismic zones [similar to those in the outdated Uniform Building Code (UBC)] to convey the seismic hazard. Although different countries might use different zone identifiers, zones are often numbered with the highest number seismic zone having the strongest potential ground motions (e.g., in the UBC, Zones 0 to 4 were used, and Zone 4 had the highest seismic hazard). Although not universally true, there is often a zone factor, Z, associated with each zone that represents the peak ground acceleration based on design earthquake ground motions having a 10 percent chance of being exceeded in a 50-year period (i.e., about a 500-year return period): For these countries, a suggested correlating adjustment is $S_S = 4.5$ Z. The 4.5 factor is determined by multiplying the peak ground acceleration by a factor of 2.5 to convert it to peak spectral acceleration and then by a factor of 1.8 to convert design earthquake ground motions to maximum considered earthquake ground motions, which are the basis for determining S_S. For example, for a Z factor of 0.4 (i.e., the highest value in the UBC), the value of S_S would be 1.8, resulting in $C_p = 0.84$ from Table 18.5.9.3. Also, for these countries, if a value of S_1 is needed, the value might be taken as 1.8 Z, which is the same relative relationship between the short-period and one-second spectral acceleration that was used in the 1997 UBC. The spectral acceleration used for seismic design is determined by Equation E.3e:

$$-S_{DS} = \frac{2}{3} S_S F_a \quad \text{[E.3e]}$$

F_a is an amplification factor based on soil conditions and the intensity of ground shaking expected, measured by S_S. Soil conditions are defined by site class in Table 20.3-1 of ASCE/SEI 7 and summarized in Table E.3(a) of NFPA 13. The values of F_a are given in Table 11.4-1 of ASCE/SEI 7, and vary from 0.8 to 1.6. For the purposes of the zone of influence (ZOI) method, the default values of F_a are taken as the maximum tabulated values for site class A through D and are summarized in Table E.3(b).

By combining Equations E.3d and E.3e, C_p can be written as shown in Equation E.3f:

$$C_p = 0.7 S_{DS} = \frac{2}{3}(0.7 S_S F_a) = 0.467 S_S F_a \quad \text{[E.3f]}$$

The site class can be determined by a geotechnical engineer. Additionally, the site class and seismic design category of a structure are separate pieces of information. Although both terms are classified by a letter ranging from A to F, the seismic design category determines when seismic protection is required for buildings and nonstructural elements, while the site class represents the type of soil underneath a structure and its ability to resist or absorb seismic forces. Each of these designations should be determined independently in accordance with local regulations.

Table 18.5.9.3 was populated by solving for C_p for different values of S_S. For example, when $S_S = 1.0$, the following in Equation E.3g is true:

$$C_p = 0.467 S_S F_a = 0.467(1.0)(1.1) = 0.51 \quad \text{[E.3g]}$$

As illustrated in Figure E.3(b), the seismic design load, F_p, includes a function of the height of the component attachment to the structure relative to the average roof height of the structure.

The most conservative seismic design load assumes the seismic attachment is at 100 percent of the average roof height, where $z = 1.0$ and $h = 1.0$. In this case, the function becomes a constant equal to 3.0 in accordance with Equation E.3h:

$$1 + 2\frac{1.00}{1.00} = 1 + 2 = 3.0 \quad \text{[E.3h]}$$

If the seismic attachment is installed at 75 percent of the average roof height, where $z = 0.75$ and $h = 1.0$, the function becomes a constant equal to 2.5 in accordance with Equation E.3i:

$$1 + 2\frac{0.75}{1.00} = 1 + 1.5 = 2.5 \quad \text{[E.3i]}$$

Since 2.5 is 83.3 percent of 3.0, the seismic design load for seismic attachments installed at 75 percent of the average roof height can be multiplied by a factor of 0.833. Because it might be difficult to accurately measure the average roof height of the structure relative to the grade plane, 18.5.9.3.4 of NFPA 13 assumes a multiplier of 0.875 is used.

If the seismic attachment is installed at 50 percent of the average roof height, where $z = 0.50$ and $h = 1.0$, the function becomes a constant equal to 2.5 in accordance with Equation E.3j:

$$1 + 2\frac{0.50}{1.00} = 1 + 1 = 2.0 \quad \text{[E.3j]}$$

Since 2.0 is 66.6 percent of 3.0, the seismic design load for seismic attachments installed at 50 percent of the average roof height can be multiplied by a factor of 0.666. Because it might be difficult to accurately measure the average roof height of the structure relative to the grade plane, 18.5.9.3.5 of NFPA 13 assumes a multiplier of 0.750 is used.

E.4 Flexural Capacity of Piping. The flexural capacity for different diameters and thicknesses of pipe were computed using allowable stress design (ASD). NFPA 13 has traditionally used ASD for design. While ASCE/SEI 7 generally uses the strength design (SD) approach, ASD is preferred for the design of piping systems. For example, the ASTM B31, *Standards of Pressure Piping*, series of piping codes are based on ASD. ASD was chosen for sprinkler piping design to limit the complexity of the analysis. Use of SD would require the use of the plastic modulus, Z, of the pipe rather than the elastic section modulus, S. Use of Z would trigger analysis of local and global buckling behavior of the pipe. SD is most appropriate when used with compact pipe sections that can develop the full limit capacity of the material, including strain hardening. Thin-wall pipes and materials without well-defined post-elastic behavior are not easily considered using SD.

Permissible stresses in the pipe for seismic loading are from 13.6.7 of ASCE/SEI 7. Assuming high- or limited-deformability pipe with threaded or grooved couplings, the permissible flexural stress under SD level demands is $0.7F_y$, where F_y is the yield stress of the material. Since seismic design in NFPA 13 is based on ASD, the SD capacity must be reduced to an ASD level.

The permissible flexural stress for ASD is determined by adjusting the SD level flexural capacity. The SD capacity is first reduced by a load factor to ASD levels, and then can be increased by the allowable stress increase for seismic loading.

N **Table E.3(a) Site Class**

Site Class	Soil Definition
A	Hard rock
B	Rock
C	Very dense soil and soft rock
D	Stiff soil

N **Table E.3(b) Values of F_a**

Site Class	Mapped Maximum Considered Earthquake Spectral Response Acceleration Parameter at Short Period				
	$S_S \le 0.33$	$S_S = 0.5$	$S_S = 0.75$	$S_S = 1.0$	$S_S \ge 1.25$
Default F_a	1.6	1.4	1.2	1.2	1.2
A	0.8	0.8	0.8	0.8	0.8
B	0.9	0.9	0.9	0.9	0.9
C	1.3	1.3	1.2	1.2	1.2
D	1.6	1.4	1.2	1.1	1

Note: Use straight-line interpolation for intermediate values of S_S.

$$F_p = \boxed{\frac{0.4\, a_p S_{DS}}{\left(\dfrac{R_p}{I_p}\right)}\left(1 + 2\frac{z}{h}\right)} W_p$$

$$\Downarrow$$

$$F_{pw} = \boxed{C_p} \cdot W_p$$

Δ **FIGURE E.3(a)   Default Seismic Factor, C_p.**

$$F_p = \frac{0.4 a_p S_{DS}}{\left(\dfrac{R_p}{I_p}\right)} \boxed{\left(1 + 2\frac{z}{h}\right)} W_p$$

N **FIGURE E.3(b)   Seismic Design Load Relative to Height.**

The use of an allowable stress increase for piping systems is typical when determining the strength of the pipe itself.

For fire sprinkler piping, the SD flexural capacity, M_{cap}, is reduced by a load factor of 0.7 to yield the ASD flexural capacity. The duration of load factor for the piping system, taken as 1.33, is then applied. Taking S as the section modulus of pipe, this yields an allowable moment capacity in the pipe, as shown in the following equation:

$$M_{cap} = 0.7\left(1.33\right)\left(0.7SF_y\right) = 0.65SF_y \qquad \textbf{[E.4a]}$$

To populate Table 18.5.5.2(a) through Table 18.5.5.2(n), which give the maximum zone of influence loads, the largest reaction (due to branch lines and the tributary mass of the main) limited by flexure for a given pipe size and span between sway braces was computed.

For example, to determine the maximum permissible ZOI for a 4 in. (100 mm) diameter steel Schedule 10 main spanning 30 ft (9.1 m), first compute the flexural capacity of the pipe.

$S = 1.76$ in.^{3} (28800 mm^3)

$F_y = 30,000$ psi (2050 bar)

The flexural capacity of the pipe is as follows:

$$M_{cap} = \left(0.65F_y\right)S = \left(0.65\right)\left(30,000\right)\left(1.76\right) \qquad \textbf{[E.4b]}$$

$= 34,320$ in.-lb (3900 kgn) $= 2860$ ft-lb (395 kgn)

For spans greater than 25 ft (7.6 m) and less than 40 ft (12 m), the branch lines are assumed to be located at ⅓-points in the span. The point load P is associated with the branch line and tributary mass of the main and L is distance between sway braces. From Figure E.2.2(b), the maximum moment in the main, M_{max}, is

$$M_{max} = 0.267PL$$

Setting $M_{cap} = M_{max}$ and solving for P, the result is as follows:

$$
\begin{aligned}
M_{cap} &= \left(0.65F_y\right)S = 0.267PL \\
P &= \frac{M_{cap}}{0.267L} \\
&= \frac{2860}{0.267(30)} = 357 \text{ lb}
\end{aligned}
\qquad \textbf{[E.4c]}
$$

The maximum permissible ZOI load $= 3P = 1071$ lb (485 kg).

E.5 Sample Seismic Calculation Using the ZOI Method. To illustrate the application of the ZOI method, the approach can be applied to a sample problem based on the sample seismic bracing calculation in Figure A.18.5(b). The sample calculation yielded a total weight of 480 lb (220 kg), which was obtained using a seismic factor of 0.5. To determine our own seismic factor, to get the total weight of the water-filled pipe, divide by the seismic factor of 0.5,

$$W_p = \frac{480}{0.5} = 960 \text{ lb } (435 \text{ kg})$$

[E.5a]

Assume the 4 in. (100 mm) Schedule 10 pipe is the main that will be braced and that distance between sway braces (span) is 20 ft (6.1 m). The installation is in a region of high seismicity, and based on the latitude and longitude of the building site, $S_S = 1.75$.

To calculate the seismic load, use Table 18.5.9.3 to determine the seismic coefficient, C_p. The value of $S_s = 1.75$ coordinates to 0.82.

The horizontal force on the brace, from 18.5.6.3, is

$$F_{pw} = C_p W_p = 0.82(960) = 787 \text{ lb}$$

[E.5b]

From Table 18.5.5.2(a), the maximum ZOI load, F_{pw} for a 4 in. Schedule 10 pipe spanning 20 ft (6.1 m) is 1634 lb (740 kg), which is larger than the calculated demand of 787 lb (355 kg). The 4 in. (100 mm) Schedule 10 pipe is adequate for the seismic load and a brace would be selected with a minimum capacity of 787 lb (355 kg).

If the sway brace was attached to the 2 in. (50 mm) Schedule 40 pipe, the ZOI demand F_{pw} of 787 lb (355 kg) would be compared to the maximum capacity for a 2 in. (50 mm) Schedule 40 pipe found in Table 18.5.5.2(c) and Table 18.5.5.2(d). For a 20 ft (6.1 m) span, this is 520 lb (236 kg), less than the demand of 787 lb (355 kg). A 2 in. (50 mm) pipe would be inadequate, and a sway brace would have to be added to reduce the ZOI demand, or the system pipe size increased.

E.6 Limitations of the ZOI Method. The ZOI approach can be used for a variety of piping materials. There are, however, important limitations of which the designer should be aware. The first is that the appropriate component response factor, R_p, must be used. To select the proper value, the piping systems must be classified as high-, limited-, or low-deformability. Definitions of these terms are given in Section 11.2 of ASCE/SEI 7. The second major assumption is that the flexural behavior of the pipe is not governed by local buckling of the pipe wall. For steel pipe, this can be achieved by observing the thickness to diameter limits given in the AISC *Specifications for the Design, Fabrication, and Erection of Structural Steel Buildings.* Establishing the local buckling characteristics of pipe fabricated from other materials can require testing.

The tables for the maximum load, F_{pw}, in zone of influence are based on common configurations of mains and branch

lines. There can be cases where the actual configuration of the piping system could generate higher stresses in the piping than assumed in the tables. For example, a main braced at 40 ft (12.2 m) intervals, with a single branch line in the center of the span, can have a smaller maximum load capacity, F_{pw}, than the tabulated value. Where the configuration of the mains and branch lines vary significantly from the assumed layout, the pipe stresses should be checked by engineering analysis.

E.7 Allowable Loads for Concrete Anchors. This section provides step-by-step examples of the procedures for determining the allowable loads for concrete anchors as they are found in Table 18.5.12.2(a) through Table 18.5.12.2(j). Table 18.5.12.2(a) through Table 18.5.12.2(j) were developed using the prying factors found in Table E.7(a) and the representative strength design seismic shear and tension values for concrete anchors found in Table E.7(b).

Δ **E.7.1 Selecting a Wedge Anchor Using Table 18.5.12.2(a) through Table 18.5.12.2(e).**

Δ **E.7.1.1 Procedure. Step 1.** Determine the ASD horizontal earthquake load F_{pw}.

Step 1a. Calculate the weight of the water-filled pipe within the zone of influence of the brace.

Step 1b. Find the applicable seismic coefficient C_p in Table 18.5.9.3

Step 1c. Multiply the zone of influence weight by C_p to determine the ASD horizontal earthquake load F_{pw}.

Step 2. Select a concrete anchor from Table 18.5.12.2(a) through Table 18.5.12.2(e) with a maximum load capacity that is greater than the calculated horizontal earthquake load F_{pw} from Step 1.

Step 2a. Locate the table for the applicable concrete strength.

Step 2b. Find the column in the selected table for the applicable designated angle category (A thru I) and the appropriate prying factor Pr range.

Step 2c. Scan down the category column to find a concrete anchor diameter, embedment depth, and maximum load capacity that is greater than the calculated horizontal earthquake load F_{pw} from Step 1.

(ALTERNATIVE) Step 2. As an alternative to using the maximum load values in Table 18.5.12.2(a) through Table 18.5.12.2(e), select a concrete anchor that has been tested in accordance with ACI 355.2, *Qualification of Post-Installed Mechanical Anchors in Concrete and Commentary,* for seismic loading and that has an allowable strength, including the effects of prying,

Table E.7(a) Prying Factors for Table 18.5.12.2(a) through Table 18.5.12.2(j) Concrete Anchors

Pr Range	Figure 18.5.12.1 Designated Angle Category								
	A	B	C	D	E	F	G	H	I
Lowest	2	1.1	0.7	1.2	1.1	1.1	1.4	0.9	0.8
Low	3.5	1.8	1.0	1.7	1.8	2.0	1.9	1.3	1.1
High	5.0	2.5	1.3	2.2	2.5	2.9	2.4	1.7	1.4
Highest	6.5	3.2	1.6	2.7	3.2	3.8	2.9	2.1	1.7

taken as 0.43 times the normal strength determined in accordance with Chapter 17 of ACI 318, *Building Code Requirements for Structural Concrete and Commentary*, as per 18.5.12.7.3.4.

E.7.1.2 Example. Step 1. Zone of influence F_{pw}.

Step 1a. 40 ft of 2½ in. Sch. 10 pipe plus 15% fitting allowance

40×5.89 lb/ft $\times 1.15 = 270.94$ lb

Step 1b. Seismic coefficient C_p from Table 18.5.9.3

$C_p = 0.35$

Step 1c. $F_{pw} = 0.35 \times 270.94 = 94.8$ lb

Step 2. Select a concrete anchor from Table 18.5.12.2(a) through Table 18.5.12.2(e).

Step 2a. Use the table for 4000 psi Normal Weight Concrete.

Step 2b. Fastener orientation "A" – assume the manufacturer's prying factor is 3.0 for the fitting. Use the Pr range of 2.1–3.5.

Step 2c. Allowable F_{pw} on ⅜ in. dia. with 2.375 in. embedment = 138 lb and is greater than the calculated F_{pw} of 94.8 lb.

Table E.7(b) Representative Strength Design Seismic Shear and Tension Values Used for Concrete Anchors

Anchor Dia. (in.)	Min. Nominal Embedment (in.)	LRFD Tension (lb)	LRFD Shear (lb)	Anchor Dia. (in.)	Min. Effective Embedment (in.)	LRFD Tension (lb)	LRFD Shear (lb)
Wedge Anchors in 3000 psi (207 bar) Lightweight Sand Concrete on 4 ½ in. Flute Width Metal Deck				Metal Deck Inserts in 3000 psi (207 bar) Lightweight Sand Concrete on 4 ½ in. Flute Width Metal Deck			
⅜	2.375	670	871	⅜	1.750	804	774
½	3.750	714	1489	½	1.750	804	837
⅝	3.875	936	1739	⅝	1.750	804	837
¾	4.500	1372	1833	¾	1.750	804	1617
Wedge Anchors in 3000 psi (207 bar) Lightweight Sand Concrete				Wood Form Inserts in 3000 psi (207 bar) Lightweight Sand Concrete			
⅜	2.375	739	1141	⅜	1.100	1358	1235
½	3.750	983	1955	½	1.690	1358	1811
⅝	3.875	1340	2091	⅝	1.750	1358	1811
¾	4.500	1762	3280	¾	1.750	1358	1811
Wedge Anchors in 3000 psi (207 bar) Normal Weight Concrete				Wood Form Inserts in 3000 psi (207 bar) Normal Weight Concrete			
⅜	2.375	1087	1170	⅜	1.100	1598	1235
½	3.750	1338	2574	½	1.690	1598	2130
⅝	3.875	2070	3424	⅝	1.750	1598	2130
¾	4.500	3097	5239	¾	1.750	1598	2130
Wedge Anchors in 4000 psi (276 bar) Normal Weight Concrete				Wood Form Inserts in 4000 psi (276 bar) Normal Weight Concrete			
⅜	2.375	1233	1170	⅜	1.100	1845	1235
½	3.750	1545	2574	½	1.690	1845	2249
⅝	3.875	2390	3900	⅝	1.750	1845	2460
¾	4.500	3391	5239	¾	1.750	1845	2460
Wedge Anchors in 6000 psi (414 bar) Normal Weight Concrete				Wood Form Inserts in 6000 psi (414 bar) Normal Weight Concrete			
⅜	2.375	1409	1170	⅜	1.100	2259	1235
½	3.750	1892	2574	½	1.690	2259	2249
⅝	3.875	2928	3900	⅝	1.750	2259	3013
¾	4.500	4153	5239	¾	1.750	2259	3013

E.7.2 Calculation for Maximum Load Capacity of Concrete Anchors. This example shows how the effects of prying and brace angle are calculated when using Table E.7(a).

Δ **E.7.2.1 Procedure. Step 1.** Determine the allowable seismic tension value (T_{allow}) and the allowable seismic shear value (V_{allow}) for the anchor, based on data found in the anchor manufacturer's approved evaluation report. Note that, in this example, it is assumed the evaluation report provides the allowable tension and shear capacities. If this is not the case, the strength design anchor capacities must be determined using the procedures in Chapter 17 of ACI 318, which are then converted to ASD values by dividing by a factor of 1.4. As an alternative to calculating the allowable seismic tension value (T_{allow}) and the allowable seismic shear value (V_{allow}) for the anchor, the seismic tension and shear values that were used to calculate Figure 18.5.12.1 for anchor allowable load tables can be used.

Step 1a. Find the ASD seismic tension capacity (T_{allow}) for the anchor according to the strength of concrete, diameter of the anchor, and embedment depth of the anchor. Divide the ASD tension value by 2.0 and then multiply by 1.2.

Step 1b. Find the ASD seismic shear capacity (V_{allow}) for the anchor according to the strength of concrete, diameter of the anchor, and embedment depth of the anchor. Divide the ASD shear value by 2.0 and then multiply by 1.2.

Step 2. Calculate the applied seismic tension (T) and the applied seismic shear (V) based on the calculated horizontal earthquake load F_{pw}.

Step 2a. Calculate the designated angle category applied tension factor, including the effects of prying (Pr), using the following formulas:

Category A, B, and C

[E.7.2.1a]

$$Pr = \frac{\left(\frac{C+A}{Tan\theta}\right) - D}{A}$$

Category D, E, and F

[E.7.2.1b]

$$Pr = \frac{(C+A) - \left(\frac{D}{Tan\theta}\right)}{A}$$

Category G, H, and I

[E.7.2.1c]

$$Pr = \frac{\left(\frac{D}{B}\right)}{Sin\theta}$$

Step 2b. Calculate the ASD applied seismic tension (T) on the anchor, including the effects of prying, and when applied at the applicable brace angle from vertical and the designated angle category (A through I) using the following formula:

[E.7.2.1d]

$$T = F_{pw} \times Pr$$

Step 2c. Calculate the ASD applied seismic shear (V) on the anchor, when applied at the applicable brace angle from vertical and the designated angle category (A through I) using the following formulas:

Category A, B, and C

[E.7.2.1e]

$$V = F_{pw}$$

Category D, E, and F

[E.7.2.1f]

$$V = \frac{F_{pw}}{Tan\theta}$$

Category G, H, and I

[E.7.2.1g]

$$V = \frac{F_{pw}}{Sin\theta}$$

Step 3. Check the anchor for combined tension and shear loads using the following formula:

[E.7.2.1h]

$$\left(\frac{T}{T_{allow}}\right) + \left(\frac{V}{V_{allow}}\right) \le 1.2$$

Confirm that T/T_{allow} and $V/V_{allow} \le 1.0$.

Δ **E.7.2.2 Example: Sample Calculation, Maximum Load Capacity of Concrete Anchors as Shown in Table 18.5.12.2(a) through Table 18.5.12.2(e).** In this example, a sample calculation is provided showing how the values in Table 18.5.12.2(a) through Table 18.5.12.2(e) were calculated.

Step 1. Determine the allowable seismic tension value (T_{allow}) and the allowable seismic shear value (V_{allow}) for a concrete anchor in Figure 18.5.12.1.

Step 1a. The Table E.7(b) strength design seismic tension value (T_{allow}) for a ½ in. carbon steel anchor with 3¾ in. embedment depth in 4000 psi normal weight concrete is 1545 lb. Therefore, the allowable stress design seismic tension value (T_{allow}) is 1545/1.4/2.0 × 1.2 = 662 lb.

Step 1b. The Table E.7(b) strength design seismic shear value (V_{allow}) for a ½ in. carbon steel anchor with 3¾ in. embedment is 2574 lb. Therefore, the allowable stress design seismic shear value (V_{allow}) is 2574/1.4/2.0 × 1.2 = 1103 lb.

Step 2. Use the applied seismic tension value (T) and the applied seismic shear value (V) based on an ASD horizontal earthquake load (F_{pw}) of 100 lb, a 30-degree brace angle from vertical, and designated angle category A.

Step 2a. Calculate the ASD applied seismic tension value (T) on the anchor, including the effects of prying, using the following formula and Figure E.7.2.2.

[E.7.2.2a]

$$T = \frac{F_{pw}\left[\left(\dfrac{C + A}{Tan\theta}\right) - D\right]}{A}$$

where:

T = applied service tension load, including the effect of prying

F_{pw} = horizontal earthquake load (F_{pw} = 170)

Tan = tangent of brace angle from vertical ($Tan\,\theta\,0° = 0.5774$)

A = 0.7500

B = 1.5000

C = 2.6250

$T = F_{pw} \times Pr$

$$T = \frac{\left\{F_{pw}\left[\left(\dfrac{2.625 + 0.75}{0.5774}\right) - 1.0\right]\right\}}{0.75}$$

$$T = \frac{\left[F_{pw}\left(5.8452 - 1.0\right)\right]}{0.75}$$

$$T = F_{pw}\left(\frac{4.8451}{0.75}\right)$$

$T = F_{pw} \times 6.46$

$T = 100 \text{ lb} \times 6.46 = 646 \text{ lb}$

Step 2b. The ASD applied seismic shear value (V) on the anchor for anchor orientations A, B, and C is equal to the ASD horizontal earthquake load F_{pw} = 100 lb.

Step 3. Calculate the maximum allowable horizontal earthquake load F_{pw} using the formula:

[E.7.2.2b]

$$\left(\frac{T}{T_{allow}}\right) + \left(\frac{V}{V_{allow}}\right) \leq 1.2$$

$$\left(\frac{646}{662}\right) + \left(\frac{100}{1103}\right) = 1.0665 (\leq 1.2)$$

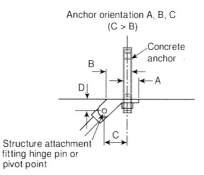

FIGURE E.7.2.2 Concrete Anchor for Sample Calculation in E.7.2.2.

Δ

Annex F Informational References

F.1 Referenced Publications. The documents or portions thereof listed in this annex are referenced within the informational sections of this standard and are not part of the requirements of this document unless also listed in Chapter 2 for other reasons.

Δ **F.1.1 NFPA Publications.** National Fire Protection Association, 1 Batterymarch Park, Quincy, MA 02169-7471.

NFPA 1, *Fire Code*, 2021 edition.

NFPA 13D, *Standard for the Installation of Sprinkler Systems in One- and Two-Family Dwellings and Manufactured Homes*, 2022 edition.

NFPA 13E, *Recommended Practice for Fire Department Operations in Properties Protected by Sprinkler and Standpipe Systems*, 2020 edition.

NFPA 13R, *Standard for the Installation of Sprinkler Systems in Low-Rise Residential Occupancies*, 2022 edition.

NFPA 14, *Standard for the Installation of Standpipe and Hose Systems*, 2019 edition.

NFPA 20, *Standard for the Installation of Stationary Pumps for Fire Protection*, 2022 edition.

NFPA 22, *Standard for Water Tanks for Private Fire Protection*, 2018 edition.

NFPA 25, *Standard for the Inspection, Testing, and Maintenance of Water-Based Fire Protection Systems*, 2020 edition.

NFPA 70®, *National Electrical Code*®, 2020 edition.

NFPA 72®, *National Fire Alarm and Signaling Code*®, 2022 edition.

NFPA 80A, *Recommended Practice for Protection of Buildings from Exterior Fire Exposures*, 2022 edition.

NFPA 101®, *Life Safety Code*®, 2021 edition.

NFPA 170, *Standard for Fire Safety and Emergency Symbols*, 2021 edition.

NFPA 204, *Standard for Smoke and Heat Venting*, 2021 edition.

NFPA 220, *Standard on Types of Building Construction*, 2021 edition.

NFPA 232, *Standard for the Protection of Records*, 2022 edition.

NFPA 259, *Standard Test Method for Potential Heat of Building Materials*, 2018 edition.

NFPA 291, *Recommended Practice for Fire Flow Testing and Marking of Hydrants*, 2022 edition.

NFPA 409, *Standard on Aircraft Hangars*, 2016 edition.

NFPA 750, *Standard on Water Mist Fire Protection Systems*, 2019 edition.

NFPA 780, *Standard for the Installation of Lightning Protection Systems*, 2020 edition.

F.1.2 Other Publications.

F.1.2.1 ACI Publications. American Concrete Institute, 38800 Country Club Drive, Farmington Hills, MI 48331-3439.

ACI 318, *Building Code Requirements for Structural Concrete and Commentary*, 2019.

ACI 355.2, *Qualification of Post-Installed Mechanical Anchors in Concrete and Commentary*, 2019.

F.1.2.2 ACPA Publications. American Concrete Pipe Association, 8445 Freeport Pkwy, Suite 350, Irving, TX 75063.

Concrete Pipe Handbook.

Δ **F.1.2.3 AISC Publications.** American Institute of Steel Construction, 130 East Randolph, Suite 2000, Chicago, IL 60601.

AISC 360, *Specification for Structural Steel Buildings*, 2016.

Specification for the Design, Fabrication, and Erection of Structural Steel Buildings.

Δ **F.1.2.4 ASCE Publications.** American Society of Civil Engineers, 1801 Alexander Bell Drive, Reston, VA 20191-4400.

ASCE/SEI 7, *Minimum Design Loads for Buildings and Other Structures*, 2016.

ASCE 19, *Structural Applications of Steel Cables for Buildings*, 2016.

F.1.2.5 ASME Publications. ASME International, Two Park Avenue, New York, NY 10016-5990.

ASME A17.1, *Safety Code for Elevators and Escalators*, 2016.

ASME B16.1, *Gray Iron Pipe Flanges and Flanged Fittings Classes 25, 125, and 250*, 2015.

ASME B1.20.1, *Pipe Threads, General Purpose (Inch)*, 2013.

Δ **F.1.2.6 ASTM Publications.** ASTM International, 100 Barr Harbor Drive, P.O. Box C700, West Conshohocken, PA 19428-2959.

ASTM A126, *Standard Specification for Gray Iron Castings for Valves, Flanges and Pipe Fittings*, 2004, reapproved 2019.

ASTM A135/A135M, *Standard Specification for Electric-Resistance-Welded Steel Pipe*, 2009, reapproved 2019.

ASTM A197/A197M, *Standard Specification for Cupola Malleable Iron*, 2000, reapproved 2019.

ASTM A307, *Standard Specification for Carbon Steel Bolts, Studs, Threaded Rod 60,000 psi Tensile Strength*, 2014.

ASTM A603, *Standard Specification for Metallic-Coated Steel Structural Wire Rope*, 1998, reapproved 2019.

ASTM A1023/A1023M, *Standard Specification for Stranded Carbon Steel Wire Ropes for General Purposes*, 2015.

ASTM B31, *Standards of Pressure Piping*, collection with various dates.

ASTM C136/C136M, *Standard Test Method for Sieve Analysis of Fine and Coarse Aggregates*, 2019.

ASTM C635/C635M, *Standard Specification for the Manufacture, Performance, and Testing of Metal Suspension Systems of Acoustical Tile and Lay-In Panel Ceilings*, 2017.

ASTM C636/C636M, *Standard Practice for Installation of Metal Ceiling Suspension Systems for Acoustical Tile and Lay-In Panels,* 2019.

ASTM D2487, *Standard Practice for Classification of Soils for Engineering Purposes (Unified Soil Classification System),* 2017.

ASTM E8/E8M, *Structural Test Method for Tension Testing of Metallic Materials,* 2016.

ASTM E84, *Standard Test Method of Surface Burning Characteristics of Building Materials,* 2020.

ASTM E119, *Standard Test Methods for Fire Tests of Building Construction and Materials,* 2020.

ASTM E580/E580M, *Standard Practice for Installation of Ceiling Suspension Systems for Acoustical Tile and Lay-in Panels in Areas Subject to Earthquake Ground Motions,* 2020.

ASTM F437, *Standard Specification for Threaded Chlorinated Poly (Vinyl Chloride) (CPVC) Plastic Pipe Fittings, Schedule 80,* 2015.

ASTM F438, *Standard Specification for Socket-Type Chlorinated Poly (Vinyl Chloride) (CPVC) Plastic Pipe Fittings, Schedule 40,* 2017.

ASTM F439, *Standard Specification for Socket-Type Chlorinated Poly (Vinyl Chloride) (CPVC) Plastic Pipe Fittings, Schedule 80,* 2019.

ASTM F442/F442M, *Standard Specification for Chlorinated Poly (Vinyl Chloride) (CPVC) Plastic Pipe (SDR-PR),* 2019.

ASTM F2164, *Standard Practice for Field Leak Testing of Polyethylene (PE) and Crosslinked Polyethylene (PEX) Pressure Piping Systems Using Hydrostatic Pressure,* 2018.

Δ **F.1.2.7 AWWA Publications.** American Water Works Association, 6666 West Quincy Avenue, Denver, CO 80235.

AWWA C105/A21.5, *Polyethylene Encasement for Ductile-Iron Pipe Systems,* 2018.

AWWA C111/A21.11, *Rubber-Gasket Joints for Ductile-Iron Pressure Pipe and Fittings,* 2017.

AWWA C115/A21.15, *Flanged Ductile-Iron Pipe with Ductile-Iron or Gray-Iron Threaded Flanges,* 2011.

AWWA C150/A21.50, *Thickness Design of Ductile-Iron Pipe,* 2014.

AWWA C206, *Field Welding of Steel Water Pipe,* 2017.

AWWA C600, *Standard for the Installation of Ductile Iron Water Mains and Their Appurtenances,* 2017.

AWWA C602, *Cement-Mortar Lining of Water Pipe Lines in Place, 4 in. (100 mm) and Larger,* 2017.

AWWA C606, *Grooved and Shouldered Joints,* 2015.

AWWA C900, *Polyvinyl Chloride (PVC) Pressure Pipe and Fabricated Fittings, 4 in. Through 60 in. (100 mm Through 1,500 mm),* 2016.

AWWA M9, *Concrete Pressure Pipe,* 2008, Errata, 2013.

AWWA M11, *Steel Pipe — A Guide for Design and Installation,* 2016.

AWWA M14, *Recommended Practice for Backflow Prevention and Cross-Connection Control,* 2015.

AWWA M23, *PVC Pipe — Design and Installation,* 2019.

AWWA M41, *Ductile-Iron Pipe and Fittings,* 2009.

AWWA M55, *PE Pipe — Design and Installation,* 2006.

F.1.2.8 DIPRA Publications. Ductile Iron Pipe Research Association, P.O. Box 19206, Golden, CO 80402.

Thrust Restraint Design for Ductile Iron Pipe, 2016.

F.1.2.9 FM Publications. FM Global, 270 Central Avenue, P.O. Box 7500, Johnston, RI 02919-4923.

Flammability Characterization of Lithium-ion Batteries in Bulk Storage, 2013.

FM Approval 1011/1012/1013, *Deluge and Preaction Sprinkler Systems,* 2009.

FM Approval 1020, *Automatic Water Control Valves,* 2007.

FM Approval 1021, *Dry Pipe Valves,* 1973.

FM Approval 1031, *Quick Opening Devices (Accelerators and Exhausters) for Dry Pipe Valves,* 1977.

FM Approval 1041, *Alarm Check Valves,* 2006.

FM Approval 1042, *Waterflow Alarm Indicators (Vane Type),* 1970.

FM Approval 1045, *Waterflow Detector Check Valves,* 2005.

FM Approval 1112, *Indicating Valves (Butterfly or Ball Type),* 2006.

FM Approval 1120/1130, *Fire Service Water Control Valves (OS & Y and NRS Type Gate Valves),* 1997.

FM Approval 1140, *Quick Opening Valves 1/4 Inch Through 2 Inch Nominal Size,* 1998.

FM Approval 1210, *Swing Check Valves,* 2004.

FM Approval 1362, *Pressure Reducing Valves,* 1984.

FM Approval 1610, *Ductile Iron Pipe and Fittings, Flexible Fittings and Couplings,* 2006.

FM Approval 1612, *Polyvinyl Chloride (PVC) Pipe and Fittings for Underground Fire Protection Service,* 1999.

FM Approval 1613, *Polyethylene (PE) Pipe and Fittings for Underground Fire Protection Service,* 2006.

FM Approval 1620, *Pipe Joints and Anchor Fittings for Underground Fire Service Mains,* 1975.

FM Approval 1630, *Steel Pipe for Automatic Fire Sprinkler Systems,* 2013.

FM Approval 1631, *Adjustable and Fixed Sprinkler Fittings 1/2Inch through 1 Inch Nominal Size,* 2006.

FM Approval 1632, *Telescoping Sprinkler Assemblies for Use in Fire Protection Systems for Anechoic Chambers,* 2006.

FM Approval 1635, *Plastic Pipe & Fittings for Automatic Sprinkler Systems,* 2011.

FM Approval 1636, *Fire Resistant Barriers for Use with CPVC Pipe and Fittings in Light Hazard Occupancies,* 2003.

FM Approval 1637, *Flexible Sprinkler Hose with Fittings,* 2010.

FM Approval 1920, *Pipe Couplings and Fittings for Fire Protection Systems,* 2007.

FM Approval 1950, *Seismic Sway Brace Components for Automatic Sprinkler Systems*, 2010.

FM Approval 1951/1952/1953, *Pipe Hanger Components for Automatic Sprinkler Systems*, 2003.

FM Approval 2000, *Automatic Control Mode Sprinklers for Fire Protection*, 2006.

FM Approval 2008, *Suppression Mode ESFR Automatic Sprinklers*, 2006.

FM Approval 2030, *Residential Automatic Sprinklers*, 2009.

FM Class Number 4651, *Plastic Suspended Ceiling Panels*, 1978.

FM Loss Prevention Data Sheet 8-9, Storage of Class 1, 2, 3, 4 and Plastic Commodities.

F.1.2.10 FMRC Publications. FM Global Research, FM Global, 270 Central Avenue, P.O. Box 7500, Johnston, RI 02919-4923.

FMRC J. I. 0X1R0.RR, "Large-Scale Fire Tests of Rack Storage Group A Plastics in Retail Operation Scenarios Protected by Extra Large Orifice (ELO) Sprinklers."

Δ **F.1.2.11 FPRF Publications.** Fire Protection Research Foundation, 1 Batterymarch Park, Quincy, MA 02169.

Antifreeze Solutions Supplied through Spray Sprinklers — Interim Report, February 2012.

Antifreeze Systems in Home Fire Sprinkler Systems — Literature Review and Research Plan, June 2010.

Antifreeze Systems in Home Fire Sprinkler Systems — Phase II Final Report, December 2010.

High Volume/Low Speed Fan and Sprinkler Operation — Ph. 2 Final Report, 2011.

Large-Scale Test Evaluation of Early Suppression Fast-Response (ESFR) Automatic Sprinklers, 1986.

Lithium Ion Batteries Hazard and Use Assessment, 2011.

Lithium Ion Batteries Hazard and Use Assessment Phase IIB, Flammability Characterization of Li-ion Batteries for Storage Protection, 2013.

Lithium Ion Batteries Hazard and Use Assessment — Phase III, 2016.

Protection of Rack Stored Exposed Expanded Group A Plastics with ESFR Sprinklers and Vertical Barriers, 2014.

F.1.2.12 ICC Publications. International Code Council, 500 New Jersey Avenue, NW, 6th Floor, Washington, DC 20001.

AC193, *Acceptance Criteria for Mechanical Anchors in Concrete Elements*, 2018.

AC308, *Post-installed Adhesive Anchors in Concrete Elements*, 2019.

International Building Code, 2018.

Uniform Building Code, 1997.

F.1.2.13 IMO Publications. International Maritime Organization, 4 Albert Embankment, London, SEI 7SR, United Kingdom.

International Convention for the Safety of Life at Sea, 1974 (SOLAS 74), as amended, regulations II-2/3 and II-2/26.

F.1.2.14 ISO Publications. International Organization for Standardization, ISO Central Secretariat, BIBC II, Chemin de Blandonnet, 8, CP 401, 1214 Vernier, Geneva Switzerland.

ISO 6182-1, *Fire protection — Automatic sprinkler systems — Part 1: Requirements and test methods for sprinklers*, 2014.

F.1.2.15 NFSA Publications. National Fire Sprinkler Association, 40 Jon Barrett Road, Patterson, NY 12563.

Valentine and Isman, *Kitchen Cabinets and Residential Sprinklers*, November 2005.

F.1.2.16 SNAME Publications. Society of Naval Architects and Marine Engineers, 99 Canal Center Plaza, Suite 310, Alexandria, VA 22314.

Technical Research Bulletin 2-21, "Aluminum Fire Protection Guidelines."

Δ **F.1.2.17 UL Publications.** Underwriters Laboratories Inc., 333 Pfingsten Road, Northbrook, IL 60062-2096.

Commodity Hazard Comparison of Expanded Plastic in Portable Bins and Racking, Project 99NK29106, NC4004, September 8, 2000.

"Fact Finding Report on Automatic Sprinkler Protection for Fur Storage Vaults," November 25, 1947.

Technical Report of Fire Testing of Automotive Parts in Portable Storage Racking, Project 99NK29106, NC4004, January 5, 2001.

UL 193, *Alarm Valves for Fire Protection Service*, 2016.

UL 194, *Gasketed Joints for Ductile-Iron Pipe and Fittings for Fire Protection Service*, 2005, revised 2016.

UL 199, *Automatic Sprinklers for Fire Protection Service*, 2005, revised 2020.

UL 203, *Pipe Hanger Equipment for Fire Protection Service*, 2020.

UL 203A, *Standard for Sway Brace Devices for Sprinkler System Piping*, 2015, revised 2016.

UL 213, *Rubber Gasketed Fittings for Fire Protection Service*, 2009, revised 2019.

UL 260, *Dry Pipe and Deluge Valves for Fire Protection Service*, 2004, revised 2018.

UL 262, *Gate Valves for Fire Protection Service*, 2004, revised 2018.

UL 263, *Fire Tests of Building Construction and Materials*, 2011, revised 2018.

UL 312, *Check Valves for Fire Protection Service*, 2010, revised 2018.

UL 346, *Waterflow Indicators for Fire Protective Signaling Systems*, 2005, revised 2019.

UL 515A, *Outline of Investigation for Electrical Resistance Trace Heating and Associated Controls for Use in Sprinkler and Standpipe Systems*, 2015.

UL 852, *Metallic Sprinkler Pipe for Fire Protection Service*, 2008, revised 2018.

UL 1091, *Butterfly Valves for Fire Protection Service*, 2004, revised 2010.

UL 1285, *Polyvinyl Chloride (PVC) Pipes and Couplings for Underground Fire Service*, 2016.

UL 1468, *Direct Acting Pressure Reducing and Pressure Restricting Valves*, 2016.

UL 1474, *Adjustable Drop Nipples for Sprinkler Systems*, 2004.

UL 1486, *Quick Opening Devices for Dry Pipe Valves for Fire Protection Service*, 2004, revised 2018.

UL 1739, *Pilot-Operated Pressure-Control Valves for Fire Protection Service*, 2017.

UL 1821, *Thermoplastic Sprinkler Pipe and Fittings for Fire Protection Service*, 2015, revised 2019.

UL 2443, *Flexible Sprinkler Hose with Fittings for Fire Protection Service*, 2015, revised 2016.

UL 2901, *Antifreeze Solutions for Use in Fire Sprinkler Systems*, 2019.

UL 2901A, *Outline for Corrosion Control Additives for Use in Fire Sprinkler Systems*, 2019.

UL Subject 723S, *Outline of Investigation for Drop-Out Ceilings Installed Beneath Automatic Sprinklers*, 2006.

F.1.2.18 US Government Publications. US Government Publishing Office, 732 North Capitol Street, NW, Washington, DC 20401-0001.

Title 46, Code of Federal Regulations, Part 72.05-5, "Definitions."

Δ **F.1.2.19 Other Publications.**

Thrust Restraint Design Equations and Tables for Ductile Iron and PVC Pipe, EBAA Iron, Inc.

F.2 Informational References. The following documents or portions thereof are listed here as informational resources only. They are not a part of the requirements of this document.

F.2.1 NFPA Publications. National Fire Protection Association, 1 Batterymarch Park, Quincy, MA 02169-7471.

NFPA 13E, *Recommended Practice for Fire Department Operations in Properties Protected by Sprinkler and Standpipe Systems*, 2020 edition.

NFPA 33, *Standard for Spray Application Using Flammable or Combustible Materials*, 2018 edition.

NFPA 850, *Recommended Practice for Fire Protection for Electric Generating Plants and High Voltage Direct Current Converter Stations*, 2020 edition.

F.2.2 AWWA Publications. American Water Works Association, 6666 West Quincy Avenue, Denver, CO 80235.

AWWA C104/A21.4, *Cement-Mortar Lining for Ductile-Iron Pipe and Fittings*, 2016.

AWWA C110/A21.10, *Ductile-Iron and Gray-Iron Fittings*, 2012.

AWWA C116/A21.16, *Protective Fusion-Bonded Epoxy Coatings for the Interior and Exterior Surfaces of Ductile-Iron and Gray Iron Fittings for Water Supply Service*, 2015.

AWWA C151/A21.51, *Ductile-Iron Pipe, Centrifugally Cast*, 2017, errata, 2018.

AWWA C153/A21.53, *Ductile-Iron Compact Fittings*, 2011.

AWWA C203, *Coal-Tar Protective Coatings and Linings for Steel Water Pipe*, 2015.

AWWA C205, *Cement-Mortar Protective Lining and Coating for Steel Water Pipe 4 in. (100 mm) and Larger — Shop Applied*, 2018.

AWWA C208, *Dimensions for Fabricated Steel Water Pipe Fittings*, 2017.

AWWA C300, *Reinforced Concrete Pressure Pipe, Steel-Cylinder Type*, 2016.

AWWA C301, *Prestressed Concrete Pressure Pipe, Steel-Cylinder Type*, 2014.

AWWA C302, *Reinforced Concrete Pressure Pipe, Non-Cylinder Type*, 2016.

AWWA C303, *Reinforced Concrete Pressure Pipe, Bar-Wrapped, Steel-Cylinder Type, Pretensioned*, 2017.

F.2.3 DIPRA Publications. Ductile Iron Pipe Research Association, P.O. Box 19206, Golden, CO 80402.

Installation Guide for Ductile Iron Pipe, 2016.

F.2.4 FM Publications. FM Global, 270 Central Avenue, P.O. Box 7500, Johnston, RI 02919-4923.

FM Approval 2311, *Pressure Gauges for Fire Protection Systems*, 2008.

F.2.5 SAE Publications. SAE International, Society of Automotive Engineers, 400 Commonwealth Drive, Warrendale, PA 15096.

SAE AIR 4127, *Steel: Chemical Composition and Hardenability (Stabilized Type), Revision A, Stabilized*, December 2015.

F.2.6 Uni-Bell PVC Pipe Publications. Uni-Bell PVC Pipe Association, 2711 Lyndon B Johnson Fwy., Suite 1000, Dallas, TX 75234.

Handbook of PVC Pipe, 5th edition.

F.2.7 U.S. Government Publications. U.S. Government Publishing Office, 732 North Capitol Street, NW, Washington, DC 20401-0001.

U.S. Federal Standard No. 66C, *Standard for Steel Chemical Composition and Harden Ability*, April 18, 1967, change notice No. 2, April 16, 1970. (Superseded by SAE AIR4127)

Δ **F.3 References for Extracts in Informational Sections.**

NFPA 14, *Standard for the Installation of Standpipe and Hose Systems*, 2019 edition.

NFPA 24, *Standard for the Installation of Private Fire Service Mains and Their Appurtenances*, 2022 edition.

NFPA 101®, *Life Safety Code®*, 2021 edition.

NFPA 5000®, *Building Construction and Safety Code®*, 2021 edition.

Index

Copyright © 2021 National Fire Protection Association. All Rights Reserved.

The copyright in this index is separate and distinct from the copyright in the document that it indexes. The licensing provisions set forth for the document are not applicable to this index. This index may not be reproduced in whole or in part by any means without the express written permission of NFPA.

Spare sprinklers, 31.2.3

System components, hardware, and use, 31.2, A.31.2.1, A.31.2.2

Valves, 31.2.6, 31.7.4.2, A.31.2.6.1

Water supplies, 31.7, A.31.7.2.7 to A.31.7.4.6

Definition, 3.3.125.10

Marine thermal barriers, 31.4.10.1, A.31.4.10(4)

Definition, 3.3.125.9, A.3.3.125.9

Measurement, units of, 1.6.1, A.1.6.1.4

Mechanical damage, protection from, 6.4.2.2, 16.2.6, 16.5

Mechanical dry pipe valve (definition), 3.3.235.4.2; *see also* Dry pipe valves

Mercantile occupancies, D.1.1.9, D.1.1.10, D.2.23, D.2.24

Metal/nonmetal mining and metal mineral processing facilities, 27.22

Meters, 5.1.6, A.5.1.6

Mezzanines, 4.4.2, 28.5.1.5, D.2.3.1.1(1), D.2.4.1.1(1)

Microbiologically influenced corrosion (MIC), 4.2(4), 7.8.2, 30.1.10, A.4.2(4)

Mines

Coal, 27.21

Metal/nonmetal mining and metal mineral processing facilities, 27.22

Miscellaneous storage, 4.3.1.3, 4.3.1.4, 4.3.1.6 to 4.3.1.8, 20.1.1, A.4.3.1.4

Definition, 3.3.130, A.3.3.130

Density/area method, 4.3.1.7.1.1

Discharge criteria, Table 4.3.1.7.1.1

In-rack sprinklers, 4.3.1.7.1.2, 25.2.1, 25.7.1

Tires, 4.3.1.6, Table 4.3.1.7.1.1

Definition, 3.3.131

Mixed commodities, 20.4.13

Mixing rooms, sprinklers for, 16.2.4.1

Mobile high bay records storage, 26.8.1, A.26.8.1

Modifications, existing system, Chap. 30

Motion picture studio soundstages and production facilities, 27.24

Motor vehicle components, *see* Automotive components on portable racks

Movable racks, 20.5.1, Fig. A.3.3.177(k)

Definition, 3.3.132

Moving stairways, 9.3.5, A.9.3.5

Multicycle systems, 8.5

Definition, 3.3.216.7

Multiple-row racks, Table 4.3.1.7.1.1, 20.5.3.1.2, 20.5.3.1.3, 25.3.2.2.1.1, 25.3.2.2.1.5, 25.3.2.2.1.6, 25.3.2.2.2.1, 25.3.2.3.2.1, 25.3.2.4.2.1, 25.8.2.1.1, 25.8.2.1.5, 25.8.2.1.6, Fig. A.3.3.177(f), A.25.3.2.2.2.1

Alternative sprinkler system designs, 24.3.1, 24.3.2

Ceiling sprinklers, 23.1.3, 25.1.11.2

Control mode density area (CMDA) sprinklers, 21.4.1.1.2, 21.4.1.3, 21.5, 21.6, 25.3.2.1.1.1(1), 25.3.2.1.1.5, 25.3.2.1.1.6, 25.3.2.1.2.1, Fig. 25.3.3.1.1.1(f), Fig. 25.3.3.1.1.2(g), Fig. 25.3.3.1.1.3(f), 25.3.3.1.1.5, Fig. 25.3.3.2.1.1(f), Fig. 25.3.3.2.1.2(g), Fig. 25.3.3.2.1.3(f), 25.3.3.2.1.5, 25.8.2.2.1, 25.8.2.2.2.1(4), 25.8.3.1.1, 25.8.3.1.5, 25.8.3.1.6, 25.8.3.2.1, A.21.4.1.1, A.25.8.2.2.1, A.25.8.3.2.1, C.22

Control mode specific application (CMSA) sprinklers, 22.1.6, 22.4, 22.5, A.22.1.6

Definition, 3.3.134, A.3.3.177(3)

Early suppression fast-response (ESFR) sprinklers, 23.1.3, 23.4.1

Flue space, 20.5.3.4.1.1, 20.5.3.4.2.1

In-rack sprinkler location, 25.6.1.1, 25.6.2.3.1

Rubber tire storage, Table 21.7.1(a), 25.3.2.5.2.1

Multistory buildings. *see* Buildings, multistory

Museums, 27.35

-N-

Net vertical force, 18.5.10

Definition, 3.3.135

New technology, 1.7

Nitrate film, 27.9

Nitrogen

Air, substituted for, 4.7

Pressurized systems, 8.2.6.2, 8.2.6.8, 8.8.2.4, 8.8.2.7, A.8.2.6.8.1, A.8.2.6.8.4, A.8.8.2.4, A.8.8.2.7.1

Nonsprinkler system components, support of, 4.8, A.4.8

Normal pressure formula, 28.2.2.3

Nozzles (definition), 3.3.215.4.10; *see also* Spray nozzles

Nuclear power plants, light water, 27.33, 27.34

Nursing homes, 9.2.4.1.2

-O-

Obstructed construction, 10.2.6.1.2, 11.2.1, Table 11.2.2.1.2, 11.2.4.1.2, 11.3.2(7), Table 13.2.5.2.1, 13.2.6.1.1, 13.2.7.1.2, 14.2.4, 14.2.10.1.4, 24.1.7(3), A.10.2.6.1.2(5), A.14.2.4; *see also* Obstructions to sprinkler discharge

Definition, 3.3.43.1, A.3.3.43.1

Obstructions to sprinkler discharge, 9.5.5, 10.2.7, 10.3.2(7), 10.3.6, 11.3.6, 14.2.11, A.9.5.5.1 to A.9.5.5.3.4, A.10.2.7.2 to A.10.2.7.4.2, A.10.3.6.2.1.3 to A.10.3.6.3.2, A.11.3.6.2.1.3 to A.11.3.6.2.2.1, A.14.2.11; *see also* Early suppression fast-response (ESFR) sprinklers; Pendent sprinklers; Sidewall sprinklers; Upright sprinklers

Alternative sprinkler system designs, 24.5

Continuous obstruction, 9.5.5.2.1, 10.2.7.3.1.1, 10.3.6.2.1.1, 10.3.6.3.1, 11.2.5.2.1.1, 11.2.5.2.1.2, 11.2.5.3.1, 11.3.6.1.4, 11.3.6.2.1.1, 11.3.6.3.1, 12.1.10.3.1, 12.1.11.2.1.1, 12.1.11.3.1, 13.2.8.2.1.1, 13.2.8.3.1, 14.2.11.3

Definition, 3.3.140.1

Control mode specific application (CMSA) sprinklers, 13.2.8, A.13.2.8

Double joist, 10.2.6.1.5

Earthquake damage, protection of piping from, 18.1.3

Extended coverage (EC) sprinklers, 11.2.5, A.11.2.5.1.2 to A.11.2.5.3.2

Fixed, 9.5.5.3.1, 10.2.7.4.2, 10.3.6.3.2, 11.2.5.3.2, 11.3.6.3.2, A.9.5.5.3.1, A.10.2.7.4.2, A.10.3.6.3.2, A.11.2.5.3.2, A.11.3.6.3.2

Hazard, discharge prevented from reaching, 9.5.5.3, 10.2.7.4, 10.3.6.3, 11.2.5.3, 11.3.6.3, 12.1.10.3, 12.1.11.3, 13.2.8.3, A.9.5.5.3, A.10.2.7.4, A.10.3.6.3, A.11.2.5.3, A.11.3.6.3, A.12.1.10.3, A.12.1.11.3, A.13.2.8.3

Isolated, 11.3.6.1.5, 14.2.11.2, A.14.2.11.2

Noncontinuous obstruction, 9.5.5.2.1, 10.2.7.3.1.1, 10.3.6.2.1.1, 10.3.6.3.1, 11.2.5.2.1.1, 11.2.5.3.1, 11.3.6.2.1.1, 11.3.6.3.1, 12.1.10.3.1, 12.1.11.2.1.1, 12.1.11.3.1, 13.2.8.2.1.1, 13.2.8.3.1, 14.2.11.2(1)

Definition, 3.3.140.2